COLOMBIA

BUILDING PEACE
IN A TIME OF WAR

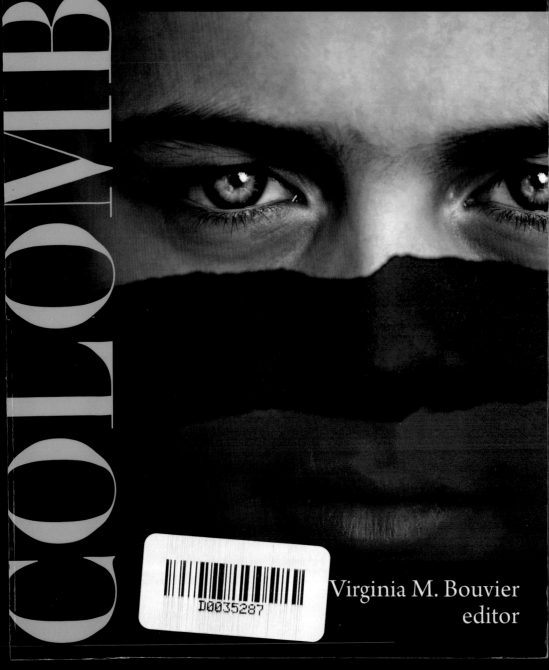

D0035287

Virginia M. Bouvier
editor

Praise for *Colombia Building Peace in a Time of War*

"This book will surely become necessary reading for all of those interested to learn or to act on peacebuilding in Colombia. This extremely useful, relevant, and timely book is the most comprehensive source available today for information, analysis and practice on non-military efforts on peace seeking in Colombia. It presents and discusses the work by a broad array of authors, academics and practitioners, national and international, representing a diversity of views from a civil society perspective. Their work covers the universe of local, regional, sectorial, gender, ethnic, institutional, national, and international initiatives for peacebuilding."

—**Jairo A. Arboleda**, World Bank

"*Rarely does a book come along to fundamentally alter our understanding of a country and the political and social dynamics at work within its borders.* Colombia: Building Peace in a Time of War *is such a volume. The contributors challenge us to look beyond the prism of drug-trafficking and terrorism that has defined—and limited—our perception of Colombian reality. What emerges is the vibrancy of civil society efforts to prevent, mediate, and transform armed conflict even as national-level negotiations with armed actors have stumbled or failed. Religious and business leaders, community organizers, local officials, women's groups—all have refused to give up in the effort to build peace. Their stubbornness and heroism deserve our closest attention.*"

— **Cynthia Arnson**, Woodrow Wilson Center

"*This book truly immerses the reader in the complex efforts to bring peace to Colombia. The thirty authors, analysts, and practitioners offer in-depth descriptions of efforts by the various sectors to find peace after fifty years of violence. Virginia Bouvier has done a masterful job of editing and collecting the essays in helpful groupings, and has included an insightful introduction and closing commentary and analysis. She makes a strong case for greater dialogue among the sectors, including more understanding of what works and what doesn't in the daunting quest for peace.*"

—**Charles Currie, S.J.**, Association of Jesuit Colleges and Universities

"*Virginia Bouvier's volume documents how different actors in Colombia's struggle for peace and security engage in preventing state failure. Lessons from this volume can serve a larger readership as the U.S. government ponders its policy options in places like Pakistan, Afghanistan, and Iraq.*"

—**Johanna Mendelson Forman**, Center for Strategic and International Studies

"The comprehensive nature of the case studies in this book lends insight into why Colombia remains one of the most intractable conflicts and what might be done about it. More importantly, the book contains a holistic evaluation of diverse initiatives to build peace in Colombia, and the lessons it highlights will aid the cause of peacebuilders everywhere."

—**Robert Ricigliano**, Institute of World Affairs

"Colombia: Building Peace in a Time of War, *allows us to appreciate a country that is daily re-inventing itself; a country of multiple resistances to violence, mass civic mobilizations, initiatives, practices, and peace communities. For the first time in decades, the legitimization of war has been radically confronted by an anti-war discourse composed of an indissoluble trilogy: peace, development, and autonomy. Virginia M. Bouvier and her contributors highlight the existence and work that this anti-war discourse performs in Colombian civil society today. A Colombia that was previously invisible has become the leading protagonist in the struggle for peace, and this book rightly calls our attention to this emergent formation."*

—**Gonzalo Sanchez**, Historical Memory Commission

"The volume offers a detailed map that Colombian government authorities, civil society leaders, and the international community can follow to help construct an enduring peace. Other societies undergoing similar conflicts will benefit enormously from this singular contribution."

—**Michael Shifter**, Inter-American Dialogue, and Georgetown University

COLOMBIA

For Jan –
With
much admiration
+ cariño,

[signature]

Oct 9, 2010
LASA
Toronto

COLOMBIA

BUILDING PEACE
IN A TIME OF WAR

Virginia M. Bouvier
editor

UNITED STATES INSTITUTE OF PEACE PRESS
Washington, D.C.

UNITED STATES INSTITUTE OF PEACE
1200 17th Street NW, Suite 200
Washington, DC 20036-3011
www.usip.org

Printed in the United States of America

The paper used in this publication meets the minimum requirements of American National Standards for Information Science—Permanence of Paper for Printed Library Materials, ANSI Z39.48-1984.

Library of Congress Cataloging-in-Publication Data

Colombia : building peace in a time of war / edited by
Virginia M. Bouvier.
    p. cm.
  ISBN 978-1-60127-038-2 (pbk. : alk. paper) — ISBN 978-1-60127-039-9 (cloth : alk. paper)
  1. Peace-building—Colombia. 2. Conflict management—Colombia.
3. Violence—Colombia—Prevention. 4. Colombia—Social conditions—1970– 5. Colombia—Politics and government—1974– I. Bouvier, Virginia Marie, 1958–
  JZ5584.C7C65 2009
  986.106'35—dc22
               2008049078

Contents

Foreword

In the last four decades the Colombian internal armed conflict has been much discussed, studied, and written about from different viewpoints. However, the multiple efforts and initiatives to resolve the grassroots of this complex conflict have been little explored.

Since the early 1990s Colombia has seen its enduring and progressive internal armed conflict decay even further. The constant battle among the parties and the number and extent of the abuses perpetrated against civilians have intensified drastically. The Colombian conflict has many dimensions that share relentless consequences. The persistence of these hostilities has contributed to new and equally disastrous situations that feed the conflict such as illicit trading, arms proliferation, drug production and trafficking, political intolerance, and ideologies that aim to legitimize violence and political, economic, and social exclusion.

The conflict, characterized by its degradation of human rights, constitutes one of the most substantial obstacles to reducing extreme poverty, fostering economic and social development, and strengthening the democratic institutions of the country. The Colombian democratic state and laws continue bearing the difficult and unavoidable responsibility of ensuring that the political will exists to put an end to the conflict.

One cannot apply isolated solutions. The multidimensional characteristics of this conflict call for joint, sustainable, and consistent efforts. In response, the Colombian state should push for economic, social, and humanitarian policymaking strategies, including those related to drug production, trafficking, and local consumption, and allow political interaction among all civil organizations, including the current opposition parties. The state should also recognize the need for discussing solutions with illegal armed groups such as FARC.

Only through a comprehensive response can Colombia reach an end to this conflict. While there is no clear recipe of how to combine these measures, Colombia's government and its civil organizations need to strictly follow the fundamental values expressed in international humanitarian law.

This book is of compelling academic and political relevance for Colombia as well as other countries that are building peace initiatives in the middle of conflict. This remarkable work details the most important projects and initiatives, which have opened up and continue to develop opportunities for peace in Colombia.

Learning from these experiences, and emerging scholarship opens the path to clear, concise strategies for addressing Colombia's unresolved challenges. Having inherited the conflict, this generation of Colombians has the moral obligation to resolve it, and not to turn it over to future generations.

Luis Eladio Perez Bonilla

Acknowledgments

It has been a delight to work with the authors of this volume. I thank them first and foremost for the work they are doing and the generosity of spirit, time, and ideas that have consistently characterized their participation in this endeavor. The personal and professional exchanges occasioned by this project have provided me with tremendous hope and an intellectual feast of the richest kind imaginable. I hope the reader will relish the fruits of their labors even a fraction as much as I have.

This project has provided an impetus for dialogue, integration, and collaboration across geographic and disciplinary boundaries; across sectors; and among those working at the local, regional, national, and international levels. The authors included in this book represent a microcosm of some of the sectors working for peace in Colombia, and their collaboration provides a model for the kind of intellectual and personal commitment that will transform the conflict in Colombia.

There are many individuals and institutions that were *imprescindible* to this book's development and publication. The United States Institute of Peace has supported the work of about half of the contributors through its Grant and Fellowship Program and provided me with the resources to hold an author's conference at Cornell University in November 2005, to publish a special report on the conference findings, and to attend the Latin American Studies Association meetings in 2004, 2006, and 2007 and the International Studies Association meeting in 2005, where I organized, chaired, or served as a discussant on panels relevant to the topic of peace initiatives in Colombia. These meetings and conferences were key to developing the ideas and the concept for this book.

I thank the executive leadership of the Institute—Dick Solomon, Chick Nelson, Trish Thomson, and Mike Graham—for these opportunities. The manuscript has been strengthened by the insightful comments provided by David Smock, the head of the Institute's Center for Mediation and Conflict Resolution. I owe a particular debt of gratitude to the various directors and former directors of the Jennings Randolph Fellowship Program—Joe Klaits, Sheryl Brown, John Crist, Steve Heydemann, Chantal Jonge de Oudraat, and Judy Barsalou. Discussions with Sheryl and John were particularly critical in coalescing my thinking about developing the multilevel peacebuilding model more explicitly. I am grateful to them, the Jennings Randolph staff—Erin Barrar, Jean Brodeur, Elizabeth Drakulich, Anne Driscoll, Shira Lowinger, and Lynn Tesser—and the senior fellows for their ongoing good humor and for providing a wonderful work environment that has nurtured this project. Thank you also to the research assistants who lent their help at critical times, especially Arshi Saleem Hashmi and Cheryl Simmons.

The authors' conference and public events on "Peace Initiatives in Colombia" at Cornell University on November 19–20, 2005, could not have happened without the enthusiastic partnership, professional expertise, and personal commitment of Mary Roldán and her team at Cornell's Latin American Studies Program, especially John S. Henderson, Treva Levine, and Andrea Matus. Conference cosponsors included Cornell's Africana Studies and Research Center, its departments of Development Sociology, Government, History, and Anthropology, the Mario Einaudi Center for International Studies, the Institute for European Studies, the Johnson School of Management, the Peace Studies Program, the Society for the Humanities, the Committee on U.S.–Latin American Relations (CUSLAR), and the Colombian Student Association, as well as Syracuse University's Program for Analysis and Resolution of Conflict (PARC). Special thanks go to each of these programs, as well as to Federico Finkel, Elisa Da Via, and other students who assisted with the transcription of the conference discussions and breakout meetings. Charlie Roberts provided outstanding interpretation services. Barbara Fraser, Andy Klatt, Barbara Gerlach, and Susan Peacock assisted in translating Spanish chapters or parts thereof into English. Thanks to the Publications Department at the Institute as well, especially developmental editors Kurt Volkan and Linda Rabben, and Kay Hechler, Michelle Slavin, and Valerie Norville.

The shape of this book owes an intellectual debt to each of its authors and to several others who have also been working to enrich foreign-policy debates on Colombia in Washington, D.C.—especially Kimberly Stanton, my first teacher on Colombian realities; Adam Isacson at the Center for International Policy; Heather Hanson at the U.S. Office on Colombia; Mary DeLorey of Catholic Relief Services; Michael Schifter at the Inter-American Dialogue; Cynthia Arnson at the Woodrow Wilson International Center for Scholars; Mark Schneider at the International Crisis Group; Natalia Cardona at the American Friends Service Committee; Rob Levinson of the

U.S. Southern Command; Lisa Haugaard at the Latin America Working Group; Cristina Esquivel at the Colombian Commission for Human Rights; and Gimena Sánchez and John Walsh at the Washington Office on Latin America.

Finally, I dedicate this book to Jim Lyons and Maya Bouvier-Lyons and to the song of life that will bring peace and justice to Colombia.

Abbreviations

ACI	Andean Counterdrug Initiative
AECI	Agencia Española de Cooperación Internacional (Spanish Agency for International Cooperation)
AET	Asociación de Entidades Territoriales (Association of Regional Entities)
AFRODES	Asociación de Afrocolombianos Desplazados (Association of Displaced Afro-Colombians)
ANUC	Asociación Nacional de Usuarios Campesinos (National Association of Peasants)
ARS	Aseguradoras del Régimen Subsidiado (Administrators of the Subsidized Regime)
AUC	Autodefensas Unidas de Colombia (United Self-Defense Forces of Colombia)
CEDE	Centro de Estudios sobre Desarrollo Económico (Center for Economic Development Studies)
CEDECOL	Consejo Evangélico de Colombia (Council of Evangelical and Protestant Churches of Colombia)
CINEP	Centro de Investigación y Educación Popular (Jesuit Center for Research and Popular Education)
CNRR	Comisión Nacional de Reparación y Reconciliación (National Commission for Reparations and Reconciliation)
CODHES	Consultoría para los Derechos Humanos y el Desplazamiento (Consultancy on Human Rights and Displacement)

CRS	Corriente de Renovación Socialista (Socialist Renewal Group)
CTI	Cuerpo Técnico de Investigaciones (Public Prosecutor's Office)
DAS	Departamento Administrativo de Seguridad (Administrative Department for Security)
ECOPETROL	Colombian Petroleum Company
ELN	Ejército de Liberación Nacional (National Liberation Army)
EPL	Ejército Popular de Liberación (Popular Liberation Army)
ERP	Ejército Revolucionario del Pueblo (People's Revolutionary Army)
ETI	Entidades Territoriales Indígenas (Indigenous Territorial Entities)
FARC	Fuerzas Armadas Revolucionarias de Colombia (Colombian Revolutionary Armed Forces)
FMLN	Frente Farabundo Martí de Liberación Nacional (Farabundo Martí National Liberation Front)
FEDEGAN	Federación de Ganaderos (Ranchers' Federation)
FRDPMMa	Fundación Red de Desarrollo y Paz de Montes de María (Development and Peace Network of Montes de María Foundation)
HRW	Human Rights Watch
ICG	International Crisis Group
IEPRI	Instituto de Estudios Políticos y Relaciones Internacionales (Institute of Policy Studies and International Relations)
IOM	International Organization for Migration
ISP	Iglesias Santuarios de Paz (Church Sanctuaries of Peace)
M-19	Movimiento 19 de Abril (April 19th Movement)
MAPP	Misión de Apoyo al Proceso de Paz (Mission to Support the Peace Process)
MAQL	Movimiento Armado Quintín Lame (Quintín Lame Armed Movement)
NCA	National Constituent Assembly

NCRR	National Commission for Reparations and Reconciliation
OAS	Organization of American States
ONIC	Organización Nacional de Indígenas de Colombia (National Organization of Indigenous Peoples of Colombia)
PDP	Programa de Desarrollo y Paz (Development and Peace Program)
PDPMM	Programa de Desarrollo y Paz de Magdalena Medio (Magdalena Medio Development and Peace Program)
PNUD	Programa de las Naciones Unidas para el Desarrollo (United Nations Development Programme)
PRT	Partido Revolucionario de los Trabajadores (Workers' Revolutionary Party)
REDEPAZ	Red Nacional de Iniciativas por la Paz y Contra la Guerra (National Network of Initiatives for Peace and Against War)
REDPRODEPAZ	Red Nacional de Programas Regionales de Desarrollo y Paz (National Network of Regional Development and Peace Programs)
SEAP	Sociedad Económica Amigos del País (Friends of the Country Economic Society)
TEVERE	Testimonio, Verdad, y Reconciliación (Witness, Truth, and Reconciliation)
UNDP	United Nations Development Programme
UNFPA	United Nations Fund for Population Activities
UNHCR	United Nations High Commissioner for Refugees
USIP	United States Institute of Peace
UP	Unión Patriótica (Patriotic Union)
USO	Unión Sindical Obrera (Employee Trade Union for ECOPETROL)
ZoP	Zonas de Paz (Zones of Peace)

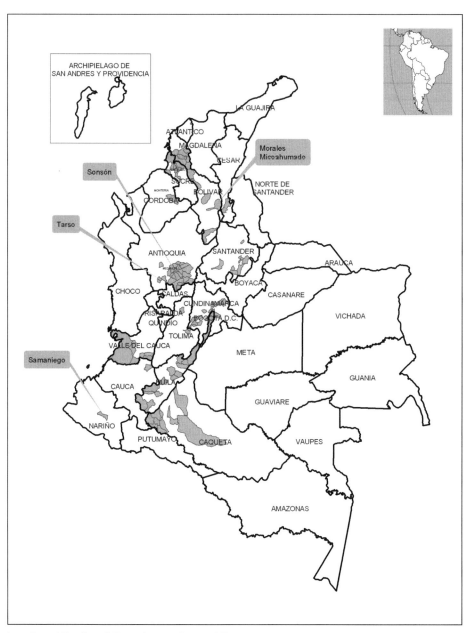

Local and Regional Constituent Assemblies

Source: Map courtesy of CINEP

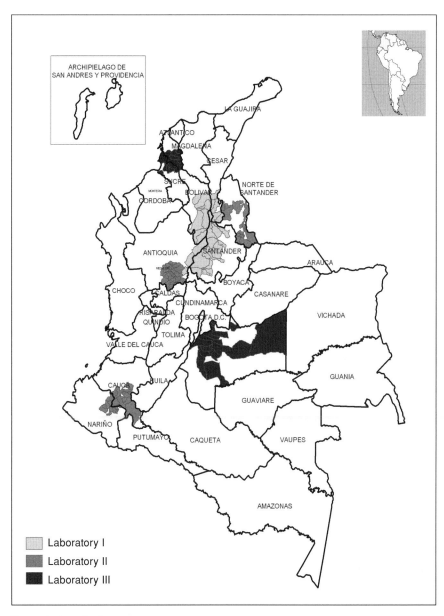

Peace Laboratories

Source: Map courtesy of CINEP

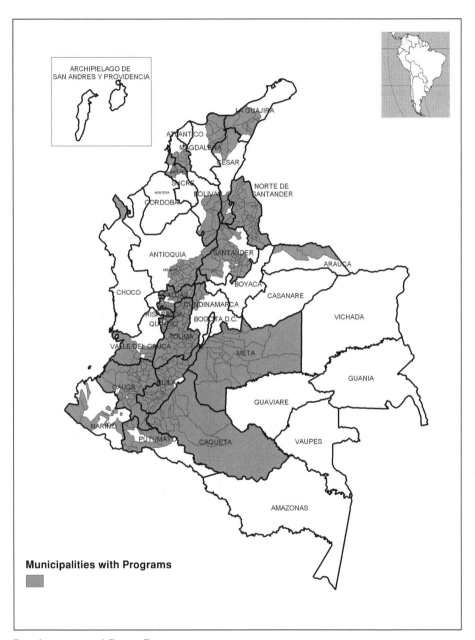

Development and Peace Programs

Source: Map courtesy of CINEP

INTRODUCTION

1

Building Peace in a Time of War

Virginia M. Bouvier

On two occasions when I was invited to talk about Colombia at the United States Institute of Peace (USIP), I asked the audiences to list all the words and images they associate with Colombia.[1] Their responses included a range of general and specific terms related to the theme of armed conflict: war, violence, drugs, kidnapping, the Revolutionary Armed Forces of Colombia (FARC)—Colombia's largest guerrilla group—arms, paramilitaries, child soldiers, corruption, sexual exploitation, and trafficking in women. Other terms mentioned—coffee, music—were less obviously related to the conflict. The audiences did not propose a single image linked to peace or to the pervasive efforts to pursue peace in Colombia. The contributors to this book seek to rectify some of the distortions created by the neglect of these nonviolent conflict actors, to consider how peace initiatives and their proponents might contribute further to a resolution of the Colombian conflict, and to assess the implications of this adjusted vision for the international community and policymakers.

The lack of attention to Colombia's peace efforts and actors, particularly in the English-speaking world, is not surprising. Colombia receives relatively little attention from the American media, the public, or the broader global community; when it does appear in the news, drugs and violence frequently dominate the headlines. Although the country's long-standing internal armed conflict involves multiple armed actors (including guerrillas, paramilitary forces, state armed forces, common criminals, and drug traffickers), agendas of violence, power, drugs, and greed have long overshadowed the political partisanship and ideologies that provided the backdrop for a guer-

---

[1] USIP, Summer Institute for Secondary School Teachers on International Peace, Security, and Conflict Management, August 1, 2006; USIP site visit of students and faculty from Ocean County Community College, New Jersey, March 17, 2008.

rilla war kindled by socioeconomic inequities and political exclusion a half a century ago. In recent decades, drugs have provided a steady source of income that has fueled the conflict and contributed to its intractability.[2] Today more than 90 percent of the cocaine and about half the heroin consumed in the United States is produced in or transits through Colombia.[3] Increasingly, Colombia's cocaine is finding markets in Brazil, Africa, and Europe as well.[4] Scholars, journalists, and others have produced a steady stream of academic and popular materials in both Spanish and English on Colombian drug cartels and drug trafficking.[5]

Besides being infamous as a leader in the drug trade, Colombia is also a leader in statistics on violence. After Sudan, Colombia has the world's largest population of internally displaced persons, estimated at between two million and four million.[6] In 2007, an additional three hundred thousand Colombians were internally displaced.[7] Labor leaders, journalists, human rights workers, church leaders, elected officials, and judicial authorities in Colombia continue to be among the most threatened on earth, and U.S. legislation linking aid to improvements in Colombia's human rights record underscores U.S. policy concerns on this front. With more than 1,100 land mine victims in 2006, Colombia surpassed even Cambodia and Afghanistan for having the most land mine accidents.[8] Colombia has long been known as the "kidnap

---

[2]Cynthia J. Arnson and Teresa Whitfield, "Third Parties and Intractable Conflicts: The Case of Colombia," in *Grasping the Nettle: Analyzing Cases of Intractable Conflict*, eds. Chester A. Crocker, Fen Osler Hampson, and Pamela Aall (Washington, D.C.: United States Institute of Peace Press, 2005).

[3]U.S. Department of State, Bureau for International Narcotics Control and Law Enforcement Affairs, *International Narcotics Control Strategy Report–2006*, www.state.gov/p/inl/rls/nrcrpt/2006/vol1/html/62106.htm (accessed October 21, 2007).

[4]Juan Forero, "Colombia's Coca Survives U.S. Plan to Uproot It," *New York Times*, August 19, 2006, www.nytimes.com/2006/08/19/world/americas/19coca.html?_r=1&n=Top%2fNews%2f World%2fCountries%20and%20Territories%2fColombia&oref=slogin (accessed August 15, 2008).

[5]See Grace Livingstone, *Inside Colombia: Drugs, Democracy, and War* (New Brunswick, N.J.: Rutgers University Press, 2004); Russell Crandall, *Driven by Drugs: U.S. Policy Toward Colombia* (Boulder, Colo.: Lynne Rienner, 2002); Robin Kirk, *More Terrible than Death: Massacres, Drugs, and America's War in Colombia* (New York: Public Affairs, 2003); Mark Bowden, *Killing Pablo: The Hunt for the World's Greatest Outlaw* (Washington, D.C.: Atlantic Monthly Press, 2001); Doug Stokes, *America's Other War: Terrorizing Colombia* (London: Zed Books, 2005); Ron Chepasiuk, *Drug Lords: The Rise and Fall of the Cali Cartel* (Preston, UK: Milo Books, 2005); Ted Galen Carpenter, *Bad Neighbor Policy: Washington's Futile War on Drugs in Latin America*, 1st ed. (New York: Palgrave Macmillan, 2003). Films include *Clear and Present Danger* (based on Tom Clancy's 1989 novel), *María Full of Grace* (2004), and *Cocaine Cowboys* (2006).

[6]United Nations High Commissioner for Refugees, *The State of the World's Refugees 2006*, www.unhcr.org/static/publ/sowr2006/toceng.htm (accessed August 23, 2008).

[7]CODHES figure cited in Washington Office on Latin America press release, "Paramilitaries, Human Rights, and the Trade Agreement," September 19, 2008, www.wola.org/index.php?option=com_content&task=viewp&id=773&Itemid=8 (accessed September 22, 2008).

[8]International Campaign to Ban Landmines, "Landmine Monitor: Colombia, 2007," www.icbl.org/lm/2007/colombia (accessed August 23, 2008).

capital of the world," with more than seventeen thousand people—including prominent legislators, government ministers, presidential candidates, businesspeople, and U.S. contractors—kidnapped in the past seven years.[9] While the number of kidnappings declined from 687 in 2006 to 521 in 2007, all of the armed actors still make use of kidnapping to sustain their war efforts. An unknown number of hostages continue to be held—750 by the FARC alone.[10]

A number of related factors contribute to the drugs-and-violence prism through which the world has tended to view Colombia. News stories are usually shaped by policy "hooks," story angles that link events of the day to government policies or to an explicit relationship to the news consumer. In the United States, policymakers have promoted three sometimes overlapping paradigms that have shaped U.S. relations with Colombia: beginning in the 1950s (and increasing especially after Fidel Castro came to power in Cuba), counterinsurgency concerns governed U.S. foreign policy toward Latin America; in the 1980s, the U.S. war on drugs dominated U.S. policy directives in the Andean producer countries; and in the aftermath of the 9/11 attacks on the World Trade Center in New York and the Pentagon building in Washington, D.C., the war on terror has driven U.S. foreign-policy concerns around the globe. These policy approaches have sometimes warranted coverage because they carried a steep price tag or because they showcased U.S. interests abroad. With the launching in 2000 of Plan Colombia, a multibillion-dollar plan to strengthen the Colombian state, Colombia became one of the top U.S. aid recipients in the world, surpassed at the time only by Egypt and Israel. From 2000 to 2007, Colombia received unprecedented levels of U.S. aid totaling more than US$5 billion, more than three-quarters of which went to the Colombian military and police for counterinsurgency and antinarcotics operations and oil pipeline protection.[11] Since most U.S. foreign aid thus far has been earmarked for the prosecution of the war, other agendas—regional stability; democracy, human rights, and the rule of law; socioeconomic development and humanitarian needs; and peace initiatives—make headlines

---

[9] Mexico surpassed Colombia for the title in 2005. See Larry Habegger, "Mexico: World's Kidnap Capital," *World Travel Watch,* August 9, 2005, www.worldtravelwatch.com/archives/2005/08/mexico-worlds-kidnap-capital.shtml (accessed August 15, 2008); Amnesty International Report 2006 (London: Amnesty International, 2006), http://www.amnesty.org/en/library/info/POL10/001/2006 (accessed October 2, 2008).

[10] *Amnesty International Report 2008* (London: Amnesty International, 2008), http://thereport.amnesty.org/eng/regions/americas/colombia (accessed August 23, 2008).

[11] Earlier levels of aid were significantly lower, reaching a high of US$50 million dollars in FY2000. Levels of aid to Colombia in 2006 and 2007, at about US$730 million per year, remained on a par with 2005 levels. Figures for 2008 and 2009 have declined slightly to about US$650 million each year, with an increase in economic and social assistance and a slight decline in military aid. See Latin America Working Group Education Fund, Center for International Policy, and Washington Office on Latin America, *Just the Facts,* http://justf.org/Country?country=Colombia (accessed September 22, 2008).

only occasionally.[12] With rare exceptions, such as the Hollywood-style rescue of fifteen FARC hostages in mid-2008, neither peace efforts in Colombia nor the conflict itself has gotten much publicity.

The relative lack of attention to the conflict in Colombia is all the more surprising given that the U.S. Embassy in Bogotá, with some two thousand employees representing thirty-two agencies, is second in size only to that in Iraq.[13] Furthermore, the U.S. presence in Colombia on the ground has grown rapidly since 2000. U.S. troops and advisers are now legally capped at eight hundred, and U.S. civilian government contractors are capped at six hundred (plus foreign contractors).[14] About a dozen U.S. citizens have lost their lives in this conflict, and three U.S. military contractors were held hostage by the FARC from February 2003 to June 2008.

If the war in Colombia has received little attention, Colombia's drive for peace has received even less. Only recently have political scientists, sociologists, and other scholars even begun to analyze the role of civil society and non-governmental organizations (NGOs) in policymaking, while the study of the violence, or "violentology," has become a sophisticated and influential scholarly discipline in Colombian academic circles.[15] To date, the literature on peace initiatives has largely been in Spanish and has tended to focus on the

---

[12] On U.S. policy interests, see Virginia M. Bouvier, "Evaluating U.S. Policy in Colombia" (policy report from the International Relations Center Americas Program, May 11, 2005), http://americas.irc-online.org/reports/2005/0505colombia.html (accessed August 15, 2008).

[13] Bouvier, "Evaluating U.S. Policy in Colombia"; Virginia M. Bouvier, "Civil Society under Siege in Colombia," Special Report 114, (Washington, D.C.: United States Institute of Peace Press, February 2004), www.usip.org/pubs/specialreports/sr114.html (accessed August 15, 2008).

[14] See Virginia M. Bouvier, "Colombia Quagmire: Time for U.S. Policy Overhaul," *Foreign Policy in Focus,* Americas Program (Silver City, N.M.: Interhemispheric Resource Center, September 2003), www.americaspolicy.org/briefs/2003/0309colombia.html (accessed August 16, 2008); and Deborah Avant, "Privatizing Military Training," *Foreign Policy in Focus* 7, no. 6 (May 2002), www.fpif.org/papers/miltrain/box4.html (accessed August 16, 2008).

[15] See Daniel Pécaut, *Crónica de cuatro décadas de política colombiana* (Bogotá: Grupo Editorial Norma, 2006); Rubén Ardila, "Violence in Colombia: Social and Psychological Aspects," in *International Perspectives on Violence,* eds. Florence Denmark and Leonore Loeb Adler, 59–67 (Westport, Conn.: Praeger, 2004); G. Guzmán Campos, Orlando Fals Borda, and E. Umana Luna, *La violencia en Colombia* (Bogotá: Tercer Mundo Ediciones, 1964); Charles Bergquist, Ricardo Peñaranda, and Gonzalo Sánchez G., *Violence in Colombia: The Contemporary Crisis in Historical Perspective* (Wilmington, Del.: SR Books, 1992); Nazih Richani, *Systems of Violence: The Political Economy of War and Peace in Colombia* (Albany, N.Y.: SUNY, 2002); Cristina Rojas and Judy Meltzer, *Elusive Peace: International, National, and Local Dimensions of Conflict in Colombia* (New York: Palgrave Macmillan, 2005); Steven Dudley, *Walking Ghosts: Murder and Guerrilla Politics in Colombia* (New York: Routledge, 2004); Mario Murillo and Jesús Rey Avirama, *Colombia and the United States: War, Unrest, and Destabilization* (New York: Seven Stories Press, September 2003); Geoff L. Simons, *Colombia: A Brutal History* (London: Saqi, 2004); and numerous World Bank studies on conflict and economics, including Andrés Solimano, ed., *Colombia: Essays on Conflict, Peace, and Development* (2000); and World Bank Sector Study, *Violence in Colombia: Toward Peace, Partnerships, and Sustainable Development* (1998).

Colombian government's repeated and largely unsuccessful efforts to negotiate peace.[16]

Although human rights practitioners in Colombia and abroad have been aware of peace initiatives, and have sometimes even taken part in their construction, they have generally focused their work on discerning the patterns of violence and abuse in the daily manifestations of Colombia's conflict. Their most pressing task is to respond to human rights violations and to violations of international humanitarian law and norms governing the conduct of the armed conflict.[17] Nonetheless, organizations such as the Jesuit Center for Research and Popular Education (CINEP), the National Network of Initiatives for Peace and against War (REDEPAZ), and the United Nations Development Programme (UNDP) have developed databases that provide not only human rights information but also much-needed documentation of peace initiatives.[18]

Ironically, within the conflict-resolution field there is an inherent bias against actors who have eschewed violence in the pursuit of peace. Conflict analysis generally is performed with "conflict actors" in mind, and they usually are limited to those engaged in the armed struggle itself. Peacemakers practicing their profession generally seek the resolution of conflicts by promoting negotiations and accords between the parties to the conflict—usually though not always between an armed group or groups and the state.[19] Thus, mediation and facilitation most frequently involve dissuading, persuading,

---

[16] See Socorro Ramírez V. and Luis Alberto Restrepo M., *Actores en conflicto por la paz: El proceso de paz durante el gobierno de Belisario Betancur 1982–1986* (Bogotá: CINEP, 1989); Miguel Eduardo Cárdenas Rivera, ed., *La construcción del posconflicto en Colombia: enfoques desde la pluralidad* (Bogotá: CEREC, 2002); Edgar Téllez, Oscar Montes, and Jorge Lesmes, *Diario íntimo de un fracaso: Historia no contada del proceso de paz con las FARC* (Bogotá: Planeta, 2002); Mauricio García-Durán, S.J., especially *Movimiento por la paz en Colombia, 1998–2003* (Bogotá: CINEP/Colciencias, 2007); and "Alternatives to War: Colombia's Peace Processes," Special Issue, *Accord* 14 (London: Conciliation Resources, 2004), www.c-r.org/our-work/accord/colombia/spanish/movilizacion.php (accessed August 16, 2008).

[17] Some of the major non-governmental groups documenting violations of human rights and international humanitarian law within Colombia include Consultancy on Human Rights and Displacement (CODHES), Colombian Commission of Jurists, CINEP, and Justapaz. International groups include Amnesty International, International Committee of the Red Cross, International Crisis Group, Pan American Health Organization, United Nations High Commissioner for Human Rights, Human Rights Watch, Refugees International, and OAS, among others.

[18] See the database compiled by CINEP at www.cinep.org.co/datapaz_resumenes.htm (accessed August 16, 2008); UNDP's National Database of Best Practices for Overcoming the Conflict (Banco Nacional de Buenas Prácticas para Superar el Conflicto), www.saliendodelcallejon.pnud.org.co/banco_bpracticas.shtml (accessed August 16, 2008); and the ongoing REDEPAZ registry of peace initiatives, www.redepaz.org.co/ (accessed August 16, 2008).

[19] See I. William Zartman and J. Lewis Rasmussen, eds., *Peacemaking in International Conflict: Methods and Techniques* (Washington, D.C.: United States Institute of Peace Press, 1997); Chester A. Crocker, Fen Osler Hampson, and Pamela Aall, eds., *Taming Intractable Conflicts: Mediation in the Hardest Cases* (Washington, D.C.: United States Institute of Peace Press, 2004); Chester A. Crocker, Fen Osler Hampson, and Pamela Aall, eds., *Turbulent Peace: The Challenges of*

and engaging those with weapons—the would-be spoilers of a peace process. Victims and proponents of nonviolent conflict resolution are frequently left outside peace talks or, in some cases, given only token representation at the table. Amnesties or other arrangements have often let known murderers and "bad guys" off the hook, although increasingly, international human rights instruments and jurisprudence reject amnesty for crimes against humanity. Demobilization, disarmament, and reintegration (DDR) programs provide incentives to the perpetrators of violence to lay down their arms and are frequently held up as a necessary cost of pursuing peace. These programs sometimes create new tensions, because they privilege the perpetrators of abuses while ignoring the urgent needs of their victims, including the displaced.

Truth commissions, sometimes established to air the claims of victims, often fall prey to political considerations that favor reconciliation over truth or justice, because they seek to appease the illegal armed actors. Such models of transitional justice often overlook the tremendous resources that civil society stakeholders bring to the table, and the urgent need for victims' interests to be represented if the peace that is negotiated is to be sustainable.

In the development field, we see a similar bias against "peace" actors. Communities that are experiencing the most violence are often the targets of international intervention and assistance—to the neglect of communities that may have been successful in preventing or curtailing violence. Ironically, attention and increased resources to these conflicted communities appear to reward or create incentives for violent behavior. The relative invisibility of Colombian peace initiatives stems in part from the general invisibility of the sectors of the population that have been most victimized by violence, economic policies, and discrimination. Women, the rural sectors in general and the rural poor in particular, youth, Afro-Colombians, and the indigenous have a history of political, social, and economic exclusion in Colombia, and they are bearing the brunt of the armed conflict.[20] About one-third of Colombia's displaced population is of African descent, more than half are women, and half are under age fifteen. Despite a general economic upturn in recent years, at least 13 percent of Colombia's rural population is now displaced, and rural poverty in Colombia appears to be growing; the World Bank estimates that 80 percent of rural Colombians live in poverty, with 42 percent living in extreme poverty.[21] Afro-Colombians (the largest minority

---

Managing International Conflict (Washington, D.C.: United States Institute of Peace Press, 2001); and Crocker, Osler Hampson, and Aall, *Grasping the Nettle*.

[20] Angela Vera Márquez, Francisco Parra Sandoval, and Rodrigo Parra Sandoval, *Los estudiantes invisibles* (Ibagué, Colombia: Universidad del Rosario and Universidad de Ibagué, 2007).

[21] United States Agency for International Development, "Budget," www.usaid.gov/policy/budget/cbj2005/lac/co.html (accessed August 16, 2008); *NotiSur*, Latin American Data Base 16, no. 9 (March 3, 2006), http://ladb.unm.edu (accessed August 16, 2008); see also Edward E. Telles, *Incorporating Race and Ethnicity into the UN Millennium Development Goals*, Race Report (Washington, D.C.: Inter-American Dialogue, January 2007).

group in the country) and indigenous communities (about 2 percent of the population) suffer disproportionate poverty, displacement, environmental degradation, ill health, illiteracy, food insecurity, and an absence of state infrastructures to promote and protect their basic human rights.

Although research is beginning to tell us how the conflict affects these groups, little scholarly research has emerged yet that focuses on the role of these groups—or of displaced groups in general—in seeking nonviolent change.[22] These marginalized groups have high stakes in the conflict's resolution and, as this book documents, are active in many of the peace initiatives being carried out in Colombia's most contested zones. They are attempting to end the violence by forming peace communities, marginalizing actors advocating violence as a vehicle for change, learning about their rights and demanding the state protections to which they are entitled, and negotiating with armed actors to prevent or resolve violent conflicts on the ground.

Of course these civil society actors are not the only key to resolving Colombia's long-standing armed conflict, nor do they act in a vacuum. The government and the armed actors provide the broader context for their actions. Government efforts to deal with Colombia's armed actors have persisted nearly as long as the conflict itself—with intermittent success in varying degrees. National efforts, including the Rojas Pinilla amnesty in 1953 and the pact that established the National Front in 1957, led to a pause in "La Violencia," an era of violence between Liberal and Conservative partisans that took the lives of some 180,000 Colombians from about 1946 to 1965 and is considered the beginning of the current conflict.[23]

In the past twenty-five years, Colombian governments have alternated between strategies of war and strategies of peace in their efforts to deal with the many illegal armed actors that have defied the state's monopoly on force. Several governments have engaged in negotiations with guerrilla groups, leading to the disarmament of at least five guerrilla groups or factions thereof.[24]

---

[22] One important exception (available only in Spanish) is Esperanza Hernández Delgado, *Resistencia civil artesana de paz: Experiencias indígenas, afrodescendientes y campesinas* (Bogotá: Editorial Pontifícia Universidad Javeriana, 2004). Faith-based groups, such as the American Friends Service Committee, have focused their programming on these sectors and have produced educational resources for popular audiences. See Gretchen Alther, John Lindsay-Poland, and Sarah Weintraub, *Building from the Inside Out: Peace Initiatives in War-Torn Colombia* (Philadelphia: American Friends Service Committee and Fellowship of Reconciliation, November 2004), www.afsc.org/colombia/learn-about/Building-from-the-inside.pdf (accessed August 16, 2008).

[23] See UNDP, *Colombia's Conflict: Pointers on the Road to Peace, National Report on Human Development for Colombia—2003* (Bogotá: PNUD, 2003), 25, www.pnud.org.co/indh2003 (accessed August 23, 2008).

[24] These included the Ejército Popular de Liberación (EPL), or Popular Liberation Army; Partido Revolucionario de los Trabajadores (PRT), or Workers' Revolutionary Party; Movimiento Armado Quintín Lame (MAQL); Movimiento 19 de Abril (M-19); and, later, the Corriente de Renovación Socialista (CRS), or Socialist Renewal Group, a splinter group of the Ejército de Liberación Nacional (ELN), or National Liberation Army.

And successive presidents, beginning with Belisario Betancur, have, to no avail, sought peace agreements with each of the two major guerrilla groups: the FARC and the Ejército de Liberación Nacional (National Liberation Army, or ELN).

After the 2002 breakdown of peace talks that President Andrés Pastrana had initiated in 1998 with the FARC, the oldest and largest of the guerrilla groups, Álvaro Uribe was elected president based on his commitment to all-out military victory over the guerrillas. Although security conditions under Uribe's program of "democratic security" improved in many of the larger cities and towns, the violence and displacement has continued, particularly but not exclusively in the countryside. Uribe's tenure has been marked by a crackdown on left-wing guerrillas and the demobilization of the right-wing paramilitary forces known as the Self-Defense Forces of Colombia (Autodefensas Unidas de Colombia, or AUC). In April 2006, High Commissioner for Peace Luis Carlos Restrepo announced that, with the demobilization of more than thirty thousand paramilitary combatants, the largest demobilization in the history of Colombia had been achieved. While the demobilization has dramatically cut paramilitary violence in many places, the demobilized AUC, like the Hydra of myth, has generated dozens of new criminal and drug-trafficking organizations and networks that include thousands of ex-combatants and that continue to terrorize the civilian population.[25] Its limitations notwithstanding, the regulation of the DDR process through Law 975 (otherwise known as the Justice and Peace Law) has also opened limited opportunities to victims of paramilitary violence. It has created the political space for investigations and activism on the part of courageous victims; journalists; judges and prosecutors; human rights defenders; and a few politicians seeking truth, justice, and reparations.[26] These investigations have confirmed the insidious links between paramilitary violence and Colombia's political elites that, as of August 2008, had put thirty-three members of Congress behind bars and led to the indictment of dozens more.[27]

In Uribe's second term, which began in 2006, there was nonetheless hope that with the AUC officially demobilized, the president might turn his attention to negotiating peace with the FARC and ELN guerrillas. In 2005, the Colombian government had accepted a proposal by European governments to create a small demilitarized zone in the Valle del Cauca that would host

---

[25] For the quarterly reports to the OAS Permanent Council on the Mission to Support the Peace Process in Colombia (MAPP), see "OEA Acompaña Proceso de paz en Colombia," www.oas.org/documents/spa/colombia.asp. See also "Se calcula que hay entre 30 y 60 'bandas emergentes' surgidas de los grupos 'paras' desmovilizados," *El Tiempo*, December 10, 2006.

[26] See Lisa Haugaard, *The Other Half of the Truth: Searching for Truth, Justice, and Reparations for Colombia's Victims of Paramilitary Violence* (Washington, D.C.: Latin America Working Group Education Fund, June 2008), www.lawg.org/docs/the_other_half_of_the_truth.pdf.

[27] Juan Forero, "U.S. Extraditions Raise Concerns in Colombia," *Washington Post*, August 19, 2008.

discussions about a humanitarian accord to secure the exchange of hostages being held by the FARC for FARC prisoners serving time in Colombian jails. Sen. Álvaro Leyva, a negotiator during previous peace talks, initiated overtures to the FARC on the viability of such discussions.[28] In October 2006, when a car bomb exploded at the war college in Bogotá, injuring twenty-three people, Uribe immediately blamed the FARC, and the talks halted.[29]

Pressures for a humanitarian accord nonetheless mounted throughout 2007 and 2008. Following the tragic killing of eleven of the FARC hostages and public mobilizations against kidnapping (including the heroic march across southwestern Colombia by Gustavo Moncayo, the father of one of the hostages), President Uribe appointed Sen. Piedad Córdoba as facilitator for such an accord. Senator Córdoba in turn secured the appointment of Venezuelan president Hugo Chávez as an official mediator for a humanitarian accord.

After a flurry of activity and far-reaching international diplomacy, in late November 2007, President Uribe suspended the process and dismissed Chávez for initiating unauthorized contact with the Colombian army chief.[30] Córdoba and Chávez's efforts, as well as ongoing shuttle diplomacy by the French and Swiss governments, the International Committee of the Red Cross (ICRC), and other members of the diplomatic community, nonetheless resulted in the unilateral release of six of the hostages in early 2008 and the announcement of the imminent release of additional hostages.[31] Chávez, perhaps prematurely, called for recognition of the FARC and the ELN as belligerent forces and their removal from various international terrorist lists, provoking a rapid outcry from the Colombian government and the international community alike and raising questions about Chávez's capacity to serve as a neutral mediator in the conflict.

In 2008, a number of developments altered the political scenario and the prospects for a negotiated solution to Colombia's conflict. In March, the Colombian army raided a rebel camp in Ecuador and killed Raúl Reyes, the

---

[28] Cynthia J. Arnson et al., eds., *Colombia's Peace Processes: Multiple Negotiations, Multiple Actors,* Latin American Program Special Report (Washington, D.C.: Woodrow Wilson Center Press, December 2006).

[29] Proof of FARC involvement was not forthcoming, however, and there was some speculation that was later confirmed that the incident was a hoax created by the military itself. See Sam Logan, "Colombia's Latest Problems with Corruption," *Power and Interest News Report,* November 9, 2006, www.pinr.com/report.php?ac=view_report&report_id=580&language_id=1 (accessed August 16, 2008).

[30] See Virginia M. Bouvier, "New Hopes for Negotiated Solutions in Colombia" (working paper, September 2007, United States Institute of Peace), www.usip.org/pubs/working_papers/wp4_colombia.pdf; Adam Isacson, "Negotiations for Colombian Hostage Release Deserved More Time," Americas Program Commentary, December 4, 2007, http://americas.irc-online.org/am/4791.

[31] See Virginia M. Bouvier, "Colombia's Crossroads: The FARC and the Future of the Hostages," USIPeace Briefing, June 2008, at www.usip.org/pubs/usipeace_briefings/2008/06_17 colomb.

FARC's number-two leader, along with dozens of others, nearly touching off an international conflagration as Ecuador and Venezuela sent troops to the border and protested Colombia's violation of Ecuador's national territorial integrity. Intervention by the Organization of American States (OAS) tamped down the escalating tensions. Diplomatic efforts for a humanitarian accord were set back at least temporarily by the incident, since Reyes had been the FARC's primary interlocutor with the international community. Accusations by the Colombian government based on information found on Reyes's laptops charged individuals who had been seeking a humanitarian accord (including Venezuelan and Ecuadorian officials, and individuals such as Piedad Córdoba, Álvaro Leyva, and Jim Jones) with complicity in supporting the FARC. Although the charges were denied by all and no proofs were forthcoming, the atmosphere of distrust and ill will dramatically limited diplomatic options (at least in the short term).

The FARC suffered other setbacks in 2008. Early in the year, FARC secretariat member Iván Ríos was killed by his bodyguard. In March, the FARC's longtime patriarch, Manuel Marulanda, died of natural causes and was replaced by Alonso Cano. Together with the death of Reyes, this meant the unprecedented loss of three of the seven members of the FARC secretariat in a short time. Venezuelan president Chávez appealed publicly to the FARC to end its forty-year struggle, noting that "an armed guerrilla movement is out of place" in Latin America. He urged the new FARC leader Cano to release all hostages, including those from the United States, suggesting that releasing the hostages in a "great humanitarian gesture" could provide the necessary condition to initiate peace talks supported by a group of friendly nations.[32] Colombian government officials, including former hostage and current foreign minister Fernando Araújo, echoed the call for the hostages' release. Additionally, hundreds of FARC militants deserted in the first part of the year, including longtime front commanders, and close to two thousand FARC combatants were killed in action. In July, a military rescue operation successfully secured the release of former presidential candidate Ingrid Betancourt, three U.S. defense contractors, and eleven others held hostage for many years by the FARC. The rescue operation involved an elaborate ruse that included the impersonation of a humanitarian rescue team and journalist, unauthorized use of the ICRC emblem (in violation of international humanitarian law), infiltration of FARC ranks, and disruption of FARC communications.[33] The operation at least temporarily destroyed the confidence that diplomats had

---

[32] Simon Romero, "Chávez Urges Colombian Rebels to End Their Struggle," *New York Times*, June 9, 2008; "Chávez pide a las FARC liberación incondicional de todos los rehenes," Reuters, June 9, 2008, www.betancourt.info/indexFr.htm (accessed August 23, 2008); and "FARC Should Free Hostages: Chávez," Agence France-Presse, June 9, 2008.

[33] See "Colombian Military Used Red Cross Emblem in Rescue," www.cnn.com/2008/WORLD/americas/07/15/colombia.red.cross/ (accessed September 22, 2008).

been building so painstakingly with each of the parties, and severely hampered future ICRC efforts to engage in prisoner-exchange dialogues.

The military rescue operation and the perceived weakening of the FARC fueled popular sentiment that military victory over the FARC just might be possible after all, deepening divisions within civil society over the best course forward. Discussions about the humanitarian accord have faltered in this new context, although efforts to secure the release of the remaining hostages may continue to provide a lightning rod for mobilization efforts.

With regard to the ELN, progress in the first decade of the twenty-first century appeared more feasible, partly because the ELN was considered militarily weakened and less beholden to drug-trafficking interests than other armed groups.[34] Civil society, including religious leaders, has spearheaded repeated attempts to bring the ELN to the negotiating table. After facilitation efforts led by Mexican government officials stalled, a civil society commission created the Casa de Paz, or House of Peace, in late 2005 to facilitate consultation between Colombian civil society and the ELN.[35] This led to eight rounds of formal exploratory meetings in Cuba between the ELN and the Colombian government, mediated by international facilitators (Norway, Switzerland, and Spain).[36] In 2006 and 2007, these talks began to address substantive issues such as forced displacement, a cease-fire, and amnesty for imprisoned ELN combatants, and the parties reached agreement on a demining initiative in Samaniego, Nariño. By the end of 2007, however, following Chávez's call to grant the ELN belligerent status, and given last-minute changes inserted by government peace commissioner Restrepo into the basic agreement that was just about to be signed, talks were put on indefinite hold. As of this writing, discussions between the ELN and the government of Colombia have halted, and there are indications that some ELN fronts, particularly in the Nariño region, have entered the drug-trafficking arena full force. As with the stymied efforts for a humanitarian accord, the impasse has left civil society grappling to find a way to move forward.

Although there is little movement toward formal negotiations between the guerrillas and the government at the national level, a variety of track II initiatives are under way as churches, other non-governmental groups, and local and regional authorities throughout Colombia seek peace—often in alliance with disempowered groups. These groups are designing and implementing programs that offer alternatives to violence and promote attitudes

---

[34] The ELN emerged in the 1960s in northeastern Colombia with the support of urban middle-class students, oil workers, and priests inspired by Catholic liberation theology and the Cuban Revolution. Its vision and revolutionary project reflect these origins.

[35] See Andrés Valencia Benavides, *The Peace Process in Colombia with the ELN: The Role of Mexico*, Latin American Program Special Report (Washington, D.C.: Woodrow Wilson Center Press, March 2006), www.wilsoncenter.org/topics/pubs/Mexico's%20Role%20in%20the%20ELN%20 Peace%20Process1.pdf (accessed September 22, 2008).

[36] See Arnson et al., *Colombia's Peace Processes*, 5.

and structures that may help create a more inclusive political system capable of managing conflict nonviolently. At the local level, Colombians have carried out delicate negotiations with armed actors to release kidnap victims, prevent the displacement of communities, and allow safe passage of foods and medicines past armed blockades. Citizen initiatives have promoted electoral debates, addressed corruption, and created institutional vehicles for local populations to contribute to the formation of municipal and national economic-development plans and to hold local authorities accountable to their campaign promises. Peace communities, peace laboratories, zones of peace, no-conflict zones, humanitarian zones, sanctuary churches, and territories of nonviolence (or peace or peaceful coexistence) are flourishing in some of the most vulnerable conflict zones in Colombia. Governors of the southern states have developed proposals for a negotiated settlement to the conflict, as well as a development plan that proposes regional alternatives—including crop substitution and the development of small microenterprises based on traditional indigenous and Afro-Colombian agricultural practices—to the current fumigation policies of the central government. Mayors are seeking paths to more participatory governance and greater community input into development decisions. Youths have emerged as a source of tremendous dynamism in the quest for peace, spearheading drives for popular education and increased citizen engagement. Dozens of "municipalities of peace" have been established that have in turn led to a proliferation of constituent assemblies at the municipal and regional levels. These new structures are increasing citizen engagement, deepening the nature of democratic governance, and enhancing accountability in Colombia.

Project Overview

This volume brings together the experiences and insights of more than thirty seasoned and emerging authors. More than half the authors of this volume hail from Latin America (especially Colombia), with the remainder from the United States and Europe. Contributors include journalists, policy analysts, church leaders, human rights and development practitioners, and scholars who have engaged in or studied peace initiatives from a variety of historical, regional, and disciplinary perspectives, including political science, anthropology, history, psychology, education, and peace and conflict studies. Documenting and drawing lessons from Colombia's persistent struggles for peace, the authors provide a veritable encyclopedia of experiences in peacemaking and peacebuilding for those seeking to transform violent conflicts in other parts of the world.

The chapters have been separated into five major sections (framed by an introduction and conclusion) that focus on the different levels of peacemaking and peacebuilding. These sections address peace initiatives involving national actors and activities, institutional and sectoral initiatives, the role of gender and ethnicity in peacebuilding, local and regional initiatives, and the multiple roles of the international community in Colombia's search for peace. These areas sometimes overlap, and the divisions between them are often porous, but this arrangement lends itself to a variety of new analytical approaches to peace initiatives.

Following this introduction, Part I provides the historical context within which the conflict and initiatives for peace have evolved at the national level. It establishes a series of frameworks for interpreting the practices of governments, civil society, and armed actors over time and evaluates national peace efforts and processes. This section includes an assessment of the evolution of a national civil society movement for peace in Colombia as well as an analysis of official government peace initiatives in the past quarter century. Finally, it provides an in-depth analysis of the evolution of the two largest guerrilla groups active in Colombia today and of the paramilitary umbrella group AUC, which has recently demobilized. It reviews how Colombian norms and laws relating to truth, justice, and reparations have evolved with changing international norms of transitional justice and human rights and discusses the implications of these trends for future negotiations with illegal armed actors.

Part II includes case studies of specific peace initiatives occurring within the context of particular institutions and sectors of Colombian society. These include studies of efforts to promote peace through education, including government and non-governmental initiatives. They analyze the role of the Colombian Catholic Church in preparing the ground for peace and promoting reconciliation, and the institutional goals and structures that have emerged from within the church in response to the ongoing violence. Finally, the section includes case studies of the private sector's current and potential role in peacebuilding.

Part III is dedicated to the ways that gender and ethnicity are mobilized on behalf of peacebuilding. These chapters analyze the development of women's organizations for peace in Colombia, the indigenous traditions of resistance and mediation in the resource-rich and highly conflictive Cauca Department, and the evolution of community-based municipal development proposals known as Planes de Vida among the Cofán people in the Putumayo region.

Part IV provides further sampling of regional and local initiatives for peace that have persisted and blossomed in the midst of conflict like desert flowers on sandy rocks. This section discusses how the tremendous variations in natural and human resources have imbued peace initiatives with regional dimensions. It analyzes the peace communities that have emerged throughout Colombia and places these local zones of peace within a broader context of current definitions and assumptions in the conflict-resolution field. This section then turns to the particular inflections of peace initiatives in four of the most conflicted regions of Colombia: the Middle Magdalena Valley, Eastern Antioquia (Oriente Antioqueño), the Montes de María region of the northern coast, and Putumayo. In the first three regions, innovative programs known as "peace laboratories" are being piloted with the support of the European Union, the World Bank, and the Colombian government. Each of Colombia's three peace laboratories builds on existing development and peace programs linked through the national Network of Regional Development and Peace Programs (REDPRODEPAZ). In the marginalized southwestern state of Putumayo, an area on the Ecuadoran border dominated by the FARC and marked by the vagaries of coca cultivation and the war against drugs, local authorities have joined forces with sectors of civil society to forge a precarious coalition in opposition to all the armed actors.

In Part V, policy analysts from both sides of the Atlantic analyze the role of internationals in the search for peace in Colombia. The first case study of this section analyzes the implementation of the UNDP's Reconciliation and Development (REDES) program in Montes de María and analyzes the complex dynamics of international and local collaboration in promoting sustainable development and peace on the northern coast of Colombia. Subsequent chapters look respectively at U.S. government and U.S. NGO policies toward and practices in Colombia, the involvement of European governments and institutions—particularly the European Union—in Colombian peace initiatives, and an ongoing project of the Norwegian government to "skill" Colombia's security forces in international humanitarian law, conflict resolution, and peacebuilding.

The Conclusion analyzes the scope and texture of peace initiatives presented in the volume. It provides a framework for evaluating these initiatives, analyzes the factors that appear to contribute to their success or failure, teases out lessons for Colombia and elsewhere, and calls on internationals to find ways to support and strengthen these fragile and innovative endeavors. Finally, it points to new avenues where further research is needed.

The contributors to this volume offer a vision and an assessment of Colombia's historical and current experiences in peacemaking, peacebuilding, and negotiating with armed actors. They explore the ways in which civil society is engaged in conflict prevention, management, and transformation; human rights protection and promotion; peacemaking (prenegotiating); negotiating; and other peacebuilding activities. They provide insights into the negotiating practices of Colombia's armed actors, and what incentives might bring them to the peace table, and they suggest the need to understand more clearly the relationship between track I and track II peace efforts, as well as the need to build on synergies between the various sectors and levels of peacemaking and peacebuilding. Attempts to transform the Colombian conflict are as complex as the conflict itself. Nonetheless, peace initiatives such as those discussed in this volume merit greater consideration than they have heretofore received, for they may well contain the seeds for the conflict's transformation.

PART I
NATIONAL INITIATIVES FOR PEACE

2

Origins, Evolution, and Lessons of the Colombian Peace Movement

Adam Isacson and Jorge Rojas Rodríguez

On July 30 and 31, 1998, more than four thousand Colombians crammed into the Luis Ángel Arango Library in the colonial heart of downtown Bogotá. They had come, a week before the inauguration of a new president who had promised to negotiate peace with guerrilla groups, to participate in a singular event: a Permanent Assembly of Civil Society for Peace. The library's auditorium overflowed with a highly unusual combination of people. Prominent politicians, church hierarchs, and business leaders rubbed shoulders with intellectuals, union organizers, human rights activists, international accompaniers, and hundreds of indigenous and campesino leaders who had spent long hours in buses from their remote localities. They had come, in the words of the Permanent Assembly's memoir of the event, "To think about the country we want so dearly: a Colombia at peace, with solidarity and kindness for our children; a Colombia that we sadly do not have, due to our own inability to resolve our differences."[1] Although it did not create a detailed road map to peace, the assembly—the first of several similar gatherings to be held over the next few years—marked a moment of optimism and signaled a new level of organization and clout for Colombia's young civil society movement for peace.

Thousands of Colombians met again during May 9–11, 2002, in the Tequendama Hotel in downtown Bogotá. Facing the likely victory within weeks of a presidential candidate who promised to intensify the war, they had come for a National Congress for Peace and Country. The crowd of participants was less heterogeneous than those who had met four years earlier. Gone were the business leaders, centrist politicians, and other elite actors. The rest had come, in what Jorge Rojas Rodríguez has written elsewhere, for "a last des-

---

[1] Asamblea Permanente por la Paz, *Memoria: Acto de instalación* (Bogotá: Asamblea Permanente por la Paz, 1998).

perate attempt by civilians to get dialogue and negotiations restarted," less than three months after the acrimonious collapse of peace talks with Colombia's largest guerrilla group.[2] Although the meeting was not a disaster, many participants were unhappy with the result of the congress; differences of opinion among participants made it difficult even to elaborate a final declaration. It would be some time before a broad-based national gathering would be attempted again.

Much took place between the 1998 Permanent Assembly and the 2002 National Congress to determine the two events' very different atmospheres and outcomes. These gatherings, however, were just two of many significant milestones in the short but remarkable history of Colombia's civil society peace movement. This history is brief: peace activism in Colombia can trace its origins back only about fifteen or perhaps twenty years. It is also tumultuous, involving a period of rapid growth, a period of daunting challenges, and, lately, a period of retrenchment.

This history is not linear, though, nor is the outlook entirely pessimistic. Colombia's civil society peace movement is currently at a crossroads, and it has a number of strategic choices and realignments to consider. When the national political context—a major determining factor—again becomes more favorable, the movement is likely to reemerge as a mature, active, and indispensable participant in Colombia's search for a way out of its conflict. Despite the frustrations of the past few years, there is reason to be optimistic about the long-term health of Colombia's peace movement.

The Rise of Colombia's Peace Movement

Little civil society peace activism existed in Colombia until the early to mid-1990s. Although the governments of Belisario Betancur (1982–86), Virgilio Barco (1986–90), and César Gaviria (1990–94) carried out talks with guerrilla groups, they did so with almost no accompaniment by organized citizens. This period did see a marked increase in non-governmental organizing, including the appearance of the first domestic human rights groups, but few were calling specifically for a negotiated end to the violence or were actively following official negotiations.

Those who did involve themselves came largely from the urban middle class or wealthy sectors, many of them moved by the traumatic aftermath of the Movimiento 19 de Abril (M-19) guerrilla group's disastrous 1985 takeover of the Colombian Palace of Justice. With women's groups playing an especially prominent role, their work focused mainly on educating the citizenry, seeking to raise the profile of negotiations and nonviolence in general without much specificity to their demands. In September 1987, citizens' groups

---

[2]Jorge Rojas Rodríguez, "Political Peacebuilding: A Challenge for Civil Society," *Accord* 14 (2004), www.c-r.org/accord/col/accord14/index.shtml (accessed August 17, 2008).

declared the first "Peace Week" (Semana por la Paz) of educational and awareness-raising events, a tradition that continues every September. Some supported the Barco government's successful negotiations with the M-19 and a few smaller guerrilla groups, a process that led to rewriting Colombia's constitution in 1991.

The Constituent Assembly that wrote this constitution had little input from citizens organized around the subject of peace. Organizations advocating human rights and the rights of traditionally excluded sectors, however, exercised much influence. A sort of hybrid human rights–plus–peace group, Viva la Ciudadanía (roughly, Long Live the Citizenry), formed in 1991 to pressure the government to comply with the new constitution's mandates for increased democratic participation and social expenditure, among other reforms.

Although these citizen efforts were small and low in visibility, they did provide space—in a polarized and violent political climate—in which to search for common ground and push for talks. At least as important, they aided the formation of informal networks linking activists throughout the country.

The external context, especially public opinion, has always been a determinant of the strength or weakness of Colombia's civil society peace movement, and it certainly explains why citizen peace activism was almost nonexistent in the 1980s and early 1990s. Not only was this a period when the idea of forming citizens' groups was rather new, it was a time when Colombia's conflict with guerrilla groups was far less prominent in the national consciousness. Although groups such as the M-19 drew episodic attention through high-profile actions in urban areas, Colombia's guerrillas were much less visible in general, and their numbers were a fraction of what they are today. (In the mid-1980s, all guerrilla groups combined had perhaps seven thousand to eight thousand members, compared with about twenty thousand two decades later.) They were incapable of carrying out large-scale actions, and they were largely relegated to neglected zones with low population density. Most were already in some sort of dialogue with the government, and once the Berlin wall fell, many Colombians expected the guerrillas simply to fade away along with the Soviet bloc. At the time, Colombia's Medellín and Cali cartels attracted far more attention (particularly from Washington) than did the guerrillas, and they appeared to pose more of an immediate security threat.

After 1992, though, the external context began to shift, and Colombia's conflict became much harder to ignore. In 1992, talks with the Fuerzas Armadas Revolucionarias de Colombia (FARC) and Ejército de Liberación Nacional (ELN) guerrillas broke down once and for all, and the Gaviria government opted for a military solution, declaring "total war." Peace activists throughout the country responded by 1993; many came together to form the

National Network of Initiatives for Peace and against War (REDEPAZ), a network of mostly local and regional peace initiatives, to push for a national agenda for renewed negotiations. REDEPAZ continues to be one of Colombia's principal civil society peace groups.

The Colombian government's "total war" strategy did not get far, and guerrillas and paramilitaries—especially the FARC and AUC, funded by the drug trade—grew enormously during the 1990s. By 1996–98, the FARC was launching frequent offensives, including attacks on municipal county seats, and battalion-size invasions of remote military bases. Guerrilla kidnappings became more brazen, making travel between cities risky by the late 1990s. For their part, the paramilitaries dramatically expanded their territorial dominions, largely by massacring or displacing civilians in the areas they sought to control.

As numbers of dead, disappeared, kidnapped, and displaced people skyrocketed, citizen tolerance for the violence wore thin. Meanwhile, the government of President Ernesto Samper, severely crippled by allegations of campaign donations from the Cali drug cartel, seemed unable to respond. As Colombia's civil society peace movement endeavored to fill this vacuum, it entered a period of very rapid growth.

The Catholic Church, whose priests and lay workers had always had to mediate with armed groups at the local level, came to play a prominent national role in the search for peace. In 1995, the Colombian Conference of Bishops formed the National Conciliation Commission, a group of notable citizens that has become the church's principal peace-promotion agency.

Secular citizen groups also rushed to fill the gap during the late 1990s. A prominent and vocal women's peace group, the Pacific Route of Women (Ruta Pacífica), formed in 1996. College students and professors formed the Network of Universities for Peace and Coexistence in 1997. Planeta Paz, a group seeking to incorporate underrepresented "popular" sectors into national peace efforts, and the Ideas for Peace Foundation, the business sector's main vehicle for peace promotion, both formed in 1999.

Assisted by REDEPAZ and UNICEF, a group of young Colombians organized an October 1996 "Children's Mandate for Peace," in which 2.7 million Colombian children cast a symbolic vote to end the fighting. A year later, civil society peace groups and business and church leaders joined forces to organize a "Citizen Mandate for Peace." On October 26, 1997, in a nonbinding ballot measure during municipal elections, the vast majority of voters—ten million Colombians in all—affirmed their support for a peaceful end to the fighting.

Although these were impressive shows of general support for negotiations in principle, they did little to indicate how, or under what conditions, a peace process should take place. Nonetheless, they signaled the birth of an active, multisector movement of concerned citizens. They also made clear to politicians (and future candidates) that any effort to open negotiations would not only enjoy the support of this movement but would also find favor among the general public.

To regularize contact with rapidly proliferating peace groups, President Samper won passage of a law creating a new National Peace Council, a thirty-member advisory body composed of half high-government officials and half civil society peace leaders representing various sectors. By law, the council was to meet once a month to help set the government's peace policy and to channel civil society's demands and recommendations.

By 1998, as news of guerrilla military victories and paramilitary blood-baths shook Bogotá, civil society peace groups began to play a more direct role. A delegation of civic leaders met with ELN commanders in Mainz, Germany; the guerrillas agreed to a prompt initiation of formal negotiations, beginning with a months-long "convention" with civil society groups to develop a negotiating agenda (an event that has yet to take place). A similar NGO delegation met with paramilitary chiefs in the northwestern Colombian region of Nudo de Paramillo, a stronghold of the right-wing groups. The paramilitaries signed a joint declaration committing themselves to modest (and to date unfulfilled) improvements in their adherence to international humanitarian law.

Large peace gatherings became a frequent tool of activism. On May 19, 1998, for example, one year after an assassin took the lives of two prominent human rights activists, hundreds of thousands of Colombians marched to demand peace. The peaceful demonstrations were the largest street protests that Bogotá had seen in decades. Candidates in Colombia's 1998 presidential elections took notice. Peace—more precisely, the perceived likelihood that a candidate could begin meaningful negotiations with the guerrillas—became a make-or-break issue in the contest between Liberal Horacio Serpa and Conservative Andrés Pastrana. What ultimately won the election for the Conservative candidate was a meeting in June 1998, shortly before runoff voting, between Pastrana aide Víctor G. Ricardo and FARC leader Manuel Marulanda, in the jungles of southern Colombia. The meeting made clear that Pastrana was the candidate with whom the guerrillas were most willing to talk. "Those guys took a big gamble and beat us," said Serpa. "It [was] a perfect political move."[3] Had it not been for intense pressure from Colombia's peace movement, it is doubtful that the Pastrana campaign would have taken such a bold step.

Peace activism continued to gather momentum as the new Pastrana government sought to get talks with the FARC under way. The Permanent Assembly of Civil Society for Peace, with extensive support from the church's

---

[3] Edgar Téllez, Óscar Montes, and Jorge Lesmes, *Diario íntimo de un fracaso* (Bogotá: Planeta, 2002), 34.

National Conciliation Commission and the oil workers' union, Unión Sindical Obrero de la Industria del Petrolero (USO), held its massive meeting shortly before Pastrana's inauguration. The Permanent Assembly would become the first of several "convergences"—huge, often chaotic, multiday, multisector meetings at which peace promoters from all over the country would assert civil society's role in negotiations and seek consensus on a common strategy.

As a tool for movement building, the convergence model had great strengths and weaknesses. Bringing together such a wide variety of activists under one roof, particularly in a country as fragmented as Colombia, was a major organizational feat. It doubtless strengthened the movement by easing networking and information sharing between groups that otherwise would have had little contact. It certainly inspired participants by demonstrating their sheer numbers and diversity. It also gave many participants—especially those from regions where speaking out is dangerous—a chance to dare to speak truths and opinions that, in another context, could get them killed. One of the greatest organizational achievements of the Permanent Assembly was to improve relations between peace activists and human rights defenders, who had differed sharply on the question of impunity.

On the other hand, it is plainly impossible to construct a coherent agenda for political action—much less a set of recommendations to guide a formal negotiating process—at an event attended by four thousand people. As one would expect, the Permanent Assembly's plenary sessions ended up producing vague statements of principle on a wide range of topics, from the importance of negotiations to the need to respect human rights and adopt a more equitable development model. All these are worthy goals, but the Permanent Assembly and other convergences usually failed to produce detailed recommendations for how to achieve them. "Beyond a 'no' to barbarity, a 'yes' to peace and a release of deeply held feelings, it has not been easy to define or to transmit specific, proposal-driven or practical messages that truly 'educate' the general public," noted one observer.[4]

Progress Slows

The peak year for Colombia's civil society peace movement may have been 1999. While the Pastrana government was taking halting steps in its talks with the FARC and ELN, organizing reached its highest levels. As Carlos Fernández, Mauricio García-Durán, and Fernando Sarmiento observed, as part of a mobilization known simply as the "No Más" campaign, "more than 2.5 million people took part in 40 marches between April and September,

---

[4] Antonio E. Sanguino Páez [director, Corporación Nuevo Arco Iris; Secretario Técnico, Colombia Va], "Colombia Va y el movimiento social de paz," *Revista Foro* (Bogotá) 40 (December 2000–January 2001): 456.

and more than 8 million people mobilized on 24 October 1999, participating in marches and events in more than 180 municipalities the length and breadth of the country."[5]

But the news was not all good. Paradoxically, the FARC-government negotiating process helped weaken the same civil society peace organizations that had struggled to get it started in the first place. The Pastrana government handled the FARC negotiations in a most exclusionary fashion: the new president chose to manage his peace policy among an inner circle of close confidants. No recognized civil society peace leaders ever served as negotiators, nor were they consulted with any frequency by the Pastrana government's high commissioners for peace. Beyond civil society leaders, even leaders of the powerful opposition Liberal Party, the military, and key ministers in Pastrana's cabinet were generally left in the dark, with few opportunities to contribute to peace policy. Pastrana hardly ever convened the National Peace Council even though its principal designers, among them the late former defense minister, Gilberto Echeverri, had intended this advisory body to be a permanent government institution, not just a program of the administration in power.[6]

The FARC, for its part, appeared to be content to leave non-governmental peace leaders out of the picture; the guerrillas tended to view activists—who, unlike them, had chosen to attempt social change without taking up arms—as either misguided, petit bourgeois enemies, or people who were simply not powerful enough to merit dialogue. As a result, as Congressman Gustavo Petro, a former M-19 guerrilla, complained at the time, "The peace process has no citizens. That is its main weakness. The process is in the hands of the masters of war, call them what they are."[7]

Civil society organizations sought to have their voices heard. They traveled frquently to the *despeje*, the clearance zone established in 1998 in San Vicente de Caguán for peace discussions with the FARC. They produced high-quality analyses and policy recommendations. Nonetheless, these efforts almost always met with a frustrating silence from the FARC and government negotiators, who were generally preoccupied with a process that appeared to do little more than lurch from crisis to crisis amid quibbling over procedural matters.

The government and the FARC did agree to create a mechanism for incorporating non-governmental groups' input: the "thematic forums" (*foros temáticos*) or "public hearings," a periodic series of discussions held in the demili-

---

[5] Carlos Fernández, Mauricio García-Durán, and Fernando Sarmiento, "Peace Mobilization in Colombia 1978–2002," *Accord* 14 (2004), www.c-r.org/accord/col/accord14/index.shtml (accessed August 17, 2008).

[6] "Consejo de Paz, en el limbo," *El Espectador* (Bogotá), February 22, 1999.

[7] "Crece apoyo para abrir el plan de paz," *El Espectador*, February 8, 1999.

tarized zone in southern Colombia, where talks were taking place. Organized by a thematic committee composed of government and guerrilla representatives, the forums were open to the public and televised nationally. They followed a sort of town hall meeting format in which citizens each had five minutes at the microphone to elaborate proposals on the day's chosen topic. Guerrilla moderators listened to the speeches. But there was no feedback and no effort to follow through on the participants' proposals. The hearings (*audiencias*), sociologist Daniel Pécaut wrote, "completely reduce civil society's capacity for expression, to the point where its representatives resemble subjects presenting letters of petition to viceroys."[8] Jorge Bernal of Viva la Ciudadanía noted, "According to the FARC's own statistics, 16,000 people have passed through the hearings in the Caguán, but to date the country has not seen any synthesis of these citizens' proposals."[9]

For their part, civil society peace groups viewed the FARC talks with widely varying degrees of enthusiasm. While some sought a greater role in the process, others saw the entire model as flawed. Seeing no point in pursuing dialogue amid conflict, some called either for a preliminary cease-fire or at least for an agreement to respect international humanitarian law in the fighting. Others saw the two groups at the table as unrepresentative and replaceable elements in a conflict with much deeper structural causes. They chose to focus their struggle on achieving a larger peace based on social justice and a culture of nonviolence. The wide divergence in these approaches to the Pastrana dialogues made it virtually impossible to hold together a broad civil society coalition. By forcing people to go beyond vague calls for peace and decide whether and how to support a concrete—and far from ideal—peace strategy, the Pastrana government's negotiations sharply divided the coalition of peace groups.

In mid-1999, REDEPAZ and Viva la Ciudadanía joined with the Free Country Foundation (Fundación País Libre, an antikidnapping organization headed by newspaper publishing heir and future vice president Francisco Santos) to organize a "Gran Marcha" for peace, to be held in October of that year. Business-sector representatives, many of them brought in through connections to the Free Country Foundation, actively funded and promoted the event. On its surface, the resulting No Más marches were an enormous success; about 10 million Colombians—one in four citizens—took to the streets on October 24, 1999. However, Colombia's mass media portrayed the march as an expression of impatience with the Pastrana government's peace talks—which had made no progress after nearly a year—and a protest against the guerrillas' practice of kidnapping. This was not the intention of the nonelite

---

[8] Daniel Pécaut, *Guerra contra la sociedad* (Bogotá: Espasa, 2001), 299.

[9] Jorge Bernal Medina [Corporación Viva la Ciudadanía], "Estado y perspectivas del movimiento ciudadano por la paz," *Revista Foro* 40 (December 2000–January 2001).

march organizers and participants, who had sought to use the event not to denounce the guerrillas but to create pressure on both sides to move the negotiations forward. The No Más marches ended up exacerbating divisions and mistrust between elite, or business, and nonelite (and usually left-of-center) participants in the peace movement, and these divisions persist to this day. Although the business sector had originally taken part in the Permanent Assembly and similar processes, by late 1999 it had broken off from nonelite activists and taken refuge in the more narrowly focused No Más campaign. Other elite sectors, such as the church hierarchy, the media, and key politicians, also began to distance themselves. The role of the Episcopal Council's National Conciliation Commission became much less visible.

This schism dealt a strong blow to the Permanent Assembly of Civil Society for Peace and similar efforts to create a broad front to exert pressure for peace. Jorge Bernal wrote in 2000 about the impact of these groups' exit on the Permanent Assembly:

> Another event that began to mark the weakening of the Assembly was the indelicate handling of relations with the Catholic Church and the National Conciliation Commission, active promoters of the Assembly, leading to their rapid withdrawal from the organization at the national level. Something similar can be noted in its relations with business sectors that were involved in the Assembly's original development.[10]

The Permanent Assembly also suffered from structural problems, a predictable consequence of a convergence—by definition a temporary phenomenon—that dared to call itself "permanent." Plenary meetings in Cali in 1999 and Medellín in 2001 drew thousands, but many were frustrated by the group's inability to make clear and specific recommendations. Although its participatory decision-making model was laudable, the assembly's insistence on consensus led either to what Bernal has called "the dictatorship of the minority" or utter paralysis. Álvaro Campos noted that "the internal discussions about how to organize itself, which armed actor deserved strongest condemnation, or the role of social reforms in peace, caused a loss of political clarity and relevance."[11] As a result, few of the group's public declarations offered timely, explicit, and operable recommendations to guide either government-guerrilla negotiations or the promotion of peace in general. As elite groups left the assembly's membership, it lost significant convening power but gained in clarity (with an evident leftward drift in its pronouncements). The Permanent Assembly remains active today, particularly in ongoing efforts to get talks restarted with the ELN.

---

[10] Ibid., 21.

[11] Álvaro E. Campos, "The National Conciliation Commission," *ReVista: Harvard Review of Latin America* (Spring 2003), www.drclas.harvard.edu/revista/articles/view/258 (accessed September 6, 2008).

The breach within the movement between left and right and between ruling-class representatives and everyone else kept widening in 2000, as the peace process continued to stumble and violence continued to escalate. The final blow was Plan Colombia, or at least the news that in mid-2000 the U.S. Congress had approved hundreds of millions of dollars in new military and fumigation assistance in the name of "peace, prosperity, and the strengthening of the state."

Business sector and other elite backers of negotiations, who were far more invested in the existing political and economic system and saw military pressure on the guerrillas as a perfectly acceptable way to speed a peace agreement, generally supported this sharp increase in military aid. But peace activists from labor, human rights, environmental, student, indigenous, Afro-Colombian, campesino, and politically similar sectors were outraged by Plan Colombia. The aid package did great damage to the effort to maintain a broad-based peace movement. Noted one peace leader, "Some [activists and groups] felt that while the plan's military strategy should be shunned, the social aid deserved support and participation. Others felt that no component of the plan merited participation. Other commentators said that whoever criticized Plan Colombia supported violence in the country."[12]

In June 2000, seventy-two human rights, peace, and "popular-sector" organizations signed a letter rejecting Plan Colombia as "part of an authoritarian concept of national security exclusively based on a strategy against narcotics," which, among other things, "leads to the escalation of the social and armed conflict."[13] They called for "an agreement among the various actors of Colombian society and the international community, where civil society can be a definite part of the dialogue so as to find solutions to the conflict and to build a stable and sustainable peace."[14]

With this goal in mind, nearly all peace organizations joined forces in a coalition called Paz Colombia (Peace Colombia), which hosted a large meeting of more than three hundred people in Costa Rica in October 2000. Unlike past convergences, this one sought to include the broadest spectrum of participants. Many representatives of the Colombian government attended, as did participants from thirty-two foreign governments and several UN agencies, and three spokespeople from the ELN. The FARC turned down the invitation, saying that it already had a space for such dialogue: the demilitarized zone in southern Colombia.

Unfortunately, Paz Colombia was unable to achieve its goal of "an agreement among the various actors . . . to find solutions to the conflict." By cast-

---

[12] Ana Teresa Bernal, "Red Nacional de Iniciativas por la Paz y Contra la Guerra," *Revista Foro* 40 (December 2000–January 2001): 27.

[13] Center for International Policy, "Statement by Seventy-three Colombian Non-Governmental Organizations," June 2000, http://ciponline.org/colombia/062001.htm (accessed September 6, 2008).

[14] Ibid.

ing its net wide to include the government, the business sector, and others who supported Plan Colombia and more military aid, Paz Colombia guaranteed that the search for consensus would be long and acrimonious. Efforts to agree on the texts of common declarations regarding issues such as human rights and land tenure dragged on into the early-morning hours, as those present refused to give ground. The resulting declarations ended up with softened language on some of the thorniest issues—or avoided them entirely.

All present did, however, appear to endorse a very concrete suggestion for moving the stalled government-FARC talks forward: they called on Pastrana and FARC leader Marulanda to meet and declare a hundred-day bilateral suspension of offensive military operations, during which the negotiators would focus on the talks' real agenda, with no procedural issues or outside combat to distract them.[15] Unfortunately, like most proposals from civil society, this one never received a response from either of the groups at the negotiating table.

Peace movement leaders were aware of the growing rifts and lack of clarity impeding their progress and ability to participate fully in the national peace agenda. With generous help from international donors, they endeavored to patch things up and develop a more coherent strategy. The Netherlands Embassy launched Colombia Va (Go Colombia), bringing together twenty peace, human rights, and sectoral groups to develop a common work plan. The three-year plan focused not just on a government-guerrilla agreement but also on a larger objective of a national peace accord. Colombia Va chose two objectives to guide its work and grant making: "the collective building of a nation-building project that could be the nucleus of a civil society peace agenda" and "political mobilization and action to develop the power and political capacity to make this project a reality."[16] This effort ultimately had little impact, however, for at least two reasons. First, some peace groups did not participate fully, out of concern that Colombia Va would duplicate what they were already trying to do, and thus put them out of business. Second, although Colombia Va had explicitly political objectives, it avoided developing a specific strategy for peace movements' involvement in Colombian politics. This contradiction—seeking to stay outside the fray while influencing what went on within it—proved unworkable.

By 2000, peace movement leaders, again with outside support, sought to change their strategic decision-making model. Instead of proposing a

---

[15] Permanent Assembly of Civil Society for Peace, REDEPAZ, INDEPAZ, et al., in a joint press release, "Reunión cumbre de Pastrana y Marulanda proponen organizaciones de paz," Bogotá, November 18, 2000, http://viejo.nuestracolombia.net/m_colombiasemanal/hechosdepaz.htm#REUNION%20CUMBRE%20DE%20PASTRANA%20Y%20MARULANDA%20PROPONENORGANIZACIONES%20DE%20PAZ (accessed September 6, 2008).

[16] Páez, "Colombia Va y el movimiento social de paz," 9.

new convergence or another effort aimed, like Paz Colombia, at providing a short-term response, groups generally agreed that they should step back, look at their larger strategy, and give a decision-making role to a smaller steering committee. Most major peace, human rights, and social movement organizations agreed that each group would continue carrying out its own peace activities without any new "umbrella" but that a seven-member linkage commission (*comisión de enlace*) would help coordinate the various groups' peace strategy. This strategy, the members agreed, would include mobilizing and educating the citizenry for peace, creating political support for the Pastrana government's sputtering dialogues with guerrilla groups, building solidarity with the conflict's victims, and encouraging international accompaniment.

The linkage commission met regularly in 2000 and especially 2001, and cooperation and coordination improved noticeably. Unfortunately, during this period, the government-guerrilla negotiations entered what turned out to be their death throes. The talks were suspended several times, while increased high-profile guerrilla attacks on civilians precipitously diminished public support for the negotiations.

Nonetheless, peace groups guided by the linkage commission worked with increasing sophistication to try to salvage the flagging talks. During fall 2001, as the process appeared headed toward oblivion, peace movement groups made public several concrete, timely, detailed proposals for getting the talks restarted. These included a proposed delegation to the negotiation zone to set up an "encounter with citizen groups," in which civil society leaders would mediate, helping the negotiators find a way out of their present impasse and returning them to the talks' agreed agenda.[17] In January 2002, intense pressure from civil society peace groups helped convince the Pastrana government—which was ready to walk away from the FARC talks—to allow James LeMoyne, the UN secretary-general's special representative for Colombia, to play a similar mediating role.

Decline

In the end, neither Lemoyne's last-ditch efforts nor the peace movement's increasingly creative and practical contributions were enough to save the Pastrana government's talks with guerrilla groups. The FARC talks collapsed in February 2002, after guerrillas hijacked a plane and kidnapped a senator; talks with the ELN—which had always received less attention from the Pastrana government—fell apart in May.

---

[17]See, for instance, Center for International Policy, letter to President Andrés Pastrana from several Colombian organizations, November 21, 2001, www.ciponline.org/colombia/01112101. htm (accessed August 18, 2008); or Center for International Policy, "Aportes ciudadanos a la mesa de negociación gobierno—Farc-Ep," November 26, 2001, http://ciponline.org/colombia/112601.htm (accessed August 18, 2008).

"It is necessary to promote civil resistance to war and to reaffirm the democratic building of peace and the nation," read a communiqué issued by several civil society peace groups the day after the FARC talks broke down. "We cannot succumb in the face of an ephemeral triumphalism from an establishment that did not understand that a negotiation takes place between two sides, nor before a guerrilla group whose political commitment to peace was belied by its own acts of war."[18] Beyond this "a plague on both your houses" rhetoric, however, the civil society peace movement knew that the talks' breakdown left their own strategy in a shambles. As Jorge Rojas Rodríguez has noted elsewhere, "Such almost unconditional support [for the talks] failed to take into account the need for a strategic proposal should the talks break down, and underestimated the population's weariness with the lack of tangible results."[19]

The peace movement not only lacked a "Plan B," it also found itself with a public relations problem. Colombian public opinion, which had played such a decisive role in encouraging the start of the talks in 1998, cheered their demise three and a half years later. February 2002 saw Álvaro Uribe move into first place in public opinion polls before the May elections. Uribe, a former governor and a third-party candidate who had been considered a right-wing fringe figure only months earlier, was one of the Pastrana talks' most vocal critics. The Uribe campaign meanwhile helped solidify the left-right split in the peace movement, recruiting many supporters from the elite/business wing of the late-1990s civil society peace effort. The Free Country Foundation's Francisco Santos became Uribe's vice presidential running mate, while Luis Carlos Restrepo, the coordinator of the 1997 Citizen Mandate for Peace, became Uribe's high commissioner for peace (chief negotiator).

Faced with an increasingly hostile public mood, space for peace activism shrank dramatically. Advocates of renewed negotiations were reviled as "soft" on the guerrillas—or, worse, as supporters of the armed groups. In February 2003, when peace activists gathered to demonstrate near the site of Bogotá's El Nogal social club, where a guerrilla car bomb had killed dozens, they were shouted down and harassed by passersby and a larger crowd of counterdemonstrators. National peace groups became subject to increased surveillance and suspicion; the most extreme example has been the Permanent Assembly, which has had its offices invaded and searched on several occasions, its staff interrogated at gunpoint, and its files and computers stolen or confiscated both by security forces and by armed men in plain clothes.[20]

---

[18] "Resistencia civil a la guerra," statement from several Colombian organizations (Bogotá: February 21, 2002), www.nadir.org/nadir/initiativ/agp/free/colombia/txt/2002/0223 resistencia_civil.htm (accessed September 6, 2008).

[19] Rojas Rodríguez, "Political Peacebuilding."

[20] U.S. Office on Colombia, letter from U.S. organizations to Colombian President Álvaro Uribe, Washington, D.C., December 22, 2004, www.usofficeoncolombia.org/signon/asambleadec04. pdf (accessed July 10, 2006).

At the local level, peace and human rights activists ran up against the Uribe government's efforts to enlist the civilian population more directly in the antiguerrilla fight. Many activists were rounded up in mass arrests and accused of supporting guerrillas; most were later released for lack of evidence. "Peace communities"—villages whose residents sought to exclude the presence of all armed groups, including the military—became a particular target of hostility from President Uribe and the security forces.

Meanwhile, the unsatisfying experience of the May 2002 National Congress for Peace and Country signaled the decline of the convergence model. Large gatherings—such as the Thematic World Social Forum gathering in Cartagena in July 2003, and the Permanent Assembly's September 2003 and October 2006 meetings in Bogotá—did occur, but these were largely confined to a rump of leftist, human rights, peace, and popular movement organizations, received little attention in the media, and produced few new ideas. Movement leaders complained about these events' near invisibility in the Colombian press, although media relations have, in fact, been a problem for civil society peace efforts for years. Worse, a more frequent feature of such meetings was the expression of dissatisfaction of organizations based in areas outside of Colombia's three or four biggest cities. They felt that these big plenary sessions did not give them sufficient voice. Resentment against members of Bogotá-based "national" organizations, with their university degrees, abstract analyses, European funding, and ignorance of the daily reality of life in conflict zones, surfaced more and more frequently at convergences.

President Uribe had made clear that he would negotiate with any armed group that first declared a cease-fire. Surprisingly, the progovernment paramilitaries—with the mediation of bishops from paramilitary-dominated areas of northern Colombia—accepted Uribe's offer, launching negotiations in December 2002. This process, which continues today, has had very little accompaniment by Colombia's civil society peace movement.

Peace organizations rooted in the business community and the church hierarchy were more accepting of the process; although they offered much criticism of the way the talks were being handled, their critiques have been largely constructive. Most peace groups, though, were alarmed by what they viewed as a negotiation "between friends," and especially by the June 2005 passage of a framework law allowing broad impunity for crimes against humanity, with weak mechanisms for reparations, return of stolen assets, and dismantling paramilitary structures. Many peace movement participants chose to stay on the sidelines or to oppose the talks entirely, although several prominent groups (including Instituto de Estudios para el Desarrollo y la Paz [INDEPAZ], or Institute of Studies for Development and Peace; REDEPAZ; and the New Rainbow Foundation, composed of former ELN fighters) took part in a "Table for Monitoring the AUC-Government Dialogues and Negotiations," which issued several strong critiques and detailed recommendations. As the paramilitary process entered its latter stages, INDEPAZ and the

New Rainbow Foundation did groundbreaking research into the emergence of "new" paramilitary groups and the extensive ties between paramilitaries and local politicians. The September 2005 nomination of REDEPAZ coordinator Ana Teresa Bernal to the government commission overseeing reparations caused some internal controversy, making clear that the rift between human rights and peace activists, which had been largely papered over for some time, was still very real.

Prospects for talks with guerrilla groups have remained low. There are two glimmers of hope, however. First, the Uribe government agreed in September 2005 to release a jailed ELN leader, Francisco Galán, for a series of agenda-setting talks with civil society leaders. These discussions gave way to formal peace talks with the Colombian government. These went through several rounds in Havana, but have yet to reach even a cease-fire declaration. As was the case from 1998 to 2002, civil society groups have been denied a direct role in this process, at the Colombian government's insistence. But groups like INDEPAZ, New Rainbow, and the Permanent Assembly have played a critical role in disseminating information about the various advances and crises in the ELN talks.

Second, bargaining and posturing continue between the government and the FARC about a possible agreement to free FARC fighters from Colombian jails in exchange for the freedom of dozens of prominent politicians and military officers who have spent years as the guerrillas' hostages. The hostages' relatives have united behind efforts to get prisoner exchange negotiations moving. The pressure they have exerted has kept the hostages' plight on the front pages of Colombia's newspapers and has forced President Uribe to take bold steps, including an August 2007 decision to allow a facilitating role for Venezuelan president Hugo Chávez, and a daring military ruse that freed fifteen hostages in July 2008.

In this otherwise difficult period, civil society groups have had some success in their dealings with the international community. At meetings of dozens of donor nations in London (July 2003) and Cartagena (February 2005), the Uribe government supported consensus language giving primacy to the fight against terrorism and the need to establish security through military means, and opposed any reference to Colombia's violence as a "conflict." Colombian NGOs, along with their North American and European counterparts, were instrumental in encouraging donor-government representatives, particularly Europeans, to exclude most of this rhetoric from the meetings' final declarations.

The Peace Movement's Current Challenges

Colombian civil society peace activism is in the most difficult period of its young existence. But it is far from moribund; the organizations founded during the movement's period of growth still exist (with the exception of Paz

Colombia), and its leaders have learned much about organization, decision making, and dialogue with the political system.

Current challenges are nonetheless daunting. Some are beyond the movement's control. Popular opinion, for instance, remains rather cold to negotiations or reconciliation with guerrillas, as evidenced by the continued popularity of President Uribe and his security strategy. But the political climate is somewhat better than it was in 2002. Leftist candidates have been elected to powerful local positions, such as mayor of Bogotá and governor of Valle del Cauca Department, and opinion polls are showing increased support for negotiations. Nonetheless, threats continue and political space for peace activism remains restricted.

Meanwhile, the FARC, the paramilitaries, and the government have not grown more receptive to the idea of civil society's input into peace policy, or its presence at a future negotiating table. (The ELN is an important exception: the smaller guerrilla group has actively sought greater civil society input into its dialogues with the government, although it has been less clear about how such input might be channeled, processed, or implemented.) The principal external power, the United States, remains largely hostile to the idea of renewed negotiations with guerrillas and has done nothing to facilitate that outcome. Meanwhile, the paramilitary process, which itself has gone far from smoothly, will continue to distract attention and energy from the civil society peace movement.

But civil society peace organizations have greater control over a host of other challenges, many of which they are currently trying to address. The first is the perennial need to overcome internal divisions. Many of these divisions, such as those over the definition of the peace being sought, are philosophical. Is the desired peace merely the military defeat or demobilization of nonstate actors? Is it a negotiated outcome with a set of reforms broadening democratic participation? Is it a cultural change based on a nationwide effort to achieve social justice? Others dispute the role of human rights and justice in a peace process: is some impunity for serious abusers inevitable, or are truth and some punishment necessary to definitively halt the cycle of violence?

Disagreement exists about whether the use of violence is justified (and thus, the guerrillas' struggle legitimate) under certain circumstances. One's view on this question strongly affects one's opinion on whether a cease-fire, a halt to kidnapping, or an international humanitarian law accord should have greater priority in a future negotiation.

Other potentially surmountable divisions are sectoral or operational. Colombia's peace movement reflects the deep divisions in society as a whole, including those based on class, ideology, geography (urban-rural), ethnicity, gender, religion, and other sector-specific splits. Getting individuals and groups on all sides of these divides to work on a common strategy is a Herculean task and difficult to sustain. Often the consensus strategy that emerges is so bland, vague, and timid that it is of little practical use. Peace groups have to decide whether it is best to subordinate group-specific interests to a larger, broader coalition and whether it is worth the effort to include elite groups—such as the business sector—that, while powerful and able to sway public opinion, have a much more minimalist definition of peace. If peace groups determine that including such groups is not worthwhile, they must decide whether it is preferable—at least for now—to allow constituencies to work separately, dedicating their energies and creativity to their own definitions of peace.

Other operational divisions may seem petty and are certainly not unique to Colombia, but they do play a significant role. One is simply the clash of strong personalities. Colombian NGOs often use the word *protagonismo* to describe individuals' and groups' tendency to place their own ambitions and desire for publicity before the success of the larger strategy. Personal dislikes and disputes make it difficult to sustain strategic discussions and to ensure that roles and tasks are performed as desired. Divisions and antagonistic behavior are exacerbated by the stubborn fact that most peace and human rights organizations, especially the Bogotá-based groups, are forced to compete time after time for the same rather small pool of funding from international foundations and donor governments. Teamwork is undermined by an unspoken but nagging sense that to make payroll, each group must prove that it is worthier than its colleagues.

Strategic Questions

Beyond overcoming divisions, civil society peace groups must address a daunting series of strategic questions. Is it possible to convince and motivate public opinion, winning back the millions who marched in the streets during the late 1990s, or is there no choice but to wait for public opinion to support peace? Does a more coherent media strategy, including a greater effort at rapid response, make sense, or is the press a lost cause since it is largely owned by some of Colombia's wealthiest and most progovernment families?

Is it a good use of resources to write proposals that might serve as draft accords for a future peace process (as the Assembly of Civil Society, a temporary coalition of organizations, did in Guatemala in the 1990s)? Could such initiatives be helpful to the Uribe government's demobilization of paramilitaries, or is it best to maintain a critical distance from that process? Does it make sense to participate in *any* government talks with an armed group, whether paramilitary or guerrilla, or should the movement aim to achieve a larger peace based on social justice, citizen participation, and cultural change? Is a humanitarian prisoner exchange with the FARC a goal worth promoting?

Are large, national-level convergences useful at this point, or should peacebuilding begin at the municipal, departmental, or regional level, with peace laboratories or local dialogues with armed groups? Should groups be excluded from coalitions if they do not reject violence as a means of social change? Should the peace movement get more involved in the political process—lobbying and pressuring politicians, backing candidates and parties, or even forming its own party or faction? How useful or necessary is international accompaniment? Should peace groups bother to sell their proposals for renewed dialogue overseas, especially in the United States?

The list of strategic dilemmas could go still further. What this sampling clearly indicates, however, is that civil society peace activism is at a crossroads. The decisions made today to answer these questions will determine not just the movement's current alignments and alliances but also its effectiveness at some future moment when public opinion and other external conditions become more favorable to a renewed peace effort.

Conclusion: A Few Bright Spots

Unlike in the peak years of the late 1990s, it is currently difficult to imagine Colombians of all social classes and political tendencies jamming into a downtown Bogotá building to demand a negotiated end to the conflict. But the picture is not as bleak as this discussion of daunting challenges and strategic conundrums might suggest. Colombians' civil society peace activism remains vibrant and creative, if less influential at the national level than it was a decade ago. Bright spots still exist, and some may indeed be the seeds of a renewed citizens' movement for peace.

As will become clear in later chapters, the most innovative and energetic peace and conflict-resolution efforts are currently most visible at the local—not the national—level. Communities have gained national recognition by saving lives through dialogue with armed groups. Indigenous groups have mobilized in nonviolent defense of their territories. Even in highly conflictual zones, women's organizations have been demanding greater participation, rejecting all armed actors, and proposing alternatives. Youth groups have sought to end gang conflict in poor neighborhoods. Peace communities have endeavored to shield themselves from the fighting by excluding all armed groups and all guns. Local elected leaders, priests, and community organizers have increased citizen participation in planning, resource use, governance, and conflict resolution.

Meanwhile, a series of regional peace and development programs or peace laboratories, combining participatory development projects and active conflict resolution, have sprung up in several localities throughout the country. The best known is the Magdalena Medio Development and Peace Program, formed ten years ago in the conflictual area surrounding the oil-refining city of Barrancabermeja. Nineteen such projects now make up Red Nacional de Programas Regionales de Desarrollo y Paz (REDPRODEPAZ, or

National Network of Regional Development and Peace Programs), a network of development and peace initiatives.

National peace movement groups have made protecting and promoting local peace efforts a major priority. Dozens of community initiatives were on display in Bogotá, for instance, at the September 2005 National Congress of Peace Initiatives, organized by REDEPAZ, the Permanent Assembly, Planeta Paz, INDEPAZ, and several other groups.

At the national level, peace activism has been less vocal. Exceptions exist, of course: women's groups have held numerous peacebuilding events; FARC hostages' relatives have been clamoring for a humanitarian exchange agreement; victims' groups have been seeking truth and reparations through the paramilitary negotiation process; and the Catholic Church remains active on all levels. But currently, no national movement on the order of what existed in the late 1990s is pressuring for a prompt return to the negotiating table, nor will the possibility of renewed talks with guerrillas be a central campaign issue.

The pendulum of public opinion is likely to swing back within the next few years, however. While guerrillas have been weakening, they—along with a growing number of rearmed paramilitaries—continue to be a major factor of violence. Meanwhile, a growing scandal surrounding politicians' ties to paramilitary groups has made it harder for the government to advance its political agenda. If these trends continue, disenchantment with a "total war" approach and weariness with violence will likely return.

When Colombians are once again ready to listen to peace proposals, civil society peace organizations will be well positioned to help lead the charge. After the successes and frustrations of the past few years, a renewed peace movement is likely to bear little resemblance to its predecessors. Having learned hard lessons from the past decade and having wrestled with the challenges and strategic dilemmas of the present, its leaders will likely be more pragmatic, more proposal oriented, more mature, more politically astute, and ultimately more successful in their endeavors.

3

Colombia's Peace Processes, 1982–2002
Conditions, Strategies, and Outcomes

Carlo Nasi

D uring the two decades from 1982 to 2002, four separate Colombian governments went to the bargaining table with rebel groups, but only President Virgilio Barco and, shortly afterward, his successor, President César Gaviria, reached negotiated settlements. These peace accords—first with the Movimiento 19 de Abril (M-19); then with the Ejército Popular de Liberación (EPL), Partido Revolucionario de los Trabajadores (PRT), and Movimiento Armado Quintín Lame (MAQL); and later with the Corriente de Renovación Socialista (CRS, a splinter fraction of the Ejército de Liberación Nacional [ELN])—can be regarded as "successful," albeit with some qualifications. As a result of the accords, 3,726 guerrillas turned in their weapons, and none of the rebel groups that signed peace agreements resumed insurrection afterward. But success was only partial in that Colombia's largest rebel groups, the Fuerzas Armadas Revolucionarias de Colombia (FARC) and the ELN, continued waging war.

Why did Barco and Gaviria succeed where Belisario Betancur, Gaviria himself (when he later attempted to reach a settlement with the FARC and ELN), and Andrés Pastrana failed? One possible explanation is that success was due to a favorable international context: the successful peace negotiations coincided with the end of the Cold War, which made several rebel groups in Colombia question the relevance and feasibility of socialism. But if we see Barco's and Gaviria's negotiations as a mere by-product of a changing international context, we miss a variety of conflict-resolution dynamics both at the domestic and international levels.

This chapter explores five factors that may partly explain the varied outcomes of the various peace processes from 1982 to 2002: (1) the military balance between the government and the rebel groups; (2) the security dilemma;

(3) the role of spoilers; (4) negotiation strategies; and (5) the political economy of war (see Table 3.1). Perhaps none of these factors individually explains a process's success or failure, but understanding their relative impacts may help us better assess what factors are likely to advance or hinder movements toward peace in the future.[1]

Military Balance

Conflicts undergo cycles and variations, and not every moment is propitious for reaching a negotiated settlement. According to Saadia Touval and William Zartman, a period of struggle, in which rival parties believe that they can get what they want without making any concessions to one another, tends to precede the search for a negotiated solution.[2] Only if the costs of war become unbearable and rival groups reach a "mutually hurting stalemate" are they likely to sit at the bargaining table and reach a peaceful settlement.

Fen Osler Hampson has criticized the notion of a mutually hurting stalemate, arguing that "the notion of 'ripeness' wrongly suggests that a conflict has reached a stable equilibrium," when the possibility of "unripening" exists in the implementation phase of any peace accord.[3] This concept is also problematic for predicting policy changes; in fact, analysts have merely inferred the existence of a mutually hurting stalemate after the warring factions have altered their policies.[4]

To these conceptual difficulties one should add that the Colombian establishment has favored a different approach, which contradicts the notion of a mutually hurting stalemate. Policymakers, entrepreneurs, and military officers—paraphrasing a line that has been attributed to former president Alfonso López Michelsen—state that the guerrilla organizations will not undertake any serious peace negotiations unless the government first "defeats" them militarily. For the Colombian establishment, "defeat" is not equated with the complete annihilation of the rebel groups, but rather with undermining their military might to the point of hindering their capacity to demand any structural transformations. Of course, the preferred scenario for the Colombian establishment would be to negotiate with (and not make any serious concessions to) virtually defeated rebel groups, but this may be wishful thinking.

For the sake of argument, the question that must be raised is whether the existence of either a "mutually hurting stalemate" or "defeated guerrilla orga-

---

[1] See also Carlo Nasi, *Cuando callan los fusiles: Impacto de la paz negociada en Colombia y en Centroamérica* (Bogotá: Grupo Editorial Norma and Departamento de Ciencia Política and Centro de Estudios Socioculturales [CESO], Universidad de los Andes, 2007).

[2] Quoted in Louis Kriesberg, *Constructive Conflicts: From Escalation to Resolution* (Lanham, Md., Boulder, Colo., New York, and Oxford: Rowman & Littlefield, 1998), 195.

[3] Fen Osler Hampson, *Nurturing Peace: Why Peace Settlements Succeed or Fail* (Washington, D.C.: United States Institute of Peace Press, 1996), 15–16.

[4] Ibid., 211.

Table 3.1. Colombia's Peace Processes: Conditions, Strategies, and Outcomes

	Betancur 1982–1986	Barco 1986–1990	Gaviria 1990–1994	Pastrana 1998–2002
1. Military Balance	Relatively weak rebel groups	Relatively weak rebel groups	Relatively strong rebel groups	Relatively strong rebel groups
2. Security Dilemma	N.a.	*Minor for the M-19, PRT, MAQL, and CRS *Major for the EPL	N.a.	N.a.
3. Role of Spoilers	Significant: All parties sabotaged the negotiations	Minor: Good faith and spoiler management techniques	N.a.	Significant: All parties sabotaged the negotiations
4. International Context	Unfavorable: Cold War	Favorable: End of Cold War	Favorable: End of Cold War	Unfavorable: Demonstration effect plus war on drugs and terrorism
5. Negotiations Strategy	Root causes of war	Power distribution plus learning process	Root causes of war	Root causes of war
6. Availability of Lootable Resources	Low	Medium	Medium	High
Results	Failure	Success	Failure	Failure

nizations" is what sets the successful peace negotiations of Barco and Gaviria apart from the rest. Was the military balance among the warring factions a decisive factor in the success or failure of the various peace negotiations?

Barco's and Gaviria's negotiations concluded successfully even though the costs of war never increased enough to make the government or the rebel groups consider serious concessions to the other necessary. Unlike the Frente Farabundo Martí de Liberación Nacional (FMLN) in El Salvador, the Colombian rebel groups did not carry out a "final offensive" before sitting at the bargaining table with the government. The FMLN's "final offensive" of November 1989, and the subsequent counteroffensive by the El Salvadoran army, produced more than a thousand casualties, which bolstered the perception of a mutually hurting stalemate.[5] The sole El Salvadoran "final offensive" produced more combat-related deaths than did the war in Colombia during the years 1988 and 1989, when the government and the guerrilla organizations were starting peace negotiations (not to mention that the Colombian guerrilla organizations never carried out a sustained attack on major urban centers).[6] These figures indicate that a mutually hurting stalemate was not a precondition for the successful conclusion of peace accords in Colombia.

Does this mean that successful negotiations occur only with defeated rebel groups, as the Colombian establishment likes to believe? The available evidence does not support this hypothesis, either. The M-19 and other rebel groups that eventually demobilized did suffer military setbacks before sitting at the bargaining table with Barco and Gaviria, but they were far from being defeated opponents. Former peace counselors and demobilized rebel leaders alike agree on the interpretation that these rebel groups, had they wanted to, could have continued waging guerrilla warfare for a long time.[7] In addition, an exclusive emphasis on military factors would hardly explain, for example, why the EPL demobilized during a period when it was one of the most active rebel groups in Colombia, particularly in strategic banana-producing areas.

This is not to say that the military situation is irrelevant for explaining the successful conclusion of peace negotiations. Guerrilla leaders know well that the stronger a rebel group is, the greater its chance to demand fundamental transformations at the level of the polity, the economy, and society. But it is virtually impossible to determine beforehand what the "right" power correlation is for reaching a peace accord. In fact, a "good" power correlation from the standpoint of a rebel organization might be deemed disastrous by a government that is unwilling to make certain concessions, and vice versa.

---

[5] Cynthia McClintock, *Revolutionary Movements in Latin America: El Salvador's FMLN and Peru's Shining Path* (Washington, D.C.: United States Institute of Peace Press, 1998), 85.

[6] Comisión Colombiana de Juristas, *Colombia, derechos humanos y derecho humanitario 1996* (Bogotá: Comisión Colombiana de Juristas, 1997), 4.

[7] Former peace counselors Rafael Pardo and Carlos Eduardo Jaramillo and former M-19 leader Antonio Navarro, interviews by author, Bogotá, 2000.

A government that is militarily strong may refuse to negotiate anything but the disarmament of rebel organizations. Conversely, a strong rebel group that believes that a revolutionary outcome is fast approaching will have no incentives to seek a bargained solution. Yet it would be wrong to equate military might with intransigence at the bargaining table. A militarily weak government might prefer a continuation of war instead of undertaking costly structural transformations as a result of peace negotiations. And weak rebel groups that have waged war for decades might refuse to negotiate if they believe that a government is demanding that they turn in their weapons with nothing in exchange. In sum, both weak and strong governments and rebel groups might successfully reach a negotiated settlement if a variety of other conditions exist.

Under what conditions, then, have peace accords materialized in Colombia? What was the military situation and offensive stance of the government and the rebel forces during the various peace negotiations?

Colombia has experienced a steady expansion of insurgency over the past thirty years. Not even Barco's and Gaviria's successful peace process that led to the demobilization of five rebel groups reversed this trend. Whereas the various rebel groups had barely 17 guerrilla fronts operating in remote rural areas in 1978, the number of fronts increased to 105 in 1994, by which time guerrilla organizations were operating in more than half of Colombia's municipalities.[8] Reportedly, the FARC comprised about 3,600 combatants in 1986, whereas nearly a decade later FARC had an estimated 16,500 combatants.[9] The ELN, in turn, went from about 800 combatants in 1986 to 4,500 in 2001.[10] (See Figure 3.1.)

While increasing their territorial reach, the guerrillas have been unable to wrest control of important urban centers from the government. Some rebel militias operate in the outskirts and shantytowns of various Colombian cities, but they pose only a minor threat to the government's stability.

And even though peasants form the bulk of the guerrilla organizations, the rebel groups can hardly claim to represent the peasantry or, more generally, the poor. In fact, peasants have joined not only left-wing guerrilla groups but also right-wing paramilitary organizations, oftentimes for practical rather than ideological reasons (for example, to increase their chances of survival in a region controlled by one armed actor or to get a regular salary). The expansion of rebel groups has been facilitated by Colombia's vast territory and the

---

[8] Daniel Pécaut, "Presente, pasado y futuro de la violencia in Colombia," *Desarrollo Económico* 36, no. 144 (1997): 896.

[9] United Nations Development Programme (UNDP), *El conflicto, callejón con salida. Informe nacional de desarrollo humano Colombia–2003* (Bogotá: UNDP, 2003), 83.

[10] Alfredo Rangel, *Colombia: Guerra en el fin de siglo* (Bogotá: TM Editores and Universidad de los Andes, 1998), 12; Alfredo Rangel, *Guerra insurgente: Conflictos en Malasia, Perú, Filipinas, El Salvador y Colombia* (Bogotá: Intermedio Editores, 2001), 383; UNDP, *El conflicto*, 83.

Figure 3.1   Expansion of Insurgency in Colombia, 1978–2004

Number of Combatants

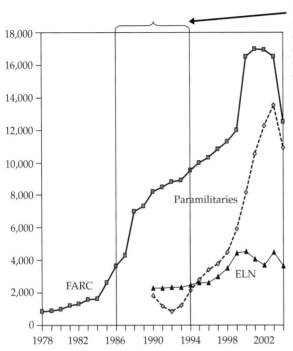

Source: Estimates by the Colombian Ministry of Defense.

abundance of inaccessible places where state institutions are virtually absent. It is there that the guerrilla organizations have established their main sanctuaries and recruited people, yet the rebels' appeal to underprivileged sectors remains quite limited.

Another crucial factor explaining why the guerrilla organizations have not been able to pose a major challenge to the Colombian regime is that the rebel groups have remained divided throughout the conflict. The guerrilla organizations attempted to join forces by forming the Coordinadora Nacional Guerrillera (CNG) in 1985, and then the Coordinadora Guerrillera Simón Bolívar (CGSB) in 1987, but despite the names, these never reached any significant coordination, which hindered their offensive capacity.[11]

---

[11] Eduardo Pizarro, *Insurgencia sin revolución: La guerrilla en Colombia en una perspectiva comparada* (Bogotá: TM Editores and Instituto de Estudios Políticos y Relaciones Internacionales [IEPRI], 1996), 214.

The expansion of insurgency has also been offset by the organizational growth of the Colombian army, the police, and right-wing paramilitary groups. The Colombian army was composed of 76,000 soldiers in 1986, 110,000 in 1991, 146,000 in 1995,[12] 158,000 in 2001, and 200,000 in 2003.[13] Also, since the Colombian police often engage in counterinsurgency operations, 160,000 police officers should be added to these calculations. In addition, right-wing paramilitary groups grew from approximately 1,500 combatants in 1988 to 4,000 in 1997, 8,000 in 2000, and 12,000 in 2002.[14]

Based on these numbers, the Colombian insurgencies are not likely to upset the numerical advantage that the Colombian military has maintained throughout recent years—not to mention its superior military technology. A rule of thumb of counterinsurgency states that governments willing to defeat rebel groups must have between five and ten soldiers per guerrilla fighter, and Colombia has matched this ratio.

Apart from this, one could argue that during two of the four governments in which a peace process was initiated, the rebel groups were on the military offensive. An unprecedented show of force took place during the government of President Gaviria before the bargaining rounds in Caracas and Tlaxcala. After the Colombian military bombed the FARC headquarters in La Uribe in December 1990, the FARC and the ELN responded in kind by launching multiple attacks throughout the country. There were 1,341 armed actions by these guerrilla organizations in 1991, compared to barely 690 in 1990, and 612 in 1989.[15] Although this may not have constituted a serious attempt to topple the government, these rebel groups did double their attacks in one year.

In a similar vein, from 1996 to 1998, before sitting at the bargaining table with President Pastrana, the FARC, for the first time ever, conducted large-scale attacks on important military battalions, winning significant victories in Patascoy, El Billar, and Las Delicias.[16] This seemed to indicate that the rebels' offensive capacity had improved qualitatively—up to that point, the FARC had conducted only hit-and-run attacks.

---

[12] U.S. Arms Control and Disarmament Agency, *World Military Expenditures and Arms Transfers 1996* (Washington, D.C.: U.S. Department of State, 1997), 66.

[13] Information from a database of the Bonn International Center for Conversion.

[14] Mauricio Romero, *Paramilitares y autodefensas, 1982–2003* (Bogotá: IEPRI, 2003), 24–26; Alfredo Rangel, "Lógicas Paradójicas," 2007, www.cambio.com.co/opinioncambio/post.php?id_blog=3396041&id_nota=3424782 (accessed October 2, 2008).

[15] Mauricio García-Durán, *De la Uribe a Tlaxcala, Procesos de Paz* (Bogotá: CINEP, 1992), 274.

[16] Ernesto Borda, "El conflicto armado y el proceso de paz en Colombia 1998–2002," in *Persistir en la paz negociada: Análisis del contexto socio-económico y político en Colombia,* eds. Astrid Martínez, Clara Ramírez, and Ernesto Borda (Bogotá: Comisión de Conciliación Nacional and Konrad Adenauer Stiftung, 2003), 177–78.

Figure 3.2   Casualties of the Colombian War

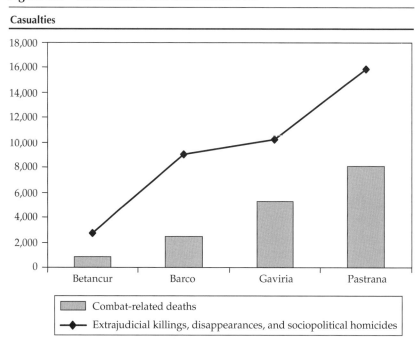

Source: Comisión Colombiana de Juristas 1997 and 2004 and CINEP database.

These offensives indicate that the FARC and the ELN were relatively strong during the negotiations under Gaviria and Pastrana, unlike during the peace processes of Betancur and Barco (see figures 3.2 and 3.3). Since neither Gaviria nor Pastrana was able to reach a negotiated settlement with these revolutionary organizations, it is tempting to conclude that the stronger the rebel groups are, the less likely it is that a negotiated settlement will emerge.

On the other hand, the guerrilla organizations were relatively weak when they went to the bargaining table with the government of President Betancur, yet no peace agreement was ever reached. This indicates that military weakness is by no means a sufficient condition for explaining the successful conclusion of a peace accord. In fact, a weak guerrilla organization may negotiate tactically, seeking to gain time, and then continue to challenge the government.

In sum, military actions do partly matter, in the sense that a rebel group whose offensive capacity is increasing will probably not sign a peace accord—especially if its leaders believe that better conditions lie ahead. But even a strong rebel organization could end up demobilizing if a government negotiates skillfully, makes some major concessions, and redresses the rebels' key concerns. Similarly, a weak revolutionary organization that has incurred

Figure 3.3   Offensive Actions by the Colombian Rebel Groups, 1986–2004

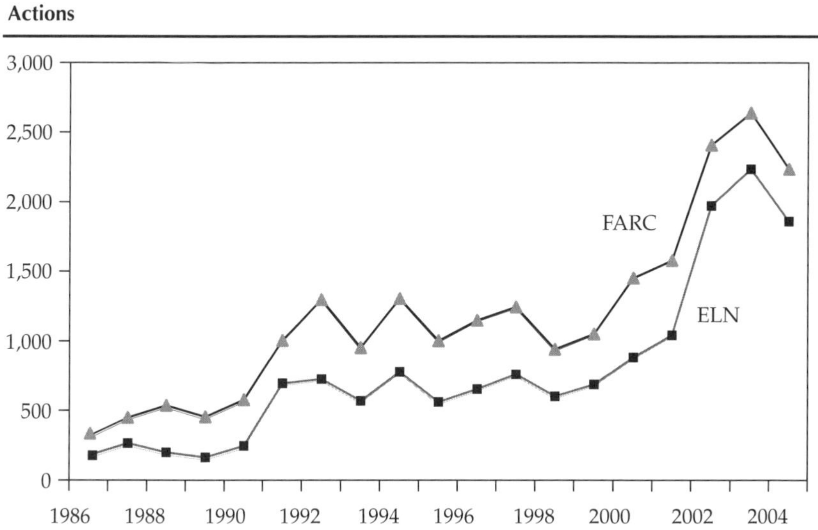

Actions

Source: DAS Bulletins

high military costs before sitting at the bargaining table may consider disarming if peace offers potential gains, even if it falls short of obtaining major concessions from the government.

Given the relentless expansion of insurgency, coupled with Plan Colombia's and Plan Patriota's only partial success in undermining the guerrillas' power base, it is likely that the government will end up bargaining with relatively strong rebel groups.[17] Perhaps the revolutionary organizations will not pose a credible challenge to the central government, but they will represent a significant force to reckon with. Under these conditions, the Colombian government will require both expertise and substantial international support if it hopes to negotiate a solution to the armed conflict.

The Security Dilemma and the Role of Third Parties

The "security dilemma" is a concept with a long tradition in the literature and debates relating to arms races and the outbreak of war in international relations. It refers to the generic notion that the measures that one state takes to increase its own security may decrease the security of neighboring (and

---

[17] Plan Colombia was a US$7.5 billion package of U.S. counterdrug/counterinsurgency military aid to Colombia, which the Clinton administration started disbursing in 2000. Plan Patriota was a military strategy of Plan Colombia, which involved deploying between fifteen thousand and seventeen thousand soldiers in southern parts of Colombia to target the FARC's top leaders. So far, Raúl Reyes is the only top FARC leader killed as a result of Plan Colombia. A joint police operation with Ecuadoran authorities led to the jailing and extradition of "Simón Trinidad," another rebel leader, but this action was not related to Plan Colombia.

other) states, which will feel threatened.[18] Barbara Walter discovered that the notion of a security dilemma also helps explain why it is particularly difficult to bring civil wars to an end.[19]

According to Walter, between 1940 and 1990, 55 percent of interstate wars were resolved at the bargaining table, but only 20 percent of civil wars were so resolved.[20] She explained such divergent outcomes in connection with the security dilemma. In civil wars, she argues, peace accords fail because an armed faction is asked to disarm without legitimate government or legal institutions in place to enforce a contract. By laying down weapons, she notes, "it becomes impossible (for an armed faction) to either survive and attack or enforce future cooperation."[21] Under these circumstances, the government might take advantage and annihilate disarmed guerrillas or not comply with the peace accords.

Third parties constitute a potential solution to the security dilemma. According to Walter, they "can guarantee that groups will be protected, terms will be fulfilled and promises will be kept."[22] But a third party "must be willing to use force if necessary, and its military capabilities must be sufficient to punish whichever side violates the treaty."[23] Walter concludes that "the only type of peacekeeping that appears to help end a war is that which is backed by a promise to use force. Observers or unarmed peacekeepers with no military backup will have little positive effect."[24]

Do these considerations of the security dilemma help explain success and failure in the various peace processes in Colombia? Did Presidents Barco and Gaviria offer better security guarantees to disarming rebel groups compared with those offered by the other governments? Were third parties a key factor

---

[18] The security dilemma was developed by theorists of classical realism. See Michael T. Klare and Daniel C. Thomas, eds., *World Security: Challenges for a New Century*, 2nd ed. (New York: St Martin's Press, 1997), 3. Walter restated the security dilemma in a slightly modified form, arguing that insecurity results when only one out of two armed rivals in a civil war turns in its weapons, leaving itself vulnerable to attack by the rival faction. Barbara Walter, "The Critical Barrier to Civil War Settlement," *International Organization* 51, no. 3 (1997): 335.

[19] The government and some analysts argue that Colombia is not undergoing a civil war, and instead prefer to use other words, such as "terrorism," "armed conflict," and so forth. But regardless of the specific features of the Colombian conflict, Colombia is clearly in the midst of civil war. See Carlo Nasi, William Ramírez, Eric Lair, and Eduardo Posada, "La Guerra Civil," *Revista de Estudios Sociales* 14 (2003): 119–24.

[20] Walter, "The Critical Barrier," 335. See also Roy Licklider, "The Consequences of Negotiated Settlements in Civil Wars, 1945–1993," *American Political Science Review* 89, no. 3 (1995): 681.

[21] Walter, "The Critical Barrier," 336.

[22] Ibid., 340.

[23] Ibid.

[24] Ibid., 361. A similar argument is found in George Downs and Stephen J. Stedman, "Evaluation Issues in Peace Implementation," in *Ending Civil Wars: The Implementation of Peace Agreements*, eds. Stephen Stedman, Donald Rothchild, and Elizabeth Cousens (Boulder, Colo., and London: Lynne Rienner, 2002), 43–69.

explaining Barco's and Gaviria's success? And have third parties been will-ing to punish defectors? The evidence is rather weak on all these counts.

Third parties have played a rather marginal role throughout the various peace negotiations in Colombia. No third party has ever acted as a full-fledged mediator, and the United Nations has never sent a peacekeeping or peacebuilding mission to help implement any peace accords. Nor has any country or international organization ever pledged to help enforce the imple-mentation of peace accords in Colombia by punishing spoilers. Admittedly, in Colombia most of the negotiations were fruitless, yielding no peace ac-cords in need of implementation; however, in countries such as El Salvador and Guatemala, the United Nations served as a catalyst for reaching partial human rights agreements before the warring factions reached a definitive settlement.

What, then, was the role of the international community in the various peace negotiations in Colombia? The international community took no part whatever in the failed negotiations of President Betancur (although the pres-ident once met with leaders of the M-19 in Spain). During Barco's partly suc-cessful peace process, the international community facilitated a few prelimi-nary meetings between the government and the M-19 and also helped in the disarmament process. The guerrilla groups were reluctant to hand in their weapons to the Colombian government, because this conveyed the impres-sion that they had been defeated. So eventually the M-19 turned over its weapons to a delegation of the International Socialist Organization, and later the EPL, CRS, and MAQL surrendered their weapons to two international verification commissions.[25] The role of the international community in the disarmament process was largely symbolic in that it did not involve any threats or sanctions if the rebel groups cheated.

During the peace talks of President Gaviria with the FARC and the ELN, Venezuela and Mexico acted as facilitators by offering to host the peace nego-tiations. The international community played a more active role during Pres-ident Pastrana's tenure, although its participation again fell short of media-tion or peacebuilding. Beginning in 1999, a group of ten (mostly European) ambassadors, along with James LeMoyne, the personal delegate of the UN secretary-general, attended the peace talks between the Pastrana govern-ment and the FARC as "observers."[26] In 2002, during the final crisis of the peace process, LeMoyne acquired greater visibility by postponing the col-lapse of negotiations for a brief time, but he was never fully empowered to act as a mediator.[27] Also, the German Episcopal Conference facilitated prelimi-

---

[25] Darío Villamizar, *Un adiós a la guerra* (Bogotá: Planeta, 1997).

[26] Socorro Ramírez, *Intervención en conflictos internos: El caso colombiano 1994–2003* (Bogotá: Uni-versidad Nacional, 2004), 223.

[27] Ibid., 226.

nary contacts with the ELN, which led to peace talks in Mainz, Germany, and later in Geneva.

Such modest third-party intervention suggests that the international community offered no better security guarantees to the warring factions during the successful peace process of the early 1990s compared to the others. In none of the four peace processes that took place from 1982 to 2002 do we see an international community willing and able to punish cheaters. Yet, as argued below, the actual security risks encountered by different rebel groups varied significantly throughout the various peace negotiations.

During Betancur's negotiations, no demobilizations occurred. The government agreed to a truce with the FARC in March 1984, and then with the M-19 and EPL in August.[28] The truce with the M-19 and EPL broke down in 1985, as did the one with the FARC in 1987, before these revolutionary organizations turned in any weapons. Perhaps the security dilemma prevented them from disarming in the first place. During the negotiations, there was an assassination attempt on the M-19's top leader, Carlos Pizarro, and later the EPL's spokesperson, Óscar William Calvo, was killed, leading to a breakdown of the truce.[29]

The FARC experienced a far more serious security dilemma. In fact, some rightist sectors of the army, as well as drug traffickers (who had been victimized by the FARC), engaged in the systematic killing of members of the Unión Patriótica (UP), a political party formed by the FARC during the peace negotiations.

The killing of key M-19 cadre Afranio Parra and chief commander Carlos Pizarro made this rebel group consider going back to war. But the M-19 resisted provocations and lobbied different parties and organizations with a conciliatory strategy, hoping that society would forgive and forget.[30] Apparently, this strategy paid off, and the M-19 did not suffer an annihilation of its cadres and militants. The same was true for other rebel organizations that demobilized during this period, including the PRT, MAQL, and CRS. Death threats were common and a few revenge killings against former guerrillas occurred, but there was no systematic effort to annihilate demobilized combatants of these rebel groups.[31]

Of all the groups that turned in their weapons during Barco's and Gaviria's successful peace negotiations, only the EPL experienced an acute security dilemma. After contentious internal debates on whether to demobilize, a ma-

---

[28] Villamizar, *Un adiós a la guerra*, 99–101.

[29] Ibid., 101–03.

[30] Former M-19 member Alberto Caycedo, interview by the author, Bogotá, July 2000.

[31] See Dirección Nacional para la Reinserción, *Los derechos humanos y el derecho internacional humanitario en los procesos de paz, 1990–2000* (Bogotá: Gente Nueva Editorial, 2000), 97.

jority of EPL guerrillas turned in their weapons, while the splinter Caraballo faction accused its former comrades of "betraying revolution" and continued waging guerrilla war.[32] To complicate matters even further, most of the EPL guerrillas who demobilized did so in the banana-producing region of Urabá, where the group had sustained a prolonged and deadly quarrel with the FARC. Since the early 1980s, these two revolutionary organizations had been attacking each other as they competed to recruit banana workers in two different rebel-controlled unions. By 1987, right-wing paramilitary groups had also entered Urabá, where they engaged in a violent territorial struggle against the EPL and the FARC. When the EPL demobilized in 1991, it suffered attacks from its splinter faction, the FARC, and paramilitary groups as well.

As a survival strategy, a number of demobilized EPL guerrillas ended up making an alliance with the right-wing paramilitary groups that were becoming the dominant warlords in Urabá, and others became part of the rural network of the Colombian secret police, the Departamento Administrativo de Seguridad.[33] The EPL paid a heavy price for this decision. Between 1989 and 2005, 321 former EPL guerrillas were murdered, 46 percent of them by the FARC, the Caraballo faction, and unidentified guerrillas; 13.4 percent by paramilitary groups; and 5 percent by the security agencies of the state. In 34 percent of the killings, the perpetrators' identities remain unknown.[34]

Accusations of "betrayal of the revolution" and the existence of splinter factions within rebel groups that negotiate peace agreements do not explain why some guerrilla organizations experience an acute security dilemma while others do not. In fact, the FARC accused all the rebel groups that demobilized in the early 1990s of betraying the revolution but undertook systematic attacks only against former EPL combatants. And whereas the Caraballo faction killed many demobilized EPL guerrillas, the ELN did not attack its former comrades from the splinter groups CRS and PRT who had turned in their weapons.

The killing of demobilized EPL combatants by the FARC was facilitated by a long history of violent retaliations between these two groups. Moreover, by deciding to collaborate with the right-wing paramilitary groups and the Colombian state, demobilized EPL combatants seeking self-protection did not fully disentangle themselves from the armed confrontation. By providing inside information to the paramilitaries and the Colombian army on guerrilla

---

[32] Villamizar, *Un adiós a la guerra*, 201–45.

[33] Former EPL commander Mario Agudelo, interview by Paola Favardo, Medellín, 2004.

[34] Fundación Cultura Democrática and Asociación de Constructores de Paz, "Elementos de diagnóstico, casos de violaciones e infracciones," in *La reinserción en Colombia*, ed. Álvaro Villaraga (Bogotá: Fucude y Asopropaz, 2006), 71–94.

operations in Urabá, former EPL combatants represented a security risk for the FARC and the Caraballo faction, thereby provoking a violent response.

During the peace negotiations with the FARC and the ELN, the governments of Presidents Gaviria and Pastrana made little progress on the issue of demobilization. Thus, the discussion on security guarantees was postponed.[35]

In sum, the Colombian experience challenges Walter's theory on the paramount importance of the security dilemma. In fact, the rebel groups that actually experienced an acute security dilemma after demobilizing constitute an exception: only the EPL suffered heavy casualties. And counterintuitively, other rebel groups (the Caraballo faction and the FARC) posed a more significant security threat to the EPL than did the Colombian state. Another important lesson that can be drawn from the experience of the M-19 is that under certain circumstances, reconciliation gestures by the rebel groups help to contain security threats—meaning that third parties do not constitute the only potential solution to the security dilemma.

What about Walter's argument that a disarmed rebel group cannot obtain compliance with the peace accords in the absence of a third-party enforcer? The Colombian Congress torpedoed a series of reforms that Barco and the M-19 had agreed to in 1989; thus, the M-19 secured no political transformations in exchange for its demobilization.[36] Still, the government attempted to deliver the political transformations that it had promised to the M-19 by promoting the formation of a National Constituent Assembly (NCA). Eventually, a popularly elected NCA was formed in December 1990 and put in charge of rewriting the constitution, which produced the deepest transformations of the Colombian polity in decades. The NCA helped change the impression that the M-19 had demobilized in exchange for nothing and was a crucial incentive that assisted in the peace process with other rebel groups.

The Colombian government was in a peculiar position in its negotiations with the M-19. If it was hoping to get other guerrilla organizations, especially the FARC and the ELN, on board with the peace process, the executive could not afford to be viewed as incompliant. The government had a special incentive to demonstrate to the remaining rebel groups that they, too, could disarm, survive, and see the peace accords implemented. An open question is whether the executive would have had the same incentive to uphold its end of the bargain had all the rebel groups disarmed simultaneously.

---

[35] Demobilization was one of the main issues discussed during Gaviria's peace talks at Caracas and Tlaxcala, but the parties never reached agreement on procedural matters, and violent acts produced a suspension of these talks. See Harvey Kline, *State Building and Conflict Resolution in Colombia 1986–1994* (Tuscaloosa, Ala., and London: University of Alabama Press, 2001), 85–118. During Pastrana's tenure, demobilization did not enter into the agenda.

[36] Former peace counselor Rafael Pardo, interview by the author, Bogotá, 2000.

The Role of Spoilers

Conflict-resolution theories highlight the role of spoilers in preventing the successful implementation of peace accords.[37] Spoiler problems are related to, but different from, the security dilemma. The security dilemma refers to a structural condition that tends to occur as a result of successful negotiations in civil wars whereby one side (often the rebel groups) must disarm completely while the other (usually the government) keeps its weapons.

The literature on spoilers, in contrast, is far less specific about who should fear whom. Anyone committing acts of sabotage—the army, guerrilla groups, splinter factions of a rebel group, or any third party that prevents the materialization of peace accords—can be a spoiler. If spoilers succeed, they can derail a peace process and lead to a resumption of war, often with disastrous humanitarian consequences. The relevant question for this chapter is whether spoilers account for the failure of various peace processes in Colombia. Conversely, did the absence of spoilers or the application of spoiler-management techniques help Barco and Gaviria keep the peace process on track?

In analyzing the various peace processes in Colombia, it becomes apparent that a number of spoilers committed acts of sabotage in each case, albeit with different rates of success. During Betancur's negotiations, all the rebel groups acted as spoilers and used the truce as an opportunity to create new fronts, expand territorially, and increase their numbers.[38] For instance, the M-19 engaged in peace talks solely to recover from some military setbacks and then resume the war.[39] Their role, as we have seen, greatly aggravated the security dilemma.

Perhaps the most problematic case of spoiling was that of the FARC. In 1984, shortly after declaring a truce but without renouncing violence, the FARC formed its own political party, the UP, to take part in the upcoming elections.[40] But the FARC did not disarm and demobilize, instead resorting to the UP as a means to attain greater power. Spokespersons of the UP openly argued that the FARC would never lay down its weapons, since arms would "guarantee" the implementation of revolutionary transformations in Colombia.[41] And in municipal elections, the FARC intimidated some locals into

---

[37] Stephen Stedman, "Spoiler Problems in Peace Processes," *International Security* 22, no. 2 (1997): 5–53; Carlo Nasi, "Spoilers in Colombia: Actors and Strategies," in *Challenges to Peacebuilding: Managing Spoilers during Conflict Resolution*, eds. Edward Newman and Oliver Richmond (Tokyo: United Nations University Press, 2006), 219–41.

[38] Jesús A. Bejarano, *Una agenda para la paz* (Bogotá: Tercer Mundo, 1995), 88.

[39] Former guerrilla commander Antonio Navarro, interview by the author, Bogotá, 2000.

[40] William Ramírez, "Las fértiles cenizas de la izquierda," *Análisis Político* 10 (May–August 1990): 38; Comisión de Superación de la Violencia, *Pacificar la paz* (Bogotá: IEPRI and CINEP, 1992), 118.

[41] Ibid.

voting for UP candidates, which cast doubt on the FARC's willingness to achieve peace.[42] From 1986 to 1995, a violent reaction by rightist sectors followed, in which private paramilitary militias financed by drug traffickers, and some army officers, killed some two thousand UP militants.[43]

The Colombian army also sabotaged Betancur's peace negotiations when it defied the president's cease-fire orders.[44] Betancur had generated a great deal of opposition from the army after he cut the military budget, reduced supplies for the troops, and did not consult the army on issues related to the peace process.[45] Thus, it is not surprising that Betancur's negotiations collapsed.

During the successful peace processes of the early 1990s, we see a decrease in numbers of both spoilers and spoiling actions. With the end of the Cold War, the M-19 engaged in a series of internal debates in which rebel leaders and rank-and-file alike became convinced of the importance of laying down their weapons and fostering social change by peaceful means.[46] The M-19 abandoned the idea of using negotiation as a means of reaping short-term military benefits, which set an example that other rebel groups followed.

The FARC, however, continued to act as a spoiler. Barco had demanded a temporary cease-fire from all the rebel groups willing to start peace negotiations. Whereas various other revolutionary organizations complied with this precondition, the FARC declared a truce on four separate occasions in 1989–90 but never backed its words with actions, as attested by the 112 armed actions it committed during that time.[47] The peace negotiations with the FARC remained stalled.

The ELN assumed a more radical stance than the FARC, since it never even considered going to the bargaining table. If the ELN acted as a spoiler, it did so by virtue of not taking part in Barco's negotiations, which prevented the full emergence of peace. This produced internal divisions, and eventually, the ELN's splinter factions CRS and PRT ended up laying down their weapons.

---

[42] Romero has offered a different take on this historical process. He argued that from the very formation of the UP, rightist sectors (especially regional elites and some military sectors) attempted to prevent the empowerment of this (and other) emerging leftist organizations by forming paramilitary groups and resorting to violence. Nonetheless, the FARC clearly opted for combining violent and electoral means to attain power, thereby acting as a spoiler. See Romero, *Paramilitares y autodefensas.*

[43] Marc Chernick, "Negotiating Peace amid Multiple Forms of Violence: The Protracted Search for a Settlement to the Armed Conflicts in Colombia," in *Comparative Peace Processes in Latin America,* ed. Cynthia Arnson (Washington, D.C., and Palo Alto, Calif.: Woodrow Wilson Center Press and Stanford University Press, 1999), 177; Comisión de Superación de la Violencia, *Pacificar la paz,* 118.

[44] Chernick, "Negotiating Peace," 176.

[45] Colombian army colonel, interview by the author, Bogotá, July 2000.

[46] Former M-19 member Alberto Caycedo, interview by the author, Bogotá, July 2000.

[47] William Ramírez, "Las nuevas ceremonias de la paz," *Análisis Político* 14 (1991): 15.

During Barco's tenure, we also see the application of spoiler-management techniques. Barco's closest aides, as well as the Peace Counselors Office (Consejería de Paz), lobbied a variety of (mainly rightist) political sectors to persuade them that making concessions to the rebel groups was a necessary condition for reaching peace.[48] More significantly, whereas Betancur generated opposition from the military forces, Barco's peace counselors worked in close cooperation with the army on any peace-related matters, which discouraged acts of sabotage by the military.[49]

Nevertheless, these initiatives did not fully prevent spoiling actions. Rightwing paramilitary groups gunned down the M-19's top leader and first presidential candidate while he was campaigning for the 1990 elections.[50] The FARC also attempted to sabotage the negotiations with the M-19, though with little success. In any event, if not for the government's spoiler-management initiatives, acts of sabotage would have reached greater proportions, perhaps undermining the peace accords.

Some analysts suggest that during Gaviria's tenure, the Colombian military did sabotage the negotiations with the FARC by launching a massive December 1990 attack on Casa Verde, the rebel organization's main headquarters.[51] But at that point, the FARC had not complied with a cease-fire in order to start negotiations, so there was little to sabotage.

Later on, Gaviria agreed to hold peace talks with the FARC, the ELN, and a faction of the EPL in the midst of war, meaning that all the parties took for granted that violent actions were inevitable during the negotiations. Nevertheless, after rightist sectors kidnapped and murdered FARC spokesperson Daniel García, and the EPL kidnapped former minister of public works Argelino Durán Quintero, who eventually died in captivity, the government and the rebel groups suspended negotiations.[52]

The role of spoilers was quite significant once again during Pastrana's peace process. As a precondition to sitting at the bargaining table, the FARC demanded the demilitarization of a large area that was supposed to provide a conflict-free zone for conducting negotiations. But the demilitarized area became a safe haven where the FARC planned attacks, traded drugs for weapons, recruited and trained new members, and also held many kidnap

---

[48] Former peace counselor Carlos Eduardo Jaramillo, interview by the author, Bogotá, July 2000. For further information on the creation and role of the Peace Counselors Office, see the section on the negotiators.

[49] Ibid.

[50] Ana María Bejarano, "Estrategias de paz y apertura democrática," in *Al filo del caos: crisis política en la Colombia de los años 80,* eds. Francisco Leal Buitrago and León Zamosc (Bogotá: Tercer Mundo and IEPRI, 1990), 118.

[51] Kline, *State Building and Conflict Resolution,* 85–86.

[52] Camilo González Posso, "Negociaciones con las FARC 1982–2002," in *Alternativas a la guerra: Iniciativas y procesos de paz en Colombia,* ed. Mauricio García-Durán (Bogotá and London: Accord and CINEP, 2004), 50.

victims prisoner.[53] The FARC turned its engagement in the peace process to its military and strategic advantage, spoiling the peace process in the meantime.

Arguably, the Colombian and U.S. governments, the Colombian military, and the paramilitary groups also sabotaged these peace talks. Shortly after starting peace talks with the FARC, Pastrana announced a "Marshall Plan" for Colombia to finance peacebuilding.[54] In the end, he did not deliver on his promise but instead jump-started Plan Colombia, a U.S.-led antidrug policy that clearly targeted the FARC and turned Colombia into the third-largest recipient of U.S. military aid in the world. Plan Colombia was not aimed at fighting either the various drug cartels or the right-wing paramilitary groups (which admitted that 70 percent of their finances came from drug trafficking) but instead targeted the FARC's strongholds in the southern part of Colombia.[55]

While the Colombian and U.S. governments may have thought that military pressure would force the FARC to negotiate seriously, instead, Plan Colombia helped escalate the war and seems to have pushed the FARC deeper into drug trafficking. In fact, the rebels increasingly resorted to drug profits to match the Colombian army's newly acquired superiority in training, technology, logistics, and intelligence.

Colombian military forces did not openly oppose Pastrana's peace talks, although they criticized some specific initiatives. The army resented the demilitarization of a large area during the peace talks with the FARC, and it later opposed a prisoner exchange with the FARC, fearing that this would encourage more kidnappings by the group. But the military eventually complied with Pastrana's orders by fully demilitarizing Caguán and by allowing a onetime "humanitarian" prisoner exchange with the FARC in 2001.

The (covert) military-paramilitary nexus was far more problematic. Some units of the Colombian army turned a blind eye to (and sometimes even collaborated with) rightist paramilitary groups. Even though the government took some measures to fight these groups, a Human Rights Watch report in 2000 referred to "abundant, and compelling evidence of continuing close ties between the Colombian Army and paramilitary groups responsible for gross human rights violations."[56] The government's failure to sever these connections undermined its credibility, since the rebel groups believed that Pas-

---

[53] "La paz armada," *Semana* 873 (February 22, 1999); "Los negocios de las FARC," *Semana* 879 (April 5, 1999); "Del despeje al despojo," *Semana* 885 (May 17, 1999); "La inocencia armada," *Semana* 970 (December 2, 2000).

[54] "Creo en la palabra de Tirofijo," *Semana* 869 (January 25, 1999).

[55] "El cheque del tío Sam," *Semana* 924 (January 15, 2000); "Guerra a la coca," *Semana* 927 (February 4, 2000).

[56] Human Rights Watch, *The Ties that Bind: Colombia and Military-Paramilitary Links* (New York: Human Rights Watch, 2000).

trana talked about peace while at the same time condoning a dirty war against sectors seeking to change the status quo.

And the right-wing paramilitary groups were major spoilers in Pastrana's peace negotiations. The paramilitaries were involved in two out of the three occasions when the FARC unilaterally suspended negotiations, thereby causing serious delays in the peace process.[57] On both occasions, the FARC demanded firmer government policies against the paramilitary groups before resuming the peace talks.[58]

The paramilitaries engaged in even more serious spoiling actions with the ELN. The peace talks with this rebel organization gained momentum at the end of 1999, when Pastrana agreed to demilitarize a small area where the ELN would carry out a national convention and define a peace agenda.[59] But right-wing paramilitary groups (since 1997 grouped under the umbrella organization Autodefensas Unidas de Colombia [AUC]) prevented demilitarization both through violence and by sponsoring mass mobilizations and blockages of highways.[60] At the end of Pastrana's tenure, the negotiations with the ELN remained stalled.

In conclusion, spoilers played a major role in all the failed peace negotiations. There was a net decrease in the number of spoilers during Barco's and Gaviria's tenures, which were the only governments that applied spoiler-management techniques. It is no coincidence, then, that these peace talks concluded successfully.[61]

The Negotiators and the Negotiation Strategy

Peace accords hardly materialize in the absence of competent, trustworthy negotiators.[62] Also, if a peace accord does not provide a relatively clear road map for the transition from war to peace, the risks of a resumption of war are high.[63] Were some personal qualities of the negotiators important for explaining the successful conclusion of Barco's and Gaviria's peace accords? Do the

---

[57] See "Ojo por ojo," *Semana* 872 (February 15, 1999); "Paras bajo fuego," *Semana* 873 (February 22, 1999); "El pulso," *Semana* 965 (October 28, 2000); "Llegó la hora de negociar con las AUC," *Semana* 966 (November 4, 2000).

[58] "Y ahora qué?" *Semana* 968 (November 18, 2000).

[59] "Se instalan mesas de trabajo en el sur de Bolívar," *Semana* 929 (February 22, 2000).

[60] Martínez, Ramírez, and Borda, *Persistir en la paz negociada*, 230–33.

[61] For a more extended analysis of the role of spoilers, see Nasi, "Spoilers in Colombia."

[62] This section refers to the government's negotiators exclusively, because the background of guerrilla negotiators (individuals who are primarily involved in illegal activities) tends to be obscure.

[63] Hartzell and Rothchild have underscored that stable peace accords are the ones that protect the vital interests of contending parties. See Caroline Hartzell and Donald Rothchild, "Political Pacts as Negotiated Agreements: Comparing Ethnic and Non-Ethnic Cases," *International Negotiation* 2 (1997): 147–71. See also Caroline Hartzell, "Explaining the Stability of Negotiated Settlements to Intrastate Wars," *Journal of Conflict Resolution* 43, no. 1 (1999): 3–22.

differences among the government's various bargaining teams help us account for success or failure? And were some peace agreements better designed than others?

Betancur formed various peace commissions that facilitated contacts between the Colombian government and the rebel groups M-19, EPL, and FARC, which eventually led to a truce. These commissions included independent experts and representatives of various social sectors who could neither speak for nor assume any commitments on behalf of the government.[64] Later, the government formed additional commissions and put them in charge of verifying the cease-fire and compliance with any accords, but they lacked the expertise, resources, and personnel to do an adequate job. And since the members of the various commissions were devoted only part time to the peace talks, their learning process was seriously marred. Not surprisingly, Betancur's peace process ended in failure.

President Barco, by contrast, concluded that the government (rather than any independent third parties) had to take direct responsibility for both the peace negotiations and any verification tasks. To this end, the president formed the Office of the Peace Counselor (consisting of a peace counselor and a number of advisers), which was put in charge of negotiating with the rebels in the name of the government.[65] The peace counselor and his advisers were devoted full time to conducting and analyzing the peace talks, transforming the very peace process into a virtual "school of negotiations."[66] The government's bargaining team devoted much time to learning about negotiating, which helped avert mistakes and conclude the peace talks successfully.

But the mere presence of competent negotiators is by no means a sufficient condition for successfully concluding a peace process. President Gaviria maintained the same institutional structure that Barco had created for the peace negotiations, appointing Jesús A. Bejarano (who had been adviser to the peace counselor during the Barco administration) and, later on, Liberal politician Horacio Serpa as heads of the government's bargaining team. This did not prevent failure in the negotiations with the FARC and the ELN at Caracas and Tlaxcala.

President Pastrana appointed two different peace counselors, Victor G. Ricardo and Camilo Gómez, who seriously mishandled relations with the military forces.[67] Pastrana also formed four successive bargaining commissions that were supposed to provide critical support to the peace counselors, but the first three commissions included public figures who were devoted

---

[64] Bejarano, *Una agenda para la paz*, 87.

[65] Ibid., 89; see also García-Durán, *De la Uribe a Tlaxcala*, 50–51.

[66] Former peace counselor Carlos E. Jaramillo, interview by the author, Bogotá, July 2000.

[67] "¿De salida?" *Semana* 871 (February 8, 1999); "Los otros damnificados," *Semana* 875 (March 8, 1999); "Nuevo round Lloreda-Víctor G.," *Semana* 886 (May 24, 1999).

to the negotiations only part time. Only the last bargaining commission—formed in July 2001, when the peace process had lost all credibility—included state officials who were devoted full time to the negotiations. To complicate matters even further, these bargaining commissions had merely a pro forma role. The peace counselors never summoned the bargaining commissions to define a negotiation strategy before meeting with the FARC, nor did they meet with the commissions in the aftermath of the bargaining rounds to debrief them.[68]

In short, what differentiated the successful peace process of the early 1990s from the others was not the presence of skilled negotiators from the very beginning. None of the negotiators (or bargaining teams) of the various governments had much experience in negotiating with rebel groups. But during Barco's and Gaviria's tenures, a fast learning process by full-time state functionaries occurred in the context of institutionalized peace structures, in contrast to other cases, where the learning process was inadequate and where part-time, amateurish (or underused) bargaining commissions contributed to failure.

The Peace Accords

Both Betancur and Pastrana placed peace negotiations at the very top of their agendas, yet they failed to reach durable accords with the rebel groups. This indicates that giving priority to a negotiated solution is not enough to bring about peace. Were there any differences in terms of the content of the various peace negotiations? And did this have an impact on success or failure?

As stated earlier, the government of Betancur and the rebel groups M-19, EPL, and FARC merely signed a short-lived truce. Apart from that, the government and the M-19 agreed to promote a "national dialogue" to find solutions to the Colombian war. Although the national dialogue did not make much progress, its underlying premise was that the Colombian government and society had to address the root causes of the armed conflict if they ever hoped to stop the war. That is, structural transformations were presented as if they were a precondition for the peace.

President Barco, on the other hand, in his Iniciativa para la Paz (Initiative for Peace) defined two parallel tracks to follow in the peace negotiations: one substantive and the other procedural.[69] The substantive track referred to the introduction of political reforms agreed on with the rebel groups, and the procedural track referred to the actual process of demobilizing the guerrilla organizations. Although the substantive track of the negotiations did not work as originally expected, it is worth recalling that Barco and the M-19 did

---

[68] Interview with two former members of the bargaining commissions, Bogotá, 2004.

[69] Presidencia República de Colombia, *Iniciativa para la paz* (Bogotá: Imprenta Nacional, 1988).

not attempt to solve Colombia's structural problems at the bargaining table. Rather, the parties agreed on a series of political and electoral reforms aimed at empowering the demobilized rebel groups. The rationale for this was to improve the M-19's chance of being elected, allowing the organization to make changes from within the system.[70]

During Gaviria's peace talks in Caracas and (especially) Tlaxcala, the FARC and the ELN returned to the notion that the peace talks had to solve Colombia's structural problems.[71] The same was true for Pastrana's negotiations with the FARC. In fact, in mid-1999, the government and the FARC agreed on a complicated forty-seven-point bargaining agenda, as if every conceivable problem could be solved at the bargaining table.[72] Of course, this was not the case, as became apparent to the FARC when the government engaged in bitter and extended negotiations with the group over relatively minor issues such as a prisoner exchange.

The bargaining agenda of the only successful peace process to date sought to empower the rebel groups and to define a path for addressing differences, rather than to solve Colombia's structural problems. Whenever the government and the rebel groups have attempted to redress the root causes of the Colombian armed conflict, they have failed to reach peace accords. This does not mean that the only desirable bargaining agenda is a minimalist one—or that under present conditions, the rebel groups would accept laying down their weapons in exchange for minor reforms. Rather, to prevent deadlock or a breakdown of the peace talks, a critical distinction must be made between negotiable and nonnegotiable issues.[73]

The Political Economy of War

Authors such as Paul Collier and Anke Hoeffler have proposed understanding rebellion as a form of organized crime while downplaying the issue of grievances.[74] In Collier's account, "perceived grievance and lust for power are found more or less equally in all societies . . . but it is feasibility of predation

---

[70] The government attempted to pass a law creating a special district for demobilized rebel groups so that they would have obtained an electoral advantage in congressional elections, been guaranteed television access, and the like. Former peace counselor Rafael Pardo, interview by the author, Bogotá, July 2000.

[71] Kline, *State Building and Conflict Resolution*, 85–108; Bejarano, *Una agenda para la paz*, 98.

[72] "Por la puerta grande," *Semana* 888 (June 7, 1999).

[73] See Carlo Nasi, "Agenda de paz y reformas: ¿qué se puede y qué se debe negociar? Reflexiones para un debate," in *La construcción del posconflicto en Colombia: Enfoques desde la pluralidad,* ed. Miguel Eduardo Cárdenas (Bogotá: FESCOL and CEREC, 2003), 137–70.

[74] Paul Collier, *Economic Causes of Civil Conflict and Their Implications for Policy* (Washington, D.C.: World Bank, 2000); Paul Collier and Anke Hoeffler, *Greed and Grievance in Civil War* (Washington, D.C.: World Bank, 2002).

which determines risk of conflict."[75] He goes on to say that the "motivation of conflict is unimportant: what matters is whether the organization can sustain itself financially."[76] This approach has offered a plausible explanation for the persistence of rebellion after the collapse of communism and the apparent loss of ideology by many present-day revolutionary groups. Arguably, many civil wars endure simply because irregular armed groups are able to loot resources.

Collier's approach has become rather popular in Colombia. In fact, some local studies noted that rebel groups expanded during the 1980s, a period characterized by a "substantial reduction of poverty."[77] Other analysts compared patterns of violence in different Colombian municipalities, concluding that during 1978–95, the guerrilla organizations opened new fronts in strategic areas characterized by dynamic economic activities, while some of the poorest municipalities remained relatively peaceful.[78]

Given these economic trends, why did the rebel groups expand? Greed and the availability of lootable resources (in particular, the cocaine trade) seemed to provide the correct answer. Authors such as Rafael Nieto Loaiza and Marc Chernick argued that the rebel groups recruited many militants in the 1980s and 1990s due to the huge sums of money that they extorted from the drug traffickers.[79]

But the greed thesis has many problematic aspects. To begin with, changes in terms of poverty reduction were reversed during 1995–99, a period when Colombia's macroeconomic crisis led to a dramatic increase in poverty and extreme poverty rates in urban areas.[80] The agricultural sector also contracted during the 1990s, and in 1999, "the percentage of poor in rural areas still stood at 79 percent while the percentage of extremely poor stood at 37 percent."[81] Rebel organizations continued to grow during this crisis, and some deprived sectors (in particular, poor peasants) joined illegal armed groups that pro-

---

[75] Collier, *Economic Causes of Civil Conflict*, 4.

[76] Ibid.

[77] Jesús A. Bejarano, *Economía de la agricultura* (Bogotá: Tercer Mundo, Universidad Nacional, IICA, and FONADE, 1998), 82.

[78] Jesus A. Bejarano, Camilo Echandía, Rodolfo Escobedo, and Enrique León, *Colombia: Inseguridad, violencia y desempeño económico en las áreas rurales* (Bogotá: Universidad Externado and FONADE, 1997), 253; Camilo Echandía, "Expansión territorial de las guerrillas colombianas: Geografía, economía y violencia," in *Reconocer la guerra para construir la paz*, eds. Malcolm Deas and María Victoria Llorente (Bogotá: CEREC, Ediciones Uniandes, and Ediciones Norma, 1999), 101.

[79] Rafael Nieto Loaiza, "Economía y violencia," in *Colombia: Conflicto armado, perspectivas de paz y democracia*, eds. Jorge Londoño de la Cuesta and Fernando Cubides (Miami: Latin American and Caribbean Center, 2001), 106; Chernick, "Negotiating Peace," 166–67.

[80] World Bank, Human Development Department; Country Management Unit for Colombia, Mexico and Venezuela, Latin America, and the Caribbean Regional Office, *Colombia Social Safety Net Assessment*, Report no. 22255-CO (New York: World Bank, 2002), 17.

[81] Ibid.

moted radical distributive policies. This suggests that grievance still plays a significant role in the expansion of insurgency.

Also, inequality is clearly associated with political violence. Six different measures of income inequality revealed worsening conditions from 1978 to 1999, a period when the insurgency expanded.[82] And a study by the Economic Planning Department of the Colombian government found that regardless of high rates of economic growth, the most unequal municipalities (as measured by the Gini index) were also the most violent ones.[83] These indicators are significant considering that Colombia has one of the highest levels of inequality in Latin America, which itself is the most unequal region of the world. On top of this, Colombia has a record of failed agrarian reforms, as well as successive episodes in which peasants have been forcefully evicted from their plots. (Some 1.7 million to 2.8 million people were forcibly displaced during 1985–2005.)[84] Under these conditions, downplaying grievances as a crucial factor for explaining the armed conflict seems a risky enterprise.

The question arises whether the rebel groups were able to loot more resources during the various failed peace negotiations than during the successful ones of the early 1990s. It is worth noting that there is much speculation about the rents that the guerrilla organizations obtain from drug trafficking and extortion. On top of this, analysts have only recently attempted to measure the financial resources owned by the rebel groups. According to Alfredo Rangel, 48 percent of the money obtained by the FARC derives from taxes on drug trafficking (and other drug-related activities), 36 percent from extortion, 8 percent from kidnappings, and the rest from robbery; by contrast, 60 percent of the ELN's income derives from extortion, 28 percent from kidnappings, 6 percent from drug trafficking, and the rest from robbery.[85] Rensselaer W. Lee III provides a different estimate, indicating that 70 percent of the FARC's income is related to drug trafficking, while only 8 percent of the ELN's income is.[86] Overall, both the FARC and the right-wing paramilitary groups have received substantial revenue from drug trafficking, whereas the "moralistic" ELN has distanced itself from this illegal activity.[87]

---

[82] Ibid., 18.

[83] Departamento Nacional de Planeación, *La paz: El desafío para el desarrollo* (Bogotá: Tercer Mundo Editores and Departamento Nacional de Planeación, 1998), 41.

[84] For a review of this, see Carlo Nasi, "Peace Accords in Colombia, El Salvador and Guatemala: A Comparative Study" (PhD dissertation, University of Notre Dame, 2002).

[85] Rangel, *Guerra insurgente*, 391.

[86] Rensselaer W. Lee III, as quoted in Francisco Thoumi, *El imperio de la droga: Narcotráfico, economía y sociedad en los Andes* (Bogotá: IEPRI and Planeta, 2002), 134.

[87] Carlos Castaño, a former top leader of the AUC, admitted that drug trafficking provided 70 percent of the finances of the paramilitary groups. "El testamento de Carlos Castaño," www .semana.com/wf_InfoArticulo.aspx?IdArt=114334 (accessed October 2, 2008).

Colombia also underwent an important change in the late 1990s. While it had long been the largest manufacturer of cocaine in the region, by 1997, the country also became a major producer of coca leaf. The United Nations reported that in 1999, "two thirds of all coca leaf was produced in Colombia."[88] Even if this did not lead to an increase in the flow of cocaine out of Colombia, the illegal armed groups benefited from this transformation, because they could now tax not only the drug traffickers but also thousands of peasants who cultivate coca bushes.[89] A study revealed that in 2000, FARC operated in 47 percent of the municipalities where coca plantations exist—prima facie evidence of the close connection between the FARC and coca-growing peasants.[90]

It appears that drug-related profits have had a growing impact throughout successive negotiations. Other things being equal, the constant expansion of the rebel organizations partly reflects a greater availability of lootable (drug-related) resources. The FARC, in particular, underwent a phenomenal expansion during Pastrana's tenure, while obtaining unprecedented rents from drug-trafficking activities. Barco's and Gaviria's peace negotiations, by contrast, were partly successful in a context where lootable resources were relatively scarce. Even though the premise that the illegal armed groups just "do it for the money" is questionable (the money could be just a means for taking power by force), a greater availability of lootable resources, coupled with relatively ineffective antidrug policies, complicates any future peace negotiations.

Conclusion

Many complex factors ultimately determine the success or failure of a given peace process. In Colombia, contrary to what some theorists argue, the military balance among the warring factions by itself does not help explain the success or failure of past peace negotiations. Failure has clearly been associated with governments that formed amateurish or part-time bargaining teams, that did not pay sufficient attention to negotiation strategy, that did not learn systematically from their own (and others') experiences, or that opted for a maximalist bargaining agenda that included too many nonnegotiable issues. Governments that neglected (or paid insufficient attention to) the security dilemma and the role of spoilers were also unable to prevent a breakdown in the peace talks. Also, governments that are attuned to the

---

[88] Office on Drugs and Crime (UNODC), *World Drug Report 2000* (New York: United Nations, 2000), 29; UNODC, *World Drug Report 2004* (New York: United Nations, 2004), 99.

[89] UNODC, *World Drug Report 2000*, 30.

[90] Ana María Díaz and Fabio Sánchez, "Geografía de los cultivos ilícitos y conflicto armado en Colombia" (working paper no. 47, Crisis States Programme, London School of Economics, 2004), 53.

shifting international context may be in a position to take advantage of unique windows of opportunity for reaching a peaceful settlement. The end of the Cold War provided an opening that facilitated the disarming of five rebel groups. Other opportunities may well emerge for the international community to contribute to a negotiated settlement in Colombia.

Finally, the availability of lootable resources has added considerable complexity to any peace efforts. This chapter rejects the simplistic notion that all problems derive from the fact that we are dealing with criminal, rent-seeking armed groups that are not interested in laying down their weapons. There may be good reasons for criminalizing some behaviors of illegal armed groups, but failure to reach a durable settlement has been due to the interaction of the many factors mentioned in this chapter, in which the government shares some of the responsibility.

4

The FARC at the Negotiating Table

Marc Chernick

The Fuerzas Armadas Revolucionarias de Colombia (FARC) is one of the most complex, most enduring, and least understood guerrilla insurgencies ever to emerge in Latin America. Founded in 1964 with roots in the earlier partisan civil war between Colombia's Liberal and Conservative parties in the 1940s and 1950s, this insurgent group grew from an initial force of forty-eight combatants to an estimated eighteen thousand by 2005. Several generations of combatants have entered its ranks. The earliest members were Liberal and communist guerrillas, mostly of peasant origins, who first took up arms in the 1940s. The second generation was made up of revolutionary students who emerged from the social upheavals of the 1960s, particularly in the wake of the Cuban Revolution. Next came a generation of political activists who had joined the ill-fated Patriotic Union party (UP) in the 1980s and then fled to the mountains in the face of an unrelenting dirty war. And in recent decades, a generation of rural and urban youth caught in the social anomie of poverty, unemployment, and lack of social and economic opportunities has entered the ranks.

As the FARC expanded, it gradually became a central player in the arena of Colombian politics and society. Every president since Belisario Betancur attempted some form of dialogue with the FARC. In five presidential elections held from 1982 to 1998, the issues of peacemaking and negotiations were at the center of each electoral campaign. During the 1998 campaign, a televised public meeting between an official of the Conservative campaign and the longtime FARC leader Manuel Marulanda helped Andrés Pastrana win the presidency. Pastrana then went on to launch another major round of negotiations.

But by 2002, the country had grown tired of fruitless negotiations. In the presidential elections of that year, Álvaro Uribe, the candidate who proposed a hard-line military strategy rather than a negotiated solution, emerged victorious. With the financial and logistical support of the United States, Uribe orchestrated a major military offensive, known as Plan Patriota, against the FARC.[1] Yet even Uribe, under strong pressure both from certain sectors of the international community and from national public opinion, halfheartedly spent his first six years engaged in ritualistic attempts to negotiate a prisoner exchange—or what Colombians call a "humanitarian accord"— with the FARC.

This chapter examines the positions of the FARC during three extended periods of negotiations with the Colombian government: during the presidencies of Conservative Belisario Betancur, in 1984–86; Liberal César Gaviria, in 1990–91; and Conservative Andrés Pastrana, in 1998–2002. What emerges from the analysis is that over the decades, the FARC has been remarkably consistent in its demands at the negotiating table, often restating positions first taken in the 1950s and early 1960s. Even as its original leadership aged or died, its basic positions did not change substantially. At the core, the guerrillas' positions have reflected their overwhelmingly peasant origins, a relatively rare phenomenon among Latin American revolutionary groups whose leadership came largely from students and urban intellectuals. Their positions also reflect the long history of social and political exclusion of the radicalized and communist-influenced peasant movements, which were repeatedly shut out during the 1930s and 1940s and were again excluded following La Violencia—the partisan civil war between Liberals and Conservatives in the late 1940s and 1950s.

Yet since the FARC's founding, Colombia has been radically transformed demographically. When its members first took up arms, the country was still primarily rural. The 1938 census placed the rural population at 69.1 percent of the population. In 1964, the year the FARC was founded, 53 percent of the population still lived in the countryside.[2] The latest census figures, from 2005, place the population living in rural areas at 23 percent.[3] The two great peri-

---

[1] Plan Patriota introduced sixteen thousand troops to attack the FARC deep in its bases in southern Colombia and to pressure and capture the senior guerrilla leadership. In January 2007, Uribe announced a new military strategy, Plan Consolidación, to replace Plan Patriota. Plan Consolidación continued this strategy with a force of fourteen thousand aimed at capturing the FARC leadership and attacking the guerrillas in their southern heartland. See "Derrota total de las Farc es el objetivo de la nueva fase de operaciones militares en el sur de país," *El Tiempo*, January 5, 2007. In March 2008, the armed forces targeted and killed a senior FARC leader, Raúl Reyes, in a controversial cross-border operation in Ecuadoran territory. This was the first time a senior leader had been killed by government forces since the FARC's founding in the 1960s. Reyes had been responsible for managing the FARC's international diplomatic effort in relation to the humanitarian accord.

[2] Colombia: Economic Development and Policy under Changing Conditions (Washington, D.C.: World Bank, 1984).

[3] Departamento Administrativo Nacional de Estadística (DANE), www.dane.gov.co/index.php?option=com_content&task=category&sectionid=16&id=269&Itemid=750 (accessed August 20, 2008).

ods of escalated violence in the past sixty years—1948–58 and 1985–2006—as well as the low-intensity conflict that existed during the 1960s and 1970s, have been focused primarily in rural areas and have accelerated this demographic transformation. By 2005, Colombia had one of the worst humanitarian crises of internally displaced people in the world, with most ending up in the nation's major cities, particularly Bogotá.

The FARC is still rooted in an earlier, more rural Colombia, and the rural areas have been the motor of the long-running war. Even in the late 1990s and early years of the twenty-first century, when the FARC made a major push into urban areas to recruit and organize urban militias in many of the poor shantytowns swollen with those fleeing the rural violence, the war remained primarily rural. Moreover, as most studies of development and violence have shown, the issues of land tenure, rural development, employment, poverty, access to state resources, and human rights have all grown worse in rural Colombia since the mid-1960s, when the FARC first took up arms.[4]

Since its founding, the FARC has focused on issues of political exclusion, access to state resources, and national security strategies such as the role, orientation, and structures of the military and police. At the negotiating table, since the early 1980s, it has called for such reforms as the direct election of mayors and of governors (eventually implemented in constitutional reforms in 1986 and 1991, respectively) and greater guarantees for minority parties at the ballot box and in the Congress. Many of its critiques of the reigning political and social system denounce corruption, clientelism, poverty, and inequality. These critiques are supported by much of the Colombian population, even as large sectors say that they reject the FARC's methods. A study comparing the political platforms of the traditional parties and those of the armed opposition groups found that programmatically there were only small differences on such issues as agrarian reform, human rights, and social development.[5] Despite the FARC's long ties, from the 1960s to the 1990s, with the Communist Party of Colombia, the FARC did not bring a revolutionary, socialist, maximalist, or intransigent agenda to the table.[6]

---

[4] See United Nations Development Programme (UNDP), *El conflicto, callejón con salida*. (Bogotá: UNDP, 2003).

[5] See Comité Internacional de la Cruz Roja and Comisión de Conciliación Nacional, *La paz sobre la mesa* (Bogotá: Cambio 16 Colombia, 1998) . This study was first released as a booklet inserted into the May 11, 1998, issue of *Cambio 16 Colombia*. The magazine cover asked in large, bold letters, "So why are we fighting?" The English-language version, *Peace on the Table,* is available at www.ciponline.org.

[6] If international communism is the prism of analysis, the FARC's agenda could be said to reflect the old dictates of the Third International after the First World War: to work with the capitalist system and the bourgeois parties against the most reactionary and fascist elements. But communism is not the best prism though which to view the FARC in its formative years. The FARC was influenced as much by Colombian liberalism at mid-twentieth century as by Soviet communism, although, to be sure, the contours of the Cold War shaped many of its earlier international positions. Since the Cold War, it has begun to speak a new language

Yet the government and the FARC have repeatedly been unable to translate relatively small and apparently bridgeable differences into agreements at the negotiating table. Each time, the talks have collapsed, not over issues and proposals, but over transgressions on the battlefield, extrajudicial killings of amnestied guerrillas and their supporters, or the kidnapping and killing of state officials. This dynamic has repeated itself, in one form or another, during each of the main periods of negotiations.

A careful analysis of the opportunities and constraints during each of these periods leads to the conclusion that failure was not inevitable and other outcomes were possible.[7] And yet, sixty years after the assassination of the Liberal populist Jorge Eliécer Gaitán—the singular event that sparked La Violencia—and forty-four years after the founding of the FARC by peasants who took up arms in the earlier violence, the long-running conflict remains intractable and destabilizing.

Over the decades, the war has been transformed. Moreover, it is geographically fluid, entering new regions and abandoning others as the actors in conflict adjust their military, political, and resource-extraction strategies. Yet the core issues of injustice and exclusion manifested in inequality, human rights violations, internal displacement, and social marginalization remain and continue to provide an endless supply of recruits to the now well-oiled military-political organization that is the FARC.

Politically, twenty-five years of intermittent peace processes have redounded more to the state's benefit than to the FARC's, despite—or perhaps because of—the great escalation of violence and dirty war from 1982 to about 2006, after which some indicators of violence began to decline. The government and the state have steadily increased their legitimacy, particularly following the 1991 Constituent Assembly that introduced sweeping democratic, institutional, and judicial reforms. The reincorporation of several smaller guerrilla groups through peace processes in the early 1990s (described by Carlo Nasi in Chapter 3) also enhanced state and regime legitimacy. Under President Uribe, the security apparatus of the state also increased its territorial reach. Combat, guerrilla actions, and large-scale counterinsurgency operations have largely been pushed farther away from the cities and have be-

---

based on the ideas of Simón Bolívar and what it refers to as *bolivarianismo*. Well before Venezuela's Hugo Chávez popularized the symbol and ideas of Bolívar, the FARC had already seized on the figure of the great liberator as a unifying concept in a post–Cold War and progressively post-Marxist world.

[7] Of course, there are risks inherent in making counterfactual arguments. William Zartman has written provocatively, "Counterfactual analysis is a minefield. . . . There are always reasons—real even if not good—why alternatives did not take place. Moreover, counterfactual propositions carry no guarantee of results, and even real events subsequent to the moment of action can no longer serve as a guide to the altered path of history. . . . Playing with history, it can be claimed, is merely creating fiction, from which few lessons can be learned." I. William Zartman, *Cowardly Lions: Missed Opportunities to Prevent Deadly Conflict and State Collapse* (Boulder, Colo., and London: Lynne Rienner, 2005).

gun to affect regions bordering Ecuador, Panama, Brazil, and Venezuela. Nevertheless, one fundamental element of the guerrilla war has not changed: neither side is capable of defeating the other militarily; neither side can impose a settlement on the other. This is so even after a string of government successes in early 2008 that included the controversial operation that killed senior FARC leader Raúl Reyes in Ecuadoran territory, the successful rescue operation of politician Ingrid Betancourt and other hostages long held by the FARC, and the death of the FARC's aging founder, Manuel Marulanda.

But this stalemate is not "mutually hurting," that is, not at the point in the conflict that Zartman famously described as "ripe" for a negotiated settlement.[8] After decades of armed struggle, and despite the military, political, and diplomatic setbacks incurred in early 2008, the FARC remains defiant and militarily as strong as any insurgency that has appeared in Latin America since the Cuban Revolution. Its presence in the Colombian political arena is a constant reminder that despite a half century of economic modernization and recent strides toward greater pluralism, the country still has not come to terms with its own past or extended its political and economic development model or constitutional protections to all its citizens.

The chapter concludes with a discussion of the FARC's likely positions toward any future negotiations on issues both of process and of substance. The FARC has shown a willingness to negotiate but has repeatedly overplayed its hand; it has also tended to view negotiations as a tactic within a wider strategy of armed struggle. Yet these factors have not been determinative in the breakdown of negotiations. More destructive have been the willful actions of spoilers determined to thwart the process. Spoilers have come from within the state, from within the FARC, and most notably from paramilitary forces that act with the acquiescence of certain state officials and social elites.[9]

A peace accord at this very late date is possible, but it will require high-level government support of a substantive reform agenda, political will, flexibility, international facilitation, and a degree of state coherence and strength that can limit the role of spoilers. It will also require a degree of calculated risk and audacity by the guerrilla leadership. The FARC views the earlier peace processes, particularly the experience of the UP, with great skepticism. The leadership is equally dismissive of the outcomes of other peace processes,

---

[8] Zartman's powerful idea of a "mutually hurting stalemate" refers to both the military balance and the psychology of the combatants, and the political relationship with their core supporters. For him, these are the key elements in determining a "ripe moment." But even when the pain may be bearable for the combatants and their supporters, this says nothing of the potential pain and devastation borne by civilian populations caught in the cross fire, or victims of the collateral damage of an ineffective, collapsed, or absent state.

[9] For a good overview of the discussion on spoilers by one of the major participants and theorists in the debate, see Stephen John Stedman, "Introduction," in *Ending Civil Wars: The Implementation of Peace Agreements*, eds. Stephen John Stedman, Donald Rothchild, and Elizabeth M. Cousens (Boulder, Colo.: Lynne Rienner, 2002), 11–14.

both in Colombia and the international arena, particularly the much-lauded experiences in Central America. In the FARC leaders' view, these "successful" peace processes led to the marginalization or disappearance of the guerrilla movement in the post-conflict society.[10]

Perhaps there are too many variables at play to ensure a successful outcome at the negotiating table. Yet, as this chapter underscores, the cost of not pursuing a political solution is even higher, since it could condemn Colombia to another half century of war. Not negotiating threatens the very real gains made by the state and democratic institutions. For the FARC, whose original leaders have already died or are at the end of their lives, the full transition to a new generation of leaders and an even younger generation of followers and combatants also poses very real challenges. Moreover, the organization's expanded involvement in criminal activities—kidnapping, "revolutionary taxes," cattle rustling, and a dominant position in the coca market—to finance its military buildup over the past few decades poses serious ethical and human rights questions. These activities have already severely damaged its support within a wide spectrum of the nation's intellectual and cultural elites, as well as with other constituencies that once were more receptive, such as middle-class students.

Indeed, many argue that the FARC no longer has a political project and that it has evolved into a criminal or drug-trafficking organization that benefits from the status quo and thus is not interested in peace. Yet this is a misreading of the FARC's history and politics, as well as of the role of resource mobilization in armed conflicts.[11] As in many post–Cold War insurgencies, the line between war and crime has become disconcertingly porous, but in Colombia it is still there. The FARC is structured and run as a military organization. It has a rigid hierarchy and command structure with the equivalents of four-star generals down to privates. It is led by a seven-member General Secretariat and a thirty-one-member command staff (el Estado Mayor). In areas where its authority is uncontested, it provides order, justice, and civil services such as matrimony and divorce. In areas where the state presence is greater, it exerts pressure on municipal governments to govern in specific ways and invest in particular needs—or, alternatively, in violation of international humanitarian law and the laws of war, attempts to make the region

---

[10] Olga Marín, FARC commander, member, International Commission of the FARC, interview by the author, Mexico City, July 2001.

[11] For an extensive discussion of these issues, see Marc Chernick, "Resource Mobilization and Internal Armed Conflicts: Lessons from the Colombian Case," in *Rethinking the Economics of War: The Intersection of Need, Creed, and Greed,* eds. Cynthia J. Arnson and I. William Zartman (Washington, D.C.: Woodrow Wilson Center Press and Johns Hopkins University Press, 2005); and Marc Chernick, "The FARC-EP: From Liberal Guerrillas to Communist Rebels to Post–Cold War Insurgents," in *Terror, Insurgencies, and States: Breaking the Cycles of Protracted Violence,* eds. Marianne Heiberg, Brendan O'Leary, and John Tirman (Philadelphia: University of Pennsylvania Press, 2007).

ungovernable by threatening or assassinating elected officials and opposition civic leaders.[12] This is all done within the framework of an ideology that draws heavily from Marxist and increasingly Bolivarian revolutionary imagery and ideas and that is sustained by a clandestine political party, the Bolivarian Movement. As this chapter underscores, the FARC has consistently articulated a set of proposals for political change at the negotiating table. The failures of past negotiations are not due to the inherent existential, that is, criminal, nature of the FARC—or, as former president César Gaviria once put it, because the guerrillas are onetime Marxist revolutionaries who have become drug traffickers and organized criminals. The failures have to do with the inability to bridge the political gaps at the root of the conflict. As President Uribe implicitly acknowledged in his reelection campaign and in the early weeks of his second administration, there is no military solution to this conflict. Moreover, the permanent war strategy first introduced with Plan Patriota and conducted deep in FARC-held areas on the periphery of the major population centers is not sustainable over time.[13] As difficult as it is to reach agreements at the negotiating table, every alternative is worse.

More than Forty Years of Negotiations: Narrow, Broad, and Thwarted

Before there was a FARC, there were negotiations. Organized in self-defense groups in the late 1950s, Liberal and communist guerrillas who had taken up arms a decade earlier refused government offers of demobilization and amnesty. These armed communities demanded a more comprehensive settlement based on land reform, rural development, and multiparty representation and participation.[14] In 1964, in the FARC's first pronouncement as an armed group—its "Agrarian Program of the Guerrillas"—it underscored its inability to find a negotiated solution: "We knocked on every door possible, everywhere, asking for help to avoid this anticommunist crusade," the document laments.[15] The moment was not propitious for negotiations with a peasant insurgency. The National Front agreement, ratified in a plebiscite, guaranteed parity between the country's two traditional parties in all branches and at all levels of governmental, as well as presidential alternation. Inaugurated

---

[12] From 2001 to 2006, 63 elected mayors and 224 elected city council members were assassinated. Many more were forced to govern from afar in safer regional capitals and under strong security measures. See Observatorio de Derechos Humanos, Vicepresidencia de la República de Colombia, www.derechoshumanos.gov.co/index.php?newsecc=observatorio (accessed December 15, 2006).

[13] See Note 1.

[14] See Jacobo Arenas, *Cese el fuego: La historia política de las FARC* (Bogotá: Editorial Oveja Negra, 1985), 81–91.

[15] FARC, "Programa Agrario de los Guerrilleros," July 20, 1964, reprinted in Arenas, *Cese el fuego*, 85.

in 1958, this constitutional agreement expressly excluded third-party participation in electoral politics for the next sixteen years. One year later, the Cuban Revolution entrenched the Cold War firmly in the politics of the western hemisphere, further excluding communist and leftist politics in Colombia and throughout the hemisphere.

The Colombian state responded to the challenge presented by a few holdout rebel peasant communities by elevating their status as a threat to national sovereignty. From the floor of the Colombian Senate in 1962, Sen. Álvaro Gómez Hurtado, son of former Conservative president Laureano Gómez, stirred up nationalistic passion by denouncing the presence of communist "independent republics." He declared, "People don't realize that in this country there are a series of independent republics that do not recognize the sovereignty of the Colombian state, where the Colombian Army cannot enter, where it is said that the state is vile and that it abuses the communities and their inhabitants."[16]

The peasant self-defense groups had sought dialogue in 1962 and 1964; the state responded with full-scale assaults by the Colombian army, assisted by the United States, leading to the occupation of Marquetalia (Tolima). Other campaigns followed against peasant self-defense communities in El Pato, Riochiquito, Guayabero, and other regions. After the second attack, these communities responded by creating a mobile guerrilla force. The bombing of Marquetalia in 1964 and the resistance of a force of "48 fighters against 16,000 heavily armed troops" became part of the iconography of the FARC.[17] The home page of the FARC Web site in 2008 read, "FARC-EP, 42nd Anniversary, 1964–2006, from Marquetalia to Victory."[18]

A year after the assault on Marquetalia and the other "independent republics" clustered in the eastern and central cordilleras, the mobile guerrillas held their foundational meeting called the First Guerrilla Conference of Marquetalia. There the guerrillas reaffirmed their rebellion and called the movement the Bloque Sur (Southern Bloc). In 1966, the guerrillas held the Second Conference, where they took the name the Revolutionary Armed Forces of Colombia and asserted that the mobile guerrillas were legitimate and that the struggle should extend to other regions of the country. Almost twenty years would pass before government leaders again reached out to the FARC.

By the early 1980s, the FARC and the other smaller guerrilla movements had moved to the center of Colombian politics. From then on, Colombian

---

[16] Reprinted in Arturo Alape, *La paz, la violencia: Testigos de excepción* (Bogotá: Editorial Planeta, 1985), 244–49.

[17] Carlos Arango Z., *FARC, veinte años, de Marquetalia a la Uribe* (Bogotá: Ediciones Aurora, 1984).

[18] FARC-EP, Fuerzas Armadas Revolucionarias de Colombia, 1964–2006, 42do Anniversario– De Marquetalia hasta la Victoria, www.farcep.org/ (accessed December 23, 2007).

politics would be defined by extended periods of negotiations and periods of prolonged and escalated confrontation.[19] The protracted nature of both the peace processes and the decades-old war produced a group of experienced government peace negotiators. It also produced a generation of military officers with deep counterinsurgency experience. Nevertheless, the empirical experiences have been interpreted differently, and there is no consensus on lessons learned. Most administrations strove to distinguish their approach from those of their predecessors, with one notable exception of continuity, in the Barco (1986–90) and Gaviria (1990–94) periods, when a core group of peace negotiators remained in place.

During these two decades of negotiating attempts, the central peacemaking framework was defined as some form of dialogue with the country's armed guerrilla movements, in search of a political solution. Two general models of peace negotiations were articulated, one based on a broad agenda, the other on a narrow agenda. A parallel terminology can be found in some of the literature on international assistance in post-conflict countries, which speaks of a "minimalist" and a "maximalist" agenda.[20] The international literature does not refer to negotiations per se. Rather, it presents a range of options in post-conflict assistance: a narrower focus on disarmament, demobilization, and reintegration (DDR); or a broader assistance program that more directly addresses the challenges facing states and society in the post-conflict period, including state capacity building, judicial reform, political reform, social and ethnic relations, poverty, human rights, security, natural resources, and other critical issues. Within Colombia, the question is whether the negotiating agenda should focus on broad political, economic, and social issues or should be constricted to agreements on cease-fire, disarmament, and reincorporation.

From 1982 to 2002, governments implemented different versions of both approaches. Presidents Betancur (1982–86) and Pastrana (1998–2002) pursued peace processes based on the broad agenda. Both processes ended in failure. Two presidents, Virgilio Barco (1986–90) and César Gaviria (1990–94), had some success with the narrower approach, reaching agreements with several smaller armed guerrilla groups, including the Movimiento 19 de Abril (M-19), Quintín Lame (an indigenous guerrilla movement), and the majority faction of the Ejército Popular de Liberación (EPL). In these processes, demobiliza-

---

[19] In February 1980, the M-19 guerrillas seized the embassy of the Dominican Republic during a diplomatic reception and held fifteen foreign ambassadors, including the U.S. ambassador, hostage for the next fifty-nine days. The action placed the issue of amnesty and negotiations into the center of Colombian politics. Following the election of Belisario Betancur in 1982, talks were opened up with the M-19, the FARC, and other guerrilla groups.

[20] See Organisation for Economic Co-operation and Development, "The Influence of Aid in Situations of Violent Conflict," *DAC Journal* 2, no. 3 (2001).

tion was accompanied by an amnesty. Barco called his approach *"mano ten-dida pulso firme"* (extended hand with a firm grip). Álvaro Uribe negotiated the disarmament of pro-state right-wing paramilitary groups within the confines of a DDR agenda that was accompanied not by an amnesty but rather by a Justice and Peace Law that held out the possibility of relatively lenient punishment for criminal actions.[21] But though the narrow approach achieved the disarmament of several smaller guerrilla movements and the demobilization of most paramilitary organizations, the FARC's position has been constant: it will accept only the broad agenda. It will negotiate peace only on the basis of political reforms and access to power.

One way to understand the dichotomy between the broad and narrow agendas is to look at the language that the FARC employs when presenting its own history, versus that used in some of the peacemaking literature and in some government pronouncements. The FARC views its rebellion as legitimate. For its leaders, armed rebellion is a response to a closed political system and a long history of repression and exclusionary social relations, particularly in the Colombian countryside. All the FARC's documents underscore the struggle against the Colombian "oligarchy" and the exclusionary bipartisan regime of the traditional parties. In its founding document declaring its agrarian program and armed insurgency, the nascent guerrilla movement pronounced:

> We, campesinos from southern Tolima, Huila, Cauca, and Valle along the ridge of the Central Cordillera, are the nerve of a revolutionary movement that first formed in 1948. Against us has been arrayed the force of the large landed estates, cattle ranches, big business, the political bosses from the official parties and the merchants of violence. We are the victims of blood and fire that have been practiced by the oligarchy. Against us, they have unleashed during 16 years, four wars. One beginning in 1948, the other in 1954, another in 1962 and another in 1964, when the high military command launched Operation Marquetalia. . . . We are revolutionaries that fight to change the regime. We wanted to fight using the least painful methods against our people: the peaceful road, the way of democratic mass struggle. But this road was closed to us violently with war, and since we are revolutionaries, in one form or another we will play the historic role that has been assigned to us, the revolutionary road of armed struggle, the fight for power.[22]

---

[21] Although the experience of the paramilitary demobilization is included here as an example of the narrow agenda, it is important to recognize that the paramilitaries, although illegal, were not armed *opposition* groups but rather organizations that took up arms to defend the state and their own interests and properties; in many cases, they had direct or indirect ties to key sectors of the state. The two classes of armed organizations—left-wing guerrillas and pro-state militias—and possible paths toward disarmament are not directly comparable, despite the similarity of the language that is often employed to describe them.

[22] FARC, "Programa Agrario de los Guerrilleros," July 20, 1964, reprinted in Arenas, *Cese el fuego*, 84–88.

Twenty-nine years later, the FARC presented the same agrarian program, only editing the original document to include the wars of the 1980s and 1990s that were "unleashed against" them.[23]

From 1964 through 1982, the FARC's strategic documents all emphasized the revolutionary takeover of power.[24] However, beginning in public and private interviews during the peace process begun in 1982, FARC leaders began to contemplate the idea of a negotiated settlement to the conflict. Jacobo Arenas, then the chief political strategist of the FARC, stated in an interview in May 1987,

> In the Seventh Conference, we had prepared a general strategy for seizing power by expanding our forces, combat capacity, and territorial presence. We had already begun to build an offensive army, moving beyond guerrilla tactics based on ambushes and small defensive units. In the Eighth Conference we changed the name to the FARC-EP.[25] But the peace process of Belisario Betancur changed everything. It forced us to change our strategy, enter into a bilateral cease-fire, and begin a dialogue on a truce, political reforms, and democratic opening.[26]

Two years later, in the conclusions of its General Staff plenum held in 1989, the FARC for the first time formally recognized in a strategic document that a negotiated settlement was possible: "The policy of the FARC is to give top priority to the struggle to find political solutions to the national problem, and, specifically, a negotiated solution to the armed conflict. . . . In the search for a new politics, the FARC will continue to bring up issues of basic change in Colombian life, which must start with the establishment of a Democratic state."[27]

For the guerrillas, negotiations must address the political and structural problems that led to the insurgency and continue to exclude millions of Colombians. In contrast, for conflict-resolution theorists and government officials who advocate the narrow agenda, the issue is not political injustice, social exclusion, and marginalization but rather the illegal recourse to arms. President Barco was very clear on this. He asserted that Colombia already

---

[23] Comité Internacional de la Cruz Roja and Comisión de Conciliación Nacional, *La paz sobre la mesa*.

[24] Jacobo Arenas, *Pleno ampliado del Estado Mayor de las FARC-EP, Diciembre 25–29, 1987* (unpublished internal FARC document); FARC-EP Octava Conferencia Nacional Guerrillera, "Plataforma para un gobierno de reconciliación y reconstrucción nacional," April 3, 1993 (unpublished internal FARC document). Both documents are excerpted in Comité Internacional de la Cruz Roja and Comisión de Conciliación Nacional, *La paz sobre la mesa*.

[25] Fuerzas Armadas Revolucionarias de Colombia–Ejército del Pueblo (Revolutionary Armed Forces of Colombia–Army of the People).

[26] Jacobo Arenas, interview by the author, La Uribe (Meta), May 1987.

[27] FARC-EP, *Conclusiones generales del Pleno del Estado Mayor de las FARC, Mayo 10–17, 1989* (unpublished internal FARC document). Excerpts can be found in Comité Internacional de la Cruz Roja and Comisión de Conciliación Nacional, *La paz sobre la mesa*.

had democratic forums as well as regular elections and other mechanisms of democratic accountability. The state could be generous (*mano tendida*) by allowing for amnesty and peaceful disarmament but must be firm (*pulso firme*) in protecting the nation's democratic institutions.[28] One approach focuses on structural change. The other focuses on disarmament and demobilization. As long as there exists an "unhurting" stalemate in military terms, the FARC will not accept a peace process that focuses on DDR.

A Broad Agenda, but How Broad?

The FARC has entered formal peace negotiations with the Colombian government on three occasions, not counting the many failed discussions and, in recent years, the extended history of contacts and negotiations on prisoner exchanges (see Table 4.1). By examining this long history, the news reports, documents, and communiqués that have accompanied the negotiations, and interviews with some of the key participants, it is possible to identify what might be called the FARC's "essential positions," that is, the most basic issues that, if substantially met, would provide a great inducement for peace.

Although the FARC has insisted on negotiating the broad agenda, the framework has been, essentially, too broad. Many issues within the general categories enumerated in the Common Agenda for Change negotiated in May 1999 with the Pastrana administration would be better left for a Constituent Assembly, congressional action, or some other forum. The Common Agenda topics included negotiated political solution, protection of human rights as a responsibility of the state, integral agrarian policies, exploitation and conservation of natural resources, economic and social structure, judicial reforms, the fight against corruption and drug trafficking, political reform and the expansion of democracy, reform of the state, agreements on international humanitarian law, armed forces, international relations, and formalizing agreements.[29]

But if this agenda is too broad and too general, there are issues, such as agrarian reform—the historical issue of the FARC—democratic opening, security, and human rights, that *are* essential for a final peace agreement. Many of the other issues have served only to obfuscate what is negotiable and what is not and thus have served to undermine the wider negotiating process.

During the Pastrana negotiations, after elaborating the agenda, the two sides chose to begin with the issue of economic reforms and, specifically, employment policies. They spent the next three and a half years on this issue. As important as economic reforms are, and however great the need, the

---

[28] República de Colombia, Presidencia de la República, *El camino de la paz,* vol. 1 (Bogotá: Consejería para la Reconciliación, Normalización y Rehabilitación, 1989).

[29] Oficina del Alto Comisionado para la Paz, *Hechos de paz V–VI: A la mesa de negociación* (Bogotá: Presidencia de la República, 1998–99), 545–48.

	Cease-fire	Amnesty/Pardon	Demobilization Disarmament	Agenda/Issues	International Context	Site of Negotiations	International Accompaniment/Facilitation	Outcome
1984–87	Bilateral cease-fire	Yes	Arms will be unnecessary in the context of democratic opening	Democratic opening and political space for new left party, electoral reform, direct election of mayors, political reform, agrarian reform	Cold War, very beginning of war on drugs	Unofficial despeje zone: La Uribe (Meta)	No	Breakdown of talks/return to war No substantive agreement
1991–92*	Failure to reach agreement on unilateral cease-fire	Proposed	Not on agenda	Cease-fire, development of a negotiating agenda (Caracas) Unrealized agenda: socioeconomic aspect, energy, and natural resources (Tlaxcala)	End of Cold War, rise of war on drugs	Caracas, Venezuela; and Tlaxcala, Mexico	Mexican and Venezuelan hosts with very limited role	Breakdown of talks/return to war No substantive agreement
1998–2002	No cease-fire	Proposed	Not on agenda	First agenda item to be negotiated: economic reforms Unrealized agenda items: agrarian policies, illicit crops, human rights, international humanitarian law, natural resources, judicial reform, political reform, state reform, armed forces, and international relations Ancillary negotiations: cease-fire, prisoner exchange (agreement reached)	War on drugs, very beginning of war on terrorism	Official despeje zone of five municipalities: San Vicente de Caguán (Caquetá), Vista Hermosa (Meta), La Macarena (Meta), Mesetas (Meta), La Uribe (Meta)	Accompaniment with limited facilitation in the final months of talks UN special adviser to the secretary-general Group of Friends: Mexico, Venezuela, Canada, Cuba, Spain, France, Italy, Norway, Sweden, Switzerland	Breakdown of talks/return to war One substantive agreement on exchange of prisoners

*Negotiations with Coordinadora Guerrillera Simón Bolívar (FARC, ELN, EPL faction) special forum that is represented by a negotiating table is not the appropriate site for this policy debate beyond a few hortatory declarations. If a negotiated settlement was the desired outcome, beginning with this issue was a recipe for failure.

There is evidence that the FARC basically understood this and chose the topic of economic issues and unemployment, not to reach agreements with the government but rather to mobilize broader popular support. Iván Márquez, member of the Estado Mayor and a former UP congressman, explained the FARC's position in an essay written during the negotiations:

> Whatever theme on the Negotiating Agenda that is chosen, the subject inevitably comes back to neo-liberalism. . . . If it's the agrarian situation, neo-liberalism together with the historical destruction of the past, is the principal cause for the current economic devastation of the countryside. . . . If it's the Armed Forces, we are speaking of the mission assigned by the new global politics to oppress the people and erase human rights. . . . If it's political economy, we see the essential savagery of neo-liberalism. . . . If it's the increase in drug production, we are speaking of a phenomenon tied to unemployment and the general injustice of neoliberalism. The issue is also used as a pretext for military intervention by the United States, which, behind the smokescreen permits them to appropriate the immense wealth of the Amazon basin, the real object of the so-called Plan Colombia.
>
> In these circumstances, it is inevitable that the Negotiating Table will be converted into the site of a confrontation of all the Colombian people against the neo-liberal policies supported by the government. . . . The Negotiating Table is an important conquest by the Colombian people that should be taken advantage of to the maximum to advance the fight for social change and the new Colombia.[30]

It is understandable that both the FARC and the government, like virtually all adversaries in a negotiation, would try to use the privileged circumstances of the negotiating table to advance their own political visions, agendas, and popular support. But if there are no mechanisms to further dialogue on concrete, attainable goals on political change *and* a negotiated end to the conflict, then the forum is bound to fail. Many in the FARC have tended to view negotiations as a means to advance the revolution, while many in the government view them as a way to advance the counterrevolution. In this maneuvering, the government has had greater success than the FARC in delegitimizing its adversary and weakening its political reach. But the cost has been high, and the strategy has not brought the conflict closer to settlement.

A more focused approach that might yield better results would still require a complex negotiating agenda. Indeed, three types of critical issues need to be engaged and considered carefully in future talks. These are (a)

---

[30] Iván Márquez, "El primer punto de la agenda, primer gran choque con neoliberalismo," Montañas de Colombia, Marzo 2000, www.farcep.org/?node=2,988,1&highlight=ivanpercent 20marquez percent20neoliberalismo (accessed January 2007).

procedural, that is, involving the rules of the game of a peace process: negotiating site, agenda, cease-fire, international mediation; (b) *substantive*, that is, involving agrarian reform and rural development, illicit crops, political reforms, political favorability and access to power, human rights and international humanitarian law, reorientation of police and military; and (c) *DDR*, that is, involving arms, demobilization and reintegration of individual combatants, truth, justice, amnesty, and reparations. The FARC has clear and consistent positions on most of these issues.

Procedural Issues

On procedural issues, the FARC has repeatedly stated that negotiations must take place in Colombia, in a zone that has been cleared of government, police, military, and intelligence forces. Of the three occasions of major talks, two followed this protocol. Negotiations during the Betancur administration were held from 1984 to 1986 in the municipality of La Uribe, in the department of Meta, an area long influenced by the Communist Party and the FARC. Without issuing a formal decree law establishing a *despeje*, or demilitarized zone, as was later done under Pastrana, the Betancur government effectively ceded the area to the FARC in the context of a bilateral cease-fire. Both sides agreed to halt military operations and refrain from attacking the other; guerrilla forces would simply remain in the locales where they were operating before the cease-fire. The cease-fire lasted from May 1984 to June 1987.

During negotiations from August 1991 to May 1992, the two sides met outside the country, first in Caracas and then in Tlaxcala, Mexico, without establishing a cease-fire, although the issue of cease-fire was the central focus of the Caracas negotiations.[31] During this period, the FARC negotiated as part of the Simón Bolívar Coordinating Body, then consisting of the FARC, the ELN, and a dissident faction of the EPL. This was the only time the FARC agreed to an international venue for formal negotiations. The ELN, by

---

[31] Between the breakdown of the cease-fire agreement in June 1987 and the initiation of talks in Caracas in August 1991, the governments of Virgilio Barco (1986–90) and César Gaviria (1990–94) escalated military operations against the FARC. The FARC rejected Barco's proposed narrow agenda, whereas the M-19 and, later, the EPL and Quintín Lame, accepted it. In December 1990, on the same day that elections were held for a Constituent Assembly—in which the M-19 received almost 30 percent of the vote—the Gaviria government ordered the bombing of the FARC headquarters in La Uribe, symbolically underscoring the difference between those guerrilla movements that had demobilized and entered the political arena and those that chose to continue the armed struggle. The effort backfired, however: the FARC, the ELN, and a dissident faction of the EPL launched a major military offensive that escalated the armed confrontation to unprecedented levels while underscoring the weakness of the state's counterinsurgency capabilities. The escalation of the armed conflict continued throughout the meetings of the Constituent Assembly from January to June 1991. In response, the Gaviria government changed course and offered renewed peace talks with the ELN, the FARC, and the EPL, paving the way for the talks in Caracas and Tlaxcala.

contrast, has met with government and civil society representatives on several occasions outside the country.[32] The FARC's preference—and in recent years its nonnegotiable position—has been to negotiate within a specially cleared demilitarized zone inside Colombia.

At the outset of the Pastrana peace process of 1998–2002, the FARC made the demilitarization of five municipalities a condition for peace talks: Mesetas, Vista Hermosa, Uribe y La Macarena in the department of Meta, and San Vicente del Caguán in the department of Caquetá. Pastrana agreed, and three months after the new president took office, the government withdrew all military and police from the five jurisdictions—a large but sparsely populated territory the size of Switzerland.[33] The area consists of municipal centers and colonization zones where the FARC had a strong presence for decades and where the state was historically weak or absent. Security functions were handed over to the FARC and to a "citizens' " police force. The few other state institutions and agencies in the area, including elected mayors and city councils, remained in place.

In these talks, the FARC accepted limited international participation for the first time; previously, it had insisted that the conflict was national and that outside mediators had no role. But both the FARC and the government consented to the naming of a UN special adviser for Colombia who was allowed to act as an observer. The FARC then accepted the naming of a "Group of Friends"—a model, used in Central America and elsewhere, bringing friendly countries into the process. The Group of Friends for the negotiations with the FARC comprised Mexico, Venezuela, Canada, Cuba, France, Spain, Sweden, Norway, Switzerland, and Italy.[34]

But neither the UN special adviser nor the Group of Friends was allowed to participate directly in the talks. When present, they generally sat outside the room in Caguán where government and FARC negotiators met. Only when the peace process was on the verge of collapse in January 2002 did the two sides permit the UN special adviser, James Lemoyne, and the Group of

---

[32] The ELN met with the National Peace Commission, consisting largely of civil society leaders, in Viana, Spain, and Mainz, Germany, in 1998; with government and civil society officials in Geneva in 2000; with government officials on Margarita Island, Venezuela, and in Caracas in 2001; and with government, civil society, and international observers and facilitators (from Norway, Sweden, Switzerland, Venezuela, and Cuba) in Havana intermittently from 2002 to 2007. For a more thorough discussion of these meetings, see Chapter 5 by León Valencia in this volume.

[33] The area contained a population of 104,729 of Colombia's total population of 42,090,500. DANE, 2005 census.

[34] A second, partially overlapping group of five nations was also created for the concurrent talks then being held with the ELN. For a discussion of the international community's participation in peacemaking in Colombia, see Marc Chernick, "Protracted Peacemaking: The Insertion of the International Community into the Colombian Peace Process," in *From Promise to Practice: Strengthening UN Capacities for the Prevention of Violent Conflict,* eds. Chandra Sriram and Karen Wermeister (Boulder, Colo: Lynne Rienner and International Peace Academy, 2003).

Friends, led by French ambassador Daniel Parfait, to play a more direct role in an attempt to salvage the process. But by then, it was too late. On February 20, 2002, President Pastrana declared the peace process over after the FARC hijacked a plane and kidnapped a prominent senator. Pastrana gave the armed forces immediate orders to retake the zone.

Under the right conditions, the policy of withdrawing police and military but increasing other state programs in a special zone, as happened during the Pastrana government, could be a net benefit for the residents and also a stimulus for the peace process. But in this case, as the negotiations stalled and the levels of national violence rose, public opinion turned against the entire enterprise.

Álvaro Uribe took office amid the ashes of Pastrana's failed efforts. Despite the escalation of hostilities between the FARC and the state after February 20, 2002, one issue remained on the negotiating table: a prisoner exchange, known as a "humanitarian accord" (*acuerdo humanitario*).

The expectations that emerged around the humanitarian accord drew in several prominent national and international facilitators/mediators. In the early days of his first administration, President Uribe requested assistance from the UN secretary-general and authorized UN special adviser Lemoyne to make contact with the FARC to facilitate a humanitarian accord. But from the beginning, Uribe presented two conditions: (a) no *despeje* and (b) guarantees that would prevent the FARC prisoners—mostly midlevel leaders and guerrilla fighters—from returning to combat after their release. His initial proposals called for a third country to take charge of the released prisoners. For the next six years, President Uribe basically did not budge from his original position.

The FARC, for its part, initially called for the *despeje* of two large departments, Caquetá and Putumayo, as the only acceptable sites for negotiations. It also insisted that there be no preconditions for the talks on the humanitarian accord. FARC leaders later lowered their demands and eventually called for the *despeje* of two relatively small municipalities in the department of Valle: Florida and Pradera. At one point, Uribe seemed to agree to these two sites, but the sides could not agree on security arrangements and the rules governing the presence of FARC arms and combatants within the zones.

In April 2005, acting on a request by President Uribe, the UN secretary-general withdrew his special adviser and eliminated the position. Numerous other potential mediators also offered their "good offices" to advance the humanitarian accord: the Catholic Church, the French government, the Swiss government, former Liberal president Alfonso López Michelson, a group of six former Colombian presidents, former Conservative politician Álvaro Leyva, Sen. Piedad Córdoba, and others.

In September 2007, President Hugo Chávez of Venezuela became directly involved in the process and allied himself with the efforts being made by

Senator Córdoba. President Nicolas Sarkozy of France, elected in May 2007, also seized the initiative, from the day of his inauguration, and reaffirmed his government's commitment to free former Colombian presidential candidate and French citizen Ingrid Betancourt. Sarkozy subsequently began to work with Venezuelan president Chávez on the issue. Such high-level international attention represented a singular opportunity to break the impasse. Uribe officially endorsed the efforts of Senator Córdoba and the Venezuelan and French governments, but he also was firm in insisting on his two original conditions.

The issue of a *despeje* has emerged as one of the FARC's central conditions for any future round of negotiations, whether on the humanitarian accord or on a more substantive agenda. Pastrana had it right on this issue: call the bluff, establish the *despeje*, and set up a viable negotiating process. Objections that the FARC would use the zone for increased military or criminal actions or that a *despeje* would undermine state authority were and are more apparent than real. The state can have a stronger nonmilitary presence, and the FARC does not need a *despeje* to launch military actions or engage in criminal activities.

The FARC's position on procedural issues related to a cease-fire has changed over time in response to the exigencies of the moment and the context of the negotiations. The experience demonstrates that the FARC does respond to serious proposals and can be engaged, although not always successfully.

In 1984, the FARC and the Colombian government signed a comprehensive bilateral cease-fire agreement, "El acuerdo de La Uribe" (the La Uribe agreement),[35] named for the municipality in the department of Meta where the accord was signed. The cease-fire was designed to take effect as a prelude to more substantive political, economic, and social reforms that were specified in the agreement and would be realized in the context of the truce. In the cease-fire accords, the FARC condemned all acts of kidnapping and subsequently provided a list of all the kidnap victims then in its custody.[36] The cease-fire was bilateral, and the guerrilla forces would remain in situ—that is, both government and guerrilla forces would mutually cease hostilities, and the guerrillas would remain geographically where they were at the time the agreement took effect.

Hostilities did not resume until June 1987, when the FARC ambushed an army convoy in Caquetá after what it declared were months of provocations by military forces, and assassination of its amnestied political leaders and militants incorporated into the UP. By then, Betancur had already left office, and the new president, Virgilio Barco, declared that he would support only a peace process that was limited to the narrow agenda of DDR.

---

[35] "Acuerdo de La Uribe," reprinted in FARC-EP, *Esbozo Histórico*. Comisión Internacional de las FARC-EP, 1998.

[36] Ibid.

Barco established new rules of the game for resuming peace talks and made a unilateral cease-fire by the guerrillas a condition for such talks. The FARC rejected these terms, stating that in effect they were a call to surrender—although the same conditions were eventually accepted by the M-19 and, later, the EPL and Quintín Lame.

During the Gaviria administration, when negotiations finally resumed with the FARC during the Caracas phase (from September to December 1991), the issue of a cease-fire became the central issue of the negotiations. The FARC demanded that the state recognize hundreds of municipalities as guerrilla-influenced and that FARC units remain in these areas, free from government attacks. The government responded that it recognized only a handful of such municipalities. The two sides eventually drew up maps and came close to an agreement involving between sixty and ninety-six municipalities, but the agreement broke down over issues such as the guerrillas' degree of mobility, their political activities, and their carrying arms in the municipalities.[37]

During the Pastrana administration, the Colombian government and the FARC agreed to negotiate amid the hostilities, without a cease-fire. This policy was a reaction both to the FARC's rejection of the unilateral cease-fire demand employed during the Barco and Gaviria years and to the armed forces' rejection of the bilateral cease-fire imposed during the Betancur administration. There also existed a strong international precedent: in El Salvador the two sides agreed to negotiate during the war and to defer discussions on a cease-fire until after substantive agreements had been reached.

But the upsurge in violence during the negotiations made most citizens increasingly skeptical of the peace process. Why was violence increasing, many asked, if the two sides were sitting at the negotiating table?

Pastrana's negotiators soon realized that the issue of a cease-fire before substantive agreements needed to be reconsidered, and the issue was reintroduced. In early 2000, both sides exchanged preliminary proposals. By October 2001, in an agreement known as the San Francisco de la Sombra Accord, the FARC and the government agreed to make the pursuit of a cease-fire a priority.[38]

The issue was daunting. The government rejected the in situ framework of the Betancur years, where all combatants would suspend hostilities but remain where they were geographically at the time the cease-fire went into effect. For its part, the FARC refused to consider the model used in negotiations with the M-19, the EPL, and Quintín Lame during the Barco and Gaviria years in which combatants agreed to unilaterally suspend hostilities and re-

---

[37] Jesús Antonio Bejarano, former high commissioner of peace and chief government negotiator in Caracas during the 1991 talks, interview by the author, Bogotá, June 1992.

[38] For the San Francisco de la Sombra Accord in English, see the Center for International Policy's Colombia Program, www.ciponline.org/colombia/100503.htm (accessed August 21, 2008).

locate to a few designated zones until agreements for demobilization and disarmament could be reached. The FARC favored the proposal discussed in Caracas in 1991 in which the state would recognize scores of municipalities where guerrilla combatants could remain unmolested by government forces during the period of the cease-fire.

Pursuit of a cease-fire was further complicated by other related issues. Principal among these were the government's concerns about the guerrillas' involvement in kidnapping and the FARC's security concerns regarding paramilitary activities against its combatants and supporters. For the government, the question was whether kidnapping should be allowed to continue during a cease-fire and in the absence of a final peace agreement. In the 2001 San Francisco de la Sombra Accord mentioned above, the FARC agreed to suspend the practice of "miracle fishing" (*pescas milagrosas*), which involves the random kidnapping of high-profile or affluent victims stopped at FARC roadblocks and control points. But the FARC was not prepared to renounce all kidnappings, as it had done in 1984 cease-fire agreements. It would only agree to study further the issue of a cease-fire that included the "cessation of hostilities, kidnappings, actions for ending the paramilitary phenomenon."[39]

No further progress was made for over a year, until January–February 2002, when the peace process was on the verge of collapse. At that point, the United Nations and the Group of Friends stepped in, and the two sides agreed to a timetable that identified benchmarks for results. The timetable stated that both sides would reach a cease-fire agreement by April 7, 2002. Negotiations began once again with the aim of identifying the total number of zones where fighters would be located, the size and location of each zone, and the rules of conduct, applicable to both sides, within and outside the zones.[40] Maps were prepared, and details began to be leaked to the press. The accords that had come so close to being signed in Caracas only to be left on the table were resurrected and updated.

But the country was in the midst of an election campaign. Candidate Uribe denounced the plans as the disguised creation of dozens of new *despeje* zones—a development that would be unacceptable for the country. The negotiations did not advance. Tensions mounted. The FARC hijacked an airplane with a leading senator aboard. Pastrana ordered the military to retake the *despeje* zone well before a cease-fire could be negotiated.

The record is clear: the FARC will accept a cease-fire that is bilateral, meaning that the armed forces must likewise agree to suspend operations against FARC forces. It prefers to quarter its forces within its areas of influence and operations, either through the in situ framework or through the negotiated development of specially prepared maps that mutually and formally recog-

[39] Ibid.

[40] Presidential adviser Gonzalo de Francisco, interview by the author, Bogotá, August 2002.

nize many of these areas. The FARC is willing to negotiate the issue of kidnapping as part of a cease-fire agreement, but it wants parallel commitments from the government to crack down on extrajudicial killings, disappearances, and other violations that are aimed at the guerrillas and FARC supporters and that have been attributed to paramilitary forces and their state allies in the past.

Substantive Issues

Regarding substantive issues, a review of FARC negotiations reveals that the organization has articulated a broad and detailed negotiating agenda several times in the past, including in its founding document, "The Agrarian Program of the Guerrillas." In at least two periods of negotiations, from 1984 to 1986 and from 1998 to 2002, the government had also basically accepted a broad agenda. The challenge has not been in defining the agenda; it has been in reaching negotiated solutions once the agenda was defined.

This subsection presents the FARC's demands in three historical periods: at its founding in 1964; as the group prepared to enter into negotiations with the Betancur government in 1984; and in a basic platform issued in 1993 after the Eighth Conference, which became the basis for agreement on a twelve-point negotiating agenda with the Pastrana administration in La Machaca in May 1999.

The FARC's positions have been consistent, although the emphases have changed over time. When the guerrillas first took up arms in the 1960s, the agrarian program dominated the agenda. In the 1980s, the FARC envisioned being the vanguard of a democratic opening and a growing leftist movement augmented by strength of arms. In the 1990s, the group's emphasis changed from political to economic and social reforms, reflecting both the aborted and tragic experience of the UP and also the significant political and institutional reforms that were made in the Constituent Assembly of 1991—in which they did not participate and, thus, did not have a stake.

The Agrarian Program of the Guerrillas, produced amid the tensions immediately after the assault on Marquetalia in 1964, remains the FARC's basic program for agrarian change and development in rural Colombia. It was expressly reaffirmed in its last general conference, held in 1993, that called for an effective agrarian reform that changes the roots of the socioeconomic structure of the Colombian countryside. The reform is based on confiscating the large landowners' properties and handing over the land, completely free, to the campesinos who work it or want to work it. Other elements of the original program include provisions for granting land titles, credits, equipment, seeds, and technical assistance to campesinos; preserving industrial structures; preserving agribusinesses and reorienting them to benefit the populace; providing pricing controls; and protecting indigenous communities and lands.

The major addition that the FARC has made to the basic agrarian program in recent years involves the issue of illicit crops. In its 1993 platform, the FARC asserted that the "production, marketing, and use of drugs and hallucinogens . . . [is] a serious social problem that cannot be treated using a military approach" and called for a "commitment to reduce demand from the major powers [that is, the United States] that are the main source of the world's demand for drugs."[41]

This issue was included in the negotiations between the Pastrana government and the FARC in San Vicente de Caguán (in the *despeje* zone), where the FARC presented various proposals, within the basic agrarian program, that supported alternative development based on a small peasant economy and sufficient financial and technical contributions from the state. Interestingly, one of President Pastrana's original proposals, the "Marshall Plan for the Coca Growing Regions," concurs with this position.[42]

The FARC has stated that it will accept the manual eradication of coca, within the implementation of the agrarian development program outlined above. In an agreement signed in Los Pozos in February 2001, the FARC was quite specific: it opposes aerial fumigation and forced eradication but will not oppose manual eradication of illicit crops in communities that have reached a common agreement with the government for alternative development assistance.[43]

In its plenum meeting in March 2000, the FARC's Central Command further articulated its position toward illegal crops: "With the extreme development of capitalism in its imperial stage . . . many people that rely on agriculture have opted to cultivate coca, opium poppies, marijuana as their only form of survival. The earnings of these peasants are minimal. Those who enrich themselves are the intermediaries who transform the crops into psychotropic drugs and who bring them to markets in the developing countries, first and foremost in the United States."

The Central Command announced its intent to "publicly reject North American imperialism and call for the legalization of drug consumption" as a means to eliminate drug trafficking. It reaffirmed the need to develop a policy of crop substitution and, in exchange, to "begin social investment in

---

[41] FARC-EP, "Plataforma para un gobierno de reconciliación y reconstrucción nacional," April 3, 1993, in FARC-EP, *Esbozo histórico*, (Comisión Internacional de las FARC-EP, 1998).

[42] This proposal was mentioned publicly by Pastrana but never formally developed or presented. It is most clearly articulated in a memo by the UNDP-Colombia following a meeting with President-elect Pastrana and key UN officials. Francisco Vicente, Resident Representative, UNDP-Colombia, "Memo: UN Meeting with the Colombian New Authorities and the Reflection Group," July 2, 1998 (unpublished internal United Nations document).

[43] Colombian government and FARC, "Acuerdo de los Pozos" (text of the Los Pozos Accord), February 9, 2001, www.ideaspaz.org/proyecto03/boletines/download/boletin03/acuerdo_los_pozos.doc (accessed August 22, 2008).

the coca-growing departments as part of the agreements for the investment of the 1.6 billion dollars [referring to Plan Colombia]."[44]

In the 1980s, leading up to the negotiations with the Betancur government, the FARC put emphasis on leading a broad democratic movement to promote a greater political opening. It also enumerated a list of political, social, and structural reforms, including its signature issue: agrarian reform. In a letter sent to the leaders of the Colombian Congress in July 1984, the FARC's leaders outlined their vision for democratic opening in the context of the peace process. They committed themselves to "lead a union of movements and leftist parties within a democratic opening demanding the return of normality in our country . . . [which] guarantees the free exercise of opposition, access to all media, freedom to organize and mobilize, and greater participation in government programs." They attested, "Within a democratic opening, the FARC, with other parties and currents of the left, and using whatever means possible, [will] fight to reform the political customs with the aim of dismantling the monopoly over public opinion held by the traditional parties for the benefit of the dominant class." Their specific proposals counseled political and electoral reforms such as the direct elections of mayors and governors, decentralization of public administration, and increased authority and funding for the municipalities, as well as tax, education, judicial, and constitutional reforms. Other topics addressed included nationalization of foreign companies, the banking and financial system, the National Coffee Federation, and the transportation sector; labor rights; reparations for the victims of the violence; the demilitarization of Colombian life and democratization of the armed forces; and the rejection of the "National Security Doctrine promoted by Yankee imperialism."[45]

The cease-fire agreement signed in La Uribe on March 28, 1984, made specific reference to many of these issues relating to the democratization of Colombian society. The FARC understood that most of these issues would be resolved not through negotiations with the government but rather in the context of a broad political struggle leading to institutional change. Some of the FARC's proposals coincided with reformist tendencies that had already won support. In 1986, two years after the agreement was signed, Congress passed a constitutional reform instituting for the first time the direct election of mayors. In the 1991 Constituent Assembly, the delegates established the direct election of governors and the decentralization of the national budget, providing ample resources to the municipalities.

---

[44] FARC-EP Pleno de Estado Mayor Central, "Tesis político militar del secretariado para la plenaria del Estado Mayor sobre el reajuste del Plan Estratégico para la toma del poder por las FARC-EP," March 21–25, 2000 (unpublished internal FARC document).

[45] Arenas, *Cese el fuego,* 11–14.

But the experience of democratic opening proved quite bitter for the FARC. In the 1986 elections, the UP won eight congressional seats and six Senate seats; in 1988, it won scores of mayorships and more than a hundred city council seats. But the UP soon faced a relentless dirty war, in which several of its leaders, including senators, congressional representatives, and the UP's candidates for president in 1986 and 1990, were assassinated.

After this experience, the FARC placed less emphasis on political participation. In 1993, after the Eighth Conference, the FARC produced a document titled "Platform for a Government of National Reconstruction and National Reconciliation." When compared with the platform leading up to the La Uribe Accords of a decade earlier, this document deemphasized the democratic opening and the creation of a political movement to work within the country's reformed democratic institutions, instead calling for structural changes to be negotiated directly with the FARC. The new list of proposals called for a negotiated solution to the armed conflict; reform of the armed forces; greater independence of the judiciary; budgetary realignments that would favor social welfare and scientific research; nationalization and state management of the energy sector, natural resources, communications, ports, roads, and public services; and progressive tax policies. Other proposals dealt with agrarian reform, land redistribution, and development policies; international relations based on self-determination and regional integration; and renegotiation of foreign debt, contracts, and natural-resource policies with multinational corporations.

This 1993 proposal became the basis of the Common Agenda, signed in La Machaca in May 1999. It is a comprehensive agenda, with both specific and general recommendations, although, given the balance of military and political power in Colombia, much of the agenda is not amenable to the realization of specific agreements within the framework of peace talks. The key is to discern what is negotiable directly with the FARC and what could become the basis for a broader process, likely a Constituent Assembly, that would incorporate other national sectors beyond the government and the FARC.

Amnesty and DDR

The third major set of issues that need to be addressed in future talks with the FARC relate to questions of DDR, including amnesty. Since the 1950s, amnesty has been a regular feature of conflict resolution in Colombia. Amnesties were granted to armed rebels in 1953, 1954, 1958, 1981, 1982, 1990, 1991, and 1994.[46] In the early 1980s, amnesty was seen by the FARC as an instrument that would facilitate the move from armed struggle to democratic par-

---

[46] See Marc Chernick, "Colombia: Does Injustice Cause Violence?" in *What Justice? Whose Justice? Fighting for Fairness in Latin America*, eds. Timothy Wickham-Crowley and Susan Eckstein (Berkeley: University of California Press, 2003).

ticipation. Jacobo Arenas stated the FARC position clearly at the outset of the negotiations during the Betancur administration. "As soon as the Amnesty Law is approved, everyone [all FARC guerrillas] will be covered. Period. There will be no need to present oneself to the authorities, no need to give declarations, no need to hand in arms, none of that. All who were accused, indicted, convicted, prisoners and those still fighting charges of political or related crimes, will be amnestied for all occurrences that took place before November 20, 1982."[47]

This amnesty was not seen as a final post-conflict measure. In this case, using the 1982 amnesty and the La Uribe cease-fire accords, the FARC founded a political party, the UP, but maintained the right to keep its arms as a guarantee, without demobilizing.

Since the mid-1990s, international human rights and international humanitarian law have increasingly rejected the idea of a blanket amnesty as a valid instrument of conflict resolution. International tribunals have already established precedent by declaring invalid several amnesties granted for war crimes and for crimes that rise to the level of "crimes against humanity."[48] There is no indication that the FARC has assimilated international experiences, although the FARC's 1984 platform did make reference to the need to compensate victims of the violence.[49]

In Colombia, the demobilization process with the paramilitary forces from 2004 to 2006 consciously changed the terms of the debate from amnesty to leniency in facing justice. Even here, the original terms of the Justice and

---

[47] Arenas, *Cese el fuego*, 57. The 1982 amnesty was unconditional and covered almost all guerrillas and prisoners, with the exception of a provision placed by Conservative lawmakers for heinous crimes outside of combat against defenseless victims. This provision was placed in the bill to exclude the assassins of former minister of government Pardo Buelvas, who were from the small guerrilla group Autodefensa Obrera (ADO).

[48] Precedents and case law include a 2001 decision by the Inter-American Court of Human Rights nullifying a Peruvian amnesty law in the Barrios Altos case. There the court ruled that the amnesty was incompatible with the American Convention on Human Rights and thus lacked juridical effect. Comparable interpretations on the reach of international law and the limits of national sovereignty have come from the special tribunals for the former Yugoslavia, Rwanda, and Sierra Leone. There is also a growing corpus of law emerging from decisions in national and international courtrooms limiting or overturning amnesties issued for crimes by individual officials and government leaders during military governments in Argentina, Chile, and Uruguay.

[49] See the exchange of letters between Human Rights Watch and Manuel Marulanda, July 2001, in which Human Rights Watch outlined its position that many of the FARC's actions, particularly the use of gas cylinders as weapons and the indiscriminate attack on civilian populations, violated international humanitarian law, specifically Common Article 3 and Protocol 2 of the Geneva Conventions. Marulanda responded, accusing Human Rights Watch of being an agent of imperialism and of the U.S. government. See Human Rights Watch, letter to Marulanda, www.hrw.org/press/2002/05/colombia0508.pdf (accessed August 22, 2008). For the FARC response, see FARC, "Las naves del intervensionismo [sic]," http://hrw.org/spanish/informes/2001/farc_apendice.html#P408_70705 (accessed August 22, 2008).

Peace Law were overturned by the Colombian Constitutional Court as being so generous as to imply impunity.[50]

The FARC expressly rejects the framework that was used with the paramilitary forces.[51] They do not accept that they have committed crimes beyond the political crimes of sedition and rebellion. Its leaders believe fervently that their cause is just and that their juridical situation in a transitional or post-conflict setting would not be equivalent to or comparable with the situation of the paramilitaries. The FARC leaders call for punishment, reparations, and an end to impunity for the war crimes committed by paramilitary forces, which they view as illegal and state-sponsored. They believe that it is the state's obligation to dismantle these groups. But in any final peace process, the FARC leaders' position is clear and unyielding on this issue as it relates to the eventual reintegration of the FARC: acts of sedition and rebellion are legitimate, and FARC will accept only a full, unconditional, comprehensive national amnesty on all activities properly classified in Colombian and international law as sedition, rebellion, political crimes, and acts of internal war. FARC's leaders also envision that amnesty will be extended to members of the armed forces and the state who were carrying out their responsibilities to defend the state and maintain public order.

The FARC has never directly addressed accusations made against it of involvement in war crimes or crimes against humanity. Nor have the armed forces or government officials directly addressed similar accusations. In the past, amnesties and pardons in Colombia covered most acts of war, legal and illegal, committed by any party to the conflict. The issues of human rights and international humanitarian law were key elements of the Common Agenda agreed to by the FARC and the Pastrana administration in May 1999 during the Caguán negotiations, but the two sides never formally discussed these issues. If the Colombian peace process is going to achieve an enduring peace within a framework of international legitimacy, these issues need to be made priorities in any future peace process.

On the related issue of disarmament, the FARC, like many insurgent groups, believes that its primary leverage is derived from its arms. Without arms, there would be no negotiations. The FARC has insisted in every negotiating period that it would not discuss the issue of disarmament. Its position in 1984 was that its arms helped guarantee the democratic opening by pressuring the government. The leadership argued then that as the system opened up, permitting the FARC to make the transition from armed struggle to democratic participation, there would be no need to use arms, and these would

---

[50] See Human Rights Watch, "Corte corrige defectos en la ley de desmovilización," http://hrw.org/spanish/docs/2006/05/19/colomb13433.htm (accessed August 22, 2008).

[51] See Chapter 7 by Arturo J. Carrillo in this volume.

become irrelevant and would disappear. Nevertheless, the leaders argued that they had to be vigilant, given the many interests opposed to negotiations and to the FARC's participation in the institutional political arena.

For the FARC, the issue is not arms but injustice and exclusion. Nevertheless, at some point in the negotiating process, the issue of arms must be addressed. It is possible that Colombia could develop a uniquely Colombian solution. The issue is not simply disarmament but the way in which disarmed groups are incorporated into the political arena. Note the emphasis on groups and not, as has previously been the case in Colombia (and in many DDR experiences around the world), on individuals. A peace that is not predicated on military defeat requires that both sides address the issue of political power and the role of a demobilized insurgent group in a post-conflict society.

With disarmament and reintegration, two issues stand out. First is the need to convert the guerrilla movement into a viable political party with access to key positions of authority. This will need to be carefully negotiated to avoid the earlier fates of the UP (physical elimination) and the M-19 and the EPL (political collapse and failure). It may be worthwhile to place greater attention on creating favorable conditions at the level of local and regional power than was the case during earlier peace processes.

Second is the need to incorporate some guerrilla units into state police and military bodies, particularly at a local and regional level. If one of the key objectives of a peace process is to build a coherent and legitimate state presence throughout all the national territory—something that has been absent since the state's founding—then such an authority could be constructed over time as some FARC fighters are gradually phased into national, regional, or local police forces. In the transition period, the FARC and state actors might share responsibilities. At the end of the transition period, the state would have significantly increased its national presence while at the same time creating conditions of security for the FARC in the post-conflict period. The timing of this transition and the end point would need to be negotiated. This could lead to a substantial increase in state authority and the institutionalization of a viable peace accord.

Conclusions

The end of the peace talks in 2002 hardened attitudes in Colombia toward a negotiated settlement to the armed conflict. Each side accused the other of not having sufficient political will or desire to end the war. The FARC denounced the exponential expansion of the Autodefensas Unidas de Colombia (AUC), the right-wing paramilitary forces, from four thousand to over eight thousand fighters during the first three years of the Pastrana government. It also repeatedly condemned the U.S.-sponsored Plan Colombia, which greatly increased U.S. military aid to Colombia and further militarized the drug war at a time when the government had publicly declared that peace was its central priority.

The government, meanwhile, condemned the FARC's stepped-up military activities in all areas of the country, as well as its increased involvement in kidnapping and other criminal activities. The peace process, as structured, was inadequate to address the concerns of both sides and eventually was overwhelmed by the issues at the negotiating table.

A careful reading of the recent record demonstrates that there is no military solution to the armed conflict in Colombia. Despite the steady increase of military capacity beginning in the Gaviria years and accelerating during the Pastrana and Uribe years, the state still cannot defeat the guerrillas. The choice, then, is to (1) escalate the war and seek military advantage at the negotiating table, (2) continue the war at current levels and try to build state capacity and institutional strength and legitimacy amid the war, or (3) attempt to reach a negotiated settlement directly.

Versions of all these options were tried over the past quarter century. From 1998 to 2002, the U.S. Department of State and many in the Pastrana administration basically argued that the first option provides the key to an eventual peace accord. From discussions with policymakers, it is clear that much of the unstated reasoning behind U.S. assistance to Plan Colombia was based on the perceived need to increase the military capacity of the armed forces and thereby pressure the guerrillas at the negotiating table. Yet the guerrillas essentially pursued the same strategy of increasing military capacity to influence the negotiations; the result was that the peace process became a stimulant for expanded war.

Álvaro Uribe chose to continue with the fundamental reasoning underlying Pastrana's strategy: increase military leverage to force greater success at the negotiating table. But Uribe opted to defer negotiations until the battlefield conditions were more favorable and the guerrillas were significantly weakened, instead of pursuing these objectives simultaneously, as Pastrana did. At the same time, the Uribe government resolved to press all political advantage to delegitimize the FARC politically, both nationally and internationally. Uribe also attempted to dismantle the illegal paramilitary groups through separate negotiations, thus more clearly defining the battlefield and, perhaps, leading to a changed equilibrium.

By 2007, this strategy had achieved only ambiguous results. The AUC had been demobilized, but paramilitarism continued. The FARC had been pushed back from the country's major cities, and the principal roadways had become more secure. Plan Patriota, the military complement to Plan Colombia, first concentrated on destroying the FARC's areas of action in Cundinamarca in the high plateaus and mountainous regions surrounding Bogotá, long a stronghold of the FARC. By late 2003 and early 2004, this objective had largely been achieved, although it is unclear whether such military gains can be sustained.[52] In December 2003, a second offensive was mounted in Caquetá and was then extended into Guaviare, Meta, and Putumayo. The push into southern Colombia reportedly involved eighteen thousand soldiers, with over eight hundred U.S. military advisers providing logistical support, as well as six hundred U.S. private defense contractors involved in the joint antinarcotics/counterinsurgency operations.[53] The military operation sought to occupy FARC support zones, neutralize their effectiveness, establish a state security presence, and capture the FARC's senior leadership. It represented the largest military operation launched by either side in more than forty years of warfare.

The initial push into southern Colombia by the Colombian armed forces fell short of its objectives. The FARC retaliated with its own Plan Resistencia and was able to absorb the blows through tactical retreats and offensive guerrilla attacks. In 2008, however, five years after the launch of Plan Patriota, the armed forces finally managed to penetrate FARC's security and communications infrastructures, leading to the death of two of the five most senior leaders of the FARC, Raul Reyes and Iván Ríos. The latter was killed by his own bodyguards, who received substantial government cash rewards for their actions. There is little doubt that the FARC has been weakened politically, symbolically, and militarily. Still, the FARC's overall military capacity and command structures remain intact. It has renovated its leadership and elevated former university anthropologist and longtime FARC political leader Alfonso Cano to replace Manuel Marulanda as commander-in-chief. Despite overly triumphal declarations emanating from Bogotá and sometimes Washington, the FARC appears to have adapted to the new political and military terrain.

Uribe's military strategy alone is insufficient to achieve peace. Moreover, the demobilization of the AUC did not succeed in removing all the paramilitary groups from the battlefield. Many have rearmed and new illegal armed groups have emerged. These shortcomings in the overall security strategy have inevitably led to a return to the search for a more comprehensive political solution. For nearly three decades, the pendulum has swung back and forth between the forces of negotiations and the forces of war. During his first term in office, Uribe emphasized the language of security (clothed in the comforting notion of democracy), of political legitimacy, and of military dominance. The great question in the last years of Uribe's second term is whether such a strategy can be parlayed into a viable peace.

In Colombia, peace basically means the construction of a more participatory and inclusive regime and of a legitimate state presence throughout the

---

[52] Thomas Marks, "Sustainability of Colombian Military/Strategic Support for 'Democratic Security'" (Carlisle, Penn.: Strategic Studies Institute of the U.S. Army War College, 2005), 14, www.strategicstudiesinstitute.army.mil/pubs/display.cfm?pubID=610 (accessed October 7, 2008).

[53] Council on Hemispheric Affairs, "Plan Patriota: What $700 Million in U.S. Cash Will and Will Not Buy in Colombia," Washington, D.C., April 20, 2006, www.coha.org/NEW_PRESS_RELEASES/New_Press_Releases_2006/06.26_Plan_Patriota.html (accessed October 7, 2008).

national territory. This will not be determined on the battlefield. A final peace agreement will need to address key economic and social reforms as well as the issue of political participation for the FARC and other groups. The broad agenda must be narrowed somewhat to discern which issues require broader societal participation and which issues can justifiably be negotiated within the special confines of a peace table. At a minimum, the refined broad agenda would include addressing agrarian reform and rural development, including the issue of illicit crops; ending the dirty war and massive violations of human rights and international humanitarian law and providing guarantees for political participation to demobilized combatants and others; reorienting the strategic mission of the armed forces and police in the context of internal peace and post-conflict; incorporating guerrilla forces and other community actors into the local and national structures of state and elective politics; and establishing broad framework agreements on social policy and natural resources.

One issue is immensely more complicated today than in earlier periods of negotiations. International human rights and humanitarian law have greatly restricted the possibilities of granting broad, general amnesties and pardons. This issue will need to be addressed directly and will need to cover all actors in the long and painful conflict: guerrillas, paramilitaries, and state actors. Justice should not be viewed as only retributive; it can also be restorative. In Colombia, a post-conflict society can be built only on a foundation of justice and national reconciliation. This will need to be addressed directly both at the negotiating table and in a larger forum.

The FARC has the political will, ideology, resources, organizational structure, recruitment network, and social base needed to continue its struggle for many years to come. It is confident that the state cannot defeat it militarily, but its leaders also understand that the FARC is not in a position to take power through force of arms. Its deliberations since the Eighth Conference reflect this reality, and it has adjusted its strategic goals to include a negotiated settlement. It understands that, under the right conditions, it can gain more through negotiations and participation within a reformed political arena than it can through armed struggle.

If peace is to be achieved, all the key political forces in Colombia essentially need to make the same determination. Over the years, the FARC has been remarkably consistent in its demands and political positions at the negotiating table. Its positions on political change fall more or less within the scope of much of the contemporary left in present-day Latin America. With the right amount of political will, audacity, and international support, a renewed and more focused negotiation strategy is the one option that could finally end one of the most protracted internal armed conflicts in contemporary history.

5

The ELN's Halting
Moves toward Peace

León Valencia

It was surprising that the National Liberation Army (ELN) would take the initiative toward the end of 2005 to begin a dialogue outside Colombian territory with the government of President Álvaro Uribe Vélez. After all, the Uribe government had stated its intention to defeat the guerrillas militarily and had mounted the largest government offensive in fifteen years. It was also surprising that the move toward dialogue would take place in the midst of the president's reelection campaign.

The ELN has said that it wanted to help change the nature of that political campaign. The central theme of Uribe's campaign in 2002 had been his promotion of a military solution, but the ELN wanted a negotiated solution to be prominent on the 2006 campaign agenda, and it determined that this could be achieved only if it made a commitment to negotiate with the president, forcing him to deal with the possibility of a peace agreement at the same time that his campaign went forward.

To some extent the ELN accomplished its goal. On several occasions during the campaign, Uribe discussed the importance of progress toward peace negotiations with the guerrillas. In his second inaugural address, on August 7, 2006, he indicated that even at the risk of seeming to contradict his hard-line Democratic Security Policy, he was willing to pursue a peace process. A few months into his second term, he expressed his willingness to go to the mountains to meet with Fuerzas Armadas Revolucionarias de Colombia (FARC) commander Manuel Marulanda Vélez. He offered a set of pardons and amnesties should the conversation take place, and he proposed holding a National Constituent Assembly if an agreement was reached.

Uribe withdrew many of these offers after a car bomb attributed to the FARC was exploded on the grounds of the Cantón Norte military base in Bogotá on October 19. This bombing shook the military's most important facility in the country, located right in the capital city, and infuriated the president, who immediately ended any talk of reconciliation.

Members of the ELN also explained their 2005 peace initiative in light of the turn to the left in Latin America and the resulting potential for their participation in politics and for the strengthening of alternative processes. The success of the Colombian left was also particularly promising, as it had elected a mayor of Bogotá, a governor of Valle del Cauca, a mayor in Bucaramanga and another in Pasto, and mayors in other, smaller municipalities. Furthermore, the municipal government in Medellín, headed by Sergio Fajardo, while not strictly of the left, was seen as providing an independent space compared to the traditional parties.

In addition to its stated reasons, the ELN's decision to propose negotiations with the government also represented a response to the fact that the ELN no longer plays a significant role in the dynamic of war in Colombia.

The ELN Stands Alone

As the dynamic of the Colombian armed conflict has evolved, the ELN has become marginalized from it. Over the past decade, the war has taken on three characteristics that the ELN has resisted, namely, the exponential growth of financing, the massive recruitment of combatants, and the displacement of inhabitants and the repopulation of regions in the ruthless struggle to control territory. While the paramilitaries and the FARC have adopted these tactics wholeheartedly, and the state, too, has done so in some respects, the ELN has fallen out of step with the evolving nature of the confrontation on each of these three fronts.

The other parties have adjusted to—and benefited from—the evolving dynamics of the war. The paramilitaries participated in drug trafficking, offered protection to rural entrepreneurs at high rates, and relied on other sources of financing such as appropriating land, stealing gasoline, pillaging state resources, and laundering money through businesses fully integrated into the formal economy. Carlos Castaño, who, until his death, was the most powerful paramilitary figure, recognized that participation in businesses related to illegal drugs accounted for 70 percent of paramilitary financing. The U.S. Department of State said that at the beginning of the new century, approximately US$5 billion in drug-trafficking proceeds were reverting to Colombia annually. Significant portions of these funds would end up in the hands of the paramilitaries and the FARC. Luis Bernardo Flórez, Colombia's vice–comptroller general, stated that paramilitaries and drug traffickers had gained control of over half the country's best land.[1]

---

[1] Luis Bernardo Flórez, *Editorial Revista Economía Colombiana* no. 309 (July 2005), www.contralo riagen.gov.co/html/RevistaEC/309.htm (accessed September 23, 2008).

This enormous resource stream allowed paramilitary leaders to enrich themselves personally and also to construct a formidable fighting force in just a few years. When the paramilitary United Self-Defense Forces of Colombia (AUC) was founded in May 1998, it had six thousand members, but by the time of the agreement with President Uribe that led to the group's partial demobilization, this number had grown to thirty-one thousand combatants, thirty-seven organizational structures, and seventeen thousand weapons.[2] Now, after the negotiated agreement, paramilitary leader Salvatore Mancuso has stated that more than five thousand men are again carrying out actions in the name of the paramilitaries.

During these ten years of expansion, paramilitaries came to be active in 223 municipalities and exercised almost complete control over areas of 12 departments. In these areas, they had a significant impact on social policy and political power. They caused thousands of deaths and displaced hundreds of thousands of people from the areas under their control.[3]

The FARC has also adjusted its practices to the dynamic of the war and energetically dedicated itself to fund-raising through drug trafficking, to the massive recruitment of combatants, and to the stubborn and violent defense of the territories under its control. Before 2003, when the Colombian state launched a major offensive in the southern part of the country, the FARC had built up its forces to more than twenty thousand combatants, and its guerrilla fronts reached into the majority of the country's departments. The organization later refocused on defending its forces, which it has done with relative success. It has lost combatants and has been dislodged from strategic positions, such as the outskirts of Bogotá and Comuna 13 in Medellín, and its finances have suffered. Nevertheless, as Marc Chernick notes in Chapter 4 of this volume, until early 2008 the FARC succeeded in keeping its command structure intact; it has preserved its strategic rear guard in the departments of Meta, Caquetá, Putumayo, and Guaviare; and it has demonstrated the ability to recover the offensive whenever this suits its purposes.

The Colombian state has continued to receive an average of US$700 million per year in assistance from the United States and has greatly increased

---

[2] See Web site for the Office of the Colombian High Commissioner for Peace, www.alto comisionadoparalapaz.gov.co/web/index.asp (accessed September 23, 2008).

[3] Between late 2004 and mid-2006, the Swedish government sponsored a study by the Corporación Nuevo Arco Iris on the paramilitary phenomenon and the negotiations at Santa Fé de Ralito. Individual monographs were produced covering Medellín, Córdoba, Urabá, Sucre, Greater Magdalena (El Magdalena Grande), Cundinamarca, Bogotá, Valle, Catatumbo, Norte de Santander, Casanare, and Meta. These studies were conducted by local researchers with the assistance of research centers at the Universidad de Antioquia, the Universidad del Valle, and the Universidad de Magdalena. A central research team in Bogotá also collected press reports, documents, and the records of public forums and interviewed people who participated in the negotiations. See León Valencia and Mauricio Romero, "Informe especial: Paramilitares y políticos," *Arcanos* 10, no. 13 (March 2007), www.nuevoarcoiris.org.co/sac/files/arcanos/arcanos_13_marzo_2007.htm (accessed September 23, 2008).

its defense spending. At the end of Pastrana's presidency, spending on defense represented 3.6 percent of GDP. By the end of Uribe's first term, according to the Ministry of Defense, defense spending had increased to 4.7 percent of GDP and security forces had grown by more than 30 percent, from 260,000 to almost 400,000 soldiers and police. The Democratic Security Policy, as the government's plan is known, has also focused on physical control of territory.

The ELN, on the other hand, has gradually lost its sources of financing. Only a few of its fronts collect taxes from the campesinos who grow coca or from those who produce coca paste. Kidnapping and extortion of foreign companies—the ELN's main sources of financing in past decades—have diminished. Few new combatants have been recruited, and some of the old ones have left the organization. Whereas ten years ago the number of armed ELN combatants was estimated at ten thousand, today there are said to be only four thousand.

Of course, this situation stems from political decisions made by the ELN in the 1990s. Under the leadership of Manuel Pérez, a Spanish priest who led the group from the 1970s until his death in 1998, the organization decided explicitly at its congress in 1996 not to get involved in drug trafficking and to dedicate more of its energies to political action than to building its guerrilla army. The ELN has paid dearly for these decisions in its confrontations with the armed forces, the paramilitaries, and the FARC.

The paramilitaries, using not only threats and intimidation but also the vast resources derived from drug trafficking and investments in mining and agriculture, consolidated their social and economic power in territories such as the Magdalena Medio and the southern Bolívar Department, where the ELN had exercised a powerful influence for decades.

Since 2006, the ELN also suffered greatly from FARC attacks in Arauca Department and in the south of the country. According to Colombia's leading newsweeklies, *Semana* and *Cambio*, more than three hundred guerrillas have died in these confrontations, and the ELN has borne the brunt of the losses. The FARC has expressed its dissatisfaction with negotiations between the ELN and the government and would like to occupy as much ELN territory as possible before the state is in a position to do so.[4]

Thus, the ELN finds itself at a great disadvantage compared to the other armed actors and must choose between two courses. Its members can either plunge back into the war by using the same sources of financing and engaging in the same practices as the paramilitaries and the FARC, thus compromising their political criteria for recruiting combatants and unleashing what would amount to an offensive within the territories they occupy, or they can take dramatic steps toward peace.

---

[4]*Cambio* and *Semana*, February 5 and 11, 2007.

Many analysts believe that the ELN is incapable of carrying out the first course, that it has suffered a strategic defeat so serious that it can no longer recover the military capability to compete in the current environment. This is not true. The ELN has been even weaker militarily in the past and has recovered. ELN commander Nicolás Rodríguez Bautista is no less skilled than the FARC's Manuel Marulanda was. He is younger than Marulanda, but he has been with the guerrillas since the 1960s, when the two organizations were formed. Nonetheless, it seems that the ELN leadership has decided against the military option and has opted to find a way back to civilian life. The boldness of proposing a negotiation process to President Uribe in the middle of his reelection campaign may be the clearest sign that they are serious about seeking peace.

The ELN Is Interested in the Colombian Left

It is clear that the ELN is favorably impressed with what is taking place within the Colombian left. At its Fourth Congress, in 2006, the organization reiterated that its primary emphasis was on political action and indicated that the most important things taking place within the popular movement were the rise of independent forces in local government and the electoral gains of the Polo Democrático Alternativo (PDA), or Alternative Democratic Pole.[5]

The ELN is aware that Colombian society is undergoing a very important transformation. For many years, the country's democracy was degraded by the withdrawal of genuinely rival political forces from peaceful competition and was governed by a coalition of clientelist forces that had no fundamental disagreements and that never debated national problems. The absence of opposition was institutionalized through the formation of the National Front in the 1960s, in which the Liberal and Conservative parties alternated presidential terms and agreed to divide between them all positions within state bodies. The National Front formally came to an end in 1978, but its spirit lives on as a deadweight on the political culture.

The vitality of political debate was revived in the 2006 presidential elections, when there actually were two opposing forces. President Uribe supported the Free Trade Agreement, and PDA candidate Carlos Gaviria opposed it; President Uribe supported his Democratic Security Policy, with its emphasis on a military solution, and Gaviria emphasized a negotiated solution; Uribe said nothing about gay marriage, while Gaviria supported it; Gaviria defended the decriminalization of small quantities of marijuana for personal use, and Uribe vehemently attacked the idea; Gaviria supported the decriminalization of abortion, and Uribe rejected it. The citizenry sat up and took notice of the unaccustomed confrontation between opponents in Colombian politics.

---

[5] Conclusions of the Fourth ELN Congress, *Revista Unidad* (*Revista de la Dirección Nacional del ELN de Colombia*) 2006.

It had become customary to designate Colombian political parties and movements as either "traditional," in the case of the Liberals and Conservatives, or "independent," to describe any others. Political leaders considered the labels "left" and "right" to be somehow deficient or illegitimate. They did not want to be categorized that way, and the terms fell into disuse. Now, however, "left" and "right" were again being used to differentiate the candidates. For the first time, the left took second place in a presidential election, winning 2.6 million votes, or 22.04 percent, and positioning itself as a credible alternative to govern after the election of 2010. Now PDA officeholders and activists are proud to be called "leftist."

The ELN understands that the existence of the PDA could be to its advantage in the negotiations. But it also knows that the existence of its own negotiating process can help the PDA in the 2010 elections. The ELN's praise for the outstanding role played by Carlos Gaviria in the presidential election campaign and the accomplishments of Bogotá mayor Luis Eduardo Garzón are testimony to their new understanding that the political positions of the PDA and the PDA's criticism of violence are well founded in this new stage of Colombian politics.

In its participation in the political life of Colombia, the electoral left is pursuing the same social goals as the guerrillas, but it is actually much more progressive on certain points of the contemporary agenda. It seems paradoxical that in this country the unarmed left—the left that criticizes violence from whatever quarter—takes more radical positions than the armed left. It is hard to imagine Rodríguez or Marulanda defending gay rights, taking any political risk to support the decriminalization of small quantities of marijuana for personal use, or openly discussing legal abortion.

The successes of the Latin American left are due in great part to the prominence of social problems in the public eye and to support for the promotion of social rights. Here in Colombia, on the other hand, we remain focused on problems of security, an area in which people put more trust in the right.

The greatest contribution that the guerrillas could make to the development of the left would be to move toward a peaceful resolution of the conflict. If peace negotiations should also provide an opportunity for reforms that strengthen democracy and address social needs in the regions, that contribution would be even greater. Putting an end to violence and bringing the war to a close would deprive the right of the pretexts it uses to justify its continued atrocities. It is possible that the ELN has begun to understand this in the light of its own political traditions, based on the thinking of its principal leader, Father Camilo Torres Restrepo.

This historical moment in Colombia provides the ELN with a great opportunity. While the left moves rapidly forward, the right is entering a deep crisis. Connections between paramilitaries and rightist politicians in the elections of 2002, 2003, and 2006 are beginning to come to light, and the Supreme

Court has implicated many congressional representatives in paramilitary-related criminal activity. The Colombian justice system seems to have begun to react honestly and conscientiously, and if investigations get to the bottom of the matter, the balance of political forces will be profoundly affected.

According to a two-year academic research project conducted by the Corporación Nuevo Arco Iris with the assistance of the Swedish government, there was a large-scale expansion of paramilitarism in Colombia between 1999 and 2003. The paramilitaries entered and established control in 223 municipalities. They established an alliance with the political class. In 2002, they elected twenty-six senators and even more representatives to the lower house. In 2003, they elected 251 mayors, 8 governors, and no less than 4,000 municipal councillors. In 2006, they raised their number of senators to thirty-three and their number in the lower house to fifty.[6]

If a significant number of these political leaders are imprisoned in the wake of current judicial investigations, the political earthquake will be devastating. Many of the parties that support Uribe and his program will collapse or suffer serious crises. An eventual peace treaty with the ELN will reinforce the idea in public opinion that the Colombian left, unlike the right, has willingly given up the use of violence. At the same time, the ELN can occupy the political space left open by these organizations in various regions of the country and can help further political change. Seizing these opportunities would require an acceleration of the negotiating process, but it is not clear that the ELN is prepared to do that yet.

The Negotiations Are Difficult

Negotiations between the ELN and the government are not easy, in particular because the two parties come to the table with very different expectations. The ELN favors and has proposed a two-phased negotiating process. The first phase would include humanitarian agreements and a mutual cessation of hostilities, financed with international assistance, and political mechanisms such as a National Convention. The second phase of negotiations would consider issues of substance. Despite its current military disadvantages, the ELN is proud of its forty years of military activities and has an ambitious set of proposals for political reform and social change that it would like to see result from these negotiations with the state.

There are several obstacles to a bilateral truce or cessation of hostilities. It would be taking place in the midst of a conflict involving other powerful armed actors: the FARC and some not yet demobilized paramilitary sectors, both of which have a history of obstructing the ELN's moves toward peace. Paramilitary forces disrupted plans for a *despeje* in the south of Bolívar for negotiations between the ELN and President Pastrana, and the

---

[6] Valencia and Romero, "Informe especial."

FARC is currently engaged in an offensive against the ELN in the latter's areas of influence.

Some elements of the armed forces, too, would prefer to see the ELN ground down by the brutal circumstances of the war and simply disappear. Among themselves, they remark that it would be best to let the ELN be quietly liquidated in the multisided war, and they do not approve of the state's generous offer of a negotiated settlement.

The ELN has small guerrilla nuclei throughout the length and breadth of the country, in no less than twenty-three departments from Nariño in the extreme south to La Guajira in the north, and from Arauca in the east to Chocó on the Pacific coast. These armed cells maintain connections with the communities and affirm their wish to stay in place and engage in social and humanitarian activities. The fact that the ELN is so dispersed, and the tendency of different nuclei to stay in their regions during any cease-fire, complicates the tasks of verification and force protection.

The problem of geographic dispersion is compounded by the ELN's internal federalism and consensual democracy. The Central Command cannot make rapid or definitive decisions regarding negotiations, because frequent consultations with the national directorate and guerrilla fronts are required. Also, individuals in many ELN structures aspire to participate more directly in negotiations. They want the process to take place within Colombia, and they want regional particularities to be taken into account. The public is beginning to be conscious of the ELN's internal disagreements and contradictions concerning these issues.

In numerous attempts at negotiations over the past fifteen years, the ELN's agenda has included political reforms (particularly in local governance), mechanisms such as a National Convention and a National Constituent Assembly, regional development projects, humanitarian agreements, and reforms responding to the aspirations of social movements and ethnic minorities. These ambitious goals will not be easy to address, especially given the compromised nature of the ELN's military force.

The government is interested in a rapid negotiating process, primarily focused on an initial cessation of hostilities and quickly followed by a demobilization with guarantees that ELN forces will be able to engage in political action once integrated into civilian life. President Uribe has stated from the beginning that there will be guarantees that political forces can join the political process once they are demobilized, but it is unlikely that any major social or political reforms will be negotiated. The president has not often varied his position on this matter, and he has done so only in the context of specific political moments, such as in the months immediately following his reelection, when he held out the possibility of a National Constituent Assembly.

Although the parties' positions are far apart, other circumstances do bode well for negotiations. Negotiations between the ELN and the government have had many willing supporters. Each time an attempt is made to initiate the process, and despite the number of past disappointments and the resulting pessimism, there are always countries, institutions, and personalities (such as Gabriel García Márquez) willing to accompany the process and extend a hand. A place always seems to be offered for talks to take place, and safe passage is always made available to ELN negotiators. But although these points facilitate the *initiation* of talks, negotiators have always run up against obstacles as soon as they tackle matters of substance.

The most contentious issue right now is the cessation of hostilities. The ELN will likely resist an early cease-fire, not because it holds any military advantage but because of the weighty implications of the step. Once a cease-fire is declared, there will theoretically be no turning back from negotiations. Also, the ELN wants to win meaningful political concessions—for example, an agreement on a National Convention and social projects to benefit the regions where it has influence—in exchange for accepting a cease-fire.

Certain civil society groups that offer their help to the ELN in the negotiating process have provided poor advice. They offer the hope that during a long, slow negotiating process, the support of social and political forces in the regions can be increased through mechanisms such as the Casas de Paz (Peace Houses, where ELN representatives are legally authorized to meet with civil society representatives) or through a succession of public events promoting the National Convention. Other groups and individuals, motivated by their fervent opposition to the Uribe government, have advised the ELN to pursue negotiations with this administration but wait to sign any final agreement with whoever is elected president in 2010. Both the ELN and Colombia deserve better than this kind of irresponsible advice.

The ELN tends to take the process and content of the negotiations in El Salvador between the Farabundo Martí National Liberation Front (FMLN) and the government of President Alfredo Cristiani as a point of reference. In the El Salvadoran process, valuable time was spent reaching humanitarian agreements and a cease-fire before entering into negotiations on demobilization and the political, economic, and social content of the final agreement. But times are different today, as are Colombia's needs.

The Government Is Not Bold Enough

Negotiations are in the interest of the ELN, but they promise desirable outcomes for the government as well. A cessation of hostilities with this guerrilla group, leading to the end of its armed uprising, would be a step toward greater national reconciliation. It would decrease the role of illegal armed actors in Colombian society, contribute to a state monopoly on the use of force, and reduce the levels of violence in particular regions.

A positive outcome to the process would also send a message to the international community and to the Colombian public. The Uribe government is frequently accused of favoring the paramilitaries and rejecting possibilities of peace with the guerrillas. Successful negotiations with the ELN would demonstrate to Colombia and the world that Uribe has a pluralist vision of peace and is able to sit down at the table with ideologically divergent political forces to reach solutions in the national interest.

Negotiations with the ELN could also serve another useful purpose by establishing a model, subject to variation, for an eventual political solution with the FARC. An internationally supervised truce with the ELN could provide a precedent for negotiations with the FARC. Humanitarian agreements with the ELN could provide a frame of reference for an eventual prisoner exchange with the larger guerrilla organization. A search could begin for solutions to the problems of coca-growing regions and for confronting demands for political reform. The negotiating process could establish a replicable road map leading from humanitarian agreements to a cessation of hostilities, the negotiation of substantive issues, and the integration of armed actors into civilian life.

But President Uribe and the high commissioner for peace have been overly cautious in moving to engage the ELN. They have not taken sufficient advantage of the favorable environment in some Colombian sectors and in the international community to advance the process.

No significant offers have been extended to the ELN, not only because the government lacks boldness in this area but also because it lacks the will to understand the ELN and its position. Despite its current political and military difficulties, the ELN is proud of its long history and especially of the role of Camilo Torres Restrepo. Priest, pioneer of liberation theology, and avatar of political change in Latin America, Camilo and his legacy occupy an enduring place at the heart of modern Colombian history. The ELN took up arms for political reasons and has struggled to maintain a set of political principles despite the degradation of the war. The organization shares responsibility for that degradation but has nevertheless upheld its political discourse and its political project. One can even say that the ELN's current military weakness is due in part to its struggle to hold on to the ideals that inspired it to take up arms over forty years ago. Its refusal to plunge headlong into drug trafficking, its commitment to work in the communities, and its adherence to the ideas of social justice inspired by liberation theology have kept it from taking steps that would have strengthened its position in the brutal form that the war has taken in recent years.

The government, the international community, and civil society must help the ELN pursue forward-looking goals and resist any temptation to respond militarily to the attacks of the paramilitaries, the FARC, or the armed forces. It must be repeatedly stressed that for the ELN, with the forces currently at its disposal, to respond militarily to the brutal dynamic of today's Colombian conflict would be suicide. It would also be an ethical and political defeat to resort to a military reactivation relying on drug trafficking, massive recruitment, and the military control of territory as a defense against other armed actors.

The ELN must be convinced of the need for a rapid bilateral cessation of hostilities, followed by humanitarian structures to protect its own combatants and the civilian populations in its zones of influence. Once the ELN definitively sets out on the road to peace, the international community, civil society, the church, and parties such as the PDA can cooperate to organize humanitarian missions and forms of civil resistance to protect the organization.

The ELN needs more than advice and admonitions, however. It needs real alternatives to confront real problems. The economic conditions of the guerrilla fronts are not good, and living conditions are difficult for the populations in its regions of influence. Finding the economic resources to establish the proposed peace zones can provide both combatants and inhabitants with the opportunity to make real commitments to reconciliation. If the practice of kidnapping can be eliminated, it will generate a great deal of confidence in negotiations and will free the guerrillas from the moral and political burden of that aberrant practice. But this will be tied to finding legitimate sources of financing for the transition of the ELN from making war to making peace.

An Agenda Was Developed over Fifteen Years

A look back at the ELN's various attempts to negotiate with the Colombian state helps explain the origin of many of the issues that the guerrilla organization brings to the table, and the nature of the mechanisms it is proposing. We can see that these issues and mechanisms have been discussed within the ELN throughout this long process, which gives us some understanding of the organization's discourse. These ideas and mechanisms include the cessation of hostilities, peace zones, regional development projects, the National Convention, the possibility of political and social reforms and of a National Constituent Assembly, possible amnesties and pardons, the legal features of a *despeje*, and the participation of civil society and the international community. Nothing has been left out.

Since 1991, the ELN has gained an enormous amount of experience in conversations aimed at a peace agreement. In that year, representatives of the ELN, the FARC, and a dissident faction of the Ejército Popular de Liberación (EPL) traveled to Caracas and to Tlaxcala, Mexico, to engage in talks on national reconciliation with the government of César Gaviria.

The participants sketched out a complex map of the country, indicating areas where the guerrillas would establish themselves in order to move toward a new cessation of hostilities and to work with the local populations in promoting moves toward peace.

These talks were broken off due to the death, while in ELN captivity, of prominent political figure Argelino Durán Quintero, but it is clear that the

ELN took away lessons from that experience, which it has used in subsequent dialogues. The concept of "humanitarian zones," or zones of peace, which are being proposed as a mechanism to facilitate the concentration of guerrilla forces in different regions within the framework of a possible cessation of hostilities, is to some extent an outgrowth of those first discussions in Caracas and Tlaxcala.

In 1997, an ELN delegation traveled discreetly to Madrid and met at the Spanish Ministry of Foreign Affairs with members of the government of President Ernesto Samper. Representatives of the Colombian National Conciliation Commission facilitated the meeting, which was fully authorized by the president, and those attending signed a detailed and ambitious document known as the Viana Preagreement, named after the palace in Madrid that houses the ministry.

This "preagreement" dealt separately with political and military topics. It established a political road map that included a National Convention and ended with a National Constituent Assembly, which would be charged with producing significant national reforms. On military issues, the participants established the goal of ending the armed uprising and explored different possibilities for dealing with the guerrillas' weapons. Discussions also included the possibility that some ELN commanders could participate in the national security forces, which would be newly reconfigured through the eventual agreement.

To be put into effect, the preagreement was to have been studied and ratified by the ELN Central Command and the Colombian president, but before these steps could be taken, news of the plan was leaked, and the resulting public debate prevented those last steps from being taken. These developments coincided with the crisis in the Samper government arising from accusations of drug cartel financing of the president's election campaign.

When the ELN engages in conversations with the state, it returns again and again to its proposals for a National Convention and a Constituent Assembly. The idea of broad civil society participation in peace negotiations is closely tied to these proposals, and the Viana Preagreement explicitly called for a complex process of engaging civil society in the negotiations between the guerrillas and the state.

Over time, the government and various social sectors interested in attempts to negotiate with the ELN have come to accept the idea that civil society participation is important and could help generate a participatory model in the context of peace negotiations. They also accept the idea that the active participation of different social sectors in the post-conflict scenario would be an important new step for Colombia.

However, the slowness of negotiations with the ELN is also tied to the difficulty of establishing mechanisms for civil society participation and the difficulty of integrating the issues that interest civil society groups into the negotiating agenda.

The ELN also moved toward conversations with the government in the summer of 1998. President Pastrana had been elected but not yet inaugurated when civil society organizations promoted a meeting in Germany, attended by representatives of the outgoing government as well as possible members of the new administration. Although the objective was to establish a transition from the outgoing to the incoming government around the status of peacemaking with the ELN, the meeting was an initiative of civil society with the assistance and sponsorship of the German government and the German Council of Bishops. Civil society participation was broad and included entrepreneurs, political leaders, members of NGOs, and a high-level church delegation. The agenda for negotiations with the incoming government was hotly debated, including for the first time the issue of kidnapping—certainly one of the most egregious human rights violations. Other humanitarian questions, including forced displacement, demining in conflict areas, and respect for the civilian population, were also discussed.

The ELN stated very frankly—or, in the opinion of some attendees, with shocking audacity—that it would be able to give up kidnapping only if another source of financing could be found through the peace process. The German government suggested establishing a fund through Werner and Ida Mauss to reduce the ELN's reliance on revenues from kidnapping and from attacks on Colombian infrastructure.[7]

This discussion was left open, but the ELN took the symbolic step of signing an agreement stating that it would not kidnap pregnant women or anyone over seventy-five years of age. This agreement unleashed a controversy in Colombia, with critics saying that the signatories to the document tacitly accepted the kidnapping of individuals who did not fall into either of the two exempt categories.

The legacy of the German meeting is strong. Since then, humanitarian concerns have played an ever-present and important role in all conversations with the ELN, and the international community and different sectors of civil society have stayed involved.

President Pastrana's government nonetheless paid insufficient attention to the results of this meeting, because reaching an agreement with the FARC consumed all the efforts of the president and his peace commissioner in the administration's first year and a half. High Commissioner for Peace Víctor G. Ricardo paid very little attention to the ELN, in some meetings even justifying

---

[7] Werner and Ida Mauss are a German couple whose role is very controversial in Colombia. Working for an international security contractor, they helped secure the release of several kidnap victims through negotiations and then took on a role in moving the ELN toward conversations with the government.

this neglect by saying that the ELN would quickly come around in the wake of an agreement with the FARC.

An attempt was made to organize an agenda for negotiations that would run parallel to the agenda being developed in San Vicente del Caguán by the Pastrana government and the FARC. On July 25–27, 2000, representatives of the Pastrana government, the ELN, and civil society gathered at Geneva's Mövenpick Hotel for a series of meetings called "Encounter for a National Consensus for Peace in Colombia." Discussions addressed the possibility of establishing a zone in southern Bolívar Department for direct negotiations between the ELN and the government and for the subsequent National Convention.

The encounter got under way with optimism and high hopes for participation by broad sectors of Colombian society. Peace Commissioner Camilo Gómez let it be known that he wanted to make progress at the meetings to stimulate negotiations with the FARC in San Vicente del Caguán, which were beginning to run into problems. The talks were thrown into crisis in the middle of the second meeting, however, when news arrived that paramilitaries led by Carlos Castaño were attacking the principal encampments of the ELN in southern Bolívar. The ELN delegation, led by Antonio García, suspended the talks, noting that the paramilitary attacks would not have been possible without the collaboration of the Colombian armed forces. ELN leaders interpreted the attacks as a provocation intended to impede progress toward an agreement.

The meetings resumed before long, however, and ended with moderate success. It opened the way toward the establishment of a *despeje* in southern Bolívar and a proposed series of subsequent negotiations to be attended by the ELN's key military commanders. But because the paramilitary attacks continued and mobilizations against the proposed *despeje* intensified, the subsequent negotiations did not materialize. Nonetheless, the talks in Geneva had generated the idea of a special zone for negotiations, which would be further discussed in Havana and again in Geneva over the course of 2001. During these discussions, the participants succeeded in drawing up a common document detailing the terms for a potential *despeje* to be established for eventual negotiations.

A declaration of intent signed in Havana on March 12, 2002, by representatives of the Pastrana government and the ELN expressed "the commitment to move forward toward a truce." The document had been prepared over several months of patient meetings in the Cuban capital, beginning in the middle of November 2001. A first agreement, dated November 24, known as the "Agreement for Colombia," established that the parties would "formally resume the process of dialogue through a transitional agenda lasting until the end of the current administration." The agenda was further elaborated at the "Summit for Peace" in Cuba on January 29–31, 2002. More than seventy people, including representatives of Colombian civil society and delegates from the international community, attended the summit. Camilo Gómez and Ambassador Julio Londoño Paredes led the government delegation, and Ramiro Vargas, Oscar Santos, Milton Hernández, Francisco Galán, and Felipe Torres represented the ELN.

Cuban president Fidel Castro took the unusual step of closely following developments at the summit. He attended the opening ceremony and catered a final reception with fine food and Havana rum. He spoke with several of the Colombian delegations, including the entrepreneurs, the governors, nongovernmental organizations, and, of course, the government and the ELN. To each of these groups he expressed his concern about the Colombian situation and stressed the need to reach peace and avoid a general conflict that could lead to a U.S. intervention—with consequences for all Latin America.

The participants at this summit were encouraged to consider immediately "the question of a truce and a cessation of hostilities that encompass respect for the life and freedom of the population" and to move forward without waiting for the installation of the new Colombian government on August 7, 2002. But the parties did not heed this call. They took no further steps until Álvaro Uribe and his first administration took office.

Uribe did not sit down with the ELN to explore the possibility of negotiations until the end of his first term. In his second term, he took up the recurring issue of a cessation of hostilities. Perhaps now it can be accomplished. Perhaps the enormous possibilities that have opened up in Colombia for the ELN to engage in legal politics will encourage the guerrilla organization to reach an agreement for a bilateral truce quickly and to sign a comprehensive peace allowing for the ELN's free participation in civilian life. But bold action is needed from President Uribe and the peace commissioner, civil society must support the process proactively, and much help will be required from the international community.

6

From Greed to Grievance
The Shifting Political Profile of the Colombian Paramilitaries

Winifred Tate

On June 28, 2004, indicted drug trafficker and paramilitary leader Salvatore Mancuso, wearing a fashionable Italian suit and tie, addressed the Colombian Congress from the podium. "The judgment of history will recognize the goodness and nobility of our cause," he told the assembled legislators and press. The day before, Mancuso, along with two other paramilitary leaders, had traveled in an official air force plane from the small northern Colombia hamlet where paramilitary leaders had assembled to begin talks with the Colombian government. After almost a decade of fighting outside the law, Mancuso was now addressing the heart of the state, his many arrest warrants—as well as the extradition order issued by the U.S. government that would land him in a jail in Washington, D.C., four years later—temporarily suspended as the Colombian government and the paramilitary leaders began negotiations intended to demobilize paramilitary fighters in exchange for state benefits.

Over the past decade, paramilitary forces under the umbrella of the United Self-Defense Forces of Colombia (AUC) transformed themselves from regional renegades to political operators and valid interlocutors, respected in many quarters as worthy of sitting at the negotiating table with the government. This metamorphosis involved changes in paramilitary tactics, as well as a substantial public relations campaign aimed at changing public perceptions at home and abroad. These groups had begun new and wider military operations in the late 1990s, dramatically expanding their numbers from an estimated 2,500 in the early 1990s to more than 15,000 by the end of the decade,

Research for this chapter was contracted in part by the United States Institute of Peace; earlier research was paid for in part by a grant from the Wenner-Gren Foundation. The author would like to thank Cathy Lutz and particularly Mary Roldán for their thoughtful comments.

and embarked on offensive military campaigns to conquer new territory. Paramilitary leaders carried out a public relations campaign employing a range of strategies to engender public acceptance of their role as political spokesmen from the government and international funders. Paramilitary groups with significant links to a growing number of congressional and local politicians were central in transforming the electoral map of Colombia.[1] These efforts were a critical component in the domestic and international support for current negotiations between the government and paramilitary leaders.

Through these negotiations, the Colombian government demobilized almost 32,000 paramilitary fighters by July 2007, using traditional conflict-resolution strategies based on the collective disarming, demobilization, and reintegration of combatants. These conflict-resolution techniques have been developed over the past several decades to bring violent oppositional groups into legal political life. However, the history and nature of the Colombian paramilitary forces, particularly their ongoing links with state security forces, involvement with violent criminal enterprises, and strategic deployment of public relations and media campaigns to increase public support of their claims without substantially altering their abusive practices, pose profound challenges to the employment of traditional peacebuilding strategies in Colombia. Unlike the insurgents who have participated in previous peace negotiations with the Colombian government, the paramilitaries were not radical leftists intent on defeating the government, but rather were led by elite ranchers and farmers—many deeply implicated in drug trafficking—who claimed to support the state. While guerrilla factions have long employed public diplomacy to further their cause, the paramilitaries have brought an unprecedented level of sophistication to their public relations campaigns. This chapter will examine how paramilitaries used new forms of technology, such as the Internet, and organizational forms including non-governmental organizations (NGOs) and foundations to increase public support and justify their negotiations with the government. These paramilitary forces offer an example of how illegal armed groups can learn political lessons from previous peace processes. This chapter begins with a brief discussion of negotiations within the Colombian conflict, outlines the history and evolution of paramilitary forces there, and then reviews the paramilitaries' efforts to bolster their legitimacy and articulate their version of the Colombian conflict, before concluding with the challenges that paramilitary groups present to the conflict-resolution models used in the current negotiations.

Negotiations within the Colombian Conflict

Measuring the degree to which illegal armed groups articulate a valid grievance against the state and represent a significant constituency is of critical

---

[1] See Mauricio Romero, ed., *Parapolítica: La ruta de la expansión paramilitar y los acuerdos políticos* (Bogotá: Corporación Nuevo Arco Iris and Intermedio Editores, 2007).

importance in assessing prospects for successful negotiations with those groups. In their analysis of illegal armed groups in entrenched conflicts, World Bank economists Paul Collier and Anke Hoeffler offered the "greed and grievance" spectrum, concluding that illegal armed groups generally move from grievance, or the articulation of complaints against the state, to greed—efforts to capture and maintain control over strategic resources. Their work was widely used in Colombia's case to explain the evolution of the guerrillas, who were seen as moving from ideologically based resistance against the state, to increasing involvement in criminal activity and drug-trade profiteering. However, Collier and Hoeffler's work has not been sufficiently analyzed in light of groups that have used the articulation of grievances against the state to further—or to mask—their violent criminal enterprises. In Colombia, grievance discourses employed against the state by violent groups have complex genealogies that do not easily translate along left-right ideological divides. While it is beyond the scope of this chapter to trace their evolution here, these discourses offer deep-rooted political resources for Colombian groups to project and claim political legitimacy and public support even while maintaining extremely violent practices. Liberal guerrillas as well as organized bandits during and following the partisan violence of the 1950s, the leadership of the major drug cartels during the 1980s, and some paramilitary spokesmen in the 1990s have all employed grievance discourses decrying state inefficiency and illegitimacy to build public support for themselves. This chapter focuses on the paramilitary leadership's use of grievance discourses and an accompanying repertoire of political practices to garner greater public support and access to official political resources (including the opportunity to run for elected office and receive state funding). By portraying themselves as motivated primarily by grievance—as victims of guerrilla violence forced to take up arms when abandoned by the state—paramilitaries attempt to counter the perception that they are motivated primarily by greed, whether defending the interests of large landowners and drug traffickers or conducting death squad operations as clandestine agents of state counterinsurgency efforts.

With a few notable exceptions, the majority of analyses of Colombian paramilitaries have focused on human rights concerns or have been journalistic accounts of their military operations. The most detailed work examining the evolution of Colombian paramilitary forces has employed the concept of military entrepreneurs to describe the shifting movement between legally sanctioned activities and illegality over time and has underscored how paramilitary forces have defended different economic interests in different regions.[2] This framework, while useful in describing those shifts, does not allow an

---

[2] See Thomas Gallant, "Brigandage, Piracy, Capitalism and State Formation: Transnational Crime from a Historical World Systems Perspective," in *States and Illegal Practices*, ed. Joseph Heyman (Oxford: Berg, 1999); Mauricio Romero, *Paramilitares y autodefensas, 1982–2003* (Bogotá: IEPRI, 2003).

exploration of how paramilitary leaders have strategically used political repertoires, discourses, and organizational forms—many traditionally employed by the left—to increase their public support. The acceptance of the paramilitaries as a negotiating partner with the government is the most significant sign of their success in reframing and legitimating their cause.

The talks begun in 2003 between paramilitary groups and the Colombian government were only the latest such negotiations in the long history of peace efforts in Colombia. Although ultimately unsuccessful in resolving the armed conflict, such efforts have allowed the demobilization of thousands of combatants from individual guerrilla groups. Amnesties and reintegration programs for bandits and Liberal Party guerrillas in the 1950s were the first such efforts. Talks with Marxist guerrillas began in the early 1980s, long before their more successful Central American counterparts would engage in dialogues for peace. By the 1990s, an international diplomatic consensus widely accepted negotiations with illegal armed groups—even for those perceived by some in the U.S. government to have employed illegal tactics or to represent unsavory ideological projects—as an established model for resolution of violent conflict. Colombia's recent paramilitary demobilization efforts are unprecedented in their size and scope; the government has moved almost 32,000 paramilitary members through its programs, while previous collective guerrilla demobilizations have involved at most only a few thousand fighters.

Previous negotiations offer many lessons to thoughtful combatants. In many cases of collective demobilization, former combatants suffered serious persecution, both from former enemies and from still active former comrades. In part because of this violence, no guerrilla force has been successful in creating a sustainable legal political party. Combatants concerned about the possible legal repercussions of demobilization may note that none of the thousands of combatants participating in these processes have faced trials or truth commissions attempting to address criminal violence or abuse that they may have committed. Indeed, many enjoyed significant economic benefits through government subsidies and reintegration programs. Finally, former guerrillas were able to return to "legal life," rejoining their home communities, and many movement leaders were able to run for political office, head foundations and NGOs, and become political commentators with respect from many quarters. Merely participating in such talks can generate public support for groups involved, even if the negotiations are ultimately unsuccessful.

Paramilitary groups participating in negotiations with the government have already obtained concrete benefits. Like demobilized guerrillas before them, demobilized paramilitary members receive a government stipend (in this case, slightly less than minimum wage for two years) in addition to employment and educational benefits. While delivery of promised benefits and services has suffered significant delays, such incentives remain an important factor, particularly for rank-and-file paramilitary members. More important for paramilitary leaders facing criminal indictments, implementation of the Justice and Peace Law passed in 2005 and discussed further by Arturo J. Carrillo in Chapter 7 of this volume has produced little accountability. While the law was significantly strengthened by a May 2006 decision of the Constitutional Court, which required a complete confession and full declaration of assets and expanded the definition of victims eligible for reparations, execution of the law has been slow.[3] Implementation depends on the 23 prosecutors and 150 investigators assigned to the Justice and Peace Unit of the Attorney General's Office, which must handle the 2,812 demobilized paramilitaries accused of crimes against humanity. As of June 2007, only forty of the accused had given their first testimony, and the investigation process was significantly delayed, with many of the accused refusing to provide information. Charges in some cases have been dismissed because witnesses recanted previous testimony; at least four prominent leaders of victims' groups calling for investigations have been assassinated.[4]

Evolution of Paramilitary Forces

"Paramilitary groups" and "self-defense groups" describe a range of different armed actors in Colombia over the past fifty years. These groups have developed according to profoundly different regional dynamics.[5] Despite regional variation, the evolution of paramilitary groups can be divided roughly into three major, at times overlapping, phases: death squad operations, in the 1970s and early 1980s; private armies funded by the drug trade, in the late 1980s and early 1990s; and the efforts to consolidate paramilitary groups under a single coordinating body represented by national spokesmen participating in public political life, starting in the late 1990s.

Paramilitary Death Squad Operations

One of the major differences between paramilitary groups and those illegal armed actors that have engaged in peace talks and demobilization programs is that paramilitaries historically have acted in concert with—and been

---

[3]See International Crisis Group (ICG), *Colombia: Towards Peace and Justice*, Latin America Report no. 16 (Bogotá/Brussels: ICG, March 14, 2006), www.crisisgroup.org/home/index. cfm?id=4020&l=1 (accessed September 30, 2008); also Human Rights Watch, *Letting Paramilitaries off the Hook* (New York: Human Rights Watch, 2004), www.hrw.org/backgrounder/ americas/colombia0105/ (accessed September 30, 2008); Latin America Working Group (LAWG), *Colombia: The Other Half of the Truth* (Washington, D.C.: LAWG, June 2008), http:// lawg.org/docs/the_other_half_of_the_truth.pdf (accessed September 30, 2008).

[4]Adam Isacson, "The 'Justice and Peace' process takes a grotesque turn," June 24, 2007, Center for International Policy, www.cipcol.org/?p=431#more-431 (accessed August 23, 2008).

[5]For greater detail on the history of paramilitaries, see Romero, *Paramilitares y autodefensas*; Francisco Cubides, "Los paramilitares y su estrategia," in *Reconocer la guerra para construir la paz*, eds. Malcolm Deas and María Victoria Llorente (Bogotá: Grupo Editorial Norma, 1999); Carlos Medina, *Autodefensas, paramilitares y narcotráfico en Colombia: Origen, desarrollo y consolidación: el caso "Puerto Boyacá"* (Bogotá: Editorial Documentos Periodísticos, 1990).

supported by—the state military apparatus rather than in opposition to the state. (An important exception to this is the paramilitary violent repression of state judicial efforts to investigate paramilitary crimes, particularly involving the drug trade.) Paramilitary groups have periodically been legally incorporated into counterinsurgency efforts, and the links between legal and illegal paramilitaries have historically been pervasive. The legal basis for state sponsorship of paramilitary organizations was Law 48, approved by the Colombian Congress in 1968, which allowed the government to "mobilize the population in activities and tasks" to restore public order.[6] International pressure and additional attacks against government officials led President Virgilio Barco to declare the creation of paramilitary groups illegal in 1989. The expansion of paramilitary groups in the 1990s coincided with the organization of legal rural defense forces, known as the "Convivir." Officially launched in 1995, the Convivir were enthusiastically supported by Álvaro Uribe during his tenure as governor of Antioquia (1995–98). Following numerous complaints of Convivir participation in human rights abuses, the Supreme Court upheld their legality in 1997 but prohibited them from collecting intelligence for the security forces and from receiving military-issued weapons.[7]

According to human rights groups and government investigators, during the first phase of paramilitary activity, there was considerable overlap between the civilians legally trained by local military forces in the 1970s and illegal paramilitary death squads, such as the American Anti-Communist Alliance, active in the Magdalena region.[8]

Expansion of Private Armies

The first qualitative shift in Colombian paramilitary groups came in the 1980s, when money from the drug trade allowed such forces to grow from small groups linked to local military commanders to private armies. Unlike the death squad operations in other Latin American countries, the paramilitaries benefited from the enormous resources provided by Colombia's most lucrative industry: drug trafficking. The fusion of counterinsurgency ideology and illegal narcotics revenue produced one of the most lethal fighting forces in Latin America. As the owners of vast haciendas (the result of money laundering and efforts to buy their way into the landed gentry, known as

---

[6] See Michael McClintock, *Instruments of Statecraft: U.S. Guerrilla Warfare, Counterinsurgency, and Counterterrorism, 1940–1990* (New York: Pantheon, 1992), 222–23.

[7] Washington Office on Latin America, *Losing Ground: Colombian Human Rights Defenders under Attack* (Washington, D.C.: WOLA, 1997); Human Rights Watch, *Colombia's Killer Networks* (New York: Human Rights Watch, 1995); Human Rights Watch, *Yearly Report 1997* (New York: Human Rights Watch, 1997); Office of the United Nations High Commissioner for Human Rights, *Report 2000* (New York: United Nations, 2000), 24.

[8] See Michael Evans, ed., "The Truth About the Triple A," an electronic briefing book published by the National Security Archive, 2007, www.gwu.edu/~nsarchiv/NSAEBB/NSAEBB223/index.htm (accessed September 10, 2008).

"reverse agrarian reform"), drug traffickers needed protection from the guerrillas, whose primary fund-raising techniques involved *boleteo* (extortion), *vacunas* ("vaccination" against guerrilla attack), and, increasingly, kidnapping of rural elites. Paramilitary groups linked to drug cartels (particularly the Medellín Cartel) worked closely with Colombian military officers to eliminate suspected guerrilla sympathizers, while at the same time attacking Colombian authorities who tried to investigate drug trafficking. Paramilitary groups were particularly vicious in targeting activists from the leftist parties, who enjoyed considerable support following the 1987 reforms, which allowed popular election of mayors and other local officials previously appointed to their posts.[9]

Paramilitary groups organized in the Middle Magdalena Valley—one of the epicenters of the drug-financed landgrab of the 1980s—became pioneers in the politicization of paramilitary activities, attempting to unify their growing military power into a grassroots base that would serve as the foundation for political control. In 1983, Puerto Boyacá mayor Luis Rubio, together with allies in the Liberal Party, created the Association of Middle Magdalena Ranchers and Farmers (ACDEGAM). As part of their political strategy to strengthen ties among local farmers, businessmen, the "self-defense forces," and the military, members set up more than thirty schools offering "patriotic and anti-Communist" education, health clinics, and agricultural cooperatives and built roads and bridges, all funded by a combination of "voluntary contributions" and government and private money. According to journalist and historian Steven Dudley, however, the ACDEGAM also served as "the autodefensas' center of operations. Recruiting, weapons storage, communications, propaganda, and medical services were all run from ACDEGAM headquarters."[10] ACDEGAM leadership worked with the support of local and national politicians, including Congressman Pablo Guarín. By the end of the 1980s, ACDEGAM, together with a sister organization known as "Tradición, Familia y Propiedad," made up the core of a new political movement called Movimiento de Restauración Nacional (MORENA). Spurred by the electoral reforms, MORENA candidates won six mayoral seats in the Middle Magdalena Valley, self-proclaimed the "National Front of Anti-Subversive Mayors." Outside its regional strongholds in the Middle Magdalena Valley, MORENA never achieved national prominence or even significant support in other regions with significant paramilitary presence. The paramilitary political movement would not emerge until the late 1990s, although the surviving

---

[9] For the history of the Patriotic Union, see Steven Dudley, *Walking Ghosts: Murder and Guerrilla Politics in Colombia* (New York: Routledge, 2004); Romero, *Paramilitares y autodefensas*.

[10] Dudley, *Walking Ghosts*, 68. See also Francisco Gutiérrez Sanín and Mauricio Barón, "ReStating the State: Paramilitary Territorial Control and Political Order in Colombia" (IEPRI working paper no. 66, Crisis States Programme Working Papers series no. 1, Development Research Centre, London School of Economics, September 2005).

leadership went on to play a major role in the new paramilitary structure. For example, Iván Roberto Duque ("Ernesto Baez"), former secretary-general of ACDEGAM and founder of MORENA, went on to be an architect of the paramilitaries' evolving political platform.

Current paramilitary leaders may also be drawing on the efforts of Colombian drug traffickers, particularly the Medellín Cartel, to bolster public support. Cartel boss Pablo Escobar used several tactics to increase his public profile and influence, including running for elected office (he was elected congressional representative alternate in 1982) and funding community development. In their unsuccessful efforts to prevent approval of extradition, the "Extraditables" (a group of drug traffickers led by Escobar) used human rights discourses and nationalism in communiqués and media interviews to frame their cause as not simply organized crime but a legitimate political and essentially Colombian enterprise. (They also resorted to extreme violence, called "narcoterrorism.") Many drug traffickers also engaged in negotiations with the central government as well as with local officials.[11] During this period, several influential leaders of the paramilitaries, including the Castaño brothers, were deeply involved in drug trafficking and active in efforts to build the political legitimacy of trafficking organizations.

Emergence of the AUC

The third phase of expansion was marked by the creation of a national coordinating body of paramilitary groups, the AUC.[12] Following a summit in July 1997, the AUC issued a statement announcing an offensive military campaign into new regions of the country "according to the operational capacity of each regional group." Newly created "mobile squads"—elite training and combat units—carried out these operations, which included numerous massacres targeting the civilian population in these areas. The July 1997 massacre in Mapiripán, Meta, was the first step in implementing this new plan. During July 15–20, 1997, gunmen from the AUC took control of Mapiripán, killed at least forty people, and threatened others. The exact death toll was never established, because many of the bodies were dismembered and thrown into a nearby river. Following a lengthy investigation, a military court sentenced

---

[11] See Mary J. Roldán, "Cocaine and the 'Miracle' of Modernity in Medellín," in *Cocaine: Global Histories*, ed. Paul Gootenberg (New York: Routledge, 1999); Francisco Thoumi, *Illegal Drugs, Economy and Society in the Andes* (Baltimore, Md.: Woodrow Wilson Center/Johns Hopkins University Press, 2003).

[12] For more detail on drug trafficking and paramilitary groups in Colombia, see Alonso Salazar, *La Parábola de Pablo: Auge y caída de un gran capo del narcotráfico* (Bogotá: Editorial Planeta, 2001); Robin Kirk, *More Terrible than Death: Massacres, Drugs and America's War in Colombia* (New York: Public Affairs, 2003), 108–09; Álvaro Camacho, "Narcotráfico y violencias en Colombia" (conference transcript from the Historical Analysis of Narcotrafficking in Colombia symposium, National Museum, Bogotá, October 30, 2003).

Gen. Jaime Uscátegui to forty months in jail for dereliction of duty because he failed to respond to repeated requests for action by local authorities and his own subordinates.[13] AUC fighters carried out similar massacres throughout the country. At the same time, paramilitary leaders gained increasing power within local and national politics. This has been dramatically demonstrated in the *parapolítica* scandal that first emerged in the fall of 2006 and caused the resignation of the foreign minister and the head of the national intelligence service.[14] As of August 2008, the investigation remains ongoing; twenty-nine members of Congress have been detained and an additional thirty-nine remain under investigation.[15]

Paramilitary Public Relations

Since its formal incorporation, the AUC has been engaged in a major public relations campaign to improve its image and represent itself as a legitimate political force. Its first communiqués copied the style of the guerrillas, issued with a dateline "from the mountains of Colombia" (previously, the guerrillas were the only armed actors inhabiting *el monte*), with a color logo in the letterhead depicting a peasant man silhouetted against a map of Colombia. In marked contrast to other forms of communication from paramilitary groups, such as the death threats intended to strike fear in the recipients (often sent in creative forms such as funeral invitations), these communiqués showcased the political nature of the organization.

In addition to written communiqués, the paramilitaries created a series of sophisticated Web pages that reflected their preoccupation with public relations. In 1999, the paramilitaries launched "Colombialibre.org," a Web site that, by 2001, rivaled official Colombian government sites in its sophistication, graphics, and content. (The guerrillas' Web sites, by contrast, languished until 2003 with only occasional flashing updates.) One of the first documents posted on the site included "proposals for structural reforms for the construction of a new Colombia," alongside diagrams outlining the AUC's structure of command, communiqués, open letters issued by paramilitary leaders, and documents outlining the history and evolution of paramilitary forces. By 2005, the still active Web site was home to daily press links to articles featuring paramilitary commanders and activities, as well as links to the home

---

[13] One of the military officers who requested assistance, Col. Lino Sánchez, was also investigated for misconduct as a result of his public testimony in the case.

[14] See John Otis, "Court Tell-Alls Tie the Elite to Paramilitary Killings," *Houston Chronicle*, May 20, 2007.

[15] These figures are from a table produced by the Colombian think tank Instituto de Estudios para el Desarrollo y para la Paz (INDEPAZ), www.indepaz.org.co/index.php?option=com_content&task=view&id=646&Itemid=1 (accessed September 8, 2008).

pages of the regional blocs making up the AUC, which featured their own communiqués and command-structure diagrams.[16]

In addition to use of the Internet, the AUC leadership, under the command of Carlos Castaño, also launched a media outreach offensive. Colombian journalist María Cristina Caballero claims to have carried out one of the first major press interviews with Castaño in 1997, following the Mapiripán massacre described above. During the interview, Castaño announced that he was "tired of fighting and ready to sit down at the negotiating table." At the time, President Andrés Pastrana had made peace talks with the FARC the major focus of his administration. In her account, Caballero reports asking Castaño to "prepare a document explaining what he wanted to achieve with his movement and proposing the key reforms the country needed for peace." His reply was later published by the Colombian newsmagazine *Cambio 16* in May 1998, along with responses from the guerrilla leadership.[17] Widespread and apparently systematic interviews with the press did not begin until 2000, however. In March of that year, Castaño appeared in his first on-camera interview in a prime-time special on Caracol network. In an apparent effort to soften his warrior image, he appeared wearing a sweater and slacks. He admitted that he often cried when thinking of the tragedies caused by the fighting in Colombia and that his troops should have "operated with more prudence." In addition to subsequent nearly weekly appearances in the Colombian press, Castaño was featured on the cover of the international edition of *Time* magazine on November 27, 2000, and profiled in the *Washington Post* (under the headline "King of the Jungle") on March 12, 2001. That same year, Castaño approved the release of *My Confession,* a fawning biography resulting from a series of interviews with a Colombian journalist. The book became a Colombian best seller. Regional paramilitary leaders also began appearing frequently in the Colombian press during this period. After Castaño's disappearance on April 16, 2004, Northern Bloc commander Salvatore Mancuso was often featured in the press, and his biography, *Salvatore Mancuso: Life Enough for One Hundred Years,* was published in late 2004; in May 2005, he launched his own Web site, highlighting his analysis and speeches. Castaño's brother Vicente Castaño Gil was featured for his first press interview on the cover of Colombian newsmagazine *Semana* in June 2005. In the interview, he clearly attempted to position himself as a long-standing power behind Car-

---

[16] As of June 2007, a much-reduced version of the "Colombialibre.org" Web site was dedicated to the "National Movement of Demobilized Self-Defense Forces," with empty pages and no links to regional groups. By the following month, the site was completely dismantled. As of this writing, Mancuso has been extradited to the United States to face drug-trafficking charges and it is unclear how this will impact the ongoing Colombian investigations into his human rights crimes as required by the Justice and Peace Law.

[17] María Cristina Caballero, "A Journalist's Mission in Colombia: Reporting Atrocities Is Not Enough," *Columbia Journalism Review* (May–June 2000), http://backissues.cjrarchives.org/year/00/2/caballero.asp (accessed September 9, 2008).

los's public face and stressed the political evolution and focus of the para-militaries under his command.

Complementing their media and Internet presence, paramilitary leaders also attempted to transform perceptions of their organizational structure and behavior through the publication of command diagrams and internal regulations, and their emphasis on the acceptance of human rights and inter-national humanitarian law standards (in marked contrast to the guerrilla leadership, which publicly rejected such norms as illegitimate and part of a neoliberal and repressive regime that does not apply to them). According to the Constitutional Statutes and Disciplinary Regime adopted in May 1998 at the AUC's second national conference, the organization had developed into a highly regimented military command structure incorporating regional groups; part of the military discipline included instructing new recruits to obey international humanitarian law, also known as the "rules of war," and to refrain from violating human rights.

This approach was partly the result of active consultation with a number of well-educated advisers. In his biography, Carlos Castaño claims to have worked extensively with Jesuit-trained intellectuals to develop the AUC's po-litical strategy. International organizations, foremost among them the Inter-national Committee of the Red Cross (ICRC), also played a role. In 1997, the ICRC negotiated a new memorandum of agreement with the Colombian gov-ernment that allowed ICRC representatives to have direct contacts with ille-gal armed groups. As a result of that agreement, the head of the ICRC, Pierre Gassmann, was one of the first international officials to meet with Castaño. One staff member at the time recalled, "It was a controversial decision, but the ICRC viewed them as an armed actor with a clear line of command, which is enough under international humanitarian law." The ICRC also offered training in international humanitarian law to combatants. The same staff member, who worked in southern Colombia during the late 1990s, gave "three or four" workshops to the paramilitaries. "They were easy to get in touch with; you had the cell phones of all the local commanders and their commanders, and they always responded quickly to requests," he told me. "Their troops were mainly young men from cities like Medellín and Cali, just guys who wanted a job," he concluded. "But they had a very clear line of command to Castaño; they knew that the ICRC boss had talked to Castaño, and were afraid of getting him mad." The impact of these classes on para-military behavior in the field was unclear. Murder and massacre rates in some regions seemed to decline, but figures are notoriously unreliable since many deaths, particularly in rural areas, are never reported.

The ICRC representatives were not the only officials to contact Castaño. Journalists, international groups attempting to promote humanitarian agree-ments, representatives of Colombian Protestant and Catholic churches, gov-ernment officials, and NGOs acknowledged holding frequent off-the-record meetings with paramilitary commanders during the late 1990s. On at least two occasions, high-ranking government ministers have met with Castaño; Minister of the Interior Horacio Serpa met with Castaño to discuss threats against Serpa's own life, and a high-ranking delegation met with Castaño to negotiate the liberation of seven members of Congress kidnapped by the AUC in May 1999. Local government officials also met frequently with paramilitary commanders in their regions.

Paramilitary groups are creating foundations and NGOs to promote their agenda. Extremely lenient Colombian legislation governing the administration of such organizations has facilitated their use by groups from across the political spectrum. One of the first such organizations was the Fundación para la Paz (Funpazcor), established in Córdoba in the early 1990s by Carlos Castaño's older brother, Fidel, and run by his sister-in-law. Set up to distribute land to demobilized Popular Liberation Army (EPL) fighters, many of whom later joined Fidel's restructured paramilitary force, then known as the Autodefensas Campesinas de Córdoba y Urubá (ACCU, a forerunner of the AUC), the foundation has been controversial. It remains unclear to what degree the entity functioned as a foundation, and how much land it distributed. The foundation has been under investigation by the Attorney General's Office for serving as a front for illegal weapons purchases and other criminal dealings, and it is currently on the U.S. State Department list of terrorist front organizations. Since the early 1990s, scores of paramilitary-sponsored NGOs have been organized. According to paramilitary commander Jorge 40, most women involved in the paramilitaries are "dedicated to social and political projects."[18] Isabel Bolaños is one such example. Originally linked to peasant organizations and guerrilla groups including the EPL, she worked closely with Carlos Castaño in development projects throughout the late 1990s before her capture in 1999, when she was charged with various paramilitary crimes.[19] In some cases, these efforts are building on more than a decade of privately organized, paternalistic land redistribution efforts, such as the proposal by the cattle ranchers' association Federación Colombiana de Ganaderos (FEDEGAN) that members donate land to peasant settlers in conflictual areas.

"They [the AUC] are preparing political proposals, including buying land and offering work, to win over people. It is very serious political work," an evangelical pastor who had been working in northern Córdoba for many years told me in 2001. These political and financial efforts have made it more difficult for grassroots and church organizations to maintain their community-based projects. "We can't respond in the same way as the paras

---

[18] Author interview, January 15, 2005.

[19] Bolaños' life history was included in a collection of testimonies by Patricia Lara, *Las Mujeres en la guerra* (Bogotá: Editorial Planeta, 2000). It is also likely that she was the woman identified as "Rosa" in Alma Guillermoprieto's article titled "Our New War in Colombia," *New York Review of Books* 47, no. 6 (April 13, 2000).

can, in terms of offering resources. It is a church of peasants—the going rate for a day's work is four thousand pesos [less than US$2], and they are offering eight thousand. They are organizing the communities, buying land; they are doubling their troops."

In another example of adopting leftist tactics, paramilitary-backed organizations in Bolívar organized a series of self-proclaimed "peace" marches and road blockades to protest a proposed "demilitarized" zone for peace talks with the ELN in 2000 and 2001. The two main organizations, Asocipaz and No al Despeje, were widely credited with shutting down the talks. AUC commander Carlos Castaño publicly supported their efforts on his Web site, where he credited the AUC with militarily defeating the ELN in the region. The AUC was also widely believed to have provided financial and logistical support to these groups.[20]

Since their demobilization as part of the Cacique Nutibara Bloc in November 2003, demobilized paramilitaries in Medellín are becoming actively involved in a number of local community projects. Their flagship organization, the Democracy Foundation, promotes community development and small-business projects for demobilized paramilitaries. Among their projects, they are organizing "neighborhood invasions," efforts by the poor and internally displaced to establish squatter settlements. Demobilized leaders have been elected to local offices. While such efforts have been common in previous cases of guerrilla demobilizations, what is significant in this case is the degree to which demobilized paramilitaries remain engaged with active paramilitary forces in the region. "The problem is not that they are doing political things—that is what happened during all the demobilization processes, with the EPL, M-19, ELN," one Medellín-based community activist told me. "The problem is their capacity for intimidation, armed and unarmed. Leaders have to submit, leave, or be killed." Reports by the International Crisis Group, Amnesty International, and the Inter-American Commission on Human Rights have all concluded that paramilitary groups maintain control over Medellín neighborhoods—and, in many cases, are working in concert with demobilized individuals.

Paramilitary leaders freely admit that efforts to increase social control in the areas where they maintain a permanent presence are part of their new strategy to expand their authority. Community and religious leaders from a number of areas where paramilitary groups have consolidated military control, including parts of southern Colombia, the Magdalena Medio region, and the northern coast, have reported over the past five years that paramilitary commanders have begun to regulate virtually every facet of social life—they are mediating domestic disputes, establishing codes of conduct and dress,

---

[20] See Omar Gutiérrez, "La oposición regional a las negociaciones con el ELN," *Análisis Político* 17, no. 51 (2004).

and meting out harsh punishments for community members who do not comply with these codes. According to Comandante Andrés, a senior member of the Norte Bloc, "We became the police in the region. If a woman says, 'My husband hit me,' we have to solve their problems. We solve money disputes and the issue of inheritances." Despite the decline in homicides in regions of consolidated paramilitary control, violence and intimidation are still employed to enforce compliance. Religious leaders in southern Colombia reported that young men who failed to obey the rules of conduct in their communities were punished, first by having their heads shaved, then by beatings, amputation of fingers, and even death. During an interview in January 2005, one such leader recounted how paramilitaries had consolidated their presence in the areas where he did pastoral outreach. He noted:

> They recruited a lot of young men from the zone, to build up the command structure in the area. Their plan is to get involved in the community dynamic, to penetrate it, gain absolute control. In the town, now everything is controlled by them, even the traditional things like rituals of baptism. If someone wants to kill someone from the town, it has to be approved [by the paramilitary leader]. They provide logistical support for the political part of the work and the social services network. Today the political component is very strong. The *personero* [municipal human rights official] himself is one of them.[21]

Paramilitary commanders also freely admit that they are closely involved with official structures of local governance in the areas they control. "We advise the authorities so they take advantage of the best opportunities for their communities," Comandante Andrés told me. Both Jorge 40 and Salvatore Mancuso made similar pronouncements during interviews.

According to Amnesty International,

> A significant component of their strategy for exercising control over the population is the imposition of rules of conduct in even the most private of spheres: intervention in disputes between family members or neighbours and the use of corporal punishment to punish transgressors. These activities have been carried out with the knowledge, acquiescence and participation of the security forces. This type of control is often preceded or accompanied by what the paramilitary groups call "social cleansing"—the killing of petty criminals, prostitutes, and others perceived as "socially undesirable"—designed to show how efficient they are at establishing "public order." Amnesty International has received testimonies that point to the persecution, disappearance, and killing of persons from stigmatized groups, including sex workers, people targeted because of their sexual orientation, and alleged carriers of STDs such as HIV/AIDS.[22]

---

[21] Member of the clergy, interview by the author, southern Colombia, January 2005.

[22] Amnesty International, *Colombia: "Scarred Bodies, Hidden Crimes:" Violence against Women in the Armed Conflict*, AI Index: AMR 23/048/2004 (London: Amnesty International, October 13, 2004), www.amnesty.org/en/library/info/AMR23/040/2004 (accessed September 8, 2008).

The Bogotá office of the United Nations High Commissioner for Human Rights and the International Crisis Group have also reported alleged links between paramilitary groups and local government agencies, including the Administrators of the Subsidized Health Regime (ARS) and a Barranquilla-based, government-contracted tax-collection service, as well as between paramilitary groups, political leaders, the Administrative Department for Security (DAS, a specialized branch of the police), and the Attorney General's Office in the department of Norte de Santander.[23]

The Paramilitary Narrative: Victims and Victors

Through interviews, Web sites, and other documents, paramilitary leaders have articulated a new version of Colombian history in which they are both the victims in the Colombian conflict, sacrificing security and domestic life to defend the nation, and the victors, able to defeat the guerrillas in areas where the military merely maintained an uneasy stalemate or ceded control entirely. In this narrative, paramilitary forces emerged as an independent force ready to step into the vacuum left by an absent state. For many Colombians, including many in the rural elite and the urban middle class, this narrative resonates with their direct experience (as well as projected fears) of guerrilla violence and the failure of the state to provide security. The role of drug trafficking in financing paramilitary operations and of other financial interests in determining the priorities of paramilitary leaders is completely erased.

I heard one version of this history from paramilitary commander Salvatore Mancuso the day before his public demobilization on January 18, 2005. Following Castaño's disappearance in April 2004, Mancuso assumed the public role of political ideologue and major promoter of paramilitary negotiations with the government. Mancuso is well known among the Colombia elite. The son of an Italian immigrant, he was raised within the cloistered world of the cattle barons of the Atlantic coast and studied in the United States. He claims to have traveled later to Vietnam to learn about counterinsurgency techniques and to have become an accomplished helicopter pilot. We met at the end of a long day as the members of the North Bloc, whom Mancuso had summoned for demobilization, were going through the preinterview and documentation phase before the formal ceremony scheduled to take place a few days later. Forty-two years old, plump, and sunburned, he was wearing the uniform of a wealthy Colombian on his day off: khaki pants with a polo shirt and deck shoes. Appearing tired and often sighing, he told

---

[23] Office of the High Commissioner for Human Rights in Colombia, "Report of the High Commissioner for Human Rights on the Situation of Human Rights in Colombia," E/CN.4/2005/10, February 28, 2005, 19, www.hchr.org.co/documentoseinformes/documentos/informe2004/documentos.php3?cat=60 (accessed September 30, 2008); ICG, *Colombia's New Armed Groups*, Latin America Report no. 20 (Bogotá/Brussels: ICG, May 10, 2007), www.crisisgroup.org/home/index.cfm?id=4824&l=1 (accessed September 30, 2008).

me, with the studied calm of someone who had related the story many times before, the story of how he joined the paramilitaries.

He began with how the government had abandoned them in the face of escalating guerrilla violence. "In the beginning, it was simple. We were cattle ranchers, *gente de bien*. But at a certain moment in life, things change." During the late 1980s, the EPL and, later, the FARC grew bolder among the vast haciendas that filled the northern coast of Colombia, promoting peasant organizations and kidnapping and extorting local landowners. Mancuso was one of many among the economic elites who sought support from the military to protect their holdings. "I worked very closely with the state," he said. "I set up a communications network for the army and the police. We set it up to get information to the army. It went well in the beginning. But the commanders changed, and they didn't want to respond to the needs in the community. They said they wouldn't go into the red zone [that is, areas of known guerrilla strength]; they were afraid that they would get the soldiers or themselves killed. They have no commitment to the country; they are just looking out for their own careers."

By the mid-1990s, some ranchers and business leaders were ready to take matters into their own hands, and they met in 1997 to plan their strategy. "The government denied us help," Mancuso explained, "so we had two options: run away or confront them. We decided to confront the problem. We sent public letters asking for help, to the national government, to the minister of defense at that time, Fernando Botero. There is a copy on the Web site. We sent copies to the armed forces, the president, the human rights ombudsman [*defensor*]. But they never answered me."

This new organization involved personal transformation from community member to leader and institutional transformation involving the creation of a parallel state structure. "Things have changed drastically," said Mancuso. "Before, I was a rancher; now I represent two hundred and fifty ranchers—I fight for them and for me. When the guerrilla came, I had to start looking out for my neighbors. It was a snowball effect. I started defending my own interests, then my neighbors' interests, now everyone's interests." Although the initial response was to provide security for landowners in the area, the paramilitary forces assumed a much larger role within the community, ultimately taking over the essential roles of the state—providing security and mediating conflicts, but also building infrastructure, establishing schools, and offering health care. "So we had to fix the roads, pay for the schools, pay for education," Mancuso explained. "We became the state. Slowly we became a substitute for the state, which had never been present. We had to pay for water [*acueductos*]; we had to pay the salary for the teachers, the doctors, the nurses. Here there were no roads. How much did we have to pay to put in the roads?"

Paramilitaries also fundamentally changed the social composition of the region by repopulating areas from which landowners and peasants had been forcibly displaced by violence. "We brought in friends to buy the land. After the displacements, the people who the guerrillas forced out—some people began coming back to their land, or we found other people to buy it." The paramilitaries also got involved in political organizing, creating the local associations that form the backbone of Colombian political life, including neighborhood associations (*juntas de acción comunal*), and successfully running candidates for local elections, including town councils, state assemblies, and mayoralties.

According to Mancuso, the paramilitaries did more than replace the state. They were *better* than the state, because of their resources and because they were unencumbered by the institutional procedures and limitations of democracy. "Social control is a simple issue when you have to resolve all the problems of the state," he said. "You become what you are trying to substitute, but we are more efficient, because the state has more bureaucracy, more limitations. We have the advantage because we don't have to deal with the bureaucracy; we can just solve problems. When we get involved, things get done. We have the resources; we put in electricity, schools."

The discourse of efficiency and organizing services, including security, without the state's help—"getting things done"—has a long history in the clientelistic relations that have characterized Colombian politics. It was a hallmark of the mafia-state structures established by the cartels that have flourished in this area of Colombia for the past two decades.

In addition to employing their own resources, paramilitary forces in the region increased local community access to state resources by shepherding development proposals through the appropriate channels. Mancuso said, "We helped communities prepare projects that were then submitted to the governmental agencies—and approved. We directly contracted the engineers for the projects."

According to Mancuso, the paramilitaries' plans for political influence extend beyond the simple demobilization of their troops to include defending the communal responsibilities they assumed as the proto-state: "After the demobilization, we are going to create a political party, because we have too much responsibility for the community, the people in the region, to abandon the work we started. We will keep working to solve the problems in the community, the economic and the social problems."

This account is notable not just for its positive portrayal of paramilitary forces as community organizers, but also for what it leaves out. Drug trafficking as a source of revenue for paramilitary groups is completely absent from Mancuso's engaging description of life on the Colombian Caribbean coast, which has been dramatically transformed by the rise of the illicit narcotics trade over the past three decades. The paramilitaries appear to act only defensively, to protect their property and rights from guerrilla attacks, with no mention of the offensive military strategy that characterized their incursions into other areas of the country throughout the 1990s. Finally, there is no mention of other political forces in the region, including legal opposition parties, grassroots organizations, and social movements.

I heard similar stories from other paramilitary commanders whom I interviewed; this version of Colombian history also appears in the documents explaining paramilitary "origin and evolution" available on paramilitary Web sites and in the fawning biographies profiling paramilitary leaders. In their accounts, paramilitary leaders borrow heavily from the genre of self-presentation known as testimonial literature, which purports to tell the collective story of oppressed groups. Most of these narratives have focused on the experience of victims of human rights violations and, in some cases, of those who resisted. The reflections of many former guerrilla commanders, particularly in Central America but increasingly in Colombia as well, fit the genre.[24] In almost all, the narrative arc remains the same: growing up innocent of political machinations, called into service by an oppressed community, frustrated by the impossibility of change through existing channels, and left with no option but organizing to defend collective interests, resulting in a personal and communal transformation. In such narratives, once the domain of leftist resistance efforts against Latin American state oppression, paramilitary leaders insert their own story of repression by, and resistance to, guerrilla forces.

Paramilitary Challenges to Conflict-Resolution Models

The shift in paramilitary tactics and the public relations campaign to bolster the paramilitaries' political legitimacy pose serious challenges for analysts and activists interested in pursuing peace in Colombia. First, it is often difficult for analysts to separate the groups' actual practices from their public relations efforts. The pursuit of negotiations with paramilitary groups as well as with the guerrillas requires clarity on many issues that paramilitary public relations efforts are designed to conceal. These issues include the degree to which paramilitary leaders represent a coherent command structure, their ongoing military operations and responsibility for human rights violations,

---

[24] For more on the testimonial genre, see John Beverley and Marc Zimmerman, *Literature and Politics in the Central American Revolutions* (Austin: University of Texas Press, 1990). Some of the best-known testimonies include Rigoberta Menchu, *I, Rigoberta Menchu: An Indian Woman in Guatemala,* trans. Ann Wright (London: Verso, 1983); Alicia Partnoy, *The Little School: Tales of Disappearance and Survival in Argentina* (Pittsburgh: Cleis Press, 1986); and Jacobo Timmerman, *Prisoner Without a Name, Cell Without a Number* (New York: Knopf, 1981). Testimonial narratives from former Colombian guerrillas include Vera Grabe, *Razones de vida* (Bogotá: Planeta, 2000) and María Eugenia Vásquez Perdomo, *Escrito para no morir: Bitácora de una militancia* (Bogotá: ILSA–Ediciones Antropos, 2000).

and their efforts to maintain paramilitary power structures in the context of negotiations and national demobilization efforts.

Public relations efforts disguise the paramilitaries' ongoing brutality. Community and religious leaders in many areas of the country report that the danger faced by those documenting violence has prevented many crimes from being registered in official tallies. The evangelical pastor I quoted earlier, who noted the increased presence of paramilitary political programs, went on to say that despite his numerous visits lobbying paramilitary leaders to respect church leaders, they continued to attack anyone they viewed as a hindrance to their efforts. "They promise to respect the work, but then, two weeks ago they killed a pastor while he was delivering a sermon," he said. "They say they know that pastors choose sides. . . . They say they do their own intelligence, and have people who were in the guerrillas who tell them who the people are and what they have done."

Paramilitary forces are also resorting to new modalities of violence that allow perpetrators to escape the scrutiny of international human rights reporting. These include incidents of "multiple homicides"—killing several people over a number of days and scattering the bodies, or dumping corpses in different locations. Such new practices circumvent being documented as "massacres," which are defined as the killing of four or more individuals in a single incident and at the same location. Similarly, a new phenomenon called "confinement" has emerged, according to the reports of some community leaders.[25] As observers count numbers of people forcibly displaced, the paramilitaries' practice of refusing to allow community members free passage or travel masks the gravity of the issue.

One of the most serious challenges to the demobilization process is to ensure that the process does not simply channel individuals through demobilization programs but dismantles the underlying structures of paramilitary power. This does not appear to be happening. Despite the ongoing demobilization efforts, paramilitary groups appear to be consolidating and expanding their political and military control in many areas of the country. Colombian officials rightly praise the reduction of violence in many communities. In many cases, however, this reduction in violence results not from the expansion of state institutions and the possibilities of genuine participatory democracy but from the social control exercised by paramilitary groups, which, in many regions, is still based on the threat of violence and the establishment of parallel authoritarian structures of governance. This danger is equally apparent in the areas hosting paramilitary demobilizations. For example, international organizations have reported that demobilized Cacique Nutibara

---

[25] See U.S. Office on Colombia, "Tools of the Colombian Conflict: Civilian Confinement and Displacement," January 2005, www.usofficeoncolombia.org/documents/confinement.pdf (accessed June 18, 2007).

Bloc (CNB) members continue to use intimidation and maintain connections with active paramilitary forces in the areas of Medellín where they are attempting to consolidate political power. For groups involved in community-development projects in the areas where demobilized CNB members are active, this presents many significant challenges. Worse, Colombian journalists and international organizations have documented the emergence of new armed groups, such as the Black Eagles and the New Generation Organization, among others. Violence from paramilitary groups that refused to demobilize, and the diverse new forms of illegal armed organizations, also pose a significant challenge.[26]

Paramilitary public relations efforts also conceal the ongoing role of paramilitary groups in criminal activities and illegal economies. Many paramilitary leaders remain deeply involved in drug trafficking, but paramilitary groups are involved in smuggling and illegal trade of other kinds as well, particularly the lucrative trade in stolen gasoline. Internal disputes over drug trafficking have resulted in divisions between "harder-line" paramilitary leaders more deeply involved in drug trafficking and a more "political line" of paramilitary leaders supporting demobilization in the name of political legitimacy. The ongoing conflict and the paramilitaries' uninterrupted pursuit of lucrative criminal activity complicate the possibility of offering incentives for demobilization and increase the risk that combatants will be "recycled" back into illegal armed groups. According to the Colombian National Police, 474 demobilized paramilitaries have been killed, although some estimates put the number at 1,000. Most were killed because of criminal activity, but some were reportedly victims of conflicts between newly organized paramilitary groups.[27] There are many additional challenges to efforts to demobilize paramilitary forces. These include the lack of centralized control, deep divisions among the paramilitary leaders, the lack of educational and economic opportunities for demobilized combatants, and administrative problems within governmental assistance programs.

Conclusion

Efforts to understand the conditions that made negotiations between Colombian paramilitary groups and the government possible must include an analysis of paramilitary campaigns to gain public support. Despite their criminal activities and brutal record, paramilitary leaders have learned to harness the persuasive power of new technologies, including the Internet, and organizational forms traditionally used by the left, such as creating NGOs, sponsoring peace marches, and developing foundations. Their leaders used the me-

---

[26] See ICG, *Colombia's New Armed Groups*.

[27] Ibid., 22.

dia to articulate a version of Colombian history that depicted paramilitary forces as both victims and heroes who took responsibility for the security and social welfare dimensions of the state that had abandoned them. Their success in these efforts, through co-opting the discourse of peace and social transformation and concealing the true nature of their agendas and their actions, poses profound challenges to conflict-resolution efforts in Colombia.

7

Truth, Justice, and Reparations in Colombia
The Path to Peace and Reconciliation?

Arturo J. Carrillo

Introduction

On July 20, 2005, Colombia's vice president, Francisco Santos, and foreign minister, Carolina Barco, addressed a public forum in Washington, D.C., organized by local think tanks to discuss key aspects of President Álvaro Uribe's ongoing peace process with the vigilante United Self-Defense Forces of Colombia, also known by its Spanish acronym, AUC. In particular, they focused on the controversial Justice and Peace Law, ratified a month earlier by the Colombian Congress, primarily to provide a comprehensive legal framework for the peace process with the AUC.[1]

In her remarks, Foreign Minister Barco described the Justice and Peace Law as "unprecedented." Vice President Santos highlighted a number of the law's innovations, especially the creation of a National Commission of Reparation and Reconciliation, with its focus on truth telling and reconciliation. It was their view that the law, which expressly acknowledges victims' rights to truth, justice, and reparations, represented the best possible vehicle for achieving the demobilization and disarmament of the AUC forces under President Uribe's peace plan.[2]

The author wishes to thank the following people for their input and support during the preparation of this chapter: Virginia Bouvier, Winifred Tate, Thomas Antkowiak, Heather Carney, and Fred Lawrence, dean of the George Washington University Law School.

[1] The official title of the law is "Por la cual se dictan disposiciones para la reincorporación de miembros de grupos armados organizados al margen de la ley, que contribuyan de manera efectiva a la consecución de la paz nacional y se dictan otras disposiciones para acuerdos humanitarios," Law 975/2005 (hereinafter the Justice and Peace Law).

[2] Woodrow Wilson International Center for Scholars (WWICS), Latin American Program, "The Peace Process in Colombia and U.S. Policy," *Noticias: Latin American Program Newsletter* (Fall 2005): 7–8.

Their statements raise a number of challenging questions. What does it mean to say that the Justice and Peace Law is "unprecedented," and why does this matter? The Colombian government had successfully negotiated the disarmament and demobilization of illegal armed groups before, most notably the Movimiento 19 de Abril (M-19) guerrillas and the Popular Liberation Army (EPL) in the early 1990s. Why was it necessary now to herald the new law as a substantial departure from prior experiences? Indeed, what are the major innovations reflected in the Justice and Peace Law, and where did they come from? In seeking answers to these inquiries, this chapter addresses another, overarching question: do the law's innovations regarding victims' rights to justice, truth, and reparations in fact contribute to promoting peace and national reconciliation in Colombia?

This chapter proceeds in two parts. The first examines the evolution of the Justice and Peace Law and analyzes the novel aspects of its technical framework with respect to the rights of victims. The second assesses the law's immediate and future implications for the pursuit of peace in Colombia. It concludes with reflections on the peace process with the AUC and on future negotiations with other illegal armed groups.

Overview of the Justice and Peace Law: What's New and Why

Since taking office in August 2002, President Álvaro Uribe has made talks with the AUC the foundation of his government's peace policy. Early in his tenure, a series of laws and decrees were enacted to facilitate the demobilization of individual members of illegal armed groups, primarily through desertion.[3] In July 2003, the Colombian government and the AUC signed a framework peace accord at Santa Fé de Ralito (Córdoba), committing the paramilitaries, among other things, to full demobilization by the end of 2005. (This deadline was subsequently extended.)[4]

As part of its obligations under the agreement, in August 2003, the Uribe government submitted to Congress a draft law intended to govern the demobilization, disarmament, and reintegration (DDR) process with the AUC. Known as the Ley de Alternatividad Penal, or Alternative Criminal

---

[3] The most relevant of these norms is Law 782/02, "Por medio de la cual se prorroga la vigencia de la Ley 418 de 1997, prorrogada y modificada por la Ley 548 de 1999 y se modifican algunas de sus disposiciones," December 23, 2002; and implementing Decree 128, "Por el cual se reglamenta la Ley 418 de 1997, prorrogada y modificada por la Ley 548 de 1999 y la Ley 782 de 2002 en materia de reincorporación a la sociedad civil," January 22, 2003; Decree 3360, "Por el cual se reglamenta la Ley 418 de 1997, prorrogada y modificada por la Ley 548 de 1999 y la Ley 782 de 2003," November 21, 2003; and Decree 2767, "Por el cual se reglamenta La ley 418 de 1997, prorrogada y modificada por la Ley 548 de 1999 y la Ley 782 de 2002 en materia de reincorporación a la vida civil," August 31, 2004.

[4] For more details on the negotiation process and the Santa Fé de Ralito Accord itself, see International Crisis Group (ICG), *Demobilising the Paramilitaries in Colombia: An Achievable Goal?* Latin America Report no. 8 (Bogotá/Brussels: ICG, August 5, 2004): 1–5.

Sanctions Law, this legislative initiative was heavily criticized in the domestic and international arenas for, among other things, being too lax and not dealing adequately with victims' rights to justice, truth, and reparations.[5] Widespread negative reactions to the initial draft law and the government's concerted efforts to respond led to a period of intense national and international debate that revolved around the Colombian Congress's deliberations. In April 2004, the Uribe administration submitted to Congress a "modified" version of its draft law, which, the administration claimed, addressed the relevant criticisms leveled against the original. Nonetheless, the revised text was again condemned as deficient by non-governmental organizations (NGOs) and international experts.[6] Consequently, the administration's April 2004 draft law was openly debated, alongside several competing proposals, for over a year by the legislature, in the media, and before the court of public opinion. Finally, after protracted political jockeying on all sides, in March 2005, the Uribe administration submitted another (and final) "modified" text of its proposed legislation.

In June 2005, after much debate, the Colombian Congress essentially adopted the Uribe government's expanded proposal for governing the DDR process with members of "illegal armed groups," in particular the AUC. The resulting statute, commonly referred to as the "Justice and Peace Law," though the product of a political consensus, was denounced by victims' groups and NGOs as still contrary to international justice standards and unworkable in practical terms. Although acknowledged as imperfect by the government itself, the Justice and Peace Law is nevertheless considered by many domestic and international observers of the peace process with the AUC to reflect a potentially viable balance between victims' rights and political necessity. This view, as noted, is not shared by many NGOs and victims, who rejected the law outright, referring to it derisively as the "Impunity

---

[5] Among the publicized international critiques of the Alternative Criminal Sanctions Law are "Human Rights and Colombia," editorial, *New York Times*, September 20, 2003, which described the proposed legislation as promoting impunity; "Más críticas para el proyecto de alternatividad penal," *Semana*, September 22, 2003; and the letter to President Uribe from fifty-six U.S. congressional representatives expressing similar concerns.

[6] See, for example, José Miguel Vivanco, "The Role of Third Parties and Issues for the International Community," in *The Peace Process in Colombia with the Autodefensas Unidas de Colombia-AUC*, ed. Cynthia J. Arnson (Washington, D.C.: Woodrow Wilson Center Press, 2005), 75, 76–79; Human Rights Watch, "Colombia: Letting Paramilitaries Off the Hook," January 2005, Section III, http://hrw.org/backgrounder/americas/colombia0105/colombia0105.pdf (accessed August 25, 2008); Inter-American Commission on Human Rights (IACHR), "Report on the Demobilization Process in Colombia," OEA/Ser. L/V/II.120, December 13, 2004, paras. 64–71, www.cidh.org/countryrep/Colombia04eng/chapter4.htm#C (accessed August 25, 2008); Colombian Commission of Jurists (CCJ), "Colombia: En contravía de las recomendaciones internacionales sobre derechos humanos" (August 2004): 71–72; United Nations High Commissioner for Human Rights (UNHCHR), "Observaciones sobre la nueva versión del proyecto de alternatividad penal," Bogotá, May 6, 2004, www.hchr.org.co/publico/comunicados/2004/cp0413.pdf (accessed August 25, 2008).

Law" and refusing to participate in the processes it established for providing reparations to victims.

In May 2006, the Constitutional Court of Colombia announced its Solomonic judgment on the challenged constitutionality of the Justice and Peace Law. The court upheld the law's constitutionality generally but struck down several key provisions favorable to the demobilizing paramilitaries that, in its view, did not meet international legal standards applicable under the constitution. The new Justice and Peace Law, including the Constitutional Court's judgment, is described in more detail below.

Comparative Analysis of Legal Norms

To understand how the Justice and Peace Law developed into its present form, one must first compare it with its predecessor, the much-maligned Alternative Criminal Sanctions Law of August 2003.[7] Identifying and contrasting the major differences between these two normative poles highlights those areas where the current law reflects significant advances over prior Colombian peace processes. It also sets up the analysis of why this evolution came about and what it portends for the search for peace in Colombia.

Content, Critique, and Context of Draft Law 85/03

The original draft law proposed by President Uribe in August 2003 set out a framework for pardoning members of illegal armed groups already convicted of crimes who demobilized and agreed to a set of minimal conditions, most of which sought to foreclose further participation in the conflict or other criminal activity. The same arrangement applied to other members of the demobilizing groups who confessed to crimes and accepted criminal charges leveled against them. This legislation defined "crimes" exclusively as those proscribed in the Colombian Criminal Code and established that all such offenses were pardonable, without exception, as long as they had been committed "in the context of the armed conflict."[8]

Under Draft Law 85/03 (Alternative Criminal Sanctions Law), judges were required to suspend punishment of eligible ex-combatants at the president's request. Instead of going to prison, the law established a range of "alternative sanctions"—largely prohibitions on the beneficiary's eligibility to participate in politics, hold public office, or bear arms. It similarly imposed restrictions on freedom of residence and movement, for example, by prohibiting pardoned ex-combatants from living or going near "victims." These alternative

---

[7] Proyecto de Ley Estatutaria no. 85 Senado, "Por el cual se dictan disposiciones en procura de la reincorporación de miembros de grupos armados que contribuyan de manera efectiva a la consecución de la paz nacional," Article 1, August 21, 2003 (hereinafter Draft Law 85/03), www.presidencia.gov.co/prensa_new/leyes/2003/agosto/penas.htm (accessed July 26, 2007).

[8] Law 85/03, Article 1.

sanctions were to be in effect for ten years, after which, assuming no violation of the terms of the demobilization agreement, they would expire.

In other words, the Alternative Criminal Sanctions Law, if adopted, would
have guaranteed a full pardon for any member of the AUC who demobilized
in conformity with the law's relatively minimal parameters, regardless of his
role in the criminal organization or the crimes he may have committed. Once
eligible through conviction or confession, to receive a pardon and probation,
a former paramilitary would have been obliged only to subscribe to an agreement (*acta de compromiso*) committing him to refrain from engaging in further
criminal activity or fleeing the country. He would also have had to agree
to appear before the presiding judge as necessary, report regularly on his
whereabouts, and carry out "acts that contribute effectively to repairing [that
is, providing reparations to] the victims, putting an end to the conflict, and
achieving peace."[9]

Finally, the aforementioned process was to be administered by the president and an executive Verification Commission to be appointed at his discretion. The Verification Commission was authorized, among other things, to collect and preserve information from official sources, with a view to establishing
a record of relevant events that would guarantee the victims' "right to truth."[10]
But although Draft Law 85/03 recognizes the existence of victims and provides for reparations to a degree, it does not contemplate a formal role for victims or their NGO allies in any of the administrative procedures established.

Criticisms of Draft Law 85/03

Draft Law 85/03 became—perhaps unsurprisingly in retrospect—the subject
of intense criticism, both domestically and internationally.[11] A summary of
the primary complaints reveals that it

- *Was prepared behind closed doors, by a small group of government lawyers,
  without consultation.* The draft law, like the AUC negotiations themselves,
  began with neither participation nor input from Colombian civil society.
  Nor did international experts play any role. The administration did not

---

[9] Law 85/03, Article 2.4. Acts listed in Draft Law 85/03 as constituting reparation were (1) direct and indirect payment of compensation; (2) carrying out social work in support of victims;
(3) charitable contributions to organizations that carry out such social work; (4) apologies; (5)
collaboration in "clarifying" the "events" that occurred during the conflict; and (6) helping
demobilize or dismantle the illegal armed groups. See also Draft Law 85/03, Article 6. It is
important to emphasize that none of these were preconditions to receiving a pardon but
merely "commitments" assumed by the beneficiary.

[10] Draft Law 85/03, Article 9.

[11] See, for example, Catalina Botero Marino (human rights adviser, Fundación Social), ed., "Ley
de alternatividad penal y justicia transicional," 2004; UNHCHR, "Report on Human Rights
Situation in Colombia," UN Doc. no. E/CN.4/2004/13, February 17, 2004, para. 30; Human
Rights Watch, "Colombia's Checkbook Impunity—a Briefing Paper," September 2, 2003,
http://hrw.org/backgrounder/americas/checkbook-impunity.htm (accessed July 26, 2007).

even consult many of its closest political allies in Congress when preparing the bill.[12]

- *Made no express reference to international law or Colombia's corresponding legal obligations,* particularly concerning human rights and prevailing standards on justice, truth, and reparations (although it did at least acknowledge the latter two). The absence of any reference to the country's international obligations in this regard was seen as especially serious, since the corresponding legal norms were already incorporated into Colombian law.

- *Promoted impunity by not recognizing or punishing international crimes.* The law made no mention of crimes against humanity and war crimes, which, under international law, are not subject to pardon or amnesty. Again, all the corresponding international norms prohibiting such crimes were already part of Colombian law.

- *Established alternative penalties that were easily accessible and patently insufficient in light of the serious crimes committed.* The law recognized no distinction among types of offenses and established penalties that were inappropriate given the gravity of many of the crimes at issue. Incarceration could be avoided in all cases by meeting a handful of relatively simple requirements and committing to comply with others in the future.

- *Failed not only to ensure justice but also to respect the commensurate rights to truth and reparations.* While nominally referring to the victims' rights to truth and reparations, the law's provisions fell far short of effectively guaranteeing them to any degree. There were few incentives or mechanisms for securing detailed information through confession from a beneficiary regarding his or the group's illegal activities or human rights abuses, in exchange for benefits. Opportunities and procedures for effectuating reparations were also grossly inadequate.

Why This Draft Law?

The political opposition that arose to the Alternative Criminal Sanctions Law and the extensive legal debates it generated raise the question of why the Uribe administration went ahead with proposing this law in these terms in the first place. But when viewed in a historical context, it becomes apparent that the government was operating along well-settled lines that had proved effective in the recent past. In particular, Colombian officials were building on the precedent set by the successful peace talks with the M-19 guerrillas in 1990, an experience that subsequently served as the inspiration and, in many respects, the model for negotiating the DDR of other important guerrilla

---

[12] Daniel García Peña (director, Planeta Paz), "The Role of Third Parties," (paper presented at the Peace Process in Colombia with the Autodefensas Unidas de Colombia–AUC forum, WWIC Latin American Program no. 13, 2005), 63, 65.

groups, such as the EPL.[13] In other words, to paraphrase a well-worn adage, the government was in many respects still "negotiating the last peace."

Clearly, there are substantial differences between the M-19 and AUC as armed actors, which this comparative exercise does not pretend to minimize. First, the paramilitary groups comprising the AUC, whose demobilized members number in the tens of thousands, had, since their inception, operated in ideological—and, frequently, operational—harmony with the Colombian authorities, especially the armed forces. Extensive ties with national and local politicians have recently come to light as well.[14] The M-19 movement, which demobilized several hundred combatants, on the other hand, was a relatively small *insurgent* organization operating in fierce opposition to the state. Second, there are substantial differences in the two groups' objectives, strategies, and modi operandi. The M-19 may arguably have committed war crimes—the systematic kidnapping of civilians for ransom and the targeting of civilian installations are actions prohibited under the laws of war applicable to noninternational armed conflicts. Yet M-19 military operations cannot generally be compared to the AUC's widespread and systematic campaigns of terror, characterized by brutal tactics such as massacres, torture, forced disappearances, and internal displacement—directed primarily at the civilian population. Finally, there is the AUC's notorious and extensive involvement in drug-trafficking activities, which are addressed below.[15]

Despite these differences, a comparison of the peace *processes* involving the M-19 and the AUC does prove instructive in understanding the approach

---

[13] The peace process with the M-19 is generally considered paradigmatic for several reasons. It pioneered a basic model of demobilization, disarmament, and reintegration that was adapted and applied effectively to the EPL, Quintín Lame, and other, smaller insurgent groups. See Mauricio García-Durán, *Procesos de paz* (Bogotá: CINEP, 1992), 67–70. In addition to being the first of the guerrilla groups to capitalize on the Colombian government's offer to demobilize in exchange for amnesty and political rights, the M-19 was the first, and by far the most successful, ex-guerrilla group to compete electorally, achieving historic voter support in the March 1991 elections.

[14] It was revealed in late 2006 that eleven members of Colombia's Congress, along with scores of local politicians, had signed a secret political agreement with the AUC leadership in 2001, unleashing the *parapolítica* scandal that snowballed in 2007. By August that year, fourteen congressmen and -women were behind bars while under investigation by the Supreme Court; in addition, twenty other national or local politicians, including six ex-congressmen and two former governors, were imprisoned. The politicians caught up in the scandal were being investigated for having benefited electorally and/or economically from their close ties to the paramilitary groups. See "23 de Julio de 2001, el día que se firmó el pacto con el diablo," *Semana*, January 19, 2007; "Corte Suprema vincula a tres congresistas de Caldas en proceso por parapolítica," *Semana*, August 1, 2007; "Vinculan a proceso por parapolítica al senador Mario Uribe, primo del presidente," *Semana*, July 11, 2007; "The Plot Thickens, Again," *Economist*, April 19, 2007.

[15] It has been suggested that the M-19 may have been acting in alliance with the major drug cartels in existence at the time, in particular during the assault on the Palace of Justice, in which the Supreme Court's judicial records, including those in ongoing cases against known drug traffickers, were destroyed by fire. The M-19 denied such a connection. See Rafael Pardo Rueda, *La historia de las guerras* (Bogotá: Ediciones B, 2004), 486.

adopted by the Uribe administration in its efforts to negotiate with the latter armed group. The motivating force behind the M-19's demobilization was that group's desire to participate in local and national elections as a legitimate political party. Like the AUC in 2003, the guerrilla group had, by 1990, announced that it intended to renounce violence and henceforth pursue its goals of political change through peaceful, democratic means.[16] Securing the guerrilla group's demobilization and reintegration was the government's main objective and the heart of its negotiating position from the outset. Nonetheless, the M-19 was able to broaden the agenda of talks to include the issue of ensuring broader democratic participation, especially its own, in the Colombian political and electoral systems.

But for M-19 leaders to run in the approaching elections, they first had to be pardoned, ideally as part of a DDR process. The administration of President Virgilio Barco took the lead in negotiating and implementing the peace agreement, with no participation and little support from the other branches of government, specifically the Congress. At the crucial moment, Congress failed to act on the political reforms agreed with the M-19 at the negotiation table, although it did pass a law authorizing the president to grant full pardons and amnesty (ley de indulto).[17] This allowed President Barco, in the end, to secure the guerrillas' demobilization by pardoning their principal leaders despite the legislature's objections to the other terms of the agreement. In so doing, he opened the door to the M-19's stunningly successful participation in the 1990 presidential elections.[18]

Despite their taking place in the midst of Colombia's worst human rights crisis to date, the final negotiations with the M-19 (1987–90) made little reference to the civilian victims of the political violence or to their rights. Accountability was simply not a factor. In the talks, general references were made to the human rights situation and the need to combat impunity, but nothing concrete came of those discussions. It is important to remember that the mid-to-late 1980s were the early heyday of the paramilitary groups, which at the time were linked to the armed forces in law and practice. It was the height of Colombia's "dirty war" against the Unión Patriótica (UP), the political wing of the Fuerzas Armadas Revolucionarias de Colombia (FARC) guerrillas, and

---

[16] See "Colombia: AUC Outlines Political Ambitions," *Latinnews Daily*, July 22, 2005; "'Paramilitares aspiran a llegar a ser un movimiento político,' Ernesto Baez confirmó," *El Tiempo*, July 21, 2005; Luis Jaime Acosta, "Feared Colombian Militias Want Political Party," *Reuters*, July 21, 2005.

[17] Pardo Rueda, *La historia de las guerras*, 512.

[18] Pardo Rueda, *La historia de las guerras*, 513. The M-19's historic electoral performance in 1990 converted it immediately into the third most important political force in the country and set it up to play a major role in the Constitutional Assembly that subsequently drafted the new 1991 constitution.

state-sponsored atrocities were rampant.[19] Nor were the guerrillas beyond reproach for abuses committed in the course of the conflict: the assault on the Palacio de Justicia in 1985 and the human tragedy it produced, for instance, continue to this day to haunt Colombians.[20] Yet no guerrilla, paramilitary, or armed forces operative was ever investigated, much less tried or punished, for violations of human rights or humanitarian law as a result of the "successful" peace process with the M-19. Nor did the negotiations even contemplate mechanisms to explore the truth about the conflict and its abuses or to determine who the victims were and how to deal with them.

Instead, the paradigm established in 1990 with the M-19 was basically this: illegal armed groups were offered pardons or amnesty for all actions relating to the conflict, and reintegrated into the social and political life of the nation, in exchange for their full demobilization and disarmament. As a practical matter, the parties negotiated autonomously among themselves to obtain what they most wanted and no more. Although the peace talks addressed the need for wider reforms, the "axis of the negotiation centered on the political space offered to [the guerrilla group] within the [existing] legal framework."[21] It is significant that the M-19 peace agreement was directly between political elites and an illegal armed actor, with little or no intervening outside interest or influence. International standards were referenced only indirectly in negotiating the agenda (for example, in proposals to ratify international humanitarian law treaties or reform the judicial system). During the negotiations, there was no participation by independent civil society or the international community. Moreover, civil society organizations' efforts to influence the talks or the agenda were studiously avoided by the government and had a minimal impact on the process.[22] On the whole, the public left the parties to negotiate peace between themselves. And the public is considered to have subsequently approved of the results, as reflected in its favorable reactions to the DDR and in the 1990 election results, which sealed the M-19's spectacular transition to political legitimacy. Several more insurgent groups were successfully demobilized soon thereafter, following a similar model of peace talks.

The Uribe administration was explicitly building on this precedent when it prepared the Alternative Criminal Sanctions Law behind closed doors and

---

[19] See Pardo Rueda, *La historia de las guerras*, 483, 502, 612–22; Comisión Interamericana de Derechos Humanos, "Segundo informe sobre la situación de los derechos humanos en Colombia," OEA/Ser.L/V/I.84, Doc. 39 rev., October 14, 1993.

[20] "Condenas por el holocausto pasarían de $10.000 millones," *El Tiempo*, November 6, 2005; "Los rostros de 10 ausencias," *El Tiempo*, November 6, 2005; "Corte designa comisión de la verdad para Palacio de Justicia," *El Tiempo*, November 3, 2005. See also Pardo Rueda, *La historia de las guerras*, 494–95 (describing other M-19 guerrilla abuses).

[21] García-Durán, *Procesos de paz*, 161.

[22] For instance, although tens of thousands of people had suffered abuses by the armed actors, the victims were virtually invisible during the negotiation process.

presented it to Congress in August 2003. Draft Law 85/03 sought to complete the legal regime governing demobilizations begun with the adoption of Law 782 in 2002, which already gave President Uribe authority to pardon or give amnesty to former combatants for political crimes, much like the *ley de indulto* passed in 1990 for the M-19 guerrillas. But unlike the *ley de indulto*, which resulted in unconditional pardons and a blanket amnesty, by 2002, Colombian law contained limitations on the definition of pardonable political offenses, which prevented history from repeating itself. As Daniel García Peña noted, "It was possible to grant amnesty for kidnapping [and other atrocious crimes] in the early 1990s, but today it is against Colombian law."[23] Since 1993, the Constitutional Court had relied on international law principles applicable in Colombia to declare that restrictions existed on the scope of political crimes that could be pardoned or amnestied, and to exclude crimes against humanity, torture, forced disappearance, and kidnapping, among others.[24] Moreover, Law 782/02, drafted in conformity with the court's jurisprudence, expressly prohibits granting pardons for heinous crimes such as kidnapping, genocide, or other "barbaric or ferocious acts of atrocity."[25]

By 2003, these legal prohibitions on pardoning serious offenses amounting to grave violations of human rights and humanitarian law operated as an obstacle to obtaining the demobilization and reintegration of the AUC leadership and many of its regular members. Draft Law 85/03 was therefore intended to overcome that impasse and restore to President Uribe the unadulterated pardoning power that prior presidents had exercised in successfully negotiating the demobilization and reintegration of the M-19 and other guerrilla groups. President Uribe argued in defense of his legal strategy that since the M-19 guerrillas had received full pardons despite their egregious crimes, he did not possess the moral authority to demand that the AUC be treated any differently.[26] But times had changed. As one Colombian expert noted in 2004, "The national and international context is different than it was ten years ago, when Colombia held talks with the M-19 and other guerrilla groups."[27] What was not yet clear was the extent to which those changes would affect the discourse of peace with the AUC and beyond.

Overview of Law 975/05

Fast-forward to 2005. In the nearly two years after its introduction, the Alternative Criminal Sanctions Law underwent a dramatic transformation in

---

[23] García Peña, "The Role of Third Parties," 66.

[24] Catalina Botero Marino and Esteban Restrepo Saldarriaga, "Estándares internacionales y procesos de transición en Colombia," in *Entre el perdón y el paredón*, ed. Angelika Rettberg (Bogotá: Corcas, 2005), 30.

[25] Law 782/02, Article 19.

[26] Iván Orozco Abad, "Reflexiones impertinentes: Sobre la memoria y el olvido, sobre el castigo y la clemencia," in Rettberg, *Entre el perdón y el paredón*, 171, 206.

[27] García Peña, "The Role of Third Parties," 66.

response—first, to the severe criticism it drew and, second, to competing versions of the same law presented by Colombian legislators. The most notable of these was the draft legislation formally submitted to Congress by Sen. Rafael Pardo and his allies in February 2005.[28] Commonly known as the Pardo Law on Truth, Justice, and Reparations, it was widely praised as adhering to international standards for transitional justice in a way that the government's proposals did not. Even before its official filing, Senator Pardo's draft legislative framework for governing the ongoing DDR process with the AUC had already become, for many, the benchmark against which all other proposals were to be measured. A third factor underpinning Draft Law 85/03's metamorphosis was the intense public scrutiny to which it was subjected and pluralistic participation in the legislative debates that followed. As one analyst noted, "Given the government's great reluctance to open up debate, the Congress's *audiencias públicas* (public hearings) were [especially] important" to improving the text of the law.[29]

Finally, in March 2005, the Uribe administration submitted to Congress an expanded version of the April 2004 proposal, itself an amended version of Draft Law 85 from 2003. This new edition of the government's draft legislation intentionally reflected many of the substantive innovations enshrined in the well-received Pardo Law.[30] In June 2005, the Colombian government succeeded in effectively pushing its modified law through Congress; despite intense debate, this final revised version supported by President Uribe suffered no major changes and was adopted as Law 975/05, the Justice and Peace Law. A side-by-side comparison of the final text of the statute signed into law with the original terms of Draft Law 85/03, however, points up a wide range of substantial changes produced during the lengthy political process that took place in the interim. The law's primary innovations are summarized below, as are the subsequent modifications made by the Constitutional Court's seminal judgment of May 2006.

Law 975/05: Principal Modifications

A distinguishing characteristic of Law 975/05 is the overarching recognition of Colombia's obligations under international law and, in particular, the detailed attention paid to victims' rights to truth, justice, and reparations. Article 2 of the law notes: "The interpretation and normative application of [the law's] provisions shall be carried out in conformity with the constitutional

---

[28] Proyecto de Ley 208/05 Senado, 290/05 Cámara, "Por la cual se dictan disposiciones para la reincorporación de miembros de grupos armados organizados al margen de la ley, que contribuyan de manera efectiva a la consecución de la paz nacional," February 3, 2005.

[29] García Peña, "The Role of Third Parties," 65.

[30] Pliego de modificaciones al Proyecto de Ley 211/05 Senado, 293/05 Cámara, "Por la cual se dictan disposiciones para la reincorporación de miembros de grupos armados organizados al margen de la ley, que contribuyan de manera efectiva a la consecución de la paz nacional," March 3, 2005.

norms and international treaties ratified by Colombia."[31] In addition to defining the victims' rights to truth, justice, and reparations in light of prevailing international standards, the law establishes specific mechanisms and procedures intended to ensure that those rights are realized. These and other innovations that set it apart from its predecessors, especially Draft Law 85/03, are discussed in this section.

Before proceeding further, two caveats are in order: Because the Justice and Peace Law is far more complex than earlier versions, this section can synthesize only the major differences relevant to the discussion. It does not attempt to reproduce in any detail the intricate structures created but only to distinguish those that are most relevant. Nor does this section purport to evaluate the law's adequacy or potential effectiveness, both of which have been seriously questioned. Rather, the objective here is to highlight the pertinent new provisions of the law that were incorporated during the legislative process as a consequence of the legal and political debates that shaped it.

Like the Alternative Criminal Sanctions Law that it replaced, the Justice and Peace Law maps out a normative and procedural framework for governing the DDR process to be applied to the AUC. But in several important respects, it dictates a more robust regime than that advanced in previous legislative proposals. First, for those individuals who have committed the worst offenses, meaning war crimes or egregious human rights violations, the Justice and Peace Law mandates punishment through prison or its functional equivalent as determined by the government. In this respect, the law offers alternative sanctions consisting of reduced prison terms for previously convicted ex-combatants or those charged with particularly heinous crimes under the terms of Law 975/05.[32] Persons found to have committed such offenses are subject to mandatory sentences of from five to eight years of incarceration, although on favorable terms that could lead to the use of alter-

---

[31] Justice and Peace Law, Article 2 (translation by the author).

[32] Law 782/02, Article 19; Law 975/05, Article 69. The Justice and Peace Law expressly incorporates by reference Law 782/02 and other norms adopted previously to regulate the demobilization and reintegration of individual ex-combatants, creating a new, tiered system for processing them. Under Law 782/02, ex-combatants facing convictions or charges of *political* crimes, such as rebellion or sedition, and related offenses, are eligible for a series of judicial benefits amounting to individualized amnesties or pardons. Former combatants who have been convicted of, or charged with, committing offenses expressly exempted from Law 782/02, namely, "barbaric or ferocious acts of atrocity," including extrajudicial killings, torture, and kidnapping, will be able to avail themselves of the new alternative penalties regime. Law 782/02, Article 19; Law 975/05, articles 62, 69. As a practical matter, then, the vast majority of ex-combatants against whom no judicial proceedings or judgments exist will most likely be allowed to demobilize and rejoin Colombian society without further criminal investigation. CCJ, "Justicia genuina para una paz creíble," Bogotá, March 10, 2005; CCJ, "La CNRR: Dr. Jekyll, o Mr. Hyde?" May 9, 2006. To date, the UN high commissioner for peace estimates that approximately 29,546 former paramilitaries have received amnesty for common crimes under Law 782/02. "Y los otros 29 mil?" *Semana*, April 19, 2006.

native venues to prison and to substantial reductions in the length of the sentence to be served.

Second, the law tightens the eligibility requirements for persons seeking to benefit from alternative penalties and establishes a judicial procedure to verify that the ex-combatant has complied (or is complying) with those requirements *before* imposing a reduced sentence. As part of this procedure, the applicant is required to testify (*rendir versión libre*) before a special prosecutor about those illicit acts, perpetrated as a member of the illegal armed group, for which he seeks application of the law's benefits. It is this "confession," along with any prior convictions or pending cases he may have, that forms the basis for the investigation and judicial proceedings to follow, culminating in the alternative sanctions sought. (Should other crimes not confessed to at the hearing be discovered later, they would still be subject to the same regime and beneficial treatment accorded by the Justice and Peace Law).

In addition to imposing some jail time on the worst offenders, Law 975/05 includes several new provisions, not found in prior drafts, that advance the victims' rights to truth and reparations. For instance, the law declares that judicial findings must be shared with the victims and/or their families to ensure their right to know the truth about what happened, and that, where possible, these findings should be made public. It specifically leaves open the possibility that the judicial proceedings that it authorizes may in the future be complemented by other "nonjudicial mechanisms for reconstructing the truth," such as a truth commission.[33] The law also creates a mechanism whereby victims can claim reparations directly from a perpetrator in the course of the official proceedings, subject to certain limitations.[34] At another level, Law 975/05 created the National Commission on Reparations and Reconciliation (CNRR) to oversee the reparations process and make recommendations on how best to implement it. The CNRR is comprised of government and state officials, as well as representatives of civil society and of the victims themselves. It has been given an ambitious mandate that includes monitoring and reporting on key aspects of the DDR and reparations processes.

A final difference worth noting between Draft Law 85/03 and Law 975/05 is the manner in which the latter attributes responsibility to a range of nonexecutive authorities for implementing its central provisions, primarily those relating to investigation, punishment, and reparations. Under the new law, these are handled by a corps of specialized judges, prosecutors, and other state officials independent of the president. The president's role in this process is limited mainly to providing a certified list of the names of those

---

[33] Justice and Peace Law, Article 7.

[34] See for example, Justice and Peace Law, Article 11.5 (requiring the demobilizing individual to turn over assets that were produced from *illegal* activity, only to compensate victims); Article 23 (indicating that the motion for reparation can be brought only by a victim or his legal representative in the course of the individualized judicial action).

ex-combatants eligible to apply for legal benefits under Law 975/05. In addition, special public agencies—the Procuraduría and Defensoría respectively—are charged with providing assistance to the victims and legal defense to the applicant defendants.

Judgment of the Constitutional Court and Implementation of Law 975/05

Notwithstanding the Justice and Peace Law's marked evolution and increased focus on transitional-justice issues, the Colombian Constitutional Court, in a landmark decision, found unanimously that certain articles were still deficient in light of international human rights norms applicable under the constitution. In Colombia, the lawmaking process is not complete until the court has ruled on the constitutionality of a new statute. This occurred with respect to Law 975/05 on May 18, 2006, when the court issued its controversial judgment upholding the general validity of the law while striking down several key provisions as contrary to international and constitutional standards on the rights to truth, justice, and reparations for victims.[35] The court held, among other things, that

- The victims' and society's right to truth required that the confessions rendered by demobilized ex-combatants be "truthful and complete," meaning that *only* those offenses testified to at the mandated hearing would be covered by the law. Contrary to the terms approved by Congress, the court found that crimes subsequently discovered but not confessed would be excluded and not made subject to the law's benefits. Since alternative sanctions would not apply to the latter offenses, these could be prosecuted and punished to the full extent under ordinary criminal law.
- The victims' right to justice required several adjustments to the law. First, victims would be allowed to participate fully in the judicial proceedings established, as opposed to only being informed of their findings once they were final, and prosecutors would be allowed more time to investigate potential criminal charges. Second, the court curtailed the benefits that would have allowed ex-combatants to reduce their alternative sentences of five to eight years even further. For example, it disallowed the provisions that would have permitted counting up to eighteen months of participation in the peace process as "time served."
- The victims' right to reparations meant that the payment of compensation could not be restricted by Law 975/05, which required that ex-

---

[35] See Jaime Córdoba Triviño (president, Colombian Constitutional Court), "Comunicado de la Corte Constitucional sobre la sentencia que declaró ajustada a la Constitución la Ley 975 de 2005," May 19, 2006; Jaime Córdoba Triviño, "Comunicado de prensa sobre demanda contra la ley de Justicia y Paz, Ley 975 de 2005," May 18, 2006.

combatants indemnify only the victims of their confessed crimes and only with funds or property illegally obtained and in their possession. The court ordered that due compensation be determined on the basis of all the perpetrator's assets and with respect to all offenses committed by the group to which the applicant belonged. It similarly nullified the restrictions imposed on the state's contributions to the reparations fund.

Before and after the Constitutional Court's decision, the Uribe administration issued executive decrees implementing Law 975/05 that sought to address several of the problems that had arisen with respect to its practical application. In December 2005, several months before the court's judgment, President Uribe adopted Decree no. 4760, which, among other things, lengthened the time that prosecutors had to investigate crimes committed by the individual paramilitaries seeking to obtain the law's benefits. It also expanded and reinforced the victims' right to participate in the criminal proceedings.[36] On the other hand, critics pointed out that Decree no. 4760 made it more difficult for victims to obtain adequate reparation for the harm suffered, not least by shielding third-party owners of paramilitary properties from prosecution.[37]

The Uribe administration continued its efforts to regulate the law's implementation through a series of decrees issued in the wake of the court's contested opinion. Decree no. 3391 of 2006 fleshed out various aspects of the judicial procedure to be followed with respect to the perpetrators being investigated, as well as the victims seeking justice and reparations.[38] Although criticized for running counter to the Constitutional Court's judgment in several respects, most notably by allowing for substantial reductions in the prison sentences for convicted ex-paramilitaries, it possessed a unique virtue: Decree no. 3391 had been published in draft form on a government Web page and subjected to public scrutiny and debate before its promulgation—a process that even the law's severest critics recognized as having led to substantial improvements in the final version.[39]

Finally, it must be emphasized that these and other key executive decrees represent only the tip of the iceberg when it comes to Law 975/05's imple-

---

[36] "Decreto 4760 por el cual se reglamenta la Ley 975 de 2005," December 30, 2005 (hereinafter "Decree no. 4760"), www.ramajudicial.gov.co/csj_portal/assets/Decreto4760%20DE%202005.pdf (accessed August 25, 2008).

[37] See Colombian Commission of Jurists, "Reglamentando la impunidad a dos manos: Comentarios al decreto 4670 de 2005," February 7, 2006.

[38] "Decreto 3391 por el cual se reglamenta la Ley 975 de 2005," September 29, 2006 (hereinafter "Decree no. 3391"), www.fiscalia.gov.co/justiciapaz/Imagenes/Documentos/DECRETO_3391_290906.pdf (accessed July 27, 2007).

[39] Colombian Commission of Jurists, "Decreto 3391 de 2006: Modifica la Ley 975, incumple la sentencia C-370 e impide el ejercicio de los derechos de las víctimas," October 11, 2006.

menting norms, most of which take the form of internal regulations adopted by the various judicial, government, and public ministry institutions charged with carrying out the law's (and the executive decrees') dictates on a day-to-day basis.[40]

Why This Justice and Peace Law?

Various Colombian commentators have observed that during the decade and a half since the 1990 reintegration of the M-19 guerrillas, the world—as well as Colombia—has changed. At the heart of Colombia's transformation has been the new constitution, adopted in 1991, which revitalized the country's ossified democracy by modernizing the state's institutions and first principles. At the same time, the international community has overseen the progressive development of a new legal and political framework for international justice. These two processes are more than interlinked; they are interwoven, thanks in great part to the 1991 constitution's inclusion of international legal norms among its most fundamental tenets.[41] And, as is evident from the foregoing sections, the Constitutional Court has been instrumental not just in enshrining basic human rights principles in domestic law but also in enforcing them.

Even so, changes to the Colombian legal framework alone do not explain the metamorphosis of the Justice and Peace Law tracked in prior sections. After all, the Uribe administration had every intention of promulgating the Alternative Criminal Sanctions Law on the theory that the "peace trumps justice" model had worked before and should be followed again. But this theory was roundly debunked in the legislative debates and public consultations that followed the debut of Draft Law 85/03. What else was happening in Colombia since 1990 that made it impossible for the old paradigms to prevail? What international developments interacted with these domestic processes and influenced them? Several important phenomena come to mind that, although mentioned only briefly here, were crucial to fueling the dynamic process behind the law's evolution. (Note that the following list is not exhaustive.)

- *The rise of a "professionalized" human rights NGO sector in Colombia, and its close articulation with domestic and, especially, international counterparts.* Beginning in the late 1980s and early 1990s, human rights NGOs in Colombia forged a new sector of social actors that sought progressively

---

[40] Two other important executive norms implementing Law 975 are Decrees no. 315 and 423 of 2007, which regulate, respectively, the participation by victims in the criminal investigation of paramilitary perpetrators and the eligibility requirements for collective and individual demobilizations.

[41] See the constitution of the Republic of Colombia, 1991, Article 93 (establishing the domestic priority of ratified international treaties and agreements recognizing human rights); Article 214.2 (stating that during a public emergency, the rules of international humanitarian law will be observed); Article 53 (incorporating international labor agreements).

to distinguish itself from the deteriorating armed conflict in an effort to legitimately monitor, denounce, and advocate on the abuses being committed by all the armed parties to the conflict.[42] Many of these NGOs formed networks to better articulate their domestic claims internationally, to great effect. As a result, by 2000, the Colombian nongovernmental human rights movement was a critical player on the national and international stages concerning governmental policies affecting human rights. Colombian NGOs had powerful allies in the Colombian Congress as well as among foreign governments, intergovernmental organizations (IGOs) such as the United Nations, and, of course, international NGOs. In particular, Colombian NGOs have been especially effective in invoking international oversight mechanisms and procedures and in reinforcing their pronouncements on the ground.

- *Increased international monitoring, reporting, and oversight of the human rights situation in the country.* The establishment in 1996 of the Office of the United Nations High Commissioner for Human Rights (UNHCHR) in Colombia represents the epitome of the international community's role in monitoring the country's internal conflict. Its annual reports and related activities provided a regular, authoritative, and highly critical commentary to the Uribe administration's efforts to implement its "democratic security" policy and promote the government's peace agenda with the AUC.[43] Similarly, the Inter-American Commission on Human Rights (IACHR) has carried out its own monitoring activities, producing country-specific reports on at least three occasions since 1990, one of them specifically criticizing the AUC peace process for its lack of compliance with international justice standards.[44] To these IGOs can be added a list of international NGOs—Human Rights Watch, Amnesty International, and the International Crisis Group, among others—that have reported closely on the peace talks and diligently denounced Colombian human rights violations for years.

- *The involvement of illegal armed groups in drug-trafficking activities and the concomitant intervention of the United States, especially through the mechanism of extradition.* The deep involvement of the AUC (as well as the FARC and the ELN) in narcotics trafficking has provoked the wrath of the United States and led to concerted U.S. efforts to ensure that some

---

[42] See Winifred Tate, *Counting the Dead: The Culture and Politics of Human Rights Activism in Colombia*, Public Anthropology Series (Berkeley: University of California Press, 2007).

[43] See reports and documents of the Office of UNHCHR in Colombia at www.hchr.org.co; Michael Frühling (director, Office of UNHCHR, Bogotá), "The Role of Third Parties" (paper presented at the Peace Process in Colombia with the Autodefensas Unidas de Colombia–AUC forum, WWIC Latin American Program no. 13, 2005).

[44] See reports of the IACHR at www.cidh.org/pais.eng.htm; the 2004 report, "Report on the Demobilization Process in Colombia," specifically criticizes the lack of compliance with international standards.

justice be done. It is difficult to overstate the importance of the United States in shaping events in Colombia; U.S. involvement is widely viewed as a primary motive for the AUC's sudden desire to negotiate its demobilization and reintegration.[45] In addition, both the executive branch, through the U.S. ambassador in Bogotá, and the U.S. Congress have exerted pressure on the Uribe administration by "emphasizing . . . the importance that the [AUC peace] process in no way prejudice the extradition of Colombians indicted in the United States, and the need to bring gross violators of human rights and major drug traffickers to trial."[46] In parallel fashion, the European Union has played a similar role in exerting a firm resistance, through diplomatic channels, to blanket impunity, especially for international crimes.[47]

• *The positive evolution of international law.* Since 1990, this refers mainly to the strengthening of international human rights law, in particular on victims' rights, and the resurgence of international criminal law. Both are primary sources for the key legal concepts on transitional justice adopted and applied by the Constitutional Court in its landmark judgment of May 2006.[48] On one hand, the robust refinement of human rights law since 1990, spearheaded by the IACHR, has established a new code of legal norms governing the rights of victims to truth, justice, and reparations.[49] The fact that those norms have been applied in half a dozen cases decided against Colombia since 1989 has further reinforced their relevance.[50] On the other hand, the criminal responsibility of individuals who commit international crimes—crimes against humanity, war crimes, and gross violations of human rights—has been codified in the Statute of the International Criminal Court (ICC), which Colombia ratified in 2002.

---

[45] See, for example, Pardo Rueda, *La historia de las guerras*, 625.

[46] William B. Wood (U.S. ambassador to Colombia), "Role of Third Parties" (paper presented at the Peace Process in Colombia with the Autodefensas Unidas de Colombia–AUC forum, WWIC Latin American Program no. 13, 2005), 48.

[47] Orozco Abad, "Reflexiones impertinentes," 201.

[48] See generally Constitutional Court of Colombia, Judgment no. C-370 of May 18, 2006, Part 6.4.

[49] See, for example, the following seminal decisions handed down by the IACHR: Loayza-Tamayo v. Peru, Judgment of September 4, 1998, Series C, no. 41 (Reparations); Barrios Altos v. Peru, Judgment of March 14, 2001, Series C, no. 75; Bámaca-Velásquez v. Guatemala, Judgment of November 25, 2000, Series C, no. 70; Myrna Mack Chang v. Guatemala, Judgment of November 25, 2003, Series C, no. 101; Moiwana Community v. Suriname, Judgment of June 15, 2005, Series C, no. 124.

[50] The most recent of these IACHR cases include Ituango Massacres v. Colombia, Judgment of July 1, 2006, Series C, no. 148; Pueblo Bello Massacre v. Colombia, Judgment of January 31, 2006, Series C, no. 140; "Mapiripán Massacre" v. Colombia, Judgment of September 15, 2005, Series C, no. 134; 19 Merchants v. Colombia, Judgment of July 5, 2004, Series C, no. 109.

- *The consolidation of peace processes in other countries confronting transitional-justice issues.* International experiences from Central America (El Salvador, Guatemala), South America (Argentina, Chile), Africa (South Africa, Sierra Leone), and Europe (former Yugoslavia, Northern Ireland) have strongly influenced the terms in which peace is discussed in the context of the Colombian armed conflict.[51] They have provided critical examples of different ways in which states dealing with past atrocities effectively do or do not address issues of truth, justice, and reparations. In general, these examples offer support for the claims made by civil society and victims for greater attention to their rights as necessary steps in the path to peace and national reconciliation.

Lessons of the Justice and Peace Law for Present and Future Peace Negotiations

When viewed in retrospect, then, the extent of the Justice and Peace Law's normative evolution is striking. The Alternative Criminal Sanctions Law initially proposed in August 2003 by the Uribe administration consisted of a scant nineteen articles. By April 2004, this revised draft law, though purporting to be merely an amended version of the original, had in reality transformed into a substantially new proposal, comprising thirty-seven articles and tellingly rebranded the Justice, Truth, and Reparations Law. And even the cursory comparison outlined in Part I of the original Draft Law 85/03 and the final Justice and Peace Law—made up ultimately of seventy-two articles—clearly illustrates the enormous advances achieved in integrating international justice and human rights standards into the domestic legal framework regulating DDR processes. Also, the Constitutional Court, in its historic decision, defined the parameters of truth, justice, and reparations as rights under the constitution primarily in terms of international law, thus confirming the extent to which these standards have become "internalized," or integrated into the domestic social, political, and legal milieus.[52] In so doing, the court not only demarcated the legal framework to be applied to the AUC demobilization process; it also "set [new] limits for future peace processes."[53]

Another revelation is the dynamic process through which the law's groundbreaking evolution took place. Riding high on the success of the Santa Fé de Ralito peace agreement with the AUC, the Uribe government submitted Draft Law 85/03 with every intention of having it ratified without major

---

[51] See Alejandro Valencia Villa, ed., *Verdad y Justicia* (Bogotá: CINEP et al., 1999).

[52] "Internalization" refers to the transnational legal process through which international norms are integrated into domestic legal systems. See Harold Hongju Koh, "The 1998 Frankel Lecture: Bringing International Human Rights Home," *Houston Law Review* 35 (1998): 623, 626–44.

[53] García Peña, "The Role of Third Parties," 65.

modifications or delay and despite an utter lack of outside (and even inside) consultation. In so doing, the Uribe administration was expressly following in the footsteps of its predecessors, who negotiated successful peace accords with the M-19 guerrillas and several other groups using a substantially similar approach. The proven model was to offer blanket amnesties and presidential pardons, along with the promise of democratic political participation, in exchange for complete demobilization and good-faith disarmament. Nonetheless, it rapidly became evident that the government had underestimated the extent to which the legal, political, and social landscapes had evolved in both the domestic and international arenas since the early 1990s.

Whereas there had been no participation by outsiders in the drafting of the Alternative Criminal Sanctions Law, the polemics unleashed by its submission to Congress opened the door to unprecedented degrees of active participation by Colombian and international civil society in the ensuing political and legal debates. Indeed, it was the widespread criticism of Draft Law 85/03, inside and outside government, that caught the Uribe administration off guard and obliged it to backtrack despite the bill's express acknowledgment—a first in the history of Colombian peace processes—of victims' rights to truth and reparations.[54] No previous legislation proposed or enacted to govern the DDR of illegal armed groups or their members had expressly incorporated substantive provisions recognizing and purporting to guarantee the rights of the illegal armed groups' victims. To its credit, the Uribe administration did not press its initial legislative proposal, opting instead to engage in the extended public debates that followed. Political allies and opponents, international and domestic civil society organizations, foreign governments, and intergovernmental bodies—all had their say, and all, in their various ways, contributed to shaping the final Justice and Peace Law and its implementing norms.

What lessons can be drawn from the foregoing conclusions? It would be premature to try to pass judgment on Law 975/05, since, as of this writing, the implementation process was still in its early stages and facing a slew of obstacles. By August 2007, over 3,500 ex-paramilitary members were in line to confess their crimes to a few dozen prosecutors, but only 44 had had a hearing so far. Tens of thousands of victims—at least seventy thousand by some accounts—had sought officially to register as victims under the Justice and Peace Law, but the vast majority had received no legal, psychological, or economic assistance to allow them to participate in a meaningful way. Scarcity of resources and expertise among the judicial, government, and public ministry institutions charged with implementing Law 975/05, as well as a lack of

---

[54] Ibid. See also García-Durán, *Procesos de paz*.

legal clarity regarding their respective responsibilities to the victims, had hampered efforts to implement the legislation effectively.[55]

In addition, uncertainty remained as to the outcome of the disarmament and demobilization of the AUC, as discussed elsewhere in this volume. Its leaders have periodically threatened to withdraw from the justice and peace proceedings or refused to collaborate, and they continue to reject several of the law's key provisions as well as the ensuing Constitutional Court and Supreme Court judgments that have run counter to their interests.[56] Several "new" paramilitary groups had arisen to take the place of those that had demobilized, and by June 2007, the Organization of American States (OAS) was warning that the "presence and activities of various illegal groups in different regions of the country continue to present one of the main risks to consolidating the peace process."[57] Already, several prominent social and community leaders had been threatened or killed for organizing and encouraging victims to pursue their claims through the justice and peace procedures, raising grave security issues for those who engaged in the process.[58]

Despite the formidable challenges facing the justice and peace process in the future, one thing can be said with relative certainty based on its past. In practice as well as in theory, peace agreements with illegal armed groups as a general matter can no longer be viably pursued based on paradigms that promote unconditional amnesty over accountability, sacrifice truth for political expediency, or utterly subordinate the rights of victims to the ideals of national peace and reconciliation. Nor, it would seem, are such agreements any longer strictly the province of governments or their armed counterparts to negotiate without regard for the interests or concerns of other sectors of Colombian and international civil society, and especially of the victims of

---

[55] See Fundación Ideas para la Paz, "¿En qué va la Ley?" no. 3, June 2007, www.ideaspaz.org/new_site/secciones/publicaciones/download_la_ley/ley_3.pdf (accessed August 26, 2008); "Demob Unhappy," *Economist*, August 2, 2007; "¿Está fracasando la Ley de Justicia y Paz?" *Semana*, July 28, 2007. See also "Justicia y Paz nos debordó," *El Tiempo*, April 29, 2007, in which it was reported that as of April 2007, approximately fifty thousand victims had come forward to denounce paramilitary crimes, at an average rate of nearly one thousand per day.

[56] Hugh Bronstein, "Colombian Paramilitaries May Opt for War over Jail," *Reuters*, June 13, 2006; "Polémica por suspensión de confesiones paramilitares en rechazo a fallo de la Corte Suprema," *El Tiempo*, July 25, 2007; "Con fuerte reacción de la oposición en contra, hoy inicia debate sobre delito de sedición para AUC," *El Tiempo*, July 29, 2007.

[57] "OEA denuncia 'clonación' paramilitary," *Semana*, March 1, 2006; OAS, "Ninth Quarterly Report of the Secretary General to the Permanent Council, on the Mission to Support the Peace Process in Colombia" (OAS/MAPP), OEA/Ser.G/CP/doc.4237/07, July 3, 2007, Para. 4, http://scm.oas.org/doc_public/ENGLISH/HIST_07/CP18719E06.doc (accessed August 26, 2008).

[58] See Comisión Nacional de Reparación y Reconciliación, "Comunicado; CNRR rechaza asesinato de Judith Vergara," April 24, 2007, www.cnrr.org.co (accessed August 26, 2008); "Tras la muerte de Yolanda Izquierdo gobierno intenta frenar cacería a víctimas de los paramilitares," *Semana*, February 2, 2007.

human rights abuses. One prominent Colombian academic, referring to the AUC negotiations, summarized it best:

> [It is likely] that in Colombia some degree of punishment and repara-
> tion will be achieved, though not historical truth just yet. It's just that
> the coalition of actors motivated by passion and retributive reason
> that are demanding punishment and reparations is [too] broad and
> powerful. In addition to important social and political actors in the
> United States and the European Union, other members of the coali-
> tion include the social democratic and "non-paramilitarized" wing of
> the [Colombian] Liberal Party, the parliamentary Left, the human
> rights NGOs and their intermestic networks, as well as important
> sectors of [public] opinion.[59]

In short, there is a new and irrevocable calculus of peace in Colombia, one that seeks to balance, through democratic processes and increased transparency, society's goals of pacification and reconciliation with victims' rights to truth, justice, and reparations. Whether it can succeed as well as the outdated paradigm it replaces depends on how and to whom it is applied.

The New Paradigm: Transitional Justice and the Search for Peace in Colombia

For all its novelty and significance, this new paradigm has limits that distinguish it from similar experiences in other countries. These limits suggest that here, as in other areas, Colombia must forge its own path to meet the particular demands of the country's political and social forces. First, unlike most other transitional-justice scenarios, Colombia is not emerging from a repressive dictatorship or the demise of the ancien régime. It is a democracy with authoritarian tendencies, locked in a long-standing internal armed conflict. Second, it is not even negotiating the end to this conflict. The country's largest and most important illegal armed actor, the FARC, refuses to initiate formal peace talks with the government of President Uribe and persists in its violent struggle. Third, the thorny issue of state responsibility for human rights and humanitarian law violations is notoriously absent from the AUC peace process and the Justice and Peace Law. But it is very much the "elephant in the room" and will plague the process down the road. These and other factors imbue the Colombian situation with a unique, multilayered complexity. For these reasons, it is unrealistic to expect foreign models of transitional justice to "fit" in Colombia, or even to compare them overtly to the country's pioneering experiment with the AUC.

Indeed, Colombia is in the process of developing a new rubric of transitional-justice analysis, one that integrates fundamental human rights norms with conventional DDR processes *during* an ongoing internal armed

---

[59] Orozco Abad, "Reflexiones impertinentes," 201.

conflict.[60] In this novel context, peace talks take place in the midst of war, between the popularly elected government of a functioning democracy and *one* of multiple armed actors enjoying elevated levels of political, economic, or military power.[61] This approach takes the country a step or two down the path to peace but leaves much to be traversed, since the war continues in effect.

An important lesson provided by the Justice and Peace Law is that in these situations, *process* matters. That is, while new rules are surely necessary, it is in fact the process through which they are vetted, debated, adopted, interpreted, and implemented that defines the degree to which they can be truly effective. Or, as Rodrigo Uprimny and Luis Manuel Lasso point out, "To the extent that any transitional justice formula is debatable and controversial, its legitimacy depends in great part on the manner in which this formula is developed and executed. . . . The design and execution of transitional justice should be participatory, seek consensus and have international support."[62]

The more democratic the process, the better the chances of securing broad and viable political consensus. Increased transparency leads to greater and more effective participation by all actors, both in and outside government. And the greater the levels of participation and consensus that can be achieved, the greater the chances that a lasting and just peace based on those rules will result, at least for the parties and stakeholders involved. In other words, it is the *integrity* of the process that defines the legitimacy of the precedent as a whole—a key consideration for when it comes time to sit down to talk with the other illegal armed groups that are still fighting. Viewed through this lens, the current Justice and Peace Law stands a much better chance than any of its predecessors of achieving some degree of peace *with* justice, notwithstanding its obvious shortcomings.

Toward the future, whether the new paradigm can succeed as well as the one it replaces depends not just on how it is applied but to whom and under what conditions. On one hand, there is concern over the extent to which the implementation of the current Justice and Peace Law has run into serious difficulties. The dictates of transitional justice and victims' rights continue to clash with the self-serving political demands of the demobilizing but still

---

[60] See Rodrigo Uprimny and Luis Manuel Lasso, "Verdad, reparación y justicia para Colombia: Algunas reflexiones y recomendaciones," *Fundación Social* (2004); Lisa J. Laplante and Kimberly Theidon, "Transitional Justice in Times of Conflict: Colombia's Ley de Justicia y Paz," *Michigan Journal of International Law* 28, no. 1 (Fall 2006).

[61] The closest precedent for such a paradigm is arguably the case of Northern Ireland, although there the peace process put an end to the political violence. For a discussion of the extent of paramilitary power, see Pardo Rueda, *La historia de las guerras*, 610–26; Mauricio Romero, *Paramilitares y autodefensas, 1982–2003* (Bogotá: Editorial Planeta–IEPRI, 2004).

[62] Uprimny and Lasso, "Verdad, reparación y justicia para Colombia," section J.1 [translation by the author].

powerful paramilitary leadership, producing intermittent crises. A sweeping political scandal has further exacerbated the tensions surrounding this process.[63] Despite these and other problems, however, the justice and peace process lumbers on, breaking new ground as it does so.

On the other hand, it is possible that down the road the new paradigm might be a victim of its own success. There is a general consensus among commentators that the standards ultimately determined to govern the AUC demobilization process must, at a minimum, apply equally to subsequent negotiations with the guerrilla groups.[64] Already, however, FARC leaders have stated that theirs is not a comparable situation and that they will never subject themselves to the conditions announced in the Justice and Peace Law, especially prison terms of any kind. It thus appears that unless significant progress can be made in combating the FARC militarily or influencing it politically, it has less incentive to negotiate its demobilization now than before the Justice and Peace Law was promulgated. In this respect, it is likely that the new paradigm under construction with the AUC may actually make it more difficult to engage in peace negotiations with the country's oldest and strongest insurgency.[65] So even though truth, justice, and reparations are today unavoidable stepping-stones on the path to peace in Colombia, the outstanding question is whether, in the long run, they will hasten or delay the journey.

---

[63] See Note 14 for details on the *parapolítica* scandal that engulfed the country in 2007.

[64] See, for example, Pardo Rueda, *La historia de las guerras*, 638.

[65] Orozco Abad, "Reflexiones impertinentes," 206–07.

PART II

INSTITUTIONAL AND SECTORAL PEACE INITIATIVES

8

Peace Education in Colombia
The Promise of Citizenship Competencies

Enrique Chaux and Ana M. Velásquez

Education has enormous potential to transform Colombian society and construct paths toward peace. First, education's fundamental mission is the development of the members of society. This development should be comprehensive—that is, it should encompass academic as well as social and cultural aspects. Such an approach emphasizes not only knowledge and information but also competencies, the capacity to perform and deal with problems in flexible and efficient ways and in changing contexts.[1] Education's well-established infrastructure makes it one of the privileged mechanisms for developing attitudes, beliefs, values, and behaviors that help prevent violence and promote peaceful *convivencia*.[2]

Second, educational institutions have high legitimacy and social credibility among local communities, especially in rural areas. Despite being located in violent environments, these institutions still have the trust of most students, parents, and the local community. Most parents value the educational system, acknowledge its authority, and think of it as a means for their children to improve their life prospects. A national public opinion survey conducted by the Institute of Political Studies and International Relations (IEPRI)

We thank María Paulina Fajardo of the Colombian Ministry of Education for helping us identify local school peace initiatives. We are also very thankful to Dora Lucía Restrepo, coordinator of the San Martín de Porras section of Institución Educativa La Esperanza in Medellín, for sharing her knowledge and insights about their school peace initiative. We thank Angelika Rettberg for her careful reading of and comments on a previous version of this manuscript. Finally, we thank Virginia Bouvier, the editor of this book, as well as three anonymous reviewers, for their insightful comments and suggestions.

[1] Carlos Eduardo Vasco, "Estándares básicos de calidad para la educación" (unpublished document, Ministerio de Educación Nacional, 2003).

[2] *Convivencia* is a Spanish word with no precise translation into English. It means peaceful interaction and coexistence among members of a social group. We use the Spanish term in this chapter.

at National University in Bogotá revealed that society places more trust in educational institutions than in most other public institutions, such as the police, the Supreme Court of Justice, the Constitutional Court, the Attorney General's Office (Fiscalía), and the Prosecutor General's Office (Procuraduría).[3] The credibility of education appears particularly strong in rural areas, where teachers usually have higher levels of education than the rest of the community. Such credibility presents an opportunity for developing initiatives that promote peacebuilding.

Finally, educational institutions are settings for social as well as academic learning. Schools are social microenvironments, where community interactions are re-created. Within schools, social hierarchies and roles are defined, groups and subgroups form, shared attitudes and behaviors are established, individuals' behavior-regulation mechanisms operate, different types of conflict occur, people are affectively connected to one another, and group identity is built. Students' experiences in those environments constitute basic learning about social life. Thus, schools have the potential to become environments where legitimacy of attitudes, beliefs, and values that encourage violence can be modified, and peaceful behaviors and attitudes can be promoted. In short, education's developmental mission and schools' credibility and status as social microenvironments underlie education's great potential to promote some of the social and cultural transformations required to confront Colombia's violence.

Although the government is leading the efforts of many in the educational sector—schools, teachers, non-governmental organizations (NGOs), secretaries of education—to offer children and youth tools for preventing or coping with violence, valuing differences and enabling civil society to transform communities using democratic and nonviolent mechanisms to promote peaceful *convivencia*, this potential is probably being wasted. Even worse, schools may be helping reinforce violence and maintain violent attitudes, abilities, and behavior. Violence, authoritarianism, abuse of power, and negligence are frequent in many Colombian schools today.[4] Thus, it is important to think about ways in which the educational sector can be used to construct peace.

Making the Most of the Transforming Potential of Education

How might one make the most of the transforming potential of education? Schools can be turned into more democratic and pacific environments that

---

[3]Instituto de Estudios Políticos y Relaciones Internacionales (IEPRI), *Programa de análisis de opinión pública. Encuesta de legitimidad institucional. Resultados ponderados*, www.unal.edu.co/iepri/images/Encuesta.pdf (accessed October 17, 2005).

[4]Francisco Cajiao, *Poder y justicia en la escuela colombiana* (Cali: Fundación FES, 1994); Enrique Chaux, "Buscando pistas para prevenir la violencia urbana en Colombia: Conflictos y agresión entre niños y adolescentes de Bogotá," *Revista de Estudios Sociales* 12 (2002): 41–51; and Rodrigo Parra, Adela González, Olga Patricia Moritz, Amilvia Blandón, and Rubén Bustamante, *La escuela violenta* (Bogotá: Tercer Mundo Editores and Fundación FES, 1992).

expose students to less violent, more participatory activities. Pedagogical interventions can be developed to promote the individual competence required to develop peaceful and constructive relationships with others and confront community violence and conflicts in critical, assertive, and safe ways.

Schools have the potential of being organized as democratic social entities, where each individual may directly (through projects and other participatory means) or indirectly (through voting and other representative means) be involved in decision making on issues of concern. Also, schools may be established as settings where members respect and take care of one another and where social-regulation mechanisms facilitate a more harmonious environment. Students then may have the experience of living in a social system that works differently from their violent environment and may realize that this alternative actually works and has benefits. Certainly this type of school context can positively influence students' development, since it provides opportunities for them to adopt peaceful attitudes and skills and practice them effectively.

Several studies show that positive classroom characteristics are related to positive behaviors and competence in students.[5] Some of the mechanisms that schools can implement include activities to (a) promote caring and respectful relationships between teachers and students and among students; (b) build norms and make decisions collectively; (c) establish clear, firm, and nonauthoritarian teaching styles for managing predefined or agreed rules in classrooms; and (d) generate collective discussion for the constructive resolution of interpersonal conflicts that emerge in the everyday interaction among the members of the school community (students, teachers, school administrators, and parents).

By using different pedagogical tools, schools may also directly promote the development of knowledge, attitudes, and abilities related to peaceful *convivencia*. These are called citizenship competencies. Some examples are (a) the capacity to stop aggression, (b) critical thinking, (c) conflict resolution, and (d) democratic participation. To stop aggressive behavior requires using different strategies to avoid hurting others (such as regulation of anger and appropriate expression of emotions) or to intervene as a third party in situations where other persons are being assaulted (asking them to stop or reporting the situation to an authority).

---

[5] J. Lawrence Aber, Stephanie M. Jones, Joshua L. Brown, Nina Chaudry, and Faith Samples, "Resolving Conflict Creatively: Evaluating the Developmental Effects of a School-Based Violence Prevention Program in Neighborhood and Classroom Context," *Development and Psychopathology* 10, no. 2 (1998): 187–213; Paul Boxer, Nancy G. Guerra, L. Rowell Huesmann, and Julie Morales, "Proximal Peer-Level Effects of a Small-Group Selected Prevention on Aggression in Elementary School Children: An Investigation of the Peer Contagion Hypothesis," *Journal of Abnormal Child Psychology* 33, no. 3 (2005): 325–38; Linda Lantieri and Janet Patti, *Waging Peace in Our Schools* (Boston: Beacon Press, 1996); F. Clark Power, Ann Higgins, and Lawrence Kohlberg, *Lawrence Kohlberg's Approach to Moral Education* (New York: Columbia University Press, 1989).

Critical thinking allows the individual to analyze the information that he or she receives, comprehend the nature of the information, and realize that it might be biased depending on the source. This citizenship competency helps people think critically about the discourses or actions that legitimize violence.

The capacity to deal constructively and peacefully with conflicts is one of the most important citizenship competencies to prevent violence in society. Although perhaps not all conflicts are solvable by means of dialogue, classroom and school benefit greatly from reinforcing the idea that every effort should be made to solve conflicts through constructive and peaceful means. And it is necessary not only to convey this message but also to provide the students with the desired conflict-solving skills. This capacity requires several specific competencies that can be promoted through educational programs, such as considering others' perspective and understanding their point of view, managing emotions that may interfere with the peaceful resolution of a conflict, listening with interest, asserting one's personal interests without invalidating others', suggesting alternative solutions to a conflict, and evaluating the different options for solving a conflict and identifying those that might fulfill everyone's interests.

The capacity to participate in democratic ways should be developed in students to empower them to transform their environments nonviolently. For example, this competence helps a person develop and use nonviolent means to state disagreements, reject situations in which human rights may be violated, and propose and promote positive changes in the social setting.

Implementing pedagogical strategies to develop competencies that will stop aggressive behavior and promote critical thinking, conflict resolution, and democratic participation is unquestionably a crucial way to contribute to peacebuilding in Colombia. Such activities contribute to societal transformation by changing individuals. Although changing individuals is not sufficient to generate broader social transformations, the impact that education can have at the individual level may be necessary to encourage those broader changes.

Structured Educational Programs

Colombia has a long history of pedagogical innovations. The best-known internationally is Escuela Nueva, a nationwide strategy that has been applied in rural public schools in almost all regions of the country and is under way in several other Latin American countries, two African countries, and India.[6] Escuela Nueva emerged in the 1970s as a pedagogical alternative to traditional rural schools. In many rural areas, population density is so low that

---

[6]See www.volvamos.org (accessed August 26, 2008).

students from different grades have to share the same classroom, with only one teacher. In traditional schools, the teacher needed to divide lecture time among the different grades and subjects, which meant that many students spent long periods without any guided learning. In addition, in the Colombian coffee region, students were frequently failing their courses because they skipped school during harvest seasons to work in the coffee fields. They needed a more flexible model, appropriate to their needs.

In response to these conditions, a group of teachers led by the pedagogical expert Vicky Colbert designed Escuela Nueva to respond to the specific needs in rural areas. In Escuela Nueva, students work at their own pace with individual booklets. Teachers concentrate on helping the youngest ones learn to read and answering unresolved questions. Older students support younger ones in their learning, too. In this way Escuela Nueva promotes citizenship competencies such as cooperation among classmates. Escuela Nueva also promotes students' involvement in issues in their own school and community. In addition to having a very active student government, students get involved in community projects that allow them to understand real-life problems and apply what they are learning.

Several rigorous evaluations of Escuela Nueva have consistently shown better performance in math and language there than in more traditional rural schools,[7] and recent evaluations have shown that students in Escuela Nueva report more peaceful and democratic attitudes and behavior.[8] These results demonstrate the potential that schools have in promoting peaceful interactions and commitment to democratic participation. Also, students learn about cooperation, peaceful interactions, and democratic participation, not by talking about it but by being involved in activities that get them to put their cooperative, peaceful, and democratic competencies into practice.

Several other structured educational programs exist for the promotion of peace and democracy in some areas. Proyecto Ciudadano (Citizenship Project) from Fundación Presencia, Habilidades para la Vida (Life Skills) from Fundación Fe y Alegría, Jóvenes Constructores de Paz (Young Peacebuilders) from the International Center for Education and Human Development

---

[7] Patrick J. McEwan, "The Effectiveness of Multi-grade Schools in Colombia," *International Journal of Educational Development* 18, no. 6 (1998): 435–52; George Psacharopoulos, Carlos Rojas, and Eduardo Vélez, "Achievement Evaluation of Colombia's Escuela Nueva: Is Multi-grade the Answer?" *Comparative Education Review* 37, no. 3 (1993): 263–76; Carlos Rojas and Zoraida Castillo, *Evaluación del programa Escuela Nueva, IFT-133* (Bogotá: Instituto SER de Investigación, 1988).

[8] Ray Chesterfield, *Indicators of Democratic Behaviour in Nueva Escuela Unitaria (NEU) Schools* (Guatemala City: Academy for Educational Development, Juárez and Associates, IDEAS Ltd., and USAID, 1994); Clemente Forero, Daniel Escobar, and Danielken Molina, "Escuela Nueva's Impact on the Peaceful Social Interaction of Children," in *Education for All and Multigrade Teaching: Challenges and Opportunities*, ed. A.W. Little (Amsterdam: Springer, 2006): 265–300; Jennifer Pitt, "Civic Education and Citizenship in Escuela Nueva Schools in Colombia" (master's thesis, University of Toronto, 1999).

(CINDE), Cultura de la Legalidad (Culture of Legality) of the Anti-Corruption Office of the Colombian Presidency, and Proyecto Hermes (Hermes Project) of Bogotá's Chamber of Commerce have been implemented in rural and urban areas for five to ten years. Ética con Inteligencia Emocional (Ethics with Emotional Intelligence) of Asesores de Proyectos Educativos, Escuelas de Perdón y Reconciliación (Forgiveness and Reconciliation Schools) of Fundación para la Reconciliación, Convivencia Productiva (Productive Convivencia) of Corporación Empresarios Convivencia Productiva, and Aulas en Paz (Peaceable Classrooms), the authors' program for promoting citizenship competencies among elementary school students, have been operating for five years or less and are still concentrated in major cities.[9] With the exception of Convivencia Productiva, which is simultaneously an education and business-cum-peace initiative, they are basically independent of peace initiatives from other sectors.

All these programs are based on theory and research, have support from different institutions or organizations, and have been or are being evaluated. Although rigorous research on the success of these programs is still preliminary, they are advancing our knowledge of how to promote *convivencia* and democratic behavior in schools and communities. Some, such as Proyecto Ciudadano, promote the development of citizenship competencies by creating a social setting where students study problems in their communities and propose projects that could bring social transformations by democratic means. Others, such as Habilidades para la Vida, are based on curricula that seek to develop specific competencies. Most share a similar pedagogical assumption: that learning citizenship competencies can be more effective if children are given opportunities to practice these skills, in either hypothetical or real-life situations.

Local School Initiatives

In addition to the structured programs, hundreds of thousands of teachers, school administrators, parents, and students throughout the whole country have been developing classroom or schoolwide strategies for promoting peace among their students and the school community. Faculty members of the Institución Educativa La Esperanza developed one of these initiatives

---

[9] More information about these programs can be obtained at presenci@unete.com (Proyecto Ciudadano); www.feyalegria.org (Habilidades para la Vida); www.cinde.org.co (Jóvenes Constructores de Paz); www.anticorrupcion.gov.co (Cultura de la Legalidad); camara.ccb.org.co (Proyecto Hermes); intemocional@yahoo.com (Ética con Inteligencia Emocional); www.fundacionparalareconciliacion.org (Escuelas de Perdón y Reconciliación); convivenciaproductiva@yahoo.es (Convivencia Productiva); Enrique Chaux, "Aulas en Paz: A Multi-Component Program for the Promotion of Peaceful Relationships and Citizenship Competencies," *Conflict Resolution Quarterly* 25, no. 1 (2007): 79–86; Cecilia Ramos, Ana María Nieto, and Enrique Chaux, "Aulas en paz: Resultados preliminares de un programa multi-Componente," *Revista Interamericana de Educación para la Democracia* 1, no. 1 (2007): 36–56.

in Medellín. This large school is located in the Comunas Noroccidentales, a violence-torn area of the city that in recent years has experienced open conflict among urban guerrillas, paramilitaries, and the Colombian military. In such a violent environment, children are learning peaceful ways of dealing with their own conflicts.

In response to an increasing incidence of aggression, intolerance, and norm violations among the students, a group of teachers and academic coordinators decided to create a peer mediation program. Instead of promoting adult interventions in children's conflicts, the basic idea was to help the students deal with their own problems. With the support of a team of teachers and coordinators, more than a hundred students from third to eleventh grade are trained each year as peer mediators. These include every class representative elected by the students in a yearly voting process, as well as some student volunteers. Whenever classmates are involved in a conflict, the peer mediator offers the possibility to resolve the conflict peacefully. The initiative has limitations. For example, not all students are willing to accept that other classmates will get involved in their conflicts. In any case, the initiative is empowering many children as peacebuilders from very early in life. If successful, they may end up contributing to peace not only in their schools but also in their families and communities.

A National Initiative: The Colombian Citizenship Competencies Program

Until recently, most school initiatives like the one at Institución Educativa La Esperanza received little pedagogical or conceptual support, and little communication and coordination took place among them. There are many initiatives, but most have been isolated. This seems to be changing with the coordination of a national initiative, the Colombian Citizenship Competencies Program, led by the Ministry of Education.

The Colombian General Education Law allows every school to determine its own curriculum and pedagogical orientation. This decentralization of educational decisions promotes autonomy and creativity, and many teachers and school administrators are making great use of it. While most schools have given a higher priority to traditional academic subjects such as math, language, or science, the National Citizenship Competencies Program is bringing more attention to heretofore isolated efforts in education for peace and citizenship. In fact, the program is giving citizenship education the same level of priority as traditional academic subjects. Since 2002, the Ministry of Education has promoted the creation of national standards and tests that seek to provide guidance, coordination, and feedback regarding schools' academic work. The standards indicate a minimum level of quality that the ministry expects of each school at different grade levels (third, fifth, seventh, ninth, and eleventh grades). The test evaluates whether and to what extent these standards are being reached. In such a strongly decentralized system, the standards and tests are almost the only mechanisms of control that the ministry has on the quality of education that schools deliver. The ministry decided in 2003 to make citizenship education one of five areas (with math, language, social sciences, and natural sciences) for which there are standards and tests. Thus, citizenship competencies gained the same importance as the other academic disciplines. This decision was made by Minister of Education Cecilia María Vélez. After several decades of high levels of violence in Colombia, several sectors were convinced that education had great potential to help promote a more peaceful society, and the education minister's decision reflected this shared feeling.

Our research group was directly involved in designing both the national standards and the National Test on Citizenship Competencies that provide the basis of the Citizenship Competencies Program.[10] The National Standards on Citizenship Competencies, published in April 2004, indicate what the ministry expects as the minimum level of performance on issues of *convivencia* and peace, democratic participation, and diversity.[11] They include knowledge (about mechanisms for democratic participation, for example), cognitive competencies (the capacity to consider other people's perspectives), emotional competencies (the capacity to identify and manage one's emotions even in stressful situations), communicative competencies (the capacity to listen accurately and with interest to others), and integrative competencies, which apply all the other competencies (peaceful and constructive resolution of conflicts).[12]

The national test, which was administered in October 2003, October 2005, and February 2006, evaluates to what extent some of these competencies are being achieved. All fifth- and ninth-grade students in every public or private school in Colombia take the test. Students report their own responses to particular situations and to their classmates' behavior. For example, empathy—the capacity to feel something similar to or compatible with what others are feeling—is measured by students' responses to how they usually feel in particular situations in which something bad happens to others. Other competencies, such as the capacity to manage anger, are measured in similar ways.

---

[10] Enrique Chaux led both teams that constructed the National Standards of Citizenship Competencies and the National Test of Citizenship Competencies.

[11] Ministerio de Educación Nacional, "Estándares Básicos de Competencias Ciudadanas. Formar para la ciudadanía. . . ¡sí es posible!" http://menweb.mineducacion.gov.co/saber/estandares_ciudadanas.pdf (accessed August 26, 2008).

[12] Ibid. See also Enrique Chaux, Juanita Lleras, and Ana María Velásquez, eds., *Competencias ciudadanas: de los estándares al aula. Una propuesta integral para todas las áreas académicas* (Bogotá: Ministerio de Educación Nacional and Universidad de los Andes, 2004); Alexander Ruiz and Enrique Chaux, *La formación de competencias ciudadanas* (Bogotá: Asociación Colombiana de Facultades de Educación, 2005).

Students' reports about their classmates' behavior (such as how often they get into physical fights) indicate classmates' integrative competencies. School results are based on the average grade of their students' reports.

The program is complemented by local, regional, and national workshops and conferences. These meetings allow teachers, school administrators, educational institutions, and national and international researchers to share experiences, concerns, insights, and research results and, in general, to learn from one another. The program also provides resources and materials from publications and a widely consulted Internet portal.[13] Finally, the program is starting to promote the implementation and evaluation of pilot programs, some of which have been adapted from foreign innovations.

Risks and Opportunities

The Education Ministry's citizenship competencies program has not been fully implemented and is still only in the beginning stages. Most schools in Colombia are probably still not conscious of its potential, or, if they are, they probably do not have the pedagogical tools or institutional support to implement it. As participants in the construction of the program, we advocate its advantages and positive potential, but implementation also involves certain risks.

Risk 1: Limited information about the program. One risk is that teachers and schools may not receive enough information about the proposal and, especially, about how to implement it. There has been large-scale dissemination of the program. All schools in Colombia received a copy of the National Standards of Citizenship Competencies, took part in the two National Tests of Citizenship Competencies, and received the results of their performance. Also, workshops have taken place in all Colombian provinces, and the program has been publicized in newspapers and on the Internet, radio, and television. But even though most teachers and school administrators now know something about the program, this may not be sufficient for them to implement it appropriately in their classrooms and schools. To be sure, this task depends not only on the Education Ministry but also on local officials and institutions such as secretaries of education, NGOs, and universities that have regular contact with schools.

Risk 2: Information received but ignored. It seems likely that many teachers and schools received information about the program but have not integrated it into their work. There are several reasons for this. The first drafts of the national standards were evaluated by a large group of teachers and researchers throughout the country, but most teachers and school administrators heard about them for the first time after the standards had already been established and published. During workshops in which we participated, some

---

[13] www.colombiaaprende.edu.co.

teachers expressed their displeasure that they had been left out of the discussions that led to the construction of the standards and that the program was being imposed by the national government without adequate consultation. To protect confidentiality and the integrity of the process, only the group of researchers who created the national test knew about its content before students took this test. This may have created resistance to the program.

Risk 3: Loss of autonomy at the local level. Resistance may also come from the perception that autonomy may be lost with adherence to the national standards and tests. The Colombian educational system is highly decentralized and grants schools a large degree of autonomy in deciding what and how to teach. The new proposal is not a mandate, but results on the national tests are one of several indicators considered in evaluating school administrators' performance. Also, the results of these tests are public, and this creates social pressures that many teachers and administrators may resent.

Risk 4: Regional variation overlooked. One of the most common criticisms that we encountered is that the program ignores the great regional diversity found throughout the country; for this reason, several teachers call into question the basic idea of a national standard. At first glance, this criticism seems reasonable, since local realities vary so much. But a closer look at the proposal shows that the competencies seem sufficiently broad to account for regional differences. For example, it is clear that the particular strategies for dealing peacefully with conflicts need to be culturally relevant, and for this reason, they vary from region to region. However, skills for peaceful resolution of conflicts are necessary throughout the country, since conflicts can and do occur in any social context, and these skills are what the standards related to conflict resolution seem to be trying to promote.

Risk 5: Competencies ineffective or inappropriate for more violent zones. A similar criticism is that some environments in Colombia are so violent that it does not make sense to try to promote competencies related to peaceful social interactions, since these skills are not adaptive in such places. Apparently, those who make this argument believe that children living in violent environments need to learn to be aggressive to survive. In fact, the proposal is based on two very different conceptions: that survival is actually increased by learning to deal constructively and nonviolently with social problems, and that these competencies are especially needed in the most violent environments because, otherwise, those places would never undergo long-lasting changes. In any case, resistance in the form of such criticisms may continue until many more realize that the proposal is sufficiently broad to account for regional diversities and that it is applicable in the most violent regions of the country. Continuing local, regional, and national debates and sharing of successful experiences could help local actors identify what is most useful in this national proposal in light of local conditions.

Risk 6: Proposal confused with earlier initiatives. The Education Ministry has promoted several educational initiatives over the past two decades.[14] These have included proposals on academic achievement (*logros*), objectives (*objetivos*), guidelines (*lineamientos*), and now standards and competencies. These may have created the sense that the new proposal is actually the same as earlier ones but with a different name. Also, some may believe that the current program will last only until a new government comes in with a new proposal; thus, they may as well continue with what they have been doing. All these factors may have created an unhelpful situation; even if the content of the program has strong potential benefits for the schools, many may have decided to ignore it completely before really getting to know and understand what the proposal is about.

Risk 7: Incorrect implementation of proposal. Even if some teachers and school administrators get to know the citizenship competencies proposal and decide to implement it, there is still the risk that they will implement it in ways that are inconsistent with the development of these competencies. This is especially likely if they do not count on the support of local secretaries of education, NGOs, or research centers and universities with access to more conceptual or pedagogical resources.

Such seems to be the case of schools that believe that their values-transmission programs—programs that schools organize around certain values that are usually defined by adults—are already developing citizenship competencies. Common activities include "the value of the day, week, or month," in which students are reminded of the relevance of a certain value by means of posters, songs, texts, and slogans. The student who best demonstrates that value (such as the most honest student of the week) receives a prize that is awarded in public. Other values-transmission programs involve students in creating portraits of ideal figures. In one Colombian school that claims to be working on the promotion of citizenship competencies, students draw human figures with hats of wisdom, shirts of tolerance, gloves of love and peace, belts of faith, pants of effort, socks of humility, and shoes of truth. Alfie Kohn has argued that these programs may actually hinder the development of certain citizenship competencies.[15] For example, they do not prepare students to deal with real-life situations where different values frequently confront one another. They may also affect the development of

---

[14] Carlos Eduardo Vasco, "¿Objetivos, logros, indicadores, competencias o estándares?" (paper presented at the meeting of the Colombian Association for Mathematical Education, Bogotá, April 30, 2002), www.socolpe.org.co/documentos/Estandaresobjetivosvasco.doc (accessed November 12, 2005).

[15] Alfie Kohn, "How Not to Teach Values: A Critical View at Character Education," *Phi Delta Kappan* 78, no. 6 (February 1997): 429–39; Chaux, Lleras, and Velásquez, *Competencias ciudadanas*; María Cristina Villegas, *Educación para el desarrollo moral* (Bogotá: Alfaomega, Universidad de los Andes, 2002).

critical-thinking skills, since students are taught to conform to the values chosen for them. Citizenship competencies are developed not by reminding students about what is good or by talking about it, but by confronting students with situations in which they need to put those competencies into practice.

Schools may also have difficulties integrating the proposal into the curriculum, and especially into academic subjects such as math, science, language, physical education, and art. The proposal states that the whole educational community, including all teachers, school administrators, and parents, needs to be involved and that citizenship competencies should be promoted in every class and academic discipline. In this way, it breaks with the belief that citizenship education is the responsibility of only a few, such as social science teachers. It is possible that this approach could diffuse responsibility throughout the educational community, although so far, very few integration strategies exist.[16]

The risks outlined above should not be understood as predictors of failure. Instead, they confirm that the task is not easy and is only in its initial phase. These issues need to be taken into account to make full use of the program's potential. For example, it seems crucial to work closely with local institutions, such as municipal or departmental secretaries of education, NGOs, and regional universities that may support interested teachers and school administrators. That is, it seems essential to support the supporters. Success may depend to a large degree on the level of coordination among local initiatives, structured programs, and national initiatives.

It is also important to guarantee stability of national priorities. Resistance to national proposals may decrease if the educational community finds that these proposals will not change once governmental officers are replaced. For this reason, relative stability and continuity of the current initiative should be made a priority and protected from abrupt changes.

Finally, a strong opportunity seems to come from the training of future teachers. Students of education and pedagogy may have the motivation required to learn new concepts and procedures, as well as the time that extremely busy practicing teachers usually do not have. If all those studying to be teachers receive training in how to promote citizenship competencies in their classrooms and schools, the educational system will be a strong promoter of peace in the future.

Conclusion

We have seen plenty of creativity and motivation among members of the educational community, especially at the local level, but we have not seen enough conceptual background and pedagogical tools to make the best use

---

[16] The proposal provides a general framework and specific pedagogical strategies about how to do this integration. See Chaux, Lleras, and Velásquez, *Competencias ciudadanas*.

of all that creativity and motivation. For example, the values-transmission programs described above sometimes reflect a lack of knowledge of their limitations in capacity to promote changes in students' behavior. Guidance and support to schools and teachers seem necessary to fulfill education's potential for social transformation.

Colombia has become a leader internationally in citizenship education. In a recent review of civic programs in Latin America, Fernando Reimers and Eleonora Villegas-Reimers of Harvard University concluded that the Colombian program of citizenship competencies is one of the most innovative and comprehensive in the region.[17] The program differs from common practice in other countries in emphasizing competencies and not only knowledge and values; it focuses on peaceful *convivencia*, democratic participation, and pluralism, not only on civics; it promotes the development, pilot testing, and dissemination of pedagogical tools; and it includes large-scale evaluation.

Although the program is only in its beginning stage and although its success depends completely on its integration with local actors and ongoing school initiatives, it seems to have enormous potential to help transform our society. In the end, the program's success should be measured not only by the number of peace initiatives implemented in schools, but by whether and how much these initiatives actually help students develop their own citizenship competencies (something that can be evaluated directly through the National Test of Citizenship Competencies) and become empowered to transform their society by peaceful, democratic means.

Many years of living in a violent situation requires substantial societal transformations in the ways we relate to one another, and education seems to hold the key to such transformations. Not taking education into account may mean that any other peace initiative will run the risk of having only short-term and limited effects.

---

[17] Fernando Reimers and Eleonora Villegas-Reimers, *Educación para la ciudadanía democrática en escuelas secundarias de América Latina* (paper prepared for the Regional Dialogue about Education meeting, Inter-American Development Bank, Washington, D.C., 2005).

9

The Colombian Church and Peacebuilding

Héctor Fabio Henao Gaviria

In recent decades, Colombians have recognized the dynamic role played by the Catholic Church in the quest for peace and reconciliation. Efforts at rapprochement between guerrilla groups and the Colombian government, which began toward the end of President Barco's administration and led to the demobilization of four thousand combatants from 1990 to early 1991, were accompanied and facilitated by offices of the Colombian Conference of Bishops. Since then, the church has taken an increasingly decisive stance on resolving the armed conflict that has wracked the country for five decades. At the heart of the concerns expressed by priests at Sunday feast day masses, by the bishops at their assemblies, and by many religious groups and pastoral workers are the problems caused by the armed confrontation; the consequences of neoliberalism, corruption, and social inequalities; and the exclusion that affects many sectors of Colombian society. The often-silent labor of pastoral workers in their parishes, in the countryside, and in the city is the most significant contribution to the quest for justice and peace. Men's and women's religious communities have played an unquestionably positive role, especially by their presence in areas that have been hard-hit by the violence and armed conflict. In many cases, pastoral workers, priests, and members of religious orders have given their lives for peace.

Church bodies often issue constructive proposals regarding internal conflicts, as well as critical statements about situations and structures that are obstacles to peaceful coexistence among Colombians. These statements are an important part of the church's role—the church's greatest strength is its ability to bear witness along with the victims and to illuminate the prospects and pitfalls along the road that society is taking. Members of the church have

This chapter was translated from Spanish by Barbara Fraser.

known the consequences of the climate of violence that has touched the lives of all sectors of the nation. A significant number of church workers have been murdered, including an archbishop, bishops, priests, men and women of religious orders, and catechists. The bishops' positions stem mainly from their reading of current events from an ethical perspective. In 2006, when the bishops stated that Colombia's institutions were in crisis, there were critics who challenged them. Nevertheless, subsequent scandals over drug traffickers who had infiltrated the highest spheres of government proved the bishops right.

The documents of the Catholic magisterium have a long tradition of examining, at the universal level, possibilities for different sectors of the Catholic community and the country. The bishops often issue statements and proposals at the diocesan level that address the local context of violence; groups of bishops, sometimes accompanied by their priests and members of religious orders, speak out collectively on common problems at the regional level; and the Conference of Bishops brings together all the bishops of the country in assemblies, where they speak with one voice. If all the bishops cannot meet, a special committee or the president of the Conference of Bishops may speak on behalf of the conference. Practically all the Colombian bishops' assemblies in recent years have addressed problems related to the conflict and prospects for peace.

Regional diversity clearly carries weight in the Colombian church and its associated bodies. Despite the country's diversity, the church has maintained a significant degree of cohesion in its position on the quest for peace, and this has given its proposals legitimacy.

Regional statements reflect the impact of the conflict in the areas of greatest confrontation. In 1998, Bishop Jaime Prieto of Barrancabermeja, president of the Social Ministry Commission, along with the director of the church's National Social Ministry Secretariat, decried the murder of a well-known human rights defender, the horrifying massacre in Mapiripán, and the murders of a local family and a former general.[1] The bishops of the Antioquia-Chocó region, meeting on August 11, 1999, issued a joint statement about the conflict affecting their region. They took a stand on the war crimes being committed, such as massacres and murders of civilians, prisoners, or the wounded; torture; abduction; disappearances; and forced displacement. They noted, "These behaviors and other, similar ones are clearly crimes against humanity and actions seriously contrary to the law of God, which cry out to the heavens."[2]

Since the 1980s, the Catholic Church has intensified its reflection on the character of the situation in Colombia and its various forms of violence. One great need has been to define the role of the Conference of Bishops, as well as the way in which the various sectors of the church join in the quest for alter-

---

[1] "Detengamos esta guerra sucia," *Documentación de Pastoral Social* (May 1998): 7.

[2] *Documentación de Pastoral Social* 186 (September 1999): 42.

natives and options for transformation amid the confrontations that have wracked Colombia for centuries.

In this quest, we have learned lessons from other countries in Latin America and the Caribbean, but in many ways, we have found ourselves facing unique situations. In Colombia, the church is not responding to the challenges of a military dictatorship, nor are the parties to the conflict differentiated into two groups, as in other countries. These differences have demanded a process of learning and reflection. Dialogue with various stakeholders in Colombian society has led the church to define the situation in the country as one of "internal armed conflict" and to take the position that the solution must come through a just negotiation.

The church's historical hegemony in Colombia has been replaced by the reality of a more pluralistic country that demands openness and dialogue. Therefore, the church has invited other stakeholders to help it define its role in peacebuilding and to identify the specific contributions it can make on issues such as public order, political negotiation of the armed conflict, and democratic security.

The recognition that Colombia is experiencing a complex conflict that requires it to respond with actions and proposals has led the church to reach out to diverse sectors. The complexity of the conflict stems not only from the multiplicity of armed actors but also from the existence of factors such as drug trafficking, the many different types of conflicts that surround the armed conflict, and, above all, the inequality and social exclusion that lie at the root of the problem.

The church has also called attention to the wealth and richness of an enormous variety of peacebuilding proposals that have emerged at the grassroots and regional levels and that give us great hope. The Conference of Bishops has highlighted that "in each Colombian there is the capacity to build something new."[3] This has enabled us to take up the cause of all sectors of society that are committed, in their own way, to building a new nation. Reading "the signs of the times" enables us to recognize the events of history and discover amid them the mystery of the presence of God and what God is asking. Therein lies much of the church's contribution to this dialogue.

As a result of its dialogues with various sectors of society, the church has been defining the options for intervention in the armed conflict. The roles of the Conference of Bishops that are best known to the public have involved facilitation, moral guidance, and mediation in several cases of negotiation between the government and irregular armed groups. Because of this, many people now consider the Catholic Church a key actor in the development of peace agreements with the various armed groups, both guerrillas and paramilitaries.

---

[3] Colombian Conference of Bishops, "Call to Unity and Hope," February 21, 2002.

The Catholic Church has lent its services to peace negotiations while calling for steps that would lead the country toward a permanent national peace policy: "In its work for peace, the Colombian Catholic Church has expressed the idea of a 'National Permanent Peace Policy' or 'Government Peace Policy' as a guide for peacebuilding. Such a policy must . . . be the fruit of a broad national consensus that takes into account the national interest and does not depend on special interests or those of particular groups. All representative sectors of the nation must therefore participate in its design."[4]

Building peace after decades of confrontation and millions of victims requires such a participatory process and pedagogy. Both the participatory process and the pedagogy that must accompany it have gradually been defined through thousands of encounters and community experiences.

In its work to promote citizen participation and pedagogies for peace, the church recognizes that there are at least three closely related scenarios for peacebuilding. There is the scenario of a negotiated settlement over the armed conflict, in which government sectors, organizations outside the law, other institutions, and facilitators participate. Another scenario involves organizing, strengthening, and building the capacity of civil society. A third scenario involves building structures at the community level that guarantee social justice and peaceful coexistence. People involved in ministry also face the daily challenge of establishing dialogue to transform the way the deepest aspects of relationships of coexistence are expressed and symbolized.

A National Project: Constructing the Public Sphere

Closely linked with this work by the Conference of Bishops is an ongoing nationwide task of building a country that can live in reconciliation and with social justice. Several years ago, the bishops held a conference, "Toward the Colombia We Want," to analyze key areas of national life, such as economics and poverty, the justice system, and security. The workshops identified inequality and extreme poverty as two of the great challenges in the area of peacebuilding. The bishops of the region concluded, "Peace is the fruit of justice; it is a construction that is always linked to development. Peace is a process; it is not merely the absence of war. It is more than the absence of war and more than peace accords."[5]

The workshops' reflections on building a new Colombia have underscored the need to contribute to the construction of the public sphere as a place of pluralism and discussion that encourages tolerance and recognizes the role of dialogue in developing a new model for society. To give impetus to the

---

[4] Colombian Conference of Bishops, "Decalogue for a Government Peace Policy," *Revista Documentación de Pastoral Social*, no. 194 (March 2002): 118.

[5] "Toward the Colombia We Want," Millennium Workshops, *Revista Documentación de Pastoral Social* (March 2002).

development of a new vision for the country and to strengthen public institutions, the Conference of Bishops has established a National Social Ministry
Secretariat to raise church members' awareness about the country's situation
and their Christian commitment; promote economic, social, and political
programs that contribute to integral human development characterized by
solidarity; and respond to current humanitarian problems. The secretariat is
under the guidance of the Commission of Bishops and includes professional
teams with expertise in human rights, the culture of peace, the rights of the
displaced population, assistance to at-risk groups, and social and Christian
formation. This entire team operates at the national level with diocesan
teams and secretariats, as well as parish committees, which motivate and
create relationships with social organizations seeking similar goals of nation
building.

The development of its role in building a sense of citizenship and a new
country has placed the Conference of Bishops in ongoing dialogue with civil
society organizations and the political community. Ecumenical encounters
have taken place with leaders of other churches and religious denominations
to discuss this shared nation-building process. Experience with ecumenical
programs with other Christian denominations has translated into regional
development projects and joint peacebuilding initiatives. Significant progress has also been made on interfaith relations. Over time, the range of ecumenical actions and campaigns has broadened.

One thing that can foster greater understanding of the Catholic Church's
role in peacebuilding is its participation in debates and the development of
consensus on a plan for international cooperation. Within the framework of
international cooperation, Plan Colombia and the spraying of illicit crops
have played an important and controversial role. On this subject, the Permanent Committee of the Colombian Bishops stated in 2000, "We believe that
the solution to the cultivation of coca and poppy crops is not indiscriminate
fumigation, which will be accompanied by other effects that harm both nature and human beings. Instead, we recommend eradication and the provision of new job opportunities."[6]

The National Social Ministry has also participated in the so-called London-
Cartagena process. This process has brought sectors of civil society together
and created conditions for dialogue with the international community and
the Colombian government about priorities and action areas for international
cooperation. According to the Conference of Bishops, "We affirm that we
need the international community's cooperation to find new paths, to take
advantage of its experience, to implement solutions to the problems of drug

---

[6] Eradication here refers to the manual destruction of coca and poppy crops. Statement on Plan
Colombia by the Standing Committee, Bogotá, September 20, 2000.

trafficking and poverty, and to promote human rights and ecology."[7] This ongoing dialogue about the country's problems and the role of the international community in the quest for peace may have a tremendous impact because of the scope of the issues being discussed.

Negotiations with the United States on the Free Trade Agreement have been accompanied by discussion about the human rights situation, peace, and vulnerable groups in Colombia. In 2004, the Conference of Bishops issued a statement highlighting its major concerns: "The Free Trade Agreement . . . is an agreement that goes beyond trade, and which is being negotiated between countries with great asymmetries in their development, capacities and possibilities. We therefore insist on the need to establish rules that ensure equality in the negotiations."[8]

Another very important activity of the Bishops' Conference has been to engage, through the National Conciliation Commission and the National Social Ministry Secretariat, in dialogue with grassroots organizations committed to peacebuilding. The National Conciliation Commission formed on August 4, 1995, in the vacuum left by the resignation and nonreplacement of the high commissioner for peace. Cardinal Pedro Rubiano, then president of the Conference of Bishops, called together people from throughout the country to seek possible paths toward peace based on a clear premise: that peace cannot be won by war. From the start, the commission had one objective: to facilitate rapprochement among the parties involved in the armed conflict and to accompany, insofar as possible, the establishment of dialogue and negotiation. The commission has sought a permanent government policy on peace and has worked to raise the country's awareness of the need to find negotiated solutions to the conflict. It is independent of the government and the guerrillas, enabling it to serve as a facilitator.

The quest to build a nation characterized by just and equitable relations and the simultaneous building of bridges with the groups involved in the conflict go hand in hand with a commitment to displaced people and victims of the armed conflict—all from the perspective of the church's mission of commitment to the Gospel and proclamation of the life that comes from the resurrected Christ.

The Humanitarian Role

Until 1996, no documents warned about the problem of internal forced displacement in Colombia. At that time, the Conference of Bishops decided to launch a national and regional study to call public and government attention to the serious situation of the victims of the conflict. Since then, the problem

---

[7] *Peace Ministry in the Current Situation of Armed Conflict in Colombia*, Final Declaration of the General Meeting of Bishops, Bogotá, March 9–13, 1998.

[8] Conference of Bishops' statement on the Free Trade Agreement, September 13, 2004.

of forced displacement has been monitored and analyzed by United Nations agencies and organizations from Colombian civil society. A law now provides a framework for government assistance to the victims of this scourge, and the Constitutional Court ordered that the urgent needs of this population be addressed immediately. These are some of the results of the church's efforts.

The National Social Ministry Secretariat's work has included a special research program on displacement and the situation of victims of the conflict, which provides input for recommendations to the national government and the international community. It guides the church's efforts to prevent human rights violations and protect victims, as well as its long-term work for the restoration of victims' rights. Studies of forced displacement drew attention to the need to provide greater assistance to two groups of victims: members of ethnic minorities and families headed by women, especially where those women have taken on this responsibility as a result of forced displacement. Meanwhile, the research has shown the need for all levels of the church to ensure that the parties to the conflict recognize, respect, and abide by the humanitarian principles enshrined in international norms governing internal conflicts.

The church works side by side with those who suffer because of the conflict. One component of this accompaniment is research, including the development of databases on forced displacement (RUT) and the recovery of historical memory (Testimonio, Verdad, y Reconciliación, or TEVERE).[9] TEVERE seeks to document and interpret the human rights situation in the country in order to contribute to national reconciliation based on clarification of the truth, recovery of dignity and the capacity to speak out, acknowledgment of victims, and reconstruction of historical memory. TEVERE produces periodic reports with case studies and witnesses' testimony. It has also produced tools for psychosocial intervention in communities affected by violence. RUT takes the Spanish name of the biblical figure Ruth, who stands in solidarity with those who suffer and feels displaced from her land. RUT is a database of situations reported to diocesan Social Ministry offices. Its goal is not to provide statistics about the number of displaced people in Colombia but to contribute to analysis and solutions for specific population groups and provide quarterly reports about the development of the situation and about new cases.

Church groups also make advocacy plans for drawing greater national and international attention to the victims. One of these initiatives was the launching of an international campaign with the Caritas network, focusing on the humanitarian crisis in Colombia. Work is also being done with other community and grassroots organizations and networks of victims to lobby

---

[9] For information about both bulletins, see Secretariado Nacional de Pastoral Social, "Cáritas Colombiana," www.pastoralsocialcolombia.org (accessed August 26, 2008).

for the drafting and implementation of a law on forced displacement. Another activity is raising awareness among Colombians through internal campaigns such as the one commemorating the Day of the Migrant. The church is also involved in direct action on the ground to prevent forced displacement, through early-warning systems and the accompaniment of displaced communities.

The church's work in assisting victims is the result of a preferential option for aiding the most vulnerable sectors and those who have suffered from armed actions. Assistance to displaced populations has aimed at the restoration of their rights and is part of a broader effort by the Conference of Bishops and the Social Ministry to defend the human rights of all Colombians. There are very close ties with Colombian and international human rights nongovernmental organizations (NGOs) for joint action to promote and defend the dignity of every Colombian man, woman, and child. A recent study by the University of the Andes and the National Social Ministry Secretariat highlights the urgency of restoring the rights of the displaced population. According to the study, 2,459,000 people, making up 554,207 households, have been internally displaced in Colombia, which means that the phenomenon has affected 6 percent of the population.[10]

The church has issued documents that highlight the regional dimensions of the conflict. The "Report on the Situation of Human Rights and International Humanitarian Law in the Sierra Nevada de Santa Marta" recognized the "grave humanitarian crisis affecting the communities living in the region of the Sierra Nevada de Santa Marta, which has been caused by the constant violation of human rights and international humanitarian law by armed organizations operating outside the law" and noted "an urgent need to implement a comprehensive emergency plan aimed at protecting fundamental rights; guaranteeing respect for economic, social and cultural rights; and reestablishing the real and effective presence of the state, taking into account the right of indigenous communities to consultation and decision making by consensus."[11]

This report made an impact by highlighting one of the most serious and unknown humanitarian crises in the country, by prompting government institutions to develop a plan for assisting the population in that area, and by creating the opportunity to address this humanitarian problem in peace processes and negotiations. It emphasized the role of humanitarian rapproche-

---

[10] As of 2007, it is estimated that 3.5 million people have been displaced in the past twenty years. See *Toward a Proactive Policy for the Displaced Population* (Bogotá: University of the Andes and Conference of Bishops of Colombia, National Social Ministry Secretariat, 2006).

[11] National Social Ministry Secretariat and Ombudsman's Office (Defensoría del Pueblo), "Situation of Human Rights and International Humanitarian Law in the Sierra Nevada de Santa Marta," Recommendations, December 2003, 96.

ment in making dialogue possible between the armed groups and the national government.

The church has also issued reports on other humanitarian problems, such as forced displacement, abandonment of high-risk populations, abduction, and the alarming number of accidents caused by antipersonnel mines.

Pastoral Dialogues

The church's role in facilitating peace processes has been strongly supported by its accompaniment of victims and its work with them in all regions of the country. The backdrop for these interventions has been the development of methods of approaching people, building trust, and establishing dialogue. Among these are pastoral dialogues—ways of listening to the parties involved in the conflict to build bridges of communication and open up possibilities for encounter. Pastoral dialogue is a mechanism that has been fiercely debated in Colombia; sometimes it has been the subject of juridical and legal debate, while at other times its relevance has been questioned. In many cases, the government has made efforts to control or limit this form of intervention. The consensus is that these dialogues are part of the church's pastoral work and that their goal is to resolve the conflict.

Pastoral dialogue is an ecclesiastical exercise growing from reflection and discernment about what the current moment demands from the local church. The bishop and members of the church community analyze the circumstances, reading them in light of the Gospel. Finally, as the leader of the church, the bishop decides the best type of pastoral dialogue. Pastoral dialogues have been carried out in the context of armed confrontation, and their goal has been eminently humanitarian. In general, they try to put an end to violence in the region and ensure that the territory, liberty, and rights of the population are respected.

In Colombia, pastoral dialogues are frequently used as a methodology for intervention in situations other than armed conflicts. They can be oriented toward humanitarian situations, such as the liberation of kidnap victims, or cases in which people have been threatened or in which communities are being pressured to abandon their homes. One bishop explains, "To speak of pastoral dialogues and community dialogues for peace is to evoke many years of working for peace in Tibú, through the dioceses of Vélez, Socorro, and San Gil in Norte de Santander and now in the south of Bolívar in Magangué. This has been the work not of one person but of many, who have put their best efforts into paving the way for peace and harmonious coexistence."[12] Pastoral dialogue presents the opportunity to explore paths creatively and with great pastoral imagination, discovering possibilities and strengths in

---

[12] Bishop Leonardo Gómez Serna of Magangué, *Pastoral and Community Dialogues*, Life, Justice, and Peace Commission, Diocese of Magangué, 2005.

the parties involved but without abandoning the prophetic voice that denounces the evil of violence and proclaims the need to find different ways to reach the desired goals and end confrontations. The church's interventions have sought to establish the legitimacy of dialogue as a means of resolving confrontations and conflicts throughout the country.

In the well-known negotiations that have occurred at a national level, including those with the Movimiento 19 de Abril (M-19), the church has always been present through the Conference of Bishops. As the church has found itself involved in new processes for bringing groups together and negotiating with armed groups, it has felt an increasingly urgent need to expand the range of interventions and respond in ways that touch the lives of communities and involve them in peacebuilding.

The Conference of Bishops recently decided to form a peace commission composed of the bishops who accompany and monitor negotiations processes with groups operating outside the law.[13] It is significant that a body such as the Conference of Bishops engages in joint reflection and action when facing a range of possibilities. The dynamics and possibilities of the approaches taken with each armed group are obviously very diverse, and there is a need for a mechanism for reviewing the lessons learned and progressing toward long-term goals.

But the church's presence goes beyond the important role played by the bishop facilitators; it includes priests, members of the holy orders, and committed laypeople working in the region to develop a culture of peace. The idea is to help communities develop values, attitudes, and behaviors rooted in respect for life, the promotion of nonviolent relationships, dialogue, and consensus building. Encounters, meetings, dialogues, workshops, and educational processes with pastoral workers, trainers, and community leaders have made it possible to extend this presence throughout the country.

Ministry for Peace and Reconciliation

What peacebuilding strategy has the Colombian church implemented since 1990? The answer lies in a series of agreements and principles expressed in documents about what can generically be called a "peace and reconciliation ministry."[14] These documents develop the principle that peace and reconciliation are central in building a society that will ensure the human fulfillment

---

[13] For example, at its February 16, 2001, meeting, the Standing Committee of the Conference of Bishops designated a commission, headed by Bishop Jaime Prieto of Barrancabermeja, to follow the peace process with the Ejército de Liberación Nacional (ELN). Archbishop Alberto Giraldo of Medellín accompanied talks between the government and the Fuerzas Armadas Revolucionarias de Colombia (FARC) during President Pastrana's administration, and a commission of bishops accompanied the talks with the Autodefensas Unidas de Colombia (AUC).

[14] Colombian Conference of Bishops, "Toward a Peace Ministry" (working paper, May 2, 1994); *Peace Ministry in the Current Situation of Armed Conflict in Colombia.*

of all its members, and that peace is central to living out the Christian message. Therefore, they speak of levels of commitment, values, principles, guidelines for action, and the role of each individual person.[15]

Having a set of decisions, declarations, and Colombian church documents on these issues has been of great practical assistance to parishes and church groups in defining their commitment to peace as an integral part of the church's work. It has also ensured that actions by the Conference of Bishops in negotiations with armed groups have had a positive impact on long-term community processes leading toward reconciliation.

Why is it now imperative to speak of reconciliation in our country? The answer is obvious if we delve deeply into the causes of the injustice and violence that we have suffered for so many years. As Archbishop Rubén Salazar of Barranquilla has noted, "We must find what lies behind these trends if we are to encounter the cause and find solutions for attacking it at the source."[16]

Creating Spaces for Encounter, Listening, Consolation, and Reconciliation

Integrating the voices of various sectors affected by the conflict and feeling the pain caused by atrocities has led the church to create spaces for reflection and action through its dioceses and local organizations. These spaces open doors for people who have no way of dealing with or expressing their sorrow, as well as those who cannot get a hearing for their proposals for peace and reconciliation. By "spaces," we mean not only physical places or moments, but also environments in which relationships that allow people to live with human dignity can be created or re-created. This vital space is very limited in regions where the confrontation tends to involve all inhabitants.

The idea of creating pastoral spaces is aimed at helping put into practice the principles that lie at the root of human coexistence and creating conditions that can enable people to live fully and with dignity amid extremely adverse social circumstances. This means being able to speak out and listen to others and expressing feelings and suffering as well as hopes and dreams. It means being able to dream with others about a future in peace. Pastoral spaces enable victims to recognize their own victimhood, experience their sorrow, and, in many cases, mourn the dead they could not bury.

These spaces of life and hope have characterized the church's presence in sectors where the state is not present and pastoral work is accompanied by various community services such as education, health care, and recreation. The question is, what must be done to ensure that each person feels that the

---

[15] "Ten Principles for the Journey toward Peace" (final message of the Seventy-Second Extraordinary Plenary Assembly of Colombian Bishops, Bogotá, March 8, 2002).

[16] Archbishop Rubén Salazar, Caribbean Region Reconciliation Congress, *Documentación de Pastoral Social* (July 2001), 22.

relationships he or she establishes are safe and fraternal? We can find thousands of examples. The TEVERE program has a methodology for recovering historical memory, welcoming victims, healing wounds, and opening up new possibilities for the victims to recover their dignity and their rights. The healing process must begin now, in social and communal terms, even though the conflict has not yet ended. Those who are serving as catalysts for this grassroots program are people from the affected communities who have participated in a national formation and reflection process implemented by the National Social Ministry Secretariat.

To reinforce these opportunities and ensure that the entire population can participate, the church has created organizations such as the Institute for Peacebuilding Foundation (Fundación Instituto para la Construcción de la Paz, or Ficonpaz), whose goal is to involve children and youth in discussions about truth, justice, and long-term peacebuilding. The "Sowers of Peace" movement that Ficonpaz promotes has involved large groups of children and young people.

At the Service of Historical Memory

One of the complexities of the problem in Colombia, from the church's standpoint, is that actions must recover and keep alive the memory of the past atrocities even while the confrontation is continuing and, in some cases, worsening. There is a constant need for more in-depth examination of the challenge posed by this work.

Archbishop Luis Augusto Castro, president of the Conference of Bishops, warns of the difficulties that accompany the current quest for memory: "Exhaustion can come when we see that the longed-for truth that labors to gain ground, instead of leading to reconciliation, a positive reinterpretation of the past, purification of memory, forgiveness between victim and perpetrator, and hope for true reparatory justice, becomes a source of vengeance and unproven accusations, a weapon against political adversaries, and a source of unhealthy hatred and lies that strike at the very value of life."[17]

The recovery of memory can have many effects in the future, because it will allow movement toward forgiveness once memory has been "purified" and will help create conditions for making reparations to victims within the reconciliation process. The call to "purify" memory is related to the need to recover memory and make it a building block of justice and peace. This means that memory must not play a merely passive role but must transcend the individual dimension; it must not lead to vengeance but must become a collective means for reconciliation and peacebuilding to ensure that the atrocities of the past are not repeated. Some of the great challenges involve returning lands

---

[17] Archbishop Luis Augusto Castro, "Without Tiring," May 13, 2007.

seized from displaced populations. In many cases, the lands are still in the hands of the perpetrators.

As the Conference of Bishops said, "We must devote ourselves to the way of truth to restore the dignity of the victims, who play a central role in reconciliation and are the privileged possessors of the grace of forgiveness, which can and must be born in them if we wish to break the cycle of rancor, resentment and revenge that sometimes becomes a burden too heavy to bear."[18]

The church has thus played a broader role than many people realize. It has facilitated working groups and negotiating processes, and because of its regional and local presence, it has responded to many social problems. A great diversity of local responses and social actions makes the church a vital presence in both evangelization and nation building.

Accompanying Those Who Suffer

What has enabled the victims of violence to express their opinions and raise their voices is the fact that they are "accompanied" in all their circumstances. Along the rivers of the Pacific region, in the rain forest of southern Colombia, and in the mountains on the borders, many pastoral organizations are in constant contact with peasant farmers, Afro-Colombian communities, indigenous people, and settlers. The idea of accompaniment has been one of placing oneself in the situation of those who have directly suffered the atrocities and who, amid so much suffering, have established their autonomy and created alternatives for themselves and their children.

Accompaniment demands an active presence that listens and helps communities explore possibilities in greater depth. It means listening and reflecting together. In many cases, accompaniment has led to a deeper understanding of situations that the armed groups do not want mentioned: the thousands of murders that communities have been forbidden to talk about or even mourn. Accompaniment has also involved the collective establishment of dialogue, taking advantage of pastoral space to pray and remember the people who have been disappeared or killed and were not buried at the time, because the armed groups prohibited it.

Reconciliation requires a new kind of communication made possible by community accompaniment. This new kind of communication, which recognizes the value of historical truth, can distinguish among the different types of truth in a peace process. It identifies and calls by name what heretofore could not be named.

In accompaniment, questions arise that must be addressed through community discernment and dialogue. These involve identifying and defining victims and perpetrators. In many cases, victims have become involved over

---

[18] Statement by the Eighty-Second Plenary Assembly of Bishops, "The Church's Commitment in the Face of the Challenges of Current Events," Bogotá, February 9, 2007.

time in actions that turn them into perpetrators, and many perpetrators also claim to be victims. In the long-term process, communities seek opportunities for reflection and clarification of such complex situations.

Encounter in a Country of Regions

Progress is also being made in encounters within the church—encounters that are characterized by regional diversity. These consultations include many voices from the academic world, other religious denominations, civil society, and the world in general. There are various ideas, even among the armed groups, about how to address Colombia's regional complexity. Our question has been, why not envision a new form of regionalization based on peace and reconciliation?

Colombia is a country of regions, and the quest for solutions must embrace its regional diversity and richness. Various regional peacebuilding models have emerged, including development and peace programs that have given rise to regional peace laboratories with an inclusive model for grassroots participation in planning and development initiatives.

When the Conference of Bishops has examined the causes of the conflict in Colombia, it has often questioned the development model that has been followed for decades and that has resulted in the exclusion of sectors of society and the concentration of wealth and power. Consequently, building a lasting peace will require regional and local proposals for development that are inclusive and characterized by solidarity. In the discussion of possibilities for peace, one step in peacebuilding that has emerged is the integration of the regional and the local. The political divisions in the country are arbitrary and obey criteria that do not reflect cultural identity, social realities, or historical needs. The country must redesign its regions to be more dynamic expressions of citizen participation and representation.

The process launched by the Social Ministry to help redefine regions has involved discussions of regional history and identity and the impact of conflicts. Based on work with displaced populations, we have seen how the regional dynamic has changed in recent years. We have also seen the need to continue building a vision for the regionalization of the country. The issue of regions and their participation in ongoing processes remains key for the church in building citizenship for peace. Many of the actions begun in the area of peacebuilding have been conceived as an expression of a regional problem, as well as an opportunity to draw together regional communities to create a climate that will allow people to live in peace.

The development and peace programs that began in the Magdalena Medio region under the leadership of the Barrancabermeja Diocese are a good example of the regions' potential for reconstructing the social fabric to foster inclusion and development. The key has been to view development as the starting point for long-term peace processes. The work has begun with dialogue about major issues in a region characterized by violence and poverty to develop a vision shared by all inhabitants of the region, setting goals by which people take ownership of their destiny and these processes. Development and peace programs have spread throughout the country and have given rise to organized community groups and the peace laboratories.

Journeying amid Hope and Cries for Justice

In 1996, after a series of reflections on how to respond to the suffering of communities dispersed throughout the country because of attacks on villages—and especially because of the humanitarian crisis in the department of Antioquia and the region of Urabá—the National Social Ministry Secretariat began a great march for peace in Colombia: the National Way of the Cross for Life, Justice, and Peace. For seven years, the Way of the Cross journeyed through the country with a huge cross that represented the people's pain and their longing for resurrection and life. It was basically a regional activity that made it possible to identify problems and raise the cry of those who suffered from multiple atrocities and had not been acknowledged by Colombian society. Along the way, Colombians made regional commitments to the defense of human rights, the construction of a just and negotiated peace, and reconciliation—including reparations for victims who appeared and were present throughout the Way of the Cross—as the long-term way to peace.

More than an isolated action or event, the Way of the Cross was envisioned as a broad process that enabled people to mobilize in support of a negotiated solution to the conflict, in solidarity with all those who have suffered and been made invisible by the perpetrators and society. In this way, the communal commitment took on a permanent, self-renewing dynamic that united communities, social organizations participating in the Way of the Cross at the national level, and the efforts of the entire Colombian church.

Along with the Way of the Cross, the Schools for Peace and Coexistence, promoted by the Society of Jesus and the National Social Ministry Secretariat, have had a major regional impact. These were originally called Mobile Human Rights Schools, but because of the danger that association with human rights studies represented for many people, they were renamed. It seemed that the mere term "human rights" had a dangerous connotation and became part of that which could not be named.

The Schools for Peace and Coexistence have paved the way for communal reflection on each community's potential for defending human dignity and building peace. This process begins with the contribution that each human being can make to peace and dignity at the personal, local, and community levels.

Formation and action require ongoing, in-depth peacebuilding processes. The church responded to this need with a Reconciliation Mission that journeyed through the same regions that the Way of the Cross had traversed, gathering hopes and plans that arose in the wake of the pilgrimage.

Communities

Throughout these decades of conflict, fear and defenselessness have marked the lives of many communities in Colombia. In many cases, bombings, threats, and wounds have engraved themselves onto the people's memories. Nonetheless, individuals have sought to rebuild relationships and propose ways to protect their dignity and ensure their survival.

Priests and church workers in the areas most battered by the violence often speak of "the communities." The term may refer to those who live in close proximity and face common problems, but "communities" especially refers to those who have a common vision of the future that involves their ability to build something new, make a contribution, and forge new paths together. The communities that try to resist the violence have engaged throughout the years in a complex process of analysis and preparation of in-depth proposals and plans, both as part of the peace ministry and in regional peacebuilding. Communities of various types are working actively for peace in their regions—some as peace communities, others as communities in resistance, and others as peace territories. Communities of resistance have taken multiple forms and have often been encouraged by the local diocese. The church has tried to ensure that many communities throughout the country distance themselves from the armed groups and plan a future in which each person's dignity and the communities' ability to contribute to peace and reconciliation are recognized. Through dialogue and a close relationship with the communities of resistance, the church has encouraged discussion on how to maintain a distance from the irregular armed groups while envisioning alternatives and drawing up proposals to safeguard the lives of community members, so that they can remain on their land and become part of the quest for peace at the regional and national levels.

Throughout the years, dioceses, religious communities, and church workers who have accompanied at-risk communities in both the countryside and the city have raised difficult questions: Should the church remain neutral? Should it take sides? How can it combine the prophetic role of denouncing violence, whatever the source, with being a builder of peace and reconciliation?

In many cases, these communities have chosen to abide by principles of autonomy and independence mentioned in documents by the Conference of Bishops, such as "Peace Ministry in the Current Situation of Armed Conflict in Colombia."[19]

---

[19]Conferencia Episcopal de Colombia, "Pastoral para la paz en la actual situación de conflicto armado en Colombia. Declaración final de la Reunión General de Obispos," Bogotá, March 13, 1998.

To gather the communities' experiences, the National Social Ministry Secretariat has convened congresses of reconciliation. The congresses of reconciliation bring together significant experiences of peace and reconciliation at the local, regional, and national levels. A great variety of viewpoints and practical visions have been discussed with victims; they include proposals for dialogue among citizens and peacebuilding efforts in the public sphere. Besides their thematic areas and formal presentations, these meetings provide a privileged opportunity for learning from the communities' experiences.

The third such gathering, in 2005, discussed how justice should be understood in processes of negotiation with armed groups. It was a rich encounter that reflected efforts to consistently apply the principles of truth, justice, and reparation as well as major international principles. It also provided the opportunity to debate the position of church workers regarding the juridical framework to make peace a reality throughout the country, with broad participation by the victims.

In August 2008, a fourth reconciliation conference was convened under the theme, "Development is the new name for peace." Each of these national conferences has been centered on key themes for the life of the country—such as justice, truth, and the conditions for achieving a sustainable, just peace.

International Support

The initiatives developed by the Colombian church have received widespread support from international organizations, especially from Caritas International's "Peace in Colombia Is Possible" campaign. This campaign has mobilized thousands of people around the world through Caritas organizations in each country. The campaign's message highlights two concepts of the Colombian church—namely, that peace will be attained through negotiations and that it will be made lasting through social justice.

Situations of serious conflict always require international solidarity that is made visible through visits, encounters, and direct relationships with the affected communities. Caritas International's campaign has enabled parliamentary groups and personalities from Europe and the United States to visit the regions afflicted by serious violations of human rights and international humanitarian law. This form of solidarity underscores the enormous challenge of doing pastoral work amid a complex conflict with multiple facets and shows that peacebuilding is a global issue.

The Journey Forward

Peacebuilding efforts in Colombia have produced many lessons for the church and for the people of Colombia. The lessons learned shed light on the demands of the long journey toward the goal of creating a world that lives in peace with social justice. First, we see the urgency of strengthening civil society and we see its ability to generate processes of local and regional transformation with high impact. The processes of citizen dialogue between the Colombian government, the international community, and civil society have helped to strengthen participation in the construction of a model of a country capable of overcoming the errors of the past. Second, local communities, especially faith-based communities, have the capacity to identify the pain of the victims and to reach out to them until the social fabric is mended. Within this communitarian exercise, it is worth underscoring the value of the commitment to recover memory and the truth of events that happened in the past. Members of the displaced communities and the "communities in resistance" are the ones who have most assisted in the search for truth and justice. By the same token, when these communities can express themselves freely, without pressure or manipulation by illegal armed groups, democracy is enriched. Third, working in the long term on processes of reparation for the victims and the restitution of goods that were seized during the conflict is important. Reparation is an essential step on the path toward reconciliation. There is still a long way to be traveled, but the sectors that have participated in peacebuilding processes have actively supported the need for reparation of the victims. Finally, not only the population of Colombia, but all of humanity, is suffering, which is why the commitment of the international community is so important. If we want to have a peace that lasts in Colombia, the local, regional, national, and international levels each have a role to play.

10

Business and Peace in Colombia
Responses, Challenges, and Achievements

Angelika Rettberg

Introduction

As suggested by the experience of other countries, the likelihood for peace to be built and consolidated in Colombia depends significantly on the domestic private sector's willingness to share the peacebuilding burden.[1] The Colombian private sector, often criticized for favoring strong-arm approaches or for remaining uninvolved in the solution to social problems, has in fact become increasingly involved in peacebuilding in several Colombian regions. This is demonstrated by the experience of Indupalma (a palm oil producer in the central Magdalena River Valley), Vallenpaz (a business-supported organization operating in the city of Cali and neighboring municipalities), and Entretodos (a splinter initiative of a private-sector think tank in Medellín).[2] Against a shared background of conflict,

Research underlying this paper was supported by grants from the Crisis States Programme of DESTIN, of the London School of Economics and Politics, and from the Colombian Institute of Science and Technology (COLCIENCIAS). Research was also supported by the Political Science Department at Universidad de los Andes. Preliminary versions of this chapter were presented at the meeting of the International Studies Association (ISA) in Honolulu on March 4, 2005, and at the Peace Initiatives in Colombia Conference at Cornell University, November 18–19, 2005. For comments, I am grateful to Virginia Bouvier, Enrique Chaux, Jonathan DiJohn, Jean Paul Faguet, Gary Hoskin, Francisco Leal, and Ann Mason. For research assistance, I thank Catalina Arreaza, Sebastián Bitar, Ana María Bustos, Marcela Jaramillo, Allison González, and Camilo Vargas.

[1] See Jean Paul Azam, David Bevan, Paul Collier, Stefan Dercon, Jan Gunning, and Sanjay Pradhan, *Some Economic Consequences of the Transition from Civil War to Peace* (Washington, D.C.: World Bank, 1994); Allan Gerson, "Peace Building: The Private Sector's Role," *American Journal of International Law* 95, no. 1 (January 2001): 102–19; and Angelika Rettberg, "Local Business and the Political Dimensions of Peacebuilding," in *Business and Peace—Unlocking the Peacebuilding Potential of Local Economic Actors*, eds. Jessica Banfield, Canan Gündüz, and Nick Killick (London: International Alert, 2006), 38–72.

[2] For a detailed description of each of these initiatives, see Angelika Rettberg, "Business-Led Peacebuilding in Colombia: Fad or Future of a Country in Crisis?" (research report,

these initiatives are investing time and resources in institution building;
supporting community organization; improving local governance; supporting education, employment, and peaceful conflict-resolution programs;
and promoting productivity and wealth creation. The initiatives described
here share the perception that peace extends beyond the silence of the
guns, but they differ in terms of where they draw the line between peace
and development.[3]

This chapter argues that business-led peacebuilding, while more an exception than the norm in the Colombian corporate response to conflict, represents innovative and quite pragmatic solutions to the specific needs of domestic companies faced with the local manifestations of conflict. In this sense,
this chapter suggests that it may be in the private sector's best self-interest to
support peace initiatives. This is good news for policymakers, since it widens
the pool of potential private-sector peacebuilding partners.

Business, Peace, and Conflict in Colombia

Until the mid-1990s, Colombian business surveys showed that conflict occupied a low spot on the list of concerns. Not surprisingly, most entrepreneurs
remained indifferent to efforts to end conflict by negotiated means during
the 1980s.[4] Only beginning in the 1990s did conflict encroach on business
interests in a significant way. National Planning Department estimates suggest that from 1991 to 1996, the conflict cost the country between 2 and 4 GDP
points per year and that in 2003 this figure rose to more than 7 percent of
GDP.[5] Business operations are likewise negatively affected by the regular destruction of infrastructure such as roads and energy and communication

September 13, 2004), http://www.crisisstates.com/download/projectnotes/rettberg.pdf (accessed August 27, 2008).

[3] For a broad review of corporate social responsibility practice in Colombia and how it relates
peace efforts to general private-sector social involvement, see Angelika Rettberg, "De la filan-
tropía a la responsabilidad social empresarial en Colombia: Una transición incipiente e in-
completa," in *Empresarios, política y responsabilidad social*, ed. Felipe Agüero (Santiago, Chile:
FLACSO and Editorial Catalonia, forthcoming 2009).

[4] See Angelika Rettberg, "The Business of Peace in Colombia: Assessing the Role of the Business Community in the Colombian Peace Process" (paper presented at the annual meeting of
the Latin American Studies Association, Dallas, Texas, March 26–31, 2003), http://lasa.inter
national.pitt.edu/Lasa2003/RettbergAngelika.pdf.

[5] See Martha Elena Badel and Edgar Trujillo, *Informe especial: Los costos económicos de la crimi-
nalidad y la violencia en Colombia: 1991–1996*, Colección Archivos de Macroeconomía, Document
76 (Bogotá: Departamento Nacional de Planeación, March 1998); Mauricio Rubio, *Los costos de
la violencia en Colombia* (Bogotá: Documentos CEDE, Universidad de los Andes, no. 11, 1997);
María Eugenia Pinto, Andrés Vergara, and Yilberto Lahuerta, "¿Cuánto ha perdido Colombia
por el conflicto?" *Cuartillas de Economía* no. 19 (Bogotá, Departamento Nacional de Planeación,
2004); and María Eugenia Pinto, Ivette María Altamar, Yilberto Lahuerta, and Luis Fernando
Cepeda, *El secuestro en Colombia: Caracterización y costos económicos*, Archivos de Economía,
Document 257 (Bogotá: Departamento Nacional de Planeación, June 9, 2004).

towers.[6] In addition, between 1996 and 2002, the number of kidnappings went up 85.7 percent,[7] and specifically those targeting the business community.[8] The private sector also faces other types of extortion from illegal armed actors. Refusal to pay has effectively prevented Colombian companies from distributing their goods in a hundred different municipalities nationwide.[9] Business has also been pressed hard for resources by the government. Since the mid-1990s, the state has collected billions of dollars from companies in security taxes and bonds.[10]

The cost of conflict to business has an important international dimension. Potential investors have been deterred by Colombia's high-risk rating (whereby investments in a given country are conditioned on the payment of extra interest on foreign loans to lending institutions to compensate investors for the added risk—for example, in a situation of armed conflict). Insecurity consistently ranks among foreign and Colombian companies' prime concerns, leading companies to spend 4 to 6 percent of their budgets on protection of their staff, equipment, and operations.[11] As should become clear to the private sector overall, the long-standing Colombian conflict has turned into a liability affecting the country's competitiveness in the region and worldwide.

Business has often been accused of indifference in the face of the escalating Colombian conflict.[12] In fact, business has produced a range of quite different, often overlapping responses. Most domestic companies have remained passive, internalizing conflict as one additional operational cost.[13] As

---

[6] Ministerio de Defensa Nacional, *Informe anual de Derechos Humanos y Derecho Internacional Humanitario 2002 y avances período presidencial 2003* (Bogotá, August 2003).

[7] Dirección de Justicia y Seguridad, Departamento Nacional de Planeación, "Costos de la paz y de la guerra," at www.dnp.gov.co/02_sec/justicia/justi.htm (accessed February 21, 2002).

[8] See Pinto, *El secuestro en Colombia*; and Jason Webb, "What Price Freedom? Kidnap Insurers Have an Answer," *Reuters*, May 15, 2003.

[9] See "Bloqueo por la '002,'" *Portafolio*, June 26, 2001.

[10] From 1994 until February of 2002 the Colombian state collected over four billion in constant 1994 U.S. dollars in the form of security taxes and bonds. See Presidencia de la República, "Informe de la Veeduría Especial. Bonos de Solidaridad para la Paz. Ley 487 de 1998" (September 2002), www.contraloriagen.gov.co:8081/internet/central_doc/Archivos/63/plan%20colombia%203.pdf (accessed September 17, 2008). Overall, tax collection has enjoyed widespread support. See Juan Forero, "Burdened Colombians Back Tax to Fight Rebels," *New York Times*, September 8, 2002.

[11] See Corporación Invertir en Colombia (Coinvertir), *Obstáculos y oportunidades para la inversión extranjera en Colombia* (Bogotá: Departamento Nacional de Planeación, 2000); "Few Friends Left for Colombia's Peace Talks," *Economist*, December 14, 2000. According to the president of the Association of Industry, Luis Carlos Villegas, 2.7 percent of company sales are invested in security. Colombian News Broadcast, December 17, 2002.

[12] For example, James LeMoyne, the adviser for Colombia to the secretary-general of the United Nations, pointed out the Colombian elites' high levels of tax evasion and their lack of support for social reform. See "El regaño de Lemoyne," *Portafolio*, May 20, 2003; and "La Frase," *Portafolio*, May 20, 2003.

[13] See Juan Carlos Echeverry, *Las claves del futuro: Economía y conflicto en Colombia* (Bogotá: Editorial Oveja Negra, 2002).

documented by the General Prosecutor's Office, many companies are involved in the financing of private militias and paramilitary groups.[14] These links were brought home by revelations regarding the conflictual relationship of business and paramilitary "protection" in the Drummond (coal mining) and Chiquita (bananas) cases.[15] Some companies have identified opportunities provided by the conflict to increase sales, as demonstrated by the boom of private security and insurance companies.[16] Many have engaged in capital flight, as reported by the president of the Bogotá stock exchange.[17] Some business members and associations took part in negotiations during the Pastrana government's peace talks.[18] One of these business responses to conflict has been an increased interest in seeking ways to precipitate an end to conflict. The underlying rationale appears simple: as one Colombian executive observed, "peace is better business."[19]

Three Cases of Business-Led Peacebuilding in Colombia

Because seeking ways to precipitate an end to conflict is still a minority response by the Colombian private sector, this section analyzes three cases in which companies have chosen to engage in peacebuilding and teases out the additional factors that are shaping businesses' preferences for business-led peacebuilding.

Vallenpaz (Valle and Cauca Departments)

A mix of recession and conflict provided the impetus for the founding of the Corporation for the Development and Peace of the Valle and Cauca departments (Vallenpaz), a business initiative led by former Cali mayor Rodrigo Guerrero aimed at supporting and rebuilding local state institutions and promoting socioeconomic development in guerrilla strongholds in the neighboring Valle and Cauca regions. Beginning in the mid-1990s, Colombia, and the Valle Department specifically, witnessed a severe economic crisis. In addition, an increase in kidnappings by leftist guerrillas reflected attacks specifically targeting the economic establishment.

---

[14] As documented in several ongoing legal processes that draw from information obtained from police searches in the Córdoba and Valle del Cauca departments. See "Cacería a finanzas paras," *El Tiempo*, May 25, 2001.

[15] "Banana 'para-republic,'" *Semana*, March 17, 2007; "Abren investigación a Chiquita y otras fruteras por pagos a paramilitares," *Noticias RCN*, April 30, 2008; "Oscuridad en la mina," *Semana*, March 24, 2007.

[16] "Los ejecutivos se atrincheran," *Portafolio*, September 16, 2002: 10.

[17] See Angelika Rettberg, "Administrando la adversidad: Respuestas empresariales al conflicto colombiano," *Colombia Internacional* 55 (January–July 2002): 37–54.

[18] See Angelika Rettberg, "Is Peace Your Business? The Private Sector and Peace Talks in Colombia," *Iberoamericana* 11 (September 2003): 196–201.

[19] President of Colombian Association of Retailers, interview by the author, Bogotá, 2002.

Guerrero and his supporters attributed violence to rampant poverty and state neglect in specific areas of the country.[20] In addition, they viewed poverty as a limit to growth. For both reasons, business-led intervention was perceived to be necessary to regain a business-friendly climate. In the words of one Vallenpaz member, Vallenpaz and other forms of corporate social responsibility represent "an insurance for personal safety."[21]

Vallenpaz's interventions are focused on 2,500 families in thirteen neighboring municipalities deeply engulfed in conflict and poverty.[22] Projects focus on promoting sustainable development in agricultural products. They require community organization and participation and offer privileged access to commercial networks provided by Vallenpaz associates.

In the absence of substantial financial support from regional business players, resources have been raised increasingly from institutional and international donors. Crucial to Vallenpaz's success in raising funds has been the positive reputation and connections of its founder and current director, Rodrigo Guerrero. In addition to serving as mayor of Cali from 1992 to 1994, Guerrero was also the director and founder of the Fundación Carvajal, one of the most reputable national philanthropic foundations, and was the former coordinator of the social component of Plan Colombia.

Guerrero's political and negotiating skills can also be partially credited with (so far) effective bargaining with local guerrilla leaders for Vallenpaz's entry into the areas under Fuerzas Armadas Revolucionarias de Colombia (FARC) and Ejército de Liberación Nacional (ELN) control and with protection against attacks by these groups. In each region, project initiation has been preceded by contacts with local insurgent commanders to seek approval and avoid delays.

Vallenpaz neatly reflects the impact of rising costs of conflict (actual and perceived) on business's willingness to engage in peacebuilding. As documented above, the sudden increase in the cost of conflict for Valle and Cauca businesses made an already unfriendly economic environment unbearable and explains widespread support of a local initiative to seek an end to conflict, with the added incentive that this initiative would specifically target areas where affected businesses operate, as opposed to, for example, nationwide approaches.

Vallenpaz points to the importance of the learning process in generating the business initiatives under study. Guerrero's diverse professional experience has provided him with the needed know-how, credibility, and contacts both for attracting local business and for negotiating with armed actors in

---

[20] Vallenpaz member no. 1, interview by the author, Cali, 2002.

[21] Vallenpaz member no. 2, interview by the author, Cali, 2004.

[22] Red Nacional de Programas Regionales de Desarrollo Integral y Paz (REDPRODEPAZ), www.redprodepaz.org/programas.shtml?x=44552 (accessed September 17, 2008).

the target regions. Similarly, some of the most active member companies have led philanthropic organizations and, thus, have institutional experience and know-how with corporate social responsibility (CSR) practices.

Third, Vallenpaz reflects the impact of company-specific traits on business-led peacebuilding: most participants are medium-size, fixed-asset (mostly agricultural) companies, which are not only context-dependent but context-specific. Few have the option to exit from the economy as a strategy when they are faced with conflict. Given their size, they are also not nationally prominent business players with the capacity to exert pressure on policy-making in conflict management; their choices are limited to locally based approaches. In the case of Vallenpaz, this choice was made easier by the ability to ride on the benefits of peacebuilding financed mainly by external—not their own—resources.

Indupalma (Middle Magdalena River Valley)

Indupalma, one of the largest companies in the palm oil extraction business, is located in the Middle Magdalena River region, long a hot spot in Colombia's violent geography.[23] Its more than ten thousand hectares of palm plantations supply the national market in fats and contribute significantly to Colombia's exports.[24] Indupalma and its host municipality, San Alberto, illustrate one more twist of Colombian business reactions faced with conflict.

Indupalma's relationship with conflict dates back almost to its founding in the 1950s, when forced colonization of the region and repressive labor practices put the company at the center of numerous disputes with its workers as well as with local guerrillas.[25] In 1977, after threats to kidnap company executives had been followed by the kidnapping of the general manager, the company signed a far-reaching labor agreement with its workers. While the agreement overcame the company's historical deficit in the recognition of workers' legal entitlements such as contract stability and health benefits, it also laid the foundations for a deep structural crisis in the company, since expenditures outweighed income, productivity was low, and possibilities for diversification were limited.

The late 1980s and early 1990s painfully brought home the need to seek drastic solutions. Beginning in 1988, the international price of palm oil dropped sharply while trade liberalization opened the national market to

---

[23] See Manuel Alberto Alonso, *Conflicto armado y configuración regional: El caso del Magdalena Medio* (Medellín: Universidad de Antioquia, 1997).

[24] Rubén Darío Lizarralde, general manager of Indupalma, interview by the author, Bogotá, 2004.

[25] See Diana Fernández, Diana Trujillo, and Roberto Gutiérrez, "Indupalma (A1): Los primeros años, 1961–1977" (case study, Social Enterprise Knowledge Network, Business School, Universidad de los Andes, May 13, 2003).

competition from foreign producers.[26] In addition, the constant threat to Indupalma staff and products caused the company to "spend 2.000 million pesos (around 900,000 dollars) per year on security and equipment . . . an important percentage of the company's income," says Rubén Darío Lizarralde, the president of Indupalma.[27]

Climbing costs of conflict and economic hardship confronted the company with the possibility of bankruptcy. Fearing that the company would close, some workers chose early retirement, and others agreed to give up some of their benefits. But even these measures proved insufficient. In what became the backbone for Indupalma's present corporate model, in 1995, the company outsourced most of its production process to its former workers in the form of cooperatives. In exchange for the commitment to buy its output (palm oil beans), Indupalma sold equipment and seeds to the cooperatives and acted as guarantor for credits allowing cooperatives to buy land. Also, the company provided training in areas including software use, accounting, strategic planning, social insurance regimes, and successful leadership practices.[28] In the period from 1995 to 1999, nineteen such cooperatives, comprising 980 workers, were founded.

Contracting out to workers allowed the company to concentrate on its core business—exporting palm oil—while shedding its labor burden, solving problems with the union, generating local goodwill, and improving its production environment. Workers gained in that they kept their jobs and income, received training, and became property owners. Quality is ensured by the company through the periodic renewal of contracts, which are crucially important in San Alberto, where one-third of the population contracts directly or indirectly with the company and where most derive at least some of their income from its presence in the town.[29]

The project is consistent with the company's peacebuilding rhetoric, which centers on promoting wealth creation and forming an entrepreneurial community—turning peasants into entrepreneurs—as the solution to both economic hardship and conflict in the region. The company's institutional presentation leaves no doubt: "Our prime interest is economical: profit."[30]

Conflict levels have plummeted. Homicides in San Alberto dropped from forty-four per year in 1990 to only eight in 2002, with the sharpest drop

---

[26] See Miguel Fadul, *Alianzas por la paz: El modelo Indupalma* (Bogotá: Programa Nacional de Alianzas para la Convivencia y la Superación de la Pobreza, 2001).

[27] Rubén Darío Lizarralde, general manager of Indupalma, interview by the author, Bogotá, 2004.

[28] See Indupalma, Departamento de Planeamiento y Control, "Indupalma S.A. ¡Sigue adelante!" (institutional PowerPoint presentation, 2000, Bogotá). Workers who fail to attend training sessions are fined.

[29] See Fadul, *Alianzas por la paz: El modelo Indupalma*.

[30] See Indupalma, "Lo social paga" (institutional presentation, 2001).

occurring from 1996 (thirty-eight) to 1997 (five). The drop was also reflected in the homicide rate per 100,000 inhabitants in San Alberto, which decreased from 296 in 1990 to 46 in 2002.[31] However, while guerrillas retreated from the region and have ceased to represent a threat to the company and its workers, the void has since been filled by rightist paramilitary groups. This leaves open the question whether violence has decreased because of company efforts or because the guerrillas have been chased out and the paramilitaries are now in charge. For his safety, Indupalma's general manager can only make unannounced visits, and worker cooperatives, once only under guerrilla pressure, now face new threats from the right, a situation that has been sustained until today.

On the economic side, Indupalma's initiative shows more encouraging results: according to company managers, productivity has climbed since implementation of the cooperative model, and the company has managed to expand its plantations up to a total of 10,345 hectares (25,606.4 acres).[32] In addition, the region has experienced economic recovery; workers can make US$300 per month, three times the minimum salary.

The Indupalma cooperative model neatly illustrates the strong link between the costs of conflict (actual and perceived), economic hardship, and a company's decision to engage in radically innovative strategies. The company would probably have collapsed in the absence of the profound restructuring effort. Hit hard by armed actors (first the guerrillas and then the paramilitaries), rich in fixed assets, extremely immobile, context specific, and highly vulnerable to international price fluctuations and market conditions, Indupalma had limited options. It was not in a position to exit—or threaten to exit—from the regional economy, nor was it big enough to force a protective response by the weak Colombian state. Corporate innovation—in this case, with a peacebuilding twist—thus became a feasible course of action.

Entretodos (Medellín)

At the beginning of the 1990s, the city of Medellín was the epicenter of urban violence in Colombia, with a homicide rate above 230 per 100,000 inhabitants, topping the list of most violent cities in the world.[33] Poor Medellín youth served as mercenaries of the drug mafias and were also becoming increas-

[31] Centro de Estudios sobre Desarrollo Económico (CEDE), Universidad de los Andes, database on conflict, crime, and political violence, 2005.

[32] See Rubén Darío Lizarralde, "Visión prospectiva de Indupalma S.A.," downloaded from the Centro de Pensamiento Estratégico y Prospectiva, Business School (Universidad Externado de Colombia, 2004), http://administracion.uexternado.edu.co/centros/pensamiento/matdi/Visi%C3%B3n%20Prospectiva%20de%20Indupalma.doc (accessed February 21, 2002).

[33] See María Victoria Llorente and Angela Rivas, "An Overview of Crime and the Criminal Justice System in Colombia," in Project on Latin American Criminal Justice Systems, eds. Tedd Leggett and Lucía Dammert (draft manuscript, February 20, 2004).

ingly attracted to urban factions of the leftist guerrillas and the rightist self-defense groups.[34]

The persistence of violence in the city, and its cost to business in terms of safety and productivity—especially its cost in economic performance—kept concern over violence high. Prior business initiatives in conflict resolution had been unsuccessful. In the early 1990s, for example, an attempt by the Colombian presidency to enlist private-sector support for local demobilization programs aimed at leftist militias, in the form of job creation and training for disenfranchised youth, failed.[35] On one hand, the lack of technical skills and poor work ethic among the militia youth turned them into a burden for companies. On the other hand, administration officials and youth criticized companies for providing only menial jobs requiring little training and responsibility and for failing to fulfill expectations of better incomes. In response, many former militia members gave up their jobs and resumed criminal activity, sometimes targeting their recent employers. Rumors spread in the business community that access to the companies and inside information had provided the former militia combatants with information they now filtered to kidnappers and thieves for purposes of extortion.[36]

When neither violence nor the economic crisis subsided, in 1996, a local business think tank and foundation, the Fundación para el Desarrollo de Antioquia (Proantioquia), or Foundation for Development of Antioquia, made a new attempt to include the private sector in local solutions to conflict, by founding Entretodos (literally, "among all"), a program inspired by corporate social responsibility principles and intended to promote peaceful coexistence (*convivencia*) in the city of Medellín. Proantioquia's members include some of the region's largest and oldest companies, many of which run philanthropic foundations.

Few of these companies had been specific targets of violence. In this sense, Entretodos was more a preventive initiative in a context of generalized and increasing violence than a response to an explicit attack. Still, the need for investing in peace as a measure of protection was intense. In the words of Entretodos's founder, "The question was clear; they [Entretodos members] came and asked, 'What do I need to do so they don't plant a bomb [in my office or factory]?' . . . Shall I bring in the army, or do I build six schools?"[37]

Lowering citywide levels of violence with a comprehensive program to promote conflict resolution and good governance overall became Entretodos's

---

[34] See Carlos Miguel Ortiz, "El sicariato en Medellín: Entre la violencia política y el crimen organizado," *Análisis Político* 14 (September–December 1991): 60–73.

[35] See Presidencia de la República, Dirección del Programa Presidencial para Medellín y su Área Metropolitana, *Medellín, reencuentro con el futuro*, 1991.

[36] Former adviser for the Consejería para Medellín, interview by the author, Medellín, 2001.

[37] Former executive director of Entretodos, interview by the author, Medellín, 2004.

goal. With the participation of non-governmental organizations (NGOs), the Catholic Church, the police, and the mayor's office, businesspeople designed the broad-based Programa de Seguridad y Convivencia Ciudadana (PSCC), or Security and Peaceful Coexistence Program. Central to the proposal was the belief that "peace and coexistence are the best investment to make social development and economic growth possible."[38] Their goal was to turn *convivencia* into local public policy's main goal. The integral proposal included the creation of a "violence observatory," programs for the prevention of violence in early childhood, programs for the resocialization of violent and criminal youth, and preventive work with families in violent neighborhoods. In all, member companies perceived the PSCC as a "strategic contribution to the city," which would pay a social debt, boost the city's productivity, and serve as protection against future violent deterioration.[39] Thus, hopes ran high when Mayor-elect Juan Gómez Martínez (1998–2000) committed to turning the PSCC into his administration's flagship program. The Inter-American Development Bank committed US$15 million, providing an important boost to the project.

But once the new administration was in office, Medellín's public bureaucracy took control of the program, delayed implementation, modified the project's components and its integral approach, and refused to meet and consult with Entretodos members. This caused Entretodos members and public officials to clash, reflecting the discrepancies between the world of business and the world of politics—where negotiation and compromise, rather than productivity and efficiency, reigned supreme. As a result, Entretodos's companies retreated into their own organizations and gave up trying to affect policy and promote good governance. Instead, they reoriented the project to focus on their workers and only a few target populations, such as youth, and on productive linkages in peripheral areas of town. As a result, while several components of the program remain in operation, Entretodos's project failed to turn into a citywide initiative. The organization's director now claims to be directly or indirectly targeting thirty thousand people in the workplace and the community (only 1.5 percent of Medellín's total population of approximately two million, the original target group of the *convivencia* program).[40]

Entretodos stands out as a difficult effort to coordinate public and private goals. In part, this failure was due to the nature of the project itself. "They [businesspeople involved in peacebuilding] need to be doing things that resemble what they normally do," said a former adviser for Medellín to the president of Colombia.[41] Designing a citywide program for *convivencia* in this

---

[38] Entretodos institutional presentation folder.

[39] Former executive director of Entretodos, interview by the author, Medellín, 2004.

[40] Ibid.

[41] Former presidential adviser, interview by the author, 2002.

case distracted companies from their core activities, failed to build on and complement company expertise, and required a significant investment of time and resources, which, when compounded by the red tape of public bureaucracy, soon caused it to run out of steam.

In addition to the bureaucratic hassles, the fact that Entretodos's members had largely been spared by local conflict helps explain the organization's narrowing the citywide scope of its *convivencia* program to more company-specific CSR activity. In the absence of direct threats, the need to pursue and persist with city-centered peacebuilding was not perceived as urgent. In fact, the Entretodos initiative closed in 2005, while its home organization, Proantioquia, is seeking to strengthen its research and public-policy impact capacity.

As in previous cases, Entretodos's most active members built on their autonomous CSR activities. In this sense, their institutional trajectories both facilitated their decision to promote citywide peaceful coexistence and provided an appropriate infrastructure to continue their work after their frustrating encounter with the municipal administration. In this way, institutional know-how in CSR provided an adequate basis for transforming while maintaining—instead of ending—member companies' commitment to addressing problems of their social environment. Today this is reflected in the participation of some of Entretodos's former member companies in state-sponsored demobilization and reintegration programs.

Finally, Entretodos's experience is important because it illustrates the many choices business has when faced with conflict. In the words of Entretodos's director, despite their commitment to peacebuilding, "[companies] will not stop paying for security or getting insurance against a bombing attack. . . . Nobody is as naive as to think that by building schools you avoid an attack on your factory."[42] This assertion puts peacebuilding as a private-sector response to conflict in perspective by underscoring the dispassionate assessment of costs and benefits undertaken even by companies in violent contexts, suggesting that peacebuilding is but one of many possible strategies.

The Context and the Company: Factors Shaping Preferences for Business-Led Peacebuilding

At least two groups of factors appear to explain business-led peacebuilding as a corporate strategy in contexts of conflict. One group of factors relates to context. In the Colombian case, these included an increase in conflict's costs to business, a severe economic downturn, and state absence both in specific regions as well as in key policy areas. In addition to these conditions, company-specific characteristics appear to influence the likelihood for business-led peacebuilding to occur. These factors are company sectoral affiliation, size, mobility, and location; philanthropic background and know-how (which point

---

[42] Former executive director of Entretodos, interview by the author, Medellín, 2004.

at the institutional trajectories and learning processes fostering business-led peacebuilding); and ability to free ride on external—financial and other—resources.

An intensification of conflict costs—actual and perceived, general and specific—was crucial in prompting the business-led peacebuilding initiatives analyzed here. In the case of Vallenpaz, rampant kidnappings, specifically of upper-class citizens, prompted the private-sector reaction in the same way that pressure by leftist guerrillas brought about a profound restructuring process in Indupalma. The urban violence epidemic in Medellín spawned Entretodos's effort to improve local governance.

When combined with bleak economic prospects or economic crisis, conflict costs became increasingly unbearable, as shown by the cases of Indupalma and Vallenpaz. More explicitly with Indupalma than with Vallenpaz, local peacebuilding was a corporate survival strategy, illustrating the potentially creative impact of crises in sparking innovation. In the case of Medellín, there was also a link between economic recession, high conflict costs, and peacebuilding, although local circumstances were less dramatic. All three cases share an expectation, within the business sector involved in peacebuilding, of a clear link between peace and increased productivity, and a corresponding resumption of economic growth.

State absence is the third element of this peacebuilding context trilogy. Without exception, the business-led peace initiatives were a response to the perceived lack of local state presence. Public authorities not only could not provide companies with protection from kidnappings, extortion, and other attacks but were also ineffective at addressing social and economic conditions, and this lack of institutional capacity was perceived to cause local populations to join or support illegal armed actors. Whether addressed explicitly, as with Vallenpaz and Entretodos, or as an indirect result of their actions, as with Indupalma, the business-led peace initiatives compellingly bring home the Colombian state's poor performance in crucial areas such as security and socioeconomic development.

Compounding these contextual factors is a group of more company-specific traits, which illustrate how conflict and economic recession hit companies and sectors differently. Notably, conflict and economic recession were most deeply felt in the two rural cases of Vallenpaz and Indupalma. In contrast, the urban Entretodos members, although concerned with growing conflict levels, had not been direct targets of conflict and reacted more in line with general CSR concerns in a deteriorating social and political environment. In addition to the rural-urban distinction, the smaller the company and the more fixed its assets, the more likely it will be tied to succeeding in the domestic market. Exit or even relocation is an unlikely option for a context-specific company.

In two of the cases examined here, business-led peace initiatives were based on and sustained by the previous philanthropic experience of their member companies. Fundación Carvajal (in the case of Vallenpaz) and the numerous foundations represented among Entretodos's corporate members indicate that the learning process associated with business philanthropy supports and facilitates decisions to engage in peacebuilding. These decisions provide obvious synergies with other aspects of the broader relationship between companies and their social, political, and economic environments while generating institutional capacity and disposition for peacebuilding activity. At the same time, philanthropy is not immune to setbacks, as shown by the Medellín case. Like any other business enterprise, peace initiatives are result dependent and reversible, which points to the importance of early and sustained efforts to improve their viability.

Finally, the ability to "ride along" and diffuse the costs of peacebuilding is an important element of private-sector participation. Most clearly illustrated in the case of Vallenpaz, peace is a public/collective good that provides actors with incentives to take advantage of international cooperation funds, which business initiatives are entrusted with managing. In the absence of a severe threat, or in the presence of improved security conditions, companies will probably abstain from investing resources in peacebuilding—again explaining the absence of business-led peacebuilding with a national scope.

The previous factors not only provide guidelines regarding what motivates business-led peacebuilding but also indicate what may cause peace initiatives to prosper in one place and not another. Clearly, an ongoing perception of threat is an important factor explaining business's commitment to peacebuilding initiatives. The reduction of threat, neatly reflected in the slimming of the public agenda on peace issues ever since violence levels have dropped and the economy has improved, makes it harder to maintain a peacebuilding momentum. Specifically, it has been increasingly hard for business-led peacebuilding promoters to obtain material—rather than merely rhetorical—support from business members. Only in those cases where a potential intensification in conflict looms over local conditions, such as in Valle and the Middle Magdalena River region, does the effort continue.

Also, peacebuilding seems to be more likely to prosper when it addresses issues of direct relevance to involved companies, such as worker training, community relations, strengthening of local distribution networks, and other forms of raising productivity and profitability. Business, after all, has a mandate to be profitable and is generally risk averse; it will not likely engage in peacebuilding behavior where this is unprofitable or unrelated to the business's core activity. As a result, business-led peacebuilding can be only a by-product, not the main purpose of corporate strategy.

Conclusions

This chapter has focused on the impacts of both context and clearly visible company traits to understand Colombian business-led peacebuilding. Specifically, the chapter suggests that context affects businesses faced with conflict in several quite distinct ways, providing constraints and facilitating conditions that make the choice to participate in peacebuilding more or less likely and that underlie organizational learning processes.

Notably, this research suggests that the relationship between business and peace is multifaceted and variable. For example, business-led peace initiatives may be independent of what goes on—or fails to go on—with private-sector participation in formal peace talks. The business initiatives described here continued even in the absence of talks and remain focused on local processes instead of national dialogue. Also, the very different ways in which these initiatives envision and pursue peacebuilding also point to the importance of considering business- and context-related factors that can explain variation.

The chapter offers important lessons for policymakers interested in attracting the private sector to the crucial but difficult peacebuilding task. As should become clear, altruism is only one of the drivers of business involvement in peacebuilding. Awareness of the facilitating conditions described here provides us with insights into how best to engage the private sector in peacebuilding, as widely recommended by the literature, while also pointing out the potential limits and obstacles.

PART III

GENDER AND ETHNIC CONTRIBUTIONS TO PEACEBUILDING

11

Women and Peacebuilding in Colombia
Resistance to War, Creativity for Peace

Catalina Rojas

Women are building a peace constituency within Colombia and creating common agendas that unite Colombians across racial, geographical, and class boundaries and highlight the root causes of the conflict.[1] But Colombian women's organizations for peace are as varied and complex as other civil society groups, raising a number of important questions: What women's groups, networks, and coalitions are working for peace in Colombia? Are they effective? What are their main limitations? And, last and very important, is their work different from that of other civil society groups?

Colombian women's groups are active at all levels of society, from small community associations to regional coalitions of women's groups and national networks such as the National Confluence of Networks (Confluencia Nacional de Redes de Mujeres), an umbrella organization that includes ten national women's networks. It is not possible to include here all the women's organizations that work for peace in Colombia,[2] but it is important to profile several organizations whose work has gained visibility inside the country and, in some cases, abroad, including Organización Femenina Popular (OFP, or Popular Feminine Organization); la Ruta Pacífica de las Mujeres, or the

---

[1] Catalina Rojas, *In the Midst of War: Women's Contributions to Peace in Colombia* (Washington, D.C: Hunt Alternatives Fund, 2004).

[2] For a more complete listing of women's networks, groups, coalitions, research centers, and think tanks that work on women and conflict in Colombia, see Michelle Guttmann and Catalina Rojas with Virginia Lambert, "Gender Assessment USAID Colombia" (report, August 2007, Washington, D.C.), www.devtechsys.com/publications/documents/Genderassessment USAIDColombiaFINAL.pdf (accessed August 28, 2008).

Pacific Route of Women; Red Nacional de Mujeres (RNM, or National Women's Network); Iniciativa de Mujeres por la Paz (IMP, or Women's Peace Initiative); Confluencia Nacional de Redes de Mujeres (National Confluence of Women's Networks); Mesa Nacional de Concertación de Mujeres (National Working Group on Women's Consensus); Mesa de Trabajo Mujer y Conflicto Armado (Women and Armed Conflict Working Group); Movimiento Nacional de Mujeres Autoras y Actoras de Paz (National Movement of Women Authors and Actors for Peace); Madres y Familiares de Miembros de la Fuerza Pública, Retenidos y Liberados por Grupos Guerrilleros (Mothers and Relatives of Members of the Public Forces Captured and Released by Guerrilla Groups); and Liga de Mujeres Desplazadas por la Violencia en Bolívar (League of Women Displaced by Violence in Bolívar).[3]

Such groups illustrate the range and diversity of women's peace groups. First, they employ a variety of methodologies. Some direct advocacy efforts to raise awareness and ensure the rights and needs of victims. Others cooperate and work with international organizations to create the conditions for future negotiations. Some work alongside grassroots community leaders to prevent further displacement in conflict-ridden areas, or document and analyze the effects of the conflict on women and children. Others promote theater, concerts, and other cultural expressions; organize public debates; disseminate reports; and participate in decision making related to issues affecting women, peace, security, and reconciliation.

Second, the majority of these organizations and networks actively work with community-based organizations in war-affected regions. Although not all women's organizations for peace are included here, most of the major ones are likely to be part of the many networks and associations described in this chapter.

Third, the groups described herein embody the diversity of class, age, ethnicity, and origin (rural or urban) characteristic of the women's movement for peace in Colombia.

Fourth, several organizations included here illustrate how gender has shaped women's relationship to conflict and peace—as both victims and protagonists for change. Such gendered experiences are emblematic of many women's peace organizations where gender has provided a common organizing identity. These include mothers organizing to protest kidnappings

---

[3] Other relevant women's groups include Movimiento Popular de Mujeres, Diálogo Mujer, Casa de la Mujer, Red de Mujeres Jóvenes Feministas por la Paz, Mujeres Unidas por una Colombia Mejor, Mujeres Artistas por la Vida y por la Paz, Asociación Nacional de Mujeres Campesinas e Indígenas de Colombia, Programa Mujer Campesina de la Asociación Nacional de Usuarios Campesinos Unidad y Reconstrucción, Corporación Casa de la Mujer, Colectivo de Mujeres Excombatientes, Observatorio de los Derechos Humanos de las Mujeres, Confluencia Nacional de Redes de Mujeres, Corporación Sisma-Mujer, Corporación de Apoyo a Comunidades Populares, Fundación Mujer y Futuro (Bucaramanga), Humanizar, Mujeres Pazíficas (Cali), Grupo de Mujeres de AFRODES, and Red de Educación Popular entre Mujeres.

and disappearances, displaced women seeking economic survival, and women's faith-based organizations seeking a role for women in peacebuilding initiatives.

Networks, Coalitions, and Alliances

Women's organizations and networks in Colombia are active at all levels and in all sectors. Women's groups are present in highly conflictual areas from Putumayo in southern Colombia to the urban neighborhoods, or barrios, of Medellín, where former paramilitaries and guerrilla groups are active. The headquarters of many of the largest women's networks are not in Bogotá, the country's capital. In fact, medium-size cities such as Medellín (Antioquia), Cartagena (Bolívar), and Barrancabermeja (Santander) host some of the main networks and organizations, giving the women's peace movement a regional and highly decentralized structure.

The Popular Feminine Organization (OFP) is a women's grassroots organization mostly of women workers, community leaders and members, entrepreneurs, youth, and female heads of household. OFP started in 1972 as a program of the Catholic Church in Barrancabermeja, a highly conflictual zone in Middle Magdalena in the northeastern department of Santander.[4] The organization has now expanded to other regions in Middle Magdalena and also to other departments, including Antioquia, as well as to barrios in Neiva (departmental capital of Huila) and in Bogotá, where significant numbers of displaced women live and where armed actors actively and forcibly recruit members to their ranks. Violence perpetrated by guerrillas, paramilitaries, and the Colombian army in Barrancabermeja has had a significant effect on women's organizations such as OFP. Gloria Amparo Suárez, a longtime member of OFP, explains: "Since the year 2000, when the paramilitaries entered the area, until now [2003], we have suffered eighty violent acts against OFP. . . . They [paramilitaries] managed to wipe out several organizations, but the ones that stayed, like us, kept resisting, raising the flag of civility, [engaging in] nonviolent resistance with lots of symbols, with lots of dignity, for our rights."[5]

OFP is a powerful example of an organization that started outside Bogotá and has progressively gained national and international recognition for its work.[6] As the organization grew, it departed from being a church program and, in 1988, began operating as an autonomous organization, developing programs on health issues, youth, and microfinance and providing assistance

---

[4] Barrancabermeja is the birthplace of the National Liberation Army (ELN) guerrillas as well as the headquarters of ECOPETROL, Colombia's major oil refinery.

[5] Gloria Suárez, interview by the author, Barrancabermeja, 2003.

[6] OFP also has links with the worldwide movement Women in Black. Through its accompaniment program, the human rights organization Peace Brigades International offers OFP leaders some degree of protection.

to victims of domestic violence. OFP's work includes housing and food security programs designed to improve living conditions of working-class and impoverished communities in war-affected regions. Beginning in the mid-1990s, OFP reached out to adjacent municipalities, where it established women's houses to provide women with spaces for meeting, socializing, and training. OFP members also participate in peace demonstrations that react to the selective violence that many of their leaders have suffered in recent years.

Symbolism is an intrinsic part of OFP's work, and even the colors in OFP's institutional flag carry meaning, with green standing for hope, red for strength, and white for utopia. Daily implements such as empty pots and pans, when publicly displayed, are transformed into symbols of protest against hunger, poverty, and marginalization. OFP members wear black robes at peace rallies as a symbol of mourning and the rejection of violence.

The Pacific Route of Women emerged in the Urabá region, which spans the departments of Chocó, Córdoba, and Antioquia. The region is rich in natural resources, and its access to the Panama Canal and the Atlantic Ocean makes it a key geostrategic area fiercely disputed by a variety of armed actors since the 1970s.[7] In 1995, in response to increased violence, including a series of particularly brutal massacres, a group of women from Bogotá and Medellín—feminist activists, women artists, and intellectuals from groups such as Casa de la Mujer (Women's House)—organized a caravan from Bogotá to Urabá to reject violent acts against the people of Urabá. This march was called the Pacific Route of Women.

What started as a onetime event blossomed into a permanent organization based in Medellín, Antioquia, with a presence throughout the country. According to Olga Amparo Sánchez Gómez, a member of the Pacific Route, the network now has 315 affiliated social groups and non-governmental organizations (NGOs) in Santander, Valle del Cauca, Risaralda, Cundinamarca, Putumayo, Antioquia, Chocó, and Cauca.

One of its leaders explains the core beliefs of the Pacific Route of Women: "No war is justified; political negotiations must include elements that transform both private and public conflicts, [wherein political negotiation] is understood as a feminist position regarding society and the political practice of women; and it is necessary to begin to construct different symbols, other than warlike symbols, [because] all that is symbolic in this society—from the use of language to the city emblems—is a celebration of all things violent."[8]

The Pacific Route of Women promotes the symbolic construction of an alternative peace discourse and the transformation of bellicose attitudes. Piedad Morales, a member, explains the importance of symbolism in the or-

---

[7] Since the 1970s, Urabá has been disputed by guerrillas (primarily the FARC and EPL) as well as paramilitaries, who appeared in the area after 1988 and expelled the FARC in 1996.

[8] Olga Amparo Sánchez Gómez, interview by the author, Bogotá, October 2003.

ganization's mobilizations: "We build objects, such as rag dolls or dream catchers, that provide symbolic protection to our actions, for we move in areas where the armed actors reside, even in actual combat areas. . . . Before going to one of the rallies, we wove a huge dream catcher that protected all the women participating in the peace rally."[9]

Colombian society is overwhelmed with cultural practices that celebrate war and violence. Although these are not exclusively a Colombian phenomenon, most of the public statues and symbols in Colombian cities are of male warriors. Colombian culture as expressed in colloquial language, the way Colombians drive, and even the lyrics of urban songs celebrates victory rather than cooperation. Peace demonstrations, such as those organized by the Pacific Route of Women, offer new cultural alternatives to the discourse of war. These new discourses and practices set the stage for the transformation of the day-to-day violence and stress that most Colombians endure, as well as the resolution and transformation of the armed conflict itself.

Based in Bogotá, the National Women's Network (RNM) defines itself as a nonhierarchical space where many grassroots organizations, NGOs, and independent women converge. RNM represents a wide range of organizations, from intellectual and academic groups to demobilized women. RNM has members in most regions in Colombia, from the islands of San Andrés and Providencia to Popayán, the southern capital of Cauca. Forty-five regional women's organizations form the RNM. Gloria Tobón, a network member, asserts, "Our common denominator is women's rights, which locates us in a key scenario: the peace scenario."[10] RNM has also been one of the leading voices demanding a place for women at the negotiating table. In fact, RNM is recognized for its work in integrating a gender perspective in peacebuilding. RNM has striven to inform and educate the leaders of the peace movement, as well as society at large, about the importance of procuring the participation of women in dialogue and negotiation. It has participated in peacemaking efforts through the Thematic Committee during the FARC-Pastrana dialogues, the 2000 meeting in Geneva with the ELN and civil society, and the National Peace Council.[11]

The RNM was one of the groups behind the preparation and implementation of the Women's Public Forum of 2000, when women from all over the country converged in El Caguán to participate in the FARC-Pastrana dialogues.[12] Also, RNM member Magdala Velázquez was nominated to represent the women's movement on the National Peace Council, established as "a

---

[9] Piedad Morales, interview by the author, Medellín, October 2003.

[10] Gloria Tobón, interview by the author, Bogotá, October 2003.

[11] United Nations Development Fund for Women (UNIFEM), *Las mujeres colombianas en busca de la paz* (Bogotá: UNIFEM, 2004), 39.

[12] See Rojas, *In the Midst of War.*

forum for consensus building on a state policy for peace, composed of civil society organizations and government officials."[13] Other RNM activities include publishing extensively on women's rights and women's agenda for peace, with special emphasis on incorporating a gender perspective on international humanitarian law.

In 2001, Colombian and Swedish trade unions jointly established the Women's Peace Initiative (IMP) as a space where women from various social sectors could design a shared agenda for peace. The idea behind the creation of this organization of women representing unions and urban- and rural-based organizations was twofold: first, to create consensus on a women's peace agenda; and second, to increase the visibility of women as valid political actors in negotiations and dialogues for peace, as called for in UN Security Council Resolution 1325. Resolution 1325 addresses protection of women during armed conflict and calls for an end to impunity for gender-based abuses during and after conflict, the integration of a gender perspective in peacemaking and peacekeeping, and the participation of women at all levels of decision making and on issues related to prevention management and resolution of conflict. It calls for action by a wide range of stakeholders, including governments, the UN Security Council, the UN secretary-general, and all parties to armed conflict.[14]

Using innovative and participatory consensus-building methodologies, the Women's Peace Initiative established the Constituyente Emancipatoria de Mujeres (Women's Emancipatory Constituent Assembly). The assembly's objectives were to create an agenda for peace so that women could influence future negotiation processes; to form a national pact among women's organizations; and to define strategies that would put the women's agenda for peace on the national agenda.[15] The assembly started with 719 women, who produced a 600-point document. After eight months of refinements, three hundred Colombian female delegates—elected from all regions, social classes, and ethnic groups—gathered at the national Capitol in Bogotá to finalize a document with five themes: economy; justice and security; politics and public life; society and culture; and land, territory, and the environment. The resulting document presents a women's unified "Twelve-Point Agenda for Peace," reflecting the consensus of hundreds of women throughout Colombia.

Based on the success of the Women's Emancipatory Constituent Assembly, various groups from civil society and regional governments organized as constituent assemblies have adopted the women's innovative, consensus-

---

[13] Ibid., 17.

[14] For a full account and explanation of Resolution 1325, see www.womenwarpeace.org/tool box/Annotated_1325.pdf (accessed August 29, 2008).

[15] Women's Peace Initiative, "The Process of Constructing a Social and Political Agenda" (internal document, Women's Peace Initiative, Bogotá, 2002). The reader can contact the organization directly for information on this document.

based methodology as a basis for their own agendas for peace. Other activities of IMP include the creation of working groups with other women's organizations to monitor the demobilization process (2002–06) and the application of the Justice and Peace Law. In 2006, a working group spearheaded by IMP published a report revealing the devastating effects of the return of the demobilized combatants on women in Santander, Antioquia, and the Caribbean.[16]

Like most women's organizations for peace, IMP is critical of the Justice and Peace Law for giving short shrift to the victims, most of whom are women and children. The women's organizations believe that the paramilitaries and any other armed actors who committed crimes should be punished. Therefore, reconciliation in Colombia requires a public investigation of the crimes and massacres that have occurred, so that the perpetrators may be brought to justice and reparations made to the victims. The IMP submitted to the Colombian Congress another report, "Violence against Colombian Women and Their Rights to Truth, Justice, and Reparation: Against Impunity and Silence," which recommended that Congress consider measures including a gender perspective in the legal framework for the demobilization and reintegration of armed groups.[17] The proposal notes that crimes against women are crimes against humanity according to international law and insists that the perpetrators cannot be eligible for amnesty.[18] The final law approved by Congress included five points from the women's proposal, relating to sexual violence against women and children, the protection of victims and witnesses of sexual aggression, representation of victims' organizations and Colombia's ombudsman on the National Commission for Reparations and Reconciliation (CNRR), and the inclusion of women on the CNRR. As a result of the proposal and pressure from women's organizations, President Álvaro Uribe appointed Ana Teresa Bernal, head of Red Nacional de Iniciativas por la Paz y contra la Guerra (REDEPAZ), and Patricia Buriticá, national director of the Women's Peace Initiative, as commissioners to the CNRR. The two peace leaders were chosen not only to bring women's interests and perspectives to the commission but to represent civil society more broadly.

Based in Bogotá since 1997, the National Movement of Women Authors and Actors for Peace gathers sixty-one organizations of women from diverse regions, representing indigenous and Afro-Colombian women, youth, and

---

[16] Mesa Nacional de Incidencia, "Por el derecho a la verdad, la justicia y la reparación con perspectiva de género" (Documento Público [Public Document] no. 2), *Tregua Incierta* (Bogotá, August 2006), www.mujeresporlapaz.org/documentos/mesadeincidencia2.pdf (accessed September 7, 2008).

[17] For the Women's Peace Initiative legal framework, see www.mujeresporlapaz.org/documentos/propuestaimp.doc (accessed August 29, 2008).

[18] Although many sectors in Colombia and abroad were critical of President Álvaro Uribe's Justice and Peace Law, except for a proposal submitted by Senators Rafael Pardo and Gina Parody, the women's proposal was the only alternative bill submitted by Colombian civil society.

urban leaders of thirteen departments, thirteen cities, and ten municipalities. The movement has participated in various initiatives of the peace movement, such as the Citizen Mandate for Peace, the Permanent Assembly of the Civil Society for Peace, the National Environmental Congress, and the National Peace Council.

In addition to the networks and organizations described above, the women's peace movement has created "meta-networks," or networks of networks, such as the National Confluence of Women's Networks. Created in 1998, the organization has brought together 10 national and international networks and almost 150 groups to advocate for women's rights. In 2000, women formed another coalition of coalitions, the National Working Group on Women's Consensus. This group facilitated the coordination of local, regional, and national women's organizations to carry out events and propose ways to increase the political pressure for negotiated solutions and for greater participation by women in peacemaking.

Since 2000, other networks and organizations have emerged with highly specific agendas. For example, the Women and Armed Conflict Working Group responded to the need to produce systematized data and analysis of the conflict's effects on women and girls.[19] In 2001, the group promoted the visit of Radhika Coomaraswamy, the UN Special Rapporteur on Violence against Women. This visit allowed the group to bring attention to the impact of the armed conflict on Colombian women and girls and to propose public policies that seek to advance the rights of women and girls. Since then, the group has produced annual reports that monitor the government's progress in applying the rapporteur's recommendations and in strengthening the rights of women and girls in the areas of prevention, protection, accountability, and reparations.

Women have organized specifically around their gender identities and the particular ways they have experienced the conflict. The mothers of some five hundred policemen and soldiers who have been held in captivity by illegal armed groups for more than six years formed a group called the Mothers and Relatives of Members of the Public Forces Captured and Liberated by Guerrilla Groups. These mothers, mostly from lower-middle-class families, have fervently tried to engage in dialogue with armed actors to obtain information about their children and to advocate a humanitarian accord.

---

[19] This working group includes many of the organizations referred to here, as well as rural women's groups such as Asociación Nacional de Mujeres Indígenas y Campesinas (National Association of Indigenous and Peasant Women), women's advocacy and research organizations such as Instituto Latinoamericano de Servicios Legales Alternativos (Latin American Institute of Alternative Legal Services), and women's human rights organizations such as Colectivo María María. International organizations such as the Bogotá-based offices of the United Nations High Commissioner for Refugees, the Office of Coordination of Humanitarian Affairs, and Save the Children participate as observers. Representing the Colombian state is the Consejería de Proyectos (Council of Projects) and the Defensoría del Pueblo.

The Cartagena-based League of Displaced Women represents millions of displaced women in Colombia. The league was founded in 1995, in one of the poorest neighborhoods of this international tourist city on Colombia's Caribbean coast, at the initiative of the Women's International League for Peace and Freedom (WILPF). The league has assisted more than five hundred displaced women—90 percent of whom are Afro-descendants and single heads of household—to articulate their demands to the Colombian state and to seek reparations, socioeconomic compensation, and, eventually, their return home.

Tendencies within the Women's Peace Movement

Approaches and philosophies differ in the women's peace movement.[20] For example, the Pacific Route of Women and the Popular Feminine Organization work from a feminist perspective. They concentrate on changing and questioning the power dynamics and their expression in the language and symbols of society. They understand peace not merely as the absence of violence but as the transformation of the cultural practices that celebrate war and violence and thus perpetuate the oppression of women and other less-privileged populations. The Pacific Route stresses the importance of mobilization and symbolic resistance to war.[21]

Other groups, such as the IMP, define women as political agents of change and press for their direct participation in negotiations and for the inclusion of a gender perspective in the reconstruction of Colombia. The main concern of organizations like the IMP is to highlight the role of women as valid political actors and to ensure their inclusion in negotiations.[22] Other women's groups work exclusively in conflict-ridden areas, dealing with day-to-day conflict-related emergencies such as massacres and internal displacement. Others, such as the Women and Armed Conflict Working Group (Mesa de Trabajo Mujer y Conflicto Armado) are dedicated to expanding knowledge through research on the impacts of violence on women and children.

Women's organizations and networks for peace can be divided into those that exert pressure from below and those that exert pressure from within. The first group opposes all forms of violence and puts direct pressure on armed actors to sit down and negotiate. Such organizations travel to conflict-ridden areas, work with victims, organize mobilizations for peace and against war, and develop a repertoire of creative symbols to raise awareness of the multiple forms of violence that are part of Colombian culture. Examples of these groups are the Pacific Route and the OFP. Such groups develop and

---

[20] See Beatriz Quintero, *Cartografía de las mujeres* (Bogotá: Red Nacional de Mujeres, 2003).

[21] See Ruta Pacífica de las Mujeres, www.rutapacifica.org.co (accessed August 29, 2008).

[22] See "Iniciativa de las mujeres colombianas por la paz," www.mujeresporlapaz.org (accessed August 29, 2008).

conduct grassroots activities and do not seek to participate directly in the various decision-making arenas.

Other organizations participate in high-level settings for peace and negotiation. Examples of organizations that work from within include the RNM, the IMP, and the National Movement of Women Authors and Actors for Peace. These networks and groups advocate for the inclusion of women and gender perspectives in all initiatives and public policies for peace and reconciliation.

Women's organizations working for peace in Colombia are united in their condemnation of all human rights violations and atrocities, regardless of who committed them. Similarly, women's groups and networks for peace agree on the fruitlessness of military solutions and are critical of international funding for military aid. They stress the need to achieve a negotiated settlement to the armed conflict and are encouraging international donors to concentrate their aid on development projects rather than on the military sector. Similarly, they all agree that women and a gendered perspective should be key components in the design, implementation, and evaluation of peace and development projects.

The presence of networks and coalitions of women working for peace is rather recent, although the participation of women's groups in the shaping of the 1991 constitution is an important historical antecedent of women's organizing for peace in Colombia. Before 1991, the Colombian constitution did not provide explicit guarantees for women's rights. Women's groups united to secure a range of such rights, including equality before the law, participation in decision-making posts, and equal opportunities, as well as the abolition of all forms of discrimination against women and the approval of state-sponsored protective programs for pregnant women.[23]

One of the most significant achievements in the work for constitutional reforms was the consolidation, in July 1991, of the RNM, the first such network to be established in Colombia. Founded by women's groups that participated in the National Constituent Assembly, the RNM was the first group to raise the banner for the political participation of women in national decision-making spaces.

Although it may be premature to judge their successes and shortcomings, it is possible to assess the strengths and limitations at this juncture. The effectiveness of women's groups cannot be measured simply by their ability to single-handedly reverse the government's policies and force the armed actors to start negotiations. Rather, effectiveness is defined here as the ability of women's organizations to gain visibility as a relevant sector within the civil

---

[23] Beatriz Quintero, "Las mujeres colombianas y la Asamblea Nacional Constituyente de 1991—participación e impactos" (Economic Council of Latin America and the Caribbean, Santa Cruz de la Sierra, Bolivia, 2005), www.eclac.org/mujer/reuniones/Bolivia/Beatriz_Quintero.pdf (accessed August 29, 2008).

society movement for peace. Their successes may be measured by examining the following indicators: women's active participation in peacemaking initiatives; their organizing capacity and ability to resist militarization; inclusion of gender perspectives in policy debates related to peace, security, and reconciliation; and the emergence and empowerment of a new female leadership for peace.

Active Participation in Peacemaking Initiatives

During the Pastrana-FARC dialogues (1999–2002), civil society actors, and peace organizations in particular, demanded active participation at the negotiating table. Women's visibility as a relevant sector within the peace movement increased during this time as they participated in the public hearings that took place in the demilitarized zone of El Caguán. Nonetheless, these hearings were relatively marginal to the formal negotiations—which excluded women. As Patricia Buriticá summarized, "War has led us to act politically, war has convened us, has gathered us. Women of a myriad of organizations reflected and concluded that in the Pastrana-FARC process we did not exist."[24]

Was women's participation any different from that of other sectors, and why did it gain visibility? Although many parts of civil society organized public hearings, the women's hearing attracted the attention of the media because they organized an event that included a coalition of women from various sectors, from businesswomen who chartered planes to the area, to campesinas and Afro-Colombian women who traveled overland for days to reach the demilitarized zone. The event also included the participation of women combatants and included plays, musical performances, and sacred ceremonies. The ability of these women to build bridges across ethnic and class sectors, and the rich mixture of speeches and cultural expressions, made their event unique. They were also the only group that left a written record and its own evaluation of the event.[25]

A more recent example of women's participation occurred in the context of the 2005 Justice and Peace Law, which provided a framework for demobilizing illegal groups and dealing with victims. Many victims and women's organizations oppose collaboration with state or government institutions and are skeptical that fruitful results for the victims can be achieved under the Uribe administration. The participation of Ana Teresa Bernal and Patricia Buriticá on the National Commission for Reparations and Reconciliation is an achievement for the women's movement, since this ensures that the commission incorporates gender in all its work.

---

[24] UNIFEM, *Las mujeres colombianas en busca de la paz*, 32.

[25] See *Memorias Audiencia Pública de las Mujeres. Economía y Empleo. Cuaderno de Mujeres en el Trabajo por la Paz* (Bogotá: Red Nacional de Mujeres, March 2001).

Organizing Capacity and Resistance to Militarization

Part of the success of women in mobilizing for peace demonstrations can be explained by their ability to establish coalitions across ethnic, class, and urban and rural lines and work toward a common goal despite the differences among groups. In the face of the collective frustration following the failure of the Pastrana-FARC negotiations, a coalition of women's networks organized a massive rally for peace on July 25, 2002. This alliance, or meta-network, was called the Movimiento Nacional de Mujeres contra la Guerra (National Women's Movement against War). It was responsible for organizing a national demonstration that gathered some forty thousand women and men in what UNIFEM called "the biggest mobilization against war and in favor of peace in Colombia in recent years."[26]

Afterward, women's networks across the country continued to mobilize, to press the armed actors to undertake negotiations. On November 25, 2003, approximately three thousand women from Cauca, Nariño, Valle del Cauca, Caquetá, Risaralda, Tolima, Huila, Santander, Barrancabermeja, Bolívar, Atlántico, Chocó, Antioquia, and Bogotá arrived in Puerto Caicedo, Putumayo. As María Clemencia Ramírez notes in Chapter 17 of this volume, Putumayo is a region where the Colombian state has historically had a weak presence and is a critical area for U.S. coca eradication programs. The purposes of the demonstration in Putumayo were manifold. First, women expressed opposition to the criminal treatment to which people in Putumayo are subjected, asserting that coca leaf producers should be treated as citizens rather than as drug lords or armed actors. Second, women criticized the government's strategy of using primarily military approaches instead of addressing historic regional problems such as poverty, and they criticized the neglect of the Colombian state. Moreover, women called for an end to fumigations, which, they argued, are destroying both legal and alternative crops as well as poisoning the population and the environment. Last, women called for the citizens of Putumayo to have a voice in the decisions that affect their daily lives.[27] Although not directly pressing for a peace process per se, women's groups are showing the government and the armed actors that civil society wants a resolution to all aspects of the conflict through negotiation and are rejecting militarization and the use of all forms of violence.

Inclusion of Gender Perspectives in Policy Debates

Women's groups have sought the inclusion of gender perspectives in policy debates related to the conflict and its resolution, and they were one of many

---

[26] UNIFEM, *Las mujeres colombianas en busca de la paz*, 32.

[27] Iniciativa de Mujeres por la Paz, "Comunicado de las mujeres desde el Putumayo" (press release, December 13, 2003), http://colombia.indymedia.org/news/2003/10/7153_comment.php#8295 (accessed September 7, 2008).

sectors of civil society that mobilized to challenge the Justice and Peace Law. Groups such as the IMP and the RNM have published reports on the demobilization processes of the AUC and the FARC as well as on truth, reparations, and reconciliation from a gender perspective. The annual reports of the Women and Armed Conflict Working Group have become a national and international reference point for understanding the armed conflict's effects on women and children. Finally, women's organizations have sought the application of international humanitarian law and have explained why a humanitarian agreement is key for women and children in conflict areas as well as for the families and victims of those captured by armed actors.

Empowerment and New Leadership for Peace

In many war-affected regions where a significant number of men have been killed or have left the area to fight, women have stepped in to assume leadership in the community. Women's new roles include conducting informal humanitarian negotiations with armed actors to open safe corridors for the passage of food, medicines, and other supplies. According to a United Nations Development Programme (UNDP) researcher for the 2003 *Human Development Report for Colombia*, "The humanitarian negotiations with certain [guerrilla or paramilitary] commanders in many regions have been done by women."[28]

Despite the evident difficulties of working for peace in areas disputed by armed actors, the work of the Asociación de Mujeres del Oriente Antioqueño (AMOR, or Association of Women of Eastern Antioquia), is an interesting case of women's leadership in the midst of violence. AMOR brings together many women's groups in eastern Antioquia, a region disputed by paramilitaries and ELN and FARC guerrillas. Women from AMOR use the perception of their traditional image as "harmless and more peaceful" to gain access to armed actors and territory considered off-limits for the society in general and even succeeded in talking directly to armed actors to obtain a short-lived peace agreement. According to a member of the Pacific Route, which has an alliance with AMOR, the humanitarian accord consisted of "persuading the armed actors to stop blocking the highway that goes from Medellín to Bogotá, in order to allow families to sell their products on the main road. It lasted about two or three months; it was a very weak agreement but quite significant." The member noted that since 2003, women from AMOR have been "working on a new partial humanitarian agreement while they

---

[28] UNDP, *Colombia's Conflict, Pointers on the Road to Peace: National Human Development Report for Colombia, 2003* (Bogotá: UNDP, 2003), http://hdr.undp.org/en/reports/nationalreports/latinamericathecaribbean/colombia/name,3213,en.html (accessed September 7, 2008).

continue demanding that the armed actors abstain from strict controls on the passage of food and medicine."[29]

The women of AMOR have also actively participated in peace laboratories sponsored by the European Union and have contributed to the Antioquia Constituent Assembly.[30] Women constitute 37 percent of the participants in the constituent assemblies of Antioquia, Tolima, Huila, and Nariño—arenas where civil society organizations and regional authorities converge to produce agendas for peace based on the specific situation of each region. Consequently, the women of AMOR have gained national visibility for these efforts. They show how the conflict has been a catalyst for female leadership for peace.

The new leadership of women is an indication of the changing nature of traditional gender roles as a result of the armed conflict. In the absence of men, women are starting to occupy the public and local political scenes that have been traditionally dominated by men. A related effect of the change in the traditional public roles on the private sphere has been noted among displaced women. In the urban areas where they tend to resettle, women are more resilient—and, thus, adapt faster—than males. Women therefore become the breadwinners of the households, causing a shift in power and decision making in the family.[31]

Limitations of the Women's Peace Movement

The work of women's networks and groups faces limitations of various kinds. Many of these limitations are not exclusive to the women's movement; they can be seen in other sectors of organized civil society groups working for peace.

First, the biggest problem for women's groups is that of security. Because of their opposition to violence by all armed actors, women peace activists are vulnerable to attacks and intimidation from multiple sources. Women's groups and civil society organizations for peace have worked under increasingly difficult circumstances since the election of President Uribe in 2002. Peace leaders in general, and women in particular, are being assassinated and threatened by all of the armed groups. According to the 2006 report of the Women and Armed Conflict Working Group, "members of women's organizations and those that belong to unions or political parties—especially those working in zones of armed confrontation—are victims of harassment, false

---

[29] Rojas, *In the Midst of War*, 26.

[30] See www.pdpmm.org.co/labpaz/laboratorio.html and the chapters by Mary J. Roldán, Christopher Mitchell, and Sara Ramírez in this volume.

[31] For an account of how displaced women change their traditional roles in urban settings, see Guttmann and Rojas with Lambert, "Gender Assessment."

accusations, threats, and even assassinations by all armed actors.[32] The report notes further that "in recent years there has been an increase in reports of attacks committed against women leaders and their organizations by state actors."[33] In addition, the work of these groups is constantly being discredited (even, on occasion, by government officials) and generally ignored by the Colombian public, governments, and international organizations.

Second, it has been difficult for women's groups to sustain national momentum after successful demonstrations. Although the major mobilizations demonstrate the capacity of various women's groups to organize and create strategic alliances, their ability to continue working together needs to be strengthened. Currently each network returns to its traditional work and constituencies, underutilizing the political advantage gained during the various events. Scarcity of funding further compromises the ability of women's groups to work together, since they often compete for funds from the same sources to sustain their projects and initiatives.

Third, the integration of gender perspectives into projects, programs, and laws related to peace and reconciliation is far from easy. One of the main obstacles to integrating a gender perspective into the legal framework for demobilizing violent groups is that gender demands tend to be overshadowed by the many other political agendas and concerns of both proponents and opponents of the 2005 Justice and Peace Law. As the sole defender of gender concerns in the Justice and Peace Law and the disarmament, demobilization, and reintegration process, the women's movement received very limited media coverage and, thus, modest support from the broader public for these issues. Moreover, despite the incorporation of some gender concerns into the law and despite the appointments of women commissioners and representatives of victims' groups, the working group led by IMP lamented that "the results are not to our satisfaction, and as other social sectors in Colombia are feeling, we are in disagreement with the general content of the law."[34]

Fourth, peace organizations and women's organizations are not exempt from personal and political problems within their groups and with other, similar organizations. Although regarded as a success for women's participation in the public sphere, the presence of women on the CNRR furthered internal divisions within certain women's networks and deepened the gap between those working outside the government and those seen as collaborators with the government by virtue of their participation in state institutions. When Patricia Buriticá, director of the IMP, accepted the appointment as a

---

[32] Mesa de Trabajo Mujer y Conflicto Armado, "VI informe sobre violencia sociopolítica contra mujeres, jóvenes y niñas en Colombia, 2002–2006" (report, Bogotá, 2006), www.mujerycon flictoarmado.org/pdfs/mca_6to_informe_2002_2006.pdf (accessed August 29, 2008).

[33] Ibid.

[34] Mesa Nacional de Incidencia, "Por el derecho a la verdad."

commissioner, her organization supported her. But given the minimal results achieved by CNRR for the victims since 2006 and despite the women commissioners' efforts to highlight gender in various programs, several member groups withdrew from the IMP in 2007 and formed the Coalición de Mujeres por la Democracia y la Paz (Women's Coalition for Peace and Democracy). The new organization will continue monitoring efforts to bring the paramilitaries to justice, establish truth, and seek reparations for the victims, eschewing links to any governmental or state institution, including the CNRR. The organizations that remain in the IMP will continue to raise the profile of women as valid political actors in the peace and reconciliation agendas of the country, as they have been doing since 2002.

Finally, despite the instances in which women's groups and networks work collectively for a common agenda for peace, such as the IMP's Twelve-Point Agenda, there is not a single unified agenda that brings together the entire women's movement. Such an agenda could be a powerful tool in an eventual political negotiation. Nonetheless, it is possible that in a future negotiation the women's movement will be much better prepared than it was during the Pastrana-FARC dialogues.

Conclusion: The Gendered Nature of Women's Peace Work and Its Contributions

Women's groups and networks are aware of the importance of gender in a conflictual society such as Colombia. Since gender relations are an expression of the relationships of power that construct the "unequal distribution of knowledge, property, income, responsibilities and rights between men and women," understanding gender's role in conflict can unlock broader understanding of the conflict as well.[35]

In Colombia, the women's sector has been especially keen on insisting that violence is the manifestation not only of the actions of individual armed men and women but also of the cultural and traditional practices that celebrate and sustain the unequal distribution of economic, cultural, and political resources. In fact, women's work for peace in Colombia is directed not only at insurgents and high-level politicians but also at society at large, suggesting that the task of ending violence and building peace is a responsibility of all Colombians. This critical stance toward the existing social order is constantly expressed in the way certain networks and organizations, such as OFP and the Pacific Route, use new discursive practices and symbols that question the hierarchical nature of relationships, and suggest new rules of coexistence for all Colombians.

---

[35] Bantaba, "Género y conflicto armado" (online course on gender and armed conflict), www.bantaba.ehu.es/formarse/fcont/genconfarm/1sesion/ (accessed August 29, 2008).

No other group working for peace in Colombia has been as effective as the women's networks in linking the transformation of gender roles in the private sphere to the transformation of women's roles in the public sphere. This is a unique contribution of the women's movement. In some areas, the armed conflict allows women to occupy local public and political roles in the absence of their male partners. Also, women have organized to search for relatives who have been disappeared, captured, or killed by armed actors. Women who joined the insurgencies or were displaced by the armed actors not only transform their traditional roles as caretakers and mothers but in some cases are empowered in their new roles as they learn new skills and become breadwinners or heads of households. Precedent in El Salvador and Guatemala shows that violent conflict sometimes opens new opportunities for women, but that once the conflict ends, society frequently demands that women return to their traditional roles.[36] What happened in Central America with women ex-combatants is a lesson that Colombian women's organizations and their leaders are integrating as they prepare for future negotiation and reconstruction stages.

Women's organizations for peace in Colombia are not only highlighting the negative effects of the armed conflict on women but also have contributed to broadening women's roles and advancing women as recognized political leaders voicing their concerns and perspective on peace and reconciliation. They protest against war, mobilize citizens for peace, and work toward the implementation of UN Security Council Resolution 1325.

Women have been very effective in building bridges across racial, geographic, and class boundaries. In a country deeply divided by class and ethnic boundaries, it is very promising to see projects in which businesswomen, urban leaders, academics, indigenous people, and Afro-Colombian leaders converge. The women's movement has been at the forefront of civil society in thinking about and creating participatory methodologies to maximize their ability to produce consensus and work across diverse sectors. Their participatory methodology has been used in other political spaces. This transfer of skills demonstrates that the contribution of the women's movement is not only content-based but also methodological.[37] In addition, groups such as the RNM and the National Movement of Women Authors and Actors for Peace have played the very important and not always welcome role of integrating gender perspectives in the greater civil society movement for peace.

---

[36] See Virginia M. Bouvier, "Crossing the Lines: Women's Social Mobilization in Latin America," in *Governing Women: Women's Political Effectiveness in Contexts of Democratization and Governance Reform*, ed. Anne Marie Goetz (New York: Routledge, 2008), 25–44.

[37] For more on women's methodological work, see Caroline Moser, Angélica Acosta, and María Eugenia Vázquez, *Mujeres y paz. Construcción de consensos* (Bogotá: Social Policy International, 2006).

What does the future hold? Women's organizations, like many other peace and development initiatives in Colombia, will continue their work despite worsening security conditions and ongoing financial limitations. Through their work as leaders of community projects or national spokeswomen pressing for humanitarian accords, members of the women's peace movement agree on the importance of a negotiated settlement of the armed conflict. At the same time, women's peace networks and groups are involved in participatory projects to sustain peace from a gender perspective, and they are contributing to the foundation of a gender-inclusive national agenda for peace. Colombian women's networks and organizations are strong enough to resist war and denounce atrocities and crimes against women, and bold enough to proclaim that peace is the radical transformation of a culture that celebrates dominance and perpetuates inequality.

12

The Power of the Bastón
Indigenous Resistance and Peacebuilding in Colombia

Leslie Wirpsa with David Rothschild and Catalina Garzón

ixty thousand people made a sixty-mile trek north on the Pan-American Highway, leaving the Andean town of Santander de Quilichao and traversing Colombia's southwestern Cauca Department. Their destination was the bustling city of Cali, population approximately two million. Shielded by five thousand "indigenous guards" who wielded only ceremonial *bastones*—wooden sticks adorned with the red and green flag of the Nasa people—this wave of indigenous women, men, and children nonviolently traversed one of the most complex war zones in Colombia.[1] They called the event a *minga*, referring to a traditional practice used by many of Colombia's eighty-five distinct indigenous peoples to collectively construct a building, hoe or plant a field, or reap a harvest.

The goal of the Grassroots Minga for Life, Justice, Joy, Freedom, and Autonomy, however, was to resist widespread physical, economic, and political aggression threatening the lives and livelihoods of Colombia's 800,000 indigenous people. Participants advocated a deepening of participatory democracy, peace initiatives, and economic justice in a country wracked by decades of civil war, rampant human rights violations, and inequity. The September 2004 *minga*, one of the largest indigenous mobilizations ever, was representative of centuries of resistance by Colombia's indigenous peoples to the imposition of physical violence and economic models threatening indigenous cultures, their livelihoods, and their sheer physical survival.

---

[1] American Friends Service Committee (AFSC) and Fellowship of Reconciliation (FOR), "Building from the Inside Out: Peace Initiatives in War-Torn Colombia" (report, November 2004, 22–25), http://forcolombia.org/publications/insideout (accessed August 29, 2008).

Indigenous Peoples: Resistance at Regional and National Levels

Indigenous peoples, representing only 2 percent of Colombia's 42 million inhabitants, have been disproportionately affected by persistent epochs of violence and civil war. As of May 2005, about 30 percent of Colombia's indigenous people were confronting problems related to the war, with 299 violent deaths of indigenous people registered from January 2004 to May 2005.[2] Attacks against indigenous communities continued in 2006 and 2007. In March 2008, the United Nations High Commissioner for Refugees (UNHCR) reported that, according to Colombian human rights groups, "many indigenous groups are now in imminent danger of extinction, with the greatest risk coming from government soldiers and army-backed paramilitaries, who threaten, intimidate and accuse them of complicity with insurgents and drive them off their lands."[3] Although statistics vary, an estimated 8 to 18 percent of all displaced persons in Colombia are indigenous. These figures become more acute regionally—one report claimed that during one period, 67 percent of all displaced people in Cauca Department were indigenous.[4] Indigenous peoples are particularly vulnerable to the effects of displacement, since indigenous culture, community, and survival are inextricably linked to the land; displacement thus provokes a dramatic deterioration of community coherence and physical health.[5] In May 2005, the Norwegian Refugee Council's Internal Displacement Monitoring Center, citing the United Nations Special Rapporteur on Indigenous Peoples, warned that violence, aerial fumigation of coca lands, and displacement put Colombia's indigenous peoples at "serious risk of extinction."[6]

Despite such challenges, Colombia's indigenous peoples have continued throughout centuries to defend their autonomy, lives, rights, cultures, and territory. They have also advocated local, regional, national, and international alternatives for peaceful coexistence, nonviolence, and environmental and economic sustainability. These efforts are even more remarkable given that

---

[2] Luis Evelis Andrade Casama, president of ONIC, presentation to the Social and Political Forum on the Humanitarian Emergency in Cauca, May 18, 2005, www.redvoltaire.net/article5259.html#article5259 (accessed March 28, 2006).

[3] Minority Rights Group International, "State of the World's Minorities 2008–Colombia," March 11, 2008, www.unhcr.org/refworld/docid/48a7eadc4b.html (accessed October 2, 2008).

[4] Departamento Nacional de Planeación (DANE), *Los pueblos indígenas de Colombia en el umbral del nuevo milenio* (Bogotá: DANE, 2004), 264; Comunicado de Prensa, "Los pueblos indígenas de Colombia le hablan al sistema de Naciones Unidas," Bogotá, April 30, 2004.

[5] Alternet, "Colombian Conflict Could Wipe Out Indigenous Groups, Warns UNHCR," April 22, 2005, www.alternet.org/thenenews/newsdesk/UNHCR/3fd7e8c082b7017e8f9893182f2c75.htm (accessed May 17, 2005).

[6] Global IDP Project, Norwegian Refugee Council, "Colombia: Government Response to IDPs Under Fire as Conflict Worsens," May 27, 2005, 7, www.idpproject.org; www.db.idpproject.org/Sites/IdpProjectDb/idpSurvey.nsf/wSummaryPDFs/B8BF79AAD24B1A71C1256E6A004C57B2/$file/Colombia_summary.pdf (accessed July 4, 2005).

this struggle to maintain autonomy and peaceful coexistence occurs frequently within territories housing strategic resources and transport corridors over which Colombia's multiple armed actors—as well as state and multinational companies—vie for control. There is much to be learned from the ongoing story of Colombian indigenous peoples' resistance to multiple forms of violence and from their historical and contemporary articulation of alternatives. This chapter examines some of the strategies that indigenous peoples employ to resist physical, political, sociocultural, and economic violence, as well as their proposals for peace. It aims to understand how indigenous voices, actions, and visions have contributed to peacemaking in Colombia and can continue to enhance it.

Although resistance and peacebuilding in the southwestern Cauca Department and development alternatives outlined in the *plan de vida* (life plan) of the Cofán people in the southern department of Putumayo provide compelling examples, the initiatives that these cases describe are national in scope. Indeed, Colombian indigenous movements have consistently influenced and shaped both informal and institutionalized peace strategies, from local to national levels. Particularly significant in contemporary peacemaking was the example that indigenous leaders set and the dynamic role they played in the broad-based Constitutional Assembly that drafted the 1991 constitution. They called on the small Cauca-based indigenous self-defense group Movimiento Armado Quintín Lame (MAQL, or Quintín Lame Armed Movement) to disarm as part of the peace agreements that were a prelude to the assembly and to indigenous participation in it. Since then, indigenous peoples, particularly in Cauca, have remarkably strengthened and expanded nonviolent participation, both from the grassroots and through electoral channels, and from local to national levels, while implementing socioeconomic strategies focused on social justice.[7]

With guidance and support from the Organización Nacional de Indígenas de Colombia (ONIC, or National Indigenous Organization of Colombia), an umbrella institution coordinating a majority of local and regional indigenous communities and organizations, Colombia's indigenous peoples have joined together to form a Mesa Nacional Indígena de Paz, or National Indigenous Forum for Peace. The *mesa* aims to respond comprehensively to economic, political, and armed violence, denouncing the ways that armed actors put at risk indigenous people's lives, territory, culture, and very existence. In general, the *mesa*'s objectives are to promote peace and a political solution to

---

[7] The MAQL was formed in 1985 in Cauca as a reaction to a rash of murders of Nasa, or Páez, leaders, including that of Father Álvaro Ulcué Chocué, the only Páez Catholic priest at the time. The MAQL consented to surrendering its arms in 1989, following through on this commitment with the ratification of the 1991 constitution, which included broad protections for indigenous rights, including territorial and legal jurisdictional autonomy of communities over formally recognized indigenous lands.

armed conflict based on indigenous principles and cultural beliefs. The *mesa* participants seek local and national negotiated solutions to the armed conflict through dialogue and agreement.

The *mesa* carries out its objectives through the National Indigenous Council for Peace. The council, organized through the ONIC, promotes the unity of Colombia's indigenous peoples and the defense of indigenous rights in the midst of armed struggle. It builds alliances with other human rights organizations, divulging through the media abuses of indigenous rights and seeking international solidarity and humanitarian assistance. The council also supports direct channels of communication with armed actors to defend the lives, autonomy, and stance of noninvolvement of indigenous peoples. It advocates and facilitates the formation of regional peace councils and committees, distributes information regarding human rights violations by armed actors, and maintains databases and analysis of the effects of the armed conflict on these communities.[8]

These actions and visions are grounded in centuries of indigenous resistance. Beginning in the early 1500s, for three centuries Spanish conquistadors devastated Colombia's indigenous peoples and their cultures through brute force and evangelization, slaughtering them, enslaving them, and forcing them to work in mines or *encomiendas*, estates granted by the crown to Spanish administrators. It is believed that when the Spaniards arrived, between 6 million and 10 million indigenous people inhabited what today is known as Colombia. Today Colombia's indigenous population is estimated at about 800,000.[9] The Spaniards pillaged resources, particularly gold and land. Indigenous peoples were broadly dispossessed of their land, taking refuge in jungle and mountain territories considered of lesser value than more fertile plains and valleys. Ironically, today many of these territories—eventually formalized as *resguardos*, or reservations—house globally sought-after resources like petroleum, natural gas, coal, hydroelectric potential, and biodiversity.

The conquest did not come without struggle. According to Roque Roldán Ortega, "Native populations confronted the conquerors with great courage and determination, making them suffer enormous losses and experience

---

[8] See www.onic.org.co/.

[9] According to 1993 census figures adjusted in 1997, the indigenous population was estimated at 701,860. Our conservative estimate of 800,000 includes a 2 percent annual population growth for 7 years. The actual number is likely higher. Spanish records show a dramatic decimation of Colombia's indigenous peoples during the sixteenth and seventeenth centuries, with deaths ranging from 70 to 97 percent of specific populations. See DANE, "Proyecciones de población según departamentos para el año 2001," in DANE, *Los pueblos indígenas de Colombia en el umbral del nuevo milenio* (Bogotá: DANE, 2004), 11. For example, in the province of Tunja, the indigenous population dropped from 53,465 to 8,610; in Pamplona, from 31,855 to 4,526; in Cartago, from 4,573 to just 119; and in Pasto, from 22,857 to 6,938. See DANE "Proyecciones de población," 20.

great difficulties in carrying out their plans for domination."[10] Several variables allowed Colombia's indigenous peoples to maintain a limited degree of
cultural, territorial, and political autonomy and physical survival. Colonial
authorities sought to preserve "human resources needed for the construction
of an economic, political and social system which allowed the conquering
nation to effectively annex a land and double the extension of the European
continent," notes Roldán.[11] Thus, colonial powers made some attempts to
lessen violence and abuses, in large part with the aim of preserving a work-
force. The *resguardo* lands—spaces where the labor force was contained and
could reproduce to meet the economic needs of the colonial empire—were
part of this strategy.

But Colombian indigenous peoples took advantage of the legal structure
established by the crown, especially the *resguardos* and *cabildos*, or governance
councils. The indigenous *cabildos* gave "communities who possessed titles to
indigenous *resguardo* lands the ability to set up their own community government and keep at least part of their traditional customs and social control
systems."[12] Although these structures evolved from within a relationship of
colonial domination, today they are essential to indigenous resistance, autonomy, and peacemaking strategies.

Independence from Spain, in 1819, brought a thrust for indigenous assim-
ilation and for privatization of indigenous lands through intensified policies
of "civilizing, settling, and Christianizing" indigenous peoples.[13] Despite an
1820 decree ordering the return of lands to the indigenous people, in 1821, the
state again authorized the division of indigenous communal lands and attempted to disband the *cabildos*. And in 1824, many indigenous territories
previously sanctioned by royal land deeds issued by the Spanish crown were
declared *tierras baldías*—empty, or no-man's-lands—and deemed free for the
taking or divided into individual plots.[14]

But indigenous resistance continued, both practically and legally, leading
to the passage of a few laws that helped form the foundation for legal recognition of indigenous rights and territories. In 1859, the Colombian government passed Law 90, the first attempt to recognize the permanent communal
nature of indigenous lands. In 1890, the government passed Law 89, which
stipulated the "way savages that are adapting to civilized life should be governed" at the same time that it recognized that indigenous peoples enjoyed

---

[10] Roque Roldán Ortega, *Indigenous Peoples of Colombia and the Law: A Critical Approach to the Study of Past and Present Situations* (London: Gaia Foundation, 2000), 8.

[11] Ibid., 8–9.

[12] Ibid., 11.

[13] DANE, "Proyecciones de población," 14.

[14] Ibid., 16–17.

specific rights as communal ethnic groups. It also recognized the communal nature of indigenous territorial reserves and, to a certain degree, indigenous peoples' right to self-governance—both key elements of current indigenous-rights legislation.[15]

But these laws and others also chipped away at indigenous rights and lands, affording local governments considerable power over indigenous peoples and maintaining the precept that indigenous lands lacking clear title could be declared public lands (*baldías*). In 1905, Law 55 authorized the outright confiscation and sale of indigenous lands.[16]

In Cauca, at the beginning of the twentieth century, threats to indigenous lands and autonomy were particularly acute as the local government attempted to confiscate extensive indigenous lands. Indigenous responses were powerful. Reacting to the debt-labor system and measures to dispossess communal landholdings, a Nasa indigenous leader named Manuel Quintín Lame began a struggle in the early 1900s for indigenous rights and the recuperation of indigenous lands. While this movement originated in the Cauca and Tolima departments, it had national repercussions, establishing key objectives that are still valued by indigenous organizations throughout Colombia—namely, recuperation of land for the *resguardos*; extension of existing *resguardos*; an end to the debt-labor system with forced payments to large landowners (*terraje*); strengthening of community-level indigenous governance (*cabildos*); publicizing and enforcement of laws protecting indigenous rights; defense of indigenous history, language, and customs; and training of bilingual indigenous teachers.[17]

Quintín Lame died in 1967, but these precepts laid the foundation for the establishment, in 1971, of the Regional Indigenous Council of Cauca (CRIC), one of the oldest organizations of its type.[18] They are reflected in the goals and priorities of contemporary regional and national indigenous organizations and movements in Colombia, as well as in contemporary legislation.

The 1991 Constitution

In 1989–90, a groundswell from grassroots and civil society movements demanding structural reforms and protesting rampant political violence led to the election of a Constitutional Assembly to draft a new constitution in Colombia for the first time in 100 years. The constitution laid out strongly progressive provisions for indigenous rights. Three indigenous representa-

---

[15] Ibid., 17–19.

[16] Ibid., 18–19.

[17] Ibid., 20.

[18] Jesús Avirama and Rayda Márquez, "The Indigenous Movement in Colombia," in *Indigenous Peoples and Democracy in Latin America,* ed. Donna Lee Van Cott (New York: St. Martin's Press, 1994), 83–105.

tives were elected to the assembly. As Donna Lee Van Cott notes, "The [constitutional] assembly provided a fortuitous 'political opportunity' for the already organized and mobilized indigenous movement to frame its particular grievances in more universalistic terms."[19] Pro-indigenous participants in the assembly relied on an evolving body of international norms regarding indigenous and human rights and the environment to shape what were regarded throughout Latin America as some of the most progressive provisions in these areas, especially the recognition of "the collective and inalienable nature of the country's existing *resguardos.*" These statutes blocked practices and provisions established in the nineteenth century that authorized the "voluntary" dissolution and sale and the involuntary reduction of *resguardo* land.

The 1991 constitution commanded the state to "recognize and protect the ethnic and cultural diversity of the Colombian Nation."[20] It guaranteed two congressional seats for indigenous representatives through special conscription and provided administrative outlines for the establishment of Indigenous Territorial Entities affording indigenous communities a moderate degree of legal, cultural, economic, and political autonomy in large extensions of territory. Within their territories, indigenous political councils were deemed legally responsible for overseeing land use, designing projects and development plans, promoting and implementing public investment strategies, receiving and distributing resources, overseeing the protection of natural resources, coordinating programs and projects, collaborating on the maintenance of public order, and representing the territory in national government forums and other entities in which indigenous peoples are integrated.

The constitution stipulated that resource-extraction projects must not harm indigenous communities and that indigenous peoples were to be able to participate in decision making about resource extraction in indigenous territories.[21] Subsoil resources, however, remained the property of the nation. The 1991 constitution earmarked a per capita percentage of federal funds to be allocated to municipal budgets and to indigenous communities.

Indigenous peoples' gains went further. In December 1990, the Colombian Congress ratified International Labour Organization Convention 169 (ILO 169) on the Rights of Indigenous and Tribal Peoples. Among other provisions, this obligated the Colombian government to guarantee indigenous peoples rights of ownership and possession of lands they traditionally occupied or used for "subsistence and traditional activities." The convention and the law ratifying it required, under international and domestic law,

---

[19] Donna Lee Van Cott, *The Friendly Liquidation of the Past* (Pittsburgh: University of Pittsburgh Press, 2000), 7.

[20] Enrique Sánchez, Roque Roldán, and María Fernanda Sánchez, *Derechos a la identidad: Los pueblos indígenas y negros en la constitución política de Colombia de 1991* (Bogotá: COAMA and Disloque Editores, 1996), 57.

[21] Ibid., 58–59.

that the government consult indigenous peoples about "legislative or administrative measures which may affect them directly."[22]

Also essential for indigenous rights—and for human rights protections and conflict mediation in general—was the creation of two new legal and oversight institutions: Defensoría del Pueblo and the Constitutional Court, as well as the establishment of a mechanism of legal recourse—a writ of protection called a *tutela*—for the protection of fundamental constitutional rights. The Constitutional Court became a judicial instrument "to protect community rights, according to the traditions of the ethnic minorities themselves."[23] Thus, Colombia's indigenous peoples have carved out considerable legal, physical, economic, and political space to sustain a strong degree of autonomy through which they attempt, in the midst of a complex war, to live peacefully and maintain distance from the influence of armed actors—legal and extralegal alike—and strengthen their cultures. This same autonomy, however, has placed Colombia's indigenous peoples in a precarious position. Indigenous territories comprise roughly 28 percent of the national territory. They are located on lands that contain valuable resources and are highly strategic.[24] Competing armed actors violently vie for control of their territories.[25] Many indigenous lands are located within—and are therefore perceived as an obstruction to—corridors that armed actors deem strategic to their physical domination of territory or to their control over activities, such as arms trafficking, the drug trade, and access to natural resources.

In this context, the urgency for indigenous communities to be supported in their stance of nonviolence, resistance, and noninvolvement with all armed groups is clear. As an indigenous leader from Cauca said,

> Although we resist war, we are always accused of belonging to one side or other of the conflict. Guerrillas accuse us of being paramilitaries, and paramilitaries accuse of us of being guerrillas. For example, when guerrilla groups came through our community, they forced me to give them food. Soon afterwards, paramilitaries came through and killed my son, supposedly because I supported the guerrillas. Paramilitaries then stayed in my house; two weeks later the guerrillas came back and killed my other son because I supposedly supported paramilitaries. Now I only have one son and no food.[26]

---

[22]James Anaya, *Indigenous Peoples in International Law* (New York: Oxford University Press, 1996), 195–96.

[23]Van Cott, *The Friendly Liquidation*, 112.

[24]Roberto Pineda Camacho, "Pueblos indígenas de Colombia: Una aproximación a su historia, economía y sociedad," in *La Tierra Profanada*, ed. Proyecto ONIC, CCOIN, GHK (Bogotá: Disloque Editores, 1995), 13.

[25]Thad Dunning and Leslie Wirpsa, "Oil and the Political Economy of Conflict in Colombia and Beyond: A Linkages Approach," *Geopolitics* 9, no. 1 (Spring 2004): 81–108.

[26]AFSC, "Views from the South: Peaceful Alternatives to the War in Colombia," www.afsc.org/colombia/peace-communities/views-south.htm (accessed August 29, 2008).

Contemporary Indigenous Resistance and Peacebuilding in Cauca

Dynamics in Cauca provide a lens through which to understand this complex scenario of violence, indigenous resistance to it, and community initiatives for peace. With more than 190,000 indigenous inhabitants from 9 distinct indigenous peoples, the department of Cauca is home to some 24 percent of all Colombia's indigenous population.[27] Since colonial times, through epochs of violence and civil war, the indigenous peoples of Cauca have been innovators of grassroots organization, resistance, and peace initiatives. In the 1980s, an indigenous armed self-defense group—unrelated to right-wing paramilitary squads also emerging at the time—took root in Cauca, naming itself after the historic leader Manuel Quintín Lame. The group organized pockets of Cauca's indigenous communities into protective forces and occupied traditional indigenous lands lost to nonindigenous landholders.[28] The Quintín Lame movement attempted to ward off attacks from large landowners and armed actors.[29] Within the provisions established by the 1989–91 peace initiatives, elections for a Constituent Assembly, and subsequent constitutional reform, the Quintín Lame guerrillas demobilized and disarmed. Marcos Yule, a 45-year-old Nasa leader, explained, "We realized that the Quintín Lame was creating more problems than it was solving."[30]

Since then, and with particular intensity since 2001, Cauca indigenous peoples such as the Nasa, Guambiano, Coconuco, and Yanacona have built a powerful movement supporting nonviolence, noninterference by armed actors in indigenous territories, recuperation of indigenous youth participating in armed groups, and peace. A *New York Times* reporter described the scope of this indigenous peace movement in May 2005: "The Indians have forced traffickers to close down cocaine-producing labs. They have faced down paramilitary death squads. When the mayor of the Nasa town of Toribío was kidnapped last year, 400 guards marched two weeks over the Andes to the rebel camp where he was being held. They won his release."[31]

The Nasa Indigenous Guard is a backbone of this nonviolent resistance. Founded in March 2001 and armed only with their *bastones*, members—women and men alike—shield communities from incursions by all armed

---

[27] DANE, "Proyecciones de población," 41.

[28] Marc Chernick, "Negotiating Peace amid Multiple Forms of Violence: The Protracted Search for a Settlement to the Armed Conflicts in Colombia," in *Comparative Peace Processes in Latin America*, ed. Cynthia Arnson (Washington, D.C.: Woodrow Wilson Center Press, 2000), 165.

[29] Manuel Santos, interview by Justin Podur, Cauca, Colombia, February 20, 2004, www.en-camino.org/caucaphotoessay/manuelsantos.htm (accessed August 29, 2008).

[30] Dan Molinski, "Indigenous Guards Face Colombian Guerrillas," Associated Press, *Miami Herald*, April 22, 2005.

[31] Juan Forero, "Colombia War Spills into Indians' Peaceful World," *New York Times*, May 2, 2005.

actors. One member of the Nasa Indigenous Guard explained, "Now when an armed group comes into our territory, the community gathers and evaluates. Then we approach the intruder and say, 'Gentlemen, you're involving us in a conflict that is not ours. You are in our territory, and here, we govern.' We've avoided many problems this way. We've saved many people—from killing and being killed. We'll let people go around our land, but they can't stay."[32]

The Nasa communities see the guard as a continuation of historical struggles of resistance from colonialism, recuperation of *resguardos*, and grassroots organization. The Indigenous Guard, in 2005 some 7,000 members strong, prevented more widespread intrusion of the armed conflict into Nasa communities. Members, trained in nonviolent security tactics, rotate shifts in groups of ten to protect each indigenous village twenty-four hours a day. Guard members must exhibit a high degree of integrity; they must not have "problems with the community or the *cabildo*"; they must be capable of offering humanitarian aid and of maintaining dialogue as "the basis of respect"; they must "be honest, respectful and not abuse authority, consider themselves part of the indigenous movement, be critical and self-reflective regarding conflict, exhibit political capacity." In addition to their task of protecting the community, guard members maintain contact with humanitarian organizations and receive and provide training in human relations, politics, *planes de vida*, or "plans of life," international humanitarian law, and first aid.[33]

One early act of resistance by the Nasa, with the participation of the indigenous guard, occurred in November 2001, in the town of Caldono, Cauca. Arriving from 6 *resguardos*, 4,500 Nasa faced a cross fire between FARC guerrillas and the police. "The guerrillas were surprised by this unusual procession of indigenous peoples," one news source described. From loudspeakers, Nasa leaders raised a clarion cry that has since characterized their mobilizations: "Our communities do not want any more war!" Indigenous women, children, and men demanded a cease-fire from both the rebels and the police. One woman leader told the press, "We will not stand for any more attacks against indigenous peoples and civilians in general. We want them to leave us alone to live in peace, and we will pay whatever price necessary to maintain our *resguardos* free of violent actors."[34]

But the Nasa's ability to keep many of the armed actors at least somewhat at bay is fragile. For example, their noninvolvement was severely threatened

---

[32] AFSC and FOR, "Building from the Inside Out," 23; AFSC, "Protector of Life: José Bernal of the Indigenous Guard," www.afsc.org/colombia/peace-testimonies/voices-for-peace5.htm (accessed August 30, 2008).

[33] See "Documento de las guardias indígenas del Cauca," Cauca, January 2002, in ONIC, *Los indígenas y la paz: Conclusiones de la mesa indígena de paz* (Bogotá: ONIC, July 2001), 70–73.

[34] "Paeces impiden ataque de las FARC," *El Tiempo,* Bogotá, November 14, 2001; see also "Colombia; indígenas y guerrilleros se enfrentan," *El Comercio,* Quito, November 14, 2001.

when the Colombian military, tutored and financed by U.S. advisers, designed and implemented Plan Patriota—an offensive that established police stations throughout communities and towns in Cauca, including in Nasa territory. Plan Patriota was arguably one of the most extensive counterinsurgency initiatives waged against left-wing guerrillas in Colombia in the past forty years. It targeted primarily strongholds of the FARC in Colombia's southern departments and the Amazonian southeastern region. While the establishment of police posts might, in some circumstances, have been conceived as a logical way to protect the citizenry, it is important to note that Colombian police are often barely distinguishable from army forces. They carry heavy weapons and often act jointly with the military, and some police officers have been implicated in cases of severe human rights abuses. Guerrillas often consider the police a military target. The Nasa communities perceived the Plan Patriota police units not as a source of protection but rather as actors exacerbating conflict.

In April 2005, a police outpost in Toribío—a town of 3,000 surrounded by Nasa *resguardos*—was the epicenter of one of the most striking challenges to Nasa peace initiatives to date. The FARC launched an attack on the town on April 14, announcing the incursion over a bullhorn.[35] They demanded that inhabitants "vacate the town because we are about to attack."[36] The army moved in, and the battle ensued for days. The FARC used gas canister bombs, and the air force, reinforcing the army, rained down bombs. An estimated 3,500 Nasa were displaced in the fighting, with some 500 choosing to take shelter in a health post on a hill overseeing the mayhem, according to the UNHCR. Illnesses like hepatitis and chicken pox spread in the makeshift camp.[37] On April 22, 2005, the Nasa communities of the Jambaló Resguardo, displaced by the violence, made a striking announcement: they would return to their communities even if the fighting had not ended. They said,

> We demand that all armed actors in the conflict respect our traditional authority. . . . We return not because of any increase of protection from public forces, but because of the difficult health situation that faces our children, pregnant women, and elders. . . . [Our] homes are left alone and some of them are being plundered, and others occupied by the police. Our domestic animals that we depend on for food are dying and disappearing. If this continues, we are at risk of becoming beggars and dependents, which we are not willing to do. We prefer to maintain our dignity.[38]

---

[35] Constanza Viera, "Caught in Colombian Crossfire, Nasa Indians Take Shelter in Health Post," Inter Press Service, April 29, 2005.

[36] Steven Dudley, "Indians Battle Rebels," *Miami Herald*, April 21, 2005.

[37] Viera, "Caught in Colombian Crossfire."

[38] *Resguardo* and municipality of Jambaló, "Comunicado a la opinión pública nacional e internacional" (e-mail received by author, May 2, 2005).

As the Jambaló declaration reveals, the Nasa—and other communities throughout Colombia—are determined to continue to promote strategies of noninvolvement and resistance, despite horrendous risk.

When the Toribío attack began, the outcry from the Nasa indigenous communities was clear and loud, and it reverberated across the country. Indigenous organizations, humanitarian agencies, non-governmental organizations (NGOs), the press, and many others were mobilized, and a solidarity network coalesced. Leaders from ONIC and the Regional Indigenous Council of Cauca arrived to provide moral, political, and humanitarian support.

Indigenous peace and resistance movements have also challenged right-wing paramilitary groups. For example, in May 2001, indigenous peoples from the town of Cajibío, also in Cauca, sent out a national and international alert regarding the presence of paramilitary and army forces near the community. Through international networking via the Internet, the Cajibío leaders called attention to the situation. During the previous six months, they had seen over a hundred people ruthlessly massacred, the majority by paramilitaries, in the region of the Naya, and they organized to create resistance to a rerun of such violence. The Nasa communities of Cajibío informed the international community that a new paramilitary incursion was pending. Leaders announced that the paramilitaries were advancing despite the presence in the region of official army troops. They specifically named the battalions present during the incursion, and the commanders in charge. The communities also requested that army personnel involved in paramilitary activity be removed from service.[39]

From time to time, government representatives have attempted to co-opt indigenous resistance as a broader sign of support for counterinsurgency strategies, especially against the FARC. In Cauca and beyond, however, Colombia's indigenous peoples have repeatedly demanded that their stance of noninvolvement not be compromised by strategic or political attempts to identify them with a specific faction of armed actors—not left-wing guerrillas, not the counterinsurgency forces of the army, and not right-wing paramilitaries.[40]

The Cauca indigenous movement has also resisted actions, accusations, and abuses from the Colombian army and police. In the aftermath of the April 2005 attacks by the FARC on Toribío, the indigenous communities denounced the police's construction of trenches in the town, claiming that these would put the civilian population at extreme risk in the case of another guerrilla incursion. The Colombian delegate from the Office of the UN High Com-

---

[39] Liam Craig-Best and Rowan Shingler, "Paramilitary Incursions in the Municipality of Caibío in the Department of Cauca, Southwestern Colombia," Colombia Human Rights Network, http://colhrnet.igc.org/newitems/june01/clmcauca.603.htm (accessed June 4, 2001).

[40] Yadira Ferrer, "Colombia: Indians Stage Civil Resistance against Armed Groups," Inter Press Service, January 8, 2002.

missioner for Human Rights supported the community's stance.[41] That same week, the communities also denounced attempts by the armed forces to take control of the distribution of humanitarian aid as part of "civic-military" campaigns. Asserting autonomy granted to them within their territorial jurisdictions under Colombian law, the northern Cauca indigenous councils demanded that indigenous traditional authorities be the sole distributors of any and all humanitarian aid arriving to the communities, citing the responsibility of said authorities to maintain equilibrium and harmony within their territories, to make sure that such goods served the collective good, and to procure a stance of noninvolvement from all sides of the armed conflict.[42]

While violence has persisted in Cauca, the indigenous communities have remained committed to strengthening these nonviolent strategies. The American Friends Service Committee (AFSC) recognized these ongoing efforts in February 2007, nominating Ezequiel Vitonás, the elder chancellor of the Association of Indigenous Councils of Cauca, for the Nobel Peace Prize.

Moreover, on a national legislative level, indigenous protests have contributed to the repeal of constitutional reforms proposed by the Uribe administration, which, according to scholars, NGOs, and human rights organizations alike, would have had severe negative consequences for human rights protections in Colombia, and particularly for indigenous rights. Indigenous actions in this grassroots resistance included the 2004 *minga*, several land recuperations in Cauca in 2005, ongoing resistance to and indigenous "popular consultations" against the Free Trade Agreement of the Americas, and another large 2006 national gathering of 10,000 indigenous people in Cauca in May 2006. The proposed reforms would have weakened writ-of-protection mechanisms (*tutela*) and constitutional provisions supporting territorial autonomy for indigenous peoples. Following Uribe's reelection in 2006, his administration took steps to revive these reforms, proposing a "rural development statute," which analysts claim would curtail the protection of indigenous groups, especially from incursions by multinational corporations.[43]

Building Peace through Economic Resistance and Holistic Alternatives

As the Grassroots Minga for Life, Justice, Joy, Liberty, and Autonomy revealed, indigenous peoples in Colombia are not only saying no to violence from armed actors, but they are also simultaneously critiquing historic and

---

[41] Asociación de Cabildos Indígenas del Cauca (ACIN), "ONU y comunidad rechazan trincheras en Toribío," May 6, 2005, http://colombia.indymedia.org/news/2005/05/25323.php (accessed August 30, 2008).

[42] ACIN, "Cabildos Rechazan Acciones 'Civicos-Militares,'" May 11, 2005, http://colombia.indymedia.org/news/2005/05/25701.php (accessed August 30, 2008).

[43] Héctor Mondragón, "Estatuto rural, hijo de la parapolítica," July 6, 2007, http://colombia.indymedia.org/news/2007/07/69053.php (accessed October 2, 2008).

contemporary development hegemony, resource policies, and economic models that, they claim, replicate a history of destructive relationships initiated through colonialism. Colombia's indigenous peoples are moving beyond denouncing violence; they are presenting new models for economic sustainability that are essential to long-term conflict resolution.

Historically, development planning in Colombia largely reflected the priorities of investors, such as multilateral lending institutions and transnational corporations. As a result, the majority of Colombians—in particular, indigenous peoples, Afro-Colombians, and campesinos—were not engaged in the design of development programs.[44] From the 1960s until the adoption of the 1991 constitution, development planning in Colombia was largely centralized through the creation of national development plans that used gross national product as the primary measure of development, while paying less attention to social indicators.[45] State policies encouraged the colonization of indigenous peoples' lands by white and mestizo settlers to "improve" rural areas, integrating them into the national economy through market-oriented agriculture, cattle ranching, and other commercialization projects. Large infrastructure projects, such as road construction and hydroelectric power, promoted expansion of corporate resource-extraction and other capital investments.[46] Indigenous, subsistence-based forms of cultivation and resource management went largely unrecognized as organic forms of self-development.[47]

Since the 1990s, indigenous peoples in Colombia have begun to transform this development legacy by devising comprehensive economic, social, and cultural strategies known as *planes de vida*.[48] The term is a deliberate counter to the framing of state-designed development plans.[49] *Planes de vida* are holistic strategies that are becoming widespread among indigenous communities. They emphasize cultural and physical survival through territorial autonomy. At the national level, ONIC promotes these *planes* as an essential element of indigenous self-determination. The *planes* advocate an indigenous-rights agenda based on communities' distinct cosmologies and lifeways, including support for education, health, ceremonial rituals and the protection of sacred

---

[44] Arturo Escobar, *Encountering Development: The Making and Unmaking of the Third World* (Princeton, N.J.: Princeton University Press, 1995).

[45] Olga Restrepo Quintero, "La institucionalización del proceso de planificación en Colombia," in *Planificación del Desarrollo*, ed. Ruth Saavedra Guzmán (Bogotá: Fundación Universidad de Bogotá Jorge Tadeo Lozano, 1998), 89–151.

[46] Escobar, *Encountering Development.*

[47] David Gow, "Can the Subaltern Plan? Ethnicity and Development in Cauca, Colombia," *Urban Anthropology* 26, no. 3–4 (1997): 243–92.

[48] ONIC, *Elementos conceptuales* (Bogotá: ONIC, 2000).

[49] ONIC, *Vida y dignidad para los indígenas y para los colombianos también: Memorias del Congreso de los Pueblos Indígenas de Colombia, Cota, 25 al 30 de noviembre de 2001* (Bogotá: ONIC, 2001).

sites, harvest calendars, and indigenous land uses.[50] *Planes de vida* are also central to the antidisplacement and peacebuilding platform articulated by Colombia's indigenous-rights movement, and they promote nonviolent alternatives both to a legal economy based on resource extraction and to the illegal drug economy.

In places like the southwestern department of Putumayo, home to the majority of Colombia's Cofán people, widespread violence fomented in part by resource extraction, particularly of oil, as well as by coca cultivation and processing, has challenged both state and indigenous designs for development. Violence has disrupted the sociopolitical fabric, complicating peace initiatives. Much of Putumayo is rural Amazonian foothills and lowlands, and the department has a long stretch of border with Ecuador. Home to 10 different indigenous peoples with a population of about 25,000, Putumayo is a fierce battleground, a territory bitterly disputed by guerrillas, paramilitaries, and the national army. Oil exploration in Putumayo, which began in 1962, has long been central to state-sponsored development plans for the region.[51] The government's strategy of militarization in Putumayo has been aimed at combating left-wing insurgents and drug interests that are damaging Colombia's relationships with major foreign investors, primarily transnational oil corporations.[52] As Colombia's leading legal export, oil is currently the source of almost one-third of the government's revenues.[53] With support from the Bush administration, Colombian president Álvaro Uribe marshaled the Colombian armed forces to protect pipelines from bombings and the bootlegging of petroleum from gas ducts by guerrillas and paramilitaries.[54]

Coca production has recently rivaled oil as the latest extractive commodity boom in Putumayo. For many campesinos and indigenous peoples, given the scarcity of alternatives, coca is often the only means to a livelihood.[55] Because it supplies the bulk of Colombia's coca production and a consistent flow of oil, the department of Putumayo has been a primary direct recipient of U.S.-backed Plan Colombia funding.[56]

---

[50] ONIC, *Planes de vida de los pueblos indígenas: Fortaleciendo la supervivencia* (Bogotá: ONIC, 1998).

[51] Mario Mejía Gutiérrez, *Amazonía colombiana: Historia del uso de la tierra* (Florencia, Caquetá [Colombia]: Consejo Regional de Planeación, 1993).

[52] Juan Forero, "Safeguarding Colombia's Oil," *New York Times*, October 22, 2004.

[53] Ibid.

[54] Ibid.

[55] Janet Lloyd and Atossa Soltani, *Reporte Sobre Plan Colombia y los Pueblos Indígenas* (Washington, D.C.: Amazon Watch, 2001).

[56] José Ramos, "Fumigaciones preocupan en el Putumayo, un enclave cocalero y petrolero," Agence France-Presse, Oct. 11, 2002; Center for International Policy, "Defensoría del Pueblo de Colombia: Informe defensorial no. 1—Fumigaciones y proyectos de desarrollo alternativo en el Putumayo, 9 de febrero del 2001," www.ciponline.org/colombia/01020901.htm (accessed

Ironically, some state-sponsored social-development programs, like illicit-crop substitution in indigenous and campesino communities, have been sabotaged by coca fumigation campaigns financed by Plan Colombia.[57] Aircraft spray a powerful glyphosate mixture that often kills not only coca plants but staple crops and tropical plants as well. For example, in 2001, the office of the Defensoría del Pueblo found evidence to support the grievances filed by indigenous communities in Valle de Guamuéz, Putumayo.[58] These communities alleged that crops planted under state-sponsored substitution activities—staples including cacao, corn, bananas, and yuca (manioc)—and cattle pastures were damaged as a result of aerial spraying. Some indigenous and campesino farmers, their livelihoods destroyed, fled to urban areas and to Ecuador, swelling the populations of internally displaced and international refugees.[59]

Thus, indigenous peoples in Putumayo have criticized both oil and coca production as de jure and de facto forms of development exacerbating violence. The Cofán Pueblo is leveraging state resources earmarked for antinarcotics programs and infrastructure development to promote indigenous visions for nonviolent development in the region through its *plan de vida*. Along with projects aimed at reducing illicit-crop cultivation, resources from government programs have also supported projects geared toward improving health, food security, and land tenure in the *resguardos* and building the capacity of Cofán leaders to identify and promote other "alternative indigenous self-development" projects.[60]

The Cofán *plan de vida*, completed in 2002, presents both a critique of Colombia's development policies and proactive strategies aimed at improving existing conditions and fomenting holistic economic and social strategies grounded in Cofán principles. The *plan* documents Cofán history from the perspective of community elders and outlines the planning process itself. It includes a thorough community self-assessment of present conditions on which to base recommendations, and it asserts that this comprehensive strategy is essential to regional peace initiatives.

The Cofán *plan de vida* attributes a massive decline in cultivation of traditional subsistence and medicinal crops, including manioc and *yagé* (a sacred

---

August 30, 2008); Lisa Haugaard, Adam Isacson, Kimberly Stanton, John Walsh, and John Vogt, *Blueprint for a New Colombia Policy* (Washington, D.C.: Latin America Working Group Education Fund, Center for International Policy, Washington Office on Latin America, and U.S. Office on Colombia, 2005), 1; Ana María Gómez López, "Talking Sense on Colombia," AFSC, September 2001, 1, www.afsc.org/colombia/ht/d/ContentDetails/i/18734 (accessed October 2, 2008).

[57] Center for International Policy, "Defensoría del Pueblo de Colombia."

[58] Ibid.

[59] Ibid.

[60] Ibid.

psychotropic plant), to colonialism, the expansion of oil development, and coca cultivation. It describes how monocultivation of coca has squeezed out small-scale farming and hunting, noting that market conditions for coca, in terms of demand, price, and infrastructure, are highly favorable in comparison to traditional crops.[61] The consequences of this transition include an increased dependence on obtaining cash to purchase food and other basic necessities, disrupting community self-sufficiency. This process not only erodes cultural cohesion but threatens the physical health and peaceful coexistence of communities: malnutrition is widespread, especially among the elderly, and illnesses related to water contamination from cocaine production and aerial eradication are rampant.

The Cofán *plan de vida* links indigenous involvement in coca production to the reduction of indigenous territories.[62] Oil exploration, the *plan* states, fed this reduction and contributed to dependence on coca. Forty years of oil exploration in Putumayo have failed to materialize in social development. Oil revenues have largely been funneled back into large-scale infrastructure projects to support oil extraction. Defining culturally based alternatives to oil and coca economies, the *plan* emphasizes the importance of land tenure in the *resguardos*, a bilingual ethnoeducation system to ground youth in Cofán culture, and a bicultural health system that incorporates both Western and traditional medicine.

The *plan* promotes spiritual practices and food security, designating areas within the *resguardos* for the protection of the *yagé* plant—instrumental in Cofán religious ceremonies—and traditional hunting grounds. It emphasizes collectively held territory as a basic premise for cultural survival, peacebuilding, and self-development. The *plan* elaborates: "For us territory is the most important thing. If we lose our territory, we disappear as a community; we lose our children, we lose everything, we become poor, we are left sad. We become transients—we and the land disappear when we don't have collective property rights. We need more land, so we are asking for more territory and legal recognition for the territory that we now have."[63]

The strategies advanced in the *planes de vida* such as the Cofán's represent an important contribution to a peacebuilding vision for Colombia, from an indigenous vantage point. Securing indigenous land rights and autonomy, in cooperation with the responsible state institutions, is a compelling alternative to surrendering de facto control over these territories to the illegal drug economy and the practices of armed actors.

---

[61] Fundación Zia-Aí, *Plan de vida del pueblo Cofán y cabildos indígenas del valle del Guamuéz y San Miguel* (Bogotá: Fundación Zia-Aí, 2002).

[62] Ibid.

[63] Ibid., 149–51.

Conclusions and Recommendations

For centuries, Colombia's indigenous peoples have resisted physical violence while simultaneously designing strategies of territorial and cultural autonomy, as well as new forms of representation and participation that challenge historical exclusions. With this legacy, indigenous peoples' struggles, in light of the current reality of war in Colombia, constitute a powerfully innovative and integral approach to peacebuilding that addresses both the political and economic roots of violent conflict, as well as viable solutions. Pragmatically, initiatives like the indigenous guard, the *minga*, and the *planes de vida* demonstrate a commitment by Colombia's indigenous communities to protect their territorial autonomy, their stance of noninvolvement with armed actors, and peaceful community coexistence.

What measures by international governments, the non-governmental domestic and international community, solidarity organizations, and the Colombian state might enhance indigenous initiatives for peace? How can policy and practice contribute to creating greater space, rather than restrictions, for the indigenous stance of nonviolent resistance and noninvolvement with armed actors?

The desire of indigenous peoples to maintain autonomy and a position of noninvolvement with all armed actors within their territories must be respected. This means respect for the inalienability of indigenous lands. They should not be used as transport routes, commercial corridors, or refuges for the activities of any armed agents, and government forces must not compromise the indigenous communities' stance of noninvolvement. Armed actors, legal and extralegal alike, must refrain from forced recruitment of indigenous peoples into their cadres and must stop associating communities with any factions, publicly as well as informally. Bombardments and raids on indigenous lands must cease, as must arbitrary detentions of leaders and community representatives. Negotiated solutions to the conflict, rather than an acceleration of the war, are essential.

Indigenous subnational autonomy, as sanctioned by the 1991 constitution, ILO 169, and corresponding legislation, requires that all state-sponsored development plans, policies, and practices be subjected to a broad consultative process with potentially affected indigenous populations. This holds true not only for domestic arrangements but also for international agreements affecting indigenous peoples. The strategies outlined in indigenous *planes de vida* must shape the government development-planning process at the municipal, departmental, regional, and national levels. Integrative approaches that combine cessation of armed conflict, negotiated solutions, and channels out of the economic and social violence feeding Colombia's war are essential for an enduring peace, as are indigenous self-development plans as conceived in the *planes de vida*.

PART IV

LOCAL AND REGIONAL PEACE INITIATIVES

13

Local Peace Communities in Colombia
An Initial Comparison of Three Cases

Christopher Mitchell and Sara Ramírez

In early 1998, the Bogotá-based peace organization Red Nacional de Iniciativas por la Paz y contra la Guerra (REDEPAZ) began a project to help establish and support new and existing local "peace zones and communities" throughout Colombia. Such communities were defined as those that had, for a variety of reasons, chosen to opt out of the struggles between guerrillas, paramilitary groups, and Colombian armed forces that were continuing to engulf the country in a tidal wave of violence impervious to national-level peacemaking efforts. Peace communities had begun to use the strategy of declaring themselves neutral, off-limits areas, no longer part of the almost fifty years of widespread violence that had afflicted their country. The REDEPAZ project was titled Cien Municipios de Paz (One Hundred Municipalities of Peace). It was to provide support, encouragement, resources, meetings, and coordination for the Colombian peace communities until the project came to an end four years later and was replaced by one that sought to develop local democracy throughout the country.[1]

In 1999, the Institute for Conflict Analysis and Resolution at George Mason University began its own research project into the varied Colombian *experiencias de paz* (experiences of peace). This project sought to describe and "map out" the various peace zones and communities in the

---

Data for this study were originally gathered during 2000–03, so the following analysis mainly concentrates on the peace communities' experience during the presidency of Andrés Pastrana and the initial year of President Uribe's first term of office. Since then, much has changed in Colombia, both nationally and locally, affecting the environment within which the peace communities operate. The final section deals briefly with some of the effects of those changes.

[1] In later years, the project changed its title to Cien Experiencias de Participación Ciudadana (One Hundred Experiences of Citizen Participation).

country. It also began to compare and analyze the histories of different types of "zones" of peace in order to discern key factors that might explain the relative success of the various *experiencias*—how and why some survived while others collapsed.

The research strategy eventually adopted was twofold. The first strategy sought out shared characteristics and major differences among a large sample of the "hundred" Colombian *experiencias* and was thus classificatory and comparative. While this was in no sense a statistical sample, we used a number of criteria in selecting peace communities for study and attempted to include in the list examples that differed according to such attributes as ethnic composition, who was in control of the surrounding region, the level of local violence, the strategic and economic importance of the community and its territory, and the degree of outside interest and support that the community enjoyed.

The second strategy adopted an in-depth case-study approach, which examined in detail eight examples of *experiencias*, seeking a "rich description" of these zones, communities, or associations. This chapter reports on some of the results from both strategies. First, we discuss our search for an appropriate framework through which to compare in the most useful way what our research revealed to be a set of very diverse experiences of local peacemaking and peacebuilding in Colombia. Second, we present some details of three local peacebuilding *experiencias* that we were able to study in some depth during 1999–2003.

Comparing Zones of Peace: Search for a Framework

An initial focus for the research arose from a preliminary review of the experiences of local communities that had established zones of peace (ZoP) in the Philippines—one of the countries that had pioneered the movement for local peacebuilding—during the late 1980s. It seemed clear that the fortunes of this first wave of peace zones had been varied, with some clearly more successful than others. This led to the question of what, exactly, constituted success for a local zone of peace. In more formal research terms, what, exactly, were we seeking to explain through our research? It seemed that given the often perilous circumstances in which local peace zones were established—including major violence, often targeting the civilian population; the determination of armed combatants to control territory and resources; and widespread zero-sum assumptions militating against the possibility of "neutrality"—simply the survival of the zone over an extended period of time could well count as a measure of (relative) success. Hence, *durability* could serve as a conceptual basis and, in formal terms, as a dependent variable. Later, as our knowledge of peace zones and communities in Colombia deepened, we came to the conclusion that the durability of an *experiencia de paz* was simply one aspect, although certainly a basic one, of success. Any evaluation would have to take into account other factors, including the objectives of the community itself at the initiation of the peace *experiencia*.

The basic research question for the overall project seemed clear: what factors had significantly affected, either positively or negatively, the durability of ZoP in Colombia? Knowing this, it might be possible to compare degrees of success in the case of the Colombian peace *experiencias* and to explain what had led to the durability of some, and the demise of others.

Determining Factors and Key Influences

Investigating accounts of the experiences of peace communities in the Philippines and, to a lesser extent, in Central America led to preliminary hunches about circumstances that were likely to affect the ability of Colombian peace communities at least to survive, if not to flourish and prosper. These hunches were plausible and could serve as a starting point. It appeared that the following factors would increase the durability of a local zone or community of peace:

- greater benefits to the armed actors because of the existence of ZoP;
- more equal distribution of such benefits among rival armed actors;
- lower levels of instability (defined as fighting between armed actors) in and around ZoP;
- lower levels of violence to ZoP members since its establishment;
- greater internal unity within ZoP, especially regarding their objectives and procedures;
- more widespread grassroots participation in the establishment and subsequent operation of ZoP; and
- greater interconnectedness of ZoP to similar bodies and to support organizations and institutions.

Later Revisions

Once fieldwork on the project had begun and some pilot interviews had been done, it became clear that many of these initial hypotheses, as well as key assumptions on which they were based, were oversimplified or plainly misleading. Many had to be modified, and others abandoned altogether. For example, it soon became evident that problems facing communities seeking to establish and maintain local zones of peace were not simply the result of violence and instability caused by combat between armed actors in the locality. If the locality of a peace zone was relatively stable for a time, clearly under the control of one or another of the armed actors, then other kinds of threats to the zone might arise. Paramilitaries might demand a switch in local forms of agriculture to coca or palm oil production or might simply eject the existing population and settle more amenable workers in their stead. The Colombian army seems to have been less than enthusiastic about initiatives that seemed to set up semisovereign entities apart from the state itself and from which the army, as a legitimate representative of that state, was excluded. In many ways, the actual world of local peace *experiencias* in Colombia was far more complicated than could be understood through simplified social science hunches or hypotheses.

More seriously, it was soon apparent that some of the assumptions underpinning our original hunches were themselves highly dubious. Our first error involved the conception of a "zone," with its implication of a territorial base. Especially with regard to those Colombian *experiencias* that had been established by internally displaced people (IDPs, of whom there are now more than three million in Colombia), it became apparent that the idea of a peace "community" implied precisely that: a group of people who were members of a *comunidad de paz* regardless of their physical location—that is, not bound by a delineated territory. Many Colombian peace communities established themselves in one location—often a refugee camp or urban shelter to which they had been driven by combat or (equally often) by being ejected from their homes by one or another of the armed actors—as a preparation for moving back to reclaim their place of origin or some new settlement in their home region. The idea of neutral "ground," or some form of sanctuary, moved with them, so that the *experiencia de paz* was based on neutral persons, not neutral territory. Hence, our research was clearly dealing with both *zones* and *communities* of peace.

Connected with this problem was the whole issue of names and terms. Finding an appropriate term to describe consistently the focus of our study proved unexpectedly difficult. Originally, we used "zones of peace," which had become familiar from the Philippine examples. But this seemed increasingly inappropriate, given that many Colombian cases involved a community of people rather than a defined territory. Some, but by no means all, described themselves as a "municipal constituent assembly," with the implication that all the members within a *municipio* (the Colombian unit of local government) were within a peace zone. Some, but not all, had formed themselves into an *asociación* of peace zones or communities. Adding to the confusion, later in our period of study, some communities began to call themselves "humanitarian zones" or "communities of resistance," or, toward the very end of the period, "laboratories of peace." For the purposes of this chapter, we have tried to adopt the Colombian habit of talking about *experiencias* of peace, although it has proved remarkably difficult to keep inconsistencies from creeping into the text.

Our second major incorrect assumption was that our study simply involved individual zones, communities, or *municipios* of peace—an assumption that seriously underestimated the political sense and organizational skills of those seeking to engage in local, grassroots peacebuilding. It rapidly became apparent that those involved in establishing local communities of peace had recognized the advantages that come from combination. Many had already taken the next step of forming themselves into associations of peace communities, so that our study would be missing an essential dimension if it simply analyzed and compared individual peace communities. By 1999, there were already a number of *asociaciones* of peace communities in Colombia, and others were forming themselves, often with the idea of obtaining slightly more bargaining power with the guerrillas, the armed forces, and even the paramilitaries.

Finally, it became increasingly apparent that we had grossly oversimplified the concept of success by assuming that the main—indeed, the only—objective that local communities had in declaring themselves a zone of peace was to obtain protection from the surrounding violence and from the depredations of the armed actors. To the contrary, while including this as an obvious aim, many communities had established themselves as peace *experiencias* for a wide variety of reasons, with a wide variety of objectives, and with a wide variety of views about what constituted "success." Some communities had initial aims of ending political corruption and patronage. In others, the aim was to provide some opportunities for local youth other than joining the guerrillas or the paramilitaries. In some indigenous communities, the aim was to protect local culture and traditional ways of life. Success was clearly a relative idea, and undoubtedly related in part to the aims and experiences of those involved in creating the peace community.

A Working Framework

Ultimately, we adapted our research strategy to take into account these initial discoveries and also the surprising number of peace *experiencias* that our initial analysis had revealed. We decided to investigate in depth eight representative peace *experiencias*, four of which would be individual communities and four of which would be associations of peace communities. When it came to selecting the eight cases for in-depth comparison, pragmatic factors played a major role in constructing the final list. Was enough background material available on the *experiencia*? Was the location reachable and reasonably safe for field visits? Would the local community be willing to allow field visits, and would such visits create dangers for the community?

Even more difficult would be to create a comprehensive report on all the characteristics deemed important for even one peace zone or community. What follows, therefore, is the application of some of the key ideas from a "working framework" to three of the *municipio*-based peace *experiencias*, selected partly because of their varied geographical locations within Colombia: Samaniego, in the department of Nariño and part of the coca-growing region in southern Colombia, near the Ecuadoran border; Tarso, in southwestern Antioquia, which seemed at first sight to have suffered much less from local combat than other regions of the country; and Sonson, in eastern Antioquia, a region that had experienced considerable violence over control of resources and routes and that had responded by forming a regional association. (See Development and Peace Programs map.)

We compare these three *experiencias* across three major dimensions: the manner in which the peace zone or community was first established, the organizational structure that was established to fulfill the *municipios'* major objectives, and the manner in which the people in the three zones attempted to deal with the armed actors that were prosecuting the violent conflict in their region.

Starting: Trigger Events and Objectives

Peace *experiencias* and communities established in the rural areas of Colombia fall roughly into two main types. The first type are established by IDP communities in exile from their own territory, usually as a means of returning to their home *municipios* or *corregimientos* (departmental subdivisions) from which they have been driven. This type usually involves prior establishment of decision-making structures, committees, and local associations before a return to the home territory. This is partly a way of signaling to the guerrillas, paramilitaries, and Colombian armed forces that on their return, the communities will no longer involve themselves in the ongoing struggle.

The second type of *experiencia de paz* is established by a community on its own original territory, either to protect the community and its territory in situ or to bring about some major change in the way the community has been managed, enabling it to create a situation of internal peace, usually linked to justice and more democratic practices. While the challenges facing the two types of *experiencias* are somewhat different, both represent, to varying degrees, efforts to establish and maintain what might be termed *external peace*, between the community and the surrounding combatants; and *internal peace*, within the community, through commitments to nonviolence, participatory decision making, and self-reliant development. Interestingly, the practical experience of Colombian peace communities illustrates the distinction between "negative" and "positive" peace first discussed by scholars such as Johan Galtung and Adam Curle.[2] But the practical combination of these two types of peace into a single overarching strategy has often proved quite difficult.

The three *municipios* to be compared in this chapter are all examples of what might be termed *continuing* rather than *returning* peace communities. All three have established themselves on their original sites, rather than dur-

---

[2]For an analysis of "unpeaceful relationships," see Adam Curle, *Making Peace* (London: Tavistock, 1971). For a discussion of the differences between "positive" and "negative" peace, see (among many other works) Johan Galtung, *Peace by Peaceful Means* (Thousand Oaks, Calif.: Sage, 1996).

ing a time of exile, when they were preparing to return to their home territory. This makes the question of their establishment an interesting one, since it raises issues about motivations that are necessarily different from the basic wish simply to "go home."

In effect, two of the three communities exhibit very clearly a pattern of establishment that seems to be emerging from our study of continuing peace zones—a pattern that is less evident in the peace community in Tarso but that may also help explain the origins of that particular *experiencia*. Both Sonson and Samaniego appear to be cases where a long period of increasing stress on the community (arising sometimes from within the community itself, sometimes from the violence in the environment, and sometimes from both) is punctuated by a crisis or trigger event that pushes the community to the point where key individuals or sectors within the population become convinced that there has to be some change, that something must be done. The trigger event then becomes a turning point for action to deal with an immediate crisis but also with underlying problems that give rise to the community's being "unpeaceful," in both the positive and the negative sense.

In Samaniego, for example, a long period of more than eight years of neglect by the state and of internal conflict and dissension—fights for political power among entrenched elites, clientelism, irresponsible management of public resources, lack of popular participation in decision making—had all led to a situation where the local left-wing guerrillas of the Ejército de Liberación Nacional (ELN) intervened constantly in the affairs of the *municipio* at all levels. This process of intervention ranged from the personal (quarrels between neighbors) to the political (who could stand for the office of mayor). As one interviewed member of the community recalled, "Practically, the guerrillas had taken determinations that they were not authorized to take. Even arranging marriages, divorcing marriages. . . . We had to live all through this situation."[3] More seriously, the ELN would intervene to remove public officials accused of incompetence or corruption. In 1994 they kidnapped and killed Luis Alejandro Bastidas, the mayor of Samaniego. While the community organized protest marches and protests against the assassination of the mayor, the trigger event for Samaniego did not come until nearly four years later, the year of the Mandato Ciudadano por la Paz, la Vida y la Libertad, or Citizens' Mandate for Peace, Life, and Liberty. The Fuerzas Armadas Revolucionarias de Colombia (FARC) guerrillas had issued a general threat against all those who intended to stand in the mayoral elections of 1997. In Samaniego, the ELN kidnapped Manuel Cellar, a genuinely populist candidate for mayor. Again there were massive protests in the *municipio*, the candidate was duly

---

[3] Unless otherwise noted, quotations are taken directly from field interviews conducted in Colombia from 2001 to 2003 and translated into English.

elected in absentia, and eventually these and other actions managed to secure the release of the now elected mayor. On assuming office, Cellar announced that he intended to conduct his administration in a transparent and participatory manner, in line with the Citizens' Mandate for Peace. He also suggested that the municipality be declared a "zone of peace." The suggestion was taken up in the community, and a declaration to that effect was made on January 23, 1998. Samaniego is thus one of the peace communities in which the initiative came from, rather than in spite of, the *alcalde* (mayor) and the local administration.

Something similar occurred in Sonson, although important additional elements figured in the formation of the "Constituent Municipal Assembly of Sonson," which came into being in July 2001. The *municipio* itself has had a history of single-party control and financial mismanagement since the mid-1980s, with one family controlling the mayorship and, through incompetence and corruption, running the administration deeply into debt. This process was halted when a new *alcalde*, William Ospina Naranjo, was elected in 1995 and, from then to 1998, instituted a series of reforms. These included a civil-training program titled the "School for Democracy," which later served as a basis for organizing the community into a peace zone. Ospina also managed to initiate an efficient and transparent local administrative system, but members of the old regime returned to power in the next election and, by 2000, had plunged the *municipio* even further into debt. Responding to popular pressure, Ospina ran again for mayor and was reelected in 2000, but he faced a crisis of governability in the *municipio*.

At the same time, the armed conflict around Sonson intensified. Since the early 1980s, this region of Antioquia, an important area for transit as well as for growing coca and poppy, had always had a major presence of both the FARC (two *frentes*, or fronts) and the ELN (the *frente* Carlos Alirio Buitrago). In early 2000, paramilitaries from the Autodefensas del Magdalena Medio began to move into the region and established a center of operations in a *corregimiento* within Sonson. Violence began to escalate, and a struggle over territory followed.

The trigger event that sparked the movement to establish Sonson as a peace zone occurred in May 2001, when Mayor Ospina was kidnapped by the ELN, ostensibly to account for the state of the municipal finances and for the increasing paramilitary control of the *municipio*'s urban areas. As in Samaniego, the community mobilized to protest the kidnapping and demand the mayor's release. This event actually started, for the very first time, an open debate about the armed conflict and what the local community could do that would not involve it, practically or ideologically, with one armed group or the other.

After the mayor was released, preparations for declaring the *municipio* a peace zone went ahead, using this event as a symbolic opportunity. But such a move had actually been planned since April 2001, and the declaration of the new peace zone and its Constituent Assembly was the result of a grassroots process influenced by three important factors. The first factor was the courses on civic participation at the "School for Democracy," conducted by a local non-governmental organization (NGO), ConCiudadanía. The second factor was the resultant development of a strong women's movement in Sonson: MAIS (Association of Independent Women of Sonson), which developed a proposal for women to fill public positions within the *municipio* as part of a "call for the different living forces of the community to become part of an assembly." The third factor was the example provided by the peace community (and the Constituent Assembly) in Mogotes, which MAIS members and others had visited previously and which provided both the inspiration and an organizational model of what a peace community might be and achieve. The *alcalde* was enthusiastic about such proposals, and a steering committee was set up. The Constituent Municipal Assembly of Sonson was declared on June 16, 2001, partly to deal with the situation where local people, "the target of the war," were "to take an active part in the solution of this conflict . . . [and] in the solution for all this crisis of governability."

The establishment of the peace zone in Tarso was less clear-cut. Although it also seems to have been in response to long-term external and internal stress and a triggering crisis, the crisis did not involve the kidnapping of a reforming local official. Tarso has a long history of conflict between peasants and landlords—a reaction to inequalities and much influenced by leftist organizations. This started in the 1950s as part of the virtual civil war known as La Violencia, when organizations such as the Movimiento por la Unidad Revolucionaria (Movement for Revolutionary Unity) and the Movimiento Independiente Revolucionario (Independent Revolutionary Movement) were active in the region. In the 1980s, there was a strong ELN presence around Tarso, and most recently, paramilitary groups have been active in the region, although until 2000 their activities in the region seem to have been sporadic and limited to collection of *vacuna* ("vaccination" against attack).

Organized resistance to involvement in the violent struggle also began relatively early, with the initiation, in the 1970s, of a campesino organization for civil resistance, under the leadership of a former priest, Ignacio Betancur Sánchez, who was murdered in 1993. Other antecedents included the ELN's assassination of one of the peasant leaders, Leonardo Gallegos. This event led to the further mobilization of the campesinos, who, in 1997, issued a declaration titled "Hamlets of Peace." Another factor in that year was the encouragement provided by REDEPAZ's proposal to create and link together a hundred Municipios de Paz.

But several respondents have argued that it was not the events of 1997 but a set of internal problems that ultimately led to the establishment of the "Constituent Municipal Assembly of Tarso" in January 2001. These included a familiar litany of issues, such as bad financial management by the local administration, corruption, political control by a small elite, and lack of transparency and of public participation. These, backed by a deterioration in the general environment, bad housing and health services, and high rates of unemployment, formed the context that led to the calling of a public forum called "Tarso: Toward a New Millennium" in October 1999 and the establishment of a committee to consider the future development of the *municipio*. These actions aimed at internal reform led to revisiting the idea of a Constituent Assembly, to production of a development plan, and eventually to establishment of the Constituent Assembly at a January 2001 meeting attended by more than three thousand people.

Why the delay from 1997 to 1999? One argument is that the trigger event that set the process in motion was not a heightened stress level occasioned by a substantial increase in violence but the very real danger that Tarso might lose its status as a *municipio* and be downgraded to a *corregimiento*, with a consequent loss of legal, fiscal, territorial, and administrative powers. Whatever the accuracy of such an analysis—and there are those who argue that Tarso is indeed a community organized for peace, even though respondents have agreed that it was not riven by armed conflict—it is certain that the declared objectives of the assembly place considerable emphasis on cooperation between all sectors of civil society, with the aim of achieving development and social stability. The opening declaration speaks of this aim: "To maintain an open space for social organization of the community for exercising the right and duty of participating in decisions and transformations that affect or comprise the economic, political, and social interests of the inhabitants of Tarso."

Moreover, the topics that the assembly has targeted for effort and activity, falling under the two broad headings of "sustainable development" and "peaceful coexistence," include democracy and public participation, employment, social security, care of the environment, education, culture and sports, and human rights, with "peace" coming at the end of the list. This is in no way to diminish the achievements of the people of Tarso, and there is a serious argument that all these activities and programs are indeed aimed at achieving *positive* peace within the community by removing many of the long-term, structural causes of internal conflict. In this, Tarso is clearly an interesting and admirable *experiencia de paz*, and one likely to provide lessons and examples for other peace zones and communities. But it does seem that the problems that the people of Tarso faced in 1999 were, at least initially, of a different order from those facing the people of Samaniego and Sonson. Thus, different priorities could be initially set out, and different structures created and activities pursued. To analyze these differences, our next section deals with a comparison of organizational aspects of the three peace *experiencias* in a little more detail.

Organizing: Decision Making

One of our very first assumptions was that two key sets of variables would affect the likely durability of local peace zones and communities. The first set consisted of aspects of internal unity and governance that would help determine the ability of those involved to present a common set of ideas and policies on behalf of their community. The question thus became one of organization and governance, how decisions were made on behalf of that community, regarding the range of activities undertaken within the community, and how the decisions were enforced and the policies carried out. The second set of variables involved issues of external relations, most particularly with the armed actors in the region but also with similar *experiencias de paz* and other institutions that might offer help and support to the community.

The penultimate section of this chapter deals with relations with armed groups, and this section briefly discusses the internal organization of the three communities: Tarso, Samaniego, and Sonson. Two fairly general points emerge from an initial review of these three *experiencias*. The first is that the durability and overall success of peace zones and communities are likely to be connected to the degree of involvement by all the community's various groups and sectors in the community's organization and operation. We may start from the hypothesis that if one views an *experiencia de paz* as a new, local political system, then support for such a system will depend largely on its success in delivering demanded "goods," whether symbolic, social, or material. (One of these goods is undoubtedly going to be an increase in physical security.) It seems appropriate, at least initially, to adopt a functional approach to understanding successful zones of peace.

The second general comment is that one of the other key sets of intracommunity variables affecting durability and success involves the relationship established with existing local power and governance structures. Many of the peace *experiencias* we have surveyed, and not merely the three that are the subject of this chapter, have in some way replaced or supplanted existing governance structures within their *municipio*. It seems reasonable to hypothesize that the nature of relations between the old governance structures and the new, grassroots organizations of the peace communities will have some effect—probably a major one—on whether the latter flourish or are relatively short-lived. In theory at least, reactions of existing local authorities and officials can range from positive to highly negative, depending on the degree to which the new grassroots institutions are seen as trespassing on existing powers, privileges, and resources—a perception that will determine the degree to which the "old guard" tries to support or undermine the new initiatives.

Relations with Local Authorities

Fortunately for the communities in the three *experiencias* reviewed in this chapter, the reactions of all three existing local governments appear to have been positive, at least initially. As we have seen in Samaniego and Sonson, a major initiative for establishing some form of zone or community of peace came from the office and person of the *alcalde*, whereas in Tarso, concerns about the possible downgrading of the *municipio* clearly played a major role in local authorities' involvement in establishing the Constituent Assembly and formulating the development plan for the future of that *municipio*.

But the changing fortunes of Sonson and Samaniego illustrate our point about the way that relations between new institutions and existing local governments can change over time, for better or worse. In Sonson, an initial move toward popular participation and grassroots decision making sponsored by one *alcalde* was reversed on the election of a member of the traditional political elite, who reverted to a policy of "politics as usual" within the *municipio*. It was only the reelection of the reforming mayor that finally— with strong internal support from the Asociación de Mujeres Independientes—led to establishment of the Constituent Municipal Assembly and the five working groups (*mesas*) that planned out the activities and organizational structure of the new peace community.[4]

A rather different dynamic can be observed in the case of Samaniego, where the establishment of the initial "Working Group (Mesa) for Peace" came initially from a reforming *alcalde* and his wife, who themselves became members of the group and who took the initiative of involving REDEPAZ in establishing the peace community. The first years of the *experiencia* thus enjoyed the full support and involvement of local government, but later administrations clearly lacked a similar level of commitment, and the full backing of the mayor's office seems to have ended with the next elections. This has led some respondents from Samaniego to question the relative benefits of too close an involvement of traditional government bodies in the grassroots organizations and to argue that having the municipal administration too closely linked to the process can be inconvenient in the long run, especially when the continuation of programs is dependent on resources from the local administration. One person lamented, "We thought that the people who would come after us would have the same mentality, and by not having institutionalized we allowed the center to lose interest even though this is the place from which the project should be continued."

The point that seems to emerge from the three cases reviewed here is that the positive involvement of municipal authorities in developing a grassroots peace project can be helpful, particularly in the initial stages, but it is important not to become too dependent on this source of support, since it can be likely to withdrawal when new administrations take office. One interviewee

---

[4] The five *mesas* were International Humanitarian Law and Public Order, Community Participation and Assemblies, Constructing a Culture of Peace, Socioeconomic Crisis, and Children and Youth.

declared, "I believe in institutionalizing and that it should be the commitment of every leader to work on this process."

Structure, Participation, and Benefits

The other set of variable factors that seemed likely to contribute to the survivability and success of local Colombian *experiencias de paz* concerned the nature of the benefits that participants derived from establishing the peace zone or community. As noted in the section on setting up peace *experiencias,* a variety of reasons led to their being established in the first place. But even though the peace *experiencia* may be born of a response to an immediate trigger event, its continued existence must be strongly related to the benefits that it provides for those involved. Clearly, in all the cases that we have examined, a major influence was the change that was anticipated (and in many cases provided) in the level of honesty and transparency in the conduct of local affairs, and this was linked to the local citizens' sense of increased participation in decisions and policies that were going to affect their lives. Many respondents mentioned an end to corruption and to *politiquería* as being one of the main goals underlying the establishment of the peace zone or community. One of the first arrangements put in place in Samaniego, for example, was a provision that the local government of the *municipio* would inform the Working Group for Peace (which represented more than twenty local NGOs) about development proposals and would both keep that *mesa* informed about the local budget and listen to proposals regarding expenditures.

All three of the *experiencias* analyzed here established institutions for as wide a participation in decision making as possible—hence the use of the title "Constituent Assembly" in each case. In each, there were opportunities for all members of the community to come together and discuss present problems and opportunities as well as future schemes and initiatives. In Sonson, for example, it became an established practice to hold open general assemblies, which anyone could attend and where anyone could speak, at least twice a year. In all three cases, the eventual decision-making structures that emerged involved such plenary meetings but also representative working committees charged with developing and reporting on particular programs and activities, coordinating such activities for the community, and liaising with municipal authorities on needed reforms and initiatives. In Sonson, the five original planning *mesas* had produced a scheme involving not merely the semiannual general assemblies but four "working committees" dealing with public relations, local *corregimientos,* general advisory functions, and "humanitarian contact." Each full working committee met every month, and each had its own coordinator and secretary as well as representatives from *sindicatos* (unions), the church, youth and women's organizations, cooperatives and community associations, and municipal NGOs. The coordinators of the four working committees met every month.

In Tarso, the Constituent Assembly involved more than 150 representatives from a similarly wide variety of social and economic sectors, including the municipal council, the mayor's office, and the local police, while the day-to-day running of assembly activities was in the hands of six working groups. A similar structure was established in Samaniego.

Aside from enabling wider participation in the overall direction of policies for the *municipio*, the establishment of such organizational structures also allowed community members to have a say in detailed policies through their representatives on committees. The structures also indicated what activities were important to local people and what the people needed from the process for their support and commitment to continue. Clearly, one of the major concerns to be addressed was the improved provision of education and training as part of overall development schemes. Programs for children and young people can be found in all three *experiencias*.[5] Another major theme was economic development, which often involved initiatives focused on improving local infrastructure on a cooperative basis. In Tarso, four of the six working groups were concerned with sustainable development and dealt with issues of employment, the environment, social security, and democracy and public management. The other two were established under the rubric of "peaceful coexistence," one dealing with education, culture, and sports, and the other with human rights and peace.

Even this brief survey of the kinds of initiatives undertaken by the organizations within the peace zones and communities provides some idea of the factors likely to be important in determining whether a particular peace community prospered or declined. Aside from reforming what seemed intolerable—corruption, the manipulation of local politics by traditional elites, and lack of public accountability—and substituting a form of open participation in local decision making, the transparent and honest use of resources for agreed ends and the successful provision of new "goods," both symbolic and material, in development, education, and other areas has helped many of the peace zones and communities to survive, even amid high levels of violence. Positive peace within seems to compensate for the lack of even negative peace without—at least to a degree. But we should recall that one of the important functions of a zone or community of peace is inevitably the reduction of violence, danger, and threat to those involved in the *experiencia*. One of the key benefits anticipated from the formation of a peace community is increased security, which in turn depends on the relations between the community and the armed actors. We end by examining this factor in the three examples of Sonson, Samaniego, and Tarso.

---

[5] Education and development initiatives shared at least one similar underlying function: providing alternatives for young people other than joining one or another of the local armed actors as the only option for any kind of socioeconomic advancement.

Surviving: Dealing with Local Armed Actors

As noted at the start of this chapter, our original conception of a "peace zone" was of an area that the local community had declared "off-limits" to the violent armed actors in an effort to create a place where "negative peace"—an absence of violence—existed. While our empirical investigation revealed that many of the peace zones and communities in Colombia (and elsewhere) had been established with at least some aspirations to create a more "positive" peace—to end corruption, establish participatory democracy, and encourage local development—there remained the generally shared goal of "insulating" the community from the surrounding violence and creating some form of sanctuary for those who wished to end the insecurity of their lives. Inevitably, this meant that the peace *experiencias* have had to devise, as best they can, some strategies for dealing with the armed actors carrying out the violence in their region—a task made doubly difficult when the community itself, or sectors of it, was the target for the violence.

Differing Environments Needing Different Strategies

Unfortunately, our analysis so far has thrown only a little light on a number of preliminary questions that must be addressed in order to begin to understand the key factors that typically make for the successful establishment of peace zones or communities. The first of these questions asks whether local communities seeking to establish a zone of peace for themselves find different problems in their relations with the three types of armed actors likely to be affected in some way by the establishment of the peace zone. What problems or obstacles are created by local guerrilla *frentes*, either FARC or ELN, compared with those raised by paramilitary *bloques* or by units of the national armed forces and police?

Evidence from our three case studies is, of course, anecdotal, but it does suggest that there are differences in reactions from each type of armed actor. The most difficult to deal with seem to be the paramilitary forces, although there have been exceptions to this. The national armed forces also frequently have strong objections to communities that try to "opt out" (in the armed forces' view) of a national struggle against rebels. Such communities are seen as denying armed forces—representing the nation—legitimate access to national territory, not to mention withholding support for those whose legitimate role (however inadequately exercised) is to provide security for loyal citizens.[6]

---

[6] Many local communities in Colombia seem to have countered this kind of argument by emphasizing the concept of *soberanía popular* (popular sovereignty), enunciated in the 1991 constitution, and by exercising this right in establishing their own form of (unarmed) security, which they see as far more effective than that—notionally—provided by the national military and police. Of course, a strong tendency among the armed forces has been to regard local communities axiomatically as supporters of the guerrillas rather than "loyal citizens" and, hence, as legitimate objects for attack by paramilitary surrogates or even directly by the security forces.

The second general issue arising from peace communities' relations with the armed actors is the nature and level of local, ongoing violence that environs the peace *experiencias*, and how this will affect the locals' ability to establish and then maintain a peace zone or community. At its simplest, the peace community's efforts seem likely to be strongly affected by whether the surrounding country is *stably controlled* by one or another of the armed actors, or *in contention* between them. In the latter case, the loss of territory, communications passages, or other valued resources, whether to an adversary or through the declaration of a peace zone, is seen as a major loss to be retrieved, by violence if necessary. There is also the question whether change makes a significant difference to the problems of peace communities. New challenges to a previously stably controlled area might make the insecurity problems of a peace community more intense, since they are seen as having "consorted with the enemy" during the period of stable control and, thus, as having become an adjunct to that enemy. Closer analysis may reveal whether different types of relational problems arise for peace communities in different types of conflictful environments, such as

1. those stably controlled by one dominant armed actor;
2. those previously dominated but now challenged by an alternative armed actor;
3. those constantly in contention between armed actors;
4. those subject to efforts to reclaim territory by a previously dominant armed actor;
5. those controlled by a newly dominant armed actor consolidating its hold.

In several of the Colombian cases we have examined, some form of stable modus vivendi between peace communities and local armed actors has been disrupted by the fresh incursions of other armed actors into the area and the resulting combat for control of territory, people, and resources. The predictable finding is that the problems for establishing and maintaining existing peace communities in circumstances of increasing violence and instability are undoubtedly made more complex and difficult, but the precise nature of these difficulties, and of any general strategies for dealing with them, remain obscure.

The same can be said about the armed actors themselves, who are likely to react to the establishment of peace communities in different ways depending on the circumstances they are facing in a particular territory. Among these circumstances are issues of whether the armed actor in question is facing unchallenged control, serious opposing violence, significant loss of dominance, or likely ejection. All these factors are likely to affect attitudes and behavior toward local communities perceived as seeking to opt out of the struggle. Moreover, the circumstances that the armed actors themselves confront due to efforts to establish local peace zones undoubtedly include the reactions of their local adversaries to those peace zones. Approval by a guerrilla *frente*, however expressed, is unlikely to sit well with a local paramilitary unit or the army brigade charged with security in the department, and vice versa.

It is also possible to overemphasize the distinction between local communities and local armed actors. Because both guerrillas and paramilitaries recruit from local people (although they find this more difficult in indigenous areas), the relationship between campesinos and combatants can be highly complex and dynamic. Attempting to draw a definite line between those who are part of a nonviolent, neutral peace *experiencia* and those who are involved in local violence can often be misleading. Certainly, the combatants themselves often make no such distinction and operate on the principle that many local people are at least supporters of the "other side," even when they claim to be members of a peace community. Thus, they are fair game for reprisals and ill treatment. On the other hand, the porous nature of the boundary between a peace community and the combatants in the environment can be advantageous on occasions. Family links can be used to aid communication and even exercise influence over combatants' decisions and tactics. How such cross-boundary relations are used depends on circumstances.

Whatever those circumstances, our initial study indicates that the reactions of armed actors can take a number of forms, including hostility, indifference, tacit or public approval, endorsement, or support. Clearly, one of the other major factors that determines what type of relationship can be established with local armed actors to increase the safety and security of members of the peace zone is the *way* that the local community establishes contacts, limitations, and agreed norms in its relations with local forces. The *experiencias* of Sonson, Tarso, and Samaniego show a variety of ways in which local peace communities have tried to increase security for their members through their dealings with the local armed actors.

Strategies and Tactics for Diminishing Insecurity

The three *experiencias* present somewhat different circumstances and, hence, different problems for community members seeking to maintain peace without as well as within and to increase their security. Tarso, for example, seems to have been firmly within the ambit of local paramilitaries after the paramilitaries' expulsion of the ELN in 1997, but the paramilitary presence consisted mainly of levying *vacunas* from the local population. In contrast, Sonson is in Antioquia, an area where illicit crops are grown and are protected by a number of armed actors, including both the ELN and the FARC, as well as the Autodefensas del Magdalena Medio, which has been increasing its control of the region since 2000. The region is heavily contested by these organizations and by the Colombian military. In Samaniego, the dominant armed actor at the time of the peace community's establishment was the ELN, which exercised considerable influence on the internal processes of the *municipio* and seems to have been the dominant armed actor in the vicinity, although the FARC was also a presence in the region. This situation seems to have lasted at least until the military and paramilitary drive to take back the south during President Álvaro Uribe's tenure.

What strategies have members of the three peace communities adopted to deal with their local armed actors, and how have these worked over time? Again, it is easier to provide examples of the strategies used at various times and places than to discern underlying patterns that explain "what works." But there are some clues that might enable some tentative generalizations. One effective strategy for local peace communities is to try to remove the justification for external armed actors to involve themselves in the life of the community—such "involvement" can run from being asked to resolve interpersonal disputes among community members to violently "removing" members seen as agents of, or sympathizers with, "the others." This particular strategy can perhaps best be seen working in Samaniego immediately after the peace zone's establishment. Before this, the local guerrilla organizations—mainly the ELN—had become thoroughly involved in the social and political life of the *municipio*, removing mayors and other officials who had been accused of corruption or malpractice by one or another political faction within the community.

After the establishment of the peace community, however, the community addressed an open letter to the local armed actors, arguing that there was no longer any need for them to involve themselves in municipal affairs and that they should allow the community to resolve its own problems within the norms of a civilized society: "We understand that one of the principal ideas of those in arms is to respect the popular will and to strive for peace with justice. This is a sufficient reason to demand respect for the decision taken by the population of Samaniego."

At least in the initial stages of this peace community, this strategy seems to have worked, and as one local respondent put it, the armed actors gave up "in the face of the popular will." Harassment of the mayor ended, and threats, kidnappings, and incursions aimed at the civil population all but ceased for a considerable time. According to local respondents, this was largely because the armed actors were left without arguments or justifications, since the local administration was being carried out in a transparent and participatory manner. One respondent noted, "When the mayor practically ran the administration however he wanted . . . the people used to go and complain to them and . . . the guerrilla with that mandate . . . used to come and impinge on administrative decisions. That is what we had to cut out at the root. How did we do it? 'Now come, the administration is all ours,' the people would go and say. 'We are happy with this situation.'"

While the examples from Samaniego show a strategy adopted to deal with a specific local situation, they also seem to represent a type of strategy for dealing with armed actors based on what could be termed the "role betrayal" of the armed actors. This strategy relies to a large degree on a process of shaming the armed actors because their actions do not conform to their stated goals or to the role that they have shaped for themselves in protecting or reforming Colombian society—for example, as "defenders of the people," "bringers of democracy and participation," or "rooters out of corruption." Basically, the peace community of Samaniego seemed to be saying that there was no longer any need for the local guerrillas to interfere in order to "correct" local social or political systems, because the people themselves were doing this very thing.

Another widely practiced version of this shaming strategy seems to be accusing particular armed actors of breaking international humanitarian law by their actions aimed at local populations, or of denying generally recognized human rights. While the strategy has had mixed results with different armed actors and has been a fragile shield in many cases, no one likes to be seen as behaving illegally or immorally, and reminders (rather than accusations) of this sort of lapse seem to have worked in some cases. One respondent from Sonson, for example, noted that on two occasions local guerrillas invaded the city center with the precisely carried-out objective of expelling paramilitaries and confined themselves to this task, deliberately avoiding any involvement with the civilian population. He noted that the community had previously adopted a nonconfrontational slogan aimed at armed actors that effectively said, "We love you like brothers; we respect you as armed actors; but we do not want your violent actions in our territory."

A second major strategy for dealing with local armed actors involves a process of negotiating agreements with them—deals that can be specific and temporary, such as ending the blockade of a route to local markets, or more general and open-ended, such as ending armed incursions onto the territory of the peace community. In either case, the question always arises regarding what type of "good" the community might possess that would be sufficiently valuable to armed actors to induce them to make a bargain with local community leaders. In the Philippines, for example, a parallel exclusion of the adversary in exchange for agreeing to keep one's own fighters from trespassing into a peace zone seems, on occasion, to have been successfully negotiated. It may be that this form of bargain—refraining from some activity provided that others can be similarly persuaded—can be a common form of agreement in some peace zones. In other circumstances, the quid pro quo can be different but a bargain nonetheless. For example, in the *municipio* of Planadas, in Tolima, an informal pact between the municipal government and the local FARC *frente* appears to have held for more than three years. The local police do not take action against the local FARC camp of Marquetalia and its surrounding poppy crops, and the guerrillas leave the town alone.[7]

In the search for strategies for dealing with local armed actors, peace communities can, at least in theory, resort to some form of sanctions, although the range available is limited. Some communities have adopted strategies such as boycotts, physical avoidance, or complete noncommunication ("sending to Coventry"). Others have tried strategies of denying needed materials to intruding armed actors unless forced to hand goods over at gunpoint. More generally, peace communities have relied on indirect pressure on armed actors, either from above or from outside: hence the importance placed on accompaniment by outsiders linked to governments or international NGOs or on the presence of outside observers.[8]

Like shame, disapproval can be a potent influence on the behavior of even the most recalcitrant armed actor, especially if the disapproval—and possible sanctions—emanates from a superior with the ability to impose costs. Moreover, revelation of reprehensible behavior, and resultant damage to reputation, can be a usable sanction, especially if the armed actor in question is at all concerned with its current image or with possible future costs—such as a decreased ability to retire wealthy and respectable.

Whether peace communities' strategies for dealing with the armed actors involve trying to hold the armed actors to their professed aims and principles, bargaining with them over specific behavioral limitations, or warning of likely sanctions, the tactics used customarily involve one of three approaches: declarations, conversations, or negotiations. In Sonson and the rest of Oriente Antioqueño, these tactics are called *acercamientos humanitarios* (literally, "humanitarian approaches"). All three have been tried at various times in Tarso, Sonson, and Samaniego. Public declarations are usually a major part of the initiation of a peace community, and these have been used in all three *experiencias* to set out the nature and aims of the new institution and also to call on the local armed actors to respect the people's sovereign right to govern themselves, free from violence and interference.[9] It seems likely that

---

[7] The ability of local governments to bargain for such local deals with the armed actors is obviously affected by the Colombian government's policy toward local peacemaking initiatives. The Pastrana government prohibited such local initiatives from 1998 to 2002, although it tolerated them. The much harder-line Uribe government has emphatically discouraged them.

[8] The role of international "accompaniers," such as Peace Brigades International, Christian Peacemaker Teams, and the Society of Friends, or some of the local Colombian church institutions is important enough to warrant a separate article.

[9] This survey has revealed very different sequences in the establishment and maintenance of peace zones and communities, and it is still unclear which pattern is the most effective. One of the two contrasting models involves the initial declaration of a peace zone or community, often though not always followed by some form of negotiation with local armed actors. In

some contacts with armed actors occur after such opening declarations, but how public and formal these are remains in some doubt. Respondents from Samaniego were very firm in their statements that Mayor Manuel Cellar did not meet with any of the armed actors once the "Territory of Peace" had been established and that the resultant tacit acquiescence to the peace community's activities in Samaniego was not the result of any negotiations or bargaining. Whether other informal contacts occurred is less clear.

More usually, contacts are made and conversations held between representatives of the peace communities and the local armed actors, although there is some debate about when and whether conversations become negotiations. In Tarso, respondents agreed that there had been conversations between representatives of the Constituent Assembly and the local paramilitaries about the payment of *vacunas* and other matters, but stated that there had never been any *negotiations* with the paramilitaries. In Sonson, a special committee for humanitarian contact was set up to deal with relations with the armed actors, but again respondents were firm in their statements that the committee did not negotiate or make agreements with the armed actors. Judging by accounts provided to us regarding the work of this committee, its activities, while apparently effective, have tended to be ad hoc and reactive—involving, for example, removal of blockades or return of displaced or kidnapped persons—and have not involved the concluding of general agreements about community–armed actor relations. One respondent noted, "In the case of the blockade that the *autodefensas* did . . . we managed to unblock this route by having chats with these gentlemen, because this region was completely idle and the *municipio* was suffering the consequences of a lack of food."

On another occasion, the committee had another chat with *autodefensas*, who had kidnapped two girls from the "Young People for Peace" who were doing community work on the outskirts of the *municipio* and who had relatives in the guerrillas: "We made contact with those people, spoke, chatted, talked with them and achieved the return of the two young people in good health, and we took them back to their homes." Another interviewee continued, "The humanitarian commission went and told them, 'And what responsibility does a person have because their relative is involved in another story?' And they managed to bring back the girl."

What is interesting about these conversations involving the committee members from Sonson is that they seem to relate directly to the strategy, mentioned above, of using norms and a discourse of human rights to put pressure on the armed actors to behave differently and decently: "They say to them, 'Do not violate the civil population.' . . . It is a community making

---

other cases, negotiations with armed actors take place *before* the declaration of a peace zone, with the declaration sometimes accompanied by some stated form of approval by at least some of the local armed actors.

claims on international humanitarian law. It is not a question of mediating with somebody; it is a question of confronting them and confronting the arguments they say they have."

Analysis of other peace zones and communities will no doubt produce further examples of successful strategies and tactics for dealing with the armed actors perpetrating violence around them and will suggest means for increasing security—even if only temporarily—for community members. Still, there is no magic formula. Measures for reducing insecurity are fragile in the extreme, and what may work for a time in certain circumstances may collapse once those circumstances change. We are dealing with probabilities of success here, and these clearly remain disappointingly low and dangerously dynamic. We can but hope that more examples and more detailed analysis will result in better insights and a better grasp of any principles underlying those strategies most likely to work.

Conclusions

This chapter is an initial attempt to analyze and understand comparatively three *experiencias de paz* in Colombia and to see if the three peace zones or communities show any common patterns in their initial establishment, subsequent organization and activities, and relationships with local armed actors.

At first sight, the most obvious feature of the three has been their very different experiences and fortunes, but even a cursory review of the three *experiencias* of Tarso, Samaniego, and Sonson suggests some commonalities, as well as some areas for closer study in these and other cases. At the very least, all three cases seem to share these common traits:

1. Initiation of the peace zone or community seems to occurr after a long period of stress and tension, followed by some trigger event that so disturbs or outrages the community that a major movement for change develops;[10]
2. Reasons for establishing a zone or community of peace are as likely to arise from the need to change problems within the community as from the need to deal with issues of violence and insecurity imposed from without;
3. The sustainability of the *experiencia* is likely to be as much a function of its success in fulfilling required functions within the community as in dealing with problems of violence and insecurity caused by the activities of armed actors;

---

[10] An important question yet to be addressed is, what sorts of local events cause such a sense of outrage among community members that they feel they cannot put up with things as they are any longer and are willing to risk retaliation to bring about change?

4. Changing external circumstances (especially the stability of the local politico-military environment) play a major role in the sustainability of the peace zone;

5. Ways of dealing with local armed actors so that they do not work to undermine the existence of the peace community can involve strategies of shaming (emphasizing their failure to adhere to their own stated goals and principles), negotiation and dialogue, and sanctions (usually but not always indirect). All are fragile and uncertain.

We advance these findings very tentatively. As noted earlier, they are based on an analysis of data from only three peace zones or communities, and even if REDEPAZ's title is not absolutely accurate, there are around a hundred other examples of peace communities to be trolled for ideas and principles of success and durability. The three peace communities chosen for this particular chapter were all established in existing *municipios*. A study of returning communities might suggest some very different findings in conclusion. From this comparative exercise, however, we are encouraged in the belief that some useful general lessons will emerge from the data that we have gathered on local peace communities and that such lessons may be of service to anyone attempting in the future to create this form of fragile sanctuary in the midst of violent civil conflict.

Epilogue

As noted at the start of this chapter, most of the data on local peace *experiencias* reported here were gathered during 1999–2003, which covered the end of the Pastrana government and the beginning months of President Uribe's first administration. It was also a period during which President Pastrana, true to his election promises, pursued some serious (although ultimately unsuccessful) peacemaking efforts with the two main guerrilla organizations in Colombia. His efforts were undermined, at least to some degree, by the operations of Plan Colombia and the later convergence of the war on drugs with the U.S.-led war on terror.

The following period, from 2003 to date, saw a marked change in both central-government policies and attitudes toward local peace initiatives, so that the opportunities for successfully maintaining them lessened while the problems they confronted multiplied. These government policies and attitudes affected all peace communities throughout Colombia and not merely Samaniego, Sonson, and Tarso, although the impacts varied from place to place and region to region, depending on local conditions. Tarso seems to have been fortunate enough to carry on its development projects relatively undisturbed, but by 2003, many peace communities had already been affected by the massive movement of refugees and IDPs coming into their areas. Especially in the south and southwest of the country, the aerial spraying that was part of Plan Colombia had already caused massive disruptions, sending people fleeing to other parts of the country. This continued after 2003 despite efforts to replace aerial spraying with locally negotiated agreements to remove coca bushes by hand in exchange for local funds and support—which often failed to arrive.

But although problems caused by fumigation and large-scale internal displacement were not new phenomena, in many regions they certainly intensified while new problems developed and made conditions harder for peace communities and other *experiencias*. Many peace communities found themselves facing intensified violence resulting from the Colombian state's efforts to gain or regain control of, or at least a presence in, certain regions, particularly after the "drive to the south"—a major military (and paramilitary) campaign in the southern departments aimed at driving out the FARC and establishing a government presence there—and the implementation of Plan Patriota. Inevitably, the first kind of state "presence" attempted in most regions involved security forces, often accompanied by paramilitary allies or surrogates. In others, the government's strategy of "democratic security" produced major pressures on local communities generally and widened divisions within those communities, even those committed to neutrality and noninvolvement in the conflict.

Underlying all this was a government philosophy that, at one level, made it impossible to establish areas or communities from which state officials were excluded, and which also denied the legitimacy of any form of peace arrangement that did not involve the central government as a party. At another level, the prevailing ideology often slid into denouncing peace communities, as well as their allies, as guerrilla supporters or sympathizers— a view that had already become widespread among the security forces. Add to this the complications caused by the government's strategy of paramilitary "demobilization," which particularly affected communities in Antioquia, Córdoba, César, and Magdalena, by fluctuating international economic help for the peace *experiencias*, and by the increasing repoliticization of decision-making processes within those *experiencias*, and it is easy to understand why their survival became much more difficult in 2003–07.

The post-2003 experience of Sonson illustrates the problems caused by intensified fighting, which affected many peace communities, particularly in Antioquia and in the south. Accounts of local people fleeing fighting between the Colombian military, the paramilitaries, and the guerrillas can regularly be found in reports from the press and from organizations such as the World Food Programme, Human Rights Watch, and the United Nations High Commissioner for Refugees. Problems with land mines, roadblocks, and forced removal continued to affect many *municipios* in Eastern Antioquia, including Sonson and its neighbors. The *municipio* has remained the operational base for at least one "demobilized" paramilitary group, a factor that continued local disruption even after 2006, when its leader, Jorge Alman, was "incarcerated" with others in Itaguí, from where he remained in contact with and in control of his fighters in Sonson. Nonetheless, in December 2004, the *experiencia* was able to host a major gathering of more than three hundred delegates from a wide variety of peace communities and constituent assemblies and subsequently to push forward its complex peace agenda. Sonson was also one of the *municipios* that benefited from the establishment of a new EU-funded "laboratory of peace" throughout Eastern Antioquia.

In the south, Samaniego experienced similar or even worse problems, compounded by an increased paramilitary presence and the spillover effects from neighboring Putumayo, including the turning of Nariño Department into a major coca-producing region. In 2004, following the death of more than sixty people from armed violence, the office of the Defensoría del Pueblo declared Samaniego a "community at risk." Moreover, data on IDPs from roughly the same time indicated that more a thousand families in the *municipio* had been displaced, and there were increasing reports of cocaine production in the *municipio's* mountainous areas.

On the other hand, the peace *experiencia* in Samaniego also has had to cope with the politicization of the process, in the sense that its decline following the early days of progress disillusioned many people and led to the establishment of other strategies for trying to achieve local peace and development. By the end of 2003, if not before, the issue of being a territory of peace had become the center of a political conflict in Samaniego. In contrast, Tarso, celebrating its sixth year as a municipal constituent assembly, has managed to avoid major internal cleavages by adhering to a policy of agreeing on, and then electing, a single candidate for mayor. This practice of having a *candidato único* has helped guarantee the continuation of the assembly and its activities, even despite the local regrouping and reemergence of "shadow" paramilitary organizations.

Even in Samaniego, however, internal political conflicts and increasingly adverse conditions in the environment have not prevented people from renewing their efforts to establish peaceful conditions, at least locally. In January 2004, under the leadership of Samaniego's *alcalde,* Montufar Andrade, a proposal for a *pacto local de paz* was put forward, which elicited a variety of responses from various armed actors, including statements of support from the ELN and—more surprisingly—from the paramilitary Autodefensas Unidas de Colombia (AUC). In January 2005, the government's response, conveyed through the Office of the High Commissioner for Peace, reiterated its opposition to such a local peacebuilding process. But the local administration continued its efforts to establish itself as neutral, autonomous, and impartial in the face of the conflict. Among other things, it demanded respect for human rights and a cessation of hostilities in "cultural spaces," including music festivals, the Samaniego carnival, campesinos' sporting events, the Week for

Culture, and various other festivals and anniversaries. In light of Montufar Andrade's efforts to maintain a distance from previous local peacebuilding efforts, it is interesting that this initiative was deliberately publicized as being different both from more conventionally established peace communities such as San José de Apartadó and from Toribío's *experiencia de resistencia civil*. Whatever these differences may be, efforts to establish a local peace agreement in Samaniego do demonstrate that some kinds of peace *experiencias* in Colombia have continued in recent years despite increasingly adverse conditions, even if they have been forced to change their shape and rhetoric. More recent evidence for these continued efforts can be found in the demining agreement, concluded in October 2006, between representatives of the ELN and the Samaniego community. To repeat the local initiative's slogan, "*La lucha para la paz local continúa*" ("The struggle for local peace continues").

14

Civil Resistance to War in the Middle Magdalena Valley

Javier Moncayo

The Program for Development and Peace in Magdalena Medio (PDPMM) began in 1995 with a broad participatory assessment promoted by the Colombian petroleum company ECOPETROL and its employee trade union, the Unión Sindical Obrera, with the backing of a consortium that included the Sociedad Económica Amigos del País (SEAP, Friends of the Country Economic Society) and the Centro de Investigación y Educación Popular (CINEP, Jesuit Center for Research and Popular Education). The SEAP-CINEP consortium formed a working group to conduct an assessment under the direction of Francisco de Roux, a Jesuit priest, economist, and soon-to-be first director of the PDPMM. The team used a methodology that included creating municipal forums in twenty-nine locations and that involved the participation of about ten thousand regional residents in municipal reflection groups. The findings led to the formation of the PDPMM and a development proposal that secured World Bank financing for two successive phases, from 1998 to 2000 and from 2001 to 2004. The two phases aimed at creating models for transforming regional development processes and the relationship between civil society and local government.

In 2001, the European Union took up the idea in its strategy to support and promote a peace process in Colombia and approved a project called the Peace Laboratory, which is still being implemented. In 2002, people involved in similar initiatives in various regions of the country formed the Red Nacional de Programas Regionales de Desarrollo y Paz (REDPRODEPAZ) to share experiences and develop coordinated activities. REDPRODEPAZ currently has 19 members and covers 447 municipalities, more than 40 percent of the municipalities in the country. Every year the members implement about 400 projects

This chapter was translated from Spanish by Barbara Fraser.

involving approximately 200,000 people. Besides the PDPMM, the network includes renowned initiatives such as the Consejo Regional Indígena del Cauca (Regional Indigenous Council of Cauca), an indigenous organization that has developed civilian resistance groups, and initiatives for enhancing democratic governance that have won national and international recognition. Seven members of REDPRODEPAZ currently receive support from the European Union to operate peace laboratories, and five have received funding from the World Bank to expand the experiment from Magdalena Medio to other regions of the country. Through grassroots organizations in the regions, REDPRODEPAZ hopes to play a significant role in promoting civil society participation in future peace dialogues between the government and the guerrillas.

In 1995, we residents of this region were resisting the paralysis that terror sought to impose on us, and we made every effort to keep society alive amid the totalitarianism of war. But we needed something to bring us together—a magnet that might organize the efforts and channel our energies and survival instincts in a way that could have an impact on the dynamic of armed confrontation. Francisco de Roux proposed to the residents of Magdalena Medio that we come together to express our opinions about the causes of war and poverty and consider how we might contribute to a solution. He called on the men and women of Magdalena Medio to reclaim their dignity as citizens and raise awareness of the power that lies in a community's joining together to express collective solidarity.

But how could this convergence be achieved in an area characterized by distrust and fear? How could men and women express their opinions and open up to one another in a region marked by terror and violence? The Pastoral Social (National Social Ministry Office) of the Catholic Church played an important role in this regard, helping create the level of trust needed to convince local residents to get involved in the collective conversation. Its workers, widely recognized by the community for their many years of service, participated in the process and formed the team that has accompanied the program since its inception. In each municipality in the region, they created safe opportunities for dialogue, with transparent rules, supported by institutions known in the area. Through these opportunities we began working to build our future. Youth groups and women's organizations, culture workers, environmentalists, human rights workers, homemakers, peasant leaders, municipal government employees, doctors, teachers, and everyone in the municipality who had been doing relatively unconnected work met in what we called "resident groups" to consider our future.

It took about a year to set up a resident group in each of the twenty-nine municipalities in Magdalena Medio, conduct diagnostic assessments with each group to determine the causes of the violence and poverty in each community, and suggest a vision of the future. This vision has to be something that moves all of us and contains each of us. No one must be left out of our dream of the region's future. We therefore had to organize delegations of the resident groups to search out people who had never participated. We had to give those people the opportunity to offer their ideas and make themselves heard and allow their voices to carry weight in our collective decisions. We climbed hills and crossed plains, rivers, and swamps to listen to the voices of people who had never been heard before. We also invited businesspeople, landowners, mayors and council members, technical experts, and teachers to join us, because our dream is of a region where there is room for all of us.

This is a diverse region, where descendants of slaves who had fled the chains of the Cartagena aristocracy settled along the banks of the Magdalena River. A mestizo peasant population has come here from all over the country; most of these peasants fled the successive wars that have wracked the nation. Peasants from Santander and Boyacá fled the Thousand-Day War in the early twentieth century, peasants from Tolima fled La Violencia of the mid-1950s, and peasants from that region fled to the mountains to escape the current violence. Cattle ranchers, agribusiness owners, petroleum workers, and people from various parts of the country also came to the Magdalena Medio to seek their fortunes, and their houses, families, and bank accounts are in Bogotá, Medellín, and Manizales.

How can a region be built amid so much diversity? How can so many conflicting interests be reconciled? We needed to look to the future, and we agreed on a common purpose: to guarantee a life of dignity and peace for everyone in the region. We defined certain principles that should guide the process of collective construction of the region. These included the belief that life comes first, that development is for the benefit of everyone and is created with everyone's participation, and that development must be sustainable.

When we had completed the assessment, defined the goal, and agreed on the principles, we began to draw up a development and peace plan for our municipality—a document that would express our vision and enable us to evaluate our efforts to attain it. We called this document the "Municipal Proposal."

The municipal proposal expresses a vision of the future of civil society in the municipality—the society we want to build, the world we want our children to live in. It requires a commitment from everyone, but it is also a means of political negotiation. Once we have agreed on what kind of region we want to build, we must begin to negotiate so that the government and civil society commit to doing their part. The obvious question was, "How can we make our vision become reality?" It was not a matter of asking the central government to deliver our dream to us, ready-made. After almost fifty years of war and frustration at the government's inability to make peace, we saw that we had to build the solution with our own hands. It was not a matter of forcing mayors to assume responsibilities they had never learned to assume. We had to transform politics in our municipalities, increase our capacity to motivate the mayors to do what was needed, and provide citizens' oversight of the public administration.

We established partnerships with national organizations that had expertise in citizenship training. We devoted ourselves to learning how a municipality operates, understanding what a development plan entails, learning how to draw up a municipal budget, understanding the limitations and rules that a mayor must recognize in running the local government, and learning to use the rights of citizens and the tools of citizen participation.

We also began to hold events never before held in our region. We sponsored debates among candidates in the mayoral and local council elections. We invited the candidates to meetings with broad citizen participation, so they could talk about the municipal budget and express their views about the dream of the future that we had developed. As a result, in many places the candidates incorporated significant aspects of the municipal proposal into their government plans, and we were able to secure commitments from them—registered before a notary public—to abide by the proposal.

Since then, we have held debates during three election campaigns for mayors and council members. The commitment that many of the mayors signed later became reality in the municipal budgets, created with the participation of broad sectors of civil society. Later, citizens organized periodic events in which the mayors were held accountable and explained how they had fulfilled the local government's commitments.

From the outset, we understood that to build the peace we yearn for, nothing can substitute for our participation. To attain our dream of a land where everyone lives in dignity and peace, we must rechannel all the energy that has stoked the armed conflict into building peace and coexistence. This requires the effort of every resident of the region.

We also understood from the start, however, that we had to develop our capacities so that we could build this dream of the future. We had to develop our ability to get things done, innovate, work together, think holistically, listen to those who have not had a voice and include them in building the dream, and establish ties with other regions of the country and the world. We had to improve our skills and abilities, and we had to learn by doing.

Following the principle that "development is done with everyone," we proposed training exercises that would not discourage residents who had never participated in development. Instead of talking about "projects," we spoke of "initiatives," because some believe that projects need to be designed by professionals, and we needed tools that would enable people to draw up their own proposals without the "intermediation" of experts who were not going to live in the region. We decided to build our skills one step at a time. With our dream before us, we evaluated our ability to attain it and drew up a plan to build our capacities in successive stages, taking small steps designed, implemented, and evaluated by the people themselves.

But once the first step was completed, our capacity had changed. And we started on the next step with something a little more complex, a little larger, a little more ambitious. It quickly became clear that different projects had common elements, because all were directed toward the same dream of the future. It was therefore possible to see the relationship between our dream of building a highly productive and environmentally sustainable region and the education of our children. It was possible to establish a dialogue between schoolteachers and farmers and between educational authorities and technical personnel; as a result, rural education in our communities began to change, becoming more appropriate for the productive projects that are the foundation of our dreams.

The work of the municipal resident groups also enabled the various stakeholders to get to know one another, breaking down barriers of distrust and stigma. In the various projects, people who had viewed each other as class enemies found common areas of interest and learned through practice that it is possible to build a world where we all have a place.

After eight years, we have barely begun our work. The war has not ended, and the government continues to waver between legality and the paramilitary mafia. Nevertheless, civil society is no longer the same. Throughout these years, we have constantly maintained space for debate in each of the region's municipalities, and we have moved from small productive initiatives to large-scale regional projects that are beginning to transform the living conditions of peasant families.

We have demonstrated that we can maintain a society capable of debating and making decisions in the midst of war and that it is possible to sustain development processes until peace comes. We know that after so many years of war, it will take at least a generation for Colombians to heal the deep wounds that have opened. We know that much work remains to be done to ensure that justice and the rule of law, dignity, and human rights prevail over the scourge of crime and the enemies of peace.

Now, however, we have a powerful weapon: now we believe in ourselves. Although many people have been killed during these eight years, and many families still live amid the uncertainty and threat of war, in many places we have been able to stop the armed groups' aggression against peasant communities. We have accompanied these communities in their decision not to leave their homes and land because of the war, to demand that the armed groups respect life, and to demand that the Colombian government recognize them as citizens and offer them the protection they are entitled to.

Many of the residents who have participated in these peace efforts are now mayors and local council members, and they work tirelessly to give dignity to government. Many of the young people now direct the regional network of community radio stations, which have become the people's voice, a place for debate and a vehicle for providing education on peace and the promotion of human rights, especially the rights of women and youth.

The road is long. We know that many years of work lie ahead before lasting peace, rooted in dialogue, participation, and mutual concessions, is achieved. We have not yet attained peace, but its seed is germinating.

15

"Cambio de Armas"
Negotiating Alternatives to Violence in the Oriente Antioqueño

Mary J. Roldán

Breaking the Silence: Oriente Mobilizes

By the beginning of the twenty-first century, Oriente (eastern Antioquia) ranked as one of the areas in Colombia with the highest incidence of violence and displacement. Villages and hamlets lay abandoned. Towns where rural people sought refuge from massacres, forcible recruitment, and economic blockades suffered from overcrowding, disease, and malnutrition. In particularly hard-hit municipalities such as Cocorná, more than half the population had fled between 2000 and 2006. Once a thriving center of agricultural production, Oriente had the highest rate of malnutrition and the greatest percentage of people under the poverty and extreme-poverty lines in Antioquia and had the highest number of antipersonnel land mine incidents in the nation.[1]

In the wake of spiraling violence, Oriente's twenty-three mayors took a decisive and unprecedented step in September 2001. They publicly announced a program of municipal solidarity and the creation of a No-Violence Movement to protest the humanitarian emergency affecting their towns. The mayors' long-term objective was to replace armed responses to conflict with dialogue and negotiation and to press for the right of local authorities to engage in humanitarian *acercamientos* (rapprochements). The mayors proposed making the entire subregion into a national Laboratorio de Paz (Peace Laboratory), where experiments in participatory democracy

---

[1] Consultoría para los Derechos Humanos y el Desplazamiento (CODHES), "La otra guerra: Destierro y redoblamiento" (CODHES report, Human Rights and Displacement Consultancy Bulletin no. 44, April 28, 2003), www.codhes.org/index2.php?option=com_docman&task=doc_view&gid=29&Itemid=50 (accessed September 16, 2008).

might serve as the basis for promoting respect for human rights and developing alternative approaches to address local security and quality-of-life issues in the region. The mayors' well-intentioned efforts at first met with little support from either the authorities or the armed groups whose violent actions they hoped to mitigate.

Oriente's mayors nonetheless persisted in their search for nonviolent ways out of a situation that local inhabitants described as *encierro* (entrapment/isolation).[2] Their efforts were rewarded when, in 2003, the region was selected as one of three groups to be included in Colombia's second Peace Laboratory. The European Union's Commission for External Relations and European Neighborhood Policy and the Colombian government agreed to commit funds for a period of five years, to promote local projects that could advance peace. The three rubrics, or *ejes*, created to fund local initiatives were the creation of a culture of peace through dialogue and respect for human rights; democratic governance and the strengthening of institutions and citizen participation; and sustainable socioeconomic development to improve communities' quality of life, in harmony with the environment.[3] The accord creating the second Peace Laboratory was signed in 2004, and the monies from Europe began to be transferred to underwrite projects in Oriente in 2005. To qualify for financing, local groups in the twenty-three municipalities were required to draw up proposals for projects that would have an impact on two or more municipalities and cost no less than 300 million pesos each.

To date, a wide variety of Peace Laboratory projects have been made possible by the collaborative support of the European Union, the Colombian government, the Catholic Church, and local non-governmental organizations (NGOs). Projects range from forest conservation, creation of seed banks, and cultivation of native species in the municipalities of San Luis and San Francisco, to fish farms and experiments in fish-food manufacturing from native vegetation in Cocorná. Marketing support and investment in materials and sewing machines has made possible the expansion of apparel and handicraft production—much-needed sources of income for women who are single heads of households in towns with high unemployment and few productive alternatives. Community radio stations sponsoring programs such as *La vida es derecho* (*Life Is a Right*), whose stated purpose is to "disseminate and promote respect for human rights through communitarian experiences," are written, produced, and managed by local youths. Rural public schools have

---

[2] Rubén Darío Zapata Yepes, "Los Campesinos del Oriente Antioqueño entre el miedo y el encierro," Agencia Prensa Rural, www.prensarural.org/ruben20031209.htm (accessed September 17, 2008).

[3] See European Union, Acción Social, "II Laboratorio de Paz," www.laboratoriodepaz.org/publicaciones.php?id=27785 (accessed September 5, 2008).

been reconceived as community centers to serve the needs both of children and of adults in hamlets where fragmented, displaced families have begun to return over the past year (2006–07).

The Peace Laboratory project represents an important step in constructing and consolidating a culture of peace in Oriente. It also promises to provide desperately needed investment to regional inhabitants hard-hit by years of violence and the vagaries of a peasant subsistence economy threatened by development-oriented megaprojects and illicit-crop cultivation. But the Peace Laboratory project's success is constrained by factors beyond either the commitment of local participants or the good intentions of the European Union, which provides the bulk of the laboratory's economic support. Like projects in other Colombian regions, Oriente's efforts to build effective economic and political alternatives to armed conflict are ultimately enabled or limited by the support or indifference of regional and national power holders. The armed actors' rejection of humanitarian overtures and alternative development projects in the areas where the laboratories function can also be an impediment to the laboratories' reach and impact. Notwithstanding these considerations, the Peace Laboratory project undoubtedly constituted what Jaime Fajardo Landaeta, peace adviser to the governor of Antioquia, called in 2003 "the best alternative" open to Oriente in its quest to escape the stranglehold of ever-escalating violence and displacement.[4] Indeed, given the highly polarized Colombian political arena and the dwindling options for social change in an ideologically fraught environment where anything resembling peasant activism could be confused with guerrilla-inspired revolutionary initiatives, the Peace Laboratory constituted perhaps the *only* alternative to armed conflict and the imminent disappearance of smallholder forms of economic subsistence and survival.

This chapter traces the trajectory of events that propelled Oriente's civic leaders and inhabitants to embrace a strategy of no violence after 1997. It discusses the difficulties in promoting bottom-up, nonviolent alternatives to conflict resolution based in broadly inclusive, deliberative, and participatory democratic venues such as the *asambleas comunitarias* (community assemblies). Civic engagement proves to be a major key allowing this region to counter armed conflict with nonviolent strategies. The conclusion considers how recent events such as the partial demobilization of paramilitary groups and the results of the October 28, 2007, elections for mayors, governors, and congressional representatives may constrain or facilitate the long-term impact of Peace Laboratory initiatives in Oriente.

---

[4] "Historia" (interview with Jaime Fajardo Landaeta regarding the objectives and future of the Peace Laboratory, March 3, 2004), www.orientevirtual.org/?2,73,es (accessed September 5, 2008).

Oriente: A Geographical and Historical Overview

The twenty-three towns that make up Oriente's No-Violence Movement are representative of only the most severely contested sites of armed conflict in Colombia.[5] Despite the internationally disseminated image of a country engulfed by violence, and national homicide rates typical of countries at war, the experience of consistent, intense violence in Colombia is more selective and concentrated than either the media or many analysts tend to represent it. Only certain Colombian areas have the lethal combination of elements that can make conflict so multidimensional as to thwart attempts at a near-term solution. Among such areas, fewer still have developed resilient, deeply rooted forms of popular participation and social mobilization that might enable the emergence of unarmed alternative responses to conflict. The towns of Oriente, indigenous groups in the Cauca and Nariño, the peace community of San José de Apartadó in Urabá, and grassroots organizations in Barrancabermeja and Montes de María form part of this select latter group.[6]

The areas in Colombia where violence is most intense have tended to be sparsely populated, hard to reach, or where significant colonization and settlement occurred or accelerated in the second half of the twentieth century. (The southern and southeastern departments of Putumayo, Guaviare, and Caquetá fit this last profile.) Migration and colonization in such areas were typically triggered by earlier cycles of violence and displacement (a pattern also true of the eastern plains regions, Meta, Amazonas, and Arauca). Some of these areas (such as the Chocó and the southern departments of Cauca and Nariño) are also places with a long history of settlement by Afro-Colombian or indigenous groups. In such areas, violence has escalated in the past decade because of the spread of illicit-crop cultivation or the emergence of the area as a contested geostrategic corridor for the conduct of illicit and armed activities. Areas of severe violence also generally have valuable natural resources such as petroleum, natural gas, and hydroelectric potential or large-scale commercial agriculture (such as African palm trees) or cattle production. Capital-intensive, extractive, or commercial agricultural production in such

---

[5] CODHES, "La otra guerra."

[6] The selective and concentrated nature of violence is recognized by international and domestic agencies collecting data on Colombia's internal war and human rights situation. See, for example, the United Nations Country Team in Colombia, "UN Situation Room—Colombia Report November 2003," November 30, 2003; Comisión Intercongregacional de Justicia y Paz, "Desplazadas forzadaman familias en Cacarica," September 12, 2003; Government of Colombia, "Desplazamientos: Informe Jul 2003," July 23, 2003; and Office of the United Nations High Commissioner for Human Rights (UNHCHR) in Colombia, *Report on Colombia* (Bogotá: UNHCHR, April 2, 2004). All documents available at www.reliefweb.int/rw/rwb.nsf/All DocsByUNID (accessed May 4, 2004). For one hypothesis of why violence has proved so intractable in the areas where it is most severe, see Nazih Richani, *Systems of Violence: The Political Economy of War and Peace in Colombia*, SUNY Series in Global Politics (New York: SUNY Press, 2002).

areas (for example, southern Bolívar, parts of Córdoba and the César, Norte de Santander, Oriente, and Arauca) is often relatively recent in origin.[7] The aforementioned variables common to areas of extreme violence characterize much, though not all, of Oriente. The towns that make up Oriente are divided into four distinct topographical and ecological zones: *altiplanos* (plateaus), *embalses* (dams), *bosques* (woods/forest), and *páramos* (moors). Towns nearest the regional capital of Medellín—such as Marinilla, Rionegro, and Guarne—have tended to be in areas where small property holding has been the dominant form of land tenure and (in the case of Rionegro) where investment in industrial and infrastructure development (airport, recreation, and tourist resources) is concentrated. In contrast, towns located near substantial forests or where abundant water resources have been dammed for hydroelectric power generation have suffered the highest incidence of displacement and violence.

In municipalities such as El Peñol, San Carlos, Granada, and Guatapé, there is competition over watersheds that have enormous potential for hydroelectric production but that are also the lifeblood of subsistence agriculture and wood extraction. In Cocorná, San Francisco, and San Luis, tropical forest coexists precariously with cattle ranching and extractive industries such as mining. For decades, struggles over the shape of development have formed the backdrop for conflict in Oriente towns characterized by valuable watersheds, woods, pasturelands, and extractive potential. Marxist guerrilla groups such as the Ejército de Liberación Nacional (ELN), in 1964, and the Fuerzas Armadas Revolucionarias de Colombia (FARC), in 1966, established strongholds in certain sections of eastern Antioquia, particularly the towns nearest the oil and gold-mining camps, but also in towns nearest Magdalena River ports. In the Magdalena River Valley, extensive cattle ranching provoked violent conflicts between squatters and absentee landlords extending back as far as the 1930s and 1940s. Municipalities with a history of disputes over resources and landholding typically emerged as the earliest areas of guerrilla organization and deployment in Oriente and elsewhere in Colombia.

This guerrilla presence, though palpable, was felt indirectly and sporadically by most of Oriente's inhabitants from the 1970s through the early 1980s. Cattlemen, businessmen, and extractive companies were "taxed" or kidnapped by the guerrillas as a way of generating income for their cause. Locals provided supplies, intelligence, and tacit political support (sometimes under pressure) for the guerrillas, but there is little evidence that many local inhabitants joined the guerrillas or that the latter conducted

---

[7] For an attempt to quantify the characteristics of particularly violent areas using data on settlement, production, location, and presence of guerrilla or paramilitary actors, see Programa de las Naciones Unidas para el Desarrollo (PNUD), or United Nations Development Programme, *El conflicto, callejón con salida: Informe Nacional de Desarrollo Humano, Colombia—2003* (Bogotá: PNUD, 2003), 23, 52–65, 73–77.

forcible recruitment among local youth, as they would come to do by the late 1990s.[8] As one woman activist with twenty-five years' experience in the region put it, "The guerrillas at that time took care of the peasants, helped the community, filled many vacuums left empty by the State. . . . You might say that that's how a close and affectionate relationship was formed between the communities and the guerrillas."[9]

The Emergence of Contemporary Civic Movements in Oriente

Since the 1950s, when Oriente's first municipal civic action campaigns protested the state's neglect of the region, residents have complained that the decision-making process underlying development projects is not "consensually negotiated" (*concertado*) but is instead "imposed upon rural folk."[10] For example, a study titled *Oriente Antioqueño: Violent Imposition of a Development Model*, published by the Spanish government agency Agencia Española de Cooperación Internacional (AECI) in 2000, concluded that a statistically significant increase in the number of human rights abuses perpetrated in Oriente began in the early 1980s. This was the period when the region's hydroelectric industry took off and local inhabitants mobilized to pressure the regional authorities to address grievances related to the policies and actions of the state electricity company Empresa Antioqueña de Energía.

Journalist Darío Zapata offers a two-stage analysis of the emergence of civic movements in response to both the development of the regional energy sector and the proliferation of armed actors in Oriente.[11] He argues that the civic movements that first emerged in the early 1980s were strongest in the municipalities where hydroelectric generating plants and dams were first developed (El Peñol and Guatapé). The main issues around which these civic movements cohered were questions of flooding and forced relocation. Civic movements in both towns organized *paros cívicos* (civil stoppages or strikes) to protest the construction of "megaprojects" and the lack of local participation or consultation in their development. These movements built broad, cross-municipal alliances. Issues such as displacement, threats to local sub-

---

[8]The rise of the drug industry in Colombia enabled guerrilla forces, whose numbers had peaked and were in decline in the early 1980s, to increase dramatically in size by the 1990s. See Frank Safford and Marco Palacios, *Colombia: Fragmented Land, Divided Society* (New York: Oxford University Press, 2002), 362.

[9]Juan Gutiérrez, "Humanization of Extremists," interview with "Guadalupe," in *Beyond Intractability*, eds. Guy Burgess and Heidi Burgess (Boulder, Colo.: University of Colorado, Conflict Research Consortium, 2004), www.beyondintractability.org/essay/humanization_extremists/ (accessed February 15, 2007).

[10]Darío Zapata, "La guerra en el Oriente Antioqueño entre dos proyectos de desarrollo," *Prensa Rural*, December 16, 2003, www.prensarural.org/ruben20031209a.htm (accessed September 17, 2008).

[11]Ibid.

sistence production, and poor energy access and service affected a broad range of people in ways that cut across partisan and even class lines.

But emergent civic movements faced a difficult opponent in their fight to gain decision-making say and recognition of local grievances. The majority shareholder in the development of hydroelectric plants and dams controlled by Interconexión Eléctrica S.A. (ISA) was and is the Colombian state, in partnership with legally independent regional public utility companies such as Empresas Públicas de Medellín.[12] Less than 30 percent of the energy company's shares are publicly traded or belong to private entities. The state's economic interests in Oriente and the imperative to maximize output and profits often conflict with its constitutional obligation to recognize and defend the right of citizens to mobilize democratically to express grievances. This tension contributes to the ambivalence that state officers charged with protecting the state's investment in infrastructure in Oriente feel toward local populations who complain of human rights violations or threats by the police or military or by the latter in collusion with paramilitary forces. At the same time, it is difficult for local civic movements to voice criticism of specific official energy policies or challenge the environmental and social impact of these policies on local communities without risking being conflated with guerrilla groups.[13]

In fact, the death blow to the first stage of Oriente's civic mobilization occurred in the late 1980s, when several fronts, or units, of what would eventually become a consolidated paramilitary presence emerged in the Middle Magdalena Valley region, around Puerto Boyacá. The arrival of a paramilitary challenge to the status quo—and, on its heels, the penetration into eastern Antioquia by the FARC from its traditional command posts along the Magdalena River—marked the turning point in Oriente's fortunes: "The paramilitaries start[ed] to look for the guerrillas, and of course they start[ed] to kill townspeople who had been helping the guerrillas. But all of them had helped, all of them, because they had lived so long with them."[14]

Among those who would eventually collaborate in these paramilitary sweeps were the now deceased Castaño brothers (Fidel and Carlos), ranchers with estates near Puerto Berrio who allegedly took up the counterinsurgency cause in retaliation for their father's kidnapping and murder by the FARC in

---

[12] For information about the company's mission, shareholders, operations, damaged infrastructure due to guerrilla attacks, and clients, see ISA, www.isa.com.co (accessed September 11, 2008).

[13] The bulk of attacks conducted against Colombia's energy infrastructure, with the exception of the oil pipeline, have taken place in Antioquia (967 towers destroyed from 1985 to 2006—837 more than in the second most affected department, Norte de Santander), especially in the Oriente town of San Carlos. For reports of attacks on electricity towers in 2005, see the *Encyclopedia of the Earth*, "Energy Profile of Colombia," August 28, 2008, www.eoearth.org/article/Energy_profile_of_Colombia (last accessed September 17, 2008).

[14] Gutiérrez, "Humanization of Extremists," interview with "Guadalupe."

1981; and Ramón Isaza Arango, founder of the now defunct Autodefensas Campesinas del Magdalena Medio.[15] The purchase of enormous tracts of land in eastern Antioquia by drug traffickers such as Pablo Escobar in the 1970s and 1980s was another factor that dramatically shifted the conflict in Oriente and paved the way for paramilitary expansion. Drug traffickers–cum–landowners or ranchers made possible the institutionalization of well-equipped and -trained private armies that could be mobilized to defend the interests of large investors in the region. Increasingly, the majority local population, who were landless or subsistence farmers, shopkeepers, or small-businesspeople, were caught in the deadly struggle for territorial domination waged by various armed groups: paramilitaries, military troops sent sporadically to "establish order" (who quickly realized they were far better off allowing the better-armed and -financed paramilitaries to do their work for them), and several guerrilla fronts of the ELN and the FARC.[16]

In the mid-1990s, survivors of Oriente's earlier civic movements regrouped around new community discussions taking place with the management of the hydroelectric plants. Colombia's 1991 constitution had introduced reforms including legal protection of cultural, ethnic, racial, and other minorities. The constitution also established that, in the interests of constructing a pluralistic society based on tolerance and respect for difference, the environmental impact of development projects had to be discussed and resolved in consultation with the communities that these policies might affect. ISA's "Environmental Policy: Toward Sustainable Development" statement makes this new imperative clear:

> ISA frames its environmental policies within the economic, political and social parameters of sustainable development. . . . From the earliest stages of planning, construction and during the operation of its transmission network, ISA develops efficient processes of education, communication, information and citizen and community participation. Consequently, all the families, social groups or ethnic and cultural sectors that must coexist with the company are included in the programs, projects, and actions concerned with environmental management.[17]

When a civic movement reemerged in Oriente to contest ISA's hydroelectric development projects in the mid-1990s, it was centered in the municipality of San Carlos. Two large plants, Playas and Calderas, had come online in

---

[15] Garry M. Leech, *Killing Peace: Colombia's Conflict and the Failure of U.S. Intervention* (New York: Information Network of the Americas, 2002).

[16] The history of guerrilla and paramilitary expansion in the Magdalena Medio region is captured in vivid and compelling detail in Steven Dudley, *Walking Ghosts: Murder and Guerrilla Politics in Colombia* (London: Routledge, 2004); and Juanita León, *País de plomo, crónicas de guerra* (Bogotá: Aguilar, 2005).

[17] ISAGEN, "Política ambiental," November 27, 2002, www.isagen.com.co/metaInst.jsp?rsc=infoIn_politicaAmbiental (accessed September 17, 2008).

the town to produce nearly half the electricity generated in eastern Antioquia, which in turn produces 30 to 35 percent of all of Colombia's electricity. The new movement expanded its linkages to include emergent human rights committees and local peasant-producer cooperatives.[18] In 1995, the mayor-elect of San Carlos was assassinated allegedly by paramilitary forces, and Antioquia's governor, Álvaro Uribe Vélez, announced his intention to appoint a military mayor for the town—an action that Oriente's civic movement opposed. The governor responded to the civic movement's protests by accusing members of San Carlos's municipal administration and other public employees of being "infiltrated by the guerrilla."[19]

"The State's first offer," one civic activist in San Carlos noted, "was to encourage us to confront the armed actors with arms." But Oriente's civic leaders, the mayor, the priest, other community leaders (members of women's groups, cooperatives, and so on), and ordinary citizens rejected the state's advice.[20] Instead, townspeople authorized their civic leaders to approach the commanders of the different armed groups (including the state's security forces) to see if, by appealing to them for suggestions on how to "bring in food, medicine, so innocent people wouldn't fall under fire, so that people wouldn't have to be displaced so much," the armed actors might cease to see the townspeople as their enemies. Every proposal to engage in dialogue with the armed actors was subjected to endless hours of consensus-based deliberation, discussion, and refinement in local *asambleas comunitarias*. Only proposals perceived to reflect values that "were very much ours, very shared, very discussed, very concerted, where we felt united and could say [to the armed actors]: 'This is our proposal,'" were endorsed.[21]

The regional government responded to the assassination of San Carlos's mayor with the largest militarization campaign ever conducted in eastern Antioquia. Moreover, paramilitaries in the Magdalena region, emboldened by the regional government's rejection of Oriente's plea for nonviolent approaches to the escalating conflict, began issuing death threats against San Carlos's civic movement leaders.[22] The first identifiable massacre in eastern Antioquia took place in 1998 in the urban center of San Carlos, a week before the town's traditional *fiestas del agua* (water celebrations).[23] The army, which

---

[18] Zapata, "La guerra en el Oriente."

[19] The hostility that has characterized the relationship between Oriente's civic leaders and Álvaro Uribe Vélez can be dated to this initial conflict over the appointment of a military mayor for San Carlos.

[20] Gutiérrez, "Humanization of Extremists," interview with "Enrique."

[21] Ibid.

[22] Zapata, "La guerra en el Oriente."

[23] The emergence of peace communities in Colombia, such as San José de Apartadó in Urabá, date to the intensification of massacres led by paramilitary forces in 1997 and 1998. See Chapter 13 by Christopher Mitchell and Sara Ramírez in this volume.

had maintained a presence in the town—in part to protect the watershed and local hydroelectric plant from possible guerrilla sabotage—abruptly decamped. Local inhabitants remember that the paramilitaries entered the town shortly after the army's departure—establishing what would emerge as a recurrent pattern in paramilitary-led massacres and forcible displacement operations. On this occasion, the paramilitaries killed thirteen people, among them several of San Carlos's civic movement leaders.

Many of those who fled or were forced by the paramilitaries to leave Oriente relocated to poor neighborhoods in Medellín. The displaced in turn became the targets of paramilitary massacres led by members of Carlos Castaño's Autodefensas Unidas de Colombia (AUC). The killers would warn people in the Medellín neighborhoods where the displaced had found refuge that "the boss [Castaño] was angry," and that even if it took going in thirty or forty times to take out people, they would do so because "they had to finish off guerrilla nests."[24]

Ironically, in the months leading up to the 1998 massacre, the San Carlos civic movement had actually managed to win support and a political presence within the town's municipal administration. It had also developed links to European NGOs and government cooperation agencies for the purpose of establishing agricultural cooperatives to foment coffee production, beekeeping, and fish farming. These measures were intended to help offset local farmers' concerns over the usurpation of their lands by ISA-directed projects to export electricity. ISA's new electrical lines were scheduled to be cut through campesino-held lands, and ISA had pushed to negotiate compensation on an individual basis with each of the affected farmers.

Civic movement leaders in the villages of Patio Bonito and El Chocó (San Carlos), where two of the regional electrical centers were located, presented ISA with a compensation counterproposal. They asked ISA to create a community investment fund that could be used to support local production projects with long-term, communitywide benefits for the affected villages. The crux of the discussions between civic leaders and the energy giant was the definition of "sustainable" practices. For ISA, "sustainability" meant barring peasants from having access to forests. For local leaders, in contrast, it meant providing communities with alternative forms of subsistence production so that they would not feel compelled to cut down trees.[25] After months of wrangling, ISA ultimately agreed to the civic movement's alternative development approach, and plans were drawn up to begin investment in small production projects.[26]

---

[24] "'Paras-Bandas, alianza mortal," *El Tiempo*, May 21, 1998.

[25] Zapata, "La guerra en el Oriente."

[26] The European-financed peace laboratories build on this model of investment in local alternative production projects.

But shortly before the agreement brokered by the San Carlos civic movement went into effect, paramilitaries abducted and killed Víctor Velásquez, the project development manager for the municipality of San Carlos in charge of implementing the ISA investment project. Paramilitaries also killed two prominent civic movement leaders who were survivors of the persecuted 1980s municipal civic movement, throwing their bodies off the local hydroelectric dam. After the paramilitary murders of these civic leaders, no one remained to implement the "alternative development farming plan." Don Alberto, a campesino from Granada and a member of the Red de Promotores Agropecuarios del Oriente (Network of Agricultural Promoters for Oriente), noted sadly when interviewed in December 2003,

> In the areas near the dams there are villages without a single inhabitant, but where production of *'rastrojo'* (plant debris or stubble) to feed the microwatersheds continues. In Granada, there may be two hamlets (*veredas*) without inhabitants and in San Carlos, they number more than fifty. This is what economic megaprojects need to fulfill their ultimate objective [that is, a depopulated, "pristine" landscape], yet many of us campesinos obstinately hold on to our lands and small production projects.[27]

Overlaying the struggle around resources and development in Oriente that lent tinder to the armed conflict was the logistical and economic importance of the Autopista Medellín–Bogotá. The highway runs through several eastern Antioqueño municipalities (Santuario, Granada, and San Carlos) and links the department of Antioquia with Bogotá. Along with the Carretera al Mar, which runs from the Caribbean Sea in northwestern Urabá to Medellín, the *autopista* constitutes the central axis along which goods (both licit and illicit) as well as people enter and leave Antioquia. Around 1998–99, inhabitants of villages along the *autopista* began to feel the brunt of intensified competition between armed actors vying to control the highway and its potential as a conduit for illicit profits. As Iván Darío Castaño, the former mayor of Granada, dryly noted, "It's a strategic point for those of us who want peace and for those who want war."[28] The ELN established obligatory roadblocks at designated points along the road, where they charged local producers who brought their goods to the road a fixed "toll" (*peaje*), and engaged in *pescas milagrosas*, or "miracle fishing," that is, random kidnappings for ransom of drivers and passengers traveling the road.[29] In retaliation, many owners of trucking and bus companies threw their considerable economic weight and influence behind paramilitary groups, which increasingly challenged the guerrillas' extortion monopoly.

---

[27] Zapata, "La guerra en Oriente."

[28] Quoted in Natalia Borrero, "Granada, una oportunidad de vida," *Semana*, July 2, 2003.

[29] The ELN's various moneymaking ploys proved so profitable that in 1999 the FARC moved its Ninth Front into the eastern town of Santuario to challenge the ELN for territorial control of that stretch of highway.

The "formal" establishment of an important beachhead of paramilitary control along the *autopista* came in February 2000, when the ELN shut down the eastern section of the highway and blocked all goods and services from entering or leaving the towns along the road. In response, members of the paramilitary AUC stationed in the Magdalena Medio forced eight thousand local campesinos to relocate from their farms and villages to the urban centers of their towns during a three-month period, creating a sanitation emergency of major proportions.[30] This was when, as one veteran local woman activist put it, "the conflict began to escalate."[31]

Fulfilling the Functions of a State without Appearing to Usurp It

In 1998, Oriente's civic leaders and mayors began to approach the regional and central authorities about the possibility of establishing a dialogue with the guerrillas to negotiate a way out of the region's growing humanitarian crisis. Several of the mayors spearheading the peace effort had come to office after defying threats by the FARC to kill any candidates who participated in the 1997 elections. Others had had to seek refuge in Medellín, where they established municipal governments "in exile" and ran municipal affairs via cell phones and the Internet. The mayors' well-meaning efforts to engage in dialogue with armed actors for humanitarian purposes were largely rebuffed by the Pastrana administration, which warned Oriente's civic leaders that only the central government had the authority to negotiate with armed groups. Indeed, local inhabitants such as "Enrique" noted that although Oriente towns had adopted *acercamientos humanitarios* (humanitarian rapprochements) as the only possible way out of an emergency situation as early as 1996, Oriente took a risk in approaching the heads of armed groups, because "from the President's office, from the [central] State, that was not allowed."[32]

Locals nonetheless persisted in pursuing the strategy of *acercamientos humanitarios* because experience had taught them that in certain circumstances humanitarian rapprochements had succeeded in deflecting possible tragedies. In San Carlos, for instance, the implementation of President Uribe's "democratic security" policy mandated that the police set up permanent residence within the local police barracks. Yet these barracks were often situated within residential neighborhoods, thus putting civilians at risk during guerrilla attacks waged against government agents. It was precisely in response to a situation where townspeople feared that an armed group's occupation of a school building would imperil the lives of civilians residing nearby that

---

[30] Borrero, "Granada, una oportunidad de vida," 66.

[31] Gutiérrez, "Humanization of Extremists," interview with "Guadalupe."

[32] Gutiérrez, "Humanization of Extremists," interview with "Enrique."

several neighbors approached the commander of the armed group to ask if they would "move over a little bit so as not to put us so strongly in the path of danger." Townspeople also appealed, in the case of the police and military, to their sense of duty, pointing out, "Look here, man, you're putting in danger the lives of our children and even the survival of the local infrastructure, the infrastructure you're supposedly charged with defending." Many townspeople felt that their use of democratic tools such as dialogue and negotiation ensured that "the number of deaths went down, the approach worked."[33] But the breakdown of peace talks and the end of the FARC's demilitarized zone in 2002 hardened the central government's opposition to Oriente's use of persuasion and dialogue to negotiate its way out of the bottleneck of repeated bombings, massacres, and economic blockades affecting the region.

Oriente's No-Violence Movement appeared to have reached an impasse when the newly elected governor of Antioquia, Guillermo Gaviria Correa, unexpectedly announced that he supported taking a new approach toward the problem of violence in Antioquia and was interested in including the Oriente mayors in a project that would become the "Plan Congruente de Paz."[34] The conversations conducted between the mayors, the governor, and the governor's peace commissioner, Gilberto Echeverri Mejía, marked an important turning point in the trajectory of Oriente's No-Violence Movement.[35] Not only were Oriente's twenty-three mayors made welcome at the gubernatorial offices in Medellín, but the mayors also convinced the governor to participate in a several-day march through northwestern Antioquia to promote solidarity for the No-Violence Movement.[36] It was during a stretch of the walk in the municipality of Caicedo that the governor, his peace commissioner, and eight other people were taken hostage by the FARC in April 2002.

The governor's kidnapping was a blow to the No-Violence Movement. Oriente's civic leadership knew from experience that without the links and effective support of regional, national, and even international interlocutors, the No-Violence Movement's dream of replacing the dynamic of coercion with one of negotiation had little hope of becoming a reality. The capture of the movement's strongest supporters, the regional governor and his peace commissioner, put the legitimacy and future of the movement's objectives in jeopardy. Moreover, the FARC, the AUC, and the Uribe administration remained

---

[33] Ibid.

[34] For a full description of the Plan Congruente's objectives and history, see www.colombianoviolencia.gov.co/html/principios.htm (accessed April 10, 2003).

[35] The year before, in his role as director of Antioquia's Strategic Development Plan, Echeverri Mejía had interceded on the mayors' behalf after they unsuccessfully appealed to the Pastrana government for permission to engage in a "humanitarian rapprochement" with the guerrillas.

[36] By 2001, most of Oriente's mayors had been forced by armed threats to relocate to Medellín, from where they conducted town business via fax, the Internet, and cell phones.

critical—for reasons particular to each group—of the Oriente mayors' use of *acercamientos humanitarios* and *asambleas comunitarias* rather than arms in the struggle to confront illegal groups. For example, less than three months after taking office, newly elected President Uribe, whose greatest concern was defeating the armed left, ordered a three-thousand-man military offensive, with U.S. Black Hawk helicopter backup, to take over one of Medellín's most violent neighborhoods, the Comuna 13, and purge the area of guerrilla support.[37] This provoked a predictably violent response from the guerrillas.

On December 30, 2002, the ELN took reprisals against the president's actions in the Comuna 13 by establishing a ten-day blockade of Cocorná, San Luis, and Granada. The guerrillas bombed the electrical towers and blew up bridges and roads to completely isolate certain villages and impede travel or communication between municipalities. Neither ambulances nor food supplies could penetrate the blockade. Only a combined effort by representatives of the governor's office, Oriente's mayors, the Sonson/Rionegro Catholic Dioceses, and civic organizations based in San Luis to negotiate with the local commanders of the ELN succeeded in bringing the blockade to an end before it could cause severe damage to the region. All the negotiating parties agreed publicly that the first step on the road to a peaceful solution was to "reduce social inequality in the area [Oriente]" and that a Peace Laboratory represented the most viable means of promoting environmental sustainability, improving the local economy, and establishing a participatory framework for achieving these goals. Consensus was reached on a working agenda for the Peace Laboratory project and the principal issues that it should address. Food security; territorial autonomy; reforming the energy sector, the environment, and ecology; and infrastructure and development were identified as the most pressing matters facing the region.

But the Colombian president's televised national declarations in September 2003 (since reiterated in national and international venues) accusing international and domestic human rights organizations and NGOs of shielding terrorist groups trained suspicion on individuals and community organizations such as Oriente's, whose movements were largely supported by the very groups that the president suggested were the apologists or accomplices of "terrorists."[38] Three years after the twenty-three mayors of Oriente launched their No-Violence Movement, the outlook for achieving even a modest détente with the armed actors in Oriente, or of institutional-

---

[37]Scott Wilson, "Urban Anti-Rebel Raid a New Turn in Colombian War," *Washington Post*, October 24, 2002.

[38]Just before his landslide reelection on May 28, 2006, President Uribe publicly accused students who criticized his democratic security policies and lenient paramilitary demobilization program of being "cryptocommunists" during a rally at the Catholic Universidad Javeriana in Bogotá. See Christian Parenti, "Colombia's Deep Divide," *The Nation*, June 12, 2006: 17.

izing nonviolent approaches to the resolution of violence, seemed increasingly bleak. Then, in an unexpected move that once more revived hope for the future of Oriente's No-Violence initiative, the government of Antioquia announced in 2004 that it had brokered a deal with the European Union, with the backing of the national government, to make the region of Oriente one of what would eventually be three national peace laboratories.

Politics and Peacebuilding: The Peace Laboratories

The stated goal of the second Peace Laboratory is to "encourage collective construction of the conditions [necessary] for lasting peace and peaceful coexistence (*convivencia*) based on life with dignity and opportunities for all inhabitants," especially in areas where violence as a result of armed conflict is most severe.[39] The twenty-three towns of Oriente, fifteen towns in Norte de Santander, and twenty-six towns in the Macizo/Alto Patía region, which straddles the departments of Cauca and Nariño, were selected as participants in the second Peace Laboratory because they share the dubious distinction of being "among Colombia's most conflictive and violent zones." (See Peace Laboratories Map.) But the presence of high levels of violence alone is insufficient to qualify a particular area for Peace Laboratory selection. What set the Oriente, Macizo/Alto Patía, and Norte de Santander towns apart from other violent Colombian areas was a history of developing "a variety of forms and experiences of civil resistance" with which to confront armed actors, as well as civil society–driven "initiatives to promote participation and peace dialogues."[40]

The Peace Laboratory's insistence on strengthening rather than creating the conditions and organizations necessary to imagining, designing, and implementing strategies aimed at peacebuilding suggests an understanding that top-down solutions, however well intentioned, are unlikely to succeed in changing the circumstances of areas with no prior history of locally rooted collective organizing and civic participation. In contrast, judicious support of existing, locally generated and led organizations with proven track records of resilience and commitment to peaceful solutions represents a largely untapped but promising avenue for effecting change in places such as Oriente. Former mayors such as Hernando Martínez, active in organizing the No-Violence Movement and putting into practice norms of accountability and transparency during his tenure in local office (1998–2002), embody the internalization of the values that underpin the Peace Laboratory project. Martínez attributed his commitment to pluralism and dialogue to his experiences as a rural schoolteacher in the 1970s and 1980s, when he was exposed to Paolo

---

[39] European Union, Acción Social, "II Laboratorio de Paz—Resumen del Proyecto," www.laboratoriodepaz.org/publicaciones.php?id=27785 (accessed September 11, 2008).

[40] Ibid.

Freire's *Pedagogy of the Oppressed*.[41] During his term in office and afterward as
a consultant to Antioquia's regional government in its negotiations to establish a Peace Laboratory, Martínez put into practice his convictions by spearheading peace initiatives shaped by participatory, open assemblies where the
opinions of all a town's inhabitants could be taken into account.[42]

"Lucía," a founding member of the Asociación de Mujeres del Oriente
(AMOR, or Women's Association of Eastern Antioquia), arrived at her commitment to organizing and civic engagement by a different path. After many
years as a barely literate rural housewife, Lucía began her career of civic participation in 1995 when she was picked as one of five people to represent
Oriente in a regional meeting. She was invited to start a regional women's
association in 1996. From there, she ran for and was elected to a city council
position, which she described as "a beautiful experience for me." "As a result"
she added, "AMOR had the idea to train more women in citizen participation
and democracy."[43] The loss of a daughter to violence, and then the disappearance of a son, convinced her that "raising our children only to give them over
to the paramilitaries or the guerrillas is a form of persecution. . . . When we
began to organize ourselves, I realized that I was not the only one suffering,
that I am not alone and that we can create a space to share our stories and our
pain." Achieving peace for "Lucía" and other members of the No-Violence
Movement is about "plant[ing] . . . seeds of peace now. . . . We are involved in
a movement, not a fight, a great movement where everyone, men and women,
must join together."[44] Individuals such as Hernando Martínez and "Lucía,"
despite the differences in their personal trajectories, are similar in their belief
that the process of peacebuilding is a long-term endeavor. "We want peace,"
"Lucía" insists, "but peace does not come quickly. We will not see it, perhaps
our children will not see it, but hopefully our children's children will be able
to experience the peace and the tranquility that we wish for."[45]

Indeed, the continued exercise of intimidation and selective killings by
former paramilitaries (now often called "emergent illegal groups") in Oriente
has interrupted the practice of *asambleas comunitarias* that formed the backbone of participatory democratic experiments. Although civic movements
and social organizations such as AMOR continue to operate and thrive, the
institutionalization of pluralism and participatory consultation secured by
the mayors committed to No-Violence between 1998 and 2002 is undermined

---

[41] Paolo Freire, *Pedagogy of the Oppressed* (New York: Continuum, 2007).

[42] Hernando Martínez, interview by the author, Medellín, August 2004.

[43] AMOR, "No One Has to Carry the Suffering All Alone," testimony of "Lucía" in *I Will Never Be Silenced: Testimonies of Hope from Colombian Women* (report produced by American Friends Service Committee and the Fellowship of Reconciliation, July 2007), 29–30.

[44] Ibid., 30.

[45] Ibid.

by repeated threats from armed groups.[46] Given the outcome of the election for mayors, town council representatives, and governors held on October 28, 2007, the *asambleas'* future reinstatement is uncertain. The majority of Oriente's towns elected mayors identified with political movements or parties sympathetic to, or perceived to be aligned with, President Uribe, but the results for town council representatives throughout Oriente were more varied. Ten of twenty-three towns elected council members aligned with local political movements committed to greater and more open local participation in policymaking.[47] In some towns, movements that were not locally generated but ran on platforms that also favor greater local and popular participation, such as the Polo Democrático Alternativo (Alternative Democratic Pole), Movimiento de Autoridades Indígenas de Colombia (Movement of Indigenous Authorities of Colombia), and Alianza Social Indígena (Indigenous Social Alliance), also won representation in town council elections. But several of the towns hardest-hit by violence and displacement—Argelia, Cocorná, Granada, Guatapé, San Carlos, San Francisco, and San Luis—all returned Conservative or pro-Uribe majorities in town council elections.[48]

In several cases, the individuals garnering the greatest number of votes on town councils belonged to movements characterized by the electoral watchdog group Votebien as being tainted by association with individuals accused of owing their electoral successes to paramilitary financial support and intimidation.[49] Eugenio Prieto Soto (the interim governor who finished out slain governor Guillermo Gaviria's term in office) and Alfredo Ramos Botero, the candidate for Alas Equipo Colombia, were the leading contenders for the office of regional governor in Antioquia. While Prieto Soto was widely perceived as being "committed to forging a cultural change [to achieve] No-

---

[46] Fernando Valencia, coordinator for the Observatorio de Paz y Reconciliación, noted that three candidates to local office in Oriente had been killed before the elections, and many others had withdrawn from their candidacies, largely because of threats from the FARC. Although several municipalities ultimately voted into town councils several individuals affiliated with local political movements committed to "a more direct participation in the administration of their towns," the possibility of fulfilling this commitment was jeopardized by continued threats by the FARC. See "En Oriente antioqueño esperan que las Farc dejen gobernar," www.terra.com.co/elecciones_2007/articulo/html/vbe1129.htm (accessed November 1, 2007).

[47] Examples of these local political movements are Marinilla Acción, Unidos por San Luis, San Rafael en Acción, and Granada para Todos.

[48] For an analysis of the sympathies and compositions of the various political movements and parties represented in the October 28, 2007, elections, see www.terra.com.co/elecciones_2006/partidos/ (accessed November 1, 2007). For results of the 2007 elections, see www.terra.com.co/elecciones_2007 (accessed September 11, 2008).

[49] See Votebien, www.votebien.com (accessed September 17, 2008). The electoral watchdog site is the result of an alliance between Caracol Radio, *Semana* magazine, Colprensa, Fescol, Congreso Visible, PNUD, and Transparency Colombia. Alas Equipo Colombia and several of its prominent members have been singled out for having paramilitary connections or receiving campaign contributions from individuals tainted by Colombia's recent *parapolítico* scandal.

Violence" and "giving great importance to processes of citizen participation such as . . . the municipal and departmental *asambleas constituyentes*," his rival and the current governor of Antioquia, Alfredo Ramos Botero, was perceived to be sympathetic to executive-centered decision making and hostile to "citizen participatory processes such as the municipal *asambleas constituyentes*."[50]

It is too soon to tell what long-term impact any of these recent events might have on Oriente's No-Violence Movement or the Peace Laboratory project. Still, the historical trajectory of peace initiatives in Oriente and an analysis of the moments when these prospered or stalled suggest that the existence of long-standing, locally led strategies of civil resistance based on broad consultation and collective consensus is an indispensable ingredient in the long-term success of peacebuilding initiatives. But strong local institutions and a collective commitment to pursuing peaceful strategies to resolve armed conflict by themselves may not be enough. Locally initiated movements like the twenty-three mayors' No-Violence Movement need regional, national, and international interlocutors and support to prosper. Oriente's mayors were able to press on with the Peace Laboratory initiative in 2002 despite the central government's opposition, in large measure because Guillermo Gaviria, Antioquia's recently elected governor, embraced the No-Violence Movement, provided it with logistical and moral support, and incorporated into the regional administration's day-to-day practice the participatory and consultative mechanisms that the mayors promoted in their municipal administrations. At a moment when the central government rejected the right of local mayors to initiate humanitarian pacts to curb violence, or to engage in dialogue with any of the armed actors, support like that provided by Governor Gaviria to the No-Violence Movement proved critical to its survival.

Local peacebuilding efforts do not and cannot exist in a vacuum. Therefore, although no newly elected governor or mayor can change the terms of an international accord such as the one that gave rise to the second Peace Laboratory, the institutionalization and short-term success of peacebuilding projects nonetheless depend on the attitude and policies of power holders external to the functioning of the peace laboratories themselves. The case of Oriente illustrates both the possibilities and the limits of seeking a *cambio de armas* (change of weapons) in a sea of armed actors in contemporary Colombia.

---

[50] www.terra.com.co/elecciones-2007/articulo/html/vhe411.htm#uno (accessed November 1, 2007).

16

The Local Community as a Creative Space for Transformation
The View from Montes de María

Ricardo Esquivia Ballestas with Barbara Gerlach

In a Land of Hope, a Culture of Violence

During the past fifty years, Colombia has experienced a grave social conflict that has degenerated into an internal armed conflict. From every point of view, the consequences of this war have been disastrous for combatants and noncombatants, the country as a whole, the state, the different administrations that have governed the country, and the economy. The prolonged conflict has helped create a political culture of violence and has whetted appetites for wealth and power, leading to administrative corruption and drug trafficking. This war, considered just or unjust by some, "dirty" or "clean" by others, has been catastrophic. Except for a handful of groups and businesses—national and international, licit and illicit—that grow rich and gain power from the war and its consequences, Colombians want peace.

That is why they have made so many efforts to end the war, including establishing an impressive array of organizations and initiatives that are working for peace. At least thirty thousand peace initiatives have been documented in Colombia. These efforts have emerged from various sectors of society, and some have been very creative.

In the late 1990s, a coalition of groups decided to gauge the level of people's interest in peace—not by telephone surveys, which are sometimes misleading because they may be biased, but by participation in certain actions. They launched a referendum with children in which some 2.5 million boys and girls expressed their desire for peace. Excited by the result, the group decided to create a ballot initiative seeking a citizens' mandate for peace; about 9.5 million people voted for peace. This coalition, supported by the Red Nacional de Iniciativas por la Paz y contra la Guerra (REDEPAZ), País Libre, churches, and other sectors, organized a massive march for peace and against war, which they called No Más (No More). Many people—12.5 million according to the organizers, 10 million according to the least optimistic estimates—turned out to march for peace.

But what happened to these good intentions and this sea of enthusiasm? Why have they not translated into changes in everyday life? The statistics are chilling. Violence and war continue to claim victims. We still have nearly thirty thousand violent deaths a year. More than three million people have suffered forced displacement. Drug trafficking continues to grow and to have a negative effect on society. Are people not sincere, and do they attend these events only out of enthusiasm? Were the demonstrations for peace in vain?

What Type of Peace Do the People Want?

The difficulty is that each person has a different concept of peace. One of the underlying problems in the work for peace is that we have to reach agreement on the kind of peace that we are building. It is important to know what we want and where we want to go, so we can discern the path, the method and strategies to follow, the tools to use, and the means to join forces and channel them toward the same goal. We need to know what kind of seed we are planting, so we can fertilize the land and use the proper tools to reap a good harvest. Or to use another metaphor, we all agree that we want to paint the house green, but what shade of green? Sea green? Parrot green? Dark green? Light green? This little disagreement can result in paralysis and frustration, and when we do not know where we are going—"any bus will do," as the saying goes—we may end up in a place where we do not want to be.

For some people, peace is the absence of war or tangible manifestations of violence. This type of peace can be achieved with weapons and violence or through pacts among the warring parties or the people who finance them. Here the main objective is to defeat or eliminate the other. As the ancient Roman gladiators said, "Your death is my life."

Ending the war is very important; it is an indispensable step. But unfortunately, it is not enough to silence the guns and subdue and demobilize the fighters. All the effort and the economic resources invested in weapons, fighter jets, training and strategizing for war, and restrictions on fundamental rights and freedoms may help the opposing parties achieve some of their goals. It may help stop the war, but it will exhaust the resources needed for building a holistic and comprehensive peace and will only produce more war and destruction. You cannot invest a little in peace and then ignore it, because peace will die and its corpse will contaminate everything around it. The crucial step is to create, beforehand or simultaneously, a social base that will sustain peace. To build a lasting peace, we must do away with the social injustices that nurture and feed the war. Otherwise, peace will be ephemeral. It will become a chimera that produces so much frustration when it fades that, sooner or later, a new war will erupt. Perhaps the leaders and armed groups will have different names, but the people will be the same and the destruction and death may be even greater.

Many government officials and citizens in Colombia take this view that peace is the absence of war and violence and that peace can be imposed by weapons and force. Thus, President Álvaro Uribe places much emphasis on strengthening the armed forces and offering military security to achieve his objective of "democratic security." Moreover, officials have come to believe that they can defeat the guerrillas or at least weaken them to such an extent that the latter will be forced to negotiate and agree to end the war. It may sound like a good idea, and it may be effective as part of a political campaign platform, but in the real practice of peacebuilding, this approach is incomplete and ineffective.

In the region of Montes de María, where I work, the armed forces have occupied the municipal centers and the main highways, providing security for the urban population. Meanwhile, people who live in the rural areas, whose daily lives are more severely affected by the dynamics of the war, lack such protection. Because of the violence, small farmers (campesinos) are unable to cultivate the land and suffer from hunger. Drops in agricultural production and army restrictions on the movement of food and medicines have caused food shortages in urban centers.

In Montes de María, democratic security has meant an increase in abuses by the police and armed forces, mass detentions, and the mining of roads by the guerrillas. Montes de María has some of the highest concentrations of antipersonnel mines in the country. Small farmers become the innocent victims of these mines because they must cultivate the land to survive. These mines, a tragic legacy of war, have a long-lasting effect, since even when the military moves its operations to other parts of the country, the countryside remains littered with mines. In addition, the concentrated military presence in the region undermines the authority of civilian leaders and results in the militarization of society. The military is smothering civil society by directing sports programs, health centers, and schools and controlling the public space. All of this increases the population's negative feelings about the government, which people associate more with soldiers and military equipment than with road repairs or facilitating the delivery of basic services.

The tension produced by the military's presence, restrictions on the movement of food, the culture of suspicion and mass detentions, the countervailing pressures of the guerrillas, and the fear of combat have increased forced displacement in Montes de María. The policy of democratic security has favored the economic development of large industries, financial institutions, and commercial businesses, but life is harder for the ordinary people who experience unemployment, hunger, discomfort, and displacement. The enrichment of the economic elites has gone hand in hand with increased poverty in Colombia.

The armed insurgency and counterinsurgency, the paramilitaries, and the gangs that produce death and destruction in Colombia—and even the war itself—are not the principal problems. All are symptoms of the same disease, branches of the same tree of social injustice.

Sacred scripture holds that peace is the fruit of justice. This view of peacemaking that seeks justice calls on us to respect and strengthen human dignity, revere life, and love others even when they are antagonistic. It requires us to protect the integrity of creation and take as a basic social and ethical framework the fundamental rights, duties, and freedoms of human beings proclaimed by the United Nations as a universal code that enables peaceful coexistence of all peoples. Working for such integral and sustainable human development—where justice is made manifest in abundant life with dignity for everyone—is thus a path toward comprehensive peace. This path implies an educational process, a way of teaching based on a methodology of learning by doing, which is democratic, participatory, communal, political, and economic. Such transformative education and active nonviolence are the ideal tools for sowing political power throughout society.

Local Protestant Initiatives for Peace in Montes de María

My own roots in this region of Colombia go deep. I was born and raised on the Caribbean coast, the son of an Afro-Colombian father and an indigenous mother. I experienced poverty and social exclusion. When my father was institutionalized for leprosy, I was taken in and educated by a Mennonite school for the healthy children of families with leprosy. From the Mennonites, I learned the practice of nonviolence, which roots my approach to peacebuilding. I also observed the potential of churches to serve as bases for community organizing and social transformation.

In 1986, I returned to Montes de María to work in the small community of San Jacinto, where I practiced law and organized small farmers. It was not long before this work for social justice and inclusion brought me into conflict with the local authorities. I was falsely accused of being an ideologue for the guerrillas, and my family was threatened. In 1988, my wife, four children, and I were forced to flee, displaced first to Cartagena and then to Bogotá. There I became the first director of Justapaz, the Center for Justice, Peace, and Nonviolent Action of the Mennonite Church, where we developed a variety of church-based initiatives for peace, including community conciliation centers, a school for conscientious objectors, programs in peace education, and training in conflict transformation.

CEDECOL and the Commission of Restoration, Life, and Peace

From our base in Justapaz and the Mennonite Church, we formed a team of about seven people who also worked with the Consejo Evangélico de Colombia (CEDECOL), or Council of Evangelical and Protestant Churches of Colombia, an umbrella organization for 70 percent of Colombia's Protestant Christians (or evangelicals, as they call themselves in Colombia), who represent about eight thousand churches and comprise about 10 percent of the population. CEDECOL was organized in 1950 to protect Protestants from religious persecution and to work for freedom of religious expression, which was finally granted in the 1991 constitution.[1]

Our emphasis as Mennonites has been on helping Protestant churches come together to assist victims of the violence and create programs for peace, justice, and sustainable development in their communities. To do this, we have created a national network within CEDECOL called the Commission of Restoration, Life, and Peace. This commission is made up of 5 regional commissions operating in 155 municipalities and involving 3,500 people. One of our strongest regional commissions is based on the Caribbean coast, an area with a high concentration of Protestant churches. This regional commission, which includes churches from the eight departments on the North coast, includes many of the Protestant churches in Montes de María.

In 2006, the Commission of Restoration, Life, and Peace organized the First Summit of Evangelicals for Peace in Colombia, which gathered more than a hundred theologians, clergy, women, academics, and denominational leaders from different regions, along with representatives from the international community, to develop a road map for Protestant churches working for peace rooted in social, economic, and political justice. The aim was to promote unity of churches in the search for peace, to design strategies to contribute to building a culture of peace that will end armed conflict, and to encourage national, regional, and local church initiatives. The commission issued a statement affirming the quiet work that Protestants have been doing at the local level, "sowing seeds of peace and welfare in our land." It urged the armed groups to "heed society's cry for an end of armed conflict," affirmed efforts at dialogue, negotiation, and demobilization, and underscored the need for a humanitarian agreement to release victims of kidnapping. It highlighted the constructive contribution that churches can make "on matters of truth, justice, reparation, forgiveness, and on reconciliation and rehabilitation for both victims and perpetrators of crimes." It committed the church to work especially on behalf of the forcibly displaced, children recruited by the armed groups, and the most vulnerable victims of the violence. Finally, it said, "Peace is not achieved simply by laying down weapons, but by building

---

[1] See CEDECOL, www.cedecol.net (accessed September 11, 2008).

conditions, a culture, and a spirituality of peace," based on a foundation of respect for human rights and economic and social justice.[2]

The commission and Justapaz also collaborate in a documentation and advocacy program. Beginning in 2002, we began to keep a record of the assassinations of Protestant pastors, the displacement of congregations, and the closing of churches because of the violence. In 2005, this program expanded. As we meet with local communities and teach them how to report human rights violations, we are producing a series of reports that document the impact of the conflict on members of the Protestant churches. The first two editions of *A Prophetic Call: Colombian Churches Document Their Suffering and Their Hope* report the violence from January 2004 to December 2006, as well as church initiatives that are planting seeds of hope in the midst of the crossfire.[3] In 2006, we documented 68 cases of human rights violations against members of Protestant churches, involving 223 victims and 289 acts of aggression. The most frequent form of violence was death threats, with 147 people threatened. Other violations included forced displacement, forced disappearances, torture, arbitrary arrests, attacks, and the use of civilians as human shields. These violations come from all sides: 131 were presumed to be committed by the paramilitaries, 126 by the guerrillas, 28 by government forces.[4] In most cases, people were targeted because they were community leaders, provided social services or human rights orientation to the displaced, witnessed a crime, denounced violence, or advocated nonviolence in the midst of the armed conflict. In 2007 there were 83 cases of human rights violations, involving 324 acts of aggression against 231 victims. This represents 5 more cases, 8 more victims, and 35 more acts of aggression against Protestant churches than in 2006. The churches that were hardest-hit in 2007 were Cristo Centro, Mennonite, and Interamerican.[5]

Sanctuaries of Peace

Justapaz and the commission also had a vision of how local churches could become sanctuaries of peace, places of refuge, and centers for local peace-

---

[2] See "Colombian Churches Commit to Peace," *Christian Solidarity Worldwide*, April 4, 2006, www.cswusa.com/reports%20pages/Reports-Colombia.htm (accessed April 25, 2008).

[3] See Justapaz and the Commission for Restoration, Life, and Peace, *A Prophetic Call: Colombian Protestant Churches Document Their Suffering and Their Hope Report* (Bogotá: Justapaz and the Commission for Restoration, Life, and Peace, August 2006); and *A Prophetic Call: Colombian Protestant Churches Document Their Suffering and Their Hope*, 2nd ed. (Bogotá: Justapaz and the Commission for Restoration, Life, and Peace, August 2007). Both reports are available at www.justapaz.org/spip.php?rubrique13 (accessed April 25, 2008).

[4] Justapaz and the Commission for Restoration, Life, and Peace, *A Prophetic Call*, 2nd ed., 11, www.justapaz.org (accessed October 2, 2008).

[5] Data from *A Prophetic Call*, 3rd ed. (Bogotá: Justapaz and the Commission for Restoration, Life, and Peace, 2008).

building in their communities.[6] Today about fifty sanctuaries of peace exist in Colombia, many with sister relationships with Protestant churches in the United States and Canada. The most developed partnership, called Sal y Luz (Salt and Light), is between three Protestant churches on the Caribbean coast and three clusters of Lutheran and Mennonite Churches and universities in Iowa, Minnesota, and South Dakota. In this joint initiative, coordinated by Justapaz and Lutheran World Relief with funding from the Ford Foundation, churches have been working together to advocate with the Colombian and U.S. governments for peace and assistance to the displaced. They have raised awareness about the threats to church leaders and the impact of the paramilitary demobilization on local communities.[7]

Each of the churches in the Salt and Light project has been a leader in its own community and has documented its local experience in peacebuilding as a way to influence public policy in both countries. Christ the King Church in Tierralta, Córdoba, in the heartland of the Autodefensas Unidas de Colombia territory, opened its building to shelter and feed displaced people fleeing massacres in the surrounding countryside. The church then purchased land to help four displaced communities rebuild and resettle. It has developed health projects, including HIV/AIDS prevention education, as demobilized paramilitaries have returned to the community.

Haven of Peace, a congregation displaced to Sincelejo by the massacre in Macayepo, has become a refuge for many displaced people who are trying to obtain government services, learn about their human rights, and organize a collective "return with dignity" to their lands. One of its leaders reflected, "We are reading about the process of voluntary return because it is our land and heritage. We have had meetings with the governors of Sucre and Bolívar. We have to recover the land of eight hundred families, four thousand people. Six hundred fifty families have signed up to return if there are security guarantees, international accompaniment, police presence, and government responsibility for security."[8]

The Peniel Church in Zambrano, Carmen de Bolívar, has been a witness for nonviolence in the midst of a "red zone" of active fighting and a high concentration of land mines. It has developed programs for food security for the many displaced people in the community and created an educational

---

[6]See Christian Center for Justice, Peace, and Nonviolent Action, "Sanctuary of Peace Churches," www.justapaz.org/-Sanctuary-of-Peace-Churches (accessed April 25, 2008).

[7]See Justapaz and Lutheran World Relief, Serie Experiencias Locales en la Construcción de la Paz, vol. 1, *Construyendo la paz: Aprendizajes desde la base, el conflicto colombiano y las iglesias santuarias de paz;* vol. 2, *Bases bíblico-teológicas del quehacer de las iglesias en la construcción de la paz;* vol. 3, *El desafío del desarrollo en zonas de conflicto;* and vol. 4, *Iniciativas humanitarias locales en contextos de conflicto armado* (Bogotá, Justapaz and Lutheran World Relief, 2006). See also the Web sites of Justapaz, www.justapaz.org, and Lutheran World Relief, www.lwr.org.

[8]Haven of Peace member, speaking with a delegation from the United States, Sincelejo, July 2004.

program on conscientious objection for youth at risk of forced recruitment by the armed groups. The pastors of all three of these sanctuaries of peace have been threatened because of their work.

Building an Infrastructure for Peace

During my eleven years as director of Justapaz, I continued to work in Montes de María on a project called "Construction of an Infrastructure for Peace Starting in Montes de María." In December 2003, I decided to leave Justapaz to work full time in Montes de María to advance this growing multilevel process of development and peace. One dimension was the creation of a small nonprofit organization called Sembrandopaz (Sowing Peace) to build a culture of peace by strengthening and linking grassroots organizations based on holistic, sustainable human development among people on the Caribbean coast. The second dimension was to work with the Protestant churches to organize the Asociación para la Vida Digna y Solidaria (ASVIDAS, or Association for a Dignified Life in Solidarity), an initiative of the Commission of Restoration, Life, and Peace to help local churches and coalitions of churches develop income-generating projects to improve economic conditions in their communities, reweave the social fabric, and create an infrastructure for peace.[9] The third dimension was the formation of the Network for Development and Peace of the Montes de María Foundation.

The time was ripe for such initiatives. Montes de María, one of the poorest regions in Colombia, located in a strategic transportation corridor for oil, drugs, and weapons, had suffered thirty-five massacres and the massive displacement of communities such as El Salado, Chengue, Chinulito, and Macayepo while four guerrilla groups, paramilitaries, and government forces struggled for control of the region. Two Colombian church leaders reported to a visiting delegation of U.S. church leaders in 2004:

> Four or five years ago we worked with a new television channel that was covering the first large displacement from El Salado. The interviews—about how people were assassinated, how they used chain saws, how the children were raped—had a great impact. When the people called for help, the churches did not know what to do. Missionaries taught about the relationship between God and the people, but not between people. The church was afraid and lacked tools in the area of social work. From that time we started to talk and be motivated to work on the social side. . . . There was a desire to come together and do something with churches, drawing on their resources for a dignified life and in solidarity with people in their communities.[10]

---

[9] See Christian Center for Justice, Peace, and Nonviolent Action, "Asvidas: Development and Peace," www.justapaz.org/-Asvidas-Development-and-Peace (accessed April 25, 2008).

[10] From notes by Barbara Gerlach from a delegation that met with ASVIDAS leaders in July 2004.

Another Sincelejo church leader described the impact of the conflict on his region and on the church. In Sincelejo, a city of some 200,000 inhabitants, 80,000 of these residents had been displaced by the conflict. He noted:

> The displacement in Sucre took us by surprise. In early 2000 thousands of persons, whole congregations of churches, fled from massacres in the rural areas to our city. We were not prepared. People were coming to us seeking economic help. . . . A majority of the people are without work. We are doing everything we can do. We began with a spiritual response, but people need help economically, emotionally, socially. We presented Jesus as a solution, but people needed housing, education, medicine, doctors. We do not have these resources. We want to do more. We created a network—ASVIDAS, the Association for a Dignified Life in Solidarity—to bring the social and spiritual activities together and to develop income-producing projects.[11]

The ASVIDAS Network of Montes de María

Over the past three years we at Sembrandopaz organized 130 local, municipal, and regional church-based associations of ASVIDAS on the Caribbean coast. These associations include 5,000 people, 230 congregations, and 29 denominations. Each association has its own organizational structure; board of directors; assembly; coordinator; committees for youth, women, and projects; and a rotating "fund for life" to support small income-generating projects.

Currently, thirty community-wide ASVIDAS groups operate in the fifteen municipalities of Montes de María (excluding the urban municipalities of Sincelejo and Corozal, which have formed their own ASVIDAS networks). Together they have formed the ASVIDAS Network of Montes de María to develop joint economic and social proposals to present to regional, national, and international funders. The central network has twelve teams to coordinate projects and provide technical assistance to local associations.

Four projects of the ASVIDAS Network of Montes de María—one in San Onofre, two in El Carmen de Bolívar, and one in Toluviejo—have been funded through the Network for Development and Peace of the Montes de María Foundation. Support has come from the Colombian government agency Acción Social and a program called "Peace and Development." Supported by a US$30 million loan from the World Bank, these projects assist displaced and vulnerable persons in the areas of food security and income generation. Each of these four projects receives about US$75,000, and they benefit a total of 3,500 families, or 17,500 people. At this point, one of our biggest challenges is to train people in the ASVIDAS network in project development, management, and oversight and to create financial policies and accounting procedures for managing large amounts of money.

---

[11] Ibid.

ASVIDAS is one of the primary ways that Protestant churches are organizing to restart the economy, provide accompaniment to displaced persons, and create an infrastructure for peace. It has caught on like wildfire and has generated unity among the Protestant churches. This work to create an infrastructure for peace is going on in the midst of a conflict that is still burning; four illegal armed groups—two fronts of the FARC, one of the ELN, one of the Ejército Revolucionario Popular (ERP, or People's Revolutionary Army), and paramilitaries—along with the armed forces under the command of the Colombian navy, continue to struggle for control of the region. In the churches, we are working for truth and justice, reparations, and reconciliation in the midst of a paramilitary demobilization that is threatening to unravel as evidence emerges tying members of Congress and other government officials to paramilitary operations and as the demobilized rearm and form gangs, mafia organizations, and new militias. We work with pastors and church members who have been displaced and tortured, who work in red zones with some of the largest concentrations of land mines in Colombia, and who live in urban areas where they are receiving the victims of the violence and responding to humanitarian crises. In the midst of the conflict, we have come together to organize initiatives for peace and justice and for integral and sustainable development.

Network for Development and Peace of the Montes de María Foundation

Protestant churches are also working ecumenically with the Catholic Church in Montes de María. Our aim is for small local communities to become creative spaces for restorative transformation, where people who have been victims of violence, abandonment, abuse, loneliness, poverty, and hunger—and the perpetrators as well—can come to be healed and to recover. There they can receive love and consolation, learn to forgive and be productive, and, above all, rebuild trust and become social actors with political influence in their region. We want to create places where "the emphasis is on promoting human potential instead of focusing only on the harm that has been done and developing the capacity to survive and overcome adversity despite the difficulties and injustices that individuals have experienced."[12]

One of the models, the Programs for Development and Peace, has been multiplying throughout the country. We have built a coalition of nineteen such programs in the Red Nacional de Programas Regionales de Desarrollo y Paz (REDPRODEPAZ). These coalitions build on local organizations, in this case, the Network for Development and Peace of the Montes de María Foun-

---

[12] Francisca Infante, *Manual de identificación y promoción de la resiliencia en niños y adolescentes* (Washington, D.C.: Pan American Health Organization, 1998), http://resilnet.uiuc.edu/ library/resilman/resilman.html (accessed September 11, 2008).

dation. Our goal is to show that it is possible to build peace from a standpoint other than the use of violence and arms. We seek to build a living model so that people will see it and realize that "it exists; therefore, it is possible." Those of us who work from a faith perspective through Catholic or Protestant churches have been giving great impetus to this kind of peacebuilding process. Spirituality and religious values are fundamental in the life and culture of a people. Religion can protect human beings and help them relate to God and to one another. It can invite us to partake of community, solidarity, mutual respect, humility, hospitality, and respect for life.

Among some peoples and cultures, religion becomes distorted and, instead of uniting people, is used as a detonator for war. That is not the case in Colombia, where religion draws people together, invites us to exercise solidarity, and renews hope. Most churches serve as bridges that unite us across the various ideological, political, economic, cultural, ethnic, and social gaps that separate people.

We have established the first ecumenical Program for Development and Peace in Montes de María, a region that includes 17 municipalities with a total population of about 800,000 people. The majority of these individuals are Afro-Colombians who suffer from extreme poverty and government neglect. We have brought together the three Catholic dioceses in the area—Cartagena, with Archbishop Carlos José Ruizseco; Sincelejo, with Bishop Nel Beltrán; and Magangué, with Bishop Leonardo Gómez Serna. I represent the Mennonite Church and the other local Protestant churches in this partnership. Setting aside doctrinal differences and working together through social ecumenism to build peace based on the message of Jesus, we developed the Network for Development and Peace of the Montes de María Foundation.[13] The foundation interconnects the various development and peace programs in Montes de María and brings together the various sectors of society in the area through a regional and ecumenical vision. Members include chambers of commerce; the Social Ministry (Pastoral Social) offices of the Catholic Church; the ASVIDAS network; universities; non-governmental organizations (NGOs); grassroots and cultural organizations; and the national, departmental, and municipal governments.

We are supported by United Nations agencies including the United Nations Development Programme and the United Nations High Commissioner for Refugees, the International Organization for Migration, and some embassies and national agencies. The European Union and the national government have asked us to serve as a nexus for Colombia's third Peace Laboratory, proposed for this area. In the process, we are aware that development is, above all, an exercise in democratic social, political, and economic participation. We

---

[13] See the foundation's Web site, www.fmontesdemaria.org (accessed September 11, 2008).

work through three mutually complementary sectors of society: civil society, private enterprise, and the government.

First, we focus on strengthening civil society, empowering citizens, and rebuilding the social fabric through citizen participation, peaceful resolution and transformation of conflicts, grassroots mediators, justices of the peace, regional peace councils, municipal planning councils, community action boards, and groups that focus on human rights education and nonviolent action. We also support the development of projects for food security and agricultural production, as well as other income-generating projects.

Second, we foster economic partnerships with local businesses to develop markets and possibilities for financing productive projects. It is important to get businesses to make a commitment to rebuild the market chains destroyed by the armed conflict. Communities must also learn how to develop businesses that are self-sustaining. This is the approach we take with the Montes de María Business Association.

Third, we support state institutions. We are not enemies of the state; we are aware that governance is needed. Governance requires a strong, legitimate state that has a constructive presence through social programs and an effective judiciary rather than through repression and military action. It requires capable public servants who can manage public assets skillfully and honestly.

Each municipality has a facilitation board, coordinated by the local government and composed of the various sectors of society. We are working with the Association of Territorial Bodies of Montes de María, which includes two departmental governors and seventeen municipal mayors. We cooperate with national government programs that foster respect and human rights, support at-risk and displaced populations, and promote culture and health.

Paramilitary Demobilization and Reconciliation on the Caribbean Coast

Colombia's Caribbean coast has been one of the regions most devastated by paramilitary influence. The paramilitaries' terrible political vision infiltrated a large part of the political and economic leadership in the region, allowing them to plunder the country like the Caribbean pirates of old—taking land, economic resources, wealth, and property from those who were massacred, displaced, assassinated, disappeared, or threatened.

In the wake of the paramilitary demobilization process and the Justice and Peace Law of 2005, communities in our region have been affected by three important phenomena. First, demobilized paramilitaries have returned to their homes without any preparation or rehabilitation. Often upon return, they encounter the victims of their violent acts: displaced people and communities who continue to live in terror in the midst of a war that has not ended and who also have not received any psychological or social care. Local authorities have not been trained or given tools or funding to work with demobilized paramilitaries and the victims of war who live together in an area of continuing armed conflict.

Second, the "truth telling" by the disarmed paramilitaries, who, to benefit from the Justice and Peace Law, are obligated to say what they know, has led to the uncovering of a vast web of complicity between local authorities and paramilitary leaders. Currently, three members of Congress from Sucre Department, four members from the departmental parliament of Sucre, and two council members from Sincelejo are in prison, and an ex-governor is a fugitive from justice. Several more members of Congress from Sucre, Córdoba, and Bolívar departments and elsewhere on the coast are expected to be summoned.

Third, as a recent report by the Misión de Apoyo al Proceso de Paz de la Organización de los Estados Americanos (MAPP-OEA), or Mission to Support the Peace Process in Colombia of the Organization of American States (OAS), has documented, and as other authors in this volume attest, many demobilized paramilitaries are reorganizing themselves into criminal gangs, others are becoming involved in drug trafficking, and still others are being recruited to form new paramilitary or "self-defense" groups or to join guerrilla ranks.[14]

Many victims' groups have been left in a sea of doubt, confusion, and fear and harbor resentment, hatred, and pain. They do not trust the process of paramilitary disarmament and demobilization or the goodwill of the Justice and Peace Law promoted by the national government. Nor do they believe in the Comisión Nacional de Reparación y Reconciliación (CNRR), whose members have been appointed by the president, or in the first Regional Commission of Reconciliation and Reparation in Montes de María, southern Bolívar, Córdoba, and Urabá. We have completed two years of an eight-year cycle under the Justice and Peace Law, yet not a single victim has received reparations, and there is little evidence of perpetrators being punished or the paramilitary criminal structure being dismantled.

In the second half of 2005, the Fundación Social, a Jesuit organization, and the Project Counseling Service published the survey *Colombians' Perceptions and Opinions of Justice, Truth, Reparations, and Reconciliation.* To a question asking which institutions would be most important in achieving reconciliation in Colombia, 70 percent of respondents said "the church," 39 percent selected

---

[14] OAS, "Ninth Quarterly Report of the Secretary General to the Permanent Council, on the Mission to Support the Peace Process in Colombia" (MAPP-OAS), July 3, 2007, www.mapp-oea.org/documentos/informes/trimestrales%20MAPP/CP18719E06.doc (accessed September 11, 2008).

the president, 20 percent mentioned the army, and 13 percent selected social and community organizations.[15]

Sembrandopaz and the Citizens' Reconciliation Commission

Sembrandopaz is a civil society nonprofit organization focused on bridging the space between church-based social service organizations and the Colombian state. Sembrandopaz's goal is to assist church-based civil society organizations in their efforts to build a culture of peace through social justice and holistic human development.

Churches on the Caribbean coast are responding to this call for reconciliation. Protestant churches, facilitated by Sembrandopaz, are joining with the Fundación Social to create community spaces of restorative transformation where people can engage in dialogue without fear and precautions; work together to reach agreements and identify joint actions; and develop proposals that can be presented to the government, the CNRR, or national and international organizations. Our hope is to bring together already existing but dispersed reconciliation efforts by civil society organizations, victims' organizations, Catholic and Protestant churches, and universities to strengthen reconciliation efforts, play a positive role in relationship to the CNRR, and become a citizens' voice for reconciliation.

We began the process of creating a Citizens' Commission for Reconciliation in March 2007, with the first of a series of workshops organized by Sembrandopaz and financed by the United States Institute for Peace. We have three objectives: to train Colombian civil society leaders on the Caribbean coast on issues related to national and regional reconciliation processes, to organize a citizens' space for dialogue and action toward reconciliation, and to support the peace process in Colombia and help push the paramilitary demobilization process in a positive direction.

In these departmental workshops, we are focusing on "Reconciliation from a Transitional-Justice Perspective." Using the "Guía sobre reconciliación: Claves para la construcción de un horizonte en Colombia" (Guide to Reconciliation: Keys for the Construction of a Horizon in Colombia), developed by the Fundación Social, participants explore definitions and approaches to reconciliation.[16] They consider different instruments that have been used to search for truth, drawing from comparative case studies in South Africa, Guatemala, and Peru. They reflect on justice as a human right and an instrument of reconciliation; explore the differences between retributive justice, amnesties, restorative justice, and transitional-justice; and then use this

---

[15] Fundación Social, *Colombians' Perceptions and Opinions of Justice, Truth, Reparations, and Reconciliation,* http://derechoshumanosypaz.org/encuesta_completa.pdf (accessed September 11, 2008).

[16] Fundación Social, "Guía sobre reconciliación," www.boletinfsocial.org/Home/tabid/36/ctl/Details/mid/375/ItemID/13/Default.aspx (accessed September 11, 2008).

knowledge to evaluate the implementation of the Justice and Peace Law. They discuss various means and mechanisms for reparations, guarantees for non-repetition, and items to be included in a national reparations agenda. Finally, participants consider different approaches and strategies for healing the wounds in Colombia and analyzing the relationships between truth, justice, reparation, forgiveness, and reconciliation. The hope is that they will use the guide and training methodology to develop workshops in their own communities and organizations.

Our long-term goal is to integrate the eight Caribbean coast departments into a network of citizens' reconciliation groups, with a loose organizational structure to coordinate the independent and autonomous actions taken in each area according to its social, political, and geographic realities. The process has begun in Córdoba, the Montes de María area of Sucre, and southern Bolívar and has continued in Atlántico, Magdalena, César, Guajira, and San Andrés. With time, we plan to connect with the other departments in Colombia to create a national network of reconciliation efforts.

Key to this process is the involvement of universities and international organizations that are studying peace processes, models of transitional justice, and truth and reconciliation commissions in other parts of the world. We began by involving the Universidad del Sinú (Unisinú) in Montería, Corporación Universitaria del Caribe in Sincelejo, and the Universidad de Cartagena. We are now developing relationships with five more universities: Simón Bolívar in Barranquilla, Atlántico; Universidad del Magdalena in Santa Marta, Magdalena; Universidad Nacional Abierta a Distancia in Riohacha, Guajira; Universidad Popular in Valledupar, César; and Instituto de Formación Técnico Profesional del Archipiélago de San Andrés. By the end of the first phase of the project, we hope to have successfully integrated eight universities in the Caribbean region, working together to further reconciliation in Colombia. Already many of these universities are providing a place for our training and a space for the monthly meetings of the Citizens' Commission for Reconciliation.

We are also consulting with Eastern Mennonite University (EMU) in Harrisonburg, Virginia, through its Center for Justice and Peacebuilding and also Strategies for Trauma Awareness and Recovery, and the International Center for Transitional Justice in New York. We think it is important to take advantage of the lessons learned on an international level to strengthen the theoretical framework of the Colombians we are training.

Because the Caribbean coast has been one of the areas most affected by the *parapolítica* scandal that has permeated state institutions, it is very significant that this is the region where we have begun a wider process of transformative reconciliation. Initially, we trained 160 leaders—20 from each of the 8 departments in the Caribbean region, including women and men, social leaders, academics, church members, NGOs, Afro-Colombian and indigenous leaders, victims' associations, and IDP organizations from the departments of Córdoba, Sucre, Bolívar, Atlántico, Magdalena, César, Guajira, and San Andrés.

We held regional Caribbean workshops in 2007–08 with leaders from the different departments to exchange ideas, share experiences, and develop proposals for joint action. We brought in experts from the CNRR, MAPP-OEA, the United States Institute of Peace, and the Defensoría del Pueblo. In addition to looking at our current situation in the Caribbean region, we analyzed our relationship to the national situation, the CNRR, and other organizations that work for reconciliation. Through this transformative educational model, we are hoping to facilitate communication and dialogue, create a collective learning experience that will lead to consensus building, and develop joint actions. Our goal is to further reconciliation in the region based on the rights of victims to justice, truth, and reparations and to encourage more citizen participation in national processes.

Conclusion

Working in Montes de María, we have found hope in community—in the ASVIDAS network, the interweaving of networks through the Network for Development and Peace of the Montes de María Foundation, and the formation through Sembrandopaz of a Citizens' Commission for Reconciliation. As churches working together with our communities to build trust, create safe spaces for dialogue and consensus building, organize development projects, and train citizens to participate in reconciliation processes, we are planting our seed of justice in this field of peace. We nurture a hope and a faith that enable us to envision the tree in the seed, watch it grow, and taste the sweet fruit of peace that it will bear.

17

Negotiating Peace and Visibility as a Civil Society in Putumayo amid the Armed Conflict and the War on Drugs

María Clemencia Ramírez

In the Colombian department of Putumayo, the defense of human rights and the search for peaceful alternatives are intertwined. Beginning in the 1990s, awareness of ways to defend against human rights violations led to proposals on how to contribute to national peace from a regional perspective. These initiatives emerged in a region that has been historically defined not only as a marginal and "empty" space but also as a destination for migrant and displaced populations. This chapter situates Putumayo's peace initiatives within a broader historical context of the history of colonization in the Amazon. It explains how the central government has constructed and perceived Putumayo as a marginal and violent region and analyzes civilian efforts to become visible in the midst of armed conflict and to participate in the central government's policies for Putumayo. After examining the nature of the state's presence in this conflictual region, the chapter considers the relationships between the civilian population and the armed groups acting in the area and reflects on the meaning of "civil society" and citizen participation in Putumayo.

This article is part of an ongoing research project in the department of Putumayo that is funded by the Colombian Institute of Anthropology and History and by Colciencias, the Colombian Institute for the Advancement of Development Science and Technology. It was translated from Spanish by Andy Klatt.

The Structural Marginality of the Amazon Region

Putumayo Department is located in the Amazon region of Colombia.[1] The colonization of the Amazon began in the nineteenth century, and the process has continued ever since as social, political, and economic upheavals in central Colombia have pushed campesinos from the Andean highlands (especially the departments of Nariño, Huila, Tolima, Cauca, and Valle del Cauca) toward the Amazon. Colonization has evolved during this time, incorporating some but not all frontier areas into the economic sphere of the centralized Colombian state in the effort to resolve structural problems of land tenure, such as smallholdings insufficient to provide subsistence. Moreover, colonization was fueled by the period of intense political violence from 1948 to 1958 known as La Violencia.

The western portion of Colombian Amazonia (Putumayo, Caquetá, Guaviare, and southwestern Meta) has received most of the population influx. While some who arrived in the area settled permanently and strongly identify as residents of the Amazon region, others have maintained their status as *colonos* (nonnative settlers), not in the sense of being rootless but as an important marker of their identity. The Amazon region has historically been seen as little more than a destination for people displaced from other parts of Colombia. This has been the defining characteristic in the formulation of state policy toward the region and is key to the sense of marginalization and abandonment that drives the discourse of the region's people when they refer to the central state. As a result, western Amazonia is now highly populated, and the *colonos* are culturally dominant.

Of the entire population of Colombian Amazonia, 86.3 percent is concentrated in the west, at a density of 2.5 inhabitants per square kilometer. In contrast, eastern Amazonia (Amazonas, Vaupés, and Guainía) has a much lower density of 0.1 inhabitants per square kilometer, predominantly indigenous people.[2] As a general rule, the state has limited its participation in the Amazon region to establishing basic services for the *colonos* located in or near the urban centers. The rest of the area lacks adequate basic services such as roads, water supply, electricity, health services, and education. The state, which has failed to provide basic needs for the *colonos*, is perceived by the

---

[1] The area of Colombia is 1,138,388 sq km, and its Amazon region is 423,473 sq km. Thus, the region comprises 37 percent of Colombian territory. The Colombian Amazon includes the following departments: Caquetá, 88,965 sq km; Putumayo, 24,885 sq km; Guaviare, 53,460 sq km; Amazonas, 109,665 sq km; Vaupés, 54,135 sq km; Guainía, 72,238 sq km; and the southwestern part of Meta, 10,125 sq km. Putumayo, Caquetá, and Guaviare have been the main producers of coca.

[2] By 1999, of a national population of 41,323,797, the Amazon region contained 981,828 inhabitants, distributed as follows: Caquetá, 410,368; Putumayo, 323,549; Guaviare, 114,083; Amazonas, 68,569; Vaupés, 29,295; and Guainía, 114,083. See Departamento Nacional de Estadística (DANE), "Proyecciones de población por área según municipios a junio 30 de 1995–2005," www.dane.gov.co (accessed July 23, 2004).

region's inhabitants as ultimately responsible for the expansion of coca cultivation in these areas. Commercial coca cultivation began in Amazonia around 1975. Five years later, it spread for the first time to the department of Putumayo and to Calamar in the department of Guaviare. Coca farming has stimulated migration. For example, harvest workers are transient in that they must constantly follow the crops. But coca has not been the only or even the main reason for in-migration.

Campesinos have been colonizing Putumayo for three generations now. When coca arrived in Amazonia, the earliest waves of migrants had long since established themselves and had already raised a generation of children. Thus, in Putumayo, coca is grown predominantly by campesino smallholders. In contrast to Bolivia and Peru, where some legal coca production has been permitted, all coca cultivation was declared illegal in Colombia and criminalized by the Narcotics Law of 1986. Although the presence of the Fuerzas Armadas Revolucionarias de Colombia (FARC) in the Amazon region can be traced back to La Violencia, in 1984 the FARC's Thirty-Second Armed Front arrived in Putumayo to stay and began to regulate coca production, processing, and marketing. The presence of these coca-related economic activities is a consequence of the marginality of the Amazon region, described earlier.

In addition to marginality, illegality, violent conflict, and state abandonment, a dirty war against popular leaders of the region has been waged since the 1980s with the acquiescence and/or cooperation of the Colombian armed forces. Many of the leaders of the coca growers' movement have been threatened or killed in this dirty war. Thus, the state has been both actively and passively exclusive, eliminating the possibility of undesired political options and maintaining the long-term structural marginality of Amazonia.[3] Moreover, certain central-government policies targeting the Amazon region are the outgrowth of this region's marginality, a condition that stems from long-term historical processes.

Indeed, aerial spraying, repressive state responses to social or civic movements and demands, increasing militarization of the area, and the criminalization of coca growers are legitimized because of the way the Amazon region has been historically constructed as a region inhabited by migrants or *colonos*, adventurers in search of easy money, and guerrillas outside the law. Both the repression of illegal activities (coca growing and insurgency) and the incorporation of this border region into the nation-state—and, more significantly, into the area subject to the rule of law—served to legitimize

---

[3] See John S. Dryzek, "Political Inclusion and the Dynamics of Democratization," *American Political Science Review* 90, no. 1 (September 1996): 475–87. Dryzek differentiates between two types of state exclusion: "Active exclusion implies a state that attacks and undermines the conditions for public association in civil society. Passive exclusion implies a state that simply leaves civil society alone."

military operations such as Operation Conquest and Plan Condor in 1996; the creation of a Counternarcotics Brigade in 1999 to operate in the departments of Caquetá and Putumayo; Plan Patriota, or the Patriot Plan, in force in the western Amazon since May 2004; and the aerial spraying of coca crops by police antinarcotics brigades with the collaboration of the U.S. military and contractors working for Dyncorp Inc. In sum, this marginal region is linked to the nation-state only because of the expanding coca economy, the war on drugs, and the armed conflict.

The implementation of Plan Colombia in Putumayo also conforms to this logic of marginality conflated with illegality. President Pastrana presented Plan Colombia as "A Plan for Peace, Prosperity, and the Strengthening of the State," designed "to ensure order, stability, and compliance with the law; to guarantee effective sovereignty over the national territory; to protect the state and the civilian population from the threats of illegal armed groups and criminal organizations; and to break the existing ties between these groups and the drug industry that supports them."[4] At that time, the department of Putumayo contained 54 percent (66,022 hectares) of the area used for coca cultivation in Colombia, 30,000 small producers with from 1 to 5 hectares of coca each, and a floating population of 50,000 people who worked in coca production and commercialization.[5] Guerrillas had long been present in the department, and paramilitaries began to arrive in 1997, when the two groups began to compete for territory, the power to regulate the coca market, and the ability to collect the illegal taxes, or *gramaje*, from the local population. All these circumstances combined to make Putumayo an ideal location for the implementation of Plan Colombia, and Putumayo became the plan's epicenter beginning in July 2000.

Since 2000, the security focus of the U.S. aid package (launched with a special supplemental appropriation of US$1.3 billion during the Clinton administration) has been maintained. In any given year, from 68 to 75 percent of Colombia's Andean Counterdrug Initiative funding has gone to the military and police, with a peak in 2001 of 99.4 percent. Additional funding through U.S. Defense Department accounts has increased the security forces' annual share of U.S. aid to Colombia to between 76 and 82 percent.[6] On the other hand, economic and social aid peaked at US$231.4 million in the first appropriation in 2000, representing 24 percent of the aid package, and remained level at

---

[4] Contraloría General de la República, *Plan Colombia. Primer informe de evaluación* (Bogotá: Contraloría General de la República, 2001).

[5] Asociación Nacional de Usuarios Campesinos, "Seminario Taller Seguimiento y Monitoreo Plan Colombia" (Putumayo, August 11–12, 2001), www.ciponline.org/colombia/01081201.pdf (accessed July 17, 2002).

[6] For a complete analysis of Plan Colombia, see María Clemencia Ramírez, Kimberly Stanton, and John Walsh, "Colombia: A Vicious Circle of Drugs and War," in *Drugs and Democracy in Latin America: The Impact of U.S. Policy*, eds. Coletta Youngers and Eileen Rosin (Boulder, Colo.: Lynne Rienner, 2005), 99–142.

US$135 million, or 18 percent of the package, after 2003 despite the efforts of some in the U.S. Congress to increase the amount. With US$757 million in total funding in 2007, a modest cut was witnessed in 2008 with US$681 million in funding; the estimated total for 2009 is US$683 million. It should be noted that the new Democratic majority in Congress reduced the proportion of military aid in the Colombia aid package from 81 percent in 2007 to 65 percent in 2008. The centerpiece of Plan Colombia, which Clinton administration documents called the "push into southern Colombia," added two more counternarcotics battalions to the one created in 1998–99. As the U.S. Embassy noted in 2001, "These units, assigned to Joint Task Force South, along with a staff headquarters, make up the Colombian army's new Counter-Narcotics Brigade." These units are based at Tres Esquinas (Caquetá), under the command of Brig. Gen. Mario Montoya.[7] The 2,300-strong brigade, equipped with 45 helicopters; advanced communications and intelligence-gathering equipment; and light infantry training, arms, and ammunition, would ease the way for the massive fumigation of coca crops in Putumayo. The Third Battalion was inaugurated on May 24, 2001, and its members were trained at the Larandia military base in Caquetá. Both the Second and Third battalions have used the Twenty-fourth Santa Ana Brigade in Putumayo as their base of operations.[8] Human Rights Watch reported that this brigade maintained a close alliance with the paramilitaries and was sanctioned for human rights violations.[9]

After the attacks of September 11, 2001, and the inauguration of Álvaro Uribe Vélez as Colombian president in August 2002, the U.S. Congress and the George W. Bush administration announced the lifting of previously applied restrictions so that Colombia could use antinarcotics resources in a unified battle against drug trafficking and terrorism.

President Uribe has wholeheartedly embraced the discourse of counterterrorism and has imbued the inherited Plan Colombia with a counterinsurgency logic resulting in an indirect legitimation of the military's violations of human rights. Uribe clearly gave counterinsurgency operations priority over social or economic investment plans to break the link between drug trafficking and the guerrillas. As the antiterrorist struggle took priority, coca came to be viewed solely as a source of financing for terrorism, and the structural economic, social, and political causes that make peasants resort to illicit crops were given no further consideration. In keeping with this approach, in

---

[7] U.S. Embassy, "U.S. Military Counter-Narcotics Training and Support for the Colombian Armed Forces," Bogotá, May 24, 2001, http://bogota.usembassy.gov/topics_of_interest/plan-colombia-full-text-documents/toipc240501.html (accessed September 12, 2008).

[8] The Twenty-Fourth Brigade was replaced by the Twenty-Seventh, which has been expanded with the addition of new counterguerrilla and infrastructure-protection units. See Center for International Policy (CIP), "A Murder in Putumayo," March 21, 2005, www.cipcol.org/?p=65 (accessed September 12, 2008).

[9] Human Rights Watch, *The Sixth Division: Military-Paramilitary Ties and U.S. Policy in Colombia* (New York: Human Rights Watch, 2001), 15–36.

May 2004, a U.S.-supported military offensive involving nearly twenty thousand troops was launched in southern Colombia (Caquetá, Guaviare, and Meta) as part of Plan Colombia. Its main objective, as Uribe described it, was to defeat the FARC by attacking its longtime strongholds and capturing its leaders. Uribe's Plan Patriota stresses the need to "conquer" and seize control of this territory from the guerrillas. An army captain called it the largest military campaign since the war of independence. In fact, Uribe has called the antiguerrilla campaign the independence war of the twenty-first century, a patriotic war of national reunification.[10]

The Colombian military's characterization of guerrilla groups as drug traffickers, or narco-guerrillas, rather than as politically motivated armed groups, legitimizes state violence and terrorism through the deployment of the armed forces against the insurgents. This policy also promotes an intensified paramilitarism, whose targets are not only the guerrillas but also the people they call "guerrilla collaborators" or "civilian supporters" of guerrilla activities. With this in mind, the following sections discuss the possibilities and limitations of the peace proposals that have emerged since the mid-1990s in Putumayo Department.

Centralization versus Decentralization

Local authorities resent the asymmetrical relationship between the center, or heartland, of the country and the marginal, conflict-ridden, colonized regions of the periphery. In Putumayo, there is tension between, on one hand, the perceived unidirectional execution of central policies designed in Bogotá and, on the other, regional expectations, or the desire of local and regional officials to be included in the central government's discussion and definition of policies that affect the region and the people under their administration. The way that decentralization has been carried out has been called "perverse" because "responsibilities are decentralized but decision making is not."[11] Moreover, the *personero municipal* (ombudsman) in Puerto Asís has criticized the stigmatization of Amazonia by the national government and the armed forces.[12] He stated, "They have wanted to deal with the social and ecological conflict by military means, thinking that they can resolve the problem in the south of our country by stationing anti-guerrilla brigades or bat-

---

[10] "La campaña libertadora de Uribe," *El Tiempo*, May 3, 2005.

[11] Mayor of Puerto Asís, interview by the author, Puerto Asís, September 21, 1998.

[12] The *personero municipal* is an official in each municipality who is charged with defending the political rights of citizens and is responsible to both the municipal council and the Ministry of Justice. He or she therefore represents a link between local and central authorities and interests.

talions or building military bases there. But what is really going on is a major social conflict that needs to be resolved."[13]

The central government and the armed forces associate local and regional governments in marginalized areas with the guerrillas, and this has impeded the authorization of regional negotiations proposed by local authorities and civil society. When Horacio Serpa, minister of the interior under President Samper, responded to the proposal for decentralized peace negotiations in 1994 by stating that peace negotiations "would be neither local nor regional, but strictly national," he was describing the way that peace negotiations have always been conducted to this day.[14]

The case of the six "Southern Alliance" governors of Putumayo, Nariño, Huila, Cauca, Caquetá, and Tolima—all elected to office in October 2000 with the support of independent political forces—illustrates this tension between the central and regional governments. In February 2001, these governors presented their proposal for a "Southern Project" that proposed "no fumigation and more funds for social investment."[15] This plan was not just to stop fumigation but also to implement an alternative regional development model as a strategy for peace. The governors insisted on the need for agrarian reform as a structural solution to the problem of the small campesinos who grow coca or opium poppies. The governors also objected to the imposition of Plan Colombia, which was developed with no input from local or departmental authorities or from the people most directly affected. For this reason, they considered the plan "dead on arrival." Finally, the governors asserted that this Southern Project was, in fact, a peace plan that proposed to constitute a large area as the "South Colombian Peace Territory."

On July 8, 2001, the Bogotá daily *El Espectador* reported that the southern governors had announced their intention to declare independence on July 19 and create a regional "Republic of the South." Their proposal was in accordance with principles that had been established (although never implemented) under Article 306 of the 1991 constitution, which allows for the establishment of decentralized administrative and planning regions by two or more departments. The governor of Tolima declared, "This is not a separatist proposal. We want the country to be organized on the basis of regional republics sharing one army and one flag. Still, they would have administrative, budgetary, and political autonomy, as they do in Spain."[16] To Orlando Fals Borda, Article 306 "is an important step toward recovering the governability

[13] *Personero municipal* of Puerto Asís, interview by the author, Puerto Asís, September 17, 1998.

[14] "No habrá diálogos regionales," *El Tiempo*, January 13, 1995.

[15] "La otra diplomacia por la paz," *El Espectador*, April 15, 2001.

[16] "La república del sur," *El Espectador*, July 8, 2001.

that has been lost in the present departments."[17] Sen. Martín Caicedo Ferrer responded that (if implemented) "this proposal would be the tip of the iceberg. It would end up undermining the way we organize the country politically. This is just demagoguery." It would be better, he said, to concentrate efforts on strengthening the departments themselves.[18] Although the proposal of the "Southern Alliance" to seek autonomy from the central government has not come to pass, it represented an alternative to the lack of regional participation in formulating national policy and a way for the governors to manifest their discontent after their proposals were not seriously considered by the central government.

The six governors presented President Uribe with the Southern Colombia Peace Proposal when he came into office. In May 2003, the governors criticized the government for its unwillingness to discuss their proposal, which called on both the government and the guerrillas to abandon their arrogance and take the road of political negotiation. The governors complained that they had been left to implement the peace proposal alone in the departments that they governed. As a consequence, they had implemented parts of it without central-government participation. For example, they promoted local assemblies and regional talks with illegal armed actors to reestablish governance, and they supported local and nonviolent civil resistance against exclusion and war.[19] The governors also complained loudly at the May 2003 meeting that their promotion of a negotiated political solution to the conflict and their defense of the rule of law (*estado social de derecho*) were not accepted by the military as a constructive proposal and that on various occasions the governors had been accused of defending the insurgency.[20]

Elections were held for governors, mayors, and municipal councilors in October 2003, contributing to a loss of momentum for the southern governors' initiative. The newly elected governor of Putumayo was Carlos Palacios, who at one time had represented great hope for the department's social organizations. Palacios was a former priest who, after leaving the clergy, was known for his commitment to the civilian population in the search for development alternatives and mechanisms to achieve peace. The election of a governor interested in representing the interests of civil society amid the armed conflict was a welcome change from traditional politics. But in August 2006, it was revealed by Ernesto Báez, the commander of the paramilitaries' Bloque Central Bolívar, that the new governor had requested economic and political

---

[17] Orlando Fals Borda, *Kaziyadu. Registro del reciente despertar territorial en Colombia* (Bogotá: Ediciones desde Abajo, 2001), 64.

[18] "La república del sur."

[19] Fifth Governors' Summit, "Propuesta de Paz Surcolombiana" (unpublished report, Popayán, May 27–29, 2003).

[20] Ibid.

support for his campaign from the armed group. This support translated into direct paramilitary influence over the new administration. For example, paramilitaries influenced the granting of a municipal contract for the distribution of alcoholic beverages to a business in which they held a 30 percent share—a contract that also involved them directly in the collection and delivery of municipal tax revenues.[21] Palacios was suspended for six months, and after an investigation, a central-government investigative body (the Procuraduría General de la Nación) found irregularities in the awarding of contracts, so he was banned from holding public office for fifteen years.[22] In December 2006, the president named Jesús Fernando Checa Mora to replace Palacios as governor, and the local press commented, "This nightmare of two years of bad government by the outgoing governor is finally coming to an end, although its negative effects continue to impact society and regional development."[23] The press also lauded the new governor for his long record of public service. Checa Mora was known and respected in Putumayo for having held several positions, including the department secretary of the treasury, and particularly for having been president of the Association of Educators and having founded the Putumayo Education Workers Cooperative (Cooperativa de los Trabajadores de la Educación en el Putumayo).[24] The new governor sought to reactivate the Alliance of Southern Governors, and after a three-year hiatus, they met again in September 2007, taking up what had been their goal from the beginning: "to establish proposals for peace and development in these regions that suffer from violence on a daily basis."[25]

The extent to which paramilitaries had infiltrated government in Putumayo is an open question. Not only was Carlos Palacios removed from office, but Ernesto Báez, the demobilized head of the paramilitaries' Bloque Central Bolívar, publicly denounced him as "an embezzler."[26] When I interviewed Palacios during his campaign for the 2003 gubernatorial election, he asserted that paramilitary dominance was so pronounced in the region that "there was no space for a political alternative." He also said that he had been taken to a paramilitary training camp in the La Pedregosa *vereda* (rural area) of Puerto Caicedo, where he was compelled to negotiate with the paramilitaries in order to continue his political campaign.

---

[21] "¿Quién manda aquí?," *Semana no. 1268*, August 21, 2006: 48–50, www.semana.com/wf_InfoArticulo.aspx?IdArt=96528 (accessed September 15, 2006).

[22] Procuradoría General de la Nación, "Boletín de Noticias" no. 388, Bogotá, October, 2006, www.procuraduria.gov.co/html/noticias_2006/noticias_388.htm (accessed September 19, 2008).

[23] Ibid.

[24] Alberto Lleras Fajardo, "Se oficializa el nombramiento del nuevo gobernador," *Putumayo Hoy* (Mocoa), December 4, 2006.

[25] "Cumbre de gobernadores de la Surcolombianidad," *Diario del Sur* (Pasto), September 8, 2007.

[26] "¿Quién manda aquí?," 48.

The Nature and Impact of State Presence in a Conflict-Ridden Region

Army, paramilitary, and guerrilla intelligence operations in the Putumayo region are pervasive, and the local population has been coerced to participate in these efforts. Each armed group is ready to label any uncooperative campesino a collaborator with its enemies. The military's call for information is particularly salient, in keeping with one of the pillars of the "democratic security" policy of President Uribe, which conceives of security as a "product of the collective effort of the citizenry: it is the responsibility of all."[27] In order to strengthen democracy and the rule of law, active support for the authorities, for the administration of justice, and for the military are expected. President Uribe's democratic security policy openly presupposes the involvement of civilians in security functions through the establishment of networks of informants.

While Uribe's goal is that "the civilian population should define its position in favor of our threatened democracy," this approach blurs the distinction between civic and military engagement by the state and between the civilian population and combatants, violating one of the fundamental principles of international humanitarian law.[28]

As Ann Mason has pointed out, "The integration of civilians into security initiatives risks promoting the privatization of security and justice, fostering military-paramilitary linkages, and undermining the rule of law and public authority."[29] Also, this privatization of security and justice runs counter to the consolidation of democracy proposed by local governments. Their proposal puts great emphasis on public participation in defining regional policies through democratic mechanisms enshrined in the 1991 constitution. Above all, though, the proposal seeks to strengthen the social contract between the state and the citizenry in conflictual regions in order to promote independence from the armed actors.

Another strategy of the democratic security policy is the "peasant soldier" program, implemented to extend the military's presence to marginal regions at a limited cost. Peasant soldiers are young people assigned to duty in their own urban and rural areas. They are issued rifles but receive only three months of training.[30] By February 2003, squads of peasant soldiers were op-

---

[27] Presidencia de la República y Ministerio de Defensa Nacional, "Política de defensa y seguridad democrática," Bogotá, 2003, 17, www.mindefensa.gov.co/dayTemplates/images/seguridad_democratica.pdf (accessed October 13, 2004).

[28] "Los vecinos encubiertos," *El Tiempo*, August 11, 2002.

[29] Ann Mason, "Colombia's Democratic Security Agenda: Public Order in the Security Tripod," *Security Dialogue* 34, no. 4 (December 2003): 401.

[30] "Campesinos armados," *Semana no. 1060*, February 28, 2002, www.semana.com/wf_Info Articulo.aspx?IdArt=65079 (accessed January 1, 2005).

erating in nine of Putumayo's thirteen municipalities. Gen. Reinaldo Castellanos, who was overseeing the Plan Patriota, commented:

> The strategy of deploying peasant soldiers has improved our relations with the civilian population. People feel closer to the military and other units rely on their presence in order to move around the area, almost always unnoticed. Civic-military activities and medical brigades are a first step toward getting closer to the community, but they are still not enough when the illegal economy on which the region depended has been shut down cold without offering any real means of survival to replace it, other than leaving the area.[31]

This commentary illustrates the difficult position of military officers who are expected to gain the support of the local population with no alternative program of social and economic investment to offer. Non-governmental organizations (NGOs), journalists, and academics insist that after three years of the democratic security policy, it is not enough for the government to establish a military presence in marginal areas characterized by a chronically weak state presence.[32] Thus, the Washington Office on Latin America (WOLA), the Latin America Working Group (LAWG), the Center for International Policy (CIP), and the U.S. Office on Colombia state that Plan Patriota "has focused primarily on the military retaking territory from the guerrillas, without a plan for extending civilian government presence in areas long abandoned by the state."[33] The provision of basic services to these marginalized communities must accompany a military presence. As the peasants have stated, "The guerrillas will be superfluous when the government provides social investment, when arms are converted to tools. Peace will bring well-being and development."[34] This echoes the main proposal of the Alliance of Southern Governors. Moreover, the recently appointed governor of Putumayo reiterated during a September 2007 meeting of the Alliance of Southern Governors that "peace will come not just with a cease-fire among the armed actors in the Colombian conflict, but with the development of the regions suffering from violence."[35] The move to concretize a Departmental Development Plan has catalyzed the initiatives of the civilian population of Putumayo to provide alternative solutions to the conflict.

---

[31] "El Plan Castellanos," *Semana no. 1176*, November 15, 2004, www.semana.com/wf_Info Articulo.aspx?IdArt=83046 (accessed January 1, 2005).

[32] See Mason, "Colombia's Democratic Security Agenda," 391–409; and "El plan antipatriota," *Semana no. 1213*, July 31, 2005, www.semana.com/wf_InfoArticulo.aspx?IdArt=88900 (accessed August 1, 2005).

[33] Lisa Haugaard, Adam Isacson, Kimberly Stanton, John Walsh, and Jeff Vogt, *Blueprint for a New Colombia Policy* (Washington: LAWG, CIP, WOLA, and U.S. Office on Colombia, 2005), 14.

[34] Agreement between the Negotiating Commission of the national government and the Negotiating Commission of the civic movement in La Hormiga (unpublished document, Putumayo, January 11, 1995), 8.

[35] "Cumbre de gobernadores."

Defining Spaces for Negotiation with the Armed Actors

The FARC is recognized as an institutional representative of authority in the areas under its control, including Putumayo. Although orders issued by the FARC are obeyed by the population, they are also challenged and negotiated. The Communal Action Committees (Juntas de Acción Comunal), which in rural Colombia have become a basic unit of social organization at the community and village levels, have established spaces for negotiation with the state and the leaders and representatives of political parties, but above all with the FARC.[36] It is important to note that the FARC's relationship with the campesinos is ambivalent. As the commander of the Southern Block observed, "We have nothing to defend but the interests of the population."[37] Yet although the FARC does promote participatory democracy, it does not always practice it. This provides the basis for the FARC's double discourse, in which it proclaims itself to be the defender of campesino interests, while also legitimizing its military actions and its authoritarianism. Unlike the paramilitaries, who impose their decisions without any popular consultation, FARC members, as self-described "representatives of the people," are obliged by their own discourse to take campesino demands into consideration.

The FARC opposed Plan Colombia along with the alternative development projects in Putumayo that it included. But the coca growers, threatened by fumigation, challenged FARC opposition to alternative development and were able to sign agreements with the government for manual eradication, thus delaying aerial fumigation for almost a year. Although the outcome of these agreements is in question, the process demonstrated the negotiation skills of the inhabitants of these areas. Moreover, their embrace of alternative development underscores their autonomy from the armed actors. This became explicit in July 2004, when Gov. Carlos Palacios of Putumayo launched a program called "A New Putumayo without Coca." Referring to the transformation to a legal economy through alternative development programs, the governor stated, "We are showing the country that we are not drug traffickers, guerrillas, or paramilitaries. We are people with the will to work, to make Colombia proud of us. With few resources, we are producing food legally and generating employment for the peasants and indigenous people of Putumayo."[38]

---

[36] Each Communal Action Committee has a president and a number of other officers called "dignitaries" (*dignatarios*), all elected for three-year terms, as well as many "affiliates" (*afiliados*)—in this case, the *vereda* residents. The *vereda* is a rural settlement composed of a number of nuclear families living about thirty to fifty meters apart. The president and the board members of the Communal Action Committee are in charge of establishing relations with state officials or any other outsider demanding services from the state and proposing projects to improve the living conditions in their *vereda*.

[37] Comandante Joaquín, chief of FARC's Southern Block, "Los soldados del Ejército sienten que esta guerra no es de ellos," interview by New Colombia News Agency, 1998.

[38] "Gobernador contra las fumigaciones," *El Tiempo*, July 16, 2004. According to DANE, 4 percent of Putumayo's population is indigenous.

Another example of peasant resistance to FARC dictates was the popular rejection of FARC armed strikes in 2000 and 2005. During an armed strike (*paro armado*), the guerrillas occupy access roads and prohibit all traffic into and out of town centers. The rejection of this tactic was so strong that both strikes were lifted even though the government had not met any of the FARC's stated demands, confirming the existence of spaces of maneuver opened by the civilian population.

In the case of the paramilitaries, who have been in the area for seven years, the imposition of their rules leaves no space for negotiation. It is expected that those who do not conform to the rules will leave the area or be killed. When the paramilitaries arrived in Putumayo, they carried out two large-scale massacres that have been etched into residents' memories: one in El Tigre in January 1999, when they killed twenty-eight people, and another in November 1999, when they killed twelve campesinos in El Placer, six in La Dorada, and seven in a rural area of Valle del Guamués. The paramilitaries accused their victims of being "guerrilla auxiliaries" and sought to demonstrate their military power and intimidate the population, setting up a base of operations in a place known as Villa Sandra in the inspectorate of El Placer.[39] Today paramilitaries have settled in the towns of Putumayo and have imposed their rules on the population. Anyone who speaks out against them risks becoming a victim of the ongoing dirty war, since paramilitaries now conduct selective killings instead of massacres. That was the fate of José Hurtado, a merchant in the town of La Dorada (municipality of San Miguel), who led a demonstration in January 2005 against the paramilitaries, denouncing them for the extortion of merchants, the killings and disappearances of campesinos in the town center, and the likely existence of mass graves in the zone. The Colombian human rights organization MINGA reported, "The protest march ended with formal complaints issued by Mr. Hurtado and forty others to the security forces, the local authorities, and the *personero municipal* in La Hormiga."[40] José Hurtado was killed in February 2005 in one of numerous killings that took place in late 2004 and early 2005, including three massacres: one in Valle del Guamués in August 2004, in which nine people were killed; one in Puerto Asís in September 2004, in which three were killed; and a third in La Dorada (San Miguel) in November 2004, in which six were killed.[41]

In July 2003, the government of President Uribe signed an agreement with the Autodefensas Unidas de Colombia (AUC) for the demobilization of the AUC's paramilitary troops and their reinsertion into civilian life. This caused

---

[39] "La presencia paramilitar," *Semana*, www.semana.com/wf_VerMultimedia.aspx?IdArt=1114 07&IdMlt=580&Res=Alta (accessed September 19, 2008).

[40] CIP, "A Murder in Putumayo" (MINGA press release, March 21, 2005), www.ciponline.org/colombia/blog/archives/000078.htm (accessed September 12, 2008).

[41] Consultoría para los Derechos Humanos y el Desplazamiento (CODHES), "Paro Armado Putumayo" (report, March 3, 2006, 1), www.codhes.org/index2.php?option=com_docman&task=doc_view&gid=52&Itemid=51 (accessed September 19, 2008).

a stir in Putumayo. People began to ask if the paramilitary Bloque Central Bolívar would demobilize. Would Southern Front commanders such as "Raúl," "El Alacrán," or "Daniel" turn in their arms?[42] In March 2006 in Puerto Asís, 504 paramilitaries of the Bloque Central Bolívar, under the command of Mario Jiménez, alias "Macaco," did demobilize. The talk in Putumayo was of "the Justice and Peace Law, the rights of the victims to reparation, and the sentences that would be given to those who had tortured, killed, and disappeared their victims. Above all, though, the talk was of the truth."[43] At the same time, word was spreading about the appearance of a new group called the Rastrojos that was emerging to fill the void left by the demobilized paramilitaries.[44]

The Rastrojos are an example of the armed groups that sprang up in Colombia when the AUC was demobilized. In fact, the very name is a metaphor for the results of that process in Putumayo. *Rastrojos* are the low weeds that grow up spontaneously in the countryside when the forest is felled or a field is abandoned, and the armed Rastrojos, a new paramilitary organization that grew in the wake of the demobilization, is made up of foot soldiers of the Norte del Valle drug cartel along with paramilitaries who remained "standing" after the demobilization.[45] In an August 2007 report evaluating the year following the demobilization process, the National Commission for Reparations and Reconciliation (Comisión Nacional de Reparación y Reconcilación, CNRR) examined "the new generations" of paramilitaries that were being formed, and drew a distinction between rearmed, dissident, and emergent groups as a function of their direct or indirect relationships to demobilized paramilitary bodies.[46] On the basis of the CNRR's criteria, the Rastrojos of Putumayo, who now have 250 members under arms, can be considered an "emergent" group.[47] This designation is based on the first definition of the term presented in the commission's report, referring to groups that had a marginal existence before the demobilization and were only minimally active or visible compared to the AUC. After that umbrella body passed from the scene, the Rastrojos began to receive increased financing from the Norte del Valle cartel and took on greater responsibility for enforcing the cartel's prerogatives in the zone. According to the mayor of Valle del Guamués, the Rastrojos include former paramilitaries of the Southern Front of the Bloque Cen-

---

[42] "La madre," *Semana no. 1306*, May 12, 2007, www.semana.com/wf_InfoArticulo.aspx?IdArt= 103590 (accessed September 17, 2008).

[43] Ibid.

[44] CODHES, "Paro Armado Putumayo," 5.

[45] Salud Hernández, "Guerra entre machos y rastrojos," *Gatopardo* 59 (July 2005).

[46] For the definitions of these groups, see CNRR, "Disidentes, rearmados y emergentes: ¿Bandas criminales o tercera generación paramilitar?" (Informe no. 1 del Área de Desmovilización, Desarme y Reintegración, August 2007), 31.

[47] Ibid., 45.

tral Bolívar who did not demobilize. Referring to the wave of violence in the municipality since July 2007, he notes, "The most worrisome part of the situation is the presence of the Rastrojos, made up mostly of ex-fighters from the demobilized self-defense forces of Putumayo, who are sowing terror among the inhabitants of La Hormiga and nearby regions in Lower Putumayo."[48]

The Rastrojos are described in the region as "paramilitaries who no longer wear uniforms but who walk the streets with handguns in their waistbands, intimidating anyone who might turn them in."[49] The restructuring going on in the country is such that this group and others like it "no longer have the territorial influence or capacity that their predecessors had, but their geographical range coincides with that of the old groups. In fact, midlevel commanders who are now working in the new groups take advantage of their close relations with the territories and the inhabitants (whom they once controlled) to maximize their mobility."[50] This is particularly significant in light of a special report by the Foundation for Security and Democracy (Fundación Seguridad y Democracia), which states, "These are relatively disarticulated armies. They do not respond to a coherent command structure, and their activities are limited to controlling the cultivation of drug crops, clandestine laboratories, and smuggling routes."[51]

The Meaning of "Civil Society" and Citizen Participation in Putumayo

When popular organizations define themselves as part of "civil society," they are presenting themselves as civilians affected by the armed conflict who do not want to be identified with any of the illegal armed actors. In this context of marginality and armed conflict, "civil society" bears redefinition. To construct civil society in Putumayo means to establish a common front against violence and to be differentiated from any armed group. Moreover, civil society initiatives have the support of state representatives, so local and regional government authorities become an active force within civil society. The population even expects state representatives to provide proposals for alternatives to the conflict. In fact, local authorities in Putumayo, with the support of civil society, have put forth a proposal for regional peace negotiations.

---

[48] "Incrementarán medidas de seguridad. Ola de violencia en La Hormiga," *Diario del Sur* (Pasto), September 15, 2007.

[49] "La madre," *Semana*.

[50] Ibid., 46. Unlike ordinary combatants, powerful commanders, or major leaders of the AUC, for whom the state has designed reintegration programs, these midlevel commanders of paramilitary structures have little to gain by demobilizing. As a result, they have resumed their paramilitary activities in the areas where they were located when the demobilizations took place.

[51] Fundación Seguridad y Democracia, "El rearme paramilitar" (Boletín no. 16, March 2007), 21, www.seguridadydemocracia.org/docs/pdf/especiales/informeEspecial16-2.pdf (accessed September 17, 2008).

Although mayors in these marginal areas have also been labeled guerrilla collaborators, lately they have also been threatened by the guerrillas, who argue that as state representatives, mayors must obey state orders and are therefore by definition considered military targets. When President Pastrana ended the peace negotiations with the FARC in February 2002, for example, the FARC high command issued a communiqué that stated, "Because the government had refused to continue with a process for peace with social justice, we have been obliged to attack its local representatives, who, although they were elected popularly, have to comply with the role assigned to them by the state, through the president." The communiqué further asserted that Plan Colombia "was designed to repress popular discontent through the work of local state representatives: governors, mayors and police inspectors," and as a consequence, FARC considered these local authorities to be "military targets."[52] In the regions under FARC control, an unintended consequence of this decision has been an intensified search for autonomy by the civilian population, which rejects FARC threats.

Germán Martínez, the *personero municipal* in Puerto Asís, repeatedly supported peace forums and open councils as ways of making civil society more visible and promoted citizen participation in the analysis and redefinition of public policy. At these events, he sought an organized response by the people to the stigmatization and insecurity that stemmed from their criminalization as coca growers or "guerrilla collaborators." As part of his job, Martínez also collected testimonies of disappearances, threats, and murders at the hands of paramilitaries and publicly denounced the link between the paramilitaries and the armed forces in Putumayo. At one such meeting in February 2000, Martínez publicly stated, "Part of the problem was that paramilitaries were 'untouchable.'" When he personally informed the police about this link, rather than investigating the charges, they rejected his accusations and threatened him.[53] As a consequence, Martínez had to leave Putumayo and seek asylum in Canada.[54]

The *personero municipal* who replaced Martínez in 2001 was not ready to support and engage in alternative proposals for peace or to report paramilitary-military ties, leaving the population on its own. In a December 2001 interview, she said, "There was a lot of conflict in 1998 and 1999 due to the arrival of the paramilitaries. But now things have changed. People are not reporting the paramilitaries, because they are afraid. People know what happened to those who have denounced abuses. Here people [illegal armed

---

[52] Red de Observación Irene, "Están armando las estrategias" (Boletín no. 28, July 11, 2002), www.viaalterna.com.co/index2.htm?; (accessed January 15, 2005). See also www.viaalterna.com.co/textos/tirene28.htm (accessed January 15, 2005).

[53] Human Rights Watch, *The Sixth Division*, 19.

[54] Germán Martínez, interview by author, Bogotá, November 13, 2000.

groups] take the law into their own hands."[55] She was also afraid of being threatened: the paramilitaries had succeeded in discouraging actions against the status quo by the civilian population.

In the context of paramilitary demobilization, the relationship between paramilitaries and the population reflects certain changes and continuities. In May 2007, a special group of judicial police investigators, acting on information previously provided to prosecutors by demobilized AUC commanders, uncovered the fifth and largest mass grave found in Putumayo that year. It was in the town of La Hormiga, in the municipality of Valle del Guamués, and contained the remains of 105 victims of the paramilitaries, bringing the total number of remains found in Putumayo since January 2007 to 211.[56] Twelve bodies had been found in a grave in the town of La Dorada, in the municipality of San Miguel, and others in the municipality of Valle del Guamués: twenty-one in the Placer inspectorate, twenty-six in the inspectorate of El Tigre, and forty-seven in the *vereda* La Esmeralda. These bodies were among nearly a thousand that had been uncovered up to that time throughout the country.[57] The existence of these mass graves confirmed earlier reports, by the mayors and residents of the municipalities of Valle del Guamués and San Miguel, of paramilitary killings such as the massacres and the murder of merchant José Hurtado, mentioned earlier.

Prosecutors reported that the mass graves were located not only thanks to information provided by demobilized paramilitaries but also with the help of victims' families and other residents. The population also participated in identifying the remains, a process that was begun immediately with the positive identification of thirteen bodies and the preliminary identification of many more.[58] Prosecutors also reported that people in Putumayo continued to be more intimidated than in other regions, and very few people came forward to provide testimony of paramilitary crimes, because they feared the new generations of paramilitaries in the area.[59] As mass graves were uncovered, Attorney General Mario Iguarán commented, "Residents opened up. In fact, relatives of the disappeared are identifying burial sites."[60] It seems that although former paramilitaries were known to be participating in the ranks of the Rastrojos, the new group was perceived to be different from the old one. People did not necessarily fear that if they cooperated with authorities

[55] Interview by the author, Puerto Asís, December 2001.

[56] "Hallan restos de 105 personas en fosas comunes en el Putumayo," *Caracol Noticias*, www.caracol.com.co/noticias/423207.asp (accessed September 12, 2008).

[57] "A 3.000 podría llegar el número de víctimas enterradas en fosas comunes en Putumayo," *El Tiempo*, May 5, 2007.

[58] Ibid.

[59] "A dos años de la ley de justicia y paz, las víctimas corren con la peor suerte," *Semana*, July 25, 2007, www.semana.com/wf_InfoArticulo.aspx?IdArt=105187 (accessed September 19, 2008).

[60] "La madre," *Semana no. 1306*, May 12, 2007.

they would be identified and marked for death. Thus, when the Justice and Peace Law providing reparations for victims of paramilitaries went into effect in July 2005, many widows from around the department came to Puerto Asís to file claims with the government. But when they learned about the extensive juridical and evidentiary procedures necessary for recognition as victims, they began to doubt the real commitment of the government to provide reparations. According to one resident of Puerto Asís, "They were very hopeful about two things: that the justice system would finally punish those responsible for the deaths of their sons or other relatives, and that they would be paid compensation. As time went by, I could see that their hope was turning to skepticism. Many of us Putumayans hope that all of this doesn't turn into frustration in the end."[61]

Suspicion of the central government was not long in returning. The state is seen as duplicitous: it promotes the search for truth and reparations for the victims of paramilitarism, and at the same time it continues to fumigate coca crops and organize their manual eradication, while paramilitarism reappears or simply persists. The armed conflict goes on as it has for years, and it is the civilian population that continues to promote initiatives for peaceful solutions through its participation in formulating local government policy.

When the Alliance of Southern Governors was reactivated in September 2007, Governor Checa Mora of Putumayo reiterated the need both to invest in community projects and to "seek a path to peace with the participation of civil society, the Church, and the regional and municipal governments."[62] Many social sectors in Putumayo have taken up this approach, in particular believing that to achieve peace and maintain neutrality toward the armed groups, the social contract between local government and the civilian population must be renewed. The governor was also referring to the social process promoted by campesinos in the municipality of San Miguel, where the Coalition of Borderland Social Organizations (Mesa de Organizaciones Sociales Fronterizas) was formed in July 2006 with the participation of twenty-three campesino leaders from eleven municipalities in the department. They organized to "formulate and execute a comprehensive alternative rural development plan for the manual, gradual, and voluntary replacement of coca crops," with the participation of all affected communities in seeking solutions "in cooperation with the national government and the international community," to achieve the "political, economic, environmental, and cultural well-being of our rural community and thus be able to live in dignity in our region."[63] The coalition

---

[61] Resident of Puerto Asís who accompanied some of the women when they filed claims, interview by the author, Puerto Asís, August 30, 2007.

[62] "Cumbre de gobernadores."

[63] "¿Qué es la Mesa de Organizaciones Sociales Campesina Fronteriza?" (working paper, San Miguel, April 2007), 2–3.

convened a three-day departmental assembly in August 2006, calling on representatives of the local, regional, and national governments to attend and debate the proposal for a departmental development plan. Several mayors, the governor, and the two representatives to the lower house of Congress attended the assembly. The mayors expressed their interest in supporting the proposal that came out of the assembly and indicated that the problem of drug trafficking would persist without an effective agrarian reform policy.[64]

In sum, the new forms of collective citizenship being constructed in Putumayo defined an emerging local civil society in opposition not to the state but to the armed actors and sought strength in constitutionally guaranteed spaces for democratic participation and, in some cases, in political representation. The struggle to construct citizenship is a demand for inclusion in the participatory democracy promoted by the state, to which Putumayans have not had access. As the *personero municipal* in Puerto Asís explained,

> The violence is getting worse every day. There are those who want to generate fear and terror in the people. Nevertheless, the people want to participate. They are tired. They want to see a different political leadership. They want to see a truly transparent administration that works for the common good, that actually builds them sewers, that provides the public services they need here. . . . The people have come to understand that peace is not just the silencing of the guns. They can see that peace is also the contribution I make as a citizen, the responsibility that I should assume in the community. People have learned to see that a disagreement is one thing and the person you are talking to is something else, that you have to have a certain respect for the other person to be able to resolve your differences and reach an agreement.[65]

Here the *personero* is stressing how people want to make use of nonviolent ways of resolving conflict, contesting the characterization that has defined this region and its inhabitants as intrinsically violent. Two peaceful campesino mobilizations against fumigation and alternative development policies were held recently in Putumayo, the first in January 2007 and the second in March. One participant commented on the March mobilization, "First a hundred fifty families came out, and then gradually more came out, but they did so peacefully so the government would see that we are not violent like they say we are, that we're peaceful. . . . That's why we came out peacefully. We were with the mobilization for two weeks. We demonstrated because the constitution gives us the right to demonstrate. The mayor and the merchants helped us with food for these people."[66]

The campesinos issued a public communiqué reaffirming their independence from armed groups: "We are not being pressured or assembled by any

---

[64] Minutes of the Departmental Assembly of Social Organizations in Orito, August 25, 2006.

[65] Personero municipal de Puerto Asís, interview by the author, Puerto Asís, September 17, 1998.

[66] Testimony of participant in the mobilization, Bogotá, May 8, 2007.

illegal armed group; thus, we hold the national government responsible for the safety of the women and men campesinos leading and participating in this mobilization."[67] To conclude the mobilization, the campesino leaders and local public officials signed a document in which Oscar Arévalo Vargas, the mayor of San Miguel, committed himself to "travel to the city of Bogotá along with Coalition of Campesino Organizations [Mesa de Organizaciones Campesinas] (three members) to help publicize the problematic situation that our municipality is currently experiencing and to negotiate toward its solution." The mayor of San Miguel also committed himself to contract two professionals to provide advice on "the proposals for integrated farms in the municipality, and the formulation of the San Miguel Alternative Development Plan," confirming the interest of local governments in working together with the civilian population.[68]

Civil society representatives from Putumayo's Mesa de Organizaciones Campesinas also spoke out in an October 2006 letter to the president, in which they expressed the idea that "the solution to the problem of coca crops in the department and in the country will necessarily require changes to agricultural, environmental, and antidrug policy." They also opposed "handouts" (*proyectos asistenciales*) and stressed their willingness to participate actively in reformulating policy.[69] Delegations of campesino leaders traveled to present their proposals to the president and presented central-government officials with proposals for a new antidrug strategy and alternative development programs. Through these participatory acts, citizens contest their supposed illegality. As Putumayan citizens, they wish to act within the law.

Conclusions

Four conclusions and recommendations emerge from the foregoing discussion. First, there is a need to strengthen local governments, both giving them greater autonomy and increasing their participation in the political decisions necessary to the search for a solution to the armed conflict. Their initiatives for peace should be attended to and put into practice. In a related sense, support should be given to the kind of citizen participation outlined in the constitution and demanded by the civilian population caught up in the conflict.

Second, greater priority should be given to social and economic investments and the presence of state institutions in regions experiencing conflict—institutions such as schools, health and justice infrastructure, and

---

[67] "Crisis humanitaria denuncian campesinos del Putumayo y se declaran en movilización permanente," *El Tiempo*, March 28, 2007.

[68] Minutes of meeting between the municipal administration of San Miguel, the *personería*, the Coalition of Campesino Organizations, and the Community Action Committees (unpublished, March 27, 2007).

[69] Putumayo Coalition of Campesino Organizations, "Letter to the President" (unpublished, October 7, 2006).

credit institutions. As long as military investment in these regions is given overwhelming priority, the presence of the armed forces will be seen as the only state presence and the only way that these marginal regions are incorporated into a central order of things. Local authorities have supported this proposal on numerous occasions. They propose social justice as a method to promote both democracy and peace.

Third, in the 2003 elections, paramilitaries sought to influence events in the department by financing political campaigns for local government positions rather than through the use of force. While we cannot know everything that took place in the case of the deposed governor, we do know that the relationship he established with paramilitaries in order to be able to campaign contributed to his inability to meet popular expectations for his administration. His vulnerability to the investigation by the Procuraduría and to being unseated may have resulted from his own lack of political experience, or it may have been due to the newness and incompleteness of the paramilitary infiltration of regional governments. The demobilization of the Southern Front of the Bloque Central Bolívar and the related disarticulation of the paramilitary central command, along with the central focus of new armed groups on the business of drug trafficking, indicate that paramilitary control of regional government was not and will not be consolidated in Putumayo. This is in contrast to the deep roots of paramilitary activity and the consolidation of paramilitary participation in regional government on Colombia's Caribbean coast. In Putumayo, the guerrillas have a more long-standing relationship with the civilian population than do the paramilitaries, and there is a long history of negotiations between the two over questions of political space and autonomy.

Finally, the civilian populations in conflictual regions propose mechanisms, such as Peace Territories, to assert their right to neutrality in the armed conflict. This neutrality should be respected. The state should not restrict the role of the civilian population to serving as informants for military intelligence. It bears repeating that linking the civilian population directly to the conflict inhibits the consideration of their proposals for a negotiated solution to the conflict and may therefore be counterproductive.

PART V

THE SEARCH FOR PEACE AND THE INTERNATIONAL COMMUNITY

18

The International Community Meets the Local Community in Montes de María

Borja Paladini Adell with Raúl Rosende, Juan Chaves, and Gabriel Turriago

Although violent conflict is a part of life, understanding it is a challenge that involves not just academics but especially those involved in different aspects of a conflict—those who work for its resolution and those more closely engaged in analyzing its causes. Sometimes this analysis results from cooperation and collective action by those living in the conflict zones and those outside. The contrary is more often the rule, with separate perceptions of multiple actors coexisting and conflicting. Still, a common understanding of the conflict is a necessary, albeit insufficient, condition for transforming it.[1]

Note the reference to "transforming" rather than "ending" a conflict. Ending conflict is a fool's errand in self-contradiction, rather like dehydrating water. But intentionally *transforming* conflict often includes thinking of, and building consensus around, ways that the conflict can be modified by getting parties to commit to new or existing rules, to change their behavior, and to set aside their narrow interests and resources, reducing human suffering and violence and addressing the root causes of the conflict.

In Colombia, peace talks and accords resulting only from negotiation between the state and the illegal military forces take place without common understanding of the conflict dynamics and seem to exclude civil society. This type of "accomplishment" is fragile, because multiple and conflicting understandings have not been integrated into peacebuilding and develop-

---

[1] Moreover, understanding conflict is not merely an analytical function (that is, breaking the whole into its parts and explaining how they interact), but a political one, as it serves as an entry point for mobilizing actors, interests, and resources.

ment, the processes are not linked to the grassroots, and public policies do not reflect a genuine consensus. Consequently, such accords are not sustainable.

This chapter makes a twofold argument. First, development is not only possible but also necessary in a setting of protracted violent conflict. Second, a comprehensive or integrated framework for peacebuilding should mainly, though not exclusively, include the following four elements: it should (1) promote social organization; (2) promote broad-based alliances; (3) manage knowledge for a common understanding of development, peace, and conflict dynamics; and (4) contribute to the transformation of social consensus into mid- and long-term policies for development and peacebuilding.

The chapter focuses on the United Nations Development Programme's (UNDP's) Colombia Reconciliación y Desarrollo (REDES, or Reconciliation and Development) program through a case study of its intervention in Montes de María, a scene of prolonged violent conflict. The REDES program shows how it is possible, even amid a protracted violent conflict, to work together with local actors to transform conflict nonviolently.

Montes de María, a natural subregion of the Colombian Caribbean region, covers 6,317 square kilometers along the border between the departments of Sucre and Bolívar. The subregion consists of fifteen municipalities, bordered on the north by the Canal del Dique (an artificial mouth of the Magdalena River), on the west by the river itself, and on the east by the Caribbean Sea. A mainly rural region, Montes de María has a population of more than 900,000 inhabitants, of which about 68 percent live in the town centers.[2] In administrative terms, the fifteen municipalities belong to either of two departments: Sucre or Bolívar. Sincelejo is Sucre's nearest city to Montes de María, and Cartagena de Indias is Bolívar's. As Chapter 16 in this volume by Ricardo Esquivia and Barbara Gerlach shows, Montes de María is one of the areas of Colombia hardest-hit by social and political conflict—particularly the struggle for land. During the 1990s, the inhabitants of Montes de María were also the worst-affected by the intensification of the armed conflict. Although security has improved somewhat, the region is still open to hostilities and institutionally weak.

In sociopolitical terms, Montes de María is a prime example of a region where a broad range of social and political actors, both armed and unarmed, have been unable to find nonviolent means to address the deep contradictions that have historically generated primarily violent processes of social change.

In 2003, as part of its democratic security policy, the government decreed a "state of internal disturbance," declared two areas in the department of Arauca and in Montes de María "Rehabilitation and Consolidation Zones,"

---

[2]Unless otherwise noted, the empirical data from this article are drawn from PNUD Colombia, "Asistencia preparatoria para la formulación de un programa de desarrollo y paz en los Montes de María," March 2003, Col/01/054 (hereafter referred to as Col/01/054).

and stationed a special military commander there to implement a state of emergency. Ann Mason writes, "Through a massive military presence, the re-staffing of police posts, roadblocks, curfews, restrictions on movement, house-to-house searches, and detention powers, the state's intention is to reinstate control over effectively lawless areas that have experienced some of the country's worst paramilitary and guerrilla violence."[3]

Some months after the army received special powers as the authority in those zones, the Constitutional Court found the open-ended duration of the special powers unconstitutional. But regardless of the legal context of government action, Montes de María is still one of the places with the most active hostilities in Colombia and is a priority zone for government efforts to restore the power of the state and its institutions. The Colombian marines (responsible for military control of the area) have taken the initiative in the past few years, forcing the irregular armed groups, particularly the guerrillas, to retreat. Also, the demobilization of the paramilitary "Heroes of Montes de María," negotiated with the state in 2005, has helped reduce the numbers of irregular armed forces in the area. The military and political offensive mounted by the Colombian government has succeeded in markedly reducing the capacity of the irregular groups to go on the offensive. Nonetheless, it remains to be seen what the result of the army offensive will be, how sustainable these military actions will be over time, whether the construction of a state of law and state institutions will accompany them, and how much the power of irregular armed groups and drug traffickers will be curtailed.[4] It is also unclear whether this government effort will produce an improvement in the human rights situation.[5]

In addition to the armed violence, other elements making up the social and political context of Montes de María include precarious local governments, weak institutions, financially insolvent municipalities, dominance of irregular armed groups, impunity, poverty, exclusion, unemployment, marginality, lack of food security, and a generally weak and fragmented social fabric.[6]

---

[3] Ann Mason, "Colombia's Democratic Security Agenda: Public Order in the Security Tripod," *Security Dialogue* 34, no. 4 (2003): 391–409.

[4] Office of the President, "Resolution 129 of 21 September 2002." On February 14, 2007, the Organization of American States (OAS) Mission to Support the Peace Process (MAPP-OEA) published its eighth quarterly report. In it, the OAS acknowledges the rearming of several paramilitary groups. In Montes de María, it identifies a rearmed group in San Onofre that includes one hundred armed individuals. See www.mapp-oea.org/node/12 (accessed September 29, 2008).

[5] See Mason, "Colombia's Democratic Security Agenda"; Office of the President, "Resolution 129"; and International Crisis Group (ICG), *Colombia: President Uribe's Democratic Security Policy*, Latin America Report no. 6 (Brussels/Bogotá: ICG, November 13, 2003).

[6] See Col/04/054. See also UNDP, *El conflicto, callejón con salida: Informe nacional de desarrollo humano, Colombia 2003* (Bogotá: PNUD, 2003); and Gobernación de Sucre y de Bolívar (Offices of the Governors of Sucre and Bolívar), *Plan integral de desarrollo humano sostenible para los Montes de María* (Sincelejo: Gobernación de Sucre, 1997).

Montes de María provides a good case study for understanding the deeply conflictive realities of Colombian history, particularly related to conflicts over land use and tenure. The historical roots of the problem of land in Colombia go back to the Spanish conquest in the sixteenth century. Successive colonial administrations set up a regime of concessions by which the crown awarded large tracts of land and estates to the local elites. Most of the indigenous population and the peasant farmers living on these lands, as well as the black slaves acquired by the beneficiaries of these grants, became dispossessed. These *encomiendas* were the original basis of the Colombian land tenure system known as *latifundio*. *Encomiendas* existed throughout the Republican era and into the twenty-first century.[7] Successive agrarian reforms have been unable to deal effectively with the land problem and the extreme poverty and deprivation of the indigenous communities, the peasant farmers, and the Afro-Colombian population that make up the majority in this region.[8]

The past fifty years have seen yet another of the severe episodes in the struggle for land. Landowners took advantage of instability and war to consolidate their holdings and, indeed, increase them at the expense of the peasant farmers on the agricultural frontier. The peasant farmers, supported first by the Liberal Party and its peasant union and guerrilla elements and later encouraged by the discourse of the revolutionary left, saw the possibility of dividing the land and turning it to subsistence farming. The testimonies of the peasant farmers in the region best explain the cycles of struggles for the land:

> We, the poor, are like ants working all day and night to build an anthill which we can use, and then when the anthill is nearly ready, along comes the anteater—the politician or the big landowner—with his long sticky tongue which he pushes down the hole and takes out the ants, destroying what has been done, and sweeps away the entrance of the anthill with his murderous claws. And then he goes away, and we—because that is our life and our destiny—madly start to rebuild the anthill in the same place, because we have no wish even to go somewhere else, because we love our land. Until the anteater comes back again to repeat the treatment, because he can see that the anthill has grown again.[9]

From 1971 to 1978, with 195 reported land seizures, Sucre had more land seizures by dispossessed peasant farmers than any other department.[10] This collision of forces over control of the land and local power, and the domi-

---

[7] See Apolinar Díaz-Callejas, *Colombia y la reforma agraria: Sus documentos fundamentales* (Cartagena: Universidad de Cartagena, 2002).

[8] See Paul Oquist, *Violencia, conflicto y política en Colombia* (Bogotá: Instituto de Estudios Colombianos, 1978); Orlando Fals Borda, *Retorno a la tierra: Historia doble de la costa* (Bogotá: Carlos Valencia Editores, 1976 and 1986); and UNDP, *El conflicto, callejón con salida*.

[9] Fals Borda, *Retorno a la Tierra*, 158a.

[10] See Col/01/54.

nance of one or another development model, explains the correlation between power and social cleavages underlying the conflicts that took shape in many parts of Colombia, particularly on the Caribbean coast. The state was absent, partisan, and often extremely weak, and no legitimate actor regulated and mediated the myriad social conflicts that have come to characterize the whole region. Here armed and violent conflict has been embedded in deep social and political divisions during the past fifty years.

In regional terms, the conflict today turns on the dispute over land and control of territorial power in the vacuum caused by the state's extreme weakness. The international phenomenon of drug trafficking and the growth of the guerrilla and paramilitary groups have aggravated this situation in recent years.

The armed conflict became endemic in the Montes de María region for a number of reasons. First, the mountainous nature of the region has made it an area of vital importance in the war. All the irregular armed actors with influence in the area—Fronts 35 and 37 of the Caribbean Block of the Fuerzas Armadas Revolucionarias de Colombia (FARC); the Jaime Bateman Cayón Front of the Ejército de Liberación Nacional (ELN); the Jaider Jiménez group of the Ejército Revolucionario del Pueblo (ERP); and the Héroes de Montes de María paramilitaries of the Autodefensas Unidas de Colombia (AUC)—have been fighting one another and the Colombian armed forces.[11] The intensity of the violence is explained by the desire of the irregular armed actors to control these natural corridors, fallback and forward zones, and access to economic resources in the farming and cattle-breeding centers and along the Troncal de Occidente highway, which carries 80 percent of the cargo transported between the interior and the Caribbean coast.[12]

Second, the armed conflict continues because the irregular armed actors have been able to maintain themselves in the region, where they promote social, political, and economic projects that go beyond military action. For example, the paramilitaries seek to control the local and regional institutions of government in addition to advancing their criminal aims. And the guerrillas strive to control territory as part of their national political design; they promote this through armed struggle and "other forms of struggle." Both groups have a certain capacity to challenge the state by undermining its role as a mediator and arbitrator of social conflict in the region; therefore, they have achieved a certain level of territorial consolidation, changing the balance of power and the evolution of social conflict by force.

---

[11] According to official sources cited by *El Tiempo*, the last remnants of the ERP were completely defeated by the Colombian army during the first months of 2007. See "'Guerrilla del Ejército Revolucionario del Pueblo (Erp) quedó desintegrada,' dijo Ministro de Defensa," *El Tiempo*, April 30, 2007.

[12] See Human Rights Observatory, *Panorama actual de la región de Montes de María y su entorno* (Bogotá: Human Rights Observatory, 2003), www.derechoshumanos.gov.co/PNA/documentos/sucre/montes.pdf (accessed October 2, 2008).

Third, the violent conflict dynamics imposed by armed actors generate cycles of renewed violence. In the struggle for territory, the irregular armed actors see civilian populations that have been under the wing of another armed actor as collaborators with that actor and therefore as a threat to their own attempts to regain control of the territory. This provokes cycles of retaliation against the civilian population and helps explain the escalation of violence in the Montes de María region. For example, according to official sources, several municipalities in Montes de María (Carmen de Bolívar, San Onofre, and Ovejas) are at the top of the list of areas in Colombia where people have been displaced by violence. In addition, some of the most notorious selective and arbitrary murders and massacres in Colombia occurred in the region (in Chengue, el Salado, Ovejas, San Onofre–Finca el Palmar, and elsewhere).[13]

Finally, drug trafficking has given enormous "added value" to the violence and armed conflict. Montes de María is not a coca crop farming region but rather a strategic zone, or transportation corridor, for inbound chemicals (for the processing of coca leaves into cocaine) and weapons, and outbound drugs. All the irregular actors have sought control of this region because of its strategic position.

The REDES Program

Given this intricate context, how can an international aid development agency such as the UNDP intervene in a way that will reduce the impact of violence and contribute to human development and peacebuilding? The UNDP's REDES program has been operating in Colombia since mid-2003. It is managed by UNDP Colombia (in Spanish, PNUD Colombia) and supported by the Swedish International Agency for Cooperation and the UNDP Bureau for Crisis Prevention and Recovery. In 2003, these organizations began to ask whether it would be possible to promote development and peacebuilding in the context of violence and protracted conflict. With some seed funding from the three institutions, a participatory process began with national and local stakeholders, including the Colombian government, to identify three territories deeply affected by violence and protracted conflict where UNDP Colombia could intervene in the field to give a programmatic and practical answer to the question. The regions of Montes de María, Meta, and Oriente Antioqueño were identified. These regions also had civil society actors who were trying to organize themselves to promote conflict transformation and nonviolent alternatives to war. The REDES program was set up to work jointly with social organizations from the actual conflict areas on initiatives responding to the problems of violence and conflict.

---

[13] On massacres, see Human Rights Observatory, *Panorama actual*; on vulnerable municipalities, see UNDP, El conflicto, callejón con salida, Annexes 3 and 4; on selective murders discovered in common graves in San Onofre, see general press coverage in *El Tiempo* (especially April 8, 2005).

The experience of the REDES program shows that work in a zone of conflict arises from deliberation and negotiation in which many actors—central and local government, local civil society, non-governmental organizations (NGOs), UN agencies, and donor countries—participate. The trend in the REDES program has been to promote processes of deliberation among all actors so that any decisions will be formulated by broad-based coalitions that express local needs and reflect local opinion.

In Montes de María, a number of civic and social initiatives for reconciliation and peace are part of the history of the region. These include, for example, the formation of the Asociación Nacional de Usuarios Campesinos (ANUC, or National Association of Peasant Farmers), in the 1960s, and the negotiation and signing of three peace accords between the government and guerrilla movements during the 1990s. Nonetheless, such attempts to organize and transform society could not offer a comprehensive response to the region's social and political problems. Many of the leading actors in these processes were affected by the exacerbation of violence in the 1990s, and yet, despite the difficulties, they left behind an accumulation of social experiences and the fabric of a culture of peace, both of which are necessary for the type of intervention needed. REDES identified these initiatives through a preliminary study, Asistencia Preparatoria, commissioned by the UNDP in 2003, and a more detailed study aimed at identifying local capacities for peace-building action.[14]

Today the REDES program in Montes de María has identified a local strategy for social organization and institutional articulation in the form of an effort to set up a Program for Development and Peace (PDP) promoted by regional representatives of the Catholic and Mennonite Churches. PDPs are regional social movements or initiatives promoted by civil society for the construction of regional peace and development. The template for Montes de María is borrowed from the first PDP, developed in the Middle Magdalena Valley in the mid-1990s, and discussed in Chapter 14 of this volume by Javier Moncayo. Nineteen such programs have been set up with diverse participants. Most involve a range of institutions and organizations, such as churches, universities, industry associations, social organizations, and NGOs. PDPs are "civil and peaceful options of social protest" for the construction of civil alternatives to war.[15]

As we have seen in other chapters of this volume, institutions that enjoy legitimacy and recognition at the local level (for example, the Catholic

---

[14] The REDES program staff, in collaboration with two well-known Colombian research institutions, the Fundación CINEP and Fundación Synergía, developed a study in Montes de María, Meta, and Nariño. See Borja Paladini Adell, Carlos Fernández, and Fernando Sarmiento, *Capacidades locales de acción para la paz en Colombia. Casos de Montes de María, Meta y Nariño* (Bogotá: PNUD, 2008).

[15] See Javier Moncayo, "Los programas de desarrollo y paz" (PowerPoint presented to UNDP Colombia, Bogotá, 2004).

Church, which tries to mobilize and unite society for peace) take on added importance in conflict settings. In Montes de María in particular, political, technical, and economic support has reinforced the efforts of Catholic and Mennonite leaders to establish the Fundación Red Desarrollo y Paz de los Montes de María (FRDPMMa, or Development and Peace Network of Montes de María Foundation), as the leading organization for the development of the PDP. The original partners in this new organization were the Archdiocese of Cartagena, the dioceses of Sincelejo and Magangué, and the Mennonite Church. The Mennonites, with the support of John Paul Lederach, were responsible in 1998 for an effort called Construcción de Infrastructuras para la Convivencia Democrática en los Montes de María (Construction of Infrastructures for Democratic Coexistence in Montes de María). This program was not implemented, but it is a clear antecedent of the PDP in the region. The original partners have been joined by the chambers of commerce of the region; some business sectors; the pastoral social groups of the Catholic Church in Sucre and Bolívar; the Mennonite Asociación para la Vida Digna y Solidaria (ASVIDAS) community network; a number of regional universities; the Bogotá-based Javeriana and La Salle Universities; and several local, regional, and national NGOs, along with community organizations such as the Colectivo de Comunicaciones Montes de María. Some of these have been described in Chapter 16 of this volume by Ricardo Esquivia Ballestas and Barbara Gerlach.

One aim of the REDES program is to create or strengthen social and institutional networks. This strategy is based on the idea that the greater the degree of social organization, the lower the level of vulnerability to armed conflict and the greater the capacity to transform the conflict nonviolently. From this standpoint, FRDPMMa, with the support of the REDES program, has defined a strategy to build a network of networks to transform the subregion of Montes de María as part of a project for peace and development.

First, the foundation has defined itself as a network of organizations that builds alternatives to violence and transforms the underlying problems affecting Montes de María through peaceful civic and political means. Second, in the framework of the PDP, the foundation has promoted a number of networks. The Red Montemariana (Montes de María Network) is the strongest one in the region. Today the Montes de María Network includes 15 municipal boards, 3 subregional boards, and at least 145 zone boards (in rural areas). The municipal boards and the zone boards are key nodes, and they comprise the nucleus of further development of the PDP.

In the framework of the Red Montemariana, sector networks are enabling a number of interest groups to organize to play a strong role in constructing new social, economic, political, and institutional dynamics in the region. These include networks of youth, women, ethnic groups, producers and peasant farmers, artisans, popular media, universities, and institutional actors in the Asociación de Entidades Territoriales (AET, or Association of Regional Entities). The AET consists of the mayors of fifteen municipalities in Montes de María and the governors of the departments of Sucre and Bolívar.

The Montes de María Network and the sector networks are designed to promote participation in defining and building subregional projects and agendas through which the local population will increase its capacity to manage public affairs and enhance community linkages. The basic intention is that the local population will lead the construction and promotion of subregional and sectoral public policy as well as agendas for peace and human development. This general objective is to be reached through varied initiatives:

- an information system documenting basic quality-of-life indicators, structured through participatory work with the communities and intended to improve the design of public policy;
- an information system documenting the land tenure situation;
- promotion of civic initiatives for local democratic governance;
- a strategy of alliances between civil society and international organizations;
- a political proposal for the creation of a regional constituent assembly;
- advancement of regional disarmament, demobilization, and reintegration of demobilized combatants;
- creation of a regional reparations and reconciliation commission;
- job creation and other income-generation projects.

Many of the networks are under construction. Nonetheless, thanks to the political, technical, and financial accompaniment that REDES provides, and the direct promotion by FRDPMMa, the capacity of social organizations that are not controlled by the irregular armed actors to draw up subregional agendas is increasing.

According to the local community, REDES's political accompaniment is the greatest asset that the UNDP is bringing to the region. A 2006 evaluation reported,

> REDES' political accompaniment has been of paramount importance to generate safe spaces for dialogue and dissent to bridge divides and provide mental and moral support that motivates all these civil society partners to gather courage and resume social mobilization activities in violent conflict environments. To imagine one's future without conflict, poverty, and fear and jointly plan interventions to that end proved a powerful and convincing idea to mobilize and motivate shattered communities to join REDES development efforts. REDES' presence as an impartial but compassionate bridge-builder has seemingly discouraged armed groups from committing large-scale human rights violations.[16]

---

[16] Elisabeth Scheper, Anders Rudqvist, and María Camila Moreno, "REDES Program Evaluation Report," Bogotá, August–September 2006.

In addition to the political alliance with the FRDPMMa, REDES encourages a set of programs to mitigate the impact of violence on vulnerable groups in Montes de María. Some programs promote initiatives to increase the protection of the individual in zones of conflict. Others include initiatives that strengthen the capacity of the inhabitants of Montes de María to construct alternatives to violence. The REDES program has developed activities that respond to the following programmatic categories: civil society, participation, and governance; human rights; truth, justice, and reparations; antipersonnel mines; prevention of the illegal recruitment of minors; productivity and employment; land ownership and alternative development; media, conflict, and the culture of peace; sexual and reproductive health; and culture.

Civil Society, Participation, and Governance

We have seen how actors in civil society (Red Montemariana, FRDPMMa) and in the international community (UNDP, or PNUD) support one another to increase their capacity to produce nonviolent social change in the region. In addition, the REDES program has promoted a "Governance Accord" for the region, signed by the governors of Sucre and Bolívar and by the mayors of the fifteen municipalities of Montes de María. One of the results of this accord has been that the signatories have created the AET. The AET is an institutional space facilitated by the UNDP, in which the participants undertake, among other things, to accompany and collaborate in the implementation and execution of the PDP, which civil society has been promoting as the central point of coordination of the Montes de María region. The AET is also a space for regular meetings, in which senior government officials regularly come together under the auspices of the UNDP and FRDPMMa.

Other outcomes of these civil society, participation, and governance programs and initiatives include a number of municipal good-governance pacts, in Maríalabaja, Morroa, Zambrano, and Carmen de Bolívar. These accords have, for the first time in history, made it possible to conduct a public rendering of accounts by elected public officials and to make proposals for participatory budget preparation exercises. FRDPMMa and the Red Montemariana have complemented these efforts by creating the first systems of municipal information that include data on the quality of life and availability of economic resources, public investment, land tenure, and other documentation to enable the real needs of the inhabitants of Montes de María to be evaluated and addressed.

The promotion of good governance in Montes de María, and the construction of rule of law as an element of peacebuilding, has come to be a difficult and dangerous process, especially in a region where the paramilitaries have penetrated local and departmental governments. Despite the mandate of the UNDP to work jointly with state institutions, the original idea to establish alliances primarily with civil society actors before partnering with local state institutions has proved wise. During the second half of 2006 and the first months of 2007, several local elected politicians were imprisoned in the *parapolítica* scandal. The political alliance between the UNDP and respected civil society actors with a long history of social mobilization for peace is a good example of conflict-sensitive peacebuilding. The alliance has become a moral standard in the region and an effective way to press for and promote new good-governance practices. Local communities, civil society actors, and the REDES program have initiated ongoing dialogue processes on participatory governance and consensus-based policies and programs to confront the Montes de María challenges. Remarkably, in a setting of weakened local authorities, these social civil processes are leading to the building of a healthier state.

Human Rights

For the first time, a human rights institution—Working Group for Human Rights (Mesa de Trabajo por los Derechos Humanos)—has been established for the region. Also, the UNDP has supported the Defensoría del Pueblo in its design of a community-based initiative to increase the presence of the state. In addition, training in human rights was initiated by REDES and conducted by the Fundación Social. This training included social and institutional actors and aimed at the recognition of participants as legal subjects, the training of staff in human rights, and the dissemination of the training through promoters. Making human rights the main focus of reflection for social and institutional organizations created favorable conditions for the Human Rights Roundtable. This permanent roundtable is meant to serve as a platform for the different peacebuilding activities in the region. Its objectives are to reflect on the human rights situation in Montes de María and to promote the adoption of a human rights approach in regional and local public policies. Although possible lines of work are only now being defined, it is clear that the participating organizations seek to articulate different efforts and build a common human rights agenda, directed initially at human rights education, with an eye toward raising the roundtable's political profile in the near future.

Truth, Justice, and Reparations

REDES is actively supporting local efforts to promote a regional strategy for reconciliation. Work is being done to support the process of organizing victims and promoting a regional branch of the Comisión Nacional de Reparación y Reconciliación (CNRR). During 2007 and 2008, REDES increased its activities to promote local and regional victims' organizations so that they might acquire the capacity and strength needed for demanding their rights to truth, justice, and reparations. As an example, REDES supported the courageous March to Commemorate the Disappeared in San Onofre, organized in August 2006 by victims' groups to call for truth, justice, and reparation and a fair CNRR process.

Antipersonnel Mines

Montes de María has an integrated action plan against antipersonnel mines, causing government institutions, for the first time, to introduce specific actions into their development plans to face this problem, and to support those plans with municipal and departmental budget funds. The UNDP and the national government have developed public campaigns to protect those people most vulnerable to mines, and support networks for survivors of antipersonnel mines are being established. In the last few years, Colombia suffered more deaths and injuries from land mines than any other country in the world. Within Colombia, those territories, such as Montes de María, that are being contested by armed actors are the most affected by the problem, with civilians suffering the majority of casualties.

Prevention of the Illegal Recruitment of Minors

REDES is promoting a number of initiatives to prevent the involvement of minors in irregular armed groups. Based on a participatory analysis of the causes of recruitment, a school for youth leadership has been created; a youth network has been promoted within the Montes de María Network; and support has been given to youth initiatives in education, culture, and productive projects.

Productivity and Employment

A set of initiatives seeks to reduce the impact and social base of illegal economies by offering productive alternatives to those most vulnerable to the violence generated by these illegal markets: peasant farmers, women, the displaced, the young, Afro-Colombians, and indigenous groups. These initiatives also promote efforts for regional development, including technical assistance in presenting projects to the state and to international cooperation programs, the creation of a regional employment council (REC), the establishment of revolving loan funds, and the promotion of productive links between small and medium peasant farmers and industries. The REC in Montes de María is a meeting space for dialogue and coordination between public and private sectors. The REC seeks to influence the formulation of local and regional policies, strategies, and projects with bearing on the economy; promote competition; create employment and income generation; and improve regional conditions for peaceful coexistence. The members of these councils are representatives from the public and private sectors; the financial sector; universities; civil society organizations; and small, medium, and large enterprises.

Based on surveys of the labor and entrepreneurial problems affecting the region, the REC has organized a series of activities (meetings, forums, conferences, participation-action workshops on specific subjects, and roundtable discussions) to highlight employment issues and contribute to departmental employment policies. More emphasis was put on microprojects and productive activities such as honey extraction, harvest and water management, marble mining, skills training and technical assistance, and microfinance, complemented by information exchange on incentives, access to markets, and state public-employment policies. One of the REC's strengths appears to be its credibility and the great progress it has achieved in creating a neutral space for convergence, where different actors express their points of view regarding regional socioeconomic development, and in finding joint alternative solutions.

Land Ownership and Alternative Development

Work on these activities began in Montes de María with an in-depth analysis of the dynamics of land purchases and sales in recent years. This study shed light on the links between the armed conflict and land ownership and has led to recommendations for a public policy that, among other things, strengthens the organizations of peasant farmers and implements processes for deeding rights of ownership to small and medium peasant farmers.

Additional work has been done supporting the peasant social movement. In Montes de María, where the peasant movement was badly hit by the paramilitaries and most of its leaders were killed or forced to flee the region due to threats, REDES has begun to establish contact with the remaining leaders in the area and to initiate a process of recovery of the movement that, in the 1970s and 1980s, was the strongest peasant organization in Colombia. On May 12, 2006, REDES held a meeting with peasant leaders from Sucre in Sincelejo. The theme was "remembering our future." Support of peasant activities in Montes de María is a priority for REDES. This project works with the most vulnerable groups—victims of the armed conflict's violence—using the United Nations' and the PDP's symbolic comparative advantage to enhance peasants' organizations and agendas and progressively address root causes of the conflict.

Media, Conflict, and the Culture of Peace

A network of popular media has been established in all the municipalities, and a clear and detailed diagnosis has been made of the various forms of popular communications in the region. An alliance with the national media has been defined, which, in addition to protecting local communicators, also facilitates the exchange of information and technical advice. At the same time, work is being done with popular communicators to enable them to transmit messages of peace and reconciliation and to be among the most important actors in transforming collective mind-sets.

Culture Program

Participatory methods are being used to construct a cultural map with the inhabitants of Montes de María. It will include the elements of culture—music and musical instruments, craftwork, oral and literary narration, festivals, the characteristic expressions of indigenous and Afro-Colombian cultures, and so on—that give the region its distinctive identity. In addition, local organizations are rotating cultural events in all the municipalities (such as *las noches montemarianas* [Montes de María nights] and public cinema screenings). In these regular events, many of them held at night, people gather again to share popular music and dancing in public spaces that were inaccessible before, because of illegal control or direct coercion by the armed actors. Expressions of culture and identity have become one of the best tools to build bridges and improve relations among divided communities and to enhance a common identity.

Sexual and Reproductive Health Program

Data gathered by United Nations Fund for Population Activities (UNFPA) show that the region of Montes de María has severe problems related to sexual and reproductive health, including high levels of child mortality, HIV/ AIDS, child pregnancy, and violence against women, coupled with a very weak or nonexistent institutional response.[17] The REDES program began in 2006 by disseminating information about sexual and reproductive health, gender, and sexual and reproductive rights in development plans in the municipalities of Montes de María. In the next phases of the intervention, the initiative aims to improve sexual and reproductive health, access to health services, and the exercise of sexual and reproductive rights in the region and is also seeking to mitigate the effects of family violence as a factor of conflict. The program is designed to target the most vulnerable groups living in critical zones of armed conflict, including the displaced and those living in extreme poverty, particularly adolescents.

International Coordination

An overall objective of the REDES program is to reduce the vulnerability of the individuals and groups in the face of violence and to facilitate processes of peacebuilding, human development, and nonviolent management of conflict at local, regional, and national levels. But REDES has also succeeded in coordinating the intervention of a number of actors of the international community in the Montes de María region. Two instances have been particularly

---

[17] UNFPA, *Diagnóstico de la salud sexual y reproductiva en la región de los Montes de María* (Sincelejo, Sucre: UNFPA, 2006).

remarkable for their originality: the United Nations Interagency Group (UNIG) and the third Peace Laboratory.

The UNIG is the vehicle through which the REDES program has arranged for the UN agencies present in the region to coordinate their activities and intervention strategies in processes of peace and development promoted from within the subregion itself. The Humanitarian Working Group promoted by REDES and FRDPMMa, for example, relies on the participation of local and international institutions and organizations with a mandate in local humanitarian matters. They constantly exchange information to give a coordinated response to humanitarian problems in the region. Also, this group has set the basis in Montes de María for the current effort promoted by the United Nations system to coordinate humanitarian intervention among its agencies and with other international humanitarian actors. Another noteworthy initiative is the third Peace Laboratory, promoted by the European Union as part of its cooperation policy for Colombia. The third Peace Laboratory was being implemented in 2008 in the department of Meta and in Montes de María, building on work that REDES has done in these two regions. Montes de María's designation as a Peace Laboratory means that the region will become a strategic target region for European cooperation and that economic resources will be available to finance projects in three major areas: culture of peace and human rights, participation and democratic governance, and sustainable productive projects. For the REDES program, this designation is a sign that its work in these two regions has been valued and recognized by other institutions and that REDES can begin to broaden its strategies to solve the problems of this region.

Toward a Strategic Framework for Peacebuilding

In conclusion, the REDES program is an integral and comprehensive intervention in regional terms. Its work in various program areas has allowed it to mitigate the effects of armed violence; increase human security; and contribute to the social, economic, and political basis for peace and reconciliation. REDES has been recognized by the UNDP Bureau for Crisis Prevention and Recovery and other donors as a valuable program concept, with "freedom from fear, want and despair" as its main objective.

Since one of the overall objectives of the program includes the facilitation of peacebuilding processes, human development, and the nonviolent transformation of conflict, REDES is a promising model of a strategic framework for peacebuilding. All the initiatives promoted in Montes de María are guided by four strategic objectives, which help obtain aggregate results for the intervention as a whole. These objectives are support for processes of community and civil society organization; support for the construction and development of alliances between institutions, between actors in civil society, and between those actors and the state; promotion of public policies for peace that address the structural roots of violence and promote opportunities for peacebuilding and prevention of violent conflict; and the creation of opportunities for deepening knowledge of the problems, challenges, and possible solutions facing the territory.

On the first objective, REDES works with endogenous civil society initiatives in the territory where it intervenes and links these initiatives to social and institutional networks. These initiatives are considered as opportunities for civic empowerment, with a capacity to reach across the territory, strengthen the social fabric, and construct nonviolent alternatives to those proposed by the irregular armed actors. In Montes de María, for example, the participants in the Red Montemariana and in the FRDPMMa are very aware of the political role that the initiative plays by encouraging people to assume the management of their own destinies and free themselves from the "protection" that the irregular armed actors attempt to impose. The strengthening of regional social networks increases the community's capacity to protect itself against the irregular armed actors and changes the balance of power in the territory. At the same time, this new strength creates the conditions for constructive dialogue between the authorities and civil society.

Peacebuilding depends to a great extent on the quality of the relationships generated between the many different actors in a given territory; and in this regard, REDES has promoted the establishment of alliances as a mechanism to strengthen social, institutional, and political networks and, thus, to increase the intervention's legitimacy and its capacity to effect transformation. Three types of alliance are fundamental in the experience of the REDES program: alliances within civil society; alliances between civil society and the state; and alliances between the territory and the international community.

Effective alliances between the state and civil society require that some progress has been made toward the first objective—that of strengthening civil society—so that the state will have an interlocutor. Likewise, civil society needs the state. Mgr. Nel Beltrán, bishop of Sincelejo and president of FRDPMMa, notes, "The state is not something we can do without. Either we stay with the state we have—which we do not like. Or the armed groups impose on us the state they want—which we like even less. Or, we build the state we want, as citizens."[18]

Robust alliances between all these actors are needed so that all might perform their mandates and responsibilities and thus work more effectively and with greater sustainability and legitimacy in each programmatic area of the intervention. Capacity of civil society actors and legitimacy of the elected authorities of the state are the keys to depriving the advocates of violence of opportunities to act and restricting the social base of the armed actors.

---

[18] Nel Beltrán, interview by the authors, Sincelejo, October 2005.

REDES's public policy objectives relate to the allocation of public resources to meet people's needs. The REDES program is promoting participation-based public policies that tackle the roots of conflict and increase the capacity of government institutions to give answers to the challenges and opportunities posed by conflict. In Montes de María, there is increasing involvement of elected officials in the initiatives promoted by the alliance between the UNDP and civil society at local, departmental, and national levels. This alliance is part of a strategy to promote processes of better local governance and conflict-sensitive development.

On the final objective, knowledge creation, the REDES program considers it essential to provide the necessary opportunities and resources for the many actors engaged in the intervention to participate fully in the process of deliberation and construction of knowledge, problem solving, and facing and transforming realities. There is one constant principle: people participate only in what they have helped to build. The building of intersubjective knowledge is an exercise that has been performed in Montes de María, not only for each line of intervention but also for the construction of collective visions of the territory, agendas, development plans, and so on.

The experience of the REDES program in Colombia has resulted in a number of observations and recommendations. First, in the midst of violent conflict and humanitarian crisis, there are windows of opportunity for constructive intervention in the nonviolent transformation of the conflict and in the support of local and transformative peace constituencies. It is important to support this type of endogenous peace initiative by increasing the capacity or power of these social and institutional actors to become active subjects and protagonists in the process of nonviolent social transformation and peacebuilding. Consequently, the actors of the international community need not wait for the end of armed conflict and the execution of a peace agreement before promoting local efforts for peace and development: they can start now, as a complement to their humanitarian action.

Second, it is possible to construct initiatives for sustainable social, economic, political, and institutional development even in settings of armed conflict. But development in the midst of conflict must be designed with a nuanced understanding of the context, including the local legitimacy of certain actors (such as the Catholic Church), the existence of and potential for various synergies or alliances, and knowledge of the territorial logic of the conflict. These actions must be linked to endogenous efforts at social organization in the territory where the intervention takes place and must accompany social, political, and cultural processes that arise as an exercise in resistance to the illegal armed actors or as an exercise in constructing alternatives in civil and nonviolent power.

Third, the peacebuilding process is not an exclusive product of accords between the state and the illegal armed actors. Peace must also be founded on stronger relations between civil society and public powers. The international community can help rebuild bridges and relations and lend added legitimacy to the state. The United Nations system can play an important role in facilitating strategic alliances between various civil actors and national government authorities, along with local and regional government leaders. In this way, the path can be prepared for a concerted design of public policies for peace, humanitarian attention, and human development, which will also contribute to increased legitimacy of the state and reduce the irregular armed actors' power and their room for maneuvering.

Finally, in academic terms, peace processes have traditionally been assumed to follow a chronological sequence: peacemaking, peacekeeping, and peacebuilding. If we follow this pattern, successful peace negotiations are a sine qua non for creating social conditions for sustainable peace. But regional initiatives in Colombia have shown the opposite. The REDES program has been a tool to promote peacebuilding in a context of protracted and violent armed conflict, and its experience challenges the chronological pattern traditionally assumed as the norm in conceptual and political thinking about peacebuilding. Even before any successful negotiations for peace, it is possible to promote social processes that will weaken the structural conditions favoring violence, and generate a context for development and peace.

19

U.S. Policy and Peace in Colombia
Lost in a Tangle of Wars

James C. Jones

Elusive peace has long chased war in Colombia, where today three wars—a war on insurgency, a war on drugs, and a war on terrorism—commingle in a seamless web.[1] Each can take on the guise of the others, as passions and interests dictate. Major warring actors include two states, Colombia and the United States; a powerful insurgent group, the Fuerzas Armadas Revolucionarias de Colombia (FARC); and a loose coalition of well-armed right-wing militias with shadowy connections to regional and national political elites, to drug traffickers, and to elements of Colombia's armed forces. The shifting policies and conduct of these actors, who often manage the media to create self-serving myths, define the dynamic of a dirty war. Sorting out actors, perceptions, and the obscure interests and myths that drive the wars, in a land where things are rarely what they seem, is a sine qua non for peace.

Dancing with Leftist Insurgents: Peace in the Time of Andrés Pastrana

Colombians yearned for peace in 1998, when Andrés Pastrana, campaigning on a peace platform in a runoff election, rode those national yearnings to power. He had met with FARC chief Manuel Marulanda in July that year to start a historic peace process. At that time, Pastrana agreed to create a demilitarized zone (*despeje*) for talks, to control right-wing militias, and to initiate "crop substitution" in the FARC-held south. The last two items were dear to Marulanda.

---

[1] This chapter is based on research conducted in part with a grant from the John D. and Catherine T. MacArthur Foundation during 2002–03, and in part during the author's work as an international consultant in 2004–05. The author translated text and interviews from Spanish as necessary.

Pastrana's primary political interest was peace. He wove drugs—a subordinate interest—into a peace plan. Meeting with international delegates in October, he announced a "Plan Colombia," a development plan that he likened to the Marshall Plan. The FARC had agreed to reduce drug crops in the south in exchange for development (that is, "crop substitution"). Pastrana saw peace as a prerequisite for drug control and drugs as a social problem. He opposed the aerial spraying of herbicides, then the centerpiece of U.S. antidrug policy. Plan Colombia squared well with FARC interests and with the July agreement between Pastrana and Marulanda.

But contrary and undermining forces were also in play. Pastrana's plan vexed important persons in Bogotá and Washington. The FARC had ravaged Colombia's armed forces in eight attacks from 1996 to 1998. Defense Minister Rodrigo Lloreda, meeting with U.S. defense secretary William Cohen in December 1998, said that Colombia risked losing the entire *oriente* (east) to insurgents. After long refusing to fight drugs, the military, keen to rally after humiliating losses, had announced in September 1998 the forthcoming creation of an antidrug unit, which Cohen confirmed. It was clear that fighting drugs would be an entrée to fighting insurgents. The first antidrug battalion debuted in December 1999, the third in May 2001.

From the moment Pastrana took office in August 1998 until mid-1999, influential U.S. Republican lawmakers, allied with elements from the Pentagon and the U.S. drug czar's office, opposed talking peace from a weak position. They favored strengthening the military, and they feared that the *despeje* would hobble aerial spraying. Drug czar Barry McCaffrey, attending Pastrana's inauguration, scolded the FARC for its drug involvement and said that spraying was the only way to fight coca cultivation. Earlier, as chief of the U.S. Southern Command, he had told Human Rights Watch that counterinsurgency and counternarcotics were "two sides of the same coin."[2] Pastrana asked the United States for crop-substitution aid in September. But an official under McCaffrey at the time told my colleague that the United States feared that the FARC might get credit for any aid. For the United States, fighting drugs nominally took priority over the peace plan, and spraying was the weapon of choice.

With the advent of Pastrana's peace process, right-wing militias, or paramilitaries, increased their activity. In an October 1998 admonitory remark, Marulanda declared progress toward peace impossible until Pastrana "calls off the dogs."[3] In a secret December meeting in Costa Rica between the State Department's Andean affairs director, Phil Chicola, and FARC "foreign minister" Raúl Reyes, crop substitution and rightist militias were major topics.

---

[2] Human Rights Watch, *Colombia's Killer Networks: The Military-Paramilitary Partnership and the United States* (New York, Washington, London, Brussels: Human Rights Watch, 1996), 85.

[3] "Colombia's Drug-Bedevilled Hopes for Peace," *Economist*, August 1, 1998.

As Reyes told me five years later, he explained to Chicola why peasants grew drug crops, and Reyes offered to help the United States eliminate them—but only after farmers had alternatives. He also asked Chicola why the United States continued, after the Cold War's end, to train Colombian soldiers who murdered civilians. He told him that Colombia's army worked closely with the paramilitaries and offered proof if Chicola wanted it. And he gave Chicola a list of names of assassinated Unión Patriótica (UP) members—four thousand names, Reyes told me.

As Reyes and Chicola met, paramilitaries launched a terror rampage of rural massacres. On December 27, 1998, the FARC stormed El Nudo de Paramillo, seat of the Autodefensas Unidas de Colombia (AUC), hoping to kill AUC chief Carlos Castaño. Castaño escaped by helicopter during a firefight—by some reports, aided by Colombia's military. The paramilitaries retaliated in January 1999, torturing alleged rebel backers, burning their homes, and killing more than 160 civilians. On January 19, only twelve days after peace talks with the Pastrana government had begun, the FARC suspended them.

The prospects for either crop substitution or control of the militias were already dim. The die for the peace plan was cast. Powerful forces deciding its fate were entrenched in both Washington and Bogotá, their course fixed, before the FARC, in an action in late February whose details are still unclear, killed three U.S. native-rights activists. The action steeled those forces and accelerated their movement toward an inexorable end. The war intensified under Pastrana.

Political feuding dominated the U.S. Colombia policy debate in 1999, only months before the 2000 U.S. elections. Republicans called Clinton (1993–2001) soft on "narco-terrorists"—despite a sharp rise in military aid under his watch. Democrats, including Clinton, the consummate politician, were sensitive to the charge. Pastrana, aware of the dangers to his peace plan and now criticizing Republicans, described Colombia in July 1999 as "the ham in the [U.S.] sandwich," and Colombia policy as a useful tool more "for hitting your government than for helping or hurting our government."[4] After months of closed multiagency Washington-Bogotá planning, in September, Pastrana announced a Plan Colombia, for "peace, prosperity and strengthening the state." According to its architect, Jaime Ruíz, the three-year plan would cost US$7.5 billion, more than half of which was for "strengthening and restructuring of the army," since "Colombia can't bet everything on the peace process."[5] As a senior U.S. official later told me, "Jaime Ruíz drafted Plan

---

[4] Karen DeYoung, "Colombia's U.S. Connection Not Winning Drug War," *Washington Post*, July 16, 1999.

[5] Larry Rohter, "Plan to Strengthen Colombia Nudges U.S. For $3.5 Billion," *New York Times*, September 18, 1999.

Colombia in English, here in Washington. Pastrana kept it under wraps; he wasn't open, and this was a mistake."

In July 2000, the United States approved almost US$1 billion dollars for this Plan Colombia II—80 percent of it for Colombia's armed forces, and most of that to support aerial spraying, which was to start in coca-rich, FARC-controlled Putumayo in December 2000. The theory held that killing coca would reduce the FARC's income, forcing it to talk peace. The logic of Plan Colombia I, with peace as a prerequisite for drug control, was thus reversed: drug control was now a prerequisite for peace. But there was also a less obvious dimension: diminishing the FARC's drug income would cripple its fighting capacity and so reduce its threat to the country's status quo. And the United States depended on that status quo for a favorable investment climate, especially for oil—whose revenues Bogotá needed to fight the war. This was Plan Colombia's counterinsurgency underside. Reyes spoke to me of this logic: "It's a big mistake by Colombia's ruling class, its government, and especially its military and the Americans, to think that once drug trafficking disappears, so will the FARC. We will live from whatever people produce, as we did before drug crops, and as we do today in areas without them." With Putumayo's fierce spraying program, coca migrated. The area planted with coca between Tame and Saravena, in Arauca, rose from 10,000 to 25,000 acres. A government ombudsman noted, "The army says that all of this coca is essentially moving up from the south because of Plan Colombia. So now we are a coca zone."[6] And the armed groups also grew. A mid-2001 report cited five thousand AUC recruits in the previous year. The FARC was growing, too.

When George W. Bush became president in early 2001, Washington's Colombia policy lacked consensus. A *New York Times* journalist noted, "Elemental questions remain. What is the basic plan? Is it a peace strategy with a military component? A counterinsurgency drive? A bulwark to salvage the Pastrana administration? A Marshall Plan for South America? And what will define its success?"[7] Pastrana may have had his own doubts, for Plan Colombia's military side had alienated Europe, leaving him entirely reliant on Washington. Seeming uneasy, Pastrana said just before a late February visit with Bush, "We are a poor country. But we are spending $1 billion a year of our money to keep drugs off the streets of Washington and New York. We need more help. This is a long-term plan, maybe 15 to 20 years." He added, "The paramilitaries are not a problem between the government and the FARC. They are a problem facing the whole country. But they are the result of

---

[6] Scott Wilson, "Wider War in Colombia," *Washington Post*, September 6, 2001.

[7] Christopher Marquis, "America Gets Candid about What Colombia Needs," *New York Times*, February 25, 2001.

the guerrillas. Once there is peace with the guerrillas, the paramilitaries will end."[8] Later events would challenge this assertion.

Pastrana and Marulanda met for the third time on February 8, 2001, and signed the Los Pozos Accord. They agreed to form a commission to study the paramilitary issue and to invite "international friends" of the peace process to talk with FARC leaders in the *despeje* on March 8. The accord's Point 10 clarified the FARC's position on drugs: "The FARC do not oppose manual eradication and crop substitution but reiterate that this should be done in agreement with local communities."[9]

On his visit to Washington after signing the Los Pozos Accord, Pastrana asked Bush to meet with the FARC to "directly exchange views. I think it's important for the United States to be there." To U.S. charges that the FARC exported drugs, Pastrana replied, "We don't have evidence, nor does the United States or anyone else, of them being a cartel."[10]

The United States refused to attend the March 8, 2001, meeting of "international friends." George Bush called it "an issue that the Colombian people and the Colombian president can deal with." Said Marulanda, "If [the United States] does not want to come and speak with us, there's nothing more to do other than extend the invitation."[11] In the meeting, the FARC condemned the paramilitaries and called aerial spraying an "aggression against 350,000 poor families who have no alternative." The rebels again proposed a crop-substitution pilot project in Cartagena del Chairá, a coca-rich Caquetá municipality under FARC control.[12]

Bush's Colombia policy crystallized. On August 29, 2001, Undersecretary of State for Political Affairs Marc Grossman led a high-level delegation to Bogotá to prepare a forthcoming visit by Secretary Colin Powell. Bush, said Grossman, supported Plan Colombia "without restrictions."[13] He said, "President Pastrana's government is engaged in a struggle that matters to everyone in this hemisphere," and the United States backed a "fellow democracy."[14] In private, officials were more blunt. Said a senior Pentagon official, "We no longer view the FARC and ELN guerrillas as an internal threat to the security of Colombia, but as a threat to the security of the United States." Said another

---

[8] Scott Wilson, "Colombia to Ask Bush for Additional Funds," *Washington Post*, February 16, 2001.

[9] Center for International Policy, "'Los Pozos Accord' between Government and FARC," February 9, 2001, www.ciponline.org/colombia/020902.htm (accessed September 15, 2008).

[10] Karen DeYoung, "Pastrana Urges U.S. to Meet with Guerrillas," *Washington Post*, February 27, 2001.

[11] "US under Fire for Colombia Boycott," *Associated Press*, March 1, 2001.

[12] "La propuesta de las FARC," *El Tiempo*, March 9, 2001.

[13] "E.U. asegura que no cambiará frente al Plan Colombia," *El Tiempo*, August 30, 2001.

[14] Andrew Selsky, "U.S. May Send More Aid to Colombia," *Associated Press*, August 31, 2001.

official, "It's time to drop the fiction of antinarcotics aid only. Americans are targets in Colombia." A State Department official said, "We want the Colombian army to be able to go and get the bad guys wherever they are." Under the new policy, said another, "we are talking about more direct military-to-military support." A onetime CIA antiterrorism expert called the *despeje* "a Club Med for terrorists."[15]

U.S. policy was speeding toward open counterinsurgency before Secretary Powell's scheduled visit on September 11, one day after the United States placed the AUC paramilitary organization on its terrorist list—and four years after placing the FARC there. But Powell never came. On the morning of September 11, the United States came under attack. The attack caused a gestalt shift in U.S. security thinking. In Colombia, it spawned a third war—a war on "terrorism." Yet the attack did not alter the shape or the course of the conflict there. Rather, it intensified it and favored peace-averse interests.

In a telling remark revelatory of U.S. eagerness to play on the attack to further its Colombia policy, which included long-standing counterinsurgency, State Department counterterrorism coordinator Francis Taylor told the U.S. Congress only days after 9/11:

> One can argue that modern terrorism originated in our Hemisphere. We date [its] advent from 1968, four years before Munich, when revolutionary movements began forming throughout the Americas. In those early years, Latin America saw more international terrorist attacks than any other region. Today, the most dangerous international terrorist group in this hemisphere is the Revolutionary Armed Forces of Colombia.[16]

Counterterrorism was a more palatable mantle than counternarcotics for waging counterinsurgency, which many in Washington feared after Vietnam. And if Washington did indeed make policy by sound bite (as one U.S. ambassador in the region told me), it was easy to make the case for drugs as a terrorist threat. Above all, the threat cleared the way for a direct assault on the FARC. Raúl Reyes addressed this semantic shift with a sense of history much at odds with Taylor's: "First, and for some time, they said that we took orders from Moscow. Absolutely false! We never received a nickel from Moscow. But beyond this, Moscow is no more. The Russian socialist camp no longer exists. So afterward they called us a narco-guerrilla. . . . And now they say we're terrorists."

With his peace process failing, Pastrana asked Bush in November 2001 to include Colombia in the global war on terrorism and allow use of U.S.

---

[15] Richard Sale, "U.S. Policy Morphing in Colombia," *United Press International*, September 11, 2001, www.freerepublic.com/focus/fr/546723/posts.

[16] "Testimony of Francis X. Taylor, coordinator for counterterrorism, U.S. Department of State, October 10, 2001," Committee on Foreign Affairs, Subcommittee on the Western Hemisphere, United States House of Representatives, www.state.gov/s/ct/rls/rm/2001/5674.htm (accessed September 16, 2008).

antidrug helicopters for counterinsurgency operations.[17] FARC commander Simón Trinidad, captured in Quito in January 2004 and later extradited to the United States, echoed Reyes's interpretation. He said, "From the beginning we said that Plan Colombia was a counterinsurgency plan. No one believed the story that it was a plan against drug trafficking. Now the mask has been taken off. [U.S. soldiers] are here to pursue a war against our own people, and they have taught the military the doctrine of state terrorism."[18]

The oil issue had also been simmering, complicating efforts to sort out U.S. interests in the region. An Occidental Petroleum executive had met with U.S. officials on May 8, 2001—the day Castaño announced that paramilitary forces would enter Arauca—and threatened to close the strategic Oxy-operated Caño-Limón pipeline for security reasons.[19] As the peace process entered a crisis, Bush divulged plans in February 2002 to equip and train a "Critical Infrastructure Brigade." To that end, U.S. troops entered Arauca in January 2003. Sen. Patrick Leahy (D-Vt.) observed, "This is no longer about stopping drugs—it's about fighting the guerrillas."[20] Meanwhile, on February 20, 2002, Pastrana terminated the peace process. In an address that evening, to history as much as to the nation, he called the FARC "terrorists" for the first time. Then, on April 16, Pastrana visited Washington for the eighth time as president and asked for aid in fighting the rebels. In a *Washington Post* op-ed piece the day before, he wrote, "The mandate I received from voters was to negotiate a political settlement with Colombia's guerrillas. The FARC did not respond to our generosity. Hence, the initial mandate has been replaced with a new and different one: to bring peace by defeating the guerrillas and the narcos on the battlefield."[21]

Closer scrutiny belies Pastrana's remarks. Indeed, he broke his word often, and his "generosity" is obscure. As a former television anchor, Pastrana understood the power of the media, which he kept at the ready. In his government's final months, that power projected a Pastrana who did all he could for peace, and a FARC that never wanted peace. This message is a disservice to the truth—and to all Colombians. It is a dangerous, self-serving myth.

As so often in Colombia, truth lay in the realm of shadows. There, where decisions of war and peace were made, the media rarely reached. An analysis of events, only snatches of which appear here, casts doubt on Pastrana's understanding of the challenges and import of his peace process—and his com-

---

[17] Juan Forero, "Asking for Aid, Colombians Cite Terror; U.S. Demurs," *New York Times*, November 11, 2001.

[18] Javier Baena, "Colombian Rebels Protest U.S. Plan," *Associated Press*, February 6, 2002.

[19] T. Christian Miller, "U.S. Troops Answered Oil Firm's Pleas," *Los Angeles Times*, December 30, 2004.

[20] Karen DeYoung, "Wider U.S. Role in Colombia Sought," *Washington Post*, February 6, 2002.

[21] Andrés Pastrana, "High Stakes in Colombia," *Washington Post*, April 15, 2002.

mitment to it beyond an electoral win. This commitment was not lost on the FARC. Raúl Reyes told me long afterward, in the din of war, as we discussed the failed peace:

> Plan Colombia gave the armed forces and Pastrana a sense of triumph. They began to think that with arms, planes, and advisers they could defeat us. They thought that with a stronger, better-trained, and reengineered armed force they could scare us and defeat us at the negotiating table. We saw during the peace process that the military took all the decisions. At one point, they opposed the high commissioner for peace [Víctor Ricardo]. He waited for Pastrana to tell him that he was wrong, or that he had misunderstood policy, or that he was right and had support, or that he should stop this or that because [the government] was on the wrong track. But Pastrana never responded, and when the chief doesn't respond, you feel you're alone. We then knew that the military was in charge.

Dancing with Rightist Militias: War in the Time of Álvaro Uribe

The battlefield role of that military would soon grow. Ultraconservative candidate Álvaro Uribe, a former Antioquia governor, won the May 2002 presidential elections, vowing to defeat the FARC. An electorate that earlier had voted for peace through dialogue now voted for peace through war. In the words of a former Chocó governor, "People see Uribe as a messiah, they're desperate." But troubling portents also hovered. The AUC openly endorsed Uribe. Militia chief Salvatore Mancuso had said prior to the March congressional elections: "We're telling people for whom they should vote. Thirty percent of congressional aspirants represent people from our zones."[22] Said a worried indigenous leader, "Uribe will govern with two armies, the regular army and the paramilitaries. For us, Uribe represents the rich. The indigenous are poor."[23]

On inauguration day, amid 25,000 soldiers and police, FARC-fired mortars fell near the ceremony, killing 14 and injuring 60. An ominous event, it spoke to rebel power and to a deep hatred of Uribe and what he stood for. Uribe had already made his policy direction clear: "What we need is to strengthen Plan Colombia."[24] Underscoring Colombia's lack of resources, he gave assurances that "with political will we can defeat these groups."[25] The United States agreed. Drug czar John Walters dismissed Vietnam fears: "We're going to see an intensification [of the conflict] and an intensification of the effectiveness of efforts. This is not a situation where we need to be afraid of ghosts."[26]

---

[22] "Sí apoyamos candidatos: 'Paras,'" *El Tiempo*, February 12, 2002.

[23] Frances Robles, "Colombians Elect Hard-Liner Uribe," *Miami Herald*, May 27, 2002.

[24] Juan Forero, "Hard-Liner Elected in Colombia with a Mandate to Crush Rebels," *New York Times*, May 27, 2002.

[25] Scott Wilson, "Colombian Frontrunner Looks to War," *Washington Post*, May 20, 2002.

[26] Angus MacSwan, "U.S. to Step Up Military Effort in Colombia," *Reuters*, August 27, 2002.

Uribe called his policy "democratic security." He would double defense spending and the size of the armed forces. He would train, arm, and deploy one million paid informers to supplement a thinly stretched military. In August 2002, he revealed plans to recruit, train, and arm twenty thousand "peasant soldiers" to defend five hundred hamlets; and in September he created the first "security zones," where the military had special powers: one in Bolívar, a paramilitary stronghold, and the other in oil-rich Arauca. He would spray until all drug crops were gone. And he would pay farmers in remote areas to remove coca and plant trees—a campaign pledge, yet one focused more on trees and the environment than on poor farmers and sustainable development. Uribe saw drug control as counterinsurgency, and poverty as a cause of neither drug crops nor insurgency. He told the World Economic Forum: "In my country there's misery and inequality, but above all there's terrorism, which is the cause of poverty, not its consequence."[27]

In November 2002, under the auspices of the Catholic Church, Uribe began secret talks with the AUC, which declared a cease-fire on December 1.[28] At the same time, he moved Colombia to the front lines of the global war on terror. He told U.S. business leaders gathered in Florida, "The Colombian conflict has the potential to spread to all of the countries in the hemisphere."[29] That movement to the front lines quickened on February 7, 2003, when a deadly car bomb wrecked Bogotá's exclusive Club El Nogal, killing 33 and injuring 160. It was a stab at the heart of Colombia's elite. And it was chilling that a 440-pound bomb could enter the high-security club, whose former board president was Uribe's minister of justice and interior, Fernando Londoño, a well-known, vocal right-wing lawyer and a fierce critic of the FARC. It was Colombia's "September 11," and Uribe blamed the FARC.[30]

The FARC denied involvement, yet called Londoño a neofascist friend of AUC-allied generals and the club the "site of meetings between political and business sectors with spokesmen for paramilitaries."[31] Subsequent government investigations tied the FARC to the event, as did circumstance. The FARC's hatred of the paramilitaries, whom it views as part of the public security forces and as Uribe allies, runs deep. That Uribe should talk "peace" with this friend was all a public show. And this only increased the rebels' odium. With acid criticism, Reyes told me,

> With Uribe, we're not surprised, because we know he's a great friend of Carlos Castaño. Uribe's now trying to do him the favor of cleaning his face from the bath in blood from all the crimes he's committed,

---

[27] "Presidente Álvaro Uribe Pide ayuda internacional contra la violencia en Colombia en Foro Económico Mundial," *El Tiempo,* January 24, 2003.

[28] "Negociación secreta," *Semana,* November 23, 2002.

[29] Phil Stewart, "Colombia Asks Neighbors to Join Drug War," *Reuters,* October 15, 2002.

[30] "Presidente Álvaro Uribe reclama al mundo por terrorismo en El Nogal," *El Tiempo,* February 8, 2003.

[31] Frances Robles, "Rebels Hint Colombia Blast Was Revenge," *Miami Herald,* February 10, 2003.

and making him a senator of the republic. This is why Castaño and the *autodefensas* campaigned for Uribe. Uribe now has to honor his commitment to these paramilitaries. The idea is to legalize them, and to make that easy, Uribe has created informant networks and peasant soldiers. Many of the paras will become peasant soldiers. Others will enter informant networks. And some will enter the army. Those with more education will become schoolteachers and perform intelligence. And yet others will work hacienda lands, some held by drug traffickers. The paramilitaries will not disappear. They will become the children of the wife rather than [the children of] the girlfriend.[32]

Uribe well knew the AUC's profile before initiating talks with them. According to a *Washington Post* journalist, he ordered a feasibility study, which determined that drugs yielded 80 percent of AUC funds—"it is impossible to differentiate between the self-defense groups and narco-trafficking organizations," the study noted.[33] It further noted that AUC chiefs saw talks with the government as a way to protect their drug earnings and that they expected security and development for their regions, legalization of their earnings, and judicial security. The study also concluded, "The Armed Forces are the principal enemy to a peace process. Opposition exists at the highest ranks." Yet peace talks with the paramilitaries, with their sporadic ceremonial demobilizations, moved forward and took center stage over the following months. Formal talks began in Córdoba in July 2004. On July 28, in a controversial gambit, AUC leaders addressed Colombia's Congress. Salvatore Mancuso, responsible for numerous assassinations and massacres and under indictment in the United States for sending seventeen tons of cocaine there, spoke at length: "I believe in God, the God of hope, of love, of forgiveness. I am a businessman, head of a family, thrown into the terrible mouth of war. I never imagined that extortion and the threat of kidnapping and death would force me to act in self-defense. The reward for our sacrifice, for having freed half the country from the guerrillas and preventing another Cuba, cannot be to send us to prison."[34] Mancuso also made it clear that he would not accept extradition—"Because it's easier to return, gather the few troops yet remaining and flee to the jungle, and die there as an old man, or be killed by the law, than to serve jail time in Colombia and then go to the United States."[35]

Bush had kept aloof from talks with the FARC but now warmed to those with the AUC. Said one U.S. official, "This is the first semi-serious show of intent on the part of one of these armed groups. I don't think it matters [that

---

[32] Raúl Reyes, interview by the author, Colombia, 2003.

[33] Scott Wilson, "Colombian Fighters' Drug Trade Is Detailed," *Washington Post*, June 26, 2003.

[34] Juan Forero, "At Colombia's Congress, Paramilitary Chiefs Talk Peace," *New York Times*, July 29, 2004; Jason Webb, "Warlords Address Colombia Congress Amid Protests," *Reuters*, July 29, 2004; Sibylla Brodzinsky, "Colombia's Paramilitaries Plead Case," *Houston Chronicle*, July 29, 2004.

[35] "Salvatore Mancuso amenaza con tomar de nuevo las armas si no hay solución radical a su extradición," *El Tiempo*, December 5, 2004.

they're terrorists]. The idea here is to take pieces off the playing board."[36] On December 10, 2004, the Mancuso-led Catatumbo Bloc, the area's major fount of violence, demobilized 1,425 paramilitaries. U.S. Embassy political officer Stewart Tuttle was there.[37] The State Department's narcotics chief Robert Charles said, "A window of opportunity has opened that will not always remain open. President Uribe has taken a huge risk, and we must do everything in our power to facilitate these peace efforts."[38]

The Colombian Congress, where Uribe had strong support, finally passed legislation to govern the demobilizations. Uribe signed the Justice and Peace Law in July 2005. Human rights groups condemned the law, stating it favored the perpetrators of human rights violations over their victims. A *New York Times* editorial called it the "Impunity for Mass Murderers, Terrorists and Major Cocaine Traffickers Law."[39] But Uribe's relations with human rights groups—he said they had guerrilla sympathies—had already soured, as had those with the United Nations, which announced in January 2005 that it would close its "special adviser" office and recall envoy James LeMoyne, who had offended Uribe by saying that the FARC had a political program. Uribe, as part of a surreal strategy in a war of verbal images as much as of guns, denied the presence of an "internal conflict"—without which the 1949 Geneva Convention was inapplicable. Said Refugees International, "By characterizing the conflict as a terrorist threat, the government is able to deny civilians protection guaranteed under international humanitarian law. In some cases civilians themselves are seen as part of the problem, rounded up in mass detentions, encouraged to act as informants against their neighbors, and formed into rural militias as "campesino soldiers."[40]

Uribe captured three important FARC rebels and extradited two of them. Extradition was now a negotiable political tool serving the interests of the armed conflict as much as a legal tool serving justice. He extradited Ricardo Palmera ("Simón Trinidad") to the United States in December 2004 and Omaira Rojas ("Sonia") in March 2005, both charged with drug trafficking—and Trinidad with hostage taking in connection with three Pentagon contractors whom the FARC captured and held after their reconnaissance plane fell in FARC territory during a mission in early 2003. Suborned Venezuelan police secretly captured Rodrigo Granda in March 2005 in Caracas and returned

[36] Wilson, "Colombian Fighters' Drug Trade Is Detailed."

[37] Yesid Lancheros, "'Pido perdón por los daños,' dijo Salvatore Mancuso durante la desmovilización más grande del país," *El Tiempo*, December 10, 2004.

[38] Sergio Gómez Maseri, "E.U. y el mundo deben apoyar con vigor y cuanto antes la desmovilización de los grupos paramilitares," *El Tiempo*, December 16, 2004.

[39] "Colombia's Capitulation," *New York Times*, July 4, 2005.

[40] Mamie Mutchler and Andrea Lari, "Colombia Cannot Deny Internal Armed Conflict," Refugees International, January 24, 2005, www.refugeesinternational.org/content/article/detail/4962 (accessed September 15, 2008).

him to Colombia in the trunk of a car. The captures and extraditions dimmed the prospects of a humanitarian prisoner swap—which was to include the three U.S. military contractors in FARC hands. Granda, with whom I met some months before his capture, was working for a swap at the time. Trinidad said in an interview on the eve of his departure for the United States, "I'm neither a drug trafficker nor a terrorist, and there in the United States courts I will not only demonstrate this, I will also fight in the political arena. [The extradition will be] a new chapter that will have consequences for the search for peace among Colombians."[41]

Yet U.S. assistant attorney general Christopher Wray said of Trinidad's extradition, "The FARC is a dangerous organization of terrorists, drug traffickers, kidnappers and murderers. Our indictments and extradition requests should send a clear message to all who participate in or support their deplorable and criminal acts: We will work with other nations to see that you are brought to justice in a U.S. court of law."[42]

The AUC was held to other standards. On the day that Uribe issued an ultimatum to the FARC—free sixty hostages, or Palmera would be extradited to the United States—Bogotá said it would not extradite Mancuso if he "complies with agreements within the peace process, abandons illicit activities, [and] contributes to the participation of other members of the AUC in the peace process."[43] The AUC's human rights crimes—paramilitary forces had murdered thirteen thousand people since 1996—dwarfed those committed by the FARC.[44] As for drug trafficking, a DEA analyst said in 2004 that the FARC "pale in comparison" to the paramilitaries.[45] A Finance Ministry study found drugs to be one-fifth of total FARC income—less than half that from ransoms.[46]

Talks with the AUC were one part of a dual strategy. In Caquetá in late 2003, Colombia launched the Patriot Plan, a secret offensive drawing on eighteen thousand soldiers and U.S. advisers—the largest military offensive ever mounted in Colombia. Its goal was to rout the FARC from the south and capture senior leaders. Said army chief Gen. Martin Carreno, "They found

---

[41] Libardo Cardona Martínez, "'Mi Extradición Afectará el Canje,'" *El Espectador*, December 23, 2004.

[42] U.S. Department of Justice, "High-Ranking Member of Colombian FARC Narco-Terrorist Organization Extradited to U.S. on Terrorism, Drug Charges," December 31, 2004, www.usdoj.gov/opa/pr/2004/December/04_crm_808.htm (accessed October 2, 2008).

[43] Steven Dudley, "Leader Won't Be Sent to America," *Miami Herald*, December 17, 2004.

[44] Steven Dudley, "Human Rights Watch Reported Colombian Government Peace Talks with Paramilitaries Are Flawed and Will Fail," *Miami Herald*, August 1, 2005.

[45] Juan Forero, "With Chief Missing, Colombia Militias Gain Leverage," *New York Times*, May 19, 2004.

[46] "Farc, Inc.," *Semana*, January 30, 2005.

Saddam in a hole, like a rat. These guys are rats too, hidden away in the jungle. And we can find them."[47] Armed forces chief Gen. Carlos Ospina said, "We finally had the political will that was lacking for so many years. The main factor is our president's attitude and the people's support. The FARC is 99 percent composed of people captured from the fields, uneducated people who don't know what they're doing."[48]

This was another self-serving myth. Toward mid-2004, after a calm that many read as a rebel retreat from Uribe's offensive, the FARC asserted its presence with small, scattered attacks. The attacks grew in 2005. February was deadly—fifteen soldiers killed and twenty-five wounded in Nariño; eight killed and four wounded in Putumayo; nineteen killed and five wounded in Urabá (near Panama); and others killed and wounded in smaller, dispersed attacks. Reyes announced the obvious on February 19: the retreat was over; a rebel offensive had begun. In April, rebels killed seventeen soldiers in Arauca and fought set-piece battles in southern Cauca. In Putumayo, they killed ten soldiers in March and nineteen more in May. By early August, attacks on security forces and infrastructure had paralyzed that province, where Plan Colombia had begun.

Colombia's military was paying a heavy price in the south. Patriot Plan casualty figures were quirky and likely much higher than reported. Mines, rebel-laid traps, and leishmaniasis disease caused desertions and low morale. FARC attacks continued to spread. On August 1, rebels killed fourteen policemen—but in the Sierra Nevada, far to the north. The FARC was clearly able to mount attacks all over the country.

The years since then, throughout 2006 and into mid-2007, have witnessed conflict and violence at alarming levels, with civilians, as always, caught in the middle. Numbers of known human rights violations, threats and intimidations, and displaced persons all remain high. And troubling reports of links between government security forces and paramilitaries continue to surface. Indeed, doubts exist about the degree of real paramilitary demobilization. Recent reports confirm the emergence of new groups, or the reemergence of old ones, throughout the country. Moreover, investigations as well as informed testimony under the controversial Justice and Peace Law have revealed disturbing links between lawmakers—most of them Uribe supporters—and paramilitaries. And there is strong evidence of widespread paramilitary penetration of government institutions.

---

[47] Vanessa Arrington, "Colombia Army Chief Vows to Get Top Rebel," *Associated Press*, December 19, 2003.

[48] Carol J. Williams, "Colombia Sees Gains in Its War with Rebels," *Los Angeles Times*, January 21, 2004.

Anatomy of a Failure Foretold: The Historical Constant

The failed dialogues under Pastrana represented a missed historic opportunity to initiate a viable peace with the FARC. Reasons for the failure are several. First, Plan Colombia II's military component signaled to the FARC a dramatic shift in the initial vision agreed to by Pastrana and Marulanda. Whereas the initial vision had wedded peace and drug control in a way that made peace a prerequisite, the new vision made drug control the prerequisite.

Second and closely related, drug control employed the military first to clear an area and then to provide protection for aerial spraying. The spraying targeted small-farm colonists, a population that had founded the FARC a half century ago and that remains its natural constituency. The spraying was a U.S. attack on those colonists, who had no sustainable economic alternative. Furthermore, the spraying's effects on human health and the environment piqued the FARC's keen nationalistic sense. It is ironic that Plan Colombia II's military aid has driven the FARC deeper into drugs to finance its war efforts.

Third, Pastrana was a weak, indecisive president and a poor administrator who failed to manage the peace process. Ministries had little executive oversight or coordination. Key appointees, while perhaps otherwise able, ill fit the positions they held. Pastrana gave wide powers to a few appointees but ignored others, such as his first director of Plan Colombia (and "crop substitution"), who resigned in frustration. An individual who knew Pastrana well told me, "He was a lightweight; he didn't recall what he had committed to. Everybody went his own way in Plan Colombia. Pastrana never led as he should have; peace was his flagship program. He's a good man, but very limited." Those limitations allowed his military and its U.S. backers to play a controlling role.

Fourth, U.S. military aid greatly emboldened influential elements of the Colombian military who had little interest in a peace process. In military minds, the aid conjured up visions, if not of victory, at least of forcing the FARC to talk peace on government terms. (The *despeje* was not the concession to the FARC that has often been argued; the FARC had long ruled the vast hinterland that included it.)

Fifth, the right-wing paramilitaries enjoyed their major growth and territorial expansion under Pastrana, more than doubling in size from 1998 to 2002.[49] Marulanda's frequent complaints to Pastrana were largely ignored. Powerful economic and political elites, who feared the concessions that peace might require of them, hedged their bets by discreetly backing the paramilitaries. And those elites, with the paramilitary leaders, saw the United States as their ally in a dirty war. The FARC, by contrast, saw the U.S. aid and this

---

[49] "'Paras': A paso grande," *El Tiempo*, September 25, 2004.

alliance as part of an unbroken historic pattern since Marquetalia.[50] In a word, they saw little commitment, from Pastrana or the United States, to a negotiated peace.

The failed peace opened the door for Álvaro Uribe, who had a mandate for war and enjoyed public support from the same political and economic elites who backed the paramilitaries. The high degree of paramilitary penetration of government became evident. Their involvement in drug trafficking, land-grabbing, and racketeering gave lie to the idea that they were a defense against rebels who threatened a weak state. A reduction in violence in the country's central core, especially the cities, combined with a sophisticated media manipulation to secure popular support for Uribe's "democratic security" policies. On the international front, that manipulation linked Uribe's war on the FARC to the global war on terror. U.S. support waxed enthusiastic; the military aid continued. But that support, and Uribe's clear paramilitary links, made any prospect for peace with the FARC even more remote. The UP experience, which has always haunted FARC leaders, and Uribe's U.S.-supported military offensive drove the insurgents into their long-accustomed guerrilla mode to await a more favorable moment.

A close consideration of the governments of Andrés Pastrana and Álvaro Uribe in a greater Colombian context suggests that they differed little on a deeper political level. It is telling that when Uribe named Pastrana ambassador to Washington in 2005, Pastrana, an opposition leader and outspoken critic only days before, accepted. The move recalls the United Front, a Liberal-Conservative power-sharing arrangement of a half century ago to end La Violencia. It also lends credence to a criticism by all major Colombian insurgent movements since: oligarchic control denies real political space to an opposition. Neither Pastrana nor Uribe wanted to confront that control and challenge the status quo.

It is useful to profile that status quo, for it remains the foundation of much of the country's political and criminal violence and forms the backdrop of the failed peace process. According to a 2004 United Nations report, Colombia was the world's ninth-most unequal country (by the Gini coefficient), with the wealthiest 10 percent earning 58 times as much as the

---

[50] Marquetalia was a small-farm collective founded in Caldas Department in 1961. One of its founders and leaders was Manuel Marulanda. The collective asked the government for roads and other services. Seeing this and other such "independent republics" as communist-inspired, and fearing the emergence of a Cuban-style revolutionary movement, Colombian president Alberto Lleras Camargo launched a surprise bombing raid and massive ground attack by the Colombian army on the community in May 1964. The United States supported the attack with advisers and equipment, including napalm. Marulanda and others, including Jacobo Arenas, escaped the onslaught. Marquetalia became part of the FARC founding myth and has been a rallying point for the group over the years.

poorest 10 percent.[51] A World Bank study two years later reported, "The inequality levels observed in Colombia during the 1990s were probably similar to those observed in 1938."[52] By the government's own statistics, nearly two-thirds (64.2 percent) of Colombians—85.3 percent of rural citizens—live below a US$3-per-day poverty line, and 31 percent live in extreme poverty on less than US$2 per day.[53] Much of the extreme poverty is "rural," a designation that includes 25 percent of Colombia by official counts. But the criteria for "rural" are now questioned in the Americas. A World Bank report, using an Organisation for Economic Co-operation and Development (OECD) classification, suggests that the "rural" sector may be more than twice the official size.[54] For Colombia, that would mean a "rural" sector far greater than 25 percent. But the issue is yet more complex. Much of the teeming population found in bands of misery surrounding Colombia's major cities is "urban" only in a geographic sense. These migrants from rural areas, often fleeing poverty and violence, do not have an urban ethos or urban survival skills. They are *in* but not *of* the city.

Related to rural poverty is the issue of land tenure, which has long been badly skewed. A United Nations report notes that in 1996, 0.4 percent of landowners (with farms larger than 500 hectares, 2,000 hectares being the average) controlled 45 percent of land being exploited. At the other extreme, 69 percent of landowners (with farms less than 5 hectares) controlled 36 percent.[55] The recent land-grabbing of right-wing paramilitaries has made this worse. By one account, paramilitaries acquired 5 million hectares of land—70 percent of land held by the armed groups—from 1997 to 2003, much of it among the more than 4 million hectares once held by those they displaced.[56] A 2003 study by the Contraloría General de la República (comptroller general) on *narcoreforma agraria* reports that drug capos (often paramilitaries) own 4 million prime-land hectares—48 percent of Colombia's best land.[57] In

[51] United Nations Development Programme (UNDP), *Human Development Report 2004* (New York: UNDP, 2004), 147.

[52] World Bank, *Poverty Reduction and Growth: Virtuous and Vicious Circles* (Washington, D.C.: World Bank, 2006), 54.

[53] Contraloría General de la República de Colombia (CGR), *Evaluación de la política social 2003* (Bogotá: CGR, 2004), 43–44.

[54] OECD defines "rural" sectors as having "population densities of less than 150 inhabitants per square kilometer and distance to major urban areas of more than one hour travel time." David de Ferranti, Guillermo E. Perry, William Foster, Daniel Lederman, and Alberto Valdés, *Beyond the City: The Rural Contribution to Development* (Washington, D.C.: World Bank, 2005), 2, 65.

[55] UNDP, *El conflicto, callejón con salida: Informe Nacional de Desarrollo Humano para Colombia—2003* (Bogotá: UNDP, 2003), 349–50.

[56] Juan Camilo Restrepo, "Los señores de la tierra," *El Tiempo*, September 22, 2004.

[57] "¿Es significativa la cantidad de tierras devueltas por los paramilitares?" *El Tiempo*, December 13, 2004.

a milieu where fewer than 1 percent of landowners own 60 percent of the land, the paramilitaries led a "reverse agrarian reform."[58]

An Escape from Madness, Maybe: Concluding Thoughts on U.S. Policy

U.S. support for Plan Colombia under Pastrana, followed by nearly blind support of the policies of Uribe, have made the United States a "spoiler" of the prospects for peace. A failure to distinguish between counterinsurgency, counternarcotics, and counterterrorism is a fatal U.S. policy flaw. There is little evidence that the wars on any of these fronts are being won or are even winnable. The logic of using guns, glyphosate, or extradition to defeat the FARC, force it to negotiate, or otherwise compel it is unsound. The logic criminalizes peasant farmers as well as insurgents, spraying the former to fight the latter. It treats them both as a law-enforcement problem while ignoring the underlying poverty and exclusion that drive them. To compound the error, this logic favors talks with right-wing militias—to "take them off the battlefield"—yet the militias never fought the Colombian state or the United States.

The cozy relationship of these right-wing militias with Uribe, and the "soft" position of the United States toward them (and toward Uribe) despite their overwhelming participation in the drug trade, recalls U.S. support of anticommunist opium-trafficking hill tribesmen in Vietnam and later support of drugs-for-arms deals to help Contra fighters in Nicaragua. The not-so-subtle message is that the United States looks less harshly on right-wing traffickers than on left-wing ones. A further message is that the United States favors Colombia's perverse status quo and its right-wing beneficiaries.

U.S. Colombia policy has made a mockery of Washington's stated concern for human rights. In a 2001 report, Human Rights Watch said that it "holds the Pastrana administration responsible for its dramatic and costly failure to take prompt, effective action to establish control over the security forces, break their persistent ties to paramilitary groups, and ensure respect for human rights."[59] As a former Colombian attorney general told me, Pastrana "was not committed to human rights, because he needed the military's support and had to concede to them." And the United States, he added tellingly, "manages human rights according to its interests."

Talks with the militias are in trouble. Socializing thousands of persons whose only skill is war—assuming that most of them will indeed demobilize—will require far more effort and resources than anything seen or promised to date. And there remain serious legal issues of immunity, im-

---

[58] Rachel Van Dongen, "Colombia's Poor Inherit Drug Estates," *Christian Science Monitor*, December 8, 2004.

[59] Human Rights Watch, *The "Sixth Division": Military-Paramilitary Ties and U.S. Policy in Colombia* (New York: Human Rights Watch, 2001), 2.

punity, and reparations for the legion of victims of calculated brutality and terror. Furthermore, these talks do not bring the FARC any closer to negotiations and may complicate its willingness to come to the table. The FARC will not accept impunity for the paramilitaries after the staggering UP losses. Nor does militia "demobilization" address insurgents' demands for change—change that long-term peace will require.

If Colombia is one day to find a lasting peace, the United States must come to a deeper understanding of the country and of the forces at play there. Colombia is not the "democracy" that many Washington policymakers think. Indeed, it has seen the emergence of more than a dozen insurgent movements over the past half century. Washington seems to have lost the capacity to craft policy based on a deeper understanding of world situations rather than on narrow domestic political calculations.

The United States, which has fought the FARC for almost half a century, should soften its inflexible and counterproductive policy of refusing to negotiate with anyone it deems "terrorists." It should engage the insurgents in a constructive fashion. I am no apologist for the FARC's egregious human rights abuses, but I am an apologist for important parts of their political program, including the twelve-point Common Agenda that was on the table during the Pastrana peace talks and that the FARC deems still viable. The FARC has a political program and will negotiate so long as needed changes in the status quo are on the table. A humanitarian prisoner swap, in which the FARC would release its political and military prisoners in exchange for rebels held in Colombia and in the United States (including "Simón Trinidad" and "Sonia") could break the ice and help open the door to such negotiations.

But first and foremost, Washington and Bogotá must abandon their futile quest for a military solution to the conflict. The United States should press Colombia's elites so that they will commit to a lasting peace. And let there be no doubt: that peace will demand substantial rather than token concessions from those elites and from Washington.

20

Weathering the Storm
U.S. NGO Efforts to Support and Protect Peace in Colombia

Neil Jeffery

Today a considerable number of non-governmental organizations (NGOs) in the United States are working on questions related to Colombia. Indeed, the number has risen significantly since the introduction of Plan Colombia in 2000, with organizations in almost every state active on the issue, and a considerable number gathered in the Washington, D.C., metropolitan area They include policy think tanks, church groups, and grassroots membership organizations.[1] Nonprofit organizations have focused their attention primarily on issues of humanitarian crisis and concomitant service delivery, human rights, security, rule of law, and establishment of peace. This chapter focuses on attempts by NGOs to establish peace and conditions for peace in Colombia, rather than on their work connected to the humanitarian and human rights crisis in the country.

Among U.S. NGOs, no one set of ideas prevails for how to respond to the many challenges facing Colombia, particularly in building a lasting peace. Over the past few years, however, two main clusters of opinion have emerged. The first broad cluster of NGOs strongly believes that the only solution to the conflict lies in a negotiated settlement between the various warring parties. They see the role of international governments as fundamental in creating the conditions to foster negotiation, with the U.S. government's diplomatic and political influence crucial to this effort.

Many, though not all, within this group also believe that the U.S. government should divert resources from military spending in Colombia to increase levels of social and economic aid as a prerequisite for fostering the conditions

---

[1] Colombia Steering Committee, interview by the author, Washington, D.C., May 11, 2005. The group estimates that in 2005, 100 to 150 NGOs had significant Colombia coverage in their programs. This compares to a mere handful in 2000.

for peace.[2] Indeed, this group succeeded in 2007—after several years of concerted and sustained effort and after the 2006 elections, in which the Democratic Party took control of both houses of Congress—in significantly influencing the direction of U.S. policy toward Colombia.[3] Both military aid and funds for aerial spraying are likely to be reduced; direct funding to victims of violence, such as displaced people and Afro-Colombian and indigenous communities, as well as to victims' legal-aid programs and resources for investigating and prosecuting human rights abuses, will probably be increased; and human rights conditions pertaining to military aid are likely to expand to cover a larger percentage of the budget.

This group of NGOs believes that increased economic assistance of this type would provide alternative employment opportunities, particularly for those traditionally drawn to the ranks of the illegal armed actors for reasons of economic need. Moreover, these NGOs argue that the role of Colombian citizens in designing, implementing, and leading local peace initiatives is crucial to the eventual success of the national peace proposals. They consider local civil society and citizen-led initiatives the fundamental blocks on which regional and national programs can be built. This cluster of organizations is best represented by the Colombia Steering Committee, a grouping of approximately forty NGOs based in Washington, D.C. Many small citizens' organizations across the United States share its core philosophy. Its principal members include the Latin America Working Group (cochair), the U.S. Office on Colombia (cochair), the Washington Office on Latin America, the Center for International Policy, and Witness for Peace, among others. Member organizations of the Catholic Church, such as Catholic Relief Services, have been among the most active in seeking to advance the peace agenda in Colombia.

The second cluster of NGOs believes that negotiation is important but only after decisive military action that will force the belligerent parties to the negotiating table. In essence, this group regards a military solution as the only realistic route to bringing about a cessation of hostilities and the best way to help Colombia's citizens achieve lasting peace. As a result, they support a continued significant level of U.S. military funding to Colombia as a means to realize that military goal more quickly. Key advocates of this position include the Inter-American Dialogue and the Heritage Foundation. Both groups of NGOs strongly support respect for human rights and the rule of law, and both have been successful in winning influential allies in the U.S. Congress,

---

[2] Lisa Haugaard, Adam Isacson, Kimberly Stanton, John Walsh, and John Vogt, *Blueprint for a New Colombia Policy* (Washington, D.C.: Latin America Working Group Education Fund, Center for International Policy, Washington Office on Latin America, and U.S. Office on Colombia, 2005).

[3] At the time of this writing, both the House of Representatives and the Senate had approved the changes, but they required confirmation in conference committee and the president's signature.

persuading uncommitted members to sign up with their cause. This has meant that Colombia, compared to other international issues, has become a highly debated issue in the U.S. Congress.[4]

Since 2002, the U.S. position has included vigorous support for President Álvaro Uribe Vélez in virtually all aspects of policy, strong backing for the Colombian military (including approximately a half-billion dollars in military aid annually), acceptance of the military solution as the most probable outcome to the conflict, a lackadaisical and insufficient approach to peace negotiations, and strong defense of the rule of law. In testimony before the U.S. House of Representatives' Committee on Foreign Affairs on May 11, 2005, Adolfo A. Franco, assistant administrator for the United States Agency for International Development (USAID) Bureau for Latin America and the Caribbean, insisted, referring to Plan Colombia, that "strengthening the capacity of the state, especially the military capability, is key to the success of any national plan." President Bush emphasized his administration's support for this approach during his visit to Colombia in November 2004. In a press conference with President Uribe, Bush affirmed his unflinching support: "If I didn't think he had an effective strategy and the willingness to fight the FARC [Fuerzas Armadas Revolucionarias de Colombia], I wouldn't be standing here in this great nation saying I'm going to work with [the U.S.] Congress to continue the support."

Many U.S. NGOs have been broadly critical of U.S. policy, particularly as it relates to strategies for a peaceful solution to the conflict in Colombia. Some have produced their own proposals, such as the "Blueprint for a Better Colombia Policy," that seek to influence U.S. policy outcomes.[5] Others reflect the suggestions and priorities of their "partners" or "constituents" in Colombia.[6] Many NGOs have undertaken relatively sophisticated efforts to inform the thinking of U.S. Congress members on these issues through regular written and oral briefings or visits by Colombian partners.

Some U.S. NGOs recognized that a proportion of what they recommended overlapped with the proposals of the European Union. The majority of EU countries have promoted strong but occasionally tempered support for President Uribe, strong backing for a negotiated settlement as the only mechanism to resolve the conflict, and staunch defense of the rule of law and human rights. This led to an unspoken alliance between EU officials and U.S. NGOs on certain policy issues for several years. Pragmatists among U.S.

[4] See debates on U.S. Colombia policy in the House of Representatives in 2000, 2001, 2002, 2003, 2004, and 2005.

[5] Haugaard et al., *Blueprint for a New Colombia Policy.*

[6] In 2003, Catholic Relief Services in the United States established its In Solidarity with Colombia program to support and represent the views and actions of the Catholic National Secretariat for Social Ministry and Caritas Colombia. For a detailed discussion, see Chapter 9 by Héctor Henao Gaviria in this volume.

NGOs accept that supporting an existing international government position provides a bigger "critical mass" on an issue, and for the EU officials it has always been useful to be able to point to domestic American support for their position when negotiating with U.S. authorities.

But in broad terms, the U.S. administration's view of how the international community should engage with Colombian authorities has prevailed since 2002. President Uribe has received strong military and political backing from the international community for his ongoing military offensive. To a large extent, he has been able to ignore criticism from the United Nations, international NGOs, and Colombian civil society on the lack of progress in peace negotiations. Peace talks with the guerrilla groups have produced little progress, while civilian casualties remain high. The Colombian government was effectively able to veto the work and appointment of the UN secretary-general's peace envoy. Demobilization of paramilitary forces has proceeded despite considerable international disquiet regarding the proposals.

Security concerns and the fight against terrorism have remained at the top of the international agenda for Colombia, to the detriment of efforts to establish formal peace negotiations. The governments of Argentina, Brazil, Canada, Chile, the European Union and its member states, Japan, Mexico, Norway, Switzerland, and the United States all confirmed this reality by signing the Cartagena Declaration of February 2005 on international cooperation with Colombia, which declared, "The governmental representatives present reaffirmed their support for the Colombian government in its efforts to improve the well-being and security of all citizens, and in the fight against terrorism and illegal drugs."

Some evidence suggests that the European Union has closed the gap between itself and the United States over the past few years, bringing its views more in line with those of U.S. authorities, in an attempt to strengthen diplomatic relations strained by the war in Iraq and by opposing views on how to tackle the emerging situation of Iran's nuclear program. The Cartagena Declaration, setting out the role of the international community concerning Colombia, more closely reflects the U.S. position than the earlier London Declaration of July 2003. These changes show the evolution of the EU position.

For example, the London Declaration's strong support for the UN secretary-general's peace envoy contrasts strikingly with the failure even to mention the existence of the position in the Cartagena Declaration. Over the period, a limited number of EU states, such as the United Kingdom and Spain, announced the beginning of military aid to the Colombian authorities.[7]

These developments point to a simple conclusion: U.S. NGOs have been unsuccessful in their attempts to bring the prospects for peace negotiations

---

[7] On October 1, 2004, the *Guardian* newspaper reported that 237 UK MPs signed a "motion, demanding that UK military help be suspended [to Colombia] because of human rights abuses and suspected links between the security forces and rightwing death squads."

in Colombia closer. Despite their recently expanded ability to influence the U.S. Congress's spending decisions on Colombia, they have been unable to persuade the U.S. authorities, the Colombian authorities, or, to a lesser extent, the European Union, to seriously consider their proposals. Many observers would argue that this outcome results from domestic political agendas, in which Colombia generally arouses scant interest among U.S. politicians—and even less among voters—and that it does not reflect the quality of U.S. NGOs' work. NGOs of the second persuasion mentioned above may argue that strong support for the Colombian military campaign is in fact a necessary step toward peace and that, therefore, their work to increase military aid has paradoxically brought Colombia closer to stability. The arguments of the two differing NGO groups can be seen regularly in the pages of serious U.S. press.[8]

Nonetheless, in several areas, the action of U.S. NGOs has been helpful in preparing the ground for an eventual peace deal or in protecting the limited efforts that exist today.

Maintaining the Debate on Peace in the U.S. Congress

Despite the deep sense of frustration and desperation among Colombians, many still believe that the conflict must be ended through negotiation. Although the guerrillas and the paramilitaries are strong enough to seriously weaken the state, neither group is capable of overthrowing the government; conversely, Colombia's military, even with U.S. aid, is unlikely to defeat either group. Colombia's fifty thousand combat troops fall far short of the 10-to-1 advantage recommended by military experts to defeat the thirty thousand members of illegal armed groups in the country.

Even persuading U.S. Congress members to listen to these arguments is a challenge, since Colombia ranks nowhere among most senators' or representatives' priorities. Despite this, U.S. NGOs have managed to keep Colombia on the radar screen as an issue for debate in the U.S. Congress over the past few years. This is no small achievement, given the many competing domestic and international issues and the recent heavy focus of foreign policy on Israel, Iraq, Iran, and China. Debates on Colombia took place on the floor of the House of Representatives every year from 2000 to 2007.[9] Although these have typically focused on the nature and development of U.S. policy toward the country, they have provided a minimal opportunity to air arguments on the possibilities for peace.

---

[8] See, for example, Michael Shifter, "'Plan Colombia' Isn't Working," *Washington Post*, December 10, 2000.

[9] For more information on these debates, see Latin America Working Group, www.lawg.org (accessed September 16, 2008).

The understanding of members of Congress of the complexities of the Colombian conflict, particularly on the House side, has increased, at least to a limited extent, over this period. Much of this increased awareness is attributable to the ongoing debate driven by U.S. NGOs. Successive votes on amendments to the Foreign Operations Appropriations Bill in the House have highlighted the growing number of members concerned about the impact of U.S. policy in Colombia.[10] In 2007, this concern culminated in both houses' approval of the proposed Foreign Operations Bill, which contained significantly revised funding figures for key U.S. government–funded activities in Colombia. Many, although by no means all, of these members of Congress also believe that the U.S. administration should instigate a proactive policy to promote peace negotiations.

Providing Opportunities for Colombian Civil Society to Speak to U.S. Policymakers

Civil society peace initiatives have gained greater relevance with time as the armed conflict has continued to hurt the civilian population in Colombia. Civil society's involvement will be crucial in any eventual negotiated settlement and in rebuilding the country after the war. The checks and balances of a strong, vibrant civil society—including journalists, human rights advocates, labor unions, women's organizations, ethnic minorities, religious institutions, academics, student groups, and community associations—are fundamental to establishing strong, transparent, and accountable government institutions and respect for rule of law.

U.S. NGOs have been particularly active, especially since the start of Plan Colombia, in providing opportunities for representatives of Colombian civil society to speak directly to U.S. policymakers. This has allowed congressional offices to meet privately with visiting Colombian experts, victims of the conflict, and representatives of civilian-led peacebuilding initiatives, to deepen their understanding of U.S. engagement in Colombia and of efforts to build peace. The prospects for peace in Colombia are increasingly bound to the policy of the U.S. government. Direct relations with U.S. policymakers can have a profound effect on Colombian peacebuilding initiatives' credibility, recognition, and ability to operate.

Groups such as Witness for Peace, Catholic Relief Services, and Washington-based NGOs including the U.S. Office on Colombia, among others, have organized frequent trips to Washington for representatives of many national and regional Colombian civilian-led peacebuilding initiatives to promote the concepts of a negotiated settlement and greater civil society participation in the official negotiation process. These individuals often visit other parts of

---

[10] In 2003, 209 U.S. House members voted in favor of the McGovern Amendment to the Foreign Operations Appropriations Bill.

the United States during their stay and frequently have enjoyed extended opportunities to talk directly to the U.S. public at church assemblies, town hall meetings, and community gatherings. Although the U.S. media generally follow government policy developments as their lead for Colombia stories, the almost constant local publicity produced by these Colombian peace representatives has fostered interest among a growing network of U.S. citizens in promoting peace efforts in Colombia. They have played an important complementary role in convincing some Congress members of the importance of civilian-led peacebuilding efforts in Colombia.

Among the many visits to Washington by Colombians are some notable examples. In 2001, U.S. NGOs provided resources for fifteen representatives of different peacebuilding organizations from the Comité de Enlace (The Linking Group) coalition to visit Washington, D.C. The Institute for Conflict Analysis and Resolution at George Mason University helped organize the event and gave the group a two-day capacity-building workshop before its meetings in Washington. The delegation met with the Department of State, Department of Defense, U.S. Congress members, the United States Institute of Peace, and a wide variety of U.S. NGOs. For almost the first time, they were able to raise with U.S. policymakers issues concerning the peaceful resolution of the conflict and a more inclusive role for civil society in the negotiation process.

In March 2005, during a visit organized by the U.S. Office on Colombia, five Colombian civil society experts were invited to attend a Washington, D.C., seminar on how best to create U.S. congressional support for civilian-led peacebuilding initiatives in Colombia.[11] The group represented a broad range of organizations from the Colombian peace movement. It included Magdala Velásquez of the National Peace Council, a formal body representing civil society in the peace negotiations between government and guerrillas during the Pastrana administration; Isabel Ortiz, director and founder of the Women and Future Foundation, an NGO focusing on women's rights and peace; Jenny Neme, codirector of Justapaz, a Mennonite Church NGO dedicated to seeking peaceful solutions to the conflict; Javier Moncayo Plata, president of the Red Nacional de Programas Regionales de Desarrollo y Paz (REDPRODEPAZ); and Moisés Medrano Bohórquez, coordinator of REDPRODEPAZ's Montes de María peace and development program. The participants attended a series of meetings with guest speakers in Washington, designed to give them an in-depth understanding of how Capitol Hill functions, the most effective way to build relationships with U.S. policymakers, and a greater comprehension of the history of U.S. policy on Colombia. At the end of the seminar, the group conducted a briefing sponsored by Rep. James McGovern (D-Mass.) and Rep. Joseph Pitts (R-Pa.) in a House office

---

[11] See www.usofficeoncolombia.org (accessed September 16, 2008).

building. The event was attended by representatives from the U.S. Congress and administration and served as an extraordinary opportunity for participants in Colombian civilian-led peacebuilding initiatives to argue their case. They welcomed the opportunity both as a practical way to learn the ropes of establishing and strengthening links with policymakers and as an excellent platform to put forward their concepts of peacebuilding. As a result of the briefing, they made a priority of identifying U.S. Congress members willing to champion local peacebuilding efforts in Colombia.

U.S. NGO groups have hosted a steady stream of Colombian civil society visitors. In June 2006, for example, the Washington Office on Latin America, Global Rights, the American Friends Service Committee (AFSC), the Inter-American Foundation, and others sponsored a delegation to Washington of fourteen Afro-Colombian grassroots leaders to attend the first-ever international conference of grassroots Afro-Colombian leaders and to meet with U.S. policymakers. The Initiative for Inclusive Security has sponsored a series of visits by Colombian women engaged in peacemaking efforts; and the AFSC has sponsored visits of civil society leaders to highlight the impact of the conflict and of U.S. policies on indigenous people, Afro-Colombians, and women in Colombia.

In late 2008, the Colombia Committee for Human Rights partnered with Consultoría para los Derechos Humanos y el Desplazamiento (CODHES, or Consultancy on Human Rights and Displacement) and the U.S. Institute of Peace to prepare a meeting in Washington, D.C., of seventy U.S. and Colombian civil society leaders to develop common strategies for a peace agenda for the incoming U.S. administration of Barack Obama.

Providing Information to U.S. Policymakers

The work of U.S. NGOs has been crucial in providing U.S. policymakers with "user-friendly" materials on Colombian civil society and civilian-led peacebuilding initiatives. The task of translating information and analytical discourse from Colombian organizations into practical, digestible, and informative chunks with bullet points and recommendations relevant to U.S. policymakers is crucial in the process of winning support and recognition in the corridors of the U.S. Congress. For example, the "Blueprint for a Better Colombia Policy" took testimony, reports, letters, suggestions, comments, and other inputs from a wide variety of Colombian civil society organizations and distilled them into succinct policy analysis and recommendations for policy change, allowing the target audience to infer the benefits of the proposed changes.

Another excellent example has been the campaign to inform U.S. policymakers about the efforts and achievements of REDPRODEPAZ.[12] This project

---

[12] See REDPRODEPAZ, www.redprodepaz.org (accessed September 16, 2008).

is the only example of a truly national civilian-led peacebuilding initiative that has the capacity to affect the lives of millions of ordinary Colombians. REDPRODEPAZ has identified the principal "added value" of the project and of the peace laboratories as their capacity to create partnerships among public, private, and community interests on the basis of an agreed regional development plan; it notes that the success of any one project in translating economic resources available into real benefits for the region depends on its ability to engage in productive dialogue with a broad range of stakeholders: NGOs, community organizations, business, and government.

This is demonstrated by the direct involvement of business in the project. Interconexión Eléctrica SA (ISA), a Latin American regional electricity and telecommunications group, has supported REDPRODEPAZ since its inception; the first meeting of the REDPRODEPAZ network took place in the company's offices in Bogotá.[13] The company finances twelve of the first seventeen programs and provides technical assistance where necessary. Ecopetrol, the state-owned oil company, provides technical assistance to the peace laboratories in Magdalena Medio through a program that encourages employees to volunteer their time. The National Federation of Cacao Growers (Federación Nacional de Cacaoteros), the National Federation of Coffee Growers (Federación de Cafeteros), and several energy companies, such as TPL and Merilectrica, are supporting the venture. The Catholic Church has also played a pivotal role in establishing and managing several of the REDPRODEPAZ programs.

An immediate and vital task for U.S. NGOs is to guarantee that U.S. policymakers have a clear understanding of the potential contribution to the construction of peace that civilian-led projects such as REDPRODEPAZ can make. The project and its present achievements are virtually unknown among U.S. policymakers, and its possible future role in peacebuilding has yet to be recognized by Congress or the administration. The two Washington visits of REDPRODEPAZ president Javier Moncayo that were sponsored by U.S. NGOs were an important start. The next great challenge for U.S. NGOs is to translate the enormous potential of this project into user-friendly policy analysis and recommendations for U.S. Congress members, enabling more locally appropriate, inclusive, and results-oriented policy creation from the United States.

Supporting the Development of Colombian Civil Society

The role of international NGOs was crucial in ensuring the inclusion of Colombian civil society at the table during international governmental donors' meetings in London in July 2003 and in Cartagena in February 2005.[14] Both

---

[13] See ISA, www.isa.com.co (accessed October 2, 2008).

[14] "Pronouncement of International NGOs to Meeting on International Coordination and Aid for Colombia, Cartagena de Indias," February 3, 2005, www.usofficeoncolombia.org (accessed October 2, 2008).

gatherings were central to establishing a framework for future international relations with Colombia.

Before the London meeting, U.S. NGOs were slower than their European counterparts to catch on to the meeting's importance for civil society and its future role in the construction of peace in Colombia. At Cartagena, however, U.S. NGOs contributed more effectively by establishing among U.S. Congress members at least a minimal level of understanding of civil society's priorities going into the conference and by working actively with U.S. policymakers to encourage the full participation of civil society in all deliberations at the meeting.

Colombian civil society demonstrated considerable dexterity in responding quickly to the opportunities arising from the London conference. Within a few weeks, they had formed the Alianza, or Alliance of Social and Likeminded Organizations for International Cooperation for Peace and Democracy in Colombia, to act as an interlocutor between Colombian and international authorities. Many international observers have recognized that the formation of the Alianza, and its subsequent work with a group of international government representatives (the G-24) to create some of the initial building blocks for the construction of peace in Colombia, is a real leap forward in the quality and sophistication of the work of Colombian civil society.[15] U.S. NGOs have strongly supported this development by providing informal advice and offering opportunities for representatives of the new Alianza to present their work to U.S. policymakers and members of Congress.

This tremendous effort by Colombian NGOs has borne fruit. At the Cartagena conference, virtually all the international government delegations praised Colombian civil society representatives for their constructive attitude and levelheaded engagement.[16] In particular, the international community acknowledged the ability and willingness of NGOs, the traditional standard-bearers of civil society opinion, to present a joint statement with other civil society representatives such as business associations, churches, philanthropic foundations, and community organizations.[17] Many international governmental delegations warmly welcomed the NGOs' recognition of the necessity to broaden their coalition for peace in Colombia. Some went further, urging NGOs to build further links with the middle classes and

---

[15] U.S. Office on Colombia, Washington Office on Latin America, Center for International Policy, Latin America Working Group, Lutheran World Relief, U.S. Labor Education in the Americas Project, Witness for Peace, Jesuit Conference USA, Colombia Human Rights Committee, United Church of Christ Justice and Witness Ministries, and Dominican Sisters of the Presentation, "Letter to Secretary of State Condoleezza Rice, January, 28, 2005," www.usofficeoncolombia.org (accessed October 2, 2008).

[16] Author interview with EU representatives to the Cartagena conference, Cartagena, February 3, 2005.

[17] Director of the Office of the United Nations High Commissioner for Human Rights in Colombia, interview by the author, Cartagena, February 4, 2005.

business as the only viable option to construct the broad coalition needed to bring peace to Colombia.[18]

Supporting and Protecting Civil Society and Civilian-Led Peacebuilding Initiatives

Amid the violence of the Colombian armed conflict, many civil society and civilian-led peacebuilding initiatives have emerged at national, regional, and local levels to complement government-sponsored proposals. These initiatives have often championed democratic participation, the strengthening of civilian institutions, and sustainable livelihoods as solutions to the armed conflict.

The late 1990s saw a flowering of peace initiatives. The Citizens' Mandate for Peace, Life, and Liberty, organized in 1997 by members of the business community, the Catholic Church and other churches, social movements, and REDEPAZ, saw nearly ten million people vote overwhelmingly in favor of a negotiated political settlement and full respect for human rights and international humanitarian law. As discussed in Chapter 2 by Adam Isacson and Jorge Rojas in this volume, this served as the first coherent expression of civil society's demand for peace and a role in the negotiation process. In 1998, the Permanent Civil Society Assembly for Peace, whose first convention drew between three thousand and four thousand members of varied sectors of Colombian society, committed itself to a negotiated political solution to the armed conflict. The assembly has sought to promote civil society as the principal protagonist in peace negotiations and to develop a civil society agenda for a peace settlement.

Colombian communities, frustrated by the failures of recent state-sponsored peace processes and by the marginalization of civil society in peace negotiations, have begun to initiate their own solutions in the form of peace communities, indigenous communities in resistance, and peace and development programs, among many other locally appropriate models for peace. Peace communities are typically isolated rural communities situated in areas of territorial dispute between belligerent forces. They have pledged themselves to active neutrality, refusing the presence of any weapons or members of armed groups in their precincts. They refuse to trade, negotiate, or interact with any armed actors.[19] Colombia's indigenous communities have resisted threats to their way of life for centuries and, most recently, have employed nonviolent resistance measures, such as the Indigenous Guard established by the Nasa people of Cauca Department. The Nasa community, caught between paramilitary and guerrilla forces vying for control of their territory,

---

[18] Author interview with European Union representatives to the Cartagena conference, Cartagena, February 3, 2005.

[19] See "Peace in Colombia," www.peaceincolombia.org (accessed September 16, 2008).

have reestablished a tradition of an unarmed civilian defense force that seeks to protect and preserve their way of life and basic human rights. In contrast to peace communities, the indigenous population has often been willing to negotiate directly with armed actors to consolidate its autonomy.[20]

The Pastoral Social of the Catholic Church has actively promoted the participation of citizens in peacebuilding and national and international solidarity with marginalized and rural populations affected by conflict.[21] Among Protestant church organizations, the Mennonite Church's Christian Center for Justice, Peace, and Nonviolent Action, Justapaz, has maintained a long-standing commitment to nonviolence, positive transformation of conflict, and peacebuilding. Since 1990, Justapaz has sought to strengthen the role of individuals, churches, and communities, through a broad range of programs and training modules.

Because of their work to protect and promote peace and peacebuilding, all the civilian-led initiatives mentioned here have been targeted by armed actors. U.S. NGO action to protect this diverse set of projects and individuals has taken many forms: performing investigative research, organizing letter-writing campaigns, participating in congressional briefings, facilitating public statements by members of Congress and congressional visits to the region, generating media coverage, making requests to the Inter-American Court of Human Rights for special protective measures, making requests to the U.S. administration to withhold military aid, and so on. Most notably, in July 2004, as a result of weeks of behind-the-scenes work by U.S. NGOs, twenty-three U.S. senators, including presidential and vice presidential candidates John Kerry and John Edwards, sent a letter to Colombian president Uribe expressing serious concerns about threats and attacks against civil society representatives and human rights and peace workers. After the letter's publication, *El Tiempo*, Colombia's major daily newspaper, described the issue of human rights and peace in Colombia as now "figuring prominently on [the senators'] agenda."

Notwithstanding such notable successes, U.S. NGO action to protect civil society peace workers has achieved only partial results; in the majority of cases, NGOs have struggled to translate increased concern or public awareness into a reduction in the number of threats or killings. For example, according to the U.S. State Department's 2005 Country Report, in May 2004, four armed and masked men forcibly entered the offices of the Permanent Civil Society Assembly for Peace in Bogotá, searched the premises, and stole a cellular phone and petty cash. Similar incidents occurred again on October

---

[20] U.S. Office on Colombia, "Colombian Indigenous Communities: Struggling for Survival," February 2005, www.usofficeoncolombia.org (accessed October 2, 2008).

[21] Director of the Pastoral Social in Colombia, interview by author, London, June 9, 2005.

18 and November 10, 2004, when armed intruders tried to retrieve information from the assembly's computer system.[22]

Local peace initiatives in conflict zones such as peace communities or indigenous communities face constant threats of persecution, kidnapping, illegal detention, and assassination by all armed groups. Since its declaration of active neutrality in 1997, the San José peace community has experienced a series of massacres, including one on February 20–21, 2005, when, allegedly, eight people were murdered.[23] Although the Nasa community has achieved some success, members of the indigenous guard continue to be killed or threatened by the illegal armed actors. According to the Colombian National Indigenous Organization (ONIC), in September 2004, the Nasa leader and mayor of Toribio, Arquimedes Vitonas, was kidnapped but later released under pressure from the indigenous guard. In April 2005, the FARC besieged the municipality and indigenous reserve of Toribio; more than a dozen civilians were wounded and a ten-year-old child was killed.[24]

Faith-based programs, too, are vulnerable to attack. According to the U.S. State Department's 2005 Country Report, both paramilitaries and guerrillas harassed, threatened, and sometimes killed religious leaders and activists. According to the Evangelical Council of Churches (CEDECOL), an umbrella organization of hundreds of Protestant and evangelical churches, as of September 30, 2004, illegal armed groups had killed eighteen church leaders.[25]

One notable exception to this litany of execrable acts is the case of Ricardo Esquivia Ballestas, founder and director of Justapaz. In 2004, Justapaz reported that Esquivia Ballestas was to be falsely accused of membership in the Ejército Popular de Liberación (EPL) and the FARC's Thirty-Seventh Front—both terrorist organizations—according to an internal memo from the government's Administrative Department for Security.[26] U.S. NGOs' coordinated letter and fax campaign, combined with clear and frequent declarations from U.S. Congress members, led to retraction of the charges. Indeed, U.S. NGO actions have had greatest impact in affecting situations that have already attained significant international recognition.

---

[22] U.S. State Department, Bureau of Democracy, Human Rights, and Labor, "Colombia: Country Reports on Human Rights Practices—2005," March 8, 2006, www.state.gov/g/drl/rls/hrrpt/2005/61721.htm (accessed September 16, 2008).

[23] See Peace in Colombia, www.peaceincolombia.org (accessed September 16, 2008).

[24] Amnesty International, "Colombia: Amnesty International Condemns Attacks against the Population of Toribio" (press release, AMR 23/011/2005, April 20, 2005), www.amnesty.org/en/related_information/1898?page=11 (accessed September 16, 2008).

[25] U.S. State Department, Bureau of Democracy, Human Rights, and Labor, "Colombia: Country Reports."

[26] Director of Justapaz, interview by the author, Bogotá, January 31, 2005.

Conclusions

At the moment, prospects for peace in Colombia look poor. They are too dependent on the domestic agendas of the United States and Colombia, and the inconsistent and unfocused foreign policy of the European Union. In this capricious and challenging environment, U.S. NGOs have managed to achieve some imperfect but significant results: first, the partial protection of some civil society leaders and civilian-led peacebuilding initiatives; second, assistance and guidance to Colombian civil society as it goes through the necessary steps of building a broader coalition to address the complex issues of peacebuilding; and finally, ensuring that peacebuilding has remained on the agenda of U.S. Congress members and other policymakers—a situation strengthened to some extent by U.S. NGOs' recent ability to influence U.S. policy toward Colombia.

All these are necessary but insufficient steps on the long road to constructing pragmatic and long-term peaceful solutions to the many challenges inherent in Colombia's conflict. For the process to have any chance of lasting success, Colombian civil society must play a central role. Without a doubt, U.S. NGOs will continue to support and protect their efforts to the limited extent possible. However, a great challenge for U.S. NGOs is to persuade U.S. and European authorities to engage seriously with Colombian civil society. They must persuade international policymakers to back civil society's efforts openly, vigorously, and enthusiastically as the only viable long-term solution to Colombia's woes.

21

The European Union and the Transformation of the Colombian Conflict

Sabine Kurtenbach

Although the European Union has developed a strategy in its relations with the Andean region and Colombia specifically, national differences have been notable in recent years due to diverging European views and readings of developments in Colombia.[1] A common EU foreign policy is in the making, but it coexists with national foreign-policy interests, strategies, and priorities, and decision making remains a prerogative of the European Council and the governments of the member states. As a result, neither European perceptions of the developments in Colombia nor the approaches of the different European actors toward Colombia are homogeneous, and European foreign policy is a mirror of the minimal consensus of the European member states' governments, which is based on a set of shared principles and norms.[2]

The main point of reference inside the European Union concerning its relations with Colombia has been Plan Colombia. The National Development Strategy of the Pastrana administration (1998–2002) was a US$7.5 billion program seeking to reduce drug cultivation by 50 percent over 6 years and addressing some of Colombia's long-standing development problems, such as the weakness of state institutions and their lack of national presence. The

---

[1] See Christián Freres, "The European Union as a Global 'Civilian Power': Development Cooperation in EU–Latin American Relations," *Journal of Inter-American Studies and World Affairs* 42, no. 2 (2000): 63–85; Christián Freres and Karin Pacheco, *Nuevos horizontes andinos. Escenarios regionales y políticas de la Unión Europea* (Caracas: Nueva Sociedad, 2002).

[2] On the European Union's Common Foreign and Security Policy, see Michael E. Smith, *Europe's Foreign and Security Policy. The Institutionalization of Cooperation* (Cambridge, UK: Cambridge University Press, 2004) and Fraser Cameron, *An Introduction to European Foreign Policy* (London: Routledge, 2007).

Clinton administration and the conservative Spanish government of José María Aznar (1995–2003) made significant contributions to Plan Colombia and supported the modernization of Colombia's armed forces and police. The European Parliament, on the other hand, took a clear stance against Plan Colombia, as did European non-governmental organizations (NGOs) lobbying at the national and European levels.[3] Although the majority of EU governments criticized Plan Colombia mostly because of the militarization of drug eradication, they and the vast majority of actors (including the U.S. government) did support the peace process that President Pastrana began with the Fuerzas Armadas Revolucionarias de Colombia (FARC) and Ejército de Liberación Nacional (ELN) guerrilla groups.

Differences inside the European Union became more obvious when Álvaro Uribe was elected president of Colombia in May 2002 and implemented his "hard hand" policy toward the guerrilla organizations. Although Spain and the United Kingdom supported Uribe, other member states, the European Parliament, media, and NGOs criticized the humanitarian costs and authoritarian tendencies of this policy. When Uribe visited Europe in February 2004, the lack of support became obvious. The change of government in Spain following the general elections in March 2004 made an important contribution to a growing coherence in EU politics toward Colombia, because the Zapatero administration is more concerned than its predecessor about Europe and is strengthening its relations with France and Germany and is following less the political priorities of the United States. This is important for the European Union's relations with Latin America due to the historical special relationship Spain has with the region, for example, via the Ibero-American Community of Nations.

Issues for the European Union in the Colombian Conflict

Neither the European Union nor the member states and NGOs see Colombia's armed conflict as one of their top priorities or perceive it as a direct

---

[3]On Europe and armed conflicts, see Organisation for Economic Co-operation and Development, *The DAC Guidelines: Helping Prevent Violent Conflict*, including the supplement from 2001, www.oecd.org/dataoecd/15/54/1886146.pdf (accessed September 16, 2008). For an overview on EU peacebuilding, see Michael Merlingen with Rasa Ostrauskaite, *European Union Peacebuilding and Policing* (London: Routledge, 2006). For an overview of the actors and the shaping of European policy toward Colombia, see Philippe De Lombaerde, Geert Haghebaert, Socorro Ramírez, and An Vranckx, "EU Policies towards the Colombian Conflict: Policy Coordination and Interregionalism" (OBREAL/EULARO background paper, April 2006), www.obreal.unibo.it/File.aspx?IdFile=450 (accessed September 16, 2008). On Plan Colombia, see Joaquín Roy, "European Perceptions of Plan Colombia: A Virtual Contribution to a Virtual War and Peace Plan?" (Miami, 2001), http://permanent.access.gpo.gov/lps12375/00023.pdf (accessed September 16, 2008); Transnational Institute, "Europe and Plan Colombia" (Drugs and Conflict Paper no. 1, Amsterdam, 2001); and Centro de Investigación para la Paz (CIP-FUHEM), *Colombia y Europa: el papel europeo en un futuro proceso de paz*, Papeles de Cuestiones Internacionales (Madrid), no. 83 (2003), 1101–64.

security challenge.[4] The European Union's conception of security is based on a broader scheme of human security and is not reduced to the absence of violent conflict. This is one of the fundamental reasons that the European Union and most member states see a military solution to the Colombian conflict as unrealistic. Although EU members have no doubts about the need to strengthen the capacities of the Colombian state, many in Europe believe that efforts to that end should not be limited to military capacities but must include strengthening the rule of law and programs for social integration and economic development.

An issue with direct security implications for the European Union is Colombia's illegal drug industry and its connection to organized crime. Although most of Colombia's cocaine goes to the North American market, Spain and the Netherlands are important entry points in Europe.[5] The European Union's antidrug strategy is based on a regional approach that aims to avoid the so-called balloon effect, in which the application of pressure on a producing country shifts cultivation elsewhere instead of reducing production.[6] Therefore, the issue of drug trafficking in Colombia is part of interregional relations. Since 1995, it has been dealt with in discussions between the European Union and the Community of Andean Nations (CAN). The Andean region is the only one with which the European Union has a special high-level dialogue on drugs, based on the assumption of shared responsibility of producer and consumer countries for the problem. There have been nine declarations of the Coordination Mechanism on Drugs since 1999, the most recent in March 2008. During President Uribe's visit to Europe in February 2004, he signed an agreement with Europol that would make it easier to share information on drug trafficking and money laundering. Inside Colombia, the European Union's antidrug strategy rests mainly on programs of voluntary eradication of illicit poppy and coca plants, and crop-substitution programs that provide support for farmers who agree to grow alternative products.

---

[4] At the end of 2003, the European Union passed its first "European Security Strategy" (known as the Solana Paper), which elaborates European perceptions of the main global challenges and threats as well as European responses. Terrorism, the proliferation of weapons of mass destruction, regional conflicts, state failure, and organized crime are seen as major global problems that the Common Foreign and Security Policy needs to address. See Council of the European Union, "A Secure Europe in a Better World," http://ue.eu.int/ueDocs/cms_Data/docs/pressdata/en/misc/78348.pdf (accessed September 16, 2008).

[5] According to the United Nation's *World Drug Report* (Geneva: United Nations, 2004), coca consumption in 2002 was increasing in Europe while slightly decreasing in North America. One hundred twenty-five metric tons of cocaine have been seized in North America; forty-five in Western Europe.

[6] In recent years, coca production moved from Peru and Bolivia to Colombia because of the eradication policies and is now moving back, as shown in the different editions of the UN *World Drug Report.*

This is one reason European governments opposed the massive fumigation that took place in Colombia with U.S. support.[7]

Another important issue for all European actors is the protection of human rights, seen as the foundation for conflict resolution and peaceful coexistence at the local and national levels. EU projects, like those of many individual member states and NGOs, support the victims of violence, such as displaced people and refugees, as well as Colombian human rights groups, programs on human rights education, and the fight against impunity. Colombia was chosen as a focus country of the EU program for promotion of human rights and democratization in countries outside the European Union. The strengthening of an independent judiciary and the promotion of the rule of law and good governance are central in the field of human rights and as instruments of the drug-control strategy. At the same time, cooperation with state agencies aims to bolster the capacities needed to fulfill the responsibility of a democratic state to protect its citizens from violent actors. Promoting respect for human rights is essential for violence reduction and conflict resolution, too. On one hand, it helps victims and protects noncombatants; on the other hand, it can serve to build confidence while the conflict is going on.

In El Salvador and Guatemala, a general agreement on human rights and the verification of its implementation in the field by external actors such as the United Nations was the first visible step toward conflict reduction and war termination. Since the mid 1990s, considerable discussion has taken place about a humanitarian agreement, which has not materialized.[8] But the topic still is on the agenda. The question of a prisoner exchange with the FARC and the ELN is discussed every now and then as a first step, but there have been no concrete results. Regarding the paramilitary groups and their demobilization, the discussion focuses on the controversial questions of truth, justice, and reparations for human rights victims and on the law passed by the Colombian Congress in June 2005.[9]

Since Colombia is one of the countries with the highest biodiversity and has a long frontier in Amazonia, questions of environment and sustainable

---

[7] On the different strategies toward the drug problem in the Andean countries, see International Crisis Group (ICG), *Latin American Drugs II: Improving Policy and Reducing Harm*, Latin American Report no. 26 (Bogotá/Brussels: ICG, March 14, 2008).

[8] On human rights, see the many reports of Human Rights Watch (Americas), Amnesty International, and the UNHCHR field office in Bogotá.

[9] For a discussion, see Adam Isacson, *Peace—or Paramilitarization?* (Washington, D.C: Center for International Policy, July 2005); ICG, *Presidential Politics and Peace Prospects*, Latin America Report no. 14 (Brussels: ICG, June 2005); Human Rights Watch, "Smoke and Mirrors: Colombia's Demobilization of Paramilitary Groups," July 31, 2005, www.hrw.org/reports/2005/colombia0805/ (accessed September 16, 2008); and Chapter 7 of this volume by Arturo Carrillo. For the text of the Justice and Peace Law, see www.altocomisionadoparalapaz.gov.co/justicia_ paz/documentos/Ley1_975.pdf (accessed September 16, 2008).

development are also issues for European cooperation with Colombia. Both are directly related to the armed conflict.[10] The attacks on the country's most important oil pipeline have damaged the environment (especially water quality), as have the chemicals used in production of coca paste and in fumigation of coca plantations. Other forms of violence have more indirect impacts—for example, when people displaced by violence clear the rain forest. Because most of the conflict takes place in rural Colombia (although attacks in the urban areas have increased in recent years), this is where the impact on the economy is felt most. A vicious cycle of underdevelopment, violence, and worse underdevelopment ensues. Addressing the root causes of armed conflict is thus a central objective for European development aid agencies.

Summing up, from an EU perspective, the issues at stake in Colombia are mostly related to long-term problems of uneven development and fragility of democratic institutions. Violence and armed conflict have their roots in Colombian history. Although influenced by contemporary political situations and economic incentives, they will not be resolved by short-term solutions that depend on military operations. The recent EU strategy paper for cooperation with Colombia (2007–13) agrees with this analysis. It states,

> There is no one solution for promoting peace in Colombia; the various components of the conflict have to be tackled simultaneously, while the results of these various measures will only become apparent after different periods of time.
>
> The EU will first of all try to bring some short-term relief to the conflict in Colombia by providing aid for victims, after which, through a medium-term contribution to a settlement, it will seek to promote peace at the local and national levels; finally, to have a long-term impact and achieve a lasting settlement of the conflict in Colombia, the EU will endeavor to attack the root of the armed conflict by promoting development for all.[11]

Supporting Islands of Civility

With the instruments available to them, EU actors intervened at different levels to support conflict transformation in Colombia. At the level of European policy, the European Union, member states, and NGOs focused their development cooperation on programs for the victims of violence and called for an enhanced role for the United Nations, especially regarding human rights, refugees, and mediation. The European Union tried to influence the armed conflict in Colombia by supporting the presence of international orga-

---

[10] Martha Cárdenas and Manuel Rodríguez B., eds., *Guerra, sociedad, y medio ambiente* (Bogotá: Foro Nacional Ambiental, 2004).

[11] See European Commission, "Colombia Country Strategy Paper 2007–2013," March 28, 2007, 6, http://ec.europa.eu/external_relations/colombia/csp/07_13_en.pdf (accessed September 16, 2008).

nizations, promoting "islands of civility" in the field, and facilitating dialogue between the conflict parties.[12] At the April 2001 meeting of the international Support Group for the Peace Process in Brussels, the European Union announced that it would spend about 335 million euros to finance projects including Colombia's first Peace Laboratory and programs that address structural weaknesses undermining peace, fight human rights abuses, and provide aid to victims of the conflict.

Since March 2002, the European Union has financed a pilot project in the war-torn Magdalena Medio River Valley, initiated by local NGOs and coordinated by the Catholic Church with funding from the World Bank.[13] The Peace Laboratory rests on four components: the promotion of peace culture and integral rights, productive activities, productive and social infrastructure, and institutional reinforcement.[14] Its objectives are to support implementation of specific agreements at the local level between parties in conflict, establish zones of peaceful coexistence through empowering local actors and supporting civil actors promoting peace, initiate economic and social development, and, as far as possible, promote alternative development models. The European Union committed 34.8 million euros over eight years for the Program for Development and Peace in Magdalena Medio.[15]

Although the Peace Laboratory is a relatively small and local effort for violence reduction and conflict transformation, it does have particularly important political significance. For decades, the Magdalena Medio has been a microcosm of the national conflict and one of the central battlefields. The FARC and the ELN, as well as paramilitary "self-defense" groups, have tried to control the region, where the Colombian oil industry has one of its bases and which is of strategic geographic importance. Consequently, civil society organizations there have come under pressure from all sides. The Peace Laboratory is an effort to protect remaining civil organizations and grassroots

---

[12] For the concept of "isles of civility," see Mary Kaldor, *New and Old Wars: Organized Violence in a Global Era* (New York: Oxford University Press, 1999). During the peace process of the Pastrana administration, the governments of France, Spain, Italy, Norway, Switzerland, and Cuba formed a "Group of Friends" of the peace process, facilitating conversations between the FARC, the ELN, and the Colombian government and offering their good offices. The talks between the Colombian government and the ELN held in Havana since 2005 are accompanied by Switzerland, Norway, and Spain. The French government of Nicolas Sarkozy supported initiatives for a humanitarian accord, hoping to free captive activist Ingrid Betancourt.

[13] See Chapter 14 of this volume by Javier Moncayo.

[14] Mauricio Katz García, "A Regional Peace Experience: The Magdalena Medio Peace and Development Programme," in *Alternatives to War: Colombia's Peace Processes*, ed. Mauricio García-Durán (London: CINEP, 2004), 30–33. For a comprehensive analysis of the Peace Laboratory, see Miguel Barreto Henriques, "Peace Laboratory of Magdalena Medio: 'A Peace Laboratory'?" (Documentos de CERAC no. 6, Coimbra, December 2007).

[15] Although conditions changed, in 2004 the European Union granted additional funds for more peace laboratories. Because of very specific local conditions in the Magdalena Medio (especially a long history of strong civil society organizations), it remains to be seen if this experience can be multiplied.

movements. On the other hand, critics believe that the vast amount of money flowing to the region has attracted violent actors even more. A final evaluation of the real contribution will be possible only in the future. An indirect success of the effort is that Acción Social (Social Action), the Colombian government's agency for international cooperation, has created a network of peace and development projects and is trying to systematize the different experiences in the field. One lesson from the Magdalena Medio for European Union development cooperation is the need to promote integrated projects that link human rights promotion and conflict transformation with the generation of income and the strengthening of democratic institutions. Otherwise, the danger is in financing a large number of different approaches at the local level that cannot make a difference beyond their target groups.

On the political and diplomatic levels, EU governments and NGOs have offered their good offices for negotiations between conflict parties and hosted conferences and meetings between them, have continued to call for a negotiated settlement of the armed conflict, and have supported a greater UN role in the search for peace. Participation in international support groups for conversations with the FARC and the ELN was also important. European academics organized several conferences with Colombian actors trying to push for negotiations.[16] Up to now, these initiatives have not shown sustainable results. Thus, the EU actors' policy on Colombia is directed mostly toward protecting civic spaces and the possibilities of civil society activities. Although they may not show impressive results in the short term, these EU efforts play a fundamental role and are a precondition for conflict transformation because they help confront the armed actors' logic and dynamics. A central challenge for the future is to link these international efforts systematically with local initiatives for peace.

The discussions of the Justice and Peace Law by Arturo Carrillo in Chapter 7 of this volume offer an interesting case in point, because they show how international criticism of a process and support for local initiatives can enhance the influence of local actors. Monitoring of the paramilitaries' demobilization by civil society groups such as Corporación Nuevo Arco Iris (New Rainbow Corporation), financed by the Swedish development agency, was an important contribution to the revelation of the links between paramilitary groups and politicians.[17] This scandal strengthened the position of human rights groups and victims in the ongoing discussion on reparations and reconciliation.

In its multilateral work, the European Union is the main financial supporter of the Bogotá office of the UN High Commissioner for Human Rights

---

[16] To mention only a few, from 2001 to 2004, the "European University Committee for Colombia," supported by the Inter-American Development Bank, met several times in Paris; European and German academics met in Hamburg to discuss possibilities for external actors; and a meeting of Colombian peace commissioners took place in Barcelona.

[17] See "Colombia: El país después de la negociación," *Arcanos* 8, no. 11 (December 2005).

(UNHCHR), which is monitoring and advising on the human rights situation in Colombia.[18] Although not all EU governments have supported or agreed with the office's reports or those of the UNHCHR, these reports have been and are an important reference point for European perceptions of Colombia's armed conflict. Over the past two years, the reports of the Organization of American States (OAS) mission monitoring demobilization, which also receives substantial European support, have also been increasingly important.

Another major focus of the European Union's multilateral initiatives for peace over the past decade has been to support regional integration and the institutional development of Community of Andean Nations (CAN). A regional approach is a consistent thread in Europe's foreign relations, based on its own historic experience that integration is an important mechanism to resolve bilateral conflicts. Such an approach was quite successful in Europe's relations with Central America during the 1980s, when the San José Process formed part of the European conflict-resolution strategy.[19] The principal idea is that political and economic cooperation and regional integration reduce the potential for bilateral conflict. The danger of conflict escalation or a spillover on the regional level in the Andes has become obvious intermittently. The most important trouble spot has been relations between Colombia and Venezuela, which have accused each other of sponsoring armed opposition groups within each other's national territory. In March 2008, Colombia's bilateral relations with Venezuela and Ecuador not only broke down but led to a militarization of the borders after the Colombian army bombed a FARC camp in Ecuador's territory. After breaking off diplomatic relations and militarizing the borders, international calls for cooperation helped to end the crisis. Thus, the EU response to the Colombian conflict is embedded in its relations with the community of Andean nations. Although the European Union does not ignore particular problems in national development, its main perception is that countries of the region share similar and interrelated problems. Underdevelopment, poverty, and a lack of social integration are common throughout the Andean region, as are drug production and trafficking, violence, and political instability. What differs from one country to another are the forms of political and social struggle. In the interregional cooperation between the European Union and CAN, Andean countries are not only included in the specialized dialogue on drugs but also have preferential access to the EU market through interregional agreements. In December 2003, CAN and the Euro-

---

[18] The UNHCHR field office is a good example of the cooperation between state and nonstate European actors, since some of the experts working in the field office came from human rights NGOs.

[19] The San José Process was an institutionalized form of interregional dialogue between the members of the Central American Integration System and the European Community. When the internal wars in Central America were in danger of escalating into a regional war in the mid-1980s, the process provided an important platform for dialogue.

pean Union signed a "Political Dialogue and Cooperation Agreement" in Rome, agreeing on a series of common principles, including respect for democratic governance and human rights and promotion of sustainable development. In June 2007, negotiations began on an agreement of association, including free trade through the promotion of social and political stability and the deepening of the regional integration process. For the Andean countries, the most important incentive for such an agreement is their wish to strengthen economic cooperation with the European Union through the opening of the EU market. For the European Union, the agreement is an instrument to promote important principles such as democracy, peace, sustainable development, and multilateralism.

The different elements of the EU approach to conflict transformation in Colombia rest on general guidelines and the principles of the Common Foreign and Security Policy to support the victims of violence and address structural causes of violence. The approach served as a minimal consensus of all EU countries and actors as long as the Colombian government followed a similar path. When President Pastrana ended negotiations, first with the FARC in February 2002 and then with the ELN in June 2002, EU governments that had been trying for a long time to save the peace process supported Pastrana's decision to break up the process, although they continued to call for a negotiated resolution of the conflict. NGOs called on the parties to resume negotiations without previous conditions.[20]

After intense lobbying during 2001 and 2002, the Colombian government even succeeded in its effort to have the FARC and the ELN placed on the EU list of international terrorist organizations that was established after 9/11. This was a diplomatic success for the Colombian government, because it delegitimized both groups on the political level. Under this classification, members of these groups are now criminalized, do not qualify for political asylum, and are not allowed to have public meetings inside the European Union, where the ELN used to enjoy some support. Financial assets such as bank accounts will be frozen if detected. This also narrows the options for EU governments (as well as the Colombian government) to begin or support talks with these armed groups, since the general assumption is that one does not talk to terrorists but combats them with the means that the rule of law provides.

When Uribe assumed office in 2002, differences inside the European Union became more obvious, and many discussions and initiatives took place to try to formulate a common policy toward Colombia that went beyond the minimal consensus of support for the victims of violence. Intense lobbying by Colombian diplomats all over the European Union succeeded in strengthening support for the government's policy of making security politics a priority,

---

[20] The presidency of the European Union issued a declaration on February 22; the European Parliament did so on March 14.

although most EU governments remain skeptical about the Colombian governments' human rights record.

Possible Roles for EU Actors

Since the Pastrana administration's peace process failed, there have been repeated calls for a greater role in Colombia for the European Union and its member states. While the Colombian government expected the European Union to make a bigger contribution to the government's own policy initiatives, such as supporting the government's talks with the paramilitaries, in some European discussion forums the European Union was called on to counterbalance growing U.S. involvement in Colombia. European support for the mediation and conflict-regulation initiatives of the Contadora Group (Mexico, Venezuela, Colombia, and Panama) and the interregional San José Process were cited as positive precedents. But because of the structure of the European Union's foreign-policymaking apparatus and the constraints that this imposes, involvement in Colombia can grow only with at least a minimal consensus—at the regional or international level—on the purposes of this engagement and the norms and principles under which it should proceed. A first step in this direction was the London donor conference on July 10, 2003, where various international actors made an effort to increase the coherence of their policies toward Colombia.[21] The resulting London Declaration reflected a consensus that could and should serve as a basis for transatlantic cooperation. The signatories to the declaration agreed on the following points:

- to support the Colombian government in its effort to cope with the problems of endangered democracy, terrorism, the illegal drug industry, the humanitarian crisis, and the violation of human rights and international humanitarian law;
- to base the struggle against violence and crime on the rule of law, human rights, and international humanitarian law; and
- to support the efforts of the Uribe government to negotiate with illegal groups willing to seek negotiated solutions.

Since the London conference, this declaration—which the Colombian government also signed—has been the central reference point for discussions at the intergovernmental level. At a follow-up meeting in Cartagena, donors repeated their willingness to increase their financial commitment under the principles of the London Declaration.

During recent years, the main question for the European Union relates to support for the demobilization of the paramilitary groups. Like the United

---

[21] The meeting was attended by representatives of the governments of Argentina, Brazil, Canada, Chile, Colombia, the European Commission and Council, Japan, Mexico, Norway, Switzerland, the United States, the United Nations and its agencies, and multilateral banks.

States, the European Union had and has serious doubts about the process in Santa Fé de Ralito, which is widely criticized because of its lack of transparency and legal basis. The Colombian Supreme Court's July 2007 verdict that paramilitaries were responsible for common, not political, crimes echoes some European concerns about the process. The qualification of crimes as political or criminal is essential for the possibility to negotiate (political) or to apply the rule of law (criminal). A democratic state can negotiate with political actors but only to a certain degree with common criminals (like reducing penalties in exchange for cooperation). One of the main points of critique toward the negotiation process between the Colombian government and the paramilitaries in Europe's public opinion was that the paramilitary's crimes were not prosecuted. It also shows a systematic problem that neither the European Union nor other state or nonstate actors has resolved up to now: how to deal with forms of violence where economic, criminal, social, and political motivations merge. Talks with groups that are to a substantial extent criminal might reduce violence, but they also undermine the rule of law. To insist on adherence to at least some standards, transparency, and a legal basis, as the European Union has done, is a minimalist approach to a complex problem.

The Colombian government tried to secure international cooperation for the demobilization, but only the OAS agreed to cooperate. As the process has continued, pressure has increased on the European Union to not stand apart and to support the process. The Colombian government has argued that it was unfair that European governments "had a drink with the FARC" but would not support the process with the paramilitaries. Using Europe's engagement then to press for an active role today is an example of how failed peace processes influence the position and perception of actors later. In the first instance, only the governments of Sweden and the Netherlands agreed to support the OAS mission. In a declaration of the European Council of December 13, 2004, the European Union formulated a series of conditions that the Colombian government had to meet before it would agree to do the same:

> A more formal EU involvement could take place through timely political endorsement for the ongoing peace process once the Colombian Government has set out a comprehensive legal framework. The Council underlined that the European Union would have great difficulty endorsing the peace talks as long as the illegal armed groups have not ceased hostilities. Following a gradual approach linked to developments on the ground, the Council also expressed its readiness to provide concrete and adequate financial support for the outcome of such talks once a comprehensive strategy on concentration, disarmament, demobilization, and reintegration of the members of the illegal armed groups in the society has been defined.[22]

---

[22] See European Council, http://register.consilium.europa.eu/pdf/en/04/st15/st15460.en04.pdf (accessed September 22, 2008).

The Colombian government did meet some of these conditions, and as the OAS mission strengthened its standing as a serious verification force, the European Union made a pragmatic assessment of the situation in Colombia and its own possibilities for participation. Member countries such as the Netherlands and Sweden contributed financially as well as with technical support for the OAS.

European development cooperation does play an important role in the field, supporting not just the peace laboratories and the UNHCHR field office but also a wide range of human rights and other civic initiatives. Pressure for compliance with human rights treaties signed by the Colombian state is important in reducing violence. A human rights agreement between the government and the armed groups, its implementation, and verification by the international community would be a significant step in the direction of conflict transformation. It could be an important element of support for the civilian population, as well as a first step to confidence building between the armed actors, and thereby contribute to negotiated solutions. Because of the wide range of actors and perceptions, joint transatlantic cooperation to support the struggle against impunity—for example, through the establishment of an independent truth commission with a much broader mandate than that of the National Commission on Reparation and Reconciliation—could help overcome suspicions in the Colombian and international human rights communities that impunity is the price for demobilization.

In the medium and long term, the reduction of violence and termination of the armed conflict in Colombia will depend on the success of a joint effort by producer and consumer countries to slash the huge profits of the drug economy. Eradication programs may show some results, but a sustainable policy has to include the broader issue of rural development. Although Colombia is one of the most urban societies in Latin America, voluntary or forced migration to the cities will not solve the historically unresolved issue of underdevelopment in rural areas. The ninth quarterly report of the OAS monitoring mission highlights the importance of rural development when discussing the complex scenarios in some regions of Colombia, "where people do not seem to notice a substantial change in security conditions."[23]

External actors do support programs for alternative development, but these programs will bear fruit only if they are competitive in the world market. An external actor such as the European Union thus needs to assume an integrated approach toward the Colombian conflict. Preferential access to the U.S. and European markets for legal products is an important step, but a general opening of agrarian markets—as discussed in the World Trade Organi-

---

[23]See OAS Permanent Council, "Ninth Quarterly Report of the Secretary General to the Permanent Council on the Mission to Support the Peace Process in Colombia (OAS/MAPP)," CP/doc.4237/07, July 2, 2007.

zation negotiations—is necessary for sustainable development. Transatlantic cooperation in this field is essential not just for Colombia but also for other developing countries. Such a policy could contribute to social and political integration.

But since the crisis in Colombia (or in other Andean countries) is not at the top of the European Union's foreign-policy agenda, a more active role for the European Union would depend on a solid regional and international coalition of those willing to transform the conflict under the norms of international law and human rights conventions. Otherwise, EU actors are likely to continue to do little more than support victims, alternative production, and sporadic initiatives.

The European Union's main contributions to the transformation of the Colombian conflict are twofold. First, the European Union is or can be a partner and supporter for a negotiated transformation of the conflict. But this is an option only when Colombian actors take the lead (as was the case at the local level in the Magdalena Medio). Second, the European Union provides those local actors with an alternative model for comprehensive peacebuilding that is based on a multilevel approach that addresses structural causes and tries to reverse violent escalation. Although, at the moment, this happens only at the local level, positive results are an important reference point for all the actors that want to resist the logic of armed conflict, showing that another Colombia might be possible.

22

A Norwegian-Supported Peacebuilding Project

Conversations among Security Forces, Former Guerrillas, and Civil Society

Jennifer Schirmer

If one of the requirements for transforming conflict into politics is a commitment to inclusiveness, then efforts toward a peaceful solution must, at an early stage, engage those actors who have the most capacity to wage war. It may not be unreasonable to assume that some of the armed actors have a stake in keeping the conflict going or that their training and experience lead them to harbor deep suspicions about the possibility for a durable peace. Yet, ironically, this very set of assumptions may well exclude armed actors from positive engagement in peacebuilding and undermine, in the end, the possibility for a durable, peaceful resolution to the conflict.

It is vital to the resolution of a conflict to set up "precursors of engagement"—often years before accords are actually signed—that bring armed actors into a dialogue that is integral to peacebuilding and peacemaking. These activities can be seen as precursors to a new way of thinking outside the traditional paradigms of war.

Colombia is not exempt from this need. It is a precarious democracy facing a myriad of contradictions. On one hand, it has a rich electoral and institutional culture and vibrant democratic discourse in the form of vigorous public and congressional debates. On the other hand, it has an enduring history of political exclusion and marginalization for a significant part of the population; profound social and economic inequality; and political assassination, forced disappearance, and other forms of repressive practices against trade unionists, journalists, human rights activists, the internally displaced, and many other vulnerable sectors. While there is vigorous political debate within socially similar sectors of society, such as the press and Congress, there has been little political engagement and dialogue between sectors. And though Colombia has in part a democratic culture, it remains a society experiencing the longest internal armed conflict in the hemisphere. It could be said that it is a democratic country at war with itself.

Fraught with these ironies and contradictions for more than forty years, Colombian society has divisions at all levels: between civil society and the military, between rebels and the government, between the left and the right, and between the rich and the poor. For the military, the reluctance to reach across dividing lines is not only ideological but also social: military and police officers live in their own segregated communities, locked into a war that breeds its own form of exclusion. For Colombian officers to have social ties, let alone informal friendships, with academics, intellectuals, and political analysts from other than conservative and right-wing persuasions is extremely unlikely.

In a similar way, most progressive politicians, intellectuals, and academics in Colombia experience their own forms of social isolation, keeping to their own circles, with little access to or interest in the armed forces, whom many hold in disdain. This sector thus lacks a "forum" generative of political debate, analysis, and reflection with officers.

Hence, officers may be seen only rhetorically as part of the citizenry: despite being referred to as "the public force" (*la fuerza pública*), they are not considered by much of Colombian civil society to be part of the "public sphere." And as a result, although officers may learn about the different ideological options available, these are often taught as operational threats to stability, not as legitimate differences of opinion open to debate. In the officers' universe, the "public sphere"—filled with politicians and polemical debates—may be viewed as a threatening and "conflictual" social and political arena and not as an arena of opportunity for informed deliberations about political choices and for a political resolution of the conflict.

There also exists a critical mass of former guerrillas from the handful of revolutionary groups in Colombia that, as a result of the multiple peace negotiations in the late 1980s and early 1990s, first chose deliberately to be outside civil society and then chose to accept peace agreements, demobilize, and "reinsert" themselves back into civil society and political debates. These *reinsertados* have made the decision to "cross" a number of social boundaries—of class, ideology, and sometimes culture and nuclear family. Although these *reinsertados* remain socially stigmatized in many ways, their experience with crossing the difficult intersectoral boundaries of Colombian society can at times be useful for peace dialogues.

With a high degree of political volatility in Colombia, with little discussion between civil society and security forces, and with peace facilitations with the Ejército de Liberación Nacional (ELN) being reinitiated in 2005 but faltering in 2007—and a potential humanitarian exchange emerging with the

Fuerzas Armadas Revolucionarias de Colombia (FARC) in late 2007 only to collapse in 2008—it would seem of the utmost importance to build sustainable dialogue between civil society and both nonstate and state armed actors if future peace agreements are to be able to be formulated. Yet little attention has been given to how to do this effectively. Seldom does one find an inclusive approach that allows for "precursors of engagement" with armed actors *in the midst of the conflict*; seldom is an action-based approach at hand that fits the conditions and demands of those involved. Too little thought has gone into developing the kind of forum in which security forces, ex-guerrillas, and civilians may begin to transform the narrative in which each side demonizes the other to one that emphasizes dialogue and collaboration to resolve the conflict and construct a democratic culture of peace. Without dialogues well before the actual negotiations begin, there may be confusion over precisely what the role of the armed forces should be in negotiated settlements as well as in post-conflict climates in which security is part and parcel of democratic nation building.

This chapter details a project I have organized together with a two-member Colombian team with the support of the Norwegian Foreign Ministry to establish sustainable dialogues involving the security forces, ex-guerrillas, and civil society, aimed at encouraging a more open perspective toward peace negotiations and an engagement in a democratically inclusive future.

The Role of Norway in Peace Processes

Norwegian efforts at global peacemaking were for the most part initiated in the early 1990s with the Oslo Peace Accords in the Middle East. It was during this period that key individuals in the Norwegian Foreign Ministry began to realize that Norway, although a small country, could use part of its significant petroleum resources to foment peacebuilding and conflict resolution and thereby play a decisive role in peace processes.[1] Today, Norway is involved in facilitating peace processes in Sri Lanka, the Philippines, Sudan, Indonesia, Nepal, the Horn of Africa, Colombia, and Palestine-Israel, among others.

These efforts are guided by a dual vision of inclusiveness and neutrality. The presence and commitment of Norway as a donor and as a third-party mediator in peace processes around the world is remarkable and serves peacemaking efforts in many discrete ways. For one, Norway supports informal avenues, such as efforts by academic institutions and/or nongovernmental organizations (NGOs), that prepare the ground and complement formal channels for peace settlements and humanitarian exchanges.

---

[1] See Jan Egeland, *Impotent Super Power—Potent Small State: Potentials and Limitations of Human Rights Objectives in the Foreign Policies of the United States and Norway* (Oslo: Norwegian University Press, 1988).

For another, it is often willing to engage the armed actors at an early stage in peacebuilding, understanding that one of the requirements for transforming conflict into politics is to include at the table those actors who have the most capacity to wage war. Norway also offers opportunities for creative triangulation with international organizations, such as the United Nations, the Norwegian government, and NGOs. Finally, it can offer an immediate mechanism of financial support to encourage dialogue between parties to help prevent conflicts from becoming violent.

In Colombia in 2005, Norway decided to participate, together with Switzerland and Spain, in facilitating the ELN–Colombian government talks in Havana. It had already, since 1998, been supporting a peacebuilding initiative titled "Skilling the Armed Actors for Peace in Colombia," which had established since 2000 important dialogues among the Colombian armed forces, civil society, and ex-guerrillas. This initiative has continued to be framed by one critical question: during negotiations for a potential peace process, can we expect armed actors, without some form of preparation in crossing boundaries, to give up isolating habits of mind in order to become part of a new democratic peace? What might a third party be able to do to make the armed actors comfortable speaking with and listening to civilians and ex-guerrillas (and possibly eventually to guerrillas) to move the discussions toward a more open perspective on a resolution of the conflict and a democratically inclusive future?

Conversations for Peace Project

As part of this "Skilling the Armed Actors for Peace in Colombia" project, I began in 2000 to hold conversations with members of the Colombian officer corps and also with representatives of government and civil society and politicians from the entire political spectrum to better appreciate the range of opinions and the sensitivity to raising conflict-resolution issues. My question was, what happens when—in the midst of a conflict—one attempts to bring armed actors of the state and civil society members into conversations in preparation for potential peace? What are the opportunities and challenges that such a complex conflict and all its attendant uncertainties offer for dialogue? How does one encourage each side to take risks and accept compromises that have made peace processes possible elsewhere?

I knew that inclusion of armed actors in such conversations could be fraught with difficulties. Career military officers do not easily forfeit their image of the guerrilla as enemy-cum-demon, and members of civil society are not usually open to meeting with officers. It takes time to build trust among parties. Taking all this into consideration, the project maintains a long-term view of confidence building and gradual engagement, and it locates the conversation in a low-profile academic setting, in an attempt to set it apart from the daily polemics of Colombian life.

If we think of conversation-as-dialogue not solely as an end product but as a continuing *process* that involves consultation, involvement, engagement, and co-ownership by both parties, the process itself becomes a significant component of the outcome, especially in the midst of a conflict. It may even be that the more that is at stake, the greater the trust that may be required: hence the need to rethink how best to undertake such a process.

Based on my initial conversations with military officers and representatives of civil society, it became clear that many were potentially open to new ways of interacting. With this in mind, the project's Colombian team established, first through the office of the vice president (who also served as defense minister) under President Pastrana and in collaboration with the army high command—and later in collaboration with each of the directors of the war college—informal, neutral, and off-the-record dialogues called "conversations" (*conversatorios*). For more than seven years now, we have worked with active-duty officers who are the elite of the officer corps—colonels who are rigorously vetted to be promoted to generals as part of the one-year promotional course (Curso de Altos Estudios Militares, or CAEM) at the war college.

Genuine conversation entails both listening and talking, and in these *conversatorios*, the primary rule has been to respect and listen to one another's opinions. All participants are encouraged to articulate their beliefs about the issues at hand and to express what they see as the issues that emanate from their experiences in the field and from their frames of reference.

The group of approximately twenty-six to twenty-eight officers participating in each year's promotional CAEM program arrives together on the bus from the airport at the particular hotel selected for each event for its quiet, retreatlike setting away from job demands and cell phones.[2] After checking in, we hold a welcoming reception and a toast, and over dinner, participants are reminded that this event is entirely off the record, with no attributions—a rule that has not been breached since the *conversatorios* began in 2001. (Many officers admit that this off-the-record style allows them to speak their mind.) I emphasize in my opening remarks that the team and I are not the "owners" of this dialogue, that if it is to be a success for them, it will be because of their own initiatives in speaking with and listening to one another: "This is *your conversatorio*, your opportunity to speak with people on an informal level about how, together, we can begin to resolve this conflict in Colombia." During dinner conversation among the officers, civilians, and ex-guerrillas, the discussion remains cordial and informal. This surprises most officers, who later admit that they expected to be "hammered by NGO types."

The next morning, the rules of the table are that the three to four civilian presenters each give a presentation on the day's topic for a maximum of

---

[2] The total number of officers varies each year, as well as the total figure from each branch of the armed forces (army, navy, air force) together with the national police.

twenty-five minutes, and then the table is open to everyone equally, with respectful questions and comments facilitated by the team. Officers may take different positions, often disagreeing among themselves or, to their surprise, even agreeing with the civilian presenters. In one instance, one officer humorously stated that he was "exceedingly worried" because he found himself in agreement with a statement by one of the former guerrillas at the table. There was a collective drawing in of breath, and then everyone laughed. Most officers and civilians readily participate by the late morning, saying how very appreciative they are of the openness and "equal making" of the methodology. The room setup is an essential element of this "leveling": it must be as tranquil as possible—no outside noise, no microphone, no PowerPoint or slide projectors inside. Each participant has a seat at the table with a name card that provides a first name in capital letters, with no title or rank; it is a rectangular table that seats about thirty people, mixed by rank, military branch, and civilian status.

Listening to and respecting the opinions of others does not mean that one has to agree with another's viewpoint. This is often a misinterpretation of dialogue, which demands neither doctrinaire agreement nor ideological opposition. Rather, dialogue here tries to step aside from ideological politics into a more continual stream of conversation that allows one to see that, through different experiences from different perspectives, we can arrive at areas of agreement, better understand the basis for our continued disagreements, and make possible new analyses and ways of thinking about the challenges of peacemaking.

By removing the conversation from the polemical world to a large extent and placing it within a world of an open discussion of ideas, in a neutral space in which ideologies are discussed in a leveling manner, some interesting concurrences of thinking and transformation of attitudes result. For example, former guerrillas have talked about their view of social justice, while military officers talk about their concerns about social inequality. From this dialogue, at times, they both come to the realization that they may have similar ideas about the need to address impoverishment and inequality, but they recognize that their ideas emanate from different perspectives.

A brief comment about how these dialogues differ from traditional human rights seminars may be useful: I tried to avoid the mistakes I had witnessed at training seminars on human rights in which an outsider, using an "outside" (and, in the officers' minds, "imposed") frame of reference, presents a monologic lecture and leaves little room for input by officers—and, thus, little understanding of what the officers may take away from it.

The project also avoids using what is often referred to as a military-to-military (MIL-to-MIL) method as the basis for working with the officers (a model used extensively by the U.S. military in their training programs). Using this model is risky, because it is unclear whether it encourages a conceptual paradigm shift or locates humanitarian principles simply as extensions of military thinking. More significantly, this approach does not appear to challenge the officers' social and intellectual isolation. It does not cross boundaries to bring them into dialogue with members of civil society, such as progressive parliamentarians and former guerrillas. And it does not provide the participants with other than military readings of the challenges that humanitarian principles set out, or with different visions of what peacemaking might entail.

Another approach avoided in the *conversatorios*, which appears to be common among various NGOs and other organizations, involves lecturing military officers from a human rights and international humanitarian law perspective based primarily on legal formulas far removed from the context of local conflict and military operations. While these seminars do bring military officers into contact with representatives of civil society, they do so in a way that tends to accentuate rather than soften the divide between the military and civil society. Lecturing suggests that one side has all the answers and that the other side should passively receive guidance. Also, the information given is often too technical; many officers complain that the lectures do little to help them, since "we are not lawyers." Such monologic talking *at* the military may produce the false impression that officers are listening and learning new ways, but without any real dialogue and with little follow-up, it is difficult to measure just what is being learned by either the military or civil society.

Our project, by contrast, eschews the idea of a single expert opinion and instead attempts to work from the viewpoints of all the participants. Preparation of all parties before a *conversatorio* is essential in the process of building confidence and trust. Before any activity goes forward, informal conversations are conducted with all participants individually, and with the military officers as a group, about their concerns and interests.

Before each *conversatorio*, discussions also take place with the individual civilian participants about how to present their ideas in ways that do not close off discussion but instead open up questions and respectful debate. (It cannot be assumed that civilians are necessarily more practiced in open dialogue than the officers merely because they are civilians or because they work, for instance, on human rights.)

Furthermore, themes and speakers of the *conversatorios* are selected beforehand in dialogue with the officers. As we know, having a say in the agenda is as important a part of the process of co-ownership and engagement as the actual event itself. In the 27 *conversatorios* organized since 2001 with more than 275 officers, themes generative of political debate, analysis, and reflection have been offered. These have included discussions of such issues as a humanitarian accord with the FARC guerrillas, paramilitarism, land reform, policies of new progressive mayors and governors regarding trade unionism, and rehabilitation and work programs for ex-paramilitary youths. Participants have explored the evolution and changes of each of the guerrilla groups from the analytical perspective of former guerrillas themselves; the historical landlessness and need for rural development as the major root cause and solution to the conflict; the social costs of war on communities; the government's demobilization talks with the paramilitaries and the issue of impunity; the violence and forced displacement of communities; and the reconciliation work that one progressive mayor's office is organizing with demobilized paramilitary and gang youth, among others. These *conversatorios* have been able to create authentic dialogue between sectors of Colombian society by using a methodology that invites former guerrillas to converse with officers. That the *conversatorios* have been able to address one of the most volatile and delicate topics in Colombia—the paramilitaries—without rancor and defensiveness is an indicator of their success.

With the demobilization of five guerrilla groups in the late 1980s and early 1990s under the governments of Barco and Gaviria, there exists today a critical mass of former guerrillas in Colombia who serve as parliamentarians of the Polo Democrático Alternativo Party (Alternative Democratic Pole), who have served as politically independent mayors or negotiators in the mayors' offices of Bogotá and Medellín and in the governors' offices in Cali and Nariño, or who write newspaper columns as political analysts.

Although the officers were very reluctant to meet with any of these *reinsertados* at first, they have come to value the former guerrillas' contributions to the *conversatorios*. Officers are also perfectly aware that the decades of experience the guerrillas have had in negotiating puts the armed forces at a distinct disadvantage. As one officer who considers himself "hard-line but pragmatic" told me before a *conversatorio*, "We don't have the years and years of experience in negotiations as do the ELN or FARC. Will we be taken advantage of at the table by all sides?" Thus, the officers know they have something to learn from these *conversatorios*, especially from the *reinsertados*.

In particular, the former guerrillas' ability to build on lessons learned from previous peace processes in Colombia has been extremely educational for the officers. To be able to meet an "enemy" face-to-face, to learn that they share similar views, and to learn that these former guerrillas, too, disagree among themselves is a critical transformation in the way the officers see the guerrillas, and vice versa. These discussions also allow officers to familiarize themselves with the history of peace negotiations in Colombia and to reflect positively on the concerns of peacemaking in general through the eyes of an ex-combatant.

Military officers are often surprised at the lack of rancor among the former guerrillas. They are surprised to hear former guerrillas or Polo Party representatives criticize another guerrilla group's agenda or oppose its illegal activities. Learning not to presume that one "knows the other side" is part of the educational process. As one air force general commented after one of the dialogues, "These *conversatorios* have been a learning experience because they represent unique neutral spaces where one can discuss themes with people with whom one is normally on an antagonistic footing. Where else can a general sit down with an *ex-guerrillero* and leftist parliamentarian and calmly discuss the conflict? Everything is off the record, and this creates trust and friendship for the necessary long-term dialogue toward peace."

The Evolution of the *Conversatorios*: Are Attitudes Shifting?

How much has been accomplished by providing this neutral space for dialogue? Do such "precursors of engagement" help to shift attitudes and predispositions? In the early *conversatorios*, we felt it was too risky to introduce either themes or speakers who were considered by the officers to be "too progressive" and outside their comfort zone. If officers suggested such "leftist" figures, it appeared to be more for the opportunity to make critical statements face-to-face than to have a respectful dialogue. When we approached certain intellectuals and certain members of the local NGO community, we were met with either a firm negative or with the mind-set that denunciatory attitudes and confrontations with the security forces were the only appropriate interaction.

Thus, we first began in 2001–03 with a generalized discussion of the roots of the conflict. Subsequently, we slowly began to include increasingly progressive participants, including moderates from various political parties who held ideas about how to resolve the conflict that differed from the officers' perspectives. We carefully calibrated how far the officers could be taken outside their intellectual comfort zones in meeting and listening to representatives from civil society. Occasionally, a former guerrilla was invited to speak on a particular topic, which opened up positive spaces for discussion on the nature of the insurgency and the potential for negotiations, and for these events, there was a special effort to prepare the participants, both civilian and military, beforehand.

With the initiation of the paramilitary demobilization talks in 2003–04 as well as the election of the new social democratic party, Polo Democrático Alternativo, we gradually began to open up our political discussions by reaching out to the new, more progressive representatives in Congress and in the mayor's office in Medellín and the governorship of Cali. Interestingly, with each subsequent *conversatorio*, the officers themselves became more insistent on having the opportunity to meet with Polo/*ex-guerrillero* representatives. In a sense, both the increasing institutionalization and legalization of the progressive party as well as the "multiplier effect" each *conversatorio* had—whereby officers from one CAEM program would highly recommend these events to the next year's group of CAEM officers—made it easier for us with each passing group to include progressive speakers and themes in the dialogues much earlier in the year.

In 2005 and 2006, we crossed a threshold by organizing *conversatorios* that began to shift the dialogues more directly and concretely into the arenas of negotiation, demobilization, and reinsertion, inviting participants to discuss the government's demobilization talks with the paramilitaries under way at the time. Another theme during this period was the potential for a humanitarian accord with the FARC. The officers told us that they found both discussions extremely productive and respectful, and this was reflected in the war college's internal evaluations of the curriculum.

Based on the positive results from these earlier *conversatorios*, we focused increasingly on the topics of conflict, negotiation, and post-conflict by giving the officers a Norwegian perspective on the constructive roles that the armed forces have played in the multiple peace processes in which Norway is engaged in the world. A key lesson for the officers from this Norwegian perspective has been that conflict, including that of Colombia, is not intractable and that the Colombian conflict is not the most brutal, nor is it as complicated as other conflicts.

Thus, we have come to a new stage of analysis and discussion, by which new brigade commanders have begun to visualize the conflict in Colombia from an increasingly international and comparative perspective. Moreover, they appear to be more able and more willing to participate in a discussion of the *resolution of conflict* and of the different "visions of peace," including those from the guerrilla side. This is a major advance in the officers' thinking and prepares them to play an effective role in building peace by supporting negotiated settlements and playing constructive roles in the post-conflict setting in Colombia.

The *conversatorios* are now seeking to encourage and sharpen this focus. The intense interest in this form of discussion and analysis has manifested itself annually in these future generals' end-of-the-year evaluations of the CAEM program, which place these *conversatorios* at the top of their list for the best course of the year. Thus, these conversations have become an organic element and play a central role in the education and socialization of these high-ranking officers in respecting differences of opinion and engaging in conflict resolution.

As the *conversatorios* have progressed, we have perceived a relaxing of the military's resistance to the perspectives of those whom they originally believed to be intrinsically antagonistic to their own and their institution's interests. We see that veterans of past *conversatorios* are fluent in conversing with "the other side" whenever they are invited to another *conversatorio*, and that they readily serve as mediators between newly invited, nervous officers and their civilian counterparts. On the other side, many ex-guerrillas, leftist politicians, journalists, and human rights lawyers have come to admit that their own prejudgments of the military were erroneous. These dialogues, then, are an ethnographic education for all parties—officers, academics, parliamentarians, human rights lawyers, businesspeople, international organization representatives, and former guerrillas—in which the participants overcome their initial predispositions and begin to see the "other" as a legitimate and ultimately helpful participant in dialogues about the future of peace in Colombia.

Conclusion

These twenty-seven *conversatorios*, begun in 2001 at the request of the officers to help make them conversant in peace issues, and still ongoing in 2008, have achieved two objectives. First, they have engaged a number of active-duty, high-level officers who are the elite of the officer corps in a setting that is democratic to the core and off the record, permitting a frank, unscripted, and respectful exchange of ideas that is unprecedented in their world. Second, the *conversatorios* have introduced the military participants to thoughts and thinkers who challenge their habits of mind and make them more comfortable with differences of opinion. This is not a one-sided dialogue in which the civilians talk *at* the military: it is a decidedly dialogic process that has also challenged the civilians' own preconceptions—and often misconceptions—of the military's mind-set and exposed them to operational issues that the civilians do not ordinarily confront.

Conversatorios, then, are not a product but a *process* of consultation and engagement that has led, at least in this instance, to a bridging of social divides. Based on years of careful engagement and discussion, of not rushing the conversation beyond the parameters of the participants' intellectual and emotional comfort zones, the project has made some progress in shifting attitudes both institutionally and individually. But as with all processes, there are questions and dilemmas about the implications of including armed actors in the dialogue about peace processes. Will they be acting in their own self-interest or for the larger good? Or will they learn, through such dialogue, how to twist the vocabulary of human rights and peace and the imagery of rule of law to create unfortunate "justificatory narratives"? While concerns about the wisdom and willingness of armed actors to engage in peacebuilding are certainly legitimate, we nonetheless must continually weigh the benefits of establishing "precursors of engagement" between security forces and civil society in an effort to influence how both parties think about peace. The inclusion of armed actors in such a dialogue is predicated on the premise that the act of dialogue with one's "enemy" is itself an important act. It humanizes and legitimizes the "other" through a democratic participatory method that provides an alternative to the operational logic of violence.

What this small Norwegian-supported project illustrates is that with the appropriate venue and form, to paraphrase a Spanish proverb, one can clear a path together by walking down it despite old enmities and divisions. These *conversatorios* have led to the discovery that quite a significant number of military officers, political representatives, and former guerrillas are more than willing to engage in meaningful dialogue about how to build peace together in Colombia.

CONCLUSION

23

Toward an Integrated Framework for Building Peace

Virginia M. Bouvier

As pervasive and complex as the internal armed conflict in Colombia has been, so, too, have been the initiatives to try to resolve it. Ordinarily when we think of peacemaking, the official "track I" negotiations at the national level are what come to mind. Colombia has a rich history of these efforts, providing us with many object lessons in what has and has not worked. And yet, a range of unofficial efforts involving many individuals, communities, and networks, sometimes organized by social and occupational sectors or institutional affiliations, coexist side by side with—or in the absence of—track I initiatives.

Juxtaposing Colombia's long history of conflict with its long history of efforts to resolve the conflict changes our images of Colombia and Colombians. Instead of seeing Colombia as a land victimized by guerrillas, paramilitaries, drug traffickers, criminals, and human rights violators and rife with violence and corruption, we see, in every sector of society and every region of the country, large numbers of people seeking ways to end the violence, address its causes, and enact mechanisms for the nonviolent resolution of conflict.

The contributors to this volume remind us that unarmed actors working for peace are both actors and stakeholders in the resolution of Colombia's conflict. By granting them greater agency, we may help diminish the power of the armed actors. And in perceiving the potential power of this sometimes diffuse movement for peace, we begin to see that conflict is not intractable, that peace is possible, and that strengthening this constituency for peace—wherever it might be—may be one of the keys not only to unlocking the conflict but also to building a peaceful future.

This concluding chapter explores the range of both complementary and conflicting conceptual visions underlying peace initiatives under way at each level of Colombian society. It proposes criteria for evaluation, elucidates the obstacles to success, and offers directions for future research. Finally, this chapter offers a framework for analyzing and strengthening peacemaking and peacebuilding and some reflections on how this volume challenges some of the conventional wisdom in the conflict-resolution field.

Visions of Peace in Colombia

The peace initiatives analyzed in this book underscore the tremendous complexity and diversity of Colombian society. Colombia's conflict involves multiple armed and unarmed actors, and complex relationships within and between heterogeneous entities. The state is a complex set of institutions from the municipal to the national level—with their own varied and sometimes conflicting interests and priorities. The armed actors, both illegal and legal, are marked by a diversity of origins, methods, and goals. Among the illegal groups, some are active, some have demobilized, and some are searching for new roles in society. Civil society includes a wide range of non-governmental actors—religious organizations, secular institutions, educators, human rights and other social organizations, business groups, journalists, labor unions, peasants, professionals, women's groups, ethnic and cultural groups, internally displaced people, and a broad range of others—that act collectively in accordance with shared interests, values, and goals but that are also heterogeneous in nature. Finally, Colombia is a country marked by regional diversity and by sometimes conflicting needs between the center and the periphery and between urban and rural areas. All these differences shape the nature of conflict and the nature of peace initiatives in particular areas of the country.

While there have been successful coalitions in the pursuit of peace, Colombians—and the internationals that wish to support peace efforts—remain divided on how to define peace; lack consensus on whether peace is a process or an endgame; and sometimes pursue conflicting strategies to attain their goals. These diverse approaches inform our analysis of the conflict and provide a context for understanding the assumptions underlying the plethora of peace initiatives, strategies, and goals at the local, regional, national, and international levels.

At a minimum, peace initiatives seek ways to end the violence. The initiatives may be track I discussions at the elite level, or they may be dialogues with the armed actors themselves to address local outbreaks of violence. At whatever level, these initiatives often seek ways for the multiple actors, armed and unarmed, to coexist, create zones that are off-limits to armed actors, or seek to restore social balance through policies and programs to disarm, demobilize, and reintegrate armed actors into civil society. Such peace initiatives assume that social organization, leadership, and public policies can protect communities from violent actors or from corruption and poor governance, and they seek to form alliances with others to strengthen a community's capacity to prevent or mitigate violence.

Many of the initiatives promoted by government, churches, businesses, and the international community support the creation of a culture of peace based on respect for human rights. The concept remains rather diffuse operationally, although its proponents generally assume that education that fosters respect for differences and facilitates the nonviolent resolution of conflict will provide an alternative to the logic of violence and help ensure a peaceful future.

Many peace initiatives focus on empowering citizens, especially disadvantaged groups, to engage with policymakers in representing their own interests and defending their rights. They assume that the conditions for sustainable peace require a broadening of democratic participation and the establishment of structures and mechanisms to address grievances, ensure accountability for past wrongs, and resolve current and future conflicts without resorting to violence. These initiatives promote the association of citizens and the participation of communities in common projects of development, local governance, protection and promotion of human rights, resistance to armed actors, and social reconstruction.

Peace initiatives such as the peace and development programs, church programs, and the three regional peace laboratories focus directly on development and human needs as prerequisites for peace. This marriage of peace and development goals seems to hold some promise, because it creates income-generating options for the economically disadvantaged and for those displaced or victimized by the conflict, and provides alternative economic livelihoods to illicit-crop cultivation or enlistment in illegal armed groups. This alternative economic development approach addresses the root causes of Colombia's conflict as well as the relatively newer dimension of the role of drug trafficking in perpetuating conflict.

Evaluating Peace Initiatives: Obstacles and Successes

So, how might we assess the nature and cumulative impact of this rich texture of peace initiatives?[1] Developing universal criteria to evaluate successes can be problematic. The initiatives promote a broad range of functions, including facilitating relationships, building trust, creating networks, and fostering local development and democratic participation. Discrete initiatives may be evaluated according to how well the articulated goals of the particular initiative are met, yet the initiatives that support processes of change are much more difficult to measure, since change often takes time to manifest.

---

[1] The conclusions of this book draw heavily on discussions with the chapter authors during the United States Institute of Peace–Cornell University conference in November 2005 and on subsequent correspondence with the authors. For a report of the conference findings, see Virginia M. Bouvier, *Harbingers of Hope: Peace Initiatives in Colombia*, Special Report 169 (Washington, D.C.: United States Institute of Peace Press, August 2006), www.usip.org/pubs/special reports/sr169.html (accessed September 18, 2008).

Short-term failures may lead to long-term success, and short-term successes are not guaranteed to hold in the long term. Nonetheless, these conclusions offer suggestions for how evaluation at each distinct level might be done, with an eye toward strengthening these initiatives and their cumulative impact across levels and ascertaining how the international community might contribute to the local, regional, and national initiatives under way.

Evaluating National Peace Initiatives

At a national level, we have seen that the Colombian state has considerable experience negotiating with illegal armed groups. Success at this level might be evaluated by measuring the incremental steps that ordinarily lead to peace: whether a group disarms and demobilizes, whether armed groups agree to sit down at the peace table, whether a peace accord is signed, whether violence resumes, whether the terms of the peace accord are respected and implemented, whether former combatants are successfully integrated or reintegrated into society, whether the state has established and implemented mechanisms to address the grievances that gave rise to the conflict and those that sustain it, whether a modicum of justice is attained, and, ultimately, whether peace and the mechanisms for peaceful resolution of conflicts hold.

Short of these clear markers of incremental success or failure, however, are a range of more nuanced and modest benchmarks. National-level negotiations may not result in signed peace accords but still may help create new mechanisms for participation or help build new relationships of trust that open the way to future dialogues. The negotiations with the Movimiento 19 de Abril (M-19) and other insurgent groups were considered successful because the Colombian government and the rebels secured the guerrillas' demobilization and created mechanisms allowing the insurgents to pursue a political agenda by participating in the Constitutional Assembly and shaping the 1991 constitution. These mechanisms, as well as the Constitutional Court, have been able to address some of the underlying injustices that gave rise to armed insurgency, and they have offered new human rights protections under national law.

Authors in this book point to a wide range of factors that have blocked Colombia's experiences with earlier peace processes. They underscore the role of spoilers, the increased militarization of the conflict through Plan Colombia, and the financial sustainability of the armed groups (through drug trafficking, extortion, and illegal trade). They note the lack of effective security guarantees, inexperienced negotiators, ineffective negotiating strategies, unrealistic bargaining agendas, and lack of political will. Also, they find that peace processes have regularly been plagued or derailed by continued violations of human rights, including physical threats to individual, institutional, and community security; intransigence of the parties; and inadequate international support for peace policies. On the other hand, Carlo Nasi analyzes the successes of the Barco administration in implementing conflict-management techniques that ensured that potential spoilers (namely, the military and the right-wing paramilitaries) were brought into the peace process, and that capable, dedicated personnel and sufficient institutional resources and mechanisms were available to support a peace process.

There is broad agreement that greater participation of civil society in various aspects of peacemaking and peacebuilding will ensure greater buy-in at the local level and will lead to a more durable peace. There is less agreement on exactly how to reach agreement or how to organize and make effective this increased participation, given the tremendous diversity of interests represented within civil society. Some authors in this volume suggest that underutilized institutional structures such as the National Peace Council could be an effective mechanism for channeling civil society participation more effectively.

While peacemaking is ordinarily a track I activity that takes place between political elites and armed insurgents, civil society can nonetheless serve as a third-party actor in helping bridge the divide between the government and armed groups. The Catholic Church has been doing this, especially at the national level, and Protestant evangelicals have similarly been conducting their own "pastoral dialogues" behind the scenes. Colombian civil society has pushed for negotiations and has mobilized public opinion on a periodic basis to create pressure for negotiations. Its direct participation in negotiations may be somewhat limited, but it can elaborate proposals, create mechanisms for citizen involvement, and articulate the costs of war for society at large and for affected regions and sectors. Civil society has the power to legitimize a national process or to withhold its stamp of approval. Finally, while peace is being waged, civil society can help the state define the needs and programs it will implement, can pressure the state to become more inclusive and more representative of marginalized groups, and can challenge the reigning culture of impunity and hold the state accountable for the promotion and protection of human rights. Civil society efforts might thus be evaluated in terms of their success in each of these arenas.

The massive mobilization of civil society in the late 1990s created momentum for peace and brought Andrés Pastrana to power in 1998 with a mandate to open negotiations with the Fuerzas Armadas Revolucionarias de Colombia (FARC). Yet despite its increased organizational capacity and participatory demands, civil society was forced to the sidelines once those talks began, and was unable to ensure that Pastrana considered its proposals or engaged the mechanisms (such as the National Peace Council) that had been set up to give civil society a voice. When the talks broke down in 2002, proposals generated during massive public hearings were shelved without further consideration, and civil society failed to establish a road map for moving ahead toward a political solution.

In more recent years, civil society discussions with the Ejército de Liberación Nacional (ELN) led to formal meetings in Cuba, mediated by international facilitators, between the ELN and the Colombian government. Civil society guarantors have been instrumental in keeping these talks on track, but by 2008, their efforts had stalled. Likewise, efforts to pave the way for peace talks with the FARC, via a humanitarian accord, were stymied by developments that year. The death of three FARC leaders, the defection of hundreds of FARC combatants including some longtime front commanders, and the Colombian army's successful hostage-rescue operation fed hopes for a military solution and deepened divisions within the populace over the best course forward. Civil society became more polarized between those who advocated a more targeted protest against the FARC's practice of kidnapping and those who rejected kidnapping by all of the actors, not just the FARC.

Evaluating Institutional and Sectoral Peace Initiatives

This book has examined a sampling of initiatives from institutional (church), occupational (business and education), and social (women and indigenous groups) sectors. Each institution or distinct social sector—in some cases by virtue of bonds of common heritage, culture, interests, values, goals, or experiences—has tremendous potential for bridging the social divides that have fostered and perpetuated violent conflict. Some of these bonds are more highly developed than others, and they contribute in different ways and degrees to peace initiatives.

The more general role of education in creating normative changes that contribute to conflict prevention, management, resolution, and transformation has been little studied. Enrique Chaux and Ana M. Velásquez describe government and non-governmental organizations' (NGOs') peace education initiatives aimed at creating national citizenship standards to ensure that students are educated and attain skills and experience in peaceful relations and coexistence. While it is still early to assess the outcomes of the national initiative for implementing curricular reform, the initiative shows tremendous promise and vision and is likely to benefit from the participation of a strong core of engaged professionals committed to education reform. Coupling this vision and national leadership with the innovative local and regional initiatives already under way opens the door for generational change that will ensure that schools provide opportunities for democratic participation and responsibility and that students can be taught to appreciate pluralism, identity, the value of differences, and respect for human rights. Curricular changes are easy to assess, but measuring long-term normative changes and other outcomes is more problematic without a clearer consensus on how to define "peace" or create a culture of peace. Further research is needed to establish the relationship between individual personal transformation and societal transformation and to draw and replicate lessons learned from current local and regional initiatives.

More than any other institution, the Catholic Church is particularly well placed to contribute to peace in Colombia. Its institutional infrastructure gives it a grassroots presence throughout the country, often in places where the state is absent, as well as a hierarchical structure that links the church hierarchy to the broader Roman Catholic community. At a local level, church people are engaged in pastoral and communitarian dialogues with armed actors that have enjoyed considerable, if not widely publicized, success.[2] These dialogues have helped avert crises on numerous occasions, with outcomes that include the rescue of kidnap victims and the prevention of violence. The Catholic Church has also played a key intermediary role in each of Colombia's peace processes. It facilitated the recent demobilization process with the paramilitaries, it has been actively engaged in talks with the ELN, and it has offered its services repeatedly as an interlocutor with the FARC. These national initiatives are ongoing processes that have yet to reach their conclusions, but clearly the capacity to engage at local, regional, national, and international levels—and to connect these levels—permits the church to perform a range of roles in both peacemaking and peacebuilding.

The Protestant churches represent a smaller constituency than the Catholic Church and lack the extensive national infrastructure and access to the government that the Catholics enjoy. Yet they, too, are developing institutional infrastructures and building constituencies and alliances for peace at the local, regional, national, and international levels. The growth of these alliances, the sustainability of partnerships, the development of action plans around which consensus can be built, and the extent to which the churches can help empower displaced and other marginalized people with knowledge about their rights as citizens will be markers of success in this realm.

The business and the military are influential sectors in elite policymaking, but they are rarely considered in terms of the potential they have to contribute to peacemaking and peacebuilding. Rather, they are usually seen in terms of their role in contributing to conflict or blocking its resolution. Private sector–led peacebuilding is somewhat sporadic, fragmented, and largely subsumed by the economic interests of individual firms. Angelika Rettberg's case studies of business-based peace initiatives, the business community's engagement in Red Nacional de Programas Regionales de Desarrollo y Paz (REDPRODE-PAZ) and peace laboratories, and business-supported think tanks such as Fundación Ideas para la Paz (Ideas for Peace Foundation) underscore the wide diversity of innovative, pragmatic models for corporate engagement beyond the corporate social responsibility model. These approaches include creation

---

[2] Comisión Vida, Justicia y Paz, Diócesis de Magangué, "Diálogos pastorales y comunitarios," 2005.

of income-generating opportunities or provision of jobs, engagement of youth and internally displaced populations in productive activities, support of educational activities and institutions, institution building, and promotion of local development opportunities. Another realm where business could play a positive role includes facilitating the reintegration of ex-combatants. Rettberg suggests that conflict levels have dropped in some areas where business-supported initiatives were implemented. An evaluation of these efforts might consider as well the unfulfilled potential of the sector.

Because the military has frequently resisted efforts to implement peace policies, those promoting peace policies should consider ways to reach out to these potential spoilers, suggest Carlo Nasi and Jennifer Schirmer. Schirmer underscores the receptivity to the conversations she facilitated on behalf of the Norwegian Foreign Ministry and suggests that such activities can contribute to the growing acceptance of alternative viewpoints among military, ex-guerrilla, and civil society participants. Further research is needed to assess how and why these mechanisms might be effective. Is it the relationship-building function of the *conversatorios* that ultimately shapes the willingness of individuals to incorporate the "other" into their conception of the nation? Is it the content of these dialogues or the exposure to other mind-sets that challenges worldviews? Are these shifts at an individual level sufficient to contribute to a shift in the broader military culture? Longitudinal studies could be helpful in identifying concrete changes in discourse, policies, and practices. They could determine whether those engaged in these dialogues assume roles in supporting (or at least not blocking) peace processes. Studies of curriculum materials and teaching practices and approaches in military educational facilities could potentially serve as barometers of change.

Evaluating the Contributions of Gender and Ethnic-Based Initiatives

The model of appealing to a constitutive identity based on commonalities of ethnicity, class, and gender may prove to be one of the most exciting innovations in the peacebuilding field, since it challenges the notion that ethnicity is inherently divisive and more likely to be a driver of conflict than a vehicle for resisting violence.[3] While Afro-Colombians, Colombian indigenous people, peasant farmers, and women all suffer from disproportionate displacement, violence, and discrimination and social exclusion, historic and cultural factors have shaped each group's capacity to challenge this structural violence as well as resist physical attack. All these groups are seeking to exercise their right to neutrality in the conflict. They are seeking to transform their roles as "victims" into new roles as active citizens advocating for their needs and rights. In so doing, their efforts have met with varying degrees of success.

---

[3]See, for example, Ted Robert Gurr, *Minorities at Risk: A Global View of Ethnopolitical Conflicts* (Washington, D.C.: United States Institute of Peace Press, 1993).

Constituencies defined by gender, ethnicity, or class have succeeded in negotiating with armed actors to achieve particular goals, including obtaining safe passage for humanitarian needs, preventing displacement of communities, and securing the release of kidnapped or captured individuals. They have found innovative ways to challenge short-term violations of their rights through collective action. Their efforts to transform the culture of war, patriarchy, and racism and, to a lesser degree, the economic inequities that they believe underlie the violence have yet to yield durable, concrete results.

Colombia's indigenous peoples appear to have had greater success than Afro-Colombian and mestizo populations in establishing and maintaining "the separation that characterizes 'successful' peace communities."[4] As Leslie Wirpsa and others note, indigenous groups have historically sought autonomy and collective rights to land as the basis of their physical integrity and cultural identity. They have picked up arms to defend themselves in the past, including in the Quintín Lame guerrilla movement, but their demobilization and participation in the national Constituent Assembly secured them new legal avenues for addressing their needs. The 1991 constitution provided guarantees of consultative status on development plans, recognition of cultural autonomy, and funds for indigenous municipal development plans (*planes de vida*). Although implementation of these guarantees is sometimes lacking, today's indigenous groups are well organized to protect and exercise these constitutional rights nonviolently through some forty-two local, departmental, and regional affiliates that form part of the National Organization of Indigenous Peoples of Colombia, and through global alliances with other indigenous and human rights organizations.

Unlike indigenous communities, Afro-Colombians do not enjoy special constitutional protections for their collectively held lands, nor has their struggle centered around defending their territory. The history of Afro-Colombians has been largely shaped by slavery, an institution that separated families and communities across continents, isolated individuals from their own language and culture groups, and made organized collective resistance untenable.[5] The organization of nonviolent resistance among Afro-Colombians is relatively new. In 1993, Colombians of African descent secured passage of Law 70, which grants Afro-Colombians legal recognition and territorial rights to ancestral lands. Implementation of the law has been frequently challenged by armed groups and corporations. More recently, the Asociación de Afrocolombianos Desplazados (Association of Displaced Afro-Colombians) formed in response to the massive displacement of Afro-Colombian communities. AFRODES and other organizations such as the

---

[4] Christopher Mitchell, e-mail communication to the author, December 9, 2005.

[5] A key exception were the *cimarrones*, runaway slaves who formed communities of resistance known as *palenques*, especially in Montes de María. See Biblioteca Luis Ángel Arango, "Palenque: Epopeya de una sociedad guerrera," www.lablaa.org/blaavirtual/antropologia/magnum/nina0.htm (accessed September 18, 2008).

Proceso de Comunidades Negras (PCN or Black Communities Process) have forged international alliances with African-American organizations, human rights groups, church groups, and the Congressional Black Caucus of the U.S. House of Representatives in an effort to highlight the disproportionate victimization of Afro-Colombians by the war.[6] There is a pressing need for serious scholarly work to document and assess the relatively recent collective efforts to shape a peace agenda.

Peasant communities, which also have few resources and even less international support, enjoy no collective protections under Colombia's constitution. Peasants, who were among the earliest to establish peace communities (such as San José de Apartadó and the Asociación de Trabajadores Campesinos del Carare [Association of Peasant Workers of Carare]), have nonetheless found ways to create mechanisms for participating in municipal and national development plans and have negotiated with armed actors to attenuate the worst effects of the violence. In places such as Micoahumado, highly organized local peasants made global headlines when they secured agreements from the ELN to remove land mines from nearby roads. These and other local-level negotiations—despite their illegal status—have proved effective and necessary to protect local populations. Addressing the needs of peasant farmers as a group—such as the longer-term structural changes related to questions of land tenure and poverty—would begin to address the fundamental roots of Colombian violence. Yet such issues, which are among the issues the FARC has historically promoted at the peace table, do not appear to be part of any recent peace policy discussions.

Gender, like ethnicity and class, can be an effective organizing tool with tremendous potential to reach across historical divides. As Catalina Rojas documents, women's groups have begun forming networks and metanetworks (or "coalitions of coalitions") that include women from both urban and rural zones, that cut across class and ethnic lines, and that create dialogue between diverse groups of women, such as peasants and academics. These alliances have succeeded in convening large numbers of people in national demonstrations in support of a political solution to Colombia's armed conflict. Women's organizations have developed organizing methodologies based on a process involving extensive consultation that has resulted in a consensus agenda for peace.[7] This process is serving as a model for local and regional Constituent Assemblies, for building consensus on a peace agenda from the ground up, and for increasing participation in governance.

---

[6] See Virginia M. Bouvier, "A Reluctant Diaspora? The Case of Colombia," in *Diasporas in Conflict: Peacemakers or Peace Wreckers*, eds. Hazel Smith and Paul Stares (Washington, D.C.: United Nations University Press, 2007).

[7] See Bouvier, *Harbingers of Hope*; and Norma Villarreal and María Angélica Ríos, *Cartografía de la esperanza: "Iniciativas de resistencia pacífica desde las mujeres"* (Bogotá: IPIS and Corporación Ecomujer, 2006), www.saliendodelcallejon.pnud.org.co/img_upload/6d6b6f733839646834623 6633233737a/Cartografia_de_la_esperanza.pdf (accessed September 18, 2008).

Beyond measuring the number and nature of the participants in their activities, women's groups will ultimately be evaluated by whether they are able to foster and sustain a consensus on a peace agenda or secure inclusion of particular points within the broader national agenda. Their success will also be measured by their ability to articulate a gendered agenda for peace; to increase women's visibility and impact on key issues; to secure inclusion of women on national peace commissions or in peace talks; to establish violence against women as a key human rights consideration and a crime under the Justice and Peace Law; to integrate gender analysis into demobilization, disarmament, and reintegration (DDR) programs and implementation of the Justice and Peace Law; and to secure women's participation in decision-making bodies, including provincial councils, Constituent Assemblies, peace laboratories, and other development projects and political venues.

Evaluating Local Peace Initiatives

At the local level, we find a range of peace initiatives, including peace communities and peace laboratories, that attempt to link diverse social sectors at the local or territorial level. These initiatives tend to emerge primarily in territories of violence and conflict where there is little or no presence of state institutions. They are fragile, vulnerable to violence, and not always sustainable. They often suffer from conflicts of interest, co-optation, incompatible agendas and personalities, and seemingly insurmountable challenges. Furthermore, their successes are sometimes undermined by the deep and long-term dynamic of the conflict, the often tenuous nature of community bonds, and a deep mistrust that individuals feel not only toward the state and some or all of the armed actors but also toward each other.[8] In this hostile environment, Christopher Mitchell and Sara Ramirez suggest that the sheer survival or durability of peace communities constitutes success.

These communities have done more than merely survive, however. Peace communities in Tarso, Sonson, and Samaniego have succeeded in removing corrupt politicians, creating new development opportunities, and participating in the creation of Constituent Assemblies and municipal development plans.[9] While the impact of these structures on levels of violence is unclear, these exercises are deepening democratic practices by increasing citizen participation and public accountability at the local level and, thus, are contributing new mechanisms for the peaceful resolution of conflict. Many peace communities have also managed to initiate contacts that go beyond the municipal level. Peace municipalities in Antioquia, Meta, Atrato,

---

[8] Jim Jones, e-mail correspondence with the author, November and December 2005.

[9] See Luis Emil Sanabria Durán, "Con la fuerza de la gente . . . Experiencias de poder popular en Colombia," December 12, 2006, www.redepaz.org.co/Experiencias-de-poder-popular-en (accessed September 18, 2008).

and the south are now forming associations of municipalities of peace that are geared toward improving development and education for peace. Their establishment is widely seen as a sign of the increased capacity of nonviolent civil society actors to become a valuable resource for conflict mitigation and future peacebuilding.

Additional criteria for judging the success of local and regional peace initiatives include whether local peace agreements are reached and whether they hold at least for a time; whether initiatives are able to prevent or mitigate violence; whether a peace community grows and is supported by civil society and national or local policies; whether peace communities are able to establish better communication with their opponents; whether the armed actors allow communities to maintain their "neutrality" amid the conflict; and whether these communities can resist favoring the interests of political sectors and continue to pursue a vision of the common good. Finally, the success of local peace initiatives is related, albeit in a rather complex way, to the relationship of the particular initiative with government officials and policies at the local, regional, and national levels. Close ties of dependency can sustain an initiative in the short term, but as Mitchell and Ramírez demonstrate in the case of Sonson and Samaniego, they can also make initiatives more vulnerable to changes in local leadership or to opposition from powerful political sectors. Moreover, in a country where drug-trafficking interests have succeeded in capturing parts of the state, additional questions emerge about the desirability of collaboration with elected officials known to have ties to criminal elements.

It has been exceedingly difficult for the local armed actors, both legal and illegal, to recognize the status of neutrals or noncombatants who choose to establish peace communities, and this contributes to their extreme vulnerability. The national government perceives the efforts of peace communities to maintain "neutrality" and to prohibit entry of the state and its agents as a threat to its ability to exercise sovereign control. Álvaro Uribe's "democratic security" policies require greater involvement of communities in the conflict, make the maintenance of neutrality in the conflict more untenable, and undermine the efforts of peace communities and local actors to avoid being drawn into the conflict. Those engaging in local and regional dialogues with armed actors do so largely without the protection of the state and, in some cases, in violation of state decrees, leaving them in a very precarious state.

In sum, the success of these local initiatives is highly contingent on the particular context and the degree of direct confrontation between local armed actors in the immediate environment. The greater the level of contention—and it seems to have increased in many regions since 2003—the less the chances for local peacebuilding, and the harder it is for civilians to disengage from the conflict dynamics to establish and sustain a local zone of peace.

Evaluating Regional Peace Initiatives

This volume begins to lay out the basis for comparative work on the drivers of conflict and peace in distinct regions of Colombia. Regional inflections of the violence, the history and presence of social movements and organizations, and the nature of local armed actors all affect a population's capacity to respond to violence in a given region.[10] In Colombia, geography and a region's relationship to the different stages of coca cultivation, cocaine production, and drug trafficking are also particularly critical in shaping a community's destiny. This helps explain the wide range of perceptions of Colombia's conflict, or lack thereof.

Regional peace initiatives must be measured against their success in marshaling and using limited resources to meet particular regional needs for peace and development. We have seen how a region's history contributes to its capacity to confront violence effectively. Conflict-related violence tends to be more highly concentrated in certain areas of the countryside and less visible in Bogotá and other urban centers.

The peace and development programs and the peace laboratories seem to be having some success in organizing civil society for violence prevention and mitigation as well as for larger development goals. Measures for such impacts are more anecdotal than quantitative at this stage, and questions of local autonomy in development decisions continue to be rather thorny.

In the Magdalena Medio region, the Catholic Church, both through individual leaders and through institutional networks such as the Pastoral Social, has built on a history of union and peasant activism to create spaces for dialogue, social organization, and heightened participation of citizens. The peace and development organizations that took root there have provided an important—and replicable—model for other regions. In Antioquia, collective identities are strong and, as Mary Roldán notes, are "based on a culture of citizenship that is not dissident, radical, or anticapitalist but that stems from a deeply ingrained understanding of the mutual obligations of the state and its citizens."[11] Where the state—defined in the case of Eastern Antioquia and many other regions as the central government of Bogotá—has failed to meet its responsibilities, we are seeing the active engagement of governors (with the support of local citizens) to hold federal officials accountable. An organized history of resistance to violence through peasant organizations and the church provided the backdrop for declaring Sonson (in Eastern Antioquia) a "hamlet of peace," establishing a municipal

---

[10] See Gustavo Montañez Gómez, ed., *Dimensiones territoriales de la guerra y la paz* (Bogotá: Universidad Nacional de Colombia, 2004). Although not available in English, the book is particularly useful on the regional variations of the conflict.

[11] Mary J. Roldán, interview by the author, Cornell University, November 2005.

community Constituent Assembly and creating mechanisms for popular participation in municipal development plans. In Montes de María, an area dominated by strong paramilitary connections with political leaders, organizing and reweaving a social fabric of trust has been harder. There, Catholics and Protestants are addressing the violence through organizations such as the Network for Development and Peace of the Montes de María Foundation, Sembrandopaz, and sanctuary churches. They are working together to build trust through the creation of a "Montesmariana" identity that draws on the multicultural identities of the region and that will, in the words of one Colombian priest, reshape Colombian society "from a culture of favoritism to a culture of rights."[12] In Putumayo and Amazonia, areas long characterized by neglect and subsequently infused with international counternarcotics programs, local and regional authorities and citizens have sought to redefine their position of marginality vis-à-vis the state through new participatory mechanisms for resolving local conflicts and through the creation of *planes de vida* that allow indigenous communities to promote the development models they feel will best allow them to secure a peaceful future.

The success of civil society groups engaged in peace work at the regional level nonetheless is sometimes undermined by a lack of consensus on peacemaking or peacebuilding strategies; long-standing class, ethnic, and regional prejudices and divides; precarious resources and unsustainable funding that contribute to a lack of institutional capacity for peacebuilding; and ongoing physical threats. Finally, local and regional interests and efforts to exercise authority and autonomy sometimes conflict with national and international interests. These tensions over different development models are being negotiated with varying outcomes. Like municipal town councils and Constituent Assemblies, regional assemblies have become a constructive vehicle for strengthening participatory democracy by encouraging broader participation in decision making. In the absence of a state presence, such vehicles can be effective in fostering accountability and a consensus on development and on the nonviolent resolution of conflict. Such mechanisms may also be used to make demands on the state. To the extent that the state can respond to these demands, regional initiatives may be able to break down barriers of distrust and alienation.

Evaluating International Contributions to Peace in Colombia

This book has also focused on international efforts to complement and support peace initiatives in Colombia. The authors have focused on the role of the U.S. government, U.S. NGOs, the European Union, European NGOs, and sectors of the international donor community (especially the REDES program of the United Nations Development Programme [UNDP] and the Norwegian

---

[12] Father Rafael Castillo, interview by the author, September 24, 2006, Sincelejo, Colombia.

government's *conversatorios*), as well as the impact of normative aspects of international transitional justice in setting the parameters of peace negotiations. The authors suggest that international actors can be most effective in the long term if they play a subsidiary or complementary role that supports and builds on local, regional, and national peace initiatives, rather than taking a lead in setting a peace agenda.

International organizations have supported peace in Colombia in multiple ways with varying rates of success. First, internationals have acted as third parties to support political solutions to the conflict. Since the FARC-Pastrana talks, every peace process or discussion about peace processes has had an international counterpart in the form of a third-party mediator, facilitator, or "Groups of Friends."[13] Some of these have had partial successes in securing agreements such as the Los Pozos Accord. "Good offices" provided by UN special adviser Jan Egeland and his successor, James LeMoyne, and the interventions of the Group of Friends were critical in prolonging the peace talks between Pastrana and the FARC, although those ultimately broke down. The Group of Friends and various member countries continue to promote the resumption of talks between the FARC and the Colombian government and have been working to facilitate an agreement on a humanitarian accord.[14] Mediation by Venezuelan president Hugo Chávez successfully secured the release of hostages by the FARC in early 2008.

The international community has also continued to support and facilitate a peace process with the ELN. In 2000, five countries—Cuba, Spain, Switzerland, France, and Norway—were the Group of Friends designated to accompany the ELN process; Mexico served as a mediator between the ELN and the Colombian government in 2004–05; and Cuba and Venezuela have provided logistical support for the exploratory talks between the Colombian government, the ELN, and Colombian civil society—facilitated by Norway, Spain, and Switzerland. All of these efforts, however, have been contingent upon the government's political will to allow and support the engagement of the international community. Once that political will has been withdrawn, international efforts have quickly fallen flat.

---

[13] See Teresa Whitfield, *Friends Indeed? The United Nations, Groups of Friends, and the Resolution of Conflict* (Washington, D.C.: United States Institute of Peace Press, 2007); and Cynthia J. Arnson and Teresa Whitfield, "Third Parties and Intractable Conflicts: The Case of Colombia," in *Grasping the Nettles: Analyzing Cases of Intractable Conflict*, eds. Chester A. Crocker, Fen Osler Hampson, and Pamela Aall (Washington, D.C.: United States Institute of Peace Press, 2005), 231–68.

[14] For the Pastrana negotiations with the FARC, the ten-member "facilitating commission" of a larger Group of Friends consisted of Mexico, Canada, Venezuela, Cuba, Sweden, Norway, France, Italy, Switzerland, and Spain. See Marc Chernick, "Protracted Peacemaking: The Insertion of the International Community into the Colombian Peace Process," in *From Promise to Practice: Strengthening UN Capacities for the Prevention of Violent Conflict*, eds. Chandra Sriram and Karen Wermeister (Boulder, Colo.: Lynne Rienner and International Peace Academy, 2003).

Sweden, the Netherlands, and Switzerland have been the countries most committed to the Uribe government's demobilization of the paramilitaries. The Organization of American States has taken the lead in establishing a verification process through the Misión de Apoyo para los Procesos de Paz (MAPP or Mission to Support the Peace Process). They have succeeded in verifying the demobilization of tens of thousands of Autodefensas Unidas de Colombia (AUC) paramilitaries but have not yet been able to assure that the demobilization is followed by effective measures to dismantle paramilitary power. Without these comprehensive measures, paramilitary demobilization may be counterproductive to the extent that it decentralizes paramilitary power and facilitates new configurations of illegal armed actors, as has already happened.

Second, internationals can facilitate intersectoral dialogue more broadly. International actors are playing a significant role in facilitating strategic alliances among diverse social actors of the peace movement and with the local, regional, and national authorities. They can facilitate participatory assessments and foster analytical consensus on the problems that need to be addressed in order to transform the conflict. The international community has exercised this facilitating role by assuming moderating functions and proposing formulas for consensus, and through observation and accompaniment. International actors can encourage civil society actors to organize themselves and to put forward proposals and agendas for action. Donors have already had some success in setting the stage for diverse agreements among civil society actors and with government authorities, and for generating consensus on peace and reconciliation proposals.[15] In the *conversatorios*, the Norwegian government is creating spaces for dialogues as a confidence-building measure between national parties. The UNDP is also playing this convening role by bringing together local groups to develop consensus on political agendas.

Third, internationals have provided direct financial and technical support for peace and development initiatives and for human rights. While U.S. government assistance to Colombia has been primarily for military assistance, it has provided some direct financial and technical assistance for social and economic development and human rights initiatives. Donors from the European Union countries, Japan, and Norway, as well as international financial institutions and multilateral development banks such as the Inter-American Development Bank and the World Bank, have dedicated resources to alternative development and to Colombian initiatives for peace, including peace laboratories. As the three peace laboratories end their pilot phase, evaluations will undoubtedly yield lessons for improving their efficacy, as well as

---

[15] At the London donor meetings in 2003, a new mechanism, the G-24, was set up as an informal group of countries to support the government of Colombia in complying with the commitments established in those meetings.

recommendations for future refinements. Since international assistance has sometimes triggered disputes over resources and occasionally overwhelmed the administrative capacities of the initiatives, it will be important to gauge how much local communities feel that their needs have been addressed and their preferences respected in the process. The trick, once again, seems to be to help local people in zones of peace develop their own resource base without fostering dependence on outside help, and to ensure that local needs are not subordinated to larger corporate interests.

Beyond technical and financial assistance, the international community can also provide moral support, visibility, and protection for peace initiatives. It can bolster local initiatives, increase institutional capacities, and help link initiatives strategically. The presence of internationals in the field can play a significant protective role for those working for peace and justice.

NGOs and faith-based groups have played a particularly important role in accompanying vulnerable communities and documenting and analyzing human rights conditions, monitoring and shaping foreign policies, and pressuring governments to pay greater attention to the human rights situation in Colombia. In 2000, Catholic Relief Services initiated a partnership with the Catholic National Secretariat for Social Ministry/Caritas Colombia, for the program In Solidarity with Colombia, which expands and strengthens coordination on humanitarian aid, justice, peace education and peacebuilding, and educating the U.S. public on issues relating to Colombia.[16] Colombian sanctuary churches have set up partnerships with U.S. communities in Iowa, Minnesota, and South Dakota through Lutheran World Relief.[17] Peace Brigades International, Fellowship of Reconciliation, the Society of Friends Peace Teams, Witness for Peace, Christian Peacemaker Teams, and the Presbyterian Church (U.S.A.) have all established accompaniment programs in Colombia. All of these programs appear to have had some success in mitigating violence as well as in generating support, solidarity, and partnerships with besieged communities and individuals in Colombia.

Fourth, the international community has an explicit role to play in norm setting and support for human rights and the rule of law. Many church groups and NGOs involved in accompaniment work see the protection of human rights as a key part of establishing the mechanisms for a sustainable peace in Colombia. As Arturo Carrillo and others have shown us, international actors have established mechanisms for addressing violations of human rights norms and international humanitarian laws and conventions at the international level. These norms are being incorporated into Colombian

---

[16] See Catholic Relief Services, www.crs.org/our_work/where_we_work/overseas/latin_america_and_the_caribbean/colombia/index.cfm (accessed January 27, 2007).

[17] See Lutheran World Relief Campaign for Colombia, www.lwr.org/colombia/salyluz/index.asp (accessed May 8, 2008).

domestic laws and have become effective organizing tools for civil society to hold the state accountable to its human rights commitments.[18]

The balance sheet for evaluating international interventions for peace has yet to be tallied. In the absence of a definitive resolution to the conflict, how might their actions be judged? The authors in this book suggest that their efforts might be measured against the progress made toward the larger goals of strengthening grassroots communities, buttressing the technical capacity of peace initiatives, developing specific social development projects, protecting and promoting human rights, increasing the rule of law and accountability for abuses committed, preventing violence, promoting sustainable alternative development, creating or maintaining spaces for dialogue, and addressing the sources of conflict in nonviolent ways.

Interdependence of Organizational Levels

The arrangement of the chapters in this book by organizational levels (local, regional, national, international) and by institutional and social sectors (church, education, business, women, indigenous) implicitly asks us to consider the relationships not only between the chapters within each section but also the relationship between the sections. This structure calls us to examine how the capacities of one organizational level might be strengthened through efforts at another level.

We have seen the impact of national policies on local and regional peace initiatives. As Christopher Mitchell notes, "At the local level it's hard to talk about conflict 'resolution' in the absence of a national level effort at peacemaking. At best, we are dealing with conflict 'mitigation,' and this can best be facilitated by a return to a recognition by the national government of local people's right to resume 'sovereignty' and to conclude local peace agreements."[19] Nationally declared cease-fires, cessations of hostilities, amnesties, DDR, and laws governing all these impact local conflict environments in different ways. National initiatives shape the conditions for increased militarization or mitigation of the violence at the local and regional levels and define the parameters under which DDR and reconciliation might (or might not) take place.

This book has also shown the many ways that the international realm—both intentionally and inadvertently—affects peace options. Among other things, international human rights and peacemaking norms and conventions

---

[18] Some of these international agencies include the International Committee of the Red Cross, the United Nations Office of the High Commissioner for Human Rights (with a field office in Colombia since 1996), the UN High Commissioner for Refugees, the OAS Inter-American Commission on Human Rights, and the Inter-American Court of Human Rights. See Pierre Gassmann, "Colombia: Persuading Belligerents to Comply with International Norms," in *Civilians in War,* ed. Simon Chesterman (Boulder, Colo.: Lynne Rienner, 2001), 67–92.

[19] Christopher Mitchell, e-mail communication to the author, December 9, 2005.

shape the kinds of peacemaking "deals" that will or will not be possible at the national level. The book has illustrated the many ways that local and regional initiatives affect international efforts and vice versa. And it has given multiple examples of the ways that civil society has contributed to shaping a national peace agenda.

A New Framework for Contemporary Peacebuilding

This book is meant to encourage greater dialogue between and within all levels and sectors, to articulate and synthesize some of the lessons from past peace initiatives, and to generate discussions of how greater integration within and across levels might be better achieved and harnessed toward a new push for peace in Colombia.

The real challenge is to put the initiatives together within a framework of mutual reinforcement. A more integrated approach to peacemaking within zones of conflict—one that builds on the tremendous energy and the variations between and across different levels of society—has the potential to be more effective in transforming Colombia's internal armed conflict. Analysis of all the conflict actors—both those striving for nonviolent peaceful change and those engaged in violence—will assist in this transformation. Armed with a better understanding of the resources that exist for peace at each level, international governments and organizations, the non-governmental communities within and outside Colombia, and the Colombian state will be better equipped to design and enact public policies that enhance peace initiatives and create or take advantage of new opportunities for peace.

John Paul Lederach has developed a pyramidal approach to understanding peacebuilding, whereby the apex of the pyramid represents the elites of society (high-level political, religious, and military leaders); the base represents grassroots leaders; and the ethnic, religious, intellectual, and social leaders constitute a middle level that engages with both the apex and the base.[20] This pioneering metaphor gives us a way to conceive of individual peace initiatives and to envision how they might be made more effective through targeted interventions at each level and construction of stronger relationships between the levels. In this model, the middle level of the pyramid takes on particular importance, for herein dwell the interlocutors and translators who move between the broad base of society and the ruling elites.

The material presented by the authors of this book confirms the importance of this middle level and suggests the beginnings of a new theoretical model. In this refined model, which builds on Lederach's work, society might be imagined as a grid of threads representing the social fabric. In conflict zones, the fabric is torn asunder by violence and war, and peacebuilding

---

[20] John Paul Lederach, *Construyendo la paz: Reconciliación sostenible en sociedades divididas*, 2nd ed. (Bogotá: Editorial Codice, 1998, 2007), 72.

efforts try to mend, reweave, and reconstruct the web and weft of the social fabric. The web of the fabric is thus made up of threads that represent local, regional, and national efforts for peace, while the weft is formed by threads representing institutions, sectors, cultures, education, ethnicity, religion, gender, and other commonalities that can bridge the different levels. These elements permeate and inform every level of Colombian society and have the potential to hold together and give cohesion to the local, regional, and national initiatives that constitute the web of the fabric. The more peace initiatives there are, the higher the density of the threads, and the stronger the fabric is likely to be. But the weft and the web must be carefully woven and well integrated. In this model, the international community provides the understitching to the fabric, reinforcing the individual threads of Colombia's social fabric but neither dominating nor departing too widely from the delicate patterns and hues of reconstruction already in place.

Challenging Conventional Wisdom

So, what are the implications of this comprehensive model? How does an appreciation for the different levels and spheres in which peace initiatives operate and interact change our understanding of Colombia's internal armed conflict and what might be needed to transform it? What are some of the reigning assumptions that are challenged by this approach?

In long-term violent conflict such as that experienced in Colombia, there does not seem to be a steady progression along a curve from a state of violent conflict to peace (however that might be defined). Instead, we see a pendulum that alternates between national efforts to achieve a negotiated settlement and efforts to win the war. When one set of peace initiatives fails or when military victory does not materialize, new administrations often reverse course. We find that executive leadership determines the direction and speed of the pendulum and that presidents can choose to ignore, seize, or create opportunities for dialogue that could lead to peace. The role of civil society at the local, regional, national, and even international levels in shaping these choices is hugely important yet widely ignored or undervalued.

A central question raised by this book is how local and regional experiences might contribute to diplomacy at the national level. Both the individuals and groups that have brokered local resolutions, and the mechanisms they have forged for resolving conflict, may be able to contribute to national strategies for peace. Colombia has a vast reservoir of accumulated experiences—negotiating agreements on humanitarian issues or for violence prevention or conflict mitigation, promoting inclusive and participatory governance, engaging in the design and implementation of municipal or regional development plans, educating for peace and nonviolent conflict resolution, and marginalizing or engaging actors advocating violence. These experiences constitute a tremendous untapped resource that may hold the keys for transforming Colombia's conflict.

In analyzing Colombia's nonviolent conflict actors, we see that one of the obstacles to peace has been the lack of consensus on the diagnosis of Colombia's conflict. To be more effective in creating a propitious environment for a new peace process, Colombians can develop a common understanding of the causes of the conflict and what is needed for its transformation. This could lead toward consensus on a common agenda for action. Civil society leaders must insist on being given space to make proposals, and the armed actors, including the state and external forces with a stake in the conflict (for example, the United States), must take these proposals seriously. The international community can provide opportunities for such conversations to take place and can encourage the Colombian government to incorporate these civil society perspectives in pursuit of a national peace agenda.

Alliance building may hold the key to greater integration in peacebuilding. Beyond the markers of success discussed at each level, peace advocates might be more effective in sustaining and advancing their peacebuilding activities if they were able to establish denser alliances and networks with others, and secure institutional and economic support from state authorities as well as from the international community. In this way, their impact could be leveraged for the design and implementation of national peace policies. Peace initiatives defined by gender, ethnicity, and religion have much to teach us in this regard, since they tend to offer opportunities based on clear organizing frameworks and structures. Many of these initiatives hold out the promise of cross-sectoral alliances and the capacity to link and create synergies between local, regional, national, and international levels.

Reflections on the Colombian experience suggest that promoting civil society peace initiatives now will help build the conditions for peace later. International aid for such initiatives, thoughtfully administered, can be well placed and effective. The REDES team suggests that the Colombian experience challenges international theories on the sequencing of peacemaking and peacebuilding activities. In Colombia, security, peace, and development are being pursued simultaneously. Concurrent pursuit of peace and development in Colombia appears to be reducing violence and mitigating conflict, and is laying the groundwork for the implementation of future peace agreements.

We see in this book how regional dimensions are central to Colombia's conflict—and likely to be central to its resolution. In the absence of strong leadership for peace at the national level, local and regional initiatives are temporarily filling the gap, with some limited success, but they have yet to be harnessed to national peace efforts.

The historical lack of trust between local and regional authorities, on one hand, and those based in Bogotá, on the other, has made collaboration difficult. The central government has tended to be distrustful of regional solutions, has sought to maintain control of all contacts with illegal armed actors, and has frequently opposed regional dialogues. As long as the national government is engaged in a policy characterized by the prosecution of a war—against the guerrillas, against the paramilitaries, and against those who object to its military approach—it will continue to view these local and regional initiatives as a threat and a challenge to its hegemony. Should efforts turn toward the pursuit of peace as a priority, however, the central government may become more open to these innovative solutions emerging outside the capital.

On the other hand, local populations are also distrustful of the center, viewing the Colombian state, which has long been absent from many areas of the country, as merely another armed actor, whose presence is no more legitimate than that of other actors. The central government's efforts to engage civilian populations caught in the cross fire of violence in helping it prosecute the war, as well as its public attacks on known and respected social leaders, have put local peace actors, already living in precarious security conditions, at even greater risk. Local and regional peace initiatives would be greatly facilitated by greater support—or less hostility—from the national level. International efforts to protect and nurture these local experiences of peace and to encourage national authorities to reach out to these local populations in a sincere search for a resolution to the conflict could go a long way in generating goodwill toward the state.

As Colombia grapples with issues of impunity and seeks policies that will ensure that the cycle of violence is interrupted, the reflections on past efforts to bring illegal armed actors to the peace table are instructive. Our analysis of peace initiatives and past negotiating efforts confirms that political will is key and that substance, process, strategy, and timing also matter. This book's insights into the past agendas and priorities of the FARC, the ELN, and the AUC have tremendous relevance for shaping future peace processes and reveal some of the fault lines between local, national, and international interests and standards.

Shifts in national or international contexts can open up new opportunities for peace initiatives. At the national level, a military impasse has held steady between the FARC and the Colombian government for nearly half a century. This impasse has outlived the many changes in administration in Colombia and continual shifts of the political pendulum since the days of La Violencia. In the second term of Uribe's presidency, while both groups of guerrilla insurgents appear to have been weakened militarily, they have not been defeated.

The international context is in flux, and global and hemispheric trends may prove auspicious for peace. Just as the end of the Cold War influenced some guerrilla groups to reconsider their options and put down their arms, so, too, is the coming to power of leftist presidents throughout much of Latin America and the emergence in Colombia of leftist electoral options shaping the political landscape within which Colombian guerrilla movements are operating. These legitimate spaces for "opposition" politics should be protected and promoted, for they provide nonviolent electoral alternatives that may be attractive to ideologically driven guerrillas in the coming years.

Furthermore, the international community, particularly the various Groups of Friends accompanying the different national peace initiatives discussed herein, has shown an increased willingness to engage on the issue of peace in Colombia. Increasingly, Colombia's conflict is having an impact on its neighbors, and international bodies such as the Organization of American States, the United Nations, and the International Criminal Court are being called upon to address violations of territorial integrity, as well as human rights and humanitarian issues related to Colombia's conflict.

U.S. policies have sought to balance concerns about insurgency, drugs, and terrorism and have rarely focused efforts on developing or supporting a peace policy per se. But policymakers may well find that making peace and development a priority addresses their other areas of concern. Working in partnership to support the communities' development needs and economic well-being can undermine the economic drivers and provide alternatives to illicit-crop production or to joining illegal armed groups. Illicit-crop production has been both a major source of jobs and a driver of conflict and displacement for affected communities in Colombia's rural hinterlands. Whereas counternarcotics efforts have done little to stem the tide of drugs entering the United States from Colombia, peace and development initiatives, ironically, may prove more effective.

The U.S. government has largely supported the Uribe administration (and, before that, the Pastrana administration) through Plan Colombia, investing heavily in strengthening the Colombian state and hoping either to defeat the FARC guerrillas militarily or to weaken them enough to force them to the negotiating table. With the death of three of the FARC's seven-member secretariat in 2008, and the rising number of FARC defections, it may be time to shift focus from the battlefield to the peace table. A peace policy that would end the war and seek the guerrillas' reintegration into society and also address the origins of the conflict might be more successful in the long term than one that disarms and demobilizes the weakened insurgents without addressing the underlying social and economic inequities that have allowed the FARC to continue to fight. Whether the FARC is driven more by ideology or by greed, Marc Chernick makes a compelling case that some of the reforms it has been seeking are far from unreasonable (indeed, some were already adopted in the 1991 constitution), and that agrarian reforms, improved social development policies, and stronger human rights protections may help break the cycle of violence.

At this point, the U.S. government has paid relatively little attention to peace efforts with the smaller ELN. Given the potential overlap in U.S. strategic objectives with the ELN's expressed interest in addressing an agenda of social issues that includes inequity, poverty, displacement, drug trafficking, and the dismantling of illicit paramilitary and criminal networks, peace talks with the ELN could serve both peace in Colombia and broader U.S. interests. Innovative models for civil society's engagement in the ELN process are being tested and may well provide lessons for other conflicted societies looking to broaden citizen participation in peacemaking.

Finally, in the paramilitary demobilization, the United States can play a role by helping ensure that illicit paramilitary structures are truly dismantled. For mechanisms of accountability and reparations to disrupt the cycle of violence once and for all, impunity for crimes against humanity cannot prevail. U.S. officials should design safeguards to ensure that the extradition of Colombia's paramilitary leaders on drug-trafficking charges does not enable them to bypass mechanisms that Colombia has established to pursue truth, justice, and reparations for victims.[21]

Our focus on past and present peace initiatives in Colombia reveals the need for a dynamic approach to conflict resolution that also considers the humanitarian crisis unleashed by the conflict. The internal displacement of more than three million Colombians and the extensive sowing of land mines by all sides as part of the war effort have left a legacy that threatens to continue the cycle of poverty and violence for generations to come. The involvement of civil society—and especially those who have been displaced by the violence—in crafting solutions to the humanitarian crisis is critical to any future peace process. Civil society's participation and engaged input will contribute to the sustainability of the peace.

This book is a testament to the ingenuity, creativity, dedication, and courage of a country blessed with resources yet plagued by violence. While Colombians have much to learn from other experiences of forging peace, it is clear that Colombia also has much to teach the international community. In its long experience struggling to transform conflict at every level of society, it has developed its own repertoire of success stories, strategies, and innovative models, particularly in the field of peace education. Understanding how to build on these experiences to advance toward peace is an urgent priority for Colombia, but these lessons will find fertile ground far beyond its borders. This book is a modest first step toward beginning that process.

---

[21] Amnesty International, "Colombia: Extradition of Paramilitary Leaders Must Not Lead to Closure of Investigations into Human Rights Violations," May 15, 2008, www.amnesty.org/en/news-and-updates/colombia-extradition-paramilitary-leaders-must-not-lead-closure-investigations-h (accessed September 19, 2008).

Contributors

Virginia M. Bouvier is a senior program officer at the United States Institute of Peace, where she has worked since 2003 and heads the Colombia Conflict Team and the Colombia grants initiative. She is the author of *Women and the Conquest of California, 1542–1840: Codes of Silence* and editor of *The Globalization of U.S.–Latin American Relations: Democracy, Intervention, and Human Rights* and *Whose America? The War of 1898 and the Battles to Define the Nation*. From 1995 to 2002, she was an assistant professor of Latin American literature and culture at the University of Maryland. From 1982 to 1989, she was a senior associate at the Washington Office on Latin America. She has also served as a consultant for the World Bank, Levi Strauss Foundation, Levi Strauss & Co., and the C.S. Fund, and as research director for the Women's Leadership Conference of the Americas, a joint project of the Inter-American Dialogue and the International Center for Research on Women.

* * *

Arturo J. Carrillo is associate professor of clinical law and director of the Human Rights Clinic Program at the George Washington University Law School. He taught previously at Columbia Law School, where he was acting director of the Human Rights Clinic in 2002–03. He joined Columbia's Human Rights Institute in 1999 as the Henkin Senior Fellow and was associate director of its Transitional Justice Program in 2001–02. From 1991 to 1994, he worked as a legal adviser and human rights monitor in the Human Rights Division of the United Nations Observer Mission to El Salvador (ONUSAL). He was the attorney for the United Nations Affairs of the Colombian Commission of Jurists in Bogotá and professor of international human rights and humanitarian law at the Escuela Superior de Administración Pública (ESAP or Superior School of Public Administration) from 1994 to 1998. He has authored numerous publications in English and Spanish on human rights, humanitarian law, and transitional justice. He contributed a chapter on the Inter-American Court of Human Rights for *The Handbook of Reparations*, published in 2006 by Oxford University Press. He is currently a senior adviser on human rights policy to the United States Agency for International

Development (USAID) in Colombia. He holds law degrees from George Washington and Columbia law schools, and a BA in politics and Latin American studies from Princeton University.

Enrique Chaux is an associate professor in the Department of Psychology at Universidad de los Andes. He has a doctorate in human development and psychology from Harvard University. He also has an MA in risk and prevention from Harvard University, an MA in cognitive and neural systems from Boston University, and undergraduate degrees in physics and industrial engineering, both from Universidad de los Andes. He has conducted research projects related to interpersonal conflicts and to the development of aggression among children and adolescents exposed to high levels of community violence, as well as educational projects related to the prevention of aggression and promotion of peaceful interpersonal relationships in schools. He led the teams in charge of designing the Colombian National Standards of Citizenship Competencies and the National Test of Citizenship Competencies. He recently coauthored the books *Citizenship Com- petencies: From the Standards to the Classroom* and *The Promotion of Citizenship Competencies.*

Juan Chaves is a political scientist who currently serves as a program officer for the United Nations Office for the Coordination of Humanitarian Affairs. He previously served as peace and development adviser at the United Nations Development Programme (UNDP) in Colombia and coordinated the Working Group for Peace, Conflict, and Development established by the Reconciliation and Development program (REDES) in 2005. His research and practice interests include conflict prevention, peacebuilding, and development within contexts of protracted deadly conflicts. He has an MA in public policy and political economy.

Marc Chernick is research associate professor in the Department of Government and the Center for Latin American Studies at Georgetown University, and author of *Acuerdo Posible: Solución negociada al conflicto armado colombiano.* He previously taught and directed the Latin American studies programs at the Johns Hopkins School of Advanced International Studies and at Columbia University, and worked for several years as a professor at the Universidad de los Andes and the Universidad Nacional de Colombia, both in Bogotá. He has been a consultant to the World Bank, UNDP, the U.S. Department of State, USAID, and the government of Switzerland on projects to promote peace and conflict resolution in Colombia and other Latin American countries and in Africa. He is currently working with a team of international scholars on a cross-regional research project sponsored by the Norwegian government and the Social Science Research Council on insurgent groups and paths to settlement of internal armed conflicts. He has written widely on drug trafficking, political violence, and negotiated settlement to internal armed conflicts and is the editor and coauthor of a 2005 study for the UNDP on conflict prevention and early warning in Latin America, focusing on the case of Colombia. He has a PhD in political science from Columbia University.

Ricardo Esquivia Ballestas is the general coordinator of the ASVIDAS network of Montes de María and Sincelejo, an organization of 130 local community groups working in the Colombian provinces of Bolívar, Sucre, Córdoba, and the Caribbean coast that has 2,500 members and a team of 30 volunteer facilitators and is dedicated to the development of sustainable peace efforts. He is a founding member of the board of directors of the Development and Peace Network of the Montes de María Foundation, and executive director of the Asociación Sembrando Semillas de Paz (Sowing Seeds of Peace Association), with headquarters in Sincelejo. He is a member of the Mennonite Church, coordinator of the Commission of Peace of the Colombian Council of Evangelical Churches, and member of the National Peace Council that advises the president of the republic.

Catalina Garzón was formerly a research associate with the Community Strategies for Sustainability and Justice Program at the Pacific Institute and, prior to that, provided technical assistance to a community-building initiative in West Oakland, Calif., as a researcher with the Institute of Urban and Regional Development. She has also served as project coordinator of Urban Habitat's Leadership Institute for Sustainable Communities. She is currently pursuing a doctorate in environmental science, policy, and management at the University of California–Berkeley and holds an MA in city and regional planning from the same institution.

Barbara Gerlach is minister of First Congregational United Church of Christ in Washington, D.C., and serves as the Colombia liaison for the United Church of Christ Justice and Witness Ministries. She is a member of the Colombia Steering Committee, Ecumenical Working Group, and Afro-Colombia Working Group, Washington-based coalitions of non-governmental organizations (NGOs) and faith-based organizations working for a more informed U.S. policy toward Colombia. She has worked closely with the peace and development initiatives of Protestant churches in Colombia and led many delegations of U.S. citizens to Colombia. She is author of *The Things that Make for Peace*, biblical meditations illustrated with her art.

Héctor Fabio Henao Gaviria, S.J., has been the director of the Colombian Episcopal Conference's National Social Ministry Secretariat/Caritas since 1996. He is president of the Ficonpaz Foundation of the Archdiocese of Bogotá and is president of the Peace and Reconciliation Working Group of Caritas Internationalis. He has headed peace and development efforts in some of the most conflicted zones of Colombia, including through Caritas' Colombia Campaign, and is known for his work negotiating the release of hostages, particularly the successful release of British and Israeli hostages following three months of negotiations with Ejército de Liberación Nacional (ELN) guerrillas. He holds a doctorate in social sciences from the Pontifical Gregorian University of Rome and a degree in sociology from the Universidad San Buenaventura of Medellín.

Adam Isacson has worked since 1995 at the Center for International Policy, an independent research and advocacy organization in Washington, D.C., where he coordinates a program that monitors security and U.S. military assistance to Latin America and the Caribbean. The program has produced numerous publications, including the *Just the Facts* series of reference books on U.S.–Latin American military cooperation. Since 1998 he has visited Colombia more than two dozen times and has traveled to twelve of Colombia's thirty-two departments. He has testified before the U.S. Congress and published extensively on U.S. policy toward Colombia. He holds an MA in international relations from Yale University and worked previously for the Arias Foundation for Peace and Human Progress in San José, Costa Rica.

Neil Jeffery was executive director of the U.S. Office on Colombia from February 2001 to May 2005. He previously worked at Oxfam GB in the United Kingdom as South America policy adviser. He is a founding member of the Peace Brigades International (PBI)–Colombia Project and served as program coordinator from 1993 until 1996. From 1991 to 1993, he worked for the PBI team in Guatemala. He has a BA in geography from the University of Cambridge and studied as a visiting fellow at the Refugee Studies Center at the University of Oxford from 1996 to 1997. He also has an MA and postgraduate diploma in forced migration.

James C. Jones is a Latin America area specialist with a PhD in social anthropology and an MS in economics. Since the mid-1970s, he has worked or conducted research in fifteen countries of the region, and has also consulted on international development issues in the areas of education, the environment, health, agriculture, and rural development in Africa and Asia. From 1997 to 1999, he served as Latin America regional adviser in alternative development to the United Nations International Drug Control Program. In that capacity, he worked closely with small farmers who were growing coca and opium poppy in Colombia, Peru, and Bolivia and with national agencies using rural development for drug control. In 2000, he received a grant from the John D. and Catherine T. MacArthur Foundation to research the impact of U.S. policy on the armed conflict and drug control in Colombia and is preparing a book based on this research. He recently completed a Latin America regional report and a major global report for the United Nations Office on Drugs and Crime to assess the use of alternative development (or "sustainable livelihoods") as a drug-control tool. He has more recently consulted for the United Nations in Afghanistan and for several European entities in the Andes. He has served as an adjunct faculty member at George Washington University's Elliott School of International Affairs.

Sabine Kurtenbach is a political scientist with a PhD from Hamburg University and is a senior researcher at the Instituto de Estudios Iberoamericanos of the German Institute of Global and Area Studies, Hamburg. She is also a consultant for various German agencies of development cooperation, including the Foreign Ministry, the Ministry of Cooperation, the German Agency for Technical Cooperation (GTZ), and the Friedrich Ebert Foundation. Her main subject areas are peace and conflict studies, development policies, and human rights, particularly in Central America, Colombia, and the Andean region. Her current research interests are the developments in post-conflict societies and the strategies of external actors toward complex emergencies.

Christopher Mitchell is emeritus professor of conflict analysis at the Institute for Conflict Analysis and Resolution (ICAR), George Mason University, Virginia, and a member of ICAR's Local Zones of Peace Working Group. He has published widely on various aspects of conflict resolution and local peacebuilding. He is author of *Gestures of Conciliation: Factors Contributing to Successful Olive Branches* and *Handbook of Conflict Resolution: The Analytical Problem-Solving Approach.*

Javier Moncayo has worked for the Program for Development and Peace in Magdalena Medio since 1996, serving as deputy director from 2002 to 2004, and he has been involved in the European Union–funded Peace Laboratory there. From 2004 to 2007, he was the coordinator of the National Network of Regional Development and Peace Programs (Red Nacional de Programas Regionales de Desarrollo y Paz—REDPRODEPAZ), and he currently serves as a consultant on development and peace issues for GTZ and continues to support the work of REDPRODEPAZ. Moncayo is also a medical doctor at the Universidad Nacional de Colombia. He worked on community health projects in Magdalena Medio for the Catholic Church's Social Ministry and was the adviser and head of the Office of Emergencies and Disasters of the Colombian Ministry of Health from 1993 to 1995.

Carlo Nasi is associate professor and director of graduate studies of the Political Science Department at the Universidad de los Andes. He has done research on conflict resolution, civil war, and democratization in Colombia, El Salvador, and Guatemala. His latest writings address the role of "spoilers" in Colombia's peace processes, the patterns of violence in the country's coffee and banana-producing regions, and the failed peace negotiations during the government of President Andrés Pastrana. He was a Hamburg Fellow and a MacArthur Associate at the Center of International Studies and Cooperation (CISAC) at Stanford University and has been awarded research grants from the Social Science Research Council, the Institute for the Study of World Politics, the International Development Research Centre (IDRC), and the Universidad de los Andes. He was also recipient of a fellowship from the University of Notre Dame and the Coca-Cola Co. and of a graduate studies fellowship of the British Council. He has a PhD in political science from the University of Notre Dame.

Borja Paladini Adell is a political scientist and peace researcher. He currently works as a field official of the UNDP in the Nariño Department of Colombia, where he is promoting the development of an integral peacebuilding and development program. He is also advising the Peace and Development Area of UNDP Colombia. His research interests include peace and conflict dynamics, conflict-related development, integrated frameworks for peacebuilding, and conflict transformation education.

María Clemencia Ramírez is the director and a senior researcher at the Instituto Colombiano de Antropología y Historia, and professor of anthropology at the Universidad de los Andes in Bogotá, Colombia. She attended the Universidad de los Andes and the Universidad Nacional de Colombia, earning a BA in anthropology and an MA in history. She also holds a PhD in social anthropology from Harvard University. Her work explores the intersections of violence and identity through the lens of public policy and state-citizen relations, especially in the Amazon region of Colombia and specifically in the department of Putumayo, where the implementation of Plan Colombia began in 2000. She has written on the intersection of drugs and war, and the *cocalero* movement in the western Amazon. She is author of the book *Entre el Estado y la Guerrilla: Identidad y Ciudadanía en el Movimiento de los Campesinos Cocaleros del Putumayo* (Between the State and the Guerrillas: Identity and Citizenship in the Putumayo Cocalero Peasants Movement). She was the 2004–05 Santo Domingo Visiting Scholar at the David Rockefeller Center for Latin American Studies at Harvard University.

Sara Ramírez is a Colombian social anthropologist who has carried out fieldwork in a large number of local peace communities in Colombia. She currently works as a researcher for the peace organization Justapaz in Bogotá, Colombia.

Angelika Rettberg is an associate professor in the Political Science Department at the Universidad de los Andes and the director of its Research Program on Peacebuilding. Her research has focused on the private sector as political actor and, more recently, on private-sector behavior in contexts of armed conflict. She has completed a comparative study on the participation of the business community in the peace processes of Guatemala, El Salvador, and Colombia and research on local-level business-led peace initiatives in Colombia. Her research has been funded by the Crisis States Programme of the London School of Economics, the Social Science Research Council, the Canadian Department of Foreign Affairs, and the Colombian National Institute for Science and Technology (Colciencias). Her work has been published in journals such as *Latin American Politics and Society, Business & Politics, Revista Iberoamericana, Colombia Internacional,* and *Revista de Estudios Sociales.*

Catalina Rojas is the director of global partnerships at Women Thrive Worldwide. Prior to joining the organization, she was a consultant on gender, conflict, and development issues with various international organizations, including the Initiative for Inclusive Security, the Organization of American States (OAS), USAID, and the United Nations Development Fund for Women (UNIFEM). She has a PhD in conflict analysis and resolution. Originally from Colombia, she has more than ten years of experience working with southern civil society organizations. She has taught and conducted research in Colombia, Guatemala, El Salvador, Peru, Bolivia, Thailand, and Indonesia. She currently lives in Alexandria, Va., and can be reached at crojas@women thrive.org. She is author of *In the Midst of War: Women's Contributions to Peace in Colombia.*

Jorge Rojas Rodríguez is the founder and president of the Colombian nongovernmental organization Consultancy on Human Rights and Displacement (CODHES). He studied social communications at the Universidad de Bogotá Jorge Tadeo Lozano and social sciences at the Universidad de Córdoba. He is researcher and author of numerous publications on migration, displacement, human rights, and peace. He is coordinator for the Consultancy on Migration and Human Rights for the Inter-American Platform for Human Rights.

Mary J. Roldán is an associate professor of Latin American history at Cornell University. She received her PhD from Harvard University and specializes in twentieth-century Colombian political, cultural, and social history. Her research and teaching interests include violence, state formation, popular culture, narcotics trafficking, and urban history. Her book *Blood and Fire: La Violencia in Antioquia, Colombia, 1946–1953* was published in Spanish as *A Sangre y Fuego: la violencia en Antioquia, Colombia, 1946–1953* and won Colombia's Fundación Alejandro Angel Escobar Prize for research in the social sciences and humanities. She has collaborated on analyses of contemporary Colombia subjects for PBS/WNYC's *The Next Big Thing* radio program and PBS/WNET's *Wide Angle* documentary film series. Her work has appeared in the *Radical Historians Newsletter, Análisis Político,* and *Estudios Sociales* and in *Cocaine: Global Histories* and *Wounded Cities.* Her current research projects include an examination of the role of radio in distance education and modernization projects in twentieth-century Colombia and an analysis of the emergence of local social movements advocating nonviolent approaches to conflict resolution in the northwestern Colombian department of Antioquia.

Raúl Rosende is the resident adviser for the UN Office for the Coordination of Humanitarian Affairs, Bogotá, and was previously adviser for the UNDP in Colombia, where he was in charge of peacebuilding programs in conflict areas, relations with civil society, and facilitating the coordination of the "Group of 24" countries engaged in development, cooperation, peace, and human rights in Colombia. Prior to working with UNDP, Rosende worked with the United Nations in Colombia, Afghanistan, and Guatemala, and with the OAS in Nicaragua. He has been involved in the design and management of peacebuilding programs, the strengthening of conflict-management capacities in countries in transition, the reintegration of war-affected populations and former combatants, and supporting negotiations and verification of peace accords. He has also worked as a consultant with the Carter Center and the Pearson Peacekeeping Center.

David Rothschild is a community-development specialist with more than twelve years of experience working with indigenous peoples and other rural communities in Latin America. He is currently working as a program officer for the Goldman Environmental Foundation. He previously worked with the Garfield Foundation to put together a grantee monitoring system for indigenous partners in the Bolivian Chaco. He recently developed, led, and documented a participatory process with one hundred and fifty indigenous communities of Bolívar State in Venezuela as part of the preparation of a four-year watershed management plan for the Inter-American Development Bank. Prior to that he served as the primary on-site manager for the Field Museum of Chicago, carrying out a participatory asset-mapping and land-use planning project with rural communities in the Pando region of Bolivia. For six years, four as the director, he worked with the Amazon Alliance, a coalition that brings together indigenous organizations of the nine countries of the Amazon Basin with environmental and human rights organizations. He holds a BA with honors in Latin American studies from the University of California at Santa Cruz. He earned an MA in international policy and practice from George Washington University and has completed the international human rights law summer program at the University of Oxford.

Jennifer Schirmer, a political anthropologist and senior researcher, directs the Program on Peace Dialogues and Reconciliation at the Center for Development and the Environment at the University of Oslo, Norway, and conducts workshops in conflict resolution in conjunction with the Department of Peace and Conflict Research at Uppsala University, Sweden. She is the author of *The Guatemalan Military Project: A Violence Called Democracy*, and has received two MacArthur Foundation research and writing grants, as well as a United States Institute of Peace grant for her research. She has written extensively on human rights, civil-military relations and reforms, and security and development in Guatemala, and was a senior fellow at the United States Institute of Peace in 2006–07.

Winifred Tate is an assistant professor of anthropology at Colby College and the author of the award-winning *Counting the Dead: The Culture and Politics of Human Rights Activism in Colombia*. She received her doctorate from New York University and has been a fellow at the Watson Institute of Brown University and at the National Security Archive. She has researched political violence, drug trafficking, and U.S. foreign policy as a consultant for a number of international organizations, including the United Nations Children's Fund, Human Rights Watch, the Centre for Humanitarian Dialogue, the United States Institute of Peace, Human Rights First, and Freedom House. She also worked as a senior fellow and Colombia analyst for three years at the Washington Office on Latin America. Her current research focuses on U.S. foreign-policy debates during Plan Colombia and their impact in the Putumayo Department of southern Colombia.

Gabriel Turriago studied political science at the Universidad de los Andes. He has been a university professor and researcher in social and political science. He has participated in negotiation and disarmament, demobilization, and reintegration processes between the Colombian government and eleven guerrilla groups. He worked with the Departamento Nacional de Planeación (National Planning Department) in the formulation of public policies for peace and the strengthening of civil society. He currently works with the UNDP's REDES program.

León Valencia was a member of the ELN Central Command in the 1980s, and in 1994 he participated in the signing of a peace agreement with the Colombian government for the demobilization of one sector of that organization. Today, he is a political analyst who specializes in themes of security and peace, and is a regular columnist for *El Tiempo* (Bogotá), *El Colombiano* (Medellín), *Semana*, *Diners*, and *Credencial*. His recent books include two volumes of collected political essays, *Adiós a la Política, Bienvenida la Guerra* (*Goodbye Politics, Hello War*) and *Miserias de la Guerra, Esperanzas de la Paz* (*Miseries of War, Hope for Peace*), and his first novel, *Con el Pucho de la Vida* (*With the Ember of Life*).

Ana M. Velásquez is a doctoral student in developmental psychology at Concordia University with an undergraduate degree in psychology and an MA in education from Universidad de los Andes. She was the academic coordinator of the emotional intelligence curriculum at Alberto Merani Foundation and is coauthor with Enrique Chaux and Juanita Lleras of *Competencias Ciudadanas: De los Estándares al Aula* (Citizenship Competencies: From Standards to the Classroom). She has been coinvestigator in projects to measure school violence in Bogotá and El Salvador. She is one of the authors of *Aulas en Paz*, an elementary-school curriculum to prevent violence and promote peaceful relationships.

Leslie Wirpsa is assistant professor of international studies at DePauw University in Chicago. She was an S.V. Ciriacy-Wantrup postdoctoral fellow in natural resource studies at the University of California at Berkeley and received her PhD from the School of International Relations at the University of Southern California. She is a former award-winning investigative journalist and is completing a book manuscript, *Shielding the Heart of the World: Oil, Contentious Politics, and Indigenous Rights*. Her work examines the geopolitics of oil, militarization, U.S. security policy, and internal conflicts and has appeared in media and scholarly outlets including *Geopolitics*, National Public Radio, *Newsweek*, *San Francisco Chronicle*, *Reuters*, *National Catholic Reporter*, *Der Spiegel*, *Cultural Survival Quarterly*, and others. She was the primary author and consultant on several human rights reports on Colombia published by the Washington Office on Latin America and the Latin American Institute for Alternative Legal Services (ILSA). She also served as the coexecutive director and primary research consultant for the U'wa Defense Project from 1998 to 2001.

Index

Board of Directors

United States Institute of Peace Press

Since 1991, the United States Institute of Peace Press has published over 125 books on the prevention, management, and peaceful resolution of international conflicts—among them such venerable titles as Raymond Cohen's *Negotiating Across Cultures; Herding Cats and Leashing the Dogs of War* by Chester A. Crocker, Fen Osler Hampson, and Pamela Aall; and I. William Zartman's *Peacemaking and International Conflict.* All our books arise from research and fieldwork sponsored by the Institute's many programs. In keeping with the best traditions of scholarly publishing, each volume undergoes both thorough internal review and blind peer review by external subject experts to ensure that the research, scholarship, and conclusions are balanced, relevant, and sound. As the Institute prepares to move to its new headquarters on the National Mall in Washington, D.C., the Press is committed to extending the reach of the Institute's work by continuing to publish significant and sustainable works for practitioners, scholars, diplomats, and students.

Valerie Norville
Director

Colombia: Building Peace in a Time of War

Text: Palatino

Display Text: Optima

Cover Design: The Creative Shop

Interior Design and Page Makeup:
BMWW: Barton, Matheson, Willse, and Worthington

Developmental Editor: Kurt Volkan

Copyediting: Michael Carr

Proofreading: Amanda Watson-Boles

Indexing: Potomac Indexing

Dreamers

On the Trail of the Nez Perce

Cover Photos:

Bear Paw Battlefield, Montana
Photo by Swallowtail

Photographs of Ollicott and other Nez Perce courtesy
Washington State University Library

DREAMERS

On the Trail of the Nez Perce

Martin Stadius

CAXTON PRESS
Caldwell, Idaho
1999

First Edition

**Library of Congress Cataloging-in-
Publication Data**

Stadius, Martin —
    Dreamers: on the trail of the Nez Perce: / Martin
Stadius.
        p. cm.
    Includes bibliographical references and index.
    ISBN 0-87004-393-5 (cloth)
    1. Nez Perce National Historic Trail
Guidebooks. 2. Nez Perce Indians--History
Guidebooks. 3. Nez Perce Indians--Relocation. 4.
Stadius, Martin--Journeys--Nez Perce National
Historic Trail. 5. Nez Perce National Historic
Trail--Description and travel.
I. Title.
E99.N5S73 1999
917.96'85— dc21   99-30863
                                            CIP

Lithographed and bound in the
United States of America
CAXTON PRESS
Caldwell, Idaho
165088

Acknowledgements

My thanks for assistance in research to the staffs of the Idaho State Historical Society Library, the Montana Historical Society Library, the Oregon Historical Society Library and the Holland Library at Washington State University. At the latter, my special appreciation goes to Jose Vargas for his knowledge and insights into the McWhorter Papers.

To the staff of the Interlibrary Loan Department at the Multnomah County Library, my gratitude for persevering in providing copies of several truly obscure source documents.

In addition to the individuals mentioned in the narrative, I add the late Grace Bartlett of Joseph, Oregon; Andy Anderson of Chinook, Montana; Web Gale at the Wisdom, Montana, Forest Service office; Lee Whittlesey at Yellowstone National Park and Arthur Currence of the Nez Perce National Historic Park to those to whom I am indebted. To Betty Regan, my companion in grammar, syntax and clarity during the writing, the word "praise" does not go nearly far enough.

My last words of profound thanks go to Max Gartenberg, my agent, and Wayne Cornell, my editor, for helping guide this novice word mariner through uncharted seas.

CONTENTS

MAPS

ILLUSTRATIONS

The Nez Perce
National Historic Trail

PROLOGUE

A few minutes after ten on a blustery and overcast June morning, I was late. My 1972 Volkswagen Westfalia struggled in third gear toward the summit of White Bird Hill on U.S. Highway 95 in central Idaho. I kept company with the eighteen-wheelers in the slow lane, practicing the patience learned by all drivers of geriatric VW vans. Passing through a cut at the top of the divide, we began the long glide down White Bird Canyon toward its juncture with the Salmon River eight miles to the south. The trucks continued to crawl from the pass as slowly as we ascended, their drivers heeding the strident warning signs about the steep descent. I slid my van into the passing lane and slipped it into fourth gear, drifting down through one sweeping curve after another.

The pavement gripped the west canyon wall as a dramatic vista unfolded 2,000 feet below. The slope from the highway fell precipitously to a sere canyon floor several miles wide, there a jumble of bare ridges and ravines, knolls and swales. White Bird Creek snaked through the dun expanse, a slender braid of green falling from its source somewhere in the mountains. Beyond the creek, the far canyon wall ramped steadily upward to a distant tree line where turbulent clouds glided across the horizon.

After several miles I spotted an overlook on the other side of the highway where a crowd of sixty or so had gathered. Braking hard, I managed to cut across the oncoming traffic. As the van lurched to a halt in the parking lot, my foot slipped off the clutch. The engine rattled noisily then stalled, and people turned to stare curiously. Graceful, Martin.

I got out with my camera and stood near the railing at the back edge of the scattered audience. Scheduled for ten o'clock, the ceremony had not yet begun, so I took in the view of the canyon floor now only 600 feet below. The opening battle of the Nez Perce War of 1877 had flared amid the contorted terrain on the near side of the canyon bottom. I struggled to imagine what it must have been like that June morning: the thin line of about 100 cavalry and civilian volunteers stretched along a ridge line, two waves of warriors advancing, led by three men wearing red blankets to draw the soldiers' fire. Seventy years of peace between the Nez Perce and whites, seventy years since Lewis and Clark had first stumbled into the homeland of the Nez Perce, disappearing in a tumult of gunsmoke and dust and shouts.

So you're from Oregon, a voice said over my shoulder. I turned to find a man probably in his fifties, fit and tall with a graying beard and thick glasses. He nodded toward the license plates on my van, and I confessed I was from Portland. He asked if I was on vacation.

Well, sort of. I'd quit my job in the spring, just before I turned forty, sold most of my household goods and put the rest in storage. I had a few dollars socked away and had been pretty much bumming around ever since, camping wherever it fit my fancy, fishing here and there on some smaller streams not overrun with anglers, hanging out in small-town saloons and lying about my fishing prowess to folks who knew yarns when they heard them and responded with some of their own, poking around little museums and historical sites, reading. The good life. I'd heard about this event last evening at the Nez Perce National Historical Park headquarters, had been headed this way eventually and just stepped on the gas a little.

His name was Denis. A farmer, he told me he was related to one of the civilian volunteers who fought beside the two companies of cavalry in the canyon below. Severely wounded in the hip during the battle, the volunteer, Theodore Swarts, eventually homesteaded on part of the battlefield. Denis pointed out to me some trees and the swampy remnant of a pond from those homestead years. I could sense the pride in his voice and perhaps a bit of nostalgia or envy.

A Nez Perce tribal leader dressed in sportcoat and slacks, his white shirt open at the collar, stepped to a podium near the overlook shelter and offered a prayer in his native language. A three-man color guard passed by, U.S., Idaho and VFW flags rippling. A stocky Nez Perce wearing sunglasses and a National Park Service uniform spoke next. His long braided hair was draped over massive shoulders and framed glasses and a gentle face. His voice was calm, melodious, but the portable public address system fought a losing battle with the wind, the roar of passing trucks and the expanse of the canyon. I heard only snippets of his speech: . . . this is not a celebration . . . first battle . . . long struggle . . . women and children . . . could have been avoided. Applause floated away in gusts of wind, and a white man approached the podium, again in the gray and green National Park Service uniform. Still, snatches of words only: . . . first in many . . . National Historical Park . . . plans for the future . . . thank the Nez Perce Tribe without whose help. . . .

A minivan with Utah license plates pulled up behind me and out poured parents, four kids and—I guessed—a grandparent. They formed a knot to my right and a hushed conversation ensued. The youngest of the boys asked what was happening. Listen and maybe you'll find out, the mother said. It's the anniversary of the Battle of White Bird Canyon, I offered. Getting blank stares in return, I added, the Nez Perce War of 1877. At that the father nodded. The one Chief Joseph fought, he explained to his kids. The youngest boy asked who won. The battle? The Nez Perce, I said, but they lost the war. Another of the boys made a gunshot sound, clutched his chest and began what promised to be a protracted death spiral until the mother grabbed his jacket and whispered, stop that!

The Nez Perce lost the war, of course, like all the native tribes eventually lost their wars. After this first battle the younger warriors were full of pepper. They had licked one batch of soldiers, bring on the rest. The older men and women knew better, though, remembered the late 1850s when war raged on the fringe of the Nez Perce homeland and American armies whipped the Yakamas, the Palouse, the Walla Wallas, the Spokanes, one defiant tribe after another; remembered the 1840s after the Whitman massacre when the Cayuse were hounded relentlessly into submission and near-extinction.

So, for almost a month after the battle here at White Bird, the Nez Perce evaded the ever-growing army, units ordered from Arizona, Nevada, California, Alaska, Oregon and Washington, from as far away as Georgia. Then came the battle at Clearwater about forty miles north, the wrenching decision to flee their homeland, the trek across the Lolo Trail to supposed safety in Montana. To the Big Hole, where another army jumped them and the Nez Perce buried eighty dead, mostly women and children.

Escaping that place grieving and enraged, they dodged south and east through the newly-designated Yellowstone National Park, leaving a wake of terrified tourists, toward the plains of central Montana, the buffalo country, where the reformed Seventh Cavalry waited, eager to kick some Indian butt as revenge for Custer's death the year before. Not this time, not these Nez Perce. They stormed north toward Canada and sanctuary until, finally, only forty miles from the border the final army caught them and Chief Joseph uttered the words that would enshrine him in memory: from where the sun then stood he would fight no more, forever.

The tribal leader returned to the microphone. He spoke passionately and in a stronger voice, but not much about the events of 1877. Instead, he mentioned the women today who held the families together through hard times, the destruction caused by alcohol and drugs, the need to protect the children, the responsibility of grandparents and parents and all adults to help the young learn how to live a good life. The women and the children, he concluded, were the reason the men fought the war over a hundred years ago, and quietly the struggle continued. A child in bright, traditional regalia wandered around the podium during the speech, and several times the speaker paused to pat the boy's shoulder. The elder offered a closing prayer in Nez Perce, and the ceremony was over. Someone later told me this simple event was the first public commemoration of the battle in years. Neither the Nez Perce nor any whites now found much to cheer about in White Bird Canyon.

One of the reasons my van proved so pathetic on hills was the library I carried with me in heavy boxes under the fold-down bed in the back. A few were paperback thrillers and mysteries, but most were histories of the American West ranging from Washington Irving's *Astoria* to Evan Connell's *Son of the Morning Star*. Among them was a 1978 work by James McDermott, a historian contracted by the National Park Service to unravel the events here at White Bird. Late into last night with a hissing lantern and a crackling camp-fire for light I had reread it and remained as impressed by his thoroughness as I had been the first time I had cracked its cover. He called the book *Forlorn Hope*.

I mentioned the book to Denis, and his gaze went distant for a few seconds. With a sudden edge to his voice he told me he remembered when McDermott was here while researching the book. Only stayed a couple of days, Denis said. Interesting, I thought. Hoping he would continue, I merely nodded. People around here have a lot of differing opinions about what really happened down there, Denis added. Old-timers once told different stories, ones they heard when they were young. I asked him if he had any of those opinions, knew any of those stories. He grinned and answered that he was a farmer, and that left little time for looking into history. He felt guilty, he said, about taking even this one day off from the stuff that needed doing on his land. His wife was at home, working, as we talked.

The white speaker from the ceremony wandered by and greeted Denis with a handshake, then me. He turned out to be Frank Walker, superintendent of the Nez Perce National Historical Park. With McDermott's book fresh in my memory I asked him to point out the specific route which two of the cavalry officers used to flee from the canyon. No one knows for sure, he told me. Somewhere along this canyon wall they made it up and out, he added, that's all we know for sure.

By now most of the casual, tourist passers-by to the commemoration had left, and a loose caravan of cars and pickups was beginning the short drive to the town of White Bird where the women of the Chief Joseph Warriors Society Auxiliary would host a picnic. Superintendent Walker said I was welcome and wandered off to shake more hands.

My van began the tedious climb back up the highway until, near the summit, I saw a narrow paved road veer off to the right. Unlike the newer highway curving downward along the west wall, this road, old U.S. 95, dropped directly to the canyon floor in a series of switchbacks then passed next to the ridge where only about seventy Nez Perce warriors thoroughly trounced the larger force of cavalry and citizen volunteers. When the brief fight was over the bodies of thirty-four dead soldiers lay strewn across the ground while the Nez Perce had suffered only three wounded. Despite the free food waiting ahead I couldn't resist slowing the van to a crawl then finally pulling over for a few minutes, the scene silent except for the wind.

As I drove the last mile to the town of White Bird, population about 100, the canyon walls closed in rapidly, squeezing the town into a narrow bottom along the creek and road. The houses were old and small, with porches and little fenced lawns. One tiny white church with a steeple, a still smaller library, a general store, two bars, an auto repair garage, a motel out of the 1930s, and not much more constituted downtown. Next to the general store was a postage-stamp-sized park, forty-odd people filling it up.

The Nez Perce women had finished setting out paper plates and plastic forks, trays of sandwiches, bowls of potato salad and chips and fruit salad, cake for dessert. Soft drinks cooled on ice. While a boy stared at me curiously, a smiling woman with streaks of gray in her black hair encouraged me to fill my plate, then take a second sandwich. I could stack it on top of that first one, she said. A long-time fan of egg salad on white bread in this age of whole wheat, I happily obliged.

I sat with Denis, who introduced me to the others at our table. Erma, across from me, wondered how I came to be interested in White Bird. Between bites of egg salad I was starting to tell her about my love of history and rambling among small towns when an image of another place flashed through my mind, a vision of a remote valley, a grassy flat beside a dark, clear stream. Rising from the grass were bare teepee poles as white as bone.

Years ago on one of my fishing trips to Montana I had chanced one stark, sunny afternoon upon the Big Hole National Battlefield in a secluded corner of Beaverhead County. The heat of the day was usually a miserable time for a dry-fly fishing, so I decided to take a look around. Skirting thick stands of willow, a path wound beside the little North Fork of the Big Hole River for about a mile to the reconstructed skeleton of a Nez Perce camp. Interspersed among the teepee poles were wooden foot-high markers planted in the grass, feathers for Nez Perce, blue hats for soldiers, brown ones for civilian volunteers. Each indicated the spot where one human had killed another. There were a lot of feathers and hats, and many of them represented Nez Perce women and children. I was chilled in the heat of the day. Walking back, near the parking lot I paused on a foot bridge over the river and slipped on my ultraviolet fishing sunglasses. The harsh, summer sunlight sliced through the surface reflection, illuminating every detail of the narrow, deep waterway. First one shadow revealed itself with the subtle flicker of a tail near a cut bank, then another. The channel teemed with trout. A sign said fishing was permitted. Not a chance. In my mind the stream still washed away blood that seeped through the soil.

Another woman named Carm suggested I stop by the county museum in Grangeville about fifteen miles to the north. Lots of Nez Perce and pioneer stuff, she said. She ran the place and planned to open it for a few hours in the afternoon. I said I would, then the conversation drifted to more important matters—commodity prices, the cool weather, the prospect for the summer hay crop.

Later that day, outside the Grangeville museum, I saw Denis again in his pickup. He spotted me, stopped, then got out carrying a rifle. I sincerely hoped I hadn't offended him somehow. Thought you might be interested in this, he said. Handing me the gun, Denis explained it was a Springfield .45-70 cavalry carbine once owned by Theodore Swarts back in the 1870s. The carbine was shorter and lighter than the rifle carried by infantry of that time, the barrel bore in this case being .45 inches, the shell loaded with 70 grains of gunpowder. To me the gun still felt substantial, heavy, lethal. Denis told me he had traced the serial number. The gun was manufactured in 1873, so Swarts probably carried it into the canyon that morning, Denis said proudly, adding that it could still fire a bullet. Racking open the chamber, I made sure the gun was unloaded, snapped the bolt shut, then pulled it up to my shoulder and sighted along its barrel into the past, wondering if Swarts had a chance to squeeze off even one round before he was wounded and the sudden rout began, wondering what really happened that day in June of 1877 down in White Bird Canyon.

Finding answers would take me years.

Washington State University Library

Nee-Me-Poo identified as members of the Dreamers faction pose for a photograph prior to the 1877 war. Several of the men have their hair in the distinctive Dreamer style.

CHAPTER ONE

THE REAL PEOPLE

I'm resting on my haunches beside a gravel road near the lower end of the Wallowa Valley in northeastern Oregon. It's near the end of July, sunny and mountain cool. In the field below the road, a solitary cow rests in verdant grass and watches me with mild interest, indulging in the bovine good life, chewing cud. The scent of the pasture, rising with the last of the night's dew, remains strong even though it's well past noon.

Beyond the field, edged by a skin of alder and cottonwood, the Wallowa River whispers past me into a canyon to my rear. Across the river a forested ridge rising several hundred feet above the bottomland defines this length of the abrupt southern edge of the valley. To the north are eroding bluffs rising to grassy, rolling hills. Pockets of trees tucked into swales and ravines suggest wooded highland beyond the close horizon. Along the base of those northern bluffs, springs feed tiny creeks which bathe the pastures and hay fields of the valley bottomland, only about a mile wide here. I feel like I'm amid a bit of paradise, and the cow benignly gazing at me seems like it might agree.

At the upper end of this valley lies the grave of a Nez Perce Indian. As was common among his people he took several names during his years. In history books he has been most commonly called either Tuekakas, which has no translation that

I've found, or Old Joseph. In 1986 Congress designated his grave as the official beginning of the Nez Perce National Historic Trail. At various points along the 1,200-mile trail are sites of the Nez Perce National Historical Park, each intended to tell some part of the story of the Nez Perce people and their eventual clash in 1877 against an inevitable white onslaught. In a few minutes I'll fire up my trusty, old VW van and head up to the grave. For the next three weeks I'll try to follow that trail from beginning to end, to White Bird and beyond, along the Lolo Motorway into Montana, up the Bitterroot Valley to the Big Hole, through Yellowstone Park and the Absaroka Mountains, finally north to a place called the Bear Paw. It's a long way from here to the Bear Paw, mostly on quiet back roads through small towns with stout names like Enterprise, Grangeville, Stevensville, Wisdom and Lewistown, others named oddly: Imnaha, Lapwai, Weippe, Leadore and Rapelje. I'll have plenty of time to tell you stories, some of which have never been told before.

My mind drifts back to that day when I held Theodore Swarts' carbine in my hands, sighted down its barrel and realized I had a lot of work to do. At least I knew where to start. Anyone seriously looking into the Nez Perce war owes a debt to a horse which cut its leg on a wire in the fall of 1907 in eastern Washington state. Its owner, a man named Yellow Wolf, consequently stopped at the home of Lucullus Virgil McWhorter to ask for help. Quite some name and quite some guy, that McWhorter. In a time when most folks thought the native peoples of America were nothing more than a fading remnant destined for oblivion, he held fiercely to the belief that they deserved respect. Yellow Wolf, who had fought as a young man in the 1877 war, picked up on this, and the two began a collaboration that lasted until the warrior's death in 1935. Yellow Wolf wanted the names and stories of the Nez Perce remembered, not only in their oral tradition, but for all people. Over the years in bits and pieces, Yellow Wolf gave his account of the war, as well as introducing McWhorter to other survivors who added their own memories. The eventual result was two books and an archive of interview notes and letters, now preserved at Washington State University. The books—*Yellow Wolf: His Own Story* and *Hear Me, My Chiefs*—are jewels themselves, narratives as told from the Nez

Perce point of view, but I hoped to find something more among McWhorter's rambling, disjointed papers. I got lucky, again and again.

My primary source for the Army was the file of letters received by the Adjutant General's Office, a compendium of all official correspondence concerning the war. In addition dozens of reminiscences, letters and diaries from soldiers and settlers reside in archives from the Library of Congress on the East Coast to the Oregon Historical Society on the West. Again, I hoped that by poking around I might find some sources both new and illuminating. Again, I was a lucky guy.

The war that began at White Bird arose over possession of this Wallowa Valley as well as other ancestral lands of the Nez Perce across the Snake River in Idaho. Tuekakas, Old Joseph, was the father of Heinmot Tooyalakekt. That name means Thunder Traveling To Loftier Heights; Thunder Rising Toward Distant Mountains or Thunder Crossing The Water And Fading On Distant Slopes. There's no single, correct translation, but you get the drift. For the sake of consistency and brevity I'll call him Thunder Rising. The whites of his time called him Young Joseph or Chief Joseph after his father, as well as a few nastier names, and they wanted him off this land. Thunder Rising and the other traditional Nez Perce band leaders in the 1870s—White Goose, Grating Sound, Looking Glass—had other ideas. So there was a war.

But much happened before that. You should know about Beringia, the Clovis, a monster named Illts-whah-tsik, Lewis and Clark and a few other things.

Slowing my van, I passed the well-kept First Indian Presbyterian Church, built before the 1877 war, then turned left off U.S. Highway 12 into a parking lot empty except for a National Park Service maintenance truck. I had arrived at the East Kamiah Site of the Nez Perce National Historical Park. Someone had recently mown the meadow grass and baled it with red twine. I hefted one, testing its weight—maybe sixty pounds—remembering the late 1960's: summers in high school, sweat, mosquitoes, getting

3

paid two cents a bale for loading, hauling and stacking the hay, a thousand bales on a good day, great money back then for a kid. Today, though, this bale was meant for sitting.

The Clearwater River remained pretty much hidden behind a shroud of trees and brush, its chant overwhelmed by traffic noise and the steady thump of a lumber mill across the highway behind the Lewis and Clark Motel. The forest and meadows on the bluffs across the river looked pretty much as they did on July 13, 1877, when defiant Nez Perce rode down those bluffs to the river a month after the fight at White Bird. It must have been a stirring sight that sunny July day: some 800 men, women and children and thousands of horses flowing down the bluffs to the water's edge in a procession that lasted for hours. They knew they had to cross the river fast. An army of almost 500 soldiers marched only miles behind them. More about that later.

About 20,000 years ago small bands of hunters and foragers gradually worked their way north and east from the Asian heartland into the region of Russia we know today as Siberia. They had no idea, of course, that their descendants would eventually populate an entire continent; they were simply tracking their primary meal ticket—the mammoth—into unknown territory. Another ice age gripped the planet, yet weather patterns left that part of the earth dry and free of ice, but bitterly cold. These people knew how to deal with cold and dry. Apparently, the land verged between tundra and steppe, with a cover of hardy grasses, maybe a few dwarf birch, alder and cottonwood. Enough mammoth, steppe bison, musk ox and saiga antelope roamed the arctic plain to sustain the humans. While some stayed in Siberia, others drifted east a few miles each generation until about 14,000 years ago the most adventurous found themselves in Alaska. They had crossed what scientists today call Beringia. Whenever I think about that land bridge, a childhood image—probably an illustration from a book—intrudes from my memory. I see a mother clutching a child in a snowstorm and teetering along an icy slip of ground a few yards wide. The reality was much different. At its peak, the Beringian Land Bridge stretched almost a thousand miles wide. Providentially, that most recent ice age waned soon after those first Americans reached Alaska, if two millennia could be called soon. As the Laurentide Ice Sheet to the east and the Cordilleran Ice Sheet near the Pacific coast slowly melted, a corridor opened from Alaska down the center of North America, enabling hunting bands to follow the mammoth south.

Just north of what is now the United States-Canadian border they found a heaven for hunters. The temperate continent teemed with wildlife: mammoth, mastodon, ground sloth, giant beaver, camel, five varieties of primitive horse, saber-tooth tiger, short-faced bear, cheetah, in all some twenty-three species of large mammals that would soon disappear forever. Archaeologist Brian Fagan wrote of those first Americans, today called the Clovis:

> *The Clovis people flourished on the Great Plains for about 500 years and then, around 11,00 years ago, they abruptly vanished, to be replaced by a multitude of different hunting-and-gathering cultures in the millennia that followed. Quite what happened is one of the mysteries of modern archaeology. By intriguing coincidence—if coincidence it be—the disappearance of Clovis coincides with one of the great mysteries of vertebrate paleontology, too—the mass extinction of Ice Age big-game animals, the megafauna. . . . Unleashed in an unpopulated, but game-rich continent, the new settlers may have become superpredators.*[1]

Abandoning the bale of hay and walking up the steps toward the East Kamiah overlook, a postmodern architectural affair of angles and oddities, I heard the murmur of voices and quiet laughter, saw paint cans, brushes, rollers. Inside the shelter, three Nez Perce men in Park Service uniforms squatted, leaning against a wall. Their conversation stopped as the closest looked up at me, eyes neutral. Break time, he said. When I told him I wasn't worried about my tax dollars, he chuckled. With that the three rose and sauntered down toward their truck, again conversing quietly. The talkative one turned and warned me to watch out for the wet paint on the wall. Then he called me "sir."

Sir? Made me feel old. Rather have been called a So-Yap-Poo, the name the Nez Perce gave to the whites. It might have meant

Long Knife People, maybe Tall Hat People. One disillusioned Nez Perce said it meant People Who Eat Everything In Sight. Maybe "sir" is okay after all.

Punching a button on the interior wall of the shelter, I heard a voice begin reciting the Nez Perce creation story. It was the voice of an elder, one who had learned to speak English in the years before television began to chip away at regional dialects. He strolled over some syllables and clipped others short. Listening to his tale, I looked out over the mown field to a large basalt rock mound about seventy-five yards away. Wildflowers sprouted from the rock as incongruously as the mound rose from the soft earth of the meadow. The rock was the remnant of the Heart of the Monster.

Here is the story of Illts-whah-tsik, the Monster:

Before there were human people, Coyote was down the Columbia River at Celilo Falls building a fish ladder so Salmon could swim upstream to become food for all the other animal people. Someone told him he was wasting his time, that all the animal people upstream had been eaten by a monster. Coyote decided to go see what was happening. Along the way he took a bath and dressed up to make himself tasty for the monster. Climbing up the ridges, Coyote looked across the land and saw here in the Kamiah valley the head of the great monster, the body looming to the horizon. Coyote had never seen anything like this. Coyote covered himself with brown clay and hid in the swaying grass so the monster could not see him. Taking rawhide ropes, Coyote tied himself to three mountains. Then he called out to the monster, "You have already swallowed all the animals. Why don't you swallow me, too, so I won't be lonely." The monster did not know that Coyote carried five stone knives, as well as flint and pitch for fire-making, so the monster inhaled like a mighty wind. He inhaled so hard that the ropes broke and Coyote was sucked right into the monster's gaping mouth. Looking around as he walked deeper into the throat of the monster, Coyote saw many bones. All the animals have been dying, he thought. Just then Grizzly Bear ran at Coyote, growling fiercely. "So, you make yourself scary only to me," Coyote said, and he hit the bear hard on the nose. That is why Grizzly Bear has a short nose today. As Coyote continued further into the monster, Rattlesnake rattled at him threateningly. "So, only toward me you are vicious," said Coyote, stepping on the snake's head. That is why Rattlesnake has a flat head today. When Coyote reached the monster's heart, the animals gathered around and Coyote cut slabs of fat from the heart for all to eat. Then he built a fire using the pitch and flint he had brought. The smoke drifted up through the monster's eyes, ears, nose and anus. With the stone knives he had brought Coyote began cutting away at the monster's heart. The first knife broke, then the second, the third and the fourth. Coyote kept on cutting. After his last knife broke Coyote grabbed the heart and tore it free. The monster died, and all the animals ran out of the monster's openings. Muskrat was the last to escape, and the others had to pull him out. That is why Muskrat has no hair on his tail today. All the animals helped carve the monster into pieces. Coyote threw the pieces in every direction. Where the pieces landed nations of people sprang up. Coyote named them: the Cayuse, the Blackfoot, the Crow, the Flathead, the Yakimas and many others. When Coyote finished, Fox came over and said, "What is the meaning of this, Coyote? You have thrown pieces of the monster all over the land. Is there nothing left for this place?" Coyote snorted, "Why didn't you mention that before? Bring me some water." Coyote then washed his bloody hands, and he sprinkled the water over the ground. From this ground sprang up the Nee-Me-Poo.[2]

The Nee-Me-Poo, Nee-Me-Pu, Nimipu. No matter how you spell the name, and there are a bunch of ways, it means The People, The Real People.

Diggings a few miles downriver from the Heart of the Monster have uncovered evidence of human activity as early as 10,000 years ago, just after the disappearance of the Clovis culture, making this part of the continent among the earliest occupied by the successors to the Clovis. Archaeologists like Brian Fagan are still puzzling over the cause of the sudden demise of those first Americans and the creation of the dazzling array of cultures that followed.

To me the answer seems clear. Coyote did it.

On September 20, 1805, Captain William Clark led six hungry and exhausted hunters of the Lewis and Clark Expedition onto the Weippe Meadows about twenty miles northeast of the Heart of the Monster. In the second year of their journey to the Pacific Ocean they had struggled through the Clearwater Mountains for the last nine days, finding little game the entire way. This advance party noticed three boys hiding in tall grass, gave them bits of ribbon as gifts, then waited as the three scampered away. Soon a man came out, greeted them in sign language and escorted Clark and his men about a mile where they found thirty double teepees arranged in two camps. The United States of America had discovered the Real People. Of course, the Nee-Me-Poo had already heard of the strange, pale people. For generations stories had drifted from the east and south, and shamans had long predicted their eventual arrival.

About 1730, a great gift had arrived from the south: the first horses. Within two generations the Nee-Me-Poo had become expert riders. Unlike most tribes, they learned the benefits of castration and selective breeding to improve their herds. The Nez Perce most transformed were the buffalo hunters. The arduous journey to the buffalo country in what is now Montana and the rigors of the hunt became much easier. Just as many of the Lakota of Minnesota abandoned their sedentary villages along the Mississippi River and migrated onto the plains with the arrival of the horse, as many as three-fourths of the Nee-Me-Poo began spending months, occasionally years at a time in Montana and southeastern Idaho, hunting the buffalo.

There they encountered hostile tribes—the Blackfoot, the Crow—armed with primitive, muzzleloading muskets obtained from Canadian trappers and traders. By 1805, the Crow counted 205 guns in their arsenal. Through trade and war the Nee-Me-Poo had managed to obtain a few weapons, but reliable sources of lead and powder were a distant dream, blocked by enemy tribes. The

Nee-Me-Poo warriors remained at a disadvantage in the sporadic, but inevitable, plains warfare. As well, for years their mortal enemies to the south, the Snake Indians, had raided and traded for white goods from Spanish Mexico. In the last decades word had filtered from the west up the Columbia River, accompanied by beads, kettles and metal knives as proof, of whites in big boats come to trade with the coastal tribes. Even the tiny Kutenai tribe living along the northern tributaries of the Columbia River in what would eventually become Canadian British Columbia had traders now providing them goods. The isolated Nee-Me-Poo homeland, it seemed, was becoming a trap rather then a sanctuary.

The men in the Weippe summer camp were wary of the strangers. Even as many of the band's greatest warriors had gone south to raid the Snake Indians in southern Idaho, here in the heart of the Nee-Me-Poo country these whites used a Snake woman, Sacajawea, as a guide. That could not be a good sign. The women and children were spread out across the meadows digging and cooking huge piles of camas root. If the white men decided to cause trouble it would not be easy to protect the families. And these men were not traders, did not come to supply the people with guns and powder and lead. The easiest course of action would be simply to kill them and take their precious weapons and other goods. Clark and Meriwether Lewis, who showed up two days later with the rest of the expedition, had no inkling of the debate swirling quietly around them.

According to Nee-Me-Poo tradition, Red Grizzly Bear was perhaps the foremost of the warriors remaining at Weippe. He listened carefully to a story told again by an elderly woman named Returned From A Faraway Country, whose name told the tale of part of her life. Kidnapped as a girl by Blackfoot in the buffalo country, she had been sold eastward as a slave, until she reached the Great Lakes area and came into contact with whites. They treated her kindly. A grown woman by then, she eventually escaped her captor and made her way westward again, carrying her baby. Although the child died during the long journey, the mother managed to make her way home. Now, on her deathbed, remembering the hospitable treatment she had received from the whites many years ago, she begged Red Grizzly Bear to spare the explorers' lives. He assented. Returned From A Faraway Country died a few days later. If she had not survived just long enough to make her final plea, President Thomas Jefferson probably would have gone to his grave wondering of Lewis and Clark: whatever happened to those guys I sent west in 1805?

Although they allowed the expedition to survive and continue west to winter at the mouth of the Columbia River, the Nee-Me-Poo did not make the greatest first impression. On October 11, as he was leaving the Real People's territory, Clark scribbled in the English of the time,

> *Their amusements appear but fiew as their Situation requires the utmost exertion to prcure food they are generally employed in that pursute, all the Summer & fall fishing for the Salmon, the winter hunting the deer on Snow Shoes in the plains and takeing care of ther emence numbers of horses, & in the Spring cross the mountains to the Missouri to get Buffalow robes . . . . They are verry Selfish and Stingey of what they have to eate or ware, and they expect in return Something for everything give as presents or the services which they doe let it be however Small, and fail to make those returns in their part.*[3]

Clark's churlish mood may have partly been due to the fact that the arduous trek through the Clearwater Mountains had dispelled the explorers' last hope of finding a convenient trade passage to the Pacific Coast, one of the primary missions given the expedition by President Jefferson. Clark's grousing is otherwise difficult to fathom. He and the rest of the whites had stuffed themselves with salmon and roots provided by the Real People. Maybe it was the subsequent indigestion they suffered after days of near-starvation in the Clearwater Mountains.

The afternoon session of the Lapwai pow-wow I attended the summer of 1993 was devoted to name-giving ceremonies for the young and memorials for the dead. The gymnasium sweltered as I slipped inside and sat near the top of the bleachers by the entrance. Many of those attending sat on lawn chairs in a circle around the gym floor. The rest, like me, were scattered on the hard wooden slats above. The master of ceremonies glanced at me as I entered during a memorial. A family member holding a blanket stood near him. Turning my attention to the crowd, I took a rough count—150 people—and guessed that a quarter were white. Cowboy boots and big belt buckles were abundant. Noticing the speaker looking in my direction again, I felt a brief panic that I was not welcome at this session, which is more personal than the evening dance competitions. Nonsense, I reassured myself, the Nez Perce woman at the Park Service headquarters had mentioned the memorials and name-givings and suggested I might find them interesting. In fact, as I tuned into the speaker's voice again, he was saying how the Nez Perce had long welcomed strangers to their land. He glanced at me again. Finally, one of the whites stepped up from the circle of chairs on the gym floor and accepted the blanket from the woman with a slight bow and a handshake.

That was a good blanket, said a man sitting a few feet to my right with his wife and daughter. Seeing that he was talking to me, I agreed. Nodding toward the master of ceremonies below, the man explained, quietly, that the elder had seen me come in and hadn't recognized me; the people here were pretty much all neighbors. He probably had wanted me to have the blanket. Giving and receiving a gift between strangers in a sincere manner shows respect both ways. Respect's important, he said. I blushed fiercely, even though my new neighbor's tone was matter-of-fact, not reproving. Still, I asked myself: why was I counting numbers instead of listening?

Various people came to the microphone and remembered the deceased, telling stories that illustrated her character. Drummers drummed and dancers danced before family members fanned out and distributed clothing and household goods to the audience from huge piles on the floor. A teenage girl, smiling shyly, handed me a gift, a red bandanna decorated with a cowboy riding a bucking bronco. Another gave me Tupperware.

A heavy-set Nez Perce sporting a Fu-Manchu mustache sitting to my left asked if I wanted some fry bread. My wife makes the best in the world, he added. Talked me into it, I answered. He went outside, returning a few minutes later with a paper bag of tennis-ball-sized loaves individually wrapped in aluminum foil. Handing

11

me one, he said, that'll be fifty cents. Hurriedly, I pulled a dollar bill out of my wallet. I had thought this was another gift situation and had been ready to receive it in a sincere manner. Sorry, out of change, he said, grinning and pocketing the money. I told him it was quite all right. After I had made quick work of the bread, my neighbor asked if I liked it. Best in the world, I told him. Reaching in his bag, he pulled out another loaf and tossed it to me. There's your change for the buck, he said.

When Lewis and Clark returned to Nee-Me-Poo territory the following spring on the homeward leg of their exploration, everyone's disposition seemed to have improved. Except for one incident in which Meriwether Lewis grabbed a hatchet and threatened to kill a warrior who had teased him for eating dog flesh, the whites and natives got along famously. Deep snow remaining in the Clearwater Mountains forced the explorers to lay over for a month at Kamiah, where they made camp a couple of miles downriver from the Heart of the Monster. They sent out hunters for deer and grizzly bear, traded freely with the Real People, smoked the pipe with them, urged peace with their hereditary enemies, the Snakes and Blackfoot, promised that well-stocked American traders would soon be coming west, held dances and running contests, even received the unsolicited gifts—fine horses—that Clark had so grouchily coveted the previous autumn. Their journals were filled with descriptions of the Nee-Me-Poo as "cheerful," "agreeable" and "amiable." Apparently so: nine months after the expedition had departed eastward a Nez Perce woman gave birth to the son of William Clark. Seventy-one years later Clark's son, Always Smoking, would fight American armies.

So how did the name Nez Perce, Pierced Nose in French, come to be attached to the Real People? Lewis and Clark were the first to attribute the practice to the tribe, followed a few years later by the earliest French-Canadian trappers to visit the region. If you suggest to the Real People today that their ancestors walked around with pieces of bone stuck through their noses, they will tell you quite firmly you are dead wrong. The collective tribal memory retains no hint of the practice. Coastal peoples, the Nee-Me-Poo insist, indeed did pierce their noses with lengths of dentalia shell, but never the Real People.

First-hand accounts of those initial meetings of the Canadian trappers and the Nee-Me-Poo apparently don't exist, but it's difficult to dismiss the journals of Lewis and Clark. Each kept a daily record of events, weather, geography, flora, fauna and, when they were hungry, their meals. Oddly, during their initial encounters with the Nee-Me-Poo in September 1805, neither mentioned nose-piercing other than noting that the tribal name was Choppunish which they translated as Pierced Nose. During the long 1806 layover waiting for the snow to melt in the mountains, though, Lewis penned this description of his hosts:

> The Choppunish are in general stout well formed active men. they have high noses and many of them on the acqueline order with cheerful and agreeable countenances; their complexions are not remarkable. in common with other savage nations of America they extract their beards but the men do not uniformly extract the hair below, this is more particularly confined to the females. I observed several men among them whom I am convinced if they had shaved their beard instead of extracting it would have been as well supplied in this particular as any of my countrymen. they appear to be cheerfull but not gay; they are fond of gambling and of their amusements which consist principally in shooting their arrows at a bowling target made of willow bark, and in riding and exercising themselves on horseback, racing etc. they are expert marksmen and good riders. they do not appear to be so much devoted to baubles as most of the nations we have met with, but seem anxious always to obtain articles of utility, such as knives, axes, tomahawks, kettles blankets and mockersonalls. blue beads however may form an exception to this remark; this article among all the nations of this country may be justly compared to goald or silver among the civilized nations. They are generally well cloathed in their stile. their dress consists of a long shirt which reaches to the middle of thye, long legings which reach as high as the waist, mockersons, and robes. these are formed of various skins and are in

13

all respects like those particularly discribed of the Shoshones. their women also dress like the Shoshones. their ornaments consist of bead shells and pieces of brass variously attached to their dress, to their ears arrond their necks wrist arms etc. a bando of some kind usually surrounds the head, this is most frequently the skin of some fir animal as the fox otter etc tho' they have them also of dressed skin without the hair. the ornament of the nose is a single shell of the wampum. the pirl and beads are suspended from the ears. beads are woarn around their wrists necks and over their shoulders crosswise in the form of a double sash. the hair of the men is cewed in two rolls which hang on each side in front of the body as before discribed of other inhabitants of the Columbia. collars of bear claws are also common; but the article of dress on which they appear to bstow most pains and ornaments is a kind of collar or brestplate; this is most commonly a strip of otterskin of about six inches wide taken out of the center of the skin it's whole length including the head. this is dressed with the hair on; a hole is cut lengthwise through the skin near the head of the animal sufficiently large to admit the head of the person to pass. thus it is placed about the neck and hangs in front of the body the tail frequently reaching below the knees; on this skin in front is attatched peices of pirl, beads, wampum peices of red cloth and in short whatever they conceive most valuable or ornamental. I observed a tippit worn by Hohastillpilp, which was formed of human scalps and ornamented with the thumbs and fingers of several men he had slain in battle. their women brade their hair in two tresses which hang in the same position of those of the men. they also wear a cap or cup on the head formed of beargrass and cedarbark. the men also frequently attatch some small ornament to a small plat of hair on the center of the crown of their heads.[4]

This journal extract is typical of the care with which the explorers described what they found around them. Exactly how Lewis came across his information concerning the private grooming habits of the women is certainly open for speculation. The comment about the nose ornament is so matter-of-fact that it seems impossible to brush off as an error. The term wampum meant native money, specifically the dentalia shell which served as a trade standard for inter-tribal exchanges. Hohastillpilp, by the way, was none other than Red Grizzly Bear, who had decided not to exterminate the expedition when it first arrived in Nee-Me-Poo territory.

Estimating the Choppunish population at 6,000, Lewis and Clark rather arbitrarily divided them into seven large bands ranging in size from 250 to 2,000. The tribal structure was in reality much more fragmented and fluid. Later estimates from 1855 identified twenty-one distinct village groupings with thirty-four headmen, at a time when the tribe was much smaller due to the ravages of smallpox, measles and other European diseases.

The villages Lewis and Clark visited varied greatly in size. The village of Twisted Hair held only two fires and twelve inhabitants. Conversely, Broken Arm's village at Kamiah boasted twenty-four hearths and fifty families with 100 men of warrior age; the total population there must have exceeded 500. In each village all lived in a single longhouse built of wood and woven reed mats, with a separate structure for menstruating women. The Kamiah longhouse extended for half a football field.

The band leaders had no power to compel their followers to obey orders, oratory being their only tool. Lewis noted an instance of this on May 12. He and Clark had met with the headmen from the Kamiah area and urged them to abandon warfare against the Snakes and Blackfoot in exchange for eventual trade with Americans:

> *The Indians held a council among themselves this morning with rispect to the subjects on which we had spoken to them yesterday. the result as we learnt was favorable. they placed confidence in the information they had received and resolved to pursue our advise. after this council was over the principal Cheif or the broken Arm, took the flour of the roots of cows and thickened the soope in the kettles and baskets of all his people, this being ended he made a harangue the purport of which was making known the deliberations of their*

council and impressing the necessity of unanimity among them and a strict attention to the resolutions which had been agreed on in councill; he concluded by inviting all such men who abide by the decrees of the council to come and eat and requested such as would not be so bound to shew themselves by not partaking of the feast. I was told by one of our men who was present, that there was not a dissenting voice on this great national question, but all swallowed their objections if any they had, very cheerfully with their mush.[5]

"Cows" in this case was not the animal, but kouse, a small root that formed a significant part of the Nee-Me-Poo diet. Clark wrote, "the noise of their women pounding the cows roots remind me of a nail factory."[6]

The explorers were impressed with the country, writing that:

. . . to its present inhabitants nature seems to have dealt with a liberal hand, for she has distributed a great variety of esculent plants over the face of the country which furnish them a plentiful store of provisions; those are acquired but little toil; and when prepared after the method of the natives afford not only a nutritious but an agreeable food.[7]

They realized the Nee-Me-Poo homeland was essentially one high plain dissected by river canyons and noted the singular effect of this on the local climate:

About noon the sun shines with intense heat in the bottoms of the river. the air on top of the river hills or high plain forms a distinct climate, the air is much colder, and vegitation is not as forward by at least 15 or perhaps 20 days. the rains which fall in the river bottoms are snows on the plains. at a distance of fifteen miles from the river and on the Eastern border of this plain the Rocky Mountains commence and present us with winter at its utmost extreem. the snow is yet many feet deep even near the base of these mountains; here we have summer, spring and winter within the short space of 15 or 20 miles.[8]

16

This abrupt geography allowed the Real People to adjust to seasonal changes in weather by moving only short distances: winters in the warm canyon longhouses, summers in the cooler, high meadows at places such as Weippe, Camas Prairie and the Wallowa Valley.

Lewis and Clark noted that the Nee-Me-Poo enjoyed fine relations with their downriver neighbors, the Walla Wallas and Umatillas, sharing the same language, but the explorers mistakenly lumped both the Palouse and Cayuse tribes into the Nez Perce tribe and assumed that the friendly Flathead tribe to the east was also related by language to the Nee-Me-Poo. No one's perfect. On the question of enemies, the Real People were perfectly clear: the Blackfoot and other tribes east of the Continental Divide had forever been implacable foes, as were the Snakes of southern Idaho. Just before the expedition departed eastward, Clark visited the village of Broken Arm for a final time. The chief informed him that the Nee-Me-Poo were taking the peace and trading proposals of the Americans very seriously. Already delegations of Nez Perce and Snakes had made contact. Producing a pipe made of stone inlaid with silver, Broken Arm announced he intended to smoke it with the Snakes. He then presented Clark with a second peace pipe as a parting gift.

During the summer of 1993 one of my visits to the Big Hole National Battlefield in Montana coincided with combined tribal and National Park Service ceremonies commemorating the events of 1877. The Nez Perce elders had decided to allow whites to witness the smoking of a pipe, and about 100 gathered to watch the ceremony. The pipe-bearer was an elder named Horace Axtell. His gray hair, twisted into long braids, fell forward over his shoulders in the style described by Lewis and Clark. He greeted us then prayed in Nez Perce. The pipe, he then explained, had traditionally been smoked by warriors. He asked Nez Perce veterans of Desert Storm, Vietnam, Korea and the Second World War to come and sit with him. About ten did, forming a small circle. The pipe bearer reminded those of us watching that many Nez Perce over the years had fought for America and had given up their lives, that the warrior remained deeply respected in the tribal culture. He went on, telling us that every act one made could be viewed as religious, and so it was with smoking the pipe. But smoking the pipe was primarily a time for reflecting and talking and telling the truth.

Holding the pipe before him, thinking deeply for a moment, he invited any white veterans who wished to join the circle to come forward and smoke with the Nez Perce veterans. The earth at the Big Hole was sacred with the blood of the victims of the 1877 battle, he explained, but the white veterans were welcome to sit on the grass and smoke the pipe. For several seconds no one moved; the atmosphere was electric. The Nee-Me-Poo inviting the So-Yap-Poo to smoke? After all that had happened over the years and especially here where so many women and children had died at the hands of white soldiers? The Nez Perce veterans widened the circle and made room for seven or eight men ranging in age from twenties to sixties. Hands shook in greeting. In the old days the Nez Perce had often smoked the pipe with warriors from other tribes, the pipe bearer explained; so it would be this day.

Pausing, for several minutes he spoke quietly with elders seated on either side of him. Then he announced: if any other Nez Perce men desired to smoke they should come forward. The circle widened. Again he conversed with those nearest him. Finally, he said, any man who wished to share in the pipe could make the circle larger. With others I sat in the grass and solemnly shook hands with my neighbors.

The pipe bearer sang in the Nee-Me-Poo language then blew a crane bone whistle. He explained that, after he lit the pipe, it would pass to the right and continue around the circle until the tobacco was completely smoked. After the last embers died, the pipe would then make another full circle. As each man held the pipe he would have an opportunity to speak, if he wished. When the pipe reached me I was deathly afraid of dropping it. It was slender, a little over a foot long and meticulously carved out of a single piece of wood. The bowl was small, maybe two inches tall and an inch in diameter. The smoke I inhaled through the long, wooden stem was cool and fragrant. Somehow, that little bit of tobacco burned through three complete turns of the circle of some thirty men.

18

A lot of good words found ears when the pipe passed the final time, the time for words. Many of the veterans, both white and Nez Perce, looking inside themselves, cleared their throats, then remembered their tours of duty and the profound relief they felt when their war ended. One, in particular, touched me. He spoke of being posted near Hiroshima just after the atomic bombs had ended the war with Japan. I could barely hear his final words: visions of the devastation still haunted his dreams, he murmured. Among the last to speak was a young Nez Perce with chiseled features and hair flowing to his shoulders, looking every bit a warrior. He stood and urgently addressed the circle and those watching. He was glad the elders had decided to smoke with the whites on this day, he said. Look around this circle, he said, and listen and remember. Go home and tell your relatives and neighbors of the day you smoked the pipe with the Nez Perce. Listen in your mind and remember. Go home, he said, and tell your relatives and neighbors and friends that the Nez Perce are a friendly people.

Notes

[1] Fagan, Brian, *The Great Journey,* Thames & Hudson, New York, 1987, p. 196.

[2] My version is slightly longer than the National Park Service recording thanks to Phinney, A., "Nez Perce Texts," Columbia University Contributions to Anthropology, Vol. XXV, New York, 1934, reprinted 1969, p. 26-29.

[3] Thwaites, Reuben G., ed., *Original Journals of the Lewis and Clark Expedition,* 8 vols., Dodd, Mead, New York, 1904-5, reprinted, Antiquarian Book Company, New York, 1959, vol. 3, p. 105-106.

[4] Thwaites, vol. 5, p. 29-31.

[5] Thwaites, vol. 5, p. 23.

[6] Thwaites, vol. 5, p.18.

[7] Thwaites, vol. 5, p. 78.

[8] Thwaites, vol. 5 p. 39

Heart of the Monster, East Kamiah, Idaho, Nez Perce Indian Reservation.

Martin Stadius

THE CENTRAL HOMELAND, 1877

**THE TRADITIONAL HOMELAND AS DESCRIBED IN THE TREATY OF 1865
INCLUDED LANDS TO THE EAST AND NORTH OF THIS MAP**

NATIONAL HISTORIC TRAIL ■ ■ ■ ■ ■ ■ ■ ■

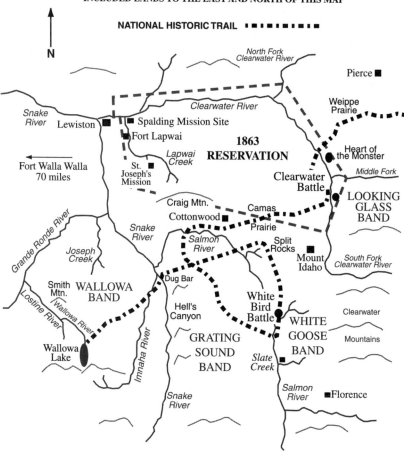

CHAPTER TWO

WALLOWA

A pickup cruises slowly past, the driver's eyes under his cowboy hat staring at me with curiosity and more than a little suspicion. It's understandable. Not many strangers would end up on this Wallowa back road staring across a field at a cow, so I give him a casual wave of the hand. He glances at my van, probably decides the cow won't easily fit in the back, finally responds with his own wave and continues on. Time for me to get moving.

Behind me the slopes of Smith Mountain climb toward a vague summit. In the immense topography of the American West it's a mountain in name only—a rugged, broad hill really—but the first white settlers followed a Nez Perce trail over one of its shoulders into the Wallowa Valley. To those settlers it seemed like a mountain, and so the name remains today. My mind drifts back.

1872

In July the Wallowa band of the Nee-Me-Poo entered the valley, almost certainly over that same Smith Mountain trail, on their annual meandering to their summer home. For generations they had enjoyed a stable existence: winters in sheltered longhouses in the low, relatively warm Grande Ronde and Imnaha canyons near the Snake River and summers in this high mountain paradise. The

23

Wallowa River brought them salmon each year. The earth provided a steady supply of camas, kouse and a multitude of other plants. Elk and deer roamed the forest and meadows, mountain sheep the canyons and peaks. In spring and autumn they might visit other Nez Perce bands in Idaho or their neighbors and friends to the west and north, the Cayuse, Palouse and Walla Walla tribes. When whites began settling the adjoining Grande Ronde Valley to the west in the 1860s, the band had welcomed them. This year they had joined the Americans at the town of LaGrande for a Fourth of July celebration before the thirty-mile journey to the Wallowa country.

A new leader guided the band this year, Thunder Rising Toward Distant Mountains. He stood a little under six feet tall with a muscular frame. His long hair fell past his shoulders, the forelock swept back from his forehead in a dramatic pompadour. One army officer, meeting him for the first time, was struck by his large black eyes, intelligent, piercing, inquisitive. The previous summer Thunder Rising had buried his father, Tuekakas, at the juncture of the Wallowa and Lostine Rivers, a few miles up the valley from here. That same summer had seen the Tully and Wright families, A. B. Findley, Ellis Jefferson, Henry Schaeffer—about fifteen whites in all—venture into the valley with their livestock. They had claimed to be interested only in summer pasture, so the Wallowa Nez Perce had tolerated the newcomers; the Creator had meant to provide for all. Still, just before old Tuekakas died, he had warned his son:

> *When I am gone, think of your country. You are the chief of these people. They look to you to guide them. Always remember that your father never sold his country. You must stop your ears whenever you are asked to sign a treaty selling your home. A few more years and the white men will be all around you. They have their eyes on this land. My son, never forget my words. This country holds your father's body. Never sell the bones of your father and mother.*[1]

Tuekakas had been nearly blind for several years, but his vision of the future was clear.

Shortly after Tuekakas' burial in 1871 and the departure of the rest of the Wallowa band for their winter longhouses in the shelter of the canyons, William McCormick began cutting timber for a cabin a few miles from Wallowa Lake in the upper valley, and Neil Keith hurriedly raised a second a little over a mile away. Believing drought in the Grande Ronde Valley threatened a shortage of feed if they returned, both men had decided to take their chances in the Wallowa with their livestock. Both men and stock survived the winter in easy fashion, so the spring and early summer of 1872 saw the Tullys, the Wrights and the others return along with newcomers: Jacob Sturgill in March; James Hutchinson and James Masterson in April; Benton Embree, Peter Flamer and William White in June. They also erected cabins and built the first fences in the valley and planted gardens of lettuce, peas, carrots, turnips, cabbage, raspberry and currants. They turned cattle and horses loose to roam on the bluffs north of the valley bottom. Charles McClure and Adam George brought mowing machines to harvest the nutritious, wild grass. By the time Thunder Rising rode over Smith Mountain in mid-July, as many as thirty homesteaders may have claimed plots along the valley floor. Thunder Rising must have been sure the Creator hadn't meant for this. His father had been right, and after only one year.[2]

I climb in the van and turn the engine over, listening carefully. The rebuilt engine sounds good. I'm in no hurry and let the van rumble at the lower end of third gear along the dusty, gravel road. A few miles on, a neatly tended graveyard appears at the edge of the road, and I pull over. The Bramlet Memorial Cemetery. Francis Bramlet and his brother, George, were among the first to move into the valley and brought in the first flock of sheep. Opening the gate, I wander among the gravestones. Most are from this century, a variety of family names, then I see an older stone for Samuel Schaeffer, born 1802, died 1893. Henry Schaeffer was a neighbor of the Bramlets, also settling near here in 1872 after initially choosing a site near the lake at the head of the valley. Was Samuel the father? An uncle? A little mystery I'll probably never solve. An inscription on another weathered stone catches my attention:

Remember, friends, as you pass by, as you are now, so once was I; as I am now, so you must be; prepare for death and follow me.

Closing the cemetery gate behind me, I continue up the valley as thunderheads begin to form over the Wallowa Mountains ahead. Turning onto Promise Road and then State Highway 82, I cruise into the town of Wallowa, population 805. Yard and garage sale signs are posted everywhere, driveways filled with knickknacks, sellers and no buyers. The entire town seems to be on the auction block. Except for a few kids pedaling bicycles furiously around a schoolyard, the few blocks of downtown are pretty much deserted.

There's no record of what Thunder Rising thought as he led his people—some 200 in all, with at least five times that many horses—past the nascent Bramlet homestead to the band's traditional campsite where Tuekakas lay buried, but the words of his father must have reverberated through the young chief's mind:

A few more years and the white men will be all around you. They have their eyes on this land. . . . Never sell the bones of your father and mother.

At thirty-two, Thunder Rising was young for the responsibility of leadership, but he knew he must proceed cautiously. Prudence suited his nature. Ever since the days of Lewis and Clark, the Nez Perce had always tried to be friendly toward the whites, and he intended to continue the practice. Still, something had to be done. For several weeks both the Nez Perce and the settlers went about their business. No doubt Thunder Rising and his brother, Ollicott—a Cayuse word that means Frog—rode the length of the valley observing the activity as still more settlers arrived. Two years younger than his brother, Frog was taller, rangier, more free-spirited, a favorite and leader of the young men of the band. Frog's exuberant personality complemented Thunder Rising's more reserved nature, and the two worked pretty much as a team in guiding the people. Eagle From The Light, a respected older chief from a band living near the Salmon River in Idaho, arrived to counsel the young brothers. In mid-August the three decided upon a course of action.

At the far edge of town in a field between the Wallowa River and the road rises a giant, open-sided, circular tent ringed by grandstands. I catch a glimpse of dancers in brightly-colored regalia circling the tent's immense center timber. Beyond the tent, near the fringe of alders and cottonwoods along the riverbank, is a line of fifteen or twenty canvas teepees. Concession stands, a line of portable toilets, sundry sizes and colors of modern tents, rows of campers and cars and pickups fill the rest of the field. The primal heartbeat of a traditional Nez Perce drum drifts in my open window and with it the falsetto wail of singers: the Fifth Annual Wallowa Band Friendship Feast and Pow-Wow. I'll be back later today. Barely a mile beyond the pow-wow encampment, the fork of the Lostine and Wallowa rivers lies hidden beyond a cover of trees. I hang a sharp left at the first side road and angle back. Here amid the pastures on this private property once was the ground where generations of the Real People spent their summers fishing and tending stock. To the right a bare, rocky ridge rises between the rivers. There Thunder Rising and Frog dug the grave of their father and surrounded it with a fence. The settlers called this place Indian Town.

On August 14, 1872, Thunder Rising, Frog and Eagle From The Light summoned the settlers to a council here. Almost all of the whites, about forty by now, showed up and were greeted by about the same number of Nez Perce men. One white participant wrote that the meeting took place in a tent 240 feet long; the band had arranged their teepee poles in a line and stretched the buffalo-hide coverings outside the poles to create a temporary version of the Nez Perce winter longhouse. Thunder Rising spoke first for his people, then probably translated to the Chinook trade jargon, a mish-mash of languages understood by at least one of the home-steaders, Joseph Johnson, who acted as spokesman for the whites. The young Nez Perce orator politely, but firmly, asked the settlers to take whatever hay they had already cut and leave the valley immediately. His exact words were not recorded, but he reminded the whites that the land had always belonged to the Wallowa Nez Perce and that the U.S. government had confirmed that ownership explicitly in the 1855 treaty signed by his father. The matter was straightforward. The whites should go.

The homesteaders understood the situation differently, Johnson responded. The Nez Perce tribe had signed another treaty in 1863, this second one relinquishing title to the Wallowa Valley. The government had surveyed the valley beginning in 1868 and declared it open for settlement. The whites had every right to be here and intended to remain. Johnson asked if the Nez Perce meant to use force to drive the whites from their new homes.

Of course not, one of the chiefs answered. For seventy years, since the first meeting with Lewis and Clark, the Nez Perce had always been friends with the Americans. That would not change. But the whites should understand that Tuekakas did not sign the second treaty, was not even present at the talks. The Nez Perce who did make their mark on the second treaty had no authority to give away this land. The whites should understand that clearly and leave.

Each group could send representatives to meet with the Indian Bureau agent on the reservation in Idaho, Johnson suggested. The chiefs refused, finding no reason to travel that far for more talk when the issue was clear. Johnson offered to send a messenger to the agent on the reservation, asking him to come to the valley to mediate. To this the Nez Perce assented, and the council adjourned.

Three days later, Agent John Monteith hurriedly arrived in the company of Reuben, a devout Christian, brother-in-law to Thunder Rising and destined to become chief of the reservation Nez Perce. Appointed to his post only a year earlier, Monteith was in his mid-thirties, tall, pale, slender, hollow-eyed, the length of his face accentuated by a dark, bushy beard. His main qualification for the job was his Presbyterian faith. After years of corrupt management of reservations all across the country by political appointees, and a brief try at it by the army, the federal government had given up and turned the matter over to various churches. Because the first missionary to the Nez Perce had been Presbyterian, the tribe had been "given" to that denomination. The son of a prominent college president in Oregon's Willamette Valley, John Monteith's instructions were to turn a people most whites considered roaming barbarians into farmers and Christians.

He met with both sides the next morning in what amounted to a repeat of the first council. Thunder Rising repeated his contention that Tuekakas had never signed the second treaty, never traded the land, never accepted any payment for the land, indeed had torn up his New Testament in 1863 and returned to the old beliefs when he found that whites had claimed the Wallowa Valley. After repeating the litany that the second treaty was valid and he had no authority to evict the settlers from the valley, Monteith cautioned everyone to keep calm and stay out of each other's way for the remainder of the summer. Returning to his agency at Lapwai in Idaho, Monteith penned a letter to his superior, F. A. Walker, Commissioner for Indian Affairs in Washington, D.C. In it he wrote:

> *It is a pity the valley was ever opened for settlement. It is so high and cold that they can raise nothing but the hardiest kind of vegetables. One man told me that the wheat was frozen after it was in the milk. It is a fine grass country and raising stock is all that can be done to any advantage. It is the only fishery the Nez Perce have and they go there from all directions . . . If there is any way by which the Wallowa valley could be kept for the Indians I would recommend that it be done.*[3]

I turn back to the main highway and continue up the valley as it widens a bit. The ridges defining the valley's southern edge rise higher and higher, split in one place by the dramatic gash of the Lostine River Canyon with the hamlet of Lostine tucked near its mouth. Beyond are a half-dozen peaks rising to 10,000 feet. I keep well back from a lumbering hay truck, its load of bales seeming to be tilting precariously to the right.

1873

When the first Nez Perce scouts and deer hunters entered the valley in mid-summer they found the settlers in an uproar. President Ulysses Grant had signed an executive order declaring most of the valley and about 2,000 square miles of surrounding land a reserve for the exclusive use of Thunder Rising's Nez Perce. The General Land Office, as a result, had issued orders forbidding any more whites from entering the new reservation. A federal commission was to appraise the current homesteaders' improvements, and once that had been completed Congress would be asked to authorize compensation for the settlers' efforts. They would have to find land elsewhere. Such was the government plan.

The settlers had their own ideas. Forming a volunteer militia, they vowed that neither Indians nor the federal government would take their land from them. At least one other militia group also formed in the adjoining Grande Ronde region to support the Wallowa whites. The first Nez Perce to approach the valley that summer were Frog, his family, and a few other young men. Two settlers calling themselves "captains" in the militia confronted the small group and suggested that Frog and his people leave. Prudently, they withdrew. Emotions calmed once the settlers realized they wouldn't be booted out of their cabins overnight. Still, when the entire Wallowa band moved up from their canyon longhouses in midsummer, they wisely avoided contact with the nervous whites as much as possible.

This stunning turn of events had been partly precipitated by the Modoc Indian war along the Oregon-California border. Rather than relocating to a reservation in southern Oregon the Modocs had been insisting on a reservation of their own in northern California, their traditional homeland. Against wiser voices, the new Oregon Superintendent of Indian Affairs, T. B. Odeneal, had decided to take a tough stand. He ordered the army to remove them to the Oregon reserve. Approximately the size of the Wallowa band, the Modocs had resisted tenaciously under the leadership of Captain Jack, defeated the first army sent at them and remained holed up in a natural lavabed fortress just south of the California-Oregon border.

Meanwhile, government officials in the nation's capital had pulled out both the 1855 and 1863 Nez Perce treaties, looked them over and decided that Thunder Rising just might have a point. Worried that a repeat of the Modoc situation might recur in the Wallowa Valley, the Secretary of the Interior had ordered Odeneal and Monteith to meet with the young chief in a final attempt to convince him to move either to the Nez Perce reservation in Idaho or to the Umatilla reservation in Oregon where the Wallowa band had relatives among the remnants of the Cayuse and Walla Walla tribes. In the likely event that approach failed, the two men had been authorized to negotiate the terms by which Thunder Rising and his people would remain both in their winter canyon homes and the Wallowa Valley.

When discussions commenced in March of 1873 at the agency at Lapwai, Thunder Rising remained firm in his commitment to his homeland. Odeneal and Monteith suggested a compromise. The Wallowa band and the settlers might share the valley, each to have part. The decision must have been agonizing for Tuekakas' son, his father's dying admonition fresh in his mind. But eventual war seemed the only alternative, and no doubt Monteith and Odeneal reminded the chief of the numbers and strength of the army. The path of resistance could lead to losing everything.

Reluctantly, Thunder Rising agreed to a compromise. The Wallowa Nez Perce would keep the eastern half of their homeland: the upper part of the valley with the lake and its fishery, the Imnaha Canyon to the northeast and the range land and hunting grounds stretching north of the lake to the lower canyon of the Grande Ronde where most of the band wintered. They would give up the western part of their homeland: the lower two-thirds of the valley, including Tuekakas' grave, the grazing and hunting ground surrounding it and the upper reaches of the Grande Ronde Canyon. On the face of it the settlement was brilliant. The Nez Perce retained enough that was vital, their winter longhouses, range for their stock, the fishery, easy access to their brethren across the Snake River in Idaho. The whites kept the lowest, warmest portion of the valley where most of the homesteads lay, retained the road across the shoulders of Smith Mountain to the settlements in the Grande Ronde, and only a few settlers inhabiting the upper valley would be required to move.

What happened to the plan in the bowels of the federal

bureaucracy between early April and June when President Grant signed the order putting it into effect remains a mystery today, but words like incompetence and stupidity are appropriate. The reservation described in President Grant's executive order bore little resemblance to the one negotiated at Lapwai. The Nee-Me-Poo received the lower valley, the whites the upper valley and lake region. Most of the settlers would be displaced with the remaining few isolated by the impassable Hell's Canyon to the east, the Wallowa Mountains to the south and the proposed reservation to the west and north. Today it's impossible to know if any reservation would have had a chance given the tenor of the times, but this one was doomed. In grand style Oregon Democratic Party politicians began raising a clamor against the Republican Grant administration and its perfidious western minions, Odeneal and Monteith. Meanwhile, the Modoc scare ended with the hanging of several of its leaders and the exile of the rest of the band to Indian Territory in Oklahoma. Privately, officials in the nation's capital began to wonder if the Wallowa reservation might have been a political blunder made in haste. Settlers voted; Nez Perce did not.

In the autumn, Thunder Rising met with Monteith again at Lapwai. Angrily, the chief listened as the agent waffled, suggesting the Wallowa band might have to move to the Idaho reservation after all. Monteith now insisted that the only alternative for the Wallowa band was to settle permanently in part of the valley and become farmers. To Thunder Rising this was an absurd betrayal. The whole point of the reservation had been to preserve the traditional lifestyle of the people: both the winter longhouses and the summer range and fishery. They just wanted to live in the old way, to be left alone, not bothering anybody and not being bothered. Thunder Rising asked Monteith to arrange for a visit to Washington, D.C., where he would make this President Grant understand what the Real People needed. Monteith prevaricated, then refused. Fuming, the young chief returned to his people.

1874

As the first anniversary of the agreement in Lapwai passed, and summer approached, hunters and scouts undoubtedly kept Thunder Rising apprised of the situation in the Wallowa: the homesteaders were staying put. He needed the counsel of other chiefs. As June drew to a close, he asked his people to pack and prepare for a special journey. Before returning to Wallowa this year they would travel to the camas grounds at Weippe in Idaho where long ago Lewis and Clark had first met the Real People. There the Wallowans met the bands led by White Goose, Grating Sound and Looking Glass. White Goose and Grating Sound lived in the rugged Salmon River Country south of the 1863 reservation. Like Thunder Rising they refused to accept the 1863 treaty as legitimate because no one representing their bands had signed the document. Close to the scene of several gold strikes, their people were being constantly hounded and occasionally killed by whites. The Looking Glass band had moved its winter village just inside the 1863 reservation boundary after their traditional site had been overrun by settlers, but they still had their problems with the whites. Looking Glass was, perhaps, the foremost of the buffalo hunters, warriors who with their families spent months and years at a time on the distant plains of Montana. There, in fights against the Blackfoot or Lakota, in horse-stealing raids against just about anybody, a man could make a name for himself. The roaming life in the buffalo country held great allure, but Agent Monteith was determined to stamp out the practice. His Indians would eventually become Presbyterian farmers, nothing else.

Monteith appeared at the Weippe encampment leading a column of cavalry, tipped off about the meeting by reservation Nez Perce. While the women harvested and cooked camas roots, children played and the young men raced horses, the chiefs met with the agent, voicing their familiar concerns. The bands then packed up and went their separate ways. As Monteith returned to the agency at Lapwai with the soldiers, the bands gathered again, this time at Split Rocks on Camas Prairie south of the reservation. Now they could hold a real council, free of the prying agent's ears. When the talk eventually turned to the possibility of war, three renowned warriors—Five Wounds, Grizzly Bear Ferocious and Rainbow—rose in turn and spoke against fighting the whites. The chiefs could have expected these fiery men to have been among those most eager for war and glory, and their caution was impressive. There would be no more mention of war.

Thunder Rising returned to the Wallowa Valley in August to find two troops of cavalry waiting. Probably he was relieved, as no doubt were the settlers, the great majority of whom continued to get along well with the Nez Perce. With the soldiers between the settlers and the Real People, trouble caused by hotheads on either side could be avoided. Captain Stephen Whipple commanding the troops, reported to his superiors in a letter dated September 5:

> *The Indians—in all about forty lodges—remained in the valley, giving no intentional cause of offence, but quietly and industriously continued engaged in preparing food for future use.*
>
> *So far as I can discover, from the most careful attention, there is no cause to apprehend any present difficulty with these Indians. The settlers generally appear to wish to deal justly by the Indians, and I have heard a majority of the former express the opinion that while that course is pursued they have no fear of hostile acts on the part of the latter.*
>
> *There is an anxious feeling with the white people who have taken up claims in the valley and commenced improvements, that the question, whether that valley is to be open to settlement or reserved for the use of Indians, should be settled at an early day; and that anxiety is fully shared by the natives.*[4]

Well-stocked with salmon, roots and game, the Real People filtered down to their warm, canyon longhouses for the long winter months, leaving the homesteaders to contend with a season of especially bitter cold, snow and wind. That year even flowing streams froze solidly, and four feet of snow reportedly fell in one day. More than a few settlers, isolated in their drafty cabins, continuously feeding their fireplaces from depleting stocks of wood, prayed the federal government would hurry up and buy them out. So both in longhouses and cabins that winter and spring, uncertainty reigned as the inhabitants waited for summer and news from the nation's capital.

From Lostine it's only an eight-mile drive for me to Enterprise. Somewhere along this stretch I pass what would have been the boundary of the 1873 reservation agreed to by Thunder Rising. The Nez Perce would have kept this upper part of the valley, leaving the rest for the newcomers. Enterprise, just ahead, is now by far the largest town in the valley, a whopping population of 2,003. Cruising past an impressive Forest Service building on a hill, I enter the short business district—a Safeway grocery store, a line of tidy motels, the county courthouse—zig and zag toward Hatchery Road and Alder Slope to the south where McCormick and Keith built those first cabins so many years ago.

1875

On June 10, bowing to political pressure, President Grant signed an order eliminating the Wallowa reservation. At a meeting with Monteith in Lapwai, Thunder Rising reacted angrily but soon calmed down. If the 1873 reservation agreement was void, he reasoned, that simply meant the 1855 treaty remained valid and the Wallowa band still owned the entire valley. They would continue their usual summer routine. When the band arrived early in August, they again found two troops of cavalry already camped in the lower valley. One was Company "H", First Cavalry, Captain Joel Trimble commanding. Years later Sergeant Michael McCarthy of that troop reminisced about that summer:

> In 1875 my company and another were ordered to the Wallowa Valley in Oregon, a mountain valley near the Idaho line. Wallowa had been from time immemorial the fishing grounds of the Nez Perces and even now the nontreaty band (Joseph's) came here every summer to camp and fish. The land along the streams was gradually being enclosed by stock men, and the Indians had a rough piece of pebbly bottom land for a permanent campground, and fished along the streams. In summer the streams of the Wallowa Valley swarmed with salmon and Redfish, a species of salmon, and the Indians took them by spearing. The men who understood spearing, mostly old men, sat on their ponies back, at edge of stream, and rarely missed a fish. The young bucks and squaws took them to camp where they were dressed and hung under a bush covered stageing to dry. . . . The banks of

35

*streams and camp presented a busy scene for about a month.
After fishing season they have a festival, dances and parades.
The tribe were nearly all domiciled in one large structure covered with skins, a sort of very long tent, with an opening at
one end where they gave their performances, as on a stage.
The rest of interior was divided off into portions and occupied
by various family groups, each with their open fireplace and
cooking utensils in front of their portion, towards centre. . . .
The parades were gorgeous affairs. The warriors were nearly
naked with immense feather headdresses (all the same as
cigar Indians). The ponies were daubed with red paint, and
the procession formed in single file, moved by the flank, and
in column of files galloped round and round the camp firing
old horse pistols, guns, etc., anything to make a noise,
singing, whooping and yelling.*[5]

As he had the previous summer, Captain Whipple made a point
of examining the length of the valley and talking with both homesteaders and Nez Perce. The brutal winter had taken its toll.
Whipple discovered that three families had already packed up and
pulled out and that others were ready to sell their improvements
if only they could find someone willing to buy. After meeting with
the Nez Perce, Whipple found his respect for them growing. "This
band of Indians are by no means a vagabond set," he wrote. "They
are proud-spirited, self-supporting and intelligent."[6]

Whipple wasn't the only soldier that summer who found himself
empathizing with the Nez Perce. Identifying himself only as
"Johnny Come Lately" another wrote his impressions in a letter to
a Portland newspaper:

*We are employing our leisure killing red fish and hunting
a little and don't anticipate any trouble whatever. In fact,
upon close inquiry, the stories of the hostile attitude of the
Indians are without foundation, and the white men of the
country are perfectly safe as far as the Indians are concerned.
I have heard white men make the most frivolous complaints,
such as, for instance, that the Indian ponies are eating the
grass off the mountain ranges; just as if it was not free to all;*

*and then again, that the Indians presumed to cross the land
claimed by the whites, which was unfenced prairie. They (the
whites) don't seem to understand the principle of living and
let live, but would appropriate to their own use even the air
the poor Indians breath . . . . the health of the troops is excellent and we are deeply grateful to the settlers of the Wallowa
valley for having us called in here, and we would be well
pleased to have the same thing occur every summer.*[7]

As another year ended placidly, in December Thunder Rising
and many of his people decided to visit friends and relatives at
Lapwai on the Idaho reservation. Meanwhile, in the Imnaha
Canyon, a dispute flared over grazing rights between a few Nez
Perce and white herders before being settled amicably.
Nevertheless, reports filtered all the way to Oregon Governor
Leonard Grover that there had been trouble. By the time he
telegraphed army authorities the dispute had ballooned in several
fertile imaginations: Thunder Rising and eighty warriors were on
the warpath. When he heard the story even the dour Monteith
thought it a hoot since the marauding chief was peacefully camped
a few miles from the agency. In the end, the only victims were the
two companies of soldiers rousted out of the comfort of Fort Walla
Walla in Washington and sent on a chilling wild goose chase as far
as the Grande Ronde Valley where enterprising settlers tried
charging the disgusted troopers exorbitant prices for horse feed
and supplies.

At about the same time, Brigadier General Oliver Howard,
army commander for the Pacific Northwest, ordered his Assistant
Adjutant General, Major Henry Wood, to look into the legalities of
the Nez Perce matter. On January 8 the junior officer gave his
report to Howard. Wood had decided:

*. . . the non-treaty Nez Perces cannot in law be regarded as
bound by the treaty of 1863; and in so far as it attempts to
deprive them of a right to occupancy of any land its provisions are null and void.*[8]

That must have raised Howard's eyebrows. With the Imnaha

37

affair fresh in his mind, Howard mulled over the report. Sooner or later an alarm coming from the Wallowa region would be real, and soldiers would be in the middle of it unless the government dealt justly with these Indians. Howard did not have long to wait for the trouble to begin in earnest.

1876

While the main band paused north of the valley to harvest the kouse root before moving on to the Wallowa fishery for the summer, hunters spread out ahead of them, searching for fresh game for their people after the long winter and its diet of dried salmon and roots. One of those hunters was Wind Blowing. With seven others he made camp near the headwaters of Whiskey Creek about six miles from Indian Town, in a swale at the verge of the immense forest stretching north. The deer hunt was good, so on June 23, leaving their rifles in camp, the men set out to collect the carcasses killed the past few days. Their ponies loaded down with venison, three returned to find two white men—A. B. Findley and Wells McNall—in the camp with the hunters' rifles in their possession. Findley and McNall accused the Nez Perce of stealing five of Findley's horses. At first the talk apparently remained coolheaded, but tempers flared and soon McNall and Wind Blowing were desperately grappling over a rifle. Wind Blowing was a powerful man. Losing the struggle for the rifle, McNall begged, cursed and screamed for Findley to shoot. Reluctantly, he did, killing Wind Blowing with a single shot. Covering the other hunters with their rifles, the whites backed out of the camp and fled toward the valley. A few days later Findley discovered his missing horses grazing near his homestead.

Many settlers now feared the worst and prepared for the coming onslaught, but the valley remained quiet. Thunder Rising had managed to quiet his increasingly angry people. After burying Wind Blowing, the chief made the trek yet again to Lapwai to meet Monteith. He found the agent quite sympathetic. Perhaps the Imnaha incident the previous winter had soured Monteith on some of the settlers extravagant claims of injustice. At any rate, he assured Thunder Rising that civil authorities in Oregon would soon deal with the killers. After the chief returned to his band the agent fired off a letter to General Howard calling the event "willful, deliberate murder" and requesting that the general send troops to the valley to protect the Indians from the settlers.

Only three weeks later, Thunder Rising and Frog returned to Lapwai, this time at the behest of the army. Waiting for them was Major Wood from General Howard's staff at Fort Vancouver. With their usual eloquence the two brothers repeated their demands for their traditional homeland and reiterated the validity of the 1855 pact and the injustice of the 1863 treaty. And now murder by white men.

The impassioned oratory impressed the army officer. Thunder Rising's brother-in-law Reuben, by now head chief of the Nez Perce faction living on the reservation, and Monteith listened sullenly. Reuben believed the army was paying inordinate attention to the Wallowa headman, and Monteith was peeved that an army officer was usurping his role as government spokesman. The tension must have been palpable, or perhaps harsh words were exchanged. At any rate Wood cut the meeting short and asked to meet privately with the brothers. If Reuben and Monteith weren't truly angry before, they were then. The army, Monteith wrote in a blistering letter to Washington, D.C., had no business interfering with his Indians. Wood met with the brothers the next day, anyway, informing them that General Howard was proposing a commission of five good men to resolve the Wallowa situation. Although he found this agreeable, Thunder Rising continued to insist the killers of Wind Blowing be brought to trial.

All summer the Nee-Me-Poo watched and waited as Findley and McNall went about their ordinary business. After meeting with Major Wood, Thunder Rising seems to have disappeared for almost a month; a discreet council with the other nontreaty headmen seems a logical supposition. At any rate, by late August he was back in the Wallowa where some of the warriors had set up a target and regularly practiced firing from atop their speeding ponies. Several times nervous settlers near Indian Town listened to the drums and chants of what they took to be war dances. On the other hand, twice in August Thunder Rising visited the Findley homestead, played with the children, sat for dinner with the family and questioned the husband in Chinook jargon about the events of June 23.

On the first day of September, warriors trotted up to most of the cabins dotting the valley and ordered the inhabitants to go to Indian Town the following day for a council. McNall and Findley must attend, they instructed. Many men, especially those with families, decided to remain holed up in their cabins, but about twenty, including Findley and McNall, gathered at the McNall place near Indian Town. After deciding the two killers should remain behind for their own safety the rest went ahead as a group. At Indian Town Thunder Rising announced his decision: since there appeared to be no prospect of white justice for Findley and McNall, they were to be turned over to the Nez Perce. If the settlers refused to give the two up, all whites had one week to pack up and get out of the valley. Although the settlers protested the ultimatum, they were in no position to carry their objections too far. They dispersed to their homesteads, more than a few beginning to pack their belongings that very evening.

The morning of September 3, seven settlers, including Findley and Wells McNall, heard the thunder of sixty ponies pounding down the surrounding hillsides then circling the McNall cabin. The riders were stripped, painted, apparently ready for a fight. Although the cabin bristled with rifles poking from windows and chinks in the wall, those inside knew they did not stand a chance if shooting began. Ephraim McNall, Wells' father, bravely stood outside the cabin door. His son was not there, he lied. Sometime during the confrontation more riders appeared, and a young woman dropped from the back of her horse. She was the daughter of Wind Blowing. Striding past the startled elder McNall, she pushed open the door and demanded to see the murderers of her father. Those inside pushed her out, but she persisted until Findley came to the door. Their eyes met. Thunder Rising asked him to come with the warriors. Trembling, Findley agreed, but the men inside pulled him back, slamming shut the door. The angry young woman stormed away, and the tension broke. After repeating the one week deadline for the rest of the homesteaders to depart if the two did not turn themselves over, the Nee-Me-Poo rode away, leaving a shaken bunch of settlers.

40

Word spread swiftly through the valley that the Nez Perce were deadly serious this time. Two-horse teams began pulling creaking wagons over Smith Mountain toward the Grande Ronde. Families on horseback and leading pack horses joined them. Others rode the opposite direction, groups of Grande Ronde militia summoned to help the Wallowa settlers. By the time the week had passed, between sixty and 100 armed men gathered at the McNall homestead, determined neither to give up the accused killers to the Nez Perce, nor to abandon the Wallowa country.

The Wallowa Mountains dominate the southern skyline as I approach Hurricane Creek, pass a tiny Grange hall and turn toward the town of Joseph, Oregon. Some 100 million years ago, when the Pacific coastline ran through what is now Idaho, the Wallowas were an island chain in the ocean. Shifting tectonic plates gradually jammed them against the shore as giant volcanoes continued to build the continent westward. Today the precipitous slopes of the Wallowas still resemble some kind of massive inland island looming above the surrounding country. Ahead, though, a more modest feature of the landscape captures my attention, a partially-wooded, knobby bluff maybe eighty feet high stretching from the mountains northward for a few hundred yards. It separates this part of the valley from Wallowa Lake and the town of Joseph. Somewhere near here lay the Wright homestead where on September 9, Thunder Rising and his warriors decided to pay a visit.

Sitting on a woodpile were a few men from neighboring homesteads who could only watch the warriors with concern. The women probably hustled children into the dubious shelter of the house, and one young man headed for the barn. A bright spot for the whites was the fact that women trailed behind the warriors; they would not have come along had a fight been in the offing.

There's no record of whether his voice was mild or angry, but Thunder Rising asked about all the Grande Ronders pouring into the lower valley, supposedly eager for war. Two settlers understood some Nez Perce and quickly responded that the settlers in the lower valley were afraid and had asked for help. If the settlers in

41

the lower valley and the Grande Ronders want a fight, my warriors will be on that bluff over there all day tomorrow, Thunder Rising answered. Now what about someone from right around here who bragged about killing all my people and then taking my scalp to decorate his bridle? the Nez Perce leader continued. One of the men hurried into the barn and dragged a guilty, quivering Gerard Cochran out of the haystack in which he was burrowed. Cochran's father pleaded with Thunder Rising to spare his son, promising to take him from the valley forever. The Nez Perce band leader agreed to let the fool keep his life. He then reminded his unwilling audience that Findley and McNall had not surrendered. He reiterated his ultimatum: either deliverance of the murderers to justice or expulsion of all whites from the valley. The deadline was a little over twenty-four hours away. All promised to leave by the next day. Satisfied, Thunder Rising led his warriors around the bluff to a traditional camping spot near the lake. Some of those upper valley settlers fled by nightfall, others departing later under glittering mountain starlight.

The army arrived in the lower valley shortly after midnight, forty-seven tired troopers of the First Cavalry's Company "E" led by First Lieutenant Albert Forse. After resting until daybreak, the command hurried upriver past wagons headed the opposite direction. Well short of the bluff Forse halted the column then coolly pushed ahead with two enlisted men and settler Tom Veasey, who spoke enough Nez Perce to qualify as an interpreter in a pinch. Silhouetted along the top of the bluff they saw a line of seventy to eighty mounted warriors with rifles in their hands. The Wallowa band had obviously been reinforced by their brethren in Idaho.

The small party reined in their horses as a single rider descended the slope. Lieutenant Forse told the warrior—Frog, according to one Nez Perce account—that he and his men were on vacation in the valley, were out looking for a good spot to camp but needed to parley first with Thunder Rising. Telling them to wait, the rider loped his horse back up the slope. After a few minutes he returned and escorted the officer and his men to the bluff. No doubt glancing at the line of painted warriors stripped to their breechclouts, Forse cautiously offered to Thunder Rising that he, as an officer of the army, would personally guarantee that the two accused men would be judged by civil authorities. Forse knew that he had no power to force the matter into a court, but his job in the few minutes ahead was to try to prevent a war. To the officer's relief the Nez Perce leader promptly agreed to give Forse a chance.

Forse next broached the confrontation of the previous day at the Wright homestead. The Grande Ronders have told several of my men they intend to kill and scalp me and my people, the chief retorted. We will defend ourselves right here on this bluff. After Thunder Rising balked at a suggestion that the Wallowa band move to the Idaho reservation for their own safety Forse suggested a line between the Indians and the settlers so there would be no more trouble. Again, Thunder Rising agreed, perhaps recalling the aborted reservation, because the boundary he then negotiated with the lieutenant was nearly identical to the line of 1873 he had worked out with Odeneal and Monteith. His people would keep to the upper valley if the settlers remained downriver. With that the young band leader instructed his warriors to "throw their bullets away" as a sign of peace, and thunder rumbled down the valley. No doubt the men of "E" Company were relieved to see their commander return unscathed after hearing the ominous gunfire.

For the next two weeks Company "E" bivouacked near Wallowa Lake and the camp of the Wallowa band. It turned out to be the vacation for his men that Forse had hoped would transpire. The army officer kept his promise to Thunder Rising; Wells and Findley surrendered to authorities in the county seat of LaGrande. Three days after the tense moments on the bluff he met again with the Nez Perce leader and told him of the fact, even convincing the reluctant chief to send two witnesses to LaGrande under the protection of a cavalry corporal. Findley was charged with manslaughter, but released when the Nez Perce witnesses apparently refused to touch a Bible to be sworn. Still, Forse's poised intervention had won another season of tenuous peace between the non-treaty Nez Perce and the whites.

It would be the last.

My van chugs along the road past the north end of the bluff where Thunder Rising and Forse parlayed. A sign on a post reads:

43

No War On The West. It's not surprising the Sagebrush Rebellion has reached this little pocket of Oregon. Although tourism plays a role in the local economy, not everyone can run a motel or restaurant or open a chi-chi art gallery. As isolated as the valley is, far from any urban populations, the highway bringing visitors is rarely crowded even in summer. Over the long winter, the tourists pretty much stay away altogether. Most of the Wallowa Mountains are set aside as wilderness, and the U.S. Forest Service controls much of the dwindling supply of available timber on the periphery of the valley. The feds don't allow as much logging as before, and mills have closed or cut back operations. Now the pressure is on in Congress to restrict grazing on public land. The ranchers and timber workers feel they're losing control of their destiny, might even have to move elsewhere if the economy keeps going south. And all because of a distant federal government and its lack of understanding about their lives. The native inhabitants felt the same in the 1870s.

Banners on the rodeo grandstand at the edge of Joseph announce the upcoming July Chief Joseph Days Rodeo. Already the town of 800 is getting spruced up, flags ready, concession stands rising in an empty lot along the placid main street. This is the kind of place where drivers stop of their own accord and wave pedestrians across the street. A sedate fifteen miles-per-hour seems about the norm for traffic, except for an occasional tourist in a rush to find that elusive something somewhere down the road.

After pulling my van over, I cross the street to an old brick bank building set on a corner, once the scene of a wild robbery and shoot-em-up right out of a western. Now it's a museum where I make a bee-line for a wall of photographs in the back. I've been here before and know what I'm looking for, a tiny pocket-sized picture of maybe thirty mounted Nez Perce men with a few women at the rear of the cluster, all in traditional clothing set against a backdrop of a barren hill-side. With my nose a few inches from the wall I stared at two grainy figures just to the left of center. One wore a headdress low on his forehead, half his face in shadow but seemingly somber. The other was taller, a little thinner, a fierce scowl on his face. I'd come across a similar photograph in another county museum amid a collection having nothing to do with the Nez

Perce, a similar print, but not identical. In the other photo the group had shifted a bit as though the photographer were taking a series of shots. What had taken my breath away at seeing the second photo were a few fading sepia words at the bottom: Lapwai . . . May 1877 . . . Chief Joseph . . . Ollokot. If those words were true then the two photographs are the only known of Thunder Rising taken before the war began. I stare at the tiny figures for the longest time. In May 1877, a year after the current narrative, at Lapwai the brothers were in the midst of a council with Agent Monteith and General Howard. They were hearing the final ultimatum that they must give up the Wallowa country or face a war. The battle at White Bird was a month away. In the photos Ollokot, or Frog, appears furious, Thunder Rising dejected.

Less than a mile south of town the road curves up a gentle slope, and I pull off onto a wide spot on the gravel shoulder. Here, a few easy steps uphill, a stone pillar on a grassy promontory just above the lower end of Wallowa Lake marks the grave of Tuekakas. His body was moved here in 1926 by enterprising locals, hoping to boost the tourist trade even then. At least they chose a beautiful spot. The placid, slender lake, dammed by the terminal moraine of an ancient glacier, stretches for three miles into the heart of the mountains, and just out of sight below this knoll, the Wallowa River gushes from the lake, adding its music to the scene. Across the river the massive hump of Chief Joseph Mountain looms abruptly some 5,000 feet above the monument. At this time of year it seems everything is green and bursts with life.

This is it, the beginning of the Nez Perce National Historic Trail. I have the place to myself and wander to the river and back, thinking of Tuekakas. When the first missionaries arrived in the Nez Perce country in the 1830s he had been among the earliest and most ardent supporters of adopting the white way of life, one of the first three to be baptized into the Christian faith, taking the name Joseph. Within a decade he had soured of the prospect of the baggage the missionaries carried with them and returned permanently to this isolated country to live in the old manner. He died with a fearful vision of what was to come.

I feel like I should do something meaningful here, the beginning of my trip, but nothing comes to mind. I simply climb back into my van, and the journey begins.

The evening dances at the pow-wow back at the town of Wallowa get going a bit late, as usual. These things seem to have a dynamic of their own, and they start when everyone is good and ready. First comes a prayer that the elders will remember the laws of the Creator, that the elders will lead the way, leaving a path for the young to follow, that all will dance with eyes and minds open, as the Creator taught. Carrying the Eagle Staff of the Nez Perce Tribe, a gray-haired man leads the procession of eighty dancers in traditional regalia into the arbor. Just behind the Eagle Staff are men bearing the American and Canadian Flags. Black hair follows gray hair in the trailing line eventually taking the shape of a circle, the young following the old. The circle stops. The staff-bearer stands motionless as drummers begin the Flag Song. He waits, listens, waits. When the moment is right, he takes a step and all the men join in, the women keeping the circle, their only movement a slight bending of the knee in rhythm with the beat. The setting sun angles under the canopy, illuminating the dust raised by the feet of the dancers and creating a mellow, golden glow.

Seven drumming groups have made the trip to this powwow. The Plainsmen, all the way from Oklahoma, lead the first of three songs in memory of the Nee-Me-Poo of 1877. The evening will be made up of circles: the drum, the singers around the drum, the dancers circling the arbor, the ring of spectators. Watching every movement, keeping it true, are the Whipman and the Whipwoman. He a descendent of Black Eagle who survived the 1877 war, she of Cayuse chief Five Crows.

The grass dancers put on their usual improbably athletic performance, spinning and jumping with outstretched arms, the long frills hanging from their regalia shimmering like grass blowing in a prairie wind. There's a reason only young men grass dance; I get tired just watching. Their bells chiming in rhythm with the heavy drums, young female jingle dancers hop as delicately as deer skittering through a forest. My favorites, though, have always been the traditional dancers: the women with their heads bobbing ever so slightly, backs as straight as saplings, epitomes of dignity and grace; and the men, more vigorous, feet pounding round and round the center pole, bending and weaving, their eagle feathers fluttering, evoking images of thundering herds of bison, hunts, war. I finally wander away and roll up in my sleeping bag about eleven that night, the drums still pounding in the distance. Sleep comes easily.

The following morning I slice up my cantaloupe and watermelon for a simple salad, my meager contribution to the Friendship Feast. Under the arbor where the Nez Perce and Umatillas and Spokanes and Yakamas danced the previous evening are nineteen tables covered with food: greens and beans and salads and desserts. Two tables with chairs are set aside for elders, both Indian and white. The rest of us will eat in the stands. Before the 400 people line up to fill their plates, a Nez Perce woman offers a traditional prayer. Ringing a bell three times, she asks everyone to raise their right arms and say Aye. It means, she explains, you respect your Creator. Four hundred people raise their right arms and say Aye.

If you've never tasted buffalo—and I don't mean buffalo burgers—you've missed a treat. Slow roasted until well done, it's lean, moist and tender with a richer flavor than beef. Frontier folk in the nineteenth century almost universally preferred buffalo to any other meat, and I understand why. And the salmon, lightly cooked, flaky, all flavor. The Nez Perce provided ten of the salmon, the Umatilla tribe another twenty. This year they had to travel hundreds of miles to the Oregon coast to find the fish. The Wallowa River no longer succors the salmon. Dams on the Snake and Columbia Rivers have made sure of that.

A couple from Spokane sit beside me in the bleachers as I balance a paper plate on my lap. They happened by on a motorcycle vacation and pulled over to check out the commotion. Already they're talking of coming back next summer for more than one day. That's one of the reasons for this celebration. With the valley's resource-extraction economy likely headed for a slow decline, many of the people here have realized that the Nez Perce heritage of the region could boost tourism. But to become a viable showcase for that heritage you have to have Nez Perce around. In 1989 a descendent of Frog returned to the valley. His name is Taz Conner, and he's co-master of ceremonies for the pow-wow this year. His dream has been for a Nee-Me-Poo cultural center in the valley. The previous day, he had spoken movingly of more and more Nez Perce returning to this land and sharing their culture with anyone with a spirit of respect for the land and all people. His words had been elegant and heartfelt.

Four Nez Perce girls, grade-school age, sit on the other side of me. One pulls a tiny, scarlet plastic warrior with headdress and rifle from her pocket. Another produces a much bigger Batman on a motorcycle. The first girl slowly stalks the kneeling warrior toward the caped crusader then pounces amid squeals of delight. It's no contest. The girl with the warrior glances up at me, shyly brushes back her hair, then replays the scenario with her friend: Warrior 2; Batman 0. This time all four look up at me with big grins.

Notes

1 Joseph, "An Indian's View of Indian Affairs," *North American Review* (April, 1879), p. 419.

2 The people and events in this chapter have pretty much been covered in: Bartlett, Grace, *The Wallowa Country, 1867-1877*, n.l., 1976. This book, while written from the point-of-view of the settlers, provides detailed accounts. Nez Perce versions are in McWhorter, Lucullus V., *Hear Me, My Chiefs!*, Caxton Printers, Caldwell, ID, 1952, p. 116-131. Also, Josephy, Alvin M., *The Nez Perce Indians and the Opening of the Northwest*, Yale University Press, New Haven, 1965, p. 445-484.

3 Quoted in Bartlett, *Wallowa*, p.14-15.

4 Quoted in Bartlett, *Wallowa*, p. 39.

5 McCarthy, Michael, "Indian Reminiscences," *Diary and Papers*, Library of Congress, Washington, DC.

6 Quoted in Josephy, *Nez Perce*, p. 467-468.

7 Letter, *Oregonian*, September 2, 1875, p. 1.

8 Wood, H. Clay, *Status of Young Joseph and His Band of Nez Perce Indians*, Assistant Adjutant General's Office, Portland, 1876, p. 45.

Martin Stadius

Wallowa Lake

CHAPTER THREE

LAPWAI

It's late afternoon before I'm ready to get going. My first camp along the Historic Trail is going to be at a place called Dug Bar. Getting there will be a sixty-mile jaunt into the depths of Hell's Canyon, the deepest gorge in America. The first forty are a piece of cake, a paved road down Little Sheep Creek to the hamlet of Imnaha on the river of the same name. From there, the defile cut by the Imnaha River provides the only road access into Hells Canyon on the Oregon side.

A few miles downstream from town the pavement ends and rutted dirt begins. My van rolls and bumps along at no more than ten miles an hour; the last twenty miles are going to take a while. By now you know of the first encounter between the Nee-Me-Poo and the United States when Lewis and Clark stumbled out of the Clearwater Mountains. You know of the tense years in the Wallowa region leading up to 1877. It's time to fill in the gap.

Until 1835 contact was pretty much limited to the fur trade. With the United States and Britain vying for supremacy in the region, traders and trappers from both countries soon filtered into the upper Columbia country bringing the prized trade goods. John Jacob Astor's Pacific Fur Company based in New York City and two Canadian firms—the New North West Company and the

Hudson's Bay Company—fought it out to see who would become top dog. Astor's enterprise faded first. Then in 1821, the Hudson's Bay Company absorbed its smaller Canadian rival. Three years before the takeover, the New North West Company had established a fort near the Columbia River on the periphery of the Nee-Me-Poo homeland. The Nez Perce quickly garnered a reputation there for being "insolent and independent," a result of their disdain for the drudgery of hunting beaver pelts.[1] When the Hudson's Bay Company took over the fort—called at first Fort Nez Perces, then Fort Walla Walla—it became the primary source of horses for that enterprise's far-flung trading empire. The Real People were more than happy to trade animals from their vast herds for guns, lead, powder and cooking utensils.

About the same time that the Hudson's Bay Company forged its monopoly over the northwest, farther east Nez Perce buffalo hunters began to run into a different kind of white man along the streams of the Rocky Mountains: the free trapper, the American Mountain Man. They were adventurers, by nature independent, spirited, profane and freedom-loving. Most were disenchanted with life in the Atlantic coast settlements, more interested in learning the ways of the West than forcing change on the natives they encountered. Within a few years, parties of Nez Perce commuted each summer to the annual trapper rendezvous in one Rocky Mountain valley or another where a year's worth of beaver pelts changed hands in return for the upcoming year's supplies packed on mule trains across the plains from St. Louis. The Real People hung out with their new friends, racing horses, gambling, listening to preposterous stories, maybe telling a few in the spirit of the occasion. Some of the trappers produced decks of playing cards, pronounced them bibles and proceeded to show the Nee-Me-Poo how to worship with them. The religion of the whites was truly something different.

In February 1834 a U.S. Army officer on official leave, a mediocre explorer and fur trader named Benjamin Bonneville, wandered into the upper end of this Imnaha Valley after finding Hells Canyon impassable. He and his three companions were on the edge of starvation, their horses shivering and exhausted after struggling down the Snake River for almost two months.

Wintering comfortably with his company of trappers near the headwaters of the Snake, Bonneville had decided to visit Fort Nez Perces on the Columbia River. It was a journey most notable for its foolishness. Bonneville's adventures during his three-year stint in the West would eventually be documented by Washington Irving, but Bonneville had neglected to read a prior work by that writer. In *Astoria,* Irving had already detailed the woes of an earlier expedition which attempted to use the Snake River as a passage to the Columbia. Still, Bonneville was lucky. He had regularly communed with Nez Perce buffalo hunters farther east, knew some of the language and convinced the Nee-Me-Poo wintering in the Imnaha Canyon to feed the helpless whites and swap a fresh horse for beads, a hatchet, gunpowder and lead.

The Imnaha is a branch canyon of Hells Canyon, but it has some pretty imposing side canyons of its own, each separated from its neighbors by towering knife-edge ridges rising thousands of feet. The names on my map for various landforms hint at stories: Mormon Prong, Axe Handle Gulch, Hangover Creek, Windy Hell Canyon, Rheumatiz Gulch. When Bonneville passed through here the canyon was home to two villages. Now there is the hamlet of Imnaha and a few isolated ranches—no more than a few hundred people in total—just as in Bonneville's time. The ranchers range their stock on the grass and sage-covered slopes, just as the Nee-Me-Poo did their horses. Some places don't change much, except for the names on the land. Bonneville mentioned the name of only one of the village chiefs he met here in the Imnaha country, Yo-mus-ro-y-e-cut. He would die in a few years, and no one in his village possessed the qualities to rise to headman. In time, both Imnaha villages would align themselves with the band who shared their summer home in the Wallowa Valley, the band led by a dynamic young man named Tuekakas.

At last, Dug Bar. The Snake River slides past, strangely quiet for the volume of dark water between its banks 200 yards apart. The dun and ocher walls of Hells Canyon recede from the river here, the reason, I suppose, it was once used as a crossing. In the distance upstream are a scattering of ranch buildings, the cause for the road I've been following. I park next to a crude outhouse in one of two sites, both empty, of what might loosely be termed a campground. Dug Bar is not the most popular tourist sight in Oregon, but it suits me just fine. It was added to the Nez Perce National Historical Park a little over a year ago, but so far there's no indication it is part of the park. After a quick dinner of a hot dog, a potato, carrot and cabbage all boiled together and topped with butter, I stroll the few yards to the river's edge in the fading light and let out a shout. No echo, but a few minutes later a coyote howls from one of the ridges rising behind me. I think back, not to Bonneville, but to the spring of 1877, the year after the confrontation in the Wallowa Valley over the death of Wind Blowing.

By May Thunder Rising had reluctantly agreed to move from his Wallowa homeland to the reservation in Idaho. In talks with government officials and army officers he had been told in no uncertain terms that the only alternative to resettling on the reservation was war, a war he had no chance of winning. He had been given a deadline of June 15 to move or fight, so part of the Wallowa band crossed into Idaho here at Dug Bar, forcing as many of their horses and cattle as they could find in the short time allotted into a current swollen by spring run-off. Some 200 animals drowned, but, fortunately, all the Real People survived the risky passage. For most of them, as they climbed the ridges on the other side and looked back at this Imnaha country and the Wallowa highlands in the far distance, it would be the last time they viewed their homeland.

Two, three then suddenly dozens of night hawks appear over the current, hunting insects. So swift is their movement I find it impossible for me to accurately count their numbers in the dying light. One of the Nee-Me-Poo was named Kosooyeen, which translates as both Night Hawk and Going Alone. I begin to think about the name. The night hawks, small angular birds, certainly don't seem to be "going alone." Rather, they sweep across the sky in squadrons. With my binoculars I try to follow the flight of one of the birds and see that what appear to be long, smooth swoops above the current are actually a series of jitterbug dips and dives, lightning jabs to the left and right scooping up one bug after another. Each night hawk truly is going alone in a furious, private hunt.

In the morning I begin the slow return trip to Enterprise. On maps the Nez Perce National Historic Trail is this nifty red line that passes effortlessly across the page. From Wallowa Lake it crosses the blue line denoting the Snake River at Dug Bar and curves northeast without a hitch to another blue line, the Salmon River, then across it to a place called Split Rocks. That's about all it really is, ink on paper. Actually, there is no trail. Even if my van could grow pontoons and float the river, the slopes rising across the water show no hint of a track for me to follow. I have a much longer road to travel, a looping detour to the nearest bridge across the Snake River at Lewiston some sixty miles downriver. Luckily, I have a great guide. In 1990 Cheryl Wilfong published a book titled *Following the Nez Perce Trail* with directions to significant sites for travelers ranging from folks who never want to leave a paved highway to people like me with a passion for dirt roads with grass growing between the ruts. It's a fine book which I recommend highly.

By eleven in the morning, I've gassed up again in Enterprise and stopped by the Forest Service office to check on another road I'm going to take later today. A woman tells me none of their people have been over that road since a series of heavy thunderstorms a few weeks ago. If I find it washed out and I make it back this way, would I please stop by and let them know? That's reassuring. After descending into the Imnaha yesterday, today I'll skirt that canyon's rim before, I hope, dropping into the depths of still another of the gorges that incise this remarkable country. Again, the pavement peters out after a few miles. But I'm now in the rolling, highland hill country north of the Wallowa Valley, heading into the hunting grounds the Nee-Me-Poo called Chesnimnus, and I fly along at a giddy thirty miles an hour, leaving a rooster-tail of dust in my wake.

Bonneville was among the last men to come west to try his hand at making a fortune in the hunt for beaver. Their skins were prized for the waterproof quality of the dense pelts—most often turned into hats for European gentlemen—but a new product called silk was beginning to find favor in all the best places.

Bonneville would spend only three years traipsing through the mountains before returning to his true avocation as an officer in the United States Army. Some historians contend his sojourn in the West was at least partially an intelligence mission sanctioned by the government to gather information in the struggle with Britain to control this part of the continent. The idea makes sense, at least as far as his winter trek through the Nee-Me-Poo homeland is concerned. His goal on the trip was the British Hudson's Bay Company fort and trading post near the Columbia River where he eventually made a feeble effort at buying supplies even though he had no means to transport them back to his trapping party on the headwaters of the Snake River some 600 miles away. After taking a good look at the fort Bonneville returned to his expedition and did just fine without any supplies from the British. If he walks like a spy, talks like a spy . . . Larger forces were swirling around the Real People, who had no clue as to the determination of the United States to someday wrest control of this country both from the British and its native peoples.

The grassy hills give way to forest as the road continues to climb. Pretty soon I see the sign for Buckhorn Springs where an old fire lookout perches above Imnaha Canyon. I walk to the edge of the precipice where the ground falls away 4,000 feet to the river where I started the day, a flight of only a few miles and minutes for the hawk patrolling the air currents, but a trip of ninety miles for me. The view is too glorious not to linger, so I make myself a sandwich and sit on the porch of the abandoned lookout.

Yo-mus-ro-y-e-cut and another Nee-Me-Poo guided Bonneville and his three companions out of the Imnaha and camped somewhere near here on the rim. The following day they descended into the canyon of the Grande Ronde River to the north. The second guide forged ahead and returned with a supply of gunpowder before the little party reached the first winter longhouse. Custom demanded that guns be discharged in the air as a sign of peaceful intent before entering a village, and Bonneville had already confessed that his supply was almost exhausted. After the last echoes of the symbolic volley rolled through the canyon, Bonneville sat down to a feast of buffalo, salmon, deer and elk, followed it with a smoke, then gave a speech about the greatness of the United States and its citizens' desire for friendship with the Real People. Criers repeated his words for those outside the longhouse. Young Tuekakas almost certainly would have been one of those listening with interest to Bonneville.

The Forest Service road follows the canyon rim for several miles through park-like country, widely-spaced stands of Ponderosa pine, some scarred by lightning, meadows thick with grass. A buck with a split rack of antlers lumbers to its feet in one meadow and bounds away, white-tail flashing. Here's the suspect road, called Cold Springs, that will take me into the canyon of the Grande Ronde River, and I make the turn past a sign that warns passenger cars away. The gravel turns to dirt and rock as the track drops into a ravine and dives like a thrill ride at an amusement park. I keep my van in first gear and my foot tapping the brake. Even though the van's going only three or four miles an hour, slower at the rockiest spots, one rear tire or the other is always slipping, the turns too tight for the differential to compensate for the varying distances the rear wheels have to travel on each curve. I watch the tenths of miles slowly pass on the odometer, praying that I meet no oncoming traffic. Once a seep from a spring runs across the ruts, turning the track to mud and rock, and hundreds of pale yellow butterflies rise from the muck and keep me company for a few yards. The forest gives way to bare rock and bunch grass. Finally, the grade seems to be leveling out, the ravine and road widening, and I know I've made it, six miles in an hour and forty minutes. The worst stretch of road I'm likely to encounter along the entire Historic Trail is already behind me, and I breathe a sigh of genuine relief.

Here's an abandoned homestead: cabin, barn, stock-loading chute. The Wallowa Nee-Me-Poo managed to successfully range cattle through this near-vertical country starting in the 1850s, and by 1877 their herds might have numbered in the thousands. The deadline to move to the reservation left too little time for a thorough round-up, so the cattle they left behind when they crossed the Snake River at Dug Bar were quickly appropriated by local whites. Another time or place and it would have been called rustling.

Beside the road now is a hand-lettered sign on cardboard from a fruit box saying: Cheif Joseph's Cave. A piece of red ribbon attached to the misspelled sign flutters in the breeze. I get out and stretch my shoulder muscles, stiff after the tension of the descent. Across Joseph Creek, barely visible through a riot of brambles, is the black mouth of Thunder Rising's birthplace. There's nothing much to see around here, no hint that a longhouse might once have stretched along the stream, that children played under watchful glances from mothers tanning hides or pounding kouse, that old men and women told stories, that young men raced horses and young women watched them appraisingly. It's all in the past now.

I pass a few isolated houses and reach the Grande Ronde River in about a mile. The immediate chasm walls must be a thousand feet high, rising almost vertically. I count fourteen layers of basalt stacked one atop another, thinking this land has taken a long time building and the river has spent a long time cutting. The Nee-Me-Poo have a story about how this country came to be:

> *Once only the Evergreen Trees atop the mountains knew about Fire until, one day, Beaver snatched an ember and dashed away. His tail slapped through the land, creating Grande Ronde Canyon. That is why the canyon is so deep. Some of the Evergreens chased Beaver toward the Snake River but grew tired a few at a time and stopped. That is why there are many Evergreens near the mountain tops but only a few down here. Finally, one last Cedar gave up the chase near where the Grande Ronde River enters the Snake River. That is why one cedar remains there to this day, high on a bluff.*[2]

The Grande Ronde joins the Snake River after five miles, and I crane my neck looking for the ancient cedar. I spot nothing, but I bet it's there somewhere, maybe an old stump scarred by lightning.

Turning north along the Snake, I'm relieved to be almost finished driving for the day. Gravel and dirt miles, as much as I enjoy them, are harder than highway miles. Pavement now, and I slip the van into high gear as the walls of the canyon begin to lose their height. I slow for the town of Asotin, population 1,020. A sign at the high school proudly announces: State Champions 1985 Baseball &

1990 Girls Basketball. This was the site of another large Nee-Me-Poo winter longhouse, the river here an important eel fishery for the Real People. Here Bonneville met a chief named O-push-y-e-cut. A son of O-push-y-e-cut named Looking Glass would become one of the leaders of Nee-Me-Poo resistance in 1877. The chief's sixteen-year-old daughter was ill and he importuned Bonneville to effect a cure. At a loss Bonneville suggested a sweat bath, a bit of gunpowder dissolved in water, colt's head soup and bed rest. Amazingly, it worked, so the chief presented the explorer with one of his best horses in gratitude. Again, Bonneville was lucky; Nee-Me-Poo shamans whose patients died occasionally got to join them in eternal rest.

And with that, I leave the army captain to his journey down the Snake River and the British outpost of his interest. Crossing the Snake into Idaho, I cough up ten bucks for a campsite at Hell's Gate State Park on the edge of the small city of Lewiston. After a swim in the river, I pull a lawn chair from my van and reflect on the last few days. The extent of the geographical isolation of the Wallowa country is crystal clear to me now, the reason it escaped white settlers' attention until the 1870's. Something Mr. Bonneville wrote also comes to mind:

The grandeur and originality of the views, presented on every side, beggar both the pencil and the pen. Nothing we had ever gazed upon in any other region could for a moment compare in wild majesty and impressive sternness, with the series of scenes which here at every turn astonished our senses, and filled us with awe and delight.[3]

He got that right.

Daylight buds with the rumble of the first RVs departing the campground. A peek outside the curtain assures me its going to be another sunny day, and hot. Lewiston's downtown is an attractive few blocks of restored brick buildings tucked between a levee and a bluff at the confluence of the Snake and Clearwater rivers. Today the 30,000 residents sprawl over the surrounding hills. In the 1870s only a few hundred folks lived in wooden houses under this bluff, praying the rivers wouldn't flood them out each spring. U.S. Highway 12 takes me out of Lewiston and up the Clearwater River, barren rounded hills rising on either side. A few miles past the immense Potlatch paper mill on the edge of town I enter the Nez Perce Indian Reservation.

In 1831, four warriors visiting the annual trapper rendezvous in the Rocky Mountains decided to accompany the supply train carrying the year's catch of beaver pelts back to St. Louis, Missouri. Eagle, Man Of The Morning, No Horns On His Head and Rabbit-Skin Leggings arrived at that bustling frontier metropolis of 5,000 souls in the fall and visited William Clark, by then Superintendent of Indian Affairs for the West. In sign language they might have asked about Clark's friend, Meriwether Lewis, and learned that he was long dead. They toured the Catholic cathedral and took in other sights like all good tourists in a foreign land. Native delegations were a common sight on the streets of St. Louis, but this group attracted attention because of the distance they had traveled. Unable to converse with the Nee-Me-Poo except in sign language, some whites decided they had come looking for the Christian religion. Perhaps it was the water or the climate or the crowded, unsanitary conditions of the settlement, but all four soon fell ill. Eagle died in October and Man Of The Morning in December. By the time No Horns On His Head and Rabbit-Skin Leggings departed with their trapper friends, on a boat headed up the Missouri River in March of 1832, word was filtering eastward to various missionary societies that some Indians of the distant Rocky Mountains were especially eager to be saved. Oblivious to the stir they would cause, the two young men simply wanted to get home. No Horns On His Head sickened again and died on the Missouri River. Rabbit-Skin Leggings almost made it back to his longhouse. Hooking up with a party of Nee-Me-Poo hunters in the buffalo country, he was nearly home when they were ambushed by Blackfoot who beheaded all thirty men they cornered.

Three years later, two missionaries appeared in the company of the yearly supply train at the rendezvous on Wyoming's Green River. They were the Reverend Samuel Parker and Doctor Marcus Whitman. Parker was in his fifties, a Congregationalist assigned by the American Board of Commissions for Foreign Missions to explore the West and find out more about these distant savages who apparently wanted to learn about God. The journal he kept during this trip, when published in 1838, became one of the classics of western history. Finding camps of Shoshones, Utes, Flatheads and Nez Perce at the rendezvous, Parker was both puzzled and a little disappointed that none of the Flathead had flat heads and none of the Nez Perce had pierced noses. He and Whitman:

> *... had an interesting interview with the chiefs of the Nez Perces and Flatheads, and laid before them the object of our appointment, and explained to them the benevolent desires of christians concerning them. We then enquired whether they wished to have teachers come among them and instruct them in the knowledge of God, his worship, and the way to be saved ... The first chief of the Nez Perces, Tai-quin-watish, arose and said, he had heard from white men a little about God, which had only gone into his ears; he wished to know enough to have it go into his heart, to influence his life, and to teach his people. Others spoke to the same import, and they all made as many promises as we could desire.*[4]

The dynamic, thirty-one-year-old Whitman decided to return immediately to the United States to report to the mission board the success of their investigation and to organize a party of believers to settle in the wilderness. The older Parker would continue on with the Real People to their homeland where he would investigate possible sites for one or more missions. The two men agreed to meet at the next rendezvous in a year's time.

For forty-five days after parting with Whitman, Parker and his Nee-Me-Poo guardians crossed mountains and deserts, pausing every Sabbath so the minister could preach the Gospel. He skirted Jackson Hole, viewing with wonder the Teton Mountains, endured a Blackfoot scare and witnessed a buffalo chase, admiring the skill and courage of both rider and pony. The mountains sheltering the Nee-Me-Poo homeland proved a formidable barrier, as always. Falling sick, Parker despaired of surviving the twelve difficult days in the mountains, but on September 28 he arrived on the Clearwater River. "These mountains were far worse to pass than the Rocky Mountains," he wrote, echoing the sentiments of Lewis and Clark.[5] His protectors hurried him along to the same British trading post on the Columbia River of such interest to Bonneville, and he spent the winter in the gentle climate of western Oregon. Although he briefly visited the Real People again the following spring, the prospect of again passing through the Clearwater Mountains to the rendezvous daunted him. Writing a letter to Marcus Whitman and entrusting it to the care of the Nez Perce, Parker headed for the mouth of the Columbia to find a ship to carry him home.

Even before the annual supply caravan arrived at the Green River Rendezvous in 1836, word spread through the sprawling camp of a momentous event: two white women accompanied the caravan. With Parker's letter in hand a delegation of Nee-Me-Poo galloped ahead to see if their missionaries had arrived. They had indeed. Dr. Whitman, his new wife Narcissa, the Reverend Henry Harmon Spalding, his wife Eliza, and William Gray had survived the long journey, although Spalding wrote to their sponsors in the East, "Never send another mission over these mountains if you value life and money."[6]

By October, Marcus Whitman and Henry Spalding had decided that the former would reside among the Cayuse and the latter the Nez Perce. Whitman picked a fertile location near the Walla Walla River for his mission. The Cayuse called it Waiilatpu, Place of the Rye Grass. He then accompanied Spalding to find a suitable spot for the second mission. As they rode up the Clearwater River from its confluence with the Snake, Spalding became despondent at the sight of the sere hills rising above the narrow river bottom. The reverend had hoped to find a green and fertile country ideal for farming, but the Nee-Me-Poo homeland was no agricultural Garden of Eden. His guides had a place in mind, though, and urged him on for ten miles until they reached a valley opening to the south. It was called Lapwai, Place of the Butterflies.

At the junction of U.S. 12 and U.S. 95, I take 95 south across an arching bridge over both the Clearwater and a junk yard on its bank. At the mouth of the valley an unobtrusive building occupies a low bluff overlooking Lapwai Creek. It's the visitors' center for the Nez Perce National Historical Park. My van joins two dozen cars and a tour bus in the parking lot. Inside, things are hopping, largely due to the folks from the tour bus. A park ranger in the standard gray and green uniform stands at a counter, simultaneously answering questions and selling souvenirs. In a room on one side, a video plays a twenty-minute overview of the Real People. My interest today is the artifact room to the left, and I wander through the glassed-in displays, taking in the details of the quilled shirts, the beaded dresses, a medal from Lewis and Clark, the high-pommeled wooden saddle, war whistles, leggings, a flute, moccasins, a rope made of bison hair. Some of the items are on loan from the Ohio Historical Society which either wants them back or a ransom of at least $600,000 from the Nez Perce Tribe. They are things of beauty and this may be my last chance to see them. After half an hour, I leave feeling steamed. Ohio, of course, has no Nez Perce, but Henry Spalding collected the goods and through some convoluted means they ended up in Ohio. I would like to think any responsible historical society would want artifacts to be displayed within the context of their original culture, not sitting 2,000 miles from the source of their creation. The notion that a dollar value can be placed on them is ludicrous, but the Ohio Historical Society is in the process of having these unique items "appraised" like some house down the street, probably so it can up the ante.

Calm down, Martin.

Henry Spalding approved of Lapwai. Arable bottomland lined the winding creek for fifteen miles. He and Eliza decided they would spend the rest of their natural days here ministering to the Real People, and at first all went well. Warriors stooped to manual labor to help build a combination house, classroom and church. They brought fish and game to allow the two to survive the first winter. Eliza became more proficient in the Nez Perce language than her husband and endeavored to teach her pupils sections from the Bible in their own language. Eleven months after she arrived at Lapwai Eliza gave birth to a daughter; three more children followed. As the first few years passed, Henry preached, sang hymns and tried to instruct men in the basics of agriculture, using hoes to break soil thick with natural roots. The Spaldings managed to procure a printing press from fellow missionaries on the faraway Hawaiian Islands and printed a portion of the New Testament using an alphabet the two developed to approximate the Nee-Me-Poo tongue. Tuekakas journeyed from the Wallowa country and spent months at a time with other men sitting in the classroom absorbing strange words about a God named Jesus who got himself killed so the Real People could be saved. After three years Henry felt that three of the men receiving instruction had learned enough of the Christian faith to be baptized. Christened Joseph, Tuekakas was one of them.

A path leads down the slope to the site of the Spalding Mission. I cross little Lapwai Creek and walk along a path under huge, old cottonwoods past picnic tables bare this early in the day. The missionaries spent the first two years a couple of miles upstream, but nothing remains of those original buildings, and that site is now on private land. Henry and Eliza had decided they needed a larger home and relief from the mosquitoes that infested their original mission, so they rebuilt here. Undulations in the grass hint at the location of their sawmill, grist mill, mill pond and race. Inside a fence put up by the Daughters of the American Revolution is all that remains of their two-story home: an outline of disturbed soil marked by the rubble of two fireplaces, one at either end of the dwelling. They built more: a student dormitory, schoolroom, woodhouse, shop, granary, storeroom. This mission was not some fleeting whimsy.

Both Spaldings were devoted to the prospect of turning a hunting and gathering society—heathens, using their word—into Christian farmers, gentlemen and gentlewomen. Their congregation swelled and dwindled with the seasons, with the years. Some Nez Perce did make a serious effort at becoming farmers and Christians and settled around the mission, but to others the buffalo country still beckoned and the camas and kouse plants sprouting from the earth each spring remained preferable to the potato. Many of those who did plant potatoes or wheat found that once the crop was in the ground they could pursue their traditional ways until harvest time.

It's hard to know exactly when and why things started to go terribly wrong for the Spaldings. The shamans certainly continued to oppose the missionaries, who, in turn, took every opportunity to denigrate the traditional ways. Henry Spalding's intemperate habit of whipping men and women for indiscretions caused resentment. A Delaware Indian named Tom Hill wandered through from the east and whispered horror stories of whites stealing the native peoples' land. A few Mountain Men contemptuous of civilization added their own tales. Perhaps some of the Nee-Me-Poo gazed at the Spalding's prosperous mission and thought it a little too grand, too large.

That seems to have been the case for Asa Smith, another missionary who arrived a few years after the Spaldings and settled at Kamiah near the Heart of the Monster. One day in 1841, he was seen marking ground with stakes. Nee-Me-Poo oral tradition recorded his departure, as told by War Singer, a tribal historian in the first part of this century:

> . . . *it was not long after when Mr. Smith was presented with a dugout boat, and all his belongings was packed up and put on the boat. So they asked Mr. and Mrs. Smith to get on the boat. When they were on, the boat was shoved down. When the pair land at Spalding place, he stated that he left Kamiah willfully, as he didn't like the place. If the Indians would have let him stay about half of Kamiah valley would have been homesteaded and that much loss to the Indians. But he wasn't as good a Real Estate man as Mr. Spalding so he failed in exchanging heaven for Kamiah valley.*[7]

The summer and autumn of 1843 saw the first large emigration across the Oregon Trail. Its guide was none other than Marcus Whitman, returning from a visit east. The settlers skirted the Nee-Me-Poo homeland and continued on to the Willamette Valley in western Oregon, but the Real People took note. Perhaps the warnings of the Delaware Tom Hill and the mountain men were coming true.

65

In December of that year, Dr. Elijah White, the first Indian agent for the Oregon country, arrived at Lapwai from Oregon's Willamette Valley to shore up the Spaldings' tenuous position. He promulgated a set of eleven laws with hanging the punishment for murder and arson, lashing for lesser offenses. More significantly, White ordered the Nee-Me-Poo to designate a head chief to enforce the new laws and to deal with the United States government in the future. The notion ran counter to the soul of Nez Perce culture with its emphasis on personal independence, equality and consensual decision-making. White insisted, and in the end a young man of thirty-two named Sparkling Horn became "head chief." He had spent several years at a school in Canada and could read and write some English, his primary qualification for the new post. Sparkling Horn apparently took his nominal position too seriously and soon earned the scorn of the tribe. The head chief departed for the buffalo country of Montana, disgraced in the eyes of his people. He would die of disease there in 1848.

By February, 1847, Spalding had become despondent and wrote back East:

> *Our prospects as missionaries have become very dark. The large and interesting school at this place which once numbered two hundred and thirty-four, has entirely ceased. Not one attends this winter, and there is not the least prospect that there ever will be another school here. The last two winters I took charge of the school myself. But more assembled to disturb, break windows, steal, create every possible confusion, than assembled to receive instruction.*[8]

On November 29 of that year, Cayuse warriors attacked the Whitman Mission at Waiilatpu. Soon Marcus and Narcissa Whitman and eleven others lay dead. The new Oregon Trail cut through the heart of the Cayuse homeland, and the Whitman Mission had become an important way station for emigrants to western Oregon. Measles contracted from the whites wiped out entire Cayuse families and ravaged villages. Some Cayuse blamed the Whitmans for the disease; a few even believed that Doctor

Whitman was deliberately poisoning their people. A bloody massacre was their only solution.

Henry Spalding narrowly avoided taking part in the Cayuse solution. He had been visiting in the area before being informed of the massacre by a Catholic priest. Evading parties of Cayuse warriors searching for him, Spalding made his way back to Lapwai over the course of five days, much of it on foot through bitter winter weather. He became so emaciated that the first Nez Perce to see him could not recognize the preacher. A Nez Perce who had taken part in the attack on the Whitmans arrived at Lapwai with a group of warriors shortly after Spalding returned. They wanted the missionary dead. Men loyal to Spalding interposed themselves, but the reverend realized he and his family were no longer safe. The eleven years he and Eliza had spent among the Real People had not resulted in a remolded culture, but a cracked one. A rent in the Nez Perce between traditionals and those intrigued by the promises of the whites had begun to form. Shortly after Christmas, 1847, a band of Nee-Me-Poo warriors escorted the Spalding family to the Columbia River where they continued down to the Willamette Valley. Their mission of a lifetime was over.

Back in my van, I turn south, up US 95 paralleling Lapwai Creek. The Nez Perce National Historical Park is something of an oddball in the park system. It consists of thirty-eight sites spread widely over Idaho, Oregon, Washington and Montana. Most are simply roadside signs describing some aspect of Nee-Me-Poo history or culture. I'm passing one right now, the approximate location of the Spalding mission during their first two years. Others such as the Heart of the Monster and the White Bird Battlefield are actual pieces of land. Recently, Congress added a bunch of new sites to the park: Tuekakas' grave at Wallowa Lake, Dug Bar, Thunder Rising's grave in Washington state, the Big Hole National Battlefield in Montana, the Bear Paw State Battlefield, also in Montana, and others.

In May 1855 the Nez Perce, Cayuse, Palouse, Walla Walla, Umatilla and Yakama peoples were summoned to a council to be held in the Walla Walla Valley not far from the remains of the Whitman Mission at Waiilatpu. In the years since 1847 the native tribes had seen the Cayuse scattered and humbled by troops exacting punishment for the murder of the Whitmans. The United States had formalized a treaty with Great Britain and now claimed all land south of the current border, sending the vaunted Hudson's Bay Company packing. Surveying parties roamed the West searching for a feasible transcontinental railroad route. Miners spurred by the discoveries in California probed the mountains for signs of gold; that spring they found it in northeastern Washington. It was time for the tribes to give up some of their land. Washington Territorial Governor Isaac Stevens and Oregon Superintendent of Indian Affairs Joel Palmer would do the taking.

Laurence Kip, an army lieutenant on leave, attended the council as an onlooker. On May 24, he witnessed the arrival of the Nez Perce delegation which he estimated at 2,500 warriors with seventy women along to tend camp. The spectacle must have temporarily overcome his counting ability, for the figure was far too high. Still, his description is fascinating:

> *Their coming was announced about 10 o'clock, and going out on the plain to where a flag staff had been erected, we saw them approaching in one long line. They were almost entirely naked, gaudily painted and decorated with their wild trappings. Their plumes fluttered about them, while below, skins and trinkets of all kinds of fantastic embellishments flaunted in the sunshine. Trained from early childhood to almost live on horseback, they sat upon their fine animals as if they were centuars. Their horses, too, were arrayed in the most glaring finery. They were painted with such colors as formed the greatest contrast; the white being smeared with crimson in fantastic figures, and the dark streaked with white clay. Beads and fringes of gaudy colors were hanging from the bridles, while the plumes of eagle feathers interwoven with the mane and tail, fluttered as the breeze swept over them, and completed their wild and fantastic appearance.*
>
> *When about a mile distant they halted, and half a dozen chiefs rode forward and were introduced to Governor Stevens and General Palmer, on order of their rank. Then on came the rest of the wild horsemen in single file clashing their shields,*

singing and beating their drums as they marched past us.
Then they formed a circle and dashed around us, while our
little group stood there, the center of their wild evolutions.[9]

It was a demonstration no doubt meant to impress upon the whites the power of the Nez Perce nation. Their nominal head chief after Sparkling Horn's brief tenure was Lawyer, an astute man from the Kamiah area who had been one of the children playing on the fringe of Weippe Prairie and had received a ribbon when Lewis and Clark first met the Real People.

The negotiations began a week later and dragged on for thirteen days. Stevens and Palmer first suggested two reservations for the peoples of the Columbia Plateau. One would embrace the Nee-Me-Poo homeland and would include not only the Nez Perce but the Cayuse, Walla Wallas, Umatillas and Spokanes, the latter a tribe from northern Washington not even represented at the council. The second reservation on a portion of the Yakama country would become home to that tribe, as well as the Palouse, Okanogans, Colvilles and a number of smaller bands of the Columbia River. None of those except the Yakamas and the Palouse even had leaders present.

Lawyer angered the other tribes and some of his own people by quickly agreeing to the proposal. He was correct in discerning that almost the entirety of the Real People's own land would be included in one of the reservations, but the Cayuse, Walla Wallas and Umatillas were astounded that Lawyer was not standing with them in an effort to help them keep at least part of their land. Some among the Nez Perce surely also wondered just where the other tribes would settle in the Nez Perce country. The other tribal speakers continued to resist, day after day, until the whites relented. There would be three reservations: one for the Nez Perce; another for the Cayuse, Walla Wallas and Umatillas; a third for the Yakamas, Palouse and the smaller Columbia River bands. Governor Stevens would treat with the Spokanes, Okanogans and Colvilles later.

It seemed like a done deal until murmurs at the edge of the watching warrior crowd turned into shouts. O-push-y-e-cut, friend of Bonneville, had returned from the buffalo country. By now about seventy years old, the respected headman was still vital, active, powerful. He rode into the encampment with three other men including Cloud Piler, a warrior whose name was feared and renowned. One of the four carried a staff bearing the fresh scalp of an unfortunate Blackfoot. Without leaving his horse O-push-y-e-cut—Flint Necklace—stared for a moment at Stevens and Palmer then turned to the Nee-Me-Poo crowd and told them to return to their fires. No one was going to sell his home. The Real People left.

Three days later Lawyer, Flint Necklace, Tuekakas and the other headmen of the Nee-Me-Poo signed the treaty. After listening to the details of the whites' proposal Flint Necklace was swayed. The clever Lawyer had done his job from the beginning, gambling that the other tribal leaders would wrest concessions from Stevens and Palmer with no consequent reduction in the Nez Perce reservation. Except for a small stretch of land along the lower Snake River, the homeland remained intact, and Stevens and Palmer had given their solemn word that the power of the United States government would forever keep whites from violating its borders. In addition, the federal government would pay the tribe $200,000 over twenty years and provide schools and a hospital, a sawmill, a gristmill, a blacksmith and gunsmith. The treaty of 1855 was a good deal. Tuekakas returned to the Wallowa and erected a line of poles along his portion of the reservation just in case some future settlers were unclear as to the boundary.

The other tribes had not been as fortunate. The Palouse and Walla Wallas had lost all their land, the Yakamas, Cayuse and Umatillas large chunks. Still, they had been told they would have a few years to adjust to the new world order. Until such time as the treaty was confirmed by Congress, Stevens and Palmer had promised that the government would keep whites out of the entire Columbia region, not just the land designated for the reservations. Just the opposite occurred; encroachments increased. Already bitter, within months the Yakamas, Walla Wallas, Cayuse, Palouse and Spokanes were at war. It took three years for the United States army to crush the resistance, three years during which the Nez Perce watched from the sideline, turning deaf ears to the pleas of their neighbors for assistance in ousting the white intruders. A few Christian Nez Perce even acted as scouts for the army.

Then came the turn of the Nee-Me-Poo. In 1860, a prospector named Elias Pierce found traces of gold on the North Fork of the Clearwater River. With the aid—the word connivance also comes to mind—of a Christian Nez Perce, Pierce searched the area until he found a rich placer lode on a creek he named Orofino only a few miles from Weippe Prairie. The solemn words of Stevens and Palmer to protect the Nez Perce homeland forever had lasted only five years. Gangs of whites numbering in the thousands spread over the land. Impromptu tent towns arose: Pierce, the site of the original discovery, and nearby Orofino, a town of 2,000.

In April, 1861, Lawyer quickly signed a new treaty ceding the affected area north of the main stem of the Clearwater River in exchange for an additional $50,000. The ink and paper were worthless. The following month saw the founding of Lewiston, south of the river, and the first prospecting parties on the South Fork of the Clearwater River. More gold sparkled in pans. By August the mining camp of Elk City on the smaller reservation also boasted 2,000 citizens. That same month came news of the biggest strike yet in the Nee-Me-Poo country, and the town of Florence was born. By 1862 as many as 20,000 miners, mule-skinners, shopkeepers, gamblers, thieves and whiskey merchants may have been squatting on the land of the Real People, outnumbering the original inhabitants six to one.

Four miles from the Spalding Mission, I reach the town of Lapwai with a population of about a thousand. It can't be mistaken for a tourist trap, which I suppose is the way the inhabitants prefer it. Except for a gas station, restaurant and grocery on U.S. 95, nothing beckons the traffic passing on the highway as I turn off and cruise through town. Most of the houses have an identical appearance hinting at some long-ago government construction, simple square structures with faded paint. Behind some are drying sheds for salmon, a reminder of the years before the dams on the Snake River obliterated the runs. Except for a discount cigarette outlet, bar and auto repair shop, the downtown buildings are boarded up. In contrast the Pi-Nee-Waus community center, schools and Northern Idaho Indian Agency are immaculate. The lawn of the city park is green and freshly-cut. Still, the town seems deserted except for a few children careening on bicycles in the mid-day heat. The silence is almost spooky as I reach the site of Fort Lapwai. The army established the post in 1862 in a belated attempt to protect the Nee-Me-Poo from the miners' onslaught. The old parade ground is instantly identifiable, about the size of a football field and surrounded by a square of more recent buildings and houses. An 1876 photograph I've seen shows officers' homes lining the west side of the parade ground with the enlisted men's' barracks on the other and the headquarters building on the south edge. Only one structure from the army years remains today, a two-story officers' duplex on the southwest corner of the parade ground.

Some Nee-Me-Poo leaders, such as Eagle From The Light and Red Owl, threatened to fight the interlopers. But the sheer numbers of the whites quickly convinced them physical resistance was futile. Many of the more settled Nez Perce, though, were quick to take advantage of the situation, establishing ferries across rivers, packing supplies, selling horses, beef, wheat and corn at healthy prices, in essence becoming part of the infrastructure of the gold rush and profiting handsomely. Others didn't fare so well, succumbing to the lure of the plentiful whiskey brought by the miners. Tuekakas' isolated Wallowa band was not harmed by the rush. Their time would come a decade later.

Talk in Washington, D.C., and the towns of the Northwest in 1862, turned to the necessity of still another council to wrest more land concessions from the Nee-Me-Poo—or even removing them entirely from their reservation to some unspecified location. The new Superintendent of Indian Affairs in charge of the Nez Perce, Calvin Hale, lobbied for a delay until the following summer. He had a little problem. Virtually none of the cash and improvements promised in the 1855 treaty had been delivered. Although government records showed that $60,000 had so far been expended, little of it had actually made its way to the reservation. Any government negotiators would sound like fools if they made more promises. Hale hurried to build the school, the sawmill, the gristmill and the promised house for Lawyer.

The interested parties met at Fort Lapwai in May 1863. At first, only Lawyer and his faction were present for the Nez Perce. Events in recent years had only worsened the rift in the tribe. Those inclined toward the traditional way had argued for aiding their brethren Palouse, Yakamas and Cayuse in their war for their land after 1855. Lawyer and his people had talked and talked that the white way was the future and eventually had prevailed; the Real People stayed out of the war. When the miners overran the Nee-Me-Poo homeland in violation of the 1855 treaty and the promised annuities failed to appear, the traditionals chided Lawyer and his people for being gullible pawns of the whites. The traditionals' words had the sting of truth, but Lawyer had seen the future and it was white. Even so, Lawyer was unwilling to roll over and play dead for Hale. Lawyer quoted the 1855 treaty and reminded the embarrassed negotiator that the God-ordained sanctity of law as preached by Henry Spalding applied to whites as well as Nez Perce. He would agree to selling the portions of the reservation where gold had been found and towns raised, nothing more.

Eventually, the traditional faction of the Nee-Me-Poo made their appearance, led by Eagle From the Light and Big Thunder, on whose very ground the council was taking place. The greatest leader of the traditionals was absent—O-push-y-e-cut, Flint Necklace, friend of Bonneville, father of Looking Glass—had died over the winter. Eagle From The Light and Big Thunder argued persuasively that selling the Creator's land was like eating the dirt itself instead of the bounty the land provided. Hale began a series of private meetings with Lawyer and other headmen who had been compliant with white intentions in the past. The specifics of the discussions were never revealed, but certain headmen eventually had houses built for them and cash payments delivered. Lawyer and his faction swung their support in favor of the new reservation, while the rest of the Nee-Me-Poo continued to resist any massive transfer of land. The inconclusive talks dragged on into June.

Present for the council was one George Currey, captain of a company of the First Oregon Volunteer Cavalry. When dissension between the white negotiators and the Nez Perce factions was at its peak, and Commissioner Hale feared outright hostilities, Currey was ordered to take twenty men and reconnoiter the Nee-Me-Poo camp late at night. In a fit of generosity, the government had footed the bill for large canvas tents to house the Nez Perce. Captain Currey found the encampment dark and quiet, except for light emanating from one tent. Curious, he entered and was allowed to sit and witness an extraordinary event:

> Here we found fifty-three chiefs and subchiefs deliberating on the propositions for treaty that had been submitted to them by the Commissioners. Lawyer's men were in favor of complying and Big Thunder's men were opposed to the proposition. The debate ran with dignified firmness and warmth until near morning, when the Big Thunder party made a formal announcement of their determination to take no further part in the treaty, and then with a warm, and in an emotional manner, declared the Nez Perce nation dissolved; whereupon the Big Thunder men shook hands with the Lawyer men, telling them with a kind but firm demeanor that they would be friends, but a distinct people. It did not appear from the tone of their short, sententious speeches that either party was meditating present outbreak. I withdrew my detachment, having accomplished nothing but witnessing the extinguishment of the last council fires of the most powerful Indian nation on the sunset side of the Rocky Mountains.[10]

This was 1863, the Civil War raging. With the Union eventually to win, how many white Americans, especially the Yankees in power in the decades after the war, would understand a nation agreeing to disagree among its parts and dissolve itself with handshakes?

With the traditional headmen no longer in the picture, Hale and Lawyer quickly concluded their business. The new reservation would be approximately one-tenth the size of the old. The ceded lands would cost the government only eight cents an acre. In an effort to add legitimacy to the new treaty, the white negotiators insisted that Lawyer round up enough adult male signatories to approximate the number of headmen who had signed the 1855 agreement. All who signed resided within the new reservation or were the benefactors of special clauses in the treaty, and all except one or two were Christians. It was a farce. Even lowly Captain

Currey of the Oregon Volunteer Cavalry at age thirty recognized the fact. He wrote to his superiors:

> *Although the treaty goes out to the world as the concurrent agreement of all the tribe, it is in reality nothing more than the agreement of Lawyer and his band, numbering in the aggregate not a third of the Nez Perce tribe.*[11]

Tuekakas, ailing, had not attended the council which ostensibly sold the land that had nurtured his ancestors. Possibly, he sent Thunder Rising in his stead, although even that has never been documented. When he heard of the revised treaty, Tuekakas destroyed the New Testament given to him by Henry Spalding and returned wholly to his traditional beliefs. If the whites could not keep their word so solemnly sworn in 1855, then their religion was not worth much.

In the early 1870s, two religious fervors swept through the tribe. One was spurred by Henry Spalding who, after a fifteen-year absence, had returned along with the miners in 1862. The elderly missionary finally succeeded in baptizing converts by the hundreds among the Lawyer faction. At the same time, a permutation of traditional religion apparently was quietly finding adherents among some members of the non-treaty bands, as well as other tribes from central California to Washington.

In 1871 a trader named Stanton Fisher accompanied some Bannock Indian friends to the buffalo country of Montana where they ran into a bunch of Nee-Me-Poo. Fisher, who later scouted for the army against the Real People in 1877 and in 1895 became their reservation agent, remembered:

> *Just before reaching the Yellowstone River we were overtaken by a small party of Nez Perce Indians from Umatilla, Ore, who said they too were after buffalo robes—but—I think the principal object of their visit was to introduce a new dogma or doctrine to the Bannock, Snake and Crow Indians, which had recently started among the Oregon and northern Idaho Indians.*

I subsequently learned that this new religion or whatever it might be called, started as follows:

One Sock-a-lie Tyhe Charlie, a Umatilla Indian, had met God somewhere on a trail; that God had informed him that a great change in the present order of things would take place the following spring towit:

That all the "pale faces" would either leave the country or die; that the buffalo and other large game would roam in endless herds where now roamed the white mans cattle, horses and sheep. A line of red and yellow dots from the outer corner of the eye extending back to the ear was the insignia worn by the believers. . . The Indians who joined us at the Yellowstone did not confide their great secret to us but shortly after reaching the main camp I noticed several of my friends among the Shoshones and Bannocks with their faces decorated with this unusual style of painting and when asked the meaning they, or rather one of them reluctantly told me the whole racket advising us three whites to leave the mountains very early in the spring even before the grass started.

I asked him if the whites who refused to leave were not to be killed by the Indians. His answer was that God had told Charley that the whites who refused to leave would surely die—but had said nothing about killing them.[12]

One of the more vocal adherents to the new doctrine was a hunch-backed shaman named Smohalla, of the tiny Wanapum tribe, whose longhouse lay beside the Columbia River at Priest Rapids in Washington state. He spoke the words that gave the new teaching its name, "My young men shall never work. Men who work cannot dream, and wisdom comes to us in dreams."[13] They were the Dreamers.

As I return to my van at the former Fort Lapwai parade ground, a Nez Perce man cruises by on a motorcycle, his long hair flowing over his shoulders. He raises one arm in a leisurely wave, the first adult I've seen on the streets of Lapwai. The day has turned brutally hot. It dawns on me that most of the people of the town have probably done exactly what their ancestors did every summer:

headed for higher, cooler country. Good idea. My van is an oven as I continue up the valley until a sign points to a side road and the St. Joseph's Mission. It was founded in 1874 by Catholic priests, adding yet another element to the religious stew bubbling over the fire. Impulsively, I wrench the steering wheel and make the turn. Cooler weather can wait a while. On my trips to the battlefield at White Bird I've always passed this road to the mission; not today. As I follow the narrow road up the valley of Slickpoo Creek, I smile at the sight of two desultory donkeys munching grass amid the rusting skeletons of cars in a wrecking yard.

An elderly Nez Perce woman greets me at the door of the tiny, tidy white church. Inside, beyond the rows of pews are a collection of brightly painted statues, detailed and ornate in their construction. Stained glass windows offer a muted light. The vivid trappings of the Catholic faith provided the Nez Perce a stark contrast to the austere Presbyterian worship of Spalding, who hated Catholicism with a passion and was never shy about making his view known. Once, when Thunder Rising was asked if he wanted churches in his Wallowa country, he responded that his people might disagree about some things but they did not argue about God as the various priests and missionaries did. Why would he want churches in which people would disagree about such a thing as the Creator?

I tell the woman I'm from Portland, and her face lights up. She has a friend there who lives on Sauvies Island. She knows my neighborhood, Sellwood, has wandered along the row of antique shops on 13th Avenue, loves the stuff but can't believe the prices. I snort in agreement. We stand outside the church and spend almost an hour talking about this and that. A hint of a breeze begins to provide relief from the heat as the whump-whump of a big helicopter fills the air. Whites logging on the higher reaches of the reservation, she tells me, looking up, obviously worried. She hopes they'll be careful. Some people don't understand, she says, what effect logging can have on the water. The Nez Perce now only own about ten percent of the land within the reservation boundary, she says. The rest was given to white homesteaders by the government around the turn of the century, another promise broken.

It's time for me to find a place to camp. After backtracking to

U.S. 95, I follow it up Lapwai Creek to the shoulder of Craig Mountain and Winchester Lake State Park. I find what might be the last open slot in the campground, change into my swimming trunks and head for the water, towel over my shoulder.

There you have it in a nutshell: two treaties, two Nez Perce factions, the farmers and the roamers, Presbyterians and Dreamers, more and more settlers, less and less open land, one young chief in the Wallowa country struggling with forces of history and human nature. The good will forged since Lewis and Clark first passed the pipe with the Real People was about to go up in smoke as Thunder Rising waited late in 1876 for the appearance of the "five good men" promised by Major Wood, the five good men who would make things right.

Notes

1 Ross, Alexander, *Adventures of the First Settlers on the Oregon or Columbia River*, Smith, Elder & Company, London, 1849, reprint, Citadel Press, New York, 1969, p. 236.

2 Based on Erdoes, Richard & Ortiz, Alfonsa, *American Indian Myths and Legends*, Pantheon, New York, 1985, p. 343-344.

3 Irving, Washington, *The Adventures of Captain Bonneville*, Baudry, Paris, 1837, reprint, University of Oklahoma Press, Norman, 1961, p. 251.

4 Parker, Samuel, *Journal of an Exploring Tour Beyond the Rocky Mountains*, Samuel Parker, 1838, Ithaca, NY, p. 77.

5 Parker, p. 116-117.

6 Drury, Clifford, *Henry Harmon Spalding*, Caxton Printers, Caldwell, ID 1936, p. 143.

7 McWhorter, Lucullus V., Papers of Lucullus Virgil McWhorter Cage 55, Washington State University, Pullman, Folder 150, item 44.

8 Drury, *Spalding*, p. 326.

9 Kip, Laurence, Indian Council at Walla Walla, Sources of the History of Oregon, Vol. 1 Part 2, p.10-11.

10 Report of the Adjutant General of the State of Oregon for the Years 1865-6, p. 18.

11 Report, p. 18.

12 Fisher, Stanton, Fisher Papers, Idaho State Historical Society, Boise, ID, MS106, unnumbered 5x8 notepad at back of miscellaneous papers.

13 Mooney, James, *The Ghost Dance Religion and the Sioux Outbreak of 1890*, GPO, Washington, DC, 1896, vol. 2, p. 708.

Washington State University Library
Thunder Rising
He refused to sell the
bones of his family.

Idaho State Historical Socirty
General O. O. Howard
A relentless adversary.

Martin Stadius

Dug Bar, Snake River. The members of Thunder Rising's band crossed here on their way to their date with history.

CHAPTER FOUR

SPLIT ROCKS

O ne of the treasures of Western history is a collection of letters written by Emily Fitzgerald spanning the years 1874
to 1878. The mother of two toddlers, Bessie and Bert, her
candid descriptions provide a vibrant and blunt view of frontier
life. After postings at Leavenworth in Kansas, the military academy at West Point and Sitka in Alaska, her husband, an army doctor, was assigned to Fort Lapwai in May 1876.

The Fitzgeralds shared an officers' duplex with the family of the
post commander, Captain David Perry. Six months after her
arrival, Emily Fitzgerald decided to take a look at the meeting
between Thunder Rising and the "five good men" taking place in
the church at the Spalding Mission at the mouth of Lapwai Creek:

> *When we got there, Joseph's band had arrived and were
> all in one side of the church, most of them sitting on the floor,
> horrible, dirty looking things all rolled up in blankets and
> robes. On the other side of the building were a lot of Treaty
> Indians who came in to hear how their wild brothers were
> treated. You noticed at once a difference in the appearance of
> the two parties. The Treaty Indians nearly all wore shirts,
> pants, and coats or jackets. Only here and there was there an
> old fellow in a blanket among them.*[1]

Fitzgerald found herself both fascinated and repelled by the garments of the traditional Nee-Me-Poo. She noted the reaction of one upon seeing the wife of the post commander:

He seemed very much amused by a little black dotted veil Mrs. Perry had over her face. By and by, he took off his headgear, which was stupendous and was made out of a whole collection of things, and took out of it an old black cotton net which he fixed over his face, like Mrs Perry's veil, and then nodded to us, as much as to ask us what we thought of it. He evidently was pleased with its effect, for he wore it nearly all afternoon.[2]

Lasting only two days in November 1876, the touted meeting between the commissioners and the Wallowa headman was a bust. Three of the government representatives were from the East—two businessmen and a bureaucrat from Washington, D.C.—and had no practical knowledge of the Nee-Me-Poo and their ways, especially their tradition of deliberate debate. Mrs. Fitzgerald described them:

They are all such good, pleasant men. One of them, a Mr. Stickney from Washington, reminds me of Uncle Essick. Then there is a lovely, old Mr. Barstow from Providence, Rhode Island, who, when he spoke to my babies, said he had seventeen grandchildren between the ages of ten years and two weeks, who were all waiting for him to spend Thanksgiving with them. Then there is a Mr. Jerome who is an exceedingly good-looking gentleman. He is President of the Commission. They are all fine looking men and men of means.[3]

And unqualified for the work before them. The few Indians they may have previously encountered would have been far different from the self-reliant, proud Wallowans they faced. The fourth commissioner was Major Wood, who had written the report the year before in favor of the rights of the Wallowa band, the last none other than General Oliver Otis Howard himself.

Oliver Howard was forty-six, tall, broad-shouldered and lean, his face dominated by a dark beard. Born in Leeds, Maine, he entered West Point in 1850 and graduated fourth in a class that included Custis Lee, son of Robert E. Lee. At the start of the Civil War, he resigned from the regular army and became colonel of a volunteer regiment. By age thirty-two, he was a major general, and the engagements he participated in read like a roll call of the entire war: both Bull Runs, Antietam, Fredericksburg, Chancellorsville, Gettysburg, Chattanooga, Atlanta and Sherman's march to the sea. At the battle of Fair Oaks he took two bullets in his right arm while leading a charge and the arm was amputated. At Chancellorsville, he was humiliated by Stonewall Jackson's army which flanked and routed his force. But he was one of only three generals Congress memorialized after the success at Gettysburg. By the end of the war, he was commanding 27,000 soldiers, respected in a Union army mostly noted for its mediocre leadership.

After the war, President Andrew Johnson appointed him to head the Bureau of Refugees, Freedmen and Abandoned Lands—a thankless position charged with aiding southerners who had remained loyal to the Union, helping the four million freed slaves in their transition to independence and administering the land confiscated from the rebels. One of the quirks of the legislation creating the Bureau was that its head was personally responsible for its funds. Naturally, in such a large bureaucracy, some of it turned up missing or misused. In 1873, a House of Representatives committee exonerated Howard of misconduct, but private lawsuits against him in excess of $170,000 were not dismissed until well after the Nez Perce war was over. That amount of money was not chump change in 1877, and Howard had a lot on his mind.

In 1872, he was given his first field assignment since the Civil War, ordered to Arizona to convince Cochise and his warring Chiricahua Apache to move onto a reservation. General George Crook, commanding officer in the region, already had a simple solution—kill Cochise and his people—but officials in the nation's capital wanted to give diplomacy one more try. With just two men, Howard penetrated into the heart of the Chiricahua territory, met Cochise and convinced him to end his struggle. It was a remarkably gutsy effort on Howard's part, but he faced criticism for offering lenient terms and for negotiating a verbal, rather than a written, treaty.

In 1874, he was given command of the Department of Columbia—Oregon, Washington, Alaska and most of Idaho—and moved his family to Portland, relieved to be out of the morass of Washington, D.C., politics. There he became president of the local YMCA, taught a Bible class at the Congregationalist church and even wrote a couple of children's books. Before the Civil War he had considered becoming an Episcopalian minister, and his faith remained a bedrock throughout his life. The profanity and drinking common to the army embarrassed and angered him. Even indulging in a cigar after dinner with fellow officers gnawed at his conscience, and he gave up the practice. Emily Fitzgerald wrote of Howard:

> *I have heard the officers discuss him and he is not very popular among them. It is owing to his ferocious religion. He is one of those unfortunate Christians who continually gives outsiders a chance to laugh and have something to make fun of. He says himself, 'You know, I am a fanatic on the subject.' He is an ordained preacher and preaches and leads meetings on all occasions—on street corners, steamboats, etc.*[4]

Such was the man who listened when Thunder Rising tried to explain once again that he and his people had both a legal and traditional religious right to their land.

The Easterners were both impressed and intimidated by Thunder Rising and apparently a little unnerved by the crowd of Real People inside and outside the church. The fledgling negotiators responded to Thunder Rising's recitation of facts and grievances with bluster and threats of military reprisal. The Nez Perce considered such talk during a council "showing the rifle," a sign of insincere intent and plain bad manners. The head of the commission, Mr. Jerome of Michigan, after warning Thunder Rising one last time to leave the spacious Wallowa and settle on a twenty-acre plot on the reservation, abruptly declared the meeting ended. He was, after all, a man of means and used to getting his way.

The following morning, four riders appeared at the back fence of the Perry and Fitzgerald duplex at Fort Lapwai where General Howard and Major Wood had stayed during the council. Emily Fitzgerald wrote to her mother:

> *I wish you could have seen them. You never saw such style . . . A ferocious looking old medicine man was with them (an old, old man). The other three were quite young chiefs. One was Joseph himself, who is a splendid looking Indian. As far as we could understand, they had come in to make terms of some sort with General Howard. They were all very smiling and pleasant and seemed very sorry about not finding him.*[5]

Thunder Rising had probably realized that the whites who had treated his people with the most respect were the army officers who would have to fight if push came to shove. From Captain Whipple and Lieutenant Forse in the Wallowa Valley in years past, to Major Wood who had appeared sympathetic in their previous two meetings, they all seemed different from the settlers and agents and preachers. The "splendid looking" young chief would soon find out that Oliver Otis Howard, the Christian General, was different.

Safely back in Fort Vancouver, hundreds of miles away from Lapwai, the five commissioners wrote their report. Significantly, their first recommendation was that the Dreamer shamans be exiled to Indian Territory in Oklahoma if they did not immediately move to the reservation and submit to the authority of the agent. They further urged that force be used to place the Wallowa band on the reservation if Thunder Rising continued to resist. Major Wood would not sign the document. In a separate report he cautiously advised that the military should move against the Wallowa band only if they initiated hostilities against settlers.

Agent Monteith hurried to force compliance with the commission's findings. Now was time for the roamers to become good Presbyterian farmers. He set an April 1, 1877, deadline for Thunder Rising to move onto the reservation. The smaller bands of White Goose and Grating Sound living south of the reservation were to comply also.

Thunder Rising appealed to Howard for still another council.

Perhaps the translators had not been good. Perhaps the whites had not understood his metaphor for the 1863 treaty:

Suppose a white man should come to me and say, 'Joseph, I like your horses and want to buy them,' he said. I say to him, 'No, my horses suit me well, I will not sell them.' Then he goes to my neighbor, and says to him: 'Joseph has some good horses. I want to buy them, but he refuses to sell.' My neighbor answers, 'Pay me the money, and I will sell you Joseph's horses.' The white man returns to me and says, 'Joseph, I have bought your horses, and you must let me have them.' If we have sold our lands to the Government, this is the way they were bought."[6]

Thunder Rising was ill when Howard was next in the area in April, so Frog met with the general at Fort Walla Walla. Also present was Young Chief of the Cayuse, a distant relation of the Wallowa brothers. Details of the council are sketchy, but Frog and Young Chief apparently tried a different tack: either the Wallowa band would move onto the Umatilla reservation, as the government itself had suggested in 1873, or the natives from Umatilla would join the Real People on a new reserve in the Wallowa country, ceding the Umatilla reservation land to the whites.

Howard rejected both proposals outright, stating he had no authority to negotiate. His orders were clear. He was to evict Thunder Rising's people if they refused to move voluntarily to the Idaho reservation. Howard did agree to meet with Thunder Rising and other non-reservation headmen at Fort Lapwai in two weeks, but if they thought they could talk their way clear of moving to the Idaho the reservation they had another think coming. In the interim, the general poised two companies of cavalry with a battery of Gatling guns to occupy the Wallowa homeland.

Mrs. Fitzgerald witnessed the raising of a large, open-sided hospital tent on the Fort Lapwai parade ground at the beginning of May. On the third, she saw Thunder Rising's band come in:

The Indians rode out from the Canyon in single file. All were on ponies and in their gorgeous array and instead of turning into the post gates, they circled the post three times, cupping their mouths with their hands, making the sound of Wah-Wah-Wah. When they finally stopped at the gate, they stacked their arms before entering the post.[7]

By leaving their guns at the gate, they were living the old way. A council was meant for talk, never a physical confrontation.

Under the tent, Thunder Rising asked that the onset of the council be delayed a day to allow the other non-treaty bands to arrive. They, after all, had been included in Monteith's edict to move to the reservation. Howard rejected the request, an indication of his attitude in the coming days. Agent Monteith stood and formally issued his instructions. Frog and a couple of the older men stood and argued against the removal, whereupon Howard announced that any who spoke in an impertinent manner would be arrested and sent to Indian Territory in Oklahoma. The general was determined not to take any more guff. The remainder of the non-treaty headmen arrived the following day, hurrying ahead of their people who were struggling over trails still slicked by rain and melting snow. Possibly Thunder Rising had sent messengers overnight with word of Howard's belligerent attitude.

Already designated as spokesman for all the bands was Toolhoolhoolzote, or Grating Sound, whose people called the rugged country between the Snake and Salmon Rivers their home. According to General Howard, he was "broad-shouldered, deep-chested, thick-necked, five feet ten in height with a heavy guttural voice." Grating Sound was reputed to be the most physically powerful man in the tribe and led about thirty families.

Another leader was Peopeo Kiskiok Hihih, White Goose, although his name has gone down in history as White Bird. Comprised of fifty families, his band ranged along the Salmon River with the side canyon of Lahmata, or White Bird, as the core of the homeland. In his seventies, White Goose was still vital and active, a commanding presence at almost six feet tall. He was a Dreamer shaman and carried an eagle wing as a symbol of his status.

Although technically not a non-treaty chief, Looking Glass also showed up. He had several names. One was Ippakness

Wayhayken, from which Looking Glass was derived. Another was Allalimya Takanin, a name McWhorter's informants had difficulty explaining in English, but which roughly meant Dwarfed Wraith Carrying A Cane Of Spirally-Streaked Blood And Traveling From East To West On A Strong Wind. I'll call him Looking Glass. Near fifty, he was near six feet tall, lean, with a striking, chiseled face. The son of Bonneville's O-push-y-e-cut, Looking Glass had moved his band from Asotin on the Snake River onto the reservation after the 1863 treaty. Forty families looked to him for leadership.

These were the headmen who joined Thunder Rising, whose band was the largest of the non-treaties at some sixty families. Although Thunder Rising would eventually become the most famous, at thirty-seven he was by far the youngest of the headmen and, accordingly, the least prominent in council. In addition, White Goose, Looking Glass and Grating Sound were all prominent buffalo hunters with reputations among the Real People as fighters, their skills honed in warfare with the Blackfoot and Lakota on the Montana plains. Thunder Rising had only once been to the buffalo country as an adult and had never been in battle.[8]

Despite the fact that the non-treaty Real People perhaps had the law on their side, when Grating Sound rose he spoke something more personal, about religion. I'm going to tread carefully here. You'd probably be surprised at the number of books and articles written on the religion of the Nee-Me-Poo and their neighbors, all of whom shared similar beliefs. I've read a bunch of them and never finished one with a final sense that it got to the heart of the matter. Even McWhorter found the traditional Nez Perce reticent when it came to discussing the details of practicing their faith. I'm positive the traditional beliefs are still followed today, quietly, out of the public eye, and I suppose I could poke around, ask questions, maybe even get a charming anecdote or two. The idea of trying to do so has always made me uneasy.

I've worked in the bookselling business for two decades now and seen too many books by folks who apparently believe sincerity, some urban drumming, a sweat lodge in the backyard and a vision quest on a long weekend are enough to qualify as an expert on Native American religion. This all seems to me a rip-off of their culture, and I want no part of it. Still, to understand the cause of the war it's necessary to apprehend one basic tenet of the Nez Perce traditional belief, the relationship between creator and land and people. Christianity has always been a portable faith: one could travel a thousand miles, open a Bible, and there it is. The Nee-Me-Poo religion seems to have been different.

Elderly Grating Sound once had this to say about leaving his land:

Who is it that lives above? Is it the First Man, or is it the second man? You are second man, I am second man. We are but children. I am a child. He who lives above set me down where the rivers flow, where the mountains stand. I must not make him angry by going elsewhere. I have no willing mind to listen to anyone telling me to move to a different place.[9]

For the Nee-Me-Poo, land and religion were inseparable. They believed in a Supreme Being or Creator who had given the land, perfect and sacred, to the Real People. They shared this belief with the other tribes of the region. In 1855, when pressed by Stevens and Palmer to sell his land at the Walla Walla council Owhi, a Yakama, tried to explain matters:

The Great Spirit gave us the land and measured the land to us, this is the reason I am afraid to say anything about the land. I am afraid of the laws of the Great Spirit. This is the reason of my heart being sad. This is the reason I cannot give you an answer. I am afraid of the Great Spirit. Shall I steal this land and sell it? or what shall I do?[10]

At the same council Young Chief of the Cayuse, the distant relative of Thunder Rising, said:

I wonder if the ground has anything to say? I wonder if the ground is listening to what is said . . . The ground says 'It is the Great Spirit that placed me here. The Great Spirit tells me to take care of the Indians, to feed them right. The Great Spirit appointed the roots to feed the Indians on.' The water says the same thing. 'The Great Spirit directs me. Feed the

Indians well.' The grass says the same thing. 'Feed the hors-
es and cattle.' The ground, water and grass say 'The Great
Spirit has given us our names. We have these names and hold
these names. Neither the Indians or whites have a right to
change these names.'[11]

McWhorter told a story about once camping with a traditional
believer. Their talk turned to the subject of death and the afterlife.
McWhorter's friend commented, "Some Indians think when they
die they will go off to a fine place in some other country or somewhere. Maybe above! But not that way for me. I stay right here in
this mountain. I like this mountain!"[12] Because God had created
the earth and all the plants and animals on it, power resided in the
earth and its living things. The Nee-Me-Poo found it possible to tap
into that power through vision quests. The results of these quests
were a helpful personal spirit, a Wyakin. War Singer tried to find
a rendering McWhorter could understand:

You want Wyakin explained? Best explanation would be to
read how Eve first woman talked with the snake. Well, it's
about the same as the snake appeared to Eve in person, it
must have been about the same as the old saying among the
Indians that any kind of animal or fowl, also fish, would
appear in person to young boys and sometimes girls sent
away at night to the buttes or mountains to receive their
Wyakin from such animals and birds.[13]

This is something of the religion and relation to the land that
Howard was to find so incomprehensible.

By 1877, both he and Agent Monteith were well aware of the
apocalyptic future foretold by the Dreamer shamans: a world without whites where buffalo, elk and deer in multitudes arose from
the earth and salmon jumped from the water to feed the people, a
world where the Real People were free to roam the dirt and grass
and trees and animals amid which their Creator had placed them.
For Grating Sound this council was a matter of the religion flowing through their veins. Undoubtedly, Howard and Monteith
noticed that many of the men facing them under the tent in front

of Emily Fitzgerald's house either combed their hair straight back from their foreheads or stiffened it vertically with grease, a sign of their adherence to Dreamer tenets.

Grating Sound stood and began to speak, his words translated by Perrin Whitman, nephew of the slain missionary Marcus Whitman. The Nee-Me-Poo preferred him to all others as a translator; he spoke the words honestly, did not shade meaning if hard words had to be said. Grating Sound apparently talked for hours. He had heard the words from Washington saying that Lawyer and the other treaty men had signed away the land of the rest of the Real People. That was a lie. He was not sure just who or what this Washington was, maybe a chief, maybe a house. If this Washington was a man, then he was a man with no brains. He did not know the Nee-Me-Poo and did not understand that the Nee-Me-Poo could never sell their land. The Creator had given the people to the land and the land to the people. It was as simple as this: the earth was his mother and Grating Sound would never abandon his mother. His words would have been a blunt reminder to any familiar with Tuekakas' last words: a man who sells the bones of his mother and father is no better than a dog; never sell our land! Grating Sound was a powerful orator who soon had the men behind him nodding and muttering in agreement.

Howard apparently was intimidated. Until now, he had faced only Thunder Rising and Frog in council. Maybe he expected at most some minor grumbling before the other non-treaty chiefs submitted, but now it was clear to him that he was wrong. It was a Friday, and the general declared the council adjourned until the following Monday. The weekend would provide time to move additional troops closer to Fort Lapwai in case trouble flared.

It's good to be camping above the heat of the river valleys. Last night was almost chilly, and the warmth of my sleeping bag is a comfort. Some people in the campground are up early, starting fires or pulling down tents, but I laze in the back of my van until nature demands a dash to the outhouse.

Howard ordered the two cavalry companies near the Wallowa Valley to hurry to the confluence of the Grande Ronde and Snake

Rivers, as far as they could hustle over the weekend, but only two days' hard march from Fort Lapwai. In addition he hoped their presence near Thunder Rising's winter village would serve as an intimidating factor. Howard also ordered Company "H" of the First Cavalry from Fort Walla Walla to Fort Lapwai to join the single companies of infantry and cavalry permanently stationed on the reservation.

The Real People would also receive reinforcements. Representing a small contingent of the Palouse tribe, two headmen essentially homeless since the 1855 treaty and subsequent war, led a total of sixteen families into the Nee-Me-Poo encampment near Fort Lapwai. One was Husis-husis Kute, Bald Head, a fierce Dreamer. The other was Hahtalekin, a name for which I've seen no translation.

First Sergeant for Company "H" of the First Cavalry was Michael McCarthy. He was thirty-two, five feet seven inches tall, born in Canada. A photo of him shows a thick, dark mustache and goatee covering his face. Eventually, his family would donate to the Library of Congress a journal of sorts, containing a brief biography of his army career, newspaper clippings, vignettes of army life and commentary on current events. In the very back of the journal McCarthy transcribed entries from a diary he kept from May through July 1877. After transcribing the diary he proceeded to scratch out portions of the entries that apparently cast an unfavorable or embarrassing light on either his conduct and that of his superiors. Even with portions of the entries illegible, it will provide vital clues to the first weeks of the war. The first entries, though, were routine and merely give a flavor of army life as Company "H" responded to Howard's order to reinforce Fort Lapwai:

May 6, 1877 Left Walla Walla about 6.30 am, halted at the upper end of Main Street about 2 hours, waiting for pack train. It commenced to rain and rained all day until late in the afternoon. We passed through Waitsburg, halting about 10 minutes, and moved on to Stan's bridge 4 miles beyond Waitsburg, and camped for the night. One of the cooks drank too much Whiskey during our 10 minute halt and reposed under a tree all afternoon and night without blankets, blissfully unconscious of rain, cold and other annoyances.

May 7 Left Camp about 6 o'clock am, (still raining) passed through Dayton, and marched to the Tucannon River, camping for the night at a place called Marengo (nicknamed Yellow Dog). still raining. our blankets getting moist and commencing to smell sour.

May 8 Left Camp at the usual time and marched to Snake river camping for the night opposite Lewiston (still raining).

May 9 ordered to remain in Camp until further orders. We received 4 days rations from Fort Lapwai and late in the evening orders to proceed to Lapwai, leaving behind 10 men and 1 commissioned officer.

May 10 Crossed over to Lewiston on the Ferry and marched to Fort Lapwai, about 12 miles. Arrived at Lapwai about noon and camped below the Post Traders store on the Lapwai Creek.[14]

By then the council was over. Grating Sound had risen again on May 7 and continued his soliloquy. Howard interrupted and told the headman that he wanted to hear no more about the mother earth religion. Barbed words shot back and forth between the two as their tempers got the best of them, Howard sternly insisting that he would use force if necessary to move the non-treaties off their land, Grating Sound adamantly refusing to budge from his position.

The general whose words had convinced the Apache chief Cochise to surrender was getting nowhere with this man. Years later tribal historian War Singer told McWhorter that the climactic moment came when Grating Sound's response to the Christian General's repeated threat to send troops to enforce compliance finally was:

I have a prick, and I will not go on the reservation.[15]

Apparently, true to form, Perrin Whitman translated accurately. Furious, Howard shouted for Captain Perry standing nearby, and the two officers hustled Grating Sound out of the tent and through the rain to the guardhouse at the north end of the parade ground. Howard later claimed that the warriors listening to the debate were secretly armed, and he feared a massacre if the orator were not stifled. When told of Howard's statement, one of McWhorter's informants simply commented, "Had there been arms among the Indians, our head speaker would not have been jailed."[16]

Camas Prairie is a twenty-mile by fifteen-mile stretch of rolling tableland, now turned to farms, bounded on the south by the canyon of the Salmon River and on the north by the canyon cut by Lawyer Creek. To the west is the unimposing, forested hump of Craig Mountain, matched on the east by its bookend, Mount Idaho. From Winchester Lake, U.S. 95 takes me across the upper reaches of Lawyer Canyon and down the gentle slope of Craig Mountain to the town of Cottonwood, population 1,000, on the edge of Camas Prairie. I've had enough of the main highway and find a side road that zigs and zags along section lines in the general direction of Mount Idaho until it reaches Shebang Creek. Here it follows the natural curves of the drainage much as an old wagon road would have done. Somewhere around here a terrible thing would happen the night of June 14, 1877. The sun is still low in the east, Mount Idaho a blue bulk on the horizon. I pass prosperous farms as the mixed odor of freshly-cut hay and fertile soil wafts through the window of my van. Someone should concoct a cologne that matches the fragrance. After a few miles, I turn south for Tolo Lake and the place the Nee-Me-Poo called Tepahlewam, or Split Rocks.

In June 1877, Cottonwood was a stop on the stage road that ran from Lewiston to the town of Mount Idaho, nestled at the base of that mountain. Owned by Benjamin and Jennie Norton, Cottonwood served as motel, restaurant, convenience store and saloon for travelers. The Nortons would have known that Thunder Rising, White Goose and Grating Sound finally had agreed to come onto the reservation, that those chiefs had decided to make their new homes on the Clearwater River above the Heart of the Monster where they would be close to the village of Looking Glass. The Dreamers would leave Lapwai and its environs to the Christians, the reservation unofficially divided. In the weeks after Grating Sound had been jailed by Howard, the Nortons would have been aware of the gradual gathering of the non-treaty bands at Split Rocks ten miles across Camas Prairie. The Nortons would also have heard ominous rumors from travelers along the stage road, rumors that many of the Real People remained adamantly opposed to the capitulation of the chiefs, rumors that councils still met nightly to discuss the future, rumors that warriors were willing to pay a premium price for bullets and gunpowder.

Howard was confident that the jailing of Grating Sound had been a smart move. While their speaker had stewed behind bars, White Goose and Thunder Rising had ridden over the reservation with the general. At first Thunder Rising had shown interest in land along Lapwai Creek above the fort, land illegally settled by two white families. He finally had decided against that site for his village, telling Howard that he would not want to take homes away from other people. The irony was lost on the general. After Thunder Rising finally had chosen a spot along the Clearwater River and Looking Glass and White Goose had promised to be responsible for Grating Sound's compliance, Howard had ordered that band leader's release from confinement. Before departing Fort Lapwai, Howard had given June 14 as the deadline for all non-treaty bands to remove to the reservation.

Company "H" of the First Cavalry remained at Fort Lapwai during the intervening weeks. With the boredom of garrison life setting in Sergeant McCarthy found time to do some sightseeing, choosing two places which I visited yesterday. He wasn't terribly impressed with John Monteith's efforts at Spalding:

June 4 Visited the Lapwai Indian Agency. Found every-thing looking dead, the ground around the Buildings littered and untidy. Rubbish even to the Agents door, a broken bridge, workshops splendid pictures of still life. The only semblance of (_ _ _ _ _) about the whole agency a few Indian boys catch-ing minnows in a sluggish millrace. If it was necessary to teach the Indians sloth and untidiness I could understand what I saw here, but if the opposite why is this place conducted in the manner it appears like. Perhaps today is a holiday, maybe the Agency folks are visiting or asleep. However it may be Uncle Sam will pay the bill in money or soldiers worthless lives. The agent and his numerous relations must have a living even if it cost somebody dear in the hereafter.

June 10 Visited the mission of Saint Joseph but was too late for Mass, remained for benediction and sermon. Had quite an interesting chat with Father Cataldo and his curate. The singing of benediction by the Indians was really beautiful and the service very interesting if not impressive.

In light of what would occur in less than a week his next entry is fascinating, even with the deletions he later felt prudent to make:

June 11 Mounted drill today. The beloved Commander drill instructor. (_ _ _ _ _ _ _ _ _ _) We passed in review before the laundresses at a (_ _ _) gait. Co. lines advanced. We dismounted, fought on foot, mounted again, charged the hospital, penetrating even to the backyard with the loss of only one trooper. We found him again. (_ _ _ _ _ _ _ _ _ _ _ _ _ _ _) after 3 hours of this returned to Camp and rested from our labors.

Apparently the cavalry wasn't at its highest possible state of readiness. Still, all was quiet, and the chance of action seemed slight:

June 12 A few days and we shall return to Walla Walla. Quiet peace reigns. Joseph has put his pride in his pocket and is now I hear crossing his stock and coming in to occupy the fine ranch the Government is giving his Serene Highness. White Bird, Chief of the Salmon River Indians, a grand looking Indian, whose headdress is decorated with an Eagles wing is present at our morning drills nearly every day for a week. He is attended by an orderly who rides the regulation distance behind him. We must be of interest to him so punctual is his attendance. It is time we were going home. We left so hurriedly that many of us forgot or had no means of packing an extra suit of clothes and the wet weather has been hard upon what we have along.[17]

It all looked good to Howard, too. The Wallowa band indeed had moved such stock as they could find across the Snake River at Dug Bar. Pro-treaty Nez Perce visiting the non-treaty bands reported that the chiefs were resigned to their fate. On June 13 Howard boarded a steamboat at the mouth of the Snake River on the journey back up to Lewiston and on to Fort Lapwai. The general who had talked Cochise into surrender wanted to be present for another peaceful triumph the following day.

Split Rocks is aptly named. The generally flat terrain of Camas Prairie appears here to suddenly have rent itself asunder, as though some primordial earthquake once shook this land and fractured the earth. These cracks eventually unite to form a narrow chasm now called Rocky Canyon which deepens until it reaches the Salmon River eight miles to the southwest and 2,500 feet lower in elevation. The fissures reveal the massive layers of volcanic rock underlying the thin skin of rich soil which nourishes the abundant grasses of Camas Prairie. Here, I've again finally hooked up with the National Historic Trail after leaving it at Dug Bar two days ago. In a shallow depression, near the head of Rocky Canyon, is Tolo Lake, another of the new additions to the National Historical Park. Today, instead of a sheet of water several hundred acres in size, I see hummocks of earth baking under the sun. With my binoculars I glass a collection of vehicles, tents and tarps at the edge of what once was the far shoreline: archaeologists working on a dig. The drained bed of the lake has proved to be the littered with the bones of prehistoric animals, mostly mammoth. Lost friends of Coyote, I find myself thinking.

The area of Split Rocks and Tolo Lake had long been a summer meeting place for the Nee-Me-Poo. Centrally located for all the bands, it provided abundant water and graze for the horses and a chance for the women to harvest the plentiful camas root for the larders. By June 12, the non-treaty families had gathered, the bands of White Goose and Grating Sound and Thunder Rising. This was to be one last time together as a free people. Looking Glass and his folks joined them for a while, as well as friends and relations from Lapwai and Kamiah.

Such an odd way for a war to explode. The warriors decided to hold a parade. Two young men, Shore Crossing and Red Moccasin Tops, were sharing a horse at the rear of the column as it wound its way through the camp. Their skittish mount trampled some roots drying outside one of the teepees. Yellow Grizzly Bear stepped out and taunted Shore Crossing who was riding in front and holding the rope bridle. "See what you do?" Yellow Grizzly Bear shouted. "Playing brave you ride over my woman's hard-worked food! If you so brave, why you not go kill the white man who killed your father?"[18]

That was all it took. Two years prior, Shore Crossing's father, Eagle Robe, had indeed been killed by a settler named Larry Ott. Eagle Robe had lingered for nine days before succumbing, and during that time he had elicited a promise from his son that his death not be avenged. Shore Crossing spent the evening of June 12 deep in thought. Early the following morning, before the rest of the Split Rocks camp began stirring, he awakened his cousin, Red Moccasin Tops, and a teenage nephew named Swan Necklace. Riding two horses, with but one gun among them, the three slipped away from camp and headed south toward the Salmon River and the homestead of Larry Ott.

After a few miles on a county road I again pick up U.S. 95 going south to the Salmon River. A steep climb takes me to the summit of White Bird Hill on the edge of Camas Prairie. After eight miles of rollicking descent past the White Bird battlefield overlook, I pass through the narrow cut formed by White Bird Creek in the Salmon River Canyon wall and catch my first glimpse of what's now also called The River of No Return. Five miles upstream the canyon widens a bit as the Salmon River curves around a hill on the canyon floor. For over a century this place has been called Horseshoe Bend.

Here Larry Ott had killed Eagle Robe. Following the murder, White Goose met with a delegation of settlers and demanded that Ott be turned over to the Nee-Me-Poo for justice. The whites flat-out refused in a scenario that would be repeated the following year in the Wallowa country with the death of Wind Blowing. After a grand jury failed to indict Ott, he returned to Horseshoe Bend and settled into what must have been an uneasy coexistence with the Real People.

The morning of June 13, Shore Crossing, Red Moccasin Tops and Swan Necklace first stopped at a store near the confluence of White Bird Creek with the Salmon River and tried to buy a rifle. The proprietor, Harry Mason, said no, and the three continued south. Perhaps it was dumb luck, perhaps some sixth sense warned him to get away, but Larry Ott was not home when the warriors arrived at Horseshoe Bend about noon. Not a problem. Plenty of whites along the Salmon River had killed or insulted Nee-Me-Poo over the years. The warriors would find another victim and come back later for Ott.

General Howard was at that moment on the steamer chugging up the Snake River toward Lewiston, supremely confident that all was well.

The canyon walls close in again as I continue south up the Salmon River. Wherever creeks enter the river, patches of flat ground allow room for houses and small farms. I pass the hamlet of Slate Creek on an alluvial bench of several hundred acres, site of a Forest Service office and a cluster of a couple dozen tidy homes.

Several ranches stood there in 1877. The warriors stopped at the house of Charles Cone, a man they considered a friend. He found it odd that they had only two horses among them and not very good horses at that. When they asked to purchase ammunition Cone turned them down and the three continued upstream as the afternoon waned. At John Day Creek, they stopped at a combination ranch, store, saloon and hotel owned by Henry Elfers, one of the whites who had protected Larry Ott after the murder of Eagle Robe. Elfer's wife, Catherine, was minding the store. The warriors browsed for a few minutes before quietly returning to their horses.

There it is—Carver Creek—slicing through the canyon wall. Across the river, a cliff rises vertically at least 500 feet from the water's edge, the granite surface so smooth and shining it appears to have been lovingly buffed by some giant hand. The road shoulder provides no room to pull off, so I continue on. At Fiddle Creek I stop at a solitary, well-stocked fruit stand and choose an assortment of peaches and plums and cherries. Across the road, I find a place to sit above the current's rumble. A procession of brightly colored rafts passes, the passengers whooping it up, most waving to me as they tip and dip and bounce downstream.

I've spent a lot of time thinking about Shore Crossing, his motives, emotions, what he and the others possibly could have been thinking. This clearly was no well-conceived venture. After finding Larry Ott absent from Horseshoe Bend, Shore Crossing had the perfect opportunity to turn around. Instead he and Red Moccasin Tops and Swan Necklace continued up the river for fifteen miles on a journey that lasted for at least eight hours. Plenty of time to reconsider. Riding only two mediocre horses, ill-armed and apparently short of ammunition, the three seemed to be the antithesis of a deadly war party. The thought must have crossed and recrossed their minds that their actions would bring the wrath of the army onto their people, their very families. They had to have known it would be a war the Real People could not possibly win. Were they recounting to each other the names of the thirty or so Nee-Me-Poo who had been murdered by whites over the years? Were they reminding each other of the lies told in so many councils, culminating in the ultimate indignity of the seizure of Grating Sound the previous month? Were they feeling in their hearts the pull of their religion that bound them to their traditional land? I'll never know.

Their choice of an alternate initial victim was careful. Richard

Devine had built a ramshackle cabin on a tiny shelf of land back at the mouth of Carver Creek. He had a foul reputation among the Real People for setting his pack of dogs loose upon any who passed by his shack, and he had been implicated in the death of a cripple named Dakoopin. Sometime after dark on June 13, Shore Crossing and Red Moccasin Tops burst open the door of Devine's cabin and killed him with his own rifle.

After appropriating the gun, ammunition and a horse the three returned to Henry and Catherine Elfers' homestead six miles away on John Day Creek. Elfers and hands Burn Beckrodge and Robert Bland died amid a volley of gunfire in a pasture at dawn. Elfers had paid for his support of Larry Ott. Taking three more horses, another gun and more ammunition, the warriors departed, leaving Catherine Elfers unharmed and obliviously churning milk beside noisy John Day Creek.

Near Slate Creek they again encountered Charles Cone who noticed that the Nez Perce were suddenly well-armed and supplied with extra mounts. Shore Crossing warned the friendly white to return at once to his home. Other settlers who had never harmed or insulted any Nee-Me-Poo also should also gather there and stay put, the warrior instructed. It was time for war. Hurrying on to Horseshoe Bend, the three took a look around for the still-absent Mr. Ott before Shore Crossing collected his wife, who had stayed absent from the gathering at Split Rocks.

With a woman present, they probably intended no more immediate hostilities. But as the four neared White Bird Creek they spotted a saloon-keeper named Samuel Benedict out searching for stray cattle. Red Moccasin Tops' eyes must have turned to fire. Two years prior, Benedict had let loose a shotgun blast at the warrior, slightly wounding him. Nez Perce accounts also implicated Benedict in the murder of a man named Chipmunk, and the settler had been another to rally to the support of Larry Ott. A bullet from one of the Nee-Me-Poo guns seared through the flesh of both of Benedict's legs and sent him sprawling. The raiders continued on.

As they neared Split Rocks, sometime early in the afternoon of June 14, Swan Necklace loped ahead on one of the stolen horses to announce their deeds. News of the murders turned the camp into pandemonium. The settled Lapwai Nez Perce quickly slipped away. Boys and young men ran for the horse herds. Women began hurriedly bundling their possessions and pulling down teepees. Some of the warriors, long frustrated that their chiefs had caved in to Howard's threats, cheered. White Goose and Grating Sound tried in vain to calm emotions and keep a semblance of order. After Shore Crossing and Red Moccasin Tops trotted their horses into camp, defiantly brandishing their purloined weapons, a warrior firebrand named Big Morning rode amid the chaos urging warriors to arm themselves and take the fight again to the whites without delay. The chiefs appealed for time. Ignoring them, warriors mounted up, including Yellow Bull, the father of Red Moccasin Tops and a noted war leader and buffalo hunter. By late afternoon, Yellow Bull led seventeen warriors back toward White Bird Creek. It's possible they had already began to liquor themselves up from bottles stashed around the camp.

Into this turmoil rode Thunder Rising, Frog and a half-dozen other men, followed closely by several women leading packhorses loaded with jerked beef. The party had spent the last few days across the Salmon River butchering cattle left there to graze and fatten. He received one bit of great news—his wife had just given birth to a girl—but he had not a moment to celebrate. Around him, his hopes for peace were crashing. Thunder Rising implored the panicked people to stay put and for the young men to refrain from any more depredations. There was still time to talk to Agent Monteith and General Howard, he urged. It was no use. White Goose and Grating Sound led their bands north toward Cottonwood Creek near its confluence with the South Fork of the Clearwater River. There the families would be within the boundary of the reservation and near the locations they had chosen to reside. Perhaps the army sure to come would not attack there. By nightfall, only the teepees of the Wallowa band remained at Split Rocks. Some of the more belligerent warriors from the other bands suspected the Wallowa brothers had another motive for not taking wing—to secretly repair to Fort Lapwai and surrender, and a party of men hovered nearby to prevent such an occurrence. The Nee-Me-Poo, already deeply divided as a tribe, threatened to fracture even further at Split Rocks.

102

I should have found some shade to park my van. The temperature inside must be 120 degrees. Within minutes, my tee-shirt becomes soaked with sweat as I retrace my route along the Salmon River from Carver Creek past John Day Creek and Slate Creek and Horseshoe Bend to the town of White Bird. After renting a room at the 1930's courtyard motel, jumping in and out of a cold shower and dumping my dirty clothes in the laundromat attached to the motel, I buy a six-pack of pop at the general store and wander next door to the shady park. Sitting on the grass, I down most of one can of soda then lay back and watch the pattern of leaves shimmering in the slightest of breezes. Damn, it's hot.

Lucullus McWhorter was a fierce advocate for the Nez Perce cause, but even he could find no justification for the actions of Yellow Bull and his raiders from about 6 P.M. on June 14, through the following morning. It was fourteen hours of sheer terror for the sprinkling of settlers who lived in this vicinity. I prefer to think the warriors were already tanked up and out of their minds when they rode down White Bird Canyon, although I've found no evidence to support that hope. That would not make their conduct excusable, but would at least account somewhat for the outrageous misconduct.

Jack and Jennet Manuel and their two kids lived about a mile up the canyon from where I'm reclining in this blessed shade. The war party overtook the family, Mrs. Manuel's father and an elderly neighbor named James Baker on the road somewhere near here. The warriors killed Baker, severely wounded Jack Manuel and his father-in-law, leaving both for dead, and wounded six-year-old Maggie Manuel with two arrows. Mrs. Manuel fell from her horse during the melee and broke her kneecap. Baby John, whom she was carrying, was battered during the fall. According to one account, Mrs. Manuel was raped. Several warriors then returned Mrs. Manuel and the two children to their ranch and stripped the place of guns and ammunition.

Continuing on to Benedict's saloon and store which was located somewhere near this little park, the warriors finished off the wounded Benedict and killed a miner named August Bacon who attempted to intervene. One warrior took pity on Isabella Benedict and her two children, protecting her and telling her to go to the Manual Ranch for sanctuary. Darkness was approaching when they arrived at another saloon and store near the mouth of White Bird Creek, about a mile downstream from here. "Hurdy Gurdy" Brown, his sister and her husband, Albert Benson, dashed for a boat tied to the bank of the Salmon River. As Benson desperately rowed for the opposite shore, the warriors unleashed a volley that wounded both men, but the three made it across alive.

After a night of looting and carousing, the raiders struck again the following morning a mile or so up the Salmon River. Surrounding the house of William Osborn, they killed him, Harry Mason and Francois Chodoze, then raped Elizabeth Osborn and Mason's sister, Helen Walsh. Six children were not harmed. McWhorter's informants told of another white killed during the rampage. This man was alone when encountered, taunted and given a chance to run for his life. An arrow in the back fired by a warrior named Strong Eagle ended his life, his name lost to history.

A second bunch of warriors was busy on Camas Prairie that same night, and, again, even McWhorter was forced to describe their actions as a "ghastly outrage."

Late on June 14, as the bands of White Goose and Grating Sound fled Split Rocks, Benjamin and Jennie Norton's roadhouse at Cottonwood was seeing its usual complement of passersby. Two teamsters, Peter Ready and Luther Wilmot, with wagons filled with goods destined for Mount Idaho were preparing to pull out after a rest stop when a rider appeared. His name was Lew Day. The inhabitants in and around Mount Idaho had noticed that something was suddenly hinky with the camp at Split Rocks, and Day was one of several couriers headed separately to Fort Lapwai to inform the army. Jenny Norton was concerned at Day's message, but her husband professed no worries. Normalcy ended when Day returned a few hours later with a bullet wound in his back. Warriors had ambushed him on Craig Mountain. About then, a wagon loaded with flour, bacon and the Chamberlin family pulled into Cottonwood, followed closely by a neighbor named Joe Moore on horseback. After a hasty conference the men pulled most of the load from the wagon. Shortly after sunset Jennie Norton, her son,

Hill, and sister, Lynn Bowers, piled into the Chamberlin wagon. Lew Day, whose wound was causing him great pain, stretched out on quilts in the back. Ben Norton and Joe Moore rode horses.

Somewhere along Shebang Creek, a party of warriors appeared. Driving the wagon, John Chamberlin loosened the reins and urged the two-horse team ahead, but the animals were exhausted after the long day and refused to pull faster than a walk. Norton and Moore tried to keep the warriors at bay with occasional shots, but the swells and swales of the prairie gave the Nez Perce plenty of chances to get close. Three or four miles from Mount Idaho, one of the horses in the wagon team was hit by a bullet, and the slow-motion run to safety was over.

Hunkering down, the men tried to keep the attackers at bay with dwindling ammunition. In desperation the Chamberlins, Lynn Bowers and little Hill Norton dashed through the darkness for their lives. After Hill Norton managed to make his way to town a rescue party from Mount Idaho rushed to the scene the next morning. They found Ben Norton and John Chamberlin dead, Lew Day and Joe Moore mortally wounded. Mrs. Chamberlin had suffered an arrow wound to her breast and had been raped. Her older child was dead, the younger suffering from a wound in the neck and a severed tongue. Mrs. Norton had taken a bullet through both legs but would survive. Lynn Bowers was safe.[19]

Two more victims remained—Jennet Manuel and baby John at their ranch on White Bird Creek. Six-year-old Maggie, who escaped, later said they were killed by a drunken warrior at the family's ranch on the evening of the fifteenth. Warriors burned the ranch, which apparently destroyed all traces of the bodies. A miner named Patrick Brice found Maggie and carried her on foot to Mount Idaho, arriving three days later.

Leaves ripple in the slightest of breezes above me.

This has been a troubling story to tell. What happened along the Snake River and White Bird Creek and on Camas Prairie was ugly beyond belief. But I realize now I've failed to tell you part of the story leading up to these days. Let me give you some names: Tennawnuhot, Hemese Wahiat, Konish Autassin, Husis Capsis, Itsiyiyi Opsun, Hias Moolmool, Yelnahhootsoot, Koosouyeen,

Motsqueh, Heyoom Totskin, Koopnee, Dacoopin, Tipyahlanah Siskan and Kitstsui Samkin. Those are just some of the Nee-Me-Poo killed by whites in the years immediately preceding 1877—years in which Nez Perce women were raped with no recourse to law, years in which the chiefs constantly counseled patience, years in which no Nez Perce retaliated.[20] Whether I find stuff like this in a newspaper or on the evening news today or read it in narratives penned by people long dead of any culture, it all makes me sick.

Obviously, Camas Prairie was no place to be the night of June 14, as Thunder Rising also found out. Whatever fitful sleep he and his people might have been getting was broken by the unmistakable sound of horse shoes pounding across the prairie. Shod horses meant white riders. A bullet rent the buffalo hides of the chief's teepee. About sunrise they heard more shots in the distance. Warriors had discovered the two wagons of Ready and Wilmot who had spent the night not far from Cottonwood. The teamsters escaped by cutting mounts loose from their teams and riding like the wind, but the whiskey included in their cargoes would provide more trouble for the chiefs. In the morning, Thunder Rising told his people to pack up. The best hope, he had decided overnight, lay in unity with the other bands. The Wallowa band safely crossed Camas Prairie and found the bands of White Goose and Grating Sound on Cottonwood Creek near the Clearwater River.

Five miles down the Clearwater was Looking Glass, who had left Split Rocks several days before the killings began. He had managed to keep his young men aloof from the depredations and was disgusted with what he was hearing. He wanted nothing to do with the non-treaty bands. Possibly, he met with one or more of the chiefs and demanded that they leave the area because on the sixteenth, Grating Sound, Thunder Rising and White Goose ordered their people to move again. On a day of intermittent skirmishing between parties of settlers and warriors which saw one white, Charles Horton, and one Nez Perce, Jyeloo, killed, the bands dashed across Camas Prairie and down White Bird Canyon. The morning of June 17 found them camped along the creek near the Manuel Ranch.

After my laundry is finished drying, I walk up main street, past the tiny library and steepled, white church, past barking dogs and a woman who waves to me from her porch, and out of town. The canyon walls widen like a funnel, the west wall almost vertical, the eastern side considerably less steep. The Manuel Ranch was right along here near the creek. Ahead are two buttes of about the same height in the middle of the canyon floor, separated from each other by a deep notch. Each rises a good 500 feet. The nearer, western one is smoothly rounded and grassy. The other is dark and volcanic. From its rugged summit a long ridge angles downward a third of a mile toward the creek to the east, ending at two knolls overlooking the creek bottom.

Battle Ridge.

Notes

[1] Laufe, Abe, ed., *An Army Doctor's Wife on the Frontier*, University of Pittsburgh Press, Pittsburgh, 1962, p.220.

[2] Laufe, p. 220-221.

[3] Laufe, p. 219.

[4] Laufe, p. 140.

[5] Laufe, p. 223-224.

[6] Joseph, "An Indian's View," p. 419-420.

[7] Laufe, p. 247.

[8] The descriptions of the leaders and their bands are from McWhorter, *Hear Me*, p. 177-186.

[9] McWhorter, *Hear Me*, p. 163.

[10] Kip, Indian Council, p. 20-21.

[11] Kip, Indian Council, p. 19.

[12] McWhorter, *Hear Me*, p. 79.

[13] McWhorter, Papers, Folder 104, item 1.

[14] McCarthy, Michael, Journals and Papers of Michael McCarthy, Library of Congress, Washington, D.C., diary entries May 6-10.

[15] McWhorter, Papers, Folder 84, item 123.

[16] McWhorter, Hear Me, p. 168.

[17] McCarthy, Diary, June 4-14.

[18] McWhorter, *Hear Me*, p. 190.

[19] For events of June 13 -15 see Kirkwood, Charlotte M., The Nez Perce Indian War Under War Chiefs Joseph and White Bird, Idaho County Free Press, Grangeville, ID, 1928, p. 40-56 and McDermott, John, Forlorn Hope, Idaho State Historical Society, Boise, 1978, p. 3-33.

[20] McWhorter, *Hear Me*, p. 116-131.

Richard Devine was killed with his own gun by Shore Crossing and Red Mocassin Tops, near this spot on the Salmon River.

Wayne Cornell

Wayne Cornell

Settler Henry Elfers and two hired hands died in a hayfield at John Day Creek, about six miles dowstream from Richard Devine's cabin.

109

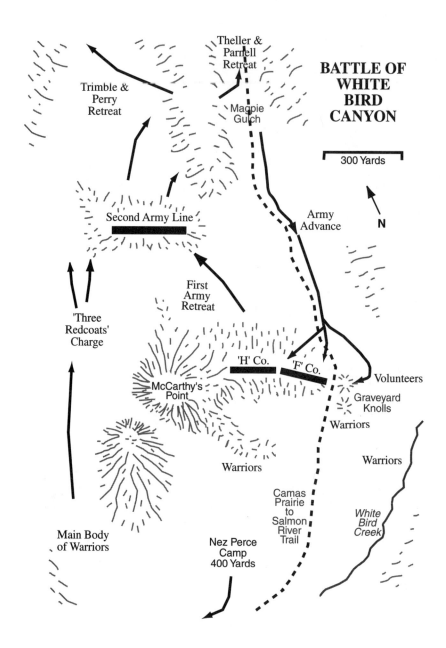

BATTLE OF
WHITE
BIRD
CANYON

300 Yards

N

Theller &
Parnell
Retreat

Trimble &
Perry
Retreat

Magpie
Gulch

Army
Advance

Second Army Line

First
Army
Retreat

'Three
Redcoats'
Charge

'H' Co.

'F' Co.

Volunteers

McCarthy's
Point

Graveyard
Knolls

Warriors

Warriors

Warriors

Main Body
of Warriors

Camas
Prairie
to
Salmon
River
Trail

White
Bird
Creek

Nez Perce
Camp
400 Yards

CHAPTER FIVE

WHITE BIRD

My travel alarm wakes me before dawn, and a quick cup of coffee and a couple of plums do me for breakfast. The terrain I'm going to walk this morning is rugged, nothing I want to tramp over with a heavier stomach than the one I already carry around. I have a couple of reasons for the early start: the battle took place about this time, and I want to avoid the heat of the day. I sip and chew outside the motel room sitting at the open side door of the van, appreciating the slow-motion light show above as the hidden sun begins to gild the eastern horizon with lemon light.

General Howard arrived at Fort Lapwai on the afternoon of June 14 and received the news from the post commander, Captain David Perry, that all seemed to be well according to the latest reports from Camas Prairie. Both their doubts began to grow that evening when a letter arrived from L. P. Brown of Mount Idaho, alleging that the non-treaty bands at Split Rocks were preparing for war. Brown had a reputation for common sense and veracity, not someone to be spreading wild rumors. Perry detailed Corporal Lytel, two privates and a civilian who spoke some Nez Perce to Mount Idaho to investigate. They returned on lathered horses about noon on the fifteenth with two friendly Nez Perce who provided the first, garbled account of Shore Crossing's initial foray along the Salmon River with Red Moccasin Tops and Swan Necklace.

Two prominent Christian Nez Perce, including Thunder Rising's father-in-law, offered to check things out further. They returned late in the afternoon in the company of two more couriers from Mount Idaho whom they had met along the road. One was a brother of Looking Glass, the other a mixed-blood named West. Each carried a letter from L. P. Brown written that same day, addressed to Captain Perry and giving details of the attack upon the Norton party and the first rumors of the murders by Yellow Bull's party at White Bird. Brown was no longer calm.

> *The Indians have possession of the prairie and threaten Mount Idaho. All the people are here and we will do the best we can. Lose no time in getting up with a force . . . . Hurry up; hurry!*[1]

General Howard took control and hurried. He ordered Captain Perry to prepare the two companies of the First Cavalry present—Perry's own Company "F" and Captain Joel Trimble's Company "H"—to ride to the relief of Mount Idaho, while one company of the Twenty-First Infantry would remain to defend the fort. The general dispatched an officer to Lewiston to engage pack mules for Perry's column and another to Fort Walla Walla and the nearest telegraph for reinforcements and supplies sufficient for a ninety-day campaign. After fruitlessly waiting several hours for the mules to arrive from Lewiston, Perry suggested to Howard that the command take the field with three days' rations packed in their saddle bags. The general agreed. Sergeant McCarthy wrote:

> *Boots and Saddles was sounded. I was ordered to have rations packed to make preparations to march. The herders brought in horses, saddled, etc, but the orders are no movement until evening. At Retreat we are in the saddle and "F" Co joined us, and together as the shades of evening are gathering we march in the direction of Camas Prairie.*[2]

Fifty-four enlisted men comprised McCarthy's Company "G" as it rode out of Fort Lapwai. Captain Joel Trimble was forty-five, tall and pencil-thin. After enlisting as a private in 1855, he had endured a lackluster military career until 1863 when he received a commission as a second lieutenant during the fury of the Civil War. The bars on his shoulders suited him, and his record thereafter was filled with commendations. His junior officer was William Parnell, a forty-one-year-old Irish immigrant who had taken part in the renowned Charge of the Light Brigade as a young British lancer in the Crimean War.

Company "F" found forty-nine men in its ranks. Captain David Perry was only thirty-six, but had been an officer of the First Cavalry for fifteen years, both in the Civil War and on the frontier. Brevet promotions for exemplary conduct had earned him the right to be addressed as Colonel. As senior officer in time served, he was in overall command of the column. Before the company departed Fort Lapwai, General Howard had attached Lieutenant William Theller of the Twenty-First Infantry in an effort to shore up the meager complement of commissioned officers. Theller was forty-four with almost sixteen years of military experience.[3]

The march along the wagon road up Lapwai Creek and over Craig Mountain took all night. Perry was prudent, posting skirmishers to either side of the column in anticipation of an ambush that never occurred. They reached Cottonwood at mid-morning and turned their horses loose in a fenced field. Some of the men napped while the cooks heated coffee and bacon. Shortly after noon, the command resaddled and continued cautiously along the wagon road, their horses kept to a walk, outriders ahead and to the flanks. About three hours later they passed dead horses and a wagon, its load strewn across the prairie, the first clear sign of the trouble brewing. McCarthy noticed an empty whiskey barrel, its head staved in.

A party of settlers led by Arthur "Ad" Chapman appeared and apprised Perry of the three bands' rush across the prairie toward White Bird earlier in the day. Chapman assured Perry that the hostiles almost certainly were planning an immediate crossing of the Salmon River after which they could secrete themselves in the rugged country between the Salmon and the Snake rivers, Grating

Sound's home territory. Chapman urged Perry to pursue and punish the bands without delay. The officer mulled over the advice as he led his troops the last few miles to Grangeville, a budding settlement consisting of several houses and a Grange hall on the eastern edge of Camas Prairie, about three miles from the much larger town of Mount Idaho.

Perry gathered his officers for a conference. His orders were to relieve Mount Idaho, but as he later stated at a Court of Inquiry, "I saw at once that if I allowed these Indians to get away with all their plunder without making an attempt to overtake and capture them, it would reflect discredit upon the army and all concerned."[4] His officers concurred. The two companies would attempt to engage the enemy at first light the following morning. If their timing was perfect, the non-treaty bands might be in the midst of crossing the Salmon River, and, divided, they could easily be crushed.

The tired troopers whiled away three hours boiling water for coffee and beans for soup, cracking hardtack bread. At 9 P.M., eleven civilian volunteers joined the command which, as quietly as possible, headed for the top of White Bird Canyon, leaving behind three troopers guarding extraneous gear. The departing soldiers carried only their arms, ammunition and overcoats. A half-dozen unarmed treaty Nez Perce rode alongside, hoping to parley with the non-treaty chiefs and avoid further bloodshed. About midnight, Perry signaled a halt above the canyon. Silence, no smoking and no sleeping, he ordered. Exhausted horses, who could not be court-martialed for insubordination, dropped to the ground beside their riders as Sergeant McCarthy prowled among his men, jostling those who dozed off. In the darkness one trooper struck a match to light his pipe. McCarthy noted in his diary the odd coyote howl that immediately followed; Lieutenant Parnell also mentioned it at the Court of Inquiry which the army would eventually convene. The element of surprise, Parnell decided, had been lost. At dawn Perry ordered the column forward. The troopers had been sleepless for forty-eight hours.

While it was still night, a rider named No Feet galloped his horse into the Nez Perce camp from his sentinel post up the canyon, shouting the alarm that soldiers were approaching. Still dreaming for some sort of peaceful resolution, the chiefs ordered a party led by Vicious Weasel to ride out with a white flag to meet the soldiers. A few men and boys gathered the horses not immediately needed by the warriors or the families, some 600 to 700 animals, and prepared to drive them to safety. Some warriors remained in camp, passed out from too much stolen whiskey, but most moved up the canyon to meet the soldiers in case the peace party failed. The fighters totaled about seventy men, some armed only with bow and arrows, determined to stop almost one hundred cavalry from harming their women and children.

Before the last of the stars wink out, I wander over to the little park across the street from the motel. Once I seriously began looking into the war, I became increasingly uneasy with the accepted version of the events of the next few hours of 1877. The primary sources for interpreting the battle have been McWhorter's two books from the Nez Perce view and the transcript of a Court of Inquiry held in Portland Oregon eighteen months after the fight. The latter file was uncovered by historian John McDermott and published as an appendix to his 1978 book *Forlorn Hope*. The Court of Inquiry was a messy affair highlighted by the testimonies of Captains Perry and Trimble who had come to hate each other's guts. The other surviving officer, Parnell, also testified, as well as four sergeants and one civilian. The result was a *Rashomon*-like series of conflicting statements which, when I examined them in detail, made me wonder if the seven had experienced the same battle. McWhorter's books followed the usual pattern of native exposition, each informant limiting his narrative to only what he did or saw with no attempt at an overview. The consensus has been that the entire clash took place on Battle Ridge, except for a running fight out of the canyon. I couldn't see how to shoe-horn all events described by the various participants into that terrain. I kept coming back and walking over the ground.

The first break happened when I overheard one Park Service employee mention to another that an archaeological survey of the battlefield had been conducted in the 1980s. That was news to me and, apparently, unknown to the several writers who had published books on the war in the intervening years. The next day found me at park headquarters at Spalding where the librarian professed no knowledge of the document and could find no record of it in the computerized catalog. She'd been there only a few months and was intrigued. Several hours' searching produced it among much more recent documents still awaiting cataloging. It was titled *A Survey and Interpretation of the Archaeological and Historical Features of the White Bird Battlefield* by David Chance, et al, dated December 1987. A quick read-through of the text and an examination of the accompanying maps convinced me that the results of the survey were potentially important.

The archaeologists had found little of significance on Battle Ridge, where the current interpretation concentrated most of the action, but spotted two areas of probable grave sites on a ridge farther to the north, indicating that serious fighting possibly had taken place there. When I returned to the library the following day to examine the document in more detail, I was informed the corresponding maps contained sensitive archaeological data, access now restricted. Well, well. One day too late. I already had a photocopy of the most significant portion of the maps in my van, and in my brain.[5]

A second break came when I finally received a microfilm copy of Michael McCarthy's diary and papers from the Library of Congress after much persistence by the interlibrary loan staff at the Multnomah County Library. In *Forlorn Hope,* McDermott quoted freely from the diary in the days and even hours preceding the battle and a detailed account of McCarthy's escape from the canyon. But there was nothing of the fight itself. I had been intrigued by the omission. I found part of the reason for excluding the material may have been the poor condition of the diary entry itself. As I mentioned previously, McCarthy scratched out portions he apparently later found embarrassing, making transcription a tedious and in some cases fruitless affair. What *was* legible, though, sent my heart pounding: the sergeant clearly placed a major portion of the battle on the same ridge where the archaeologists had unexpectedly discovered the probable grave sites.

My final break came when I was tracking down an obscure reference in the papers of Walter Mason Camp, a western history buff in the first part of this century who seemed to have spent all his spare time interviewing and corresponding with survivors of the frontier wars. In the index to his papers, I noticed the names of two of the volunteers who took part in the battle and immediately realized that no reference to these letters existed in any published accounts of the Nez Perce war. One proved to be a bust—Theodore Swarts, whose gun I had held, was aging and unable to respond personally—but the second was a jewel. Frank Fenn had herded stock over the battlefield in the years after the war and remained intimately familiar with the terrain. His letter and map pinned down the location of the volunteers at the beginning of the fight, only seventy yards from where historians thought, but critical yards.

With this new information I went back to the Court of Inquiry transcript and to the words of McWhorter's informants and found a coherent story finally emerging from accounts which had previously seemed hopelessly in conflict.

I fire up the van, let it warm up for a minute, then creep out of town in the lower end of second gear, keeping the engine as quiet as possible as main street turns into narrow, old U.S. 95. After passing the site of the Manuel Ranch I pull over near the more southerly of the two grassy knolls that mark the eastern terminus of Battle Ridge. Both knolls once were used as graveyards by the Nez Perce. In years past, I've had to struggle over the wire fence here, and I appreciate the new gate I now find. Signs along the fence warn against hunting or trapping, but the park service is finally going to encourage walking. Only a few yards from where I pause is a flat, grassy bench extending from the end of the southern knoll.

Yellow Wolf and others waited on that grassy bench for the soldiers to appear. They heard gunfire from the north, beyond Battle Ridge. They could not see it, but Ad Chapman, accompanying the advance party of Perry's command, had fired on Vicious Weasel's peace party which had tried approaching the column from the west, waving a white flag. The Nee-Me-Poo emissaries wheeled their horses and galloped away down the western canyon. There would be a fight.

A moment later, Chapman appeared far up Battle Ridge. With the settler were eight or nine soldiers commanded by Lieutenant Edward Theller. Chapman looked over, spotted Yellow Wolf and the others and snapped off a long, wild shot. Lieutenant Theller ordered Trumpeter John Jones to sound the bugle, which would bring the rest of the cavalry forward. As the thirty-year-old private lifted his bugle to his lips, Fire Body, reclining in the grass next to Yellow Wolf, took careful aim with his rifle and pulled the trigger. Jones slumped from his horse. The Nez Perce later agreed Fire Body had made a very lucky shot from a quarter-mile away. As Chapman led the soldiers on a reverse charge back toward the rest of the command, Jones' riderless horse loped along with them. "Chapman ride too fast," one of McWhorter's informants remembered. "Injun bullet not catch him."[6]

Following the trace of an old wagon road up the face of the ridge toward a notch in the crest beside the second graveyard knoll, I notice little flags stuck discreetly in the dirt. My guess is the Park Service is preparing a walking trail for visitors. In 1877, this faded wagon road was a wide horse trail used by generations of Nee-Me-Poo to travel between Camas Prairie and the Salmon River. I spook a fawn out of the dry, thigh-high grass and thistle that covers the entire battlefield. It bounds ahead of me, pauses and turns to watch, then trots a few yards farther. I scan the ridge for its mother but see nothing. The fawn and I play a long-distance game of tag until I reach the notch where the old road crosses the top of Battle Ridge. As he followed the trail down the canyon, this is where Captain Perry got his first clear view of its lower reaches. I turn to see what he saw.

Just before reaching this spot, Perry ordered Company "F" to move from column into line and sent word back to Captain Trimble that his company should do the same farther up the ridge. Sergeants maneuvered the troopers into a thin chain along the ridge crest. Perry's fifteen years of training and experience as a cavalry officer told him to order a charge: a swift shock, the unexpected blow—that was cavalry at its best. The previous evening the settlers on Camas Prairie had told him the hostile Nez Perce would certainly flee at the sight of soldiers. Perry had entered the canyon with that assumption in mind. Now, he hesitated. His eyes took in several hundred yards of broken ground, then thick brush edging the creek which angled across his front. The village was farther down and still hidden by brush and trees. Perry could see that once his troopers approached the creek they would be perfect targets for marksmen stationed in the brush. An occasional bullet whistled by, and he could see a few warriors dodging about, taking advantage of even closer rough ground for cover. Many others he could not see waited for him down there, gut instinct told him. If his line went forward it could be cut to pieces.

Captain Perry was probably correct, but the decisive blow would have come not from the warriors hidden in the brush to his front and left, but from the right where the main body of mounted warriors, led there by Frog, waited hidden behind the rounded butte. Glancing around, Perry noticed some of the volunteers had just arrived on the knoll to his left, protecting that flank. Trimble's "H" Company was moving into line farther up the ridge to his right. The crackle of gunfire began to swell, a few of his troopers foolishly returning ineffective fire from atop their dancing horses. As puffs of acrid white smoke belched from their gun barrels, then drifted in the breeze, Perry made his decision. With Trumpeter Jones already dead and Trumpeter Daly having somehow dropped his instrument during the night march, Perry was forced to shout his orders. Dismount to fight on foot, he yelled to Lieutenant Theller, every fourth man to take the horses to the low ground in the rear. Let these Indians come to him if they dared.

Oh, they dared all right. In many ways this battle is quite easy to describe: in the period of less than an hour, fewer than seventy Nee-Me-Poo warriors routed about 100 soldiers and civilian volunteers, killing thirty-four and sending the rest fleeing in terror while suffering only three wounded themselves, all of whom recovered from their injuries. Walking the thirty yards to the top of the northern graveyard knoll, I murmur my apologies to the Nee-Me-Poo dead perhaps underfoot and peer over the other side into the creek bottom.

While the two cavalry companies were forming into line on the ridge, George Shearer, a former Confederate army officer, led nine civilians around the base of the graveyard knoll. Gunfire from a few warriors farther down the creek bottom scattered them. According to Frank Fenn, Theodore Swarts accidentally shot himself in the hip while drawing his revolver from his holster. The discharge of the black powder set fire to his clothing and Fenn hastily helped Swarts bat out the flames. A few of the civilians wheeled their horses and headed back up the canyon at a gallop; war was no fun when the opponent fought back. The rest dashed to the top of the northern graveyard knoll, finding the left end of the "F" Company skirmish line touching the trail below. The civilians watched as the soldiers began dismounting, every fourth man hustling the horses away. The thirty-five or so remaining troopers knelt and began exchanging fire with warriors hidden among the nooks and crannies of the rough ground slanting toward the Nez Perce camp. The knoll looked like a good place for the civilians to make their stand.

Shouting and shooting, several of the warriors who had been waiting with Yellow Wolf and Fire Body below the other graveyard knoll swarmed on foot toward the volunteers. Other warriors ran for their horses and began making their way up the creek bottom, flanking the volunteers' position. One warrior yelled at a citizen he recognized, "You, Charley Crooks: take your papa's hoss and go home!" When Herman Faxon took a bullet in the thigh and the unlucky Swarts another in the leg, that's exactly what the volunteers did. One warrior who took part in this attack remembered, "They did not stay there any time, and I, Two Moons, hardly saw them at all."[7]

According to all accounts from surviving soldiers, the battle turned when the volunteers fled. Warriors reaching the knoll poured a devastating flanking fire into the dismounted "F" Company line and into the milling horses and holders in the ravine behind the line. Between six and ten troopers were hit in the first few volleys. Captain Perry had begun to ride up the ridge to confer with Captain Trimble and to find a trumpeter to sound further orders. As he later said:

. . . a Cavalry command on a battlefield without a trumpet is like a ship at sea without a helm.[8]

Realizing that the Nez Perce had flanked his line, Perry dashed back and with Lieutenant Theller and the company sergeants attempted to keep order. Seeing the position was no longer tenable, Perry ordered a retreat up the ridge toward Company "H" on more defensible ground. Some of the troopers panicked and bounded down the back slope of the ridge toward the horses. Others followed Perry up the ridge on foot, perhaps helping the wounded and dragging the dead with them.

I amble from the knoll back down to the old wagon road. Poor Theodore Swarts. With two wounds in the first seconds of battle, I seriously doubt he did any shooting. As I head up the bare slope where "F" Company deployed, a hard climb of forty yards brings me to a rocky knob along the rising ridge line. A solitary hackberry tree stands on the point. I look back. According to army accounts, the troopers in the skirmish line were about three yards apart. No more than about thirty-five men formed the line, another twelve or so having taken the horses to lower ground behind me. About half the line would have been between this tree and the wagon road. It's no surprise they broke and ran. They had absolutely no cover and were sitting ducks. The upper part of the line was more fortunate. The crest of the ridge flattens out here, and irregularities in the terrain would have provided more protection. Puffing, I continue up the ridge line toward the Company "H" position.

Approaching the ridge, Captain Trimble had noticed the Nee-Me-Poo horse herd, guided by a half-dozen or so men, thundering up the canyon to the right of his line. Trimble picked Sergeant McCarthy and six men and rode with them up the ridge to the top of the butte farthest to the right where Trimble instructed McCarthy to prevent any more Nez Perce flankers from riding around the butte and getting in the rear of the command. Back at the skirmish line, Captain Trimble had failed to order the rest of his company to dismount, although a few did so on their own.

Those who remained on horseback were unable to return fire accurately and, of course, made better targets for the scattered Nee-Me-Poo marksmen below the ridge. Corporal Roman Lee was hit first, a painful groin wound. Fellow troopers helped him from his saddle, then lost track of him in the smoke and noise and confusion. Dazed, perhaps thinking it was time to return home far away in Pennsylvania, Lee wandered down the face of the ridge in the direction of the Nez Perce camp and a final Nez Perce bullet.

Meeting up with Trimble, Captain Perry got more bad news. Trumpeter Marshall of Company "H" had managed to lose his instrument also, the last in the command. By now Perry must have had a feeling this was going to be one of those days. Around him, troopers from both companies on horseback and afoot milled aimlessly, the sergeants on the verge of losing control. Briefly, the two captains reviewed their options. Trimble suggested a charge through the Nez Perce camp. Perry thought Trimble had gone batty. Perry was now thinking the unthinkable—retreat. Focusing on the next ridge to the rear, he ordered Trimble to withdraw in column and reform on the ridge. Perry then raced off to save what he could of the rest of scattered "F" Company.

Up to this point, about twenty Nee-Me-Poo warriors had joined the battle. Hidden from the soldiers' view by the second, rounded butte on the canyon floor, almost fifty warriors had remained close to the village, waiting to determine the direction the battle would take. When word came that the soldiers were in retreat, these warriors cantered their horses forward. In a few minutes they would deliver a crushing blow.

A steep climb takes me up from the ridge onto the volcanic butte where Trimble deployed McCarthy and his squad. They were soon joined by one volunteer and a few men from "F" Company fresh from the mess down the slope. It's easy to understand why they ended up here. Except for the other, rounded butte across the ravine, which is only a few feet higher, this point is the highest on the canyon floor. Only the northern, rear slope is unprotected and vulnerable, the other three sides being rimmed by dark volcanic rock with steep slopes dropping off hundreds of feet at places. A natural fort. This is where I would have wanted to be.

For several minutes McCarthy's attention was directed to the front and sides. He detailed his best marksmen to take positions to the west to cover the low ground directly below the prominence on which he was posted. The fifty warriors who had held back now began to pass the butte with most riding up the canyon between McCarthy and the west canyon wall. Three warriors led this charge: Shore Crossing, Red Moccasin Tops and Strong Eagle. The first two, you remember, had begun the killing of settlers a few days before. They had brought the soldiers upon the Real People, so it was now their duty to protect the elders and women and children. The sergeant's few men on the butte above proved helpless to stop them. Finally looking around as his position began to be flanked, McCarthy was astounded to see that the rest of the command had fallen back some four hundred yards to a second ridge where the officers had managed to rally most of the panicky men.

This was the way civilian George Shearer remembered it:

> *We reached the first ridge that was susceptible of being held after the retreat commenced. It was there I said to Captain Perry we had a good strong position, thinking he was not acquainted with the country. He remarked we would hold that ridge and immediately took steps to organize a line, and about the time I thought a very fine line organized the Indians made their appearance . . .*[9]

During the minutes before the warriors struck the flank of the second line, Captains Perry and Trimble were again in a quandary as to their next move. For a few moments they considered advancing to the butte where McCarthy was ensconced. Its height and rocky outcroppings clearly made it the most defensible position within view. In indecision, they first signaled for McCarthy to retreat, then waved him back to his promontory. Trimble managed to get a few troopers to advance with him across the low ground toward McCarthy's point, but turned back when the sergeant waved and pointed out the first warriors riding up the canyon west of his position.

As the final attack began, Perry's horse became exhausted and refused to move. Perry mounted behind a trooper for a short time, moving along the line and encouraging the sergeants to hold the men. He apparently did not order the troopers to dismount and form an effective skirmish line. McCarthy wrote in his diary:

> *The line meanwhile was mounted, and looking back towards the line I could see the men firing from their horses backs and they appeared half the time enveloped in the smoke of their own guns and they also appeared to recede, a sway-ing motion to the right and left being perceptible, and the cit-izens seemed to have disappeared completely. The one who had advanced to the bluffs had long since disappeared. The Indians had got past my position in the bluffs on both sides, almost between me and our line . . . .*[10]

The back of my T-shirt is soaked with sweat even though the sun has yet to clear the canyon wall. The earth seems to absorb the summer heat and radiate it back through the night and these early morning hours. Or maybe I'm just getting old and out of shape. At any rate, I'm relieved to be going downhill again, along the back slope of McCarthy's Point toward the ridge where Perry tried to make a stand. I find the differing perspectives on the battle between the whites and the Nee-Me-Poo fascinating. The soldiers who testified at the court of inquiry felt the fight had already been lost once the initial Company "F" skirmish line had been flanked and shot up on Battle Ridge. They barely mentioned the second stand they made on the ridge to the north. Any retreat meant defeat, I guess, and no use talking about it. On the other hand, the warriors who spoke with McWhorter seemed to pay little attention to the first portion of the battle, perhaps because so few warriors were involved and it was over so quickly. To Yellow Wolf and oth-ers, the fight around the ridge ahead was the heart of the fight.

Weyahwahtsitskan, a warrior, had this to say about the attack by the force riding up the canyon past McCarthy:

> *It was truly a startling scene. Unlike the trained white sol-dier, who is guided by the bugle call, the Indian goes into bat-tle on his own mind's guidance. The swift riding here against*

the troops was done mostly by the younger men. All the warriors, whoever gets ready, mounts their horses and go. In this charge against the soldiers' right flank Wahlitits, Sarpsis Ilppilp and Tipyahlahnah Kapskaps (Shore Crossing, Red Moccasin Tops and Strong Eagle) *were the first to start in the charge, all of the three wearing full-length red blanket coats of same make and pattern. These coats were to show their contempt, their fun-making of the soldiers, to draw their rifle shots, of which they were not afraid. Other warriors follow after them riding singly, and many hanging on the side of their horses, shielded thus from soldiers' sight. There is fast shooting and wild yelling and whooping as the horsemen stream by, an occasional horse shot down. It is a bad mix-up for the soldiers. They do not stand before that sweeping charge and rifle fire of the Indians. Their horses go wild, throwing the riders. Many of their saddles turned when the horses whirled, all badly scared of the noisy guns. Soldiers who can, remount, and many without guns dash away in retreat. It was a wild, deadly racing with the warriors pressing hard to head them off.*[11]

A boy of twelve named About Asleep followed the warriors into the battle and in 1912 told McWhorter what he saw:

Warriors rode one by one scattered out in long lines. Soldiers were close together, and the first shots—one— three—then the clatter of many shots coming fast and unbroken. Many soldiers went to the ground at the first volley, their horses rearing and whirling every way. Indians and soldiers are close together. The war-whoop is heard above the guns, and there was shouting from the soldiers. The soldiers do not hold more than five or ten minutes. Now running from the battle, they are dropping like hunted birds.[12]

In 1930, Yellow Wolf visited White Bird Canyon with McWhorter. The old warrior was nearing the end of his years and tired easily. The first day of the visit he explained to McWhorter what he remembered of events by the graveyard knolls. The second day he took McWhorter to the second ridge and said:

> *The warriors charging up the west canyon struck that flank hard. Hanging on the sides of their horses where not seen, they gave the soldiers a storm of bullets. Warriors dismounted, and from hiding dropped soldiers from their saddles . . . In the meantime our smaller party, sixteen in number, attacked the enemy's left flank. It was just like two bulldogs meeting. Those soldiers did not hold their position ten minutes.* [13]

I reach a cluster of volcanic rocks partway between McCarthy's butte and the ridge where much of the rest of the command had reformed. The archaeologists who conducted the surface survey decided the rocks were piled in an unnatural manner and might be associated with the battle.

McCarthy's diary entry provided a clue as to what might have occurred, although some words were illegible:

> *The order to get back was signalled to us, all who had horses mounted, a quick run over the boulders through a hail of bullets and (_ _ _ _ _ _ _ _ _ _) the line had been, not more than two had got back even that far, some were driven from their horses riding down the slope among the boulders, some F Co men had no horses and some were killed running on foot, nearly all were struck, so close and heavy was the cross fire. Arrived where the line had been, I found several wounded or dismounted men trying to get back, a little further back Colonel Parnell, the only officer in sight was trying to rally about a dozen mounted men to save the wounded and dismounted men.* [14]

My guess is that a few of the troopers on foot with McCarthy during the rush for the line, piled up these rocks and tried to make some kind of stand here. With warriors on all sides the soldiers wouldn't have had a chance. I reach the west base of the second ridge where the second line formed then broke. It's maybe sixty feet high, smoothly rounded and covered with high grass. This is where Red Moccasin Tops and friends struck one end of the line. According to the archaeologists who examined the battlefield, there are probably eight or nine gravesites hidden under the grass at this end of the ridge.

By the time McCarthy had raced his horse, Harry, back to the second line it had disintegrated. During the Court of Inquiry, Perry and Trimble each insinuated cowardice on the other's part. Apparently, both fled with the mass of troopers, Perry possibly on foot. Lieutenant Parnell remained near the ridge waiting for McCarthy and the men with him to make their escape. Although both McCarthy and Parnell would eventually be awarded Congressional Medals of Honor for their efforts to save fellow soldiers during the next few minutes, McCarthy later scratched out much of the following passage in his diary. Still, with the aid of an especially helpful staff member at the Multnomah County Library—thanks, Jenny—I was able to decipher some of what McCarthy had tried to eradicate:

> *Small parties of Indians were still riding up our right and left, not even pausing to fire at us. Some semblance of a stand was made by us and Colonel Parnell begging me to hold them said he would ride to the rear, overtake the fugitives and "bring me help." Here again the most desperate part of the business fell to my share. For a few minutes I managed to hold them and some of the wounded and dismounted men were almost saved. I scolded, swore and abjured the (_ _ _ _) men to deploy and make a stand if for no other reason than to breathe themselves, some yet not touched continued on and even passed us but many wounded do not reach us. They are paralyzed with fear or exhausted with fatigue or loss of blood and are killed unresistingly before our eyes (_ _ _ _ _ _ _ _ _ _ _ _) no help appeared. We could look back half a mile and not see a blue coat, and my line melted from me and joined the fugitives, and (_ _ _ _ _ _ _ _ _ _ _ _ _ _ _ _ _ _) Up to this time I didn't begin to realize that there was a disaster. The*

excitement and the (_ _ _ _ _) that terrible (_ _ _ _ _ _ _ _ _ _ _) fight, and the occupation of encouraging, rallying and looking after others had dulled any sense of fear or danger. It did not seem at all possible that I could be (_ _ _ _ _ _ _ _) the dismounted (_ _ _ _ _ _ _ _ _ _ _ _ _) considerably in our rear and are I thought out of danger. There must I thought surely be another line at the next raise.[15]

There was no line anywhere, only soldiers dropping like hunted birds.

I walk east along the base of the ridge to where the smaller party, including Yellow Wolf, attacked the wavering line. Here the archaeologists found four or five probable grave sites, and this is where Yellow Wolf stood as he described the climax of the battle to McWhorter. I can imagine the somber face of the seventy-five-year-old warrior, his graying hair still braided and draped over his shoulders, his forelock still swept back in the traditional manner of an unrepentant Dreamer. I wonder if he smiled a bit as he described the action, the two wings of warriors hammering the wavering line. Somehow, I think not.

One of the three Nez Perce wounded during the battle caught a bullet somewhere around here during a hand-to-hand fight with a trooper over his rifle. The warrior's name was Bow And Arrow Case. I don't know the name of the trooper. During the struggle, Bow And Arrow Case heard the voice of Thunder Rising saying, "be careful!" This is the only mention of him during the battle. Thunder Rising was never a general giving orders: you go here with those fifty men, you attack there with the others. When he fought he was like any other warrior. The idea that he was some kind of Napoleonic military mastermind does no justice to him nor to the other Nee-Me-Poo fighters who used their own skills and minds.

I'm glad no one's around to witness my effort to get over the wire fence and back to the highway. Charlie Chaplin would have been proud of me—slapstick in its purest, unrehearsed form: flailing arms and legs to accomplish the apparently simple, followed by subtle adjustments in posture and clothing to regain a semblance of dignity. After it's over, I wonder why I just didn't hike back to the nifty new gate by my van.

The two companies had disintegrated into individuals and squads fleeing the canyon. Both Captains Perry and Trimble eventually climbed the steep west canyon wall on a game trail, Perry on Trumpeter Jones' horse which he caught along the way. With them were some of the citizens and soldiers. Here and there Perry would convince a few of the terrified men to stand and fight for a minute or two, but it was a hopeless cause. Trimble apparently had no interest in stopping for anything. Sergeant McCarthy, meanwhile, was wondering where the hell Lieutenant Parnell was with the promised aid. In fact, the lieutenant had been unable to halt any substantial number of soldiers and was now trying to get those he could out of the canyon along the trail they had entered. McCarthy's diary gives the flavor of the panic that had taken over:

My horse was wounded. It was time to get me back before he gave out, besides my saddle had slipped back and in danger of turning. I feel certain a short gallop will bring me back to the new line which I expected to find just beyond the next swell of the ridge and (_ _ _ _ _ _ _) of the selfish (_ _ _ _) passed the dismounted men (_ _ _) (the Indians seemed to have halted I didn't hear their yells) (_ _ _ _ _ _ _ _ _ _ _ _ _ _ _) his gait to a walk. I dismounted thinking (_ _ _ _ _ _ _ _ _) to save time I just (_ _ _ _ _ _ _ _ _ _) It is getting a little scarey to be left so far behind with a wounded horse but "Harry's" gait does not improve (_ _ _ _ _ _ _ _) so I dismount, turn him loose and take it afoot and get over the ground quite lively, for I am now thoroughly scared. a half mile dismounted and I am almost exhausted. I overtake a man of my Company (Fowler) (_ _ _ _ _ _ _) Fowler took me on behind, and a few hundred yards further a friendly Indian catched a loose horse, but I was so exhausted that they had to help me on. I am all right again and in a few minutes we overtook a party of our own men with Colonel Parnell. I reported the result of my attempt to save the wounded and that we could

129

again hear the Indians yelling behind us that they were probably all killed. He said "I could not help you Sergeant you see how everything is going." We were now almost 10 men strong in column of files all the rest had disappeared officers citizens and men and the Indian (_ _ _ _ _ _ _ _) coming up the road behind us and we were not yet quite as safe as we could wish, but our only safety lay in moving back slowly and keeping up a fire. So each man loaded and fired as he saw anything to fire at, and our fire had a very good effect for the Indians appeared to keep a respectable distance. They also fired wild and did us little harm wounding several of the horses, however not dangerously. A couple of more miles were made in this manner and we reached a place where the road is graded. We are getting near the head of the canon. We over-take two of our men that are apparently mortally wounded, one is lying on his horses back with his hand convulsively clasped around the pommel of the saddle. The Indians, fear-ful of losing their prey are getting bolder and are closing in around us like the jaws of a trap. all discharge their pieces and quicken the gait. (_ _ _ _ _ _ _ _ _ _ _ _ _ _ _ _) I am again unfortunately the last file we have been riding in a column of files, a shot from the Indians following up the road disables my 2nd horse and he stops in the road (_ _ _ _ _ _ _ _ _ _ _ _ _) I dismount and try to run up the road but I am so exhaust-ed from previous effort that when I try to run up the very steep incline I fall on my face several times. The Indians on the road see my situation and when within almost fifty yards give me a volley. The bullets striking the bank about the height of my knees. I cannot go any further, so turning part-ly towards them I staggered to the side of the road my foot slipped and I fell all abroad (_ _ _ _) by the side of the road. My fall must have decieved the Indians into the idea that they had killed me in the last volley for as I lay (_ _ _ _ _ _ _ _ _ _ _ _ _ _ _ _ _ _ _) and the whole party passed me at a gallop in the pursuit and so as far as I am concerned the battle of White Bird was over.[16]

Back in my van, I drive up the old highway as it skirts the pond and trees that mark Theodore Swarts' homestead after the war. The narrow lane loops over the shoulder of a ridge into Magpie Gulch where McCarthy decided his role in the battle was done. About a mile farther on, the road begins its abrupt climb out of the gulch onto a ridge leading to the top of the canyon. One switchback after another takes me higher and higher.

Two bicyclists whiz past me, the first people I've seen today. One lifts her fingers from the grips and gives me a tiny wave, but they're zipping downhill so fast that they need total concentration. I pull off the road at a point where I can look back at the battle-field, now a good two miles down the canyon, and into Magpie Gulch. Although it's only nine in the morning, the air temperature must be above seventy by now, and not a hint of a breeze. Glad I got my hiking done early in the day, I sit by the edge of the road and chew on a long stem of grass, gazing into the past.

When the two companies of cavalry had been entering the canyon before the battle, the horses at the front of the column had shied from movement in the thick brush beside the trail near the top of Magpie Gulch. As the nervous troopers had struggled to control their mounts, a white-haired woman had stepped out, followed by two children clinging to her skirt. It was Isabella Benedict, still hiding three days after the Nez Perce raiders had killed her husband at the bottom of the canyon. She had begged the officers to turn around and get out of the canyon. You'll be massacred, she had insisted. Perry had offered her an escort out of the canyon, a few of the Nez Perce scouts. She had refused, perhaps not trusting any Nez Perce by then. A trooper named Shay had leaned over and handed a loaf of bread to the shivering, frightened woman before the column had continued along the trail.

The thunder of the battle must have reached Isabella Benedict, echoing up the canyon walls. She and her children watched in dismay as the first soldiers streamed by, their horses lathered and panting. Civilian Charlie Crooks jumped from to the ground long enough to sweep up her children and hand them to passing cavalrymen. He then grabbed the reins of one of the unmounted horses galloping along with the fleeing throng and thrust her in the saddle, but the frightened horse soon threw her into the brush. A warrior named Wounded Head spotted Mrs. Benedict as she struggled to reach the top of the canyon on foot. He'd gone on a bender the night before and woke up too late for most of the fight. He put her behind him and rode back toward the battlefield where Nee-Me-Poo women searching the canyon for dead or hiding soldiers convinced him it was best to release her. She would reach Camas Prairie and safety after one more harrowing night.

When the army returned to the canyon to bury the dead, they found the bodies of Lieutenant Theller and seven other men in a brushy side ravine in Magpie Gulch. One of the oddities of the Court of Inquiry was the fact that the presiding officer made no attempt to account for the fate of Lieutenant Theller, the one officer killed, an omission I find astonishing. Trimble casually mentioned seeing him during the initial retreat from Battle Ridge to the second line. Theller was on foot, carrying a carbine, then was helped onto a horse and galloped to the rear, according to Trimble. Without being asked, Parnell offered that Theller "seemed to have lost all control of himself." Perry merely stated that as he climbed up the canyon wall he knew Theller was attempting to leave the canyon with a squad of men along the same trail used by Parnell, adding that Theller "seemed much excited and did not seem to know what he was doing." The court asked no follow-up questions to any of the officers, and Theller's reputation remained impugned in the official record.

Civilian Frank Fenn remembered a totally different Edward Theller. According to Fenn, just before the main mass of fleeing soldiers reached Magpie Gulch, Perry begged Theller to stop and form some kind of rear guard to hold off the pursuing warriors until the rest of the troopers could make it out of the canyon. Theller succeeded in stopping about twelve men, including Fenn. Fenn remembered:

The party with Theller was well in hand and he directed their fire with such good effect that the Indian advance was thoroughly checked . . . After thus checking the Indians Theller very quietly directed his men to take to the road again

*with the view of getting ahead of the Indians a second time
and in that way cover the retreat as well as possible.*[17]

At that point Fenn and the two or three other civilians abandoned Theller's party and high-tailed it directly up the canyon
wall. Theller's diminished squad would make it only another half-
mile up Magpie Gulch. Yellow Wolf remembered them:

*Keeping after the runaway soldiers, we made a stop to
fight seven or eight who had dismounted. Their horses were
played out. They were in a ravine where grew thornbushes.
Those soldiers put up a fight.*[18]

On the evening of the battle General Howard received a note
from Captain Perry written in Mount Idaho. In the dispatch Perry
informed Howard that Theller was dead and asked the general to
break the news to Theller's new widow. That dispatch had to have
been written no later than mid-afternoon for the general to have
received it by evening. At that time, soldiers were still straggling
in from the battle; Sergeant McCarthy, for instance would not
reach safety for three days. Yet Perry was so sure that Theller was
dead that he could positively ask Howard to break the dreadful
news to the officer's widow, something Perry would not request
unless he was absolutely sure of Theller's fate. How was that possible given the confusion which attended the aftermath of the fight
and the fact that Perry had taken a different route out of the
canyon? The court of inquiry testimony was silent. The answer
might reside in McWhorter's papers. One of the officers present
during the campaign, Lieutenant Harry Bailey, sent McWhorter
copies of all his correspondence home. One of them was this fascinating letter written five days after the battle:

June 22, 1877
    *DEAR HOME—In camp en route to Mt. Idaho, I. Ty.,
Tomorrow we expect to reach Mt. Idaho, and Capt. Perry's
command. 1st Lieut. Edward Russell Theller, 21st Infantry,
and thirty-three men of the 1st Cavalry killed (june 17th).*

Theller was hit three times and begged officers to leave him, as he could not live.[19]

Such was the nature of the scuttlebutt around the army campfires in the days after the battle. Could that have been how Perry was so sure Theller was dead? If so, there was only one officer who could have spoken with a wounded Theller: William Parnell. First Trimble, then Perry had turned away from the trail before reaching Magpie Gulch and climbed the canyon wall well before the location of Theller's last stand. Parnell's squad, though, followed the trail up Magpie Gulch out of the canyon right past the spot where Theller and his compatriots fell. Yet in his testimony Parnell never mentioned seeing Theller once the retreat began. The scratched out sections of McCarthy's diary describing his escape from the canyon become all the more fascinating for what might be there. The exact circumstances of the last minutes of the lives of Theller and the troopers with him will probably remain forever a mystery, but the men who chose to stay with their wounded officer rather than continuing to flee up the canyon deserve a whole bunch of respect.

My stomach is rumbling. I grab some more of the fruit I bought at the stand along the Salmon River yesterday and munch as I continue the steep ascent out of the canyon. Before long I'm 2,000 feet above the site of the battle. The troopers' horses must have been ready to drop by the time they made the climb. The old highway connects with new U.S. 95 near the top of the grade, and in a couple of minutes my van is gliding downhill toward Camas Prairie. I watch for a side road to the west. One of the park rangers for White Bird showed me the location of my next stop a few years ago, but my memory is a little vague. There it is, and luck is with me; a break in the oncoming traffic lets me turn smoothly. That eighteen-wheeler barreling down the hill behind me won't get to squash my van like a bug.

After wandering around county roads for a while, I find the site of Henry Johnson's ranch in 1877. The location of the horse trail in and out of Magpie Gulch remains something of a mystery, as does the route that Perry, Trimble, most of the volunteers and a few of the soldiers took directly up the west canyon wall. Johnson's ranch, though, was a landmark in all accounts left by participants, and here it's possible to pick up the story on the actual ground where events took place. A couple of sheds, a massive tree that looks old enough to have been around during the war and rows of gigantic round bales of hay are about all there is to see now. In 1877, Johnson had some kind of a house here and probably a barn. About 100 yards beyond the ranch site to the west is a rocky hill maybe thirty feet high, then fields of grass extend over undulating hills to the horizon with no hint that the terrain precipitously drops into White Bird Canyon within a few miles. Between the hill and the ranch is a swale. That rocky hill, I think, is where Perry tried to make his next stand.

When he reached the top of the west canyon wall, Captain Perry had ten or fifteen men with him, including two volunteers. Few warriors had followed them up the imposing grade and for a time the beleaguered troopers enjoyed a respite from attack. They made their way around toward the head of the canyon, finding Lieutenant Parnell emerging with his squad.

The unified command now totaled between twenty-five and thirty men. The warriors who had been dogging Parnell soon resumed pressing the cavalry's rear and flanks. Before reaching Johnson's ranch, the bluecoats had to cross a ravine where the column would be vulnerable. Perry asked Parnell to keep his men in a skirmish line before the ravine until Perry's force had crossed. Perry's men, in turn, would cover Parnell's men from the other side.

It was a good plan, theoretically. Parnell became a bit peeved, though, when he witnessed Perry's force keep right on going after making it across. The two civilians had panicked the soldiers into believing any halt was foolish, and Perry again had been powerless to stop the flight. Lieutenant Parnell and his squad made it safely, though, to Johnson's Ranch where they found Perry dismounting his troopers and forming a line.

Of course, the warriors promptly flanked the position. Several slid from their mounts and began working their way toward the army horses in the swale behind the line. Others took possession of a somewhat higher knoll about 200 yards east. It didn't take Perry long to figure out that he was going to be in deep trouble within a few minutes and ordered his command to remount. As they passed the ranch buildings, a scrawny black and white mongrel scampered out and joined them. The surviving troopers of "H" Company would eventually adopt it and name it White Bird.

For the next four miles across Camas Prairie Perry kept his unreliable portion of the command in a tight column of fours while Parnell's men formed a mounted skirmish line at the rear, occasionally turning to fire at their circling tormentors. The Nee-Me-Poo were not especially eager to press their attack by this time, content to herd their opponent along like cowhands on a cattle drive. When a party of civilians appeared across the prairie coming from the direction of Mount Idaho the warriors wheeled their ponies and broke off the pursuit.

The battle of White Bird Canyon was over.

In the afternoon I meet one of the two park rangers assigned to White Bird at her office tucked in the Forest Service building at the edge of Grangeville. Her name is Teresa Seloske. She knows I disagree with the official interpretation of the battle but always finds time to listen. I 'd given her a copy of McCarthy's full diary a year ago, and she's been intrigued. She's walked over the battlefield a couple of times with me in years past, and I appreciate that she always managed to keep a straight face when I offered a particularly ludicrous observation. Some sort of special training, I suppose.

I've brought with me a copy of Frank Fenn's letter and map and give it to her. She has some new stuff for me to take a look at: photos that didn't make it into *Forlorn Hope* which shed some light on the location of the trails in and above the upper portion of the canyon, and the results of sweeps with a metal detector of three other war sites by two amateur archaeologists thirty-five years ago. Normally, that kind of off-the-cuff activity destroys more than it saves, but these guys were careful about documenting their results. I spend a couple of hours in a conference room, happily reading and taking notes. It's aggravating to find that the two with the metal detector also scoured White Bird, but that data is missing.

I spend the rest of the afternoon playing tourist at Tolo Lake. It's another of the sites just added to the National Historic Park, but this summer attention is devoted to the ancient fossils discovered in the lake bed. A fence keeps spectators like me at the edge of the ground the archaeologists and trained volunteers are working. A graduate student from Idaho State University tells me there might be from twenty to 200 mammoth preserved here. They were Columbia mammoth, twelve to thirteen feet tall at the shoulders, considerably larger than the more well-known woolly mammoth. So far, she says, there's no indication any were killed by humans. When I ask if I can help for a few hours, she laughs. It takes time to train rookies in even the basics of the proper procedures, she tells me. I'd undoubtedly do much more harm than good.

It's time to find a campsite, anyway.

Warriors searching the battlefield missed Sergeant McCarthy hiding in the thick brush of Magpie Gulch. He would slip to safety and reach his compatriots at Mount Idaho. Women and boys scoured the battlefield for weapons dropped by soldiers who had fled, as well as those carried by the dead. It proved to be quite a haul. According to Yellow Wolf, the chiefs tallied sixty-three Springfield carbines and a small number of Colt pistols. That meant, that in addition to the dead, half the troopers who had made it out of the canyon must have dropped their weapons. Warriors who had gone into battle carrying muzzle-loaders or bows and arrows would now have rifles. Three of the treaty Nez Perce with the army were found but released with a warning never to aid the military again.

The day after the battle, a squad of warriors fresh from the buffalo country of Montana rode into the jubilant camp at the Manuel Ranch. Among them were Rainbow and Five Wounds, renowned as fighters. Remember those names. The Real People were stronger than ever. The chiefs knew, though, that another army would eventually follow. Two days after the victory, the bands forded the Salmon River so the families could hide in the mountains while warriors watched the river crossings for the first sign of danger.

From here on out the primary goal of the chiefs would be evasion from the troops and the safety of the women, children and elders.

The first hint General Howard received of the disaster was the arrival on the afternoon of June 17 at Fort Lapwai of a corporal and private from Company "F" who had fled from the battlefield as soon as the first bullets started flying. Howard listened to their breathless descriptions of massacre with disgust. In his mind they were little better than outright deserters and their claims nothing more than an attempt to mask cowardice. But when several of the treaty Nez Perce who had accompanied Perry also returned with similar stories, Howard must have had a sinking feeling in his gut. Full realization hit when the note written by Perry arrived by courier that night. As the survivors had straggled into Grangeville and Mount Idaho, the sergeants had kept count. A third of his command was missing and presumed dead, Perry reported. And Lieutenant Edward Theller. Shortly after reading the report, the general made the difficult walk to the door of the Theller quarters and knocked. The look on Howard's face told the new widow more than she wanted to hear.

Over the next four days, the two cavalry companies patrolling the Wallowa country, two infantry companies from Fort Walla Walla and a mixed command of one company of artillery and three of infantry which had been bivouacked on the Columbia River all arrived at Fort Lapwai. Other troops were on the way, but Howard was itching for the field and revenge. On June 22, he gave the order to march.

Notes

[1] Howard, Oliver O., *Nez Perce Joseph*, Lee & Shepard, Boston, 1881, p. 96.

[2] McCarthy Diary, June 15th.

[3] officers' biographies from McDermott, *Forlorn Hope*, p. 57-68

[4] quoted in McDermott, *Forlorn Hope*, p.197.

[5] The bodies of the soldiers and there effects were long ago disinterred and reburied at another location, so foolish souvenir hunters should leave their tools at home and not even think about desecrating an historic site.

[6] McWhorter, Papers, Folder 66, item 12.

[7] McWhorter, *Hear Me*, p. 247. McWhorter's confusing series of photographs following page 54 in Yellow Wolf were a real problem in unraveling the battle, especially in locating the volunteers. In the end I was forced to discount them. In the text Yellow Wolf stated that the main battle took place on ground to the north of Battle Ridge not visible from the cemetery knolls (page 56). Yet McWhorter in the photo titled Panoramic View, taken from the south cemetery knoll, nevertheless identified ground (Point E) on the upper reaches of Battle Ridge and visible in the photo as the main scene of the fight, a serious blunder. McWhorter also mistakenly identified Point A as being the rounded butte on the canyon floor behind which the majority of the warriors waited. Point A is a portion of the west canyon wall. He even got the location of the camera wrong; on the back of the original photo which I examined he wrote that it was taken from the north cemetery knoll. It was taken from the south. McWhorter further confused matters with the final photo in the series, supposedly a close-up of Point F in the panoramic view. The low, rocky outcropping in the last photo is actually some 500 yards from Point F.

[8] quoted in McDermott, *Forlorn Hope*, p. 198.

[9] quoted in McDermott, *Forlorn Hope*, p. 190.

[10] McCarthy, Diary, June 17th.

[11] McWhorter, *Hear Me*, p. 248-249.

[12] McWhorter, Papers, Folder 28, items 49-5.

[13] McWhorter, *Yellow Wolf, His Own Story*, Caxton Printers, Caldwell, ID, 1940, p. 57.

[14] McCarthy, Diary, June 17.

[15] McCarthy, Diary, June 17.

[16] McCarthy, Diary, June 17.

[17] Fenn, Frank, Letter of September 19th, 1915, Walter Mason Camp Papers, Brigham Young University, Provo, UT.

[18] McWhorter, *Yellow Wolf,* p. 59.

[19] McWhorter, Papers, Folder 101, item 109.

Wayne Cornell

Soldiers and volunteers reached the left butte, center, before being driven back by Nee-Me-Poo warriors. Some of the fleeing troops managed to climb the nearly vertical bluffs west of the battlefield, passing near the point from which this photograph was taken. The Nez Perce camp was located on White Bird Creek, just out of the photo on the far right.

Martin Stadius

Soldiers rode down Magpie Gulch to attack the Indian camp on White Bird Creek. Some of the terrified troopers and volunteers fled back up the draw, after being routed by the Nez Perce defenders.

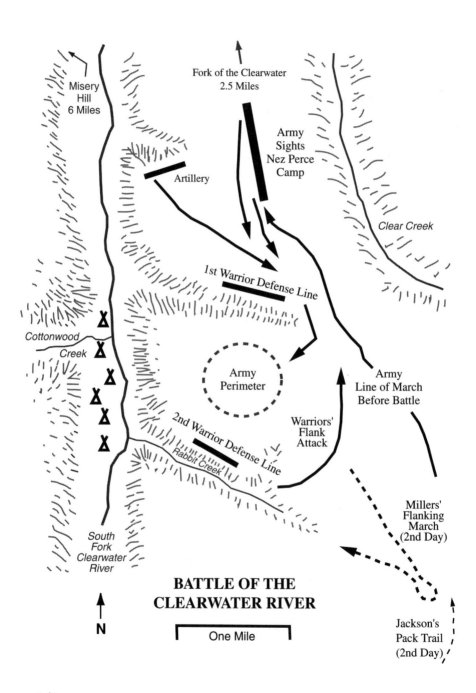

Misery
Hill
6 Miles

Fork of the Clearwater
2.5 Miles

Army
Sights
Nez Perce
Camp

Clear Creek

Artillery

1st Warrior Defense Line

Cottonwood
Creek

Army
Perimeter

Army
Line of March
Before Battle

2nd Warrior Defense Line

Rabbit Creek

Warriors'
Flank
Attack

Millers'
Flanking
March
(2nd Day)

South
Fork
Clearwater
River

**BATTLE OF THE
CLEARWATER RIVER**

Jackson's
Pack Trail
(2nd Day)

N

One Mile

CHAPTER SIX

CLEARWATER

T he morning is cool and I laze in my sleeping bag past 8 A.M. When I finally step out of my van at Fish Creek campground, on the slopes of Mount Idaho, my shoes touch asphalt. The Forest Service must have had funds to burn at the end of some fiscal year and decided to pave this place. I'm not one of those taxpayers who automatically objects to every government expenditure, but give me a break. A paved campground?

With General Howard and his force of 230 men marching from Fort Lapwai for Camas Prairie and things quiet around Mount Idaho and White Bird, this is probably a good time to tell you a bit about the army of 1877 and give you a sense of the United States as a whole at that time.

The population of the country was approximately forty-seven million, but the Pacific Northwest—the states of Oregon and Washington and the territory of Idaho—could claim only 228,000 citizens—less than one-half of one percent of the national total—with almost all clustered in Oregon's Willamette Valley and to a lesser extent around Washington's Puget Sound. Eastern Oregon and Washington and virtually all of Idaho remained frontier.[1]

A Republican, Rutherford Hayes, was president, having been elected in 1876 in a race notable for the highest voter turnout in

American history, as well as the most dubious outcome of any presidential election. Okay, fraud. Hayes lost the popular vote to Democrat Samuel Tilden, but some last-minute backroom bargaining swung the Electoral College votes of three southern states to Hayes. I can still imagine the stench of cigars and whiskey.

One of the terms of the deal was that President Hayes would remove the last of the federal officials and troops overseeing the southern states in the wake of the Civil War, the so-called Reconstruction. The mostly-southern Democrats who controlled the House of Representatives didn't exactly trust Hayes, so when they met in 1877 they applied added pressure by refusing to appropriate any money for the army. As they marched toward battle, Howard and every officer and enlisted man in his command had not received paychecks for three months and would receive none until well after the war was over. It wasn't quite so bad for the privates and corporals and sergeants; the terms of their enlistment guaranteed room and board. For the officers it was another matter; they were expected to pay for the upkeep of themselves and their families with their wages.

Congress had authorized a minuscule army of 2,000 officers and 27,500 enlisted men. But, due to the difficulty of recruiting privates for a measly theoretical wage of thirteen dollars a month it rarely approached that number. The oceans provided an effective barrier to most foreign threats, and a large standing army had never been popular with elected officials. Canada was friendly, and the only real threats from Mexico were gangs of bandits prone to dashes across the border for loot. The only major action was out West where a few native people still insisted their homelands were theirs.

In a time when the Secretary of Defense was called the Secretary of War, President Hayes appointed George McCreary of Iowa to the post. His nominal subordinate was General of the Army William Tecumseh Sherman, whose middle name, oddly enough, derived from a Shawnee leader killed in 1813 by American troops. Like all armies, Sherman's was comprised partly of the necessary support units: Signal, Ordnance, Engineer, Payroll (just keeping tabs at this time), Medical, Quartermaster and so forth. The guts were the infantry, cavalry and artillery line units.

As far as the army was concerned, the nation was comprised of three parts: the Division of the Atlantic with Major General Winfield Scott Hancock commanding from New York; the Division of the Missouri with Lieutenant General Philip Sheridan commanding from Chicago; and the Division of the Pacific with Major General Irwin McDowell commanding from San Francisco.

Each division was cut into departments, one of those being General Howard's Department of the Columbia. The other departments in the Pacific Division were the Department of California and the Department of Arizona. The Division of the Missouri had four departments—two you should know about: the Department of the Platte, headed by Brigadier General George Crook from Omaha in Nebraska; the other the Department of Dakota headed by Brigadier General Alfred Terry from Saint Paul, Minnesota.

The 1870s had seen the Lakota and Cheyenne on the northern plains prove particularly troublesome, so the Department of Dakota was further divided into districts. Colonel John Gibbon and his Seventh Infantry watched over the District of Montana from Fort Shaw. Gibbon was responsible for the western portion of Montana where most settlers resided. Colonel Nelson Miles held sway over the District of Yellowstone from Tongue River Cantonment in eastern Montana. In overall command of the Fifth Infantry, the Seventh Cavalry and a battalion of the Second Cavalry, Miles had forced the Lakota and Cheyenne into either surrender or exile in Canada in the months after the Custer fight at the Little Big Horn, and that officer was a rising star in the army. It hadn't hurt that he had married the niece of General of the Army Sherman.

It strikes me that you might be wondering why in the world I'm giving you all these names and details that have nothing apparent to do with the Nee-Me-Poo holed up in the Salmon River country. The answer is that those few Real People would soon have everybody I've mentioned scrambling. The names you're reading will pop up here and there later in the story, and this might help you make sense of it all.

The primary unit of the army was the regiment, comprised of

twelve companies and commanded by a full colonel with a lieutenant colonel, three majors, adjutant and quartermaster as support staff. The latter two were usually either captains or lieutenants, although one of the majors sometimes took the added duty. Each company theoretically consisted of a captain, first lieutenant, second lieutenant and a varying number of sergeants, corporals and privates depending upon whether the regiment was cavalry, infantry or artillery.

In reality, no regiment was ever at full strength in either officers or enlisted men. Regimental staff regularly found themselves detached for extended tours of recruiting duty. At the company level a captain and one lieutenant was the norm. The situation was even more critical among the enlisted ranks. After the Custer debacle, Congress had authorized an expansion of cavalry companies from fifty-four privates to 100, yet when Perry led the two, ill-fated companies toward White Bird on June 15, Company "F" could claim only forty-one privates and Company "G" forty-four. Infantry and artillery companies were even smaller, rarely exceeding thirty-five enlisted men, corporals and sergeants included.

General Howard's Department of the Columbia consisted of seven companies of the First Cavalry Regiment, ten companies of the Twenty-First Infantry Regiment and five of the Fourth Artillery Regiment. Headquarters for the First Cavalry was Fort Walla Walla, but only three companies were permanently stationed there. The rest were scattered about California, Nevada, Oregon and Idaho, mostly at isolated posts. Eventually, ten of the twelve companies would gather to fight the Real People, including three released from detached duty in the Department of California.

Regimental headquarters for the Twenty-First Infantry was Fort Vancouver near Portland. Again, most units manned smaller posts. Eight companies were all Howard could scrape up for duty in the field against the Nez Perce. With headquarters in San Francisco the Fourth Artillery's primary assignment was defense of the Pacific coastline. Secretary of War McCreary had recently ordered the abandonment of several posts in Alaska, and three artillery companies already en route from there to Fort Vancouver would leave their heavy guns behind and soon find themselves tromping across Idaho with rifles slung across their backs.

The Pacific Division commander, Irwin McDowell, dredged up a few more units: Companies "C" and "L" of the Fourth Artillery and the men of the Presidio Light Battery, all previously protecting San Francisco Bay, and Companies "C" of the Twelfth Infantry and "H" of the Eighth Infantry, both stationed in distant Arizona. General of the Army Sherman did his bit by ordering the entire Second Infantry from Georgia to Idaho. With the army out of funds, though, a number of railroads balked at transporting the regiment, and the Second Infantry would not arrive at Lewiston until the end of July.[2]

The weapon lugged by the infantry and artillery doing duty as infantry in Howard's column was the Springfield .45-70 rifle. Reliable and accurate as long as it was kept clean, the Springfield was a single-shot breechloader. Repeating rifles were on the market, but the army ordnance honchos figured soldiers who had to load rounds one at a time were more likely to make that shot count. The cavalry carried the shorter carbine version of the same gun.

After dropping off the mountain, I reach what's left of the town of Mount Idaho, a few houses scattered near a bend in a county road. Somewhere around here in 1877, the town and Camas Prairie residents built a circular barricade of logs, fence posts and sandbags as they waited for General Howard to appear. On a hillside above is a cemetery, and I go up to take a look. Hoary headstones and some familiar names.

Jonathon Chamberlin, born 1847, killed by Nez Perce Indians June 14, 1877. The inscription reads:

> *My heart once heavy now at rest, my groans no more are heard. My race is run, my grave you see. Prepare for death and follow me.*

Benjamin B. Norton, died June 14, 1877, aged forty-two years, two months and sixteen days:

147

*A brave spirit has rested here who died a glorious death in
his country's course.*

Lewis Day, born July 10, 1821, died June 20, 1877:

A victim of Indian barbarity.

Off in a distant corner is James Baker, killed by Indians June
15, 1877, aged seventy-four years:

Gone but not forgotten.

Jennet D. Manuel, killed by Nez Perce Indians June 1877, aged
twenty-eight years. Of course, there's no coffin under that stone.
Her body was never found. As I drive the three miles to
Grangeville, I remember that scattered throughout the region are
dozens of graves of equally-innocent Nee-Me-Poo who have no
headstones.

General Howard's column stalled on June 24 near Cottonwood
and cautiously probed for signs of non-treaty warriors. Captain
Perry rode out from Grangeville to deliver what must have been an
embarrassing report on the White Bird fight. Lieutenant Thomas
Knox and ten men returned to Grangeville with Perry, Knox carrying instructions to reinforce Trimble's Company "H," fully arm
that company with weapons from Perry's company; the combined
units then to proceed to the relief of settlers from the Salmon River
area forted up at Slate Creek. According to Sergeant McCarthy's
diary, the company departed Grangeville on the evening of the
twenty-fourth, following a circuitous mountain trail to avoid White
Bird.

After spending two days talking with the fifty or so settlers
gathered at Slate Creek and reconnoitering up and down the river,
McCarthy made a diary entry I find astonishing given the times:

*The Indians, White Bird's Band were raised around here
and had lived and trafficked with the whites (who were nearly all shopkeepers) for a great many years. Many causes of*

dissension had grown up against them, and in nearly every case the whites were to blame. They were in fact crowding the Indians, taking forcible possession of every little plot of ground that would grow anything along the river and the creeks flowing into it and covering the hills with their stock. I would not for anything be the apologist for the Indians, but I could not shut my eyes to what I saw and close my ears to what I heard and in my opinion the white people were to blame for the trouble.[3]

I wonder exactly what he heard and saw that made McCarthy, in fact, become a private apologist for the Real People.

After a day's halt at Cottonwood (a Sunday, which reinforced in many peoples' minds the image of Howard as the Christian General) the main column split. The infantry and artillery veered toward Johnson's Ranch at the southern edge of Camas Prairie, the cavalry continuing along the road to Grangeville and Mount Idaho in a move meant to show the flag and uplift the spirits of the settlers gathered there. The following day as civilian scouts kept watch over warriors distantly visible across the Salmon River, the cavalry descended White Bird Canyon and began the miserable task of burying the dead.

After nine days of stultifying heat mixed with occasional rain the bodies tended to fall apart at the touch and release odors that would gag the hardest man. The best method the unlucky soldiers detailed to the duty could improvise was to quickly scratch a shallow hole adjacent to the corpse, roll it in and cover the remains with dirt and rocks. Amazingly, troopers searching for bodies found settler Jack Manuel, one of the victims of the June 14 rampage, in the outhouse of his ranch, clinging to life despite his wounds and twelve days of starvation.

After locating and interring the last of the remains on the twenty-seventh, the column moved on to the Salmon River. Warriors across the current shouted insults at the Christian Nez Perce scouts leading the way. Desultory gunfire followed, but no one on either side was hit. That evening four companies of artillery, and one of infantry that had departed Fort Vancouver on the twenty-first, arrived. With about 400 men now gathered, General Howard

149

felt confident he could engage and defeat the nontreaty bands. With only three rowboats available, he began the tedious process of ferrying his troops across the Salmon River at Horseshoe Bend as warriors watched from bluffs thousands of feet above.

On June 29, Howard made a monumental blunder. He ordered Captain Steven Whipple to take his and Captain Winters' company of cavalry and the battery of Gatling guns to arrest Looking Glass and his people at their village on the reservation. The captain was then to turn the captives and their livestock over to tender mercies of the citizens of Mount Idaho. In *The Flight of the Nez Perce*, historian Mark Brown did a fine job of dissecting the general's various self-serving explanations—more correctly, obfuscations—and put together a likely account of events. Although Howard later claimed that treaty Nez Perce had asked him to act because Looking Glass was about to join the nontreaty bands, Brown traced the false rumors back to Mount Idaho itself. It seems a group of men there cleverly concocted a ruse to use the army to help them confiscate Looking Glass' considerable horse and cattle herd. The general fell for it hook, line and sinker. In reality Looking Glass wanted nothing to do with a fight against U.S. troops.[4]

I turn north at Grangeville, away from White Bird Canyon. After a few miles the highway hairpins down into the canyon of the South Fork of the Clearwater River, a stream whose crystalline waters do justice to its name. The winding, picturesque drive under the narrow canyon walls takes me past the mouth of Cottonwood Creek, where the non-treaty bands had initially sought refuge, to the town of Kooskia (pronounced koos-kee) at the juncture of the South and Middle Forks of the Clearwater. A mile east is a federal salmon hatchery on the right, or eastern, bank of the north-flowing Clear Creek. I hope to see the fish, but the concrete tanks are empty. This time of year the smolts are already struggling past the gauntlet of dams on the Snake River, stalling in the lakes, getting chewed in the turbines and falling prey to squaw fish. Across Clear Creek a wooded bluff rises abruptly. That's where the Captain Whipple and his soldiers appeared.

Although Looking Glass spent much of his time in the buffalo country, some of his people were stay-at-homes. Gardens of corn and potatoes and melons and cucumber flourished on the periphery of the camp. There must have been several hundred people here on July 1, a Sunday. In addition to the Looking Glass band the families of several other minor bands had gathered, those of Red Owl, Red Heart, Timpoosman and Kilkil Choosling. All were opposed to war and had come together to talk and stay out of harm's way.

In 1930 McWhorter visited this place with an elderly warrior named Bird Alighting. Bird Alighting had been sitting in Looking Glass' teepee that July morning as the chief ate breakfast. When the cavalry and about twenty Mount Idaho volunteers rode over the bluff and stopped in sight of the village, the chief asked Bird Alighting to deliver a message: we are peaceful, leave us alone. The young warrior did as requested, but one of the volunteers jammed the business end of a rifle in his gut in response. Another volunteer who spoke some Nez Perce told the warrior to bring Looking Glass. Bird Alighting hurried back across the creek. The chief ordered that a white flag be raised on a pole, but he wasn't about to go to the bluff and be poked with a rifle, or worse. Again, Bird Alighting made the trip, this time in the company of an elder named Kalowet. Both men implored the whites to leave the village alone. The volunteer, whom Bird Alighting suspected was drunk, again stuck his rifle in the young warrior's stomach. Finally, one of the army officers and two or three troopers and the civilian interpreter rode with Bird Alighting and Kalowet into the village. No sooner had they reined in their horses near the white flag than a shot fired by a Mount Idaho volunteer rang out from across the river. Red Heart fell wounded. As the officer and his men dashed back toward their compatriots, several volleys poured into the village. Luckily for the Real People, the whites were lousy shots. Among all the people fleeing pell-mell from the camp, only Bird Alighting, Broken Leg and Black Raven were hit, the latter fatally. A young woman carrying her baby drowned as she tried swimming the Clearwater River to safety. The soldiers and volunteers trashed the village and gardens and attempted, mostly unsuccessfully, to burn the teepees. After rounding up some 700

151

horses and all the cattle they could find, they returned, the civilians gloating, to Mount Idaho. Howard's prediction that Looking Glass intended to join the warring bands would shortly become self-fulfilling.

I return to Grangeville, and by noon I'm barreling down White Bird Canyon on the new highway above the battlefield. At Salmon River I take a narrow bridge across the torrent and begin a tedious hairpin climb up a gravel county road. Eventually, I'm rewarded with a stunning view: the river a blue and white and green ribbon shrinking and shrinking until it's thousands of feet below; the ravines and slopes of the knife-edge ridge separating Salmon and White Bird canyons perfectly revealed in the clarity of the light; the Seven Devils Mountains to the south and the Clearwater Mountains to the east. I stop the van and get out to stretch. Add the smell of dirt and wildflowers, the silence, and I think I'm in heaven.

By July 2 Howard's army was across the Salmon five miles upriver from here and had been joined by Trimble's company from Slate Creek. With Perry's remnant of a company delegated to guarding a pack train trudging from Fort Lapwai to Mount Idaho and Whipple and Winter off antagonizing Looking Glass, Trimble's company became the only cavalry unit with the column. They forged to the head of the line and took the lead. In a way.

As you might have noticed already and you'll surely see throughout this narrative, the actual vanguard into dangerous terrain was a squad of scouts from whatever native tribe was available. Next in line, usually, were civilian volunteers who found it temporarily thrilling to be part of a war, many reliving what they remembered as the glory days of the Civil War. Accounts left by these individuals often described themselves as being captains or some other commissioned rank. I've yet to find one who called himself a private. If no native scouts were available the civilians took the point. After them came the real army units. Such a line of march made sense in several ways. The tribal scouts and civilians would have possessed greater knowledge of the countryside than soldiers recruited from some eastern city. Native scouts, of course, would have been adept at finding and interpreting sign found along the trail, the white civilians somewhat less so. I suspect, also, that army officers considered Indians and civilians somewhat more expendable than regular soldiers. If an ambush lay ahead and not all the point men made it out safely, well, the regulars following up would do their best to exact revenge.

The drizzle of July 2 turned to rain as Trimble's company reached the top of the canyon at nightfall after losing two pack mules to falls from the slippery trail during the day. Most of the command spent a miserable night strung out along the muddy path, huddled under wet blankets on whatever patch of semi-level ground they could find. As the bulk of the column struggled out of the canyon on the third, the scouts and cavalry reconnoitered the plateau between the Salmon River and the Snake River to the west. The broad, three-day-old trail left by the non-treaty bands split after a few miles, one continuing north toward a ford across the Salmon River and back to Camas Prairie, the other to the northwest and the Snake River at Dug Bar. Treaty Nez Perce later told officers at Fort Lapwai that the band leaders had disagreed in council as to the proper course of action. Thunder Rising had argued for a dash to the Wallowa country where they would fight it out once and for all. White Goose and Grating Sound had urged a return to Camas Prairie and continued evasion. The scouts discovered that the two trails reunited after a few miles and turned toward Camas Prairie, mute testimony to the result of the deliberations. Several of McWhorter's informants, though, denied any dissension among the bands. The two trails could simply be explained as a temporary separation to provide adequate water and forage. At any rate by July 2 the bands had recrossed the Salmon at Craig's Ferry, again placing that formidable natural barrier between the families and the soldiers.[5]

The Fourth of July brought no fireworks for the soldiers struggling behind the nontreaty bands. It did bring a courier and a rumor of a squad of cavalry cut off and killed on Camas Prairie near the Lapwai-Mount Idaho road. Howard ordered his volunteers, led by Ed McConville, to hustle across the Salmon to support Captain Whipple, who had moved his two companies of cavalry to

Cottonwood after his foray against Looking Glass. Howard continued to dog the actual trail of the Real People.

This plateau isn't as flat as it seemed at first sight. It's incised by drainages and pocked with hills and ridges. Stands of pine mix with open country. I bet those scouts were pretty cautious riding through here. I won't be taking you to the ford used by the Nee-Me-Poo on the second of July. There's supposed to be some sort of track down to there, but it's nothing my van can negotiate. The only bridge across the Salmon that will take me back to Camas Prairie is some twenty-five river miles upstream from there at the mouth of Rocky Canyon. It's the same spot McConville chose to cross his eighteen volunteers over the river. Here I go another time, down an insane series of switchbacks. I'm beginning to feel sorry for the horses and mules of 1877. Once across the bridge and headed up Rock Creek, I'm on a paved road, albeit one with potholes worthy of individual names on the map. I'm glad oncoming traffic's non-existent; I'm swerving my van from one lane to another to avoid the biggest of the pits. More fun than any video game.

I pull over at the Weis Rockshelter. According to archaeologists it was home to over 200 generations of humans. It's not really a cave, more like an eroded gap under an overhang of basalt. Water dripping from the ceiling provides a clue as to its creation. It looks awfully damp inside, not my idea of a great abode. Still, the folks who lived here for 7,400 years until 600 years ago must have discovered charms not immediately apparent. Were they here all year long, or did they move with the seasons? It's too small to hold much more than an extended family. Did generation after generation of the same family live here, or did some fade away to be replaced by others? The shelter's darkness holds secrets.

Howard reached the Craig's Ferry crossing of the Salmon River late on the fifth. The ferry boat, naturally, was nowhere in sight, and the general found himself confronting one hundred yards of roiling water. On the opposite bank two treaty Nez Perce plunged their horses into the torrent. Emerging dripping, they informed Howard that Lieutenant Sevier Rains, ten soldiers and two civilian scouts indeed were dead, and Captain Whipple had been skirmishing with warriors all day. At that very moment the non-treaty bands were crossing Camas Prairie for a rendezvous with a seriously peeved Looking Glass. One white scout kicked his recalcitrant horse into the river to test the current. A few seconds in the swift water convinced the rider that dry land was the place to be. The Nee-Me-Poo might be able to cross the river with ease, but the army was going nowhere unless someone came up with a brilliant idea.

I can imagine Howard, his officers clustered about him, standing at the edge of the river saying, darn it, darn it. darn it. A few of his subordinates might have wandered away and uttered stronger expletives before returning to the Christian General.

Lieutenant Harry Otis of the Fourth Artillery came up with the brilliant idea. A gang of soldiers spent the evening tearing down the nearby cabin of a friendly Nez Perce named Luke Billy. From its logs they fashioned a raft held together with lariats. Tying more lariats together end to end, they came up with a rope long enough to stretch across the river. Once the first passengers had paddled to the far bank, Otis reasoned, the rope could be used to haul the raft back and forth. The maiden voyage took place the morning of the sixth. Otis received the honor of being admiral and shoved off with a doughty crew of six. A knot on the long rope slipped, as other officers had already predicted, and Otis and company became some of the first recreational rafters on the River of No Return. Some hours later the soaked and abashed lieutenant and crew slunk back into camp after a three-mile ride and equally long hike, his naval career at an end. Howard had already ordered an about-face. By July 8 the column had successfully recrossed the Salmon at White Bird and found themselves at the same spot they had camped on June 27. The general had been seriously outwitted and embarrassed.

After another night at Winchester Lake I'm up bright and early, rolling into Cottonwood. Low bluffs on the east and southwest overlook the sleepy town where Norton's Ranch and stage stop stood in 1877. Captain Whipple arrived here on July 2, one day after his attack on Looking Glass and the same day the non-treaty bands recrossed the Salmon River fifteen miles away at Craig's Ferry. General Howard had two motives for placing the cavalry companies here: reconnaissance and, more importantly, protection for a supply train making its way from Fort Lapwai with Perry's reduced and demoralized Company "F" as its only escort.

That evening the troopers dug breastworks on the bluffs above the ranch and sighted their Gatling guns outward. The following day Whipple asked two civilians to scout toward Craig's Ferry. In the afternoon only one, William Foster, lathered his horse back into camp. He and Charles Blewett had run into a warrior named Red Spy, the resulting exchange of gunfire proving fatal to Blewett. Whipple ordered his command to prepare to move, except for a detail of twenty men who would remain with the Gatling guns and in the breastworks. Lieutenant Sevier Rains, civilian Foster and ten troopers formed an advance party. Captain Whipple cautioned the green lieutenant to keep to high ground and retreat at the first sign of hostiles. The rest of the soldiers were still saddling and moving into formation five minutes later when the crackle of gunfire erupted from the direction Rains and his squad had disappeared. The sound lasted only a few minutes.

I turn out of Cottonwood on a county road leading to the Northern Idaho Correctional Institution. Two miles later in rising, rolling country of mixed meadow and forest on the lower reaches of Craig Mountain I pass William Foster's grave. In a pasture just ahead, a jumble of innocuous boulders catches my eye, and I pull over on a side lane.

The shootout between Red Spy and Charlie Blewett had attracted a number of warriors, including Five Wounds, Rainbow, Yellow Wolf and Two Moons. Lieutenant Rains, only a year out of West Point, perhaps too eager for glory, maybe just raw, led his detachment right into their gunsights. Warriors shot six out of their saddles. The remainder took cover behind the rocks in the pasture. While Strong Eagle decoyed the soldiers, other warriors circled a low ridge north of the rocks and finished off the doomed bluecoats with one irregular volley. It was over in no time, and twelve more rifles fell into the hands of the Nee-Me-Poo.[6]

A pickup with two men in the cab and a couple more in back roars down the road from the direction of the Correctional Institution. It turns out to be a posse of sorts. The vehicle skids to a stop near me, and a tall fellow in his late fifties jumps out of the cab and bluntly asks me my business here. After I tell him, he nods and asks me to move my van. They have a fugitive to catch. He points farther up the side lane. A cow I hadn't noticed before peers at us from around the corner of a small house, aware the jig is up, I suppose. Relaxed now that he knows I'm not a cattle rustler, the rancher tells me that fifteen years ago two men from Montana swept the area around the rocks with a metal detector. About fifty feet from the rocks they found what they thought was conclusive evidence, buried four or five inches in the soil, of the spot where Lieutenant Rains fell. Watched 'em myself, he says. I ask if he knows what artifacts they uncovered. He shakes his head. By now the heifer is down the lane and trotting in the direction of its own correctional institute. As the rancher jumps into the pickup, he points to a gate at the far side of the pasture and tells me I'm free to take a look around. I wander among the boulders, thinking of a remarkable story.

The warriors found a soldier leaning against one of the rocks. He had been shot once in the head and twice in the chest, but still lived, making a clucking sound, wiping blood from his face, looking around in agony. The warriors felt sorry for him and discussed among themselves what to do. They decided the white warrior was much like them. Unlike most whites, they decided, this one had a Wyakin, the personal power given by the Creator. He was calling his Wyakin with the clucking noises. They finally agreed that the man's injuries were mortal and he should not suffer more. They killed him with respect.[7]

Captain Whipple was too late, of course, by a few minutes. His seventy-five troopers and the warriors faced each other from a half-mile apart, but nothing much happened. As darkness fell both groups retreated, one jubilant, the other distraught. The following morning Whipple and Perry hooked up and brought the supply train safely into Cottonwood. As senior officer, Captain Perry took command and decided against continuing across Camas Prairie. He had already suffered one disastrous encounter with warriors and was not eager for another. The rest of the day must have been a nervous one for the isolated soldiers as warriors circled at a safe distance, probing, taunting, preparing the way for the families of the Real People. Early on the morning of July 5, the Nee-Me-Poo families began their dash across Camas Prairie to the South Fork of the Clearwater River where, this time, Looking Glass was waiting for them with open arms. Simultaneously, seventeen citizens from Mount Idaho decided the time was right to ride to the aid of the troops at Mount Idaho. Bad idea.

Now I'm at a turnout about a mile on the other side of Cottonwood from the site of the Rains fight. This is typical Camas Prairie, a quiet sea of grass with swells that appear innocuous until you realize a tall man could easily disappear in one of the swales. Nearby is a stone which lists the names of the citizens from Mount Idaho.

Led by "Captain" D. B. Randall, the seventeen had crossed most of the prairie, keeping their mounts at an easy canter, when they sighted the Nee-Me-Poo family caravan. The whites watched it pass well to the south near Rocky Canyon. The main body of Nez Perce fighters kept close to the families while other squads variously scouted ahead, observed the soldiers holed up at Cottonwood, watched for trouble from Mount Idaho and kept an eye on the trail from White Bird Canyon. About fifteen warriors detached themselves to handle the threat from Randall and his volunteers. One group dropped from their ponies and prepared an ambush, another lining up across the road to Cottonwood. Randall shouted an order to charge through their line. The stunt took the warriors by surprise, and the line parted. A frantic ride across the prairie ensued, men on each side firing from racing ponies, the warriors from the ambush party belatedly joining the chase. A bullet winged White Cloud in the thigh and killed his horse. Frank Vansise's mount dropped, too, but Henry Johnson, following behind, stopped long enough to scoop him up. D. H. Hauser was hit in the chest but managed somehow to stay atop his horse. The wound would eventually prove fatal. When both Randall and his mount were shot, the volunteers halted, only a mile and a half from safety at Cottonwood. Taking command, Lew Wilmot dispatched two men to hurry on to the army camp for assistance. Warriors pressed close until one of the whites felled a middle-aged man named Wounded Mouth. The seventeen were no longer a threat to the families, so the warriors backed off, wishing to avoid further casualties. A long-distance sniping contest followed, lasting at least an hour, maybe longer. Sometime during the fight Nez Perce bullets killed Ben Evans and wounded another volunteer. Wilmot later claimed to have fired his rifle seventy-six times, all the while wondering where in hell was the cavalry?

The sound of the gunfire during the chase carried all the way to Cottonwood where Captain Perry watched the distant action from the bluff to the east of the ranch. He muttered that whoever was out there would not last a minute, that anyone should know better than to travel Camas Prairie at a time like this. As the gunfire diminished, Perry turned and walked away. George Shearer, the civilian who had fought beside Perry at White Bird, heard the officer say that he couldn't bear to watch any more, that the sight of it made him sick. Shortly after, the two riders dispatched by Wilmot galloped into Cottonwood, but Perry was convinced that the slackened fire meant the others still out there were goners. He refused to send a relief party.

Perry reasoned that if he detailed a force large enough to defend itself on the open prairie, the remaining soldiers would be inadequate to guard the vital supply train should warriors choose to assault Cottonwood. His orders were to deliver the train safely to General Howard, and he would not jeopardize that mission. The crackle of occasional rifle fire continued and continued. Finally, George Shearer saddled his horse, commenting that he might be a damned fool for going out there, but at least he was no damned coward. Perry relented and ordered Captain Whipple to proceed cautiously with about forty troopers and a Gatling gun. The relief force reached the beleaguered civilians at mid-afternoon, the remaining warriors withdrawing with a few parting shots, one of

159

which left George Shearer on foot. D. B. Randall died from his wound just as the soldiers arrived.

The final casualty of the skirmish was Captain Perry's reputation. Idaho newspapers soon filled with letters and editorials questioning his judgment and bravery. Lew Wilmot, for one, was hopping mad that assistance had taken so long, and Yellow Wolf commented to McWhorter that even the warriors were surprised at the length of time it took for soldiers to appear. Although a Court of Inquiry would eventually exonerate him of misconduct, Perry would never regain the trust of the settlers of Camas Prairie and Mount Idaho.[8]

I head due east on gravel roads for Cottonwood Creek and its confluence with the South Fork of the Clearwater. Several white accounts of the Camas Prairie skirmish estimated the number of warriors engaged in the hundreds and Nee-Me-Poo casualties as high as thirty. It's a fine example of the exaggeration and outright lies I've found so common as I've looked into the war. Every adult male in the non-treaty bands from the age of fifteen to ninety would have to have been present to account for that many fighters, a ridiculous notion. The warriors had a number of possible threats to contend with as the families crossed the prairie, and the idea that every able-bodied Nee-Me-Poo male took off after Randall and his buddies just doesn't hold water. The thirty casualties would have been twice as many as the entire number of warriors actually present.

Twenty crooked miles following section lines brings me to the bluffs overlooking the South Fork of the Clearwater, the defile cut by Cottonwood Creek to my left. The non-treaty bands, joined by Looking Glass, camped along the river and creek bottom from July 5 until the twelfth, resting while the chiefs counseled. Atop the bluff across the river I can see a flat piece of ground a little over a mile square defined on the north and south by wooded ravines. That's where General Howard finally got his chance for a battle on July 11. First, though, you need to know what Lew Wilmot and the rest of the volunteers were up to between the fifth and the eleventh.

I descend the bluff to State Highway 13 and turn north for

twelve miles past the fork of the Clearwater to the Heart of the Monster and Kamiah. County Road 62 takes me back up the bluffs west of town. I backtrack south until I find two hills about four miles northwest of the fork of the Clearwater. The hill closer to the river is named Misery.

By July 8 Perry, the pack train, the three cavalry companies and the volunteers had crossed Camas Prairie to Grangeville, meeting Howard and the vanguard of the army column returning from their fruitless jaunt through the Salmon River country. All was not well that day in nearby Mount Idaho. Citizen Eugene Wilson had shot a volunteer from Dayton, Washington, during a drunken dispute, and friends of the wounded man were talking of a lynching party. Cooler heads decided it would be prudent to get the volunteers out of town, and the call went out for an impromptu scout down the South Fork of the Clearwater River. About seventy-five men responded. Such a majestic force required more than a mere captain, so Ed McConville of Lewiston found himself elected "Colonel." Mounted on horses stolen from Looking Glass, the volunteers departed town on the eighth. Incredibly, they managed to miss the trail of the Real People down Cottonwood Creek, and nightfall found the whites on the hills above the fork of the Clearwater near present-day Kooskia, some five miles beyond the nontreaty camp.

That night they thought they heard drums coming from the area of the river fork. Lew Wilmot, fresh from the Cottonwood fight, would later write that at first light he and "Captain" James Cearley crept to the edge of a bluff overlooking the fork. There they:

> . . . counted 72 teepees. We counted over 150 horses tied at different places around the teepees. Soon life began to show. First squaws began to come out. Fires began to start and once in a while men began to move around. Boys began to start out onto the hills on the opposite side of the river. Finally we went back to our camp and reported.[9]

McConville ordered a courier to return to Mount Idaho to

161

inform General Howard that the hostiles had been located. L. P. Brown wrote to Alonzo Leland, the editor of the Lewiston *Teller*:

> *Yesterday Capts. Hunter, McConville and Cearley left with 80 men for the Clearwater to ascertain where the Indians are. By messenger who has returned from them they found the Indians in force at the forks of the Clearwater on the east side of the South Fork. They learned from a Kamia Indian that they had a large drove of stock on the north side of the Middle Fork, which indicates they are to fall back towards the Lolo Fork trail. The volunteer companies mentioned before are camped back from the river opposite the Mouth of the Middle Fork, and are waiting the arrival of General Howard's force . . .*[10]

With that intelligence in hand Howard quickly formed a plan. He would march his column down the east side of the Clearwater, ending up on the bluffs above the fork and the nontreaty camp. The unseasonable rains of the past two weeks had swollen the rivers, and the hostiles would be trapped with high water at their backs. Howard sent George Shearer and a few more volunteers to apprise McConville of the line of march and plan of attack. As the army column fell upon the Nez Perce camp, McConville and his men would descend to the west bank of the Clearwater and mop up those that might escape across the river. A plan classic in its simplicity with only one problem: Wilmot and Cearley had given Howard the wrong location.

I can't imagine how Wilmot and Cearley could have got it so wrong, except to conjecture that after leaving the volunteer camp the two didn't actually go as far as the bluff overlooking the river. I would have been scared, too. Wilmot later wrote that he was convinced as early as the evening before that the non-treaty bands had to be at the river fork. Why put oneself in unnecessary danger by getting too close to so many warriors? Just stay out of sight of the rest of the volunteers long enough to make it look good, then report back with a few juicy details like the number of teepees you saw. In one of his reminiscences Wilmot offered the lame suggestion that the non-treaty bands subsequently moved their camp upriver to Cottonwood Creek where Howard actually found them. That's not what the Nee-Me-Poo said.[11]

Mid-morning of the ninth one of the volunteers accidentally discharged his big .50 caliber Springfield rifle. Two Nee-Me-Poo happened to be riding within earshot and investigated. Sighting the volunteers, the two spun their horses and galloped away. The whites realized instantly they were in for it and hustled for the top of a nearby hill, the one they would soon call Misery. About twenty warriors showed up first, but contented themselves with climbing the adjacent hill, scoping out the nature of the threat and shouting taunts at the volunteers busy digging holes and piling rocks. As the day progressed more warriors appeared and encircled the hill at a safe distance. When George Shearer and his companion messengers came into view about twenty volunteers dashed on horseback down the open south face of Misery Hill and escorted them back to safety. The warriors were biding their time until darkness. After hearing Shearer's report McConville dispatched Lew Wilmot and Ben Penny to Howard with the news that the volunteers had been discovered. McConville added a request that the general light a bonfire at the onset of the attack on the village so the volunteers could coordinate their attack with the army's. The two departed shortly after nightfall without incident.

A gravel road descends the ravine between the hills, and I ease in my clutch and let the van roll down. The forested north hillside of Misery Hill comes into view. This is where the warriors struck about midnight.

Led by Rainbow, Five Wounds and Frog, a party of warriors crept up through the brush and pine as others began a covering fire from the adjacent hilltop. Most of the volunteers laid low, but a few popped their heads up to return fire. One warrior likened the whole thing to a nighttime fireworks show. The warriors in the trees found it a simple matter to slip among the citizen horse herd and liberate fifty animals. One Nez Perce named Paktilek lost a finger to a volunteer bullet as he was leading away two mounts, the only casualty the Nee-Me-Poo suffered. With the whites now unhorsed the warriors backed off, content with the knowledge the volunteers no longer posed a threat to the camp. About noon the following day, seeing that the warriors had withdrawn, McConville ordered his men to stack their saddles on the remaining animals, and the citizens began the long walk back toward Mount Idaho, taking care to stay well away from the river.

A story has sprouted that the volunteers departed Misery Hill at exactly the same moment that General Howard discovered the actual site of the Nee-Me-Poo camp at Cottonwood Creek on July 11. It makes for a touching example of historical synchronicity, except that it seems not to be true. Wilmot's *Misery Hill* manuscript makes clear that he and Ben Penny arrived at Howard's camp on the morning of the tenth, a date confirmed in Michael McCarthy's diary. There Wilmot spotted Captain Perry and, remembering Perry's reluctance to go to the aid of D. B. Randall's crew on Camas Prairie, threw a conniption fit. After cussing out both Perry and General Howard and being threatened with arrest, Wilmot returned to Misery Hill, arriving about 11 P.M. on the June 10 to find the hilltop abandoned.[12]

As I make my way down to Kamiah and retrace my route south along the river, I ponder what was going on in the Nez Perce camp in the days since arriving at Cottonwood Creek on July 5. This was the longest pause they would make at any one location during the entire campaign, and it seems a dangerous one. It's plausible the chiefs were already discussing a proposal put forth by Looking Glass. In 1873 he and a few of his warriors had fought on the side of the Crows in the buffalo country of Montana against a larger war party of Lakota and helped win a victory that drove the Lakota from Crow territory. At that time Crow chiefs and leading warriors had promised Looking Glass that they would help the Real People if ever push came to shove with the United States government. Five Wounds and Rainbow, just returned from the buffalo country, reported that the Crows continued to avow their support. Looking Glass' proposal, if indeed it was made during this time, surely would have created dissension among the bands. Meanwhile, the warriors were inexplicably lax in scouting the country around the Cottonwood camp. Probably they were expecting any approach to come from their back trail across Camas

Prairie. Had they been more thorough, they would have easily discovered General Howard's column bivouacked almost at their back door on the night of July 10, a mere six miles away on the bluffs east of the river.

Which is where I'm headed. I return to Kamiah and turn south again past the forks to Cottonwood Creek. Back and forth. I'm beginning to think of myself as a human yo-yo today, but such is the lot of the intrepid storyteller. I continue on for eight miles to the tiny burg of Harpster. In 1877 it was called Jackson, and a bridge here allowed Howard to cross his units over the churning Clearwater. I turn east and begin to climb. Here among the hills and draws above the river Howard paused until his army, still strung-out from the tedious recrossing of the Salmon River at White Bird, gathered.

By the evening of the tenth Howard's force consisted of four cavalry companies, six infantry companies and five artillery companies with the latter mostly consigned to infantry duty. Including scouts, both Nez Perce and white, and packers, the column would boast some 500 men and stretch for well over a mile in length. The following morning Howard gave the order to march on the enemy camp he confidently thought to be at the fork of the Clearwater.

I zig and zag northward again, roughly following the route the column followed that day. This is broken terrain, a broad ridge top with a mix of pine forest and field. It's really quite pretty, some of the fields nice and square, others contoured, this one a lush green, that one a shorn yellow. It reminds me of something Van Gogh might have turned into one of his remarkable landscapes. Off to the right is the canyon formed by Clear Creek, to the left the one formed by the South Fork. Dead ahead is the fork of the Clearwater.

The scouts and cavalry at head of the column had probed to within three miles of their destination with no sign of the Nee-Me-Poo ahead, naturally, when Howard's aide-de-camp, Lieutenant Robert Fletcher, on a whim loped his horse to the edge of the bluff overlooking the South Fork. Fletcher looked back upriver and was

165

stunned. The entire column had already passed the nontreaty camp which was about a mile and a half south. He gesticulated frantically, drawing the general's attention, who rode to the top of the precipice and saw with his own eyes. At about the same time four warriors guided their mounts up the bluff. It only took them a second to realize what was up, and Many Coyotes whipped his horse down the slope to warn the Real People that danger was imminent. Howard later wrote:

> *I rode to the bluff to the left, where Fletcher was, and saw plainly the hostiles, who, judging from their motions, had just discovered our approach. By one o'clock a howitzer and two Gatling guns, manned by a detachment under Lieutenant Otis, Fourth Artillery, were firing towards the masses of Indians below. The Indians were running their horses up the south fork of the Clearwater, on both banks, near the river, and driving their stock, as fast as possible, beyond our range.*[13]

The shells fell well short of the Nee-Me-Poo camp where the chiefs were dividing the fighters into three units, two to linger until they could determine the course of the upcoming battle, one to meet the soldiers head-on. Grating Sound led the twenty men of the last group up the bluff.

A century of farming has turned this battlefield from a rock-strewn benchland into flattened fields which mask the details of terrain as it once was. Today I turn short of the ravine cut by Rabbit Creek and follow a winding lane, hoping to find a good overview of the ground on which the battle occurred. No luck. Back at the road along the ridge top I continue north. Here I find a fair view of the fields where the major portion of the battle took place, but that's not what I'm looking for right now. Another side road takes me closer to the river, and I slow my van to a crawl with periodic stops, peering for a view similar to one witnessed by McWhorter when he visited here with elderly Yellow Wolf. A teenager on a bike pedals by, staring at me curiously. Finally, at the ravine at the northern edge of the battlefield, I think I see the area where Grating Sound and his men, racing this direction, deflected the advance of the army.

On the advice of Ad Chapman, Howard ordered the command to reverse direction rather than attempt to descend directly to the river. The most feasible route down from the heights lay several miles to the rear at Rabbit Creek. The general instructed Winter's company of cavalry to escort the howitzer and Gatling guns in a hurry to the bluff directly above the Nee-Me-Poo camp. Captains Perry and Whipple were also to take their cavalry to the new point of attack to the south, while Trimble's troopers remained as a rear guard. Meanwhile, the rear of the column had already become the van, and the first soldiers Grating Sound and his few men encountered were infantry. While four held the horses in the ravine, the remaining warriors crawled ahead and opened fire, Grating Sound with an old muzzle-loader. Yellow Wolf later said:

> *Soldiers were strung out a long ways and advancing.*
> *Some were close to us. Indians and soldiers fighting—almost*
> *together. We could not count the soldiers. There must have*
> *been hundreds. Bullets came thicker and thicker.*

The Nee-Me-Poo could not hold their position without being wiped out, and Grating Sound ordered them to retreat. It must have been rough. Yellow Wolf, never one to exaggerate, admitted to McWhorter, "I thought it my last day."[14] But he and the others had bought enough time for the rest of the warriors to respond.

At Rabbit Creek the second contingent of forty or so warriors led by Rainbow had arrayed themselves among rocks along the edge of the ravine and prepared to blunt the army advance once and for all. Against a force with huge superiority in numbers they succeeded with the advantage of their cover in contrast to the mostly open terrain the soldiers were forced to traverse. The third bunch of warriors circled east in a flanking maneuver. General Howard on the second and third groups of warriors:

> *Around the head of the ravine our distance was over a*
> *mile, the enemy having less than a third to go. So beyond the*

*second bluff we found Joseph and his people, dismounted,
and already in position, on our approach, while some thirty
or forty mounted Indians had galloped just beyond our range,
to compass our left . . . My line I extended to the left by the
cavalry, and to the right by the infantry and artillery battalions, gradually refusing my flanks, until the whole bluff was
enveloped.*[15]

The maneuver wasn't as neatly executed as Howard suggested.
Lieutenant Harry Bailey of the Twenty-First Infantry had this to
say:

*I saw that the artillery and my company, and some others,
were jumping up and shooting at each other, at a range of
some one hundred to two hundred yards. Although bullets
were flying, I rushed out between the artillery and my own
company, yelling, "Cease firing! You are firing into your own
men!*[16]

The detachment of warriors circling east across the plateau
found a juicy target, a small, straggling train of three mules and
men coming from the south in a desperate attempt to overtake the
main army force. Easy pickings. Howard sent the cavalry of Perry
and Whipple to their aid, too late. The warriors continued on after
killing one teamster and making off with the loads of two mules
bearing ammunition. Well over a mile to the north, those same
Nee-Me-Poo spotted the main supply train. Taking it would have
been a great victory and something to boast about around campfires to come, but Trimble's rear-guard cavalry and another company of artillery arrived just in time to surround the braying
mules and their frightened guides and lead them to the safety of
Howard closing wings.

Howard at first tried to form part of his circle near the edge of
the bluff where his two howitzers and two Gatling guns could rake
the village, but desperate charges by warriors, both mounted and
on foot, to within yards of the big guns forced a retreat from the
brink. Counter-charges by the infantry and artillery units pushed
warriors back from the army line. By late afternoon the opposing

sides had settled into positions as much as a quarter-mile apart. Most warriors occupied the south edge of the plateau along the lip of Rabbit Creek ravine with a sporadic cordon on the other three sides. The army position consisted of entrenchments almost a half-mile in diameter in the center of the plateau. The four cavalry companies manned the northern and eastern portion of the line, leaving the more dangerous southern and western sides to the infantry and artillery with their longer and more accurate rifles. A barricade of supply boxes and saddles in the center of the circle provided a haven for General Howard.

Michael McCarthy's diary provides a sense of those hours:

> We could not see what was going on, but there was one continual peal of musketry and the howitzers and gatlings were being used freely, and the yells of the Indians, shoutings of our men and the brayings of our packmules made a terrible din. For a while the Indians covered with their fire the only water accessible. It was a spring in the hollow we had crossed and was about 200 hundred yards in front of our side of the line. The hospital attendants came down, looking for water for the wounded, but were afraid to venture to the spring. A man of my Company (Fowler) the same man who gave me a lift at White Bird, went down and filled the canteens, and brought me some also. We were terribly thirsty by this time. The hospital attendants said that there was a great many killed and wounded. The day wore along but we were yet all right on our side, nobody hurt. About sundown the firing became dreadful heavy and the yells of the Indians something terrific. This continued until about 9PM. Some Indian was haranguing the warriors, and his voice could be heard above the din of the battle. He kept it up long after the firing had slackened, which it did about ten o'clock.[17]

As the afternoon wore on this was what it was like for Yellow Wolf at the southeastern extremity of the Nez Perce defenses:

> I came where four men were fighting. They were my uncle, Old Yellow Wolf, Otstotpoo, Howwallits (Mean Man), and

169

Tomyunmene. The three older men's faces were bleeding. Rock chips from flying bullets were doing the work. These warriors had rifle pits among some boulders. Not too big, the rocks, but about the right size for concealment. I dropped down behind one of them. We were now five, all fighting in thick smoke. Like smoke rolling up from burning woods. . . . Most shooting was now from the whites. I heard the cannon guns and was scared. I lay close to the ground. I did not know to shoot or not. . . . Soldiers, armed, were about thirty steps from me. I grew mad to see them so close. I showed myself brave. I now was not afraid of death. From between the boulder rocks, I pushed my rifle. I fought like a man, firing five or six shots. [18]

And Roaring Eagle:

There were around thirty of us, all stripped for battle. When we made the mount the chief called, "Forward!" We made a charge but not as soldier cavalry. In this battle I put myself as a brave man where we stood our ground the best we could. We pushed those soldiers back on the pack-saddle fort, where General Howard stayed with his chief officers, away from bullet danger. But we could not stand before the soldiers' big guns. We were forced back from that part of the field. The Indian way of fighting is not to get killed. Killed today, there can be no fighting tomorrow. [19]

Thomas Sutherland, a newspaper correspondent:

Wishing to enjoy all the experiences of a soldier, I took a rifle and crept out to the front line of pickets prepared to take notes and scalps. My solicitude in the former direction was nearly nipped in the bud, for the moment I inquisitively popped up my head, a whine and thud of bullets in my proximity and a very peremptory order to "lie down, you ——— fool." taught me that hugging mother earth with my teeth in the dirt was the only attitude to assume while in that vicinity. [20]

170

Sometime during the afternoon a Nez Perce army scout named Joe Albert made a dash on his pony across no-man's-land and reached the Nee-Me-Poo line, unscathed despite gunfire from both sides. His father had been the sole casualty among the Real People during the skirmish on Camas Prairie with Randall's volunteers. Once among his kin Joe Albert stripped his blue clothes from his body and again became Elaskolatat, Animal Entering A Hole. He refused to find a hole and hide, becoming one of six warriors seriously wounded during the battle. Yellow Wolf told McWhorter that Animal Entering a Hole proved himself a brave fighter.

Sunset found General Howard in an embarrassing position. About 100 warriors had surrounded and pinned down his far larger force. While the soldiers dug deeper in the rocky earth and Howard and his staff pondered their next move, many warriors took advantage of the darkness to return to the village and their families.

As I prowl the perimeter of the plateau, I encounter the teenage bike rider again and stop to talk with him. He eagerly volunteers information about entrenchments he's found, including more than a few in improbable directions. Three horseback riders stop and chat with me. Two profess total ignorance of the past, but one woman tells me that, yes, a battle did occur here. She points in the right direction.

I find it incomprehensible that the Real People failed to take advantage of the efforts of their warriors. The teepees remained in place through the afternoon, evening, night and following day, the children and women and old folks vulnerable. What were the chiefs thinking? That the soldiers were total cowards and would eventually just slink away? That their warriors were such hotshots there was no danger? The Nee-Me-Poo would soon pay the piper.

The morning of July 12 Howard consolidated his line, withdrawing the five artillery companies to form a reserve. Some of the warriors who had departed for hearth and home the previous evening never returned, a different sort of reserve unit, I guess. The soldiers expended ammunition freely, leaving Yellow Wolf with a lead slug in his forearm which McWhorter would feel beneath the skin decades later. As the day wore on, still other Nez Perce decided to take a break. The adrenaline rush of the first day of battle had long since drained. This fight was becoming boring, no chance for glory. Noon passed with no initiative from either side.

In response to Howard's first directives after the debacle at White Bird, Captain James Jackson had marched his Company "B" of the First Cavalry nearly 250 miles from remote Fort Klamath in southern Oregon to Fort Vancouver on the Columbia River. There he had loaded his troopers and horses on a paddle-wheel steamer for the ride up the river to Lewiston. After arriving at Fort Lapwai, Jackson picked up a pack train loaded with supplies and headed for the latest confirmed location of Howard's army. About 2:30 in the afternoon the dust to the south kicked up by the horses and mules of Jackson's caravan caught the attention of Howard, who had been expecting it. He ordered Captain Marcus Miller, commanding the artillery reserve, to rush his column to their support. Miller skirted the east flank of Rabbit Creek ravine and began to escort the supply train into the army lines. As he again passed the head of the ravine, he abruptly ordered his column to face left into line and charge.

A few warriors rushed to their horses and attempted to flank the oncoming soldiers, but Miller had kept Company "D" in reserve. Bullets from their Springfield rifles drove the feeble attempt back. Nee-Me-Poo resistance wilted under the hot sun. The remaining warriors guarding the Rabbit Creek trail to the river fled for their lives, Yellow Wolf among them. Thunder Rising had sensed the impending disaster and rushed to the village shouting with all the power in his lungs for the women and children to drop whatever they were doing and skip for the hills. White Goose tried to rally warriors at the river, but the panic had become general. The men scattered with their families.

The only road to the river these days is down not Rabbit Creek, but rather the ravine at the northern end of the battlefield. The remains of a soldier were found while building the road. I cross the river at the Stites bridge and let my van chug in second gear for a mile past scattered houses, some with old cars in the yard and horses out back. This had been the village site.

The infantry jumped from their trenches with a cheer and charged into Rabbit Creek ravine on the heels of the artillery companies chasing the routed warriors. The cavalry saddled their mounts and followed. Howard ordered the howitzers and Gatlings brought to the edge of the bluff where their crews began firing into the village. Yellow Wolf was the last warrior to reach the camp, having paused to retrieve his horse. After crossing the current he dashed past the now-deserted teepees as artillery shells began raining down. He heard a voice, a woman crying, and found her. It was Springtime, wife of Thunder Rising, on a rearing, frightened horse. On the ground nearby was a cradleboard with the baby girl born at Split Rocks. Yellow Wolf reached down, scooped her up and handed her to Springtime, then the two lashed their horses up Cottonwood Creek to safety. Only one Nee-Me-Poo remained at the village for the soldiers to find, an elderly, ailing woman in her nineties who lacked the strength to ride a horse.

The foot soldiers found the river a daunting barrier and halted at its edge. Perry's cavalry arrived and began the time-consuming task of ferrying the artillery and infantry troops across the rain-swollen current. Once in the village the soldiers discovered kettles heavy with food still simmering over cooking fires, teepees filled with clothing and underground caches containing tons of camas and flour.

The looting and burning began, with the civilians accompanying the soldiers especially proficient at these tasks. Howard arrived but failed to organize any pursuit. He was convinced he had just won the decisive battle that would break the spine of Real Peoples' will to fight. Fifteen enlisted men and two civilians died as a result of the clash. Twenty more were seriously wounded, including two officers, Captain George Bancroft of Company "A" of the Fourth Artillery and Lieutenant Charles Williams of Company "C" of the Twenty-First Infantry. A heavy price to pay, but worth it to end a war. The abundance of captured supplies seemed to Howard further evidence of total victory. Stripped of their belongings, he thought, the non-treaty Nez Perce could not continue to resist. He was wrong.

The warriors had suffered ten casualties, four dead and six wounded. Those killed were Going Across, Grizzly Bear Blanket, Red Thunder and Whittling. The families had their horses and more caches of provisions and supplies to fall back on. The Nee-Me-Poo had long been an industrious and wealthy people in quiet ways that most whites had little ability to understand. Their will to survive as a free people would eventually amaze the nation.

The road takes me up the bluff to Camas Prairie. A young Nez Perce man with long hair stands just off the road, staring upward. He's not near any houses or even a lane leading to some ranch away from the road. I stop and ask him if he wants a ride somewhere. He regards me for a few seconds, says no thank you, politely, then resumes his communion with the sky. I continue west until I find a county road that takes me north toward Kamiah. I don't know where the bands spent the night of July 12, somewhere around here. McWhorter's informants had nothing to say about the matter, but the evening must have been filled with talk, plans and a few recriminations. I wonder if this was the first time Looking Glass offered his plan to travel to the buffalo country or if he had broached it before the battle. Tonight I'll get a motel room in Kamiah and jump in a shower. So far I've been criss-crossing the Nez Perce homeland, but tomorrow I begin to travel the Nez Perce National Historic Trail in earnest.

It's a long way to Bear Paw and the end of the trail, a distance that would come to both astound and dispirit General Howard. The war he thought was over had just begun.

Notes

[1] These statistics and those that follow are from: Austin, Eric W., *Political Facts of the United States Since 1789*, Columbia University Press, New York, 1986.

[2] See Brown, Mark, *The Flight of the Nez Perce*, Capricorn Books, New York, 1971, reprinted University of Nebraska Press, Lincoln, 1962, p. 142-154 & p. 211-214 for a more detailed account of troop movements.

[3] McCarthy, *Diary*, June 27.

[4] Brown, *Flight*, p. 164-166.

[5] Wilfong, Cheryl, *Following the Nez Perce Trail*, Oregon State University Press, Corvallis, 1990, p. 101, quotes volunteer Ed McConville on the split trail and Brown, *Flight*, p 171-172, quotes Captain Birney Keeler on reports at Fort Lapwai. McWhorter, *Hear Me*, p. 276-280.

[6] McWhorter, *Yellow Wolf*, p. 70-72 and McWhorter, *Hear Me*, p. 282-286.

[7] McWhorter, *Yellow Wolf*, p. 73-74.

[8] McWhorter, *Yellow Wolf*, p. 75-83; McWhorter, *Hear Me*, p. 287-293; Brown, *Flight*, p. 178-183; Wilfong, *Following* , p.105-107.

[9] Wilmot, Luther, *Recollections of 1877 Campaign*, Luther Wilmot Papers, Nez Perce National Historical Park Manuscript Collection, Spalding, ID.

[10] Lewiston *Teller*, July 21, 1877.

[11] See Wilmot, *Recollections*, and Wilmot, Lew "Battle of the Clearwater," in Adkison, Norman, *Nez Perce Indian War and Original Stories*, Idaho County Free Press, Grangeville, ID, 1966.

[12] McWhorter, *Hear Me*, p. 294-297 and *Yellow Wolf*, p. 78-84, also McConville, Edwin *Fifteenth Biennial Report of the State Historical Society of Idaho*, p. 64-67 and Wilmot, Luther "*Recollections*"

[13] Howard, *Nez Perce Joseph,* p. 158.

[14] McWhorter, *Yellow Wolf*, p. 88-89.

[15] Howard, *Nez Perce Joseph*, p. 159.

[16] McWhorter, *Hear Me*, p. 302.

[17] McCarthy, *Diary*, July 11th.

[18] McWhorter, *Yellow Wolf*, p. 89-91.

[19] McWhorter, *Hear Me*, p. 303-304.

[20] Quoted in Brown, *Flight*, p. 191 from *San Francisco Chronicle*, July 20, 1877.

Wayne Cornell

Lieutenant Sevier Rains and his squad were killed in these rocks on a hillside northwest of Cottonwood. Modern-day Cottonwood is visible in the background, about two miles east. The grave of civilian scout William Foster is beyond the larger boulder, about a half mile away.

Wayne Cornell

The Battle of the Clearwater was fought on this grassy bench above the river valley. Soldiers huddled behind makeshift breastworks in this open meadow, trading shots with Nee-Me-Poo warriors hidden in the trees to the front and in ravines on both flanks. The Indian camp was located to the east in the valley beyond the trees. The mouth of Cottonwood Canyon is visible in the distant bluffs.

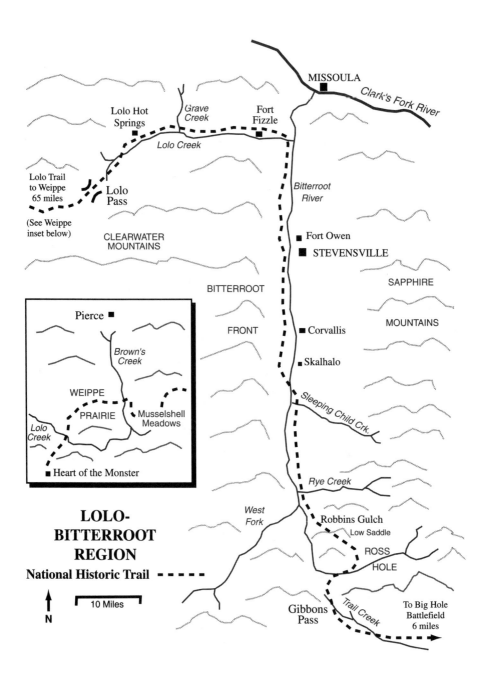

MISSOULA

Clark's Fork River

Lolo Hot Springs

Grave Creek

Fort Fizzle

Lolo Creek

Bitterroot River

Lolo Trail to Weippe 65 miles

Lolo Pass

(See Weippe inset below)

CLEARWATER MOUNTAINS

Fort Owen

STEVENSVILLE

SAPPHIRE

BITTERROOT

Pierce

Brown's Creek

FRONT

MOUNTAINS

Corvallis

Skalhalo

WEIPPE

PRAIRIE

Musselshell Meadows

Lolo Creek

Sleeping Child Crk.

Heart of the Monster

Rye Creek

West Fork

Robbins Gulch

Low Saddle

ROSS HOLE

**LOLO-
BITTERROOT
REGION**

National Historic Trail - - - - -

↑
N

10 Miles

Gibbons Pass

Trail Creek

To Big Hole Battlefield 6 miles

CHAPTER SEVEN

LOLO

After my usual hearty breakfast of bacon and eggs, fried potato with onions and tomato, all cooked on my Coleman at the riverside park near the motel, I lounge at a picnic table with a cup of coffee and a plum for dessert, letting it all settle. A city cop car cruises by, and I give the occupant a wave. He responds with a flick of his hand on the steering wheel and continues on to fight crime elsewhere. Blue sky and only the hint of a breeze suggest another scorching afternoon. By then I'll be in the mountains and out of the valley heat. I wander down to the river and take in its depths.

In 1877 this left bank of the Clearwater River remained farmland. Across the river and a mile upstream near the Heart of the Monster sat the houses and fenced fields of some treaty Nez Perce, a Presbyterian church, a sawmill, flour mill, smithy and the cabin of missionary Kate McBeth. The vanguard of the Nee-Me-Poo column arrived in mid-morning on July 13 to find the settlement abandoned and spent the next six hours getting everybody across the river with the help of two canoes found on the bank. About 3:30 in the afternoon, just as the last of the people and horses were crossing, scouts on the backtrail waved blankets, signaling bluecoats on the bluffs above the river. Warriors hid among the rocks and trees along the riverbank and prepared to greet the soldiers.

General Howard ordered Captains Whipple and Jackson to occupy the valley floor with their cavalry companies, taking along a Gatling gun and crew under the command of Captain Wilkinson for support. Perhaps the three junior officers expected a cowed and submissive opponent after the success of the day before because they recklessly charged their troops in two columns down the slope toward the Clearwater. General Howard described the result as well as anybody:

> . . . a brisk fire from Indian rifles was suddenly opened upon them. It created a great panic and disorder; our men jumped from their horses and ran to the cover of the fences. Little damage resulted, except the shame to us and a fierce delight to the foe.[1]

Major Edwin Mason, Howard's Chief of Staff, viewed this display of ineptitude with disgust. In his next letter home he wrote:

> The Indians are very much afraid of our 'foot' troops but hold the cavalry in profound contempt as well they may, for the truth is they are almost worthless. They cannot fight on horseback and will not fight on foot. I feel safer with a dozen foot soldiers than with all the cavalry in the field.[2]

The artillery crew wheeled the Gatling gun into position and sprayed a barrage of bullets across the water, apparently clearing the opposite bank, as return fire from the invisible warriors gradually slackened then halted completely.

Still, Howard wisely ordered camp set up for the night over a mile back from the Clearwater. Others weren't quite so smart. A few soldiers decided to take their pipes and indulge in a leisurely after-dinner smoke by the river. As they slouched and chatted, the crack of a rifle shot split the air. One of them, Harry Bailey, remembered the incident:

> The soldier wounded as we sat about on the River bank

was of the Artillery, and I was at his side almost at once, the wound proving a red ridge where the hair parts on top, only superficial, but it shocked the man considerably, and caused a lot of vomiting for a few minutes.[3]

It's safe to assume no more smokers enjoyed the sounds and sights of the riverbank that evening.

Earth Blanket summed up the harmless day's fighting for the Real People:

The firing was across the river, the soldiers not trying to cross to our side. I was in this skirmish. A gun had been given to me, one captured at the White Bird fight. It was the short gun used by the horse soldiers cavalry. We had war most rest of that day. It was fun war for the Indians.[4]

Councils took place both in Howard's tent and in the Nee-Me-Poo camp in the hills four miles from the river. Both were inconclusive. Rumors reached the army that Thunder Rising had advocated giving up the war only to be opposed by the other band leaders. As at the Salmon River, Howard found himself stymied by water. A safe crossing would be impossible until the warriors could be forced away from the river. Howard came up with a plan.

Soon after sunrise on July 15, the general with the cavalry and McConville's volunteers climbed out of the Kamiah Valley, intending to deceive the Nee-Me-Poo into thinking the force was returning to Fort Lapwai. Instead they were heading for Dunwell's Ferry sixteen miles downriver, there to cross the Clearwater, swing east, then descend on the non-treaty camp from the rear in a classic pincer exercise right out of a West Point textbook. When lookouts brought news of the column's departure, though, the chiefs figured something was fishy and promptly decided to move their camp. About six miles along the trail to the ferry Howard noticed dust clouds across the Clearwater and correctly surmised his strategy was doomed. Just then James Lawyer and James Reuben galloped up with startling news that sent Howard rushing back to Kamiah: Thunder Rising was ready to surrender.

Time to get moving while the air's still cool. My van rumbles across the bridge and up a back road climbing the precipitous bluffs overlooking the Clearwater. Before long, I've geared down to first as my tires spin and toss gravel in an effort to grip the surfaces of hairpin curves.

A warrior identified by Yellow Wolf as No Heart rode to the river and yelled across to pickets that Thunder Rising had sent him to parley. Someone, maybe an officer, more likely a treaty Nez Perce such as Lawyer or Reuben, held a brief shouted conversation during which No Heart asked about terms of surrender. Someone on the army side of the river took a shot at the warrior, who wheeled his horse and galloped away, slapping one bare buttock in derision, the Nez Perce version of giving the finger.

This encounter sent Reuben and Lawyer dashing after Howard. Yellow Wolf told McWhorter that No Heart was sent by the chiefs to sow confusion among the whites. Sometime after the general returned, another rider appeared carrying a white flag, swimming his horse across the current. Thomas Sutherland, the newspaper correspondent from Portland, reported his name as Kulkulsuitim. Meeting with Howard, he said that the rest of the chiefs had forced Thunder Rising to move to Weippe that day, but that the Wallowa leader intended to give up the following morning. Again, gunfire erupted, this time from the non-treaty side of the river. Kulkulsuitim explained, presumably after taking cover along with the general, that the other band leaders remained adamantly opposed to any surrender. Neither Yellow Wolf nor any other survivors of the war said anything to Lucullus McWhorter about this second exchange, but it had the effect of freezing the army in place for a day while Howard exultantly waited for Thunder Rising to come in.

The one-lane dirt road into Lolo Creek Canyon drops 800 feet in a mile, a twisting, muddy, slippery, twenty-percent grade where pine branches occasionally slap both sides of the van simultaneously. I should be used to this by now, but I find myself forgetting to breathe and reciting the most sincere, silent prayers that I neither meet oncoming traffic nor slide off the road. My prayers are granted. The road up the north side of the canyon to Weippe has been dried by the sun, the going a little easier. When Howard's column finally pushed this way the muddy descent into Lolo Canyon would cause them grief.

Long a summer hangout for the Nee-Me-Poo, Weippe Meadows had in recent years been invaded by ranchers. When the hostilities had broken out, the newcomers had thoughtfully retired to the mining town of Pierce a few miles north. So, while the Nez Perce women hurried to gather what camas they could that July 15, the young men cheerfully made bonfires of the whites' cabins, slaughtered some of the settlers' cattle for the evening meal and made short work of the hated hogs that rooted among the precious camas grounds. Warriors checking out the Lolo Trail ahead found two Montana men, Billy Silverthorne and Pete Matte, on their way, so they claimed, to buy horses in Lewiston. The two may have been interested in horses, but probably had no intention of paying for them amid the confusion that was Idaho. Matte was just out of prison for horse-stealing. At any rate they became unwilling guests of the Nez Perce for the next week.

The camp saw quite a few comings and goings over the next day. An old man, Accompanied By Cyclone, rode up from the reservation to try to talk his son into going home. Thunder Rising's brother-in-law, Black Eagle, made the trip also, and rode among the cooking fires pleading with the Real People to surrender. A warrior severely wounded at the Clearwater battle by an artillery shell departed with a friend. Three Feathers and some others left for the safety of the reservation, intending to blend in with relatives and friends. A few more Palouse warriors with their families showed up to bolster the fighting force. One was Hahtalekin, the respected band leader from Wawawai, who took a prominent role in the discussions that evening. Red Heart (not the same man wounded during the attack on Looking Glass' village) and his small band were returning over the Lolo Trail from the buffalo country of Montana. After visiting friends in the non-treaty camp they pulled up stakes for Kamiah.

The evening council was momentous. Looking Glass ridiculed the notion of surrender, then spoke again in favor of seeking sanctuary in the buffalo country among the Crows. If General Howard pursued the Real People, he argued, the Crows would help in the fight. The whites of Montana were friendly, and after a while it might be safe to return to Idaho. The buffalo would provide meat and hides for the families. Looking Glass said in the end:

> *Listen to me, my chiefs! The Crows are the same as my brothers! If you go there we will be safe!*[5]

He was seconded by Rainbow and Five Wounds.
Thunder Rising thought Looking Glass missed the main point:

> *What are we fighting for? Is it our lives? No. It is this fair land where our fathers are buried. I do not want to take my women among strangers. I do not want to die in a strange land. Some of you tried to say once that I was afraid of the whites. Stay here with me now and you will have plenty of fighting. We will put our women behind us in these mountains and die in our own land fighting for them. I would rather do that than run I know not where.*[6]

The lure of safety in the familiar buffalo country swayed White Goose, Grating Sound and Hahtalekin. All knew that to stay and fight would mean eventually to die. They knew they had been lucky at the Clearwater battle. If Howard had not blundered past the camp, giving the warriors time to mount a defense, the war would have been over. Better to live another day, month, year. Eventually, the whites might come to their senses. It was decided: the buffalo country. The wife of Geese Three Times Alighting On Water, a member of Thunder Rising's band, remembered well, fifty years later, the departure for Musselshell Meadows and the beginning of the Lolo Trail the following morning:

> *Joseph's camp was about the last to break and was plainly seen that he hesitated to follow the others.*[7]

A few farmhouses scattered among fields of cut hay, a cemetery, groves of pine that somehow have avoided the sawmill so far,

Weippe Prairie today doesn't seem like a place steeped in history, the spot where the Real People decided their future in 1877, where Lewis and Clark stumbled out of the woods, where generations of women dug camas for their families. A gray-haired Nez Perce woman once told me that if I came to Weippe at just the right time I might see the blue flower of the camas still rising here and there among the fields, a faint reminder of the past when the ground could easily be mistaken for ponds reflecting the azure sky. Not today. Finding pavement, my van chugs into the modern town of Weippe. The downtown consists of a school, a bar, a pizza joint and Mary Anne's grocery store with a couple of old gas pumps in front.

When Red Heart and his little entourage of thirty-five inno-cents from the buffalo country arrived at Kamiah instead of Thunder Rising, General Howard angrily ordered them chained and held as prisoners of war. Eventually, he would have them marched on foot to Lapwai, then sent on to Fort Vancouver where they would languish in cells for nine months.

Then he ordered his Chief of Staff, Major Mason, to prepare the five troops of cavalry and McConville's volunteers for a three day reconnaissance-in-force to Weippe and beyond. The civilians crossed the river that evening and prepared for a pre-dawn depar-ture. Eugene Wilson remembered:

> . . . it was short work swimming our horses over, a task accomplished without further incident than the arrest of a few packers who had offended the ears of the General by swearing at their animals, and that night we were encamped at the edge of the little fields of grain belonging to the Mission Indians. There was no grass for our horses and strict orders were issued forbidding us to cut the Indians' grain for forage. A hard march ahead of us for the morrow with a probable skirmish with the hostiles was not to be considered with fam-ished horses and, despite the orders, as soon as it was dark dozens of crouching forms might have been seen bobbing around in the grain fields as the boys cut and gathered the coveted feed for their horses.[8]

185

Their horses sustained, the civilians followed several Nez Perce scouts out of Kamiah before first light on the seventeenth, the cavalry trailing behind. Late morning found them at deserted Weippe, the trail of the Real People eastward wide and plain on the earth. After a brief rest and a bite to eat, Mason ordered the command to follow the broad swath toward Brown's Creek. The Nez Perce scouts—among them James Reuben, Abraham Brooks, Captain John, Sam Morris and John Levi—probed cautiously ahead.

After filling both the van's tank and a spare gallon can to the brim, I buy ice for my cooler and head east toward Brown's Creek and the Musselshell Meadows. The hundred miles of the Lolo Motorway wait beyond. Ten miles on, the gravel road crosses a densely forested saddle between the Weippe Meadows and the Brown's Creek drainage. I pull over. It happened somewhere around here.

Waiting along the trail were two groups of warriors guarding the families at Musselshell Meadows, the first a squad of seventeen led by Rainbow, the second larger and closer to camp. When army scouts Reuben, Brooks and Levi bumped into Rainbow's bunch and found themselves surrounded, a parley ensued. The scouts described the size of the soldier column, hoping, I suppose, to intimidate the warriors. Rainbow sent one of his men, Heyoomtamalikinma, rushing to warn Looking Glass at the meadows of this development. As the messenger passed the larger force he, of course, informed them that Rainbow had captured some reservation scouts who were leading soldiers to the Real People. This second group decided not to move forward, but to prepare a surprise for the bluecoats if they somehow made it past the formidable Rainbow. As Heyoomtamalikinma briefed Looking Glass in the Musselshell Meadows camp, they heard the distant crackle of gunfire like fireworks. Heyoomtamalikinma kicked his horse back the way he had come. He arrived at his destination to find John Levi, also known as Sheared Wolf, dead. The other army scouts had fled, James Reuben shot in the hand and Abraham Brooks through the shoulder. As Red Spy crouched at the base of a nearby tree, deep in thought, distraught at killing one of his tribe, the others told Heyoomtamalikinma what had happened. Red Spy had berated his companions for listening to the traitors. The arrogant John Levi had smirked at Red Spy's angry words, prompting that warrior to raise his repeating rifle and begin firing. It had been over in a few seconds. Rainbow quietly gathered the men and they melted into the woods toward camp. This killing of kin was not a good thing.[9]

Major Mason also heard the gunfire. As the surviving Nez Perce scouts came barreling back, Mason ordered a few men forward to investigate. Ed McConville, leading the volunteers, remembered:

> *Immediately after the firing began I dismounted my men, and in a few minutes Capt. Winters Co "E" 1st Cavalry, came up dismounted and gave me an order to advance into the woods with Capt Winters to reconnoitre. Myself and Capt Winters marched through the dense underbrush and fallen timbers, until we found one of the wounded Indian scouts. We then with our own command skirmished through the woods until we found the body of "Levy" (also one of the scouts). We then returned to the edge of the timber, where I met Lieut Forse 1st Cav. coming out of the timber above me with his men. I found upon coming into the Prairie that, Col. Mason had his whole command dismounted and deployed as skirmishers, it being utterly impossible for a mounted man to make his way through the timber.[10]*

Major Mason's lack of confidence in the fighting ability of his cavalry again became evident; he decided to beat a retreat. Having ascertained that the non-treaty bands had indeed taken the trail to Montana, he reasoned that the purpose of the reconnaissance had been accomplished. After camping for the night in the canyon of Lolo Creek, the five companies arrived back at Kamiah the morning of the eighteenth, the surviving reservation scouts having buried Sheared Wolf along the way. The war in the Nee-Me-Poo homeland was almost over.

I cross into Clearwater National Forest, and immediately the trees are smaller than on the private land I've been passing. This edge of the Clearwater Mountains has been pretty well worked over; second or third growth predominates. Musselshell Meadows, just inside the boundary, is one of the few spots where camas continues to thrive in relative abundance. A split-rail fence surrounds part of the marshy meadow, keeping the cattle grazing in the national forest by permit from trampling and chowing down on the plants. I'm sorely tempted to hop over the fence and dig one or two of the roots as a souvenir, but some Nez Perce women still come up from the reservation and harvest for their tables. It seems better to leave what little is left of the traditional plant for them.

So, away I go into the mountains which almost spelled the doom of the Lewis and Clark expedition. The first fifteen miles take me up semi-maintained logging roads to Beaver Saddle. Here, I'm on a ridge which stretches eastward for eighty miles, already as high as Lolo Pass on the Idaho-Montana border, so you'd think I'd be home free as far as steep terrain for my van to traverse. Hardly. From here the road climbs toward Snowy Summit, dips into Beaver Dam Saddle, loops up across Rocky Ridge then dives toward Green Saddle. At Pete Fork Junction an old sign informs me I'm on the road to Missoula, Montana. From the 1930s when it was built until the 1960s when U.S. 12 was completed along the Lochsa River to the south this one-lane track with turnouts for passing was the only way to get from Lewiston to Missoula unless you made a long detour north through Spokane and Coeur d'Alene. Today, it's another thorough education in the three "Rs"—rocks, roots and ruts—and I've had enough learning for the day. I stop at Rocky Ridge Lake, a jewel nestled at the base of a cliff below the ridge, and swim with the trout, letting the cold, crystal water absorb the kinks of hours behind the wheel.

General Howard had been ordered to follow the non-treaty Nez Perce bands even if they fled the jurisdiction of his Department of the Columbia, but he had been concerned all spring and summer that other tribes in eastern Washington might also go to war. With Major Mason's report that the Nee-Me-Poo were truly on their way to Montana and out of his department, the one-armed general decided to march most of his force back to Fort Lapwai for a quick resupply. Then he planned to move north through the Spokane country, showing the flag to the Spokane and Coeur d'Alene tribes. The Mullan Road would then take him into Montana. Such a roundabout detour would leave him far behind the hostile Nez Perce, but he believed that dealing with them had become the primary responsibility of General Sheridan in Chicago and his Division of the Missouri. Leaving one company each of infantry, artillery and cavalry at Kamiah, Howard and the remainder of his army departed for Lapwai on July 18 and 19.

They didn't make it far. Warriors raided around Kamiah and stole off with several hundred horses, despite the presence of the rear guard. Had the Real People really departed, or were they merely pausing in the mountains until the opportunity came to return and wreak havoc? The sixth-ranking general in the army couldn't take that chance and look like a fool. He decided his only recourse lay in delay until sufficient additional troops arrived. Then he could divide his army into three units—one to swing north through the Spokane country, a second to follow directly on the Lolo Trail and a third to remain in Idaho should the Real People loop back to their homeland. The first of the reinforcements disembarked from a river steamer at Lewiston on July 19, two companies of artillery from San Francisco and two of infantry from Arizona. Still, Howard's new plan meant waiting until Colonel Frank Wheaton and the twelve companies of the Second Infantry appeared from Georgia, until Major George Sanford and his four companies of First Cavalry arrived from Boise and until Major John Green with three companies made it from Nevada. Howard would not begin his journey across the Lolo trail until July 30.

In the meantime, he heard of newspaper articles criticizing his conduct of the campaign and of rumors that Secretary of War McCreary was ready to order him replaced. On the seventeenth, after receiving reports detailing the battle above the Clearwater, General McDowell felt compelled to write to Howard:

Immediately reported them to Washington to be laid before the Secretary of War and the President. These despatches came most opportunely, for your enemies had raised a great alarm against you which the press reported had not been without effect in Washington.[11]

Howard's blood pressure shot up, and he telegraphed back to McDowell:

> *Sorry for need to defend me. Would like to put a few of lying rear enemies on these mountain trails under a boiling July sun. Have put the command to the limit of human endurance and with success.*[12]

At the same time events in little Martinsville, West Virginia, began to mushroom into a national crisis that would overshadow events in Idaho and Montana and divert the attention of the army from the Nez Perce for the next two weeks.

The national economy had gone south, and corporate leaders had seized the opportunity to slash workers' wages while maintaining a healthy profit for shareholders and an opulent lifestyle for themselves. Sound familiar? Only the railroad unions retained enough clout to protest with some effect. Protest they did. On July 17, militiamen protecting a cattle train killed a striker in Martinsville, inflaming emotion throughout the East. The next day an alarmed President Hayes authorized the use of federal troops to protect the mail, and, not coincidentally, the railroads on which it was carried.

On the twentieth, a crowd of 15,000 attempted to burn the B&O railroad station in Baltimore and fought it out with the police and state militia. At the end of the day ten people lay dead. Similar violence spread through every major city in the northeast in the following days, most notably in Pittsburgh where the railroad station and a good part of downtown burned. The riots even reached as far as the Pacific Coast where they took a distinctly anti-Chinese tone. For a tense week the country seriously threatened to fall into anarchy as the federal army scrambled to help local police and state militias restore order.

It's a pleasant ramble on foot of less than a mile from Rocky Ridge Lake to Weitas Meadows. From the name you might suppose the meadows are named after some illustrious Mr. or Ms. Weitas of bygone years. You'd be wrong. About three football fields in size and well-watered by springs feeding a rivulet maybe a foot wide and a foot deep, they used to be called Wet-ass Meadows until some Forest Service functionary decided maps needed cleansing of such a crude, if accurate, moniker. The Forest Service has built a gravel path along the north edge of the meadows, complete with boardwalks and bridges over the marshy areas, more to protect the wetlands, I suppose, than to protect my butt from a soaking. I'm surprised to see the winding stream supporting a population of tiny trout and can't imagine how they survive the winters.

Howard's men slept here the night of August 2. The locations of the army camps along the trail are pretty easy to find based on mileages and vivid descriptions left by members of the column. For them the trek across these mountains was a memorable ordeal, just as it had been for Lewis and Clark. The whereabouts of the Nee-Me-Poo camps are a different story. For them the journey was no big deal, and little information about the week they spent making the trip found its way into McWhorter's papers. White Hawk did mention to McWhorter that he herded some cattle liberated from the Weippe ranches as far as Chipmunk Basin before slaughtering them, Chipmunk Basin being one of the names used by the Nez Perce for these meadows. Others, though, denied taking any cattle at all along the Lolo passage.[13]

My first stop the next day is Deep Saddle, where two years ago I helped in a volunteer effort rebuild part of the actual trail used by the Real People and the army in 1877. For decades everyone had assumed that the last traces had been wiped out over the years. After all, it had been nothing more than a horse trail used for only a few months each summer. Then an electrical engineer from Iowa, Steve Johnson, using bearings recorded by a party of whites in the 1860s, began tramping through these mountains. To everyone's amazement, over several years he discovered the entire length of the trail.

Two years ago I was at first unconvinced that the track we were improving at Deep Saddle was over a century old with a past that merged with prehistory. On relatively flat ground it looked to me to be nothing more than some disused hiking path. A quarter-mile on, the faint trail disappeared into a thicket of brush and pine branches cascading down the fifty-degree slope of a ravine. Somewhere, water gurgled over rocks. By the time we paused for

191

lunch we had cleared enough of the ravine of undergrowth to uncover the distinct furrow of the ancient trail, a few feet wide and concave. I became a believer that Steve Johnson was right. The thick brush had protected the earth from erosion, and the rut worn by generations of hooves and feet was still as plain as day. I see now the Forest Service has improved on our work, widening the path and building simple stone walkways over the streams cascading down the side of the ridge. The water tastes as cold and bracing as ever.

I had a chance to talk with Steve Johnson for a while back then, and he agreed with a hunch I had that the Real People probably split into smaller groups going over the trail. There are a few big meadows like Weitas, but he told me he had found a string of small meadows along the way which would have been suitable for a few families and their horses, but not for the entire caravan. The scenario makes sense considering what happened as soon as the Nee-Me-Poo reached Montana. Now, with another fifty miles of slow dirt road still to traverse I can't linger long.

As General Howard stewed and waited at one end of the trail in Idaho, folks at the other end in Montana were getting sweaty palms. As early as July 13 Montana Territorial Governor Benjamin Potts had wired President Hayes for authority to raise a militia of 500 to be funded federally. He received a polite brush-off from Secretary of War McCreary, who assured him that General Philip Sheridan in Chicago was monitoring events closely and had plenty of soldiers at hand to deal with any Nez Perce who might show up in the region.

That same day Captain Charles Rawn, commander of newly-established Fort Missoula a few miles from the town of the same name, ordered Lieutenant Francis Woodbridge and four men to scout the eastern reaches of the Lolo Trail. Three days passed with no word from Woodbridge. Hearing via telegraph that the non-treaty Nez Perce were definitely somewhere on the Lolo, Rawn became concerned and sent Lieutenant Charles Coolidge with one soldier and a couple of civilians to find the first party. The two little groups met up late on the twenty-first with Woodbridge reporting he had penetrated into Idaho with no sign of the Indians.

The motorway finally descends from the ridge to the Lochsa River and joins U.S. Highway 12. I wander down to the water and toss pebbles. Woodbridge probably came about this far and missed sighting the Nez Perce by a day. The Nee-Me-Poo passed here uneventfully about July 21 through 23. When Howard's force finally arrived the evening of August 5 the sound of gunfire at the head of the column caused a brief alarm. The general initially thought his cavalry van had run into the rear guard of the non-treaty bands. Instead, troopers were splashing their horses through the salmon-choked river, gleefully shooting spawning fish. Today the shallow, crystal water runs undisturbed. The salmon are gone from this stream, probably forever, victims of the dams downriver on the Snake and Columbia rivers.

A short, three-mile haul in third gear brings me to Lolo Pass and Montana. I slip the transmission into fourth and glide downhill for seven miles beside the East Fork of Lolo Creek (there are two Lolo Creeks, one back in Idaho near Kamiah and this one in Montana) to the Lolo Hot Springs Resort. Across the highway from the pool and motel I pay ten bucks at the private campground and park well away from an ominous horde of grade-schoolers romping around a church bus and some concrete teepees. After setting up my tent to stake my claim on a patch of grass for the night, I continue down the narrow canyon past Howard Creek and Chief Joseph Gulch, past Grave Creek, where the Nee-Me-Poo families spent July 26 and 27, to a wayside rest stop and picnic ground. Fort Fizzle.

On July 22 the advance guard of Nez Perce warriors released Pete Matte and Billy Silverthorne, their guests since Weippe Meadows, at the hot springs. The two scurried down the creek and soon ran into Lieutenant Woodbridge. The officer dispatched a courier to Captain Rawn with this first firm news of the impending arrival of the Real People, then beat a judicious retreat himself.

An informal militia had been forming in the town of Missoula, and one of its officers, "Captain" E. A. Kenney, and four men were also scouting up Lolo Creek. Late on the evening of July 24 a Delaware Indian named John Hill rode into their camp, an emissary from the Nee-Me-Poo chiefs. The following morning Kenney sent this message to Missoula:

> *A messenger from Joseph's band reached our camp last night at 10:00 o'clock. He is instructed to find out whether he can leave the pass and go through Missoula to the buffalo country. Says he will go peaceably. I have sent him back this morning to tell Joseph and his Chiefs to come to our camp and have a talk.*[14]

Kenney soon found himself surrounded by warriors and decided that waiting around for a talk with the chiefs wasn't such a bright idea after all. After promising that someone with authority would treat with the Nez Perce the following afternoon, "Captain" Kenney executed a swift tactical withdrawal.

That same day, Captain Rawn received orders all the way from General Sheridan in Chicago. They were simple: he was to disarm and dismount the Nee-Me-Poo. Right. Still, good officer that he was, he gave it a try. With all the infantry he could muster—about thirty men—he immediately marched in the company of fifty Missoula volunteers. At a narrow neck of the Lolo Creek Canyon, they set out felling trees. By nightfall they had managed to construct a simple log and dirt breastwork stretching from the timbered southern slope to the grassy northern one. Then they hunkered down to wait.

I'm pleased to see that the Forest Service has improved the historical information at the wayside. Previously a sign had stated that General Howard was "hours" behind the Real People as Rawn tried to block them from entering the Bitterroot Valley. That was technically correct, I suppose, if you put the number of hours in the hundreds. Now a more accurate sign is in place beside a reconstructed section of the breastwork.

On July 26 more volunteers and about twenty Flathead Indians bolstered the little force, bringing the total to about 125. The Flatheads were an especially welcome addition. The settlers of western Montana had been more than a little nervous about the loyalty of that tribe, who for generations had been allies of the Nez Perce. In the afternoon Captain Rawn ventured out and met with White Goose and Looking Glass. The Nez Perce leaders promised to pass through the western Montana settlements peaceably. Rawn stated the demand for the unconditional surrender of their guns and horses, tantamount to total capitulation. Looking Glass and White Goose told the officer that they would meet with him the following day after the band leaders had a chance to talk among themselves. Rawn, in turn, told the chiefs that Governor Potts would be present for the next talk.

The Nee-Me-Poo had several options besides surrender of their horses and guns, which was a laughable proposition. The least palatable was fighting their way past the barrier. As an alternative, a low pass from the head of Grave Creek to Petty Creek offered an easy passage northward to the Clark Fork River. The drawback to that route was that the families would have to pass near the town of Missoula after reaching the Clark Fork. Perhaps there was another way.

By Friday, July 27, the force opposing the Nez Perce at the barricade had grown to the neighborhood of 200 with still more civilians expected. Governor Potts had visited in the morning, conferred with Rawn, then returned to Missoula to divert further reinforcements to the vulnerable pass at the head of Grave Creek. That afternoon Captain Rawn and 100 volunteers left their little fort and rode toward the Nez Perce camp. Unarmed, Looking Glass came out alone to talk to Rawn. According to white accounts, the Nee-Me-Poo leader offered to give up their ammunition, but not their guns or horses, in exchange for safe passage past the settlements. The captain, of course, had no authority to negotiate. Surrender or fight, he responded, make up your mind. Looking Glass readily agreed to meet again the following noon.

Many of McWhorter's informants were aware of only one meeting with the whites, and none seemed to know of any offer by Looking Glass to turn over the ammunition. One arrived at the camp only on the twenty-seventh, supporting the idea that the Real People had split up over the Lolo Trail, the first group having arrived at Lolo Springs as early as the twenty-second. In all likelihood, Looking Glass' ammunition proposal was designed to stall for time until the People were united and ready to move. His acceptance of another parlay the next day was certainly a deception. The Nee-Me-Poo women were already prepared to be on the move early the following morning, and the warriors also knew exactly what they would have to do.

The attitude among the whites in western Montana the evening of the twenty-seventh was one of cautious optimism. Newspapers reported that most whites felt confident the stymied Nez Perce would surrender. Those manning the barricade were not so sure. The promise by Looking Glass that the Real People would harm no person or property carried weight with some of the defenders. He was a familiar figure whose words the whites of Montana had learned to trust. In the trenches at the barricade and around the cooking fires behind it, a surrender would have been welcomed by all, but some of the militia were wondering whether provoking a fight was such a good idea. The volunteers from the Bitterroot Valley were the most concerned. Many lived on isolated farms and ranches and were particularly vulnerable. If the Nez Perce prevailed and forced their way past the barrier, they might take their anger out on the people of the valley. What to do? The decision would be made for them early the next day.

Back at the hot springs I cross the road from the campground to the swimming pools. Early visitors described a bucolic scene here: steam rising from the mineral water as it poured from a field of boulders, the pungent water flowing into shallow, translucent pools before wedding with Lolo Creek. The boulders are still here, but a series of pipes with peeling paint siphons off the water for the swimming complex even before it reaches the surface. The natural basins have been replaced by a parking lot. Poking around the rocks, I locate a trickle of water which has eluded capture. On my hands and knees I manage a few sips. Tasty, just like Lewis and Clark wrote in their journals.

Notes

[1] Howard, *Nez Perce Joseph*, p. 167.

[2] Davison, Stanley A., "A Century Ago: The Nez Perce and the Tortuous Pursuit," *Montana, The Magazine of Western History*, October, 1977, p. 6.

[3] McWhorter, *Papers*, Folder 101, item 71.

[4] McWhorter, *Papers*, Folder 104, item 9.

[5] McWhorter, *Hear Me*, p. 334.

[6] Wood, Charles, E. S., "Chief Joseph, the Nez Perce," *Century Magazine*, May 1884, p. 138. Wood's account of the speech, taken from an unnamed Nez Perce informant, should be considered an approximation rather than a verbatim quote.

[7] McWhorter, *Papers*, Folder 34, page 73.

[8] Wilson, Eugene T., *The Nez Perce Campaign*, manuscript, Washington State Historical Society, p. 11.

[9] McWhorter, *Papers*, Folder 344, item 57.
 McWhorter, *Papers*, Folder 104, items 19-20.
 McWhorter, *Papers*, Folder 62, items 93-94.
 This account varies from previously published versions. Recent writers have placed this encounter on Incendiary Creek some twelve miles closer to Kamiah than Brown's Creek and on the other side of Weippe Prairie. This interpretation flies in the face of every Nez Perce narrative of the event, as well as the reports of Mason and McConville. McWhorter's informants unanimously placed the event near Brown's Creek.

[10] Chaffee, Eugene B., "Letters of the Nez Perce War to Governor Mason Brayman," *Fifteenth Biennial Report of the Board of Trustees of the State Historical Society of Idaho*, Boise, 1936, p. 68-69.

[11] Adjutant General's Office, *Records of the Adjutant General's Office, Letters Received, 1877*, reel 338, item 645.

[12] Adjutant, *Records*, reel 337, item 402.

[13] McWhorter, *Papers*, Folder 166, item 17.
 McWhorter, *Hear Me*, p.335.

[14] *New Northwest*, July 27.

Martin Stadius

The Lolo Trail

CHAPTER EIGHT

BITTERROOT

The Nee-Me-Poo made their move at first light. Protected by a line of warriors and shielded from view of the whites by a bend in the canyon, the women and children advanced to within a half mile of the barrier. There they climbed the hills to the north, passing another bunch of warriors who had their rifles trained on the exposed and helpless whites below. Two miles beyond the barricade they descended to the canyon floor where a third cordon of warriors waited.

The question now became: who had whom trapped? A few of the volunteers began sneaking away from the barricade to try to make their way home. Lieutenant Rawn discreetly waited a little over an hour before ordering forty-five volunteers onto their horses to scout the situation down Lolo Creek. Three of these men, ahead of the others, ran into the screen of warriors protecting the rear of the family cavalcade now proceeding sedately downstream. Seeing the three, Looking Glass waved his hat in a friendly manner, rode up and again told the whites that his warriors would harm no one if the whites went home and minded their own business. To Rawn's amazement twenty volunteers from Phillipsburg arrived, having ridden through the Nez Perce caravan blissfully unaware they were among the "hostile" Indians. Just whom the Phillipsburg men supposed them to be is beyond answer. Rawn ordered the barricade abandoned, and thus ended the short life of what soon became known as Fort Fizzle.

One of the civilians, John Humble, claimed many years later that the whole affair had been quietly arranged with Captain Rawn's tacit approval. Humble stated that he had been in command of a squad of pickets on the northern hill. Prior to the arrival of the Nez Perce he had ordered his force back to the barricade as part of a surreptitious agreement reached between a few of the civilians and Looking Glass the previous day. These settlers had been convinced by the chief's professions of goodwill. Most of the volunteers had been unaware of the deal, but the conspirators had received Captain Rawn's private consent.[1] The unsubstantiated story has the ring of truth to it. As I survey the scene again this warm summer morning I can't imagine Captain Rawn neglecting to post guards above his vulnerable breastworks. We're talking about a lesson he would have learned the first week in Army Procedure 101. At any rate the Nez Perce movement went off without a hitch.

It's only about five miles along Lolo Creek until the canyon opens up to the Bitterroot Valley and a stop sign at U.S. 93. If I were to turn left and head north for ten miles I would find Missoula. That's the direction Rawn, his infantry and most of the volunteers took. The Nee-Me-Poo turned right for a few miles and camped near the ranch of a settler named McClain, some of the volunteers trailing after them and passing through the Nez Perce camp to their homes without incident. When a break in the traffic finally allows, I head south and shift rapidly through to fourth gear. No more moseying along; parts of the Bitterroot Valley are becoming like a bit of California plopped down into Montana, and many of the drivers are a little crazed. People with dreams of that ranch out in the wild West seem to find this valley irresistible. Oh-so-cute, one-horse ranchettes with Land-Rovers in the driveway are popping up all over the place on acreage that used to produce something tangible.

A few miles of this traffic is enough. Even though I'm going as fast as the line of cars in front of me, a guy in what looks to be a Blazer crowds up on my rear bumper, weaving like he's preparing for a suicidal dash. Signaling well in advance and cutting across the oncoming lane, I pull into the Chief Looking Glass Recreation Area, a shady sanctuary on the banks of the Bitterroot River. Four miles to the west the Bitterroot Mountains rise spectacularly without foothills some 6,000 feet above the valley floor. Even a geological idiot like me can see that a major fault at the base of the mountains has thrust them upward. The Sapphire Range seven or eight miles to the east is lower, seemingly unformed and lumpy. One of my guide books tells me they once rested atop the Bitterroots, but slid off as the western mountains rose. The Nee-Me-Poo camped several miles from here up against the base of the Bitterroots.

That night they held a council. Duncan McDonald, the son of a Scots trader and Nez Perce mother, arrived in the evening from Missoula where he had witnessed the initial reaction to the fiasco at Fort Fizzle. After the war he would write the first account of the entire conflict from the Nez Perce perspective for the *New Northwest* newspaper in Deer Lodge. In it he made no mention of his presence at the council, but McWhorter's sources detailed his attendance. McDonald probably recounted, humorously, the sorry-looking chain the citizens had stretched across the Clark Fork River bridge into Missoula, guarded by one man who intended to halt the Real People in their tracks if they moved in that direction. He must have mentioned how Governor Potts, upon hearing a rumor of approaching Nez Perce, nearly bowled McDonald over in a rush for cover in the town hotel.

McDonald offered to guide the non-treaty bands north to the Flathead reservation, where his father was agency trader. From there the People could continue on to safety in Canada. Red Owl strongly seconded the proposal, as did White Goose and Grating Sound. Looking Glass held out for traveling to the buffalo country and the Crows as agreed at Weippe. The Flatheads could no longer be trusted, he said. They had stood beside the whites at the barricade. Only the Crows remained true friends of the Real People, Looking Glass argued. If there was trouble in the buffalo country the Nee-Me-Poo could always go to Canada, but no need for that right now.

Thunder Rising, the least senior of the chiefs, had little to say; they had abandoned their homeland, the bones of their ancestors, and it mattered little to him where they wandered. The oratory of Looking Glass again won the day. He would continue to lead the Real People toward the land of the Crows. The next morning the bands continued south past the former trading post of Fort Owen and the town of Stevensville, both on the other side of the river.

Looking Glass and a few warriors went ahead to pick the next campsite, but a courtesy visit to the village of Charlo, the chief of the Flatheads, turned tense when Charlo refused to shake the hand of Looking Glass. The Nez Perces' hands were bloody, Charlo said, and he had no intention of touching them. Like the Nez Perce, the Flatheads had signed a treaty in 1855, theirs guaranteeing them the Bitterroot Valley. Their thief treaty came in 1872. To the end Charlo swore that he had not signed the paper. Historians have pointed the finger at negotiator James Garfield, later president of the United States, as the probable forger. Still, Charlo steadfastly refused to take up the gun against the whites, so in 1891 his people would be forced from the Bitterroot. After the cool reception by Charlo, the Real People camped two miles south of Stevensville on Silverthorne Creek. Remember Billy Silverthorne captured on the Lolo trail? It's a safe bet the young man kept close to his family homestead nearby.

At Kamiah General Howard was finally ready to move. The Second Infantry, fresh from Georgia, and Captains Perry's, Trimble's and Whipple's cavalry would swing north then east to Montana under the command of Colonel Frank Wheaton. Major John Green with two companies of cavalry and two of infantry would remain near Mount Idaho in the event the non-treaty Nez Perce swung back toward their homeland. The direct pursuit force consisted of eight companies of infantry with Captain Evan Miles as battalion commander, seven companies of artillery acting as infantry under Captain Marcus Miller and four of cavalry, Major George Sanford commanding. Twenty Bannock warriors from southern Idaho led by Buffalo Horn acted as scouts, and a few treaty Nez Perce signed up as herders. About 150 civilians joined the column as packers, couriers, scouts and engineers or trailclearers. In all almost 750 men departed Kamiah with General Howard for the Lolo Trail on July 30.

Back on the U.S. 93 again, but thankfully only for a few more miles. State Highway 269 takes me across the river to Fort Owen and off the beaten path. Now a state monument, the fort was named for John Owen, who arrived in 1850 and bought the place from Jesuits priests who were giving up after nine years in the wilderness, disheartened by the constant warfare between the Flatheads and the Blackfoot. Today, the adobe walls surrounding the structure have long since melted away, but the east barracks remains. I wander through the cool dark interior of the four rooms, Owen's bedroom, office, guest room and a dorm for his workers. Wall displays describe Owen's many accomplishments over the twenty-odd years he lived here. By 1877, despondent over the death of his Shoshone wife, Nancy, Owen had drunk himself into oblivion, been declared insane and shipped back to Pennsylvania. When most of the men of the valley rushed off to Fort Fizzle as the Nee-Me-Poo approached the Bitterroot, over 200 women and children crowded into the adobe safety of the trading post, nicknamed Fort Brave.

From Fort Owen it's less than a mile to Stevensville. Intending to find a laundromat, I'm surprised to find Main Street blocked off and swarming with people, traffic detoured onto Buck Street. Squeezing into a parking spot on Buck, I wander into the middle of the three-day Eighty-third Annual Creamery Picnic. It seems the local creamery burned down back in 1911, and the locals helped get it up and running again. Ever since then it's been party time once a year. I've missed the grand parade, but the music stage, cake walk and the dunk tank are going great guns. Sitting on the plank over the dunk tank, a pretty teenager sasses the crowd while her mother stands back and feeds dollar bills to a steady stream of boys eager to hit the target with a softball and shut her up.

Wandering along, I indulge in roasted corn-on-the-cob dipped in butter, the shucks still attached for convenient handling, then wash it down with lemonade squeezed fresh before my eyes in a contraption that looks straight from the pioneer days. I top it off with a free dish of ice cream maybe five minutes young, compliments of the Lutheran Church and a couple of Clydesdales by the name of Mike and Marshall who take turns providing the horsepower for the old ice cream maker. I pull out of Stevensville grinning. Nothing like an old-fashioned celebration to improve one's mood. The valley citizens also threw themselves a bash after the Real People had passed.

Buck Street had to have been named after the Buck Brothers—Fred, Amos and Henry—proprietors of a general store in 1877. Henry Buck left the most complete account of the Real People's visit to Stevensville. Henry, one of the fifteen men guarding Fort Brave under the leadership of his brother, "Captain" Fred, watched the Nez Perce pass by and camp a couple of miles south of town:

> As was always customary with Indians traveling on horseback, they jogged their ponies along on a little dog trot. Being curious enough to gain some idea of their number, took out my watch and timed their passing a given point. It took just one hour and a quarter for all to move by and there were no gaps in the continuous train. There was no unusual confusion or disorder and none came over on our side of the river. Developments afterward showed that their herd of horses numbered more than three thousand, many of them being of very fine stock.[2]

Henry Buck and his brothers, ever the practical shopkeepers, decided it was safe to return to town and reopen the general store. Mustn't lose business. They loaded up a wagon with goods and had no more put them back on the shelves when:

> . . . low and behold a band of squaws from the Nez Perce camp, accompanied by a few armed warriors, appeared. They soon made known their wants to us, saying they needed supplies and had money to pay for them, but if we refused to sell, would take them anyway. Our stock comprised but a handful of such articles as they wanted. However, we held a

consultation over the matter and decided that "Prudence was the better part of valor", so decided to trade with them. Flour was their main desire and we had none; but near Fort Owen was located the flour mill to where they repaired for a supply.[3]

In the weeks that followed, Buck and the other Stevensville merchants would take a lot of heat, both from military officers and private individuals all around Montana Territory, for trading with the Nez Perce.

Fred, Amos and Henry decided to leave the rest of their goods in the fort the next day, but went into town to watch events unfold:

... about ten A.M. were surprised by the appearance of one hundred and fifteen warriors, well armed with Henry Rifles, riding into our little village under the leadership of White Bird. We were lost to know what this day would bring forth. Never shall I forget their formidable appearance, their stern looks, their aggressiveness and their actions, which in themselves placed us immediately on the defensive. This added another stimulus to our present fear, which made a life-long impression.

They were all well dressed with apparently new showy blankets, well armed and rode the finest of horses. Many of these horses, I well remember, were branded "B" and said to have been taken from a man by the name of Baker who lived near their old home in Idaho. The Nez Perces were by far the finest looking tribe of Indians I have ever seen and so much superior to the Flatheads in intelligence, physique, manner of dress, equipment and arms, that they were hardly to be compared. We had always considered the Nez Perces as a wealthy tribe and on this visit they seemed to have plenty of money, all in gold coin, but they did not come to trade this day, nor did they buy anything to my knowledge except some whisky sold them by unscrupulous individuals who had no care of the well-being of our community.[4]

This account of the Nee-Me-Poo sojourn through the Bitterroot

Valley contradicts the assertions of General Howard and others in Idaho that the seizure of their camp after the Clearwater battle had impoverished and crippled the non-treaty bands. The Nez Perce that Buck encountered on the dusty main street of Stevensville were by no means on their last legs.

Buck's adventures that day had just begun:

> *Finally it was noticed that some of the Nez Perces were getting drunk and on investigation found that a white man by the name of Dave Spooner, who tended bar in the Reeves saloon was selling the whisky. The liquor was seized by a party of us and transported on a wagon to the Fort. Strong talk of lynching the dispenser of the firewater was indulged in, yet at the same time we were afraid that if we enforced the vigilante act, it would incite the Indians to violence. The next move was to enter the general store of Jerry Fahy, the only other place in town where liquor was sold.*
>
> *I might explain that in those days it was customary for storekeepers to have a barrel of whisky, not especially for sale, but to treat customers, thereby retaining their trade and good-will; but Fahy like Spooner in his eagerness for the almighty dollar, forgot the graveness of the situation and it developed upon a party of our citizens that "his barrel be given up". Fahy at first resented and wished to know, "By what authority we had for making such a demand". One man amongst our number—a South Methodist minister by the name of Reverend T. W. Flowers—stepped forward with his pistol in hand, leveled it and said, "By this authority". Jerry, realizing the situation, remarked, "That's pretty good authority all right; there is the barrel, take it.[5]*

They rushed Fahy's whiskey to Fort Brave, but the damage had already been done. The older Nee-Me-Poo evinced nothing but good will and tried to keep the younger warriors under control. It didn't work. Luckily for the whites, Chief Charlo's Flatheads showed up, determined to keep the peace. When one drunken Nez Perce warrior entered the home of the town blacksmith and pointed a gun at the smithy's wife, a Flathead pulled the gun away and

ejected the perpetrator. Another performed a similar service outside the Buck business when a Nez Perce warrior aimed his rifle
at the store window and muttered, "See me kill that man in the
store." White Goose happened to witness that scuffle. He jumped
from his horse, smacked the hapless offender with his quirt and
sent him packing back to camp. The remainder of the warriors
soon followed, and Henry Buck retreated to the fort.

> *Upon arriving my nerves gave way to the awful strain and
> I collapsed, trembling like a leaf, when I looked back over the
> scene which we had just passed through, and realizing how
> near we came to the close of our earthly careers.*[6]

The Missoula newspaper reported that a week later the people
of Stevensville put on a celebration for Charlo and his people in
gratitude for their assistance.

After a two-night layover Looking Glass instructed the Nee-Me-
Poo women to pack their camp, and the caravan continued south
up the valley. It apparently took them two days to travel the twelve
miles to the tiny hamlet of Corvallis, where the settlers had hastily constructed a sod fortification 100 feet square with walls twelve
feet high, dubbed Fort Skedaddle. It would have been at one of
these stops that Shore Crossing dreamed of impending disaster.
The morning following his dream he rode about the camp loudly
informing the others of its contents:

> *My brothers, my sisters, I am telling you! In a dream last
> night I saw myself killed. I will be killed soon! I do not care.
> I am willing to die. But first, I will kill some soldiers. I shall
> not turn back from death. We are all going to die!*[7]

Looking Glass ignored the young warrior's foreboding.

A noted Nez Perce buffalo hunter named Lean Elk—whites
called him Poker Joe—was camped just south of town with his
band of eight lodges, probably sixty people in all. After listening to
stories of the situation in Idaho another buffalo hunt
sounded like just the ticket to Lean Elk, so he hooked up with the

nontreaty bands as they continued on their way from Corvallis on August 2.

With the Real People peacefully making their way up the valley, it's a good time to go to the war of the telegrams, where some real action was taking place. On July 23 General McDowell in San Francisco ordered General Howard to send two companies of artillery back to California to assist in quelling the riots there. Howard protested the order and, probably imprudently, suggested alternate troop movements to his commanding officer. He added an unfounded rumor to shore up his objection: the bands of Smohalla and Old Thomas from central Washington had joined the nontreaty bands on the Lolo Trail. McDowell swallowed the insubordination for the time being as he mulled over another message just in from Howard, "I have signified acceptance of two hundred volunteers from Governor of Washington Territory."[8] That was followed a few days later by a third from Howard, this one truly pitiful in light of his reluctance to give up the two artillery companies from his large command still stalled beside the Clearwater River:

> *Cannot troops at Missoula or vicinity detain Joseph till I can strike his rear. The two companies there with a little help from volunteers ample considering present condition of hostile Indians. My troops will push through rapidly.*[9]

McDowell apparently found himself at a total loss for words on how to respond to the last communication, but not the first two. On August 3 he replied through his adjutant:

> *The Division Commander directs me to say that as you had up to July 26th regarded your forces, present and assembling, sufficient to contend with the hostile Indians in your Department, and had so reported, he thinks your acceptance of 200 Washington Territory volunteers unnecessary. So far as he can judge, the need for such troops passed away with your defeat of Joseph's band on the 11th and 12th of July. He cannot therefore approve of your action in this respect.*[10]

McDowell's separate telegram concerning the artillery companies, also dated August 3rd, was even more blunt:

> *The Division Commander directs you will at the earliest moment comply with the orders heretofore given you, to send back Cushing's and Field's Companies to their Stations. It is supposed this order will reach you at Missoula. If so, return them from that place. Acknowledge receipt and telegraph compliance.*[11]

Acknowledge and comply. Couldn't get much simpler than that, could it? We'll see.

Meanwhile in Montana Governor Potts was obviously relishing his martial duties. After the fiasco at Fort Fizzle, Plan B involved raising a militia from Butte, Deer Lodge and surrounding mining camps to cross over into the Big Hole Valley and again confront the leisurely Nee-Me-Poo caravan after it departed the Bitterroot settlements. By July 29 about 200 men had mustered into "companies." Apparently, they were a ragtag lot, many without horses and crowded into wagons, about half armed only with ancient muzzleloaders. Potts took one look at his "army" and moved on to Plan B, Version 2. Perhaps he could induce the federal government to sanction his militia, in which case the territory would not end up paying the tab for the sorely needed guns, ammunition and supplies to make the force respectable.

On July 31 he telegraphed Secretary of War McCreary:

> *The hostile Nez Perces from Idaho are in Bitter Root valley in force. They have not, as yet known, committed hostilities, but avow their determination to pass through to the buffalo country. General Gibbon has asked assistance under the circumstances. I am powerless without authority and most earnestly urge authorization from the War Department to call 300 volunteers, furnishing their own horses, for not exceeding thirty days. Believe I can organize in three days. Please answer immediately.*[12]

Potts' mention of Gibbon requesting assistance apparently was

209

a fiction designed to bolster his case. Delegate Maginnis, Montana's representative to Congress, seconded the request in another telegram then took off for Fort Ellis in central Montana hoping to intercept General Sherman, who was headed west on a combination inspection tour and vacation, and enlist his support for a federalized militia. With General Sherman out of touch, McCreary passed the request on to Adjutant General Townsend in New York, who, in turn, sent it to General Sheridan in Chicago. Sheridan's response is notable for his lack of understanding of events about the location of the nontreaty bands:

> *I have not been able to realize that Joseph's band of Nez Perce is coming through the Bitter root Valley to Central Montana; there are no buffalo this year south of the upper Missouri river except a small band of five or six thousand on the headwaters of the Powder River too far to the eastward for Nez Perces hunting and the Indians are always well posted about where the buffalo are. I have no information from the dept of Dakota to warrant the alarm of the Governor of Montana, so I do not feel gratified in recommending the three hundred volunteers. General Sherman will be at Fort Ellis tonight and being on the ground could give the most reliable opinion. Would it not be best to consult him—if I thought the People of Montana were in danger I would not hesitate to recommend the three hundred volunteers but at present I am without official or unofficial information sufficient to justify me in approving the request. I will consult with General Terry and ascertain his opinion. Should the Indians come through and go to the Buffalo grounds General Miles has not less then one thousand men at a reasonably convenient distance to attack them.*[13]

In his August 2 telegram to Potts denying the militia, Secretary McCreary didn't mention that Sheridan refused to believe the nontreaty bands were yet in Montana, instead merely reassuring the territorial governor that the army had things well in hand.

That same day delegate Maginnis reached Fort Ellis and found Sherman just-arrived and sympathetic, but the telegraph line from the outpost was down, and the head of the army was unable to communicate with the Secretary of War. Unwilling to delay his Yellowstone Park vacation, the best Sherman could do was give up his escort company and order in three companies of the Second Cavalry from eastern Montana. In a letter to Potts delivered by Maginnis, Sherman wrote:

> *Arrived yesterday. Escort of 1 company will get in today. Riots in the East have ceased and I am authorized to go on as first planned. I shall take four men, and start for the Geysers the day after tomorrow by the Mammoth Springs. Thinking to get back to Ellis in fifteen days. Howard has orders to follow up the Nez Perces. I will leave subject to Genl Gibbons orders the Escort Company and have instructed Genl. Terry to send up the other three Companies. This is about all we can do. These Indians should not be allowed to traverse Montana for the Buffalo Country but should be Captured, or forced back on Howard. I approve what you are doing. And if your volunteers act under the Regular officers, I am sure Congress will pay for the necessary stores for their maintenance. Also pay them in time. I have no authority to issue stores, unless the citizens act immediately along with the Regular troops. In such cases arms and ammunition could be loaned and bills for forage and provisions could be certified. I know it is the office of the General Government to protect its citizens, but you know the extent of our territory, the great diversity of local dangers, and the fewness of soldiers allowed by law.*[14]

Potts faced a quandary. His militia would not be deployed directly with regular army units, so Sherman's "approval" was meaningless. His only recourse lay in spending territorial funds to equip his militia, so he conferred with several territorial notables. The consensus formed that the necessity defending the citizens of Montana from the Nez Perce stopped short of actually spending any local taxpayer money. If the feds wouldn't come up with the cash, forget the whole thing. Pott's Big Hole militia was a dead duck, and the men dispersed to their homes.

Cruising toward Corvallis at a sedate forty-five miles per hour, I pass a sign for the Bitterroot Turf Farm. I guess that sod the settlers used to build Fort Skedaddle turned out to be worth something. Corvallis boasted about 100 inhabitants in 1877 and hasn't gotten any bigger since. There's a school and an old Methodist church in "downtown" and that's it. When the Real People passed by, Corvallis included a general store whose proprietor, one P. R. Young, slammed his door in the faces of some Nez Perce who came to trade. Nothing came of it. The chiefs had the young men in hand again after the drunken confrontations in Stevensville. From Corvallis it's only about five miles to the town of Hamilton, called Skalhalo in 1877 with about eighty citizens. Their citadel from the rampaging savages—nicknamed Fort Run—was a sorry affair with sloping walls only five feet high. A party of warriors rode their horses up those embankments and curiously peered inside, much to the dismay of its doughty defenders. Fort Fizzle, Fort Brave, Fort Skedaddle, Fort Run. A different kind of war here in the Bitterroot.

State 269 dead ends in Hamilton, and I'm back in the traffic mess of U.S. 93. I need to do my laundry and buy ice and food, but Hamilton with its population of 3,000 and string of fast food joints and chain stores with absurdly large parking lots doesn't suit my fancy. I'll spend my money in little Darby up the road a way, one of my hangouts from my fishing years. A few miles farther south I flee 93 for Sleeping Child Road. On the side of the road sits a ranchette with a sign proclaiming its name: IHAVENO RANCH. They do have a sense of humor.

The Bitterroot and Sapphire ranges are closing in now, the valley only a few miles wide. A road sign warns of livestock on the road, open range, then I cross the Bitterroot River on a bridge with rattling wooden slats under my wheels. My kind of road.

Back in Missoula the settlers were struggling with the events of the week. The initial reaction to the failure to halt the Real People at Fort Fizzle had been universal disgust all over western Montana. Captain Rawn and the Missoula volunteers were forced to defend themselves against charges of cowardice. The Missoula newspaper pointed out, reasonably, that bravery and cowardice were characteristics evenly distributed throughout the territory's citizenry. Those howling with contempt knew the exact location of the Nez Perce and were welcome to have at them.

McWhorter reported that a few Missoula residents under the nominal command of a "Lieutenant" Andrews, but under the actual leadership of an excess of whiskey, rode up the valley and placed themselves in front of the Nee-Me-Poo line of march. When the first warriors appeared at the head of the column, this bunch of heroes promptly sobered up and lit out for safety. One of them later commented ruefully that the Nez Perce probably figured the whites were putting on a racing demonstration for the enjoyment of the warriors.[15]

Colonel John Gibbon, commander of the Seventh Infantry, arrived in Missoula from Fort Shaw a few hours before sunset on August 2. All the soldiers he could muster from the area around Fort Shaw—only about eighty men—followed a day later. Gibbon had expected the Nez Perce to turn north at Lolo, skirt Missoula, then cross the Continental Divide into the Missouri River buffalo country at Cadotte Pass. Like all senior officers in the 1870s army, he had been a general in the Civil War and, as commander of the Iron Brigade, had earned a reputation for unusual fearlessness. Still, approaching Cadotte Pass, he must have been a little apprehensive, knowing his puny walking outfit would be no match for numerically superior and mounted warriors. When the anticipated confrontation failed to transpire and a messenger brought word of the actual movement of the Nez Perce up the Bitterroot, Colonel Gibbon pushed rapidly ahead to assess the situation.

With Gibbon was Lieutenant James Bradley, the Seventh Infantry's chief of scouts and a fascinating character. An avid and accomplished student of history and veteran of a decade in the West, Bradley had written several accounts of the early years of the white settlement of Montana. The previous year he had been the first soldier to arrive at the Little Big Horn and discover the corpses of Custer's battalion scattered over the slopes above that stream. Since then in his spare time he had been writing a memoir of his role in that Sioux campaign of 1876. When the order arrived at Fort Shaw for the Seventh to pursue the Nez Perce,

Bradley had completed the manuscript up to the day prior to finding Custer's body. He would not finish it. Bradley had six days to live. His memoir of 1876 would eventually be published and acclaimed for its detail and accuracy, but scholars and Custer aficionados have ever since regretted the loss of that unwritten entry for June 26, 1876.

On the third of August from Missoula, Bradley penned a letter to his wife back at Fort Shaw. In it he wrote:

> *It has not yet transpired what we are to do, but it is probable we will remain inactive for a few days till Howard comes up from the west side of the mountains and the 2nd Cavalry battalion from the Yellowstone, and then we will push for the Indians.*

He ended the letter with:

> *Kisses for the babies and love for yourself.*[16]

Something happened in Missoula that evening to stir the fifty-year-old, bearded Gibbon to immediate action rather than waiting for reinforcements, but no record apparently remains of what occurred. Captain Rawn, stung by criticism, had been recklessly ready to pursue the Nez Perce on the second with portions of three infantry companies, maybe sixty men, but delayed upon hearing of Gibbon's imminent arrival. In all likelihood he pressed Gibbon: honor, glory and all that stuff awaited. The citizens of the town almost certainly pestered Gibbon to no end: do something, the whole state, the entire country is watching and laughing. Someone may have mentioned the campaign of 1876 when rumors of over-caution on Gibbon's part spread through Montana. At any rate, after dispatching a messenger named Pardee up the Lolo Trail with a note urging General Howard to hurry up, on August 4 Colonel Gibbon ordered his newly-combined command of fifteen officers and 146 soldiers into wagons provided by local citizenry and began the rattling ride up the Bitterroot in pursuit of the Real People.

After a quick stop at the Darby National Forest district office to check road conditions ahead, I spend a pleasant hour in the shade on a bench in front of a laundromat watching the traffic slowly pass the quaint log and false-front buildings of town. Darby didn't recently dress up this way for the tourists; a book I came across written in the 1930s described this street exactly as it looks today. Heading out of town, I notice the Darby city cop sitting in his car next to a 25 MPH speed limit sign motioning with his hand for incoming traffic to slow down. Imagine that, a cop who prefers not to hide then race out and write tickets. That's why I like this place.

The same afternoon that Colonel Gibbon departed Missoula, the Nee-Me-Poo traversed this section of valley, camping a few miles ahead. That evening Lone Bird, a noted warrior, mounted his gray horse and walked it about, shouting:

> *Why the idea these chiefs travel slowly? Maybe our enemies are now overtaking us, and we get whipped! We should keep going! Keep watch everywhere. Each chief look after his own warriors! Be ready for fighting any time! Keep going! Move fast! Death may now be following on our trail.*[17]

Looking Glass remained unmoved, confident General Howard was far behind and the ineffectual force that had opposed the Real People at Fort Fizzle posed no further threat.

Also on August 4, General Sherman departed Fort Ellis for Yellowstone Park in the company of a guide, his son, two military aides, three drivers for the wagons and four soldiers for protection. Before setting out he wrote a cable to Secretary of War McCreary for transmission as soon as the line was repaired:

> *I do not suppose I run much risk, for we are all armed and the hostile Indians rarely resort to the park, a poor region for game, and to their superstitious minds associated with hell by reason of its geysers and hot springs.*[18]

The General of the Army would learn something different about those superstitious minds in a few weeks.

Rye Creek flows into the Bitterroot four miles south of Darby. Myron Lockwood ranched here in 1877, the last homestead the Real People passed in the valley. Some of the young men got rambunctious and pretty well tore up the contents of Lockwood's cabin, hauling away the flour and coffee they found and probably slaughtering several cattle also. Hearing of this, Looking Glass was not amused, considering it a violation of his promise that the Nee-Me-Poo would pass through the Bitterroot without harming the settlers in any way. He compelled the culprits to give up seven horses, mark them with Lockwood's brand and leave them in his corral.

The Ponderosa pine forest and hills are closing on the river and road now, the valley at an end. Ahead the river passes through a steep, cramped canyon. Beyond are Ross Hole and the headwaters of the river in the surrounding mountains. The builders of U.S. 93 dynamited their way through, but earlier travelers took to the hills.

I pass a dirt road heading up Robbins Gulch into those hills, remembering with embarrassment getting lost a couple of years ago near the head of the gulch. I'd been searching for traces of an old wagon road that might have crossed from the Bitterroot Valley into Ross Hole, the route Gibbon and his wagons took while following the Nez Perce. I'm used to tramping off-trail and usually have a pretty good sense of direction and terrain, but that day I managed to get completely turned around. Luckily, after an hour or so I was able to get my bearings and find my van. No sign of an old wagon road, though. The builders of the current logging road appeared to have dynamited their way through a rocky bottleneck at the lower end of the gulch, and I should have known right away that Robbins Gulch did not contain Gibbon's trail. Above that barrier, though, the ground did open up and offer easy access to the top of the divide leading to Ross Hole.

Five more miles brings me to another side road following Warm Springs Creek into the hills. I cruise through a Forest Service campground looking for an RV with Delaware plates, but Sam and Carol aren't here. I first met them a few years ago in the library of the Montana Historical Society. Serving as hosts for this campground, they had also volunteered to research events in the Bitterroot Valley for a Forest Service pamphlet on this part of the National Historic Trail. I camped with them several times that summer and found them delightful company around a crackling fire. Disappointed at not being able to say hello, I return to U.S. 93 then take Spring Gulch Road up the mountain east of the highway, a precipitous, twisty three-mile climb in first gear to Low Saddle on top of the divide into Ross Hole.

Sam and Carol were almost positive the old wagon road had followed this route. After I walked over this area following the Robbins Gulch debacle, I had to go back and admit to them they were onto something. The present-day road climbs another mile to a fire lookout atop Sula Peak, but from here at Low Saddle the vestige of another much older dirt road is unmistakable descending into Ross Hole. The upper portion hugging the side of Sula Peak clearly was graded and improved at one time, probably for logging. Further down, though, the terrain flattens, and I enter the spacious, park-like atmosphere of an old-growth Ponderosa pine forest. The presence of the rotted trunks of decades-old fallen trees across the faintest remnant of the track strongly suggest history. After a day of noise and traffic the silence of this old forest is a balm. Choosing the shade of a venerable ponderosa pine, I sit in the soft grass at its base and lean back. The highest branches sway in some breeze that doesn't reach me on the ground.

People have assumed that both the Real People and their pursuers followed the same trail into Ross Hole, but one summer evening, camped up on the Continental Divide ahead, I had one of those Aha! moments. Gibbon enlisted the aid of a Bitterroot settler named Joe Blodgett to guide his wagons because Blodgett had once managed to force the first wagon train through these hills. The colonel later recalled the arduous struggle to repeat the trick:

All that afternoon was occupied in climbing that steep mountain and dragging our wagons up behind us. The trail was almost obliterated in places, and but for Joe's knowledge of the features of the country, we must have been lost in the mountains, and all our labor would have gone for naught.[19]

217

Having been lost in these mountains myself, I can empathize, but if the 800 Nee-Me-Poo with their thousands of horses had preceded the army, the trail would hardly have been difficult to find, certainly not almost obliterated. Gibbon could have closed his eyes and found his way just by the smell of horse manure. In addition, when General Howard crossed into Ross Hole five days after Gibbon, he somehow missed a courier returning from the colonel.

There had to have been two trails.

The Real People must have taken a route unsuitable for wagons, probably up Robbins Gulch with its bottleneck at the bottom. Blodgett guided Gibbon to the one he had previously hauled wagons over, here at Low Saddle. Howard, his command without the impediment of wagons, followed the much more obvious Nez Perce trail. Gibbon's return courier took the trail he was familiar with over Low Saddle, thus missing Howard. So simple.

I drop back to U.S. 93 and turn upriver into the two miles of canyon which forced Gibbon's wagons into the miserable detour. Dynamite can work wonders. The highway skirts the southwest edge of Ross Hole, rolling rangeland watered by streams pouring out of the circling mountains. Unlike the agricultural Bitterroot Valley, this region is too high for crops, but it looks to be cattle heaven. The highway follows Camp Creek into the mountains, the Continental Divide only five miles ahead as the eagle flies.

The Nee-Me-Poo camped somewhere along here the night of August 5. By now Colonel Gibbon's army was only thirty-five miles behind, stopping for the night at Sleeping Child Creek south of Hamilton. Since leaving Missoula the afternoon before, their steady progress had cut more than half the distance between the two groups. During the day the arrival of a squad of mounted volunteers had bolstered the command. Apparently, Gibbon was dubious of their worth, and some did indeed drop out and return to their homes. The Yankee colonel's reluctance may have had as much to do with their accents as their potential fighting abilities. Andrew Garcia wrote to McWhorter:

One side of the Bitter Root valley was settled mostly by

Missourians. The other side of the valley mostly by Georgeians. So in all this bunch of Jeff Davis's Orphans, it could not be expected that their Civil War record, from a union man's point of view was good.[20]

About thirty of Jeff Davis' Orphans ended up sticking with Gibbon.

It's been a long, hot day, but I have only a few miles to go. At the Sula Ranger Station I leave the highway for Forest Road 106 and the 2,500-foot climb to the Continental Divide. I'm blessed with a fine view of the patchwork of clear cuts on the side of Saddle Mountain across Camp Creek. Cattle dot the sloping meadows beside the road. One cow, planted firmly in my path, seems enchanted with the bleating of my horn and stares at my dusty van as if it might be some long-lost calf now grown and come home to mama. It reluctantly moves only when I climb out and shoo it away, waving my arms like a maniac. Finally, Gibbons Pass, altitude 6,951 feet. The green alpine landscape turns black and white, the charred remnants of the forest rising from pale ash and soil. A lightning fire at this altitude, probably. The little valley formed by Trail Creek widens, the stream meandering through meadows thick with brush. This side of the Continental Divide is easy traveling, a gentle counterpoint to the rugged grade of the western slope. Somewhere along here the Nee-Me-Poo spent the night of August 6. Gibbon and his infantry spent a thirsty night partway up Spring Gulch going into Ross Hole, only twenty miles behind the Real People. I come to a paved road, Montana 43, and a few miles later a forest service campground.

Clustered together in five or six adjacent units are Nez Perce families here for the following day's events down at the Big Hole battlefield. I nod and say howdy as I walk back to the campground entrance to pay the fee. A few folks look up and give me waves in return, but I don't stop to chat. I've learned over the past years that a white man writing about the war is met with distance, and my presence today is about the war and writing. I've never met a Nez Perce who hasn't treated me with courtesy. But for them the 1877 war is a grief that is their own, their Civil and

219

World wars rolled into one. Imagine you were already a nation divided, and you were in the process of losing most of your remaining land to another people. Some of your kin acquiesced in the taking, others fought. You might not want one of those other people to write about it yet again. From my point of view, though, the war is now a part of a larger American history. I try as much as I can to understand it all. A dog barks from one of the Nez Perce campsites as I go to sleep.

Notes

[1] McWhorter, *Hear Me*, p. 351.

[2] Buck, Henry, "*The Story of the Nez Perce Campaign During the Summer of 1877*," Montana Historical Society, Helena, p. 26.

[3] Buck, "*Story*," p. 27.

[4] Buck, "*Story*," p. 28-29.

[5] Buck, "*Story*," p. 30-31.

[6] Buck, "*Story*," p. 32-33.

[7] McWhorter, *Yellow Wolf*, p. 108.

[8] AGO, *Letters,* roll 337, page 406.

[9] AGO, *Letters*, roll 338, page 410.

[10] AGO, *Letters*, roll 337, page 420.

[11] AGO, *Letters*, roll 337, page 418.

[12] *New Northwest*, August 10, 1877

[13] AGO, *Letters*, roll 337, p. 208-212.

[14] *New Northwest*, August 10, 1877

[15] McWhorter, *Yellow Wolf*, p. 108.

[16] Bradley, James H., *Letters, SC#1612*, Montana Historical Society, Helena, P. 5-7.

[17] McWhorter, *Hear Me*, p.363-364.

[18] Sherman, William T., *Travel Accounts of General William Tecumseh Sherman to Spokane Falls in Washington Territory in the Summers of 1877 and 1883*, Ye Galleon Press, Fairfield, WA, 1984, p. 49.

[19] quoted in Brown, *Flight*, p. 247.

[20] McWhorter, *Papers*, Folder 186, item 5.

Washington State University Library

Fort Fizzle, site of a comic interlude in the Nez Perce saga. Soldiers and Montana volunteers manning the barracade at the east end of the Lolo Trail allowed the Nee-Me-Poo caravan to pass without firing a shot.

BATTLE OF THE BIG HOLE

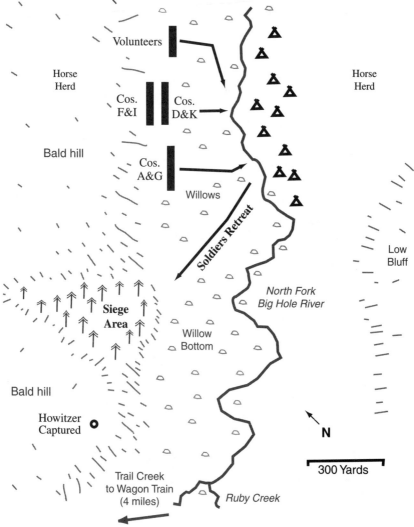

CHAPTER NINE

BIG HOLE

Birds chirping, cool air, the smell of pine, another perfect morning. As I laze in my warm, blue cocoon, I realize I'm not looking forward to this day. The Big Hole National Battlefield always has this effect on me. Still, I crawl out, roll the sleeping bag, stow it and my pillow and the blue ground tarp in the van, pump the Coleman stove and heat water for coffee. Routine is good.

On August 6, General Howard with the four troops of cavalry in his command arrived at Lolo Hot Springs. His eight companies of infantry and seven of artillery having fallen behind on the Lolo Trail. There the general met a courier from Missoula with General McDowell's peremptory repeat order to return Cushing and Field's artillery companies to San Francisco. Howard's response:

> *Please telegraph me permission to retain these companies till arrival of Wheaton's column if the General can possibly spare them that long. I shall not retain them a day for your answer, but as I know that this detaching imperils the whole expedition, it is proper for me to so report.*[1]

McDowell received this telegram two days later. He must have been livid. His adjutant wasted no time answering:

As you say you know your compliance with the orders given you to send back Cushing's and Field's Companies will emperil the whole expedition, you are authorized by the Division Commander to retain them as you desire, but he will require that you hereafter satisfy him that the expedition would be incurring such danger as you represent.[2]

Howard's claim was untenable on the face of it, but McDowell's insistence is likewise a little hard to fathom. Quiet reigned in San Francisco. The fury fueling the urban riots had subsided as quickly as it arose and with it the dire need for the two companies who could not possibly make it back to California for weeks. The generals were acting like children arguing about who gets to play with a toy. McDowell had the ultimate advantage, though. He was Howard's superior.

On August 7 the Real People made the short jaunt from their Trail Creek layover to the floor of the Big Hole Valley. On the western edge lay a traditional campsite they called Place of the Picket Pins after a small ground squirrel that, when standing alert for danger at the entrance to its hole, resembled the little wooden stakes used to tie horses. The women began to cut and strip lodgepole pine from the forest edge for teepee poles. The People planned to drag the poles to the buffalo country and no longer sleep in crude shelters. The hunters didn't have much luck, only one elk, but the stream teemed with trout and the children had plenty to eat.

Some of the young men rode fifteen miles across the valley to the foothills of the Pioneer Mountains where a white man, E. M. Doolittle, and his Nez Perce wife had built a dugout cabin. Doolittle must have been something of a hermit, living in such splendid isolation. After a brief flurry of gold fever on French Creek at the northern extreme of the valley, the Big Hole had reverted to wilderness, except for the brief summer months when cattlemen sometimes brought stock to graze. The young men hoped to find a jug of whiskey at Doolittle's to liven up their feet at the dances the people would hold to celebrate their freedom, but they returned empty-handed.

Colonel Gibbon's little army crossed into Ross Hole on the seventh and camped at the base of the Continental Divide. Overnight, Lieutenant Bradley led sixty mounted men, a mixture of soldiers and volunteers, over the mountain and along Trail Creek. He hoped to find the Nez Perce camp before sunrise and stampede the horse herd, but daylight found him several miles short of his goal. As Bradley's party neared the Big Hole the morning of the eighth, the lieutenant sent two soldiers ahead to reconnoiter. They soon returned with the news that they had heard the unmistakable crack of axes striking wood, the sound of the women hard at work preparing hundreds of lodge poles. Bradley himself then went forward in the company of Lieutenant Joshua Jacobs. Climbing a tree, Bradley saw the Nez Perce camp laid out below him at the near margin of the valley. It took the shape of an irregular flattened V, the point facing west, mirroring the contour of a slender dark stream. Bingo. Committing the terrain around the camp to memory, Bradley slid down the tree and retreated.

After a quick breakfast of a sliced peach with cereal and milk, I hit the road which quickly leads out of the forest and into the Big Hole. Grassland stretches for twenty miles ahead to the Pioneer Mountains silhouetted beneath the rising sun. I turn into the entrance of the Big Hole National Battlefield. About a square mile in size, it's one of the recent additions to the Nez Perce National Historical Park, though it's been in the park system as a national monument since 1910. This battle has been studied and dissected for decades, and I have nothing new to add. A Park Service employee wearing the signature pointed hat with the flat brim greets me and hands me a brochure detailing the day's activities. Ahead is the visitor's center, a one-story structure, muted in color and blending with the terrain. I hang a left and take a side road to a parking lot already half-filled with thirty cars. Crossing the bridge over the river, I begin the walk to the site of the camp Bradley had viewed. Ahead, I hear the compelling chant of Nez Perce singers. When I'm almost there, a midget squirrel, a picket pin, pokes its head out of a hole and chatters at me furiously, indignant over all the commotion.

Despite the general relief among the Real People at having passed the white settlements of western Montana safely, some of the best warriors were nervous. The urgent speeches of Shore Crossing and Lone Bird about danger on their heels remained fresh in their minds. Now a new voice, Hair Combed Over Eyes, added concern. In the night he had dreamed of soldiers coming fast. A bunch of fighters got together and decided that a scout over the back trail would be prudent. They were Five Wounds, Red Moccasin Tops, Rainbow, Yellow Wolf, Strong Eagle, Muscles in Back Thigh, Lone Bird, Hair Cut Upward, Woodpecker, Red Spy, Bird Alighting, Rattle On Blanket and Travelling Alone. Two of these men, Red Moccasin Tops and Red Spy, had only jaded mounts, so their wives went to an old man rich in horses, Coals of Fire, and asked for help. He refused. Looking Glass got wind of the proposed reconnoiter, maybe from Coals of Fire, and upbraided the warriors. The Montana whites had been friends to the Nee-Me-Poo, he told them, so you must not go back to the Bitterroot and perhaps cause trouble. Reluctantly, the warriors bent their wills to the objection of the man designated to lead the Real People to the buffalo country.

The women had accomplished much during the day. By nightfall eighty-nine hide-covered teepees stretched along the stream two to four deep. Time for fun, then rest. The Real People drummed and sang and danced late into the night, their first chance for amusement and celebration in months. They then curled into their sleeping robes, looking forward to a long, relaxed snooze.

Colonel Gibbon's main force spent all the morning of the August 8 hauling their wagons up the Continental Divide. In the afternoon they hurried down Trail Creek, meeting the advance party at dusk only four or five miles from the Nez Perce camp. Bradley described the layout of the camp and the surrounding terrain to Gibbon and the other officers. They settled upon a plan of attack, an assault along the length of the camp at dawn. Companies "D" and "K" led by Captains Comba and Sanno would form the center of the line, while Captains William Logan and George Browning with Companies "A" and "G" would charge on the right. The left flank would consist of the volunteers and a squad of six or eight troopers of the Second Cavalry, all commanded by Lieutenant Bradley. Companies "F" and "I" under Captains Williams and Rawn would form a reserve. At the first glimmering of light the line was to move forward to the river, fire three volleys into the camp, then charge. Each of the four wings consisted of about forty men, not including officers.

After a cold dinner of salt pork and hardtack the men rested until 11 P.M. Each took ninety rounds of ammunition from the supply wagons. Then, while twenty men remained with the wagons, the rest—seventeen officers, 133 soldiers and about thirty-two civilians—followed Lieutenant Bradley along the trail. Only Colonel Gibbon and his adjutant, Lieutenant Charles Woodruff, were mounted. The stealthy march took two hours and ended with the troops stretched in a long line along the base of the hill across the river from the teepees spread along the bank.

To Gibbon's surprise he found part of the Nez Perce herd above the soldiers on the grassy hillside. He whispered instructions to civilian guide Henry Bostwick to take several men and run off the horses. Bostwick talked him out of it, convincing the colonel the task could not be accomplished without alerting the sleeping camp. Watch the fires outside the teepees, Bostwick said. If women came out and stoked the cooking fires, the colonel would know the troops had not been discovered. Sure enough. In the distance shadows emerged periodically from the teepees, and embers flared. Gibbon and his men settled down to wait in silence for dawn.

As I hurry down the path toward the camp site, I step aside several times to allow Park Service minivans ferrying elders to pass. A crowd of 100 has already gathered, milling about quietly as they wait for the ceremony to begin. It's almost nine o'clock, but I know from experience these things have their own kind of time. It will begin when the elders are ready.

My first stop is a pyramid of teepee poles with five wooden feathers planted in the earth inside. They mark the place where five Nez Perce died. When I first visited this battlefield years ago

I sensed the markers represented women and children. In my research I've found I was right. During my first visit I also wondered who thrust aside the flap of the teepee and methodically killed those innocents. I think I know the answer. He was a sergeant, but some names are best not remembered. I stroll along the circular path among the teepee poles and other markers for the dead—Nee-Me-Poo, soldier and civilian—then stop and gaze across the river toward the base of the hillside 200 yards away where the whites waited out the night. Nearer, the river has eroded eastward since the war and is beginning to encroach on the campsite. Several clumps of willows on this side of the river have washed away in the intervening years, but otherwise the terrain appears much as it did on that August morning.

On the face of it, Gibbon's plan looked good, right out of a textbook, but he blundered in assigning only one officer out of seventeen—Lieutenant Bradley—to the left wing of the attack. A good thing for the Nee-Me-Poo. Historians have debated whether Gibbon ordered that women and children be shot. It seems to me that when an officer directs that 400 rounds of ammunition in three volleys be fired indiscriminately into tents containing noncombatants the answer is obvious. Volunteer Tom Sherrill later said that John Catlin, head of the civilians, asked Gibbon what to do with prisoners after the attack. Gibbon's response was, he didn't want any prisoners. Catlin related Gibbon's answer to his men then somberly added, "Boys, you know what to do now."[3]

Before the first hint of light on August 9 began to turn the scene shades of gray, Bradley sent some civilian skirmishers forward to cover the advance of the rest of his unit. At about the same time Gibbon ordered the center companies under Comba and Sanno to move ahead.

Some of the Real People were stirring also, men rising to check on the horse herds around the periphery of the camp. One of them, Natalekin, mounted a gray pony tethered for the night outside his teepee and splashed across the river at the northern, lower edge of the village. Another, Hahtalekin, removed his moccasins and waded through the chilly water behind the horseman. After climbing out he noticed in the first dim light of day movement among the soldiers at the base of the hill, possibly "D" and "K" Companies beginning their advance, and rushed back to warn the People of possible danger. An older man with poor vision, Natalekin guided his horse directly toward the line of volunteers. At close range three or four of the civilian pickets rose up and blew him from his saddle.

Gibbon had ordered the command to fire the three volleys at once if they were discovered before reaching the river, and for the next few seconds a hailstorm of lead ripped through the buffalo hide coverings of the teepees. But the fusillade came from two hundred yards in dim light and lost much of its killing punch. Then the entire line charged.

Pandemonium, confusion, fear and anger struck the Nee-Me-Poo along with the bullets. As warriors groped for their weapons, some of the women and children and old people ran or crawled toward the river and the dubious sanctuary of the willows. Others fled across the open ground eastward toward a bluff a quarter mile away. Some remained in their teepees, unsure what was happening or what to do. Most of the horses picketed in the camp fell in that first barrage.

Companies "D" and "K" forded the river first and struck the middle of the village, apparently meeting little initial resistance. Captains Logan and Browning led Companies "A" and "G" into the south end of the camp a moment later. Shore Crossing, who with Red Moccasin Tops precipitated the war, met them, his pregnant wife at his side. He was no match for forty. His wife, already wounded, grabbed his gun and killed the man who had shot her husband. Captain William Logan was one of the first soldiers to fall at that end of the village and may have been her victim. Other soldiers quickly dispatched her.

Hahtalekin's warning provided the crucial seconds needed for a few warriors to prepare themselves at the north end of the camp. Lieutenant Bradley took the lead in the charge. He and volunteer Davis Morrow died rushing forward. Leaderless, the attack by the volunteers faltered short of the river. Watching the action from the hillside, Gibbon had already committed the two reserve companies to the assault on the center and right, leaving him unable to reinforce his wavering left. Warriors soon sensed that portion of the village was safe and headed upstream to help their kin.

For twenty minutes a brutal melee ensued in the willows skirting the stream and amid the teepees in the southern half of the village. Both white and Nez Perce accounts detail savage gunfire at short range and hand-to-hand combat with children, women and the elderly helplessly in the middle of it all. Finally the six companies cleared that portion of the camp. Carrying his two-month-old child, Thunder Rising had managed to escape, but two of his wives were not so fortunate. Fair Land, one of Frog's wives, was also mortally wounded. In all, the bodies of about twenty Nee-Me-Poo men of varying ages, ten women and perhaps as many as forty children and elderly lay on the ground or in the willows or drifted in the river current. Many more, of course, were wounded.

Following on horseback close behind the reserve companies, Gibbon ordered the teepees and possessions inside burned. The heavy buffalo hides wet with dew proved resistant to fire, and soldiers began merely to pull the teepees to the ground. For a few moments it appeared the battle was almost won, but, as the volunteers drifted in from across the river to the north, Gibbon realized that almost half the village remained in control of the warriors. The fight was nowhere near over. The soldiers heard the voices of Looking Glass and White Goose shouting encouragement. White Goose said:

> *Since the world was made brave men fight for their women and children! Are we going to run to the mountain and let the whites kill our women and children before our eyes? It is better we should be killed fighting. Now is our time. Fight!*[4]

Before Gibbon had much chance to consider his options, the intensity of sporadic sniper fire from outside his lines increased. In short order both he and his adjutant, Lieutenant Woodruff, were hit, each in the leg. Awkward on foot because of an old Civil War wound to his hip, the colonel nevertheless decided remaining on horseback was no longer prudent. Gibbon ordered charges into the willows to the west and south and toward the unoccupied half of the village to the north.

Captain Browning's company briefly sallied southeast across the valley floor toward the grassy bluff where the fire of distant snipers was particularly galling. Nothing seemed to work. Realizing that the Nez Perce fighters would remain free to indulge in target practice from several sides and that the gradual annihilation of his command would result, Gibbon ordered a retreat. He set his sights on a copse of trees in a ravine cutting the hillside to the southwest almost a half-mile away. The command had passed it earlier in the night, and Gibbon apparently remembered it as adequate for defense. With Captain Rawn's "I" Company deployed as a rear guard, the Seventh Infantry fled, taking their wounded they could find but leaving the bodies of their dead. The infuriated warriors refused to let up. Corporal Daniel McCaffrey of the rear guard took a bullet, then Sergeant Michael Hogan. Both were left behind.

McWhorter visited the battlefield in 1927, 1928 and 1935, fascinated by the prodigious memories of Yellow Wolf, Bird Alighting, Black Hawk and Sam Lott, the son of Hair Combed Over Eyes, each determined that names and stories not be forgotten, that they should be passed from generation to generation. They were able to remember and stake the precise locations of most of the teepees along the stream. They were able to remember the battle in such detail that to me, gazing across the river, that day seems all too real.

A few warriors dogged the rear and flanks of the column, among them Rainbow. He and a straggling volunteer surprised each other in the maze of willows, suddenly face-to-face only a few feet apart. Rainbow's rifle misfired. The tall volunteer's did not, and one of the greatest warriors was dead. Dashing after the retreating column, that same volunteer ran into Bad Boy Grizzly Bear. Each swung the butt of his rifle at the other's head and connected. The clash turned into a wrestling match with the powerful volunteer gaining the edge until another warrior, Rattle On Blanket, stuck the barrel of his gun in the side of the volunteer and pulled the trigger. Bad Boy Grizzly Bear carried the impression left by the volunteer's rifle butt on his forehead for the rest of his life.

On his way back to the camp Rattle On Blanket found another volunteer hiding. The warrior hustled his prisoner, Campbell Mitchell, into the camp. Looking Glass ordered that he not be hurt, but a woman whose brother and children lay dead stepped up and slapped the volunteer's face. Mitchell tried to kick her. Going Out, a warrior with a reputation for a bad temper, raised his rifle and killed the settler. Going Out shouted:

> *No use! The difference is, had he been a woman, we would have saved him. Sent him home unhurt! Are not warriors to be fought? Look around! These babies, these children killed! Were they warriors? These young girls, these young women you see dead! Were they warriors? These young boys, these old men! Were they warriors?*[5]

Looking Glass could not blame Going Out for his impulsive act.

As soon as the soldiers had departed, surviving Nee-Me-Poo rushed from their hiding places and began searching the camp and nearby willows. Shore Crossing and Five Fogs, dead; also Circling Swan and his wife; Allezyahkon, sixty years old; Woodpecker, dead; Sun Tied, a young woman who had given birth overnight, the baby, too; Granite Crystal, an old woman; I Block Up, whose son watched soldiers kill her; Patsikonmi, an old woman; Weksookahaukt, whose young sister grabbed a rifle and fought in his name; Illatsats, a boy; Likinmi, a woman who sought shelter near Fair Land with three other women, all five of them dead or mortally wounded.

The names and the grieving went on and on and on. Even the soldiers heard it from afar. Gibbon later wrote:

> *Few of us will soon forget the wail of mingled grief, rage and horror which came from the camp four or five hundred yards from us when the Indians returned to it and recognized their slaughtered warriors, women, and children.*[6]

The soldiers already had their own losses to bear: Captain

Logan, Lieutenant Bradley, Corporal Domminick O'Connor, Private Gottlieb Manz, Trumpeter Francis Gallagher, Sergeant Frederick Stortz, Private Herman Brotz; McCaffrey and Hogan protecting the retreat. There would be more.

Shore Crossing and Red Moccasin Tops had touched off the war with their vendetta against the Salmon River settlers. During the height of the assault on the village the voice of Looking Glass had pierced the air, upbraiding the two for bringing this destruction to the people. Shore Crossing and his wife lay dead. Filled with rage and grief, Red Moccasin Tops knew he was not done with the soldiers and was among the first to slip away from camp and dodge among the willows toward the hillside. When word of the death of Rainbow reached the camp, Five Wounds hurried to the scene and knelt over the body of his fallen friend. Five Wounds and Rainbow had grown up as close as brothers, their fathers dying together in the buffalo country. Each had sworn to the other they would die on the same day, as had their fathers. Five Wound's knew it was his time. He thought about things for a while then he, too, deliberately made his way toward the soldiers' hasty fortifications.

The pipe ceremony begins. A Nez Perce veteran asks that no cameras or sound recording devices be used. Sitting to the left of the pipe bearer is a middle-aged woman, her back as straight as a lodgepole pine, pride and strength visible in the features of her face. The pipe man discusses the importance of the role of the women in preserving and protecting the Nez Perce culture in the past and in modern times. The pipe man introduces her, saying she had been an army nurse in Vietnam. Today, she, as a veteran, will smoke with the men. The pipe bearer invites any other white female veterans present to join the circle. One observer says, hesitantly, that she had been an MP in Europe. Did that count, she asks? One of the Nez Perce veterans mutters, "Sounds like combat to me." Amid quiet laughter she steps forward and sits.

There are two long pipes filled with tobacco this year. A Nez Perce boy with matches crouches in the center of the circle ready to relight the pipes if they go out. After everyone has smoked, the pipe bearer passes a bundle of eagle feathers to his right, announcing that the smokers may speak when the feathers reach them, if they wish. As every year, a lot of good words. The pipe man sings a song in memory of the dead as five young men lead Appaloosa horses around the circle. The riderless horses symbolically carry those lost in 1877. When another song begins, five drummers clustered around a single large drum add their beat. Forty or so descendants of participants in the war, many in traditional regalia, fall in line behind the horses and slowly march three times around the circle, one old man hobbling with painful determination, occasionally stumbling, staying the course. The music rises to a crescendo, then all is suddenly silent. Three veterans in an honor guard aim their rifles toward the sky. The first volley is impossibly loud, and most of those watching, including myself, flinch. The sound echoes off the hills and rolls across the valley two more times. "Pick up your arrows, men," the head of the honor guard says. They find the spent shells in the grass, and the ceremony is over.

Gibbon's battered force made it to its destination in the trees at the base of the hillside in fairly good order, although some of the men were on the verge of panic. One enlisted man wildly urged his compatriots to continue fleeing into the mountains. Gibbon, who was nearby, calmly reminded the fellow who was in charge, much to the amusement of those within earshot. A few Nez Perce warriors who had stationed themselves nearby slipped away when they saw the entire army column coming their direction. It may have been one of them whose bullet hit Lieutenant William English soon after the soldiers reached their destination.

The army had recently begun experimenting with a combination bayonet/trowel, and those who had been issued the new tool put it to good use. To the north lay the open hillside where the Nez Perce horse herd had grazed in the night. A charge would probably not come from that direction, and fortifications on that side were relatively few. A steep, twenty-foot embankment to the willow-covered river bottom marked the south-eastern extremity of the shelf. Soldiers gouged a line of trenches just back from the lip. The west side presented a problem. Gently sloping, forested, it provided no natural barrier from attack, and, consequently, the soldiers dug in deep along that line. And then there was the ravine leading up the mountain. If warriors made their way around to its upper reaches and attacked from there, real trouble.

After the memorial I take the trail to the siege area. As at the site of the camp, the Park Service has marked significant locations with feathers and hats with numbered posts keyed to an accompanying brochure explaining what happened and where. As I stroll with others from the ceremony along the circular, dappled path among the lodgepole pines, a few hushed conversations break the still, cool air. Remains of the trenches the soldiers and civilians hurriedly scratched from the earth are still plainly visible almost 120 years later. I try to imagine the scene, the shouts of the officers, the crack of occasional bullets rending the air, the dull thuds of lead striking a tree, the moans of the wounded helped from the village, dirt flying upward propelled by adrenaline. Fourteen months before, Gibbon's Seventh Infantry had seen the bloated bodies of more than 200 of Custer's Seventh Cavalry scattered on a hillside beside the Little Big Horn where they had paid the price for a failed attack on a Lakota and Cheyenne village. More than a few must have wondered if they would suffer the same fate August 9, 1877.

Few of the warriors had any intention of attempting to overrun the army position. Most wanted only to protect the families from any further threat. About sixty men in all left the village to pursue the fleeing infantry, the others staying to care for wounded, dying and dead relatives. Thunder Rising found a horse and hurried across the river to round up the herd on the hillside. Returning, he and White Goose supervised the burial of the dead and the breakup of camp. The grim task took up the morning. Most of the bodies were brought to the river, wrapped in buffalo hides, placed beside the water, then covered by caving in the cutbank. By noon the grieving Real People had said their good-byes to the dead. The freshly-cut lodgepoles became travois for the injured. One of those, White Feather, a woman of eighteen years who had been shot in the left shoulder and clubbed in the face with a rifle butt, later remembered that the chiefs carefully led the people north, away from the soldiers' refuge, before circling to the east then south far beyond the range of any more bullets.[7]

Most of the fighting at the siege area occurred at a distance. Nee-Me-Poo sharpshooters watched from the cover of the surrounding forest on the hillside above the soldiers. Any sign of movement, a head bobbing up or a scramble for better cover, elicited the squeeze of a trigger. Other warriors climbed trees in the river bottom and waited for a quick shot. One sniper using two isolated trees on the otherwise bare hillside north of the trenches for protection proved particularly effective.

From the southwest the soldiers heard two loud booms, the higher crackle of a few seconds of small-arms fire, then silence. Colonel Gibbon remembered the previous evening. He had ordered a detail waiting with the wagon train to bring up a mountain howitzer and a pack animal loaded with additional ammunition at first light. The silence after the gunfire was not a good sign for the fate of the men with the gun and mule. They had, indeed, been found by warriors both on horseback and afoot, scouting the back trail for signs of army reinforcements. Corporal Robert Sale was dead. Sergeants Patrick Daly and John Fredericks were wounded but managed to escape along with two or three other enlisted men and civilian Joe Blodgett, who all scampered back toward the supply train. Two more soldiers lit out in the opposite direction and showed up a few days later in the town of Virginia City over 100 miles to the east. One of them by the name of McGregor urgently wired ninety miles further east to Fort Ellis for an ambulance. Thinking the soldier must be badly wounded, the post commander, Captain Benham, quickly complied with the request. His reaction when McGregor showed up at Fort Ellis without a scratch was not recorded but can be imagined.[8]

Yellow Wolf, Band of Geese, Dropping From A Cliff, Sun Tied, Calf Of Leg, Stripes Turned Down, Red Spy and Light In The Mountain were among those who captured the howitzer and, more importantly, 2,000 rounds of ammunition. Many stories have swirled around the howitzer in the decades after the battle: whether the soldiers had disabled the firing mechanism before fleeing; could it still have been used by the Nez Perce against Gibbon's surrounded force; how it finally ended up down in the river bottom from its original position on the hillside west of the siege area. The one I like best was told to McWhorter by War Singer:

> *I have this neighbor that run the cannon into the water at the Big Hole fight . . . him and another man about his age were looking over the cannon and some way it started down-hill, he said they never done it for purpose, this man wasn't much of a warrior, he attended more to his uncle's horses, but he saw a lot of fighting.*[9]

Oops.

Shortly after the capture of the howitzer and the ammunition, Red Moccasin Tops, wearing a wolfskin cape, determined to kill and die, crawled close to the army line on the south and was badly wounded, as were the first two warriors who tried to rescue him. Eventually, Strong Eagle succeeded in carrying him partway back to safety before taking a bullet below the ribs. Finally, Bighorn Bow, urged on by Yellow Bull—Red Moccasin Tops' father—succeeded in retrieving the warrior. By then he was dead. Some of the heart for heavy fighting left the Nee-Me-Poo warriors.

Five Wounds, friend of the dead Rainbow, had been fighting from the willows in the river bottom. Sometime after hearing of the death of Red Moccasin Tops he recklessly charged and made it almost to the trenches before he was cut down. Another warrior was somehow able to reach for his gun, which apparently slid down the slope, but his body was too close to the army line to rescue. His was the only one left unburied by the Real People.

In the late afternoon a stiff breeze came down out of the mountains. Warriors on the hillside above the ravine lit a line of grass on fire. It began to burn down the slope toward the trenches. The soldiers and volunteers could do nothing but watch it creep closer, imagining a horde of warriors behind the screen of smoke. Before the fire reached the flat and torched the defenders out, the wind died. There must have been a collective sigh of relief in the trenches.

As the long day drew to a close, most of the warriors

surrounding Gibbon's force slipped away to join their families heading south. Only Frog and twelve others remained, dodging from one position to another before firing in order to create the illusion of a larger force. Around midnight they heard someone far away shouting in English. Frog whispered to others nearby to be still. Eventually, a rider galloped through the darkness into the ring of soldiers and volunteers, and a moment later the army position erupted with cheers. Reinforcements were near, the warriors guessed, no sense in sticking around. After firing two good-bye volleys they melted into the darkness, leaving some of the soldiers so spooked they continued firing at phantoms the rest of the night and into the day.

Company "A" two dead and five wounded. Company "D" three dead and four wounded. Company "F" two dead, six wounded. Company "G" six dead and six wounded. Company "I" three dead and five wounded. Company "K" also three dead and five wounded. Five volunteers dead, four hurt. Gibbon wounded. Bradley dead. Guide Bostwick dead, also Sergeant Page from the Second Cavalry. Gutshot, Lieutenant William English would linger for eleven painful days. More than a thirty-percent casualty rate. It had been a helluva twenty-four hours, not the way Gibbon must have imagined it would end when he first gazed upon the sleeping camp of the Real People.

The drive up to the Visitor Center on the bluff overlooking the battlefield only takes a few minutes. This was one of the places from where Nez Perce marksmen poured fire into the soldiers occupying the camp. I luck out and find a parking space in the crowded lot next to a strip of grass where members of the Frontier Soldiers Association have set up tents and army gear from the 1870s. A squad of five marches up and down the length of grass demonstrating basic army drill, attracting a small crowd with cameras. None of the Nez Perce present are watching.

Wandering around, I see Superintendent Frank Walker over from the park headquarters at Spalding and we say our hellos. Sue Buschel, in charge of the Montana and eastern Idaho park sites, is here, of course, busy, and Otis Halfmoon, Site Ranger at the Bear Paw Battlefield. I tell him I plan to be in his neck of the woods in about ten days. He won't be there then, he says, but I should look up Jim Magera, a new seasonal ranger who's long had a special interest in the Bear Paw battle and its aftermath. After scarfing down an Indian taco and a can of soda pop, I go inside the Visitor Center and catch most of a presentation on plants used by the Nez Perce. A park naturalist passes around samples of edible roots and medicinal herbs. Fascinating stuff, and the crowd gives her a good hand of applause at the end.

Outside, Ranger Halfmoon is getting ready to give a talk on Jackson Sundown, so I pull my lawn chair out of my van and sit at the edge of the audience. The day is turning windy from the south, one of those big Montana blows that you can feel in your bones. I scrunch my baseball cap down to my ears and take a listen. Otis Halfmoon is descended from the Five Wounds family and has a deep interest and knowledge of the Big Hole battle. Today he talks about Jackson Sundown, a boy at the time of the battle, who became the world-champion bronco rider thirty-five years later at the Pendleton Roundup at an age when most riders had long since retired all stove-up. Halfmoon is one of the best impromptu speakers I've ever heard, and he takes the crowd on a wild, informative, often humorous ride from all-Indian rodeos in out-of-the-way towns through sign language to Lewis and Clark. The folks Lewis and Clark saw with pierced noses back in 1805 and 1806, he says, were tourists from downriver.

Before the Flag Song begins I find time to stand in line for another piece of fry bread smothered with hamburger and sauce and tomato and onion. Proceeds from the food sales go to support the Lookingglass Powwow held in Kamiah every summer. I'm not making a pig out of myself, just helping a good cause. Really. The wind must be howling a sustained thirty miles an hour through the clear skies when the drummers and singers begin the Flag Song. An elder in full regalia carries a six-foot staff with a line of eagle feathers along most of its length, another the U.S. flag. The Eagle Staff is the flag of the Nez Perce tribe. They enter the circle of visitors followed by a line of men dancing a slow, deliberate two-step in rhythm with the drums. After greetings from park service and tribal officials comes the Honor Song. Women and children in traditional dress join the men in the slow, clock-wise dance, backs straight, knees bending and heads bobbing in unison. Following the Honor Song an elder speaks of unity and the need to mend fences, both between whites and Nez Perce and among the Nez Perce themselves.

Now, the Friendship Dance. Onlookers can join in, and soon two circles form, an outer one facing inward and moving clockwise, the inner one facing out and moving in the opposite direction. The drumbeat and dance step are simple enough that even klutzes like me catch on after a few seconds, but it really doesn't matter how well one can keep the rhythm. The heart of the dance rests in greeting and touching hands with everyone in the other circle. After a complete rotation, I bounce into the inner ring and continue shaking hands, my index finger for shy, tiny pre-schoolers, firm grips and hellos with the men, a brief touch for elder women. I'm reminded of descriptions from the last century from whites who witnessed the meeting of Nee-Me-Poo bands in the buffalo country. Each band leader would arrange his people in a dismounted line with the warriors at the front, then the elders and women, followed by the children arranged by age. The two bands would then file past each other, shaking hands with everyone, friends not seen for months or years, relatives perhaps, until everyone had greeted all in the other band, the greatest warrior touching the youngest child. So it is today until the drummers end their song with a resounding flourish. After we return to our seats we remain standing as the elders retire the eagle standard and U.S. flag. The Big Hole commemoration is over for another year.

The wind blows me all over the road the ten miles east to Wisdom. Turning south, the van can manage no more than forty miles-per-hour into the gale. Luckily, traffic is light this late weekend afternoon, and I have only a few miles to go before the turnoff to Twin Lakes. The view is spectacular after I turn west on the side road. The ragged, snowy peaks of the Continental Divide stretch for sixty miles in front of me and to the north, their abrupt rise accentuated by the flat valley floor. The soil here is about 15,000 feet deep, the valley filling over millions of years with eroded earth from the surrounding mountains. Big Hole, indeed.

The afternoon and evening of the battle, the Real People made about eighteen miles before halting to take care of the wounded. Warriors constructed rock rifle pits to protect this camp, one night too late. At a council of the head men Lean Elk took over the leadership of the daily march from Looking Glass. Lean Elk and his band had spent the last eight years in the buffalo country, and his knowledge of the trails in the area they were to traverse was invaluable. It might seem surprising that a man who had only joined the non-treaty bands the week before in the Bitterroot Valley would be chosen to take the lead, but such was the fluid nature of Nee-Me-Poo tribal structure. The chiefs—including Looking Glass, who many blamed for the lack of vigilance that contributed to the Big Hole disaster—would continue to meet in council almost every evening, but they now trusted Lean Elk to take care of each day's movements.

That night Fair Land died of her wounds, and in the next few days, Gray Eagle and Red Heart, certainly others. The total number of Nez Perce killed as a result of the attack at the Big Hole is lost in time. Estimates range from about sixty to more than 100. Thunder Rising's best guess was thirty men of all ages and fifty women and children, about one in ten of the People. In the days ahead the young warriors ranged far and wide seeking fresh horses, food, cloth for bandages, revenge. Every white man they met would regret not fleeing to some town for safety. The young Nee-Me-Poo fighters were seriously angry.

The road to Twin Lakes takes me somewhere close to that first camp. I'm not convinced anyone will ever be able to pinpoint the location, if there indeed was a single location. Family groups or bands might have halted wherever the wounded could take no more travel. Some historians place the location near Swamp Creek north of here toward the battlefield where thirty-three rifle pits were once found. The problem with that spot is that it is only about five or six miles from the battleground, which does not jibe with most Nez Perce accounts of the distance traveled that first day. Perhaps thirty-three warriors stopped there the first night to protect the back trail. In terms of mileage a more likely location is somewhere along Lake Creek which flows out of the

Twin Lakes in the mountains to the Big Hole River. I just don't know.

The road wastes little time in turning miserable. Usually, I prefer these byways, but this is ridiculous. Beaverhead County officials must have gotten a bargain price on some oversized gravel that other jurisdictions refused to touch with a fifty-foot pole. The washboard rattles my teeth, and everything inside the van bounces around. I try varying my speed anywhere from five miles-an-hour up to thirty-five, but nothing seems to help. Finally, given the choice of shaking my van to pieces slowly or quickly, I opt for getting it over with as soon as possible. After twelve excruciating miles I turn onto Forest Service Road 183. Yes! The rutted dirt and occasional big rocks leading to the campground at Twin Lakes are like heaven.

Before falling into a dreamless sleep I remember a joke Otis Halfmoon told. It went something like this:

This cavalry lieutenant was leading his company along a road when they came upon a Nez Perce warrior lying flat on the ground, one ear pressed to the earth.

"What's going on?" the lieutenant asked.

"One wagon, moving fast, pulled by four mules, carrying the driver with dark brown hair and one passenger, red hair, followed by three riders in single file. Two of the horses sorrel, one gray, all shod," the warrior slowly said.

"That's amazing!" the lieutenant answered. "You can tell all that about who's coming this way just by listening to the ground?"

"Hell, no," the warrior answered, still not moving. "They all just ran over me."

Notes

[1] AGO, *Letters*, roll 338, p. 412-413.

[2] AGO, *Letters*, roll 337, p. 419.

[3] quoted in Beal, Merrill D., *I Will Fight No More Forever*, University of Washington Press, Seattle, 1963, p. 126.

[4] McWhorter, *Hear Me*, p. 383.

[5] McWhorter, *Yellow Wolf*, p. 130.

[6] Beal, *I Will Fight*, p. 138.

[7] McWhorter, *Papers*, Folder 186, item 57.

[8] *Bozeman Times*, August 23, 1877.

[9] McWhorter, *Papers*, Folder 34, item 110.

Martin Stadius

The Big Hole.

Martin Stadius

Tepee frames mark the site of the
Nee-Me-Poo camp at Big Hole.

Washington State University Library

Rifle pits at Big Hole battlefield

245

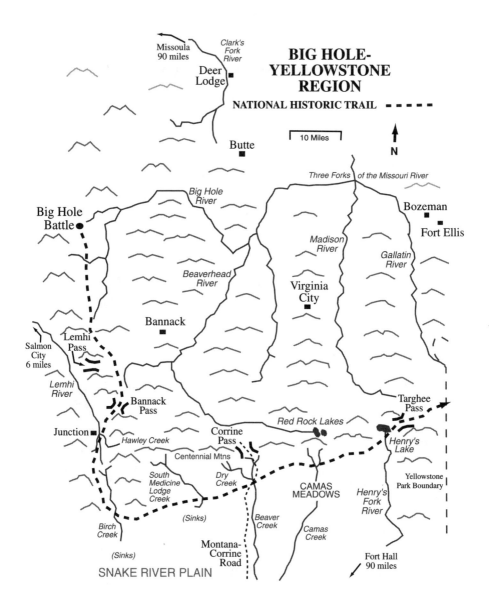

BIG HOLE-
YELLOWSTONE
REGION

NATIONAL HISTORIC TRAIL

CHAPTER TEN

BIRCH CREEK

I wake with first light, but doze off again in the warmth of my sleeping bag in my van. It's after seven before I convince myself it's time to get up. I'll do without coffee this morning, having decided while cozy in the bag to eat back at Fetty's in Wisdom. Their breakfasts have always been too good to pass up. I also make up my mind to try a different route back to the highway.

Once I reach the valley floor there's a track that follows Lake Creek. On the map it doesn't look promising—dashed lines indicating at best unimproved dirt—but I'm willing to try anything to avoid the county road I took yesterday. I can also take a close look at the country where the Nee-Me-Poo might have camped. The first half mile isn't bad, rutted and rocky and slow-going, infinitely preferable to that washboard gravel until I come to a stream crossing that doesn't show on the map. The ford is maybe five yards wide but looks like it might be too deep for my van, so I replace my hiking boots with tennis shoes, roll up my jeans to my knees and step into the creek. The icy water wakes me up faster than any caffeine possibly could, quickly rising and soaking my pants above my knees. There's no way the van can make it. Back to the county road. Damn.

In his official report on the Big Hole battle to General Terry in

St. Paul, Colonel Gibbon wrote that sniping continued a second day with the final volleys from the Nez Perce coming late in the evening of the August 10 or very early in the morning of the eleventh. This stands in direct contradiction to the memories of the Nez Perce that the last warriors departed a full twenty-four hours earlier. Gibbon also stated in his report that a courier from General Howard arrived that first night, having passed the wagon train in the darkness without spotting it. This man, probably a civilian named Nelse McGillian, was the rider Frog allowed to pass into the trenches with the resulting cheers when he informed the beleaguered force that General Howard was near. A second courier from Howard, Sergeant Oliver Sutherland of the First Cavalry, arrived shortly after the first. Following down Trail Creek, he had found the wagon train about midnight and brought the welcome news to Gibbon that it was safe. Nez Perce narratives make no mention of a second rider, so it is likely the last warriors departed in the interim. The fact that Gibbon sent a detail back to the train and had it brought forward without incident the afternoon of the tenth, as he also stated in his report, seems to belie his contention that the siege was still underway that day.

General Howard arrived at the battlefield about 10 A.M. on the August 11, the end of a grueling forced march. After receiving word August 6 at Lolo Springs of Gibbon's arrival at Missoula and immediate pursuit of the Nez Perce, Howard and the four companies of cavalry covered twenty-two miles on the seventh and thirty-four on the eighth, reaching just beyond Stevensville. The evening of the August 9 found them at the southern end of the Bitterroot Valley, having traversed its length in less than two days.

While passing through the Bitterroot, Howard somehow found time to pen a response to the newspapers criticizing his conduct of the campaign, a waste of ink that only provided more ammunition for ridicule. He also sent back orders to the trailing infantry and artillery battalions to halt once they reached the Bitterroot Valley, pending further instructions, and directed Cushing's and Field's companies of artillery to detach themselves from the command and return to San Francisco via the freight road over Corinne Pass to the transcontinental railroad in Utah. Finally, the one-armed general issued orders to Colonel Wheaton's column of the Second

Infantry, making its roundabout way through the northern Spokane country to Montana, to turn back. Howard must have thought that, with Gibbon and the Seventh Infantry close on the heels of the Nez Perce, the end of the war was near.

Major Edwin Mason, Howard's chief of staff, was not happy with what he encountered in the Bitterroot. He also found time to write to his wife his impressions of the valley's settlers:

They have bought watches and jewelry taken from the people killed in Idaho, sold them goods from their stores, sold them ammunition, and are now cursing us, some for not coming faster, and other for coming at all, saying this is not our Department and we are not wanted. . . . It is for such cattle that we risk our lives.[1]

Most of the army horses were becoming jaded after eleven straight days of travel. Indian ponies were used to living off graze, but the bigger army horses needed massive amounts of fodder and oats to keep going for extended periods. Howard wanted very much to be in on the final blow, even if it meant leaving his command far behind, so he and thirty-nine men with the best mounts took off at a trot at sunrise of August 10. Seventeen of the thirty-nine were Bannock Indians led by Buffalo Horn, longtime enemies of the Nee-Me-Poo who had joined Howard as scouts at Kamiah. They made an astonishing fifty-three miles that day, reaching the Continental Divide and camping on the upper reaches of Trail Creek. During the night seven volunteers, who had slipped away from Gibbon's command, walked into Howard's camp with stories of disaster.

So much for the end of the war.

The general sped a rider back toward Major Mason with instructions to hurry up. Realizing his tiny escort could easily be overwhelmed, Howard ordered that downed timber be piled into barricades and extra fires be built to simulate a larger force. They spent a restless night before cautiously winding their way down Trail Creek to the battered Seventh Infantry.

The night after the battle and siege Gibbon had sent out three messengers, one to the wagon train and two toward the nearest mining town of Deer Lodge. The first made it to the wagon train then continued on the back trail, missing Howard's little party in the mountains near Ross Hole. He ran into Major Mason and the bulk of the cavalry the evening of the tenth and gave the major a note that ended:

> *We are near the mouth of Big Hole pass with a number of wounded and need medical attendance and assistance of all kinds, and hope you will hurry to our relief.*[2]

Mason dispatched a courier back to the infantry and artillery column in the Bitterroot Valley, ordering them forward with all possible speed. With Mason were two army surgeons, Drs. Alexander and Fitzgerald. Mason gave them a small guard and told them to ride through the night to the aid of Gibbon. The rest of the cavalry followed the next morning.

The first of the two messengers to make it to Deer Lodge was a civilian, Billy Williams, who covered the eighty-mile distance in about thirty hours, arriving early the eleventh on a horse he had borrowed at a mining camp along the way. Williams carried two messages, one to Gibbon's army superiors stating only that the colonel's infantry had sustained losses while capturing the Nez Perce camp— the other to Montana Governor Potts urgently requesting medical assistance and any other help the territory could provide. For a day or two, Gibbon's superiors, Generals Terry in St. Paul and Sheridan in Chicago, were under the impression that the Seventh Infantry had won a decisive victory. It soon became clear, though, that the message to Governor Potts pleading for help more accurately represented the situation.

In his version of events written after the war, General Howard described the scene when he arrived at Gibbon's camp as "all right and cheerful." The wounded were "doing well." The colonel himself had a "bright face" and greeted Howard with a casual, "Glad to see you." Army surgeon Fitzgerald who got there the next morning had a different take on the situation. He wrote to his wife:

> *We found a horrible state of affairs. There were 39 wounded men . . . many of them suffering intensely.*[3]

250

The Bannocks with Howard wasted no time. Riding to the deserted Nee-Me-Poo camp, they easily located many graves. Pulling the bodies out of the earth, they methodically began scalping and mutilating. One body of a woman they hoisted in the air, tied to an abandoned teepee pole they found nearby, before hacking at it. Howard watched and did nothing. After the war he claimed to be saddened by the event and described a touching scene in which the officers present tenderly reburied the bodies after the Bannocks were finished. No one else remembered this act of compassion. As at all the previous battles, the Nee-Me-Poo had not scalped or abused any of the bodies of the white dead left on the field.

By August 13 Gibbon and Howard were ready to part company. Word had come of the approach of a caravan of twenty-eight wagons bearing food, medical supplies and civilian doctors from the towns of Deer Lodge, Butte and Helena. Gibbon, with the wounded in the wagons brought from the Bitterroot Valley, would head north and meet that relief party. Howard would turn south on the trail of the Real People. One company each of infantry and artillery from Howard's lagging foot column showed up in time to join the cavalry. With the addition of fifty men from Gibbon's Seventh Infantry under Captain Browning, Howard's force numbered more than 300 as it followed the wide swath of hoof prints and travois gouges across the Big Hole Valley. Scouts quickly brought him word that the Nee-Me-Poo had crossed through a pass from the Big Hole into another valley farther south called Horse Prairie. To the northeast of Horse Prairie on Grasshopper Creek lay the mining town of Bannack, once the territorial capital of Montana. Howard ordered his column in that direction. The first night, camped at the south end of the Big Hole, he received words from two excited messengers from Bannack that several settlers in Horse Prairie were dead.

The revenge had begun.

Wisdom, with a population of about 200, is an isolated little town some sixty miles from the nearest school. There's one gas station, two motels, a church, the Antler Bar, an art gallery, a grocery, a hardware and sporting goods store with a huge depiction of a reclining Indian maiden with Barbie-doll curves on the front of its building, and Fetty's Restaurant and Bar. I've missed the Fetty's morning rush, if there is one on a summer weekday, and have the place to myself. These days the Big Hole Valley is cattle country, and 8:30 in the morning before the weather heats up is prime time for work. The vacationing trout hounds are either already out beating up the water or nursing hangovers in dark motel rooms. Breakfast costs me $4.85 for a plate piled to the rim with eggs, country sausage, hash browns and toast perched precariously on top. It's going to take a while, but I'm determined to eat it all.

The first summer I looked into the war, I spent a Friday night bellied up to the bar in the room next door getting acquainted with McGillicuddy's Peppermint Schnapps, courtesy of a couple of friendly locals who had just discovered this obscure delight and were eager to share their good fortune with a stranger. Their names escape me, although the one without the bushy beard might have been Dave. I assume the information was imprinted on some of the brain cells that didn't survive the evening. Anyway, the conversation eventually turned to the battlefield ten miles to the west.

My new buddies told me that a certain famous country singer had bought a ranch in the valley, some sort of an investment. He showed up now and then to admire his property and decided to apply for a resident permit to hunt elk. Sorry, the state said, he didn't meet the requirements to qualify as a resident of Montana. The famous singer was offended. Here he'd spent all this money for a big ranch, helping the local economy and all, and the state couldn't just wink and give him his permit? Nope, the state said, he could take his chances in the non-resident lottery just like the regular folks. The famous singer didn't have to put up with that kind of crap, so he donated money for an archaeological study of the Big Hole Battlefield. The National Park Service gladly accepted the loot, and the Nez Perce tribe let him shoot his elk on their reservation in Idaho. The park service and tribe got valuable new information. The famous singer got a rack of antlers for his wall, and it only cost him thirty grand. Everybody was happy, except the elk and a few residents of Montana. Sometime during the evening I asked the fellow who might have been Dave: what do you'all think about this famous country singer? Well, he said, if the famous singer was to walk through that door right now, I doubt if anyone in this bar would bother turning a head. The bushy-bearded guy who wasn't Dave nodded sagely. Except maybe to spit, he added. Not all cowboys respect famous country singers.

Yesterday's stiff south wind kicks in again with a vengeance as I drive the twelve miles to Jackson, a little resort village at the site of a hot springs. Billowing clouds sail along the crest of the Continental Divide, but the sky over the valley floor remains clear. The head wind blows me down into third gear. It's a good thing I'm in no hurry today.

Camped a few miles southeast of the hot springs the evening of August 13, General Howard studied his maps and listened to his scouts. He was aware that his reputation continued to suffer in both the regional and national presses. With the exception of the battle above the Clearwater, for almost two months he had followed and followed and followed but simply could not catch his prey. His men and horses were tired and could not go on forever. What to do now?

The Nez Perce now in Horse Prairie had three alternatives. They could turn east, skirting Bannack. That would be too good to be true. By heading directly toward Bannack Howard was cutting the chord of an arc and would be in position within a day to pounce. Or, they could recross the Continental Divide at Lemhi Pass and turn north back toward their homeland. Once they passed the settlement of Salmon City a trail would eventually debouch them near Mount Idaho where Major Green and his force were waiting. If the Nez Perce took that route Howard could follow and squeeze them into a trap between the two armies. He must have felt some satisfaction that the strategy he formulated at Kamiah of three separate commands might finally pay off. Colonel Wheaton's northern party had certainly proved useless. On the other hand, the Nez Perce might cross out of Horse Prairie to the southwest over Bannack Pass. From there they could continue south to the Snake River Plain then head east toward Yellowstone National Park and the buffalo country beyond.

The safest course for Howard would simply be to follow the non-treaty bands. The troops would remain a couple of days behind the Nez Perce but would be in no danger of losing them. If the fugitives did turn north toward their homeland such a straight pursuit would be the correct decision. His two Nez Perce scouts, though, were positive the non-treaty bands would take the third alternative. Accepting their judgment, Howard formulated a plan to move his command southeast from Bannack along a freight road beside the Red Rock River to Corinne Pass eighty miles distant. With a little luck he could intercept the Nez Perce on the Snake River Plain beyond Corinne Pass.

That same day General Sherman was leaving the Upper Geyser Basin in Yellowstone Park after being properly impressed with the sights. His subordinates in charge during his absence—Adjutant General Edward Townsend in New York, General Sheridan in Chicago and General McDowell in San Francisco—remained in constant telegraphic communication with each other and with outposts in Montana, attempting to get a grasp on the situation around the isolated Big Hole. They preferred not to believe the newspaper reports from Montana detailing the battle and the casualties suffered by Gibbon's force. Sheridan wrote to Townsend:

> *There is no further official news from Montana this morning. Gen. Terry thinks that the published dispatches from Gen'l Gibbon to Gov. Potts are not genuine. . . . Gibbon had doctors and medical supplies and did not lose his train or howitzer.*[4]

He was right about only one thing: Gibbon had not lost his wagon train. Sheridan was facing up, though, to the fact that the campaign against the Nez Perce was nowhere near over. He sent another telegraph on August 13, this one back to Terry in St. Paul:

> *Cooperate with Howard even to temporarily placing such troops as you may have to spare under his command if necessary and notify him there are no hostile Sioux for the Nez Perces to join south of the line of the Manitoba and such junction is preposterous.*[5]

Two weeks before, Sheridan had refused to believe the Real People had made it as far as the Bitterroot Valley. In the coming weeks he would learn what else they could accomplish, preposterous or not.

At Jackson I turn southwest on County Road 181 encountering more of the damn washboard and oversize gravel. It's time to introduce another character in the story, one John W. Redington who you'll hear from periodically from here on out. He corresponded extensively with McWhorter and also wrote a memoir, somehow both brief and wordy, of his experiences he called "Scouting in Montana." Of all the people involved in the war he's definitely one of the more interesting. His personalized stationery bore a photograph in the upper left corner of a man, presumably Redington himself, with some kind of ship behind him. Below the photo is the explanation:

> *In the N.W. background*
> *UC the prairie schooner*
> *Belle of the Buffalo*
> *Wallow—formerly flagship of*
> *the Swiss Navy.*

To the right of the photo was a printed salutation:

> *Dear Sir, Madam or Mlle:*
> *(He or She, as the case may be)*
> *In answer to your thrilling letter of so-and-so, which came to hand afterwards, would like to say:*

Above the salutation lay Redington's motto:

> *Veracity First!*
> *Safety Second!*
> *Loquacity Last!*

Despite his alleged devotion to veracity, in his correspondence with McWhorter he kept insisting his middle name was

Watermelon. Needless to say, I found it prudent to verify his version of events as much as possible. It turns out he was pretty much accurate.

When the war started, Redington was an itinerant printer in Salt Lake City. Itching for excitement, he first wired to Idaho Governor Mason Brayman, volunteering his services for the mere price of a stagecoach ticket to Boise. The governor regretfully declined. Some weeks later, Redington talked the *Salt Lake Tribune* into naming him a "Special Correspondent" and headed north to Montana, arriving in Deer Lodge about the time of the battle at the Big Hole. Hooking up with a force of volunteers mobilizing to aid Howard, he rode part-way with them then took off on his own. As a scout he was a bust. He easily found the broad swath of trail leading south from the battlefield, but somehow missed the point where Howard's shod army horses veered off toward Bannack. He thus gained the dubious distinction of being the only white to follow the Nee-Me-Poo over the divide into Horse Prairie. Warriors watching the trail wasted no time in teaching him the error of his ways.

Here is his version of what happened:

> But my sticking to the trail and admiration of the country was rudely broken in upon by a bunch of about seven Indians dashing at me across a meadow. As an act of courtesy I also dashed off into a wooded swamp, and their bullets hit high on the trees close by. They might have been soft-nosed bullets, but they sounded like hot tamales or scalded snowballs the way they spattered out when they struck and mussed up the woodland.
>
> By changing my course and coming to another edge of the swamp I could look out and see the Indians sitting on their horses and firing a few shots into the swamp at the point where I entered it. It was rather tough travelling through the swamp, but after a horse had sunk half way to his knees he found firm bottom, so I took a southerly course, aiming to again strike the trail further on, which I finally did.
>
> ### AS A SWAMP ANGEL
>
> Being a swamp angel in a miry morass was a strange and

sloppy stunt, but if the swamp cover had not been there the hostiles would soon have made some other kind of angel of me and sent me climbing the golden stair, which might have its compensations, for I could throw down the top step for filling the teeth of some of the boys who could not keep up with the high cost of dentistry. The two hours delay was a lucky strike for me, and kept me from rushing up on the hostile camp without a letter of introduction.

It was very kind of the beavers who had dammed up that creek and flooded that piece of timber, for it certainly gave me the cover that saved my scalp. They must have known I was coming.[6]

The swamp where Redington had his first encounter with the Real People is probably off to my right at the base of the Continental Divide. It's an easy 600-foot climb over seven miles through forest to Skinner Meadows where the Nee-Me-Poo camped the night of August 11 near the top of an unnamed pass into Horse Prairie. I pull off the road just short of the meadows. The clouds I'd seen earlier scudding along the Continental Divide, just four miles to the west now, are overhead, leaving the air damp and chilled. Profligate wildflowers wet with dew are blooming violet and ruby and white amid clear rivulets flowing from the top of the continent. I hop across one channel, then another and another, landing in natural perfume, a carpet softer than any you can find in the best of stores, until I reach the river. Somewhere around here the Nee-Me-Poo buried two more victims of the Big Hole assault. On the bank leading to a ford the Real People would have used, the prints of deer and cattle are etched sharply in the mud. After taking off my boots I cross and follow twin tracks upstream onto higher ground covered with a mixture of sage and grass. The ghost of a road disappears into a narrow band of trees. The parallel tracks are probably the remnant of an old pioneer road which succeeded an Indian trail, which itself followed a game path. The forest gives way to a field of green, brilliant even in overcast. Skinner Meadows.

It was here that Redington met his first Nez Perce face-to-face:

257

At the next Indian camp I came to the still-warm ashes showed that the Indians were not far ahead. I was pretty hungry, and was lucky enough to find a piece of Indian bread about as big as your hand that had been overlooked in the ashes. It was made of straight flour and water, but just then it was a sweeter morsel than any angel-cake that ever happened.

The saddest sight at this camp was an old, helpless Indian lying on a few old buffalo robes, with only a bottle of water alongside. He looked as though the snows of a hundred winters had fallen on his head, but still there was no trace of baldness. He volunteered a wan smile at the sight of a human being, and made a feeble motion with one arm, pointing to his forehead, making a mumble with his poor old toothless mouth. My compulsory schooling had not embraced his language, but I could understand that he was inviting me to shoot him in the forehead and end his misery. Instead of accommodating him I fed him half of the piece of bread I had found, which he ate ravenously. He seemed quite disappointed when I made a motion of flapping my wings to indicate that I must skiddoo and be on my way.[7]

I wonder what the old man, whose name has been lost in time, must have thought as he watched the crazy white man waving his arms in the air. I try to imagine the scene when he told his family he wanted to be left behind to die at this beautiful place. As an elder his wishes would have been respected. There must have been tears, hugs, memories. Or had his relatives all been killed a few days before?

Crossing back over the river, I continue on in my van as Forest Road 181 dips into Horse Prairie by following Bloody Dick Creek. One of the first settlers along the stream was an Englishman named Richard with a penchant for the adjective "bloody." Horse Prairie ranges from east to west for about twenty miles, pinched like a wasp in the middle by converging bare hills, getting its name from the time of Lewis and Clark. On the westward leg of their journey they met a band of Shoshones here and found it was led by Sacajawea's older brother, Cameahwait. After a joyful reunion

Cameahwait was more than happy to provide horses to the explorers who had recently cached their canoes after paddling up the length of the Missouri River. Once out of the forest my van again feels the brunt of the wind. I head east, then north again through fields of grass and hills of sage, my sights set on the ghost town of Bannack.

In 1877 the settlers and miners in the area had listened for news of the errant Nez Perce with trepidation. The locals also had cause for concern about their own Indian troubles. Leading a small band of warriors, a Snake Indian called Major Jim by the whites had been prowling the periphery of Horse Prairie for weeks, waiting, many believed, to hook up with the Nez Perce. Major Jim bore a long-standing antipathy against the whites, held in check only by his chief, Tendoy. Isolated ranchers had found it prudent to send their women and children to Bannack for safety.

Nee-Me-Poo warriors with blood in their eyes swept across Horse Prairie on August 12. Soon William Montague, James Farnsworth, Thomas Flynn, James Smith and Alexander Cooper lay dead. Others escaped to the hills on foot and eventually made their way to Bannack. The warriors ransacked houses for supplies and added several hundred horses to the Nez Perce remuda. Remembering the Bitterroot volunteers who had joined the army to attack the village and shoot women and children, the warriors looked upon these civilians as fair game. The main Nee-Me-Poo caravan arrived late in the day and set up camp along the upper reaches of the prairie. Bedding from the settler's houses became bandages for the wounded.

General Howard arrived at Bannack to a hero's welcome on the fourteenth, just after the burial of four of the Horse Prairie settlers on Boot Hill above town. Men, women and children streamed a mile out of town to cheer the passing column. After so much abuse in Idaho and in the Bitterroot Valley from civilians and the press, the adulation must have been heartening for the beleaguered officer. The troops camped on Horse Prairie Creek after marching another four hours. Citizen militia from Butte and Deer Lodge joined the general that day, the same volunteers that Redington had abandoned in his rush to find Howard. Redington, meanwhile,

259

was over in Horse Prairie about to lose his horse, but not his life, to Nez Perce raiders. In a few days someone would find a letter from the Special Correspondent of the *Salt Lake Tribune* in an empty cabin. His exact whereabouts would remain a mystery for ten days.

General Howard could not keep his foot out of his mouth. Bannack was the terminus for a telegraph line, and he found time to wire General McDowell in San Francisco, updating his superior in a long, rambling telegram which included the following comments:

> . . . *if they escape into the Buffalo country beyond me is it worthwhile for me to pursue them further from my Department unless General Terry or General Crook will head them off or check their advance. . . . Please advise me that I may not wear out our troops to no purpose. We have made extraordinary marches and with prompt and energetic cooperation from the Eastern Departments may yet stop and destroy this most enterprising band of Indians, without this cooperation the result will be as it has been, doubtful. If Gibbon had 100 more men the work would have been complete. Surely he might have had more from all the Territory, three times as many.*[8]

McDowell was furious. His junior officer was questioning his standing order to pursue regardless of boundaries. Add to that, the thinly-veiled criticism of other officers from a man who had dallied for two weeks waiting for the Second Infantry to arrive all the way from Georgia. McDowell's blistering response would not reach Howard for a week because early on August 15 Howard and his weary column departed Horse Prairie for Corinne Pass.

Bannack is now a state park, so I hand over a few bucks for admission before strolling down the dusty main street toward the red-brick bulk of the Meade Hotel. On either side are the dun, weathered, wood and adobe forms of saloons and shops and homes from another century. This was a town built on gold, a town of miners, thieves, vigilantes, gamblers, shopkeepers, teamsters, whores, entrepreneurs, confidence men, preachers, mothers and kids. As the wooden sidewalk resonates to the rhythm of my boots, dust-devils swirling ahead, it's easy to imagine the clatter of wagons, the pervading pungency of manure, the monotonous pounding of stamp mills, music and laughter emanating from the honky-tonks. Many of the buildings are sealed, but the door atop the steps leading to the Meade Hotel is open and I step inside.

The interior is cool and dark, specks of dust floating in the beams of light angling down from the windows. Ornate woodwork and generations of graffiti adorn the walls. Upstairs, the rooms are tiny cells of plaster. One of them would have been home to the wife of Daniel Winters during the scare. When word came of the attacks on the Horse Prairie homesteads, she strapped a holster and revolver around the waist of her dress, mounted a horse and set out to find her husband. In the company of twenty-four men including a Methodist preacher, Brother Van, she stoically inspected the bodies of the dead. She didn't find her man. Daniel Winters stumbled into Bannack the following day. Outside, I climb Boot Hill past the site of the gallows used to remove incorrigibles from frontier society. The townspeople buried Smith, Montague, Farnsworth and Flynn here, but no traces of their graves remain. The fifth victim found his final resting place near the spot he was killed, a mining sluice box for a coffin.

The day is getting along, and I have a good distance to go. Hurrying downhill, I fire up my van and retrace my route back to Horse Prairie. The road turns to well-maintained gravel and aims like an arrow for a treeless notch on the Continental Divide. Bannack Pass. Although the upward grade seems slight, I'm forced to floor the gas pedal to maintain thirty miles-per-hour in third gear. Dust kicked up by a pickup traveling in the other direction tells me why. The pickup must be doing forty miles-per-hour, but the driver can barely keep ahead of the dirt cloud surging behind him. The grit strikes my windshield like sandpaper, and one of my wipers flutters as if it intends to abandon ship. At the top of the pass I pull over at elevation 7,672 feet. Opening the door is a chore, and I barely get my fingers out of the way before the wind slams it shut for me. My baseball cap goes flying. I chase it for a thirty feet before stomping on it with a boot. It needed cleaning anyway.

Black and gray clouds roil past in fantastic shapes, seemingly only fifty feet overhead, but there's no smell of rain in the air. I can't even guess the wind speed, forty, fifty miles-per-hour sustained, gusts higher.

The road dives into Railroad Canyon and a respite from the wind. Ahead is the Lemhi Valley and the town of Leadore, as in the heavy metal. In the 1870s the town was called Junction, where Canyon, Hawley, Eighteenmile and Big Timber creeks unite to form the Lemhi River, a branch of the same Salmon River which rolls through the Nee-Me-Poo homeland. At that time the valley was home to a few hundred settlers and a band of Shoshones led by Tendoy.

About the time of the Big Hole battle, settlers in the Lemhi Valley and Salmon City to the north passed the hat and collected about $350 which they used to buy out the owner of a fish trap near Salmon City. The trap, which had prevented salmon from reaching Tendoy's village farther upriver, became driftwood. This act of brotherly affection occurred solely because the settlers were scared silly Tendoy would join the Nee-Me-Poo in the war. The chief had been complaining vociferously for months about the trap and the failure of the government to deliver promised annuities to his people. The settlers could do nothing about the federal government, but the fish trap was another matter. The chief was delighted.

August 13 found the Real People crossing Bannack Pass and arriving at Junction about 8 A.M. As the families turned south and went into a day camp a few miles away, warriors inspected from a distance a small but formidable fort settlers had erected. About sixty feet square, with vertical timbers entrenched firmly in the ground, it bristled with rifles sticking from loopholes. Inside, the defenders had erected a second set of timbers about five feet high flush with the outer wall as additional protection against gunfire.

Accounts of what happened at Junction are all over the map. One witness, J. P. Clough, said that two men, Ed Swan and John Hays, went out and met with White Goose:

The Chiefs wished to assure us of the great love they had

for ranchers especially, and asked that we return to our homes that they might come and eat with us as evidence of their friendship. Captain Swan declined their kind invitation. They asked about the number of men in the stockade and Capt. Swan replied about one hundred.[9]

Actually about fifteen, and a story possibly rooted in reality.

From the top of the stockade H. C. McCreary claimed to have watched a chief harangue 400 warriors gathered in a large circle. Eventually, they mounted their ponies, formed a line and charged the fort, every warrior flat on the back of his horse. At the last second the line split in half and circled the fort before riding away, daunted by the imposing walls. Huzzah! Almost certainly the product of a fertile imagination.

An aspiring politician and eventual governor of Idaho added his modest two-bits. According to supporters spreading the word in newspapers, George Shoup of Salmon City, riding to the aid of his outnumbered compatriots and fellow voters, valiantly and fearlessly rode into the Nez Perce camp and demanded they leave the vicinity forthwith or face the sternest consequences, etc, etc. Cowed, the heathens slunk away. Political fantasy.

A Nez Perce, Shot In The Head, told McWhorter a slightly different story, one totally lacking in drama and heroics. After a brief conference between Tendoy and the Nee-Me-Poo headmen, the bands continued south as they had planned. They liberated a few horses from ranches in the area on general principle. No big deal.

My first stop in Leadore, population seventy-four, is the gas pump in front of the grocery store, then the district office of the Salmon National Forest just before it closes for the day. The permanent building is undergoing renovation, so I storm into the temporary quarters, find three employees and roar,

"Who's in charge of the wind around here?"

Silence. Suspicious stares. Then laughter. A woman tells me the guy in charge of the wind is in the back room. Actually, I tell them, I'm just looking for directions to the side canyon where the Nez Perce camped their first night in the Lemhi Valley. I'm following the trail, you see. She tells me the guy who knows that kind of stuff is the same one who's in charge of the wind today. In the back room. Feeling a little bit like Dorothy in Oz, I go back and find the wizard's name is Dana. He quickly pulls out a map and shows me Cold Springs Road off State Road 28. The road's a piece of cake, he says.

The view is breathtaking as I take leave of Leadore. At thirty-five miles-per-hour into the headwind I have time to take a lot of breaths. I visually soak up the scenery, the Beaverhead and Lemhi ranges towering above the narrow sage-covered valley, the tops of the 11,000-foot peaks and sky hidden by dark clouds fleeing north. I feel like I'm driving in some majestic, slightly malevolent, tunnel.

Six miles out of town I turn right, following the wizard's directions. Five minutes and a couple of turns later the road turns to rock going over a bluff, then to deep mud on the flat on the other side. Uh-oh. I back up until I can find a place to turn around. According to my map, once I get back to the highway I can take another unimproved road five miles further along and backtrack to Nez Perce Canyon tucked into the base of the Lemhi Range. I find the road with no problem and jump out to inspect the ford across Texas Creek. The bottom looks firm, the water only a few inches deep. Across the creek, though, is a ramshackle house right out of a Depression-era photograph, the dirt road running between the house and an outhouse. A barefoot girl of ten or eleven in a print dress steps out of the outhouse and stops, staring across the stream at me. There's no sign of a vehicle, but a curtain rustles inside a window. I give the girl my friendliest wave. She runs to the house, disappearing around the back, and I hear a door slam. I suddenly know I'm not going to disturb their privacy. Backing the van onto the highway, I continue my snail's pace toward Gilmore Summit and Birch Creek beyond.

Needing accurate information about the route of the non-treaty bands, General Howard dispatched six civilians to follow them into the Lemhi Valley. The six, including Alex Cruikshank, prudently elected to take Lemhi Pass, twelve miles north of Bannack Pass, in order to avoid any warriors watching the back trail. The morning after the Nee-Me-Poo crossed the Continental Divide, Cruikshank and the others arrived at Fort Lemhi, the agency for Tendoy's

Shoshones, then turned south to Junction. Three of the whites headed back over Bannack Pass to inform Howard of the direction the Nez Perce had taken. Howard's Nez Perce scouts had been correct: the non-treaty bands were still bound for the buffalo country, not turning back toward their homeland.

In the company of Major Jim and thirty other warriors, the remaining whites rode southeast up Hawley Creek, angling toward the Continental Divide south of Bannack Pass. This was an intriguing direction for Major Jim to take, an old-time trail over the divide into the Sheep Creek drainage of Montana, over another pass to South Medicine Lodge Creek, finally to the Snake River Plain. The mountainous shortcut was Major Jim's best chance to intercept the Nee-Me-Poo. Cruikshank, who provided the only narrative of Major Jim's whereabouts at this time, turned back after a few miles.

Cruikshank next met up with George Shoup, Tendoy, about forty settlers and as many Shoshone warriors holding a hasty council. Two Chinese men had arrived from Birch Creek farther south with disturbing news. Their English language skills were minimal, but the two managed to get the bare bones of their story across. A wagon train carrying goods intended for Shoup's store in Salmon City had been accosted by Nez Perce warriors on Birch Creek. White men were dead. Shoup discreetly decided to halt for the night, hoping the Nez Perce would clear out of the area by the next day.

Tendoy, however, figured the time was ripe for a little horse-stealing from his Nee-Me-Poo brethren and headed south with fifteen warriors, including his sons, Jack and Tendim. Cruikshank and two other whites named Falkner and Jarvis decided to trail along and see if they could help the men in the wagon train. In the middle of the night they heard horses milling about ahead, and Tendoy's son, Jack, slipped away into the darkness. Tendoy explained to Cruikshank what to expect next:

Nez Perce pretty soon. Dog bow-wow. Horses come. Maybe Nez Perce come quick, too. All keep close together, shoot Nez Perce, then run to the hills.

Soon they heard the thunder of hooves. Tendoy decided to skip the part about "shoot Nez Perce" and jumped on his horse yelling "Heap run!" When they finally stopped, Jack came along with about sixty-five horses, seven of which Cruikshank recognized as having been stolen from his ranch on Horse Prairie.[10] Nee-Me-Poo memories of the encounter were limited to Shot In The Head:

> *We continued on towards the Lemhi Valley, passing the Lemhi Indians. They told us not to remain longer near their place, and we kept going, crossing through the mountains. Short days later the Lemhis overtook us and put up a fight with us. We had a fight with those Lemhis in the mountains, but no one of our band was hurt."[11]*

Gilmore Summit is 7,186 feet. The crest of the Lemhi Range paralleling the highway is only four miles off to my right and soars almost 4,000 feet above the road, disappearing into swirling thunderheads. My odometer rolls over to a line of zeroes a few miles later. The old beast has made it 300,000 miles. Please, at least a thousand more.

The garbled story told by the Chinese was correct. Warriors had discovered the four sets of doubled wagons about mid-morning on August 15 and ordered the drivers to continue ahead to where the families had stopped for a mid-day rest. Lean Elk had adopted a routine of moving at first light, stopping late in the morning for several hours to cook the only meal of the day and to graze the horses, then continuing on until darkness. The children were given cold snacks through the day. It was a plan designed to outpace any pursuit and depended on fresh horses for success.

Mules pulled three of the freight outfits, but the fourth was drawn by eight horses. As the teamsters lit a cooking fire and tried to remain calm, some of the warriors began to inspect the horses' teeth. One Nez Perce remembered a teamster leaning against a wagon, whistling nervously, looking from left to right. Some warriors demanded that the whites sell bags of flour, to which they rapidly acquiesced, although the cargo belonged to Shoup. This was not a time to worry about petty details of ownership.

The wife of Geese Three Times Alighting remembered that one of the whites grabbed a bucket and started toward the creek as the families began to pull out. Her father motioned the man to vamoose. Al Lyons was that man, a rancher out looking for stray cattle. Happenstance had him chatting with the teamsters when the warriors came upon the wagon train. Lyons floated downstream until he was out of sight then lit out for the hills, reappearing a week later, his mind addled from fear. The chiefs ordered Dan Coombs, Al Green, Jim Haydon and two other whites onto horses and told them to ride north toward Junction. The headmen could not control their angry young men, though. The wife of Geese Three Times Alighting recalled distant gunfire soon after the families left the wagons. All five teamsters were dead.

Rifling the contents of the wagons before burning them, the warriors found ten barrels of whiskey and more in bottles. Some proceeded to get drunk. When the chiefs said, enough, and ordered sober men to smash the barrels, a brawl broke out. Five Snows shot Stripes Turned Down who was trying to pour the booze onto the ground. The wound would prove fatal in a few days. Chelotokiktkin and Red Elk fired at each other, the latter receiving a wound in one hand. Coyote With Flints stabbed Heyoom Pishkish in the side. The Real People were divided again. It was an ugly end to an ugly episode.[12]

The site of the Birch Creek massacre is marked by a monument erected by a Lions Club from Dubois, fifty miles away. A few picnic tables are scattered along the willows lining the creek, along with an outhouse. I'll camp here alone tonight, not a favorite place for the occasional tourists who find this remote valley. I change into my old tennis shoes and roam up and down both sides of the creek, chilled. A downpour begins, and the willows thrash with the gale. Thunder echoes from peak to peak across the narrow valley as darkness drops. My van eventually rocks me to sleep. Big country, big weather.

Notes

[1] Davison, *A Century Ago*, p. 7.

[2] Howard, *Nez Perce Joseph*, p. 199.

[3] Howard, *Nez Perce Joseph*, p. 203.

 Laufe, *Army Doctor's Wife*, p. 302-303.

[4] AGO, *Letters*, roll 337, p. 260.

[5] AGO, *Letters*, roll 337, p. 394.

[6] Redington, John W., *Scouting in Montana & Miscellaneous Papers SC683*, Montana Historical Society, Missoula, p. 2.

[7] Redington, *Scouting*, p. 3.

[8] AGO, *Letters*, roll 338, p. 554-556.

[9] Clough, J. P., *Recollections of the Nez Perce Indian War of 1877*, Idaho State Historical Society, Boise, p. 2.

[10] Cruikshank, Alexander, *Birch Creek Massacre SC584*, Montana Historical Society, Helena, p. 4-5.

[11] McWhorter, *Papers*, Folder 28, item 28.

[12] McWhorter, *Papers*, Folder 34, item 99.

 McWhorter, *Yellow Wolf*, p. 165.

Stevensville

Martin Stadius

Martin Stadius

A roadside attraction.

Martin Stadius

Skinner Meadows

CHAPTER ELEVEN

CAMAS MEADOWS

A t the first hint of light I'm up after a fitful night's sleep, warming my hands around a cup of coffee and stamping my feet to get my blood circulating. After the storm front passed about one in the morning the winds began to die down, until now a gentle breeze from the northeast is all that remains. The clouds have mostly dissipated, only white pillows left to adorn the mountain tops, and the rain has washed fresh color into the sage on the valley floor.

Five miles down the road I note a singular rock formation several hundred feet high and about a mile in circumference detached from the base of the Beaverhead Mountains. Passing here in 1835, the missionary Samuel Parker noted it in his journal. According to the mileages he gave, he and the Nez Perce accompanying him camped at the exact site of the murder of the teamsters on Birch Creek. It must have been a traditional stopover for Nee-Me-Poo traveling this country. What a different situation it was in 1835:

> *About eight in the morning some of the chiefs came to me and asked where they should assemble. I asked them if they could not be accommodated in the willows which skirt the stream on which we were encamped. They thought not. I then enquired if they could not take the poles of some of their*

lodges and construct a shade. They thought they could; and without any other directions went and made preparation, and about eleven o'clock came and said they were ready for worship. I found them all assembled, men, women, and children, between four and five hundred, in what I would call a sanctuary of God, constructed with their lodges, nearly one hundred feet long and twenty feet wide; and all were arranged in rows, through the length of the building, upon their knees, with a narrow space in the middle, lengthwise, resembling an aisle. The whole area was carpeted with their dressed skins, and they were all attired in their best. The chiefs were arranged in a semicircle at the end which I was to occupy. I could not have believed they had the means, or could have known how, to have constructed to convenient and so decent a place for worship, especially as it was the first time they had had public worship. The whole sight, taken together, sensibly affected me and filled me with astonishment; and I felt as though it was the house of God and the gate of heaven. . . . I never spoke to a more interesting assembly, and I would not have changed my then audience for any other upon earth; and I felt it was worth a journey across the Rocky Mountains, to enjoy this one opportunity with these heathen who are so anxious to come to a knowledge of God.[1]

Some of the Nee-Me-Poo in 1877 might have been present that day forty-two years before. Now they were running for their lives and fighting among themselves.

The mountains on either side of the Birch Creek corridor terminate in a stunning display of abrupt geology. The both lines of peaks simply end, and the Snake River Plain stretches before me, dotted with a few low cinder cones. According to geology books I've read, hot spots of magma exist relatively close to the surface at various places under the earth's crust. As the tectonic plates move above these hot spots, volcanic eruptions occasionally occur along the line of movement. The Hawaiian Islands, as an example, are the result of the periodic activity of a hot spot under the Pacific Ocean. Millions of years ago a hot spot formed under what is now southeastern Oregon, perhaps the result of a giant meteor slamming into the earth and weakening the crust. As the tectonic plate that forms this continent moved westward, the hot spot remained stationary, but to an immortal observer above the surface it would have had the appearance of moving east. It's now under Yellowstone National Park creating the geysers and hot springs that elicit oohs and aahs from so many visitors. Every 600,000 years or so this monster of a hot spot erupts from a caldera tens of miles across, creating not picturesque volcanic mountains, but a level expanse of total devastation. Today the Snake River Plain, the remnant of the wandering apocalypse, stretches sixty miles wide the length of southern Idaho. The rich volcanic soil produces the famed Idaho potatoes.

A sign informs me I'm entering the Idaho National Engineering Laboratory, Quality People Doing Quality Research. Smaller signs warn me of the illegality of leaving the highway. Miles ahead, shimmering in the desert air in a shallow depression where Birch Creek sinks forever into the earth, are a cluster of white buildings, one with the distinctive cone shape of a nuclear cooling tower. The folks over there are busy busting atoms. With pleasure I reach a crossroads and turn east on State 22, toward Yellowstone Park. Under the park the hot spot that erupts every 600,000 years last blew about that long ago. I'd rather take my chances with nature than that cone-shaped tower.

Colonel Gibbon and his mangled command arrived at the town of Deer Lodge the same day as the massacre on Birch Creek. There Gibbon found the two artillery companies led by Cushing and Fields who had been released by Howard in the Bitterroot Valley, now on their way to Corinne, Utah, to find a Union Pacific train back to San Francisco. Gibbon ordered them to rejoin General Howard's column. There's no record I've found of General McDowell's response when he heard the news. First his own general does his best to ignore instructions and now a mere colonel from another department was feeling free to get in on the fun. Boarding wagons, Cushing and Fields set out the same day. Also present in Deer Lodge was Lieutenant Henry Benson. In Maryland on recruiting duty when newspapers reported the approach of the Nez Perce to Montana, he had scrambled madcap across the continent to rejoin his Seventh Infantry. Gibbon also ordered him to join General Howard, ostensibly to command whatever civilians might be with Howard, more likely to give the young officer his chance for glory.

As he made his way toward Corinne Pass, Howard could have used Lieutenant Benson. The Deer Lodge and Butte volunteers were proving to be a major pain in the butt. The concept that they might have to coordinate their actions with the army, even obey instructions, had apparently eluded them when they set out from their homes. Late on August 16 they left in a snit, offended that the general had told them to remain close to the army column instead of charging ahead on their own and alerting the Nez Perce to the approach of the soldiers. Howard wasn't to remain without civilian "help" for long. The following day "Captain" James Callaway and some fifty citizens showed up from Virginia City. They hauled along a Civil War cannon they had faithfully fired once each year on the Fourth of July, intending to give the Nez Perce a dose of heavy lead.

As usual, the Nee-Me-Poo were a step ahead of Howard's army. Roaming far in advance of the family caravan, the first warriors struck the Montana-Corrine road near Hole-in-the-Rock Stage Station on August 16, cutting the telegraph line linking Montana to the rest of the country, running off horses, forcing teamsters to abandon their wagons and sending agents at the various way stations up and down the road fleeing for safety. For the next four days the most important travel corridor in and out of Montana would be closed.

Thirty miles will take me to Interstate 15, the modern version of the old stage road. To the north are the Centennial Mountains, an anomaly in the Rocky Mountains where most of the ranges line up north and south. The Centennials stretch east-west for eighty miles from Birch Creek to Yellowstone Park. Although they form the Continental Divide, they are unprepossessing viewed from here, a lumpy line of big hills. A notch at the head of South Medicine Lodge Creek is plainly visible. That would have been where Major Jim and his Snake warriors had been heading when

Alex Cruikshank left them. What were you up to, Major Jim? Far to the east are the ragged peaks of the Tetons. Last night's rain has cleared the air, and the outline of that impressive range is distinct even though they must be eighty miles away. I pull into Dubois ("Do boys") on I-15 a little before eight and top off the van's tank at the fancy gas station and convenience store just off the freeway interchange. I haven't been near an interstate highway for nearly two weeks. The frantic rush of one man to get the gas pumped, the windshield cleaned, the wife and kids in and out of the store with their morning snacks makes me smile.

It also makes me wonder how Lean Elk managed to get 700 people going in some semblance of order day after day. One disappointment for me when reading through the McWhorter archives was the lack of reminiscences from the women—and the men, too—about their daily routine. Probably the Nee-Me-Poo method of leadership was not much changed since Reverend Spalding first noted it in 1836:

> *The Nez Perce camp was divided into small bands of some 50 or 100 with four times as many horses, each band under a sub chief, the whole tribe directed by three war chiefs, who gave their orders or directions every evening for the next day, riding slowly around among the lodges, with a crier by the side repeating every sentence in a distinct loud voice. . . . The labor of the Indian camp, while in a dangerous country, was pretty well divided between the women and the men. The latter having the fighting to do, the hunting and scouting and the constant watching; the driving horses to grass and bringing them in at night. While the women do the packing and driving the horses by day, the putting up and taking down lodges and poles, the gathering wood and digging roots and the pounding seeds for food and making moccasins.[2]*

But other mundane details intrigue and elude me. Who got to go first in the line of march and who had to breathe dust all day? How did so many people take a crap without creating a wretched stink around their camp? Did each family have a fire or did several share? In barren country like this how did they even manage to gather enough wood? What did they talk about late in the evening, or were they too blasted sore and tired to do anything other than crawl into the folds of a blanket or buffalo robe and sleep? Were husbands and wives still fooling around?

And what were the Real People doing between the August 15 when they camped along the southern reaches of Birch Creek until the eighteenth when they reached Camas Meadows, ahead? The total distance they had to cover was only about fifty miles through level country. At the three mile-per-hour gait of a walking horse on easy terrain they were only looking at sixteen or seventeen hours of travel time. Were the horses played out? Had Lean Elk and the other chiefs halted early each day to talk to their people about the need for unity, an end to the madness that had reared its ugly head at Birch Creek? McWhorter's archives are silent about these days, except for noting that Stripes Turned Down, wounded at Birch Creek, died.

I ponder all these questions while methodically scarfing down an omelet, toast and hash browns at the counter of the Legion Bar and Cafe. Coffee carafe in hand, the waitress is gabbing with locals. This, the only culinary establishment in Dubois, is just a few blocks from the freeway, but it's a different world. Here the waitress knows every customer except me by name. She knows what's happening with their families and friends, knows how to make them laugh and how to take a ribbing. People at tables listen to the surrounding conversations and feel free to break in and comment on the topic of the moment. Small-town real people.

Concern was mounting for the whereabouts and safety of General Sherman since it was becoming clear the Nez Perce were heading for Yellowstone Park. On the seventeenth General McDowell in San Francisco tried to get through to Captain Benham at Fort Ellis in Montana:

> *Did General Sherman when he left Fort Ellis say when and by what route he would return from the National Park. The hostiles under Joseph crossed Corinne Road yesterday and must be near Henry Lake today, apparently making for the Buffalo Country thru the National Park.*[3]

An article in the *New York Times* echoed the worry, couching it in bravado:

> *There is no little alarm felt at headquarters for the safety of General Sherman who is supposed to be at the present moment in the Yellowstone Park. He has only five men with him. The squad is well armed, however, and might worry Joseph and his band fearfully if the two commands should happen to come together.*[4]

Sherman's party would have worried the warriors fearfully for about five seconds, but the general was fine. He had already left the park and would arrive at Fort Ellis on the eighteenth, but the telegraph lines the warriors had cut along the Corrine Road would keep him out of touch with the wider world for two more days.

As General Howard approached Corinne Pass on August 17, the reports he was receiving indicated he might be falling a day behind the non-treaty bands yet again. His command could go no faster, though. The heads of his cavalry horses were drooping as the animals plodded along, and no amount of spurring increased their weary gait for more than a few steps. In a battle they could very well lack the stamina necessary for rapid maneuver, and, unlike the Nez Perce warriors, his troops had no spare mounts to ride into a fight. The men atop the horses were in better shape, but only marginally. Their summer-issue clothing was no match for chilly mountain nights. Their daily meals of the cheapest bacon, boiled beans and hardtack—small bricks of flour, some of which had been baked during the Civil War and "preserved" since—were barely enough to keep them going each day. Each morning they pounded on coffee beans, sometimes with the butts of their pistols, and dumped the grounds into a pot of boiling water for that morning cup of java. Many troopers had been city dwellers or recent immigrants before they had signed the recruitment papers. Drill had consisted, at most, of an hour or two a day of mounting, moving from column into line, charging and dismounting in some semblance of order. Nothing in their brief training or the routine at their assigned forts had prepared them for week after week of swaying in the saddle with no respite.

So Howard again pored over his maps the evening of the seventeenth. The only logical approach to Yellowstone Park was past Henry's Lake and up the Madison River. If he turned left short of Corinne Pass and followed up Red Rock River, he could shorten his march to Henry's Lake by a full day. The Centennial Mountains would shield his movement from the non-treaty bands heading on a parallel course to the south. He stood a good chance of arriving at Henry's Lake simultaneously with his foe where one more battle could end the war. Howard wavered then inexplicably split his force. He ordered Lieutenants George Bacon and George Hoyle to pick forty of the best men and horses. In the company of Rube Robbins and a few of the Bannock scouts they were to depart before morning directly for Henry's Lake. The general had Major Mason prepare written orders for Bacon, who would be in command. The orders read:

You will proceed with your command to the vicinity of Henry Lake and Reynolds Pass. The object of this expedition is to ascertain whether the hostile Indians are passing into the buffalo country by the above-mentioned route. Should you find the Indians you will take a defensible position and while observing their movements do all you can with your force to harass them. Exercise at the same time prudence and caution. You will send a courier back to these headquarters with information as soon as you discover the Indians and form an opinion of their intended movement. Should you not at the expiration of 48 hours discover any trace of the hostiles, you will return to this camp by easy marches, sending a courier in advance.[5]

The little party rode into the darkness about 1 A.M. on August 18. Fifteen hours later Bacon was forced to call a halt on the shores of Red Rock Lake. The exhausted horses and men could go no further after covering fifty-five miles. Bacon was confident, though, they could reach Henry's Lake the following day. His orders had been clear; he was on a scout, not on a mission to engage and turn the enemy back on Howard. Little could the lieutenant guess that years later the general would try to make him the scapegoat for the events of the next few days.

I head north from Dubois on a quiet road paralleling Interstate 15 and Beaver Creek. The creek forms at present-day Monida Pass—the Corrine Pass of 1877—then flows south across this plain where it has cut a channel some thirty feet deep into the lava. The vertical walls of the channel prevent passage across the creek for most of its length. A few miles from town I see a golden eagle perched on a fence post beside the pavement. As I brake, the eagle and I stare at each other for a few seconds. It hops from the post and with slow, powerful strokes climbs skyward directly over my van. For an instant its wings span my windshield, its bright eyes glaring down. I see a faint track veering off the road and bounce along it in my van for about a quarter mile. I'm heading for the Dry Creek Crossing where the Real People forded Beaver Creek either late on the seventeenth or early on the eighteenth. Sure enough, the steep lava walls along Beaver Creek have given way to a pass-able slope. The old Corinne Stage Road forded the creek here, and a way station for changing horse teams stood somewhere close. Remains of the road are distinct on both banks leading to the ford. If General Howard's column could have beaten the Nee-Me-Poo caravan to this spot, the general could have forced a decisive bat-tle. After the Nee-Me-Poo had passed, returning whites found the bodies of two Nez Perce women in the area. They had been wound-ed at the Big Hole and made it this far before dying. Their names have been lost.

I continue north to the hamlet of Spencer at the base of Monida Pass, find Kilgore Road and head east toward Camas Meadows where the Real People paused the night of the eighteenth. The road is gravel but beautifully maintained. Thank you, Clark County, Idaho. I'm traveling along the foot of the Centennials now and spot the white gash of the Spencer Opal Mine on the slope above, peer into a series of picturesque little canyons on one side, gaze across the Snake River Plain on the other and remember why I love driving the back roads of the American West. The cool air wafting in my window bears the scent of sage and freshly-cut hay. Red-tailed hawks sit on fence post after fence post, impassively

observing my passage. They must be waiting for the air to warm
so they can soar on the updrafts with ease.

In an incident that bordered on the ludicrous, General Howard
crossed Corinne Pass in a wagon on August 18, far ahead of the
rest of the column and almost ran into the Nee-Me-Poo. With him
were only Lieutenant Robert Fletcher, a wagon driver and one
civilian on horseback. That morning the general had asked
"Captain" Callaway's Virginia City volunteers with their fresh
horses to escort him in advance of the main column. With some
reluctance they agreed, telling the general they would be along in
a few minutes. After the cavalry had grazed their horses for several hours, the army units were to follow. Off the general went in his
wagon, no doubt glancing back every now and then, expecting to
see his escort hurrying to catch up. No volunteers appeared. The
wagon passed over the summit into the headwaters of Beaver
Creek, a green oasis called Pleasant Valley. Civilians from the Dry
Creek area hurried by, saying warriors were only a few miles away,
and Howard quickly ordered the wagon driver to halt. The four
men nervously waited. And waited. Late in the afternoon the army
column showed up. The good news was that Captain Randolph
Norwood and his Company "L" of the Second Cavalry had finally
found the command. At Fort Ellis nearly two weeks before,
General Sherman had ordered Norwood to reinforce Howard. The
Virginia City volunteers, though, were nowhere in sight, having
decided after much deliberation that their horses needed even
more rest than the cavalry mounts who had come all the way from
Idaho. Disgusted, Howard finally continued out of the mountains
to the Dry Creek stage station, arriving after dark.

Black Hair, wounded at the Big Hole, had slept only fitfully
since. The night of the eighteenth he had a dream. In it he saw
warriors riding silently through darkness. They came to a place
with lush grass and two streams. There, cavalry horses, grazing,
ripe for stealing! Whooping, dream warriors charged through the
meadow, driving the horses before them into the night. When
Black Hair awoke in the morning he saw that the verdant grass
and twin creeks of his dream were none other than Camas

Meadows where the Real People were camped. Puzzled, he told others of his dream.

Later that day, as Lean Elk led the family cavalcade eastward, a scout named Bull Bait galloped from the back trail. Soldiers coming, he said, lots of dust, lots of soldiers. A party of warriors halted, cut their war ponies out of the herd, checked their rifles, then sat. Rattle On Blanket arrived from the rear, his horse snorting from exertion. Still coming, he said. A few of the warriors pulled out pipes and filled them with tobacco. They smoked, waiting for battle. Eventually, other scouts reported that the army column had halted at Camas Meadows. Word of Black Hair's vision reached some of the leading warriors and the chiefs. The dream was a good thing, they agreed. Perhaps it meant the time was right to get the army off the backs of the People once and for all. Without horses the cavalry would be crippled.

General Howard seemed destined to get in trouble with his superiors. As Major Mason supervised the setting of camp and the location of picket posts at Camas Meadows, the general sat down with pen and paper to compose another message to General McDowell in San Francisco. Because the Nez Perce had cut the telegraph line on the sixteenth and it was not yet repaired, Howard had no idea McDowell had sent a stinging rebuke to the last plea from Bannack to give up the chase. Howard's latest words were:

> *Have driven the hostile Indians from the Clearwater to the Yellowstone without regard to Department or Division lines; Shall I rest, resupply and pursue them further or return. I wish the General for instructions or opinion. Will return via Fort Hall and Boise.*[6]

That night about thirty men left the Nee-Me-Poo camp, now just eighteen miles ahead of Howard. Thunder Rising stayed with the families while Looking Glass and Frog led the warriors. The weather was cool and dreary, no stars or moon visible through the cloud cover. As the raiders approached Camas Meadows just before dawn, they split into three groups, some warriors slipping from their horses' backs and easily bypassing sleepy pickets.

Zigging and zagging on back roads, I pass within a mile of the location of Howard's camp, now private property and off-limits. Camas and Spring Creeks create a natural oasis in the surrounding dry, flat lavalands. It's easy to understand why both the Real People and the army chose to spend a night here, one after the other.

A gunshot from just outside the army camp broke the night air. Howard later wrote it was an alert picket. The warriors, he claimed, had approached the camp in a column of fours in an attempt to fool the guards into thinking the warriors were actually Captain Bacon and his scouting party returning from Henry's Lake. Interesting story, General, but not terribly likely, since the Nee-Me-Poo were completely unaware of the existence of the lieutenant and his forty men. Warriors told McWhorter that Going Away, nervously fingering the trigger of his rifle, accidentally fired the shot. "Otskai was always doing something like that," Bird Alighting noted, wryly.[7]

Pandemonium erupted. Soldiers rolled from their blankets and groped in the darkness for their weapons as flashes from Nez Perce rifles randomly lit the night. The warriors who had sneaked into camp desperately cut tethers, waved their arms then skipped away. Those on the periphery let out a chorus of shouts. In a few minutes it was all over. The pounding of hundreds of hooves receded into the distance. Soon it began to grow light. Yellow Wolf's reaction:

We could begin to see our prize. Getting more light we looked. Eeh! Nothing but mules—all mules![8]

A shocked Howard ordered three of his five cavalry companies to pursue the raiders. Major George Sanford led them forward at dawn, two units from the First Cavalry under Captains Carr and Jackson and Norwood's fresh troopers from the Second Cavalry.

I continue east for another six miles to a barbed wire gate beside the road. I pop it open, drive through and go back to close it. This is a Bureau of Land Management holding, and ranchers have grazing leases for the range. It wouldn't do to let the cattle out on the road. Although generally level, the terrain is broken up by long, volcanic pressure ridges from ten to twenty feet in height. I pass one near the road—this, I think, is as far as the cavalry advanced—and continue about a quarter-mile back toward the Camas Meadows camp site to two shorter ridges running almost at right angles to the first. The narrow depression between them is shaded by a few aspen. Sparse sage and a few hardy grasses make up the remaining vegetation struggling to grow amid the chunks of volcanic rock.

While Howard sat down to breakfast, Sanford's cavalry chased the thundering herd of 150 mules and a few horses, retrieving about thirty that fell away from the mass. After seven miles the warriors decided the troops were getting too close to the family camp for comfort. A few continued on as herders while the rest peeled off, dropped from their horses and waited for the soldiers to come into shooting distance. Their first long-range volley sent the troopers scrambling from their mounts and taking cover behind a lava ridge. Major Sanford formed the companies into a skirmish line with Norwood's in the center, Carr's on the left and Jackson's on the right. Taking advantage of the uneven terrain, warriors worked their way around either side of the line and began an effective enfilading fire. Trumpeter Bernard Brooks was riding behind the line with Captain Jackson when a bullet knocked him from his saddle. As at White Bird, the Nee-Me-Poo warriors knew the value of denying an army commander of his means of communication. Realizing the precariousness of his position, Major Sanford ordered a retreat. The two companies of the First Cavalry on the flanks wasted no time in complying. Captain Norwood, incredibly, refused to obey the order and soon found himself and his troopers alone. After Lieutenant Benson, detailed to Norwood's company by Howard after the long trip from Maryland, was hit, Norwood decided retreat was a pretty good idea after all. Quickly his men

283

were running for their lives across the lava plain toward the depression where the horseholders had sheltered the animals.

This is the place. Leaving my van in the hollow between the two lava pressure ridges where the horses were kept, I scramble up one of the slopes. Rock shelters hastily thrown up by the troopers are still visible along the edge of the ridge, along with a few obvious frauds built more recently by clowns who lack the sense and respect to leave historical sites untouched.

For the next few hours troopers paid dearly for their captain's lack of judgment. Several young women from the Nee-Me-Poo camp rode out and watched from a distance as warriors made life miserable for the soldiers in the impromptu fort. A few warriors crawled to within yards of the rock shelters, but most were content to keep their distance, poised to fire at anything that moved. Sergeant Henry Wilkins, Corporal Henry Garland and Privates Samuel Glass, Harry Trevor, Wilford Clark and William Jones all moved. Glass would succumb to his wound within days, Trevor a little longer. Garland, perhaps the least fortunate, lived in unrelenting pain for a couple of years before taking his own life.

When Major Sanford reported back to Howard and was unable to account for Norwood's whereabouts, the general mustered a relief force of three companies cavalry and one of infantry. As this column approached, the Nee-Me-Poo warriors slipped away. Hair Combed Over Eyes and Bird Alighting had been wounded, slightly, during the latter stage of the skirmish.

I'm surprised to hear the sound of engines. This place is off the beaten path, to put it mildly. I'd wandered a few yards away from the ridges, trying to imagine how warriors had managed to sneak close, as both Nez Perce and white accounts attested. Suddenly remembering I've left the door of my van open and the key in the ignition, I hurry back and peer into the depression. Seven or eight people pour out of the doors of two minivans. Ah! One of them is Sue Buschel, the Park Service boss for Big Hole and all points east. I trot down the slope to say hello. She tells me she's heading a management team on a survey of significant sites along the trail, coming up with a long-range plan for the newly-expanded National Historical Park. As her crew spreads out to look things over, she takes a few minutes to chat. Like me, she was surprised to see another vehicle here but soon recognized the white VW van and Oregon plates. I tell her I'm finally following the trail from beginning to end, straight through. She mentions the new seasonal ranger at Bear Paw, Jim Magera. He's a real history buff, she assures me, and I'll enjoy talking with him. By the way, she casually adds, if I don't mind waiting around a while, she's gotten permission from the landowner to take a look at the site of Howard's camp. I can tag along if I want.

My eyes light up.

An hour later I follow the two government vehicles along a rutted ranch road. We spread out through a pasture east of the Camas and Spring creeks, searching for the grave of Trumpeter Brooks. According to historical accounts he was buried at the site of General Howard's tent, and once we find it we'll be at the center of the army camp. Before long I hear shouts and hurry toward the noise. The grave is in the middle of a slight elevation with higher lava outcroppings a few yards away on three sides. Enclosed by a rusting iron fence, the white granite headstone is about two feet high and overgrown with sage. Rest in peace, corporal. The next job for the Park Service team is a quick survey of the surrounding area for signs of rifle pits the soldiers may have dug in the tense minutes after the raid when a full-scale attack was feared. I wander about, finding one or two unusual piles of rock, then find a place to sit. Never in my wildest dreams had I imagined I would be here, and I find myself trying to drag details of the layout of the camp from my memory.

General Howard definitely chose the safest available spot for his tent, the surrounding lava outcroppings making it a three-sided fort. Spring Creek is a good three hundred yards west of Howard's tent, a much greater distance than I imagined. The mules, I think, were between Howard and the creek as were the two units of infantry and artillery. The cavalry horses and one company of troopers remained on the other side of the stream where thick grass provided forage. The other cavalry companies ranged outward from the general's tent. The perimeter of the camp must have been huge, I realize. No wonder the warriors were able to bypass the sentries so easily. And the hapless volunteers. Definitely near the creek, also. Scurrying for cover, several had jumped or fallen into the water when the bullets started whizzing. I add another sound to the crack of gunfire, war whoops, whinnying horses, braying mules and shouted orders to my mental reconstruction of the attack. Kersplash, kersplash. It's a good thing the volunteers never got their cannon unlimbered and ready to fire; they probably would have shelled the general's tent in confusion.

On our way out, the ranch owner sits at the wheel of a highway-sized grader beside the dirt road. He had noticed the cars going in and has smoothed out the ruts for us. I give him a wave and a toot of my horn. At the county road Buschel and her team turn in the direction of Dubois, I in the other. Thanks, Sue. It's mid-afternoon before I'm rambling east on Shotgun Road toward Henry's Lake and Yellowstone Park beyond. The lava fields give way to aspen, pine and willows interspersed with meadows and a multitude of rivulets flowing from the Centennials. I'm beginning to get worried about where I'm going to spend the night. My plan to find a motel in the town of West Yellowstone is down the drain, I'm sure. The neon NO VACANCY signs all will be lit by now. I know better than to bet my marbles on a campground in Yellowstone this late in the day. I'll try the state park at Henry's Lake first.

Two brown, furry things trundle across the gravel fifty yards ahead, and I hit the brakes hard. My first guess is marmots, but these critters seem to be equipped with legs too small for their bodies and their fur is darker than other marmots I've seen. Also, the countryside here is a mixture of forest and soggy meadow, and marmots prefer drier, open, rocky slopes where they can whistle their warnings when unfriendly neighbors come calling. My van skids to a halt only ten yards away. While the first disappears off the road, the second briefly pauses near the edge and stands on its hind legs and broad, flat tail to give me the once-over. Beaver.

Late in the day of the Camas Meadows skirmish, the infantry and artillery battalions, which had separated from General Howard and the cavalry clear back on the Lolo Trail, finally caught up. With them again were Field's and Cushing's San Francisco artillerymen, still in the role of military yo-yo's. His entire command united, his supplies packed on the remaining mules and piled high on the newly-arrived wagons accompanying the foot soldiers, Howard once more resumed his pursuit on August 21. He wasn't taking any chances with a surprise daylight attack, improbable as that may have been. Henry Buck from Stevensville was among the teamsters who arrived with the foot soldiers and provided a description:

> *This morning we were late getting started, but when we were ready, we sure did move in military style. The wagon train and the pack animals were placed in the center; ahead of us was a company of cavalry to lead the way, while another company of cavalry brought up the rear. The infantry marched on either side of the wagons about one hundred feet distant, while on the outside of these the balance of the cavalry took their places in the grand parade across the prairie following Joseph's trail.*[9]

Howard needn't have worried. The Real People were hurrying ahead and laid over at Henry's Lake that night.

Two adventurous whites from the town of Bozeman, near Fort Ellis ninety miles to the north, deeming themselves "scouts" of the first order, had decided to lend a hand in the war. They apparently viewed the Nee-Me-Poo camp at a safe distance from one of the ridges above Henry's Lake. The 2,000 horses impressed them, spread out over three square miles. Of course, if you're scouts of the first order you have to report your findings to someone, so George Herendine and Jack Bean high-tailed it back to Bozeman and the *Times* newspaper.

Lieutenants Bacon and Hoyle and their meager reconnaissance force of forty had already missed the spectacle. Arriving in the area early on the August 20, they ran into not the Nez Perce but a herd of cattle being driven south by a man named Watkins and a few cowboys. After Bacon informed them of the proximity of the non-treaty bands, Watkins and his crew departed the vicinity with appropriate speed. Apparently, they decided at least some of the cattle were an impediment to their healths because Henry Buck recalled dining well on freshly slaughtered beefsteak smothered with butter, salt and pepper then broiled on a stick over an open campfire when the army column reached the lake. The Nee-Me-Poo had undoubtedly relished similar fare when they passed through, although they certainly hadn't bothered to note the brands on the cattle to later compensate the owners, as the army did.

Lieutenant Bacon had seen no Nez Perce in the forty-eight hours since leaving Howard. His orders were to return to the same camp from which he had departed, and so he did with easy marches north of the Centennials, also as his instructions stated. What had Howard meant when he said to return after forty-eight hours? From the time of departure as Bacon interpreted the words? Or had Howard intended Bacon to remain at Henry's Lake for two days rather than the half-day he did? The orders were ambiguous. Writing in 1907, Howard remembered:

> *He was to head off the Indians and detain them by his fire till we could come upon them from the rear. Bacon got into position soon enough, but did not have the heart to fight the Indians on account of their number.*[10]

Come on, General, you had instructed him, . . . *while observing their movements do all you can with your force to harass them. Exercise at the same time prudence and caution.* Bacon exercised prudence and caution. If he had tried to stop the Nee-Me-Poo with his puny unit Howard would have found forty dead troopers somewhere near Henry's Lake.

I pass a nascent pod of ranchettes on the edge of Shotgun Valley, ugly real estate weeds in beautiful cattle country. The wind must have blown the seeds over from the Bitterroot. There's no sign of any cowettes or sheepettes or horsettes yet, thank God. I cross the Henry's Fork River at McCrea Bridge, another of my old stomping grounds for fishing.

Before dawn on August 22, halted for the night in Shotgun Valley, Howard's pickets challenged a group of seventy horsemen approaching the camp. It was not a repeat of the Camas Meadows raid. Captain Augustus Bainbridge with an escort of ten soldiers had brought about sixty Bannock warriors from the Fort Hall Reservation 100 miles south. General Sheridan in Chicago had ordered them enlisted as scouts for two reasons: to help Howard chase down the Nez Perce and to get the warriors away from the reservation where the agent feared an uprising was imminent. What better way to blow off a little Bannock steam than to send the young men to war against their ancestral enemies?

Hired to lead the Bannocks was a tall, pale, reticent white man dressed in buckskin named Stanton Fisher. The quiet, daring Fisher was to make quite a positive impression on Howard and others with the command. It had been Fisher in 1871 who had been one of the first whites to hear some sketchy details of the apocalyptic new religion sweeping through the traditional believers of the Columbia plateau. In 1895 he would become the agent to the Nez Perce. In 1877, though, his job was to hunt them down in some of the wildest country remaining in the United States. He would prove quite adept at it, and the notes in the diary he carried would become the best record available of the route the Nee-Me-Poo took through Yellowstone Park.

The following evening, camped on the banks of the Henry's Fork, the Bannocks held a war dance. The singing and drumming kept the entire command awake and maybe a little nervous until midnight when the general ordered the Bannocks to knock it off. Sometime that evening Buffalo Horn and a few others came to Howard with a suggestion. They were there to kill Nez Perce, so why not start with the three herders with the command? Howard nixed the idea, but one of the Nez Perce decided his presence was required back home. The other two, Captain John and Old George, stuck it out. Both had family with the fleeing bands.

I turn north on U.S. 20 for ten miles into the Henry's Lake bowl. The Continental Divide surrounds it on three sides, but the mountains hold three easy passes across the divide, Red Rock to the west, Raynolds to the north and Targhee to the east, the latter leading to Yellowstone Park. The round lake is about three miles in diameter with a state park and campground tucked onto a peninsula on the south end. Whitecaps rip across the surface beneath a gusty north wind and increasing clouds.

The army column arrived at the lake early on the August 23 after a march of only a few hours. In a conference with his officers Howard came to the conclusion that the men and horses could go no farther without a rest. His chief surgeon, Major Charles Alexander, was particularly outspoken in arguing that the soldiers required fresh supplies of shoes and warmer clothing or disease would soon decimate the ranks. That evening Major Mason wrote to his wife, Frances:

> *The command is completely worn out and the chase should end here, but the General is disappointed at not reaching a brilliant end and is disposed to push on into the Yellowstone country . . . This is a most disagreeable day, blowing a gale, throwing dust over everything in clouds.*[11]

Howard, himself, did not rest. Late in the afternoon he climbed aboard a wagon along with his son, Lieutenant Guy Howard, and Lieutenant John Adams and began an exhausting, all-night journey to Virginia City seventy miles north. Pack animals, clothing and communication with his superiors were on his mind.

The campground on the shore of Henry's Lake looks raw, windswept, dusty and desolate, much the same as Mason described it in his letter. I hope I can do better. Amid a steady flow of traffic I continue on, up the easy grade beside Howard Creek past Howard Springs to Targhee Pass. Over the top the valley of the Madison River spreads out before me, Hebgen Lake filling the center. Somewhere under the blue surface was a campground of the Real People. The national park boundary just to the east is unmistakable; much of the forest outside it has been clearcut.

The army had stopped, but not Stanton Fisher. He had already pushed ahead to Targhee Pass where a courier from the army camp arrived with a verbal message ordering him back to Henry's Lake. There, Fisher had a short, sharp discussion with Howard and his chief of scouts, Lieutenant Fletcher. Fisher reminded the officers that he could read and write and suggested that if they wanted him to stay on the trail of the Nez Perce that it might not be appropriate for them to order him back to camp every time they had a message. Something about the newcomer impressed Howard because Fisher received what he termed a "roving commission."

That same afternoon—with the addition of Buffalo Horn's Bannocks to his own force—Fisher led some eighty warriors back toward Targhee Pass. At the divide he climbed a tree and spotted what he thought might be the Nez Perce camp on the opposite side of the Madison River. Leaving the trail for the dense forest, he and his men approached to within a few miles by sunset. Fisher sent scouts ahead on foot who soon returned and reported seeing the Nez Perce in camp. Fisher considered simply sending word back to Howard of the proximity of the prey and letting the army handle the problem, but his Bannocks assured him they could handle the Nee-Me-Poo. That was fine with Fisher. Sending out more scouts to get closer to the Nez Perce and to find a ford across the river, he sketched out a simple plan of attack. They would charge through the camp firing volleys to stampede the horse herd. Most of the Bannocks would then turn back to fight off any pursuit while a few would rush the captured stock back toward Targhee Pass. The Bannocks were stripped, painted and ready to proceed when the latest scouts brought back the bad news: the fires were cold, the Real People gone, only a few lame horses and mules wandering around.

At the Baker's Hole Forest Service campground, on the Madison River, a few miles north of West Yellowstone, I find one of the last unoccupied sites, pay my fee, sign the required waiver that I won't blame Smoky the Bear if one of his grizzly cousins eats me during the night. The grizzly waiver proves unnecessary. Next morning with an early start I've beaten the rush out of Yellowstone Park and have the road pretty much to myself. The first leg of this side trip from the National Historic Trail puts me on U.S. 287 along the north shore of Hebgen Lake, the Madison River Canyon dead ahead. My mind drifts back to 1959 and an August morning when I awoke to the earth shuddering. I was seven at the time, living some 120 miles from here as the eagle flies. There the quake did little more than rattle dishes and scare unsuspecting kids. Here the south side of the fault dropped almost twenty feet in an instant, or the north side rose that far. It's a matter of perspective, I suppose, this business of making mountain ranges. The thunder of the planet shifting like a restless dreamer must have been deafening for the tourists sleeping in their tents along the shore of the lake or the banks of the river downstream. Past Hebgen Dam the gray ghosts of trees protrude from the surface of narrow Earthquake Lake in the Madison River Canyon. Ahead, the scar of a massive landslide dominates the south canyon wall. The highway climbs over rubble a hundred feet deep on the canyon floor. The debris forms a natural dam creating Earthquake Lake, the Madison River cascading over a spillway it has created amid the massive boulders. Under the thousands of tons of rock are the remains of some forty tourists who had been sleeping in a Forest Service campground that morning in 1959.

The canyon walls widen then give way. Having cut directly through the Madison Mountains, the river curves north through a broad valley between the Gravelly Range on the west and the Madisons on the east. The highway follows the river and so do I, picking up Howard's route to Virginia City from Henry's Lake. I see a fresh dusting of snow on the dark peaks of the Madisons. White cloud-fingers explore the highest crags.

Howard missed by a hair running into a band of Nee-Me-Poo raiders during his night-long wagon trip to Virginia City. A party of seven whites headed by Thomas Carmin from the mining town of Pony some sixty miles north were camped in the Madison Valley that night when warriors swooped down and relieved them of their horses about 10 P.M. Carmin and his buddies had been boasting that they intended to lift some Nez Perce scalps. After giving the matter careful consideration the seven decided to return home and just talk about a scalping expedition.

After breakfast in the ranching and tourist town of Ennis, it's a steep ten-mile haul up State Road 287 to the summit of the Gravelly Range. Virginia City is scrunched into the narrow confines of Alder Gulch just on the other side of the pass. After prospectors discovered gold in the gulch in 1864 the population boomed to 30,000 in a series of towns stretching for eight miles. Of course, the numbers plummeted almost as quickly as the gold began to play out. Today, Virginia City's population is about 200, and you better bring your credit cards. This place survives on extracting gold from tourists' pockets.

While Lieutenant Adams began buying out virtually every store in town, paying exorbitant prices because he was forced to issue government vouchers of dubious worth, General Howard got busy at the telegraph office. He wired General McDowell in San Francisco, mentioning that Colonel Samuel Sturgis and part of the Seventh Cavalry were waiting for the Nez Perce to appear in the buffalo country and wishing to "hear from you in answer to telegrams sent," by which Howard meant his request to return home.[12] McDowell's adjutant was brutal in response:

> *The Division Commander thinks you need no further instructions on this subject, and advises you that the United States have no body of troops so near the hostile Indians as those immediately with you and you, it seems to him, will certainly be expected by the General of the Army, the War Department and the country, to use them in carrying on the most active and persistent operations practicable, to the very end.*
>
> *You say that with prompt and energetic cooperation from the Eastern Departments, you may yet destroy these Indians, and without cooperation, the present result will be, as it has been, doubtful. It is not understood by the Division Commander nor is it believed in the country, that you have not had prompt and energetic cooperation. It is on the contrary held that Gibbon's aid from Terry's Department whence only effectual aid could come, was prompt, energetic and effectual, and as abundant as the state of the Army in the Department permitted. The General in all kindness asks me to suggest to you to be less dependent on what others at a*

distance may or may not do, and rely more on your own forces and your own plans.[13]

The General asks in all kindness? I don't think so.

The beleaguered Howard had no better luck with Sherman, who had by now left Fort Ellis and arrived at Fort Shaw north of Helena. Sherman wired:

> *Don't want to give you orders as this may confuse Sheridan and Terry, but that force of yours should pursue the Nez Perces to the death, lead where they may. Miles is too far off and I fear Sturgis is too slow. If you are tired give command to some energetic officer and let him follow them, go where they may, holding his men well in hand and subsisting them on beef gathered in the country with coffee, sugar and salt on packs. For such a stern chase infantry are as good as cavalry; leave to Sturgis to head them off if he can. I will be at Helena on Tuesday next. No time should be lost. I don't know your officers, but you can select the commander and order accordingly.*[14]

Howard's response was emphatic:

> *You misunderstood me. I never flag. It was the command, including the most energetic young officers, that were worn out and weary by a most energetic march. You need not fear for the campaign. Neither you nor General McDowell can doubt my pluck and energy.*[15]

That same day Sherman telegraphed General Sheridan in Chicago:

> *I don't think Howard's troops will catch Joseph, but they will follow; trusting to your troops heading them off, when they come out east of the mountains.*[16]

Sherman was simultaneously hedging his bet, playing one officer's ego off against another's misfortune.

"Captain" Callaway's volunteers returned to their home town from their great adventure at Camas Meadows the same day Howard arrived. Lacking even enough horses for riders, they had temporarily abandoned their cannon. Their spirit and sense of humor were intact, though, because they marched into town singing a song they called "Brave Boys Are We." The first few lines went something like this:

> *Lay low, boys, it's a general attack.*
> *Down in the grass, or you'll get shot in the back.*
> *I pledge you my word I wish I hadn't come,*
> *And I'll bet ten to one we have to hoof it home.*[17]

By the following morning Howard and his lieutenants had procured all the supplies, horses and mules available. After making arrangements for their transfer to Henry's Lake, the general climbed back in his wagon with an improbable new passenger. The editor of the Virginia City newspaper noted on August 25:

> *We acknowledge call from Mr. John W. Redington, special correspondent of the Salt Lake Tribune, with Howard's army. Mr. Redington has been following up the command, not exactly lost, but, as the Virginian would say, 'somewhat bogued' most of the time since he reached Montana. He left this morning for camp with General Howard and staff.*

"Bogued" is an old nautical term that means "off the wind." Drifting. Out of control. Still, Redington had gotten his chance to become a scout for the army. Why hire this guy?

The Thompson-Hickman Memorial Library and Museum sits on the edge of town. When "Captain" Callaway's son corresponded with McWhorter in the 1930s he remembered the day the volunteers left to join Howard and recalled them dragging along the cannon the townspeople fired every Fourth of July as part of that day's festivities. When the younger Callaway wrote to McWhorter the cannon then sat just outside the museum. A quick look by me around the sides of the building reveals nothing. I trot up the

295

steps. Inside the door a white-haired, friendly woman looks up from a book, smiles and asks me to sign the visitors' register. The room is filled with household items from generations past, mining tools, faded photographs, doo-dads. And a tarnished brass cannon barrel resting on a white counter. It's about three feet long with a bore of five inches. The letters U.S. are engraved on the curved top. There's more on the face of the muzzle: C.A.M. Co. 223 1863 TJ 332. Yup, 1863 means Civil War.

I ask the woman if she happens to know if this cannon was ever on display on the lawn outside. Why yes, she says, years and years ago. I smile. The old cannon played no real part in the 1877 war. Finding it adds nothing to my understanding of what happened, but, as I run my hand up and down the mottled metal, I feel reassurance that something tangible remains of the times and events I've spent so much time researching. The texture of this old cannon warms my hand.

Notes

[1] Parker, Samuel, *Journal*, p.97-98.

[2] quoted in Warren, Eliza Spalding, *Memoirs of the West: The Spaldings*, Marsh Printing Company, Portland, Oregon, 1916, from a lecture printed in the Albany Democrat 1867-1868.

[3] AGO, *Letters*, roll 338, p. 561.

[4] *New York Times*, August 20, 1877.

[5] Davison, *A Century Ago*, p. 12.

[6] AGO, *Letters*, roll 338, p. 568.

[7] McWhorter, *Yellow Wolf*, p. 167.

[8] McWhorter, *Yellow Wolf*, p. 168.

[9] Buck, "Story," p. 63.

[10] Howard, *My Life and Experiences Among Our Hostile Indians*, A. D. Worthington & Co., Hartford, 1907, p. 292.

[11] Davison, *A Century Ago*, p. 12.

[12] AGO, *Letters*, roll 338, p. 545.

[13] AGO, *Letters*, roll 338, p. 562-564.

[14] AGO, *Letters*, roll 338, p. 174-175.

[15] quoted in Brown, *Flight*, p. 306.

[16] AGO, *Letters*, roll 338, p. 545.

[17] Virginia City *Madisonian*, August 25, 1877

Martin Stadius

Camas Meadows. A rock shelter built by a nervous soldier.

Martin Stadius

Dry Creek ford of Beaver Creek, Idaho. The trace of the Corrine-Montana stage and freight road is visible at the upper left. If the army had arrived one day earlier, the conflict might have ended here.

Martin Stadius

The Meade Hotel, Bannack State Park, Montana. Settlers sought refuge here from Nez Perce raiders after the Battle of the Big Hole.

299

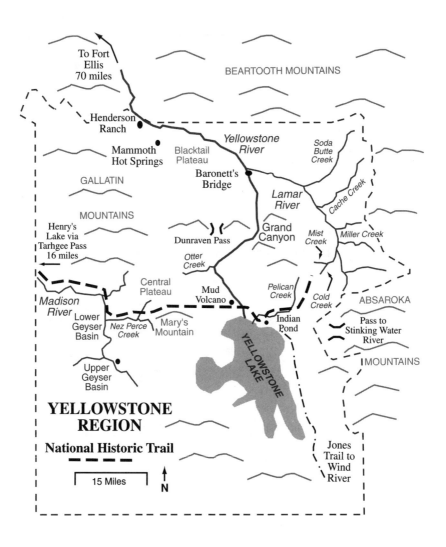

To Fort
Ellis
70 miles

BEARTOOTH MOUNTAINS

Henderson
Ranch

Mammoth
Hot Springs

Blacktail
Plateau

*Yellowstone
River*

*Soda
Butte
Creek*

Baronett's
Bridge

GALLATIN

*Lamar
River*

Cache Creek

MOUNTAINS

Henry's
Lake via
Tarhgee Pass
16 miles

Dunraven Pass

Grand
Canyon

*Mist
Creek*

Miller Creek

*Otter
Creek*

*Madison
River*

Central
Plateau

Mud
Volcano

*Pelican
Creek*

*Cold
Creek*

ABSAROKA

Lower
Geyser
Basin

*Nez Perce
Creek*

Mary's
Mountain

Indian
Pond

Pass to
Stinking Water
River

Upper
Geyser
Basin

YELLOWSTONE
LAKE

MOUNTAINS

YELLOWSTONE
REGION

National Historic Trail

Jones
Trail to
Wind
River

15 Miles

N

CHAPTER TWELVE

YELLOWSTONE

The Nee-Me-Poo entered the park on August 22 and followed the rudiment of a wagon road beside the Madison River upstream toward the geyser basins. In the years since President Grant had set aside Yellowstone as a National Park in 1872, visitors probably numbered only in the hundreds. It was still one of the wildest, most isolated spots on the continent. But visitors there were in August 1877. A few were prospectors who could have cared less about some new-fangled idea called a national park if they could find gold or silver in the hills.

At least one cattleman thought the pristine meadows made crackerjack summer pasture for his stock. One party of tourists consisted of an Irish nobleman—the Earl of Dunraven—a doctor friend, a scout named Texas Jack and a camp helper. Nelson Story headed another group of four. Story got out of the park a day ahead of the first warriors and would eventually leave his name in history books as one of the great cattle barons of the plains rather than as a victim of Nez Perce acrimony. Another tourist was a Canadian Mounted Policeman and still another was a soldier just roaming and enjoying himself after the end of his enlistment. Two tourists in the park were women, members of a nine-person outing mostly from the town of Radersburg in Montana. Another contingent of ten from Helena rounded out those whites who should have chosen another time for their Yellowstone adventure.

I join the parade of vehicles entering the park and moving at a sedate pace through a forest burned in the massive fires of 1988. Wildflowers and verdant grass counterpoint the black and gray lodgepole pine skeletons rising from the earth. Trumpeter swans glide across the glassy, green surface of the Madison River as it curves through the narrow valley. Despite being part of a throng every time I visit, I love this place. It's the element of wildness that still exists away from the roads that brings me back. I'll never forget a morning almost twenty years ago on Slough Creek, sitting on the sunny bank, sated after hours of catching and releasing Yellowstone cutthroat when I noticed a slender black shape darting through the water toward me. A tiny black face with shiny dark eyes popped up from behind a log after the creature clambered out of the water. A mink, fewer than ten feet from me. We stared at each other for the longest time, it seemingly patient and fearless, my heart pounding with surprise and delight. Or the afternoon a bear rose out of meadow grass onto its hind legs and inspected me as I froze, scared spitless. Even though it was 200 yards away, its broad face was unmistakable. A grizzly. After a few seconds it dropped and lumbered into the forest at the far edge of the meadow. Or the evening I spent crouched behind a fallen log in the mountains west of Mammoth watching a family of beavers cruise the still waters of a pond, their round heads leaving wakes like speed boats. And the eerie moonlit hike back to camp.

At Madison Junction I turn south through the Firehole River Canyon into the Lower Geyser Basin, an open bowl several miles wide dotted with pools and springs spurting plumes of steam. I'll never forget one evening here over a decade ago, casting a mayfly imitation over a cautiously feeding trout in the Firehole River, trying to match the drift of my fly and the flow of my breath and rod to the rhythm of a single trout's rise and descent. A scattered herd of elk kept me company a hundred yards away across the river. I'll never understand how I happened to sense the young bull which suddenly raised its head in the midst of its grazing companions, as if noticing my presence for the first time. We stared at each other in the fading light. It began walking toward me, head high, sniffing the air, snorting. I forgot about the fish and began reeling in my line, watching the elk all the while. It began to trot directly toward me. I scrambled out of the water and dropped my tackle, ready to run. It stopped at the opposite bank, prancing and tossing its impressive rack of antlers back and forth for my edification, reminding me this was not my river, not my country.

I pull my van off the road at the Nez Perce Creek trailhead. The trail goes upstream to the east, away from the geyser basin, but I make my way on foot downstream toward its confluence with the Firehole River. The ground near the creek is soft and soggy, but I find better footing a little higher up. Across the creek a solitary bison grazes. Somewhere around here was Shively's camp.

John Shively had lived in the West for twenty years. The spring of 1877 found him in the mining town of Deadwood in the Black Hills. After prospecting west to the Big Horn country, south through the Bridger Range and west again to the Wind River Mountains, he decided to try his luck in Yellowstone Park. Provided with a map of the region by a Shoshone Indian, Shively worked his way to Yellowstone Lake. He had found nothing in his pan all summer. He was fifty-five years old, his hair was turning white, and he was almost broke. On the shore of the lake he heaved his prospecting gear into the choppy water, his search for his golden bonanza over. Heading west he camped at the northern edge of the Lower Geyser Basin on August 23.

Yellow Wolf and Going Away were among the warriors in advance of the families late that day when they heard the sound of someone chopping wood. It was easy to sneak up on the old man as he cooked his evening meal. Each of them grabbed an arm, but he didn't put up a fight. The Nee-Me-Poo were in an unusual position that day. Since their accustomed trails to the buffalo country lay well to the north, they were unsure of the best route through the park. Another warrior named Bunched Lightning spoke a little English and asked Shively if he could show the People the way to the land of the Crows on the other side of the Absaroka Mountains. Shively quickly assured them he would be an excellent guide, so a party of warriors escorted him back to meet the council of chiefs.

The bison has wandered across the creek and closer to the road, creating the usual Yellowstone traffic jam that occurs whenever a wild animal gets close enough for folks to get a photo without taking a hike. I circle a good fifty yards wide of the shaggy beast, but others are approaching much closer. I hope a ranger shows up soon and shoos the tourists away. The bison's horns combined with its powerful neck and shoulder muscles can toss a full-grown human in the air like a toddler playing with a Raggedy Ann. My van is parked beside the mess on the highway. Drivers have abandoned their cars on the road, completely halting traffic in both directions. I cross over and pull my knapsack, binoculars and water bottle from the van. Climbing a low bluff, I scan the basin to the south with my binoculars. The Radersburg tourists camped somewhere along its eastern edge near the Fountain Geyser.

Yellow Wolf and four others continued ahead after capturing Shively. As darkness descended on the geyser basin, the glow of another fire appeared across the open country. Night made the unstable ground, thermal pools and hot springs of the basin too dangerous to traverse, so the five picketed their ponies, rolled up in their blankets and waited for morning. At first light Yellow Wolf, Bunched Lightning and Bowstring cautiously approached the camp of the Radersburg tourists. One of the whites rose from his bedding, grabbed a water bucket and began walking in the direction of the three warriors, oblivious of his watchers. The three held a whispered conference. Yellow Wolf wanted to kill him and everyone in the camp. The People had their guide in Shively; all other whites could now be simply classed as enemies. Not yet, said Bunched Lightning, let the chiefs decide if these whites live or die. Bill Dingee did the right thing. When he saw the mounted warriors he calmly waved. They waved back and walked their horses into the white camp. A. J. Arnold, too, had risen and also proved himself a man of good sense. He stepped forward and shook hands with each of the warriors. At that moment Yellow Wolf decided he would not kill him or any of the others in the camp. Shaking hands was like making peace. Arnold cemented his friendship with the Nez Perce by climbing into a wagon and handing down sacks of flour and sugar and two hunks of bacon.

For every person of common sense such as Dingee or Arnold nature apparently has to balance the world with a fool. One of them, George Cowan, stormed out of the only tent in camp and bellowed for Arnold to get off the wagon and for the warriors to depart pronto. Yellow Wolf and his companions were not impressed. Cowan's own wife later drolly commented, " . . . I think this materially lessened his chances of escape."[1] When Cowan demanded to meet Chief Joseph, Yellow Wolf hesitated. Using Bunched Lightning as an interpreter, he tried to explain that not all the warriors guarding the main group would be friendly, that some would want to kill the whites. If they kept away from the families, Yellow Wolf said, perhaps he could protect them. Nevertheless, at Cowan's insistence the Radersburg party proceeded to break camp and load their goods into their wagon. They had intended to depart from the park that very day through Targhee Pass to Henry's Lake, and Cowan remained determined to pursue that course. When all was ready, to Yellow Wolf's surprise, a woman and a teen-aged girl emerged from the brush behind the wagon and hastily clambered aboard a two-seater carriage. The woman was Emma Cowan, the twenty-three-year-old wife of George. The girl was Ida Carpenter, Emma's thirteen-year-old sister.

Big steps take me down the side of the bluff to Nez Perce Creek, and I turn upstream away from the highway. The creek is about fifteen feet wide, shallow, clear. Low forested hills line its narrow, open valley guiding me east toward the park's central plateau. I pass two fishermen then have the country to myself. I'll only hike a few miles in since the Park Service has pretty much closed the central plateau ahead to human activity, allows no overnight camping whatsoever. Hard-core grizzly country. Every quarter of a mile or so I stop and pull up my binoculars and scan the side slopes and valley ahead for sign of bear. Hiking alone has lots of advantages. It's much easier for one quiet, careful person to get close to wildlife than a larger group, not that I'm terribly interested in running into a grizzly today. Conversation is natural with companions, but the sounds scare off animals. In a group it's sometimes easy to get distracted, to miss little things, a low clump of cactus with a flower nestled inside, the shimmer of mica, faint bird songs, the smell of sage, silence.

Somewhere along here is where the Radersburg tourists got into real trouble.

Yellow Wolf's concern about other warriors was justified. Forty soon surrounded the two wagons and six horseback riders and forced them to turn up Nez Perce Creek and join the cavalcade of non-treaty bands. After a couple of miles, rough terrain prevented the wagons from going further, so the wagon passengers cut the horse teams loose and mounted as warriors proceeded to ransack the wagons. When the Nee-Me-Poo halted for their long mid-day break, Lean Elk informed the Radersburg people that they were free to turn back once they exchanged their good horses for slower, broken-down animals and gave up their rifles and ammunition. Emma Cowan remembered:

> . . . I immediately slipped out of the saddle to the ground, knowing I would never see my pony again, and went over to where Mr. Cowan was being persuaded that an old rack-abone gray horse was a fair exchange for his fine mount. He was persuaded.[2]

As soon as the hapless tourists were away from Lean Elk's protection, the shooting started. It lasted only a few seconds. George Cowan, who must have continued being obnoxious, was hit first, a bloody leg wound. He slid from his horse. Al Oldham, Charles Mann, Bill Harmon and D. L. Myers dashed for the relative safety of nearby woods. A warrior rode up beside Oldham and shot him in the head, but the others made it. Emma Cowan jumped to the ground and bravely tried to shield her husband's body with hers, but a warrior named Big Joe dismounted, pulled her away and fired a revolver point-blank at George Cowan's head. Emma fainted. Her little sister, Ida, bit the hand of a warrior who grabbed her, but she had no chance of escape. Frank Carpenter, alone of the men, stayed with his two sisters. Red Scout prevented the milling young warriors on horseback from killing him. Lean Elk hurried back, too late, and encountered trouble with some of the young

306

men led by the irascible Going Away. One of McWhorter's informants remembered:

> *This Ots-kai* (Going Away) *was cross-eyed, tall and raw-boned and ugly. They say he was a murderer, he is the one that threaten shoot Lean Elk if he interfered them with the white women, but Lean Elk got better warriors to take the white women away from the Indians that didn't want to give them up.*[3]

The site of the shooting is only a few miles ahead, but I'm turning back. That cliche about hairs standing on the back of the neck is real in this case. I feel like I'm being watched. By chipmunks, probably, but I'm going no further. Standing and glancing around, I eat a granola candy bar, the kind which is supposed to be healthy. It tastes just mealy enough that it might be true.

A few years ago I dropped in at park headquarters at Mammoth and chatted with the park historian at the time, Tom Tankersley. He showed me a grungy revolver someone had found near where George Cowan was shot. Cowan, miraculously, had remained alive. The bullet fired by Big Joe was defective, the slug imbedding itself in Cowan's forehead but doing no real damage. I wonder if Big Joe threw away his weapon in disgust once he learned Cowan had escaped, and that was how the revolver ended up with Tankersley. Speculation only.

Back at the highway my van is intact, and the bison has moved on, the traffic jam with it. Twenty minutes later I find a parking spot at Old Faithful and drop in at the backcountry office. The usual bear closures are in effect—the Central Plateau, the Hayden Valley, the Pelican Creek drainage—all areas the Nez Perce traversed. This time of year the bison are rutting, an event occasionally fatal for bulls competing for the carnal favors of their damsels. The carcasses of the unfortunate males attract grizzlies out of the higher, more remote areas of the park. The best news is that the Lamar Valley remains open. The ranger warns me, though, that the Lamar is pretty crowded with visitors this year. The release of wolves in the valley has attracted people hoping for a glimpse of the elusive creatures. He asks how many would be in my party if I decide to go into the Lamar country. One, I tell him. He looks at me dubiously. We recommend groups of four, never fewer than two, he tells me. I tell him I'll think about it.

It takes a little over an hour to circle south of the Central Plateau to Buffalo Ford on the Yellowstone River. The road twice crosses the Continental Divide then hugs the shore of Yellowstone Lake up to Fishing Bridge. The day remains cool and breezy, the atmosphere unsettled. Every now and then sunlight pops through a hole in the clouds and provides a moment of warmth, but I wish the van's heater worked. The Buffalo Ford picnic area occupies part of a large, mostly open flat on the edge of the Yellowstone River. The Real People nooned across the river on the twenty-fifth after spending the previous night somewhere on the Central Plateau. While I'm fixing my tomato and avocado sandwich, three fishermen in fancy waders and vests stroll by the No Fishing signs at the edge of the water and make their way toward an island in the middle of the river. Where's a ranger when you need one?

Emma Cowan and Frank Carpenter spent their first night in captivity under Thunder Rising's protection while John Shively and Ida Carpenter stayed with Lean Elk. Lean Elk told Shively that two of the chiefs were extremely angry over the attack on the tourists and were talking of splitting off from the rest of the non-treaty bands. Frank Carpenter remembered Thunder Rising reacting with disgust at mention of the unprovoked attack back along Nez Perce Creek. According to Mrs. Cowan, Thunder Rising:

> . . . *sat by the fire, sombre and silent, forseeing in his gloomy meditations possibly the unhappy ending of his campaign. The 'noble red man' we read of was more nearly impersonated in this Indian than in any I have ever met. Grave and dignified, he looked a chief.*[4]

She remembered him smiling only once, when Frank took a baby from one of the Nee-Me-Poo women and gave it to Emma to hold. It was not Thunder Rising's "campaign," of course, as Emma Cowan thought. His heart was back in his homeland, not on this tortuous trail away from the bones of his mother and father in the Wallowa earth.

The following morning Nez Perce scouts captured another white, James Irwin, a discharged soldier from Fort Ellis wandering through the park, enjoying the sights. Bartering for his life, he informed the warriors of the presence of another tourist group farther down the Yellowstone River. For that Emma Cowan held him in contempt, noting that many warriors soon departed to hunt down the party from Helena. The chiefs decided the time was right to release the women and the voluble Irwin. Emma Cowan flat out refused to go with him, and the chiefs relented to the gutsy woman; Frank Carpenter would be the escort. The wife of Geese Three Times Alighting remembered:

The two sisters had freckles in their faces and were shivering. The girl had short dress and had buttoned shoes, the older had lace shoes, one of the shoes on the younger girl was torn and an Indian woman tied it with a rag to keep it from coming off, each were given a pair of moccasins[5]

The Nee-Me-Poo woman pinned a shawl over Ida Carpenter's shoulders and gave them some camas and kouse roots.

Lean Elk provided jaded horses to both women, took Frank Carpenter on the back of his mount and reforded the river to Mud Volcano. There he urged the three to travel night and day until they reached Bozeman. If they did stop at night they should sleep in open country, not brush, to avoid an encounter with a grizzly bear. He gave them matches in case they wanted to build a fire along the way. Finally, he asked them to tell the citizens of Bozeman that he wanted no more war. With that, Lean Elk set them free, Frank Carpenter on foot, and the three took off down the river as fast as the two broken-down horses would allow.

In McWhorter's papers is a statement by Yellow Wolf suggesting that there was still another group of whites in the park, one that has never made it into the history books. McWhorter chose not to include the passage in either of his works, perhaps because no corroboration ever arose from another source. Still, Yellow Wolf was a strictly truthful man and his words deserve airing:

After we captured that bunch in that camp and day after in the evening we run onto four fellows three of them got away and one was captured this fellow we gave him some food and told him to go right away for there were some more in our party coming and some of them might kill him.[6]

Whatever this unknown man's name, he probably owed his life to Bill Dingee and A. J. Arnold who greeted Yellow Wolf in a friendly manner back at the Lower Geyser Basin.

All three fly fishermen I'm watching beyond the No Fishing signs are hopelessly inept. They cluster together in the center of the wide river, safety in numbers in case the fish attack, I suppose. Their lines hit the water on almost every backcast, and they spend much of their time untangling their leaders. Ever since Robert Redford made a movie out of Norman Maclean's *A River Runs Through It* there's been a lot of this on western rivers. It's not a pretty sight. Over the past few years I've talked with more than a few serious fly fishers who wouldn't mind running into Redford in a dark alley and making him pay for what he's done. Safe in the knowledge the trout have nothing to worry about, I fire up my van and head back to Fishing Bridge.

Just past Pelican Creek's outlet into Yellowstone Lake I stop at a small body of water now called Indian Pond, slightly more politically correct, I suppose, than its older name, Squaw Lake. An elderly aunt to Looking Glass, shot twice at the Big Hole, finally died here.

After leaving Buffalo Ford midday on the August 25 the Nee-Me-Poo families advanced only a couple of miles before stopping for the night. On the twenty-sixth they moved just four miles before Lean Elk called an early halt at Indian Pond. Something was up. The Nee-Me-Poo were only nine miles from the pass at the crest of the Absaroka Range toward which Shively had been leading them. Beyond the Absarokas lay the Stinking Water River leading to the southern reaches of the buffalo country in the Big Horn Basin, exactly where they wanted to be. In his most complete account of his stay with the Nez Perce, published in the Deer

Lodge *New Northwest* newspaper on September 14, Shively told the editor:

> *At this camp Mr. Shively showed them the mountains they must pass going to the Crow country and pointed out the trail to Stinking river. But there was a Snake chief (formerly in jail in Boise) with a few men along, who said he had now found the old Snake trail and they would follow that. Mr. S. was therefore released from service as a guide and kept back while the Snakes went ahead.*

The pond is about twenty acres in size, fed by underwater springs and filling a hole created by some kind of thermal explosion. Adjoining is a meadow of a hundred acres surrounded by dense thickets of lodgepole pine. The 700 Real People would have filled the meadow up with their temporary hide and canvas shelters, their cooking fires and a few of the horses. Most of the herd would have grazed along Pelican Creek about a mile away, I guess.

Shively's "Snake chief" was perhaps none other than Major Jim, whom we last saw twelve days ago leaving Alex Cruikshank shortly after the Birch Creek massacre and hurrying after the non-treaty Nez Perce over the mountain shortcut. Major Jim disappeared from mention in Montana and Idaho newspapers until late September when he was reported again roaming his old haunts around Horse Prairie, this time harboring several Nez Perce wounded at the Big Hole. His absence from his usual country corresponded with the sojourn of the Real People through the park. McWhorter apparently suspected Major Jim might have been the "Snake chief." He wrote War Singer during the 1930s and asked the tribal historian if any of the few survivors of the war remembered Major Jim. War Singer responded in the negative, although he wrote back that one of the old people did remember that a Bannock named Zu-Koop was with the Real People. Yellow Wolf was of no help, either. During this time he and many of the young men were away from the families, scouting ahead and behind. In the end, McWhorter devoted only one sentence in *Hear Me, My Chiefs!* to the actions and whereabouts of the families over the next two, crucial weeks and skipped over the families entirely in *Yellow Wolf, His Own Story*. The silence of McWhorter's informants is intriguing because the decision to follow the advice of the Snake chief to ignore the nearby route out of the park and turn north for another trail led to near-disaster for the Real People. The extra days the Nee-Me-Poo spent struggling through the tortured terrain of the Absarokas allowed six companies of the Seventh Cavalry under Colonel Samuel Sturgis time to position themselves within sight of the spot where the non-treaty bands would eventually emerge from the mountains onto the buffalo plains. Only a miracle there would save them.

A short walk takes me to the Pelican Creek trailhead. The backcountry is closed, so I only hike in a mile or so to a low bluff overlooking the valley. Pelican Creek meanders through incredibly lush meadows covered with grass that must be at least waist-high. The valley floor is flat, the calm water of the creek flowing without a ripple. The tired Nez Perce horses must have thought they had found heaven here. My topo map shows similar country stretching for about eight miles along the creek. The route the families took from there remains something of a mystery to this day and is still debated by the obsessed.

In the early 1970s, a fellow named Daniel Goodenough collected a team of hikers and thoroughly scouted all the possible routes the 700 people and 2,000 horses might have taken. He came to the conclusion that the Nee-Me-Poo had, in fact, been headed directly across the Absaroka Divide to Stinking Water River, although over an alternate route to the one suggested by Shively. Disoriented and believing he had already crossed the Absaroka Divide, the Snake chief turned down Cold Creek, a tributary of Mist Creek, which flows in turn into the Lamar River. In Cold Creek Canyon the Real People found the worst terrain they would encounter during their long flight from their homeland toward Canada. Lean Elk put Shively and Irwin to work with axes, clearing the way through choked timber. Accustomed to long days digging prospecting holes to bedrock, the old miner still called August 28 "the hardest work he ever did." Following the trail a few days later, Stanton Fisher had this to say:

312

We broke camp this morning at daylight and were off on the trail, following it through the roughest canyon I ever undertook to pass through. About every foot of it was obstructed with dead and fallen timber and huge blocks of granite which had fallen from its rugged sides. We found plenty of dead and crippled horses which had been left by the enemy. They evidently had a hard time getting through this place for the trees and logs were smeared with blood from their horses.[7]

According to Goodenough, of all the drainages flowing from the Pelican Creek divide into the Lamar River, only Cold Creek's canyon possesses that kind of terrain.[8]

In 1990 a historian named William Lang published an article disputing Goodenough's conclusions. The Nez Perce, he contended, were never on Cold Creek but followed Mist Creek all the way from its headwaters to the Lamar.[9] I've examined Fisher's original journal in the archives of the Idaho Historical Society, and it contains this sentence about the terrible, choked canyon, "We were several hours makeing down to the Main creek, one of the branches of East Fork."[10] (The East Fork was Fisher's name for the present-day Lamar River.) To me that sentence strongly buttresses Goodenough's argument, not Lang's. Clearly, Fisher was describing a tributary of a tributary of the Lamar: Cold Creek.

I like Goodenough's conclusions, except his contention that the direction taken down Cold Creek was inadvertent. My topo maps show the Absaroka Divide rising 2,000 feet directly in the path of the Nee-Me-Poo before they turned sharply to the left down Cold Creek. It seems to me impossible that the Snake chief guiding the Real People could have erred in recognizing the divide. More likely, I think, they took the most difficult route imaginable in order to make pursuit by Howard as daunting as possible.

The Nee-Me-Poo were perfectly aware of the presence of Fisher and his scouts dogging the heels of the families and must have known that sooner or later Howard's army would be following. If they hadn't already done so, the chiefs would soon be sending emissaries to the Crows to judge their mood and discuss the possibility of an alliance between the tribes to fight the whites as the

Crows had promised Looking Glass in 1873. Until those men returned, the Real People would need a sanctuary for the families. The Lamar Valley and its environs were to be that safe place. The plan worked. On September 3 Stanton Fisher sent John Redington—who had brought hardtack, bacon and dispatches to the scouting party—back to Howard with the suggestion that the general abandon direct pursuit of the Nez Perce due to the difficulty of the terrain and find another route across the Absaroka Mountains.

While all this was transpiring, young warriors far from the calming influence of the elders were searching for the party of tourists that Irwin had mentioned. It's time to go take a look at the area where the warriors found them. Returning to my van, I drive back to Fishing Bridge and turn north again past Buffalo Ford and Mud Volcano into the Hayden Valley. Just before the road begins the climb to Dunraven Pass, an innocuous stream gurgles under the asphalt and flows into the Yellowstone River. Otter Creek. A service road follows it up, but a locked gate bars the way and a sign says the area is closed to both vehicular and pedestrian traffic.

The Helena party spotted the Nez Perce camp at Buffalo Ford about the same time ex-soldier James Irwin was giving away those same tourists in an effort to save his hide. Why these ten guys from Helena didn't high-tail it out of the park as fast as their horses could take them will forever remain a mystery. Charles Kenck, the only married member of the party, was actually in favor of doing just that. He applied spurs to his horse and stopped near Dunraven Pass only when he noticed that none of his companions had followed him that far. Returning, he easily found the others' "hidden" camp up Otter Creek after spotting smoke from their fire. One member, Andrew Weikert, lamely wrote in a journal later published by the Historical Society of Montana that they figured "they were afraid of us and we were afraid of them, so it was mutual on that score."[11] Dumb, dumb, dumb.

The warriors struck about mid-day on August 26, as the whites lounged about waiting for the black cook, Ben Stone, to fix their meal. Kenck started running up the slope away from the creek, but took several bullets, one in the back of the neck. He died almost instantly. With him was Jack Stewart who was hit twice, once in the side and once in the leg. Joe Roberts and August Fuller dashed upstream and made it to safety. Ben Stone and Richard Dietrich somersaulted into the creek and hid in the water for the next three or four hours. Fred Pfister and Leonard Duncan escaped into the woods. The warriors appropriated horses, saddles, clothing, food, weapons and the $263 in Stewart's pocket, not bothering to expend another bullet on the wounded man.

Andrew Weikert and Leslie Wilkie were not in camp, having decided to ride toward Buffalo Ford for another look at the Nee-Me-Poo. Warriors soon spotted them and sent a hail of bullets in their direction. Leaning flat on his galloping horse, Weikert took a glancing bullet along one shoulder blade that nicked the bone but luckily did not enter his back. Another slug smashed the butt of the rifle he carried across his lap before he and Wilkie made their escape. Scattered and unsure of the fate of the other members of their party, the surviving whites began to make their way singly or in small groups toward safety.

It's just a few miles to the Grand Canyon of the Yellowstone, but I don't dally to gawk at the falls. It's afternoon, and I still have to find a place to spend the night. With a bit of luck the campground at Mammoth will still be open. The road north takes me up the side of Mount Washburn to Dunraven Pass, named after the Irish earl who was in the park in 1877. On his second trip to Yellowstone, he had already written a book published in England describing his first visit in 1874. He seems to have been a likable guy. Unlike many of the European nobility who came to the American West, Dunraven disdained the creature comforts and a retinue of servants, preferring to live as westerners did, sleeping in a crude tent or under the stars, hunting each day for food and sometimes not eating at all, tipping a jug of cheap whiskey at night beside a bonfire. Like the Helena party, he and his scout, Texas Jack, had sighted the Real People as they were crossing the river at Buffalo Ford but they, being individuals of some intelligence and discretion, vamoosed.

About the time Nez Perce warriors were shooting up the Helena party, Lieutenant Charles Schofield stood atop Mount Washburn off to my right, scanning the country to his south with a field glass. He and a few men had scouted up the Yellowstone River from Fort Ellis for the past four days. He could see no activity in the river valley and decided to withdraw. In a few hours he would find Emma Cowan and her brother and sister and thus gain firm intelligence as to the location and direction of the non-treaty bands.

The road drops toward Tower Junction where I head west toward Mammoth over the Blacktail Plateau. Since passing Buffalo Ford I've pretty much been following the route taken by Emma Cowan and her kin after their release by Lean Elk. Here the land falls away to the north toward the Yellowstone River hidden in Black Canyon before rising again to the massive Beartooth Mountains just outside the park. This is my favorite part of the park, a patchwork of pine and fir and spruce and aspen interspersed with meadows and ponds. One minute the rolling terrain is intimate, the next expansive. I'd like nothing better than to stop in one of the many meadows, find a rock warmed a bit by the intermittent sunlight and soak in the immense prospect and billowing sky, but there's no time. I wonder if Emma Cowan spent a few seconds or minutes enjoying this view. If she did, there's no indication in her memoir.

Somewhere short of Mammoth she and Frank and Ida noticed fresh pony tracks on the trail they were following and soon came in sight of men and horses in a distant meadow. Frank dodged cautiously ahead on foot, then came hurrying back with the welcome news they were soldiers. Lieutenant Schofield quickly fed the exhausted refugees then piled them on fresh horses. He had already set up camp for the night, but the news that the Nee-Me-Poo were near convinced him to make tracks. To add impetus to the move, the fleetest afoot of the Helena survivors, Fred Pfister, soon stumbled into the camp with the first tidings of that attack. Schofield shepherded the civilians the seventeen miles to Mammoth in darkness, arriving about midnight.

I make it to Mammoth about five in the afternoon, cruise through the hotel and park headquarters complex and find one of the last open spaces in the campground perched on a slope below the springs. For some reason the Mammoth campground always seems to be the last to fill in the park—a free travel hint for the vacationing tardy. I need to stretch my muscles after spending most of the afternoon hunched over my steering wheel in heavy traffic and take the foot trail back up to the springs. At the northern edge of the travertine cliffs formed by the springs is an innocuous wooded ravine opening onto a shelf of grass. Some of the grass is a rich emerald, the earth underneath lumpy, all that's left of Mack McCartney's Resort. In 1877 it consisted of a tiny hotel— really a log cabin—a couple of log bathhouses with roofs so low you had to duck to get inside, an outhouse and some sort of miniature barn.

Schofield and company found McCartney, the Earl of Dunraven's party and a few other men at Mammoth. At dawn on the twenty-eighth, four more members of the Helena group arrived, sharing three horses: Stone, Wilkie and the two wounded men, Stewart and Weikert. Dr. George Kingsley, Dunraven's English sidekick, treated the injured while Schofield sent a courier scurrying down the Yellowstone River to Fort Ellis with news of the location of the non-treaty bands and the rescue of the tourists. Later in the day Duncan and Dietrich came in, exhausted after traveling on foot for fifty miles, which left only three of the Helena party still missing. Kenck, of course, lay dead at Otter Creek, but Roberts and Fuller had lit out in a different direction than their companions. Setting their sights on Virginia City, they would run into Howard's column and safety, but concern at Mammoth over their whereabouts would lead to the death of another of the Helena party.

On August 28 most of the sundry folks at Mammoth departed downriver toward Fort Ellis. Mack McCartney, Andy Weikert, Dick Dietrich and Ben Stone remained, hoping the missing men would appear and tending to Jack Stewart's wounds until a wagon arrived from downriver to ferry him home. On the twenty-ninth, McCartney and Weikert saddled up and began the long ride to Otter Creek, trusting the Nez Perce had moved on and they could safely discover the fate of Kenck and the others.

A raiding party of eighteen to twenty warriors passed them that night and arrived in the vicinity of Mammoth late in the afternoon of the thirtieth. The wagon for Stewart had come and gone. Dietrich and Stone were supposed to have departed with Stewart, but Dietrich had been feeling pangs of guilt the last three days; he had convinced the twenty-year-old Roberts to make the trip and could not face the prospect of meeting the young man's mother without knowing her son's fate. Reluctantly, Stone agreed to stay with Dietrich, and one of the men with the ambulance wagon, Jake Stoner, decided to keep the two men company. While Ben Stone was fixing dinner, Dietrich took his horse down to the Gardner River to stake it near good grass and water for the night. Stoner took a walk to the top of the springs but soon came running back. He had seen riders in the distance, two groups of about ten and they didn't look like white men. While Stoner hurried to the river to warn Dietrich, Ben Stone fled out the back door of McCartney's "hotel" and secreted himself in the trees adjoining the ravine. He soon saw figures wearing blankets circling the building on foot and decided it was time to make himself even scarcer but in his rush to get away stepped on a dry branch. The loud crack in the silence of the evening sounded like a gunshot. He ran for his life. Hearing the sound of a horse behind him, Stone hoisted himself into the branches of a tree and held his breath as a warrior reined in his mount almost directly beneath him. After a few seconds the warrior continued on, and Stone breathed a huge sigh of relief. He climbed further up the mountain, crawling on his hands and knees, once coming face-to-face with a bear which, fortunately, crashed away through the underbrush. Sometime in the night he heard the sound of gunshots below, and he could see fires near McCartney's place. Stone spent the next day hiding on the mountainside, pondering the fate of his comrades, scared half to death, until about three in the afternoon he was startled by a burst of gunfire coming from the direction of McCartney's Resort; he later estimated the number of shots at fifteen. Richard Dietrich, a mild-mannered music teacher originally from Germany, now lay dead.[12]

Under clearing skies I fix myself a fancy dinner back at the campground: potato, carrots and onion wrapped in foil bake under the coals of a fire I let flare and die; a rib-eye steak I bought in West Yellowstone waits its turn. My stomach is rumbling.

General Howard's army remained halted at Henry's Lake until August 27, the day of the attack on the Helena party at Otter Creek. By then the Nee-Me-Poo were far ahead at Indian Pond. Stanton Fisher, meanwhile, was having problems with his Bannock scouts. Buffalo Horn, who had been with Howard since Kamiah, had tired of the endless chase and the soldiers' inability to match the pace of the Real People. He deserted on the twenty-fourth after the abortive attack on the abandoned Nee-Me-Poo camp on the Madison River, taking half the warriors with him. Fisher persisted and entered the national park with the remaining, discontented scouts.

Late on the August 25, one of the scouts reported seeing two white men along the Madison River but refused to disclose the location until Fisher paid him ten dollars. They proved to be Bill Harmon and Charles Mann from the Radersburg party. When Fisher sent them back to the camp at Henry's Lake the news that the Nez Perce had captured white women caused a sensation. Captain Robert Pollock wrote in a letter:

> *Oh, how I pity those poor women in the hands of fiends. . . . (Harmon) runs a gnarled paw through long locks all the time. Lt. Weeks joshed him about this, asking him if he was making sure the renegades had not lifted his hair. It isn't very funny, the man has the shakes and jumps.*[13]

The following day Dingee and Arnold of the Radersburg party walked into the army camp, having evaded the Bannocks, thinking they were Nez Perce watching the back trail. Of the Radersburg party that left Al Oldham, Andrew Myers, George Cowan and the three captives unaccounted.

When Howard ordered the command forward again, it was a refreshed column. Not only had McDowell's and Sherman's telegrams received in Virginia City stung the general and his staff with their criticisms, but the thought of the two women in the hands of the Nez Perce put fire in the eyes of the soldiers. Even

319

Major Mason, who had for weeks been writing privately to his wife of the folly of continuing the pursuit, had felt a change of heart. He wrote:

> *I am perfectly willing to follow these felons until the last one is disposed of—they should be killed as we kill any other vile thing.*14

In the meantime, General Sheridan in Chicago was plotting. The war against the Nez Perce had entered his jurisdiction, despite his earlier, embarrassing prediction that the Real People could not be heading for the buffalo country. In addition the nation-wide labor riots had been quelled, and the newspapers were once again focusing attention on the 700 or so Nez Perce who were continuing to confound the army. Public opinion in the East was even beginning to sway in the direction of the nontreaty bands as personified by Chief Joseph.

The most recent army map of the Yellowstone region had been drawn by Captain William Jones of the Corps of Engineers who had spent the summer of 1873 on a reconnaissance of the remote area. To Sheridan it appeared the Nez Perce had four possible avenues of escape from their last known location in the center of the national park: north down the Yellowstone River toward Fort Ellis, an unlikely alternative; north then east along a miners' trail to the Clark's Fork River; due east to the Stinking Water River; or southeast to the Wind River. According to Jones' lengthy report to which the map was appended, the Wind River route was by far the easiest to traverse.15 The Nee-Me-Poo had just struck that trail to the Wind River. Sheridan outlined his moves to block the escape of the Nee-Me-Poo to General Sherman in a telegram of August 28:

> *Col Gibbon telegraphed on 27th that Nez Perce crossed Yellowstone River in the National Park just south of Canyon. Col Sturgis with 7th Cavalry is at Crow Agency and will cross to Clarks Fork and go up that stream to intercept them. Lieut. Doane with 1 Company of Cavalry and 100 Crow Indians left Fort Ellis for Bridge on Yellowstone North of Canyon and a trail across to Clark's Fork. Genl Howard is*

not mentioned but I presume is following up. The Indians say they are going to Wind River and it looks a little as though this may be so. To meet it I have sent Col Merritt to Camp Brown where he shall have 4 companies of Cavalry and I have ordered 5 companies more to go by rail to Green River and from there to Camp Brown. This will give Merritt at Brown 9 companies of cavalry. Major Hart is on head of Tongue River, 40 miles east of Fort C. F. Smith, with 5 companies of Fifth Cavalry. In case the Nez Perce come down Stinking Water Major Hart will be sent there. If they go to Wind River I will cross him over the Bighorn Mountains to Wind River.[16]

In a telegram dated the following day Sherman approved of the plan and added his own twist. With him in Helena was Lieutenant Colonel Charles Gilbert, second-in-command of Gibbon's Fifth Infantry. It was time, Sherman decided, to relieve Howard. Penning a letter to Howard on the twenty-ninth, the General of the Army gave it to Gilbert and told him to find the pursuing column. After describing Sheridan's forces soon to be converging on the Nee-Me-Poo the letter ended:

Tomorrow I start for Missoula and Walla Walla. There are many things in your Department about which I would like to consult you, and I will feel your absence much. Really I do not see much reason for your commanding a Detachment, after having driven the hostile Indians out of your Department across Montana, and into Genl Sheridan's command. I find (General) Lt Col CC Gilbert here, who has served long in this territory, and is familiar with the Indians, and the country in which they have taken refuge. I don't want to order you back to Oregon, but I do say that you can with perfect propriety return to your command, leaving the troops to continue till the Nez Perces have been destroyed or confined, and I authorize you to transfer to him, Lt. Col Gilbert, your command in the field and to overtake me en route or in your Department.[17]

It was actually quite a gentle letter, closing with "I am, with

321

great respect, your friend." The two men's friendship went back to the Civil War when Howard had commanded the 27,000-man Army of Tennessee, part of Sherman's famous—or infamous—march from Atlanta to the sea. Colonel Gilbert departed Helena for Fort Ellis with instructions to push up the Yellowstone River, rendezvous with Lieutenant Doane's command of cavalry and Crow scouts, then find General Howard.

By August 30 Howard's column had reached the Lower Geyser Basin and found Andrew Myers, Al Oldham and George Cowan, the latter two with incredible stories to tell. The bullet fired at Oldham's head had passed through both cheeks, knocking out a couple of teeth and tearing up his tongue. The wound was bloody and extremely painful but far from fatal. He managed to play possum even when a warrior kicked him to make sure he was dead. Once night came he began crawling. He found he could drink a little water, but eating was impossible. Now, after five days of constant pain, hunger and exposure Oldham was weak but soon would be mending. Cowan was similarly lucky or unlucky as the case may be. He, you might remember, had been shot in the leg then again at close range in the forehead with a handgun, the latter bullet lodging in his skull. He lost consciousness, not reviving until late in the day. When he got to his feet with the aid of a stick the first thing he saw to his dismay was a mounted warrior only twenty-five yards away, raising a rifle. This bullet hit him in the side above one hip and exited his abdomen. Down he went, of course. Again, this warrior assumed Cowan was a goner, and again a warrior was wrong.

Crawling at night, Cowan reached their last camp in the geyser basin after four days and found matches and coffee. John Redington was the one who found him on the twenty-ninth and remembered:

> *Cowan had very black hair, and had lost so much blood that his face was deathly pale, and the contrast between face and hair was so striking that I will never forget it.*[18]

After first taking a look at the geysers in the area Surgeon Fitzgerald removed the bullet from Cowan's forehead and dressed his wounds. Cowan to the end of his days held a grudge against the army physician for playing tourist before tending to a patient. It's difficult to disagree.

Life soon got better for him. Courier Frank Parker rode into Howard's camp late on the thirtieth after a long ride from Bozeman. He saw Cowan sitting alone and:

> . . . asked some of the soldiers what was wrong 'with that feller?' One of the men replied: 'If you were in his place you would feel the same way. That is Cowan.' 'What?' I replied, 'Why I just came from Bozeman, and both his wife and his sister Ida are there unharmed, as well as their brother Frank Carpenter.' I then went back to Cowan and said, 'Now you see here! I have the best news in the world for you, but I won't tell you a word until you take a good drink of this whiskey.' He seemed to gather hope at once, and begged to hear, but I made him take the whiskey first, and as he drank I told him the glad news. I never saw such a change come over any one man in my life as manifested by Cowan at that time.[19]

Howard's column continued up Nez Perce Creek over the Central Plateau and found the going increasingly difficult for the wagon train. As they began to ascend Mary's Mountain, axemen had to hack a primitive road through dense thickets of standing and fallen lodgepole pine, slowing forward movement to a snail's pace.

Stanton Fisher had been doing his job, staying close to the non-treaty bands without getting himself or his Bannock scouts killed. By the August 28 he and one of his men had reached the abandoned camp at Indian Pond. That evening he alone followed the trail up Pelican Creek and reached the Lamar Divide about sundown. Before turning back he saw smoke from the fires of the Nez Perce camp in the valley below, but it would be another five days before Fisher poked ahead into the Lamar drainage. Lack of food, the flu and disgruntlement among his scouts would keep him occupied around Mud Geyser until September 2. When he finally, cautiously nosed ahead he again found the Real People within a few miles of where he had seen them on the twenty-eighth. They were going nowhere fast.

I'm cleaning up after that fine steak dinner. My stomach is comfortably stuffed, and I'm tempted to put my feet up and watch the day end. Across the Gardner River to the east the shadow cast by the setting sun rises inexorably up the side of Mt. Everts, named after a man who spent thirty-seven days lost in Yellowstone and weighed only about sixty pounds when rescued. The mountain is a flat-topped geologic layer cake with enough colors of volcanic rock to be the centerpiece of any party. Around me the sounds and sights of families returning after a day exploring the park provide a comfortable bustle. Instead, I climb in my van and drive five looping miles a thousand feet down to the boundary of the park and the town of Gardiner straddling the Yellowstone River.

After a visit to a gas station and grocery store I take a gravel National Park service road along the west bank of the river. The valley's about a mile wide here, flat and barren except for a scant cover of hardy grass, dark mountains rising on either side. The river itself remains out of sight, hidden beneath rocky banks fifty feet deep. A couple of miles on I spot two old trees—one splintered and dead, the other barely hanging on—just off the road. Henderson's Ranch, or what little is left of it.

The ranch location was pointed out to me three years ago by Tom Tankersley of the National Park Service (In one of the few errors in Cheryl Wilfong's fine trail guide she places the ranch several miles farther downriver on the opposite bank). Between the trees and the river lies a field of boulders, some as big as two feet high. I wander among them for a few minutes, crouching behind three or four, imagining bullets coming my way, making myself small. Six distant antelope are the only witnesses, and they are only mildly curious about my antics.

Beyond the two trees, lonely in this spartan landscape, is a low ridge. I walk the 200 yards or so to the trees and on to the ridge. It's only twenty feet high and covered with smaller rocks and boulders. Choosing the most comfortable-looking one, I take a load off my feet.

While Ben Stone spent his miserable night and day on the mountain above McCartney's Resort, Richard Dietrich and Jake Stoner somehow managed to evade the Nez Perce raiding party. Stoner never told his story to anyone who left a record; since he apparently abandoned Dietrich sometime during that twenty-four hours, it might not have been a pretty tale to tell.

Meanwhile, rancher Bart Henderson had sent his wife and seven of their children downriver when word spread of the Nez Perce depredations in the park. He, along with one son and two hired hands, stayed to protect his cattle ranch as best they could. On the morning of the August 31, Henderson and one man strolled down to the river to catch some fish. The remaining hand soon noticed mounted warriors coming down the valley. He and Henderson's son grabbed all the available guns and ammunition and scampered for the river. As soon as all four whites were armed and had gotten their courage up, they dodged up to the boulder field and spotted eight warriors dismounted and milling about the ranch house. Ten more warriors watched from the low ridge beyond the ranch. Henderson and his men squeezed off a volley, sending the warriors near the house scrambling for cover. Most of their horses bolted, coming to a halt midway between the ranch and the boulders.

What followed for a while was an old-fashioned stand-off: the warriors unable to dislodge the whites from their rocky redoubt and unwilling to retreat and hoof it all the way back to the family camp forty miles away, the whites unable to press the advantage of their initial surprise. Henderson's nerve broke first. He and his little group eventually crawled away and paddled a boat across the river to safety. The warriors quickly ransacked the house, set it afire, rounded up about fifteen horses, scattered several hundred head of cattle and turned back. Passing Mammoth they noticed Richard Dietrich standing near the door of McCartney's hotel and delivered the barrage that Ben Stone heard from his sanctuary in the forest above.

Coming up Yellowstone Canyon at that very moment was Lieutenant Gustavus Doane leading a company of the Seventh Cavalry along with about forty Crow warriors and a contingent of settlers from Bozeman. Spotting the smoke from the burning

Henderson Ranch, Doane ordered Lieutenant Hugh Scott and ten men to press ahead and investigate while the Crows dropped from their horses, stripped and began to adorn themselves for battle.

Scott, the troopers and civilian Jack Baronett galloped their horses forward. Meeting up with Henderson, who had returned to his ranch, they received a hurried recount of the day's events before continuing on the warriors' fresh trail. At Mammoth, Scott discovered Dietrich's body, still warm. As familiar with this country as any man alive, Baronett warned Scott against pursuing the Nez Perce across the Blacktail Plateau at night with only ten men. Suicide. Prudently, Scott retreated to Henderson's ranch where Doane was setting up a heavily guarded camp.

That evening a thoroughly frightened Ben Stone slipped into the camp. He would not, he said, be taking any more pleasure excursions soon. Not long after Stone made his appearance, foot-sore Andrew Weikert and Mack McCartney hobbled into the light of the cavalry fires. That morning they had been jumped by another bunch of warriors on the eastern edge of Blacktail Plateau. After Weikert's horse had been shot and McCartney's horse had bucked him off, the two men had raced on foot for the shelter of some brush where they had managed to hold off their attackers. After that came an all-day, hair-raising hike across Blacktail Plateau.

The following morning Doane ordered Scott and twenty troopers to scout across Blacktail Plateau as far as a bridge Jack Baronett had built a few years back across the Yellowstone River below the Grand Canyon. The Crows' ardor for a fight with the Nee-Me-Poo had diminished considerably overnight, but Scott managed to bribe one to be his eyes and ears. Arriving at Baronett's Bridge safely, Scott's men set fire to the grass in the area then wasted no time in beating a retreat. They must not have crossed the river because Scott failed to notice that some of the bridge timbers were scorched, the result of an attempt by the Snake chief traveling with the Nee-Me-Poo to destroy the bridge two days earlier.

On the way back Scott's contingent ran into two frontiersmen named Groff and Leonard who had been sent across the Absaroka Mountains by Colonel Samuel Sturgis of the Seventh Cavalry who was now on the Clark's Fork River east of the mountains, waiting with six companies of his cavalry for the Real People to leave the park. Groff was bleeding from a bullet wound in the neck, the result of an ambush by Nez Perce warriors that also resulted in the death of a Warm Springs Indian boy in the company of the two whites. Scott escorted them back to Doane's camp. In a few days Lieutenant Doane would send Groff and Leonard back to Sturgis bearing a message with the latest intelligence on the whereabouts of the Nez Perce. They were never heard from again, presumably suffering lonely deaths somewhere in the Absaroka Mountains. After the battle at the Big Hole most of the angry young men of the non-treaty bands still had no mercy in their hearts.

Notes

[1] Cowan, Mrs. George F., "Reminiscences of Pioneer Life," *Contributions To The Historical Society of Montana*, Vol. 4, p. 167.

[2] Cowan, *"Reminiscences"*, p. 169.

[3] McWhorter, *Papers*, Folder 164, item 184.

[4] Cowan, *"Reminiscences"*, p. 172.

[5] McWhorter, *Papers*, Folder 34, item 73.

[6] McWhorter, *Papers*, Folder 84, item 108.

[7] Fisher, S. G., "Journal of S. G. Fisher," *Contributions to the Historical Society of Montana, Vol II*, Helena, 1896, p. 275.

[8] Goodenough, Daniel, "Lost on Cold Creek," *Montana, the Magazine of Western History*, Autumn 1974.

[9] Lang, William, "Where did the Nez Perce Go in Yellowstone in 1877?" *Montana, the Magazine of Western History*, Winter 1990.

[10] Fisher, Stanton, *Journal*, p. 8. Idaho Historical Society, Boise.

[11] Weikert, Andrew, "Journal of the Tour Through Yellow-Stone National Park in August and September, 1877," *Contributions to the Historical Society of Montana, Vol. III*, Helena, 1900, p. 159.

[12] Bozeman *Avant-Courier*, Sept. 6, Sept. 13. My version of the events surrounding Dietrich's death varies considerably from other accounts. I've decided to rely on Ben Stone's fresh recollection published on the dates noted, while most writers apparently have used Andrew Weikert's second-hand version published much later which telescopes events into a few hours instead of two days. I've also omitted any mention of Yellow Wolf's narrative on pages 177-180 of *Yellow Wolf, His Own Story*. Although he details the death of a white man at the door of a structure, the size of the warrior party, the mention of willows near the building, the presence of another party of whites with whom the warriors had a fight and the proximity of a second house with five or six men inside all argue against Yellow Wolf describing Dietrich's death. A reader can construct a time line of Yellow Wolf's activities from the day of the Dietrich incident until the fight at Canyon Creek on September 13. The inescapable conclusion of such a time line is that the events described by Yellow Wolf took place no earlier than September 5th. By then all Nee-Me-Poo were well out of the park and Yellow Wolf was scouting the area around the Stinking Water River. A number of miners were indeed killed about that time in that area as you will read in the next chapter. I'm convinced that McWhorter erred in placing Yellow Wolf at Mammoth.

[13] Pollock, Robert W., *Grandfather, Chief Joseph and Psychodynamics*, Caxton Printers, Caldwell, ID, 1964, p. 92-93.

[14] Davison, *"A Century Ago,"* p.13.

[15] Jones, William A., *Report Upon the Reconnaissance of Northwestern Wyoming Including Yellowstone National Park Made in the Summer of 1873*, Government Printing Office, Washington, 1874.

[16] AGO, *Letters*, roll 337, p. 510-513.

[17] AGO, *Letters*, roll 338, p. 506-507.

[18] McWhorter, *Papers*, Folder 50, item 86.

[19] McWhorter, *Papers*, Folder 158, item 117.

Martin Stadius

Pelican Creek, Yellowstone National Park. The Nee-Me-Poo families rested here while their horses grazed and their leaders talked.

Martin Stadius

Henderson Ranch, Yellowstone National Park. From behind these rocks settler Bart Henderson, his son and two hired hands exchanged shots with warriors ransacking his house. The house was located between the two trees in the distance.

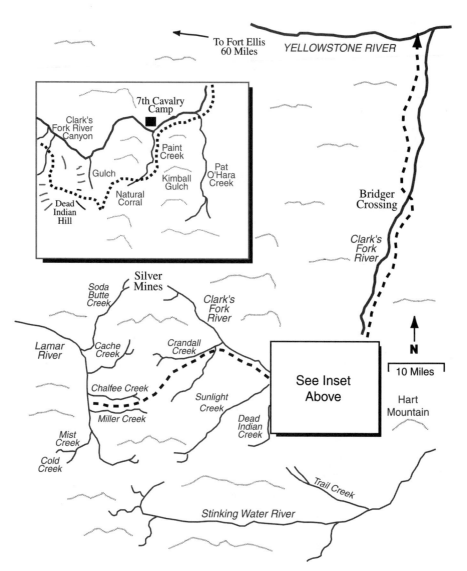

ABSAROKA REGION **National Historic Trail** ▪ ▪ ▪ ▪

CHAPTER THIRTEEN

ABSAROKA

G o back a few days in your mind. The Real People had arrived on the Lamar River on August 28 after their arduous trip down Cold and Mist Creeks. The next day, according to John Shively, they moved only four miles downstream, and on the thirtieth they shifted another few miles, just enough to provide fresh grass for their horses.

The party which raided Henderson's Ranch trotted out of camp that day. Another group of warriors scouted up Soda Butte Creek toward the silver mines atop the Absaroka Divide; their presence would eventually be reported in a Bozeman newspaper. The Snake chief and a few men decided to burn Baronett's Bridge across the Yellowstone River to hinder the approach of any troops. On the back trail no soldiers were anywhere close to the families. It was looking good. On the thirty-first they moved three miles, leaving the river bottom and ascending a high ridge to the east between two creeks flowing from the Absaroka heights where they found more meadows and springs and an abundance of elk. As a precaution warriors built log breastworks atop the ridge. Now they had a refuge and time to rest, time to hope and grieve, time to wait for word to come from their emissaries to the Crows.

After climbing to the divide separating the Pelican Creek and Lamar River drainages on the evening of the August 28 and sighting the smoke from the Nez Perce camp in the valley below, Stanton Fisher had retreated to the Yellowstone River. For the next two days he stayed in camp at Mud Volcano, nursing a mild case of the flu and considering giving up the chase. By the third day both his stomach and his mood had improved, and he was ready to continue; most of his remaining Bannocks weren't. They had signed on assuming it would be a simple matter to find the Nez Perce and steal a bunch of horses to bring home as trophies, just like in the old days. These Nee-Me-Poo were proving a hard nut to crack, and the prospects for the future weren't sanguine. It was time to go home. Fisher had no choice but to relent. He signed a paper releasing twenty-two scouts. Passing General Howard's column on the central plateau, the returning Bannocks absconded with forty horses belonging to civilian teamsters—the warriors, after all, couldn't show up at home with absolutely nothing to show for their time—but quick action by the general forced the return of all forty by nightfall.

His force now down to eighteen men, far too few to risk any direct encounter with Nez Perce warriors, Fisher was on the move again on September 1. Along the upper reaches of Pelican Creek he spotted a man hurrying toward him on foot in the half-light of sundown. Fisher covered the stranger with his rifle, demanding his name and business. It was James Irwin, the ex-soldier captured by the Real People who had slipped out of the Nez Perce camp atop the ridge early that morning. Here was reliable intelligence concerning the location of the Nee-Me-Poo, and Fisher hurried Irwin back to Howard the following morning.

Poring over his maps in light of the information Irwin provided, General Howard realized the Nez Perce could not possibly be heading for the Wind River to the southeast along the Jones Trail, likely not the Stinking Water River due east. The best bet was clearly the Clark's Fork River where Colonel Sturgis with the Seventh Cavalry should soon be waiting, if not already there. Howard's heart might have beat a little faster. If he moved his column north along the Yellowstone River to Baronett's Bridge then took the miners' trail up Soda Butte Creek to the upper reaches of the Clark's Fork, he and Sturgis could crush the hostile bands in unison. The end of the campaign was surely near.

The weather has turned delightful overnight, the chill of yesterday blown north. After recrossing the Blacktail Plateau in easy traffic I reach Tower Junction and continue east, cross the Yellowstone River over a high, modern bridge and pull into a deserted parking lot just off the highway. The confluence of the Yellowstone and Lamar Rivers is about a mile downstream, the site of Jack Baronett's old bridge a bit closer. I follow a faint path along the edge of a cliff above the Yellowstone. The river here is compressed between two walls, the current swift and roiling. Angling down the opposite bank is the faint but unmistakable trace of an old wagon road. I find where the remains of the road climb up this side of the river and start down. Massive pines cling to the slope above and below the old roadbed, their trunks curving toward the sky once free of the rocky ground. Decades of erosion have washed away much of the narrow road, and what remains tilts toward the water. I turn an ankle on the loose scree. Landing hard on my butt, I manage to grab a pine sapling before I slide over the edge, down the cliff and into the river. Pulling myself up, I find a convenient rock and have a seat. My hands are shaking a bit after the fall, and I light a cigarette. Blue smoke swirls in the still air as my adrenaline level slowly drops toward normal. The heel of my right hand is bleeding a bit from an abrasion, and that wrist and my right ankle feel slightly sprained. I squeeze as much blood as I can from my hand and work my ankle to keep it loose.

Jack Baronett anchored his wooden bridge to stone abutments on each bank; fragments of these are all that remain for me to admire, really not much to see in exchange for almost ending it all. I'd been daydreaming when I took the spill, imagining how Baronett managed to build the bridge. I envisioned him choosing a tree near the bank tall enough to span the river, building the abutments below the trunk, hacking away just so with an axe, feeling a surge of satisfaction as the trunk crashed down exactly as he planned, methodically chopping away the hundreds of branches as the green water slid below him, using that massive trunk as a base for his bridge. I was stupid, I tell myself. I'm old enough to know that I have to keep my mind on the important stuff when I'm out alone like this, things such as where I'm putting my foot. If I don't, there will be a little article in some newspaper saying Hiker

Missing In National Park, followed in a week or two by another saying Missing Oregon Man Presumed Dead.

Given Irwin's report on the location and direction of travel of the non-treaty bands, General Howard abandoned his direct pursuit. His new goal was Baronett's Bridge and the wagon road leading to the Clark's Fork mines at the head of that river. His column turned north from Mud Volcano on September 3 but only made ten miles before going into camp on the rim of the canyon near the Lower Falls. The wagon train continued to impede their progress, traveling only a few miles and stopping short of the army camp at nightfall. Major Mason penned a disgusted letter to his wife. General Howard, he wrote, had no idea how to move an army.

But the army trap indeed was getting into place. Colonel Sturgis with six companies of his Seventh Cavalry arrived at the mouth of the canyon where the Clark's Fork River debouched eastward from the Absaroka Mountains on the same day Howard departed from Mud Volcano. Sturgis had been able to enlist only a few Crow scouts at their reservation agency, but promptly began sending patrols to the south and west looking for signs of the Nez Perce exiting the mountains. At this time he had no idea if the bands would use the Yellowstone, Clark's Fork, Stinking Water or Wind River corridors. His latest communication from General Howard, dated August 24, from Virginia City, included Howard's surmise that the Nez Perce were heading for the Stinking Water, but Major Hart with his five troops of cavalry and two hundred Lakota auxiliaries, assigned to block the Stinking Water, would not arrive from the other side of the Big Horn Mountains for another two weeks. For the time being Sturgis was on his own to watch both the Clark's Fork and Stinking Water and be ready to quickly strike wherever the Nee-Me-Poo appeared.

That same day Colonel Gilbert arrived at Henderson's Ranch on the Yellowstone and found Lieutenant Doane with his company of cavalry and collection of civilians and Crows. In the colonel's pocket was the letter from General Sherman advising Howard to give up his command. Doane urged Gilbert to press ahead across Blacktail Plateau. At Baronett's Bridge they could either cross to the east and scout out the non-treaty bands or turn north and find

Howard. Gilbert listened to a recounting of the events in the park the last few days, hesitated, then made his decision. Retreat. Doane begged and pleaded to no avail. Later, in his official report Gilbert called his actions just a detour. Maybe he thought that explanation looked good on paper, but his detour consisted of back-tracking down the Yellowstone before taking a trail west away from the action, turning north and eventually coming upon Howard's trail after it crossed Targhee Pass near present-day West Yellowstone. Originally only about thirty miles from Howard at Henderson's Ranch, Gilbert quadrupled the distance with his decision. Perhaps he was trying to make a fellow officer look good.

The fellow officer was setting no records for travel. On the fourth, General Howard's column again laid over, waiting for the wagons which finally lumbered into the canyon camp about noon. Finally doing the obvious, perhaps at Major Mason's urging, Howard ordered as many supplies as possible transferred from the wagons to the mules. The wagons would divert to Fort Ellis at their own pace, so for Henry Buck of Stevensville, pressed into service a month earlier, the war was almost over. Howard's column moved ahead again on the fifth and finally made good time, reaching Baronett's Bridge late in the day after a march of twenty miles. Finding the timbers at the east end burned, Howard ordered Jack Baronett's cabin torn apart and the wood used to repair the bridge.

I carefully make my way up the grade to the top of the cliff and follow the faint ruts across a meadow. Baronett's cabin was somewhere around here, but if any trace of it remains it's well hidden in the yellow grass. About a hundred yards ahead in a grove of aspen I spot a female moose with her head down, chomping away. If she's got a youngster anywhere close I want nothing to do with her. My wrist and ankle aching a bit, I edge back until I'm in some trees then begin working the half mile to the van. Her head jerks up and she trots out of the aspens, sniffing. I walk faster. She turns away and crashes through the trees, and I breathe a sigh of relief. Back at the parking lot, a pickup with Montana plates is parked next to my van. Two guys with knapsacks spot me coming through the rocks and give me a wave. It turns out they've heard stories about caves in the area where miners used to store supplies in the

1870s and 1880s and they're here to see if they can find them and get some souvenirs. Sounds like fun, if only it were legal in a national park.

I continue east up the Lamar River Valley for fifteen miles along the same route that Howard took on September 6. Traffic's light, the air's clear and cool, the scenery delightful. Across the open, rolling valley Specimen Ridge rises abruptly. There's supposed to be a bunch of petrified trees up there, a part of the park I've never explored. The highway turns northeast up Soda Butte Creek while the Lamar River veers to the south. I see a half-dozen horse trailers parked in a lot at a trailhead. That means a lot of folks up the river, packed in by professional guides with permits from the Park Service. That also means a lot of horse manure on the trail. The trailhead for hikers is a little farther on, and I pull into a parking lot jammed with cars. It's the lure of the wolves, I'm sure, but the people here are staying near the highway or playing in Soda Butte Creek. I fill up my knapsack and take off. The hikers' trail hooks up with the horse trail, and my nose is assaulted with a certain ripe odor as dozens of black flies leave the piles of crap to check me out. This won't do at all. The undulating valley floor is covered with low grass and sage, easy walking even with my sore ankle. I move off the trail about fifty yards and continue upriver parallel to the trail. Much better. I suppose I could remain on the trail, thereby gaining a greater historical appreciation of the daily plight of the infantry slogging along behind the hundreds of cavalry horses. On the other hand, momma didn't raise no fool.

According to John Shively, on September 2 he took Lean Elk to the top of the Absaroka Divide. From there the two could see the plains of the Big Horn Basin twenty miles to the east—the southern reaches of the buffalo country. Lean Elk told Shively that the families would remain at their camp on the bluff another four days. By then the emissaries sent to the Crows would have returned and the future course of the Real People determined by the chiefs. Shively claimed that the Nee-Me-Poo had been lost since arriving on the Lamar, and until he showed Lean Elk the buffalo country that day, the Nee-Me-Poo had no idea where they were. Historians have gone around and around on this issue, but to me it seems plainly untrue: if the Nez Perce could send men to council with the Crows and know how many days the journey would take, they could not have been lost. Shively might have mistaken a discussion among the chiefs about the best route out of the mountains for an indication they were astray.

Shively decided that evening he had tired of Nee-Me-Poo hospitality. The weather was beginning to turn sour, dark clouds promising rain. Lean Elk offered the comfort of the shelter his wife had fashioned, but Shively demurred and put on a great show of constructing his own brush abode. Once inside he kept his boots on. After darkness fell and the downpour began, Shively slipped away. He would miss Howard by two days at Baronett's Bridge, trudge by Mammoth and Henderson's Ranch until, finally, running into a settler who took him downriver to Bozeman and Fort Ellis. His story created a sensation, and he went from town to town, repeating it for the press and no doubt earning more than a few free drinks in more than a few saloons.

A herd of about fifty bison graze close to the river a quarter of a mile away, paying me no mind. Almost a third are this year's calves; the wolves will have plenty to eat. After three miles the valley narrows and the forest closes in. I climb a bluff, pass through a screen of trees and find silvery Cache Creek pouring from the Absaroka Mountains. Beyond the stream is a pine-covered bluff with a ramp-like meadow running up its tip to a grassy summit. The big fires of 1988 raced through here, leaving a gray swath along the creek and fingers of charred trunks climbing the bluff. Still, there's almost as much green visible as gray.

I find a dry branch that will suffice for a wading stick, tramp down to the water's edge, sit in the soft grass and exchange my hiking boots for my running shoes which I pull out of my knapsack. Cache Creek's a good eighty feet wide here, shallow, riffly, an easy ford. And arctic cold. Oh, well, I can splash across in a minute or two. The water's almost to my knees when a rock shifts under my right foot and the damn ankle doesn't take even a little sideways pressure. I go down. The branch I picked up for a wading stick floats downstream along with my cap as I crawl, sputtering, on my hands and knees back to the bank, undergoing a thorough, chilling, soaking on the way. Collapsing in the grass, I shrug away my knapsack. Off comes my dripping shirt and, carefully, my shoes and socks. Sitting with my left leg crossed, I plunge my afflicted ankle back in the icy current; the cold should keep the swelling down. The thick material of my knapsack—thank you, Jansport—has protected its contents: my hiking boots, spare socks, camera, tape recorder, canteen, lunch and cigarettes. I light up and consider my options. What options? It's obvious I'm not going any farther today. A wave of anger and disappointment washes through me.

Stanton Fisher followed the bloody trail with its carcasses of horses and mules down Cold Creek to Mist Creek and the upper Lamar River on September 3. Early the following morning he sent John Redington, who had come up with supplies, back to General Howard with the advice that the general find a different route through the Absarokas. Howard, of course, had already come to the same conclusion and was moving north toward Baronett's Bridge.

Later in the morning Fisher and a white scout from the Bitterroot Valley named Gird descended the Lamar for a few miles before climbing one of the bluffs to the east. Irwin's description of the location of the Nee-Me-Poo camp had been accurate; the two men found themselves looking across a side canyon of the Lamar directly into the Nez Perce camp on the opposite bluff. From about a mile away Fisher could see men and boys gathering up horses and women pulling down the buffalo robes and pieces of canvas they had used for temporary shelters. (John Redington later claimed to be with Fisher when he spotted the camp, but this appears to be one instance when Redington embellished history a bit. Redington undoubtedly picked up details of Fisher's story when the two met again a few days later.) As the Real People began moving east along the ridgetop, Fisher and Gird followed along with them on their own ridge. About 2 P.M. they heard the rattle of gunfire in the canyon below. They tried to scramble on foot to the creek bottom but found the terrain too steep to negotiate. After Fisher returned to his Mist Creek camp he discovered that several of his Bannocks had stumbled upon Nez Perce warriors guarding the moving families. Neither side had felt much like pressing the matter in the narrow confines of the canyon, and the Bannocks had withdrawn, the only casualty a horse nicked in the lip by a bullet.

Clearly, the Nee-Me-Poo had pulled up stakes midway through the four-day rest mentioned to Shively by Lean Elk. Although the Nee-Me-Poo record is silent on these difficult days, the emissaries to the Crows must have returned. The news was not good. According to Thomas LeForge, a white living with the Crows, Looking Glass himself led the delegation that met with several Crow chiefs near the reservation agency. It must have been a day of brutal disappointment for the Nez Perce chief. The years since 1873 when the Crows had promised to join the Real People in any war against the whites had been real eye-openers, especially the last fourteen months. Since the Lakota and Cheyenne had over-whelmed Custer along the Little Big Horn River in June of the previous year, the full force of the American army had made itself manifest on the plains of the buffalo country. Sitting Bull had fled to Canada. Crazy Horse had surrendered. The mighty Lakota nation had been defeated, and the Crows were not about to take on the soldiers who had just swept the most powerful of the native peoples from the plains. The vows of 1873 were like the wind. The Real People were on their own.

In an ironic twist the army had just asked Crazy Horse to fight again, this time against the Nee-Me-Poo. Crazy Horse angrily responded that he had promised never to go to war again, but if the whites wanted him to take that path one more time he would fight until every Nez Perce warrior lay dead. A translator interpreted the statement as: until every white lay dead, and a Lakota police-man ordered to arrest Crazy Horse bayoneted him on September 4. He died the following day, an unwitting casualty of the campaign against the Real People.

I'm munching on Ritz crackers and peanut butter, my right foot completely numb in the water, the alpine sun beating down on my shoulders and face. I can almost feel my skin turning darker. If I have to be laid up with a bum ankle I can definitely think of worse places to be than this.

Fisher's journal is ambiguous as to the location of the Nez Perce camp on some ridge above the river. Three creeks flow from the Absaroka Divide to the Lamar River from north to south: Cache Creek, Chalfee Creek and Miller Creek. In one way the bluff between Cache and Chalfee creeks is the most logical choice for the camp. Across the stream from me, the grassy ramp up the end of that bluff is part of what historians call the Great Bannock Trail, an ancient path used by those natives to travel from Idaho to the buffalo country. It continues along the top of the bluff for fifteen miles through mostly open meadow to the Absaroka Divide and could have been the trail the Snake, or Bannock, chief shepherding the Nee-Me-Poo had found when he turned them away from the Stinking Water route at Indian Pond.

Daniel Goodenough in the 1970s, though, decided their trail went up Miller Creek Canyon. In his journal Fisher described the route the Nez Perce took from the Lamar to the Absaroka divide as a "trap" some fifteen miles long with no escape except at either end. Goodenough assumed the trap had to be low ground and settled on Miller Creek. Discounting Shively's account of the Real People moving down the Lamar River in easy stages, William Lang later suggested they split into two groups with most actually turning up the Lamar River after descending Mist Creek. The upper Lamar Canyon, he proposed, provided an easier route to the divide than tangled Miller Creek. There is, however, no hard evidence to support Lang's theory.

I'm thoroughly unconvinced that the Real People took either route. A ridge with deep canyons on both sides is just as much a trap as a canyon with steep ridges on either side. Once the families had ascended to whichever bluff or ridge they did—and both Shively and Fisher clearly stated they had—it would have been downright foolish for them to go back down again. Just as in the Clearwater Mountains with the Lolo Trail, the easiest terrain to traverse was the highest. In Fisher's papers at the Idaho Historical Society I found a piece of paper which tends to put their route on the ridge between Miller and Chalfee Creeks. Having already examined Fisher's original journal, I was leafing through a file containing miscellaneous papers when I noticed a single sheet about four by six inches. Clearly Fisher's scrawl, it read:

Keep on trail through down timber till the East Fork of Y.S. is reached—follow that till a small stream coming from the east is found—follow up this stream a 2 or 3 miles, then climb the high bald hills on left till their summits are reached when the Nez Perces trail will be visible and their old camp will be found.[1]

The "East Fork of Y.S." is the Lamar River. Going down the Lamar from Mist Creek, the first stream flowing into the Lamar from the east is Miller Creek. My topo maps show high, unforested hills between Miller and Chalfee Creeks on the left of Miller Creek, and those "bald hills" are the beginning of a long ridge leading to the Absaroka Divide. I think the Real People climbed those hills and kept going up that ridge.

That was supposed to be my destination today, only a few more miles. I could probably make the flat terrain along the river, but ascending the bald hills seems out of the question; the three miles back to my van is my decision. Time to get going. I lift my foot out of the current and massage it slowly until circulation and feeling return. The swelling isn't bad yet. I pull an extra sock over the bum ankle to make the fit in the boot extra tight. Finding another dry stick for walking, I strip away a few twigs and set off down the valley.

After the encounter with the Nee-Me-Poo warriors on the September 4, Fisher and his crew stayed in their Mist Creek camp the following day. Fisher was homesick, spending much of the day thinking of his wife and little daughter, Maud. He was, he wrote in his diary, "becoming tired of trying to get the soldiers and the hostiles together. 'Uncle Sam's boys are too slow for this business.'"[2] The morning of the sixth, the courier he had sent back to Howard returned with the news that the army column had turned north down the Yellowstone River. Guessing at Howard's intentions, Fisher ordered his men to saddle up. They would go down the Lamar and hopefully hook up with Howard. Along the way he found the butchered carcasses of several cattle from the herd a man named Beatty was running in the park. Near Cache Creek one of the Bannocks got a deer in his gunsight and the men hurriedly built a cooking fire in a steady, chilling rain. At Soda Butte Creek they found the hours-old trail of Howard's army wending upstream, but darkness fell before they could catch the command.

Back at my van I dig into my first-aid kit and wrap the ankle with an Ace bandage, something I should have done earlier if I weren't so lazy or proud or stupid. Some character flaw, anyway. Tomorrow I absolutely must take another hike, this time over much more difficult ground. I'm just going to have to suck it up and deal with whatever pain the nerves in my ankle jet up to my brain. A half-hour drive up Soda Butte Creek takes me to the northeast exit from the park and the towns of Silver Gate and Cooke City nearly atop the Absaroka Divide. The 1988 fires also blew through this narrow valley, and the lifeless trunks of hundreds of blackened trees only yards from homes and businesses stand as mute witnesses to the desperate efforts of fire fighters that summer. With an afternoon now on my hands I decide it's time to take care of chores. While my clothes are churning away in Betty's Laundry, I hobble up to Betty's Grocery and buy a few supplies, then on to a saloon for a bottle of booze. Medicine for my ankle.

Howard arrived here September 7, Fisher catching up later in the day. They found about twenty miners "resolute and well-armed" according to Howard. The whole bunch signed on as scouts; apparently the search for mineral riches wasn't going so well. The never-tiring Stanton Fisher, two army officers and one of the miners, George Huston, forged ahead ten miles the next day and found the Nee-Me-Poo trail coming down a tributary of the Clark's Fork River named Crandall Creek. Fisher judged the sign to be two days old. Howard's army was again close to its prey. The bulk of the scouts, following some miles behind the leaders, spotted a solitary rider watching from a promontory near the headwaters of the Clark's Fork. Soon he and two others cautiously made their way down to Howard's scouts. His name was Roque, a French-Canadian. His companions were Siebert, an American prospector, and a Crow warrior whose name was never recorded. They had been sent by Colonel Sturgis to warn the Cooke City miners of the proximity of the non-treaty bands. The Crow had probably shown the two whites a bypass named the Lodgepole Trail, and they had successfully evaded the Nez Perce traveling down the Clark's Fork. Soon, Howard was reading the letter Sturgis had written dated September 6, only two days prior. It must have brought a smile to the general's face:

HEADQRS 7th CAVALRY
Mouth of Canon of Clark's Fork
Sept 6, 1877
To the Miners and others at the Smelting Works:
The Nez Perces are now on the East Fork of the Yellowstone and will probably reach your place very soon by way of Soda Butte creek; and as they are hostile and murdering all the unarmed people who are in the way. I send you this to put you on your guard; so that you may be on the lookout for them and take timely precautions for your safety.

My command will be encamped in this vicinity, or near Heart Mountain, for some time, and I will be glad to receive from any of you the earliest possible information of their advance and of the direction which they may be moving.

S. D. Sturgis
Col. 7th Cavalry
Bvt. Mag. Gen'l Commanding[3]

The Nez Perce were sandwiched between two armies. The end of the campaign was near. It would be short, bloody and ohhh, so sweet.

I cross 8,000-foot Colter Pass into the Clark's Fork drainage, a big, open country of 10,000-foot peaks, massive boulders sprinkled among hardy evergreens and broad meadows, spring-time in August. I turn off the Beartooth Highway onto Wyoming 296, the Chief Joseph Memorial Highway, past a smattering of summer homes, down into the upper reaches of the Clark's Fork Canyon. Even my geologically untutored eye can see that a massive glacier once was at work here. The canyon deepens into an immense, U-shaped void sculpted through the successive ridges of the eastern Absaroka Range. Ahead I see the canyon reaching proportions approaching 3,000 feet deep and three miles across, as though some giant had taken a gargantuan ice cream scoop and swiped it through the mountains. At the bottom of the U, the river has churned even deeper into the volcanic rock, a precipitous, narrow V only a few hundred feet wide and some eight hundred feet deep. There's a bunch of breathtaking country in the West, but the Clark's Fork rivals all I've seen.

Ten minutes after turning down the canyon I pull over at Crandall Creek. The 1988 fires escaped the park and licked their way another twelve miles east to here, torching one slope, sparing another, until finally succumbing to exhaustion here like some briefly living thing. The route the Nee-Me-Poo took from the Absaroka divide to this point remains even more of an enigma than their route inside the park. There are theories about them going down this or that branch of Crandall Creek, but given the silence of the Nee-Me-Poo and the lack of either the jottings of someone like Stanton Fisher or the memories of someone like John Shively the days the Real People spent getting here are forever to remain shrouded in the smoke of history.

Half an hour later I pull into a Forest Service campground along the banks of Dead Indian Creek, a tributary of the Clark's Fork. It's a tiny place, five sites, only one already occupied. Just ahead a precipitous thousand-foot ridge juts from the side mountains, blocking what has so far been a pretty easy drive down the canyon. The rumble of heavy machinery reaches my ears from up the ridge, and the ground along Dead Indian Creek is filled with pickups and temporary trailers. A water truck tears down the road, parks across the stream from me, and a pump roars to life and begins sucking water from the current. Ten minutes later the water truck heads back up the road to where the Wyoming highway department is turning the last stretch of gravel on the Chief Joseph Memorial Highway to asphalt. Howard arrived here the afternoon of September 9, confident the campaign was in its last hours.

At Crandall Creek the column had divided. Fisher and thirty-two scouts, mostly whites, followed the trail down the canyon, the soldiers veering into the mountains along the Lodgepole Trail. The scouts reached Dead Indian Creek first and found an elderly Nee-Me-Poo man too sick to continue with his people. Three bullets from a Bannock pistol mortally wounded the helpless man. The Bannocks this time refrained from mutilating the body, but one white scout had no such reservations. According to John Redington, a fellow named Loud Mouth Moore scalped the old man while he was still barely alive, then one of the Bannocks took the scalp from Moore and stretched it over a willow stick to dry. Before long General Howard arrived at the head of the army column. Wishing to question them, Howard had given strict orders that no captured Nez Perce were to be harmed. Fisher distracted the general until another of the scouts managed to sidle over to the willow stick and kick it down into the grass. Howard eventually found out about the incident. It, he later wrote, filled his breast with horror.

Work on the highway ceases at five o'clock, and workers pile into their pickups and cars. After letting the traffic clear, I chug my van up the hairpins of Dead Indian Hill, as the ridge is now called, to the summit. Spectacular vistas of wave after wave of the Absaroka Mountains receding in the distance, the depths of the Clark's Fork gorge and the imposing 12,000 foot Beartooth Plateau to the north keep me awed.

As they arrived at Dead Indian Creek on September 9, Howard's scouts had seen Nee-Me-Poo warriors at the top of the ridge. Everyone from the general down to the greenest private expected a battle at the crest of the ridge where the Nez Perce warriors would have a distinct advantage. The following morning Stanton Fisher took the lead several hundred yards in advance of the rest of the scouts, well ahead of any soldier. Cautiously approaching the summit, he was both relieved and surprised to find no sign of the Real People except for their broad trail turning southeast toward the Stinking Water River. As the army column struggled up the slope, Fisher and his scouts probed ahead until they came in view of the end of the mountains. Ten miles out on the plains Hart Mountain rose, a solitary, rocky monolith. The non-treaty bands were nowhere in sight. Once atop the ridge Howard ordered his signalmen to wave their flags as he and his officers desperately scanned the countryside below with telescopes and binoculars for Sturgis and the Seventh Cavalry, the smoke of a battle, anything. Nothing.

I reach Dead Indian Pass and let the van glide ahead a mile or so across the broad ridgetop until I get a fine view of the buffalo country. The Absarokas don't peter out into foothills; they simply end. Almost 3,000 feet above the Big Horn Basin, I have an unobstructed view eighty miles east to the Big Horn Mountains and forty miles northeast to the Pryors. The basin floor to the southeast toward Hart Mountain must be a geologist's dream, a dry jumble of red and gray and black earth, folded and pushed and pulled, layer after layer tilted and exposed, the story of creation revealed. For General Howard it must have been a bitter view.

Stanton Fisher followed the obvious trail for about two miles in a southeasterly direction along the ridgetop until he came to a spot where the Nee-Me-Poo had apparently milled their horse herd in an effort to confuse their pursuers. His Bannock scouts told him that if the Nez Perce continued in that direction for about ten miles along the ridgetop they would reach a trail dropping into the Stinking Water drainage. Unconvinced, Fisher wandered back north and eventually found the path of the Nez Perce. It led along the top of the ridge until plunging into a steep ravine. Soon he was leading the army on a wild, hairy ride downward.

Back at the campground I soak my ankle in the chill stream, slap at the first mosquitoes I've encountered on the entire trip and sip a cupful of scotch I've splashed over ice chipped from the block in my cooler. It's not so much a sprain as a strain, I tell myself.

Dead Indian Hill blocks the morning sunlight, but I can tell it's going to be another glorious day of weather. I've gone light on breakfast: one of those little boxes of granola cereal that always make me wonder why I didn't buy Wheaties. My ankle's wrapped tight, and I'm as ready as I'll ever be. The trail down and around the face of Dead Indian Hill into the Clark's Fork Canyon begins only half a mile down Dead Indian Creek, but I take the van anyway, through a parking lot for the construction workers then along a pair of bumpy ruts.

It's been the conventional wisdom ever since people began writing about the Nee-Me-Poo and their remarkable flight that they evaded Sturgis and Howard by descending a slit in the Clark's Fork Canyon wall. These days the slit is called Dead Indian Gulch. It begins near the summit of the hill of the same name and drops a little over 3,000 feet to the floor of the canyon. The bottom of that gulch is my destination today. A pack trail that winds into the canyon and will cross the gulch about a thousand feet above the canyon floor. On topographic maps the top three-fourths of the gulch above the pack trail appears relatively benign, a slope of about twenty-five percent. The portion below the pack trail looks to be a different matter, eventually falling off to a forty-five or fifty percent grade. That angle of terrain would be difficult for horses to descend, but not impossible. The latest book written about the Nez Perce, Bruce Hampton's *Children of Grace*, proposes in a footnote that the Nee-Me-Poo probably could not have taken the gulch, that the last few hundred feet were a rockfall too steep for horses.[4] I'll try to find out for sure.

Two miles along, I leave the side canyon formed by Dead Indian Creek and enter the Clark's Fork Canyon proper. The panorama almost makes me forget my bum ankle. I've reached the bottom of the broad U-shaped upper canyon and now can look almost a thousand feet down into the impenetrable V cut by the river. I'm standing above the point where the fist of Dead Indian Hill punches the water into its narrowest extreme. Out of sight directly below, Dead Indian Creek pours into the river, and just upstream I can see Sunlight Creek gushing from its side canyon over a foaming, white fall into the river. The roar of rushing water echoes up the sheer walls. Across the way the Beartooth Plateau climbs to the sky.

Finally, Dead Indian Gulch. I turn away from the trail and carefully make my way downward. Soon the walls narrow and the angle of descent steepens. Freshets have stripped the surface to white bedrock. I clamber from one smooth boulder down to another. General Howard described the ravine his force used to descend to the Clark's Fork as being twenty feet wide at its narrowest, but already I can almost touch each brush-tangled side with outstretched arms. Before I've slid down two hundred feet, I'm carefully dropping on my butt from one rock to another. I reach a point where my only option is only eighteen inches wide, a notch between two massive, white boulders. Peering through the tiny V, I find a vertical drop of at least eight feet to more slick rock. Beyond is a series of similar steps, a staircase suitable only for giants. There's no way even the Nee-Me-Poo could have taken horses down here, certainly no way Howard's men followed. Dead Indian Gulch is a dead end. What one soldier called the Devil's Gateway must be someplace else. I turn around, mystified. When I reach the pack trail, instead of turning back toward my van, I continue down the canyon until I reach a promontory with a fine view toward the mouth of the canyon. Pulling a bruised peach, crackers and my binoculars out of my knapsack, I snack and scan the 3,000-foot south wall. No alternative path presents itself. The river is a unique color of green below, not emerald, not pea. I lie back and let the sky take over my mind, feel the sun relax my muscles. It's okay to be stumped, I tell myself, not to know all the answers.

By one in the afternoon I'm back in my van, then past Dead Indian Pass into the Big Horn Basin, the road zig-zagging down the terminus of the Absarokas in dizzying turns. The Chief Joseph Memorial Highway ends, and I turn north on Wyoming State Highway 120. After seven or eight miles I spot a county road leading back toward the mountains which takes me to the top of a range of hills now called the Kimball Bench, sparsely covered with sage. The mile-wide mouth of Clark's Fork Canyon is just to the north, the 3,000-foot wall of the Absarokas rising directly in front of me. Based upon Stanton Fisher's diary, possibly the Nee-Me-Poo and then Howard's army descended about two miles south of the canyon mouth. I scan the slope with my binoculars, searching for any kind of deep ravine that might fit the bill. Nothing.

I take another side road toward the Clark's Fork Canyon mouth. A few miles from the highway it crosses a narrow, dark stream edged by thick brush, and I pull over beside two white wooden crosses jutting from piles of stone and surrounded by plastic flowers, memorials to victims of a traffic accident. One year after the Nez Perce conflict, war flared between the Bannock tribe

led by Buffalo Horn and the American army over settler encroachments on traditional tribal land in southern Idaho. Does the name
Buffalo Horn sound familiar? He was the leader of the Bannock
scouts enlisted by General Howard for the Nez Perce campaign. In
a series of engagements in southern Idaho and eastern Oregon,
Howard crushed the uprising with relative ease. In an eerie
reprise of the Nez Perce flight, one Bannock band fled through
Yellowstone Park and emerged here. Instead of Colonel Sturgis
and the Seventh Cavalry, Colonel Nelson Miles and a mounted
contingent of the Fifth Infantry waited for them. Miles pounced on
that sleeping Bannock band while it was ranged along this creek.
When it was over some thirty men, women and children lay dead,
most of the rest captured, a few escaping on foot to wander the buffalo country before dying or surrendering.

A few miles farther on, outside the mouth of the Clark's Fork
Canyon is a pile of rocky rubble some 800 feet in height and almost
two miles in length, the terminal moraine of that humdinger of a
glacier that scoured out the gorge. Beyond the moraine the rocky
portals of the canyon rise almost vertically, Bald Peak on the south
rising more than 4,000 feet above me. After it exits the mountains
the river swings south of the moraine before looping around in a
wide 270-degree curve and turning north. What a sight.

Howard's army reached the mouth of the Clark's Fork Canyon
by nightfall on the September 10 and went into camp somewhere
along the curve of the river. Major Mason wrote to his wife that,
Yellowstone Park notwithstanding, he was amid the most majestic
mountain scenery he had ever seen. Howard's mind must have
been filled with a different thought: what the heck had happened
to Sturgis?

That same day two men rode into Bozeman, some 100 miles distant, and excitedly told anyone who would listen their story: they
and about twenty others had been prospecting along the Stinking
Water when Nez Perce warriors had attacked. The others were
dead. The editor of the Bozeman *Times* dutifully reported the news
while expressing doubts as to the veracity of the tale, but Yellow
Wolf and a group of warriors indeed had been in the area. They
had encountered an unsuspecting white man standing at the door

of a cabin. Naked-Footed Bull and Shooting Thunder quickly dispatched him. The following morning Yellow Wolf stole four horses from under the eyes of half a dozen whites who fired a couple of shots at him but remained holed up in their cabin. War Singer told McWhorter that warriors also shot up another camp of whites, the survivors fleeing into the surrounding woods with the exception of the cook who fell to his knees and begged Going Away not to kill him. The warrior put a bullet between the pleading man's eyes. These events took place somewhere along the upper reaches of the Stinking Water River on the fifth through the seventh as the main body of the Real People made their way down Crandall Creek and the Clark's Fork.[5]

At dawn on September 8 near the divide between the Stinking Water and Clark's Fork drainages, Yellow Wolf and Going Away ran into two prospectors acting as scouts for Sturgis. A few minutes later one white lay dead, the other wounded, and Yellow Wolf had endured his closest call of the war. A bullet had glanced off his skull, knocking him senseless. Later that morning, a Seventh Cavalry patrol led by Lieutenant Luther Hare stumbled upon the two prospectors. After making the wounded man as comfortable as possible, Hare hurried back to Sturgis to report news of the attack along with the intelligence that the trail of the warriors came from the Stinking Water River. Another patrol commanded by Lieutenant Alfred Fuller dashed into the army's Clark's Fork camp on the heels of Hare with the news that they had spotted fires and a big horse herd on the Absaroka ridges some eighteen miles to the southeast. Prospectors familiar with the area assured Sturgis that the Nee-Me-Poo had to be headed for the Stinking Water. Sturgis became a believer.

According to Private Theodore Goldin, many of the soldiers were spread out over the countryside either fishing or goofing off when the trumpet urgently sounded. It took time for the six troops of cavalry to gather and strike camp. The smoke of a fire high on Bald Peak directly above the army camp caught the private's attention; not until later was Goldin to realize that it might have been a signal lit by Nee-Me-Poo scouts warning the chiefs of the proximity of the Seventh Cavalry. Instructing his wagon train to return to the relative safety of the Crow Agency, Sturgis prepared for a hard march and a lightning strike against the Nez Perce. It was growing dark when the column followed Lieutenant Hare south toward the Stinking Water River.

Returning to the main highway, I turn south along the generally route they followed. Twelve miles takes me to the headwaters of Pat O'Hara Creek where it splits into three tributaries amid the naked, broken terrain along the Clark's Fork and Stinking Water divide. Rattlesnake country. Sturgis' first camp would have been close to here.

Darkness forced the column to halt before finding the wounded prospector. That night sentries blasted away at Nez Perce phantoms circling the camp. Although Private Goldin claimed that troopers found the prints of unshod horses nearby, Yellow Wolf told McWhorter that the soldiers must have been dreaming. No Nee-Me-Poo were close. The next morning troopers located the wounded prospector and loaded him upon an improvised travois. Five civilians volunteered to transport him north to safety while Sturgis continued south over the divide to the Stinking Water River. It was September 9. Later the same day the Real People descended from the Absarokas—not down to the Stinking Water River and not down Dead Indian Gulch—and scampered north safely out of sight of the over-eager Sturgis. So easy.

About noon the following day Yellow Wolf and a few other warriors jumped the five men escorting the wounded prospector. The injured man did not survive his second encounter with the Nee-Me-Poo. Yellow Wolf reported to McWhorter that, as far as he knew, only one of the other whites was killed, but Stanton Fisher's Bannocks eventually found three more bodies. Papers in their pockets indicated one man was named Oleson, another Anderson. The third went into his shallow grave nameless. Yellow Wolf was unrepentant in describing the affair to McWhorter. "Every white man in those mountains could be counted our enemy," he said.[6]

From the divide it's an easy drop for me over the ten miles to the town of Cody on the Shoshone River, the sanitized name these days for the Stinking Water. Private Goldin remembered the troopers filling their canteens with its clear, cold water only to find the liquid smelling like rotten eggs when they next unscrewed the caps. Now, I guess, the old name might put off the tourists streaming in and out Yellowstone Park. My hopes of finding a motel in Cody and a hot shower for my ankle are quickly dashed, too late in the day for me to see anything other than NO VACANCY signs. I cruise through town past the Buffalo Bill Cody Museum until I can look up the valley of Trail Creek angling into the Absarokas toward Dead Indian summit. Sturgis would camp near here on the ninth and cautiously probe up Trail Creek on the tenth, convinced he would encounter the Real People at any moment. On the eleventh he would find the trail of both the Nee-Me-Poo and Howard's column up on Dead Indian Hill. He would follow the obvious sign down to the Clark's Fork River right to his old camp at the mouth of the canyon. I wonder what he had to say to his scouts and lieutenants Hare and Fuller; wouldn't have been pretty. Tired, I turn north and set my sights on Montana.

McWhorter's informants were excruciatingly silent on the route by which the Real People evaded Sturgis. For them it was no big deal. One, though, did tell a story of the situation of the families during these dangerous days. A vignette related by White Hawk, a boy of about twelve in 1877, indicated that Lean Elk was again pushing the families hard:

> *Riding rough trails in the night was bad, especially for the wounded, and old people and children. Passing through the Hart mountain country in the night, my mother looked back and saw my horse following with empty saddle. Turning back, she found me lying on the edge of the trail sound sleeping. The fall from my horse did not awake me. Had she not missed me, General Howard's Bannock scouts would have found and killed me the next morning. They killed all the sick who had to be left on the trail.*[7]

On September 11 Sturgis met up with Howard camped on the Clark's Fork and let loose with an explosion of expletives. The Seventh Cavalry, their angry colonel promised, would push ahead until they either caught those damned Nez Perce or the troopers or their horses dropped from exhaustion. The Christian general disapproved of the language but approved of Sturgis' pluck. Howard added fifty of his cavalrymen with the fittest horses and two mountain howitzers on mules to Sturgis' column. It marched early on the twelfth and made an incredible fifty miles in one day under a steady, chilling rain.

The modern highway follows the Clark's Fork River north for some sixty miles until it joins the Yellowstone River in southern Montana, mimicking the trail the Nee-Me-Poo and army took. The Crows called the Clark's Fork the Rotten Sun Dance River. I guess not every tribal ritual could be perfect. Ten miles beyond the Wyoming-Montana border I slow for the hamlet of Belfrey—no motel. The next town is Bridger, another twenty miles down the river. (Somewhere along here a Nee-Me-Poo woman dropped out of the caravan to deliver her baby alone. Some Crows noticed her horse tethered near some brush and investigated. Luckily for the woman, the Crows were friendly, taking her and the baby in tow and harboring them for the next several months.) Bridger Crossing was where Howard's force stopped the night of the September 12, lagging some twenty miles behind Sturgis, but still traveling thirty miles that day. The valley here is flat and would have been easy going even for Howard's exhausted horses and infantry. With a little bit of good fortune this is where I'll spend the night, too. It's not a big town—fewer than a thousand people, I'd guess—but there it is, the Bridger Motel, and the parking lot is mostly empty.

In the evening I make notes about the day's events. My microcassette recorder has gone on the fritz, maybe from its dunking in Cache Creek, and all the words of wisdom I poured into it during the day are lost. No big deal. Then, glancing at my USGS topo maps of the Clark's Fork Canyon region, my heart suddenly starts pounding. I limp out to my van and come back with a pair of scissors. After cutting away the white borders of the Deep Lake, Clark, Cody and Pat O'Hara quadrangles I fit the edges together, just to confirm what I suddenly know. So obvious! The Devil's Gateway, the route the Nee-Me-Poo took out of the mountains, at the intersection of the four maps. I groan and flop back on the bed, staring at the ceiling. In my van are the files where I've kept copies of all the old narratives—Fisher, Goldin, Mason, Howard—but I don't need them now. The pertinent words from the past float above me. How could I have missed this?

Notes

[1] Fisher, Stanton, *Papers*, MS 106, Folder 17, unnumbered sheet, Idaho Historical Society, Boise.

[2] Fisher, *Journal*, p. 275.

[3] Bozeman *Times*, September 13.

[4] Hampton, Bruce, *Children of Grace*, Henry Holt, New York, 1994, p. 364-365.

[5] McWhorter, *Yellow Wolf*, p 177-183.

McWhorter, Papers, Folder 34, item 84.

As I wrote in a footnote at the end of the last chapter, McWhorter placed Yellow Wolf at Mammoth at this juncture. The timing, the specifics of the terrain and the number of whites present are all wrong for it to have occurred there.

[6] McWhorter, *Yellow Wolf*, p. 184.

[7] McWhorter, Papers, Folder 104, item 14.

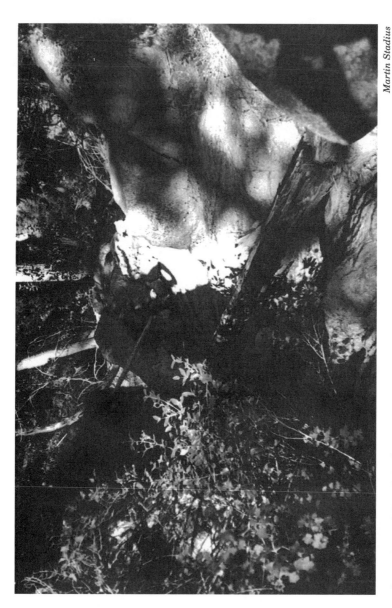

Martin Stadius

A section of Dead Indian Gulch in the southern wall of Clark's Fork Canyon. Only a few yards wide, with vertical drops of eight feet, the gulch could not have been the route taken by the Nee-Me-Poo.

Martin Stadius

Lower Clark's Fork Canyon, Wyoming. Some researchers assume the Real People and General Howard's Pursuing army passed through here.

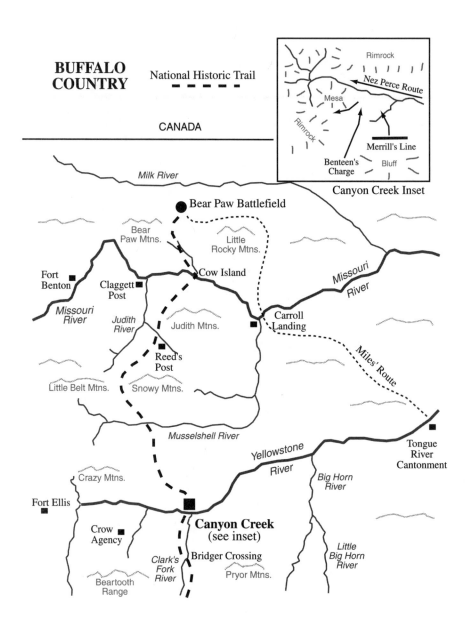

BUFFALO COUNTRY

National Historic Trail

CANADA

Milk River

Bear Paw Battlefield

Bear Paw Mtns.

Little Rocky Mtns.

Fort Benton

Claggett Post

Cow Island

Missouri River

Missouri River

Judith River

Judith Mtns.

Carroll Landing

Reed's Post

Miles' Route

Little Belt Mtns.

Snowy Mtns.

Musselshell River

Yellowstone River

Tongue River Cantonment

Crazy Mtns.

Big Horn River

Fort Ellis

Crow Agency

Canyon Creek
(see inset)

Clark's Fork River

Bridger Crossing

Pryor Mtns.

Little Big Horn River

Beartooth Range

Inset:

Rimrock

Nez Perce Route

Mesa

Rimrock

Merrill's Line

Benteen's Charge

Bluff

Canyon Creek Inset

CHAPTER FOURTEEN

BUFFALO COUNTRY

In the morning, cooking breakfast at a rest stop outside Bridger, I consider turning back to take a look at the place where I now think the Nee-Me-Poo made their descent from the Absarokas. That's not how this trip works, I finally decide. The Nez Perce and army columns forged ahead, and so will I.

Here's what I think happened back there:

From the area where the Real People milled their herd up on Dead Indian Hill they moved only about two miles north before descending into what is now called the Natural Corral. The upper entrance is at the 7,000-foot level, the exit two miles away at 5,400 feet where it forms Paint Creek. From there they continued almost five miles north in the low ground of the Paint Creek drainage between the Absaroka Wall and the Kimball Bench, striking the Clark's Fork River at the southern end of the terminal moraine. That's two miles from the canyon's mouth, the distance, Fisher noted in his journal entry of September 10, from the canyon mouth to the location they left the mountains and struck the river. In Fisher's mind, I think, the Kimball Bench was still part of the Absarokas, and they hadn't exited the mountains until they reached the point where Paint Creek emptied into the river.

Lieutenant Charles Wood likened the descent from the Absarokas as being through the "spout of a funnel," an apt description of the Natural Corral as it narrows from its half-mile width near the top down to its tiny exit. Most convincing, though, is Private Theodore Goldin's statement that the exit was less than five miles above Sturgis' camp, a perfect fit if he was describing the Natural Corral and Paint Creek rather than Dead Indian Gulch and the Clark's Fork River itself. Goldin also stated that one of the scouting patrols of the September 8 had passed the exit. Both patrols out that day probed south toward the Stinking Water River. Lieutenant Hare's patrol definitely went up Pat O'Hara Creek since that was where he found the wounded prospector; logically, Lieutenant Fuller's patrol would have gone up the only other drainage coming from the south, Paint Creek. It's extremely embarrassing not to have put this together long ago. On the other hand, I console myself, no one else has in the last 120 years.[1]

The evening of September 12, while at Bridger Crossing, Howard found time to pen two dispatches. One was a gloating report to McDowell in San Francisco, noting that Colonel Gilbert, the "energetic" officer designated by Sherman to replace Howard, still lagged some seventy miles behind the command, unable to catch up. The other was a plea for help. Howard had come to the reluctant conclusion that neither he with his force nor Sturgis and the Seventh Cavalry would probably catch the non-treaty bands. It was time to call in still more troops for one last, desperate attempt to corral his slippery, ingenious adversaries. This dispatch was addressed to Colonel Nelson Miles, commander of the District of Yellowstone based 175 miles down the Yellowstone River at Tongue River Cantonment. It read:

Colonel:
 While Colonel Sturgis was scouting towards Stinking water, the Indians and my force in close pursuit passed his right, and they after a short detour turned to Clark's Fork, and by forced marches avoided Sturgis completely.
 I have sent Sturgis with Major Sanford, 1st Cavalry, and Lieutenant Otis, 4th Artillery, with howitzer battery, in fast pursuit and myself following as rapidly as possible with the remainder of my own immediate command. The Indians are

reported going down Clark's Fork, and straight towards the Musselshell. They will in all probability, cross the Yellowstone near the mouth of Clark's Fork and make all haste to join a band of hostile Sioux. They will use every exertion to reach the Musselshell country and form this junction, and as they make exceedingly long marches it will require unusual activity to intercept or overtake them. I earnestly request you to make any effort in your power to prevent the escape of this hostile band, and at least to hold them in check until I can overtake them.

Please send me return couriers, with information of your, and the hostile's whereabouts, your intended movements, and any other information I ought to know.

Yours respectfully,
O. O. Howard
Brig Genl Cmdg Expedition against hostile Nez Perces[2]

Howard sent a courier bearing this message downriver to Sturgis, who added his own comments headed "Crossing of the Yellowstone Near mouth Clark's Fork 13th September 9am." After blaming a lack of reliable scouts for the embarrassing blunder at Clark's Fork, Sturgis confessed himself mortified and determined to make amends until his troops reached the end of human endurance. Then he wrote:

My animals are shoeless and broken down, and my command without rations, yet we made fifty miles yesterday, and will try to do so until we overtake them, but whilst we are now crossing the river their scouts are on the hills opposite watching us, and, I fear, their main body has some thirty six hours the start.[3]

Sturgis forwarded one copy downriver toward Tongue River Cantonment by mounted courier, another by a small boat belonging to a settler living nearby. Little could Sturgis guess that his fifty-mile march had caught the Nee-Me-Poo by surprise. The families were less than ten miles away, and the scouts watching from the hills opposite were concerned. Within three hours the Seventh Cavalry and the Real People would be in a fight.

Half an hour after leaving Bridger I reach Laurel, Montana, on the banks of the Yellowstone River. Sturgis wrote his message to Miles somewhere around here. Traffic on I-94 whizzes east and west with efficiency, but I've made it this far without touching an interstate. I'm not about to start here. Wandering through the sprawling town of 6,000 with its smelly oil refinery and massive railroad switching yards, I find a country lane that I hope will take me east toward Billings.

After crossing the Yellowstone River, for some reason the Nee-Me-Poo caravan trailed downriver about six miles before reaching an intermittently dry tributary of the river called Canyon Creek. They crossed the unimposing channel and followed it upstream back to the northwest. In effect they traversed two sides of a triangle; the army would shortly charge along the third side and almost, almost catch the Real People. Half an hour would make the difference.

I cross dry Canyon Creek over a narrow bridge, passing small ranches with a few horses or cattle in pastures. The houses grow closer together, livestock gives way to dogs and within a few miles I'm on the outskirts of Billings, population 70,000 and the largest city in Montana. Turning south, I find Riverfront Park without much trouble. The freshly-cut grass releases its scent as I walk to the edge of a little lake and sit on cool green.

Only one year after the Lakota and Cheyenne taught Custer the last military lesson of his life just fifty miles from here, whites were beginning to settle this area permanently. A stage line had begun running from Tongue River Cantonment in eastern Montana beside the Yellowstone River to Bozeman near Fort Ellis. This stretch here was known as the Clark's Fork Bottom, and Perry McAdow had just built a lumber mill a mile or so upstream in anticipation of new arrivals. Nearby was a saloon, that necessity for any aspiring town. Downstream a few miles was a stage station manned by Elliott Rouse and H. H. Stone. Nearby were two shanties occupied by Bela Brockway and Edward Forrest, hunters and trappers. John Alderson had begun erecting his cabin somewhere nearby, and Joseph Cochran claimed this land that would someday become Riverfront Park. Nee-Me-Poo warriors were about to come visiting.

Rouse and Stone noticed riders approaching and correctly surmised they might be unfriendly. The two hurried upriver, running into Brockway, Forrest and a westbound stage driven by Frank Eastwood. One passenger was Fanny Clark, an entertainer fresh from relieving the soldiers at Tongue River Cantonment from the boredom of frontier life. Another may have been a dentist. Intriguingly, a tough thirty-five-year-old woman named Martha Canary also may have been on the stage. She was better known as Calamity Jane. When they noticed smoke rising from the stage station and about a dozen warriors drawing near, all scrambled into the thick brush bordering the river. As Brockway's haystack went up in flames, the warriors shouted for the whites to come out and talk. They declined. Four warriors appropriated the stage coach and took it back toward Canyon Creek, delivering mail to clumps of sagebrush along the way. The others continued on and ran into Joseph Cochran and a few hired hands cutting lumber. Cochran cocked his repeating rifle, and the warriors moved on after borrowing the whites' horses. At Cochran's homestead, two men were not so alert. Clinton Dills and Milton Sumner died quickly. The men at McAdow's Mill forted up inside, and the warriors contented themselves with burning the saloon and taking the horses corralled nearby.

For a half-hour I tour parts of Billings most tourists never bother to check out: wide thoroughfares lined with strip malls and shopping centers; new subdivisions mixed with a few older houses; the places where regular folk live, work and play. I'm sort of lost. Finally, I'm headed west again on a road I hope will take me to my next destination. Now that I'm out of town it shouldn't be too difficult to find. The northern limit of the Yellowstone Valley is defined by a line of rimrock several hundred feet high. For miles the only break in the cliff is where Canyon Creek cuts through on its journey from its headwaters to the river. That was where the Real People were headed, and so am I.

As Sturgis' cavalry struggled across the deep ford of the Yellowstone, his scouts spread out both down the river, where smoke from the burning buildings and haystacks was plainly visible, and north toward a low bluff about four miles from the river where Nee-Me-Poo warriors watched the scene at the crossing. The warriors on the heights skirmished only briefly with the army scouts before retiring. By two o'clock Stanton Fisher and a few of his men looked north from the height toward Canyon Creek and the rimrock beyond. The bunched Nez Perce caravan stretched for over a mile between the creek and the cliff. Behind them the stage coach bounced along the rough ground, the four horses of the merry riders tied to the rear.

I'm at about the spot where the Real People were when Stanton Fisher and his scouts spotted them, the gully of Canyon Creek to my left, the rimrock to my right, quite high here—almost 400 feet. Two miles dead ahead is the opening into the rimrock, its mouth maybe a half-mile wide, the southern wall formed by an isolated butte, or mesa, about a mile square, again about 400 feet high. Two miles to the south is the low bluff from which the army scouts first sighted the families and horse herd. These days the intervening ground is smoothed-over fields; back then it was scarred by gullies and washes and covered with greasewood and sage. Cutting across the benchland between Canyon Creek and the bluff was an especially deep ravine cut by Dry Creek.

The chiefs had known of the proximity of the soldiers for at least an hour. Now they only needed a few more minutes for the women and children and stock to reach the relative safety of the canyon. Some warriors hurried ahead to climb the rimrock flanking the canyon entrance while others fanned out in the nooks and crannies along Dry Creek. Still more remained with the families. The thirty or so army scouts spread out and charged. A few warriors might have noticed one rider falling behind while desperately flogging and kicking a recalcitrant mule: Fisher, whose horse had played out the day before. Well before reaching Dry Creek the scouts dismounted and sought cover as Nez Perce bullets began to sing through the air. Then over the crest of the bluff came the first bluecoats, three companies in column and moving fast.

Colonel Sturgis had split his command into two battalions, and this first to charge was led by Major Lewis Merrill. Before reaching even the scouts' position, Merrill's squadron—Companies "F," "I," and "L"—dismounted and formed a skirmish line some 500 yards from the first Nee-Me-Poo warriors. Caught in the middle, the army scouts retreated into the cavalry line. Sturgis arrived on the bluff in time to see this initial charge stall. He probably uttered a profanity or two over the next few minutes as he watched the Nee-Me-Poo families and herd edge ever closer to the canyon mouth.

The warriors along Dry Creek mounted and began a deliberate retreat, turning to fire from atop their ponies as the line of soldiers advanced cautiously, firing volley after volley. Yellow Wolf remembered:

> . . . a big noise in my head. I did not hear anything separate. It was the sound of many guns all roaring at once.[4]

But it was one of those typical Montana days with a fierce wind sweeping out of Canada, so accurate shooting at a distance was impossible. Only two warriors were hit by the thousands of bullets fired by the troopers on the skirmish line. One was Eeahlokoon, a flesh wound in the right leg below the knee. The other was Animal Entering a Hole, Joe Albert, the army scout who had switched allegiances in the middle of the Clearwater battle. A bullet passed though his left hip and thigh, his second wound of the war.

Captain Frederick Benteen's battalion had already unsaddled and begun to prepare cooking fires along the Yellowstone when news of the proximity of the Real People arrived. Now they came up, and Sturgis ordered Benteen to lead a charge to the left of Merrill's line. At the same time Sturgis dispatched an aide to Merrill with instructions to remount and also move to the left toward the canyon mouth after Benteen had passed his flank. Watching from Merrill's line, Stanton Fisher thought he saw one company of Benteen's battalion make it across Canyon Creek before wilting and hurriedly retreating. They would have been taking crossfire from both the warriors with the families and those on the rimrock above the canyon mouth. Benteen's battalion dismounted and returned fire from an arroyo a quarter mile short of the canyon mouth, the fire from above and the flank too galling to advance.

Lieutenant Guy Howard, the general's son, appeared leading a mule carrying the barrel of one the field howitzers on top its back. Howard turned the unsuspecting mule, loaded a shell and fired. It exploded harmlessly near the Nez Perce herd. The mule did not appreciate the recoil, but braced itself for Howard's second shot, which, likewise, did no damage.

On his own initiative, Benteen tried a different tack: flank the warriors on the butte. Ordering his men to remount, he led the troopers back almost a mile and turned up a ravine south of the butte. Company "G" with Lieutenant George Wallace commanding was at the point. Private Goldin remembered:

> *Away we went, plunging into the narrow opening, and we were just at the narrowest point, when evidently, having just discovered our purposes, we were assailed by a rattling volley from the edge of the cliffs just above our heads. Wallace never paused; one or two of his men went down, and soon reached the open space beyond. Fortunately for us the Indians were so nearly directly over us that their fire was high, most of their shots passing over our heads.*[5]

Benteen, following Wallace's company, ordered companies "H" and "M" to dismount and charge up the steep face of the butte.

I reach the mouth of the canyon, turn south and pull over on the shoulder after a mile. This is all private land, and I have to settle for a look-see from here. To the east stretches the flat where Merrill dismounted his troops for a long-range shooting match. Merrill's horseholders had failed to follow the advancing skirmish line, and the major was unable to remount his battalion in any kind of timely manner. The ravine where Benteen tried to flank the warriors is plainly visible to the west. His men made it to the top of the mesa, a few minutes too late. The families and herd had already scurried into the canyon.

I turn my van back and enter the wide mouth of the canyon. It's mostly open now, but in 1877 cottonwoods lined the creek and provided protection for the warriors who fought a rear-guard action here. A mile ahead I pause at an intersection of ravines. One fork of the creek comes from the south where Lieutenant Wallace halted about a mile and a half away. Warriors had shot eleven horses from under his troopers, and Wallace had had enough. A second fork of the creek comes from the west, a third from the north. The Real People turned up this north ravine. The rimrock rises 300 feet above the narrow opening, only about 100 yards wide. Just inside the entrance the ravine splits, and there another eminence overlooks the passageway. Anyone attempting to follow the families would face guns aimed down from three directions.

As Merrill's line cautiously approached the mouth of the canyon, still on foot after three miles, Benteen's men skirmished across the top of the butte. The last few warriors atop the height ran for their ponies and disappeared. Reaching the edge above the canyon, Benteen's troopers sighted the warriors of the rear guard below. Cavalry carbines barked: two Nez Perce horses fell dead and Silooyelam took a bullet in the ankle, the final Nee-Me-Poo casualty of the day. Unwilling to expose his men to fire from the heights across the canyon by descending the slope in front of him, Benteen ordered a withdrawal. One of his troopers lay dead and five were wounded. In addition to the eleven horses lost from Wallace's company, another thirty fell in the rest of the battalion. Meanwhile, Merrill halted his force at the mouth of the canyon. Two of his soldiers had been killed, six wounded. Fisher, Redington and a few other civilians ventured into the canyon, making it as far as the fork of the creek. There, warriors perched among the rocks to the north drove them back, slightly wounding Redington in the leg. A plug of tobacco sufficed to stop the bleeding. The gutsy printer from Salem, Oregon, was seeing all the action he possibly could have wished.

It was nightfall, and the battle was over. Stanton Fisher and a few members of the Seventh Cavalry later declared themselves disgusted with Sturgis' timid conduct of the battle. It's clear to me, however, that Sturgis never ordered Merrill to dismount his battalion to fight on foot, the one action that certainly aided the Nee-Me-Poo in making their escape unscathed. Further, Sturgis almost immediately ordered Merrill to remount, which he failed to do. Stanton Fisher also groused in his diary that Sturgis ordered only half the command into the battle. Untrue. Fisher must have been ducking too many bullets to realize all that was happening.

The only unit not engaged immediately upon its arrival on the scene was Major Sanford's company of the First Cavalry, the one detached by Howard to accompany Sturgis. It remained behind to guard the supply mules until Sturgis ordered it, too, into action to support Benteen's belated foray onto the bluff above the canyon. That may have been Colonel Sturgis' only mistake of the day. Long reputed to be the most accomplished thieves of all the Plains Indians, some Crows hanging about the rear managed to make off with a few animals from the supply train, including Stanton Fisher's spare mule carrying his bedroll, extra clothing and meager supply of food.

The cavalry camp at the mouth of the canyon was a miserable place the night of September 13. The creek was dry, the only water available a few alkali pools seasoned with buffalo manure. With the command virtually out of rations, dinner consisted of horse steak cut from dead animals. The wounded were suffering, their cries occasionally piercing the air. According to Private Goldin, Calamity Jane, dressed in men's clothing and armed with a knife and pistol, made her appearance in the company of the others who had hidden in the brush near the stage station earlier that day. He remembered:

> She paid not the slightest attention to the crowds of staring soldiers, but stalked over where the wounded were, visited each one of them, questioning them as to the nature of their wounds and laughing and joking with them in a rough, hearty way. . . . I never saw her again, but the men of our outfit were ever ready to give a cheer whenever her name was mentioned.[6]

Neither Fisher nor Redington nor any official reports mentioned Calamity Jane, but if she did show up at the time, she took a look around and liked what she saw. Within a few years she built a cabin here and with two worthies named Rattlesnake Jake Fallon and Longhair Ed Owen set up a profitable horse-stealing business. They used the flat top of the mesa where Benteen and the warriors skirmished to stash and graze the proceeds of their endeavors. It's still known today as the Calamity Jane Horse Cache.

Driving up the road beside the North Fork of Canyon Creek, I see a faded billboard:

CHIEF JOSEPH ESTATES
VARIOUS SIZES
CHOICE ACREAGE TRACTS
GOOD RESTRICTIONS
LOW DOWN PAYMENT
EASY TERMS

Apparently, the terms aren't quite easy enough. Not a new house in sight. The gravel road winds its way up the ravine for several miles until it reaches a high plain. The next sixty miles will take me over a turtleback hump between the Yellowstone and Musselshell Rivers, a distance the Real People would cover in less than two days. I pass fields of hay and wheat and barley amid widely scattered, prosperous ranch houses. Only big spreads can survive here, but around the turn of the century railroad builders criss-crossed this country thus garnering land grants from the government. The railroads then placed glowing ads in eastern papers and magazines, suckering immigrants and American dreamers into buying small farms which didn't stand a chance of growing enough grain to support a family. It was all a big con.

The Seventh Cavalry was in no shape to continue. Men and horses were exhausted and hungry, but Sturgis didn't care. He was determined to force another fight with the Real People. On the morning of the fourteenth, the tired troopers found the north

369

ravine blocked by downed timber and piled brush, the handiwork of Nee-Me-Poo warriors, so the first order of business became clearing a trail. Overnight, as many as 200 Crow warriors had arrived at the army camp. Now they swept across the plain ahead of the plodding cavalry. Decades later Yellow Wolf remained bitter about the day:

> *I looked one way and saw strange Indians. I looked good! Then I thought, They must be either Walk-around Sioux or Snakes. I will go see. I rode closer. Eeh! Crows. A new tribe fighting Chief Joseph. Many snows the Crows had been our friends. But now, like the Bitterroot Salish, turned enemies. My heart was just like fire.[7]*

The Crows hounded the Real People for two days in a running, long-distance fight. Yellow Wolf and Earth Blanket told McWhorter that one Nee-Me-Poo warrior named Over The Point died when his skittish horse bolted too close to the enemy. The Crows also killed two unarmed, older men who strayed from the caravan. They were Fish Trap and Surrounded Goose. Another unidentified informant confirmed those names and added the latter's wife and grandson. The total number of Nee-Me-Poo dead was probably five. On September 20 the Bozeman *Avant-Courier*, quoting an army officer, reported that same number of bodies on the trail.

The Crow coveted the horse herd of the Real People more than they wanted a hard fight. By now the Nee-Me-Poo stock was tired, and many had developed sore feet. As the families pressed forward, the animals that could no longer keep up were abandoned. The first mention of Nez Perce horses rounded up by the Crows came from their agent, George Frost, on the fourteenth. Warriors brought in about 100 head on the twelfth and thirteenth, animals left behind during the dash down the Clark's Fork River. A later report in the *Avant-Courier* added another 200, followed by another claiming still 200 more. Yellow Wolf told McWhorter that about forty good horses fell into Crow hands, as well as an unknown number of broken-down animals.

As the Real People neared the Musselshell River, the Crows

counted themselves fortunate to have lost no men and gave up the chase. Trailing, Sturgis reluctantly did the same. His column was spread out for miles, many troopers leading exhausted horses, others trudging along with their mounts left behind. When his command suddenly had been ordered to the Clark's Fork it had already been in the field for four months, far from its home post in North Dakota. Supplies had been a continual aggravation. His men had devoured corn meant for the horses which had made do with whatever grass they could munch whenever troopers weren't slinging saddles over their backs. Unlike the Nee-Me-Poo, the cavalry had no spare mounts, and, now, the desperate chase from the Devil's Gateway had taken its toll. For Colonel Sturgis this had been sort of a last hurrah.

After taking command of the Seventh Cavalry in 1869, he had seen his lieutenant colonel, George Custer, garner all the attention and glory. Then Custer had led the regiment into disaster at the Little Big Horn, and one of the dead as a result was Sturgis' own son Jack. At fifty-five, Sturgis was probably too old to have taken command in the field again, but he did. Private Goldin once called him a "granny" better suited for a swivel chair. When the granny colonel finally called a halt on the banks of the Musselshell one relieved private was a certain Mr. Theodore Goldin.

In the hamlet of Rapelje I stop at the Stockman Bar & Cafe for a quick burger. Several hundred rattlesnake tails adorn one wall, courtesy of ranchers in the region. One set boasts twelve rattles and is over two inches long. I'm glad I don't have to do any hiking around here. A few miles ahead I reach the summit of the divide between the Yellowstone and Musselshell rivers. The air is clear and breezy from the west. Sixty miles to the south and southwest the Beartooth Mountains rise to 12,000 feet in a solid wall seventy miles long. The same distance to the southeast is the humbler Pryor Range. Fifty miles due west the Crazy Mountains climb a respectable 11,000 feet. To the north and northwest are the dark slopes of the Snowy and Little Belts, a mere 8,000 feet each, fifty miles away. Turning to take in the panorama, I try to calculate the square miles of Montana within my view. I think it comes to a little over 5,000 square miles. I'm impressed.

General Howard and a small escort reached the scene of the Canyon Creek fight mid-morning of September 14 to find Sturgis already departed in pursuit of the Real People. Backtracking to the Yellowstone, Howard waited for his column to catch up. A tired, dirty and hungry bunch of soldiers arrived the following day. Major Mason in a letter to his wife:

> *They are moving 35 and 40 miles a day while we are drag-ging our worn-out horses and leg-weary men along at the rate of 12 and 15 miles a day. It looks like a perfect farce, one of those foolish things that can occur in the military profession when a man a thousand miles from the scene of action con-trols. . . . All this must not be repeated—I must not be quoted as growling about the actions of my chief.*[8]

Another officer writing home the following day found a closer target than General Sherman to blast. Captain Robert Pollock in a rambling, bitter letter:

> *Our Christian General often forgets there should be a day of rest. . . . He is the first Professor I have had to follow and I hope he may be the last. He says that nobody likes him and this is truer than he thinks. Too timid a pursuer; pickets, patrols and flankers spread all over the line of march, likes to give us talks about the hostile peril in the day and evenings when he isn't lying on a blanket on clear nights looking at and studying the stars. . . . A dedicated army man, everything done by the book down to the last period. We had an inspec-tion this morning, as useless as this eternal marching.*[9]

My, my, weren't tempers getting short. Captain Pollock appar-ently had forgotten that the orders for eternal marching had come from a higher rank than General Howard, who would have gladly returned his men to Idaho yet was unwilling to return alone even with the approval of General Sherman. After the full day of rest so coveted by Captain Pollock—and no doubt the rest of the men—and the arrival of supplies from Fort Custer on the Big Horn River, the command headed for the Musselshell River.

It was probably fortunate for Howard's ego that he was far beyond the reach of newspapers, for he continued taking a beating. One example from the Fort Benton *Record*:

> *Howard's bureau containing manuscript copies of his replies to the newspaper critics was captured with his pack train, and it is said Sturgis would never have caught up to Joseph if the latter had not stopped to read the voluminous documents.*[10]

Aahh, frontier wit.

From the Yellowstone-Musselshell divide I drop on a gravel road into Big Coulee. This is one strange bit of geology to my amateur's eye. Earlier I described the terrain between the rivers as similar to a turtleback sixty miles across. In its shell is this abrupt oval gouge about eight miles in diameter and several hundred feet deep. Water must have done the work, but for the life of me I can't figure out why here and nowhere else in this country.

Off to my right I spot another rarity, and I turn onto a side lane. A faded-white, one-room schoolhouse, perfectly preserved but abandoned, sits on a quarter-acre lot amid the hayfields. Off to one side is a tiny house, no more than fifteen by fifteen feet. In back is an outhouse, toppled by decades of north winds. The rusted remains of a teeter-totter and swing inhabit the lawn. I know from reading a history of Montana that the first settlers arrived in Big Coulee only two years after the Nez Perce passed through. I wonder how many years later isolated ranching families got together and built this school for their kids. I wonder about the first teacher—a young woman from back east, perhaps—and how she dealt with the long winter nights and snow and wind. I imagine several generations of kids playing at recess, their screams floating away under this big sky. Ever onward I go until I reach the Musselshell River at Ryegate, population 275. The Musselshell's a small, sluggish stream winding through a narrow emerald and amber valley topped by rimrock. Early on September 20 Howard found Sturgis and the Seventh Cavalry in a pleasant camp somewhere near here along its bank.

For five days the Seventh had lounged under the cottonwoods lining the stream, fishing, picking tart buffalo berries and hunting antelope and bison while their horses recuperated on the hills above the river. Howard's men joined in the same for two more relaxing days while the general and the colonel planned their next move. A courier arrived from Colonel Miles at Tongue River Cantonment, who had received Howard's request for assistance on the 17th. The short reply was not encouraging:

Dear General:

Acting on the supposition that the Nez Perce will continue their movement north, I will take what available force I have, and strike across by the head of Big Dry, Musselshell and Crooked Creek and Carroll, if I do not get any information before. I fear your information reaches me too late to intercept them, but I will do the best I can. Please send me information of the movement and course of the Indians.[11]

Even though Miles had an additional hundred miles to cover and lacked the knowledge of the Nee-Me-Poo route that following their trail provided, Howard and Sturgis decided to pin their hopes on him. They would continue their pursuit, but slowly, hoping the Nez Perce would respond in kind and give Miles time to bring his force to bear.

I'm tempted to head east for sixteen miles to the hamlet of Lavina and enjoy a slice of the world's best pie at Richard's Cafe, but the day is getting on. I'll have to content myself with the memory of that crisp crust and the apple-cherry filling. It's still ninety miles to Lewistown and a motel, most of it on gravel roads. My van climbs the hills north of Ryegate, and I set my sights for Judith Gap, a wide, low pass between the Little Belt and Snowy Mountains. The wind is picking up out of the west, and thunderheads are forming over the mountains. I could be in for some weather.

After crossing the Musselshell sometime on September 15, the Real People spent eight days reaching the Missouri River at Cow Island 120 miles farther north, an average of fifteen miles a day.

Their pace was slowing. Two months of unrelenting travel since leaving Weippe Prairie on July 16 must have been taking its toll. McWhorter's informants had little to say about this time. Yellow Wolf remembered happening upon a camp of four whites while scouting ahead of the families. After killing two in a brief gunfight he took the four horses. He was matter-of-fact in telling the story to McWhorter. The People needed all the horses the warriors could find. Other than that single anecdote, the eight days were a blank slate in the Nee-Me-Poo story.

For Colonel Nelson Miles at Tongue River Cantonment it was a busy time. After receiving Howard's plea the evening of the seventeenth, he kept the men at the post hopping overnight. By 10 A.M. the following day, four mounted companies of the Fifth Infantry and two companies of the Seventh Cavalry were crossing the Yellowstone River. Close behind was another foot company of the Fifth, guarding a supply train of both wagons and mules. Miles dispatched one courier down the Yellowstone to the Missouri River with a request that rations for 60,000 meals be sent up the Missouri by steamboat to supply his command as well as Howard and Sturgis. Miles also requested 250 tons of forage for the army horses. Another courier hurried on the trail of three companies of the Second Cavalry and another of the Seventh which had departed for Fort Benton to escort a commission headed to Canada to treat with Sitting Bull.

Miles was thirty-eight years old, brash, competent and extremely ambitious. Before the Civil War he had taught himself military history and doctrine while clerking in a Boston crockery store, of all places. Enlisting as a volunteer lieutenant in 1861, he rose to major general by the time he was twenty-six and won himself a Congressional Medal of Honor. After the war he transferred to the regular army as a full colonel and assumed command of the Fifth Infantry. In 1874-75 the Fifth played a major role in the campaign on the southern plains that ended native resistance there. Moving to Montana after the Custer debacle, Miles immediately plunged into a brutally effective and relentless winter war against the Lakota and Cheyenne, the campaign which sent Sitting Bull fleeing to Canada and forced the surrender of Crazy Horse.

The column that marched from Tongue River Cantonment on

September 18 was tough and confident. By September 23 it had united with the four companies of cavalry called back from the trek to Fort Benton and had reached the Missouri River at the mouth of the Musselshell River. They had covered 125 miles in five days and were only eighty miles from the unsuspecting Nee-Me-Poo caravan. With them were about thirty Lakota and Cheyenne warriors. The previous summer they had fought Custer, but now they joined the army in the hunt for the Real People.

Two other columns sent out by General Sheridan in Chicago were nowhere near. The same day that Miles departed from Tongue River Cantonment, Major Hart and his command arrived at their assigned blocking position on the Stinking Water River east of Yellowstone Park. Colonel Merritt and the nine companies of cavalry from Camp Brown had moved north after it became obvious the Real People would not strike the Wind River in central Wyoming. Merritt joined Hart on the Stinking Water where their scouts soon told the officers they were way too late.

The wind from the west blows me all over the highway as I cross Judith Gap into the Judith Basin, location of, not surprisingly, the Judith River. The gap is seven or eight miles wide, defined by thickly forested heights to the east and west. Spread out ahead of me is the basin, some fifty miles wide, stretching to a low horizon. Isolated cells of flat-bottomed thunderheads float from west to east, gray rain angling from them toward the earth, their brilliant white tops mushrooming tens of thousands of feet in the sky. Beautiful. I should be off this highway and on another gravel road in a few minutes. Then this gale will be at my back, great for gas mileage and no danger of being blown into the path of an oncoming truck.

The Crow nation consisted of two large bands, the Mountain Crows who hung around the Yellowstone River region and the River Crows who preferred the Judith and Musselshell country. At the time of the Canyon Creek fight and subsequent chase by the Mountain Crows, their government agent confidently predicted the River Crows would finish the job of stripping the Real People of their stock which the Mountain Crows had begun. It didn't quite work out that way. While Sturgis lay over on the Musselshell, George Huston, John Redington and a few other scouts kept on the trail. Redington:

> In one part of the Judith we found the remains of a wrecked Indian camp, and wondered how it happened. From the way things were torn up around there, there had certainly been quite a little battle. George Huston figured out that the camp had been occupied by Dumb Bull's outfit of River Crow Indians, who were drying buffalo meat and were attacked by the Nez Perces. There were tons of dried and partially-dried meat lying around, and a flock of Poe's ravens rose gracefully from where they had been holding inquests on the rigid remains of several Indians . . . and when we passed Reed's Fort later in the day we found that the scout's conclusions were correct. Dumb Bull was there, and was feeling pretty sore about the way the hostiles had cleaned him out of all his horses.[12]

I pass an abandoned ranch house, a sprawling, two-story, multi-gabled affair with seven outbuildings, the paint fading on all, a perfect picture of good fortune gone sour. What went wrong? I arrive at Lewistown a little after five o'clock, too late to check with the Bureau of Land Management about the next leg of my trip. Nestled near the base of the abrupt Judith Mountains, this is a prosperous, picturesque town of 6,000, its Main Street lined with sturdy red brick and gray sandstone buildings, the massive county courthouse sporting a golden cupola.

After checking into a motel I decide to find the remains of the Reed's Fort mentioned by Redington. It was actually run by two men in 1877, Alonzo Reed and John Bowles. No softies could survive in an isolated frontier trading post, and these two apparently were as tough as any men in the West. They preferred to settle differences over etiquette with guns. A scout for Howard named Gird, who had joined the column way back in the Bitterroot, met his end here. By 1884 a rough town had sprung up, and on July 4th Calamity Jane's partners, Longhair Owen and Rattlesnake Fallon rode into town to celebrate the holiday. They proceeded to get drunk and shoot up the town. Area settlers had long suspected them of rustling and took advantage of the situation to administer frontier justice. Longhair was shot eleven times, Rattlesnake only nine.

I'm having a little trouble finding the remains of the Reed and Bowles fort until I figure out that Lewistown has a First Avenue and a 1st Avenue, a Second Avenue and a 2nd, and so on, a stunning lack of creativity among the early townspeople. With that information tucked in my brain I manage to find a sod-roof cabin beyond the edge of town on the bank of Big Spring Creek. Constructed of logs squared-off with an axe, everything about it is slightly askew. The cabin shares a small pasture with a sway-backed, piebald horse who moseys over to the fence to find if I've come bearing gifts. Its breath is humid on my hand as it sniffs for carrots or some other treat.

As I step out of my motel room in the morning, the air is delightfully cool. A few wisps of cloud clinging to the Judith and Snowy ranges are all that remains of yesterday's sporadic thunderstorms. At the BLM office I ask the woman behind the reception desk about access to Cow Island, where the Nee-Me-Poo crossed the Missouri River. She gets a worried look on her face and disappears into the back room. After a few minutes a stocky, sandy-haired man appears and gruffly asks me why I want to go to Cow Island. After I tell him, he relaxes a bit but shakes his head. Been having a bit of trouble with someone down there, he says. He notices the uncomprehending look on my face and adds, it's just not a good idea for anyone to be poking around down there right now. It may not be safe, he finally says. Now I get it.

The land around there is a mix of private and public land, and some folks take property rights pretty seriously. This is Montana, after all. It's a disappointment. I'd tried to get to Cow Island two summers ago but had been turned back by Missouri River gumbo, a particularly gooey mud that turns any unpaved road impassable after a rain. Okay, I tell him, I'll take the McClelland Ferry across the river upstream from Cow Island. That road's open, isn't it? Another shake of the head. Ferry's shut down. Two Calf Road? He shrugs. Depends on if it rained much there yesterday, he says. At the first sign of mud you'd better turn back, he warns me. If you get into the gumbo you won't get out.

After that heartening conversation I steer north for the village of Winifred and the Missouri Breaks beyond. The road to Cow Island would have been on the other side of the river, but that's a definite no-go. I have a thorough aversion to having guns pointed at me. My second choice, the ferry, would have crossed me over the river about twenty miles above Cow Island, and from there a gravel road would have taken me to the upper reaches of Cow Creek which debouches into the Missouri near Cow Island. The Nee-Me-Poo followed the creek to its headwaters in the southern reaches of the Bear Paw Mountains. From there they cut directly through the mountains on their way to Canada. My third choice, Two Calf Road, winds along the top of the Missouri Breaks on the south side of the river. If I'm lucky I can catch a glimpse of the Cow Island crossing below.

On September 21 Major Guido Ilges in command of Company "F" of Gibbon's Seventh Infantry at Fort Benton received a plea for assistance from Fort Claggett, a trading post at the mouth of the Judith River on the Missouri. The traders feared the Nee-Me-Poo were heading their way. Company "F" had been severely roughed up at the Big Hole battle, and Ilges could only muster fifteen men to send downriver by boat with Lieutenant Edward Hardin and a mountain howitzer. By evening, though, twenty-four mounted civilian volunteers had gathered, and Ilges himself led them out of Fort Benton. Ilges and Hardin reunited at Fort Claggett the following day to find all quiet. Two scouts the major sent into the Judith Basin returned at 2 A.M. on the twenty-fourth with news they had struck the Nez Perce trail, heading for Cow Island. Hardin's men pushed their boat into the current at first light, and Ilges again set off cross-country.

The settlements of western Montana depended upon two supply routes for goods bound in and out of the region. One was the Corrine road from the Union Pacific and Central Pacific railroad north to the settlements in the western part of the state. The other was the Missouri River where fifteen steamboats plied up and down the current. In spring and early summer the head of navigation was Fort Benton, but as the river level lowered the boats stopped at Cow Island to unload their cargoes. From there wagon trains hauled the goods overland to Fort Benton and points beyond.

Ilges arrived opposite the Cow Island landing after sunset, Lieutenant Hardin beaching his mackinaw boat a little later with bad news. Midway between Fort Claggett and Cow Island lay the Dauphin Rapids where Company "B" of the Seventh Infantry guarded army engineers attempting to create a permanent channel for the steamboats. A squad of Company "B" had also been detailed to Cow Island to protect army supplies awaiting transport to Fort Benton. Below Dauphin Rapids Hardin had spotted the Cow Island detail hurrying upstream. Sergeant William Moelchert reported the news to Hardin: thirty tons of government supplies and twenty tons of private goods burned by the Nez Perce.

Yellow Wolf called the events at Cow Island "nearly like play." Preceded by twenty warriors, the Nee-Me-Poo caravan forded the river several miles above the landing, which was on an extensive bottomland. The twelve soldiers and four civilians, huddled behind an entrenchment far from the stacked supplies, posed no threat to the families as they passed sedately up Cow Creek and went into camp. Late in the afternoon while a few warriors kept the whites' heads low with desultory target practice, the women brought pack horses back and went shopping. Yellow Wolf: "Each family took maybe two sacks flour, one sack rice, one sack beans, plenty coffee, sugar, hardtack. Some took bacon. . . . We did not starve that sun, that night. Whoever wanted them, took pans, cooking pots, cups, buckets. Women all helped themselves. When everybody had what they wanted, some bad boys set fire to the remaining. It was a big fire!"[13] Two civilians and one warrior suffered nicks during the exchange of gunfire in the afternoon and overnight. Less fortunate was a Company "B" private named Pearse traveling from Dauphin Rapids to Cow Island. He died alone.

At Winifred the asphalt turns to gravel as the road follows section lines north and a little east toward the Missouri River. After twenty miles comes the dirt and probably the last ranch house I'll see. Someone in a heavy pickup with wide tires has been on the road since the last rain, leaving deep, hardening ruts. I have to keep out of those, or I'll risk high-centering my van. This could get tricky, but at least the surface seems pretty firm.

Using the mackinaw boat, Ilges crossed his force the morning of September 25 and with the mounted civilians immediately started up the Cow Creek trail. The day before the Nee-Me-Poo appeared, a party of four women and seven men had departed the landing for Fort Benton, the women riding in a light wagon. Also on the trail was the Cooper & Farmer bull-train, hauling a mixed load of government and private cargo. Ilges probably believed he could do little more than bury the bodies if the warriors had found them. The first party had made good time, reaching the head of Cow Creek and turning west toward Fort Benton without mishap. The freight train made slower progress, the trail crossing and recrossing the creek, often requiring the teamsters to double up the oxen. About noon, eight warriors caught up, causing no trouble, passively watching the whites struggle up the grade. About the time the teamsters paused to cook lunch, the family caravan came into sight and flowed around the halted wagons. It took about an hour. O. G. Cooper, co-owner of the outfit, noticed that the Nee-Me-Poo horses were jaded, many with sore backs and feet. At least a dozen had brands, and a few of the army mules captured at Camas Prairie still tagged along. Most of the younger warriors appeared to be short of ammunition while the older men had hoarded their cartridges and remained better supplied. Just beyond the whites' nooning spot, the Real People halted and prepared to stay the night. Cooper and Farmer decided not to push through their camp.

Throughout the afternoon warriors came to visit, offering to buy ammunition and asking when dinner was going to be served. Cooper turned them away as gently as possible. Late in the day one of the chiefs, probably Looking Glass, dropped by and chatted for a few minutes in good English. Cooper remembered him as being about forty-five years old, "good-natured" and "spoke very kindly." The chief mentioned the People were on a buffalo hunt and casually asked if Cooper knew if any soldiers were nearby, to which Cooper presumably responded in the negative. Before departing the chief casually remarked that his scouts had spotted some Sioux in the area and the whites should consider abandoning the train.[14]

I doubt if Cooper and the other eight teamsters slept well that night, but I have my own problem right in front of me. The road ahead drops into a swale which has collected water. A quick scout reveals the dirt road has turned to gumbo. How much more is there ahead? The truck tracks veer off cross-country, so I follow for a hundred yards, still on foot, checking out the soil under the grass. Spongy. That pick-up might very well be stuck somewhere out of sight ahead. I light a cigarette and squat, considering my options. Paved road and the bridge across the Missouri are only about twenty miles away. If I back-track and detour the distance is over one hundred miles. I'm reminded of Colonel Gilbert's dilemma at Henderson's Ranch when he was trying to reach Howard and relieve him of command, whether to take the direct, hazardous path or the roundabout, safer way. I can't, I finally decide, take the chance of spending days marooned out here. Cluck-cluck.

The following morning, the twenty-fifth, Cooper and Farmer discovered their oxen had wandered through the Nee-Me-Poo camp overnight. The two men passed through the impromptu shelters, cooking fires, rising families and bunches of horses and rounded up their stock. Suddenly, they noticed a commotion among the Real People, a chief shouting instructions and warriors mounting their horses. Scouts watching the back trail had spotted Major Ilges and his well-armed companions, suddenly close on the trail. Cooper and Farmer scurried for the bluffs above the creek, while the teamsters back at the wagons suddenly became fair game and Fred Barker paid the ultimate price. The others dashed to safety. As small parties of warriors rode down the creek to deal with the threat, others stopped at the wagons, took whatever ammunition they could find, then struck matches. Dark smoke soon billowed upward.

The skirmish between Ilges and the Nee-Me-Poo rear guard proved to be strictly a long distance affair, conducted at a range of up to a thousand yards, but the whites discovered the warriors could be lethal even at that range. After Ed Bradley was killed and John Tatan was scared out of his wits when his belt buckle deflected a bullet, Major Ilges ordered a retreat. The civilians complied with remarkable speed.

After my own forty-five-mile retreat to U.S. 191 I'm headed northeast again with a splendid view of the Judith Mountains to the south. The wind is kicking up again, straight out of the north. I notice a hawk perched on a fence post ahead and an RV coming my way in the opposite lane. The hawk spreads its wings and lifts off just as another violent gust buffets my van. Caught by the wind, the hawk drifts in front of the RV. My last view of the bird is it striking the grill of the vehicle, its beautiful wings outstretched as if on display. I feel slightly sick as my van gains momentum down a long slope toward the Missouri River and a bridge some twenty-five miles downstream from Cow Island.

The evening after the skirmish with Ilges, Looking Glass lit into Lean Elk during the nightly talks among the headmen. Many Wounds explained what happened:

Looking Glass upbraided Poker Joe (Lean Elk) *for his hurrying; for causing the old people weariness; told him that he was no chief, that he himself was chief and that he would be the leader. Poker Joe replied, 'All right, Looking Glass, you can lead. I am trying to save the people, doing my best to cross into Canada before the soldiers find us. You can take command, but I think we will be caught and killed.'"*[15]

The distance from that camp to the Canadian border was only about seventy-five miles. Over the next four days the pace under Looking Glass' tutelage slowed to less than ten miles a day.

Howard was crawling at a similar snail's pace. After he and Sturgis left the banks of the Musselshell, they spent five leisurely days reaching the Judith Basin, pausing for a Sabbath rest along the way. Upon reaching the basin he noted that someone—presumably the Nee-Me-Poo—had set fire to the grass. Thousands of acres had burned, obliterating the trail of the Real People. At their first camp in the basin on the September 27 the general decided to send the First Cavalry companies to their home posts in the Department of the Columbia. The Idaho scouts and packers turned back with them. Once he reached the Missouri River Howard also planned to ship his foot soldiers downriver on a steamer then back across the continent by rail. With the Nez Perce only a few miles from the sanctuary of Canada the chase seemed over for the Department of Columbia column.

Not for Colonel Miles. After arriving at the mouth of the Musselshell on the Missouri River on September 23, he split his force. With the assistance of a passing steamer, the *Fontenelle*, the Second Cavalry battalion crossed to the north shore of the Missouri, while the three companies of the Seventh Cavalry began probing upstream on the south side of the river. The Fifth Infantry units remained at the mouth of the Musselshell, prepared to follow up in whatever direction might prove fruitful. On the twenty-fifth a small boat drifting down from Cow Island brought the news that the Nee-Me-Poo had crossed the river two days before. By September 27 the three wings of Miles' command had reunited some twenty miles north of the Missouri River. The colonel ordered eight days rations packed on mules, and at 4 P.M. the mounted units cut loose from the wagon train and began to march along the eastern slope of the Little Rocky Mountains. The Real People and this last army were following parallel trails north, some forty miles apart, headed for a collision.

I'm driving north on State Highway 66 smack dab between those two paths. The Bear Paw Mountains rise fifteen miles to my left, an unprepossessing bunch of hills and buttes, really. A few miles to my right lie the forested humps of the Little Rockies, the scar of a giant mine pale amid the dark slopes. I cross into the Fort Belknap Indian Reservation, home of the Assinoiboine tribe, whom the Nee-Me-Poo called the "Walk-around Sioux."

Passing herds of bison and antelope, Miles' column reached the northern end of the Little Rockies and camped in cold rain and wind on September 28. At the same time Nee-Me-Poo hunters stalked buffalo just north of the Bear Paw Mountains. The families would need the meat and hides in the coming cold Canadian winter. The camp of the Real People shifted north only three miles on September 29, to a spot along Snake Creek where men had downed several of the shaggy beasts. Dark, low clouds almost touching the ground dropped intermittent rain all day as the Real People rested and the army column crossed the open plain between the Little Rockies and the Bear Paw. The soldiers went into camp near two conical buttes which defined the northeast corner of the Bear Paw Mountains. The two camps were now only about twelve miles apart the night of the twenty-ninth, each unaware of the other's location.

A gravel road takes me west and north out of the reservation through open range. Cattle have replaced the bison and antelope of 1877, and several times I slow my van to a crawl while passing clusters of the animals foraging beside the road. Sunflowers bursting yellow carpet the roadside, turning their faces skyward. Ahead are the two abrupt conical hills, each about a thousand feet high. These days one is called Miles Butte.

The evening of September 29 brought a chilling rain to the Indian camp, and the hides and canvases draped over the brush frames probably filled early with sleepers eager for the warmth of their blankets. A dream of disaster had visited Hair Combed Over Eyes in the darkness before the attack at Big Hole. This night brought another disturbing vision. Years later he remembered:

> *I saw, and recognized where our camp was pitched. I saw the waters of the stream all red with the blood of both Indian and soldier. Everywhere the smoke of battle hangs dark and low. I awoke! That vision is strong on my mind. I put on leggins and moccasins and with the blanket walk all over the grounds. I note it just as seen in the dream. The level meadows, the creek, the washout-gully, the surrounding bluffs. Yes it is true what I saw while sleeping. I go back to my poor, torn canvas shelter and sleep. The same dream-vision, and more, passed before me again. The mingled blood on the running water, the smoke-darkened air, but with it all came falling leaves, withered flowers, followed by spring-time grass and bursting buds, sunshine and peace. These signs I understood, and knew we would very soon be attacked.*[16]

385

Sometime in the early morning hours before dawn the storm passed and the sky cleared. Shortly before dawn, women crawled from the shelters to rekindle their buffalo manure fires against the sharp cold.

In the army camp the men were also up early, heating their coffee and bacon and hardtack. Before the sun brought its first dim light the fires were extinguished, no tell-tale smoke left to alert Nez Perce watchers. Colonel Miles hoped his rapid march had placed him between the Nez Perce and the Canadian border, so the line of march he ordered was west across the northern limits of the Bear Paw Range. Lieutenant Marion Maus and his Cheyenne, Lakota and white scouts spread out, probing ahead along the fringe of the mountains. After about an hour some of the Cheyenne, spotting two or three Nez Perce men on horseback, chased the riders farther south until they were lost in the mountains. The Nee-Me-Poo watching for Howard's command on the back trail would not be able to warn the Real People of Miles' approach.

Miles believed these riders were advance scouts for the northward moving bands and turned the steadily moving army column more to the south and west. Then, just twenty minutes after the Nez Perce outriders had been chased away, more Cheyenne galloped in to report a wide, obvious trail, two days old, just ahead, going north. The colonel responded quickly, sending scout Louis Shambow north with ten Cheyenne to follow the sign. For tense minutes the command waited for the verdict of the scouts. With the Canadian border only fifty miles away a two-day lead could mean that the Nee-Me-Poo were already under the protection of the Queen of England.

Hair Combed Over Eyes was not the only one to have a premonition of the future that cold September morning. While the army column waited for news, the three captains of the Seventh Cavalry battalion—Owen Hale, Myles Moylan and Edward Godfrey—grouped together to pass the time. Captain Godfrey later remembered that out of the blue Captain Hale suddenly blurted out:

> . . . *with a rather cynical smile, 'My God! Have I got to be killed this beautiful morning!' Then his smile passed, his*

*countenance became serious and his eyes to the ground. Not
a word was spoken for several minutes; then the Adjutant R.
W. Baird rode up with orders to mount. The scouts had sent
the message that they had located the Nez Perce village.* [17]

Notes

[1] Fisher, Journal, September 10.

Wood quoted in Brown, *Flight*, p.351.

Goldin, Theodore, *A Bit of the Nez Perce Campaign*, privately printed, Bryan, TX, 1978, p. 9-12.

[2] AGO, Letters, Roll 338, p. 350-352.

[3] AGO, Letters, Roll 338, p. 352-253.

[4] McWhorter, *Yellow Wolf*, p. 186.

[5] Goldin, *A Bit*, p. 15.

[6] Goldin, *A Bit*, p. 16-17.

[7] McWhorter, *Yellow Wolf*, p. 187.

[8] Davison, "A Soldier Writes," p. 16.

[9] Pollock, *Grandfather*, p. 100.

[10] Fort Benton Record, September 28.

[11] quoted in Brown, *Flight*, p, 365.

[12] Redington, *Scouting in Montana*, p. 10.

[13] McWhorter, *Yellow Wolf*, p. 199.

[14] Fort Benton Record, October 5.

[15] McWhorter, *Hear Me*, p. 473-474.

[16] McWhorter, Papers, Folder 56, p. 46-48.

[17] Godfrey, Edward S., Papers, Library of Congress, p. 22.

Washington State University Library

Nee-Me-Poo sharpshooters made a stand at the mouth of Canyon Creek Gorge and stopped pursuing 7th Cavalry troopers cold. This photograph was probably taken in the early 1930s.

Martin Stadius

Buffalo Country

Martin Stadius

A vigilant caretaker watches over the remains of the Reed and Bowles trading post, now Lewistown, Montana.

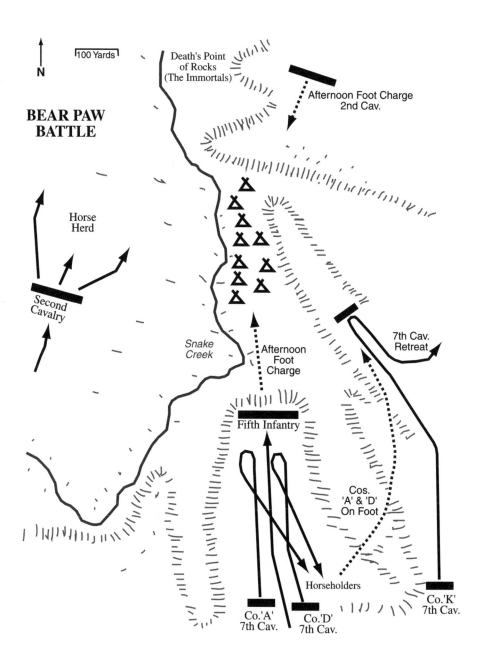

100 Yards

N

Death's Point
of Rocks
(The Immortals)

Afternoon Foot Charge
2nd Cav.

**BEAR PAW
BATTLE**

Horse
Herd

Second
Cavalry

7th Cav.
Retreat

Snake
Creek

Afternoon
Foot
Charge

Fifth Infantry

Cos.
'A' & 'D'
On Foot

Horseholders

Co.'A'
7th Cav.

Co.'D'
7th Cav.

Co.'K'
7th Cav.

CHAPTER FIFTEEN

BEAR PAW

The road passes between the two conical buttes then turns west and a little south for five miles along the northern limit of the Bear Paw Mountains, a route virtually identical to that taken by the army before word came of the location of the Nez Perce camp on Snake Creek. At Cleveland crossroads I turn north over a plain broken by coulees and ravines. The Real People came out of the mountains right about here. Eight miles to go.

Louis Shambow had not actually sighted the Nez Perce camp tucked under the bluffs along Snake Creek, but had seen about a dozen hunters chasing buffalo, some of the riders draped with a distinctive striped blanket commonly only worn by the Real People. Then Shambow had spotted the horse herd and figured he had found his quarry. Close enough for government work, anyway.

Miles ordered his troops to advance at the trot. Henry Tilton, a surgeon with the Fifth Infantry destined to earn a Congressional Medal of Honor for tending the wounded under fire in the upcoming hours, provided this romantic description:

We soon came upon the broad Indian trail. Our Cheyennes and Sioux undergo a sudden transformation: they are painted, stripped for a fight, on their favorite chargers, and are a study for the artist. The picture lasts but a moment; they are bounding over the plain on either side of the column, which is now in rapid motion. To be astride a good horse, on the open prairie, rifle in hand, has an exhilarating effect on the majority of men. To be one of four hundred horsemen, galloping on a hot trail, sends a thrill through the body which is seldom experienced.[1]

Captain George Tyler with his three companies of the Second Cavalry took the lead, followed by the battalion of the Seventh Cavalry, Captain Hale commanding as the senior officer. The four-company squadron of the mounted Fifth Infantry with the light Hotchkiss artillery gun and the pack train shadowed the two cavalry battalions. Colonel Miles rode near the Seventh. The terrain the column traversed undulated gradually from the Bear Paw Range down toward the Milk River to the north, but the scant vegetation provided little protection to the earth from the effects of water and wind. The long slope was cut by numerous ravines so that in close view the land appeared much like a stormy sea. Three miles from where Shambow believed the camp of the Real People to be, Miles ordered the column from the trot to the gallop. The Second Cavalry drew their pistols and prepared to charge through the Nez Perce camp, the Seventh Cavalry to follow right on their heels, the Fifth holding back as a reserve. The 1,500 horse hooves pounding the damp soil sounded like a continuous peal of thunder.

I top a low ridge, drop into the drainage of Snake Creek and park in a lot overlooking the creek. Gesturing animatedly, a man in a National Park Service uniform speaks to a cluster of a half-dozen people near an interpretive sign at the edge of the parking lot. He must be Jim Magera, the new seasonal ranger Otis Halfmoon mentioned back at the Big Hole and Sue Buschel told me about at Camas Meadows. Across the creek is a level piece of ground about 300 yards from north to south, anywhere from fifty to 100 yards wide. Two shallow gullies divide it into three sections. Thunder Rising's band built their fires farthest south, Grating Sound's to the north. In between were Looking Glass, the little Palouse contingent and White Goose. To the north, east and south bluffs from forty to fifty feet high rise to a relatively flat tableland above the campsite. Like the lower ground near the creek, the tableland is cut by ravines. On this side of the creek and extending to the west, is a sloping grade where the Nee-Me-Poo herd grazed that morning.

As dawn broke in the camp, some of the men and boys splashed across the stream to tend the horses, while others loitered near the meager fires of buffalo manure. One fellow produced a deck of cards and got a desultory game of poker going with a few others. A boy, Red Elk, remembering he had left moccasins on a nearby bluff, left to retrieve them. For the women cooking, it must have been a good morning. The supplies taken at Cow Island and the buffalo killed in the previous days would provide good meals for all. Hair Combed Over Eyes, though, was extremely troubled:

> *It was coming daylight but dimly when I awoke and went out from the broken wind-break of canvas. Going through the camp, I called out everywhere. "My people, I have been delayed in this my dream. In Idaho, when I joined the war, I knew, and in vision was directed beforehand. Listen well to my words, to my dreams of last night. I dreamed! And when I woke up, here, where we are camped, is the very ground I saw in vision. Above was the thick smoke of battle. On the stream from which we drink was the blood of both Indian and white soldiers. Very soon we shall be attacked." . . . Chief Looking Glass answered my talk. He called to the people: Do not rush! Build fires, cook breakfast! Go slowly! Give the children time to eat! After all have eaten we will get horses, pack up and start moving![2]*

And so the Real People took their time, even after two scouts galloped in from the south, reporting stampeding buffalo, a sign of something amiss on the back trail.

I wander to where Magera is answering questions and soon realize he is telling a different version of the battle than what has long been "common knowledge." I feel like doing a little dance; thought I was alone on this.

About two miles from the camp the Second Cavalry suddenly veered to the left. Captain Godfrey with the Seventh wrote a few days later:

> *The Cheyenne scouts saw the Nez Perce pony herd out grazing and made for the herd. Capt. Tyler commanding the 2nd Cav. probably mistook the Nez Perce herders and Indians running for the herd for the main body and made in the direction of the pony herd which took him far to the left of the village. The 7th Cavalry was now ordered to make the charge on the village with pistols.*[3]

The Seventh's Company "K" with Captain Hale was now in the van. He ordered his troopers from column into line and gave the order to charge. Companies "A" and "D" under Captains Moylan and Godfrey then also moved into line, took to the trot, the gallop and finally the charge, pistols drawn, no doubt shouting encouragement to one another.

About an hour after the first two Nez Perce scouts reported possible danger from the south, a third came galloping from the same direction. As soon as he came within view of the camp, he circled his horse while desperately waving a blanket in the air, a signal which could mean only one thing—the Nee-Me-Poo were about to be attacked once again. Yellow Wolf remembered well the scene:

> *A wild stir hit the people. Great hurrying everywhere. I saw this uncle, Chief Joseph, leap to the open. His voice was above all the noise as he called, 'Horses! Horses! Save the horses!' I grabbed my rifle and cartridge belts and ran with others for our horses. Warriors were hurrying to the bluffs to meet the soldiers. Soon, from the south came a noise—a rumbling like stampeding buffaloes. Reaching the higher ground north of our camp I looked back. Hundreds of soldiers in two, wide, circling wings.*[4]

Some of the women had already packed their gear and now fled northward with a small guard of men. Many men and some women and children raced across Snake Creek just before the flanking charge of the Second Cavalry descended on the herd. Here the army had great advantages: shock and discipline on open terrain perfect for maneuver. Thunder Rising was among those who made it to the horses:

> *About seventy men, myself among them, were cut off. My little daughter, twelve years of age, was with me. I gave her a rope and told her to catch a horse and join the others who were cut off from camp. I have not seen her since, but I have learned she is alive and well. I thought of my wife and children, now surrounded by soldiers, and I resolved to go to them or die. With a prayer to the Great Spirit Chief who rules above, I dashed unarmed through the line of soldiers. It seemed to me that there were guns on every side, before and behind me. My clothes were cut to pieces and my horse was wounded, but I was not hurt. As I reached the door of my lodge, my wife handed me my rifle, saying, 'Here's your gun. Fight.'*[5]

The other wing Yellow Wolf saw enveloping the camp was Hale's Company "K" which had gotten a head start over the other two Seventh Cavalry companies. Hale took his troopers across the tableland east of the camp, where, led by Frog, warriors waited at the lip of the eastern bluff. When the cavalry line was about 200 yards from striking the northeast corner of the camp, the warriors rose and unleashed a devastating fire that stopped the charge cold. Hale hurriedly ordered his men to dismount with every fourth trooper taking the horses to the rear. The rest formed a skirmish line and returned fire with their carbines. Taking advantage of the creek bed and a ravine cutting into the tableland, sometime in the next few minutes warriors flanked the soldiers and reached the horseholders, where a hand-to-hand struggle ensued. The horseholders apparently fled. Captain Hale, realizing he and his men were in a world of trouble, ordered a retreat, abandoning their dead and wounded, among them young Lieutenant Jonathan Biddle, just a year and a month out of West Point.

Meanwhile, the other two Seventh Cavalry units charged directly from the south. It must have been an unnerving sight for the few warriors crouched at the lip of the southern bluff: eighty bluecoats with pistols in hand on massive army horses, the officers in front, the sergeants slightly behind the line to "encourage" any stragglers, the line stretching for almost 200 yards. McWhorter's informants remembered the names of some of the waiting warriors: Hair Combed Over Eyes, Many Coyotes, Red Spy, Shooting Thunder, Lone Bird, Akhtailaken, Soo-Koops and Peopeo Ipceewet. They waited and waited, sighting along the barrels of their rifles. Captain Moylan, writing eleven months later:

> *After repulsing Company "K", the Indians turned their attention to the other two Companies, ("A" and "D"), which charged them in front. These two Companies charged up to within twenty yards of a line of Indians that was concealed behind a high bank which overlooked their village (the village being situated in a deep ravine through which Snake Creek ran), and owing to the fact that this bank was at the point charged by the companies almost perpendicular, they could not dislodge the Indians, neither could they charge through them owing to the nature of the ground. Taking in the situation at once and seeing the hopelessness of being able to do anything at this point mounted, I gave the order for the Companies to fall back. . . . The loss of the Companies in the action thus far was not so great as might have been expected for the reason that a heavy depression in the ground between them and the Indians protected them somewhat, the Indians overshooting them.*[6]

I believe Captain Moylan's memory was less than totally accurate about a few details. The "heavy depression in the ground" that protected the soldiers is about 400 feet from the edge of the bank where the warriors waited. I think it also extremely unlikely that the Nez Perce would have allowed the cavalry within twenty yards before firing their first shots; they were not foolish fighters. The charge of Companies "A" and "D" probably stalled about 150 yards from the northernmost edge of the low bluff overlooking the camp.

At any rate Moylan ordered the line to reform into a column of fours and retreat. Captain Godfrey had his horse shot out from under him about this time, and he pitched to the ground and somersaulted, ending up on his feet with his pistol still in his right hand but unable to raise it, having dislocated his shoulder in the fall. As the rest of the column continued to fall back, Godfrey thought "affairs were looking pretty squally" for him, but his trumpeter, Thomas Herwood, turned back and rode between the officer and the Nez Perce positions. Godfrey remembered that earlier in the day Herwood, a new recruit, had commented nervously, "There'll be a good many of our saddles emptied today, won't there?" Godfrey had responded that if Herwood stayed close to the officer everything would be all right. Now, Herwood took a bullet in his side and cried out, "Well, Captain I got it!" Godfrey ordered the trumpeter to get the heck out of there and find a doctor. Another trooper returned with the blood-spattered horse just ridden by Sergeant James Albert, who would have no need for it again, and Godfrey made his escape. A Congressional Medal of Honor awaited Thomas Herwood.[7]

Captain Moylan, meanwhile, halted the two companies just out of effective range of the Nez Perce warriors' rifles, probably about 200 yards south of the point where the charge had stalled. Up to this point they had lost three men killed and four wounded. Colonel Miles, who had been watching the action, ordered the troopers to dismount, leave their horses with holders and double-time it on foot to the aid of Captain Hale and Company "K" to the east of the Nez Perce camp. Captain Godfrey, dislocated shoulder and all, arrived just in time to lead his men. They had almost a quarter-mile to run in their heavy overcoats, down one ravine, up to the tableland, down a second ravine, then up again before they could reach their beleaguered comrades. All the way they were running across the gunsights of Nee-Me-Poo marksmen, like targets in a carnival game. Moylan later wrote, "It was during this movement that Companies "A" and "D" suffered their heaviest losses."[8]

One of many who did not make it was Captain Godfrey. Still on horseback, he was urging his men forward when he:

> *. . . felt a shock as if a stone or club on my left side. I was just congratulating my good fortune in having turned enough to have the bullet strike my cartridge belt and glance off, that the cartridges had turned it away, but just then I felt my body swaying forward and a stinging pain in my body. I was powerless to prevent going over my horse's neck. My horse stopped, stood instantly still and then, as if knowing the situation, gently lowered his head and I slid down to mother earth.*

Grasping the pommel of his saddle and guiding his horse, Godfrey made his way back to the held horses where surgeon E. F. Gardner probed the wound and consoled Godfrey, saying:

> *Well, I see your backbone, a quarter of an inch more to the right and it would have been all up for you!*[9]

A concoction of brandy and opium brought relief from the pain.

Many of the warriors from the southern defenses also rushed toward the melee to the east. Three of them, according to Yellow Wolf:

> *. . . were too far toward the enemy line. Husishusis* (Naked Head, the Palouse headman) *thought them enemy Indians and killed them all. He had a magazine rifle and was a good shot. With every shot he would say, 'I got one!' or 'I got him.'*[10]

They were Lone Bird, Koyehkown and elderly Kowwaspo.

As the dwindling Companies "A" and "D" neared the remnant of Company "K," the warriors retreated to the edge of the bluff overlooking the camp and began to dig in. Soon after the troops united, Captain Moylan was wounded in the leg and taken from the field. Captain Hale was killed by a bullet through the neck. All three First Sergeants lay dead. Only one officer remained, Lieutenant

Edwin Eckerson, who ordered the battered battalion to retreat further east.

The fight had been short, ferocious and costly. Company "K" suffered eleven men killed and twelve wounded, almost sixty percent of the unit. Aside from the horse holders left behind south of the camp, about fifty men from Companies "A" and "D" went to the rescue of their fellow soldiers. Six died and another seventeen were wounded, almost fifty percent of the total. None of McWhorter's informants were on that part of the battlefield early in the day. Still, they named the dead they could: Red Star, Red Legs, Wichlatapalatsin, Yalmee and Tehomitskon. They were sure there were at least four others. And Frog, brother of Thunder Rising.

Meanwhile, the four mounted companies of the Fifth Infantry thundered past the Seventh's horseholders. Since most of the warriors originally defending the south had rushed to the east, Miles' infantry seized control of the bluff overlooking the camp with little trouble. After a warrior named Soo-Koopt fell in short-range combat, the remaining warriors retired. Soldiers brought up the Hotchkiss artillery gun and attempted to fire into the camp, but Nee-Me-Poo marksmen hidden in the camp below soon forced the gunners to retreat and the infantry skirmish line in general to keep a very low profile.

At the other end of the camp as the Second Cavalry swept west and north, nine Nee-Me-Poo warriors rushed north for several hundred yards along the creek bottom and began constructing three hasty rock shelters at the base of a forty-foot-high outcropping. One soon slipped back toward safety, but eight remained, determined not to give ground. They were tough old Grating Sound, Eagle Necklace and his son of the same name, Tahtahhaliihken, Timlikpoosman, Lakoiyee, Heyoom Eekahlikt and Tomyahnin. They would be remembered a generation later in the oral history of the Real People as the Immortals, the outcropping they defended as Death's Point of Rocks.

When the Second Cavalry had finished rounding up what they could of the horse herd, the battalion moved on the camp, only to find themselves blocked by the Immortals. Several Cheyenne scouts crawled to the top of the point and attempted unsuccessfully to roll rocks down on the defenders. One Cheyenne, peering over the edge, was wounded, his rifle sliding down into the Nez Perce position. One by one the defenders began to fall, but the others hung on, preventing the army from advancing up the creek bottom into the camp.

On the tableland to the east, an act of remarkable bravery was taking place. The warriors dug in along the edge of the bluff were running low on ammunition. One remembered a young Nee-Me-Poo woman who came to help:

First day, while the fighting, she went out on the field among the dead soldiers, unfastened their cartridge belts, and brought ammunition to the warriors. Soldiers fired at her but she escaped unhurt.

Red Wolf also kept her in his memory:

While fighting, our cartridges get low. We think we need more cartridges. One woman had certain power. She performed and talked, telling of her power found in younger days. This woman's name was Ah-tims; and her power had been given her by the bird called by the whites prairie chicken. It was daytime, when the woman went out to where the dead soldiers lay. She did not run, but went slowly along. Soldiers fired at her, but none hit her. She gathered all the cartridges she could find there and came back with them to our trench. She distributed the cartridges among us all, about ten to each man. I think she went for cartridges two or three times.[11]

The group clustered around Magera breaks up, so I introduce myself and tell him I've been doing some research on the war and this battle. He's heard that before, no doubt, but he humors me and asks me what I think happened here. For one thing, I say, pointing across the creek, the Seventh Cavalry mostly got roughed up over there east of the camp not down to the south. A big grin breaks out over Magera's face. He asks for my name again and shakes my hand vigorously. He's thought that for years, he tells me, despite the Noyes map. I nod.

In 1935 a local historian named C. A. Noyes drew a detailed map of the battlefield and placed the Seventh Cavalry action entirely on the tableland to the south of the camp. Writers since have been reluctant to contradict Noyes despite compelling archaeological and documentary evidence to the contrary. Earlier in the summer, Magera says, a National Park Service historian visited as a result of the addition of the battlefield to the National Historical Park, and Magera convinced him to write a revised interpretation of the battle, finally placing the major Seventh Cavalry action to the east where it belongs.

I mention that I've spent quite a bit of time going through the McWhorter Papers and came across some interesting stuff, especially the field notes from McWhorter's first trip here in 1928 with Yellow Wolf, Bird Alighting and Sam Lott. The warriors staked significant locations across the battlefield while McWhorter made notes about persons and events at each stake. A local surveyor was supposed to follow up and map the stakes, but that never happened. By the time McWhorter returned in 1935 the wooden stakes were gone, informant Bird Alighting was dead and Yellow Wolf was too infirm to travel.

McWhorter, Sam Lott and another Nez Perce named White Hawk restaked the battlefield as best they could, but Lott had not taken part in the war and White Hawk had been a boy of twelve or thirteen and had fled north at the beginning of the battle. The 1935 material became the basis for the Noyes map that has caused so much confusion, while the older material has languished forgotten in a folder. When I found the 1928 data I was pleasantly startled to find considerable new information, including detailed descriptions of a series of rifle pits dug by warriors on the tableland east of camp. They were a major part of the defenses as outlined in the 1928 notes but totally missing from the 1935 map. Magera immediately nods. He was unaware of the existence of the pits, he tells me, but he knows why they were there to be staked in 1928 but gone by 1935. Let's go take a look, he says.

By mid-afternoon Colonel Miles decided to give another assault a try— a simultaneous foot charge by all three battalions: the Fifth from the south, the remains of the Seventh from the east and the

Second from the north. He ordered Lieutenant Henry Romeyn with his Company "G" of the Fifth to move east to reinforce the shocked and depleted Seventh. Lieutenant Thomas Woodruff described the first attempt:

> When the order to charge was given, only a part of two companies of the 5th Infantry went forward; this little handful was composed of 15 men of Co. "I" Capt. Carter commanding, and 10 men of Co. "F", and two or three odd men. I went forward with the line. We yelled and cheered, went over the steep bluffs across a deep ravine and right into the village. After getting in we could not stay and had to fall back to the ravine with a loss of eight wounded (two afterwards dying).[12]

Thunder Rising was one of the warriors who repelled this attack.

Colonel Miles was not amused by the lackluster effort and sent word to the various companies that when he gave the command to charge that meant *everybody* should charge. Captain Godfrey, who was lying wounded in the hospital camp immediately behind the Fifth Infantry line suggested to Miles that he have a trumpeter sound the charge since that would be much easier for everyone to hear. Godfrey got the impression that the colonel was in no mood to listen to suggestions from a wounded lieutenant, but he did have a trumpeter sound the next charge. Still, the infantry line failed to budge. To the east, when he heard the bugle call, Lieutenant Romeyn stood, waved his hat and gave out a rousing cheer. The Nez Perce responded with a fusillade that struck his field glass case, cut away the hunting knife and pistol on his belt and struck him square in the right lung. The rest of the infantry and cavalry line dropped back down, and the charge from the east quickly ended. The Second Cavalry on the north surged to within 200 feet of the main line of Nee-Me-Poo defenders before the hail of bullets turned them back. Two Nez Perce were in more forward positions and paid the price. Naked Legs, whose position was overrun, was killed in hand-to-hand fighting, but not before he dispatched Private John Irving, the only fatality suffered by the Second during the day. Lean Elk was one hundred feet west of Naked Legs and became the fourth warrior to fall from "friendly fire."[13] Had Looking Glass not usurped Lean Elk's leadership, the Real People might have been crossing the border the day of the battle.

As darkness descended, the Fifth Infantry survivors of the failed assault from the south abandoned their two dead and scrambled to the safety of the bluffs. At the other end of the battlefield, Death's Point of Rocks, Tomyahnin and the younger Eagle Necklace likewise slipped back to the relative safety of their camp. Both were severely wounded, Tomyahnin hit five times. Grating Sound and the five other Immortals lay dead. Leaving a line of sentries around the camp, Colonel Miles pulled the two cavalry battalions back to the safe ground behind the infantry line. Officers and enlisted men alike were muttering that those Nez Perce were fighters from hell and the best marksmen anyone had ever encountered. Miles would order no more charges. He would simply wait the Nez Perce out, until fatigue or hunger or common sense forced a surrender. The Battle of the Bear Paw was essentially over. Losses to each side had been virtually identical—about twenty-three dead with twice that many wounded—but for one side little hope existed. The end of the war was five days away.

Ranger Magera and I cross a footbridge over Snake Creek and make our way across the southern tableland past the mass grave where the fallen soldiers were eventually buried. Farther on to the east and north, the ground over which Hale's Company "K" charged has the appearance of a long, flat, narrowing tongue with the creek bed to the left and a ravine to the right. About 650 feet short of the tip of the tongue an amateur archaeologist with a metal detector once found a distinct line of shell casings, almost certainly the point where the cavalry attack faltered and the Company "K" skirmish line formed. Magera and I continue on quietly to the abrupt promontory at the tip of the tongue and a memorial column placed by McWhorter and his Nee-Me-Poo guides in 1928. Nearby are the remains of a rifle pit scratched out by Nez Perce defenders and the rock behind which Frog waited to blunt the shock of the cavalry attack. The rock wasn't big enough.

That first night the Real People dug in, deep. Warriors

improved their rifle pits along the higher land to the north and east and near the creek to the west and south while the families constructed about seventy shelter pits concentrated at the base of this promontory. From then on, the Nee-Me-Poo would find themselves almost impervious to fire from the soldiers. The remains of most of those pits are still visible today, but not the ones on this east tableland. Now I see why. It's been a wetter than normal summer, and Magera points out to me the disturbed ground of an old roadbed marked by slightly brighter grass. Folks driving their Model T's to the memorial shaft in 1928 and later years obliterated the pits, a shame. Yellow Bull and Many Coyotes defended their families here, and Sun Falling and Grizzly Bear Home. From here Ah-tims strolled toward the soldier line to find bullets for the warriors.

During the initial minutes of the battle almost 200 Nee-Me-Poo made their escape, those already packed and ready for the day's move and those who made it to the horse herd before the Second Cavalry cut it off and drove it away. Decades later Yellow Wolf remained bitter that the Cheyenne and Lakota scouts fought on the side of the army against the Real People. He remembered:

> *At the head of his warriors, that Cheyenne chief rode toward Heyoom Iklakit, who threw him the command, 'Stop right there! You are helping the soldiers. You have red skin, red blood. You must be crazy! You are fighting your friends. We are Indians. We are humans. Do not help the whites!' The Cheyenne chief stopped as told. He answered by signs: 'Do not talk more. Stop right there! I will never shoot you. I will shoot in the air.' . . . The Cheyenne chief lied to Heyoom. He rode south about forty steps from where he had talked, and met a Nez Perce woman mounted. He caught her bridle and with his six-shooter shot and killed the woman.*[14]

Heyoom Iklakit translates as Grizzly Bear Lying Down. A trooper of the Second Cavalry would kill him within minutes.

One large group of escapees fled northeast for a few miles to the base of a butte where about twenty warriors decided to make a stand while the women and children continued to the top. Only Lieutenant McClernand's Company "G" of the Second Cavalry with some of the Cheyenne scouts had followed this far, the rest of the battalion being occupied securing the horse herd and investing the northern end of the Nez Perce camp. A short, sharp fight ensued in which two warriors, Alute Pouyeen and Weas Simlikt, were killed. McClernand, having suffered no casualties, decided to retreat. Some of the Real People were safe, at least for a while.

It's late in the afternoon, and Magera says he has some old maps and photos to show me at the National Park Service office in in Chinook, Montana, on the Milk River fifteen miles north. After a brief stop there Magera takes me to a secluded spot along the Milk River where a wooden staff rises from the grass, placed there with quiet ceremony by Nez Perce elders a few years ago. More sacred ground. As the Real People struggled toward Canada, they occasionally stumbled upon other native peoples. If they met Crees or Metis or Chippewas they were welcomed, clothed and fed. If they met Assiniboines they were killed. Seven died here. Magera suggests we don't linger.

After I find a motel room and a Chinese dinner in the town of Havre I return to the battlefield alone, remaining at the overlook across the creek from the camp. I've never really been comfortable walking the ground at White Bird or Big Hole or here, any of the battlegrounds. I get the sense that interrupted lives somehow remain, ghosts. Names and stories live in the land.

The siege lasted from the evening of September 30 until the afternoon of October 5. Mixed snow and rain began to fall the first night and continued intermittently throughout. With no wood and just a few buffalo chips available for fires, conditions in the shelter pits must have been miserable. About 450 Nee-Me-Poo remained invested, but only about forty or so could have been listed as men of prime warrior age. The cordon surrounding the Real People was loose, and the able-bodied could have escaped on foot in darkness, though few were willing to abandon the aged and the children and the wounded. After spending the first day protecting those fleeing north, Yellow Wolf actually slipped back through the army line to

405

be with his trapped people. Here, on a bleak, wintry prairie far from home he:

> *. . . felt the coming end. All for which we had suffered lost! Thoughts came of the Wallowa where I grew up. Of my own country when only Indians were there. Of teepees along the bending river. Of the blue, clear lake, wide meadows with horse and cattle herds. From the mountain forests, voices seemed calling. I felt as dreaming. Not my living self.*[15]

Thunder Rising was disconsolate over the unknown fate of his daughter, Noise of Running Feet, whom he had sent fleeing northward at the onset of the attack. He also must have taken a look at the damp, cold shelter pits and realized that the children and the elderly and the wounded could not stand the conditions for long. Several of the leading warriors believed that Sitting Bull at the head of his warriors might soon arrive from Canada, fresh for another fight with the army that had forced them into exile, a feeble dream. When Colonel Miles raised a white flag on October 1, Thunder Rising decided to talk. Lieutenant Lovell Jerome of the Second Cavalry rode between the lines and escorted the chief to Miles while other soldiers took advantage of the lull to retrieve the bodies of those who had fallen near the Nee-Me-Poo lines. Jerome then ventured into the Nez Perce camp and walked his horse among the shelter pits, observing conditions among the Real People.

Details of the meeting between Thunder Rising and Miles are murky, but Miles apparently demanded the surrender of all weapons while Thunder Rising held out for keeping half so the People could continue hunting as they returned to Idaho. The result of the talks definitely reflected poorly on the colonel's honor. Despite the white flag, he ordered the Wallowa headman detained; soldiers possibly hobbled him, rolled him in a blanket and left him to spend the next night on the ground next to the mules of the pack train. When word of the arrest reached the Nez Perce camp, warriors pulled Lieutenant Jerome from his horse and stashed him in one of the shelter pits. The following day Jerome wrote a note to Miles reporting that the Nee-Me-Poo were treating him well, providing food and water, warm blankets and, occasionally, freedom to walk around. The note shamed Miles into ordering Thunder Rising's release. Shortly after the two prisoners were exchanged on the afternoon of the second, the gunfire renewed.

Sometime during the five-day siege army scout Milan Tripp spotted a warrior rise from a rifle pit on the tableland at the northeast corner of the Nez Perce camp. Tripp squeezed off a long-distance shot and hit the stationary figure square in the left forehead. Looking Glass was dead. He had spotted a solitary rider far in the distance to the northeast and had hoped against reality that it was the first of Sitting Bull's Lakota warriors coming to the aid of the Real People. Throughout, the army continued to lob shells from the Hotchkiss gun randomly into the camp. On the fourth day a shell landed directly in a shelter pit, killing two women and a girl. According to Frog's widow, they were Bear In The Evening, Intetah and Its Peepeetin. Sometime during the siege, Ah-tims performed her magic once again, dodging through the soldiers' fire for a hundred yards to retrieve a cache of ammunition abandoned during the initial army attack. The Real People, though, had pretty much run out of luck.

The day of the battle Colonel Miles had sent couriers searching for his lagging wagon train and for General Howard or Colonel Sturgis and their armies. Bringing desperately needed tents, medical supplies and rations, the supply train arrived a few hours after the exchange of Thunder Rising and Lieutenant Jerome. Early on the same day Howard, Sturgis and their combined column arrived back at Carroll Landing on the Missouri River where the general co-opted a steamer, loaded the artillery battalion and set course upriver for Cow Island. Reaching there early on the October 3, Howard pushed ahead with an escort of seventeen mounted men and arrived at the battlefield after sunset on the fourth. Way back at Virginia City, on August 24, he had promised General Sherman he would "never flag," and he was keeping his word. Now, he magnanimously allowed Colonel Miles, once his aide-decamp during the Civil War, to retain command of the final moments of the long campaign.

The following morning the two Nez Perce who had accompanied

Howard through the entire ordeal, Captain John and Old George, entered the besieged camp carrying a white flag. They informed White Goose, Thunder Rising and the Palouse headman, Bald Head, that more soldiers were on the way, more than enough to overrun the defenses. They assured the chiefs that Miles and Howard had good hearts and delivered a promise that the Real People would be allowed to return to Idaho. After sending the messengers back to the army lines, the chiefs and elders and leading warriors talked it over for hours.

According to McWhorter's informants, few had much use for General Howard, not after his conduct at the council at Lapwai in May. Despite his treatment under another white flag three days ago, Thunder Rising thought Colonel Miles might be a different kind of man. The promise to return the Real People to their homeland was tantalizing to the Wallowa headman, who had never wished to leave in the first place. Finally, Thunder Rising decided to give up and face whatever the future might bring; the others, of course, could do as they wished. When Captain John and Old George returned, Thunder Rising asked them to relay his decision to Howard and Miles. Back at the army lines, Captain John repeated the gist of Thunder Rising's words:

> *Tell General Howard I know his heart. What he told me before — I have it in my heart. I am tired of fighting. Our chiefs are killed. Looking Glass is dead. Grating Sound is dead. The old men are all dead. It is the young men, now, who say yes or no. Frog, who led on the young men is dead. It is cold and we have no blankets. The little children are freezing to death. My people—some of them—have run away to the hills and have no blankets, no food. No one knows where they are—perhaps freezing to death. I want to have time to look for my children and see how many of them I can find; maybe I shall find them among the dead. Hear me, my chiefs; my heart is sick and sad. From where the sun now stands I will fight no more forever.*[16]

About two in the afternoon Thunder Rising with Bald Head and a few warriors met the officers on neutral ground. Miles assured

Thunder Rising that his people would be allowed to return to their homeland in the spring after the snow had melted and travel was easy, saying through an interpreter:

I will take you to a place for this winter; then you can go to your old home.

The colonel continued:

No more battles and blood! From this sun, we will have good time on both sides, your band and mine. We will have plenty time for sleep, for good rest.

General Howard added his two bits:

Same is here. I will have time from now on, like you, to rest. The war is all quit. You have your life. I am living. I have lost my brothers. Many of you have lost brothers, maybe more on your side. I do not know. Do not worry anymore.[17]

Thunder Rising surrendered his rifle to Colonel Miles. As the day waned, more warriors straggled out of their hiding places and stacked their guns.

After dark White Goose and a few others slipped away on foot, refusing to believe the words of any white man. One was Wetatonmi, Frog's widowed wife, who later said, much later:

It was lonesome the leaving. Husband dead, friends buried or held prisoners. I felt that I was leaving all that I had but I did not cry. You know how you feel when you lose kindred and friends through sickness-death. You do not care if you die. With us it was worse. Strong men, well women, and little children killed and buried. They had not done wrong to be so killed. We had only asked to be left in our homes, the homes of our ancestors. Our going was with heavy hearts, broken spirits. But we would be free. Escaping the bondage sure with the surrendering. All lost, we walked silently on into the wintry night.[18]

About 430 Real People did give up, only about eighty of them adult men, half of those wounded. Escorted by Miles and the Fifth Infantry battalion, they arrived at Tongue River Cantonment on the Yellowstone River on October 23 where Howard and Miles had decided to hold them until spring. Six days later, though, when a message arrived from General Terry with orders to transport the Nez Perce east to Fort Abraham Lincoln, Dakota Territory, Thunder Rising might have felt the first foreboding of the coming betrayal. A portion of the prisoners, mostly the women and children, piled into all the available boats for the journey down the Yellowstone River to the Missouri and on to Fort Abraham Lincoln and the town of Bismark adjacent to the post. Thunder Rising, Colonel Miles and those who could not fit in the boats traveled on horseback and in wagons with a small military escort. The colonel's admiration for the Wallowa headman was growing, and he would eventually state that Thunder Rising was, "a man of more sagacity and intelligence than any Indian I ever met . . ."[19]

The two rode side-by-side at the head of the overland column when it reached Bismark on November 19. A brass band and almost the entire population of the town turned out to greet the chief and his people. Cheering townspeople broke through a cordon of soldiers and thrust food and gifts into the hands of the startled Nee-Me-Poo. Two days later the front page of the local newspaper blared "the admiration we have for your bravery and humanity," topped off by an invitation to Thunder Rising to a formal reception and dinner at the local hotel.[20] Thunder Rising, the young and inexperienced headman from the isolated Wallowa country, was well on his way to becoming Chief Joseph, the myth.

A new set of orders, these from General Sheridan in Chicago, arrived. Miles was to arrange transport for the prisoners on the railroad, destination Fort Leavenworth, Kansas. On November 23 Chief Joseph stood on the rear platform of the train bearing his people and waved good-bye to the citizens of Bismark. One woman darted from the crowd and impulsively kissed him on the cheek. Still, Joseph knew the train was bearing him farther from his homeland. The promises made by Howard and Miles at the surrender to return him to be near the bones of his father and mother seemed to be blowing away in a chill wind.

Troops sequestered the Nee-Me-Poo on a soggy, mosquito-infested piece of Missouri River bottomland near Leavenworth. Soon the Real People began dying of malaria, cholera and despair. In 1878 the War Department turned them over to the Department of the Interior, which resettled them on the Quapaw Reservation in Indian Territory, Oklahoma, farther yet from the homeland. The Real People soon had a name for their new home: Eeikish Paw, the Hot Place. An agent for the government told them they would stay in the Hot Place forever, and by the end of the year, one in seven was dead.

It's almost dark here at Bear Paw, the ravines completely in shadow, the higher ground an amber glow. I walk back to my van and sit in the driver's seat for a few minutes.

About 230 Nee-Me-Poo eventually made it to Canada. According to one count, 140 were men and boys, ninety-three women and girls. Yellow Wolf was one who decided not to give up his gun, easily bypassing the sentries around the camp the day after Thunder Rising's surrender. He and the others found haven with Sitting Bull's Lakota on the plains and hills of Saskatchewan. The Nee-Me-Poo and Lakota had long been enemies in the buffalo country, but now they forged a bond, a friendship based on retaining freedom, even if in exile. Descendants of the Real People still live north of the border.

For many, though, it was not home. Elderly White Goose made one brief foray toward Idaho, a journey on foot with his family. Rejected on the way by the Flatheads in Montana, he returned to Canada and was killed there a few years later, reportedly at the hands of one of his own people. Bird Alighting stayed with the Lakota for a year, then wandered west and spent two years with the Spokanes of eastern Washington before turning east again and finding solitary refuge in the Dakota country. He told McWhorter:

I dreamed, and the thought came to my mind. How of my time? I shall now drift alone here and there—all alone—

411

unfriended and without a home. Nowhere to sleep in comfort,
hungry every day, wandering as a chased coyote. Skipping
from mountain to mountain, seeking for a shelter not found.[21]

Yellow Wolf spent only eight months in Canada before slipping
south across the border with about twenty-five others. After several skirmishes with settlers and soldiers he surrendered at Lapwai
and joined the exiles in the Hot Place, one of about eighty
returnees who eventually made the long journey under guard to
Oklahoma. Chief Joseph's daughter, Noise of Running Feet, also
returned with Yellow Wolf and turned herself in to authorities.
Cruelly, they refused to send her to Oklahoma. She died a few
years later, never reunited with the father who wanted nothing
more than to see his daughter once again.

Sympathy for the exiled Real People continued to flourish in the
Eastern States. Nelson Miles, to his credit, still pressed for the
return of the banished bands to Idaho. In 1879 Chiefs Joseph and
Yellow Bull traveled to Washington, D.C., to plead for the return of
the People to their homeland. While there, Joseph spoke before a
large crowd in Lincoln Hall, his words ironically translated by Ad
Chapman, the civilian who had fired the first shot of the battle at
White Bird. Joseph's impassioned plea for justice brought the audience, cheering, to its feet. That same year the Indian Bureau
moved the Nee-Me-Poo again, this time to the Ponca Reservation
in Oklahoma. The dying continued, suicide added to the causes of
death. Their agent thought them doomed. Charles Wood, the
young lieutenant who had written down Joseph's surrender
speech, left the army to become a lawyer and a poet. He and others kept peppering Congress with letters and petitions demanding
justice for the exiled Nez Perce.

Finally, in May 1885, the 268 surviving Nee-Me-Poo in
Oklahoma boarded a train, leaving hundreds of graves in the Hot
Place. The train headed west, eventually halting at Wallula,
Washington, on the Columbia River. The People stepped down onto
familiar soil, breathed familiar air, only about thirty miles from
the site of the 1855 council where their homeland had been
promised them forever. Bald Head, the Palouse headman, led 117
of the Real People on the short, bittersweet journey to Lapwai. But

a ludicrous state indictment for the murders along Salmon River and on Camas Prairie at the onset of the war awaited Chief Joseph in Idaho, the price of fame. At the federal government's insistence for his safety, Joseph departed for the distant Colville Reservation in northern Washington state. With him rode about 150 others who would not abandon their chief.

Joseph was allowed to return to the Wallowa Valley for a brief visit in 1900. He wept at the grave of his father, paused by the deep blue waters of the lake, visited the town named for him and pleaded for a bit of land for his people. Just a little of the Wallowa country. The answer was no. So, one autumn day in 1904 Joseph sat before his Colville teepee fire. He could have lived in a house the government provided him, but Heinmot Toolyalakekt, Thunder Rising Toward Distant Mountains, preferred to remain true to the old ways. While staring at the embers he pitched forward to his mother earth. His people called for the agency physician, but it was too late. Joseph, the doctor decided, had died of a broken heart.

It's time for me to go home.

Notes

[1] Remsen (Tilton, Henry Remsen), "After the Nez Perces," *Forest and Stream and Rod and Gun*, December 27, 1877.

[2] McWhorter, *Papers*, Folder 56, p. 46-48.

[3] Godfrey, *Papers*, p. 7-8

[4] McWhorter, *Yellow Wolf*, p. 205.

[5] Joseph, "An Indian's View, " p. 428.

[6] Moylan, Miles, *Battle of Bear Paw Mountain, M.T.*, MG5165, University of Idaho Library, 1878.

[7] Godfrey, *Papers*, p. 9-11.

[8] Moylan, *Battle*.

[9] Godfrey, *Papers*, p. 12-16.

[10] McWhorter, *Yellow Wolf*, p. 209.

[11] McWhorter, *Papers*, Folder 62, item 19 and Folder 28, item 59.

[12] Woodruff, Thomas, "We have Joseph and All His Prople," *Montana, the Magazine of Western History*, October, 1977, p. 32.

[13] McWhorter, *Papers*, Folder 110, items 40-43. Although Thomas Woodruff in "We Have Joseph," a letter to his mother, assumed the courier delivering the order to Captain Tyler of the Second Cavalry to make the foot charge was wounded and failed to reach Tyler, McWhorter's 1928 Field Notes support the existence of the charge from the north. Naked Legs died "where 100 soldiers and Cheyennes charged from the north in a flanking movement. (First days' fighting)" McWhorter went on to write that Lean Elk, too, died "opposing onslaught from the north."

[14] McWhorter, *Yellow Wolf*, p. 206-207.

[15] McWhorter, *Yellow Wolf*, p. 212.

[16] based upon Wood, Charles E. S., "Chief Joseph, The Nez Perce," *Century Magazine*, May, 1884, p. 141. The notion that Thunder Rising delivered the speech directly to Howard and Miles while surrendering his gun is nothing more than romantic fiction.

[17] McWhorter, *Yellow Wolf*, p. 224-225.

[18] McWhorter, *Hear Me*, p. 511.

[19] quoted in Wilfong, *Following*, p. 320.

[20] quoted in Wilfong, *Following*, p. 339.

[21] McWhorter, *Papers*, Folder 31, item 67.

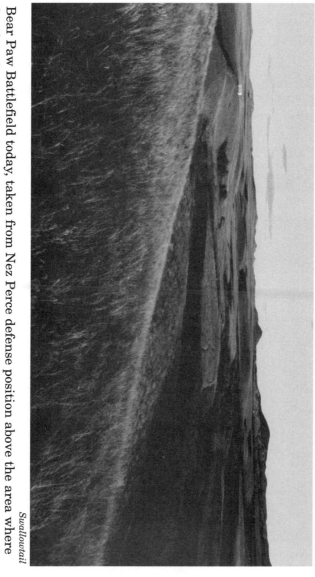

Swallowtail

Bear Paw Battlefield today, taken from Nez Perce defense position above the area where families dug in. Miles' troops came from the southeast (left of center of picture).

BIBLIOGRAPHY

Adjutant General's Office, *Records of the Adjutant General's Office, Letters Received*, National Archives, Washington, D.C., 1877-1887.

Adkison, Norman, *Nez Perce Indian War & Original Stories*, Idaho County Free Press, Grangeville, ID, 1968.

Alcorn, Rowena, "Jackson Sundown, Nez Perce Horseman," *Montana, The Magazine of Western History*, Helena, Autumn 1983.

Alt, David, *Roadside Geology of Idaho*, Mountain Press, Missoula, MT, 1989.

Alt, David, *Roadside Geology of Montana*, Mountain Press, Missoula, MT, 1986.

Alt, David, *Roadside Geology of Oregon*, Mountain Press, Missoula, MT, 1978.

Annual Report of the Secretary of War, 1876, 1877, National Archives, Washington, D.C., 1877-1878.

Aoki, Haruo, *Nez Perce Texts*, University of California Press, Berkeley, 1979.

Ault, Nelson, *The Papers of Lucullus Virgil McWhorter*, Friends of the Library of Washington State University, Pullman, 1959.

Austin, Eric W., *Political Facts of the United States Since 1789*, Columbia University Press, New York, 1986.

Bailey, Robert G., *River of No Return*, Bailey-Blake Printing Company, Lewiston, ID, 1947.

Bartlett, Grace, "Ollokot and Joseph," *Idaho Yesterdays*, Spring 1977.

Bartlett, Grace, *Wallowa Country 1867-1877*, n.l., n.p., 1976.

Beal, Merrill D., *"I Will Fight No More Forever"*, University of Washington Press, Seattle, 1963.

Bismark *Tri-Weekly Tribune*.

Bond, Fred G., *Flatboating on the Yellowstone*, American Library Association, New York, 1925.

Bonney, Orrin & Lorraine, *Battle Drums and Geysers*, Swallow Press, Chicago, 1970.

Bozeman *Avant Courier*.

Bozeman *Times*.

Bradley, James H. *"Letters,"* Manuscript #SC1612, Montana Historical Society, Helena.

Bradley, James H., "Statistics of Various Tribes," *Contributions to the Historical Society of Montana, Vol IX*, Helena, 1940.

Bradley, James H. & Stewart, Edgar, ed., *The March of the Montana*

Column, University of Oklahoma Press, Norman, 1961.

Brady, Cyrus T., *Northwestern Fights and Fighters*, Doubleday, New York, 1907.

Brown, Mark H., *Flight of the Nez Perce*, New York, Capricorn Books, 1971, reprinted University of Nebraska, Lincoln, 1982.

Brown, Mark H., "Chief Joseph and the Lyin' Jack Syndrome," *Montana, The Magazine of Western History*, October 1972.

Brown, Mark H., "The Joseph Myth," *Montana, The Magazine of Western History*, January 1972.

Brown, Mark H. "Yellowstone Tourists and the Nez Perce," *Montana, The Magazine of Western History*,, July 1966.

Bruce, Robert V., *1877: Year of Violence*, Bobbs-Merrill, Indianapolis, 1959.

Buck, Amos, "Review of the Battle of the Big Hole." *Contributions to the Historical Society of Montana, Vol. VII*, Helena, 1910.

Buck, Henry, *The Story of the Nez Perce Indian Campaign During Summer 1877*, Manuscript # SC492, Montana Historical Society, Helena.

Butte *Miner*.

Camp, Walter M. *Interviews*, Brigham Young University Library, Provo, UT.

Catlin, John B., *Reminiscences*, Manuscript # SC 520, Montana Historical Society, Helena.

Carpenter, John A., *Sword and Olive Branch*, University of Pittsburgh Press, Pittsburgh, 1964.

Chaffee, Eugene B., "Letters of Nez Perce War to Governor Mason Brayman," *Fifteenth Biennial Report of the Board of Trustees of the State Historical Society of Idaho*, Boise, 1936.

Chittenden, Hiram M., *Yellowstone National Park*, Robert Clark Company, Cincinnati, OH, 1904, reprinted University of Oklahoma Press, Norman, 1964.

Clark, Robert A., *The Killing of Chief Crazy Horse*, A. H. Clark, Glendale, CA, 1976.

Clough, J. P., *Recollections of the Nez Perce Indian War of 1877*, Idaho State Historical Society, Boise, nd.

Connell, Evan S., *Son of the Morning Star*, North Point Press, Berkeley, CA, 1984.

Coues, Elliott, ed., *History of the Expedition Under the Command of Lewis and Clark*, New York, Dover Books, 1965. Reprint of 1893 Francis Harper Edition.

Cowan, Mrs. George F., "Reminisences of Pioneer Life," *Contributions to the Historical Society of Montana, Vol. IV*, Helena, 1903.

Cruikshank, Alexander, *untitled manuscript*, MS 70 #2, Idaho State Historical Society, Boise.

Cruikshank, Alexander, *The Birch Creek Massacre*, Manuscript # SC584, Montana Historical Society, Helena.

Davison, Stanley A., "A Century Ago: The Nez Perce and the Tortuous Pursuit," *Montana, The Magazine of Western History*, October 1977.

Deer Lodge *New North-West*.

Drury, Clifford, *Chief Lawyer of the Nez Perce Indians, 1796-1876*, Arthur H. Clark Company, Glendale, CA, 1979.

Drury, Clifford, *Henry Harmon Spalding*, Caxton Printers, Caldwell, ID, 1936.

Ege, Robert J., *After the Little Bighorn*, Werner, Great Falls, MT, 1982.

Erdoes, Richard and Ortiz, Alfonsa, *American Indian Myths and Legends*, Pantheon, New York, 1985.

Evans, Steven R., *Voice of the Old Wolf: Lucullus McWhorter and the Nez Perce Indians*, Washington State University Press, Pullman, 1996

Fagan, Brian, *The Great Journey*, Thames & Hudson, New York, 1987.

Federal Writers' Project, *Montana, A State Guide Book*, Viking Press, New York, 1939.

Fee, Chester A., *Chief Joseph: The Biography of a Great Indian*, Wilson-Erickson, New York, 1936.

Ferris, Warren A. *Life in the Rocky Mountains, 1830-1835*, Old West Publishing, Denver, 1940.

Fisher, Stanton G., "Journals of S. G. Fisher, Chief of Scouts to General O. O. Howard During the Nez Perce Campaign," *Contributions to the Historical Society of Montana, Vol. II*, Helena. MT, 1896.

Fisher, Stanton G., *Papers* , Idaho State Historical Society, Boise.

Foley, William E., *The Genesis of Missouri: From Wilderness Outpost to Statehood*, University of Missouri Press, Columbia, 1989.

Fort Benton *Record*.

Godfrey, Edward Settle, *Papers and Correspondence, 1863-1933*, Library of Congress, Washington, D.C.

Goldin, Theodore W., Brininstool, E. A. and Carroll, John M., eds., *A Bit of the Nez Perce Campaign*, privately printed, Bryan, TX, nd.

Goodenough, Daniel, "Lost on Cold Creek," *Montana, The Magazine of Western History*, Autumn 1974.

Grillon, Charles, *Battle of Snake Creek Between U.S. Troops and Indians*, Montana State University, Bozeman, 1877.

Guie, Hester D. & McWhorter, Lucullus V., *Adventures in Geyser Land*, Caxton Printers, Caldwell, ID, 1935.

Guie, Hester D., *Papers*, MSS2511, Oregon Historical Society, Portland.

Gulick, Bill, *Chief Joseph Country*, Caxton Printers, Caldwell, ID, 1981.

Haines, Francis D. "How the Indian Got His Horse," *American Heritage*, February 1964.

Haines, Francis D., *The Nez Perces*, University of Oklahoma Press, Norman, 1955.

Hampton, Bruce, *Children of Grace: The Nez Perce War of 1877*, Henry Holt and Company, New York, 1994.

Hardin, Edwin, *Diary, 1874-1888*, Manuscript # SC1006, Montana Historical Society, Helena.

Hendrickson, Borg and Laughy, Linwood, *Clearwater Country!*, Mountain Meadows Press, Kooskia, ID, 1989.

Howard, Helen A., *War Chief Joseph*, Caxton Printers, Caldwell, ID, 1941.

Howard, Oliver O., *My Life and Experiences Among Our Hostile Indians*, A. D. Worthington & Co., Hartford, CT, 1907.

Howard, Oliver O., *Nez Perce Joseph*, Lee & Shepard, Boston, 1881.

Hutton, Paul A., *Soldiers West: Biographies from the Military Frontier*, University of Nebraska Press, Lincoln, 1987.

Irving, Washington, *Adventures of Captain Bonneville*, Baudry, Paris, 1837, republished University of Oklahoma Press, Norman, 1961.

Irving, Washington, *Astoria, Or Anecdotes of an Enterprise Beyond the Rocky Mountains*, 2 vols, Carey, Lea & Blanchard, Philadelphia, 1836.

Jocelyn, Stephen P., *Mostly Alkali*, Caxton Printers, Caldwell, ID, 1953.

Jones, William A. *Report Upon the Reconnaissance of Northwestern Wyoming Including Yellowstone National Park Made in the Summer of 1873*, Government Printing Office, Washington, D.C., 1875.

Joseph, "An Indian's View of Indian Affairs," *North American Review*, April, 1879.

Josephy, Alvin M., *The Nez Perce Indians and the Opening of the Northwest*, Yale University Press, New Haven, 1965.

Kelly, Luther S., *Yellowstone Kelly*, Yale University Press, New Haven, 1926.

Kip, Laurence, *Indian Council at Walla Walla*, Sources of the History of Oregon, Vol. 1 Part 2, Contributions to the Department of Economics and History at the University of Oregon, Star Job Office, nl. 1897.

Kirkwood, Charlotte, *The Nez Perce Indian War Under War Chiefs Joseph and Whitebird*, Idaho County Free Press, Grangeville, 1928.

Lang, William L. "Where Did the Nez Perces Go in Yellowstone in 1877?" *Montana, The Magazine of Western History*, Winter 1990.

Larocque, Francois, *Journal of Francois Larocque*, Ottowa, Government Printing Bureau, 1910, reprinted Ye Galleon Press, Fairfield, WA, 1981.

Fitzgerald, Emily, Laufe, Abe, ed., *An Army Doctor's Wife on the Frontier*, Univiversity of Pittsburgh Press, Pittburgh, 1962.

Lavender, David, *Let Me Be Free: The Nez Perce Tragedy*, HarperCollins Publishers, New York, 1992.

LeForge, Thomas H., *Memoirs of a White Crow Indian*, University of Nebraska Press, Lincoln, 1974.

Lewiston *Teller*.

Long, Denis G., *One Family's Indian War*, privately printed, Grangeville, ID, nd.

Madsen, Brigham D., *Bannock of Idaho*, Caxton Printers, Caldwell, ID, 1958.

Magera, James, *Private Communications, Maps and Photographs*, Nez Perce National Historical Park, Chinook, MT, 1995.

Mayer, Frederic, "The Nez Perce War Diary of Frederick Mayer," *Seventeenth Biennial Report of the Idaho State Historical Society*, 1940.

McBeth, Kate C., *The Nez Perces Since Lewis and Clark*, Fleming H. Revell Company, New York, 1908.

McCarthy, Michael, *Diary and Papers*, Library of Congress, Washington, D.C.

McClernand, Edward J., *With the Indians and Buffalo in Montana, 1870-1878*, Arthur H. Clark Company, Glendale, CA, 1969.

McCreary, H. C., *untitled manuscript*, Idaho State Historical Society, Boise.

McDermott, John D., *Forlorn Hope*, Idaho State Historical Society, Boise, 1978.

McDonald, Duncan, "The Nez Perces, the History of Their Trouble and the Campaign of 1877," *New Northwest*, April, 1878 — March, 1879.

McWhorter, Lucullus V., *Hear Me, My Chiefs!*, Caxton Printers, Caldwell, ID, 1952.

McWhorter, Lucullus V., *Papers of Lucullus Virgil McWhorter Cage 55*, Washington State University, Pullman.

McWhorter, Lucullus V., *Yellow Wolf: His Own Story*, Caxton Printers, Caldwell, ID, 1940.

Missoula *Missoulian*.

Moelchert, William, *William Moelchert Letter*, Manuscript # SC491, Montana Historical Society.

Mooney, James, *Ghost Dance Religion and the Sioux Outbreak of 1890*, GPO, Washington, D.C., 1896.

Moore, Rae Ellen, *Just West of Yellowstone*, Great Blue Graphics, Leadore, ID 1987.

Moylan, Miles, *Battle of Bear Paw Mountain*, Manuscript # MG5165, University of Idaho Library, Moscow, 1878.

Mueller, Oscar, "The Nez Perce at Cow Island," *Montana, The Magazine of Western History*, April 1964.

Myers, Rex C., "The Settlers and the Nez Perce," *Montana, The Magazine of Western History*, October, 1977.

New York Times.

Parker, Samuel *Journal of an Exploring Tour Beyond the Rocky Mountains*, Ithaca, NY, Samuel Parker, 1838.

Parnell, William R., "The Nez Perce Indian War — 1877," *United Service*, October, 1889.

Phillips, Paul C., "The Battle of the Big Hole," *The Frontier*, November, 1929.

Phinney, Archie, "Nez Perce Texts, *Columbia University Contributions to Anthropology*," Columbia University Press, New York, 1934.

Pollock, Robert W., *Grandfather, Chief Joseph and Psychodynamics*, Caxton Printers, Caldwell, ID, 1964.

Portland *Oregonian*.

Pouliot, Gordon L. & White, Thain, *Clearwater Battlefield, The Nez Perce War-1877*, manuscript at Nez Perce National Historical Park, Spalding, ID, 1960.

Pouliot, Gordon L. & White, Thain, *Possible Site of the Rains*

Scouting Party Tragedy, manuscript at Nez Perce National Historical Park, Spalding, ID, 1960.

Redington, John, *Scouting in Montana & Miscellaneous Papers*, Manuscript # SC683, Montana Historical Society, Helena.

Relander, Click, *Drummers and Dreamers*, Caxton Printers, Caldwell, ID, 1956.

Rickey, Don, *Forty Miles a Day on Beans and Hay: the Enlisted Soldier Fighting the Indian Wars*, University of Oklahoma Press, Norman, 1963.

Report of the Adjutant General of the State of Oregon for the Years 1865-1866.

Romeyn, Henry, *The Capture of Chief Joseph and the Nez Perce Indians*, Manuscript #SC693, Montana Historical Society, Helena; also same title, *Contributions to the Historical Society of Montana, Vol II*, 1896.

Ronda, James, *Astoria and Empire*, University of Nebraska Press, Lincoln, 1990.

Ross, Alexander, *Adventures of the First Settlers on the Oregon or Columbia River*, Cleveland, 1904, reprinted New York, 1969.

Ross, Alexander, *Fur Hunters of the Far West*, London, 1855, republished University of Oklhoma Press, Norman, 1956.

Ruby, Robert, *Cayuse Indians: Imperial Tribesmen of Old Oregon*, University of Oklahoma Press, Norman, 1972.

Russell, Steve F., *Private Communication*, Letter of March 6, 1995, also conversation of July 17, 1993.

Samples, John, *Battle of Cow Island*, Manuscript # SC715, Montana Historical Society.

Sandoz, Mari, *Crazy Horse, the Strange Man of the Oglalas: A Biography*, Alfred A. Knopf, New York, 1942.

Sarris, Greg, *Keeping Slug-Woman Alive*, University of California Press, Berkeley, 1993.

Scott, Hugh l., *Some Memories of a Soldier*, Century Company, New York, 1928.

Seloske, Teresa, *Private Communications*, Nez Perce National Historical Park, Grangeville, ID, 1993 and 1995.

Shambow, Louis, *Reminiscence*, Manuscript # SC715, Montana Historical Society, nd.

Sherman, William T., *Travel Accounts of General William T. Sherman to Spokan Falls, Washington Territory, in the Summers of 1877 and 1883*, Ye Galleon Press, Fairfield, WA, 1984.

Slickpoo, Allen P. & Walker, Deward E., *Noon-Nee-Me-Poo: Culture and History of the Nez Perces*, Nez Perce Tribe of Idaho, Lapwai, ID, 1973.

Snyder, J. A., *Map of the U.S. Military Reservation of Fort Assiniboine Montana Territory*, provided by James Magera, Nez Perce National Historical Park, Chinook, MT., n.d.

Space, Ralph S., *The Lolo Trail*, Printcraft Printing, Lewiston, ID, 1972.

Spier, Leslie, *The Prophet Dance in the Northwest and Its Derivatives*, George Banta Publishing Co., Menasha, WI, 1935.

Spinden, Herbert J. *The Nez Perce Indians*, New Era Printing Company, Lancaster, PA, 1908.

Sproull, Harry V., *Modoc Indian War*, Lava Beds Natural History Association, n.l., 1969.

Stern, Theodore, *Chiefs and Chief Traders: Indian Relations at Fort Nez Perces, 1818-1835*, Oregon State University Press, Corvallis, 1992.

Stout, Tom B., *Montana, Its Story and Biography*, 3 vols., American Historical Society, Chicago, 1921.

Sutherland, Thomas A., *Howard's Campaign Against the Nez Perce*, A. G. Walling Steam Book and Job Printer and Bookbinder, Portland, OR, 1878, Facsimile Reproduction by Shorey Bookstore, Seattle, 1966.

Thwaites, Reuben G., *Original Journals of the Lewis and Clark Expedition*, 8 vols., New York, 1905, reprinted Antiquarian Book Company, New York, 1959.

Tilton, Henry R., "After the Nez Perces," *Forest and Stream and Rod and Gun*, December 27, 1877.

Urwin, Gregory J., *The United States Cavalry*, Blandsford Press, England, 1983.

Van West, Carroll, "Coulson and the Clark's Fork Bottom," *Montana, The Magazine of Western History*, Autumn, 1985.

Victor, Frances F., *River of the West*, R. W. Bliss, Hartford, CT, 1870, Reprinted Brooks-Sterling Company, Oakland, CA, 1974.

Virginia City *Madisonian*.

Walker, Deward E., *Conflict and Schism in Nez Prece Acculturation*, Washington State University Press, Pullman, 1968.

Warren, Eliza Spalding, *Memoirs of the West: The Spaldings*, Marsh Printing Company, Portland, OR, 1916.

Weikert, Andrew, J., "Journal of the Tour Through Yellow-Stone

National Park in August and September, 1877," *Contributions to the Historical Society of Montana, Vol. III*, 1900.

White, Thain, *Relics From Misery Hill, Nez Perce War, 1877*, manuscript at Nez Perce National Historical Park, Spalding, ID.

White, Thain, *Relics From the Bear's Paw Battlefield, 2 vols*, manuscript at Blaine County Historical Society, Chinook, MT.

Whittlesey, Lee H., *Yellowstone Place Names*, Montana Historical Society, Helena, 1988.

Wilfong, Cheryl, *Following the Nez Perce Trail*, Oregon State University Press, Corvallis, 1990.

Wilmot, Luther, "Recollections of 1877 Campaign," *Luther Wilmot Papers*, Nez Perce National Historical Park Collection, Spalding, ID.

Wilmot, Luther, *Narratives of the Nez Perce War*, Manuscript # MG5481, University of Idaho Library, Moscow.

Wood, Charles E. S., "Chief Joseph, the Nez Perce," *Century Magazine*, May 1884.

Wood, Henry C., *The Status of Young Chief Joseph and His Band of Nez Perce Indians and the Indian Title to Land*, Assistant Adjutant General's Office, Portland, OR, 1876.

Woodruff, Charles A., "Battle of the Big Hole," *Contributions to the Historical Society of Montana, Vol VII*, 1910.

Woodruff, Charles A., "Communication Concerning the Battle of the Big Hole from General Woodruff to Amos Buck," *Contributions to the Historical Society of Montana, Vol VII*, 1910.

Woodruff, Thomas M., *Letter to Mother, October 15, 1877*, Manuscript # SC18, Montana Historical Society, Helena, MT; also "A Soldier Writes Home About the Final Battle," *Montana, The Magazine of Western History*, October, 1977.

INDEX

434

The Author

Born in Thermopolis, Wyoming, Martin Stadius grew up in a family where history was important. His mother was a member of the board of directors of the Wyoming Historical Society.

The Stadius family moved to Klamath Falls, Oregon, in 1964, where Martin graduated from high school in 1970.

Relatives owned a cattle ranch in the Klamath Falls area and Martin said he became a willing part-time cowboy, "riding only Appaloosa horses, the

Kan Okugawa

breed supposedly descendant from Nez Perce war ponies (not true, I've discovered; the Nez Perce word for spotted horses is 'meinem' or 'meinske' meaning stubborn or mule-headed, hardly a good horse during a fight)."

After "escaping" from college in 1978, Martin began a career in the book business that lasted more than twenty years. He said he began looking into the Nez Perce war in 1988 after reading about the new National Historic Trail. In 1992, "I quit my job, took to the back roads and ended up at White Bird talking to a guy named Denis who showed me a rifle belonging to Theodore Swartz."

Martin currently works for the Portland State University Bookstore as coordinator for the satellite bookstore at Marylhurst University. He is a Portland, Oregon, resident.

437

Other suggested reading material
on Nez Perce history

Hear Me, My Chiefs!
Nez Perce Legend and History
Lucullus V. McWhorter

6x9, 48 illustrations, 5 maps, 640 pages,
bibliography, footnotes, index,
ISBN 0-87004-310-2   paper $19.95
ISBN 0-87004-316-1 cloth $27.95 (limited quantities)

Yellow Wolf: His Own Story
Lucullus V. McWhorter

6x9, 48 illustrations, map, 328 pages,
bibliography, footnotes, index,
ISBN 0-87004-315-3   paper $16.95

Chief Joseph Country
Land of the Nez Perce
Bill Gulick

9x12, 231 illustrations, 27 maps, 316 pages,
bibliography, index,
ISBN 0-87004-310-2   Cloth, boxed $39.95

Voice of the Old Wolf
Lucullus Virgil McWhorter
and the Nez Perce Indians
Steven Ross Evans

Washington State University Press
Pullman, Washington 99164-5910
6x9, 200 pages,
chapter notes, bibliography, index,
ISBN 0-87422-128-5   Paper $19.95

For a free Caxton catalog write to:

CAXTON PRESS
312 Main Street
Caldwell, ID 83605-3299

or

Visit our Internet Website:

www.caxtonprinters.com

Caxton Press is a division of The CAXTON PRINTERS, Ltd.

WC